D0101227

# Understanding Child Development

SEVENTH
EDITION

Join us on the web at

**www.EarlyChildEd.delmar.com**

# Understanding Child Development

## For Adults Who Work with Young Children

SEVENTH EDITION

**Rosalind Charlesworth, Ph.D.**
Weber State University

THOMSON
DELMAR LEARNING™
Australia Canada Mexico Singapore Spain United Kingdom United States

THOMSON
DELMAR LEARNING

**Understanding Child Development, Seventh Edition**
by Rosalind Charlesworth, Ph.D.

**Vice President, Career Education Strategic Business Unit:**
Dawn Gerrain

**Director of Learning Solutions:**
John Fedor

**Managing Editor:**
Robert L. Serenka, Jr.

**Senior Acquisitions Editor:**
Erin O'Connor

**Editorial Assistant:**
Alison Archambault

**Director of Production:**
Wendy A. Troeger

**Production Manager:**
Mark Bernard

**Content Project Manager:**
Angela Iula

**Director of Marketing:**
Wendy E. Mapstone

**Channel Manager:**
Kristin McNary

**Marketing Coordinator:**
Scott A. Chrysler

**Art Director:**
Joy Kocsis

© 2008 by Thomson Delmar Learning, a part of the Thomson Corporation. Thomson, the Star Logo, and Delmar Learning are trademarks used herein under license.

Printed in United States of America
1 2 3 4 5 6 7 XXX 10 09 08 07

For more information contact Thomson Delmar Learning, 5 Maxwell Drive, Clifton Park, NY 12065-2919
Or you can visit our Internet site at http://www.delmarlearning.com

ALL RIGHTS RESERVED. No part of this work covered by the copyright hereon may be reproduced or used in any form or by any means—graphic, electronic, or mechanical, including photocopying, recording, taping, Web distribution, or information storage and retrieval systems—without the written permission of the publisher.

For permission to use material from this text or product, contact us by
Tel (800) 730-2214
Fax (800) 730-2215
www.thomsonrights.com

Library of Congress Cataloging-in-Publication Data:
Charlesworth, Rosalind.
Understanding child development : for adults who work with young children / Rosalind Charlesworth.
p. cm.
Includes bibliographical references and index.
ISBN-13: 978-1-4180-3810-6
ISBN-10: 1-4180-3810-5
1. Child development. I. Title.
HQ767.9.C436 2007
305.231—dc22
2006030562

**NOTICE TO THE READER**

Publisher does not warrant or guarantee any of the products described herein or perform any independent analysis in connection with any of the product information contained herein. Publisher does not assume, and expressly disclaims, any obligation to obtain and include information other than that provided to it by the manufacturer.

The reader is expressly warned to consider and adopt all safety precautions that might be indicated by the activities described herein and to avoid all potential hazards. By following the instructions contained herein, the reader willingly assumes all risks in connection with such instructions.

The publisher makes no representations or warranties of any kind, including but not limited to, the warranties of fitness for particular purpose or merchantability, nor are any such representations implied with respect to the material set forth herein, and the publisher takes no responsibility with respect to such material. The publisher shall not be liable for any special, consequential, or exemplary damages resulting, in whole or part, from the readers' use of, or reliance upon, this material.

# CONTENTS


Preface ix

**SECTION I**
**The Young Child: Birth Through Age Eight • 1**

1 A Brief Look at the Young Child . . . . . 3
2 Developmental and Learning Theories . . . . . 12
3 Studying the Young Child . . . . . 28

**SECTION II**
**Learning: Birth Through Age Eight • 41**

4 How Learning Takes Place . . . . . 44
5 Learning Through Play . . . . . 72
6 The Adult Role in Learning: General Characteristics . . . . . 90
7 The Adult Role in Learning: Family and Sociocultural Factors . . . . . 120

**SECTION III**
**Prenatal and Infancy Periods • 153**

8 Conception and Prenatal Development . . . . . 154
9 Heredity, Environment, and Development . . . . . 170
10 Birth and the First Two Weeks . . . . . 182
11 Infancy: Theory, Environment, and Culture . . . . . 197
12 Infancy: Health and Physical and Motor Skills Development . . . . . 219
13 Infancy: Affective Development . . . . . 242
14 Infancy: Cognitive Development . . . . . 260

**SECTION IV**
**The Toddler: Developing Toward Independence • 275**

15 The Toddler: Autonomy and Physical and Motor Development . . . . . 276
16 The Toddler: Affective Development . . . . . 295
17 The Toddler: Cognitive Development . . . . . 313

**SECTION V**
**Physical and Motor Development: Ages Three Through Six • 333**

18 Physical Development, Health, Safety and Nutrition: Ages Three to Six . . . . . 335
19 Motor Development: Ages Three to Six . . . . . 349

**SECTION VI**
**Cognitive Growth and Development: Ages Three Through Six • 371**

20 The Cognitive System and Concept Development . . . . . 374
21 Oral Language Development and Use . . . . . 407
22 Written Language: Development and Everyday Use . . . . . 438
23 Intelligence and Creativity . . . . . 459
24 The Adult Role and Cognitive Development . . . . . 477

**SECTION VII**
**Affective Growth and Development: Ages Three Through Six • 503**

25 The Nature of Affective Development: Theory, Emotion, and Personality . . . . . 505
26 Social Development . . . . . 545
27 The Adult Role in Affective Development . . . . . 570

**SECTION VIII**
**The Primary Child: Growth and Development Ages Six Through Eight • 591**

28 Preschool to Primary: Bridging the Gap . . . . . 593
29 The Primary Child: Physical and Motor Development . . . . . 611
30 The Primary Child: Affective Development . . . . . 624
31 The Primary Child: Cognitive Development and Schooling . . . . . 647

SECTION IX
The Whole Child • 671

**32** A Look at the Whole Child . . . . . 675
**33** Action for Children . . . . . 691

Glossary 705
References 715
Index 757

# PREFACE

***Understanding Child Development*** is designed for teachers in training and teachers in service whose major interest is the prekindergarten, kindergarten, and primary child. It is also a valuable tool for social service workers, special educators, parents, home visitors, and others who require a practical understanding of the young child. For students, it introduces the uniqueness of the young child as distinguished from the older child and shows how to work with young children in a way that corresponds with their developmental level. For teachers in service, this text offers an opportunity to evaluate their views of the young child and compare them with the views presented in the text. For all adults who work with young children, this book presents a picture of the child in the context of family, school, culture, and language.

The young child, the theories of child development, and the methods of studying the young child are introduced first in the text. Next, the means through which children learn from birth to age eight are described. The following sections follow the child from prenatal to infancy to preschool to primary, focusing on physical motor, health, affective, and cognitive development.

Finally, the whole child is considered, along with the role of the adult who works with young children in the development of public policy that supports child development and family.

The text contains many examples. Each chapter, "Time to Reflect" and "Looking Further" boxes offer practical learning applications that enhance individual experiences and add to classroom excitement when shared with other students.

Work with young children is a challenging activity today. Those who work with young children agree that development and education are inseparable at this age. In this text, developmental concepts are placed in a practical perspective. Theory, research, and practice are mixed in a no-nonsense fashion that applies to everyday interaction with young children.

What's new in the seventh edition?

Organizational changes:

- New chapter on how children learn through play has been added.
- New chapters on physical/motor, health, and safety have been placed in developmental sections.
- New chapter on adult role in cognitive development.
- Affective chapters have been consolidated.
- New material in every chapter (2005 MyPyramid Food Guidance System, obesity information, streamlined theory presentations, and new developmental assessment charts).
- Current resources are included throughout the text to reflect changes in the field of early childhood education.

- New key terms have been added to the text and comprehensive glossary, and are listed at the end of each chapter.
- New material has been added concerning special needs and brain development.
- The "For Further Reading" sections of each chapter have been updated and expanded.
- New full-color photographs and illustrations bring child development to life.
- New review questions have been added to help students review new material.
- The Online Companion™ has been enriched with case studies, Web links, and updated content to reflect the changes to the text.

## ABOUT THE AUTHOR

Rosalind Charlesworth, Ph.D., is a professor and chair in the Department of Child and Family Studies in the Vickie and Jerry Moyes College of Education at Weber State University in Odgen, Utah, where she teaches Child Development and Early Childhood Education courses. She has also taught developmental courses to students in home economics, education, and behavioral sciences. Her career history includes experience in teaching young children in laboratory, public school, and child care settings and in research in social and cognitive development, developmentally appropriate practices, and teachers' beliefs and practices. Originally, this text grew out of several years of experience in teaching child development courses for adults who planned to work with preschool children. It has been expanded with Dr. Charlesworths' further experience teaching both preservice and graduate-level students who work with young children from birth through age eight.

## ACKNOWLEDGMENTS

The author wishes to express her appreciation to the following individuals and early childhood education and development centers:

The following students at Bowling Green State University in Ohio, the University of Houston at Clear Lake City, and Louisiana State University at Baton Rouge, who provided many examples from their projects and contributions to class discussion: Donna Jolly, Zheng Zhang He, Stacie Ducote, Rhonda Balzamo, Deneé Babin, Lisa Kirk, Pattie Guidry, Gay Koenig, Jill Ochlenschlager, Jill Evans, Donna Wendt, Tammy Overmeyer, Jill Flaugher, Kathleen Roberts, Sue Heestand, Beth Leatherman, Elizabeth M. Schumm, Nancy Miller, K. Weber, Adrienne Rossoni, Susan Rollins, Carol Roach, Kristine Reed, Kathy Kayle Bede Hurley, Linda Boone, Ruthie Johnson, and Carolyn Nattress.

The following Weber State University students kindly gave permission for anecdotes they collected to be included in this text: Christi Allan, Britnee Allred, Jodie Bennett, Jennifer Benshoof, Rebecca Burt, Elizabeth Cook, Sherrae Flanders, Misty Francis, Marianne Gill, Melissa Ginter, Amy Goodwin, Brenda Hagen, Stacy Hair, Andrea Halls, Faith Hedges, Jill Hess, Rebecca Hansen, Susan Houston, Carole Lane, Alicia Madsen, Kimberly Morgan, Brooke Murdock, Jennifer North, Annie Peterson, Brooke Peterson, Stacy Roubinet, Cynthia Sheffield, Stephanie Scholes, Amy Simpson, Mary Stokes, Crystal VanArle, Jaclyn Wintle, and Cindy Winward.

Those Louisiana teachers whose students provided writing and/or drawing samples: Joan Benedict, Cleator Moore, Robyn Planchard, and Lois Rector.

To the many users of the text, especially the reviewers of this and previous editions, who offered numerous valuable suggestions and helped shape the final work:

**Audrey Beard, Ed.D.**
Albany State University
Albany, GA

**Nancy H. Beaver, M.Ed.**
Eastfield College
Mesquite, TX

**Amy Huffman, M.A.**
Guilford Technical Community College
Jamestown, NC

**Rebecca Mangin**
Colorado Community College Online
Denver, CO

**Michelle Rupiper, Ph.D.**
University of Nebraska, Lincoln
Lincoln, NE

**Trisha Smith, M.S.**
Oklahoma State University
Oklahoma City, OK

**Kellie Jo Sullivan, M.Ed.**
Brazosport College
Lake Jackson, TX

**Elaine VanLue, Ed.D.**
Nova Southeastern University
Orlando, FL

The staff at Delmar Learning: Erin O'Connor, Acquisitions Editor, Alexis Breen Ferraro, Developmental Editor, Stephanie Kelly, Editorial Assistant, and Ken Karges, Content Project Manager.

And last, but not least, to my daughter, Kate, for her tolerance and understanding through seven editions of this book.

## Ancillaries

The following ancillary materials are available to accompany *Understanding Child Development, 7th edition:*

### Instructor's Manual

The Instructor's Manual provides general guidelines for using the text and instructor's manual; overhead transparencies; suggestions for films, videos, and filmstrips that can be used in the classroom; selected Web sites and Web site information; selected computer software; journals for further reading; and answers to the review questions in the text.

### Computerized Test Bank

The Computerized Test Bank comprises true/false, multiple–choice, short–answer, and completion questions for each chapter. Instructors can use the computerized test bank software to create sample quizzes for students. Refer to the CTB User's Guide for more information on how to create and post quizzes to your school's Internet or Intranet.

### Online Companion™

The Online Companion™ that accompanies the seventh edition of *Understanding Child Development* is your link to early childhood education on the Internet. The Online Companion™ contains many features to help focus your understanding of child development.

- Critical Thinking Forum—In this section, you have the opportunity to respond to "Time to Reflect" and "Looking Further" concepts. Various child development scenarios and thought-provoking questions will test your understanding of the content provided in the text. You can share your ideas with classmates and interact informally with your instructor online.
- Student Journal—The student journal can be downloaded to your computer, where you can keep a daily journal. You can print the journal pages to hand in to your instructor.
- Matching Exercises—Interactive matching exercises reinforce concepts ranging from child development theorists, prenatal development sequence, toddler play behaviors, adult roles in learning, and gross and fine motor development skills from birth to age eight. You can go online and test your knowledge in this fun and interactive section.
- Child Development Assessment Forms—These forms can be printed and used during your observation of cognitive, physical, and affective development for children from birth to age eight.
- Online Early Childhood Education Survey—This survey gives you the opportunity to point out the features you like and the features you want to see improved in the Online Companion™.
- Case Studies—A new feature of the Online Companion™, the case studies are designed to reinforce important concepts presented in each chapter.
- Web Links—a multitude of Web links are provided for student research on the Internet.

You can find the Online Companion™ at www.earlychilded.delmar.com.

### WebTutor™

The WebTutor™ to accompany *Understanding Child Development, 7th edition,* allows you to take learning beyond the classroom. This Online Courseware is designed to complement the text and benefits students in that it enables them to better manage their time, prepare for exams, organize their notes, and more. Special features include Chapter Learning Objectives, Online Course Preparation, Study Sheets, Glossary, Discussion Topics, Frequently Asked Questions, Online Class Notes, Online Chapter Quizzes, and Web Links related to chapter content. Printing features allow students to print their own customized study guides.

A benefit for instructors as well as students, the WebTutor™ allows for online discussion with the instructor and other class members, real-time chat to enable virtual office hours and encourage collaborative learning environments, a calendar of syllabus information for easy reference, e-mail connections to facilitate communication among classmates and between students and instructors, and customization tools that help instructors tailor their course to fit their needs by adding or changing content.

WebTutor™ allows you to extend your reach beyond the classroom and is available on either the WebCT or Blackboard platform.

### Professional Enhancement Text

A new supplement to accompany this text is the *Child Development Professional Enhancement* booklet for students. This supplement, which is part of *Thomson Delmar Learning's Early Childhood Education Professional Enhancement* series, focuses on key topics of interest to future early childhood directors, teachers, and caregivers. Students will keep this informational supplement and use it for years to come in their early childhood practices.

## DEDICATION

To Edith M. Dowley, Ruth Updegraff, Shirley G. Moore, Willard W. Hartup, and Ada D. Stephens, who nurtured my professional development, and to my daughter, Kate, and now my granddaughter, Summer, who have provided a rich source of developmental information and inspiration.

# SECTION I

## The Young Child: Birth Through Age Eight

Our children are our hope for the future and our responsibility for the present. Knowledge of their growth and development will aid adults who work with them to provide the most supportive environments possible.

The United States is a potpourri of many cultural and ethnic groups. These groups provide children with a diverse and complex environment in which to develop. Throughout the text, you will meet children, parents, and teachers from many different cultural backgrounds, such as Native American, European, Latino, Asian, and African.

Children live in a variety of family configurations. Besides the traditional mother, father, and one or more children, there are single parent families, adoptive families, blended families, families headed by two parents of the same sex, families headed by grandparents, etc. Family heads have in common the objectives of providing love, food, shelter and other necessities of life while teaching values and cultural traditions. Reaching these objectives is a challenge for all family heads. It is a greater challenge for many families due to an increasing number of risk factors for children.

Many changes have occurred in our population of young people since the field of child study first became a major focus in the early twentieth century. For example, the numbers of what are termed **high-risk children** have increased dramatically. High-risk children are at risk for school failure and possibly survival as a result of various environmental, mental, physical, and/or emotional problems. Some of these problems have hereditary causes, but many have environmental beginnings that can be addressed. These children need to be helped as early as possible to meet the challenges of child development. All who work with young children, such as parents, teachers, doctors, nurses, psychologists, speech therapists, and physical therapists, need to collaborate when possible. The challenge for those who work with young children is to provide each child with the best developmental opportunities.

**high-risk children**
Children who are at risk for school failure and possibly even for survival due to various environmental, mental, physical, and/or emotional problems.

Several factors have increased the high-risk population. One factor is the progress of medical advances. For example, many infants who in earlier times would not have survived the prenatal period survive prenatal and consequent postnatal difficulties today. Cultural changes, such as the dramatic increase in the number of teenage pregnancies and increased use of abusive substances (e.g., alcohol, drugs, tobacco), have added further to the numbers of our young children who are at risk. Other children are at risk because they come from non–English-speaking families; they need help making the transition while maintaining their first language. A serious problem that carries many risks is that millions of our young children live in poverty. Among children, those under six are most likely to be living in poverty, according to federal statistics (Federal Interagency Forum on Child and Family Statistics, 2001).

In spite of the many risk factors in the world, there are also many assets that can offset these negative factors (Unique strengths, Shared strengths, 2003). The Search Institute defines developmental assets as "positive factors in young people, families, communities, schools, and other settings that have been found to be important in promoting young people's healthy development" (Unique strengths, Shared strengths, 2003). The Search Institute identified 20 external and 20 internal assets. The external assets are categorized as support, empowerment, clear boundaries and expectations, and opportunities for constructive use of time. The internal assets are categorized as commitment learning, positive values, social competencies, and positive identity.

This first section provides an overview of child development followed by an introduction to the theories of development that guide child study. Finally, there is a brief overview of the methods used to learn about children.

CHAPTER

# 1

# A Brief Look at the Young Child

## OBJECTIVES

After reading this chapter, you should be able to:

- List settings in which professionals work with young children.
- Begin to recognize typical and atypical infants; toddlers; three-, four-, and five-year-olds; and six- through eight-year-olds.
- Begin to discuss the similarities and differences among infants; toddlers; three-, four-, and five-year-olds; and six- through eight-year-olds.
- Identify the essential adult role with young children.

**NAEYC**
National Association for the Education of Young Children.

**young children**
Children from birth through eight years of age.

Who is the young child? According to the National Association for the Education of Young Children **(NAEYC),** children from birth through eight years of age are considered to be **young children** (Bredekamp & Copple, 1997). They are usually grouped into approximate age categories:

| | |
|---|---|
| Infants: | birth to one year |
| Toddlers: | one year to three years |
| Preschoolers: | three years to five years |
| Kindergartners: | five years to six years |
| Primary: | six years through eight years |

The young child is a small person who is complex and at times puzzling. Jerry Tello (1995) describes how children come into the classroom as reflections of their diverse family backgrounds. Some are not prepared to take full advantage of what it has to offer. Some children may "speak an entirely different language, practice different customs, expect different kinds of nurturing, embrace different values, be surrounded by people who look different, or have a variety of special needs" (p. 38). This unit defines the early childhood age span and presents diverse examples of young children's behavior.

**infants**
Children from birth to approximately one year of age.

What does the young child do? The newborn is interested in personal comfort: being warm, being well fed, and having a dry diaper. Very quickly, the newborn learns to expect attention and cuddling from the caring others in his or her environment. Soon the **infant** becomes aware of his or her own body and of things

**toddler**

Children from age one to age three.

**preschoolers**

Three-, four-, and some five-year-olds who have not yet entered elementary school.

**kindergartners**

Children enrolled in kindergarten classrooms; usually between the ages of four-and-a-half and six years.

**primary period**

Children ages six through eight or grades first through third.

in the environment that he or she can control. By age one, the infant moves into the **toddler** period, and from age one to three, the infant is most interested in moving about and exploring everything. By the time the child is a preschooler, paint, clay, balls, games, dolls, trucks, and books all serve as raw material for the young child's play. By age three, the child accomplishes many routine tasks, such as eating, sleeping, bathing, using the toilet, and dressing. Young boys and girls can walk, run, climb, yell, speak conversationally, and whisper. They can express their feelings clearly—happiness, sadness, contentment, anger, and irritability.

Three- and four-year-olds are usually called **preschoolers,** meaning they have not yet entered elementary school, although many five-year-olds have not yet entered kindergarten and are still preschoolers. Five-year-olds are usually labeled as **kindergartners** even though kindergartners may be four, five, or six, depending on their birth dates and when they entered school. Ages six through eight, or grades first through third, are in the **primary period.** These age labels are rather arbitrary and do not necessarily tell us where a child is developmentally. Therefore, the following descriptions are examples; not every child is exactly like the ones described.

Infants are, as already mentioned, very dependent. Between ages one and three, the young child moves toward increased independence. Preschoolers are ready to "strike out on their own" beyond the safe confines of home and parents. Many children have spent extended periods away from home before age three—in a child care home, at a relative's home, in a center-based infant and/or toddler playgroup or full-day child care group. By age three, however, children have skills that enable them to function well without the almost constant adult attention needed in the infant and toddler years.

For the adult who works with young children in full-time child care, part-time preschool programs, elementary schools, medical settings, social service centers, or at home, questions constantly arise regarding these small people and the best educational and care practices. This unit develops an initial picture of young children through descriptions of their characteristics and actions and by presenting essentials of the adult's role in working with them.

## VIEWS OF YOUNG CHILDREN

The children described on the following pages come from diverse backgrounds and have a variety of capabilities and needs. The following descriptions include young children at different age levels (from birth to primary grades), children with typical and atypical development, and children from various cultures.

### The Infant

Maria (three months old) is on the floor happily sitting in her car seat. Dad is kneeling on the floor talking with her at eye level. Dad begins making one syllable sounds of various pitches. Maria smiles at him, raises her fists, and kicks her feet as she mimics the sounds he makes.

Andy (nine months old) is in his stroller with the back propped up so that he can sit up more easily. The family is at a fast-food restaurant seated at a table in the corner. His stroller is facing his mom so she can feed him. She is facing the play area so she can keep an eye on the two older children. She sets out the two older children's food and her own and gets out crackers for Andy. Andy is happily babbling and looking at his mom. His arms wave around, and he wiggles around animatedly in his stroller. He sees the food and seems excited to begin eating. Mom gives him a cracker to munch on, but he will not accept it. He clamps his

FIGURE 1–1 The infant is engrossed in the activity in the environment.

mouth shut, turns his head away, and furrows his brow. His arms begin to wave even more, and he begins to whine. He appears to want to eat what everyone else is eating. Mom breaks off a soft piece of French fry and offers it to him. He opens his mouth. He looks surprised at the taste and texture. He gums the piece down and eagerly accepts another fry.

Ann (nine months) is crawling into a little cubby hole. She sits there for a moment and then crawls back out. She then picks up a toy and then drops it, and then picks it up again. She repeats this process several times. Next, she crawls over to Susie and yanks on her hair. Susie starts crying and the teacher tries to soothe her. Ann looks at Susie and the teacher and also starts to cry (see Figure 1–1).

## The Toddler

Summer is 17½ months old. She's sitting on the floor looking at books. Her Dad tells Wolf, their German Shepherd, to get a toy. Summer jumps up, goes to Wolf's toy basket, picks up Wolf's favorite toy, and takes it to him. Then, she gets him another toy. Wolf wags his tail and chews on one of the toys, obviously delighted.

Donna positioned Haniya, a toddler with cerebral palsy, in her special seat on the countertop so that Haniya could hold her hands under the faucet. Jonathan came in from the adjoining play area to wash his hands before snack. Donna said to Jonathan, "Please turn on the faucet for Haniya." Jonathan did. Haniya glanced at him and gave a faint smile. She stuck her hands under the faucet of running water, seeming to enjoy the cool feeling on her hands. Jonathan stuck his hands under the water also, and they splashed the water together (Bredekamp & Copple, 1997, p. 65).

FIGURE 1–2 Young children enjoy dressing up as adults.

## The Three-Year-Old

Columnist Dave Barry is in charge of his three-year-old daughter Sophie while his wife is away on business for a few days (Barry, 2003). He writes several anecdotes about the experience including the following. Sophie has a mermaid doll named Ariel. She has beautiful hair! She gets married a lot. She also takes a bath with Sophie every night. Ariel's hair gets very wet. But Sophie wants to sleep with her. So Daddy has to blow-dry Sophie's hair. And brush it out. Every night! Imagine how Daddy feels styling a mermaid's hair, while the other daddies are watching *Sports Center* (see Figure 1–2).

Josh was a three-year-old boy with lively brown eyes, a ready smile, and dark curly hair. . . . Pat, his teacher, was concerned about Josh. She had noticed that he walked and ran awkwardly, stumbling often. He didn't talk much and was difficult to understand. He frequently drooled. He had not yet mastered simple puzzles that were done with ease by other children in the class (Chandler, 1994, p. 4).

Tamika [age three], her sweet face framed by golden ringlets of hair, sits silently in a wicker chair watching her 34-year-old mother prepare for her daily sustenance. . . . Her mother's friend, Dorene McDonald, picks several rocks of cocaine out of her belly button, then positions a milky white pebble in a pipe. As the women alternately take hits off the small glass tube, crack smoke envelops Tamika, who blinks sleepily in her mother's arms (Nazario, 1997).

FIGURE 1–3 Four-year-olds like the companionship of other children and are more independent of adults than three-year-olds.

## The Four-Year-Old

Four-year-old Jorge and three-year-old Hamako are on the playground in the fort. The fort is an enclosed area with windows. Inside it contains steering wheels on two sides and a slide on another side. Jorge is pretending the fort is a ship, and he is the captain. As Jorge steers the ship, Hamako imitates him using the other wheel. Jorge tires of the ship theme and sits down on top of the slide. He tells Hamako to slide with him. She sits down behind him. Together, they form a train and go down the slide (see Figure 1–3).

[Four-year-old Mindy] was a bright and inquisitive girl who chatted readily with the teachers and other children when she and her mother visited the preschool during enrollment week. Mindy had spina bifida and had no feeling below her waist. As a result, she needed to be catheterized several times a day to prevent urinary tract infections. She wore braces on her legs and used a walker. . . . Mindy wanted to be independent. She refused assistance in negotiating the environment or in caring for herself. . . . She didn't want special attention and took pride in doing things for herself (Chandler, 1994, p. 34).

Four-year-old Cedric came into teacher Cathy Main's room one day anxious to tell a story. The night before, he told his classmates at Circle Time, his dad took him riding in the car. His dad's friend was in the front seat, Cedric and his mom in back. Cedric's dad and his friend were drinking and smoking reefers. The cops started chasing them so his dad got on the expressway and drove really fast. His mom was yelling, "Stop! Stop!" Finally the cops pulled them over. They yanked his father out of the car and threw him onto the hood. Then, they cuffed him and dragged him to the police car. [This incident was the focus for dramatic play for several days. Cedric and his classmates acted out all the parts.] (Teaching Tolerance Project, 1997, p. 173).

## The Five-Year-Old

Charlie is putting together a puzzle with two other boys in his kindergarten class. The puzzle is a picture of a box of crayons. The boys open the lid and begin to take out the pieces. Charlie suggests that they begin with all the pieces that have straight edges. While putting the puzzle together, Charlie says, "Green, green I need green." He then commented, "This thing is too easy." He is finally stumped on a part and says to Taylor, "Let me see the lid!" When the puzzle is finished, Charlie puts his hands on the puzzle and smiles. Kofi says, "Let's do another one!" Charlie replies, "Kofi, you have to help us clean up this one first" (see Figure 1–4).

FIGURE 1–4 Kindergartners are more independent than preschoolers.

[Mrs. Johnston explains Kwanzaa to her daughter's kindergarten class]. . . . Mrs. Johnston puts both arms around her daughter and sings out: "Kwanzaa is the time to celebrate, The fruits of our labor, ain't it great! Celebrate Kwanzaa, Kwanzaa!" By the second repetition, many of us are singing also while the teacakes are passed around (Paley, 1995, p. 8).

## The Six- Through Eight-Year-Old

The children [in the primary years] seem to be in a stage of developmental integration. [They] can take care of their own personal needs. . . . They

FIGURE 1–5 Primary age children enjoy board games with rules.

observe family rules about mealtimes, television, and needs for privacy. They can also be trusted to run errands and carry out simple responsibilities at home and at school. In other words, these children are in control of themselves and their immediate world (Allen & Marotz, 2003, p. 140) . . . they enjoy being challenged and completing tasks. They also like to make recognizable products and to join in organized activities (Allen & Marotz, 2003, p. 142). See Figure 1–5.

[In the primary class, the students are painting self-portraits with People Colors multicultural paints. Each child is asked to select the paint color that matches his or her skin tone.]

"I'm gingerbread," says Rodrigo.

"I'm melon and terra cotta," boasts Millie.

"Raise your hand," Debra says, "if your color is close to Millie's."

April volunteers.

"April's a little darker than Millie," someone comments (Teaching Tolerance Project, 1997, p. 12).

In these brief descriptions of child growth from birth to age eight, an increase in independence and self-confidence is evident. At the same time, there seems to be a cycle marked by calmness at three, to increased activity at four, to calmness again as the child reaches five. The adult who works with young children must be aware that these changes are typical. Also exemplified are the diversity of backgrounds, experiences, and special needs evident in young children's lives.

Think about the special needs of the children in the descriptions just mentioned. Describe your reactions and interpretations. Do you think there is a "typical" child at any age? What are some factors that put some of the children described "at-risk"?

## THE ADULT ROLE

Relationships with adults are critical to young children's healthy growth and development. According to child psychiatrist Stanley L. Greenspan:

> . . . good relationships and emotional interactions are the most critical primary foundation for social and intellectual growth, including communication and thinking. Relationships teach children which behaviors are appropriate and which are not. (As quoted in Greenberg, 2001, p. 7)

**developmentally appropriate practices (DAP)**

Instructional practice that is age, individually, and culturally appropriate as defined by the NAEYC (Bredekamp & Copple, 1997).

Young children need to be nurtured and stimulated by adults. Pediatrician T. Berry Brazelton believes that there is power in numbers. He suggests that schools take the lead in "organizing teachers, parents, related professionals, and caring citizens in their communities to develop policies, practices, and services that are good for children (Greenberg, 2001, p. 14). See Chapter 33 in this text for ideas on how to develop community action (Figure 1–6). Throughout the text, adult roles are described relative to ages, stages, and settings.

FIGURE 1–6 Reading enriches both mental and emotional development.

## SOCIOCULTURAL FACTORS

The American population has changed greatly over time. The typical citizen can no longer be defined as being of white, European descent. The non-European American population is growing rapidly and includes six main groups: Latinos, African Americans, Pacific Islanders, Asian Americans, Caribbean Islanders, and Middle Easterners. In addition to these main groups are Native Americans. It is important to keep in mind that these major groups are not homogeneous. Within each group, cultural variation exists. Adults who work with young children and their families must recognize that the "new complex diversity mandates programs that positively affect the learning processes and social adjustments of all school children . . . we know that providing children with **developmentally appropriate practices (DAP)** is at the core of" the early childhood education profession. Educators must be sensitive to children's cultures (de Melendez & Ostertag, 1997, chap. 1). Okagaki & Diamond (2003) caution early childhood educators regarding the importance of developing sensitivity to parents' beliefs and practices. They explain that adults should not make assumptions about any families child-rearing practices but should make the effort to learn what each family's needs and expectations are. Throughout the text, sociocultural factors are related to child development.

## SUMMARY

The text describes growth and development from the prenatal period through the eighth year of life. The study of child development helps adults understand the general ages and stages of young children. Adults work with young children in a multitude of different settings. In this chapter, examples of child behaviors at a variety of ages and stages have been presented in order beginning with the process of reflecting on their similarities and differences. It is through our interactions with young children and their families that we come to know and understand them. The major role of adults is to nurture and stimulate children. Adults also need to attend to the beliefs and practices of families and their cultures. Throughout the text, we describe the relationship of adult behavior and child development.

## FOR FURTHER READING

Alanen, L., & Mayall, B. (Eds.). (2001). *Conceptualizing adult-child relationships.* New York: Routledge-Falmer.

Bornstein, M. H., & Lamb, M. E. (Eds.). (2005). *Developmental science* (5th ed.). Mahwah, NJ: Erlbaum.

Elkind, D. (1993). *Images of the young child.* Washington, DC: National Association for the Education of Young Children.

Gonzales-Mena, J. (2005). *Foundations of early childhood education: Teaching children in a diverse society* (3rd ed.). Boston: McGraw Hill.

Hartup, W. W., & Weinberg, R. A. (Eds.). (2002). *Child psychology in retrospect and prospect: In celebration of the 75th anniversary of the Institute of Child Development.* Mahwah, NJ: Erlbaum.

Kehily, M. J. (Ed.). (2005). *An introduction to childhood studies*. New York: Open University Press.

Landy, S. (2005). *Early intervention with multi-risk families*. Baltimore, MD: Brookes.

Maynard, T., & Thomas, N. (Eds.). (2005). An introduction to early childhood studies. Thousand Oaks, CA: Sage.

McCartney, K., & Phillips, D. (Eds.). (2005). *Blackwell handbook of early childhood development*. Williston, VT: Blackwell.

Paley, V. G. (1988). *Bad guys don't have birthdays: Fantasy play at four*. Chicago: University of Chicago Press.

Sroufe, L. A., Egeland, B., Carlson, E. A., & Collins, W. A. (2005). *The development of the person*. New York: Guilford.

Wolpert, E. (2005). *Start seeing diversity*. St. Paul, MN: Redleaf Press.

## SUGGESTED ACTIVITIES

1. Start a child development journal. A journal is a record of daily actions and reactions. In this case, it is a record of your activities and reactions regarding children and your role with them. Use a spiral notebook for the journal. Each day as you read, attend class, observe, and interact with young children, store your reactions in your memory. Each evening, take out the journal, write the day's date, and record whatever you feel is important. Start by recording your present feelings about children. As a start, think about your past experiences as a child and with other children and write down whatever seems important. As you go through the course, record any changes or confirmations that occur because of your new experiences. A journal entry might appear as follows:

| Date | Entry |
|---|---|
| 1/23/06 | Today I observed at the child development center. Johnny, who I find very irritating because of his constant whining, was lying on the floor screaming and kicking. I had a chance to speak with one of the teachers later and found out that Johnny's parents have just separated after a long period of fighting and bickering. No wonder Johnny is such a sad person. I can see now where you need to know the whole picture to make an accurate judgment about a child. Johnny's situation makes me feel very sad. A happy note!: Terry moved away from the blocks today and painted a picture. In class we talked about the value of play for young children—I'll never again feel that play is a waste of time. I'm really beginning to see its value. |

2. Arrange a visit go to a child development center by calling the director. Observe an infant, a toddler, a three-year-old, a four-year-old, and a five-year-old. Spend 20 minutes watching each child. Compare their behavior with the general descriptions in this chapter. Were these children the same or different from what you expected from your reading in the text? In what ways? List questions regarding the comparison and/or additional things you would like to know about the specific children observed and about child development. Share the experiences in class.

3. Go to an elementary school. Observe children in kindergarten through third grade. Spend 20 to 30 minutes at each grade level. Compare the behaviors you observe with the descriptions in this unit. Were these children the same or different from what you expected from your reading in the text? In what ways? List questions regarding the comparisons and/or additional things you would like to know about the children you observed and about child development. Share your experiences in class.

4. Observe two or three children for 1 hour at school and for 1 hour at home. Write a description of each interaction the child has with an adult. Compare similarities and differences between the child's home and school behavior. Compare similarities and differences between the behavior of the adults at home and at school. If differences were observed, speculate on the reasons for those differences. Share your experience in class.

5. Interview a teacher of young children. Ask the person to talk about characteristics of typical infants; toddlers, three-, four-, and five-year-olds; and six- to eight-year-olds. Ask the teacher if there is any preference as to which age she or he would rather teach. Compare these pictures of "typical" young children with those in this book. Discuss your findings with the other students in class.

6. Interview two of the following: a nurse, a pediatrician, a social worker, a dentist, a camp director, a psychologist, or another professional who works with young children in a nonteaching role. What differences do they see in infants; toddlers; three-, four-, and five-year-olds; and six- to eight-year-olds? What kinds of special techniques, if any, do they use with young children that are different from those they use with older children and adults? What do they find most rewarding and most frustrating about working with young children?

## REVIEW

1. List five settings in which adults work in a professional capacity with young children.
2. Decide whether each of the following incidents involves an infant, a toddler, a three-year-old, a four-year-old, a five-year-old, or a six- through eight-year-old child.
   a. Tom and Larry are playing nicely together with blocks. They have built a large fort. Suddenly Bill comes along and tries to knock it down. "Mr. Jones! Mr. Jones! Help! We need you!" shouts Tom.
   b. Five children are cuddled up against one teacher as she reads them a story. Each seems to need a part of her lap.
   c. The dentist announces he is ready to see Mary. She enters the office with confidence and a cheery smile. "Climb up in this big chair, Mary." Mary climbs up agilely and confidently.
   d. Mrs. Cohen is concerned. What *was* a sweet and agreeable child just a short time ago is now bossy, rude, and testing limits. Mr. Jones assures her that this type of behavior swing is normal at this age.
   e. Bill and Derrick are putting LEGO® airplanes together. They are in deep concentration, discussing where each of the small parts belongs and sharing information they have read about different kinds of aircraft. They are both saving up their allowance to buy a model space shuttle building kit.
   f. Billy is racing around the house laughing and yelling. Mrs. Garcia, his child care provider, believes he is taunting her and trying to show his superiority.
   g. As spring approaches, Mr. Woods suddenly finds the children in his group are becoming more creative and thinking of more projects on their own. He finds he needs to provide more materials and activities to support their ideas than he had to do in the past.
   h. Mrs. Hopkins finds Kate has pulled herself to her feet and is cruising around the living room, holding onto each piece of furniture as she goes.
3. Why are relationships with adults critical to young children's healthy growth and development?

## KEY TERMS LIST

developmentally appropriate practices (DAP)
high-risk children
infants
kindergartners
NAEYC
preschoolers
primary period
toddlers
young children

Additional resources for this chapter can be found on the Online Companion™ to accompany this text at http://www.earlychilded.delmar.com. Respond to "Time to Reflect" and "Looking Further" concepts, review various child development scenarios, and answer thought-provoking questions in the Critical Thinking Forum. Keep a daily journal by downloading the student journal available on this Web site. Complete the interactive matching exercises to reinforce concepts, and print out the child development assessment forms to use during your observation of development for children from birth to age eight. In addition, read the case studies on the Web site to reinforce the important concepts in each chapter, and take a look at the multitude of Web links that are available for student research on the Internet.

CHAPTER

# 2

# Developmental and Learning Theories

## OBJECTIVES

After reading this chapter, you should be able to:

- Define the term *theory* and identify developmental and learning theories, including the normative views.
- Recognize definitions of cognitive, affective, physical, motor developmental, and learning areas.
- Name important theorists/researchers.
- Identify some practical applications of theory.
- Describe cautions that should be used when applying theory to the lower socioeconomic level and/or minority group child.
- Define and apply sociocultural theory.

The study of children has been a subject of great interest during the twentieth century. Scholars have gathered information about and from children and have used this information to formulate ideas about how children grow and develop. Most scholars are researchers who mainly gather information. However, some scholars are researchers and theorists. Theorists/researchers go beyond their data to develop broad ideas that attempt to explain how children learn and grow. These ideas are called **theories.** A theory is designed to show one plan or set of rules that explains, describes, or predicts what happens when children grow and learn. Several popular theories are described in this unit.

**theories**

Ideas designed to show one plan or set of rules that explains, describes, or predicts what happens and what will happen when children grow and learn.

## TYPES OF THEORIES

Child development theories have conventionally been the foundation of educational and child-rearing practices. The guidelines for practice in early childhood education published by the NAEYC are called Guidelines for Developmentally Appropriate Practice (DAP) (Bredekamp, 1987; Bredekamp & Copple, 1997). DAP is age appropriate and individually and culturally appropriate. In recent times, the cultural relevance of these theories has been questioned by developmental psychologists (i.e., Coll et al., 1996; Greenfield & Cocking, 1994; Goodnow, Miller, & Kessel, 1995) and highly criticized by those concerned with the care and education of minority and lower–socioeconomic-level young children (i.e., Mallory & New,

1994; Lubeck, 1998). The basis for this criticism is that the theories were developed by European Americans from a European American point of view. Therefore, they do not necessarily apply to other cultures, ethnic groups, and races such as Asian, African, Latino, and Native American, both in the United States and in their native countries. Thus, theorists have moved toward applying a strong sociocultural theoretical foundation to early education and development. For example, Hyun and Marshall (1997) have proposed a model that combines DAP and a multicultural perspective. This model is labeled **developmentally and culturally appropriate practice (DCAP).** After describing the major developmental and learning theories and the views of those who propose a stronger cultural basis for child development theories, this unit concludes with some cautions in applying the conventional child development perspectives to early development and education.

**developmentally and culturally appropriate practice (DCAP)**

An elaboration of DAP that focuses more strongly on cultural appropriateness (Hyun & Marshall, 1997).

## Theories of Child Development and Learning: The Developmental Psychology View

Some theorists identified with child development focus on growth, some on how learning takes place, and some on both. The term **growth** usually refers to a sequence of changes or stages that takes place on the way to adulthood and is controlled, for the most part, by an inherited timetable. For example, a child's head reaches full growth before his or her trunk. **Learning** refers to behavioral changes caused by environmental influences. A child in the United States might learn English or Spanish as a first language, whereas a child in Germany learns German. **Developmental theories** usually explain changes in the child that result from interaction between growth and learning. Every child develops in a similar manner. For example, infants explore objects by sight, taste, touch, sound, and smell before they learn that these objects still exist when out of their sight. Theories emphasizing change that originates in the environment through learning are called **behaviorist theories.** For example, if children hear language, imitate it, and are rewarded for making sounds, they will learn to talk. Behaviorist theories explain how the child learns regardless of his or her age or stage. Some learning-oriented theories explain what is happening in the mind. Others look only at behavior that can be seen. To sum up, behaviorists focus strongly on external environmental factors as they affect learning and development. Developmentalists focus on the interaction between internal genetic factors and environmental factors as children learn new concepts and skills that enable them to transition from one developmental stage to the next.

**growth**

A series of steps or stages a child goes through on the way to becoming an adult.

**learning**

Behavior change that results from experience.

**developmental theories**

Ideas that explain changes in a child due to interaction between growth and learning.

**behaviorist theories**

Ideas emphasizing change that originates in the environment through learning.

The normative/maturational view is another way of looking at development. **Norms** define what most children do at a certain age. The **normative/maturational view** stresses certain norms, such as the time when most children can sit up, crawl, walk, talk, count to 10, or play cooperatively with other children. Other norms define the average size, shape, weight, or height of a child at a specific age. Furthermore, norms can suggest typical behavioral characteristics, such as the fact that toddlers are naturally negative because they try so hard to be independent. Theories and norms are related in that theories try to explain why norms occur as they do.

**norms**

What most children do at a certain age.

**normative/maturational view**

A way of looking at development that stresses certain norms.

Theories differ regarding the specific part of growth and learning they try to explain and describe. For purposes of study, child growth is usually divided into four areas: cognitive, affective, physical, and motor.

**Cognitive growth** centers on the mind and how the mind works as a child grows and learns.

**cognitive growth**

Centers on the mind and how the mind works as a child grows and learns.

Jenny, age 14 months, points to her pet cat and says,"Ki Ki." Jenny is learning to speak and has learned the concept *cat* ("Ki Ki").

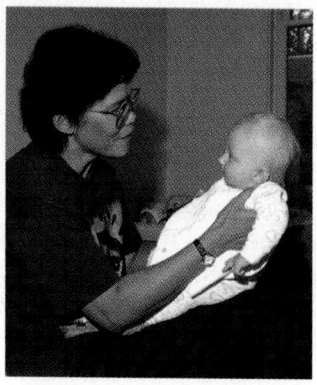

FIGURE 2–1 Emotional support from a warm, concerned adult helps the child develop in the affective domain.

Javier, age three, wants a cup. He tries but can't reach. He pulls the kitchen stool over, climbs up, and gets the cup. Javier has solved a problem.

Lai, age five, is given a plate of cookies and told to give the same number of cookies to each child in her class. She goes from one child to another, giving each child one cookie at a time. Lai understands that by using the idea of one-to-one correspondence, she can divide a group of things into groups of equal size.

Bill, age six, takes three red blocks and four blue blocks and combines them into one group. Then, he picks up his pencil and on a sheet of paper he writes 3 + 4 = 7. Bill is making the connection between concrete objects and abstract symbols.

**affective growth**

Centers on the self-concept and the development of social, emotional, and personality characteristics.

**Affective growth** centers on the self-concept and the development of social, emotional, and personality characteristics (Figure 2–1).

Mrs. Smith holds Tony, age one month, in her arms, rocking him and softly singing a lullaby. Mrs. Smith is helping Tony experience the attachment necessary as the basis for later independence.

John, age four, almost always smiles and looks happy. Other children like him and want to play with him. He is always kind to other children and tries to find a place for them in his play. John has a positive self-concept and has developed well in the affective area.

Louisa, age five, takes whatever she wants and hits children who try to defend their property. She has not yet acquired the skills to interact positively with others.

Thuy, age six, would like to have a candy bar before dinner. However, her mother has told her she will have to wait until after dinner. Just thinking about taking a candy bar makes her feel guilty. At six, Thuy has developed a conscience that tells her not to disobey her mother.

**physical growth**

Development of the body and its parts.

**Physical growth** has to do with development of the body and its parts (Figure 2–2).

John, age four, weighs 36.6 lb (16.6 kg) and is 3.4 ft (104 cm) tall. This is average for his age.

Kerry, age two-and-a-half, weighs 35.5 lb (16.1 kg) and her height is 2.95 ft (90 cm). She is below average in height and above in weight. She appears short and chubby.

Carlos, at age seven, is well proportioned. His legs have outgrown their toddler stubbiness.

**motor development**

The development of skill in the use of the body and its parts.

**Motor development** refers to the development of skill in the use of the body and its parts (Figure 2–3).

Pete, age three, does well at lunch. He eats his soup with a spoon, spilling very little, and easily pours milk from a pitcher.

Rosa, almost age five, hasn't yet learned to skip, can hop on one foot only three times without losing her balance, and can't walk a straight line.

Azam, age seven, and several of his classmates have joined an after-school soccer team. Azam can now coordinate his body and his mind and is ready to engage in team sports with rules.

Child development theorists attempt to describe basic processes that explain how children learn and when they are more likely to learn specific concepts and skills. Some theorists believe that people learn in much the same way, whatever their age. Others believe that learning is done in a different way as the person progresses

FIGURE 2–2 The preschool child has reached a stage of physical/motor development in which he can participate and enjoy complex activities, such as playing catch.

through different stages. It is important for teachers of young children to be familiar with a variety of theoretical approaches to understand, explain, and respond to young children's behavior.

Some theorists whose ideas have been very influential are Jean Piaget, Lev Vygotsky, Sigmund Freud, Erik Erikson, B. F. Skinner, Albert Bandura, Carl Rogers, and Abraham Maslow. The normative/maturational view of Arnold Gesell has also added a great deal to our knowledge of child development. Figure 2–4 outlines the areas that these theorists attempt to explain through theory development and research.

Each theorist is interested mainly in one area of development and/or learning. Skinner is the exception. His theory offers an explanation for any learned behavior, whether cognitive, affective, physical, or motor. Bandura is known for his work on social learning, Piaget for his work on the development of logical thought and sociomoral knowledge and behavior, Vygotsky for his contributions to our view of how children learn to think and speak and the importance of adult and peer social interaction to the young child's learning, and Freud and Erikson for their theories of social and personality development. Rogers focuses on the development and organization of the self-concept, Maslow on the hierarchical nature of human needs, and Gesell on the development of growth and development norms and their practical applications for child-rearing and teaching.

Several of these theorists/researchers view growth and learning as proceeding in an orderly fashion from birth to adulthood. Figure 2–5 shows the stages associated with each theorist. The data gathered by Gesell indicate that physical and motor growth develop at a continuous, rapid rate that levels off at approximately six years of age. According to Piaget, the young child proceeds through two periods of cognitive and sociomoral development from birth to about age seven. In the affective area, Freud and Erikson each look at different aspects of development. Erikson was Freud's student. Therefore, it is not surprising that the three-step structure of their early childhood stages is similar. However, whereas Freud's stages focus on the child's psychosexual interests, Erikson's focus on the psychosocial side. Vygotsky believes that child development proceeds through a series of five stages. He focuses on the social aspects of learning, that is, the role of adults and older children in supporting cognitive, self-regulation, and language development.

FIGURE 2–3 The kindergartner is nearing the time when motor control can be used to play simple group games, such as bounce the ball with a parachute.

Maslow and Rogers are neither strictly learning nor strictly developmental theorists. Their ideas focus on the process of achieving a positive self-concept. Love from parents and positive interaction with peers help the child move toward adult self-actualization. The self-actualized adult's basic needs for survival, security, belonging, and esteem are fulfilled. The adult is then able to fulfill intellectual and aesthetic needs and become a fully functioning person.

Piaget's and Vygotsky's theories are the most popular guides to early childhood education and development. Their ideas focus on both the cognitive and affective views

| | Type of Theory | |
|---|---|---|
| Tries to Explain Changes in: | Developmental: Growth and Learning Interact | Behaviorist: Learning Is the Main Determiner of Behavior |
| Cognitive Area<br>language<br>concepts<br>problem solving<br>intellectual needs | Cognitive-Developmental<br>Development Leads<br>(Jean Piaget)<br>Language/Communication<br>Learning Leads<br>(Lev Vygotsky)<br>Normative/Maturational<br>(Arnold Gesell)<br>Self-Actualization<br>(Abraham Maslow)<br>Example: A supportive adult and a rich environment with freedom for exploration will allow learning and intellectual growth. | Behaviorist (B. F. Skinner)<br>Examples: Learning to speak. Learning red, blue, and yellow are colors.<br>Social Cognitive Theory<br>(Albert Bandura)<br>Example: The child observes the language users of his or her culture and imitates what he or she sees and hears. |
| Affective Area<br>aggression<br>dependency<br>cooperation fears<br>self-concept<br>affective needs<br>motivation | Psychosexual<br>(Sigmund Freud)<br>Psychosocial<br>(Erik Erikson)<br>Self-Concept<br>(Carl Rogers)<br>Self-Actualization<br>(Abraham Maslow)<br>Sociocultural (Vygotsky)<br>Sociomoral (Piaget)<br>Examples: Through play, the young child learns the benefits of cooperation. Dependency must develop first for the child to become independent later. | Behaviorist (B. F. Skinner)<br>Examples: Learning to hug and not to hit. Learning to help others.<br>Social Cognitive Theory<br>(Albert Bandura)<br>Example: The child observes another child being praised for helping to set the table. The child imitates what he or she has seen and heard. |
| Physical and Motor Areas<br>body size and growth rate<br>motor skills (e.g., creeping, walking, grasping) | Normative/Maturational<br>(Arnold Gesell)<br>Example: The head and thus the brain have the fastest growth rate during early childhood; therefore, neurological growth is rapid and determines cognitive and motor growth. | Behaviorist (B. F. Skinner)<br>Examples: Complex skills, such as riding a bicycle or skating, and physically related behavior, such as eating nutritious food.<br>Social Cognitive Theory<br>(Albert Bandura)<br>Example: The child is told to watch while the coach kicks the soccer ball and then is asked to try to kick it the same way. |

**FIGURE 2–4** Theories of child development and learning. On the left side are the three major areas of development. The headings across the top indicate the two types of theories: developmental and behaviorist.

| | Areas | | | | |
|---|---|---|---|---|---|
| | Physical Motor | Affective | | Cognitive | |
| Age | (Gesell) | Social/ Personality (Erikson) | Personality (Freud) | (Piaget) | (Vygotsky) |
| Birth<br>16 mo | The body develops rapidly from head to toe (lifts head, then shoulders, then sits up) and from the center out (reaches, then grasps). | **Crisis I: Trust versus Mistrust** The relationship with the caretaker during feeding is central. | **Oral Stage:** The mouth is the source of pleasure; feeding and teething are central. | **The Sensori-motor Period:** The child's sensory (hearing, tasting, touching, seeing, smelling) and motor skills develop and are the means for learning. | **Infancy** (2 mo–1 yr) Leading Activity: emotional com-munication. Private Speech: public cooing and babbling. |
| 18 mo–2 yr<br>3 yr | | **Crisis II: Autonomy versus Shame and Doubt** The child strives for independence. | **Anal Stage:** Bowel movements are a source of pleasure. Toilet training is a critical area. | **The Pre-operational Period:** Language and cognitive development are rapid as learning takes place through imitation, play, and other self-initiated activities. | **Early Childhood** (1–3 yr) Leading Activity: manipulation of objects. Overt private speech develops self-regulation. |
| 6 yr | By age six, the rate of development levels off. | **Crisis III: Initiative versus Guilt** The child plans and carries out activities and learns society's boundaries. | **Phallic Stage:** Sex role identification and conscience development are critical. | | **Preschool Age** (3–7 yr) Leading Activity: play. Overt private speech develops self-regulation. |
| 7–13 yr | Child can engage in activities requiring more physical strength and coordination. | **Crisis IV: Industry versus Inferiority** The child needs to be productive and successful. Failure results in feelings of inferiority. | **Latency Stage:** The child consolidates previous stages' developments. | **Concrete Operations:** Abstract symbols and ideas can be applied to concrete experiences. | **School Age** (7–13 yr) Leading Activity: learning. Silent private speech serves to regulate task-related behavior and performance. |

**FIGURE 2–5** Stages of development from birth to age 13.

**constructivist**

A believer in the idea that children construct their own knowledge through interaction with the environment.

of learning and are the foundation of the **constructivist** approach that is the basis of DAP. Initially, the constructivist approach grew out of Piaget's theory (DeVries & Kohlberg, 1987, 1990; DeVries, 1997; DeVries, Zan, Hildebrandt, Edmiaston, & Sales, 2002; Papert, 2004). Later, Vygotsky's theory was incorporated (Bodrova & Leong, 1996; Berk & Winsler, 1995). For those working with children with special needs, behaviorist theory is also widely used. Behaviorist theory is useful in analyzing behaviors and creating programs aimed at specific developmental and instructional needs.

## Theories of Development and Learning: The Sociocultural View

Since the publication of the DAP guidelines, increasing attention has been given to the appropriateness of applying developmental theory to early education and the development of children from diverse cultures and with diverse capabilities. Critics believe that because the most popular theories were created by white males of European heritage, they may not apply beyond the populations studied by these theorists/researchers (New & Mallory, 1994). NAEYC has addressed this critique in the revised guidelines (Bredekamp & Copple,1997). However, these efforts have not satisfied critics.

Early childhood educators who do not accept developmental and learning theories as the foundation of understanding and planning for young children believe that sociocultural factors should provide the basis for the education of young children. Lubeck (1998) believes that the traditional early childhood developmental view causes pressure to conform and decreased respect for diversity by presenting universal developmental stages that suggest universal methods of instruction. Lubeck also believes that early educators should be less firm in their convictions and should avoid formulating guidelines based on consensus. Instead, planning for children should grow out of cultural and community beliefs and interests. Ryan & Grieshaber (2004) believe that a developmental knowledge base is not adequate for teaching children in today's world. They question whether culturally appropriate practice can be based on research done with homogeneous white, middle-class populations. They believe that the conventional child development view is out of date and doesn't recognize the issues faced by children in current society. Ryan and Grieshaber view children from a **critical theory** perspective. Critical theorists look at the power relationships in the classrooms. They encourage teachers to "make sense of the ways their practices can contribute to unequal opportunities for students" (Ryan & Grieshaber, 2004, p. 45). They believe knowledge is socially constructed and that there are no universal truths, principles, or laws that can be applied to everyone as implied in developmental and behaviorist theory. Thus, it can be seen that there is a major difference between the developmental and behaviorist and critical theory views. This author (Charlesworth, 1998) believes that developmental universals exist and that the developing child should be the focus of educational planning, with cultural and community interests being an essential consideration. This view does not preclude, but supports, flexibility in specific planning. Child development and learning should be viewed for individual children within their cultural context as suggested by a variety of professionals in the field (see Mallory & New, 1994).

**critical theory**

Encourages teachers to examine the power relationships in the classroom.

## Ecological Theory

An interest has developed in recent years on person-in-context views (Miller, 2002). This type of theory is closely related to the sociocultural views in that individuals are viewed within their cultures. Bronfenbrenner's *ecological-systems* approach has been very influential. A diagram of Bronfenbrenner's system is included in Chapter 3. His theory is made up of layers which range from the child's immediate environment, such as home, school, and peer group, which links with societal institutions, such as an economic system, government, and mass media, which in turn links with the beliefs and values of society. The layers interact with each other and with the child.

The last part of this chapter includes descriptions of the cultural view of child development from the author's standpoint, as well as from a group of minority child-development researchers. From this material, the reader should formulate a personal view of how, and if, child development theory and research provide a foundation for educational practice.

## THEORY APPLICATION

To clarify the ideas of these important theorists, a brief example of an application of each theory follows.

### Application 1: Piaget

A teacher of young children wants to know whether preschool children really need to role-play. From reading Piaget, the teacher finds that Piaget believes that dramatic play is essential to cognitive development. Through pretending to be someone else and through the use of objects for purposes other than their original intent (e.g., sand used to make a pie), children have their first symbolic experiences. These experiences are the basis for more abstract symbol learning, such as when children learn to use letters, numbers, and words as symbols (Figure 2–6). The teacher also investigates Vygotsky's view of play. Vygotsky emphasizes learning self-regulation through play; that is, children learn the rules of social interaction.

**scaffolding**

A process through which an adult supports the child's learning, providing support as the child moves from the current developmental level to a higher level.

### Application 2: Vygotsky

A child care provider wonders why it is important to provide support for children's language development through activities such as conversation and storybook sharing. At a professional meeting, the child care provider attends a session about **scaffolding.** Scaffolding is a process through which an adult supports the child's language development, thus reinforcing the child's efforts at verbal expression. It can be used during storybook sharing when the adult extends the experience by asking the child questions. The process continues by encouraging the child to ask questions and relating the story to the child's personal experiences.

FIGURE 2–6 Primary-level students enjoy working together on long-term, complex projects.

### Application 3: Erikson

A preschool teacher wonders how much freedom four- and five-year-olds need to work on their own. From Erikson, the teacher finds that the child must learn to take initiative when appropriate but, at the same time, learn the rules for the kinds of behaviors that are not allowed. The teacher realizes a delicate balance must be found between being too permissive and too restrictive.

## Application 4: Freud

Mrs. Ramirez, a child care mother, is concerned that two-year-old Tasha is not responding to toilet training. Mrs. Ramirez talks to a Freudian-trained psychologist at the health center. The psychologist explains to Mrs. Ramirez that toileting is a significant activity for a child Tasha's age and should be handled gently and patiently.

## Application 5: Maslow

Mr. Ogden, a kindergarten teacher, is concerned that the breakfast program at his school may not be funded next year. A good breakfast, he believes, is necessary not only for health reasons but also to give the child the security of knowing his or her basic needs will be met in a predictable fashion. A child who is concerned about where the next meal is coming from will not be able to concentrate on the social and cognitive needs that the school program is designed to fulfill.

## Application 6: Rogers

The local early childhood education professional group is contacting state legislators to gain their support to lower the adult/infant ratio in child care centers in the state. This group of educators supports its stand with the ideas of several experts, including Carl Rogers. According to Rogers, children must be loved and feel secure to grow into loving adults. This love and security comes through their relationships with their caregivers. Infants, especially, need a great deal of individual attention; a low adult/infant ratio helps fulfill this need.

## Application 7: Skinner

A child care provider is worried about a very aggressive child she has in her home each day. She seeks help from a psychologist who suggests a Skinnerian approach. The child care mother observes the child carefully each day for a week. She keeps a count of each time the child hurts another child or breaks a toy. She also notes each incident in which he does something that is not aggressive. The next week, she makes a point of giving him attention when he does anything positive and ignoring his bad behavior unless he is hurting someone, in which case he goes to the "cool down" chair until he regains control. After three weeks, she counts incidents of aggressive behavior and positive behavior. She finds that the positive behaviors have increased and the negative behaviors have decreased.

## Application 8: Bandura

A parent is concerned about her child's use of unacceptable language. She speaks with his teacher, who probes to find out where he might have learned such language. The mother realizes that her father, who lives with the family, peppers his speech with a great deal of profanity. Her son spends a lot of time with his grandfather and has observed and imitated his vocabulary.

## Application 9: Gesell

A mother is concerned about her three-and-a-half-year-old daughter's behavior. Her daughter's teacher reads to her from a book by Gesell and his coworkers:

> Something unexpected and confusing seems to happen to the smooth, conforming three-year-old as he turns three-and-a-half. Where did all this turbulence and trouble come from? Why is there such opposition, so much refusal to obey or even to try? (Gesell et al., 1974, p. 191).

The mother reads on and is relieved to find her child is a typical, if negative, three-and-a-half-year-old girl.

## Application 10: Sociocultural

John Hughes is principal of a school on a Navajo reservation. He is feeling frustrated because the parents of his students are not cooperative in seeing that their children attend school regularly. A friend recommends that he learn more about Navajo culture. He reads a chapter by Jennie R. Joe (1994) that explains Navajo customs regarding formal instruction. Mr. Hughes discovers that the Navajos divide learning into three different levels. Learning is lifelong and begins at birth. Initial instruction is informal and focuses on language, religion, customs, and other areas that are necessary for becoming a useful member of Navajo society. At the next level, an occupation is acquired and the necessary skills are learned through an apprenticeship. Formal instruction, the third level, is restricted to young adults who are interested in becoming healers or religious leaders.

This view explains why, when the U.S. government introduced formal schooling for children, most Navajos misunderstood the intent and refused to send their children. Also, because Navajos believe in individual autonomy, they did not force their children to go to school. On the other hand, the government prevented parental involvement in education so communication and information sharing were not instituted. After obtaining this information, Mr. Hughes sees that he needs to share information with parents and let them know that he wants schooling to be culturally relevant. He decides to meet with community leaders to develop a plan encouraging more parental involvement in classroom activities and policy and decision making. Parents would then see the value of formal education and support regular school attendance.

Figure 2–7 is a summary of the major developmental and learning theories applied to practice.

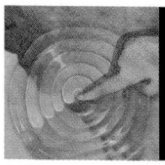

**LOOKING FURTHER**

Interview two or more teachers of young children. Find out whether they apply any theories of Piaget, Vygotsky, Skinner, Freud, Erikson, Gesell, Bandura, Maslow, and/or Rogers to their everyday interaction with young children. Use the following questions and/or some that you devise:

1. How are you influenced by developmental and/or learning theory? (Name some theorists if the teacher cannot think of any.)
2. Describe how you apply theory. What is a specific application?
3. Describe your teaching practice. What goals do you have for your students? Which kinds of activities are most important for your students? How important is it for students to have opportunities for exploration and for play?

Adults who work with young children must have a sound, underlying theoretical basis to support their actions (Glascott, 1994). Throughout this book, theory is applied to practice. However, caution is also taken to clarify some of the limitations of taking any theory too literally. Theory should always be considered within the child's sociological context of family, community, culture, and language.

| Theory | Adult Role | Environmental Factors |
|---|---|---|
| Cognitive-developmental/constructivist (Piaget and Vygotsky) | Guide; provider of scaffolding; sets the stage for learning | Some freedom and choice; concrete materials and activities; opportunities for social interaction |
| Psychoanalytic (Freud, Erikson, Rogers, Maslow) | Guide; especially focuses on the affective areas; sets the stage for learning | Some freedom and choice; concrete materials and activities; opportunities for social interaction; environment is therapeutic (nurturing and comfortable for expression of feelings) |
| Behaviorist (Skinner) | Director; sets the stage for learning; provides reinforcements and punishments; manages behavior | Allows for maximum positive reinforcement of appropriate adaptive behaviors |
| Social cognitive (Bandura) | Models appropriate behavior | Provides appropriate social models; clarifies appropriate behavior |
| Sociocultural (Lubeck, Ryan) | Facilitators and interventionists; assist children in recognizing their views of race, gender, and sex | Provide a varied environment that encourages children to develop their personal interests and examine their personal views |

**FIGURE 2–7** Summary of the major developmental and learning theories applied to practice.

## APPLYING DEVELOPMENTAL AND LEARNING THEORY AND RESEARCH WITH CAUTION

Stott and Bowman (1996) provide a thoughtful view of the relationship between theory and practice. They point out that theory and research are only one set of data that may shape teaching practice. The individual's personal experience and the children's roles in family and community are also important to the total picture. Therefore, theory and research should be applied with caution.

> What makes theories worth reading and discussing is not the assumption that they mirror reality but that they serve as suggestions or estimations—they help us arrange our minds. Theories are helpful in that they organize and give meaning to facts, and they guide further observation and research (Stott & Bowman, 1996, p. 171).

Stott and Bowman also point out that theory and research from other areas, such as anthropology, sociology, mathematics, various sciences, and the arts, contribute to ideas that may guide teaching practice. Furthermore, each person and each cultural group holds individual values regarding the goals of education. It is for this reason that teachers must be able to integrate multiple perspectives.

Developmental research can also be viewed from different perspectives. A group of minority child development researchers have developed a model for studying minority children's development (Coll et al., 1996) (Figure 2–8). This model is set up in a linear fashion, moving from the sociocultural variables to the child's competencies. Coll, et al. state that the primary developmental processes operate in the same fashion for children of color as for Caucasian children. However, it is very important to consider their special circumstances, such as racism, social position, culture, etc. Rather than accepting white, middle-class child-rearing approaches as applying to all children, child-rearing practices appropriate for children of color need to be considered. Equally important are the characteristics of the child. Age, temperament, health, maturational timing, and race are essential characteristics to consider. Coll, et al. also explain that there is evidence that children of color may have distinct biological factors that are important influences on their development. The Coll et al. model places these diverse factors at the core of many developmental influences. In Figure 2–9, the model is rearranged to

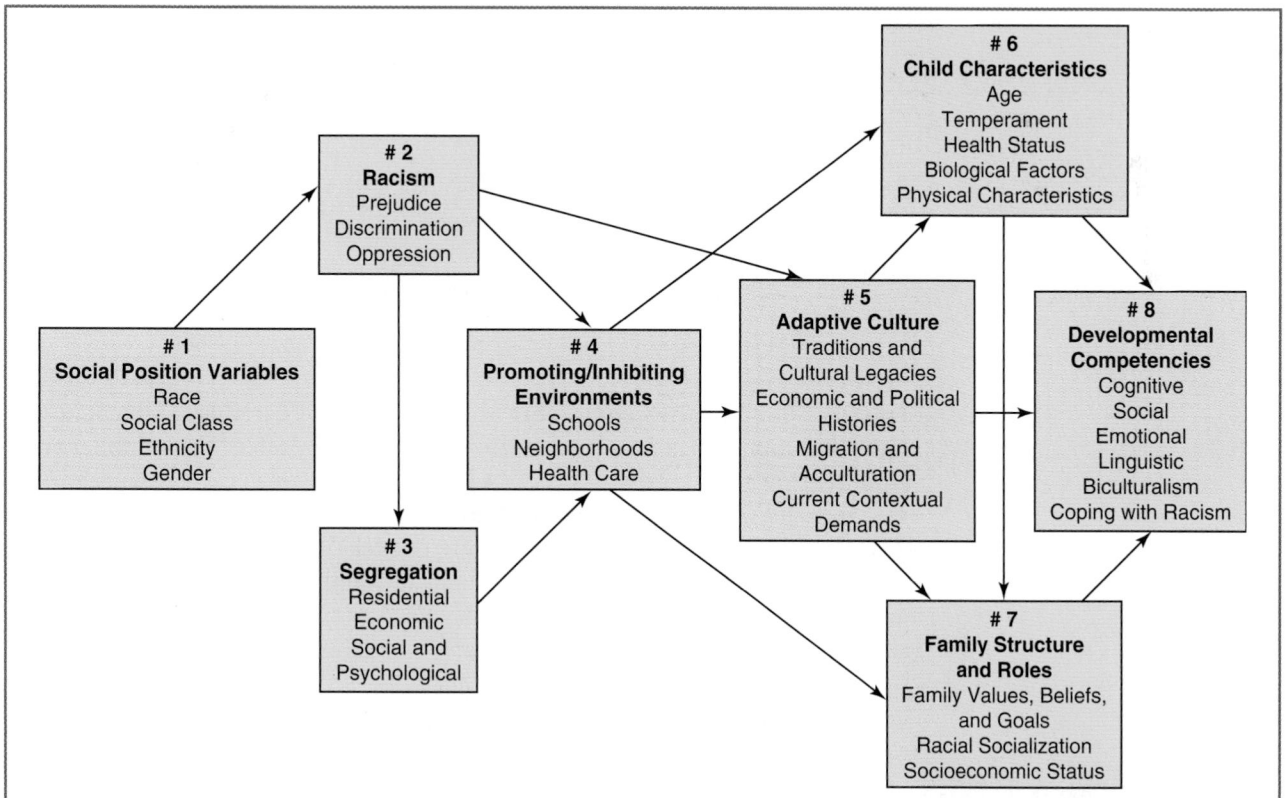


**FIGURE 2–8** Integrative model for the study of developmental competencies in minority children (Adapted from Coll, C. G., Lamberty, G., Jenkins, R., McAdoo, H. P., Crnic, K., Wasik, B. H., & Garcia, H. V. [1996]. An integrative model for the study of developmental competencies in minority children. *Child Development, 67,* 1891–1914. Reprinted with permission from Blackwell Publishing.).

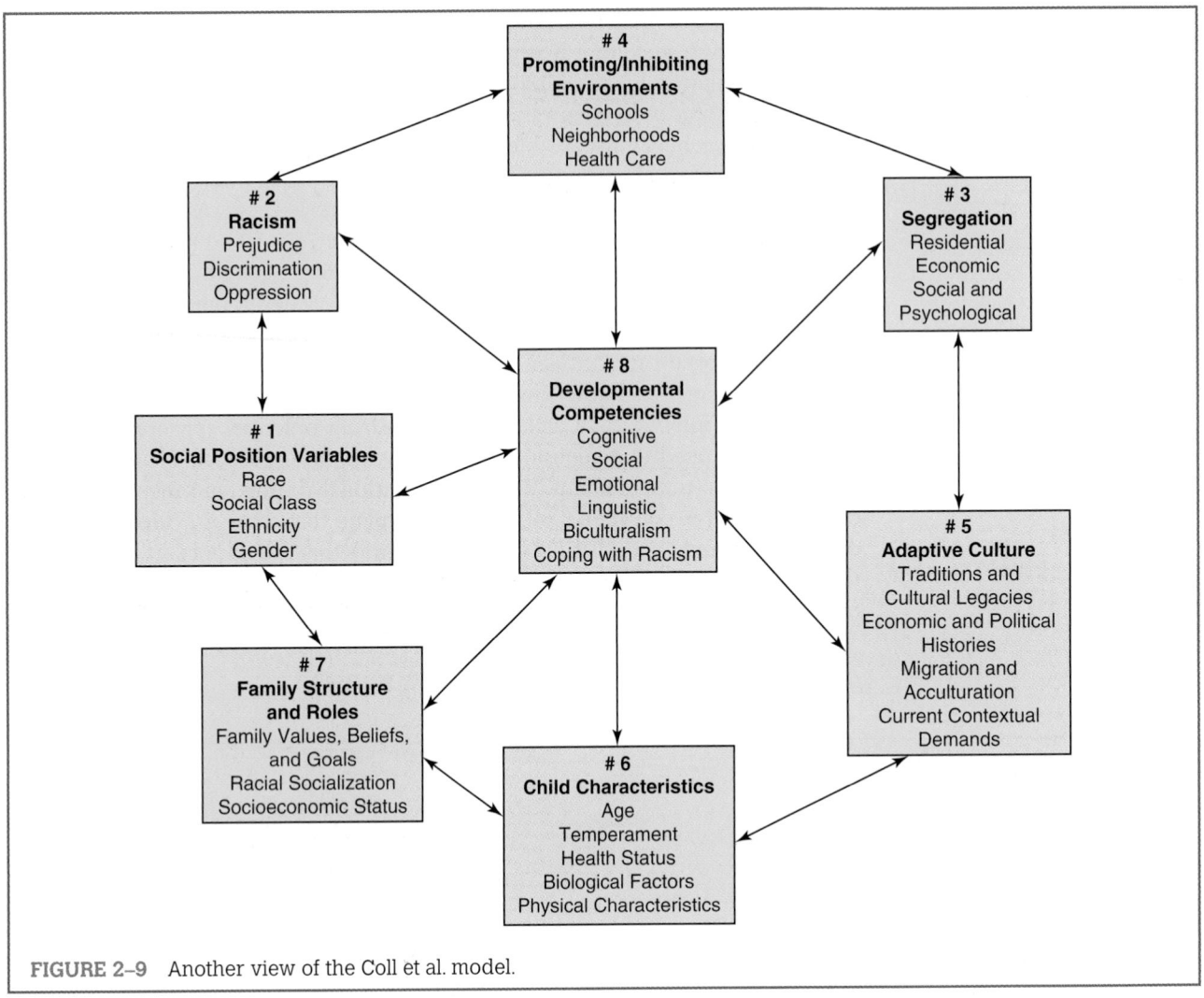


**FIGURE 2–9** Another view of the Coll et al. model.

depict the child at the center, with the sociocultural variables influencing the child's development and each other. Readers are free to select either model or develop their own.

Sociocultural and curriculum content views of behavior and development are woven in throughout this text to illustrate the relationships between culture and content, and development. To understand any individual child's development, adults who work with young children may need to select, combine, and integrate various theories and values.

From this overview of theories, which one(s) do you find most appealing? Why? Why must we be cautious in applying developmental theories and research to teaching practice?

## SUMMARY

Both developmental- and behavior-oriented theories attempt to explain what happens as children develop mental, social, physical, and motor skills. Sociocultural theory provides explanations from a more diverse view. Each type of approach to explaining early development can be applied to everyday work with children. More details regarding the views of these theorists/researchers and their application to everyday practice are included in following chapters. Ideally, child development and early childhood education should work as one (Elkind, 1993). This text is designed to demonstrate how this goal can be achieved.

## FOR FURTHER READING


DeJong, L. (2003). Using Erikson to work more effectively with teenage parents. *Young Children, 58*(2), 87–95.

Dickinson, D. K. (2002). Shifting images of developmentally appropriate practice as seen through different lenses. *Educational Researcher, 31*(1), 3–12.

Elkind, D. (2001). *The hurried child* (3rd ed.). Boulder, CO: Perseus.

Friedlmeier, W., Chakkarath, P., & Schwarz, B. (2005). *Culture and human development*. New York: Psychology Press.

Kozulin, A., Gindis, B., Ageyev, V. S., & Miller, S. M. (Eds.). (2003). *Vygotsky's educational theory in cultural context*. New York: Cambridge University Press.

Leonard, D. C. (2002). *Learning theories A to Z*. Westport, CT: Greenwood.

Lerner, I. M. (2002). *Concepts and theories of human development* (3rd ed.). Mahwah, NJ: Erlbaum.

Lewis, V. (2002). *Development and disability* (2nd ed.). Williston, VT: Blackwell.

Miller, P. H. (2002). *Theories of developmental psychology*. New York: Worth.

Oates, J., Grayson, A., & Wood, C. (Eds.). (2005). *Psychological development and early childhood*. Williston, VT: Blackwell.

Salkind, N. J. (2004). *An introduction to theories of human development*. Thousand Oaks, CA. Sage.

Scholnick, E. K. (1983–current). *Jean Piaget symposia series*. Mahwah, NJ: Erlbaum.

Thomas, R. M. (2000). *Recent theories of human development*. Thousand Oaks, CA: Sage.

Tryphon, A., & Voneche, J. (Eds.). (2001). *Working with Piaget: Essays in honour of Barbel Inhelder*. Philadelphia, PA: Psychology Press.


## SUGGESTED ACTIVITIES

1. Go to the library. Find an article in a journal, such as *Young Children*, *Dimensions*, *Early Childhood Education Journal*, or *Childhood Education*, that describes a way to apply the theories of Piaget, Vygotsky, or other theorists to your work with young children. Discuss the article and share your evaluation of the article with the class.

2. Go to a curriculum resource center and interview the director. Ask the director if there are any theory-based materials at the center. If so, examine them. Share a list of the materials and an evaluation of them with a small group of fellow students.

## REVIEW

1. Explain what a theory is.
2. Name one or more theorists/researchers associated with each of the following areas:
   a. cognitive development
   b. normative development
   c. affective development
   d. all areas of learned behavior
   e. affective learning
3. Match the names in Column I with the application descriptions in Column II.

| Column I | Column II |
|---|---|
| a. Gesel | 1. Johnny is playing nicely. His teacher compliments him. |
| b. Rogers | 2. Mary is pretending to make a pie from wet sand. |
| c. Maslow | 3. Mr. Jones tells the children they can plan and carry out an activity of their choice today. |
| d. Piaget | 4. Bill and Kate's father shares a storybook with them. He encourages them to ask questions and to relate the story to their own experiences. |
| e. Skinner | 5. "How old are children usually when they begin to walk?" |
| f. Erikson | 6. Five-year-old Theresa is very concerned about being female. |
| g. Freud | 7. Chan is a loved and secure four-year-old who is loving toward other children. |
| h. Bandura | 8. Every evening Liu Pei watches her mother fix dinner. One day she asks if she can help. Her mother is surprised to see how much Liu Pei has learned from her observations. |
| i. Vygotsky | 9. Jason Goodbird is identified by his teachers as a child who gets the most out of the activities at preschool. They note that he comes from a secure and loving home environment. |

4. Compare sociolcultural theoretical perspectives such as Ryan and Lubeck's or Coll et al.'s with conventional developmental theories.

## KEY TERMS LIST

affective growth
behaviorist theories
cognitive growth
constructivist
critical theory
developmental theories
developmentally and culturally appropriate practice (DCAP)
growth
learning
motor development
normative/maturational view
norms
physical growth
scaffolding
theories

Additional resources for this chapter can be found on the Online Companion™ to accompany this text at http://www.earlychilded.delmar.com. Respond to "Time to Reflect" and "Looking Further" concepts, review various child development scenarios, and answer thought-provoking questions in the "Critical Thinking Forum." Keep a daily journal by downloading the student journal available on this Web site. Complete the interactive matching exercises to reinforce concepts, and print out the child development assessment forms to use during your observation of development for children from birth to age eight. In addition, read the case studies on the Web site to reinforce the important concepts in each chapter, and take a look at the multitude of Web links that are available for student research on the Internet.

CHAPTER

# 3

# Studying the Young Child

## OBJECTIVES

After reading this chapter, you should be able to:

- Explain important historical factors in child study.
- Identify these methods of child study: anecdotal records, diary, observations, and interviews.
- List examples of current child study research questions and the focus of developmental research in the twenty-first century.
- Explain how teachers can be researchers.
- Compare developmentally appropriate and inappropriate assessment methods.
- Explain the need for a professional code of ethics.

Adults who work with young children have become more aware in recent years of the need to know how young children develop. Adults now realize that knowledge of child development is necessary to understand, interact with, and plan for children. However, this has not always been the case. Only during the twentieth century did the study of how children grow and learn develop into an area that stands on its own merit. Before the twentieth century, most adults did not feel there was anything special to be known about young children.

## A BRIEF HISTORY OF CHILD STUDY

Child development researchers study a host of questions and problems to find answers that will help those who work with young children. Examples of concerns relevant to child study in the twenty-first century include the effects of child care experience on young children's development, the effects of formal early education on children and their families, the influence of technology on the child's behavior and development, the characteristics of infants, the rate of brain growth, the effects of prenatal maternal substance abuse on children, literacy development, and the role of the father in the lives of young children.

Prior to the twentieth century, there was interest in child growth and development but little research. People proposed ideas about how a child grows and learns. They did little, if anything, though, to check if their ideas were supported in the real world of children and the adults with whom they interact.

**baby biographies**
Diary records of interesting things a particular child does each day.

In the late 1800s, **baby biographies** began to appear. These biographies were the first kinds of recorded child research. Parents kept diary records of interesting things their children did each day. These diaries inspired much of early child research. As the twentieth century approached, G. Stanley Hall performed the first organized research project on a large group of children. He asked parents all over the United States to fill out questionnaires about their children. This project was the beginning of child development as the field of study we know today.

In his presidential address to the members of the Society for Research in Child Development (SRCD) in 2003, Ross D. Parke (2004) provided a historical overview of the study of children as reflected in the work of historical figures in the field. With the organization of the SRCD in 1933, the study of child development became recognized. During the early years from 1933 to 1943, the major achievement in the field was the establishment of research institutes at the University of Iowa, University of Minnesota, Columbia University, Yale, Berkeley, and Fels. These institutes were modeled after the agricultural research stations on the premise that if hogs could be improved through research so could children. During this period, Arnold Gesell began his studies of children's motor development. Freud's psychoanalytic theory was very influential and Watson's behaviorism was still an important factor in the field. Piaget was becoming recognized in Europe. The important theorists in the 1933 through 1943 period were Freud, Watson, Gesell, and Piaget. From Freud came a focus on aggression, dependency, moral development, and gender roles. Watson provided the foundation for experimental child psychology. Piaget's influence didn't come to North America until the 1960s. Although Gesell's focus was mainly on motor development, he recognized that all areas of development are interdependent.

From 1943 to 1963, the interest in applying theories of learning to the study of development gained prominence. The objective was to translate Freud's areas of interest, such as aggression, sex-typing, and dependence into learning theory terms. John Whiting attempted to relate early child-rearing practices with later personality development. Robert R. Sears examined the relationships between early child-rearing practices, such weaning, toileting, punishment, dependency, etc. During this time, B. F. Skinner developed operant conditioning, which has been widely applied in the study of children. Sears's and Skinner's work reflected an interest in practical application. During the 1943 through 1963 period, there was an increased awareness of the influence of biology on behavior and the importance of the earliest experiences on development.

Parke (2004) describes the period from 1963 to 1983 as one dominated more by themes than theories. Major themes were concerns about cognitive development, infant sensitiveness, social leaning, social interaction, and the area of emotion. Sputnik made Americans concerned about our educational system, Piaget's work was translated into English and interpreted by J. McVicker Hunt and John Flavell. Piaget's view of the interaction between nature and nurture became popular. SRCD members became interested in social policy. In 1977, a Social Policy Committee was formed as a liaison to government as it became evident that child development knowledge could have important applications on finding solutions to social problems. Through Bronfenbrenner's work (described in this chapter), the importance of context became a major focus. Another major advance was the discovery of the tremendous learning capacity of infants.

From 1983 to 2003 Parke (2004) identified several themes that influenced research and theory: genetic and neurological bases of behavior, the interdependence of cognition and emotion, recognition of the role of culture, and a move toward more interdisciplinary research. Interest returned to some of the areas that were the focus of some of the early scholars in the field of child development. There was a return to interest in consciousness, reflection intention, motivation, and will. The interaction between cognition and emotion brought a focus on emotions, such as shame, guilt, pride, empathy, and social emotions, such as jealousy. The search for a grand theory of development was abandoned and more eclectic, flexible models of theory application were adopted. Theories became flexible guides for understanding development. Among the important discoveries, it was found that there are changes in the cortical function in the brain between five and seven years of age, which occur at the same time that there are shifts in children's learning and memory; there have been exciting findings in the area of genetic and hormonal influences on behavior and development. In the past, there were conflicting arguments regarding the evidence for heredity and for environment as influences on development. Currently, an interactionist view is more popular. This area is discussed in Chapter 9. For the future, Parke (2004) sees the need for more interdisciplinary research, more focus on solving childhood problems, and more cultural sensitivity. The study of child development has made much progress since it began, but there is still room for more progress. As time goes by, we see that children are complex and that we tend to come up with more questions than answers.

## THE IMPORTANCE OF CONTEXT

In the study of young children, we have a desire to learn everything. David G. Smith (no date) reminds us that we cannot define what a child is. We have to look at each child in relation to others, such as parents, teachers, and peers. Each one who has contact with a child has a personal picture of that child. Even when these pictures are assembled into one portrait, we still do not have all the pieces. As we consider child research and its applications, we need to be cautious and keep in mind that although it tries to explain all, it really cannot. Smith (p. 4) reminds us that "because the aim of Child Psychology's effort is to understand the child more completely, to contain him, and to control him, it misses the point. Children are always beyond our understanding because they are beyond us." Keeping this caution in mind, we can benefit from the bits and pieces of understanding gleaned from research in child development.

**ecological research model**

Viewing children in all their roles in all the areas of their environment.

**microsystem**

A child's relationship to home, school, neighborhood, peer group, and church.

**mesosystem**

The interactions and relationships between and among the child's home, school, neighborhood, peer groups, and church.

**exosystem**

A child's interactions and relationships with local government, parents' workplace, mass media, and local industry.

**macrosystem**

A child's interactions and relationships with the dominant beliefs and ideologies of the culture.

Although we will never know everything about any child, we want to know as much as we can. To accomplish this, Bronfenbrenner (1979, 1989, 1992) developed an **ecological research model** (Figure 3–1). Bronfenbrenner stresses the importance of viewing children in all their roles in all areas of their environment. Children must be studied within their **microsystem,** which includes their relationship to home, school, neighborhood, peer group, and church. Of equal importance are three other ecological systems that impact children's lives. Surrounding the microsystem is the **mesosystem.** The mesosystem includes the interactions and relationships between and among home, school, church, peer group, and neighborhood. Moving farther out into the world, additional influences come from the **exosystem,** which includes influences such as the local school board, local government, parents' workplace, mass media, and local industry. Beyond this system is the **macrosystem,** which encompasses the dominant beliefs and ideologies of the culture.

Within any microsystem component such as the classroom, "the structure and content of the setting, and the forms of developmental process that can take place within it, are to a large extent defined and delimited by the culture, subculture, or other macrosystem structure in which the microsystem is embedded" (Bronfenbrenner, 1989). As you look at children daily in the classroom, it is essential to consider these other outside factors as they influence children's behavior.

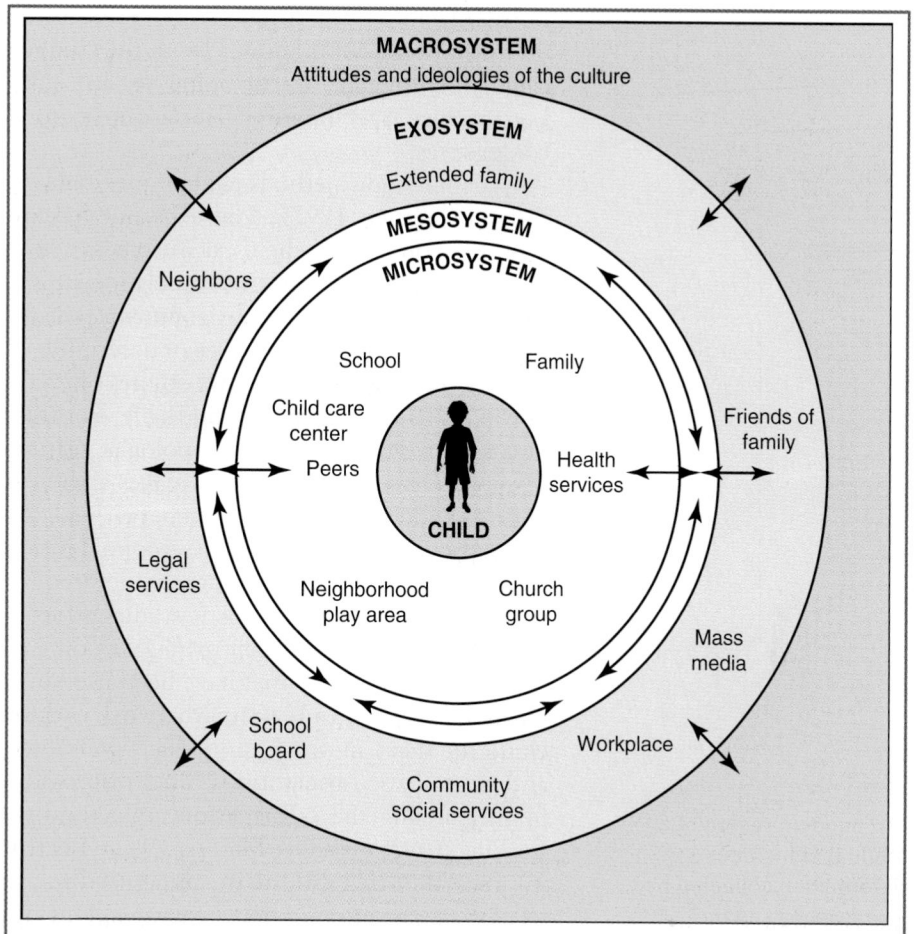


**FIGURE 3–1** Ecological research model (Reprinted by permission of Addison-Wesley Educational Publishing).

Cultural context is a critical consideration in the study of children (New, 1994). James P. Comer (Goldberg, 1997) says that in planning curriculum, instruction, and assessment for children, "I argue that it should be development first and that development should guide everything else" (p. 559). It is vital that adults who work with young children and their families study each child and family within their unique cultural context.

The developmental research field in the twenty-first century is very different from its beginnings in the twentieth century. Fabes, Martin, Hanish, & Updegraff (2000) summarized and evaluated some of these differences. From the narrow focus of descriptive studies and later experimental laboratory studies, the field has expanded out into topics influenced by the systems outlined by Bronfenbrenner (1979, 1989, 1992). More emphasis is placed on topics that will help improve the lives of children and have an effect on public policy (see Chapter 33). For example, the tragic school shootings that took place at the turn of the century were an impetus to more research on violence.

## METHODS OF CHILD STUDY

Each adult who works with young children needs to study those children in much the same way a researcher does. Adults need to know as much as possible about each child to plan appropriate learning environments. It is important that what is learned from a child development course is checked against and applied to children whom the adult knows. From the study of the children in their care, adults can obtain valuable information to use in planning for children and their families. For instance, specific information can be obtained to share with parents during conferences.

Child-study methods fall into two main categories: experimental and naturalistic (Pellegrini, 1991). The experimental approach sets up environments designed to control and elicit specific types of behavior. Experiments are designed to look at specific cause-and-effect relationships. The naturalistic approach looks at children in their everyday environments. Currently, naturalistic methods are gaining in popularity. Various types of descriptive studies of children's everyday activities are increasing. Descriptive studies offer a broader and more in-depth picture of what is happening in the child's life. For this type of study, the researcher takes on a role like that of the anthropologist visiting a new and unknown culture. The researcher takes detailed notes, makes audio and videotapes, and interviews those persons under study. The researcher either stays in the background or becomes an active participant within the classroom. This type of descriptive information supplements information from more structured observations in either naturalistic or laboratory settings. Naturalistic studies afford increasing opportunities for teachers to be researchers in their own classrooms.

Several methods that have been used in childhood research can be used by teachers, parents, and others who work with young children. These methods include the diary method, individual interviews with caretakers and/or children, and naturalistic observations. **Portfolio** systems are being developed as guides for organizing the information collected by teachers and students (Gelfer & Perkins, 1992; Grace & Shores, 1992). Portfolio systems also provide an ongoing record of the child that can be used to assist in making smooth transitions to new classrooms and new programs. During the course of your study of child development, numerous activities will be suggested that offer you the opportunity to try these techniques. Taking advantage of as many of these opportunities as possible will prove beneficial later in your career. The following are examples of these methods:

**portfolio**

An ongoing record of a child that includes information collected by the teacher and the student.

## Anecdotal Record

1. Child: Sam, it is his second day in the toddler room.
2. Setting/Activity: The children are finishing breakfast. Sam is still sitting at his place.
3. Anecdote: Sam was chewing on his napkin. He actually bit pieces off and was chewing with great energy as he glanced around at the rest of the room. Suddenly, teacher Heidi apparently noticed that he was finished and chewing on his napkin. She bent down and calmly indicated to him that he should spit the sodden remains of the napkin into the garbage tub. Sam turned, stood up, and willingly followed Heidi's directions as she demonstrated how to scrape his bowl and place it in the dirty dishes tub.

The anecdote is a short story that describes a significant incident. In this case, it is documentation that Sam appears to be comfortable starting school and is content to wait patiently (although eating the napkin may indicate some stress) until the next step in the breakfast routine is explained. An adult can jot down a brief note at the time of the incident and write a more detailed account later.

## Diary Method

Grandma is keeping a record of Summer's development.

> *June 15.* Today Summer [four years old] ran into the house eager to show me a book she was holding. She told me to sit in an armchair. She then perched on one arm and told me she would read me the story of *The Cat on the Mat*. She was very pleased with her accomplishment. She pointed to each word as she read and demonstrated a good understanding of the print to oral language relationship.

## Parent Interview

A parent is interviewed about her child's experience in child care (Paulsell & Nogales, 2003, p. 34).

> My son, he loves to go to school. If one day I can't take him to school or something, he will get mad at me. He says, "No Mama, I want to go to school. I have to go to school." We had spring break and all he talked about was going to school, but I'm like, "Honey, there's nobody at school." So it was pretty funny, he really wanted to go to school, and I knew he enjoyed his class.

## Interview with a Child

> Interviewer: What makes the clouds move along?
>
> Child: God does.
>
> Interviewer: How?
>
> Child: He pushes them . . . [the clouds] stay [in the air] because God wants them to stay (Piaget, 1966, p. 63).

## Running Record

It's the first day of toddler preschool after the holiday vacation. Teacher Ann is the head teacher and there are two new student teachers: Kate and Sandy. Summer's mom brings her in at 10:30 AM (half an hour after class has started). The other children are busily involved in center activities: water pouring, mini-trampolines, writing center, easel painting, playdough, home center, library, and tables with a variety of manipulatives. Summer looks around the room as her mother signs her in. Mom leaves. Summer heads right for the easel, grabs a paint brush and begins to paint. As she holds the paint brush, her attention goes toward the trampolines. She walks over and observes. A teacher asks if she would like to try one and steers her toward one, but she indicates she wishes to stand back and observe and then goes to a table where there is bright green playdough. A teacher invites Summer to sit. Summer grabs a lump of dough and pounds it on the table at the same time observing the rest of the activities. She gets up and scoots to the trampolines. While she appears to be making a decision, two of the bigger boys jump on to the vacant spaces. Summer returns to the easel.

From the diary record, we learn what a parent or other adult believes is important enough to write down. Thus, the information is very selective. However, an adult who understands and applies a thorough knowledge of child development to making selections can learn a great deal about what is happening with children as individuals and as a group. A teacher does not have time to write a detailed diary entry on each child every day but can write descriptions of individual incidents or anecdotes that seem of special importance (Bentzen, 2001; Nicolson & Shipstead, 1994).

Parent and child interviews are used to obtain information that is specific to something the interviewer would like to know. The parent interview information depends on the accuracy of the parent's memory of past events and the parent's

FIGURE 3–2 From an interview with parents, information is obtained on the parent's current child-rearing attitudes and current and past child-rearing methods.

FIGURE 3–3 Specific facts can be learned during a one-to-one child interview.

FIGURE 3–4 Naturalistic observation is used to find out what children do during their normal daily activities.

opinion of the child's behavior. It can be quite subjective, but it is still important and can yield information that would otherwise not be available (Figure 3–2). Child interviewing is critical to the process of teaching (Figure 3–3). Informal questioning (described more in later chapters) is a necessary means for finding out what young children know and how they think. Observation and interviewing are two of the teacher's most important tools.

In the example given, the running record observation was done by an outside person and describes what the child did in a detailed, factual way (Figure 3–4). The reader is left to decide what is important about the incident. This type of record is usually called a **running record** or a **specimen record** (Bentzen, 2004; Nicolson & Shipstead, 1994). It is time-consuming to gather information in this manner, but the yield can be very revealing. Developmental and educational researchers are turning more to naturalistic observations and interviews to gather information on children and teachers (New, 1994; McLean, 1993). Naturalistic observation can be done in a more structured and less time-consuming fashion using some predetermined categories or a checklist of behaviors (Bentzen, 2004; Nicolson & Shipstead, 1994).

Besides naturally occurring settings, such as the home, school, or playground, observations can also take place in laboratory settings where experimental studies are done. Laboratory settings are environments specially structured to elicit a certain type of behavior. For example, we may want to know how children behave with certain kinds of materials or people, such as peers or strange adults. By setting up the environment in a special way, there is more assurance that the type of information desired will be obtained.

Adults who work with and who gather data from young children must be skilled observers. For example, with the increasing diversity of our school population, teachers need to research each of their students to plan for them in a culturally relevant way. New (1994) suggests three roles teachers can take. First, using photographs, videotapes, audiotapes, children's work samples, anecdotal records, and other observation data, teachers can document children's daily activities. Second, teachers can experiment with a variety of teaching strategies and materials, seeking practices that promote motivation and learning for their students. Third, teachers can take on the role of anthropologists as they study the culture of each of their students. In early childhood education, the use of methodology involving collaboration between researchers and teachers, and teachers as researchers of their own practices, has been expanded.

## TEACHER RESEARCHERS

A **teacher researcher** is a classroom teacher who does a carefully planned, systematic, and documented study of activities designed to solve a classroom instructional

**running record**

A naturalistic observation done by an outside person that describes what the child did in a factual way and in great detail; also called a specimen record.

**specimen record**

See *running record.*

**teacher researcher**

A classroom teacher who does a carefully planned and documented study of action designed to solve a classroom instructional problem or introduce a new teaching practice; often done in collaboration with university personnel.

problem or introduce a new teaching practice. The study is often done in collaboration with university personnel, but this is not a prerequisite. Teacher researchers become constructors of knowledge and, thus, gain feelings of empowerment. Curriculum development emerges from the classroom instead of being handed down from the administration. Teachers may use quantitative or qualitative methods for their action research (McLean, 1997). McLean (1997) maps a sequence from conceptualization to implementation to interpretation.

The role of teachers as researchers is becoming increasingly important (New, 1994). Teachers are gathering information about their students, their students' families, their students' communities, and themselves. Teachers are becoming more reflective about their own practices and writing their own stories (McLean, 1993). Case studies, oral histories, and other narratives documenting teachers' life experiences are rapidly appearing in print. Teachers' stories provide in-depth information upon which others can reflect. These stories provide whole pictures in contrast to the more specific, but less colorful, information that has conventionally been the result of research on larger groups of subjects.

For most teachers, research involves gathering information regarding their instruction and their students. It may include gathering information for student portfolios, recording the results of a new instructional method, or collecting detailed information on an individual child.

Whether engaged in formal or informal projects, adults who work with young children can and should be researchers who systematically collect information about children and their ecological systems to answer questions that will make their work more effective.

## THE CHALLENGE OF INAPPROPRIATE ASSESSMENT

The pressure of required standardized testing is frustrating to teachers at all levels (Kohn, 2001). Even in prekindergarten programs, such as Head Start, a multitude of assessments are required. Teachers are pressured to meet standards of achievement that force them to use more developmentally inappropriate instructional practices in order to prepare for narrowly focused, developmentally inappropriate tests (Popham, 2005). Young children do not develop at exactly the same pace at every age. Even if they have mastered a concept or skill, they may not be able to show it on a group-administered test. Even individually administered assessments can present problems. Often, such an assessment can be too narrowly focused and consume valuable instructional time. For example, the current Reading First Initiative requires assessment of early literacy skills using Dynamic Indicators of Early Literacy Skills (DIBELS), which has a narrow focus and takes up time that might be better used for more appropriate assessment methods. DIBELS focuses on subskills, ignoring skills such as comprehension of the material (Gordinier & Foster, 2004/2005).

These mandated testing requirements can be very stressful for both teachers and students. The challenge for teachers is to do the minimal amount of specific test preparation so that most class time can be spent on meaningful learning and appropriate assessment. In addition, teachers and parents need to take action to change the system (Kohn, 2001) (See Chapter 33). Appropriate assessment methods for young children include observation records, interviews, collections of children's work samples, checklists, rating scales, and rubrics (a defined assessment guide) (McAfee, Leong, & Bodrova, 2004). These strategies and tools can become a part of everyday instruction. Throughout this text, these types of assessment tools are provided for you to use.

Think about your experiences with testing. How do you feel when you have to take a test? Can you remember any of your early experiences in elementary or high school? Have you spoken with any teachers or children about their experiences? Compare your experiences with those of other people in your class.

## PROFESSIONAL ETHICS

Whether a teacher, a researcher, or a student of child development, one must always follow the principles of professional ethical conduct. The NAEYC has adopted such a code (Feeney & Freeman, 1999; NAEYC's Code of Ethical Conduct, 1996). This code is designed to assist teachers and others in solving ethical dilemmas. The code focuses on the daily practice of those adults who work with young children ages birth through age eight and their families. However, "many of the provisions also apply to specialists who do not work directly with children, including program administrators, parent educators, college professors, and child-care licensing specialists" (NAEYC's Code of Ethical Conduct, 1996, p. 57). The code also applies to students of child development and early childhood education. The code addresses professional responsibilities in four areas: (1) children, (2) families, (3) colleagues, and (4) community and society. The code includes ideals and principles for each area. The **ideals** reflect the goals of practitioners. The **principles** are guides for conduct and can help solve ethical problems. Ethical problems are those for which there is no clear answer for reaching a solution. The key, most critical principle is:

**ideals**
These are the goals of practitioners.

**principles**
These are guides for conduct and can help solve ethical problems.

> **P.1.1—Above all, we shall not harm children. We shall not participate in practices that are emotionally damaging, physically harmful, disrespectful, degrading, dangerous, exploitative, or intimidating to children. *This principle has precedence over all others in the code.*** (NAEYC, 2005)

The American Educational Research Association (AERA) has *Ethical Standards* (AERA, 2005) for its membership. These standards are designed for researchers in the field of education. "A main objective of the code is to remind us, as educational researchers, that we should strive to protect these populations [children and others], and to maintain the integrity of our research, of our research community, and of all those with whom we have professional relations." Standards pertain to responsibilities in the field of education, to research populations, educational institutions and the public, and other areas that demand ethical consideration.

Consider how you might handle the following dilemma. Identify the stakeholders and the possible solutions. Obtain a copy of the NAEYC Code of Ethical Conduct and identify the ideals and principles that might guide the solution to the problem.

*A parent, Mrs. Brown, comes into your classroom. Her son Matthew is following her, looking tired and red-eyed. Mrs. Brown appears angry and upset. She explains that Matthew pinched and punched his three-month-old sister Cassie. Mrs. Brown gave him a good whipping with a belt buckle. She wants you to back her up. What will you say? What will you do?*

## SUMMARY

The study of child development is a fairly new area of research. The field of child study came into prominence in the twentieth century becoming a recognized field of study in 1933. In recent years, cultural context has become a greater focus in the study of child development. Teachers and others who work with young children must gather information using methods such as observation and interview. Of great concern are the mandates to use inappropriate methods for assessing young children's achievement. There are still many unanswered questions regarding how children grow and learn. Meanwhile, adults who work with young children can make the most of what is known and can contribute new knowledge from their own experiences. Teachers and other child practitioners can use methods, such as observation and interviews, to record information for child study. Those who work with young children and their families must do so in an ethical manner. Child development research has examined many areas of behavior and development. As you proceed through this text, you will become more familiar with these areas.

## FOR FURTHER READING


Bentzen, W. R. (2004). *Seeing young children: A guide to observing and recording behavior* (5th ed.). Clifton Park, NY: Delmar Learning.

Billman, J., & Sherman, J. A. (2006). *Observation and participation in early childhood settings: A practicum guide* (2nd ed.). Boston: Allyn & Bacon.

Boehm, A. E., & Weinberg, R. A. (1997). *The classroom observer* (3rd ed.). New York: Teachers College Press.

Brooks-Gunn, J., Fuligni, A. S., & Berlin, L. J. (Eds.). (2003). *Early child development in the 21st century: Profiles of current research initiatives*. New York: Teachers College.

Cohen, D. H., Stern, V., & Balaban, N. (1997). *Observing and recording the behavior of young children* (4th ed.). New York: Teachers College Press.

Elliott, B. (2002). *Measuring performance: The early childhood educator in practice*. Clifton Park, NY: Delmar Learning.

Gober, S. Y. (2002). *Six simple ways to assess young children*. Clifton Park, NY: Delmar Learning.

Krechevsky, M. (1998). *Project Spectrum: Preschool assessment handbook*. New York: Teachers College Press.

Marian, M. (2004). *Using observation in early childhood education*. Columbus, OH: Merrill.

McAfee, O., & Leong, D. (2002). *Assessing and guiding young children's development and learning* (3rd ed.). Boston: Allyn & Bacon.

Nadelman, L. (2004). *Research manual in child development* (2nd ed.). Mahwah, NJ: Erlbaum.

Nicolson, S. A., & Shipstead, S. G. (2002). *Through the looking glass: Observations in the early childhood classroom* (3rd ed.). Columbus, OH: Merrill.

Nutbrown, C. (2003). *Research studies in early childhood education*. Sterling, VA: Trentham Books.

Pellegrini, A. D., with Symons, F., & Hoch, J. (2004). *Observing children in their natural worlds: A methodological primer* (2nd ed.). Mahwah, NJ: Erlbaum.

Reed, J. S., & Bergemann, V. E. (2005). *A guide to observation, participation, and reflection in the classroom* (5th ed.). Boston: McGraw Hill.

The science of early childhood development. (2001). *Zero to three*. [Focus issue], *21*(5).

Shores, E. F., & Grace, K. (1998). *The portfolio book*. Beltsville, MD: Gryphon House.


## SUGGESTED ACTIVITIES

1. Start collecting information for a child case study and portfolio to be assembled at the end of the course. Suggestions for observation and interviews are included in the Suggested Activities sections at the end of each unit.

**Case Study Report**

Your name:
Child's name:
Child's age/date of birth:
Inclusive dates of study:
Location of study:

I. Reason for choosing this child. Describe how you happened to select this child (e.g., physical appearance, convenience).
II. A brief description of the child's outstanding characteristics.
III. History and background. Include any information you can obtain about the child's family, ethnic/racial background, health history, birth and prenatal periods, and so on.
IV. Physical and motor growth and development.
V. Cognitive growth and development.
VI. Affective growth and development.
VII. Summary and interpretation.
a. In what ways has the child changed since you began your study?
b. In which aspects of development is the child most advanced for his or her age? In which areas does the child show the slowest development? In which areas is development most typical?
c. If you were assigned to work with this child as a teacher, what kinds of experiences would you plan to facilitate his or her development?
d. How well do you feel the child's school program and family is meeting his or her needs?
e. Include any other conclusions or recommendations.

In writing your case study summary report, use *it seems, the evidence indicates, it may be*, and other qualifiers freely. Remember, you have only studied a small time period in the child's life span.

## PORTFOLIO

A portfolio contains the case study report and supporting information and artifacts. Information might include anecdotes, conference notes, interview reports, checklists, rating scales, and assessments. Artifacts might include a collection of the child's work (drawings and paintings, writing samples, schoolwork, photos of completed projects [e.g., block or LEGO® constructions, Unifix Cubes® used to solve a math problem, science projects], and videotapes). Children three or older should help select the artifacts. The portfolio may be used as the basis for a parent conference.

**1.** Read each of the following examples carefully. Note which are examples of the (1) diary method, (2) running record or anecdote, (3) parent interview method, (4) child interview method, or (5) laboratory observation method.

a. Adult A: Tell me about John's infancy. Did you always pick him up when he cried or did you wait a while?
Adult B: I always picked him up right away. I found he usually didn't cry unless he wanted something.

b. Enrique said his first word today. He jumped out of the car when we arrived home from the store. He turned and pointed at our car and said, "Car!" What a big day for us.

c. Adult: Where do dreams come from?
Child: They fly in the window when I am asleep.

d. Adult A: How do you feel about punishments and rewards?
Adult B: For punishment, I usually have Mary take time out and sit in a chair until she cools off. Once in a while, she loses a privilege like dessert or going to her friend's house. Fortunately, she loves praise. I find if I give her a lot of attention for all the good things she does, I seldom have to punish her.

e. Maria looked at the vase of flowers on the table and then at her mother. She was on her hands and knees. Her right hand slowly left the floor and moved in the direction of the flowers. "No, No!" said her mother firmly as she got up and went over to her. She handed Maria a toy horse saying, "Play with this." Maria turned and smiled. She took the horse and immediately put it in her mouth and rubbed it against her gums.

f. Tony went for his checkup today. The doctor was very pleased. He weighs 12 pounds and is 23 inches long. He can now have rice, oatmeal, pears, peaches, and applesauce. We tried applesauce for lunch, and he loved it.

g. Isabel and Kai were playing with blocks and cars. Derrick smiled broadly as he sat back on his heels and looked at the structure they were working on. "We made a big parking garage. Just like the one downtown!" He looked at Isabel and suggested, "Let's park all the cars inside, Okay?" Isabel silently began collecting cars and passing them over to Kai.

h. Mrs. Tanaka was interested in finding out what her three-year-olds said to each other when they played at the sand table. She set the sand table up in a corner of the room where the children could play in private while she observed unobtrusively. She got this idea from one of the research methods she learned about in her child development course.

**2.** Explain how a teacher might also be a researcher.

**3.** Explain the purpose of the NAEYC Code of Ethical Conduct.

**4.** Provide examples of developmentally inappropriate and appropriate assessment strategies to be used with young children.

## KEY TERMS LIST

baby biographies
ecological research model
exosystem
ideals
macrosystem
mesosystem
microsystem
portfolio
principles
running record
specimen record
teacher researcher

Additional resources for this chapter can be found on the Online Companion™ to accompany this text at http://www.earlychilded.delmar.com. Respond to "Time to Reflect" and "Looking Further" concepts, review various child development scenarios, and answer thought-provoking questions in the Critical Thinking Forum. Keep a daily journal by downloading the student journal available on this Web site. Complete the interactive matching exercises to reinforce concepts, and print out the child development assessment forms to use during your observation of development for children from birth to age eight. In addition, read the case studies on the Web site to reinforce the important concepts in each chapter, and take a look at the multitude of Web links that are available for student research on the Internet.

# SECTION II

## Learning: Birth Through Age Eight

Of major concern to those who work with young children is discovering how they learn and in what kinds of settings they will be able to reach their potential. As you already know, the NAEYC has developed guidelines for developmentally appropriate practices in programs serving children from birth through age eight (Bredekamp, 1987; Bredekamp & Copple, 1997). This section looks at how young children learn. Instruction should fit children's individual learning styles, developmental stages, ages, and sociocultural backgrounds. Knowledge of child development should serve as guidelines for instruction that promotes children's learning. As you read the environmental descriptions that follow, think about whether these settings are developmentally appropriate.

### AN INFANT AT HER GRANDPARENTS' HOME: ANNIE, AGE SIX MONTHS AND TWO WEEKS

During this observation, Annie spent most of her time in the room where the dining table was located. She also went into the kitchen, bathroom, and hallway. Each of these rooms had beige carpet. The dining room had French doors with light pink blinds. One of the blinds was drawn. The walls were painted white. In the dining room, pink, white, and blue print wallpaper was on half of the wall. The dining table had two benches, each covered with forest green upholstery. Annie smiled and giggled a lot. After her parents left, her grandfather watched Annie for about an hour. Then the grandmother came home and took over. Annie's parents had brought her Johnny Jumper, a rattle, a toy key ring, a blanket, diapers, clothes, several bottles, and cereal.

This home was warm and comfortable. Everything Annie might need was available. She was never exposed to any danger. Her grandparents are very kind and caring people. You can tell that they adore their first granddaughter. It is also obvious that Annie adores her grandparents. There is a definite positive bond between them. Annie usually sees her grandparents two to four times each week. Her grandparents love to play with Annie and see her smile. They also take a very positive approach when Annie is not feeling happy. The grandmother likes to feed her and hold her when she is upset, and she can get her to go to sleep faster than anyone else. The grandmother is the mother of seven and is also a preschool teacher. She is a confident and experienced child care provider, as is her husband. It is clear they both love children because they are so at ease with them.

## THE TODDLER AREA AT A HIGH SCHOOL CHILD CARE CENTER

The center was large and was divided into three separate rooms. On this particular day, the toddlers were playing in the playroom. In the playroom, there was a climbing toy with a slide; a hiding box set up so the children could climb on top, jump off, and land on a group of brightly colored mats; and an open area for dancing. Six toddlers and three high school students participated. First, the toddlers had their circle time. They sang, performed finger plays, and read stories. Circle time lasted about 10 minutes, after which they climbed and jumped on the equipment and danced in the open space.

The room was well-organized. It allowed the children to climb, jump, dance, and exert energy without bothering the infant or preschool groups.

## UNIVERSITY CHILD CARE CENTER, THREE- AND FOUR-YEAR-OLD CLASSROOM

Three tables, each a different shape, were situated in the center of the classroom. One was a circle, another was shaped like a rainbow, and the third was like half of a rainbow. The carpet was an orange color and the walls were decorated with posters and pictures. Many different learning play centers were situated around the room, including blocks, dress-up or dramatic play, painting/art, and computers. A fish tank and a bowl with tadpoles were on a table against one wall. The bathrooms were along another wall. The children sat down to eat lunch, which consisted of meatballs, rolls, cheese, and milk. When they were done, they cleared their places and participated in a variety of activities at the different centers.

The room was full of activities that were developmentally appropriate for young children. They were having a good time playing and interacting with each other. The centers were set up so that the noisy areas were not next to the quiet areas. The children in the reading center were not being distracted by those who were playing with building blocks because they were across the room from each other. The children could select from a variety of books. Many posters and other items were hung up in the room. These provided the children with visual stimulation. A big private-space box was set up in the reading area. A child might sit in it if he or she was sad or wanted to be alone for a moment. The children were being creative and using their imaginations with the building toys and blocks. The atmosphere was conducive to learning and encouraged independence and initiative. Children asked questions or made comments at any time.

## KINDERGARTEN IN A PUBLIC SCHOOL: WOODHAVEN ELEMENTARY

There were 21 children and one teacher in the classroom. Learning centers were arranged throughout the classroom, predominately on the perimeter areas. They contained an abundance of highly meaningful concrete materials that children were able to pursue, manipulate, and actively explore.

The environment was print rich. Each center was labeled. The reading center was filled with books made by the children containing many of their drawings and writings. The writing center was equipped with many materials the children could play with to learn about concepts of print.

The day began with a group activity. The class was working with the letter *T*. A large *T* cutout was spread out in the center of the floor. Each child had brought an object from home that began with the letter *T*. The children and the teacher were seated around the letter. The children placed their objects on the *T* and said the name. Mrs. A wrote the name on a big chalkboard for all to see. The children all participated in handling and talking about the objects. Then, they did a movement exercise, pretending their bodies were *T*s.

Next, the children got their toothbrushes and a graph was made of colors of the toothbrushes. This large-group activity integrated reading, language, mathematics, physical, and social development tasks. During the discussions and the center time, Mrs. A used many open-ended questions. She accepted more than one answer when posing questions to her students. She also asked individuals and groups questions pertaining to their work. She often initiated questions that required complex ideas and thinking strategies.

Particularly impressive was the science center. It was abundant with materials, such as scales and other measuring devices, rocks, charts, terrariums, a bone collection, a preserved snake collection, and many other materials.

The children were provided with many opportunities daily to develop social skills. Their group time was a cooperative venture in which all played an active part. The tables and chairs were arranged so that areas were provided for children to work together and share materials. Both child-initiated and teacher-initiated activities took place. Children made many of their own decisions and choices. The prevailing atmosphere was one of curiosity, exploration, and peaceful appreciation for the teacher and each other and from the teacher toward the children.

## FIRST GRADE PUBLIC SCHOOL: SOUTHSIDE ELEMENTARY

To get to the classroom, you walked through a courtyard. In the courtyard were a few benches, trees and flowers, and a cement walkway around the edges. The classroom doors were on the outside edge of the walkway. The classroom had both a front and a back door. The back door went to the playground, and the front door opened into the courtyard. By the back door was a short hallway that led to the bathrooms and the other first-grade classroom. The classroom carpet was rust colored and the brick walls were beige. The classroom had many windows and a vaulted ceiling, which gave it a light, airy feeling. Chalkboards were on one wall. The other walls were covered with bulletin boards. Some of the bulletin board materials included birthdays around the year, colors, a calendar, the alphabet, numbers to 100, the seasons, the days of the week, helping hands, a "something to smile about" area with children's artwork, shapes, and illustrated emotions. There was a sink inside the classroom. Each student had his or her own desk and in the back of the room were two rectangular tables. Beside the door was an area for the children's coats and book bags. Each space had a name tag for each child. The room also had two computers, a piano, a VCR/TV, a film projector, an overhead projector, and a world globe.

The observer liked the room overall. The room had an abundance of materials; however, in some areas, it looked too cluttered and overloaded with information. The classroom had one teacher and 23 children. It had a nice atmosphere, and the children seemed to get along with the teacher and the other students. An assembly had been held earlier in the day, and the children were a bit restless. The teacher would periodically have them get up and jump around for a minute. Displaying the children's artwork was a great idea, as it made the children feel that their work was something special.

Note how the settings described in this introduction relate to the items in the "Learning Environment Checklist" found at the end of Chapter 6.

CHAPTER

# 4

# How Learning Takes Place

## OBJECTIVES

After reading this chapter, you should be able to:

- Define *learning, perception, reflex,* and *memory.*
- Define the parts of the brain.
- Discriminate between the developmental and behaviorist views of learning.
- Apply the concepts of perception, learning, and memory.
- Recognize examples of perceptual, learning, and memory concepts.
- Understand the importance of action and concrete sensory experiences in young children's learning.
- Describe the changes in motivation from infancy and toddlerhood to elementary school.
- List criticisms and positive aspects of television as a learning tool for young children.
- Describe how computer instruction relates to the constructivist and behaviorist points of view.
- Realize the importance of video games in the lives of young children.
- Recognize how television can enhance the child's imaginative play.
- Explain what is meant by special needs and at-risk.
- List at least 10 types of special-needs conditions.
- Recognize the major benefits of inclusion.

**learning**

Behavior change that results from experience.

**Learning** may be defined as behavior change that results from experience. Learning experiences involve many kinds of activity, as the following examples show:

**Six-year-old:** Carla, age 6, is sitting on the sofa next to her sister Becky, age 13. They are kneading a gooey substance. Becky has taken the gooey substance and separated it into two equal pieces for them to work with. Carla is watching Becky as she creates designs using her forearm as a table for the goo and the palm, wrist, and forearm of her other arm to shape the material. Carla asks Becky to help her do the same. Carla follows each step as Becky gives her directions. First, she extends her arm out and places the goo on the forearm. Next, she uses her palm to flatten the material. She sees Becky use her wrist and other forearm in a twisting motion to extend the material into an oval shape. She is unable to duplicate the motion and asks Becky to show her how it's done. Becky takes Carla through the steps and movements of the wrist and forearm. She has Carla repeat the movements and Carla is successful.

**Five-year-old:** Pablo, age five, exclaims, "I can ride my bicycle and, look, it only has two wheels!" Aunt Sara responds, "That is so cool!" "Yup, watch me," says Pablo as he starts to ride on the sidewalk in front of the house. He rides out of sight and comes pedaling back about three or four minutes later. He looks very proud.

**Four-year-old:** Kate, age four, points to a small creature that is walking on the sidewalk and asks, "Dad, what is it?" "That's a big, red ant," answers her dad.

**Three-year-old:** Chan, age three, grabs Ginger's truck. Ginger hits Chan. Mrs. Clark steps over and says, "Wait a minute. This has to stop." She puts an arm around each of them and looks at each in turn, explaining, "Taking other people's toys is not allowed, but hitting is not allowed either. Chan, next time you ask Ginger to let you use the truck when she is done with it. Ginger, when someone takes something from you, you ask for it back. If they won't give it back, come and ask Mrs. Clark for help."

**Toddler:** Summer, almost 15 months, is moving Grandma's refrigerator magnets around on the refrigerator door. Apparently satisfied that the objects will stick to the refrigerator, she moves around the kitchen checking on whether the magnets will stick on the wooden cupboards.

**Infant:** Sonja, nine months, selects a small bucket and then a small cow and sticks it into her mouth and makes a noise with it. She picks up another toy and as she plays with it, she says, "Ma ma ma ma ma and aaaah."

In the experiences described, each of the children involved has learned a new behavior. Carla has learned through supportive scaffolding to work with the goo. Pablo has learned to ride his two-wheel bike. Kate has learned to name a red ant. Chan and Ginger have been told how to solve problems peacefully. Summer has learned that while the magnets will stick on the refrigerator, they don't stick on the wooden doors. Sonja is learning the attributes of objects and is practicing the sounds included in conventional language. Future behavior will demonstrate whether they have learned how to do it.

FIGURE 4–1 Children construct their own knowledge about the class guinea pigs as they observe their daily activities.

Different theorists have different views of learning. The developmentalists emphasize the interaction between growth and learning.

Behaviorists emphasize the effect of the environment on learning. Kate learned "red ant" because she has a responsive father who answered her question. Chan and Ginger learned how to negotiate because they wanted Mrs. Clark's approval.

The developmentalists emphasize stages and readiness for learning. They view learning as an active process that takes place as the young child acts upon (Bodrova & Leong, 2003) the environment and constructs his or her own knowledge (DeVries & Kohlberg, 1990; Kamii, 1986; Winsler, 2003) (Figure 4–1). They view changes as part of a process more than as an end product. Behaviorists, on the other hand, emphasize the end product (i.e., learned behavior), and view the process as the same, no matter what the child's age and current developmental stage.

This author takes the position that both points of view are helpful to adults who work with young children. Unfortunately, traditional education, has taken a behaviorist view and ignored the constructivist view (Larkin, 1993; Lauritzen, 1992). That is, emphasis is on the product of learning more than on the process. David Elkind (2005) states that when planning for children, too many grownups fail to consider what research tells us about how children learn. This has resulted in curriculum being pushed down from elementary grades to preschool and kindergarten and the elimination of adequate time to play. In this chapter, how children learn is examined. In Chapter 5, the role of play is discussed.

**neurons**
Small cells that are the building blocks of the brain.

**axon**
An output fiber that sends information to other neurons.

**dendrites**
Short, hair-like fibers that receive information.

**myelin**
A white fatty material that protects axons.

**synapses**
The connection of cells to each other.

**plasticity**
Abundance of synapses accounts for why the young child's brain learns new skills quickly.

## HOW THE BRAIN FUNCTIONS

Starting from conception, brain growth and development moves at a rapid pace. The advent of new technology in the latter part of the twentieth century enabled the brain to be studied in detail (Shore, 1997; Thompson & Nelson, 2001). The PET scan enables observation of the structure of the brain and the activity in the brain. The brain is a part of the central nervous system. It has two hemispheres (or halves) each of which has four lobes (Shore, 1997). Different parts of the brain have different functions (Porter, 2006). The upper portion or cortex is where most of our mental activity, such as thinking, planning, and remembering, takes place. Small cells called **neurons** are the building blocks of the brain. Infants are born with about 100 billion brain cells. Each neuron has an **axon,** an output fiber that sends information to other neurons. Each neuron also has **dendrites,** which are short, hair-like fibers that receive information. As children grow, the number of neurons stays about the same, but each cell increases in size and grows more dendrites. Axons transmit messages to other neurons. Axons are protected by a white fatty material called **myelin.** The key to brain development is the connection of cells to each other. These connections are called **synapses.** Children's experiences provide increased connections. Any one neuron may be connected to as many as 15,000 other neurons. During the early years, children's brains develop more synapses than are needed. This abundance of synapses accounts for the **plasticity** of the young child's brain which allows it to learn new skills much more quickly than the pruned adult brain (Murray, 2006). After the first year, pruning takes place, that is, unused synapses are lost. The ones that remain as a permanent part of the brain connections are the ones that are used repeatedly. If they are not used, they are eliminated. Dendrites also increase rapidly in number. During the first five years, the greatest growth of synapses and dendrites takes place. By five, the child's brain weighs as much as an adult's (see Figures 4–2 and 4–3).

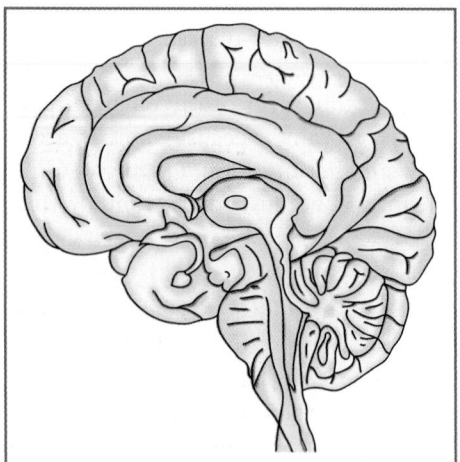

FIGURE 4–2 The brain.

## PERCEPTION

"In its simplest sense, perception is the brain's interpretation of physical sensations. . . . Sensation is what happens when physical stimuli are translated into neural impulses that can then be transmitted to the brain and interpreted" (Lefrancois, 1992, p. 225).

The senses of taste, touch, sight, hearing, and smell, and proprioceptive messages, such as muscle contractions, transmit messages to the brain. The meaning of these messages to each individual is different, depending on individual perception of the information. For instance,

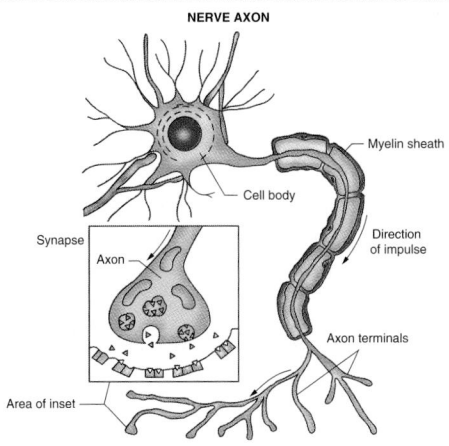


FIGURE 4–3 Diagram of a synapse and a nerve axon.

Melissa tastes some beans that have a lot of hot pepper sauce in them. She frowns, says "Awful," and runs for a glass of water. Mario takes a bowl of beans from the same pot. He tastes them, smiles with satisfaction, and says, "Bueno, bueno!" Melissa and Mario each have a different interpretation of the taste of hot pepper sauce.

The importance of perception is emphasized by seeing what might happen if messages were interpreted in ways different from the way other people in the culture interpret them. For example, consider the following incident:

> Richie looks at the word *cat* and says, "That says 'bat.'"

Perception is related to the processes of learning, cognition, and language. A child with a problem in perception has difficulty in other areas.

The senses begin to develop before birth. By five months in utero, the fetus has some sense of motion and sound (Cole, Cole, & Lightfoot, 2005). Normal full-term infants are born with all their sensory systems functioning to some extent. Up until about age five, children tend not to perceive the totality of the available information, as their attention centers on the most obvious (Cole, Cole, & Lightfoot, 2005). Younger children become distracted and lose their train of thought when presented with loud and flashy stimuli. They also tend to explore new things in an unsystematic way and, thus, miss some of the details. They often miss the most important and relevant information. In addition, they may overestimate the effects of specific sensory experiences (O'Neil & Astington, 1990). For example, O'Neil and Astington asked children to decide whether sight or touch would have to be used to answer a question about a hidden object. The children under five overselected feeling as the means to solve the problem. Infants and toddlers in the sensorimotor period favor their senses of touch and taste when exploring new materials. This need to touch seems to carry over through the early preoperational period.

## Attention

**attention**

A critical aspect of perception that involves ignoring irrelevant information and finding relevant information.

**Attention** is a critical aspect of perception. Attentional processes involve ignoring irrelevant information and finding relevant information (Ault, 1983). At first, infant attention is captured by whatever is novel in the environment. Soon, attention becomes voluntary; that is, infants can choose the focus of their attention. As children grow older, they become increasingly skilled at being able to ignore what is not important and to attend to what is important. As they become more adept at attending to things and avoiding distractions, their attention span for any specific task increases.

**attention deficit disorder (ADD)**

A condition in which most of the hyperactivity symptoms are present with or without hyperactivity.

The ability to attend is an extremely important factor in learning. Children who experience difficulty maintaining attention have difficulty in a traditional school setting where students are required to sit still, listen to lectures, and work at abstract activities. These students have difficulty interpreting information because they may miss segments as their attention wanders. Some may withdraw and daydream, whereas others are more active, roaming around and talking out of turn. They may also be disorganized and have difficulty forming relationships with others. The more active, inattentive students are often identified as having behavior problems. These children are labeled as having **attention deficit disorder (ADD)** and as being hyperactive. Those children who daydream and fade into the background are labeled hypoactive. Both types of ADD students are more likely to achieve success in a developmentally appropriate classroom environment, but they are usually doomed to failure in the more traditional school setting (Landau & McAninch, 1993). Divoky

**individual education plan (IEP)**

A set of objectives that must be written for every special education student.

(1989, p. 600) describes the **individual education plan (IEP)** for a third grader identified as having ADD, which includes the following statements:

- "Casey is able to learn in a regular classroom situation only when he is heavily invested in the activity."
- "For most academic instruction, he needs one-to-one or small-group instruction with realistic expectations, clear behavioral limits, and frequent change of activities."
- "He also needs to be able to move around during the day to burn off excess energy."

Look carefully at these prescriptive statements. They identify behaviors that would easily fit into a developmentally appropriate classroom.

**sensory involvement**

Using all the senses as a bridge from the concrete to the abstract.

**sensory integrative dysfunction**

A condition where the senses do not provide accurate or clear messages.

## Learning through Sensory Involvement

Because young children seem to favor and appear more skilled at learning through touching and feeling than through vision, it would appear that this is a characteristic that could be used to an advantage. Maria Montessori (Humphryes, 1998) noted this characteristic in young children and applied it to instruction. The materials designed by Montessori all involve manipulation of objects as a means to develop all the senses. Materials used in this approach encourage perception of color, shape, size, texture, sound, and other attributes through the manipulation of concrete materials. In **sensory involvement,** all the senses are used to bridge the concrete with the abstract. For example, children trace sandpaper letters and numerals while saying the name of each one, thus making use of touch, sight, and sound at the same time. Montessori was creative in developing multisensory materials for young children (Figure 4–4).

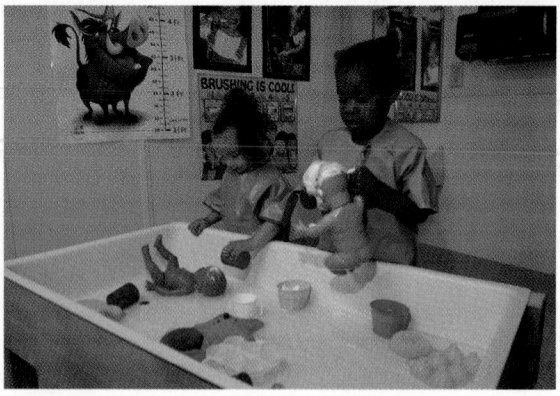


**FIGURE 4–4** Young children learn actively through their firsthand sensory experiences.

Those who support Piaget's cognitive developmental view also believe that children learn best through manipulation of objects. Williams and Kamii (1986) point out that young children's manipulation of objects is not mindless but involves mental and physical action. For example, Isabel puts another block on her block tower because she thinks it will balance. Jason rolls his clay because he thinks he can make it look like a snake. No one has told these children what to do. They have figured it out for themselves.

Multisensory learning is especially critical during the first three years, when the brain is developing at its most rapid rate (Shore, 1997). The brain of a one-year-old looks more like an adult's than a newborn's. By age three, children's brains are two-and-a-half times more active than adult brains. They continue to be even more active during their first 10 years. Besides caring for basic needs, such as health, safety, and nutrition during the infant and toddler periods, it is important to provide sensory stimulation (Shore, 1997, pp. 26–27), such as the following:

- Talk, read, and sing to the infant/toddler.
- Encourage safe exploration and play.
- Limit television.

Unfortunately some children do not react to sensory information in a constructive manner. Some young children have a disorder known as **sensory integrative dysfunction**

(Stephens, 1997). Children with this disorder are unable to carry out ordinary activities because their senses do not provide accurate or clear messages. They cannot integrate new information with memories and make a response that makes sense. Sensory information seems to travel around the brain in a random fashion. Symptoms vary and may include problems in attention and self regulation, over sensitivity, over- or under-activity, and/or behavior problems.

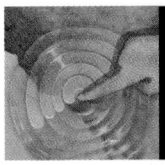

**LOOKING FURTHER**

Complete one or more of the interview tasks on perception and/or the effects of rewards, which can be found in the "Suggested Activities" at the end of this chapter (Activity 1, 2, and/or 3).

## MEMORY

**memory**
The mental capacity of retaining and reviving impressions.

**Memory** is the mental capacity of retaining and reviving impressions. Some information is perceived through the senses and stored away for further use. The information may be retrieved later through one of four different processes.

Four types of memory are recall, recognition, paired associates, and reproductive. Recall is remembering something pulled directly from the mind's storehouse.

> "What is your name?" "My name is Carlos."
>
> "Who are your friends?" "Sam, Stephanie, Justin, Maria, and Mark."
>
> "How old are you?" "Four."

Recognition is easier than recall in that the choices are given, such as, "Are you three or four years old?" "Look at those animals. Pick out the dog," and "Show me which child is your friend, Sam." Paired associates involves placing two things together, such as a name with a face, an object with a color or shape, or some other characteristic, as in, "This is my friend, Sam," "The red sweater is mine," or "Triangles have three sides; rectangles have four sides." Reproductive memory is more difficult than simple recall. In this case, what is recalled must be reproduced. For example, Kate writes her name, draws a picture of her friends, and holds up four fingers to represent her age.

Memory can be aided by a number of factors. The more senses involved in the original learning experience, the easier it is to remember. The Montessori method is one example of learning through more than one sense at a time. Learning through experience is another example. The child is told that a small cup holds less water than a large cup. The child remembers better if he or she can pour water from cup to cup and experience through sight and action the fact that the small cup holds less.

Memory is best when the items to be remembered are meaningful. Three is more easily remembered as an amount if you are three years old or looking forward to being three years old, or if three objects are explored and held while someone says, "There are three rocks: 1, 2, 3." If a child likes long hair, he or she will remember the names of people with long hair more easily than those with short hair. As the child reaches the preschool years and learns more about categorizing or grouping things, he or she also can use this skill to aid memory.

Metamemory ("the ability to think about one's memory processes"—Cole, Cole, & Lightfoot, 2005) has been of interest to researchers. Researchers have been interested in finding out at which age people begin to have some idea about how they remember things, what kinds of things are easiest to remember, and how well they memorize. Young children tend to have faulty views about how things are remembered and, therefore, use inefficient strategies to help them memorize.

Around five years old, children have some ideas about their own methods of memorizing, but it is not until about eight that children begin to understand how memory works and are aware of strategies for memorizing and how and when to use them (Cole, et al., 2005).

## LEARNING

When a change in behavior occurs as a result of experience, learning has taken place. Reflexes, such as blinking the eyes, pulling back from a hot flame, or crying are not learned, although experience may increase or decrease the frequency with which they occur. Some learning depends on maturation. For example, a newborn cannot walk, talk, play tag, or solve arithmetic problems. We will look at several aspects of learning: classical conditioning, operant conditioning, observation and imitation, some specifics of learning, adult and peer support of learning, and activity and learning.

### Classical Conditioning

**classical conditioning**
Learning takes place through the association of a stimulus and a response.

In **classical conditioning**, learning takes place through the association of a stimulus and a response. For example, a child will startle at a loud noise. If something else is paired with the loud noise, the child may also learn to respond with a startle at the new stimulus. In Watson's classic experiment with the infant Albert (cited in Miller, 2002, p. 216), Albert was naturally startled by a loud noise but was not afraid of white rats. However, when Albert was shown the white rat along with the loud noise, he became afraid of the white rat. Much learning takes place through these simple and usually accidental associations. For example, baby says, "Mama" when mother happens to be around. Mother responds with a smile and a hug. *Mama* becomes associated with *Mother*.

### Operant Conditioning

**operant conditioning**
Behavior is shaped by careful use of reinforcements (rewards) for appropriate behavior and, at the same time, inappropriate behavior is ignored so that it is not rewarded with attention.

Learning also takes place through **operant conditioning**. Through operant conditioning, behavior is shaped by careful use of reinforcements or rewards for appropriate behavior. At the same time, inappropriate behavior is ignored so that it is not rewarded with attention. In Chapter 15, it is suggested that operant conditioning or behavior modification techniques are especially useful with the toddler. For the preschooler, there is a wider variety of choice for managing behavior.

### Observation and Imitation

Throughout the preoperational period, much of the child's learning is achieved through processes of observation and imitation. The child can learn through imitation in two ways. Children can act at the same time as the adult and receive an immediate reward. They also can learn when they see someone else receiving a reward for a behavior. The following is an example of the first type of learning:

> Mark comes into the bathroom. His dad is brushing his teeth. Mark says, "I want to do that, too." Dad responds, "We have a little toothbrush we've been saving for you." He gives it to Mark, saying, "Now watch me and do what I do." Mark watches. He then does what he saw his dad do. Father says, "Good for you, Mark. You're a big boy."

Next is an example of the second type of learning:

> Isabel notices that other children in her preschool class are complimented for sharing. She decides to share, also.

FIGURE 4–5 As children work with a variety of materials, they note similarities and differences.

**generalization**
The process of finding similarities among things.

**discrimination**
Perceiving differences.

**shaping**
Gradual acquisition of a learned behavior.

**successive approximation**
Gradual learning in discrete steps.

**extinction**
Unlearning; if a behavior is not rewarded, it gradually is no longer used.

**habituation**
A feature of getting used to something.

**assimilation**
An incorporation process in which new ideas and concepts are fit into old ideas or concepts.

**accommodation**
The means for changing the old concepts to fit a new piece of learning.

**equilibration**
Brought about through the balance between assimilation and accommodation.

In the first example, Mark simultaneously copies his dad's action and receives an immediate reward. In the second example, Isabel's peers serve as models. She sees what brings approval to other children and then does the same thing on her own. She has the expectation that she will also receive a compliment from the teacher.

## Some Specifics of Learning

What is learned in one situation may be applied later in another situation (Figure 4–5). There are several basic features of learning (Yussen & Santrock, 1978). Some of these features are generalization, discrimination, shaping, extinction, and habituation. **Generalization** is the process of finding similarities among things. For example, balls, tires, and coins are round. Or, girls, boys, moms, and dads are people. **Discrimination** has to do with perceiving differences. One ball is red and one is blue. One tire is big and the other is small. One person has long hair and another has short hair.

**Shaping** has to do with gradual acquisition of a learned behavior. This is accomplished through **successive approximation**, or gradual learning. For example, it is not unusual for a child who is new in a group situation to refuse to join in large-group activities. The first day or so, he or she sits apart from the group and may even do another activity. The next day, he or she sits near the group but just watches the activity. Soon, the child moves into the group but is not an active participant. Finally, he or she participates along with the other children. **Extinction** has to do with unlearning. If a behavior is not rewarded, it gradually is no longer used. **Habituation** is a feature of getting used to something. That is, when an event is novel or uncommon, the child is more likely to pay attention to it immediately than if it occurs often. If an adult who never speaks sharply to a child suddenly does so, the child attends immediately. The child who is often spoken to sharply becomes accustomed to the harsh tone of voice and does not pay attention.

Classical conditioning, operant conditioning, and observational and imitative learning are behavior-oriented approaches to explaining how learning takes place. Piaget (Miller, 2002) has developed a theory that addresses unseen behavior, that is, what is going on in the mind as learning occurs. He views learning as a continuous process of adaptation. The child adapts through the processes of assimilation and accommodation. **Assimilation** is an incorporation process. New ideas and concepts are fit into old ideas or concepts. For example, the child knows that the big, red, round object is a ball. The child then sees a small, blue, round object that he or she also assimilates as *ball*. **Accommodation** is the means for changing the old concepts to fit a new piece of learning. The child sees another big, red, round object that he or she calls *ball*. The child is told that this object is a *balloon*. Accommodation enables the child to modify his or her concept of ball and add a new concept, balloon. Through adaptation, the child maintains equilibrium or balance between himself or herself and the environment. A balance between assimilation and accommodation brings about **equilibration**. The child can, to his or her satisfaction, make sense out of the world.

## Adult and Peer Support of Learning

Vygotsky's view of the importance of adult support for learning in the zone of proximal development has been described (Winsler, 2003). Adult support, or scaffolding, is always critical to children's learning. That is, when the child is ready to move ahead, the adult can support development through asking the right questions and providing appropriate materials and explanations. Although, as described next, active learning through child-initiated activities is essential, so is skillfully initiated adult support and guidance. Peers can also positively affect each other if encouraged to work together toward common goals (Cannella, 1993; Tudge, 1990).

From the Vygotskian view, scaffolding is an essential element that supports children's learning through play (Berk & Winsler, 1995; Bodrova & Leong, 2003). Development of children's pretend play is supported through social collaboration with adults and older peers. "Vygotsky-based research on play emphasizes that make-believe is, from its beginnings, a social activity" (Berk & Winsler, p. 63). The caregiver is the expert who initiates and supports fantasy activity by taking on pretend parts in games and fantasy. Adult-initiated turn-taking games, such as peek-a-boo and pat-a-cake, support the social exchange that is basic to conversation later on. Physical games that involve bouncing, lifting, and wrestling also build a foundation for communication, emotional development, and social skills that are a part of representational play. Once children enter the preschool period and are able to engage in fantasy play, adults can continue to provide support by taking an active role as play partners. For example, the adult can be the baby while the child is the mother or father, the adult can be the passenger in the car while the child drives, or the adult can be the patient while the child plays doctor. Make-believe supports not only overall mental development but also the development of creativity (Figure 4–6).

The following dialog took place one week before a presidential election. Kate is three years and ten months of age. She has cut out pictures of the candidates from the cover of a magazine, and she and her mother are using them for paper dolls.

| Mother | Kate |
|---|---|
| What do they say to each other? | Nothing. You're not gonna vote for me. I want to vote to your no. |
| You're not gonna vote for me? | Yeah. |
| Who are you gonna vote for? | May I have this one, Mom? I want this. |
| I'll have this one. Okay. I've got C. Who have you got? | President F. |
| Okay. What does President F. say to C.? | No, I'm not gonna kiss you. I'm gonna kiss myself. 'Kay? I'm not gonna kiss you, I'm gonna kiss myself. |
| You are, huh? Well I'm not gonna kiss you either. | Oh, beans! |
| Ah! Ooh! He hit me. Ouch! | (Take) that! |
| Ouch! Why did you hit me, President F.? | Because I think you are mean. |
| You, oh, I'm not mean. What makes you think I'm mean, President F.? | Because you are icky. |
| Ah, but I just want to move into your White House. | Okay, come on. |
| Can I come and move in with you? Where can I stay in your White House? | In my bed. |

Mother asks questions and goes along with her assigned roles. The play theme is more sustained and complex than previously. The content reflects the young child's view of the presidential election as she perceives it.

**FIGURE 4–6** Example of adult support of a child's play.

## Activity and Learning

An appropriate environment for young children supports active learning. It includes many opportunities for child-initiated learning (Bullock, 1990). Children do not wait for an adult to arrive before they engage in learning. They are continuously acquiring knowledge. "They are busy trying to make sense out of everything they encounter" (Kamii, 1986, p. 71). According to DeVries and Kohlberg (1990), the Piagetian **constructivist** view perceives the roots of educational practice "in his theory of the role of action in development" (p. 19). Spontaneous activity is the foundation of mental development. DeVries and Kohlberg (1990) summarize Piaget's point of view in the following three "interdependent characteristics of early education aimed at fostering development"(p. 20):

**constructivist**
A believer in the idea that children construct their own knowledge through interaction with the environment.

1. Methods appeal to the child's spontaneous mental activity.
2. The teacher acts as a companion who minimizes the exercise of adult authority and control over children and as a guiding mentor stimulating initiative, play, experimentation, reasoning, and social collaboration.
3. Social life among children offers extensive opportunity for cooperation, including conflict, in situations inspiring children to desire coordination with others.

The third characteristic cannot be overemphasized. Social interaction is extremely important as a vehicle for learning. Cooperation for Piaget is not mindless submission but refers to individuals interacting with each other in both harmony and conflict (Figure 4–7).

FIGURE 4–7 These children are learning through interactions with each other and with the materials.

Whereas Piaget focuses more on the child's emerging development through self-initiated learning and Vygotsky more on the social elements, it is important for adults who work with young children to consider both views. Although it is important for children to have time to develop their own play activities for learning, they also need the support of adults and older peers. It is also important for children to have the opportunity to develop play through a variety of vehicles or resources which are described in Chapter 5.

# LEARNING STYLES

All children do not learn the same way. There are many **learning styles.** Each child has strength in different modalities. Fagella and Horowitz (1990) describe seven styles identified by Howard Gardner in his book *Frames of Mind* (discussed in Chapter 23). Gardner (1999) later added an eighth intelligence, naturalist intelligence. Two contrasting examples are the linguistic learner compared with the bodily/kinesthetic learner. Children who learn best through words do well in our schools because they like to read and write, are good at memorizing, and learn best by saying, hearing, and seeing words. In contrast, the bodily/kinesthetic learner does poorly in the sit-still classroom. Bodily/kinesthetic learners like to move around, touch things, and talk. They excel at physical activities and crafts; learn best through touching, moving, and interacting with space; and process knowledge through their bodily sensations. Some children learn best on their own; others work better in a group. Style is an extremely important variable in school learning. See more on multiple intelligences in Chapter 23.

**learning styles**
The methods by which a child acquires knowledge.

## THE DESIRE TO LEARN

An important task for those who work with young children is being sure that these children are assisted in every way to maintain the desire to learn. The desire to learn appears to reflect a natural motivation that children have to "solve problems, figure out how objects work, and complete tasks they set out to do" (Hauser-Cram, 1998, p. 67). Learning is built on the desire to find out about the world. Infants and toddlers are strongly motivated to learn, but the desire seems to dwindle in many children as they proceed through school. Hauser-Cram (1998) describes how motivation shifts as children proceed through different age levels. The infant under six months explores through reaching, mouthing, and visual exploration. By nine months, infants usually become more goal directed and want to study cause and effect (e.g., shaking the rattle results in a noise). As children enter the toddler period around eighteen months, they become imitators of standards (e.g., Dad shaves, so will he; Mom puts on lipstick, so will she). Toddlers are very motivated to do what they see others do. Preschoolers take on more complex tasks that involve thinking through problem solutions. Strongly motivated infants and toddlers take advantage of all opportunities for exploration and thus learning. Some research has explored motivation in children with developmental or physical disabilities. At the infant and toddler stages, levels of persistence to reach goals is about the same for children with and without disabilities. Evidence suggests that as these children get older, adults may become directive and interfere in their play. Thus, they have less autonomy and independence for mastering tasks that interest them.

Besides a general concern with motivation, there is also concern with motivation from the cultural perspective. McInerney, Roche, McInerney, and Marsh (1997) examined whether goals held by students from diverse cultural backgrounds differ and whether cultural background affects school motivation and achievement. They administered a school motivation inventory to high school students from five diverse cultures. The results indicated that, by high school age, these groups were similar in terms of motivation and, therefore, did not fit some of the typologies that have been identified in studies within cultures, as are described throughout the rest of this text. Their responses were in line with the Western view of valuing task orientation, individual work, and competition. The authors suggest that, by high school, these students may be socialized into the Western cultural view of school. However, the authors raise an important question as to whether "academic achievement could be enhanced in other, more culturally appropriate ways, that is, by developing learning structures that are more consonant with cultural values" (McInerney et al., p. 233). This goal of making education culturally appropriate is a major element of developmentally appropriate practice with young children (Bredekamp & Copple, 1997).

Research has shown that by the third or fourth grade, many children can be identified as having acquired what is called "learned helplessness" and have lost their natural curiosity and motivation to learn. What do you think might cause this to occur?

Providing programs that fit learning styles and make children feel good about themselves has been increasingly difficult as early childhood instruction has become increasingly less developmentally appropriate. Unfortunately, instruction has become more oriented toward paper and pencil, workbooks, and work sheets so as to fit with standardized tests. Geist & Baum (2005) describe the challenges teachers face in resisting the pressures to use developmentally inappropriate instructional practices. Much inappropriate practice is test driven. That is, teachers, parents, and administrators may view work sheets and drill and practice as the most effective test preparation. Hopefully, some of the current efforts at assessment reform, which are discussed later in this text, will take hold. The curriculum for young children should be designed to fit the child's developmental level and learning style rather than reshaping the child to fit the curriculum (Charlesworth, 1989).

## TECHNOLOGY AS A VEHICLE FOR LEARNING

In the twenty-first century, technology is advancing at a rapid rate. Technology will undoubtedly be an ever-increasing element in young children's learning in the future. Technology will continue to present a multitude of challenges for adults who work with young children in both homes and schools. Although technology is becoming less expensive, much of it is still beyond the reach of many schools and homes. However, as television was available to most families by the end of the twentieth century, computer technology will probably be more common in most homes by the end of the twenty-first century. Teachers, parents, and other caregivers are challenged to explore new technologies and their effectiveness as vehicles for children's learning. In a special focus section of *Young Children* (E-learning for educators, 2004) the challenges for educators are described. Educators need to keep up with technological innovations in order to improve their own knowledge and that of their students.

> Interactive media have come of age. The range of interactive entertainment products, intended to be used by children in and out of school settings is growing: CD-Roms, computers, the Internet, video games . . . , interactive toys . . . , and a variety of wireless software for cell phones and other wireless devices. (Watella, Caplovitz, & Lee, 2004, p. 1)

Technology in the workplace is far ahead of technology in the school and home. The challenge for the future is to help our children become experienced in learning from and using technology so they are ready to handle the technological requirements of their future occupations. This part of the chapter examines what we know about technology as a vehicle for young children's learning.

### Learning from Television

There is no argument regarding the power of television as a vehicle for children's learning. Although many high-quality programs and videos are available, there are also opportunities for children to learn many inappropriate behaviors and to be exposed to unsuitable content from television, DVD, and video games. Numerous criticisms have been leveled at these technological tools.

In 1990, the NAEYC published a position statement on media violence in the lives of children (NAEYC, 1990):

> NAEYC CONDEMNS VIOLENT TELEVISION PROGRAMMING, MOVIES, VIDEOTAPES, COMPUTER GAMES, AND OTHER FORMS OF MEDIA DIRECTED TO CHILDREN. NAEYC supports efforts to use media constructively to expand children's knowledge and promote the development of positive social values. NAEYC also supports measures that can be taken by responsible adults to limit children's exposure to violence throughout the media (p. 18).

NAEYC suggests that policy makers put stronger limitations on broadcasts and that teachers help children learn prosocial behaviors and limit violent play activities. NAEYC also suggests that parents censor their children's television viewing and watch television with their children so they can explain what is good and bad. Parents are encouraged to write sponsors about advertisements for poor-quality products and the abundance of violence.

In 1993, NAEYC published a position statement on the overall violence situation in our society (NAEYC Position Paper on Violence, 1993). Included was the following recommendation for action (p. 82):

> Regulate children's television programming to limit media exposure to violence and restrict practices that market violence through the linkup of media, toys, and licensed products.

NAEYC also joined a national task force on media violence (NAEYC joins, 1993). The task force's purpose is to continue and increase government regulation of television violence.

Levin and Carlsson-Paige (1994) outline the need for developmentally appropriate television that puts children first. Action must be taken to educate parents, teachers, and legislators. Levin and Carlsson-Paige describe several ways children are being damaged by spending too much time viewing developmentally inappropriate media content. Children need to develop a sense of trust and safety that is undermined by violent and scary content. They need to develop a sense of autonomy and connection, while the media depict that independence and dependence cannot work together. Children also need to develop a sense of empowerment and efficacy, while television does not provide models that use peaceful means for gaining these characteristics. Television still gives a distorted picture of sex roles and does not support the acquisition of gender identity. Television does not support the development of an understanding and appreciation of how people are alike and different but continues to promote stereotypes. Children need to develop a sense of morality and social responsibility (see Chapter 26). Television undermines healthy development in this area by showing violence as a justifiable way of solving problems and not showing enough positive models. Levin and Carlsson-Paige describe the need for action to support reform of children's television and television-viewing habits.

A great deal of research has been conducted on the television viewing habits and effects of television viewing on children over age three. For example, Anderson, Huston, Schmitt, Linebarger, & Wright (2001) followed children from preschool to adolescence. Their data indicated that adolescents who viewed educational programs as preschoolers had higher grades, read more books, placed more value on achievement, and were more creative and less aggressive than those who did not watch educational programs. The pattern was especially strong for boys. Girls who watched more violent programs had lower grades. While we know quite a bit about television and children over three, we know very little about the experiences of infants and toddlers with media. Jordan & Woodward (2001) report a small-scale study done by interviewing parents of two- to three-year-olds. Their study supports the need for more research with children under three. Their study documents that most two-year-olds have access to and spend time each day with television, VCRs, and other technology. However, what infants and toddlers understand, how they interpret what they see, and the effects on their learning are not known. The results of a study by a pediatrician in Seattle indicated that children who watch two hours per day of television before age three were 20 percent more likely to have attention problems by age seven than children who never watched television. The American Academy of Pediatrics recommends no television for children under age two. (O'Brien, 2005)

Television's power as a learning tool can be turned in positive directions. Many programs present positive models and useful information. *Barney* the purple dinosaur is beloved by toddlers and younger preschoolers. *Sesame Street* provides opportunities to learn basic skills, such as counting and reciting the alphabet; presents positive, culturally diverse role models; and supplies many types of good information. The slow-paced, reflective *Mr. Rogers' Neighborhood* is conducive to learning. Other examples of programs that provide positive learning experiences for young children are *Reading Rainbow*, *Bill Nye the Science Guy*, *The Magic School Bus*, *National Geographic Specials*, and concerts and other musical programs. It is up to adults to control the amount of time children watch television, to monitor the types of programs they watch, and to view programs with children and discuss the content afterward.

## Video Games

Video games, a combination of video and computer technology, were introduced in the 1980s. They now have a firm foundation in almost every home with children. Children may be spending more time with video games than with television programs. Video games offer opportunities for problem solving and eye-hand coordination experience, but they also usually include violent content (Rogers, 1990).

In 1992, it was estimated that one in three homes owned a video game system (Veciana-Suarez, 1992). In his book *Video Kids: Making Sense of Nintendo*, Eugene Provenzo is quoted as stating that too many video games are crude and violent. Even though some nonviolent games are available, children spend too many hours playing with them when they should be involved in more large-muscle motor activity, preferably outdoors, or reading a good book. Veciana-Suarez reports that Jason Rich, author of *A Parent's Guide to Video Games*, suggests that parents play the games with their children to monitor content and to spend some interactive time with the children. Furthermore, a limit should be set on playing time. Parents should preview games and read reviews before making a purchase. Provenzo warns parents to stay away from games that use terms on the box such as *shoots*, *destroys*, or *kills*. Rich says to look for descriptors, such as "dozens of hidden places to explore," that indicate challenging multilevels, no violence, and color.

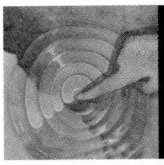

**LOOKING FURTHER**

Do a survey of television programs designed for young children. View one show on public television, such as *Sesame Street, Mr. Rogers' Neighborhood, Barney, Where in the World is Carmen San Diego?* or *Square One Television*. View one on a commercial or cable network and one hour of Saturday morning or weekday afternoon cartoons. When viewing each program, list how many of each of the following kinds of behaviors are depicted:

A. violence, aggression, or other antisocial behavior (see lists in this chapter and see Chapter 26)

B. positive social acts or moral lessons (see Chapter 26)

C. cognitive concepts (see Chapters 20–23)

D. number and length of commercials and types of products advertised

E. sex-role stereotypes (see this chapter and Chapter 27)

Which programs would you recommend to parents? Which would you not recommend? Which, if any, would you use if you were working in an all-day child care program? A kindergarten? A primary classroom? Report the data you collected regarding each program and your recommendations to the class.

## Learning with Computers

Computers can be motivational for children and enhance their learning. However, questions have surfaced as to the age at which children should be introduced to computers, how they should be introduced, and what kinds of activities young children should use them for. Silvern and McCary (1986) discuss three issues:

1. Can computers change the way children think?
2. Is it worth the effort to include computers in the early childhood curriculum?
3. How does the computer fit into the constructivist view of child development?

Silvern and McCary believe computer software will not enable children to learn any more than they would through some other instructional method. Children are limited in what they can learn through drill and practice. Working in a small group with a teacher may be as effective as working individually with a computer. However, thought can be changed qualitatively; that is, children may learn to think differently. There is some evidence that experience with LOGO helps children think more divergently and reflectively.

In considering whether computers in the early childhood classroom are worth the trouble, Silvern and McCary consider the most common criticisms. First, computers limit the child to working with two dimensions. Silvern and McCary accept this limitation but believe that even three-dimensional materials have limitations and that the experiences offered from color graphics, touch screens, a mouse, and a joystick offset the two-dimensional limitation. A second criticism is that computers are too abstract for preoperational children. Silvern and McCary believe that this is the fault of the software, not the computer. However, they believe that software appropriate to the preoperational child's level of development can and will be developed. A third criticism is that working with a computer limits mobility to simple eye-hand coordination. Silvern and McCary point out that this is not true at the beginning levels of LOGO, where children actually imitate the turtle and go through motions with their own bodies that they will later use in manipulating the turtle on their computer screen. However, Silvern and McCary also remind us that many valuable activities, such as drawing and painting, require limited body movement.

Next, critics find that working with a computer limits social activity. This point is true only if adults make it so. Children have been observed socializing by sharing responses and working together to solve problems. Computer programs have been criticized for being in a format in which only one answer is right. Again, Silvern and McCary say the software is to blame. Adults have to be careful in their choice of software. Computer time is criticized because there is no linguistic response, thus, depriving children of time for language development and causing frustration for nonreaders. This problem can be solved initially by having older children help the nonreaders. Voice synthesizers have become less expensive and are available at a reasonable price. Critics also believe that computers restrict freedom and creativity. However, software that facilitates creativity, exploration, and even dramatic play is available. Finally, critics question the value of drawing or typing on a computer screen when these tasks can be accomplished with less expensive equipment. Silvern and McCary believe that the computer offers a new medium for these activities that provides a different and rich experience.

Silvern and McCary suggest the following guidelines to facilitate overcoming the criticisms just described:

1. Do not use the computer as a means for accelerating achievement.
2. Consider the computer an additional piece of media material that can enrich, not replace, experience with other media.

3. Be sure experience with the computer relates to children's real-life experiences.
4. Provide opportunities that enable children to construct knowledge.
5. Allow free access, not forced access, to the computer. Children who are developmentally ready and interested can use the computer while other children choose other activities.

The third problem dealt with by Silvern and McCary centers on how constructivist theory relates to computer use. The question regarding computers is whether they are real or representations. Silvern and McCary believe that computers can be considered real and, thus, concrete if the software allows the child to learn and build on experiences, versus the right-and-wrong point of view and if the activities are matched to the child's ability. Concreteness depends on the adult choosing appropriate software and the ability match of the children who choose to use the computer. However, keep in mind that when the ratio of computers to children is unequal, timid children will sometimes avoid the computers and let their more aggressive classmates dominate the equipment. One way to ensure that everyone has equal access is by having the children sign up for turns and using a timer to limit the amount of time each child spends on the computer. Silvern and McCary conclude that computer use can be compatible with constructivism if handled correctly by adults. However, we need to be careful not to think computers can replace concrete materials and experiences, which are the core of knowledge construction. The nature of computer programs sets limitations that are not present in the natural environment. Haugland and Shade (1990) define the computer component of early childhood education as follows:

> Computers are an essential tool for young children. Like crayons, paints, blocks, and/or any other learning resource we provide young children, computers are neither good nor bad.
>
> The potential benefits and the dangers of computers in the hands of young children depends on how they are utilized. The potential of computers depends upon the wisdom of adults to make wise choices regarding appropriate experiences for young children (p. vii).

As technology has taken over more of our lives, a large number of child development experts have expressed concern over young children spending too much time with computers (Alliance for Children, n.d.). There is concern that computers contribute to health hazards and present risks that include "repetitive stress injuries, eyestrain, obesity, social isolation, and, for some [children], long-term, physical, emotional, or intellectual development damage." They point out that the Surgeon General is concerned that children are spending too much time staring at screens. There is no evidence that use of technology increases academic achievement. Young children, especially, need face-to-face contact with other human beings to develop language, conceptual, emotional, and social skills. The Alliance for Children paper contributors believe that today's technology will be obsolete by the time today's young children join the workforce. They believe creativity and imagination will always be valuable. Hands-on learning is still most valuable in early childhood. Further, as with television, computers should not be introduced to infants and toddlers except in the case of those with disabilities who can benefit from **assistive technology** (Wilds, 2001).

**assistive technology**
Tools and services that help a child with disabilities engage in everyday activities.

## Technology in the Future

In the commentaries section of *The Future of Children* (Five commentaries, 2000) in an issue devoted to computer technology, five experts in the field provided their

FIGURE 4–8 The computer supports social learning as these children share responses and take turns.

views on the future of technology. The question posed to the experts was, "How can we help to ensure that computer technology is used equitably, effectively, and ethically to promote positive child development?" (Five commentaries, 2000, p. 168). Regarding equity, all children not only need access to state-of-the-art equipment but also need motivation and a positive attitude. The best equipment, to be effective, needs to provide improved graphics, images, and sound. Better and more equipment means more funding is needed. Online content must be geared more to children's interests and ages. Further, adults need more training, since children are often more computer literate than adults.

More applications are needed to develop children's reflective and problem-solving skills versus just "fun." Computer labs shouldn't be installed at the expense of cutting out art and music programs, guidance counselors, or reading specialists. We need to be cautious because, as already mentioned, concerns exist about children's physical health and how exposure to technology may affect brain development. One commentator suggested that children under seven should not be using computers, and there is some evidence that preschoolers' creativity can be depressed by using some readiness software.

For the future, developers of technology equipment and software should focus more on the creative aspects of computer technology. One commentator suggests that, "Computers, like finger paint, blocks, and beads, can be used as a material for making things" (Five commentaries, p. 174). Children can design graphics and even machines (with the LEGO® programmable bricks). Expert conclusions indicate that technology needs to be viewed and used with caution, and that there is a long way to go and much to learn about the effects of technology on young children's development.

Daniel Shade (1996) identified several major issues to consider in the twenty-first century:

- Computers could potentially have a positive impact on children's social, emotional, language, and cognitive development.
- Rather than using the commonly used drill and practice software supplied by the school system, teachers should be able to select software that integrates into the curriculum and allows exploration, discovery, and creativity.
- Rather than being placed in computer labs, computers should be housed in each classroom and should be available when needed.
- All children should have access to computers with appropriate software. Too often, it is the lower socioeconomic status (SES) students who only have drill and practice software. Both boys and girls should have equal access.
- Technology changes so rapidly that it is difficult to keep up; however, young children should have the opportunity to work with the most up-to-date equipment.
- Many teachers have not had long-term exposure to computers. They must be encouraged to learn.
- Parents need to be informed that the computer is not a cure for all our educational problems and that drill and practice programs are not developmentally appropriate (see Figure 4–8).

Finally, Hilari A. Hinnant (1997), a first-grade teacher, presents us with some food for thought. As she watches young children glued to computers searching the World Wide Web for information, she ponders the concrete, real-life learning experiences that are so important in providing sensory input for young children. Outdoors, many wonders—grasshoppers, snakes, flowers, and more—are being missed. She reflects on how the Internet cannot teach many things, such as what it is like to catch a fish, hold a baby, or watch kittens being born.

> Yes, I have computers in my first-grade classroom. My students take incredible journeys on the Internet gathering exciting new information and viewing the diversity of the world. But children need someone to turn off the switch and let the real world back in. We hug, we laugh, ask questions, and learn by making concrete connections as our world becomes alive again (Hinnant, p. 17).

Compare how well the constructivist and behaviorist points of view fit the use of computers in the classroom.

## LEARNING AND CHILDREN WITH SPECIAL NEEDS OR DISABILITIES

Many children have special needs or disabilities that may make learning a special challenge. These children may need special help because of conditions that make their developmental patterns different from those of most children. However, children should be looked upon as children first and as having some special needs second:

> A child is first of all a child, regardless of how smart or delayed or troubled that child may be.
>
> Every child is unique, different, and therefore exceptional in one or more ways (Allen & Schwartz, 2001).

Allen and Schwartz (2001) point out that, although it is not always easy to define normal and abnormal, or typical and atypical, development, general developmental milestones can be used as guidelines. These milestones are a major focus in this text. Furthermore, the means by which all children learn follow the same models as already described in this unit. The challenge for those working with children with special needs is just greater in terms of finding their strongest modalities for learning and for strengthening their weaker modalities.

There has been a great deal of change in philosophy, governmental mandates, and accepted terminology over the years. **Children-first language** involves mentioning the child before the disability.

**children-first language**
Involves mentioning the child before the disability.

Children with special needs such as those listed in Figure 4–9 are often labeled **at-risk.** Hrncir and Eisenhart (1991) concede that this term is convenient and descriptive, but warn that it should always be used with caution. It is too often used indiscriminately for making placement decisions. The criteria for labeling a child at-risk should be carefully delineated. Furthermore, Hrncir and Eisenhart (1991) describe three limitations on the use of the term:

**at-risk**
Children with special needs.

1. Risk is not static. The rate of development varies and so do environmental characteristics, causing the degree of risk to vary also.
2. Test scores are not effective predictors of risk. As described in Chapter 29, test scores obtained during early childhood are not good predictors of later functioning and may not be valid and reliable measures of current functioning.

| Condition | Description |
|---|---|
| Mental Retardation | Intellectual challenge based on multiple criteria, including IQ test score, level of functional adaptive behavior (e.g., dressing, toileting, feeding), and level of social adaptive behavior. |
| Polydrug Exposed | Cognitive, motor, and perceptual deficits. Possible behavior problems. Central nervous system damage. |
| Visual Impairment | Ranges from total lack of vision to correctable vision. |
| Hearing Impairment | Ranges from total hearing loss to correctable hearing. |
| Learning Disability | Average or above intellectually but has difficulty learning. Characterized by attentional, memory, and perceptual problems. |
| Neurological Impairment | Neuromuscular disorder, such as cerebral palsy, or neurological disorder, such as epilepsy. |
| Attention Deficit Disorder (ADD) | Inattentive, disorganized, off task; may be overly active and lacking in self-control. |
| HIV-Positive | May lack immune system that will fight diseases. |
| Orthopedic Handicap | May have one or more missing limbs or limbs that do not function properly. |
| Physical Weakness | Has to conserve strength due to heart condition, bronchial problem, blood condition, etc. |
| Speech and Language Disorders | Speech difficulty may be an articulation problem. Language problems include slow or delayed speech development, lack of comprehension, etc. |
| Emotional and Behavioral Disturbance | Unable to adjust, unhappy, has behavior problems. |
| Autism | Effects communication, imagination, and socialization; child appears to avoid social interaction. |
| Giftedness | High intelligence and/or creativity and special talents. |
| Cultural Differences | Child's culture is not the mainstream model. |
| Environmentally Induced Disabilities | Abusive treatment, malnutrition, cultural differences. |

**FIGURE 4–9** Special-needs conditions.

3. Children are not isolated entities but develop within an ecological context. The situation both at home and at school affects children's behaviors. Children may operate well in a developmentally appropriate setting but appear at-risk in a developmentally inappropriate setting.

These authors conclude that the term *at-risk* must be used with care and not just applied indiscriminately.

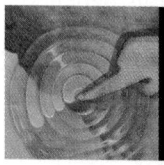

**LOOKING FURTHER**

From the list in Figure 4–9, pick one type of special-needs condition. Try to learn as much as you can about the condition through:

A. reading books and articles

B. talking to professionals who work with that type of child

C. visiting programs that deal with that type of condition

## Learning in Inclusive Settings

The major concern for children with special needs or disabilities is defining the type of setting that will provide the best and most appropriate learning environment. It is generally accepted that children with special needs should be included in settings with typical students. The general definition of inclusion is provided by Richey and Wheeler (2000, p. 23):

> . . . inclusion [is] an approach and process of including young children with various types and levels of severity of disabilities in the same services, programs, and settings as young children without disabilities.

**inclusion**

The commitment to educate each child, to the maximum extent appropriate, in the school and classroom he or she would otherwise attend; involves bringing the support services to the child and requires only that the child will benefit from being in the class.

**full inclusion**

All of the services and support needed by children are present and available in the schools they would normally attend.

The terminology of inclusion is continuously changing. Fuchs and Fuchs (1998) explain the current tension between those who favor **inclusion** versus those who favor **full inclusion.** Inclusionists believe that regular classrooms have a finite capacity to change and handle children's special needs. Therefore, a continuum of specialized services must be designed to deal with each student's special educational requirements. This continuum is illustrated in Figure 4–10. Full inclusionists believe that educators' major responsibility is the social development of children with special needs. They believe it is imperative that children with special needs establish friendships with typically developing children. This scenario can happen effectively only with full-time placement in regular classroom settings, which gives legitimacy to the student with special needs as a member of the class. The student with special needs does not have to come and go out of the class for special instruction, which highlights that the student does not completely belong. Furthermore, self-contained special classes provide educators with a place to send difficult students rather than forcing them to develop responsive teaching methods in responsive classrooms that include all children with special needs. Fuchs and Fuchs (1998) describe the apparent weaknesses in both the inclusionist and full-inclusionist points of view. A major weakness is the lack of extensive research. Most research pertaining to full inclusion has been done at the preschool level and has yielded many positive results (e.g., Rafferty & Griffen, 2005). Little research has been conducted in elementary schools regarding full inclusion or the continuum-of-services model. Statistics indicate that once children are placed in a special education classroom, it is a dead end for them. They are rarely sent back into a regular classroom. Fuchs and Fuchs (1998) favor the continuum-of-services approach, as long as it is designed to help students move up into regular classrooms.

Using Bronfenbrenner's ecological systems model (see Chapter 3), Odom and Diamond (1998) summarize the research on the classroom as a microsystem. Some of the findings include the following:

- When children with special needs are included in classrooms where teachers offer a broad selection of activities, they are more likely to engage in peer interaction at a higher social level. They also appear to stay on task with greater frequency and to be more persistent in mastering selected tasks.

| Regular Classroom | Regular Classroom with Consultative Assistance | Regular Classroom with Part-Time Resource Room | Regular Classroom with Part-Time Special Class | Full-time Special Class | Full-time Special Day School | Homebound Instruction | Hospital or Residential Placement |
|---|---|---|---|---|---|---|---|

FIGURE 4–10 Continuum of services.

Form a discussion group with a few fellow students. Discuss your feelings about and experiences with young children with special needs. Ask the group the following:

a. Has anyone ever had any experiences with special-needs young children? At home? In a school setting?
b. What happened? How did you feel about the child(ren)? Did the child(ren) enjoy the experience? Did the child(ren) have any difficulties?
c. How would the others feel about teaching in an integrated class? A class for special-needs children only?

- Opportunities to work in small groups provide a setting for more peer interaction.
- Placement in mixed-age groups appears to provide more social opportunities for children with special needs.

Overall, research evidence supports the conclusion that children with special needs gain a social development advantage in regular classroom placement.

## SUMMARY

Young children learn through their experiences. They learn through constructing knowledge as they interact with the environment and through various forces that exert outside controls on their activities.

Young children perceive the world differently from older children and adults. They use all their senses but tend to be selective in the information they take in. They learn best through manipulation and handling of concrete objects in contrast to passive listening or using workbooks or work sheets. Young children are still in the process of developing memory strategies. Their memory processes are relatively inefficient, but they remember more if the input has been from concrete experiences rather than from abstract instruction.

The rapid growth of the brain during the first five years provides the connections for children to store the wealth of knowledge constructed during the early years. The five-year-old's brain weighs as much as an adult's. However, some children have dysfunctional memory, which results in an inability to make the best use of the information they store and to respond appropriately to new sensory information.

Learning may occur through classical conditioning, operant conditioning, and observation and imitation, combined with interaction with the environment.

Motivation is another important element in learning. Children need to have a desire to learn. Infants and toddlers have a natural curiosity that motivates them to explore their environments. Maintaining this motivation is the challenge as children grow older.

Other critical factors in learning include adult support and activity-based learning in an appropriate environment. Opportunities to work with peers also enhance learning. Through instruction that fits their learning styles, children can achieve greater success and maintain their desire to learn.

The growing technological world provides new tools and new challenges for learning as well. Television, video games, and computer technology open up new vistas for learning but must be handled with care, with content and time allotments controlled.

Children with special needs and abilities follow the same developmental steps as more typical children but need special assistance due to problems with perception, memory, motor abilities, physical development, and/or general pace of development. There is general agreement that children with special needs should spend as much time as possible in regular classroom settings to learn how to live in the larger social world. However, opinions differ as to whether students with special needs should be included full time or part time in regular classrooms.

Overall, the question of how learning takes place is complex. Finding answers for the individual child is a complex problem. In Chapters 6 and 7, the roles of adults are examined more closely.

## For Further Reading


Bailey, D. (Ed.) (2002). *Children with special needs* [Special issue] *6*(2). (Publication of the FPG Child Development Institute, University of North Carolina at Chapel Hill.)

Blakemore, S., & Frith, U. (2005). *The learning brain: Lessons for education*. Williston, VT: Blackwell.

Bryant, J., & Bryant, J. A. (Eds.). (2001). *Television and the American family*. Mahwah, NJ: Erlbaum.

Byrnes, J. P. (2001). *Minds, brains, and learning*. New York: Guilford.

Chang, F., & Burns, B. M. (2005). Attention in preschoolers: Associations with effortful control and motivation. *Child Development*, *76*(1), 247–263.

Cortes, C. E. (2000). *The children are watching: How the media teach about diversity*. New York: Teachers College Press.

Duckworth, E. (1996). *"The having of wonderful ideas" and other essays on teaching and learning*. New York: Teachers College Press.

Eichenbaum, H., & Cohen, N. J. (2001). *From conditioning to conscious recollection: Memory systems of the brain*. New York: Oxford University Press.

Fisch, S. M. (2004). *Children's learning from educational television*. Mahwah, NJ: Erlbaum.

Fosnot, C. T. (Ed.). (2005). *Constructivism: Theory, perspectives, and practice* (2nd ed.) New York: Teachers College.

Gargiulo, R. M., & Kilgo, J. (2005). *Young children with special needs* (2nd ed.). Clifton Park, NY: Delmar Learning.

Gibson, E. J., & Pick, A. D. (2000). *An ecological approach to perceptual learning and development*. New York: Oxford University Press.

Goldstein, E. B. (Ed.). (2004). *Blackwell handbook of sensation and perception*. Williston, VT: Blackwell.

Goldstein, J., Buckingham, D., & Gilles, B. (Eds.). (2004). *Toys, games, and media*. Mahwah, NJ: Erlbaum.

Grisham, J., Hemmeter, M. L., & Pretti-Frontczaj, K. (2005). *Blended practices for teaching young children in inclusive settings*. Baltimore, MD: Brookes.

Hauser-Cram, P., Warfield, M. E., Shonkoff, J. P., & Krauss, M. W. (2001). *Children with disabilities. Monographs of the Society for Research in Child Development*, *66* (3, Serial No. 266).

Hayne, H., Barr, R., & Herbert, J. (2003). The effect of prior practice on memory reactivation and generalization. *Child Development*, *74*(6), 1615–1627.

Helm, J. H., Berg, S., & Scranton, P. (2004). *Teaching your child to love learning*. New York: Teachers College.

Holyoak, K. J., & Morrison, R. G. (Eds.). (2005). *The Cambridge handbook of thinking and reasoning*. New York: Cambridge University Press.

Livingstone, S., & Bovill, M. (Eds.). (2001). *Children and their changing media environment: A European comparative study*. Mahwah, NJ: Erlbaum.

Marlowe, B. A., & Page, L. M. (2005). *Creating and sustaining the constructivist classroom* (2nd ed.). Thousand Oaks, CA: Corwin.

McNary, S. J., Glasgow, N. A., & Hicks, C. D. (2005). *What successful teachers do in inclusive classrooms*. Thousand Oaks, CA: Corwin.

Papert, S. (1994). *The children's machine*. New York: Basic Books.

Price, M., & Verhulst, S. G. (2002). *Parental control of television broadcasting*. Mahwah, NJ: Erlbaum.

Prior, M. (Ed.). (2005). *Learning and behavior problems in asperger syndrome*. New York: Guilford.

Richey, D. D., & Wheelen, J. J. (2000). *Inclusive early childhood education*. Clifton Park, NY: Delmar Learning.

Sandberg, J. (2000, Fall/Winter). Multimedia childhood. *Newsweek*, 78–79.

Silver, L. B. (2004). *Attention-deficit/ hyperactivity disorder*. Arlington, VA: American Psychiatric Publishing.

Van Evra, J. (2004). *Television and child development* (3rd ed.). Mahwah, NJ: Erlbaum.

Wall, K. (2004). *Autism and early years practice*. Thousand Oaks, CA: Corwin.


## Suggested Activities

1. One aspect of perception is visual discrimination and observation. Find out how skillful children are at some visual discrimination tasks. Try the tasks on at least three young children. Three children of the same age may be used to get an idea of the variation in skill at one age. Or, pick children at different ages (e.g., one three-year-old, one four-year-old, one five-year-old, and/or

one six-year-old) to get some idea of developmental differences. The following tasks may be used.

Warm-up task: Concept of *same*

To accomplish the following skill tasks, the child must be able to understand and use the concept *same*. Show the child a group of three familiar objects, such as a cube block, a penny, and a toy animal. Have an exact duplicate of each object. In turn, show the child each duplicate object.

Say, "What is this?"(If the child cannot name it, you name it and respond, "This is a block. Now you tell me what it is." )

Hold up the block, point to the three objects and ask, "Which one is the same as this?" (If the child does not answer correctly, show him or her which one is the same. Then have the child show you.)

Repeat with the other two objects. If the child does not understand *same*, going on to the skill tasks would be frustrating and meaningless. If the child does understand *same*, go on to the following skill tasks.

**Skill 1: Shape—Keep color and size constant, varying shape only.**

a. Present three shapes and ask, "Which is not the same?"

b. Present a square to the left and a square, triangle, and circle to the right. Point to square number 1, and ask, "Which of the other shapes is the same as this one?"

Present a circle on the left and repeat.

**Skill 2: Color—Size and shape are kept constant and only color varies.**

a. Present three objects and ask, "Which is not the same?"

b. Present three objects.

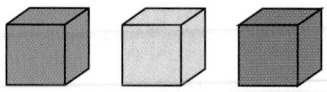

Show the child a fourth object that matches one of the three, and ask, "Which is the same?"

**Skill 3: Size—Shape and color are kept constant with only one size varying.**

a. Present three objects, asking, "Which is not the same?"

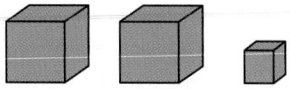

b. Present three objects of different sizes.

Show the child an object that is the same as one of the three and say, "Find one that is the same as this one."

**Skill 4: Detail**

Card a.  "Which is not the same?"

Card b.  "Which is the same as this one?" (Point to the figure on the left.)

Contrast and compare the responses from each of the children. What were the similarities and differences? Did you find any reflections of age difference? Compare your results with those obtained by other students in the class.

**2.** Examine visual memory by using the following tasks. Find three children between the ages of three and seven, either all the same age or three different ages.

**Task 1: Real Objects**

Have a collection of 8 to 10 common objects, such as toy cars, small dolls and animals, buttons, crayons, pencils, and spoons. Include some duplicates.

a. Have the child name each object.
b. Put the duplicates aside.
c. Tasks
   1. Show the child four objects. Show him or her a duplicate of one, saying, "I'm going to hide this." (Hide it.)
      "Find one like I showed you."
      The task can be increased in difficulty by using more and similar objects.
   2. Show the child three objects. Say, "I'm going to hide one. Cover your eyes or turn your head."
      Hide one. "Open your eyes. What is missing?"
      Task difficulty can be increased by showing more objects and hiding more.
   3. Show the child two or more objects. Say, "Look carefully before I hide them." Cover (or remove) the objects. Say, "Name as many as you can remember."

**Task 2: Pictures**

Administer the same tasks, using pictures instead of objects.

**Task 3: Sequence**

Place pictures of objects in a simple sequence on a card. Let the child study the sequence and then hide the pictures. Say, "Name the pictures in order."

Contrast and compare the responses from each of the children. What were the similarities and differences? Were there any differences according to age? Compare results with those obtained by other students in the class.

3. Auditory memory can be examined using a digit span task. Present the child with several numbers, such as 1–3–5–9, and ask the child to recall the numbers in the order presented. Work with a three-year-old, a four-year-old, a five-year-old, a six-year-old, and/or a seven-year-old. Present the following sets of digits each in turn. Say to the child each time, "Listen carefully to what I say because I want you to repeat some numbers after I say them."

   Warm-up task: "One. Now you say 'One.'"
   "Four. Now you say 'Four.'"
   Task 1: 2–5–8
   Task 2: 1–4–5–9
   Task 3: 3–5–7–9
   Task 4: 1–3–5–7–9
   Task 5: 5–1–9–4–2

   Were there differences in the number of digits recalled by each child? Did the children seem to have any special way of trying to remember the number sequences? Write a description of each child's response to the tasks.

4. Children can learn through observing other children being rewarded for some behavior. Arrange to work with two groups of four-, five-, six-, or seven-year-olds. Have four children in each group. Work with one group at a time. Give each child paper and crayons. Say to them, "Draw a picture of things you see outdoors." With the first group, wait until everyone is working and approach one child and comment on his or her picture (e.g., "What nice clouds," "What a nice tree," or "Pretty flowers"). Say nothing else to either group during the drawing sessions. Count how many in each group drew the object you reinforced in the one child's picture. In which group's pictures did that item appear more often? Did it appear more often in the pictures of the group that was reinforced? Did the individual whose picture was commented on respond (e.g., by drawing more of the item mentioned)?

5. Watch one or more children's television shows with young children. Note each child's interest level, the kinds of questions he or she asks, and the responses the child gives. After the program, ask the children questions about the content of the program. What was it about? What did they like? What did they learn? Why did the characters do what they did (if some kind of story or plot was included)? Report the results to the class.

6. Visit two or more preschool, kindergarten, and/or primary classrooms where computers are being used. Through observation and teacher interviews, obtain the following information:
   a. How is computer use managed relative to room placement, time scheduling, turn taking, number of children working at the same time, and so on?
   b. What types of programs are being used (e.g., tutorial, drill and practice, simulation, or as a tool; commercial and/or teacher made)?
   c. How are the students responding? Do they seem motivated? Are they anxious to get a turn? Do they have choices? (Observe at least two students, closely following them through the whole process.)
   d. Write a report including all the information you obtained and an evaluation of the effectiveness of the computer as it is used in these classrooms.

7. Visit a child developmental center or an elementary school with inclusive classes for students with special needs within the age span birth through age eight. Interview the director or principal and one or more teachers. Ask about the following or other questions you might devise:
   a. the objectives of the program
   b. the screening and placement procedures

c. the criteria for admitting a child to the program
d. the staffing of the program and the training required for the staff
e. the types of activities and services offered

Visit at least one classroom in each center/school and record what you observe. Write down your observation of the children, the teachers, and their relationships, and your feelings about what you observed. Compare and contrast the two classrooms.

**8.** Make an entry in your journal.

## REVIEW

**1.** Match each of the terms in Column I to their correct definitions in Column II. Put the answers on a separate sheet of paper.

| Column I | Column II |
|---|---|
| a. learning | 1. An inborn, unlearned behavior. |
| b. perception | 2. The mental capacity of retaining and reviewing impressions. |
| c. reflex | 3. A change in behavior that occurs as the result of experience. |
| d. memory | 4. The interpretation of what is sensed. |
| e. synapses | 5. Small cells that are the building blocks of the brain. |
| f. plasticity | 6. An output fiber that sends information to other neurons. |
| g. neurons | 7. Short, hair-like fibers that receive information. |
| h. axons | 8. A white fatty material that protects axons. |
| i. myelin | 9. The connection of cells to each other. |
| j. dendrites | 10. Abundance of synapses accounts for why the young child's brain learns new skills quickly. |

**2.** Write the number of each statement that describes a part of the developmentalist view of learning.
a. The process of learning, rather than the product, is emphasized.
b. The interaction between growth and learning is emphasized.
c. Learning is emphasized more than growth.
d. The product of learning (what is learned) is emphasized more than the process.
e. Stages of growth and readiness to learn are viewed as key factors.
f. The child constructs his or her own knowledge.

**3.** Read the following description. What seems to be the problem?
Johnny is working on a task that involves sorting letters of the alphabet into different piles. He has put all the *p*s and *b*s in the same pile.

**4.** Label the types of learning that Pablo and Terry experience in the following story. Pablo is four-and-a-half years old and attends an all-day child development center program. Pablo is working with a puzzle. Terry, four, is working with Tinker Toys®. Mr. Carter stops by. He smiles and says, "Big tower, Terry." Pablo glances up at Terry as Mr. Carter speaks. Pablo puts aside his puzzle and starts to build with Tinker Toys®; Pablo says to himself, "I need more of those orange things." The lights flicker twice. This is the signal to clean up for lunch. Pablo suddenly feels hungry.

**5.** Decide which of the following are examples of generalization, discrimination, shaping through successive approximation, and extinction.

a. One of the mothers brings the family dog to school to visit. He is a friendly basset hound who loves children. Most of the children are delighted to pat him and hug him. Patrice runs into the bathroom and refuses to come out. Her teacher finds out from her mother that Patrice has been afraid of dogs since a big dog jumped on her when she was two years old.

b. The next time Hound visits school, Mr. Hernandez encourages Patrice to sit where she can see the other children playing with him. A couple of weeks later, the dog returns. This time, Mr. Hernandez is able to get Patrice to sit closer to the other children. When the dog visits again, Patrice is willing to let him come within two feet of her. With each step that Patrice takes closer to the dog, Mr. Hernandez commends her for being so brave. Eventually, she sits next to Mr. Hernandez while he pats the dog. Finally, when Hound returns for his final visit of the year, Patrice pats him on the head.

c. After that, Patrice never runs away at the first sight of a dog, although she is still cautious until she is sure the dog is friendly.

d. Patrice tells Mr. Hernandez that Joe's dog, Hound, is nice. She says, "He's not mean like the dog that jumped on me."

**6.** Name the three processes that, according to Piaget, enable the child to adapt to and make sense out of his or her environment.

**7.** Match the types of memory listed in Column I with their descriptions in Column II. Put the answers on a separate sheet of paper.

| Column I | Column II |
|---|---|
| a. recall | 1. "Name all these animals for me." (A bear, a mouse, and a deer are on the table.) |
| b. recognition | 2. "Here are three animals. Now, I'll cover them with a cloth. Next, I'll show you one and put it back. Okay, now I'll take off the cloth. Which animal did I show you?" |
| c. paired associates | 3. "Now, I'll cover the animals again. Draw a picture of one of the animals." |
| d. reproduction | 4. "With all the animals covered, tell me what kinds there are under the cover." |

**8.** Mrs. Jones is teaching the children the concepts of hard and soft. She shows them a piece of cotton, a ball of Play-Doh®, a piece of fur, a piece of wood, a cube of metal, and a plastic box. She asks which are hard and which are soft. How could this experience be improved to help the children remember hard and soft?

**9.** List five criticisms of television.

**10.** Discuss the positive values of television for young children.

**11.** Select *all* the statements that are correct.

a. Computers can never be expected to change the qualitative aspects of young children's thinking.

b. Although computers are two dimensional, they provide worthwhile and unique experiences that cannot be obtained through other media.

c. It is possible to develop software that is not too abstract for young children to use.

d. Computers inhibit social development because they can be used by only one child at a time.

e. Software is available that promotes creativity, exploration, and even dramatic play.

f. Computers should be treated as just another type of classroom media that can assist in individualizing and motivating learning.
g. Computers should be used primarily to try to accelerate achievement.
h. Computer programs are teacher proof. That is, the teacher has no effect on how well they work.
i. A teacher who dives in and becomes knowledgeable can find a multitude of uses for computers in his or her classroom.
j. Children as young as two years of age can become interested in exploring the computer, especially if they see their parents using one.
k. Video game technology is about to expand into more powerful and creative formats.

**12.** What are the issues concerning the future of computer technology?
**13.** Explain the terms *special needs* and *at-risk* as they apply to young children.
**14.** List at least 10 special-needs conditions.
**15.** Give your opinion regarding the concept of inclusion. Consider the definitions given in the text and the skills required for teaching an integrated class.

## KEY TERMS LIST

accommodation
assimilation
assistive technology
at-risk
attention
attention deficit disorder (ADD)
axon
children-first language
classical conditioning
constructivist
dendrites
discrimination
equilibration
extinction
full inclusion
generalization
habituation
inclusion
individual education plan (IEP)
learning
learning styles
memory
myelin
neurons
operant conditioning
plasticity
sensory involvement
sensory integrative dysfunction
shaping
successive approximation
synapses

Additional resources for this chapter can be found on the Online Companion™ to accompany this text at http://www.earlychilded.delmar.com. Respond to "Time to Reflect" and "Looking Further" concepts, review various child development scenarios, and answer thought-provoking questions in the Critical Thinking Forum. Keep a daily journal by downloading the student journal available on this Web site. Complete the interactive matching exercises to reinforce concepts, and print out the child development assessment forms to use during your observation of development for children from birth to age eight. In addition, read the case studies on the Web site to reinforce the important concepts in each chapter, and take a look at the multitude of Web links that are available for student research on the Internet.

CHAPTER

# 5

# Learning Through Play

## OBJECTIVES

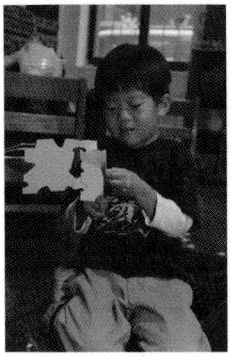

After reading this chapter, you should be able to:

- Define *play* and provide examples.
- Identify theories of play.
- Categorize play examples according to resources used.
- List the functions of play.
- Identify play accommodations made for children with disabilities.
- Identify and use Parten's and Smilansky's play categories.
- Apply the factors involved in the sociocultural apects of play.
- Describe the three areas of research that support a play-based environment for young children.

*I tried to teach my child with books,*
*He gave me only puzzled looks.*
*I tried to teach my child with words,*
*They passed him by often unheard.*
*Despairingly I turned aside,*
*"How shall I teach this child," I cried.*
*Into my hand he put the key,*
*"Come," he said, "play with me."*
—Author Unknown

Play is the major activity through which children learn. It is also a natural, biological function (Elkind, 2003). Both human and animal children enjoy play and learn about the world through play. Elkind (2003) reminds us that play is not academic work but a spontaneous and creative activity. True play is joyful and pleasurable. Elkind (2005) emphasizes that play is not an optional activity for children as it is for adults but is an essential activity needed for healthy growth and development. "Play is a child's right, and protecting it is everyone's responsibility" (Schmidt, 2003). Research on play and brain development supports that "active, physical, and cognitively stimulating play" provides a place for cognitive skills to advance (Stegelin, 2005).

## THEORIES OF PLAY

The major theories of play are the psychoanalytic theories of Freud and Erikson and the constructivist theories of Piaget and Vygotsky. The psychoanalytic perspective focuses on the expression of emotions and the mastery of difficulties that children meet. The constructivist view focuses more on the intellectual function of play as the means through which young children construct knowledge. Through fantasy, the child experiences both pleasant and unpleasant feelings in a safe way. The child takes care of his or her baby doll just as the child's parents took care of him or her. The child fights feared monsters and kills them without fear of reprisal or punishment. From Freud's point of view, the child is free to engage in self-expression while the adult stays out of the way.

Erikson emphasizes the importance of play as a vehicle for children to find their identity. Play is a means for facing reality and mastering the skills needed for living. Toddlers use play to master skills. Preschoolers who have attained a sense of autonomy use their initiative to attack problems creatively through play. From Erikson's view, the adult can take a more active role in play. The adult must provide real experiences, such as washing dishes, setting the table, folding laundry, sweeping and feeding a pet, washing the car, and mowing the lawn. These real experiences enrich the child's spontaneous play.

Piaget views play as it relates to mental development. Play serves the functions of assimilation and accommodation. The three stages in the development of play are defined by the type of assimilative acts the child uses:

1. *Practice play:* The child repeats the same activities over and over. This behavior is typical of the toddler.
2. *Symbolic play:* The child pretends to be something that he or she is not (e.g., a superhero, a parent) or uses a material as something that it is not normally used for (e.g., sand for food, a block for a car). This behavior is typical of the preschool preoperational child.
3. *Games with rules:* This type of play is typical of the school-aged child.

For Piaget, the child must have some degree of control over his or her own activity to develop properly through play.

Vygotsky (Berk & Winsler, 1995; Bodrova & Leong, 2003a & 2003b) emphasized representational play. He viewed the make-believe play that emerges during the preschool period as a critical factor in development. This representational play evolves into the games with rules that are the focus of children's activity during middle childhood. For Vygotsky, play created a zone of proximal development (ZPD) where children could behave older than their age. Vygotsky identified two critical features of play (Berk & Winsler, 1995, pp. 53–54):

1. All representational play creates an imaginary situation that permits the child to grapple with unrealizeable desires. The appearance of imaginary play coincides with the time when children are expected to learn to delay gratification. Through fantasy, children can have immediate, if imaginary, gratification.
2. Representational play contains rules for behavior that children must follow to engage in and complete the play scenario. Every fantasy activity follows social rules that develop during the course of the developing script.

Berk and Winsler (1995, p. 54) conclude:

> According to Vygotsky, make-believe supports the emergence of two complementary capacities: (1) the ability to separate thought from actions and

objects and (2) the capacity to renounce impulsive action in favor of deliberate and flexible self-regulatory activity.

Fantasy play then serves both a cognitive and a social function.

Play includes some of each of these theories. Freud addresses the emotional aspects of play, Erikson the social, Piaget the cognitive, and Vygotsky both the cognitive and social.

This chapter describes some basic learning processes with applications from both the developmentalist and behaviorist points of view. It also provides detail on the adult's role in the young child's learning.

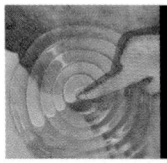

**LOOKING FURTHER**

Watch *Mr. Rogers' Neighborhood.* Describe what kinds of things in the program you think might inspire interesting fantasy and imaginative play in young children. Tell how you might watch this program with a small group of children, interpret the program for them, and follow up on what was viewed in a way that would support and enhance the children's play. Do the same activity watching *Sesame Street* and *Dora the Explorer.* Compare the results.

**vehicles for play**

Play with motion and interaction, objects, language, and social materials.

## THE DEVELOPMENT OF PLAY

Play develops into different forms at different levels as children age and pass through their stages. Johnson, Christie, & Wardle (2005) see play and development in a two-way relationship. "Development is served *by* play, and development is seen *in* play" (p. 56). That is, play supports development, and it is the arena in which we can observe developmental changes.

Play takes on many forms. Catherine Garvey (1990) described and categorized these **vehicles for play** by identifying four sets of vehicles or resources: play with motion and interaction, objects, language, and social materials.

**FIGURE 5–1** Play with motion involves high spirits and gross motor activity.

### Play with Motion and Interaction

This is described by Garvey (1990, p. 25):

> The kind of play that most clearly reflects exuberance and high spirits is based on the resource of motion. The running, jumping, skipping, shrieking, and laughing of children at recess or after school is joyous, free, and almost contagious in its expression of well-being.

An interest in interaction with other children is evident in infants and toddlers, but it is during the preschool period that social interaction begins to develop and mature at a rapid rate (Figure 5–1).

Eventually, play with motion becomes integrated with games with rules. From about age six or seven on, we see children participate in activities such as jump rope with accompanying rhymes, chasing games such as cops and robbers, and other games with rules, like red rover come over, hopscotch, and hide-and-seek.

## Play with Objects

Children use objects as links between themselves and their environment. They do this in several ways (Garvey, 1990, p. 41):

- They provide a means by which a child represents or expresses his or her feelings, concerns, or preoccupying interests.
- They provide a channel for social interaction with adults or other children.
- An unfamiliar object tends to set up a chain of exploration, familiarization, and eventual understanding, an often-repeated sequence that eventually leads to more mature conceptions of the properties (e.g., shapes, textures, sizes) of the physical world.

Interaction with objects begins in infancy. The nine-month-old infant grasps an object and puts it in his or her mouth. The child waves the object and bangs it. By twelve months of age, the child usually looks at the object, turns it over, touches it, and then puts it in his or her mouth, waves it, and/or bangs it. By fifteen months, the child visually inspects an object before engaging in other activities with it. By the time he or she reaches three years of age, the child is acting out themes with objects, such as feeding a doll using a toy cup and saucer or having a doll drive a toy truck. By the time the child is three, Garvey indicates that the child interacts with objects in the following ways (1990, p. 44):

1. The child uses objects in the way they are intended. The child no longer, for example, puts every toy in the mouth but only those that are supposed to go in the mouth, such as a spoon or fork.
2. The child organizes objects so that things that belong together are used together, such as horse and rider, cup and saucer, doll and doll clothes.
3. The child performs sequences of actions, such as cooking a meal, eating the meal, and washing the dishes.
4. The child uses objects appropriately for himself or herself, such as brushing his or her teeth with a real toothbrush; on others, such as a doll; or has others use objects, such as a doll brushing its teeth.
5. Where the child does not have a needed object, he or she can pretend it is there, such as eating pretend soup with a toy spoon.
6. The child uses objects for things that he or she may need but does not have. For example, the child stirs coffee with a stick when a spoon is not available.

The three-year-old is well into the period of symbolic representation. Garvey has found that younger children need realistic types of toys to get started in the world of pretend. As the child gains skill at pretending and imagining, he or she then makes use of abstract items, such as big cardboard cartons that can be used as a house, a cave, or a castle.

When a child meets a new object, he or she usually goes through a sequence of four activities: exploration, manipulation, practice, and repetition. Garvey presents the following example. A three-year-old boy approaches a large wooden car he has never seen before. Garvey indicates that the child goes through the following sequence (1990, pp. 46–47):

1. *Exploration:* He paused, inspected it, and touched it.
2. *Manipulation:* He then tried to find out what it could do. He turned the steering wheel, felt the license plate, looked for a horn, and tried to get on the car.
3. *Practice:* Having figured out what the object was and what it could do, he got to work on what *he* could do with *it*. He put telephones on it, took them off,

next put cups and dishes on it. Now he knew what could be done with the car.

4. *Repetition:* He then climbed on it and drove furiously back and forth with suitable motor and horn noises.

The first three activities are clearly not as playful as the last is. The first three are more experimentation than play.

The young child gains in several ways from playing with objects. As Garvey shows, highly imaginative players are also excellent at solving problems involving the use of objects. Much of the young child's social life centers on objects. Toddlers' social activity centers on exchanging objects. Three-year-olds spend time deciding who things belong to, as in "This is yours and this is mine. "Things are passed out: "One for you and one for me."

Emotional attachments to toys can be very strong. Often we see a young child who goes everywhere carrying a scruffy stuffed animal or find a child treasuring a set of toy cars. Children also express emotion through objects. A doll may become the child's own little brother or sister.

For older children, play with objects becomes complex. Intricate structures are built with building materials."All through these changes, however, objects continue to arouse curiosity and the desire to learn. They provide enjoyment in mastering their use or in understanding the properties of things, and they also continue to facilitate social contacts and to assist in the expression of ideas and feelings" (Garvey, 1990, p. 57).

## Play with Language

Play with language includes play with noises and sounds, playful use of the linguistic system, and social play with language. Play with noises begins with the babbling stage. Older children also play with sounds and syllables in a rhythmic way. A child two years and two months of age says, as she builds with her toys:

Go, bib bib bib, bib bib bib.

Go, bib bib bib.

She finds her "sleepy time" book and chants:

Sleepy time a sleepy time.

Sleepy sleepy time.

Sleepy time.

Between the ages of two and three, children begin to use noise words when playing with objects or pretending to be an animal, such as *bow-wow* for a dog, *ding-a-ling* for a phone, or *pow-pow* for a gun. Children also begin to change their voices to fit different characters, such as using a deep voice for a father and a high, squeaky voice for a child. Sound play is found most often when the child is playing alone. This child talks as she plays alone in the bathtub with an assortment of objects:

Water is in this water is in this water is in this water is in this water is clear.

Water in the cup. Water in the cup there . . . put some shampoo in water.

I put shampoo on it.

I put shampoo on it.

I put shampoo on it.

FIGURE 5–2 Dressing up in adult clothing is a favorite part of dramatic play.

She repeats phrases and sentences in a rhythmical way, as if experimenting with the language.

During social play, language play falls into three categories: spontaneous rhyming and word play, play with fantasy and nonsense, and play with conversation.

## Play with Social Materials

Play with social materials is play that centers on the social world and, according to Garvey, provides the principal resource of make-believe or pretending. When this type of play includes characters, dramatic themes, and story lines, it is called **dramatic play.** This type of play is very complex and integrates all the child's resources into one whole. It is seldom seen before the age of three.

Certain themes are used by young children. Two popular ones are treating/healing, in which someone is hurt and is helped to get well, and averting threat, in which some danger, such as a monster, is posed and the children save themselves. Other popular plans are packing for and taking a trip; shopping, cooking, and dining; repairing; and telephoning. Objects often influence the choice of themes. That is, the kinds of dramatic play props available may provide inspiration. Dress-up clothes, kitchen equipment, or vehicles may inspire a theme or plan (Figure 5–2).

The play of younger children usually follows rules, not in the sense of a formal game but in the sense that the children involved put some specific limitations on what can be done during the play activity. Some teasing may be allowed, for example, but it cannot get mean or the play breaks up.

**dramatic play**

Play that centers on the social world and includes characters, dramatic themes, and a story line.

Young children's play also contains ritual, that is, some kind of controlled repetition. A ritual usually includes some kind of turn taking, with each person's contribution being a turn. Two turns, one by each participant, is a round. Look at this example from Garvey:

| | First Child | Second Child |
|---|---|---|
| Round 1 | You're a girl. | No, I'm not. |
| Round 2 | You're a girl. | No, I'm not. |

These rituals rarely occur in the busy preschool room but often occur when a pair of children play together in privacy.

## Dramatic Play

The dramatic play of preschoolers at ages three, four, and five has some distinct characteristics. Three-year-olds usually have no preconceptualized theme or plot (Brown, Curry, & Tittnich, 1971). Much of their play involves a display of fear due to the appearance of some threatening, aggressive character who may be imaginary or one of the other children pretending. When a three-year-old becomes a character, he or she *is* that character. The child's play is not the conscious pretending of the older child. For three-year-olds, roles are fluid and constantly changing. They do a lot of collecting and gathering and carry things around in purses and suitcases. These containers must be searched daily for clothes, kitchen equipment, and manipulative toys that have been packed and carried around. Play is very repetitious. The child may do the same thing in the same way every day for long periods.

Four-year-old dramatic play involves the management of aggressive impulses (Brown, Curry, & Tittnich, 1971). It usually involves aggressive heroes who attack and rescue. A monster or a ghost may attack, and the rest of the children respond by running. There is typically a safe or cozy place where those attacked can hide and be protected. For some children, the open aggression is too threatening, and they vent their hostile feelings by being silly or using bad language. Masculine and feminine traits are exaggerated, and props, such as cowboy outfits; firefighter, police, and medical equipment; dresses; veils; coats; ties; and grown-up shoes, are needed. A lot of gross motor activity takes place, especially running and jumping. More roles are used, and groups are set up according to some criteria. For example, the author had a group of four-year-old boys who had a leather sole club; only the children with leather soles on their shoes could belong. Fantasy and reality are now more clearly separated and the four-year-old can role-play and consciously pretend. Hiding is often a part of the action.

The five-year-old uses complex dramatization (Brown, Curry, & Tittnich, 1971). He or she works through his or her fears and hostilities in play. Roles are not only real-life types but also cultural folk heroes, such as superheroes and characters from fairy tales.

In the primary grades, children continue to enjoy dramatizing (Wasserman, 1990). "Opportunities to dramatize—either purely inventive scenarios or those stories read and loved in class—should be part of the daily life in a primary classroom" (Wasserman, 1990, p. 175). An accessible supply of props, such as dress-up clothes, hats, shoes, crowns, scarves, tools, and flashlights, are essential materials for the primary classroom. Spontaneous dramatic play should be encouraged. It is not unusual for the dramatization of a favorite story to evolve into a new plot. Puppets and a puppet stage should also be available to further stimulate spontaneous dramatic play.

## THE FUNCTIONS OF PLAY: WHAT CHILDREN LEARN

Over the years, an increasing amount of research and experimentation has been done to document the functions served by play. The functions of play include supporting cognitive development, supporting language and literacy development, learning social roles, and supporting the development of children with disabilities.

### Play and Cognitive Development

Advances in brain development research are providing increased knowledge of how the brain develops. The brain is developed only 25 percent at birth, so 75 percent is still developing during early childhood and later years (Bergen & Coscia, 2000). According to Bergen and Coscia, play development is closely related to brain development. Infant play begins with sensorimotor activity, which provides for growth and development in the sensorimotor area of the brain. During the toddler period, language develops rapidly and pretend play (where young children can practice the language they are learning) supports this development. From ages three through eight, play is very elaborate and engages children in problem-solving, processing of information, and memory, thus, enriching brain development in the related brain areas. We can observe children's brain development in their spontaneous play, therefore, they should be provided with a wide range of materials and experiences. Neurons are the basic materials of the brain, and synapses connect neurons during infancy and later life. Synapses enable messages to be carried around the brain (Gallagher, 2005). In infancy, synapses develop very rapidly. Play activity helps maintain the synaptic connections.

Elena Bodrova and Deborah Leong have written extensively on the Vygotskian view of play and its relationship to cognitive development (Bodrova & Leong, 2003a, 2003b, & 2004/05). Vygotsky viewed make-believe (or dramatic) play as the leading activity for preschoolers that creates their ZPD. He identified three major features of make-believe play:

1. An imaginary situation is created.
2. Roles are taken on and acted out.
3. The roles determine a specific set of rules that are acted out.

The features have important roles in the development of the mind. Make-believe play supports the development of thinking and imagination. It develops the ability to think ahead and plan and to follow rules and regulating behavior. Vygotsky's student, Daniel Elkonin, elaborated on Vygotsky's theory (Bodrova & Leong, 2003b). According to Elkonin, in order to be prepared for the primary grades, children must achieve four outcomes through play (Bodrova & Leong, 2003b, p. 13):

1. Play affects motivation. As they develop self-regulation, they learn to delay gratification.
2. Play facilitates *cognitive decentering*. Children learn to take the other person's point of view.
3. Play advances the development of mental representations. That is, children gradually move on to use object and verbal representations for the real objects.
4. Play fosters the development of deliberate behaviors—physical and mental voluntary actions. As children learn to follow the rules for play (e.g., animal role-players must crawl on all fours), they develop mental processes, such as memory and attention.

Henry Petroski (2004/05) describes how "children are born engineers." That is, they love to build with sand, blocks, and boxes and to draw, paint, and write. They naturally like to invent and design in a playful way. He believes young children need to be encouraged in engineering activities. These early childhood engineering projects can lead to further creative projects in later childhood and adulthood. Elizabeth Jones (2003) defines *smart* as being skillful in curiosity and critical thinking. Children grow smart through play.

Dramatic play is built on fantasy and imagination. When engaged in make-believe, children escape reality, make their own rules, and have power over their activity (Klein, Wirth, & Linas, 2003).

## Play and Language and Literacy

Development in language and literacy is supported by play activities of many kinds. Symbolic play and literate behavior are closely related. Story reenactments facilitate comprehension and retention (Pellegrini, 1985). The first stages of reading and writing are enhanced by teacher extension of children's literacy-related symbolic play through supplying literacy props in centers (e.g., paper and writing implement, maps, magazines, *TV Guides*, and menus) and encouraging children's attempts to write, such as writing a shopping list in the housekeeping center (Campbell & Foster, 1993; Morrow, 1990; Neuman & Roskos, 1993; Perlmutter & Laminack, 1993; Schrader, 1990). Play facilitates language and social development (Monaghan, 1985). The social interaction during play facilitates social development by helping children become less self-centered and more able to see other children's points of view. It supports language development through opportunities for applying language to real-life situations.

## Play and Learning Other People's Social Roles and Supporting Social Development

Young children's role-playing provides a window into their view of other people's social roles (McLoyd, Ray, & Etter-Lewis, 1985). Role-playing also provides a view of children's language development (Sachs, Goldman, & Chaille, 1985). Social play promotes maturity: children act more mature when engaged in pretend play than when engaged in nonpretend play (Berliner, 1990b). By elementary school, children usually select playmates of the same sex. They also may have contests with the boys against the girls, pollution rituals (i.e., one sex is contaminated if touched by the other), or invasion rituals, such as when one sex teases or interrupts the other sex's games. Overall, boys engage in more play with motion and include more conflict in their play. Girls tend to solve their problems in more low-key ways (Garvey, 1990).

## Play and Children with Disabilities

Play is a medium for expression and learning for all children, including those with disabilities. Because of their disabilities, children may have difficulty participating in some of the usual play activities enjoyed by children of their age (Sandall, 2003). However, it is possible to make modifications and adaptations that will let the children with disabilities participate with children without disabilities. Sandall and her colleagues (2003) identified eight types of modifications: environmental changes, materials adaptation, simplification of an activity, providing the child's preferred play material, providing special adaptive equipment, providing adult support, or providing peer support, or providing invisible support (modifying naturally occurring events).

Francke & Geist (2003) provide an example of adult support in their study of a structured instruction curriculum designed to increase the level of play of a three-year-old child (Jay) identified as autistic. As already discussed, children are biologically wired to engage in play. Children who are autistic tend to lack social and communication skills and the imagination needed to acquire important learning through play. Jay was enrolled in an integrated preschool setting with both children with disabilities and children without disabilities. Jay couldn't engage with toys in a typical three-year-old manner. Jay was put through a series of structured play lessons that took him to a higher level of interaction with toys. The researchers observed Jay during structured teaching, free-choice time, and whole-group activities. Following the instruction, they observed Jay playing with toys in a more complex way, increasing interaction with peers, and generalizing social skills to new play settings.

Murata and Maeda (2002) provide an example of individualizing instruction. Physical activity is essential for all young children. Murata and Maeda (2002) created a developmentally appropriate approach for teaching physical education to preschoolers with and without developmental delays. Preschoolers with developmental delays need extra instruction and teacher direction. They may need more time and repetition than their peers without disabilities. The Murata and Maeda approach provides these necessary procedures so that children with developmental delays can engage in the physical development experiences enjoyed by their peers.

By making adaptations and modifications to instruction, adults can provide children with disabilities with appropriate play experiences.

You are teaching in a child development center, a kindergarten, or a primary classroom. A parent comes to you and says, "Why do the children spend so much time playing? They can play at home. Why should I have to pay money for my child to play?" How would you respond?

## THE CONTEXTS OF PLAY AND PEER GROUP ENTRY

**context of play**
Interaction with peers that takes place within a play context.

Interaction with peers takes place within a play context. Kenneth H. Rubin and his colleagues have done research on the developmental **context of play** from two points of view:

1. *Social Participation:* They used M. B. Parten's (1932) play categories to distinguish the amounts of social interaction children have during play activities.
2. *Cognitive Level of the Play Activity:* They used the Piaget-based categories developed and used by Smilansky (1968).

Rubin and his colleagues developed a two-dimensional category system (Figure 5–3). The six play categories defined by Parten (1932) are as follows:

1. *Unoccupied Activity:* The child is not playing. The child may glance around, not focusing on any one activity for very long; he or she may play with his or her clothing; wander around; or follow the teacher. Overall, the child shows little interest in and gives little long-term attention to any one activity.

| | Cognitive Level of Play Activities | | | |
|---|---|---|---|---|
| **Social Participation** | **Functional** | **Constructive** | **Dramatic** | **Games with Rules** |
| Unoccupied and Onlooker | No | No | No | No |
| Solitary | Yes | Yes | Yes | No |
| Parallel | Yes | Yes | Yes | No |
| Associative | Yes | Yes | Yes | No |
| Cooperative | No | Yes | Yes | Yes |

**FIGURE 5–3** Play categories used when observing free play activity: possible combinations.

2. *Onlooker Activity:* The child observes other children as they play. The child may speak to the other children but does not get involved in their activity. This type of activity differs from the unoccupied in that the child's attention is strongly focused on a particular activity, and he or she is physically close enough to see everything and to participate verbally.
3. *Solitary Play:* The child plays alone and is independent of other children. He or she uses materials that are different from those of any children around.
4. *Parallel Play:* The child plays independently but is with other children. The child is using the same or similar kinds of play materials as the others. He or she does not try to control what the other children are doing in any way.
5. *Associative Play:* Children play with each other. They talk about what they are doing: They exchange play materials, follow each other around, and control who is allowed in the group. Everyone is participating in a similar type of play activity; there is no division of labor or working together toward some goal or end product. Everyone does pretty much whatever he or she wishes to do. The group comes together because of a common interest in the materials or activity, not because they want to work together.
6. *Cooperative or Organized Supplementary Play:* The child is in a group that is organized for a particular purpose, such as making some product, achieving a goal, dramatizing some aspect of life, or playing a formal game. There is definitely a situation of belonging to the group or of not belonging to the group. One or two leaders control the group's activities. Children take different responsibilities and/or roles within the group. The group is organized and controlled by children.

During unoccupied activity, solitary play, and parallel play activities, there is by definition no interaction with peers. During onlooker, associative, and cooperative play, peer interaction does take place.

As described by Rubin (1977), the cognitive play categories are broken down as follows:

- *Functional Play:* Simple repetitive muscle movements with or without objects.
- *Constructive Play:* Manipulation of objects to construct or to create something.
- *Dramatic Play:* The substitution of an imaginary situation to satisfy the child's personal wishes and needs.
- *Games with Rules:* The acceptance of prearranged rules and the adjustment to these rules.

The categories are listed developmentally from functional play, which is seen in infancy, to games with rules, which usually appear in the concrete operations stage. Peer relationships can develop during any of these four types of play if the child is involved in associative play or cooperative play activity at the same time. The possible combinations can be seen by looking again at Figure 5–3. The activities are listed from top to bottom as the least social to the most social, and from left to right as the lowest to highest cognitive level play.

Through collecting observational data on lower- and middle-class four-year-olds in a preschool setting, Rubin and his colleagues found that the lower the socioeconomic class child's play tended to be at a lower level both socially and cognitively. When they compared preschool and kindergarten children, they found a developmental difference in free-play behavior. Probably the older children's less egocentric view allows them to engage in more reciprocal, give-and-take activity. As children participate in more social play, peers become more important and vice versa. Shim, Herwig, & Shelley (2001) found that preschoolers engaged in more complex sociodramatic play outdoors as compared to indoors, indicating the importance of both indoor and outdoor playtimes.

Researchers have been especially interested in how children enter cooperative and associative play groups, and how relationships are maintained in these contexts. For example, peer relationships can be examined as settings for social problem-solving situations. "Social problem-solving (SPS) behaviors are attempts to achieve personal goals within social interaction" (Krasnor, 1982, p. 113). For example, when playing together, children will often want to change the theme of the play. To achieve this goal, they may try any number of strategies, such as threatening to leave the scene, offering a bribe, sharing a prized toy, making a polite request, crying, or hitting. The strategy chosen is probably influenced by the child's previously used strategies and by the particular situation. A child who is capable of accurately processing social information will probably show more variability in strategies as situations vary.

Group entry techniques have been the focus of much study (Hart, McGee, & Hernandez, 1993). Children who gain entry with ease are those who have techniques relevant to what the group is already doing. The most successful group entry tactic is to hover for a short time and then copy the behavior of the group members. Classrooms of children form unique cultures that develop their own patterns for successful social group entry and participation (Kantor, Elgas, & Fernie, 1993). For example, object sharing will be successful only if the object offered is of value to the group and is used with "the appropriate gesture, tone, and language" (Kantor et al., 1993, p. 143). Socially competent children are skilled at interpreting the social positions of their peers, are good at reading peer social cues, and can readily pick up sociocultural knowledge.

Using the play criteria just described, analyze the following social play descriptions:

- The three girls (Betty, age three; Susan and Maria, both age five) went into Maria's apartment and dressed up in adult clothing that is available for play. Maria and Susan had on "princess" dresses, and Betty came out with a pink boa and some matching heels. The princesses walked around the yard, as if in a trance, with Betty following close behind.
- Susan and Jackie (both age five) are in the living room of Susan's home. Susan is wearing a beat-up old taffeta dress with some plastic "dress-up" shoes, and Jackie is wearing an old set of Susan's pajamas, which she must have found to be beautiful, as they are adorned with a necklace, and she also has on some plastic high heels. They pretend to be princesses, and as they play, they act out a story that they narrate. They both provide input to the plot and cooperate very well.

## SOCIOCULTURAL VIEWS OF PLAY

Play is a "common feature of children's lives; children everywhere play" (Frost, Wortham, & Reifel, 2005, p. 190). Johnson, Christie, & Wardle (2005) remind us that from the sociocultural view we need to consider race and ethnicity as being one of many factors that influence development in general and play in particular by keeping the ethological model in mind (see Chapter 3). Johnson, et al. (2005) focus on the importance of the context of play. Three factors must be considered: the physical environment, the social ecology, and the cultural context.

From the sociocultural view, development and environment blend with culture into a closely linked whole (Johnson, et al., 2005). All three elements work together to influence development, including development of play. Rather than viewing play as fitting in the center of a series of concentric circles as in the ethological model, the sociocultural view depicts play as a blend of community, interpersonal, and personal influences. Johnson et al. (p. 160) conclude, "The relationship between play and context is far from simple!" The following are brief descriptions of some of the factors that influence play according to Johnson, et al. (2005).

Geography and climate are important factors that influence play. In tropical climates, the school buildings are open with minimal differentiation between indoors and outdoors. In the United States, schools in the north are built with a clear demarcation between indoors and outdoors—indoors is educational, outdoors is recess and play. Some schools have a more transitional plan with doors from classrooms leading to a covered area. Outdoor play is very influenced by climate with much less outdoor access in places where there are cold winter days as compared with mild climates where outdoor play is a year-round activity.

Neighborhoods and communities also vary. Many areas provide only adult-directed play opportunities with very little opportunity for the freedom of outdoor neighborhood play. There may be no trees to climb, sidewalks on which to skate, backyards to explore, or neighborhood parks to roam. Johnson, et al. (2005) describe recent studies that document the shrinking and disappearance of neighborhood play areas.

The family setting also influences children's play opportunities (Johnson, et al., 2005). Parents have increasing anxiety regarding children's performance in athletics, the arts, and academics; they believe play is a waste of time. Thus, playtime decreases, and time in structured activities increases. Parents also may find they have little time to engage their children in play because of job and career time overwhelming their waking hours. Research supports that parental scaffolding of play is invaluable for child development. Social class and culture also influence parental beliefs about the value of playing with their children.

Culture influences play. In different parts of the world as well as within a country, play takes on different forms. Johnson, et al. (2005, p.185) include the following example:

> In the highlands of Guatemala, girls and boys as young as eight years old are expected to help their parents in working in the fields, grinding coffee, and preparing meals, and girls as young as five and six years old help to wash clothes in the stream. But these children do not seem to have our Protestant concept of work, often playing tag through the corn, splashing each other with water in the stream and running around between the adults as they prepare the meal on a community fiesta day. And sometimes the adults drop their work and play with them.

In the areas of psychology and child development, there is no agreement on whether certain play behaviors are common to every culture or whether each culture determines how play is defined and how play relates to learning (Johnson, et al., 2005). Johnson, et al. (2005) believe that play is a universal activity that all children in all cultures engage in but that it takes on different forms as defined by each particular culture. For example, the American middle-class, believes play stimulates early cognitive and social development, which prepares children for school and for later life. They place a high value on imaginative play. In other cultures, values could be quite different.

Think back to your personal childhood play experiences. Compare your experiences with those you are acquainted with today. What were the family, neighborhood, community and cultural values that influenced the play you engaged in? What is similar and/or different today?

## RESEARCH BASE FOR THE VALUE OF PLAY

Dolores Stegelin (2005) summarized the three major research areas that support the rationale for play-based environments for young children. The three areas are (1) active play and health indicators; (2) brain research; and (3) the link between play, early literacy, and social competence.

Stegelin (2005) describes the conclusions from research on active play and health-related indicators that suggest that the rising frequency of childhood obesity and weight-related health problems is related to the lack of physical activity and a lifestyle that is too sedentary. Further, physical activity can alleviate anxiety, depression, and behavior problems in young children. Both indoor and outdoor active play are essential to children's health. Play that involves running, jumping, climbing, and other large muscle experiences builds coordination and muscle, increases metabolism and energy consumption, decreases weight and heart-related problems, reduces chronic stress levels, and increases feeling of success, self control, and competence.

Stegelin (2005) believes that the research on the brain indicates that the brain is the critical link between play and cognitive and physical development. During the first 36 months of life, children in stimulating environments have more quantity and quality of brain development than children in nonstimulating environments. As infants and young children explore and solve problems with play materials, their cognitive skills increase. As they use their fine motor skills, they enrich their cognitive skills.

Steglin (2005) summarizes the research results that link play, early literacy, and social competence. Research has shown a relationship between active social play and early language and literacy development. Children learn social skills, such as cooperation, turn taking, and playing according to rules during socio-dramatic play with peers. They learn to communicate with others, and their language skills increase. The inclusion of literacy props, integration of art activities, emphasis on environmental print, inclusion of poetry, songs, chants, storytelling, and book sharing, and adequate time to play with these materials provides skills that add to children's print knowledge and sound/symbol relationship knowledge.

## SUMMARY

Play is the major activity through which children learn. A variety of theories of play support its importance as being critical in emotional, social, cognitive, and language development. Play develops through several stages. Children use several types of resources as vehicles for play: motion and interaction, objects, language, and social materials. Children learn concepts, language and literacy skills, and social behavior through play. Play materials and environments can be modified to accommodate the learning needs of children with disabilities. Parten and Smilansky created categories that are helpful in identifying types of social and cognitive play. From the sociocultural view, community, neighborhood, family, parental values and beliefs, culture, and race influence play activities. Research also supports the importance of active play contributing to a healthy body: both mentally and physically.

## For Further Reading


Axline, V. A. (1964). *Dibs: In search of self.* Boston: Houghton-Mifflin.

Cooney, M. H. (2004). Is play Important? Guatemalan kindergarteners' classroom experiences and their parents' and teachers' perceptions of learning through play. *Journal of Research in Childhood Education, 18*(4), 261–277.

Duncan, R. M., & Tarulli, D. (2003). Play as the leading activity of the preschool period: Insights from Vygotsky, Leont'ev, and Bakhtin. *Early Education and Development, 14*(3), 271–292.

Fromberg, D. P. (2002). *Play and meaning in early childhood education.* Boston: Allyn & Bacon.

Frost, J. L., Brown, P., Sutterby, J. A., & Thornton, C. D. (2004). *The developmental benefits of playgrounds.* Olney, MD: Association for Childhood Education International.

Frost, J. L., Wortham, S., & Reifel, S. (2001). *Play and child development.* Upper Saddle River, NJ: Prentice-Hall.

Gil, E., & Drewes, A. A. (Eds.). (2004). *Cultural issues in play therapy.* New York: Guilford.

Gmitrova, V., & Gmitrov, J. (2003). The impact of teacher-directed and child-directed pretend play on cognitive competence in kindergarten. *Early Childhood Education Journal, 30*(4), 241–246.

Gotz, M., Lemish, D., Aidman, A., & Moon, H. (2005). *Media and the make-believe worlds of children.* Mahwah, NJ: Erlbaum.

Isenberg, J. P., & Jalongo, M. R. (2001). *Creative expression and play in the early childhood curriculum.* New York: Merrill/Macmillan.

Koralek, D. (Ed.). (2004). *Spotlight on young children and play.* Washington, DC: National Association for the Education of Young Children.

Paley, V. G. (1988). *Bad guys don't have birthdays: Fantasy play at four.* Chicago: University of Chicago Press.

Pellegrini, A. D., & Smith, P. K. (Eds.). (2005). *The nature of play.* New York: Guilford.

Price, M., & Verhulst, S. G. (2002). *Parental control of television broadcasting.* Mahwah, NJ: Erlbaum.

Russ, S. W. (2004). *Play in child development and psychotherapy.* Mahwah, NJ: Erlbaum.

Scarlett, W. G., Naudeau, S., Salonius-Pasternak, D., & Ponte, I. (2005). *Children's play.* Thousand Oaks, CA: Sage.

Widerstrom, A. H. (2005). *Achieving learning goals through play: Teaching children with special needs* (2nd ed.). Baltimore, MD: Brookes.

Wolfgang, C. H. (2004). *Child guidance through play.* Boston: Allyn & Bacon.

Zigler, E. F., Singer, D. G., & Bishop-Josef, S. J. (Eds.). (2004). *Children's play: The roots of reading.* Washington, DC: Zero to Three.


## Suggested Activities

1. Compare your memories of your childhood play activities with a small group in the class. What did you learn from your childhood play experiences?
2. Observe some young children engaged in sociodramatic play. Record the themes they use, the roles they take on, and the dialog. Does each role seem to have special rules?
3. Visit an inclusive early child program or a self-contained classroom for young children with disabilities. Describe the available play activities. Describe any accommodations or modifications for play that you observe.
4. Visit a child development, child care, or preschool center or a kindergarten or primary classroom. Observe one or more teachers for a total of 60 minutes during playtime. Write down everything the teacher(s) does (do). Evaluate each teacher's behavior by answering the following questions:
   a. Did the teacher get involved in the play in a directing way ("Now we will do this")?
   b. Did the teacher get involved by offering guidance (suggest a toy or prop, suggest an idea)?

c. Did the teacher get involved by becoming a part of the activity as a model or as a participant?
d. Did the teacher spend time observing the children's play?
e. Was there any evidence that the teacher had planned in some way to support spontaneous play (e.g., supply special materials or props, read a story, show a film, or take the children on a trip that might expand their role-playing)?
f. How effective was each teacher in any or all the roles observed? Do you think the teacher was more supportive or directive?

**5.** Make an entry in your journal.

## REVIEW

**1.** Define *play.* Give at least three examples.

**2.** Match the theories in Column I to their descriptions/definitions in Column II.

| Column I | Column II |
|---|---|
| a. Freud's theory | 1. Through play, children gain their identities. |
| b. Erikson's theory | 2. Through play, the child expresses emotions and masters problems, especially fears. |
| c. Piaget's theory | 3. Play provides an opportunity to develop social skills and practice adult roles. |
| d. Vygotsky's theory | 4. Play develops through three stages: practice, symbolic, and games with rules. |

**3.** Categorize each of the following examples as play with motion and interaction (*MI*), play with objects (*O*), play with language (*L*), and/or play with social materials (*SM*).
a. Dot is playing with clay, "Gooky, gooky, cooky. Cooky, cooky, gooky."
b. Lee Kwan says to Isabel, "Let's cook dinner."
c. The children come running out to the playground, laughing and shrieking as they race toward their favorite piece of play equipment.
d. Kate laughingly says to Bill, "You are a super-duper-pooper."
e. Bill says, "This is my truck, and that is your truck."
f. Theresa says, "Derrick, you be sick, and I'll be the doctor."

**4.** Read each of the following play descriptions carefully. Decide whether each child is probably five, four, or three years of age.
a. Derrick pretends to be a ghost and "attacks" the other children, who run off screaming.
b. "Let's get dressed up like grown-ups and then hide in our house so the bad guys can't get us."
c. An assortment of empty food containers is set up on the shelves of the grocery store by the teacher. The children spend the morning packing the containers into bags and carrying them to the housekeeping area.
d. "Don't let any boys touch you—they are poison!" shouts Shelly to the other girls as they all run screaming across the playground.
e. "Come on. I'll be the police, and you guys be the robbers."

**5.** List 4 major functions of play.

| Categories | | |
|---|---|---|
| **Parten** | **Smilansky** | **Incident Example** |
| | | a<br>b<br>c<br>d<br>e<br>f |

**6.** Categorize each of the following examples of child play behavior. Rate each according to the category systems of Parten and Smilansky.

a. Janie comes over to the block area and moves one of the blocks. Aaron sees her and exclaims, "Janie wrecked it!" They argue between themselves until Janie walks away. Aaron goes on building with the blocks. Two other children are building near him.

b. The blocks have fallen down. Aaron sees Andy start to build, and he does the same next to Andy. They share the blocks and compare buildings.

c. As Carmen watches the children fish, she blurts out, "Get the hook in him, David!"

d. Miguel gives the yellow car to Bill. Bill then follows Miguel.

e. Ronnie suggests that they all pile leaves. "Come on, get in here," he shouts. Six children are piling leaves.

f. Maria and her friends are all riding bikes. She slows herself by dragging her feet. Her friends do, also.

**7.** The most successful group entry technique is:

a. Push in and demand attention.

b. Say politely, "May I play with you?"

c. Hover around the edge of the group and then move into a role in the group that fits with what is already going on.

d. Hover around the edge of the group and then move into the group with a new idea.

**8.** Select the correct answer(s) to the following. There may be more than one correct answer or no correct answers.

a. Parten's play categories can be used to find the level of children's

(1) cognitive play. (3) social participation.
(2) dramatic play. (4) functional play.

b. A child who can accurately process social information will most likely

(1) find a social strategy that works and stick with it in all situations.
(2) use a variety of strategies with choice depending on the situation.
(3) select the most appropriate strategy, positive or negative.
(4) use only positive strategies, such as asking or showing.

c. Smilansky's play categories can be used to find the level of children's

(1) cognitive play. (3) social participation.
(2) cooperative play. (4) associative play.

d. A small group of children is playing house. One is the father, one the mother, one the big brother, and one the baby. Each plays his or her role in relation to the others. This is categorized as

(1) cooperative play by Parten. (3) dramatic play by Smilansky.
(2) functional play by Smilansky. (4) associative play by Parten.

e. A child is playing alone away from the other children. He appears to be making a building out of building toys. His play would be categorized as
(1) parallel by Parten. (3) solitary by Parten.
(2) functional by Smilansky. (4) constructive by Smilansky.

**9.** Respond to the following statement. "Play is the same the world over."

**10.** List the factors that influence children's choice of play activities.

**11.** Briefly describe the three areas of research that support a play-based environment for children.

## KEY TERMS LIST

context of play
dramatic play
vehicles for play

Additional resources for this chapter can be found on the Online Companion™ to accompany this text at http://www.earlychilded.delmar.com. Respond to "Time to Reflect" and "Looking Further" concepts, review various child development scenarios, and answer thought-provoking questions in the Critical Thinking Forum. Keep a daily journal by downloading the student journal available on this Web site. Complete the interactive matching exercises to reinforce concepts, and print out the child development assessment forms to use during your observation of development for children from birth to age eight. In addition, read the case studies on the Web site to reinforce the important concepts in each chapter, and take a look at the multitude of Web links that are available for student research on the Internet.

CHAPTER

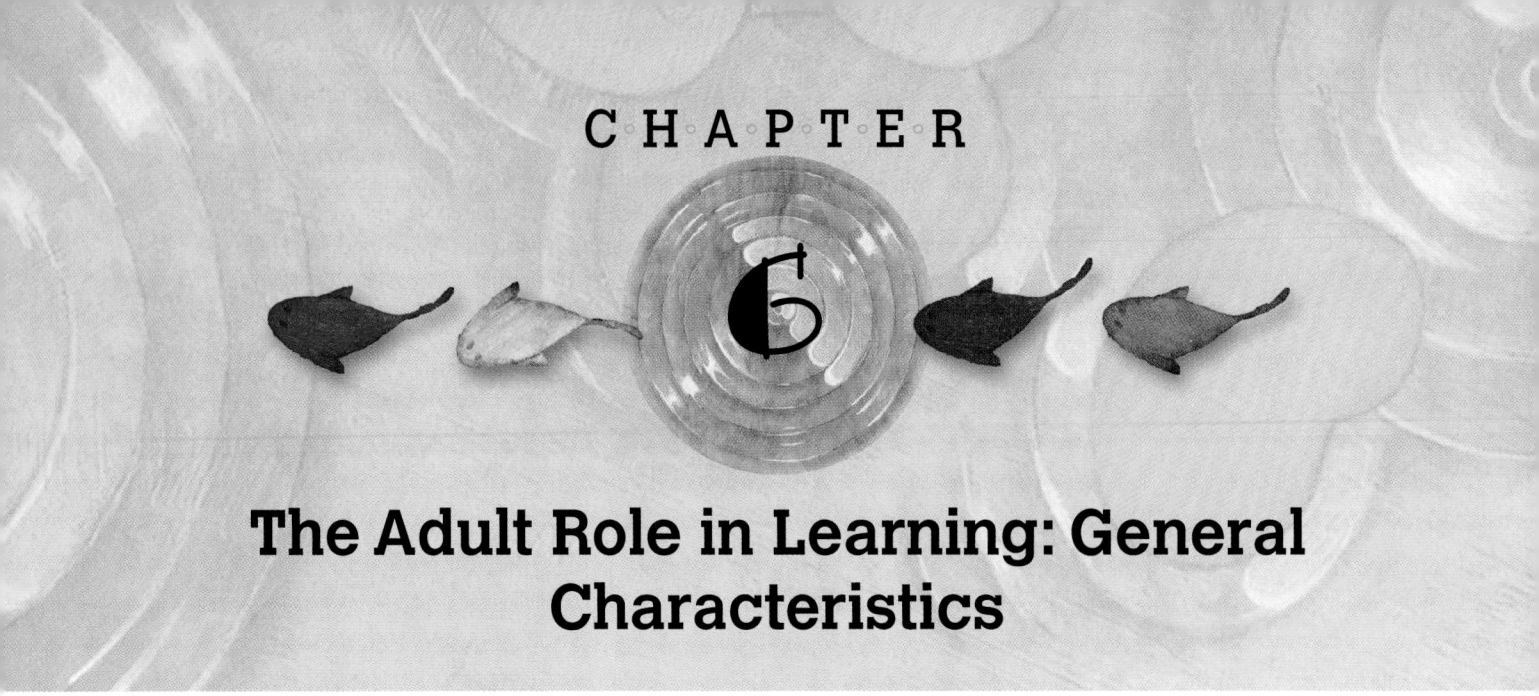

# The Adult Role in Learning: General Characteristics

## OBJECTIVES

After reading this chapter, you should be able to:

- Observe adults and children and describe the adults' roles in the children's learning.
- State the two basic roles of the adult in children's learning.
- Identify the adult role in learning as it might be defined by Piaget, Vygotsky, and Skinner.
- Discriminate between the characteristics of a constructivist teacher role and a behavioristic teacher role.
- Evaluate whether an adult is using behaviorist techniques well.
- Identify the behaviors and comments of a teacher that help children think and learn.
- Develop activities that promote cooperative learning.
- Describe the development of motivation in young children.
- Describe how peer and teacher presence and activity type use relate to the development of social and cognitive competence.
- Evaluate the adult's role in play.
- Identify the role of the teacher in providing materials, equipment, and space for play.
- Describe the responsibilities of adults in helping young children get the most value from technology.
- Explain the importance of legislative amendments PL 94–142, PL 99–457, PL 101–476, and the Americans with Disabilities Act (ADA).
- Describe how an adult can avoid burnout.

Chapter 4 described many factors involved in how learning takes place. This chapter examines the major roles of adults in providing the environment and experiences that promote young children's learning. It is apparent that adults have a critical role in children's learning. The adult role has two basic aspects: interaction with children in their daily lives and provision of the physical environment in which children operate. The two most prominent views of the adult role come from the constructivists, Piaget and Vygotsky, and the behaviorists, Skinner and Bandura. Other theoretical views have enjoyed less prominence but contribute important elements. This chapter looks further at the adult role from these views. Also, this chapter explores other areas relevant to learning: motivating children, selecting practical applications of theory, encouraging thinking and problem solving, developing competence, playing, using technology, helping children with special needs, and providing a quality environment and quality instruction.

## APPLYING THEORY TO PRACTICE

Each of the theorists—Piaget, Vygotsky, Erikson, Freud, Rogers, Maslow, Bandura, and Skinner—view the adult role in learning a little differently. From the Piagetian cognitive-developmental point of view, the adult takes the role of a guide and sets the stage for learning. The adult questions the child to encourage the development of thought and to assess the learner's stage of development. The adult then provides appropriate learning experiences. From the Vygotsky-based cognitive developmental view, the adult takes a more prominent and somewhat directive point of view in providing the scaffolding children need to move through each zone of proximal development to reach their learning potential (Figure 6–1). Interaction with others is essential to learning in both cognitive-developmental views.

From the psychoanalytic point of view offered by Erikson, Freud, Rogers, and Maslow, the adult is also a guide. However, more emphasis is placed on emotional and personality development than on cognitive development. The adult is emotionally supportive; an interpreter of feelings, motives, and actions, and assists the child in solving social problems. The adult assesses the emotional makeup of the child and his or her progress through each developmental crisis.

The maturationist, such as Gesell, sees the adult as a guide who supports the child through the cycles of growth. The adult support is considered especially important in getting through rough spots. The adult is understanding, tolerant, and calm. The child's development in the cognitive, affective, and psychomotor areas is assessed to supply him or her with experiences at his or her developmental level.

**observation**

A means through which children obtain information about social behavior.

Behaviorist Skinner emphasizes the importance of the environment to learning. In contrast to the cognitive-developmental, psychoanalytic, and maturationist views, Skinner perceives the adult as a director rather than as a guide. The adult sets the stage, dispenses reinforcements and punishments, and manages observable behavior.

FIGURE 6–1 From Vygotsky's point of view, the supportive adult provides the scaffolding that assists the child to higher levels of development.

Bandura refers to his theoretical point of view as "social cognitive theory" (Perry, 1989). From Bandura's perspective, adults serve an important function as models of appropriate behavior. Bandura focuses less on direct imitation or exact copying of the behavior of others but more on what children learn from **observation** of others' behavior. Observation is a major tool for learning about social behavior. Adults are also a resource, at a more abstract level, for instruction on how to accomplish the tasks needed to survive and thrive in the social world (Miller, 2002). The cognitive label is meant to emphasize the importance of the mental work needed to coordinate and integrate various aspects of learning. For example, children learn to throw and catch a ball, bat a ball, and run. They also learn the rules for baseball. To play the game, they have to mentally integrate the skills and the rules of the game. Much of this learning takes place simultaneously through observation of older children or adults playing baseball. However, not every child will choose to play baseball because he or she may not be interested or motivated to become involved. Observing and learning particular social behaviors does not guarantee that children will perform them. They also need the motivation to do so.

The environment provided by the adult is viewed differently relative to each of the theoretical positions. Common to all the developmental approaches is the importance of some degree of freedom. For the cognitive-developmentalist, freedom occurs within limits. Choices are offered. Concrete materials and experiences are the basic learning activities. Opportunities for social interaction exist, and the child is encouraged to observe, study, and manipulate the environment.

From the psychoanalytic view, the environment has a somewhat therapeutic aspect. Outlets and avenues are available for expressing feelings, such as hostility, doubt, shame, pride, and happiness. The maturationist emphasizes broad limits to allow room for growth. It is considered important that activities fit the particular behavior stage. For the behaviorist, the environment permits maximum positive reinforcement of appropriate adaptive behaviors. The environment provides the control and the behavioral models. This area is discussed further at the end of this chapter.

## THEORY-BASED APPROACHES

Piaget's and Vygotsky's constructivist views of cognitive development and learning and the behaviorist view of learning are the most widely applied to the development of approaches to the instruction of young children. Bodrova and Leong (1996) describe the similarities and differences between Piaget and Vygotsky. Both studied the development of thought processes. Both identified qualitative stages in development, but Piaget's stages were more distinct than Vygotsky's. Both men also believed that children play an active role in their own learning and construct knowledge in their minds. However, they differ in their respective views of the role of culture. Vygotsky believes that the "cultural context determines the very type of cognitive processes that emerge" (Bodrova & Leong, 1996, p. 28). "While Piaget emphasizes the role of the child's interactions with physical objects . . . Vygotsky focuses on the child's interactions with people" (Bodrova & Leong, 1996, p. 28). Therefore, from Vygotsky's view, compounded with Piaget's, the adult role is more directive and much more involved in the child's learning. The behaviorist view places even more emphasis on the adult as the director and controller of learning. Some of the elements of adult roles were mentioned in previous chapters and are examined further in the following sections.

### Piaget's Constructivist View of Learning

The applications of Piaget's views of cognitive development to practice are numerous. For Piaget (1971, pp. 151–157), "To educate means to adapt the individual to the surrounding social environment. The new methods [referring to open education], however, seek to encourage this adaptation by making use of the impulses inherent in childhood itself, allied with the spontaneous activity that is inseparable from mental development." Piaget indicates that the child is capable of diligent and continuous research, springing from a spontaneous need to learn (Figure 6–2). Intelligence is an "authentic activity." For Piaget, both physical and

FIGURE 6–2 The teacher can sit back, observe the children solving problems on their own, but join in when needed.

social activity is the key to learning and development. Spontaneous play is the vehicle for this activity.

As already pointed out, many early childhood educators have adopted Piaget's concept of **constructivism.** Constance Kamii (Kamii, 1986; Kamii & Ewing, 1996) and Rheta DeVries (De Vries, Zan, Hildebrandt, Edmiaston, & Sales, 2002; DeVries & Kohlberg, 1990) are two outspoken constructivists previously referred to in Chapter 4. Kamii and Ewing (1996) emphasize that children assimilate experiences and construct knowledge from within. Adults must provide the proper experiences for assimilation and construction to take place. DeVries (DeVries & Kohlberg, 1990) defines the role of the teacher as first assuming that, "The teacher is child centered, relates well to children, knows how to manage a classroom smoothly and how to provide traditional nursery school [or other early childhood level] activities" (pp. 83–84). In addition, the teacher's role includes the following:

**constructivism**

A belief that learning takes place based on the process of stage change brought about as the child constructs knowledge.

1. Creating an atmosphere conducive to learning. The atmosphere promotes positive child development through encouraging independence and initiative so that the child can speak out, ask questions, and experiment and explore.
2. Providing materials and activities and assessing what the children are thinking. Children are encouraged to explore materials on their own. When new ideas are needed, the teacher models ideas that flow naturally into what the children have been doing. The adult picks up on the children's interests and follows their lead rather than imposing ideas on them.
3. Encouraging children to keep trying and to construct their own knowledge rather than imposing one "right" answer.
4. Helping children extend their own ideas.

Rather than trying to modify young children's preoperational thought, Kamii and DeVries (DeVries & Kohlberg, 1990) value it, plan for it, and teach in terms of it. Kamii (1986) states that **autonomy** is the goal of education envisioned by Piaget. That is, children will be able to explore and think through problem solutions and construct knowledge independently through their own actions.

**autonomy**

Children will be able to explore and think through problem solutions and construct knowledge independently through their own actions.

## Vygotsky's View of Learning

Moll (1990) describes Vygotsky's view of the adult role in children's learning. Vygotsky's theory of cultural transmission joins development and learning. Vygotsky viewed education not only as central to cognitive development but also as the core sociocultural activity of humans. His work focused on the social origins and cultural basis of individual development. Vygotsky saw the cooperative relationship between adult and child as the main part of the educational process.

For Moll (1990), the zone of proximal development (ZPD) is the concept at the heart of Vygotsky's theory. Bodrova and Leong (1996) define the ZPD as bounded at the lower end by what the child can accomplish independently and at the upper end by what the child can accomplish with assistance (Figure 6–3). These

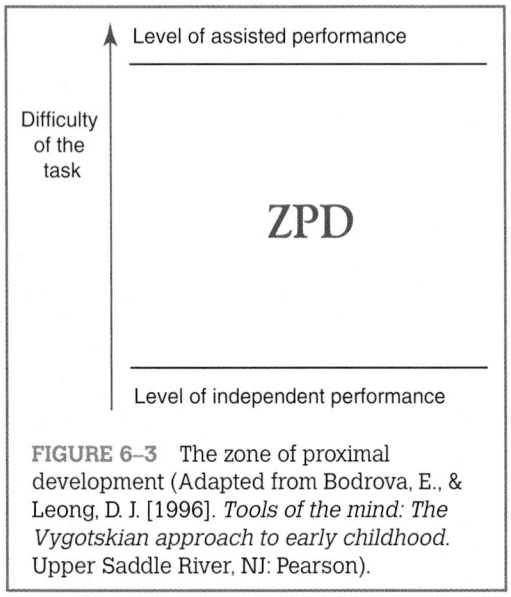


FIGURE 6–3 The zone of proximal development (Adapted from Bodrova, E., & Leong, D. J. [1996]. *Tools of the mind: The Vygotskian approach to early childhood.* Upper Saddle River, NJ: Pearson).

boundaries are constantly changing as the child reaches new levels of accomplishment. The level of assisted performance includes actions done with the assistance of an adult or an older and/or more accomplished peer. Interactions may include "giving hints and clues, rephrasing questions, asking the child to restate what has been said, asking the child what he understands, demonstrating the task or a portion of it and so on" (Bodrova & Leong, 1996, p. 35). Indirect help, such as setting up the environment to support the practice of a skill, would also be included. For example, the teacher might provide many types of writing implements and paper to support the development of writing. With time and learning, the zone keeps progressing to higher levels.

For Vygotsky, developmentally appropriate instruction should include what the child can learn with assistance. Teachers should provide activities just beyond the independent level but within the ZPD. A vital role for adults is gauging where to provide an appropriate level of challenge that is within the child's current zone. The adult should use **amplification** to appropriately make best use of the ZPD. Amplification is not the same as acceleration, which is teaching something that is out of the child's realm of understanding. For example, many three-year-olds may learn to recite the alphabet but may not have reached the level where they can actually apply this knowledge to reading and writing. In this case, the alphabet is an isolated bit of information with no useful context. Amplification builds on the children's strengths by increasing development while staying within the ZPD. The assistance provided is called **scaffolding.** The ZPD is the area within which knowledge construction takes place (Bodrova & Leong, 1996).

**amplification**

The provision of greater challenge within the zone of proximal development.

**scaffolding**

Assistance supplied by an adult or older child that supports movement through the ZPD.

From Vygotsky's view "a major goal of schooling is to create social contexts, (or zones of proximal development) for mastery of and conscious awareness in the use of these cultural tools" (Moll, 1990, p. 12). These cultural tools are our means of communication: reading, writing, and speech.

Change takes place within the ZPD when a child demonstrates that he or she can do something independently today that he or she could not do yesterday without assistance. Vygotsky viewed classroom learning as being intertwined with the relationship between thinking and the social organization of classroom instruction. "The role of the adult is not necessarily to provide structured cues but, through exploratory talk and other social meditations such as importing everyday activities into the classrooms, to assist children in appropriating or taking control of their own learning" (Moll, 1990, p. 13). Learning is a joint experience between an adult and child, not just transmission of knowledge from an adult into the head of a child.

## Behaviorist Views of Learning: Skinner and Bandura

The behaviorist views of learning grew from the learning theory tradition in America. Learning theorists tend to be interested in how to change behaviors at any time rather than in stage-related behaviors. According to Miller (2002), Skinner viewed only observable behavior to be worth studying. He found that behaviors became more frequent if they were reinforced. While Skinner's research focused mainly on rats and pigeons, his theory led to an interest in exploring applications to human behavior. The result was an approach to changing children's behavior called behavior modification or behavior analysis. The basic view of behavior modification as a technique is that if adults want to increase the number of times the child behaves in a certain way, a positive consequence must follow each

**rewards**

Positive consequences that are likely to increase positive behavior; reinforcements.

**reinforcements**

Positive consequences that are likely to increase positive behavior; rewards.

positive behavior. Positive consequences that are likely to increase positive behavior are called **rewards** or **reinforcements.** Adults who are skilled at behavior change are constantly alert for opportunities to follow desired behavior with positive consequences and thus increase the frequency of desirable behaviors. These reinforcements include verbal and nonverbal approval and praise, physical contact, activities, and privileges or material objects. Undesirable behaviors are generally ignored unless they are dangerous in nature. Behavior modifiers also use techniques such as shaping and substituting an incompatible behavior. A whole classroom system called behavior analysis (Bushell, 1982) uses behaviorist principles.

A theory that developed from a combination of learning theory and Freudian theory is social learning theory. Bandura's social cognitive theory is an offshoot of social learning theory. Bandura began with studying children's observational learning. Bandura's research made us aware of the importance of observation and imitation as vehicles for children's learning. In his later work, Bandura studied the thinking underlying observation and imitation. For adults who work with young children, application of Bandura's social cognitive theory would emphasize that children select information through their observations and come up with general conclusions. That is, for example, when they observe another child being rewarded for a behavior, they consciously put this information together to formulate the conclusion that if they act in the same manner, they will also be rewarded.

Behaviorist theory provides adults with the following major guidelines:

- Reward appropriate behavior
- Ignore inappropriate behavior (unless it is dangerous)
- Be aware of the power of observational learning.

## The Effects of Rewards on Child Behavior

**extrinsic rewards**

Concrete and social rewards.

**intrinsic rewards**

Used in the development of a desire within the child to learn through internal motivation.

A growing body of research indicates that adults need to proceed with caution in using **extrinsic rewards,** which are both concrete and social. That is, providing concrete rewards, such as food, money, or toys or too frequent praise, provides motivation to behave appropriately in order to get the rewards rather than performing appropriately because it makes the child feel good. That is, children should do the job, paint a picture, learn in school, or behave in a socially acceptable way because it makes them feel good inside; it gives them a feeling of pride and accomplishment. The goal has been to develop a desire within the child to learn through the development of **intrinsic rewards,** or internal motivation. Infants and toddlers have an internal drive to learn about the world. As they move beyond infancy and toddlerhood, it is important to keep that natural curiosity alive. Gottfried (1983), after reviewing research on intrinsic motivation, concluded that it is important to encourage intrinsic motivation during the early years as the basis for later academic motivation. She further suggests that the early childhood learning environment should be as free of anxiety as possible because high anxiety is associated with low motivation.

Even verbal praise can be carried too far according to Alfie Kohn (2001). First it is manipulative. It is often given for the adult's benefit in that it makes the adult's life easier. For example, Kohn suggests that instead of saying "good job" when a child puts his toys away, there should be a discussion about the importance of keeping the room neat and taking good care of the toys. Second, children may come to rely on adult approval for measuring their worth rather than doing self-evaluation. They may become over dependent on praise from adults to evaluate their accomplishments. Third, too much praise can steal child's pleasure. They lose the opportunity to feel joy in their own accomplishments. Fourth, children may lose interest in an activity when the praise is not present. They may be motivated only to receive praise rather than to complete the project for the fun of it. Finally, too much praise may result in a decrease in achievement. Children may think they won't do as well the next time. Thus, they may do poorly due to anxiety that they may not be able to keep up the standard or they may give up.

Kohn (2001) states that adults need to consider cutting back on praise. He states "*we praise more because we need to say it than because children need to hear it*" (p. 27). Children need unconditional love and acceptance with no strings attached. Rather than manipulating children with praise, we should spend time explaining and helping them to develop appropriate behaviors and good values. Kohn suggests that when a child does something impressive, adults have three reactions from which to choose:

1. Say nothing. Let children enjoy the moment.
2. Say what you saw. Make an evaluation free statement such as "You dressed yourself," "You did it," "You spent a lot of time on your picture," or "You made your friend happy." These kinds of statements emphasize the child's accomplishments rather than the adult's evaluation.
3. Talk less, ask more. Ask the child, "How did you figure out how to do that?"

The objective is to provide encouragement and support the children's feelings of control over their own lives.

## Maintaining Natural Motivation to Learn

From their reviews of the research on young children's motivation to learn, both Hauser-Cram (1998) and Carlton and Winsler (1998) formulate several similar conclusions. If infants' and toddlers' natural intrinsic motivation to learn is maintained into school age, they will be more likely to seek challenge and persist at solving difficult problems. They will maintain the needs for competence, relatedness, and autonomy or self-determination. If their natural curiosity and need to explore are not maintained, they may avoid challenges and give up easily when faced with a difficulty. This condition is called "learned helplessness" and results from repeated failure that leaves children feeling helpless and unable to succeed. The critical task for adults during children's early childhood years is to promote mastery-oriented behavior by focusing on the development of a variety of problem-solving strategies rather than on right answers.

Hauser-Cram (1998) and Carlton and Winsler (1998) suggest several ways that adults can support young children's mastery motivation. They can supply more sensory stimulation, as this factor seems to be critical in supporting persistent exploration of objects. Adults also need to step back and not interfere in children's autonomous activity as long as no danger is involved. It is through autonomous activity that children gain confidence in their ability to master the problems they meet. Hauser-Cram (p. 71) and Carlton and Winsler (p. 165) suggest guidelines for supporting mastery motivation, which are summarized here:

1. Provide a moderate, not overwhelming, choice of activities. Experience with making choices gives children control over their own learning (Hauser-Cram).
2. Provide activities that allow problem solving and exploration rather than correct or incorrect responses (Hauser-Cram). The environment should be filled with toys and activities that provide children with an opportunity to see the results of their actions (Carlton & Winsler).

3. Support children's activities, but do not interfere with their autonomy. When children are having difficulty with tasks, adults should be patient and wait before offering comments or suggestions. If the children show frustration, say, "What about . . . ?" rather than giving a direct command (Hauser-Cram). Scaffold problem solving (Carlton & Winsler).
4. Foster self-evaluation. Ask questions such as, "How do you feel about . . . ?" or "Are you happy with that or do you want to do more?"
5. Provide challenging activities and materials (Carlton & Winsler).
6. Teachers should talk with parents to find out children's interests and the kinds of activities they enjoy (Hauser-Cram).

Note that these suggestions center on children and their developing competence as learners. Stipek, Feiler, Daniels, and Milburn (1995) compared children who attended didactic, teacher-directed preschool and kindergarten programs that stressed basic skills and academics with children who attended child-centered programs. Although the children from the highly teacher-centered programs did well on letter and reading achievement tests, they performed no better than the child-centered group on knowledge of numbers, and their outcomes were negative on measures of motivation. Drill and practice appear to be effective for learning letters and word recognition but not for learning mathematics concepts. Drill and practice appear to adversely affect children in the motivation area. Children in child-centered programs "rated their abilities higher, had higher expectations for success on school-like tasks, selected a more challenging math problem to do, showed less dependency on adults for permission and approval, evidenced more pride in their accomplishments and claimed to worry less about school" (Stipek et al., 1995, p. 220). In the book *Motivated Minds*, Stipek and Seal (Alexander, 2001) describe how they promote their children's enthusiasm for learning. Like Kohn, they emphasize the importance of not trying to control too much from the outside. Motivation is supported by providing children with opportunities to make choices. Adults should be models by showing their enjoyment in learning new things.

Our goal with young children is to maintain their natural motivation to learn so that as they proceed through school they continue to find learning intrinsically motivating and exciting. Children can learn fairly early to be helpless and powerless, with no control over their learning. Motivation goes down, and by fourth grade, they may lack the motivation to succeed in school.

## Selecting Theory for Practical Application

In Chapter 2, examples were provided to demonstrate how different theories can be applied to different problems. Teachers often avoid adopting a theory as a tool because promoters of particular theories usually support only one point of view and leave the practitioner the problem of making a choice. Teachers are often left in a state of confusion as they try to sort out the claims made for each theory as the guide to instruction. When theories are viewed as complementary rather than contradictory, they can be used to develop a framework to guide instruction. Each new early childhood educator needs to consider this idea. Cowles (1971) sums up the view that no one theory answers every educational question by suggesting that theories "are in many ways far more complementary than competitive, in the same way that neither the trunk or the leg describes the whole elephant."

> Don't become wedded to one theoretical model or another. Be flexible and perceptive (Honig, 1986, p. 10).

Keep in mind that each theory addresses a different aspect of development. We might first want to consider the problem to be dealt with, then choose the theory that seems to apply best to that problem. Look back at the examples in Chapter 2 and you will see how this approach works.

Applying what you have read about motivation relative to research, comment on the following guidelines for developmentally appropriate practice for three- through five-year-olds as suggested by NAEYC (Bredekamp & Copple, 1997, pp. 126–127):

- Teachers plan a variety of concrete learning experiences with materials and people relevant to children's own life experiences and that promote their interest, engagement in learning, and conceptual development.
- Teachers provide opportunities for children to plan and select many of their own activities from a variety of learning areas and projects that the teacher makes available based on program goals and information gathered about children's varying interests and abilities. Following their own interests, children choose from a variety of activities.

Now, consider the following procedures identified as inappropriate practice (also pp. 126–127):

- Learning materials are primarily workbooks, ditto sheets, flash cards, and other materials that focus on drill and practice.
- The program provides few or no opportunities for children's choices.

## THINKING AND PROBLEM SOLVING

To promote intrinsic motivation for learning, emphasis is placed on children developing thinking and problem-solving skills through exploration and experimentation. Campbell and Arnold (1988) point out that most questions asked in classrooms are literal. They ask for direct informational feedback that requires memory skills but not thinking skills. The developmental approach to questioning suggested by Campbell and Arnold involves going step by step from simple to complex questions. Start at the literal "What is?" level. Then move on to "What else?" questions that associate the new information with previous information. Next, move on to cause and effect with "What?" and "Why?" questions. These questions take the children further from the immediate situation. At the next level, the imagination is brought into play with "What if ?" questions. These questions take the children's thinking into the possible and provide room for a variety of responses. There is no "right" answer.

Vygotsky's concept of scaffolding supports the value of good questioning for children's learning (Cassidy, 1989). Questions such as "How can we find out? "What will happen when we. . . ?" and "What should we do to . . . ?" open the way for children to think and to solve problems. Carr (1988) specifically addresses critical thinking skills. She points out that students need to learn how to question, analyze, and look beyond the obvious to find possible answers. Promotion of critical thinking skills should be an integral part of everyday learning experiences.

Tudge and Caruso (1988) found that cooperative problem solving can enhance young children's cognitive development (Figure 6–4). That is, in line with

FIGURE 6–4 One important aspect of the adult role is to provide children the opportunity to work cooperatively in small groups.

Piaget's thinking, when children work together to solve problems, their cognitive growth is supported. In natural situations, one or more experts and one or more novices are typically in the group. Tudge and Caruso were interested in what would happen when children were paired based on their problem-solving abilities and were presented with a balance beam problem to solve together. They found that when they paired a higher-level and a lower-level child, and the higher-level child was sure of the solution, the lower-level child moved up. If the higher-level child was unsure, the lower-level child did not change and sometimes influenced the higher-level child to select the lower-level solution. If the children were allowed to try out their predicted solutions, they improved in further problem-solving situations regardless of whether their partner was at the same or a different level. Tudge and Caruso suggest a number of ways teachers can ensure that true cooperative problem solving occurs in their classrooms. These include the following (pp. 50–51):

1. Plan activities in which children have a shared goal. For example, encourage them to collaboratively plan how to build a zoo for the toy animals.
2. The goal should be intrinsically interesting to the children. Encourage children to solve problems they have selected, such as how to share the available blocks or how to fill the water table.
3. Children should be able to achieve their goal with their own actions. They need to have the opportunity to try their solutions.
4. The results of the children's actions should be both visible and immediate. Then, if they are not satisfied with one solution, they know right away and can try another way.
5. The teacher's role is to encourage and suggest, not to direct.
6. Encourage children to interact with each other by introducing activities as problems that need to be solved by two or more children working together.
7. Help the children clarify or adapt their shared goals. The teacher can help the children think through what they plan to do before they act by rephrasing their solution and giving them time to reflect on it.
8. Involve children who are less likely to initiate problem solving, that is, the quieter, more reserved children, to contribute to the discussion.

Tudge and Caruso point out that problem solving may occur in any curriculum area. It may occur during play or during open-ended activities designed by the teacher. By encouraging cooperative problem solving, teachers can greatly enhance cognitive development.

## Competence

A major goal for children during early childhood is to promote both cognitive and social competence. Adults have the role of providing environments that serve this function. Kontos and Wilcox-Herzog (1997b) examined classroom influences on preschool children's social and cognitive competence. Teachers and children were observed during indoor playtime. The observer focused on children's interactions with objects and with peers, as well as teachers' behavior when they were in the children's presence. The highest levels of cognitive competence were observed when children were involved in activities such as art, blocks, and dramatic play. Such activities make the most demands on cognitive skills. Teacher presence showed no positive effect in the cognitive area. Social competence was related to peer and teacher presence but not to activity type. Social competence necessitated active peer interaction but only when teachers kept out of the situation or provided stimulating involvement. The authors concluded that "for early childhood classrooms to enhance children's cognitive and social development, teachers need to be particularly attentive to the types of activities they select for free play and to the potential of those activities for contact with peers as opposed to adults" (p. 260).

Katz and McClellan (1997) believe that teachers can play a significant role in promoting social competence. They recommend individualized guidance that promotes active involvement through warm and supportive teacher-child relationships. The adult role in social and other areas of affective development is addressed in future chapters.

## ADULT SUPPORT OF LEARNING THROUGH PLAY

This section looks more closely at the adult's role as a supporter of play through classroom behavior and through providing the environment to do so.

### Adult Intervention in Play

As with other areas of child activity, adults can intervene, join in, and/or be directive in play. They also can step back, stay out, and serve as guides when needed. Research has indicated that adults can enhance child play directly. There are two basic types of sociodramatic play training: **outside intervention** and **inside intervention** (Christie, 1982). During outside intervention, the adult stays outside the play but offers questions, suggestions, directions, and clarifications that will help the children enhance their dramatic play roles. For example, "What else can doctors do?" or "Firefighters use hoses to get the water to the fire." Inside intervention involves the adult in the play activity. The adult actually takes on a role. The adult can then demonstrate various types of play behaviors, such as imitation, using objects for make-believe, performing make-believe actions, showing how to enter already established play situations, using appropriate verbal communication, and extending the story line. For example, as a patient, the adult might say, "Oh doctor, I have a headache and a stomachache. Please help me." As the children pick up the play techniques, the adult can gradually phase out. The adult needs to be cautious about not dominating the play (Trawick-Smith, 1985). Trawick-Smith (1998b) developed a model for play training through adult play intervention. He demonstrates that several intervention strategies may be selected after thoughtful reflection "based on careful observation and an understanding of diverse theories of play" (p. 127). Adults must tailor their strategies to fit child behavior and play contexts. Adults must be flexible, changing strategies as situations change. The following are examples of some of the research that supports the value of using play-training techniques.

**outside intervention**
Sociodramatic play in which the adult stays outside of the play but offers questions, suggestions, directions, and clarifications that will help children enhance their dramatic play roles.

**inside intervention**
Sociodramatic play in which the adult is involved in the play activity.

Studies by Morrow (1990), Neuman and Roskos (1993), and Schrader (1990) all involved enhancing literacy knowledge and concepts by providing both literacy props and adult support during play activities. Morrow (1990) found that including reading and writing materials in dramatic play centers increased the frequency of observed literacy play. Morrow compared the frequency of literacy behaviors observed with and without teacher guidance.

The frequency of literacy play behaviors was higher with teacher guidance than without. All experimental classrooms were supplied with a special container filled with literacy materials: book-making materials, different sizes and types of paper, ready-made blank booklets, magazines and books, pencils, felt-tip pens, crayons, and colored pencils. In two sets of experimental classrooms, one with teacher guidance and one without teacher guidance, a thematic center was set up as a veterinarian's office. In the no-guidance classrooms with literacy materials only and with the veterinarian centers, the teachers introduced the materials the first day, discussed how they might be used, and did not refer to them again. In the classrooms with teacher guidance, the teachers discussed potential uses of the materials at the beginning of each play period. In addition, the children were told that they could pretend to read and write. Addition of the literacy materials increased the frequency of literacy dramatic play compared to control groups where no intervention occurred. When teacher guidance was used, there was a greater increase in literacy behaviors than under the no-guidance conditions.

In a study by Schrader (1990), four prekindergarten teachers participated in a workshop designed to acquaint them with how to determine children's intentions in their play activities, particularly as related to literacy. Schrader was interested in whether the teachers would be able to follow the children's literacy interests rather than impose their own ideas. Each classroom had three centers designed for symbolic play: the post office, the office, and the house. Each was stocked with a supply of literacy materials. The teachers were observed to determine whether they used their knowledge regarding the determination of children's intentions to extend and expand the children's play or whether they ignored the children's intentions and redirected them in other directions. Examples of an extending style would be, "Did you write the address on the envelope? You could buy a stamp. You could write a check for it. You could fill out the order form. Why don't you look it up in the phone book?" (pp. 87, 89). A redirecting style would be one like the following in which the teacher ignores what the children are doing and redirects their attention to a writing activity that he or she selects, "I'd like you to write me a story. Okay? Write me a story." Schrader found that literacy play based on extending the children's natural activities was much richer than that which came from teacher suggestions and preconceived ideas. Teaching from the children's natural inclinations requires spontaneity and creativity on the part of the teacher. "This requires teachers to focus not on teaching per se but on the process of learning that belongs to the child. Consequently, teachers must exercise self-control when participating in children's symbolic play. They must refrain from pressuring children to cooperate with the teacher's own preconceived priorities" (p. 99).

Neuman and Roskos (1993) focused on children enrolled in Head Start classes. They found that classrooms in which materials were provided and a parent/teacher was actively involved in assisting the children resulted in an increase in the children's ability to read environmental print (e.g., office signs, such as *Exit*, *Come in*, *Open*, and *Closed*) and label functional print items, such as *telephone book* and *calendar*. "These findings suggest that adult interaction in literacy-enriched play settings may represent an important opportunity for assisting minority children who live in poverty to think, speak, and behave in literate ways" (p. 95).

**self-regulation**

The behavior control needed to be accepted by peers into a play activity.

Play not only supports literacy development but also **self-regulation** (Bodrova, Leong, Hensen, & Henninger, 2000). To engage in a play activity, children must follow the rules set up by their peers. Thus, to be accepted into the peer group, one must accept the roles and behaviors set up by the group. Bodrova et al. (2000) emphasize the importance of the adult role as a facilitator of children's play. Adults provide scaffolding, space, and materials.

FIGURE 6–5 Nonthematic play equipment inspires a variety of dramatic play roles.

## The Adult Role in Provisioning the Play Environment

Adequate play materials and play space are necessary for promoting play activities (Frost, 1992; Hart, 1993). Adults are responsible for providing materials and equipment that fit the development levels of the children; arranging and rearranging furniture, equipment, and materials as needed; and providing new materials as required.

Whether settings are **thematic** or **nonthematic** can affect dramatic play (Figure 6–5). Dodge and Frost (1986) explored ways to set up dramatic play areas that would encourage role-playing but not dictate the roles to be taken, such as would be the case with a home center, a medical center, or a firefighter center. They and others noted that as children neared age five and their thinking extended outside their immediate experience, the usual housekeeping area became less enticing as a setting for role-playing. They found five-year-olds were inspired by more open-ended props, such as empty cardboard cartons, spools, planks, and crates. Along with these open-ended materials, various types of realistic props were available to use in whatever roles the children chose. In this type of nonthematic setting, the children engaged in more dramatic role-playing using many different themes. When structured play centers were available, the play was richer in content if more than one center was available, such as a home, a grocery store, and an office, and if things in each center interested both males and females.

**thematic**

The use of set play centers that suggest specific roles to be taken, such as a home center, medical center, or firefighter center.

**nonthematic**

The use of open-ended materials and various types of realistic props.

McLoyd (1983) compared three-and-a-half-year-olds' and five-year-olds' play with high- and low-structure objects. High-structure objects are realistic items, such as a tea set, ironing board, tool kit, or telephone. Low-structure objects are open-ended items that do not have any predetermined use relative to a specific role, such as pipe cleaners, cardboard boxes, metal cans, foam cups, and blocks. High-structure objects increased the frequency of parallel and solitary pretend play for the three-and-a-half-year-olds. Overall, the quality of the play with the two types of toys was about the same at each level. McLoyd concluded that one type of toy cannot be recommended as better than the other at this point.

Thomas (1984) found that the toy preferences of early readers (children who read at age four) were different from those of four-year-old nonreaders. Early readers preferred reading readiness toys, such as books and alphabet cards, whereas those who did not read early preferred gross motor, construction, and fantasy toys.

Rogers and Sawyers (1988) reviewed research on the effects of toys and materials on play. When too few or no toys are available for children, the number of aggressive acts is much greater. More negative interactions occur when children are playing with small toys than when they are playing on large pieces of equipment, such as slides and climbers. Art materials, manipulatives, clay, sand, and water inspire less social pretend play than dress-up outfits, other dramatic play props, small cars, and blocks. The kinds of materials adults provide can determine the type of play in which children will engage. Children's interest is enticed by novelty, variety, and complexity. Toys should be rotated so that the same things are not available every day. Open-ended toys, such as blocks and LEGOS®, grow in complexity with children's cognitive growth and ability to use them in more complex ways.

Rogers and Sawyers (1988) also examined research on the effects of space on children's play. Space needs to be adequate, and equipment and materials should be placed for maximum stimulation of the most complex, advanced forms of play. The smaller the space, the more social interaction takes place. Aggression also increases. However, in a larger space, more rough-and-tumble play and more running takes place. Small groups are more conducive to friendships and imaginative play. The younger the children, the smaller the group should be. Everyday outdoor play is also important. The more mobile the outdoor equipment is, the more frequently imaginative play activities will occur.

## Adult Provision for Appropriate Use of Technology

In Chapter 4, a variety of views were presented relative to young children and the role of technology in their lives. This chapter describes the adult role in using technology appropriately as a learning tool for young children.

### Television

Levin (1998) outlines the hazards of the "remote control childhood." Adults have the responsibility for helping children make sense of what they see on television. The challenge for adults is to help children explore the ideas they see depicted on television, explore their understanding of them, and make connections to their own ideas and behaviors. Children need help in making sense of the violence they see. For example, they can discuss alternative ways to solve problems and identify the difference between fantasy and reality. They also must become informed consumers by critically analyzing commercials. Adults should talk to children and encourage individual and group discussion. Primary age children can develop questionnaires and surveys and collect data from peers and adults regarding television viewing habits.

Levin provides many procedures that adults can use to help children take charge of the media in their lives. Children need to become media literate, and adults must teach children how to make informed choices. Children and adults need to discuss the programs viewed and identify the positives and negatives. Most important, adults need to teach children how to plan ahead so they do not impulsively turn on the television or a video game. Adult guidance can be used to do the following:

- Help children develop guidelines regarding how much television and/or video game time they will be allotted. Then, help them select the programs and/or games they will use in that time.
- Discuss all options: television programs, video games, and computer time.
- By kindergarten or first grade, children can keep a personal log to plan their television and/or video game time. Adults can help them make their own log book.

If viewing time is limited, it is the adults' responsibility to provide alternative activities for children. Children can brainstorm ideas from which to select.

As Levin suggests, fostering creative play is an excellent means of counteracting the negative impact of media culture. Open-ended, unstructured play materials like clay, blocks, construction toys, trucks, trains, balls, puzzles, sand, generic or nonviolent dolls, and play figures encourage imaginative play. Sets of dramatic play materials can be placed in shoe box kits. Levin suggests themes, such as office, play dough, rescue and first aid, and others. Avoid media-related toys that encourage violence and/or repetitive, limited pretend play.

Video cameras offer many exciting opportunities in the classroom. For example, students and teachers can record activities. The videotapes can serve as a source of data for teachers to include in portfolios of work to be shared with parents, as vehicles for students and teachers to evaluate experiences, and as records of student activities to be enjoyed again. Students can even write scripts for programs, record the programs, and show them to other classes and at parent meetings.

An innovation in in-service education was using *Mr. Rogers' Neighborhood* for effective staff development (Marazon, 1994). Mr. Rogers provides a model that respects young children and focuses on affective development. Included in the Mr. Rogers' programs are behaviors that exemplify virtue, values, morals, and self-concept themes. Some examples are "kindness, sharing, compassion, caring, joy, peace, love, confidence building, success, forgiveness, understanding, trust, autonomy, uniqueness, patience, honesty and goodness" (Marazon, p. 35). After only one month of viewing Mr. Rogers, the teachers had begun to reflect and modify their behaviors so they were calmer, slower paced, and more patient. As the in-service sessions progressed over the year, they became more self-aware.

## Computers

Haugland (1999) asserts the importance of using computers in a developmentally appropriate manner that emphasizes creativity and problem solving. She recommends that computers not be introduced to children before age three and cautions that they should be used differently with three- and four-year-olds as compared with kindergarten and primary age children. For the preschoolers, computers should be used for exploration. They should be available in a learning center where children can choose to use them and where they have adequate time to explore developmentally appropriate software. Fischer and Gillespie (2003) describe a Head Start class where students can select from one desktop and five laptop computers during their center time. Kindergarten and primary classrooms should continue to include a computer center with developmentally appropriate software, but teachers can suggest more directive projects and activities that focus on creativity and problem solving.

**software**

The individual programs installed for use on the computer.

Selecting good **software** is a critical part of preparing to use computers in the classroom. Haugland and Shade (1990) provide guidelines for software selection. Haugland and Shade (1990) suggest the following criteria:

1. The concepts and the method of presentation should be appropriate for young children.
2. The child should be in control of the pace and direction of the activity.
3. The instructions should be clear.
4. The program should provide for increasingly complex activities.
5. Children should be able to operate the program independently.
6. The activities should be process rather than product oriented, thereby encouraging exploration and discovery.
7. The software should be a simple model of some aspect of the world. Graphics should be realistic and proportional to real-world objects.
8. Technical qualities should be good: bright colors, clear pictures, animation, and sound.
9. The software should provide unlimited opportunities for trial-and-error problem solving.
10. There should be opportunities for children to make transformations that they cannot make in real life, such as changing a scene from city to country or the weather from sunny to cloudy.
11. Software should "reflect the diverse backgrounds, cultures, and experiences of young children" and maintain the anti-biased point of view (Haugland, 1992, p. 44).

The variety of computer-related materials and activities available is changing rapidly. Upgraded and new software is continuously coming onto the market (Haugland, 1993, 1994; Haugland, Bailey, & Ruiz, 2002a; Haugland & Ruiz, 2002b; Shade, 1993, 1994). Software evaluation tools and software evaluations can be found on the Internet. For example:

- Haugland Developmental Software Scale at www.childrenandcomputers.com.
- Super Kids Educational Software Review at http://superkids.com
- EMC 300, Software Evaluation Form at www.Seamonkey.ed.asu.edu

**CD-ROM**

Compact disc software that contains great varieties of information and activities in an easy-to-store format.

**CD-ROM** technology can provide more exciting and versatile programs. New vistas have opened with the availability of networks and information services (Brett, 1994). A wealth of information is available through these online services.

Computers can be valuable tools for the classroom if they are set up at a center where children can choose to go when they are interested. Too often, they are set up in a laboratory where everyone has to go for a certain prescribed period of time and where the activities are not necessarily integrated with those in the classroom. Hopefully, in the school of the future, every classroom will be equipped with two or three computers, and every student will have equal opportunity for access.

**Web sites**

Internet sites that offer opportunity for many activities.

**Internet**

The worldwide computer connection.

In addition to commercially available software, a multitude of **Web sites,** Internet sites, which offer the opportunity for many activities, are available on the **Internet,** the worldwide computer connection. Haugland (2000) points out that, while the Internet has been researched less extensively than software due to its relatively recent growth, "it provides children with a variety of learning opportunities that appear to enhance problem solving, critical thinking skills, creativity, language skills, knowledge, research skills, the ability to integrate information, social skills, and self-esteem" (Haugland, 2000, p. 13). The quality of sites ranges from excellent to terrible. Haugland and Gerzog (1998) have developed a scale for evaluating Web sites (cited in Haugland, 2000). Haugland (2000) describes four types of children's Web sites: information, communication, interaction, and publication. Information sites provide references that support student and teacher research. Interaction sites are those that allow for communicating with friends, relatives, and people in other cities, states, and countries. Interaction sites are much like software games and activities. Publication sites are places where children's work can be published. It is important to use only high-quality sites that integrate with classroom learning objectives. Haugland (2000) cautions that a screening device should be used to ensure that children do not have access to sites that are harmful and that children understand that they should not share any personal information. She suggests they should even use a pen name, such as their dog or favorite doll's name. Finally, adults are responsible for selecting computers. Unfortunately, changes in computer technology are moving so fast that computers can become obsolete in a relatively short time. Therefore, it is important to select equipment that can be easily upgraded. While there is some disagreement regarding when computers should be introduced to young children, when they are introduced, it should happen through a gradual training process that gets them off to a good start (Haugland, 2000).

Buckleitner and Kalinowski (2005) provide an overview of trends in software for young children. The number of new CD-ROMs produced has gone way down. Children have many more options such as videogame systems, Web sites, and interactive toys, such as LeapPad®, Leapster, Pixter®, and Power Touch®. Computers are becoming smaller and less expensive and, thus, more available. Teachers are using digital photography and ink jet printers to obtain portfolio documentation. They are constructing classroom Web sites and using E-mail and cell phones to communicate with parents. It's important for adults to keep up on the latest technology developments.

### Technology and the Disabled

Whereas there is much controversy relative to the value of technology for the general population of young children, support is strong for the value of its applications for assisting children with disabilities (Hasselbring & Glaser, 2000; Wilds, 2001). Even infants and toddlers can benefit from assistive technology (AT) activities that promote healthy development (Wilds, 2001). Equipment is available that can help them interact and improve their functional capabilities, [and Web sites exist that can provide information for their families.] A toddler who may not have the necessary motor skills to turn the pages in a book can use a software version where touching a key or the screen turns the book page. "Specialized computer software, large trackballs, tough windows, alternative customized keyboards, and authoring software for overlays are AT supports that can help infants and toddlers with disabilities communicate and interact during playtime" (Wilds, 2001, p. 39). Older children with disabilities can also be aided with the use of AT (Hasselbring & Glaser, 2000). They can use computer technology for word processing, communication, research, and multimedia projects. Nelson and Fritschi (2004) outline a plan for school-wide assistive technology. They point out that many students not identified as having a disability could benefit from AT. Teachers and family members need equipment and training in the use of the equipment for children at all age levels.

Technology presents us with new ways to learn and communicate. Adults have the responsibility for ensuring that children know how to use it sensibly and with accountability.

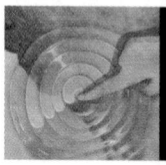

**LOOKING FURTHER**

Find three articles in current periodicals that discuss the adult role with technology and young children. Look through periodicals, such as *Young Children, Early Learning, Early Childhood Education Journal, Childhood Education, Dimensions of Early Childhood, Instructor,* and *Pre-K Today*. Also check current issues of magazines designed specifically for parents. Write a summary and a reflective reaction to the articles you read. Be sure to include the following:

a. The title of the article, the author(s), and the name of the periodical

b. The date of issue and the inclusive page numbers

c. A short summary (less than a page) of the major points included in the article

d. Your reaction to the content of the article. Did you feel you learned something worthwhile?

Do you agree or disagree with the author(s)? What alternatives would you suggest? Share what you learned with the rest of the class.

## HELPING CHILDREN WITH SPECIAL NEEDS LEARN

To understand their role in supporting learning for children with special needs, adults must be acquainted with the laws that specifically pertain to this population. Following is an overview of this important legislation.

**PL 94–142**

The Education of All Handicapped Children Act of 1975, which ensures that all children with special needs, ages five to twenty-one, have equal opportunity education.

**PL 101–476**

Revision of PL 94–142. IDEA 97 made further improvements.

**IDEA 97**

The Individuals with Disabilities Act Amendments greatly improved educational opportunities for children with disabilities.

**PL 99–457**

The Education of the Handicapped Act Amendments, Title I, Programs for Infants and Toddlers with Handicaps, gave states five years to institute a program for serving children with disabilities ages three through five.

**Americans with Disabilities Act (ADA)**

States that people with disabilities are entitled to equal rights in employment, state and local public services, and public accommodations, such as child care and early childhood education programs" (Chandler, 1994).

**haptic**

Sensing through touch.

**task analysis**

A procedure through which learning tasks are broken down into smaller steps for children with learning disabilities.

The Education of All Handicapped Children Act of 1975 (**PL 94–142**, now revised as the Individuals with Disabilities Education Act (IDEA), **PL 101–476**) was a landmark in legislation for children with special needs ages five to twenty-one years. Its purpose is to ensure that all children with special needs receive equal educational opportunities. The act was implemented in the fall of 1978. Unfortunately, the federal law was not made as strong for children ages three, four, and five, as it was for the school-aged child (Cohen, Semmes, & Guralnick, 1979). In 1997, Individuals with Disabilities Act Amendments (**IDEA 97**) greatly improved educational opportunities for children with disabilities. The role of parents in educational planning and decision making was strengthened (McLean, 2002).

Weaknesses were rectified in 1986 when Congress passed **PL 99–457**, the Education of the Handicapped Act Amendments. PL 99–457 amended PL 91–230, the Education of the Handicapped Act, which was passed in 1970. Two new programs were authorized by PL 99–457. Title I, Programs for Infants and Toddlers with Handicaps, gave states five years to institute a program for serving children ages three to five with disabilities. Incentive monies were provided for children birth to age three. Title II, the Preschool Grants Program, directed at children three through five years of age, extends the rights that PL 94–142 gave to older children to younger children. Since the fall of 1991, states applying for funds under PL 94–142 must show that they provide free and appropriate education to all handicapped children ages three through five, as well as for older children. Thus, services for three- through five-year-olds are no longer optional. (See *Journal of Early Intervention, 15*(1), Winter 1991, for a thorough discussion of the law and its implications and implementation.)

In 1992, the **Americans with Disabilities Act (ADA)** went into effect. This law "states that people with disabilities are entitled to equal rights in employment, state and local public services, and public accommodations, such as child care and early childhood education programs" (Chandler, 1994). Thus, preschool programs were not just encouraged to include children with disabilities, but were required to do so.

## Teaching in the Inclusive Classroom

Like all teachers, adults who teach in inclusive classrooms need an in-depth knowledge of the typical growth and development of young children. They also need specialized knowledge of the various exceptionalities with which they must work.

New curriculum and teaching skills must be learned to aid those teaching an inclusive class. According to Allen and Schwartz (1996), the developmental and behaviorist approaches can be blended in the inclusive classroom. Young children with special needs learn by the same principles as typical children, but because of their specific disabilities, they may have to learn with a greater emphasis on specific modalities. For example, the child who is hearing impaired relies on sight and the child who is visually impaired relies on kinesthetic and **haptic** modalities. Their tasks may have to be broken down into smaller steps through a process called **task analysis**, and successive approximations may have to be used to arrive at a particular learning objective. For example, Melissa has been diagnosed as having autism. Melissa, at age three, demonstrates no recognizable speech. The initial objective is to connect vocalization with positive, desired consequences. Melissa loves the daily snacks offered in her classroom. Melissa must make a sound to receive her snack. The teachers and other children model this desired behavior. They give Melissa her snack accompanied by verbal praise after she makes her sound. Teachers of special-needs children must also have excellent skills for working with parents and identifying family needs. This aspect is discussed in Chapter 7.

The role of teachers in the placement of and successful educational programming for young children with special needs is critical. They spend several hours each day with the children, in contrast to specialists who spend a limited time and parents who may have difficulty maintaining objectivity. Teachers must be objective and factual. They must be able to document classroom behavior in accurate, objective language. Their records should withstand the test of careful scrutiny by other professionals. Keeping up with these heavy demands can be very stressful for teachers. White and Phair (1986) describe a wide range of negative emotions experienced in the integrated classroom: denial, sadness, anger, guilt, fear, overprotection, defensiveness, jealousy/competition, frustration, exhaustion, and fatalism. These feelings must be faced and discussed to alleviate the effects of stress. Eventually, as they observe the future progress of their former students, teachers may feel more secure, and their jobs will become less stressful.

## Preparation for Elementary Grades

Prekindergarten and kindergarten teachers play an especially important role in preparing special-needs children for the transition to the elementary grades. The rapid growth of inclusion has brought a focus in the prekindergarten program not only on the development of social, cognitive, and motor skills but also on the development of classroom participation skills. In kindergarten, participation skills for first grade are developed (Carta, Atwater, & Schwartz, 1991). Researchers have gathered data on kindergarten teachers' expectations for success (Beckoff & Bender, 1989; Rule, Innocenti, Coor, Bonem, & Stowitschek, 1989). Carta, Atwater, and Schwartz (1991) designed an intervention strategy for two groups of special-needs students: one group attending a special education preschool and one attending a regular kindergarten. The intervention strategy focuses on three sets of skills found previously to be essential for moving early childhood students from special education programs to typical elementary classrooms. These skills included the following:

1. participating appropriately during group instruction
2. completing individual work with a minimum of teacher direction
3. managing in-class transitions independently

Teachers and students were observed during the intervention period to assess how well teachers were implementing the intervention and to assess any immediate effects on the students. The first-year results showed positive changes in all three skill areas. Achievement measures improved, and problem behaviors decreased. The intervention's effects carried over into the students' regular kindergarten and first-grade placements.

Teaching children with special needs requires the same knowledge of development and learning as teaching typical children. In addition, knowledge of special needs and techniques for teaching children with specific disabilities is also necessary. The final part of this unit focuses on research that has been conducted on a variety of elements affecting how adult behavior relates to children's learning.

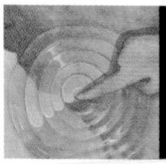

**LOOKING FURTHER**

Do a survey in your community. Find out what kinds of services are available for young special-needs children. Who is eligible for each program? Do all children who need services seem to be receiving them? Do you think your community is doing a good job for its young, special-needs population? If not, what more is needed?

## PROVIDING A QUALITY ENVIRONMENT AND QUALITY INSTRUCTION

Adults have a complex role in providing quality learning experiences for young children. Two prominent, and in some ways conflicting, theoretical views have been formulated in regard to the adult's role. There are also considerations of motivating children, selecting practical applications of theory, encouraging thinking and problem solving, developing competence, playing, using technology, helping children with special needs, and providing appropriate environment and instruction when it comes to providing a quality learning environment. The aspects of quality discussed in this part of the chapter include overall quality, the important factors in teachers' and parents' interactions with children, teachers' beliefs and practices, and relevant principles from the NAEYC. Other aspects of quality are discussed in later chapters.

### Overall Quality

Phillipsen, Burchinal, Howes, and Cryer (1997) performed a multistate study designed to identify structural characteristics of center child care that are associated with observed child care quality. Overall quality of process in classrooms was higher in states with more stringent child care regulations, in nonprofit centers, and in preschool classrooms compared with infant/toddler classrooms. In infant/toddler classrooms, process quality was higher in classrooms with moderately experienced and better paid teachers. In preschool classrooms, process quality was higher in classrooms with moderately experienced and better paid teachers and more experienced directors. The authors conclude that state child care regulations need to be increased, and child care programs' budgets rearranged so that a larger proportion is invested in staff wages. For preschoolers, they recommend better adult/child ratios, lower enrollment, lower proportions of infants and toddlers, and subsidized children in each center, because these factors predicted higher process quality for preschoolers. Staff turnover decreases if they receive higher wages. Generally, infants and toddlers receive lower-quality, minimal care. Furthermore, legislation is needed to control infant, toddler, and preschool teachers' salaries and to make educational requirements for teachers more stringent. Kontos and Wilcox-Herzog (2001) found that overall classroom quality correlated with the degree of the teacher's formal education.

### The Significance of Teacher-Child and Parent-Child Interactions in Children's Learning

Kontos and Wilcox-Herzog (1997a) reviewed the research on teacher-child interactions and their relation to learning. Interactions with adults are critical to development. Yet research indicates that attention to individual children does not occur frequently in early childhood classrooms. Teachers are interacting with children 71 percent of the time, but one-third or less of the children are receiving individual attention. Developmentally appropriate program teachers tend to have more warm, stimulating interactions with their students. When children have sensitive, involved interactions with teachers, their development tends to be enhanced in the cognitive, socioemotional, and language areas. More positive interactions, which provide stronger attachments, are associated with greater social and cognitive competence. Also, children in classrooms filled with warm, positive interaction exhibit less stress than children in classrooms where teachers use harsh, critical, and detached interaction techniques. Kontos suggests several implications for teachers. First, it is difficult to provide individual attention for each child when class sizes are too large. The NAEYC suggests the following adult/child ratios:

| Age of Children | Adult/Children |
|---|---|
| 0–1 year | 1:3 |
| 1–2 years | 1:5 |
| 2–3 years | 1:6 |
| 3–5 years | 1:8 |
| 3–6 years | 1:10 |

Second, specialized training is strongly connected to sensitive teacher-child interactions. Most states require minimal, if any, educational standards for child care teachers. Third, teachers in developmentally appropriate classrooms tend to display more warmth, sensitivity, and verbal stimulation. Finally, teachers must consciously distribute attention equally among all their students. Kontos concludes, "Quality in early childhood programs is, in large part, a function of the interactions that take place between the adults and children in the program" (p. 11).

A study by Pianta, Nimetz, and Bennett (1997) provides insight on the teacher-child and mother-child relationship and children's school success. The subjects of this study were mothers and teachers of preschool and kindergarten students predicted to be at high risk for future school problems. The quality of both mother-child and child-teacher interaction predicted children's performance on a measure of concept development. The quality of mother-child relationships was a stronger predictor of success than was the quality of teacher-child relationships. However, a similarity existed in both sets of relationships. The same characteristics that characterize secure mother-child relationships also characterized secure teacher-child relationships, such as keeping track of the adult, using the adult as a secure base from which to explore, being reassured and comforted by the adult, and being in tune to adult facial expressions and emotions. Children with secure relationships with their mothers also had the most secure relationships with their teachers. Mothers who had control struggles or lacked control had children who formed conflicted, dependent, and insecure relationships with teachers. Positive mother-child relationships predicted positive relationships with teachers and higher levels of concept development.

## Teachers' Beliefs and Practices

Many studies have focused on teachers' beliefs and practices, most of which have focused on kindergarten teachers. Therefore, Stipek and Byler (1997) selected preschool, kindergarten, and first-grade teachers as subjects on a study designed to explore relationships among teachers' beliefs about how children learn; their views on the goals of early childhood education; their positions on policies related to school entry, testing, and retention; their satisfaction with current practices and pressures for change; and their actual practices. Stipek and Byler found that preschool and kindergarten teachers' beliefs, goals, and practices and, to some extent policy positions, were in line with current debates among experts on child-centered versus more didactic, basic-skills approaches to instruction. First-grade teachers displayed few of the predicted relationships. The teachers who were not able to implement their beliefs felt that the current school policies mandated a curriculum that was too oriented toward basic skills. Parents were most often identified as the greatest source of pressure. Administrators were also identified by the kindergarten teachers as a source of pressure. First-grade teachers also had more mixed beliefs and practices. Possibly, they see child-centered practices as working best for some goals, whereas drill and practice work better for others. Many benefits have been documented for child-centered approaches to instruction (see review by Hart, Burts, & Charlesworth, 1997).

Play is emphasized as the major vehicle for young children's learning. Kemple (1996) looked at prekindergarten and kindergarten teachers' beliefs and practices concerning dramatic play. She found that although play opportunities were readily available in most prekindergarten classrooms, the opportunities decreased in kindergartens. Even when teachers had sociodramatic play materials available, they tended not to see play as contributing to cognitive development and academics. The teachers did not see the benefits of intervening in children's play. Many of the teachers were not educated regarding play and its contribution to learning. Teachers generally do not take advantage of the many methods available for encouraging children's sociodramatic play. They mainly set the stage but do not intervene to enhance the play. The teachers cited social and emotional benefits from play, but not academic ones. They mentioned that one reason they did not have much playtime was because too much aggressive play inspired by television programs occurred. They did not appear to consider intervening to provide other play choices.

## Avoiding Burnout

Providing for children's learning can lead to burnout or a desire to give in to exhaustion and depression resulting from overwork. In her article, "Dedication Doesn't Have to Mean Deadication" (2005) Paula Jorde Bloom provides cautions for administrators, which also are excellent advice for teachers to help avoid burnout. Bloom sets forth the following questions (p. 74):

- Do you dread leaving your center [or school] for a long weekend or a vacation because of the mountain of work that will pile up in your absence?
- Do you feel you do the work of several people and many things not in line with your job description?
- Does your work consume your whole life, rarely allowing you time to pursue outside interests?

An affirmative answer to these questions indicates a prime candidate for burnout. Bloom suggests the following things to do to be happy and healthy (pp. 74–76):

- Be aware of your own reactions to stress. Recognize your personal stress indicators, which might be physical (i.e., aches and pains), psychological (i.e., worry), or behavioral (i.e., yelling, eating, drinking). Be aware of what gives you energy and what drains you.
- Strive for balance. Find a "balance between giving and receiving, talking and listening, planned and spontaneous, alone and together, now versus later, variety and routine, seriousness and silliness" and other tensions. Emotionally close the door when you leave work each day. Diversify your interests.
- Embrace a new mantra— "Simplicity is power." Do less of what doesn't matter. Focus on what does matter. Streamline your life.
- Accept the fact that you can't please all the people all the time. Know your core values and weight suggestions and criticisms against them.

- Carve out time for positive self-indulgence. Take time to renew your body and spirit. Do something that makes you feel special.
- Learn how to advocate for yourself. "Learn to say no with sensitive assertiveness." Set high but realistic standards.

Construct a deliberate game plan and follow these guidelines. Control events, rather than letting events control you.

## The NAEYC Principles for Development and Learning

In the NAEYC guidelines for developmentally appropriate practice (Bredekamp & Copple, 1997), quality is associated with 12 principles of child development and learning. Principles that particularly relate to learning include the following:

- Children are active learners, drawing on direct physical and social experience as well as culturally transmitted knowledge to construct their own understandings of the world around them (p. 13).
- Play is an important vehicle for children's social, emotional, and cognitive development, as well as a reflection of their development (p. 14).
- Development advances when children have opportunities to practice newly acquired skills, as well as when they experience a challenge just beyond the level of their current mastery (p. 14).
- Children demonstrate different modes of knowledge and learning and different ways of representing what they know (p. 15).
- Children develop and learn best in the context of a community where they are safe and valued, their physical needs are met, and they feel psychologically secure.

To live up to these principles, we have a long way to go.

Look back through this chapter and reflect on how you relate to the adult roles in children's learning. Evaluate each factor. Can you think of any other factors not mentioned? Which factors seem to be most important? Describe how you perceive your role with young children as learners. The next chapter examines parent and culturally influenced adult roles.

## SUMMARY

Whichever theoretical position is examined, adults have a definite role in children's learning. The adult has the responsibilities of interacting appropriately with children and providing the physical environment. The major difference among theories is the degree to which adults serve as guides as compared to serving as directors. The Piagetian and Vygostkian, or constructivist and behaviorist, views have been the most widely applied to education. The constructivist sees the adult as a guide who sets up the environment and supports the children's active construction of their own knowledge. Support is called scaffolding and assists children in moving up through their ZPD. The behaviorist views the adult as a director who directly shapes the child's behavior and gives him or her specific knowledge that the adult believes to be important.

For the behaviorist, extrinsic rewards shape behavior and gradually give way to intrinsic rewards for learning. For the constructivist, the child is by nature a learner and acquiring knowledge is intrinsically rewarding. Research indicates that rewarding children for things that they already like to do can possibly decrease their performance. It has also been found that specific encouragement is more effective than general praise and helps maintain children's natural motivation.

While theorists in every camp may tout their own points of view, the most practical approach to the selection of a theoretical framework appears to be to fit the theory to the problem. No one theory can answer every question.

A vital aspect of the adult role is supporting children in the development of their thinking and problem-solving skills and keeping them motivated to learn. Provision of open-ended activities, asking open-ended questions, providing needed scaffolding, and encouraging group discussion and cooperative problem solving in all areas of the curriculum are essential support for children as they reach their learning potentials and acquire competence. Adults also have the responsibility for intervening appropriately in support of play, providing appropriate access to technology, supporting the learning of children with special needs, and providing high-quality learning environments. To meet all the role requirements and avoid burnout, adults need to take control of their lives.

## For Further Reading


Anderson, D. R., Huston, A. C., Schmitt, K. L., Linebarger, D. L., & Wright, J. C. (2001). *Early childhood television viewing and adolescent behavior. Monographs of the Society for Research in Child Development, 66* (1, Serial No. 264).

Brett, A., & Provenzo, E. F., Jr. (1995). *Adaptive technology for special human needs.* Albany, NY: SUNY Press.

Chambers, C. R., & Childre, A. L. (2005). Fostering family-professional collaboration through person-centered IEP meetings: The "True Directions" model. *Young Exceptional Children, 8*(3), 20–28.

Fisch, S. M. (2004). *Children's learning from educational television.* Mahwah, NJ: Erlbaum.

Fosnot, C. T. (2005). *Constructivism* (2nd ed.). New York: Teachers College.

Grisham-Brown, J. Hemmeter, M. L., & Pretti-Frontczak, K. (2005). *Blended practices for teaching young children in inclusive settings.* Baltimore, MD: Brookes.

Goldstein, J., Buckingham, D., & Brougere, G. (Eds.). (2004). *Toys, games, and media.* Mahwah, NJ: Erlbaum.

Haugland, S. W. (1997). *The developmental scale for software.* Cape Girardeau, MO: K.I.D.S. & Computers.

Haugland, S. W., & Gerzog, G. (1998). *The developmental software scale for websites.* Cape Girardeau, MO: K.I.D.S. & Computers.

Haugland, S. W., & Wright, J. L. (1997). *Young children and technology: A world of discovery.* New York: Allyn & Bacon.

Hauser-Cram, P., Warfield, M. E., Shonkoff, J. P., & Krauss, M. W. (2001). *Children with disabilities. Monographs of the Society for Research in Child Development, 66* (3, Serial No. 266).

Helm, J. H., Berg, S., & Scranton, P. (2004). *Teaching your child to love learning.* New York: Teachers College.

Herbert, M. (2002). *Typical and atypical development: From conception to adolescence.* Williston, VT: Blackwell.

Lesar, S. (1998). Use of assistive technology with young children with disabilities. *Journal of Early Intervention, 21*, 146–159.

Odom, S. L., & Diamond, K. E. (Eds.). (1998). Inclusion in early childhood settings [Special issue]. *Early Childhood Research Quarterly, 13*(1).

Palmer, E., & Young, B. M. (Eds.). (2003). *The faces of television media.* Mahwah, NJ: Erlbaum.

Richey, D. D., & Wheeler, J. J. (2000). *Inclusive early childhood education.* Clifton Park, NY: Delmar Learning.

Roopnarine, J. (Ed.). (2001). *Conceptual, social-cognitive, and contextual issues in the fields of play.* Westport, CT: Ablex.

Sailor, W., & Roger, B. (2005). Rethinking inclusion: Schoolwide applications. *Phi Delta Kappan, 86*(7), 503–509.

Sanger, J., with J. Wilson, B. Davies, & R. Whittaker. (1997). *Young children, videos, and computer games.* Bristol, PA: Falmer (c/o Taylor and Francis).

Sansone, C., & Harackiewicz, J. M. (Eds.). (2000). *Intrinsic and extrinsic motivation.* San Diego, CA: Academic Press.

Shade, D. D., & Haugland, S. W. (1996). *Young children and computers: A world of discovery.* Boston: Allyn & Bacon.

Watkins, D. E. (2005). Maximizing learning for students with special needs. *Kappa Delta Pi Record, 41*(4), 154–158.

## SUGGESTED ACTIVITIES

1. The objective of this activity is to look at the teacher's role as one who provides an environment for learning. Some classrooms offer opportunities for the child to express individuality, explore, and experiment. Other classrooms are highly structured and offer little room for the child to act as an individual. Visit a preschool, kindergarten, or primary classroom; categorize the environment's physical, social-emotional, and intellectual aspects; and decide whether it promotes children's learning. The following learning environment checklist, adapted from Harms (1970, pp. 304–308), can be used.
   a. Write a description of the room you visited.
   b. Write a summary of everything you saw.
   c. Write a summary of what you learned, using the learning environment checklist.
   d. Do you think the teachers do a good job in their roles as providers of a learning environment? Why?

2. Read descriptions of four Head Start/Follow-Through or Transition model programs or other early education program models. Compare the descriptions of the teacher's role in each model. Which do you think is best in promoting learning? Why?

3. In your neighborhood, at a child care center or in an elementary school, question six children ages three, four, five, six, seven, and eight regarding their play activities and preferences. You might ask the following:
   a. What do you do when you play?
   b. What do you like to do the most when you play? At home? At school?
   c. When you are not playing, what are you doing?

   Compare the children's responses by age and whether their answers pertain to home or school. Report on your results in class.

   Question four parents and/or teachers about how they feel about play. Do they value play? In what ways? Some questions to ask include the following:
   a. Describe play in your own words.
   b. Does play have value for children? If so, what is the value (are the values)?
   c. What kinds of things support children's play? What kinds of things discourage children's play?
   d. What is the role of play at home? at school? (If interviewing a parent, ask specifically what he or she does to promote play at home; if interviewing a teacher, ask what he or she does to promote play at school.)

4. Visit a curriculum materials center and/or look through some materials catalogs that specialize in materials for young handicapped children. Categorize the kinds of materials available for various kinds of children with special needs. Compare these materials with the kinds you would use with children without special needs. What are some differences you find between materials for children with and without special needs? Can you find any similarities? If possible, bring some materials to class to share with the other students. Give a report on your findings and use the materials as examples to illustrate what you discovered.

5. Contact six families with at least one child between the ages of three and eight. Provide the parents with a chart set up as shown below. Have the parents keep a one-week record of the child's television viewing on the chart.

## Learning Environment Checklist

| Characteristic | Yes | No | Comments |
|---|---|---|---|
| **The Physical Environment** | | | |
| Is there a place for quiet and noisy activities to go on at the same time? | | | |
| Are a variety of materials available and easy for children to obtain? | | | |
| Is it clear where each type of material may be used? | | | |
| Can children choose to use material alone or in groups? | | | |
| Are children allowed time to explore, experiment, and discover? | | | |
| Do the adults observe carefully, intervening to expand an activity by providing additional material or providing some scaffolding by making a suggestion, asking a question, or helping to settle a dispute as necessary? | | | |
| **The Interpersonal Environment** | | | |
| Is there a feeling of mutual respect between adults and adults, adults and children, and children and children? | | | |
| Do the adults spend more time observing and interacting with the children than setting limits? | | | |
| Do the adults have specific objectives for each child's learning? | | | |
| Is cooperation rather than competition reinforced? | | | |
| Do the adults model the kind of behavior they want the children to learn? | | | |
| Do the adults give ample appropriate positive reinforcement and encouragement? | | | |
| **Activities** | | | |
| _____ art materials | | | |
| _____ writing materials | | | |
| _____ musical instruments | | | |
| _____ record or CD player | | | |
| _____ computer(s) | | | |
| _____ book center | | | |
| _____ puzzles and games | | | |
| _____ math manipulatives | | | |
| _____ hands-on science materials | | | |
| _____ construction toys (e.g., LEGOS®) | | | |
| _____ blocks and accessories | | | |
| _____ dramatic play area with props | | | |
| Are there opportunities for field trips? | | | |
| Are there materials of different difficulty levels? | | | |
| Do the children do some of the planning? | | | |
| Do the teachers pick up on the children's interests? | | | |
| Are parents invited to share their talents in the classroom and/or assist with activities? | | | |

ONE-WEEK TV RECORD

Child's name _____ Sex _____

Date of birth _____

| Date | Program | Length |
| --- | --- | --- |
| | | |
| | | |

Evaluate each child's viewing habits. Are there any improvements you feel could be made?

**6.** Make an entry in your journal. As a parent (or future parent) and/or a teacher (or future teacher) reflect on your feelings about your role in supporting children's learning.

## REVIEW

**1.** What are the two basic roles the adult has in the child's learning?

**2.** Match the theorists in Column I with the adult roles in learning described in Column II.

| Column I | Column II |
| --- | --- |
| a. Piaget | 1. The adult guides the child through the cycles of growth and gives support when the child goes through a difficult stage. |
| b. Vygotsky | 2. The adult is more of a director than a guide. The environment controls learning. |
| c. Erikson, Maslow, Rogers, Freud | 3. The adult guides the child's healthy emotional, social, and personality development and assists the child through developmental crises. |
| d. Gesell | 4. The adult guides the child through the stages of mental development by providing the appropriate environment, the right kinds of questions, and an opportunity for exploration and discovery. |
| e. Skinner | 5. The adult is a model of appropriate behavior. |
| f. Bandura | 6. The adult provides support for the child through the zone of proximal development. |

**3.** Write a *P* for each statement that describes a Piagetian teacher role, a *V* for a Vygotskian teacher role, and a *B* for a behaviorist teacher role.

a. Teachers are people who change learners.

b. What the teacher does immediately following a behavior is a critical factor in determining whether or not the behavior is learned.

c. The teacher asks questions that help the child solve the problem on his or her own.

d. The teacher provides assisted performance within the child's realm of understanding.

e. The teacher needs to be alert so that he or she can follow up desired behaviors with positive consequences for the child.

f. The teacher provides a variety of experiences in which the child is encouraged to explore and experiment.
g. The teacher feels free to stand back and let the child discover for himself or herself.
h. The boundaries within which children can be successful independently and within which they can be successful with assistance are constantly changing.

**4.** Read the following description of teacher behavior. Decide whether this teacher is using good behaviorist techniques by reinforcing only desired behaviors and using a variety of reinforcers.

Paul R. is the head teacher for a group of four- and five-year-olds. The children are busy in several learning centers set up around the room. Julie comes in, goes to her cubby, hangs up her coat, and comes over to greet Paul. He gives her a hug and tells her to look around and decide what she would like to do this morning. Paul moves about the room, smiling at children as they work. Throughout the observation period, we note that Mary Lou always lets Paul know when she needs something by yelling across the room, "Teacher! Teacher! I need you." Paul always goes to her immediately. Each time he reminds her not to yell.

**5.** Describe an activity that promotes cooperative problem solving.

**6.** Briefly describe the development of motivation in young children.

**7.** Describe how peer and teacher presence and activity type affect social and cognitive competence.

**8.** Select the correct answer to the following. There is only one correct answer for each.

a. When children are playing, adults sometimes suggest how a toy can be used more imaginatively or how a new role or scene might make the play more interesting.
   1. An adult should definitely not take that role.
   2. Sometimes an adult might take that role.
   3. It is appropriate for an adult to take that role often.

b. Mrs. Goodbird and Jason are sitting at the kitchen table. Jason is playing with his clay and some toy trucks. He fills the trucks and moves them around the table. His mother unloads the trucks for him and then he drives them back and fills them up again. They talk about what they are doing as if they were really a truck driver and a truck unloader.
   1. This is a good example of how a parent can teach her child about how to pretend.
   2. To help Jason, his mother should be more directive and have him play her way.
   3. Getting involved in a child's play like this is undignified for the adult and of no help to the child.

c. Mrs. Tanaka brings in some new props for the children: dress-up clothes, fire hats, construction worker hats, and medical kits. When the children do not seem to know what to do, she gets out a medical kit and says, "I feel sick. Who will check me?" Isabel says, "I will. I will be the doctor. Theresa, you be the nurse."
   1. This teacher is being too directive.
   2. This teacher has done a good job of bringing in materials and presenting an idea, while leaving it up to the children to elaborate on it.
   3. The teacher should be more directive. She should tell the children what to do. She should assign roles and make them play with the props so they will all know what to do with them.

d. Mr. Brown sits near where the children are playing with blocks. He observes closely but does not intervene in any way.
   1. Observing is one of the roles an adult may take in child's play.
   2. Observing is not a role that the adult should take in child's play.
   3. Mr. Brown must be tired today or he would be more involved.

e. Mrs. Kirk has set up a medical center. Among the many dramatic play props are pads and pencils to write prescriptions, a book to record appointments, a clipboard with paper to record the patient's progress, telephones, telephone book, Post-it® notes for messages, and magazines in the waiting area. To get the highest rate of literacy behaviors from her class:
   1. Mrs. Kirk should sit back and let them use their imaginations.
   2. Mrs. Kirk should explain everything the first day and then let the children use them in their natural way.
   3. Mrs. Kirk should discuss the possibilities and materials in the center each day to provide guidance for their activities.

f. Schrader found in her research that one style of teacher interaction produced much richer literacy play in the classroom:
   1. Extending the play by building on the children's natural intentions.
   2. Redirecting the play so that the children were sure to do what she believed they should do.
   3. Keeping out of the play so that the children could engage in their natural ways of learning to be literate.

g. If Joan, a teacher, provides appropriate and adequate play materials, equipment, and space for play:
   1. She has done her job. The children can take it from there.
   2. That is only the beginning. She will have to follow up with rearranging and bringing in new things when needed, and play a number of roles, such as observer, reflector, or elaborator.
   3. Children really don't need many raw materials. She could have saved herself a lot of trouble.

**9.** Match the terms and phrases in Colums I with the definitions/examples in Column II.

| **Column I** | **Column II** |
|---|---|
| a. violence on television | 1. Some examples are toys, clays, blocks, and dramatic play. |
| b. commercials | 2. This is a program that provides a model of calm, patient adult behavior. |
| c. planned television viewing | 3. Children must learn to be informed consumers. |
| d. alternatives to television | 4. It is the adult's responsibility to interpret. |
| e. *Mr. Rogers' Neighborhood* | 5. Limit time and make up a schedule on a calendar. |
| f. computer drill and practice | 6. A twitch of the cheek or blink of an eyelid can control the action. |
| g. technology holds great promise for the disabled | 7. This type of computer software has very limited value. |
| h. PL 94–142 | 8. This provided for the education of three-, four-, and five-year-old children with special needs. |
| i. PL 101–476 | 9. This was a landmark in legislation for those with special needs. |
| j. PL 99–457 | 10. This law protects equal rights for employment, social services, etc., for people with disabilities |
| k. Americans with Disabilities Act (ADA) | 11. This is a revision of PL 99–142. |

**10.** Mark each statement *T* for true or *F* for false.

a. No specialized knowledge is needed to teach children with disabilities in inclusive settings.

b. When faced with the prospect of teaching in an inclusive setting, it is not unusual for a teacher to feel many strong emotions.

c. It is important to teach special-needs children the basic survival skills they will need when they enter the primary grades.
d. Because children with disabilities are different from typical students, knowledge of typical development is not valuable in planning for their instruction.
e. Overall program quality is related to the amount of specialized education of the teachers and the level of teacher wages.
f. For the most part, preschool programs tend to be higher quality than those for infants and toddlers.
g. The quality of the mother-child relationship is a critical element in children's learning.
h. Most of the best early childhood teachers manage to give special individual attention to each student every day.
i. Parents and administrators are always supportive of child-centered instruction.
j. Recently, it has been observed that adequate opportunities for play are available in most kindergartens.
k. The adult role as a facilitator of children's play is to provide scaffolding, space, and materials.
l. Potential benefits of Internet use include enhanced creativity; critical thinking, problem solving, language, research, and social skills; knowledge; self-esteem; and the ability to integrate information.
m. Children can never receive too much praise.

**11.** Explain how adults can avoid burnout.

## KEY TERMS LIST

Americans with Disabilities Act (ADA)
amplification
autonomy
CD-ROM
constructivism
extrinsic rewards
haptic
IDEA 97
inside intervention
Internet
intrinsic rewards
nonthematic
observation
outside intervention
PL 94–142
PL 99–457
PL 101–476
reinforcements
rewards
scaffolding
self-regulation
software
task analysis
thematic
Web sites

Additional resources for this chapter can be found on the Online Companion™ to accompany this text at http://www.earlychilded.delmar.com. Respond to "Time to Reflect" and "Looking Further" concepts, review various child development scenarios, and answer thought-provoking questions in the Critical Thinking Forum. Keep a daily journal by downloading the student journal available on this Web site. Complete the interactive matching exercises to reinforce concepts, and print out the child development assessment forms to use during your observation of development for children from birth to age eight. In addition, read the case studies on the Web site to reinforce the important concepts in each chapter, and take a look at the multitude of Web links that are available for student research on the Internet.

CHAPTER

# 7

# The Adult Role in Learning: Family and Sociocultural Factors

## OBJECTIVES

After reading this chapter, you should be able to:

- Analyze and evaluate your own feelings about parenting styles, parent education, and parent involvement.
- Identify adult caregivers and teachers who are doing well at supporting children's learning.
- Evaluate whether an adult caregiver or teacher has a positive or negative teaching style.
- Describe the role of the family in planning for children with special needs.
- Identify adult responsibilities for children's access to technology.
- Give examples of how families within the same culture may differ.
- Discuss multicultural and antibias education.
- Discuss why adults must adopt different roles and behaviors when they work with children and parents from different social and cultural backgrounds.

Family, community, and culture have profound influences on children and their development. Bronfenbrenner's model (see Chapter 3) shows that the various domains of persons in the family, the community, and the culture are always interacting with each other and influencing children. In this chapter, a variety of factors that influence child development are examined. These elements include the role of the family and sociocultural influences.

## THE ROLE OF FAMILIES IN CHILDREN'S LEARNING

Families of young children play a critical role in their learning. This chapter examines several parts of the family role: parent-child interaction, nonparental care, parent education and school involvement, and technology in the home. Bradley, Corwyn, Burchinal, McAdoo, and Coll (2001) looked at how various home environmental factors affected children's well-being from birth through age 13. These researchers examined outcomes related to motor, social, and vocabulary development; achievement; and behavior problems. The children in the study were members of both poor and nonpoor European American, African American, and Latino American families. Three aspects of the environment were the major focus of the study: materials and experiences that stimulate learning, parental responsiveness, and spanking. Stimulation of learning had positive relationships across all three ethnic groups with motor and social development during the first three years, language competence, and kindergarten achievement. Both parental direct instruction and responsiveness showed positive developmental effects. The negative effects of spanking during the preschool period grew stronger as children reached adolescence. That is, behavior problems increased more for students who had experienced more spanking. The higher the overall quality of the home physical environment, the stronger the children's competence and the lower their levels of behavior problems. In considering families and parents, it is important to recognize the changing nature of American families (de Melendez & Ostertag, 1997). The concept of traditional family has changed as diversity among families has become more recognized.

De Melendez and Ostertag divide family structure into traditional and nontraditional. Traditional families are two-parent families, with the father as the head of the family, and extended families, which include other relatives, such as grandparents, aunts, uncles, and cousins. Nontraditional families include step-families, parenting grandparents, blended families, reconstituted families, single-parent families, unmarried families, homosexual families, families headed by siblings, and foster families. For convenience, the term *parent* is used in this unit in a generic way that may be applied to other caregivers in the family. De Melendez and Ostertag (1997) describe the family "as being a basic social and human unit instrumental for individual and social survival." The family provides economic support, recreation, socialization, self-identity, affection, and education. Each cultural group has its own expectations of family responsibilities regarding education and child-rearing. Examples of such expectations are examined in the next part of this chapter, and family roles in learning are looked at in a more general way.

Research has supported the basic findings that positive, cooperative interactions between parent and child when completing a task at the preschool level predict higher academic achievement in elementary school (see Figure 7–1) (Bradley, et al., 2001).

Shared book reading is a parent-child activity that has been closely examined. Pellegrini, Perlmutter, Galda, and Brody (1990) found that low-socioeconomic-scale African American mothers used the same kinds of strategies as the middle-class mother-child pairs in previous studies. The mothers seemed to operate in the ZPD as they demanded higher-level cognitive responses when engaged with a familiar book rather than with a new book.

FIGURE 7–1 "You can do it for yourself." The adult helps the child be independent and responsible.

Hyson, Hirsh-Pasek, Rescorla, Cone, and Martell-Boinske (1989) found that upper-middle-class mothers' beliefs regarding mastery were related to their interactions when working on a problem-solving task with their children. Those mothers who believed strongly in skill mastery were much more directive than those whose beliefs about skill mastery were less strong.

Okagaki and Sternberg (1993) found differences in beliefs regarding school performance among parents from different cultures. Immigrant parents from Cambodia, Mexico, the Philippines, and Vietnam, and native-born European

FIGURE 7–2 Respect for adults is an important value for Mexican Americans.

American and Mexican American parents were questioned regarding their beliefs about child-rearing, what should be taught in the first and second grades, and what characterizes an intelligent child. The immigrant parents favored conformity over autonomy, whereas the American-born parents favored autonomy. European American parents related cognitive characteristics, such as problem-solving skills, verbal ability, and creative ability, to intelligence. The other groups placed more importance on noncognitive characteristics, such as motivation, social skills, and practical school skills. Okagaki and Sternberg (1993) suggest that the immigrant parents' emphasis on conformity, although negatively related to school performance, is probably a practical approach for children who must learn to live in a new culture (Figure 7–2).

Takanishi (2004) reviewed the status of the education needs of immigrant children in the United States. She focused on the period from birth to age eight when the foundation for the future should be built. She found that immigrant children tend to be disadvantaged in the three areas needed for child well-being: family economic security, access to health care, and access to sound early education. Immigrant children could benefit from prekindergarten and after-school programs and yet are less likely to participate. This is especially true for Mexican American children and is very strong in the area of center-based child care. The reasons for this lower level of particpation by racial/ethnic and immigrant children is not well understood. The reasons could relate to differences in parental and cultural preferences or to a lack of affordable and accessible care. These questions need to be explored. Takanishi recommends that high-quality early childhood education programs should be available for all children.

Most studies have focused on the mother's role in learning. What about the father's role? As already described, the types of groups that constitute "family" have changed greatly over time. As families have become more diverse, so has the definition and the role of **father.** The definition of a father has become broader, since there are biological fathers who live in the child's home and those who don't, stepfathers, fathers who were never married to the child's mother and those who were, etc. (Tamis-LeMonda & Cabrera, 1999). A father may be biological and/or social, legal, or nonlegal (Tamis-LeMonda & Cabrera, 1999). The important factor is to examine the roles that males take in children's lives. Tamis-LeMonda and Cabrera point out that the father role has moved beyond the traditional one of breadwinner into more child care–related roles. Father involvement has three major components. **Direct engagement** involves direct contact through play, caretaking, and leisure time activities. **Accessibility** refers to the father's degree of availability to the child. **Responsibility** includes meeting emotional, social, and economic needs. More research is needed on how these roles affect child outcomes. However, there is evidence that fathers' emotional investment, attachment, and provision of resources are all associated with young children's degree of well-being. A father's care during the child's first year has a relatively positive impact on developmental outcomes. When children are in elementary school, father involvement with them is correlated to school success. Attending school meetings and parent-teacher conferences, and volunteering in school all correlate with academic achievement and enjoyment of school. For out-of-home fathers, providing financial support and having a good relationship with the mother have positive effects on children's development. Overall, there needs to be just as much focus on father figures as on mothers and their effect on child development. Overall, we know that children do better when their fathers are involved.

**father**

The primary adult male figure in a child's life; may be related legally or nonlegally.

**direct engagement**

Direct contact through play, caretaking, and leisure time activities.

**accessibility**

Degree of availability to the child.

**responsibility**

Degree of meeting emotional, social, and economic needs.

In the past very little was known about how fathers in low-income communities contribute to their children's development. Research by Daria Zvetina (2000) revealed that although only a small percentage of African American fathers in low-income communities may live with their children, more than half provide some financial support and visit their children at least once a month. White and Hispanic low-income fathers tend to visit their children less frequently than do African American fathers. In a study of African American families in the most destitute area of Chicago, 95 percent of fathers of toddlers were described by the mothers as "attached" or "strongly attached" to the toddlers. Fifty-nine percent of the mothers reported that the fathers of the toddlers were very much involved in caregiving. Mothers reported that fathers were involved in protecting their toddlers from harm, teaching them right from wrong, and disciplining them. Two-thirds of the mothers said the fathers did best in playing with their toddlers. These research studies break the stereotype that all fathers in low-income communities abandon their young children.

## Nonparental Care

Quality factors in nonparental, out-of-home care were described in Chapter 6. These nonparental, out-of-home caregivers also have an influence on young children's learning. Alison Clarke-Stewart (1984) has done extensive research in this area. Clarke-Stewart identified a continuum of child care arrangements that ranged from full time at home with parents to full time in a child care center. In addition, she identified an arrangement in which children were cared for part time at a nursery school and part time at the caregiver's home or their home. Seven child care arrangements were identified:

1. at home with parents
2. at home with parents and siblings
3. at home with baby sitter
4. child care home
5. nursery school, part time
6. child care center, full time
7. nursery school and baby sitter

Children were observed in these settings, and mothers, fathers, and caregivers were interviewed. Clarke-Stewart found that child care center children were more competent than children in the other types of situations during interactions with parents, strangers, and unfamiliar peers. They were also more advanced in intellectual abilities and social knowledge. Child care center children were also more independent of their parents. The center-based child care settings tended to have more highly trained caregivers than did the other settings. The results indicated that high-quality, out-of-home care can have beneficial effects on child development.

Thornburg, Pearl, Crompton, and Ispa (1990) found that full-time child care had no apparent detrimental effects on children's social and intellectual development as measured when they were in kindergarten. Child care participants tended to be somewhat more aggressive than non–child care attenders, but not to the point of being viewed as problem children by their teachers. African American children appeared to receive some intellectual benefits from having attended child care programs.

Votruba-Drzal, Coley, and Chase-Lansdale, (2004) did a study on child care and low-income children's development. Unlike previous studies that looked at children enrolled in center-based care, the child care settings included in this research were quite varied: regulated and unregulated homes, for-profit centers, nonprofit centers, and Head Start. The results indicated a positive relationship between quality and social-emotional development. Low-quality care appeared to be harmful for the social-emotional development of these low socioeconomic status (SES) children, especially the boys. Burchinal, Lee, and Ramey (1989) found that lower-socioeconomic–scale African American children who were enrolled from infancy in a high-quality intervention child care program were significantly ahead in cognitive development compared to similar children who attended lower-quality community child care, who were ahead of similar children who experienced little or no child care. Caughy, DiPietro, and Strobino (1994) found this same protective factor for impoverished children who entered child care as infants. Phillips, Voran, Kisker, Howes, and Whitebook (1994), reporting the results of a national child care study, found that upper-class children received the highest-quality care, middle-class children the least-quality care, and lower-class children more variable care. Most of the low-socioeconomic-scale programs are government funded, and there is a government responsibility to evaluate some of these programs and provide increased quality. Support is increasing for the belief that quality child care during early childhood not only is nondetrimental but also can enhance the development of young children.

## Parent/Caregiver Education and Involvement

Research has demonstrated that some kinds of parent-child interactions are effective in enhancing children's learning, whereas others may thwart normal development. Therefore, early childhood educators have sought means to help parents and other caregivers become more effective teachers of young children. A great deal of attention has focused on parent and caregiver education and involvement. The Head Start program (Celebrating Head Start's 25th Anniversary, 1990) has effectively included both the educational and the involvement components. Head Start focuses as much on the education and involvement of parents as on education of the children. Although preschool educators have long recognized the value of parent education and involvement, educators at the elementary and secondary levels are recognizing the importance of getting parents more involved in the education of their children (Epstein, 1991).

Fitzgerald and Goncu (1993) and Christie (2005) point out the importance of a collaborative parent-teacher relationship in which both teachers and parents contribute to decisions regarding what children learn and how they learn it. They believe that this is especially important for low-income parents and children whose backgrounds are different from the school personnel. In their study of parent involvement in low-income urban public schools, they found very little parent-teacher collaboration. The school personnel set the agenda for parent involvement, deciding what forms it should take, where it should take place, and what the focus should be. Fitzgerald and Goncu (1993) suggest that it is essential for school personnel to stop viewing themselves as the experts who tell parents what is best for their children and, instead, learn to respect parents' opinions and negotiate with parents regarding what is best for their children in a partnership relationship.

Increasingly, early childhood educators are seeing the importance of developing numerous involvement strategies that fit parents' and caregivers' time frames, interests, and talents. The objective is to develop parents and caregivers who are active supporters of children's education (Rockwell, Andre, & Hawley, 1996). Joyce Epstein has created a popular model of parent involvement (Epstein, 1997). Her model includes six types of parental involvement: parenting, communicating, volunteering,learning at home, decision making, and collaborating with the community.

FIGURE 7–3 High-quality, nonparental care can be very beneficial for the child.

*Parenting:* The goal is to help all families establish home environments that provide for the health and safety of children to support learning and positive parenting. Schools and community agencies can provide support through parent education, parent support groups, parent rooms and spaces in schools, social service directories, and parent resource libraries.

*Communicating:* The goal of this strategy is to design effective forms of communication to reach parents. These types of communication include parent handbooks, newsletters, audiotapes and videotapes, yearbooks, parent meetings, parent conferences, activity calendars, surveys and questionnaires, health and other screenings, orientation meetings, home visits, notes, letters, and phone calls. Schools must also communicate regarding transitions to higher levels and must consider the importance of communications that are understandable to all parents, including those whose first language is other than English.

*Volunteering:* The goal is to recruit and organize parent support. Volunteering might take place in the school but out-of-school jobs are also possible. Some types of activities include telephoning other parents when needed; coordinating volunteers; fundraising; constructing games and other materials; volunteering in classroom, library, or office; supervising on the playground; maintaining and constructing playground equipment; and sharing talents, skills, hobbies, and resources (Figure 7–3).

*Learning at home:* The goal of this strategy is to provide ideas and materials to parents on how to help their children at home. Parents are helped to apply their knowledge of their children to selecting materials and activities that will support their learning. These strategies are developed through parent meetings, book and activity bags for use at home, workshops and seminars, and loaning out parenting books.

*Decision making:* The goal of this strategy is for schools to give parents meaningful roles in the school decision-making process. Schools need to provide training and information so they can make the most of these opportunities.

*Collaborating with the Community:* Schools can help families gain access to support services offered by other agencies, such as health care, cultural events, tutoring services, after-school child care, etc. Schools can also promote service to the community, such as sponsoring recycling programs and collecting supplies for food pantries.

Christie (2005) suggests that parent involvement can be viewed from several levels of parental influence:

1. Volunteering at the child's school.
2. Faithful attendance at school conferences and activities.
3. Serving on committees and tutoring.
4. Making sure their children do their homework, that children have a quiet place to study with needed materials, and that children get to school on time every day.
5. Most important, parents have high expectations for their children's effort and behavior.

In summary, Christie suggests there should be mutual accountability between parents and schools that all children are reaching their academic potential.

Think about your own family experience. Evaluate it as a setting for learning. If you are currently in a family setting with young children, describe it and evaluate its strengths and weaknesses as a setting for learning. If you have not yet had a family of your own, describe how you imagine your future family.

## Involvement of Families of Children with Special Needs

With the advent of PL 94–142, the family became an integral part of planning for the education and placement of children with special needs through participation in the development and evaluation of the individualized education program (IEP). This involvement has been included in the regulations for PL 99–457, Part H, through parent involvement in the **individualized family service plan (IFSP).**

**individualized family service plan (IFSP)**
A plan with specific objectives that must be developed for all families enrolled in birth to three-year-old special education programs.

It is mandated that every child with special-needs have an IEP. This plan is designed to ensure that the child receives the education to which he or she is entitled. It is developed cooperatively through a committee made up of school personnel and the child's parents. No child can be placed in any kind of special education program unless the IEP has been written. To receive federal funds, the school must follow through on the services stated in the IEP.

The development of an IEP and the placement of the child with special needs are achieved through a specifically defined process. The process can be undertaken only with the parents' signed permission. With the parents' permission, the assessment team proceeds with the assessment task. The assessment team is composed of the teacher and other professionals, such as a nurse, physician, social worker, speech and language therapist, psychologist, and special educator. Test and observational data are collected, evaluated, and discussed by the team with the parent, who then becomes a member of the planning team. The parent has final authority regarding placement.

Whereas PL 101–476 IDEA focuses on the child, PL 99–457 focuses on the family. This focus is operationalized through the IFSP (McGonigel, Kaufman, & Johnson, 1991; Widerstrom, Mowder, & Sandall, 1991):

> The IFSP venture involves family and early intervention professionals working together to develop a plan that includes services and supports that will enhance the development of the child and the capacity of the family to meet the special needs of the child (Widerstrom, et al., 1991).

The IFSP must contain information on the child's current level of functioning, a statement of the family's strengths and weaknesses, the expected outcomes for the child and the family, the intervention services that will be needed, the number of days and sessions for which the service will be provided, the length of time of each session, and whether the service is individual or group. The location for service (e.g., home, early intervention center, hospital) must be designated. Any services needed that are not specified under the law will be described with steps to be implemented to acquire the services. Anticipated dates of service initiation and duration must be specified. If the child is nearing age three, a plan for transition out of infant/toddler services must be included. Meetings with the family, case manager, and interdisciplinary team members should be planned with the family and take place in a situation that is comfortable for the family. The IFSP must be reviewed every six months. "The message of PL 99–457 is that early intervention for children with special needs must respect the family" (Widerstrom, et al., 1991).

**family-centered practice**
Educational plans and practices developed from the family's point of view (versus the professionals').

With the focus on the whole family through development of the IFSP, researchers became interested in looking at **family-centered practice.** McBride,

Brotherson, Joanning, Whiddon, and Demmitt (1993) identified three major principles of family-centered practice that reflect the beliefs and values that serve as a framework for practice (p. 415):

1. establishing the family as the focus of services
2. supporting and respecting family decision making
3. providing intervention services designed to strengthen family functioning

McBride, et al. (1993) interviewed professionals and families regarding their experiences with family-centered practice using these three principles as criteria for evaluation of practice. The results indicated that although the families were satisfied with the services received, the professionals varied in their degrees of family centeredness. The professionals also varied in the degree to which they had switched their focus from the child to the whole family. The authors conclude that both preservice and inservice education programs need to focus more strongly on family-centered delivery of services.

## FAMILIES AND TECHNOLOGY

In Chapters 4 and 6, the power of technology and cautions regarding technology were discussed. In this chapter, a more detailed look is taken at technology in the home.

### Television at Home

Children are watching three to five hours of television per day. Even children as young as nine months old are watching up to 90 minutes of television per day (Cohen, 1993/94). Public television and educational commercial television offer many excellent programs. However, these are not necessarily the programs our children are watching. They spend a lot of time watching violence, commercials, and even "steamy sex" (Notar, 1989). In the 1980s, the time networks spent showing commercials increased from what it was in the 1970s to 12 to 14 minutes per hour. Moreover, during commercials, the sound level is increased to attract the viewer's attention. Many children are at home unsupervised after school with access to adult programming available on cable and satellite systems.

Opinions differ regarding young children's television viewing. Daniel McGinn (2004/05) suggests that television for children is improving. There are many programs from which to choose. Programs, such as *Sesame Street*, *Dora the Explorer*, and *Blue's Clues* are researched as to appropriate content and child interest. Most parents agree that television is okay for children as long as they are

Think about the pros and cons of television watching by young children. Consider the following description:

> Summer, four-and-one-half years old, loves television and videos. She has learned to count from *Ernie*, to recite the alphabet from *Barney*, and some Spanish vocabulary from *Dora the Explorer*. She's only allowed to watch PBS, Noggin, Disney, children's specials, educational programming, and G-rated movies.

Is this good or bad? What do you think? If you are (or expect to be) a parent how do you (or would you) handle television and video viewing?

viewing appropriate programs. Research shows that children prefer longer, more conceptual segments, which contrasts with earlier beliefs about children's television. The American Academy of Pediatrics (AAP) (2005) Web site provides up-to-date information and recommendations from the pediatrician's point of view. If children watch noneducational television, they will see violence, sex, alcohol, tobacco and other drugs, and a multitude of commercials. The AAP suggests parents consider the following when their children are viewing television:

- Time. Children in the United States spend about four hours a day in front of the television, watching movies on tape or DVD or playing video games. Consider whether much of this time might be spent playing or reading.
- Nutrition. Children who watch too much television tend to be overweight. Commercials are filled with ads for unhealthy foods that children may beg their parents to purchase.
- Learning. Children can learn important concepts from educational television. They tend to do better on reading and math tests. However, AAP advises that since we don't know the effects of television on children under two, they can benefit more from interaction with other people. Beyond age two, AAP recommends no more than one or two hours per day in front of the television.

AAP also provides several tips for parents:

1. Set limits on time, don't allow children to have the television on while doing homework, and do not put a television in children's bedrooms.
2. Use a program guide to plan viewing with your child.
3. Watch television with your child. Discuss what is viewed. Explain what is fantasy, what is reality, and how commercials are trying to sell merchandise.
4. Find the right message. If stereotypes are shown, discuss why they are bad and why tolerance and understanding of diversity is important.
5. Help children resist commercials. Explain that they are designed to get people to buy things they don't need. Consider only watching public television or videos.
6. Look for quality videos and DVDs. Check reviews.
7. Provide other activity options, such as playing, reading, sports, art, or learning an instrument; and spend time with family and neighbors.
8. Adults should set a good example by limiting their television viewing and making careful program selections.
9. You can express you views by writing the local station, the network, or the program's sponsors.
10. Get more information by checking with your pediatrician, the AAP, public service groups, your local PTA, and other parents.

AAP states that television can be a valuable learning experience for children if parents handle it in an informed manner.

An important area for family discussion is the presence of stereotypes on television (Williams, 2004). Children may see Native Americans in buckskin, war paint, and feathers waving tomahawks; super-smart Asians; a black basketball player; or a mysterious villain in a turban. Parents should discuss with their children how these stereotypical characters relate to the people they see and know in their world. Discuss whether the show writers and producers really know and understand the group their characters represent. Consider other media, such as newspapers, magazines, and billboards. How are different groups depicted? Why are certain ethnic groups representing particular products? Check the real history as compared with the filmed version, such as the movie *Pocahontas*. Parents can also participate in the annual TV-Turnoff Week.

## Computers in the Home

Increasing numbers of children are entering prekindergarten and kindergarten with home computer experience. Most young children who learn to use computers at home do so because they see their parents using them. For example, as a parent is word processing, his two-year-old climbs in his lap. He lets the child try the keys. The child is delighted with the response on the screen and is soon experimenting on his own. Although many parents already have hardware, others will need advice regarding what kind of hardware to purchase. Resources such as the magazine *Computer Shopper*, friends, or computer experts in the community can provide advice. Parents also need advice for purchasing appropriate software. The NAEYC (1996) provides the following guidelines for parents to use when looking for good software for children:

1. Software for young children should use pictures and spoken directions rather than written ones so that children will not need to ask for help.
2. Children should be able to control the level of difficulty, pace, and direction of the program.
3. The software should offer variety, enabling the children to explore a number of topics on different levels.
4. Feedback should be quick so the child's interest is maintained.
5. Programs should use the capacities of today's computers by appealing to children through interesting sights and sounds.
6. Parents should preview the product before purchasing it to ensure that it fits the interests and developmental level of their child.
7. The software should engage children's interest through humor and encourage their imaginations and desire to explore.
8. The program should allow children to experience success and feel empowered through learning.

The number of new software programs produced each year has decreased as more free material is available on the Internet. The major networks provide sites, such as PBS Kids, Noggin, and Disney, which provide games, teacher activities, and parental advice and activities.

As described in Chapter 4, there is some difference of opinion regarding when children should be allowed to use a computer and how much time they should spend on the computer. For preschoolers, computer use should probably begin as a family activity with the young child exploring in collaboration with an adult or older child. Inappropriate sites can be blocked and appropriate sites can be bookmarked. Interested preschoolers learn fairly quickly to turn on the computer and use the mouse to find their favorite games and activities. A study by Bers, New, and Boudreau (2004) is an example of parent and child learning technology together. Bers, et al. documented the behavior of pairs of four- and five-year-old preschoolers and their parents as they learned to program and build robots using a LEGO® Mindstorms Kit and art materials in a project combining math, science, engineering, and technology. Some parents were concerned that their children were too young to engage in such a complex project, but when they saw the children's eagerness and openness to try, they went ahead with the project. The objective was not to build the perfect robot but to explore the material and construct a culturally relevant product.

### Video Games

We discussed video games in Chapter 4. We must emphasize that many of these games contain violent content and that parents must closely monitor their selection and use.

Design a technology family information pamphlet that could be distributed in your community. Have two parents of young children read the pamphlet and give you their reactions. Distribute copies to members of the class for their reaction and discussion. Revise the pamphlet. Share it with some adults who work with young children in your community (i.e., a Head Start director, a child care center director, and a kindergarten or primary teacher). Ask them if they might be interested in distributing copies to their families. Offer to help them design a parent meeting with the subject "Young Children and Technology."

## SOCIOCULTURAL FACTORS

We cannot assume that all children are the same and that they will react the same way to every adult or to the same adult at all times. The United States is a diverse nation with a variety of cultural groups. It has always been a nation of immigrants and continues to be so today (Banks, Cookson, Gay, Hawley, Irvine, Nieto, Schofield, & Stephan, 2001; Boutte, 2000; Shields, 2004; West, 2001). De Melendez and Ostertag (2000) describe the history of immigration in the United States. The United States has welcomed **immigrants** from all over the world, and the result is a multicultural, pluralistic society. Our current society began with the immigration of Europeans who systematically eradicated the Native Americans and who imported slaves from Africa. The Mexican Americans who settled in the West and Southwest were also purged and disenfranchised. All these events have made it difficult to truly unify our land and provide equal opportunity for all children. Recent immigrants include Latin Americans, Asians, and South Pacific Islanders. According to future projections, the current minority ethnic groups will become the majority by about 2040 (Hernandez, 2004). This nation also varies greatly in terms of locales (rural, urban, and suburban) and social classes (West, 1986). All these factors affect the adult role in the child's learning. Each adult will view children differently depending on that adult's cultural group, social class, and locale. Children will react differently based on the same factors.

**Immigrants**
Individuals from one country who settle in another country.

The sociocultural aspects of children's learning are extremely important considerations when children enter an out-of-home setting, whether for pre-elementary school child care or for more formal schooling. Adults need to be informed to avoid stereotypes and misconceptions (Slaughter-Defoe, Nakagawa, Takanishi, & Johnson, 1990). Lack of cultural understanding can lead to misinterpretation of children's language and cognitive competence (Banks, et al., 2001; Boutte, 2000; West, 2001; Mukhopadhyay & Henze, 2003). For example, Bloch, Tabachnick, and Espinosa-Dulanto (1994) present a picture of some of the unfair assessments made regarding children's academic progress and social behavior based on teachers' incomplete and biased information. Even the best-intentioned teachers "still had too little knowledge of all of their children's backgrounds to understand all of the different ways in which children's competencies could be utilized in the classroom and [in] their learning" (p. 245). Bloch, et al. (1994) found there were school norms that did not leave room for the strengths that might be found in the non–European American students. They believed that there was too much pressure for assimilation and not enough openness to the strengths and talents the non–European American children brought with them to school.

Perez (1994) called for diversity to be responded to with respect. He proposed that schools look upon diversity not as a problem but as an opportunity to experience other peoples and cultures. He suggested several steps that could be taken. For example, children's names should be respected by learning to pronounce them correctly as given rather than changing them to English equivalents. Furthermore, students' primary languages can be respected. Teachers cannot become fluent in all the languages currently represented in our schools, but they can learn at least a few basic terms and phrases. Students should be free to speak their primary languages at school if English is not a particular focus of the instruction. Teaching English should be viewed as adding a second language, not as replacing the primary language. Finally, teachers can demonstrate respect for the students' cultures. Students' cultural beliefs, values, histories, and experiences can be integrated into the curriculum. This should not be done in a fragmentary way but through real integration that looks at different cultural perspectives on various issues.

**multicultural education**

Teaching with respect to the diversity within our culture.

In education, we face a number of problems in our efforts to respect the diversity within our culture. **Multicultural education** was established to support equality of education for all children (Banks et al., 2001; de Melendez & Ostertag 1997). Multicultural education is the goal we strive for, but it has also brought about some concerns that are not yet answered. Knutson (1993) points out two multicultural challenges. First, there is the problem of "teaching *to* diverse populations—migrants, immigrants, refugees, and minorities," and second there is the problem of "teaching *about* these populations." Clabaugh (1993) describes a third problem. In our quest for multiculturalism, how far do we go? For example, if a student comes from a community that does not value education, do we have the right to encourage that student to pursue his or her studies? If a student comes from a culture in which corporal punishment is the norm for misbehavior or in which women are looked upon as property, do we have the right to propose alternatives? A fourth problem is put forth by Ryan (1993). According to Ryan, a peril of multiculturalism is that schooling to the group may bury individuality. Multiculturalism can perpetuate stereotypes, thus, overlooking that members of a cultural group each have their own individuality. Ryan believes that multicultural education should focus on both integration (what needs to be done to network and relate to those who are different) and differentiation (the individual's talents, skills, strengths, weaknesses, likes, and dislikes). Although teachers need to be aware of some of the prevalent attributes of diverse cultures, they also need to be aware that not every member of a group will fit these attributes exactly. A final consideration is the question of balancing our respect for diversity with the major mission of our schools, which is to promote the following (Rozycki, 1993, p. 127):

1. the nonexclusive distribution of power (i.e., democracy)
2. the reduction of stereotyping (i.e., destroying prejudice)
3. equal opportunity for all persons to any role in society

Rozycki (1993) points out that this apparent inconsistency is very confusing to immigrants who have come to this country to become American. Hilliard (1994) believes that questions of race, socioeconomic status, and gender equity should be treated as political rather than educational and pursued on that level. On the other hand, Hilliard sees culture as something real that includes the shared creativities and experiences of groups of people. For most people, socialization and learning begin in a primary culture. It is this cultural diversity that should be understood and inform educational decision making to provide the best education for each individual. Hilliard believes that, to accomplish this goal, educators must distinguish between what is political and what is educationally relevant.

Ogbu (1994) takes still another view of differences within cultures. In studying peoples of the same racial heritage within and across countries, he has identified two major groups that can be found within the minority cultures in the United States:

1. Voluntary or immigrant minorities who voluntarily come to a new country seeking new opportunities. They do not feel that they were forced to come to the new country.
2. Involuntary minorities who are forced to come to a new country against their will, such as the Africans brought to the United States as slaves or the Mexicans incorporated into the United States by conquest.

He has found that voluntary minorities tend to achieve more academic and economic success in the United States than involuntary minorities. He believes that because accommodation to the majority culture is compatible with their goal for coming to this country, they are able to accommodate without assimilating. That is, they adopt the customs of the new country needed to achieve their goals but do not assimilate in that they maintain their own culture, language, and identity. Involuntary immigrants were forced to give up their original culture and forced to conform to the majority culture without all the benefits. Being forced to conform may cause involuntary minorities to avoid acquiring any majority cultural characteristics and customs. Hence, they become oppositional rather than accommodating.

Keep in mind that every cultural group is represented by a diverse collection of individuals, and we need to avoid stereotypes. At the same time, there are some cultural attributes that need to be understood and considered by adults to work with young children and their families from a culturally respectful point of view. We will look next at some of the unique characteristics of the major cultural groups in the United States.

## Hispanic Americans

Our largest minority group is composed of people whose origin is a country where the major language is a dialect of Spanish. The United States has large numbers of Mexican Americans, Cuban Americans, Puerto Rican Americans, and immigrants from many other Central and South American countries. The Mexican Americans comprise the largest group. In 2003, the Hispanic population became the largest minority group (Perez, 2004). This is our fastest-growing minority population. It is also our most undereducated group, has the highest dropout rate, and is the most segregated (Hyland, 1989). But this group is a youthful group and could be a major source of leadership in the future if these issues are addressed. The greatest problem for this group is becoming fluent speakers of English. The methods being used to solve this problem are discussed in Chapter 21.

The Mexican Americans, the largest group, have received a great deal of attention. An important question for research is identification of factors that account for academically successful Mexican American students. Losey (1995) examined the research in this area. Losey (p. 312) concluded that successful classroom environments for Mexican Americans appear to have the following characteristics: "collaborative learning, lesson plans designed around student interests, a sense of belonging to classroom community, flexibility in language usage and a challenging curriculum. . . ." Losey finds that these characteristics are compatible with a Vygotskian theoretical framework for the social context of the classroom, in which there are multiple opportunities to use language communication.

Another area of research focuses on the teaching techniques used by Mexican American mothers. Moreno (Scholars, 1994) had 17 Chicano and 12 European American mother-child pairs videotaped while the mothers taught their children to tie their shoes. He found that, whereas Chicano mothers used more commands than European American mothers during the first three minutes of instruction, this number decreased over the next six minutes observed and turned out to be less overall than exhibited by the European American mothers. Although European American mothers increased their praise over time, Chicano mothers use of praise was constant. Moreno concluded that Chicano mothers do not actually overuse commands as has frequently been reported. Within any cultural/ethnic group, variation exists. For example, research comparing the views of child development of Mexican American mothers who had various degrees of acculturation into mainstream culture found that different groups within the Mexican American culture varied in their views of how children develop (Gutierrez & Sameroff, 1990; Gutierrez, Sameroff, & Karrer, 1988).

A good example of the differences that result in interactions between two types of families from the same ethnic background is the study done by Delgado-Gaitan (1994). Delgado-Gaitan studied family socialization observed in first-generation Mexican American families and Mexican immigrant families in Carpinteria, California. The first-generation parents were born in California and attended the Carpinteria schools when the system was segregated. The immigrant parents were educated in Mexico, but their children attended the Carpinteria schools when special programs for Latinos were instituted but before the creation of a community organization. Delgado-Gaitan was interested in comparing the parent-preschool-age-child interactions and the child development outcomes in these two types of Mexican American families with such different backgrounds. One of the points of comparison was how the families handled the apparent contradiction in values between the expectation for critical thinking skills and respect for adults. In school, critical thinking skills are emphasized. Children are expected to use verbal analysis, verbal questioning, and verbal argument. They are encouraged to question and even argue against adult and peer points of view. In the Mexican culture, respect is emphasized. Children are expected to show respect toward their elders, to greet them politely, and to not argue. Children are not included in adult conversations and are expected not to interrupt or offer an opinion. Respect is an important value in both sets of families. In the community group, the parents were instructed to read stories or write letters and numbers at home with their children. In the immigrant families, the parents allowed some questioning and statement of opinion during school-related activities, but at other times, full respect was expected. In second-generation families, the mothers asked more questions to elicit children's opinions during story reading. They also allowed children to state an opinion and to negotiate rules, such as bedtime or watching television. Critical thinking had attained a broader scope, whereas respect took on a narrower scope. The immigrant families were more accommodating, accepting critical thinking in the school domain but maintaining strict respect in the family domain. In the area of language, the first-generation families spoke English at home and had almost lost the ability to speak Spanish in one generation. The immigrant families spoke

Spanish at home and their children attended bilingual educational programs that encouraged maintenance of their primary language. This brief example shows how discontinuity may develop within the same cultural group.

## Native Americans

Lee Little Soldier (1992) describes how Native American preschoolers have been observed to be enthusiastic and talkative in their informal Head Start preschool classes in contrast to their uncommunicative behavior in most kindergarten and elementary classrooms. The pressure for individual achievement and performance demanded in the traditional elementary school is in conflict with Native American family values. Native Americans grow up in an extended family with a strong group orientation. Individual public attention makes them feel uncomfortable. When working with Native American children, several sets of values should be respected (Foerster & Little Soldier, 1978):

- the dignity of the individual
- cooperation
- sharing
- time as having no beginning and no end
- the wisdom of their elders
- independence

They respond poorly to both a traditional structured situation with the teacher as the director and a completely free situation where the teacher is always in the background. "Teachers are there to offer assistance when needed but should encourage the children to be self-reliant"(Foerster & Little Soldier, 1978, p. 56).

Little Soldier (1992) cautions that, beyond these core values, not all Native American families fit one stereotype. There are more than 250 recognized tribes in the United States. Each tribe has its own history, culture, and language. Within each tribe, diverse levels of acculturation and education determine what Native American children bring to school and what level of comfort they will feel in school. To succeed academically, they may acculturate to school expectations and even become alienated from their primary culture. Eventually, they may find that although they act like non–Native Americans, they are not accepted as equals and find themselves alone, angry, hostile, and frustrated. Schools need to help Native American children learn to live comfortably in both cultures, that is, to be bicultural.

Little Soldier (1992, pp. 18–20) suggests five value areas where home and school may conflict:

1. Direct personal criticism and harsh discipline that might negatively influence a child's self-esteem are avoided at home.
2. Native Americans may feel indifference toward acquiring material goods.
3. Many Native Americans tend to view time as flowing and relative; things are done as the need arises rather than by the clock or according to some future-oriented master plan.
4. Not all children, certainly not all Native American children, learn best in the logical, linear, and sequential teaching style typical of today's elementary school.
5. Physical modesty should be considered; the need for privacy in toileting, dressing/undressing, and showering in physical education classes must be taken into account.

Little Soldier (1992, p. 21) concludes, "We have to begin where children are and not where we feel they ought to be." This is a basic position in early childhood education.

An important factor in support of children's learning is respect for their culture and their learning styles. For example, Tharp (1994) shows how a curriculum designed for native Hawaiians had to be modified when used on a Navajo reservation. The Navajos are wholistic thinkers in contrast to the Hawaiians, who are analytical thinkers. Although the Hawaiians were comfortable learning in small steps, the Navajos preferred to see the whole first, then consider the details. When learning styles are not considered, children may not learn as well and as much as their capabilities allow. They may then be labeled *at-risk* and *disadvantaged* when "it is clear that the risk or the disadvantage emerges from the institution," not the children (White, 1995, p. 176).

## African Americans

Carol Brunson Phillips (1994) promotes an interactive approach to African American child development. From this view, the social, political, and economic characteristics of the school interact with what the children bring from home. African American children bring some specific core values and experiences to school. For example, they bring a personal orientation that comes from their infant experiences. As infants, they are held and played with rather than given a wide array of toys; they are encouraged to play with their caretaker's face, thus, developing a close interpersonal relationship. African Americans have developed some unique language usage, which results in verbal performances through narration of myths, folktales, sermons, joke telling, and other special kinds of talk. Talk is used to learn about life and the world and to achieve group approval and recognition. African Americans have also developed a unique language system that has continued African language traditions as adapted to European English. Thus, African American children enter school equipped with these and other cultural attributes. School traditions and values have grown from a different historical tradition, with its basis in European culture, which stresses individuality and competition. Thus, African American students are placed in a conflict situation between home and school values and traditions. As with other cultural groups, they either fight the system and fail, give in and acculturate completely, or learn to operate in both places, fitting their style to each setting. Teachers can support children in making the transition into school and into a bicultural mode by learning more about African American history and culture, capitalizing on the learning styles they bring to school, and discussing openly the conflict situation in which they find themselves.

African American children enter school with a style of learning that can be capitalized on to bring about success. They tend to have a relational cognitive style that contrasts with the analytical cognitive style of most European American, middle-class-designed schools (Hale, 1981). That is, African American children tend to thrive where freedom, variation, creativity, novelty, uniqueness, and affective and other humanistic patterns describe the school situation. Children with an analytic cognitive style fit into situations that emphasize rules, standardization, conformity, regularity, precision, and other factors that support a strict structure for learning. African American children are oriented more toward other people than to things and need a lot of interpersonal interaction in their learning. Many African American children enter school with energy and enthusiasm that is often labeled as hyperactivity and is then squelched (Hale, 1981). School becomes sterile and boring. The African American child's assertive style of problem solving tends to be viewed negatively by teachers (Holliday, 1985), so that, by age 9 or 10, "we speculate that teacher attitudes transform young black children's achievement efforts into learned helplessness" (Holliday, 1985, p. 128).

FIGURE 7–4 Asian Americans represent wide cultural variability.

Vann and Kunjufu (1993) believe that African Americans should have an Afrocentric, multicultural curriculum. That is, they should not have just a European American viewpoint, but also African American, Native American, Asian American, and any other relevant viewpoints, in every area of the curriculum. Janice Hale-Benson (1990) reports on a preschool program designed specifically for African American children and their special characteristics. Visions for Children is a program ". . . offering a teaching method and curriculum that encourages children to learn the information and skills necessary for upward mobility, career achievement, and financial independence in the American mainstream" (p. 199). The curriculum also teaches ethnic cultural pride and the importance of contributing to the development of African American people. The curriculum is infused with black history and culture while at the same time emphasizing cognitive skills, such as reasoning, memory, problem solving, creativity, and language. Expressive language skills are a major focus. The daily schedule has a balance of teacher-directed and child-selected activity periods.

As a group, African American mothers have high aspirations for their children (Washington, 1988). They want their children to be learners and to have a good education. Washington (1988) suggests that African American mothers learn to appreciate and apply the people and movement orientation of young African American children to enhance their learning at home, just as is suggested for enhancing school instruction.

African American single mothers make up a large portion of the urban poor. Cook and Fine (1995) document the clever ways in which these women provide their children with survival skills for coping with violence, drugs, and poverty. They support their children's educational efforts despite many obstacles. Arnold (1995, p. 146) points out the core strengths in African American families:

1. strong kinship ties
2. strong work ethic
3. adaptability of family roles
4. strong achievement orientation
5. strong religious orientation

These core strengths are what keep African Americans striving to overcome the racism that tries to keep them down.

## Asian and Pacific Islander Americans

According to the 2000 census our Asian population is 3.6 percent and our Native Hawaiian/Pacific Islander population is 1 percent. The Asian population includes Chinese, Filipino, Japanese, Korean, Vietnamese, East Indian, Cambodian, Guamanian, Hmong, Indonesian, and Laotian groups (Pang, 1990). Our country's Asian and Pacific Islander population is rapidly increasing. The two Pacific Islander groups with the highest U.S. populations are the Hawaiians and the Samoans (de Melendez & Ostertag, 1997).

Just as with other ethnic groups, Asian Americans represent wide cultural variability (Figure 7–4). Some pride themselves on being highly assimilated and may even refuse to speak their ancestral language or practice any of their ancestral customs. Others may take a more bicultural approach by maintaining pride and involvement in their ancestral language and customs while also appreciating the need to adapt to the mainstream culture to move up socioeconomically. Families with long-standing roots in this country may be at odds with new immigrants or with immigrants from other Asian countries. For example, Pang (1990) describes an incident where a Cambodian American student would not accept help from a Vietnamese American student because of a long-time antagonistic relationship between Cambodia and Vietnam.

Many of our Southeast Asian immigrants have achieved great success in the United States but many have also had great difficulty (Yang, 2004). Many have had difficulty with the English language. Even the American-born children have had problems because their parents may not have been literate in their primary language and did not have the time to attend English as a Second Language (ESL) classes.

Kitano (1982) cites one study that looked at the learning characteristics of preschool-age Asian American children, formulating the following conclusions:

- The Asian American cultures are not all the same.
- Within and between groups, background experiences differ, and teachers must treat each child individually.
- Group achievement rather than competition should be emphasized.
- Korean children seem to possess a low self-concept.
- Learning styles differ among groups, with Samoans and bilingual Chinese children tending to be less creative, Filipino children more field dependent, Chinese more reticent about answering questions posed individually in front of the class, and Vietnamese children more passive.
- Overall, the Asian American preschoolers rank well on school readiness.
- Teachers need to keep in mind that each Asian and Pacific Islander group has its own culture and customs and does not fit into one stereotype.

Research, such as that reported by Holloway (1988) and Stevenson and Lee (1990), indicates that the higher achievement levels of students in Japan and Taiwan compared to American students may be related to parental beliefs and practices. Not only do Japanese and Chinese parents tend to set higher standards for achievement, they also tend to believe that effort is just as important, if not more important, than native ability. In this country, parents tend to believe that native ability is more important than effort. There is also a tendency to believe that Asian Americans are all high achievers. Pang (1990) cautions that this assumption does not hold true because, within each group, there is wide variability. All Asian Americans are not "whiz kids." Also, all Asian and Pacific Islander Americans do not hold the effort-over-ability belief. Mizokawa and Ryckman (1988) reported a study done in the Seattle public schools comparing the beliefs about school achievement effort and ability held by Chinese, Filipino, Japanese, Korean, Vietnamese, and other Southeast Asian American students. They found that, overall, Asians attributed success more to effort than to innate ability. However, when broken down into the various subgroups, they did not fit into one global stereotype. Koreans attributed significantly more to effort than the other groups. All except the Japanese attributed more of their successes to effort than they did failures to lack of effort. The lower socioeconomic–status students found more value in working hard to achieve success. On the other hand, they also were more likely to perceive math or science failure as resulting from lack of ability. The authors of this study emphasize the variability that pervades the Asian cultural groups in their beliefs about academic achievement.

We are gaining a better understanding of our Southeast Asian immigrants. Before the 1970s, we had very few Thai, Laotian, Cambodian, and Vietnamese immigrants (West, 1983). West agrees with others that teachers need to be aware that Southeast Asians cannot be considered one homogeneous group. Each group is a separate culture with different languages, customs, and religious beliefs. Morrow (1989) describes the cultural importance of Southeast Asian names. Each of the groups he describes (Vietnamese, Cambodian, Laotian, and Hmong) have distinctive rules regarding how names are sequenced and used. An understanding of name customs would be a good first step in learning the cultures and customs of Southeast Asian students.

Southeast Asian parents and children often have trouble communicating with each other. Both groups may have difficulty communicating with teachers and other school personnel (Yang, 2004) because language is a problem. Parents also tend to lack formal education and, therefore, are not much help to their children. Whereas teachers usually expect parents to come to them with questions, Southeast Asian parents tend to be shy and not assertive in approaching teachers. Young people may pick up the more assertive American style that conflicts with their parents' traditional cultural practice. Some areas have community based organizations that provide support to families. Unfortunately, many Southeast Asian students don't have this support and feel alienated from their schools.

More Koreans are also immigrating to the United States (Lee, 2003). Their children find life very different. Korean teaching is mostly direct instruction through lecture while in the United States, instruction often includes participation in games and group projects. Their parents usually promote biculturalism, but achieving it is difficult. Korean children are expected to obey and respect their parents. In this country, children learn to question adult authority, and this leads to conflict. Korean parents expect high academic standards. Children may study more academics after school, beyond school requirements. Korean parents and children need understanding support from teachers.

Asian Indians are increasing in number in the United States. They are usually highly educated and speak excellent English (Joshi, 2005). In the Indian culture, it is more important to learn correct conduct and habit than to be involved in play-based education. They believe early childhood education programs should stress academics, and education is equated with status. Indian families emphasize homework drill and practice. Indian parents highly respect teachers and expect the same from their children. They emphasize family solidarity and loyalty and stress interdependence rather than independence. They are guided by the concept of *Karma*—every action has a consequence. Parents use punishment to form behavior and offer few rewards, which might spoil their children. In school, Indian children will wait to be called on. They usually look at the other's point of view rather than their own. Teachers can support parents' strong belief in homework by providing developmentally appropriate home activities. Parents will need frequent face-to-face conferencing to obtain details on their children's academic progress. Parents may be reluctant to volunteer in class because they believe they should not interfere.

## European Americans

Historically, European Americans have been the dominant group in our society. Howard (1993) proposes that it is time for European Americans to rethink their role in a multicultural country and in the development of multicultural education. As with other Americans, European Americans all came from somewhere else originally. However, there is great diversity within the European American culture. Many of our diverse European American cultural groups were pressured to take on the Anglo-Saxon Protestant image to be "real" Americans. Howard (1993) points out that, as the dominant group, European Americans were not forced to learn about minority group cultures to survive. Now times are changing, and we need to honestly face the inequities of the past and look forward to supporting changes in the future. Howard (1993) further suggests that European Americans must become more humble and not insist they know it all. They should stop forcing their ideas onto other groups. Furthermore, he believes European Americans need to develop respect for other groups and their right to be themselves. Howard's first suggestion for European Americans is that they define who they are as a people. Then, they can begin to become a part of new multicultural partnerships.

Within the European American culture is contained the largest nonmainstream group that lives at or below the poverty level: the lower-socioeconomic-scale Anglos (Garber & Slater, 1983). These Anglo families are under constant economic threat. Their income is always insecure because of the changing economy and employment in seasonal industries, such as construction. Their children's cognitive style, language patterns, and motivation make it difficult for them to meet the challenges offered by the middle-class mainstream.

De Melendez and Ostertag (1997, p. 30) remind us that:

> . . . we cannot neglect the fact that European Americans, from thirty-seven European countries speaking ten different languages, helped settle this continent and created this country. They are the original creators of the pluralism that has always been a part of the United States.

Today, our immigration patterns are increasingly less European and more global. Forty of our fifty states have a youth population that is more than 10 percent non-European in origin. The results of the 2000 census show that both native born and new immigrants are much more dispersed around the United States than they were in 1990 (Tilove, 2003). It is evident that adults who work with young children must recognize the influence of culture on child development.

## Interracial Children

As the multicultural population increases, so does the population of interracial children (Morrison & Bordere, 2001; Pang, 1990; Wardle, 1987; West, 2001). According to Wardle (1987), the 1983 census counted 632,000 interracial marriages, of which 125,000 were African American/Anglo. There are also many Asian-American/Anglo and Native-American/Anglo children. Other intermarriages include Eurasian, Asian/Latino, Asian/African American, and Asian/Native Americans, according to Pang (1990). Also, many children conceived during the Vietnam War have emigrated to the United States (Pang, 1990).

According to Wardle (2001), while the concepts and methods of multicultural and antibias education have spread since the late 1980s, biracial and multiracial children have been left out. Since the 1970s, the number of multiracial babies has increased more than 260 percent compared to an increase of 15 percent for single-race babies (Wardle, 2001). Programs for young children need to respect the heritage of these children and provide a curriculum that provides for their interests, talents, and cultures. West (2001) refers to these children as third-culture children, meaning that they are a bridge between two (or more) cultures, providing them with a rich background that can be a classroom asset.

Morrison and Rodgers (1996) point out that biracial children's development continues to be greatly ignored in both the research and educational arenas. Morrison and Rodgers focus particularly on children of one Anglo and one African American parent, believing that their problems are similar to those encountered by all biracial children. Historically and currently, these children are usually viewed by the larger population as African American. However, ethnic identity is an important aspect of children's self-concepts, and it is difficult for them if they are not accepted as being of two races. According to Morrison and Rodgers (p. 30), the racial identity of biracial children should be viewed as a combination of their dual ethnic parentage. Although changes are currently being made, this dual parentage is not commonly recognized. For example, when asked to fill out personal information forms, biracial categories are not included in the list of possible ethnic groups. Morrison and Rodgers provide a description of a third grader's concern about which category to select:

> Both my mother's grandmothers were Native Americans from south Texas and both grandfathers were African American. My father's father was a Cuban whose family had settled in western Louisiana, where he met and married my grandmother, a Creole (with a mixed heritage of French, Spanish, Native American, and African).

Those who work with young children and their families need to be prepared to recognize and accept dual parentage.

## Connecting Cultural Style and Education

**cultural style**
The personality of a group.

**cultural stereotyping**
Believing that all members of certain groups have identical beliefs and behaviors.

Previously in this unit, descriptions of varying learning and teaching styles were suggested as being applicable to various cultural groups. Although it is true that cultural groups have certain beliefs and practices that apply to most group members, each person and each family have their own unique qualities within each group. Hilliard (1989) notes that conflict is posed between **cultural style** and **cultural stereotyping.** Cultural style refers to the personality of a group. Hilliard defines style as "consistency in the behavior of a person or of a group that tends to be habitual" (p. 67). Style is learned, not innate, so it can be changed or modified. A person can learn more than one style and switch styles when appropriate. Cultural style becomes deeply rooted during early childhood. It is then generalized to later learning experiences when the child enters school. Posey (1997) has carefully analyzed the teaching styles of three Native American cultures and two Pacific Islander cultures and has shown how the models used in these cultures are different and more complex than the Western or European American model. The result is that children arrive in school having learned through a mode of instructional practice that is most likely different from the traditional school practice. According to Hilliard, the difference may not be caused by the mismatch between teacher and student styles but poor delivery of the instructional style the teacher uses. This point of view is supported by other authors, such as Donmoyer and Kos (1993), Swadener and Lubeck (1995), and Tabachnick and Bloch (1995). Teachers may have a stereotyped view of their students. For example, teachers tend to demand less from students they believe to be low achievers; wait less time for them to respond to questions; provide less support through repeating questions, giving clues, or asking a new question; and treat them differently in a number of other ways than those students perceived as high achievers.

Hilliard (1989) believes that style becomes a problem when teachers misread style differences as signs of poor potential or when style differences cause problems in communication. Misreading style differences may cause the teacher to "teach down" to the children and not provide an opportunity for them to fulfill their potential. Teachers need to understand style differences that are not stereotyped but are based on firsthand observation and use this information to better understand and communicate.

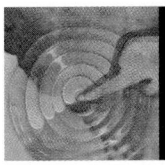

**LOOKING FURTHER**

Do you know which non-European American groups reside in your area? Identify these groups and write down what you know about each one. If you are a non-European American, you might write down what you know about European Americans or some other non-European American group in your area. If you are acquainted with one or more members of these other groups, check the accuracy of your knowledge. Was your level of knowledge accurate and detailed? Did you learn anything new about the other cultures? How can this information help you as an adult who works with young children and their families?

Irvine (1990) suggests several characteristics that teachers need to develop. They need to be reflective practitioners who are open-minded, observe their students, and make informed decisions. They need to acquire an understanding of their students' cultures, including their language and history. Teachers also need to include their students' families and communities in the education process. Hauser and Thompson (1995) describe the first-grade classroom of a teacher named Paula. The students come from diverse cultures and speak a variety of primary languages, including Hmong, Lao, Khmer, Russian, Mien, and Spanish, and have limited or no English language facility. An overview of Paula's classroom presents a busy, active, relatively noisy scene of industrious students hard at work. All of Paula's students come from families where parents believe school and home are separate or from homes where schooling is foreign to the parents. Therefore, Paula has no initial opportunity to inquire into the students' backgrounds and, instead, focuses on discovering her students' strengths. She begins with the belief that all children can learn:

> I think my students have potential, motivation. They're not turned off to anything. They have motivation from themselves and from the group. They have determination and will. They haven't been handed everything on the proverbial silver platter. Everything we do is new and great . . . every book, every piece of art (Hauser & Thompson, 1995, p. 213).

Paula puts her theory into action in the classroom by emphasizing collaboration, autonomy, communication, and collegiality. Children are encouraged to work together in self-selected groups, make choices, and contribute to group discussions. Paula works cooperatively with the two language tutors. Paula's overall goal for her students is the development of socialization skills, communication ability, and a strong sense of self. She provides a setting where children from diverse cultures can apply their previous learning and acquired perceptions of how to learn.

Multicultural education should be provided for every child through their daily experiences (de Melendez & Ostertag, 1997). It is not a "topic" presented one week and then forgotten. It is an attitude and an instructional approach that should pervade the whole early childhood program and enhance child development, especially in the areas of self-concept and social concepts. Derman-Sparks (1989, 1993, 1993/94) points out that young children are already aware of cultural biases (p. 1):

- They notice differences and construct classificatory and evaluative categories very early.
- There are identifiable tasks and steps in the development of identity and of attitudes.
- Societal stereotyping and bias influence children's self-concepts and attitudes toward others.

The early childhood curriculum needs to be not only multicultural but also antibiased. "Bias is any attitude, belief, or feeling that results in, and helps justify, unfair treatment of an individual because of his or her identity" (Derman-Sparks, 1989, p. 3). Antibias (Derman-Sparks, 1989, p. 3) is defined as follows:

> An active/activist approach to challenging prejudice, stereotyping, bias, and the "isms." In a society in which institutional structures create and maintain sexism, racism, and handicappism, it is not sufficient to be nonbiased . . . nor is it sufficient to be an observer. It is necessary for each individual to actively intervene, to challenge and counter the personal and institutional behaviors that perpetuate oppression.

The antibias curriculum uses the ideas of the multicultural curriculum but goes beyond the "tourist" approach in addressing all types of prejudice and working with children's developing identity and attitudes by dealing directly with stereotyping, bias, and discriminatory behavior. The antibias curriculum is not an add-on, but an integral part of the regular curriculum.

## SPECIAL CIRCUMSTANCES THAT INFLUENCE LEARNING

Two factors that increasingly affect children's development and learning are the increase in reported cases of child abuse and the number of homeless families with young children. This chapter closes with a look at these two problem areas.

### Abuse and Neglect

According to the Children's Defense Fund (2005) approximately 3 million children were reported as possible victims of child abuse and neglect and referred for investigation or assessment in 2003. Nationally approximately 900,000 children were confirmed as victims of maltreatment. About 63.2 percent were victims of neglect. The largest group of victims are children between birth and age 3 (29 percent). Over half of the victims are 7 years and younger. A study of the long-term effects of early childhood physical maltreatment was done by Lansford, Dodge, Pettit, Bates, Crozier, & Kaplow (2002). The results indicated that children maltreated in early childhood experienced many psychological and behavior problems in adolescence.

Increased family stress from drugs and violence is believed to be related to the increase in abuse and neglect. Increasing numbers of children are in foster care or are living with relatives other than immediate family members. The loss of parents to acquired immunodeficiency syndrome (AIDS) is increasingly becoming a cause of parentless children. Of the approximately three million children who have serious emotional disturbances, only about one-third are receiving adequate care. Advocates for emotionally disturbed children are trying to move toward more family-focused, community-based approaches, which have more money to invest in keeping early identified disturbances from intensifying. Children who are abused and neglected are at a disadvantage for reaching their developmental potential.

Every state has laws mandating that suspected cases of abuse be reported by professionals, such as teachers (Gootman, 1993). English (1998, p. 41) outlines the definitions of the major forms of abuse:

- *Physical abuse:* An act of commission by a caregiver that results or is likely to result in physical harm, including death of a child. Examples of physical abuse acts include kicking, biting, shaking, stabbing, or punching a child. Spanking may be classified as abusive if the child is bruised or injured.

- *Sexual abuse:* An act of commission, including intrusion or penetration, molestation with genital contact, or other forms of sexual acts in which children are used to provide sexual gratification for the perpetrator. Also included are sexual exploitation and child pornography.
- *Neglect:* An act of omission by a parent or caregiver that involves refusal or delay in providing health care, nutrition, shelter, clothing, affection, and attention; inadequate supervision; or abandonment.
- *Emotional abuse:* An act of commission or omission that includes rejecting, isolating, terrorizing, ignoring, or corrupting a child. Examples are confinement; verbal abuse; withholding sleep, food, or shelter; exposing a child to domestic violence; allowing a child to engage in substance abuse or criminal activity; refusing to provide psychological care; and other inattention that results in harm or potential harm to a child. An important component of emotional or psychological abuse is that it must be sustained or repetitive.

Some signs of abuse and neglect that can be easily spotted include the following:

- *Poor physical care:* Child comes to school dirty and dressed in dirty clothing; child is weak and ill and not taken to the doctor; child is hungry and shows signs of undernutrition; child is tired and cranky.
- *Battering:* Child has bruises, broken bones, etc.

Other types of abuse, such as sexual abuse and emotional abuse, may be more difficult to spot. However, watch for signs, such as reluctance to leave school, sophisticated sexual knowledge or play, radical behavior changes or regressive behavior, withdrawal or standing back and watching adults, or events that are revealed through discussion, stories, or drawings (Meddin & Rosen, 1986).

Unfortunately, children with special needs are most likely to be victims of abuse and neglect (Disabled children, 1994; Goldman, 1993). Their vulnerability is sometimes masked by their disabilities. For example, they may have limited communication abilities. Children with orthopedic problems are likely to fall and injure themselves, which can be used as an excuse for an injury that was actually caused by physical abuse. Parents may expect too much from the child with special needs and abuse him or her out of frustration, or expect too little and neglect his or her needs. Young children with special needs are especially vulnerable to sexual abuse because they may be much more dependent on caretakers than other children are. Goldman (1993) suggests that child care personnel can be an important line of defense for these children.

Child abuse can be reported anonymously. Most cities have a child abuse hotline. Parents Anonymous groups, which are growing in number, help parents face their problems and find ways to handle them. Survivors of child abuse suffer from both immediate and long-term negative effects (English, 1998; Leiter & Johnsen, 1997). They may have retarded physical growth, be infected with sexually transmitted diseases, or suffer from severe psychological problems and evidence serious maladaptive social behaviors. Leiter and Johnsen (1997) found that school performance declined among abused and neglected children, grades worsened, absenteeism increased, the rate of expulsion increased, more were retained a grade, and more were placed in special education.

Data from the Chicago Longitudinal Study (Reynolds and Robertson, 2003) indicates that a supportive preschool/kindergarten/primary level program for low-income parents and children can lessen the frequency of child maltreatment.

Children and parents who participated in the Title I Child-Parent Centers (CPC) programs had lower rates of maltreatment than a comparison group. Preschool participation was an especially strong factor. Important components were parent involvement and staying in the same elementary school.

## Homelessness and Poverty

The Children's Defense Fund reports that in many parts of the country, families with children are the fastest-growing group within the homeless population (Children's Defense Fund, 2004). According to a 2005 report (Children's Defense Fund, 2005) children constitute 40 percent of the homeless, up from 32 percent in 1992. These figures indicate that an increasing number of America's children are likely to face the risks associated with unstable, inadequate housing or actual **homelessness**. These children "typically develop more severe health, developmental, and nutritional problems than other poor children and are more likely to suffer lead poisoning, educational disruption, emotional stress, and family separation" (p. 37). It is estimated that 100,000 children are homeless every night. Within this group, minorities, especially African Americans, are disproportionately represented. The shortage of low-rent housing has reached the crisis stage.

**homelessness**
Having no stable place to call home.

Overall, homeless families reflect great diversity: unemployed couples who cannot afford housing, mothers leaving relationships (often abusive ones), Aid to Families with Dependent Children (AFDC) mothers who cannot manage on the amount they receive, and mothers with a history of homelessness and poverty. The conditions they live in, in shelters and homeless hotels, are usually squalid and dismal. The children are at high risk for eventually being placed in foster care. The families are under stress, which may increase the chance of child abuse and neglect. Many homeless families are not in shelters or homeless hotels; they live in vacant buildings or cars, or are temporarily sharing a home with friends or relatives.

The homeless suffer from both poor mental and poor physical health. Solarz (1988) reports on a Boston study that found that homeless children had serious developmental and emotional problems. For example, half of the homeless preschoolers had at least one serious developmental lag compared to 16 percent of those living in subsidized housing. Other researchers observed two-and-a-half to five-year-old homeless children in child care centers and found that they had many problem behaviors: short attention span, weak impulse control, withdrawal, aggression, speech delays, and regressive behaviors. Affective relationships with mothers were likely to be detached, with stronger bonds to siblings. The Children's Defense Fund continues to pursue the abolition of homelessness (see http://www.childrensdefense.org).

It is estimated that 40 percent of school-aged homeless children do not attend school. A large portion of those who do attend school are very likely to have repeated grades. They may have to stay out of school to care for younger siblings while their parents are job hunting. When they move, which they do frequently, they may have to change schools and break the continuity of their schooling. Often, they cannot be enrolled because they do not have necessary documents, such as birth certificates. Therefore, they are at-risk educationally.

Eddowes (1994) suggests that schools can provide a safe haven for homeless children during the part of the day they attend. The school can provide support services and outreach programs. Some school systems have opened schools in shelters. Other school systems have special classrooms just for homeless children. Still others provide special services within regular classrooms. Eddowes suggests that, no matter where the program is located, special services can be provided, such as bathing facilities, clean clothes, toothbrushes, and nutritious meals. Like other programs, the educational component should be individualized. Gaining the trust of homeless families in order to open lines of communication is difficult (Swick & Bailey, 2004). Swick and Bailey state that the key to working with homeless families is identifying and nurturing their strengths.

The Children's Defense Fund (Children's Defense Fund, 2005) calls on the government for housing relief for the poor (Children's Defense Fund, 2005). Housing costs for low-income families are increasing faster than wages so that more families cannot afford housing. In addition, the government has not followed through on promises to build more low-income housing. Poverty is still an increasing problem (Children's Defense Fund, 2005). One in six children live in poverty in spite of the country's overall prosperity. Income growth has been unequal, so that today a child is more likely to be poor than he or she might have been 20 or 30 years ago.

## Migrant Children and Families

Every year, nearly a million migrant farm workers and their families follow the harvest across the country (Duarte & Rafanello, 2001). These workers are mainly Latino. They travel in extended family groups that provide strength and support. Their pay is low and their housing is often substandard. Migrant children live in a cycle of poverty and often begin work in the fields as preschoolers. Frequent home changes result in a lack of stability. Migrant Head Start is a program designed to respond to the unique needs of migrant children and their families. Migrant Head Start serves many infants and toddlers (over 40 percent of the children served). Unfortunately, only one-third of eligible children are served because of the limitations on funding.

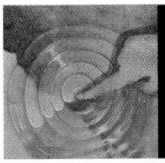

### LOOKING FURTHER

Using the background information in this chapter and some further reading on multicultural and antibias curriculum, locate or devise a list of criteria that indicate a classroom is meeting multicultural and antibias standards. Visit several preschool, kindergarten, and primary classrooms. In each classroom, note which cultural groups are represented among the students. Using your multicultural/antibias criteria, note any evidence that the class curriculum is multicultural and antibias. If possible, interview each teacher regarding how multicultural and antibias curriculum is included in planning for instruction.

1. Evaluate the multicultural and antibias curriculum in each classroom using the criteria you used.
2. Compare the classrooms. Which met the greatest number of your criteria? Which met the least number of your criteria? Overall, did you find that the teachers had cultural and bias awareness?

## SUMMARY

Children's well-being has roots in infancy and early childhood learning. Families are increasingly diverse in membership. Parents and other caregivers have critical roles in supporting optimum child development. Adults vary in their styles of teaching young children. Some approaches enhance learning more than others. Children seem to thrive when taught in a positive manner with clear communication, high expectations for achievement, mature language, rule-based discipline, and self-regulated control. Both

*(continued)*

mothers and fathers tend to offer more cognitive stimulation to boys than to girls. As more mothers work, fathers are taking a greater part in child care. Parent and caregiver education and family involvement in young children's learning are becoming increasingly important areas for program development. Legislation for children with special needs mandates collaboration between families and professionals. Technology provides media for learning through the use of audio-, video-, and computer-assisted methods. Adults must exercise their responsibilities in selecting videos, television programs, and computer software and in limiting children's time for use of these materials.

Cultural and social variations also influence the young child's learning. The adult who works with young children must be knowledgeable regarding their sociocultural background and incorporate this knowledge into curriculum and instructional planning. Our major cultural groups include Anglo or European Americans, African Americans, Hispanic Americans, Asian and Pacific Island Americans, and Native Americans. Within and among groups, variation is increased due to specific regional background, length of time in this country, socioeconomic status, and local differences.

Poverty is increasing, and along with it, homelessness. Abuse is a problem that is also increasing in frequency. Migrant families and their children also face many difficulties.

Teachers need to understand style differences and incorporate these differences into their instruction in ways that enhance learning for children. Curriculum for all children should be multicultural and antibias.

## For Further Reading


Adelizzi, J. U., & Goss, D. B. (2001). *Parenting children with learning disabilities.* Westport, CT: Greenwood.

Arnold, M. (2005). *Effective communication techniques for child care.* Clifton Park, NY: Delmar Learning.

Banks, J. A., & Banks, C. A. M. (Eds.). (2001). *Handbook of research on multicultural education.* New York: Jossey Bass.

Banks, J. A., & Banks, C. A. M. (Eds.). (2001). *Multicultural education: Issues and perspectives.* Boston: Allyn & Bacon.

Batshaw, M. L., (Ed.). (2001). *When your child has a disability: The complete sourcebook of daily and medical care* (Rev. ed.). Baltimore, MD: Brookes.

Berk, L. E. (2001). *Awakening children's minds.* New York: Oxford University Press.

Borkowski, J. G., Ramey, S. L., & Bristol-Power, M. (2002). *Parenting and the child's world.* Mahwah, NJ: Erlbaum.

Bornstein, M. H., & Bradley, R. H. (Eds.). (2003). *Socioeconomic status, parenting, and child development.* Mahwah, NJ: Erlbaum.

Day, R. D., Lamb, M. E. (Eds.). (2004). *Conceptualizing and measuring father involvement.* Mahwah, NJ: Erlbaum.

Edmiaston, R., Dolezal,V., Doolittle, S., Erickson, C., & Merritt, S. (2000). Developing individualized education programs for children in inclusive settings: A developmentally appropriate framework. *Young Children, 55*(4), 7–10.

Eggers-Pierola, C. (2005). *Connections and commitments: Reflecting Latino values in early childhood programs.* Portsmouth, NH: Heinemann.

Gay, G. (2000). *Culturally responsive teaching.* New York: Teachers College Press.

Golombok, S. (2000). *Parenting. What really counts?* Philadelphia, PA: Psychology Press.

Gunter, B., Oates, C., & Blades, M. (2004). *Advertising to children on TV.* Mahwah, NJ: Erlbaum.

Hamner, T. J., & Turner, P. H. (2001). *Parenting in contemporary society* (4th ed.). Boston: Allyn & Bacon.

Helm, J. H., Berg, S. & Scranton, P. (2004). *Teaching your child to love learning.* New York: Teachers College.

Hiatt-Michael, D. (Ed.). (2001). *Promising practices in family involvement.* Greenwich, CT: IAP, Inc.

Huntsinger, C. S., Huntsinger, P. R., Ching, W., & Lee, C. (2000). Understanding cultural contexts fosters sensitive caregiving of Chinese American children. *Young Children, 55*(6), 7–12, 14–15.

Jacobson, T. (2003). *Confronting our discomfort: Clearing the way for anti-bias in early childhood.* Portsmouth, NH: Heinemann.

King, E. W., Chipman, M. F., & Cruz-Janzen, M. (1994). *Educating young children in a diverse society.* Des Moines, IA: Longwood Division, Allyn & Bacon.

Kostelnik, M. J., Onaga, E., Rohde, B., & Whiren, A. (2002). *Children with special needs.* New York: Teachers College Press.

Matsumoto, D. (Ed.). (2001). *The handbook of culture and psychology.* New York: Oxford University Press.

Naseef, R. A. (2001). *Special children, challenged parents* (Rev. ed.). Baltimore, MD: Brookes.

Okagaki, L., & Diamond, K. E. (2000). Responding to cultural and linguistic differences in the beliefs and practices of families with young children. *Young Children, 55*(3), 74–80.

Palkovitz, R. (2002). *Involved fathering and men's adult development.* Mahwah, NJ: Erlbaum.

Quisenberry, N. L., & McIntyre, D. J. (Eds.), & Duhon, G. (Case author). (2002). *Racism in the classroom: Case studies.* Olney, MD: ACEI.

Ramsey, P. G. (1998). *Teaching and learning in a diverse world: Multicultural education for young children* (2nd ed.). New York: Teachers College Press.

Rogoff, B. (2002). *The cultural nature of human development.* New York: Oxford University Press.

Sternberg, R. J., & Grigorenko, E. L. (2001). Learning disabilities, schooling, and society. *Phi Delta Kappan, 83*, 335–340.

Tamis-LeMonda, C. S., & Cabrera, N. (Eds.). (2002). *The handbook of father involvement.* Mahwah, NJ: Erlbaum.

Tilove, J. (2003). *Migration Patterns Point to a Nation of "Three Americas".* Newhouse News Service, July 30, 2003, Retrieved September 14, 2006 from http://www.newhousenews.com. 7

Turbiville, V. P., Umbarger, G. T., & Guthrie, A. C. (2000). Fathers' involvement in programs for young children. *Young Children, 55*(4), 74–79.

## SUGGESTED ACTIVITIES

1. Visit the home of a friend or relative in which there are one or more preschool, kindergarten, or primary children. Observe the mother for 30 minutes and the father for 30 minutes. If the father is not available, observe the mother for one hour. Write down everything the parent and child do when they interact. Analyze and evaluate the material relevant to the following behaviors:
   a. Does the parent participate in activities as a guide and partner?
   b. Is the child allowed to explore household materials, such as play with pots and pans or a tub or sink of soapy water, or help cook a meal?
   c. Does the parent trust the child to try things, such as cut some fruit or a carrot with a sharp knife, climb a ladder, pour his or her own milk, do a simple errand?
   d. Does the parent talk to the child a lot and listen to what the child has to say?
   e. Does the parent show an interest in the child's accomplishments?
   f. Does the parent provide materials and activities?
   g. Does the parent encourage the child to do things on his or her own but give help when needed?
   h. Does the parent present imaginative suggestions to the child when he or she runs out of play ideas?
   i. Does the parent reward the child for learning and for doing tasks well?
   j. Does the parent set clear and consistent limits?
   k. Does the parent redirect behavior of the child?

   Write a summary profile of each parent observed. If two were observed, compare the behaviors observed. Were there any differences? What were they? Would you conclude that these parents are supporting the children's learning?

2. Find four mother-preschooler or father-preschooler pairs with whom to work. Visit them at home and have each pair do a structured teaching/learning task, such as those used by Epstein. For example, you could bring the ingredients and have each pair bake cookies, or you could bring a new puzzle the child has never seen before and ask the parent to teach the child to put the puzzle together. While the parent and child complete the task, write down everything they do and say. Afterward assess whether the parent has a positive or negative way of interacting. A positive style with the puzzle task is one in which the parent helps the child by expanding on what he or she says, asks questions that help him or her think about what to do, and encourages him or her to solve the problem on his or her own. A

negative style is one in which the parent says "no" and "don't" a great deal and tells the child what to do. A positive approach in the cookie-baking task is one in which the parent and child work cooperatively and talk constantly about many subjects, or in which they work cooperatively, but talk centers on the baking activities. A negative style is one in which the child is passive; neither parent nor child says very much, the child has little if anything to do in making the cookies, and the parent does most or all of the work while the child watches. Categorize the information obtained from each observation.

a. Which parents use positive styles?
b. Which use negative styles?
c. What would you predict regarding these children's future success?

**3.** Brainstorm some ways to involve working parents in their child's educational program.

**4.** Looking at Epstein's model, give real-life/realistic examples for each of the six types of parental involvement: parenting, communicating, volunteering, learning at home, decision making, and collaborating with the local community.

**5.** There is a movement among many minority groups to provide space on information sheets, such as job and school applications and census reports, for people of mixed racial ancestry to list their complete accurate racial background. For example, this list would include check boxes for someone who is part African American, Native American, and European American, Japanese American and European American; or Mexican and Native American, etc. Considering all the diverse racial heritages in our pluralistic nation, create a plan for solving this dilemma. Consider how many categories can be realistically included and/or some other ways to make categories inclusive. Compare your selections with those used in the 2000 U.S. Census (see http:// census.gov).

**6.** Survey parents on their children's television viewing. Ask parents how long their children watch television, when they watch, and which programs they watch. Record the answers and make a graph with the answers to see the relationships.

**7.** Make an entry in your journal.

## REVIEW

**1.** Define *family.*

**2.** Decide whether the following examples are positive in teaching style or negative in teaching style.

a. Mother is trying to teach Matt how to put his trousers on correctly. "First, find the front." Matt turns them backward. "How do you know which is front and which is the back?" Matt examines the trousers. "Oh, the zipper is in the front." "Good, Matt, that's right. Now put your legs in." He gets both legs in the same pant leg. "What happened, Matt?" He looks at the situation and pulls one leg out and puts it into the other pant leg.
b. Mother is trying to teach Mark how to put his trousers on correctly. "This is the front," she reminds him. Mark starts to put them on backward. "No, Mark! Not that way. The zipper goes in the front." Mark gets both legs in the same trouser leg. "Don't do it that way, Mark. Here, let me do it for you."

c. Dad is showing Patty how to hammer in a nail. Patty hits the nail and it bounces out. Dad says, "No, Patty, you must hold the nail like I showed you. Don't do it that way again."
d. Mother and Mario are making pizza. Mario watches as Mother rolls out the dough and puts the sauce and the other ingredients on.
e. Dad and Johnny are making biscuits for Sunday breakfast. "This is a two-cup measure, Johnny. Measure out two cups of flour while I get the milk and the baking powder." Dad returns with the milk and baking powder. Johnny asks "O.K., Dad?" Dad says, "Yes, great. Pour it in the bowl."

Go back to the negative comments and suggest alternative ways to handle each situation.

**3.** Describe at least three parent-involvement strategies.

**4.** Select the correct answer to each of the following. There is only one correct answer for each.

a. The IEP is
   1. a plan the teacher devises to provide an educational program for the young child with special needs.
   2. an individualized education plan developed cooperatively by teachers, support personnel, and parents.
   3. an individualized education plan prepared by diagnosticians.
   4. not required but recommended by federal and state laws.

b. The IFSP is
   1. an individualized family service plan prepared by a transdisciplinary team and the parents.
   2. an individualized family service plan that gives direction for finding families in need.
   3. an individualized family service plan prepared by an interdisciplinary team and approved by the parents.
   4. an individualized family service plan recommended by each state's human services office.

c. Abused children come from
   1. only the lowest-income families.
   2. all kinds of families at all economic levels.
   3. families that lack religious conviction.
   4. mostly families with a history of mental illness or alcohol or drug addiction.

d. When it comes to being responsible for reporting cases of child abuse, teachers should
   1. mind their own business and keep their suspicions to themselves.
   2. report cases if they think no one will find out they were the ones who told.
   3. be careful not to get involved in lawsuits.
   4. know that laws in at least 43 of the 50 states require them to report any suspected cases of abuse.

e. The frequency of child abuse cases
   1. can never be cut down.
   2. can be lowered with preschool programs that include parent involvement.
   3. cannot be determined since Reynolds and Robertson found that the child participants in the Parent-Child Center Program were abused as frequently as the comparison children.
   4. is higher for children who live in poverty because they cannot escape being abused.

**5.** Match the terms and phrases in Column I with their definitions and/or examples in Column II.

| Column I | Column II |
|---|---|
| a. commercial network | 1. Doing what one has seen someone else do. |
| b. PBS | 2. Behaviors and ideas that are thought to be good or bad. |
| c. imitation | 3. A television network supported by public funds and private donations. |
| d. Migrant Head Start | 4. Watch television with a child. |
| e. values | 5. A television network supported by money from advertising. |
| f. co-observe | 6. Cartoons, adult soap operas, and detective shows. |
| g. shows that depict positive social behavior | 7. Watch high-quality PBS and commercial programs. |
| h. shows that depict negative social behavior | 8. Cartoons, quiz shows, and soap operas. |
| i. shows that present a variety of people and cultures in apositive way | 9. *Sesame Street* and *Arthur.* |
| j. television viewing habits of well-developed children | 10. A program designed to meet the unique needs of migrant children and their families. |
| k. viewing habits of less well-developed children | |

**6.** How should a parent or teacher handle the following problem situations?

a. You are a teacher of young children. The parents of one of the young children in your class tells you that they think television is harmful but they don't know how to go about regulating their child's viewing. How would you help them?

b. One of the children in your preschool class comes in every day with a cape made out of a towel pinned around his shoulders. He says he is Superman and runs wildly around the room "flying," climbs on anything available, and jumps off. He "saves" other children who don't want to be "saved," and the children become very angry with him. What could you do?

c. Mrs. Nguyen finds that all her young children want to do is watch television. She believes that they should go out to play. What can she do?

d. Mrs. Ramirez usually allows the children in her child care home to watch television in the afternoon just before they leave while she cleans. She limits their viewing to the local public television channel. Evaluate her procedure.

e. Seven-year-old Raymond, one of your second-grade students, comes in bleary-eyed every morning. He tells you that his favorite television show is a late-night program. What, if anything, should you do?

**7.** Discuss your opinion of multicultural and antibias education. Do you think that adults have to take on different role behaviors in teaching children from different sociocultural groups? Apply the ideas discussed in this unit.

## KEY TERMS LIST

accessibility
cultural stereotyping
cultural style
direct engagement
family-centered practice
father
homelessness
immigrants
individualized family service plan (IFSP)
multicultural education
responsibility

Additional resources for this chapter can be found on the Online Companion™ to accompany this text at http://www.earlychilded.delmar.com. Respond to "Time to Reflect" and "Looking Further" concepts, review various child development scenarios, and answer thought-provoking questions in the Critical Thinking Forum. Keep a daily journal by downloading the student journal available on this Web site. Complete the interactive matching exercises to reinforce concepts, and print out the child development assessment forms to use during your observation of development for children from birth to age eight. In addition, read the case studies on the Web site to reinforce important concepts in each chapter, and take a look at the multitude of Web links that are available for student research on the Internet.

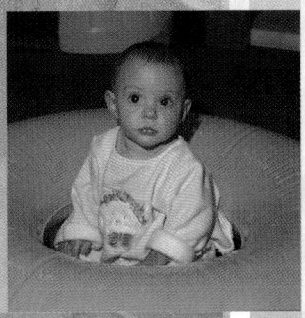

# SECTION III

## Prenatal and Infancy Periods

We have become increasingly interested in conception and prenatal development. Researchers have been looking into many questions in this area. For example, conception has been looked at closely to solve problems of infertility. The effects of various substances and experiences during the prenatal period are the focus of inquiry. Nutrition is one of the most critical aspects of prenatal maternal health care. Given the richness and advanced knowledge available in the United States, the rates of infant mortality, low birth weight, and premature births are quite high. A major contributing factor is the relative lack of attention given to prenatal medical care for pregnant women who are living near or at the poverty level. The effects of various methods of delivery on mother and newborn have also been the focus of some attention.

As we interact with infants, we find ourselves curious regarding what they understand and how they understand what is happening in their environment. We often communicate with them through speech and gesture as if we were carrying on a two-way spoken conversation while they respond with expressions and movements that communicate their interest in what we say and do.

In this section, we look at the beginnings of life: conception, prenatal development, and the influence of heredity and environment on the developing child. Next, we look at the development of the typical newborn and infant, and finally at social and cultural factors that may affect development.

CHAPTER

# Conception and Prenatal Development

## OBJECTIVES

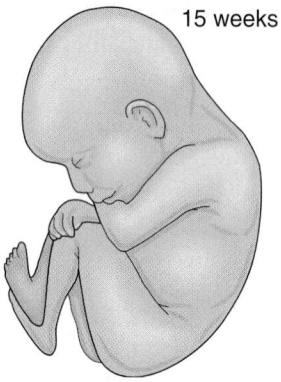


After reading this chapter, you should be able to:

- Describe the sequence of events that results in fertilization and conception.
- Recognize the three stages of prenatal development.
- Recognize the functions of the placenta, umbilical cord, and amniotic fluid.
- Describe the highlights of fetal development.
- Recognize the sensitivities of the fetus.
- List and discuss environmental factors that can affect the developing fetus.
- Discuss the problems associated with teenage pregnancies.
- Identify the most effective methods for preventing teenage pregnancy.

As you read this text, you will meet a number of young children at different ages and stages of development. This chapter explores life before birth, beginning with the joining of the sperm and the egg at conception and following development through the prenatal (prebirth) period. We will also look at some of the environmental factors that can affect the developing child prior to birth. Finally, the responsibilities of adults in caring for the prenatal infant are discussed.

**ovum**
Female egg cell.

**follicle**
Fluid-filled sac that houses the ovum.

**semen**
Liquid ejaculated from the male's reproductive organs.

**sperm**
Male reproductive cell.

## CONCEPTION

About every 28 days, at the midpoint of the menstrual cycle, a female egg cell or **ovum** housed in a fluid-filled sac called a **follicle** leaves one of the female's ovaries and journeys into the abdominal cavity and then into a fallopian tube. The ovum is the largest cell in the human body. Once it reaches the fallopian tube, there is a period of between 10 and 24 hours in which it can be fertilized by a sperm from a male (Berk, 2003).

The male system produces many millions of sperm. When orgasm is reached during sexual intercourse, the male ejaculates a liquid called **semen** that may contain more than 300 million **sperm.** These sperm are only 1/600-inch long and are shaped like tadpoles. Their life span is only 24 to 48 hours. Sperm have a long route to travel to reach the ovum in a relatively short time. They must race from

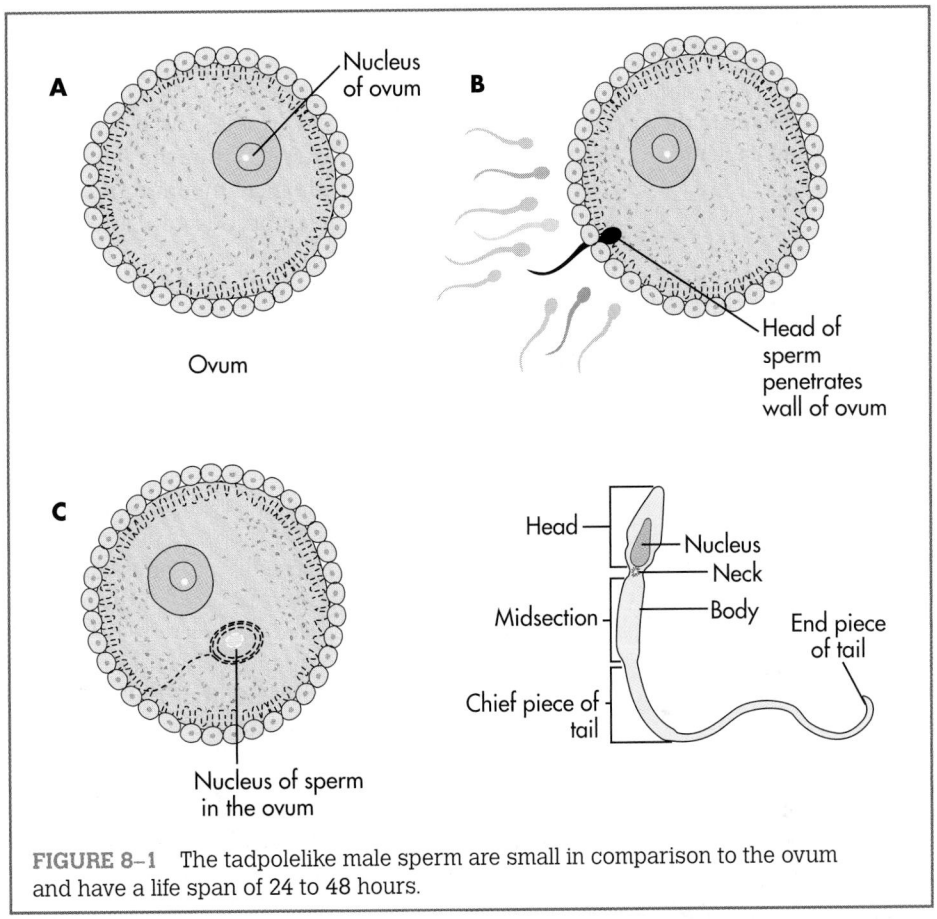


FIGURE 8–1 The tadpolelike male sperm are small in comparison to the ovum and have a life span of 24 to 48 hours.

the vagina, through the cervix, into the uterus, and then up the fallopian tube, which may or may not have an egg ready for fertilization. All sperm are not equally strong or equally fast. From the millions of sperm that are initially released, usually 300 to 500 reach the egg. If one sperm makes it through the outer membrane into the egg, a chemical reaction takes place that prohibits any more sperm from gaining entrance (Berk, 2003). The moment when **fertilization** takes place is referred to as **conception.** Child development begins with the ovum and sperm uniting into one cell called the **zygote** (Figure 8–1).

**fertilization**
The joining of sperm and egg.

**conception**
The moment when fertilization takes place.

**zygote**
The cell that is formed by the ovum and sperm uniting.

**fertility**
The ability to contribute successfully to fertilization or conception.

**Fertility** is the ability to contribute successfully to fertilization or conception (Fogel, 2001). According to Fogel, about one in six couples is infertile and unable to conceive successfully during the female childbearing years. Female infertility may be caused by failure of the ova to ripen and ovulate or by a blockage in the fallopian tubes that prohibits the ova from reaching the uterus. Failure of ovulation may result from treatable factors such as "excessive exercise or weight loss, obesity, excessive alcohol use, exposure to toxic chemicals, and hormonal imbalances" (Fogel, 2001, p. 77). Both drugs and surgery have been used to correct blockages. Use of fertility drugs may lead to multiple births. Male infertility may be caused by use of "marijuana and cigarettes, wearing excessively tight underwear, taking hot baths or saunas, inability to maintain an erection, and premature ejaculation or failure to ejaculate" (Fogel, 2001, p. 77). These causes can be treated through behavior change or sex therapy. Some causes, such as underdeveloped testes, injuries, and some childhood diseases, may be untreatable.

Fogel (2001) describes several natural methods for fertility enhancement. For example, timing of sexual intercourse can be monitored by noting when the

**IVF (in vitro fertilization)**
Egg and sperm are united in a sterile medium in the laboratory and implanted in the uterus.

**sperm microinjection**
A process through which sperm are injected directly into the ovum.

woman's temperature goes up, indicating the onset of ovulation. If neither natural methods nor drugs or surgery work, several other methods are available. **IVF (in vitro fertilization)** has rapidly increased in popularity since the first so-called "test tube baby," Louise Joy Brown, was born in 1977 (Ubell, 1995). IVF is accomplished by removing ovaries from the female and joining them with sperm from the male in a sterile biological medium. If successful, the ova and sperm unite, the zygote divides, and the embryo is implanted in the female's uterus for normal prenatal development (as described in the next part of this chapter). If the sperm are too weak to break through the wall of the ovum, they may be injected directly using a method called **sperm microinjection** (Fogel, 2001, p. 78).

Many infertile couples have turned to egg donation as a way to become parents (Hamilton, 2000). College and university campuses have become hunting grounds in the search for intelligent, physically attractive egg donors. Unfortunately the donor business is unregulated and often results in unexpected tragedy:

> For eight agonizing weeks last Fall, Calla, a 22-year-old college graduate slipped in and out of a coma in the intensive care unit. As her mom sat in the hospital lounge she flipped through a campus magazine where she saw ads seeking egg donors and offering up to $25,000 to the right candidates. Calla had answered one of these ads and agreed to donate eggs for $15,000. Unfortunately, she had a negative reaction to Lupron, a synthetic hormone administered to prepare her body for egg donation (Hamilton, 2000, p. 52).

RESOLVE is a national association that provides support for infertile couples and has called for a fee ceiling of $5,000 and national control over egg donation. From the scientific view, there is no assurance that couples will get a child with the characteristics they have paid for.

Which method or methods do you believe are best for dealing with infertility: adopting a healthy lifestyle, adopting a child, drug therapy, or egg donation? Why? You may want to research this topic further.

**natural family planning**
A form of contraception; the couple charts ovulation and avoids intercourse during that period.

Sometimes there is a need or desire to control fertility through some method of controlled contraception. The simplest and least expensive method is **natural family planning** (Fogel, 2001, p. 80). For this method, the couple charts ovulation and avoids intercourse during that period. Other methods include sterilization, birth control pills, condoms and diaphragms, spermicides, the birth control patch, the ring, or continuous abstinence (Planned Parenthood, 2005). Some countries have a need to control the birth rate. The United States has a relatively low birth rate, whereas other countries such as Brazil, Kenya, and India, have relatively high birth rates (Fogel, 2001, pp. 116–117). India has a population that includes a large proportion of illiterate people who live in poverty and cannot adequately care for their children. However, they resist control of fertility because they need large numbers of children to support their livelihood. China has been more successful in lowering its birth rate through implementing a policy of one child per family. Family planning has to be adapted to fit each individual culture.

**gestational period**
The period of pregnancy; usually lasts about nine-and-a-half calendar months.

**embryo**
The second stage of the gestation period; usually lasts from about three to eight weeks.

## THE PERIODS OF PRENATAL DEVELOPMENT

The period of pregnancy is referred to as the **gestational period.** It usually lasts about nine-and-a-half calendar months (Berk, 2003). The gestation period proceeds in three stages: the zygote (conception to two weeks), the **embryo** (three to

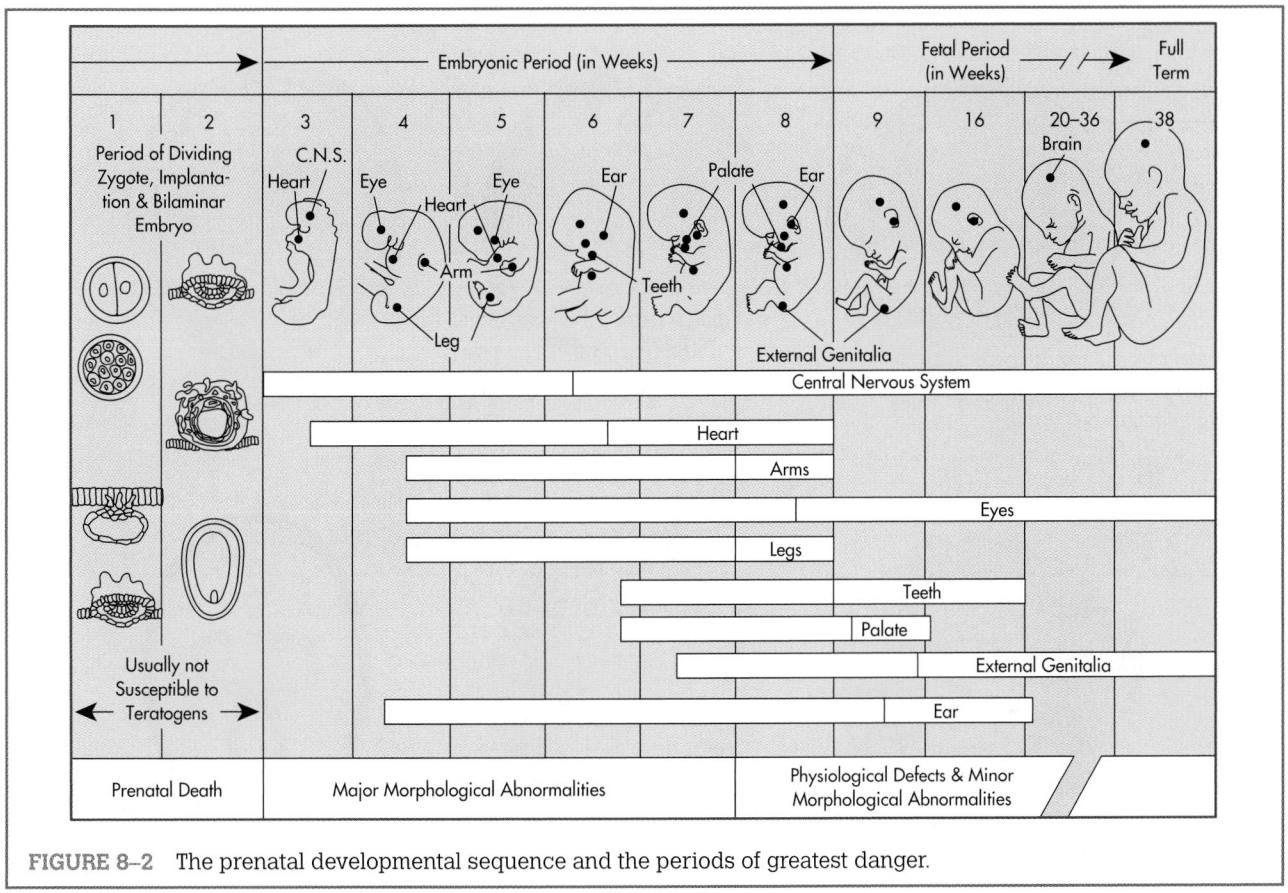


FIGURE 8–2 The prenatal developmental sequence and the periods of greatest danger.

**fetus**

The third stage of the gestation period; usually lasts from nine weeks until birth.

eight weeks), and the **fetus** (nine weeks until birth) (Figure 8–2). During the time in the womb, many changes take place, and many environmental factors influence development (Nash, 2004/05). The air the mother breathes, the water she drinks, the food she eats, the drugs she takes, diseases she may contract, and any hardships she suffers will affect the developing child. Modern technology, such as CT scans, (magnetic resonance imaging (MRIs) and sonograms, enable us to follow the developmental process from conception to birth. Scientist also have learned more about the chemical signals and switches, which control fetal development.

## The Zygote

**placenta**

The covering that protects the developing infant and serves as a medium of exchange for food and oxygen.

**umbilical cord**

The cord that connects the developing child to the mother.

The first stage begins when the sperm and ovum unite into one cell, which floats freely down the fallopian tube. This stage lasts for about two weeks. During this period, cell division takes place very rapidly, with one cell dividing into billions. By about day six, the cell arrives in the uterus, where it begins to implant or attach to the uterine wall so it can obtain nutrients. The **placenta,** the covering that protects the developing infant and serves as a medium of exchange for food and oxygen, and the **umbilical cord,** which connects the developing child to the mother and is his or her lifeline, are beginning to develop (Nash, 2004/05 & Pekkanen, 2004/05) (Figure 8–3). By the fourth day after conception, the zygote begins to change form. Two new layers of cells form. One layer shortly becomes the placenta and amniotic sac and the other the embryo.

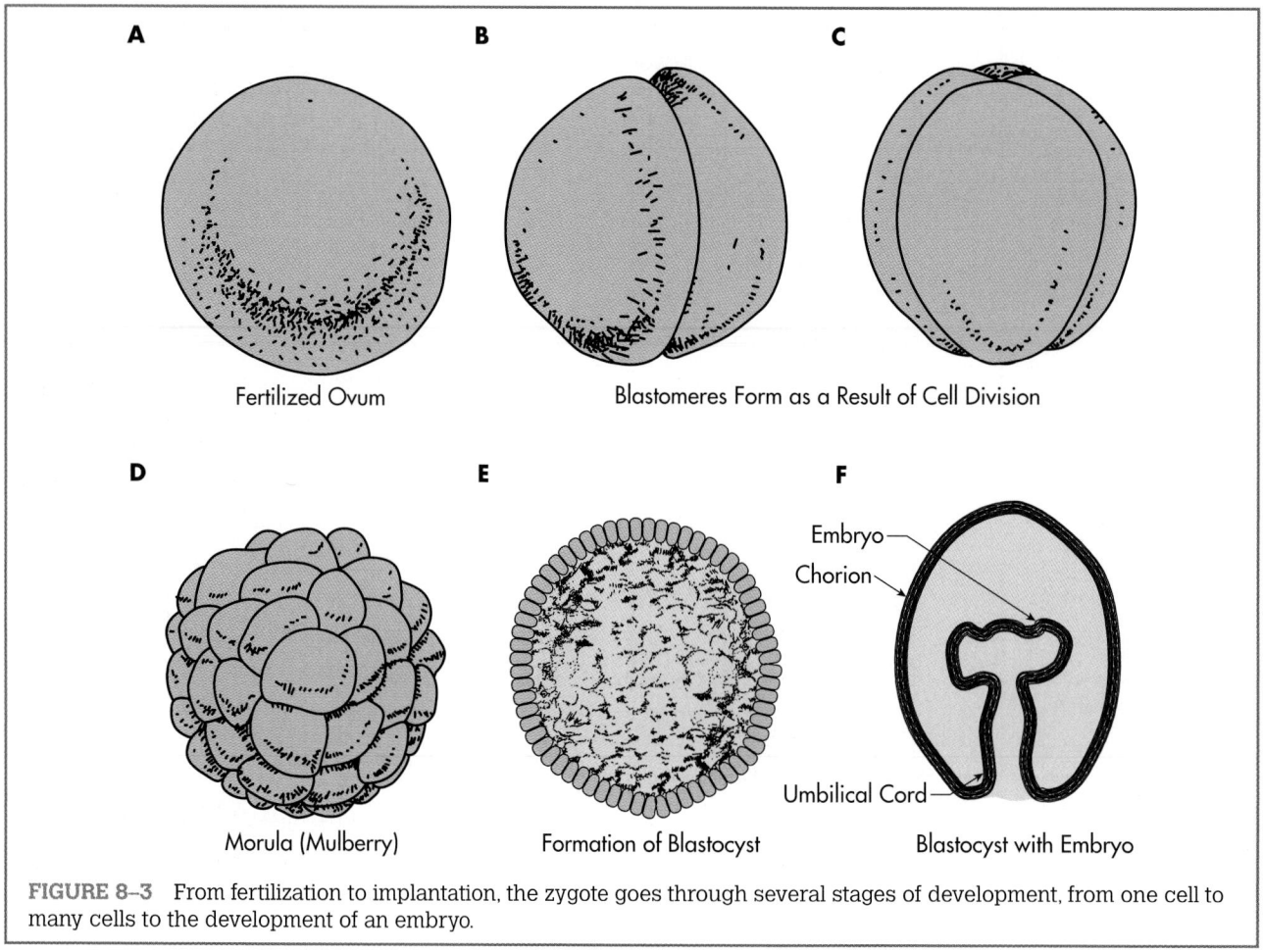


FIGURE 8–3 From fertilization to implantation, the zygote goes through several stages of development, from one cell to many cells to the development of an embryo.

**amnion**

A sac lining the uterus.

**amniotic fluid**

The liquid that fills the amnion.

## The Embryo

The second stage begins when the zygote is implanted in the uterine wall and continues until about the eighth week. This stage is critical because 95 percent of the body parts appear during this stage (Nash, 2004/05). By the end of this stage, the developing embryo begins to resemble a miniature person (Figure 8–4). It is during this stage that the prenatal child is most vulnerable to damage by drugs, alcohol, disease, infection, radiation, and poor nutrition (Berk, 2003). The woman who contracts German measles, who uses cocaine, or who is poorly nourished places her child at high risk. For example, if a woman contracts German measles during her pregnancy, her child stands a risk of being born deaf, blind, or with heart disease.

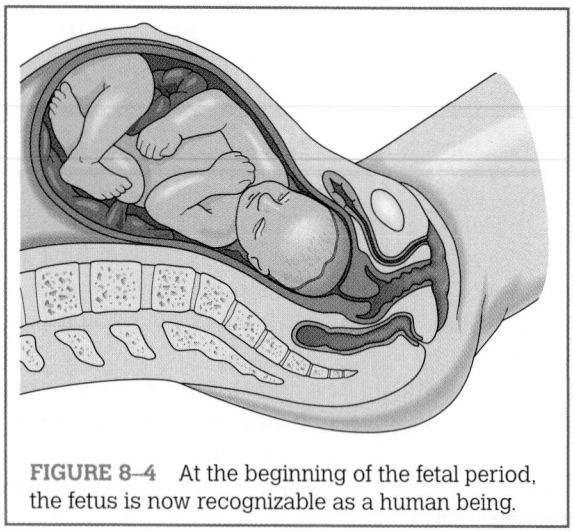

FIGURE 8–4 At the beginning of the fetal period, the fetus is now recognizable as a human being.

The development of the placenta takes place during the embryo stage. The placenta is the vehicle through which the fetus receives nutrients and oxygen and disposes of waste. The umbilical cord connects the fetus and the placenta. The uterus is lined by a sac called the **amnion,** which contains **amniotic fluid.** The fluid serves several purposes. It protects the fetus from injury and provides room for movement and growth.

The amniotic fluid maintains a constant temperature and provides oral fluid. The fluid also collects waste products (Berk, 2003).

During the embryonic period, a great deal of development takes place. A neural tube that is the beginning of the spinal cord and brain and the head-to-tail axis is determined. The head-to-tail axis is established by the **HOX gene**. This development ensures that the body parts will be at the right ends of the body. The upper and lower limb buds appear (*About pregnancy/birth*, 2005).

**HOX gene**

Establishes the head-to-tail axis.

## The Fetus

The fetal period begins at about nine weeks and extends until birth. As mentioned earlier, the child now begins to look like a human being. All the organs that began development during the embryonic stage will grow and develop rapidly during the fetal stage. The head becomes more proportional to the rest of the body, and the limbs are more clearly differentiated. By the fourth month, the placenta is fully operational. A few of the highlights of fetal development (Berk, 2003 and About Pregnancy/ Birth, 2005) include the following:

- During the twelfth week, the baby's bones begin to ossify or harden.
- External ears form and external genitalia begin to differentiate.
- The placenta has taken over production of the hormones, which sustain the pregnancy.
- All the teeth have formed during the sixteenth week.
- By the twelfth week, male and female external genitalia are visible.
- By the twenty-first week, the fetus could survive outside of the uterus.
- By the twenty-fourth week, the fetus has eyelashes and eyebrows and the eyelids are open.
- Toenails and fingernails are formed by forty weeks.
- During the twenty-eighth week, the baby begins to turn its head down.
- About one or two weeks before delivery for the first child and at the time of delivery for subsequent babies, the baby drops down into the pelvis and is ready for birth.
- During the thirty-sixth week, the limbs and organs are fully formed, and the lungs make their final preparations for birth.

## Fetal Sensory Capacity and Learning

Modern equipment and techniques have enlightened us as to the sensory capacities of the fetus (Cole, Cole, & Lightfoot, 2005).

> Pregnant Kate is reading stories to Summer, who is six months from conception. Kate notices that when she reads the rhythmical books by Dr. Seuss, Summer becomes very active. Summer appears to be responding to the rhythm of the story.

We do know that the senses begin to respond during the prenatal period (Cole & Cole, 2001). There is even some evidence that newborn babies respond to stories they have heard while in the womb. At about five months prenatal, the vestibular system in the fetus's middle ear, which controls balance, begins to function. This indicates that the fetus may be able to sense changes in the mother's posture and can orient itself as it floats in the amniotic fluid. By 26 weeks, fetuses respond to light. And, by five to six months after conception, the fetus responds to sound. Tiny microphones have been inserted into the uterus next to the head of the fetus. The noise level is about the same as that in an automobile with the windows up. In spite of the internal noise, fetuses respond to and discriminate among outside noises.

## ENVIRONMENTAL EFFECTS DURING PRENATAL DEVELOPMENT

As shown in Figure 8-5, several types of prenatal environmental influences can affect the fetus. These can be classified as nutritional; maternal characteristics, experiences, and personal habits; and drugs and disease (Annis, 1978).

### Nutrition

Nutrition is an exceptionally important factor during pregnancy. "... of all the long-term threats, maternal undernourishment—which stunts growth even when babies are born full term—may top the list" (Nash, 2004/05, p. 20). Improper prenatal nutrition is one of the greatest dangers to the fetus. Annis (1978) lists a number of factors associated with prenatal maternal malnutrition. These complications include "stillbirths, low-birth-weight babies (babies weighing less than 5 $^1/_2$ pounds or 2,500 grams after a normal period of prenatal development), short-gestation-period babies, and neonatal deaths, as well as many difficulties appearing in the offspring after birth, such as mental deficiency, rickets, cerebral palsy, epilepsy, speech defects, general physical weakness, and susceptibility to illness and disease" (Annis, 1978, p. 63). Not only does a woman need to eat a healthy diet during pregnancy, but also she should

| Maternal and Environmental Conditions | Possible Effects on the Child |
|---|---|
| **Poor Nutrition** | ■ Stillbirth, neonatal death, low birth weight, short gestation<br>■ Mental deficiency, rickets, cerebral palsy, epilepsy, speech defects, general physical weakness |
| **Maternal Characteristics** | |
| ■ Depressed emotional state | ■ Crankiness |
| ■ Small physical size | ■ Difficult delivery |
| ■ Over age forty | ■ Retardation |
| ■ Rh incompatibility | ■ Stillbirth |
| ■ Low blood-oxygen level | ■ Nervous system damage |
| **Maternal Experience and Personal Habits** | |
| ■ X-ray exposure | ■ Tissue damage, retardation |
| ■ Smoking | ■ Low birth weight, death |
| ■ Substance abuse (e.g., alcohol, caffeine, cocaine, heroin) | ■ Slow growth, retardation, miscarriage, fetal alcohol syndrome, heroin addiction |
| **Disease** | |
| ■ AIDS | ■ Mental retardation |
| ■ Genital herpes | ■ Miscarriage, physical malformations, mental retardation, low birth weight, prematurity |
| ■ Syphilis | ■ Miscarriage, physical malformations, mental retardation, low birth weight |
| ■ Rubella (measles) | ■ Miscarriage, physical malformations, mental retardation, low birth weight, prematurity |

FIGURE 8–5 Prenatal maternal and environmental conditions that may negatively affect the child.

begin pregnancy in a good nutritional state. If the pregnant woman is not in good nutritional health, nutritional improvement during pregnancy does have a positive effect. For example, Joos, Pollitt, Mueller, and Albright (1983) found that supplying a nutritional supplement to pregnant undernourished women had a positive effect on the motor development of their infants. The effect was small, probably because there was no postnatal supplement. Nutritional deficiencies continue to be a major worldwide health problem that place women's successful reproductive capacity at risk (*Infants and children at risk*, 1992).

## Maternal Characteristics and Experiences

Maternal characteristics, such as a mother's emotional state, age, physical size, possible Rh incompatibility with the fetus, low blood-oxygen level in the bloodstream, and state of fatigue, can affect the fetus. Personal habits that include the use of alcohol, drugs, tobacco, and caffeine may also be harmful (Nash, 2004/05; & Pekkanen, 2004/05). A long period of emotional upset on the part of the mother can have a negative effect on the fetus. A relationship exists between tense, anxious pregnancies and the delivery of cranky infants.

The mother between the ages of 20 and 30 has the best chance of having a normal, healthy child. Teenage mothers may have relatively poor eating habits and, thus, may not be in good nutritional condition for nurturing a developing infant. Among the large numbers of unwed mothers, a large proportion are teenagers. These young unwed mothers and mothers from impoverished environments are more likely to have infants who are at high risk because of poor maternal nutrition. In addition, the adolescent girl's body is not yet fully mature and ready for childbearing. This adds another factor that results in infants of teenagers being much more likely to be born at-risk than those of fully mature women. These teens' infants are more likely than those of adults to be subject to low birth weight, mental retardation, birth defects, or possibly death before infancy is completed (Nash, 2004/05; & Pekkanen, 2004/05). The reproductive system of mothers older than 30 may be on the decline. The possibility of having a child with Down syndrome is much higher for the older mother who is experiencing her first pregnancy. The mother's size also may be an influence on the pregnancy. Short, small women generally have more difficult pregnancies. Infants of overweight mothers are also more at-risk.

**Rh factor**

A substance found in 85 percent of humans; when present, it is referred to as Rh positive; when absent, Rh negative.

**anoxia**

The stage in which the oxygen supply in blood dips below the safe level.

When the blood types of mother and father are incompatible, denoting the presence of an **Rh factor,** the infant may develop severe anemia, which can result in stillbirth, brain damage, or birth too early for survival. The prenatal infant must have an adequate supply of oxygen in his or her blood. **Anoxia** is the state in which the oxygen supply in the blood dips below the safe level. In this case, the nervous system and the brain are likely to receive damage resulting in cerebral palsy, epilepsy, mental deficiency, and/or possibly behavior problems, such as hyperactivity and learning difficulties. Anoxia is most likely to occur during the birth process, when the child is most in need of an adequate oxygen supply. Anoxia may also be related to maternal fatigue. Radiation, such as X-rays, is another danger to the developing fetus. Both mental and physical retardation from tissue damage can result. Death may result from large doses of radiation.

The mother's personal habits are another important factor to consider. Cigarette smoking is associated with low birth weight, spontaneous abortion, stillbirths, and neonatal death. Smoking may slow the fetal heart rate and affect the fetus's circulatory system. Some research has indicated that if smoking is light or stopped by the fourth month, the baby will not be damaged. Overall, however, pregnant women are urged not to smoke at all. Alcohol, especially in large amounts, presents another danger to the prenatal child. Children of alcoholic mothers show slow physical growth and generally retarded development. Even small amounts of alcohol increase the risk to the infant. Caffeine, found in coffee, tea, cola drinks, and chocolate, is thought to have possible negative effects on the amniotic fluid, which might be associated with a greater chance of miscarriage. In general, any woman who is or suspects she is pregnant is wise not to smoke or drink alcoholic beverages, coffee, tea, cola, or any other beverages that contain caffeine.

The large number of adolescent pregnancies brings with it an increasing number of infants who may suffer the effects of prenatal maternal experiences and habits (Honig, 1984). More teenage girls are smoking. Smoking is habitual among 15 percent of girls between 12 and 18 years of age. The younger a smoker starts, the heavier a smoker she tends to be. Therefore, the chances that the teen mother will be weak and unhealthy puts her infant at even greater risk. Alcohol use has also increased in frequency and amount among adolescents. Pregnant teenagers are very likely to suffer undue stress because of fear regarding their situation, abandonment by the baby's father, or a negative response from parents (Honig, 1984).

Prevention of adolescent pregnancy is one of our major challenges. Children's Defense Fund (1998) reviewed the period from 1973 to 1998. Although the teen pregnancy rate declined, it is still much too high. "Teen pregnancy is a major contributor to, as well as a consequence of, the poverty that victimizes more than 14 million American children" (Children's Defense Fund, 1998, p. 93). Not only is the rate of teen births down, so are the absolute numbers. In 1996, the rate was 54.7 births per 1,000 girls, with a total of about 505,000. In 1998, the rate fell to 51.1 births per 1,000 girls between ages 15 and 19 (Children's Defense Fund, 2001). By 1999, the rate for girls 15 to 17 was down to 29 per 1,000 (FIFCF, 2001). The rates varied for different racial groups: 12 per 1,000 for Asian Pacific Islanders, 17 for white non-Latinos, 41 for American Indians/Alaska natives, 54 for black non-Hispanics, and 61 for Latinos (FIFCF, 2001). However, there are still a large number of teens having babies. A news release from the American College of Obstetricians and Gynecologists (ACOG, 2002) reported that a study showed 15-year-old girls' healthy firstborn infants face a three-to-four times higher risk of dying before age one. When compared with a similar group of infants born to women ages 23 to 29 possible neglect or abuse as a cause of death was found to be much higher, and the rate of SIDS (Sudden Infant Death Syndrome) deaths was higher for the teens' babies. These statistics refer to preventable deaths that might not have occurred if the young mothers had some postnatal training and support. The rate of abortion has also gone down. The proportion of births to unmarried teens has steadily increased to about 44 percent. It is believed that teens are delaying sexual activity and using contraceptives more often. Looking at the global perspective, our rate of teen births is much higher than that of other Western, industrialized countries. For example, the United Kingdom's rate is 32 per 1,000; Canada's is 26 per 1,000; France, 9 per 1,000; and Japan, 4 per 1,000. The difference appears to be due to two factors: first, teens in the United States have more difficulty getting contraceptive supplies, and second, they are taught about sex in a less detailed way and at a later age than in other countries. Looking at the demographics, most teen mothers are white, next black, with much fewer belonging to other minority groups. However, in 1995, blacks had the highest teen birth rate, but that rate has dropped considerably.

"The reasons teenagers become pregnant include lack of knowledge or skills to avoid sex or use contraceptives and lack of motivation to avoid childbearing" (Children's Defense Fund, 1998). It is not clear what kind of approach to prevention works best. However, programs that focus on the reasons teens become pregnant seem to be the most effective. It is essential to educate children before they get involved in high-risk activities. These types of programs include the following:

- helping teens postpone parenthood by working on the major precursors of teen pregnancy—early school failure, early behavioral problems, family dysfunction, and the pressures that come with poverty
- working with males to make them understand that, although it is not good to become a father as a teenager, if they do, they have the responsibility to become a good one

## Drugs and Disease

Drugs and disease are sometimes damaging to fetal development. The effect can be particularly severe during the first three months—the time when the woman is least likely to be aware that she is pregnant. No drug should be taken by a pregnant woman except under a doctor's prescription. One of the most disastrous drug episodes concerned the use of **thalidomide** by pregnant women in Europe in the early 1960s. This drug, taken for the relief of morning sickness, caused retarded limb development when taken during the embryonic period. Children were born without arms and legs or with undeveloped arms and legs similar to those of an embryo. Limb malformations have also been related to the ingestion of hormones, such as those in birth control pills, by pregnant women. Tranquilizers and even aspirin have been shown to be unsafe. Drugs taken during and before delivery should be kept at a minimum because they may also have negative effects on the infant.

**thalidomide**

A drug taken by pregnant women in the early 1960s for the relief of morning sickness that caused retarded limb development when taken during the embryonic period.

Drug addiction presents another danger to the pregnant woman. Cocaine appears to be first on the list of illegal drugs used by women of childbearing age. Although it is widely believed that cocaine-exposed infants are severely damaged, research indicates that most of these infants are not significantly impaired. However, in the long run, they may evidence problems that will require many special services. Probably the most essential element in ensuring cocaine-exposed infants a healthful life is treating their mothers to overcome their addiction so that they can create a healthful home environment. Heroin-addicted mothers appear to have delivery complications. The children of addicts are sometimes born exhibiting behavior similar to that of a person withdrawing from heroin. Cocaine and crack addiction among pregnant women has resulted in the birth of addicted and damaged infants. A 1988 study in 36 hospitals indicated that 11 percent (375,000) of infants born were affected by substance abuse (Weston, Ivins, Zuckerman, Jones, & Lopez, 1989). The drugs affect not only the fetus directly but also the fetal environment and the mother. For example, marijuana retards the development of the placenta, which results in reduced blood flow to the fetus.

Drugs affect the mother's central nervous system, placing the fetus at additional risk. In their review of research, Weston et al. (1989) describe a variety of possible drug effects (Weston et al., 1989). The drug may be addictive to the infant, but after withdrawal, the infant may develop fairly normally. More likely, the drug may also be toxic. That is, it may directly affect the fetus in many ways that will retard or modify infant development. The endocrine or central nervous systems may be damaged. Resulting abnormalities may include reductions in pain threshold, ability for self-control, attention, interpersonal relationships, and bonding with other humans. The genitourinary system and the cardiovascular systems can be damaged. Other dangers include effects from maternal seizures, which may result in death; mental problems, such as delusions and paranoia, which might lead to suicide; aggressive behavior, which might result in injury; or impaired motor coordination, which may result in an accident. Many doctors advise that the safest approach is not to take any drug during pregnancy unless there is a specific medical need for it.

**fetal alcohol syndrome (FAS)**

A group of child behaviors associated with maternal alcohol intake during the fetal period.

**fetal alcohol effects (FAE)**

A condition related to FAS where children do not usually have the identifiable physical characteristics but may be hyperactive as infants.

Another danger to the developing infant during the prenatal period is **fetal alcohol syndrome (FAS).** Each year, 50,000 babies are born to mothers who drink alcohol during pregnancy. It has been estimated that FAS is responsible for 20 percent of all cases of mental retardation (Hymes, 1990). Children with FAS typically have distinctive facial characteristics, especially widely spaced eyes, thin upper lip, short eye openings, a small turned-up nose, and a small head, which reflects an underdeveloped brain (Berk, 1998). **Fetal alcohol effects (FAE)** is a related condition where children do not usually have the identifiable physical characteristics of FAS but may be hyperactive as infants. These are usually children of mothers who drank alcohol in smaller quantities.

Chemicals may find their way into the environment and endanger infants. The toxin PCB (polychlorinated biphenyl) has been found in some of our food and water supplies and has been ingested by pregnant women. Jacobson, Fein, Jacobson, Schwartz, and Dowler (1985) studied 123 mothers and their newborns who had been exposed to PCBs. The mothers had eaten PCB-contaminated fish. When tested at age seven months, the infants were found to have deficits in visual recognition memory.

As discussed earlier in this chapter, diseases may be damaging. German measles can seriously damage the fetus. The effects of chickenpox, mumps, measles, and hepatitis are not as well documented. The common cold does not seem to have an effect on the fetus, but influenza appears to. Syphilis, gonorrhea, diabetes, iron-deficiency anemia, and sickle-cell anemia all present dangers to the unborn child. The total number of children affected by these diseases and disorders is small, but it is still important that pregnant women be under a doctor's care and avoid these dangers if possible.

**acquired immunodeficiency syndrome (AIDS)**

A communicable disease caused by a virus that attacks the immune system.

Another threat to prenatal development is **acquired immunodeficiency syndrome (AIDS)** (*The AmFAR Report*, 1993). AIDS is a communicable disease caused by a virus that attacks the immune system. The AIDS victim is left without normal bodily disease-fighting mechanisms and is susceptible to death from diseases that ordinarily would not be life threatening. The disease is carried in the person's blood. It may be transmitted to sexual partners, those who share drug needles, through blood transfusions, and to unborn children through transfer of blood from pregnant woman to unborn child (Skeen & Hodson, 1987). About 80 percent of HIV-infected children younger than 13 have a parent with AIDS or AIDS-related complex or a parent who is at risk for AIDS (Weston et al., 1989). Because teens are most likely to be indiscriminately sexually active and to share drug needles, AIDS is a clear and present danger to their unborn infants.

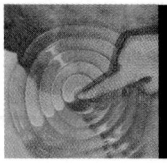

**LOOKING FURTHER**

Consider the many factors that can adversely affect the prenatal development of children. Describe the method or methods you would advocate for protecting them from environmental dangers. Research programs that appear to be successful.

**genetic counseling**

Assessment of maternal and paternal genetic makeups and their possible effects on offspring.

## ROLE AND RESPONSIBILITIES OF THE ADULT

The steps suggested by Apgar and Beck map out the roles and responsibilities of adults with regard to unborn children. First, planning ahead is important. **Genetic counseling** (to be discussed in Chapter 9) can be considered before pregnancy.

Next, a woman contemplating pregnancy should have a complete physical checkup. During the checkup, the many factors that might endanger an unborn child should be discussed to be sure she understands their importance. During pregnancy, the woman should have regular medical checkups. Parents can attend childbirth education classes so they know what to expect during labor and delivery. Brazelton (1992) recommends that at seven months of pregnancy, the parents become acquainted with their **pediatrician,** the physician who will care for their child after birth. He believes that if the parents wait longer, they will be more concerned with delivery and will not take the time to get acquainted with their child's future doctor. He especially encourages fathers to come in, even if it is only for 10 minutes. He has found that even a short visit seems to make fathers more interested in coming in with the child for future well-baby checkups.

**pediatrician**

A physician who specializes in the care of children from birth to age 21.

Expectant mothers should have access to the services of a **perinatologist,** a physician who specializes in the care of women who are at high risk during pregnancy. High-risk factors include age of the mother, diabetes, high blood pressure, lupus, sickle-cell anemia, or a previous history of birth problems, such as multiple births, miscarriages, stillbirths, or physical deformities. Unfortunately, poor and unwed mothers, who are often in their teens, usually do not have access to this type of prenatal medical care.

**perinatologist**

A physician who specializes in the care of women who are at high risk during pregnancy.

The problems associated with poor, unwed, teen pregnancies can be alleviated through programs that focus on teen pregnancy prevention. The Children's Defense Fund (1998, pp. 99–100) identified an effective program designed to reduce teen pregnancy. The Teen Outreach Program (TOP) has been implemented at 107 sites in 16 states. The objective of TOP is to reduce rates of teen pregnancy, school failure, and school suspension. The TOP approach focuses on a cluster of four interrelated strategies:

1. To support *youth development,* TOP sets standards and expectations high, provides meaningful activities, and fosters positive and lasting relationships with caring, supportive adults.
2. The teenagers provide service to their communities through *community involvement* assignments and receive community support for their work.
3. *Education is learner-centered,* with adults offering guidance and providing hands-on classroom activities.
4. *Academic extensions* provide opportunities to apply what is learned in school to workplace requirements in service assignments.

TOP is unique in that it does not focus directly on the problems it wants to prevent, but instead works to enhance the teenagers' competence in decision making, interacting with peers and adults, and identifying and handling their own emotions (p. 100). The results have been positive. Comparing a TOP group with a randomly selected control group, the TOP teens demonstrated an 11 percent lower rate of school failure, 14 percent fewer school suspensions, a 60 percent lower dropout rate, and 30 percent fewer pregnancies. Students who feel confident and respected appear to be able to make better decisions about their lives.

The teen pregnancy rate and the number of wed and unwed teen parents is still high. Many professionals believe that these pregnant girls must have an opportunity to have prenatal and postnatal care and parent education in order to have healthy, happy babies who are well cared for. The Birthing Project (Ryan, 1997) is an exemplary project with these objectives. The program is located at 46 sites around the country. The focus is on one-to-one contact with sister-friends who help pregnant women get prenatal care and proper nutrition, listen to their problems, and assist them in getting available health care and housing. The pregnant women and their sister-friends are organized in groups of 10, called baby bunches. They meet for support and for social activities, such as baby showers. The sister-friends commit to provide support to their "little sisters" for at least one year after the birth of the baby. Although the program began initially for African Americans, it is now multicultural, including Asian Americans, Christians, Jews, and others.

The adult who works with the young child must be alert to past influences that may affect the way a child acts today. When Billy is exceptionally active and disorderly, his behavior may not be under his control. A look at the past may reveal that mild anoxia occurred during delivery. The adult will then realize that Billy needs more than the usual amount of help to develop self-control. A good medical history should always be part of a school intake application. With the increase in AIDS-infected and substance-addicted infants, we face a future with an increasing number of young children who have serious health, behavioral, and emotional problems. We are still searching for methods of working with them and their families.

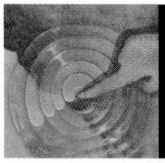

**LOOKING FURTHER**

How do you feel about the large numbers of teenagers becoming parents? List the major problems this situation creates. Explain what you believe is the best plan for dealing with this situation. Research programs that appear to be successful for pregnancy prevention, for prenatal care, and for teaching child care.

## SUMMARY

The prenatal period, which extends from conception to birth, is a time of phenomenal development but also a time when there are many potential threats to normal healthful growth.

Gestation is divided into three stages. The first stage, the zygote, lasts about two weeks. The second stage, the embryo, begins when the zygote is firmly implanted in the uterine wall and lasts until about the eighth week after conception. The third stage is the fetal period, which begins at about nine weeks and extends until birth. This is a period of rapid development.

The fetal environment can be threatened by many outside factors that can intrude and damage the developing child. Because the developing infant receives all nutrients and oxygen from the mother's system, the mother's health is critical. Her health is affected by her nutritional status; her use of alcohol, drugs, or tobacco; and her contact with communicable diseases. These factors can directly affect the baby and can have a negative effect on growth and development. Pregnant teens who are unwed and/or from lower-socioeconomic-status (SES) levels are especially at risk. Some programs encourage avoidance of pregnancy, whereas others assist already pregnant teens and low SES women.

## FOR FURTHER READING

Banhidy, F., Lowry, R. B., & Czeizel, A. E. (2005). Risk and benefit of drug use during pregnancy. *International Journal of Medical Science, 2*(3), 100–106. Retrieved July 20, 2005, from http://www.pubmedcentral.gov

Brazelton, T. B. (1992). *Touchpoints: The essential reference.* Reading, MA: Addison-Wesley.

Brazelton, T. B., & Greenspan, S. I. (2000). *The irreducible needs of children.* Boulder, CO: Perseus.

Duckworth, S. V., & Norton, T. L. (2000). Fetal alcohol syndrome and fetal alcohol effects: Support for teachers and families. *Dimensions, 28*(3), 19–23.

Glink, P. (1998, April/May). The Chicago Doula project: A collaborative effort in perinatal support for birthing teens. *Zero to Three, 18*(5), 44–50.

Harwood, M., & Kleinfeld, J. S. (2002). Up front, in hope: The value of early intervention for children with Fetal Alcohol Syndrome. *Young Children, 57*(4), 86–90.

Herbert, M. (2002). *Typical and atypical development: From conception to adolescence.* Malden, MA: Blackwell.

Leitch, M. L. (1998). An essay for practitioners. Contextual issues in teen pregnancy and parenting: Refining our scope of inquiry. *Family Relations, 47*, 145–148.

Lewis, V. (2003). *Development and disability* (2nd ed.). Malden, MA: Blackwell.

McCall, R. B., & Ingram, A. (1995). Special report: Preventing teenage pregnancy. *Developments, 9*(1), 5–7.

New approach to prevention gives county a closer look at fetal and infant mortality. (2003). *Developments, 17*(4)2, 1–2.

Rodrick-Athans, L., & Bhavnagri, N. P. (1996/97). Strategies for overcoming obstacles in AIDS education for preteens. *Childhood Education, 73*(2), 66–69.

Stewart, I. (1998). Prevention programs that work for youth: Pregnancy prevention. In *Education and development of American youth* (pp. 49–54). Washington, DC: Aspen Institute.

Streissguth, A. (1997). *Fetal alcohol syndrome.* Baltimore, MD: Brookes.

Sutton, A. L. (Ed.). (2004). *Pregnancy and birth sourcebook* (2nd ed.). Holmes, PA: Omnigraphics.

United States Department of Health and Human Services. (2005). *News release: U.S. surgeon general releases advisory on alcohol use in pregnancy.* Retrieved July 20, 2005 from, http://www.hhs.gov

## SUGGESTED ACTIVITIES

1. Find out how knowledgeable your friends are regarding conception and prenatal development. Ask the following questions:
   a. How does conception take place?
   b. After conception, how long is the gestation period?
   c. What is a zygote? Embryo? Fetus?
   d. What are the purposes of the umbilical cord? The placenta? The amniotic fluid?
2. Ask five friends to list as many factors as they can think of that may enhance or endanger prenatal development. Compare their lists with the items described in this book. How many did each list? Do you feel well informed or need more information? Give them a list of the dangers described in this book. What are their reactions?
3. Make an entry in your journal.

## REVIEW

1. List some of the issues related to infertility.
2. Put the following events in the correct sequence by listing the letters in their appropriate order on the right side of the page.
   a. The male ejaculates semen.
   b. The ovum reaches the fallopian tube.
   c. The menstrual cycle reaches its midpoint.
   d. A sperm enters the membrane of the ovum.
   e. The ovum, in the fluid-filled follicle, leaves the ovary and heads for the fallopian tube.
   f. The sperm race toward the waiting ovum.

**3.** Match the prenatal stages in Column I with the descriptions in Column II.

| Column I | Column II |
|---|---|
| a. germinal stage | 1. Third stage of prenatal development, from about two to nine months. |
| b. embryonic stage | 2. First stage, which lasts until ten days to two weeks after conception (zygote). |
| c. fetal stage | 3. A very critical stage during which defects are most likely to develop. |

**4.** Match the functions in Column II with the terms in Column I.

| Column I | Column II |
|---|---|
| a. placenta | 1. Connects the fetus and the placenta. |
| b. umbilical cord | 2. Substance that protects the fetus from injury and provides for movement and growth. |
| c. amniotic fluid | 3. Vehicle for receiving nutrients and oxygen. |

**5.** List four highlights of fetal development.

**6.** Select the statements that are true.

a. The fetus is sensitive to light.
b. The uterus provides the fetus with a quiet environment.
c. The fetus has no sense of the mother's movement when suspended in the amniotic fluid.
d. The fetus responds to outside noises.
e. No learning takes place in the uterus.

**7.** List and describe at least five prenatal environmental dangers.

**8.** Mark an *X* by the methods that work best in preventing teenage pregnancy.

a. Threaten teens with the dire consequences of sexual activity.
b. Reach and educate children before they become sexually active.
c. Work on the precursors of teen pregnancy, such as early school failure, early behavioral problems, family dysfunction, and the pressures that go with poverty.
d. Do not explain too much about sex and pregnancy because it might tempt the teens to explore the area firsthand.
e. Work with young males to help them understand the responsibilities of parenthood.
f. Start early helping young people to develop logical decision-making skills.

## KEY TERMS LIST

acquired immunodeficiency syndrome (AIDS)
amnion
amniotic fluid
anoxia
conception
embryo
fertility
fertilization
fetal alcohol effects (FAE)
fetal alcohol syndrome (FAS)
fetus
follicle
genetic counseling
gestational period
HOX gene
IVF (in vitro fertilization)
natural family planning
ovum
pediatrician
perinatologist
placenta
Rh factor
semen
sperm
sperm microinjection
thalidomide
umbilical cord
zygote

Additional resources for this chapter can be found on the Online Companion™ to accompany this text at http://www.earlychilded.delmar.com. Respond to "Time to Reflect" and "Looking Further" concepts, review various child development scenarios, and answer thought-provoking questions in the Critical Thinking Forum. Keep a daily journal by downloading the student journal available on this Web site. Complete the interactive matching exercises to reinforce concepts, and print out the child development assessment forms to use during your observation of development for children from birth to age eight. In addition, read the case studies on the Web site to reinforce the important concepts in each chapter, and take a look at the multitude of Web links that are available for student research on the Internet.

CHAPTER

# Heredity, Environment, and Development

## OBJECTIVES

After reading this chapter, you should be able to:

- Explain why it is important for the adult who works with young children to know the children's histories.
- Explain what is meant by the *nature-nurture (heredity-environment) controversy.*
- Understand the point of view of heredity and environment having mutual effects.
- Identify hereditary predispositions and environmental dangers that may hinder children's optimal development.
- Define the terms *gene, chromosome, DNA, gene therapy,* and *genetic discrimination.*
- Recognize when a genetic counselor's services may be needed.

**hereditary**
Factors determined at conception.

**environmental**
Factors that begin to play a role as soon as conception occurs.

**monozygotic (MZ) siblings**
Twins who develop from one egg that has divided into two or more parts after fertilization, so the same hereditary characteristics are present in each.

Both hereditary and environmental factors influence the course of child development. **Hereditary** factors are determined at conception. **Environmental** factors begin to play a role as soon as conception occurs. The adult who works with young children needs to understand the development of the child from the time of conception. With this knowledge, adults can gauge where children are in their development. When speaking with parents, the adult can also ask questions that will provide information on critical background factors that have influenced the child's development prior to the time the child comes under the adult's care. This information can be used to evaluate and interpret the child's current behavior.

## THE MOMENT OF CONCEPTION: HEREDITY

At the moment the sperm enters the ovum and the child begins to form, characteristics from both the mother's and the father's sides of the family are merged into one or more new individuals. In the case of multiple births, **monozygotic (MZ) siblings** develop from one egg that has divided into two or more parts after fertilization, so the same hereditary characteristics are present in each. **Dizygotic (DZ) siblings** develop from separate eggs fertilized at the same time. Characteristics such as skin, hair, and eye color; potential physical size and proportions; and even potential temperament and cognitive characteristics are included. Once the instant of conception has passed, environment begins to exert a strong influence on what children will be like as they grow and learn. As in the past, concern and curiosity continue regarding the relative influence of heredity and environment. Historically, interest and discussion focused on the relative influence of heredity and environment. This **nature versus nurture** controversy went on for many years (e.g., Baumrind, 1993; Jackson, 1993; Kagan, 1994; Scarr, 1993; Wolfe, 1972, 1977) with more developmental psychologists leaning toward an **interactionist** view (Horowitz, 1989; Kagan, 1994).

**dizygotic (DZ) siblings**
Twins who develop from separate eggs fertilized at the same time.

**nature versus nurture**
The relative influence of heredity and environment on a child's development

**interactionist**
One who views the child as entering the environment with a variety of potential behaviors that may or may not develop depending on the process of development and the opportunities presented in the environment.

This interactionist position views the organism as entering the environment with a variety of potential behaviors that may or may not develop, depending on the process of development and the opportunities presented in the environment. It is neither the genetic factors in the organism nor the environment that controls development but the process of development itself that is the critical and controlling factor. What happens prenatally has an important role in determining the probability that any particular set of behaviors will emerge, rather than another set of behaviors. Horowitz (1989) points out that there are some universals in all human development. That is, there are regularities in the development of all typical human beings. Differences appear in just how these regularities appear in a particular individual. For example, language is a universal, but its exact construction depends on experiences in the social and cultural context as they relate to individual differences. The environment may or may not facilitate development. The organism may be vulnerable to or protected from outside forces. The organism may reach the optimal developmental outcome or only the minimal. The organism may be impaired or unimpaired. Development has many dimensions. As we look at a particular child or at research on numbers of children, we need to examine all the evidence and not naïvely accept simple cause-and-effect or simple heredity/environment answers to our questions about development. Jerome Kagan (1994, p. A64) suggests the following relationship between biology (heredity) and behavior (environment):

> Fortunately, no human psychological profile is a product of genes alone. To rephrase a graceful sentence by the philosopher W. V. O. Quine, every behavior can be likened to a pale gray fabric composed of black threads, for biology, and white threads for experience, but it is not possible to detect any purely black threads nor any white ones.

Most recently, the National Research Council commissioned a review of the research on early childhood development which looked at the relationships among the neurobiological, behavioral, and social sciences (Shonkoff & Phillips, 2000). Scientific knowledge has provided a deeper appreciation of:

1. The importance of early life experiences, as well as the inseparable and highly interactive influences of genetics and environment, on the development of the brain and the unfolding of human behavior.
2. The central role of early relationships (*From Neurons to Neighborhoods*, 2005).

The reviewers coordinated a rethinking of the nature and nurture relationship, which resulted in a new appreciation of the coactivity of nature and nurture in development. That is, nature and nurture are no longer viewed as antagonists, but are viewed as partners based on the newer research. No longer is it nature versus nurture, but it is nature through nurture. Heredity is no longer viewed as placing limits on development but heredity and environment are viewed as working together. Parents and other caregivers must learn to read children's behavior and create environments that meet the children's needs and temperaments. For example, a highly active child needs a setting that provides for physically active play whereas a shy child may need a quiet place to go away from the more active children. Hereditary characteristics can be controlled by environmental factors. Brain development is no longer viewed as highly genetically controlled. While basic processes of brain development are controlled by genes, the information that the brain must store, use, and create comes from the environment. When the brain is ready to learn, the environment must provide the necessary experiences.

With this in mind, we can now look at some of the ways heredity and environment have been studied.

## AFTER CONCEPTION: ENVIRONMENT AND HEREDITY

As already mentioned, scientists continue to be intrigued by the complexities of heredity and environment. Although in the past researchers focused on the determination of just how much each factor contributes to human behavior, today the process of interaction between the two is seen as the direction in which to go. Even children with identical heredity, the monozygotic (single-egg) twins, start out in different surroundings during the prenatal period depending on their positioning in the womb and the relationship this may have to their prenatal development (Wolfe, 1977). The twin process of prenatal development may be different due to a variety of factors. For example, they each wait for birth in a different area of the uterus with their umbilical cords attached to different parts of the placenta. They each have their own circulatory system and may receive different amounts of nutrients from their mother. The twin who is born first may have a more difficult time getting out into the world because the birth canal is tighter. The second twin may suffer from a short supply of oxygen while waiting for the first twin. Even identical twins, starting with the same hereditary background from the moment of conception, live in different environments (Figure 9–1). Peter Wolfe concludes the following:

**behavioral geneticists**

Those who are concerned with heredity and environment as a two-way interaction and influence.

> From the moment of conception to the moment of birth, heredity and environment contribute to development as inseparable factors. Although the distinction between heredity and environment may be useful for some technical discussions, it is an artificial abstraction that has no direct reference to actual developmental processes (Wolfe, 1972, 1977, p. 15).

FIGURE 9–1 Identical twins have the same heredity, but the environment offers opportunities for them to be different in many ways.

Today there is ongoing contact and cooperative research between developmental psychologists and **behavioral geneticists** (Shonkoff & Phillips, 2000; *From Neurons to Neighborhoods*, 2005). Behavioral genetics is a major research focus. Developmental behavioral genetics combines the study of heredity (genetics) and the effects of the environment on the development of behavior. As described above, behavioral geneticists are concerned with heredity and environment as a two-way interaction and influence. That is, they look for the influence of heredity on environment as well as environment on heredity. They view genes as active, not static. They are particularly interested in individual differences in children and how the environment can accommodate these differences, rather than trying to change the child to fit the environment.

In the past, nature/nurture research focused on adoptive studies and twin studies as a way to find the contribution of heredity and environment to behavior. Quantitative formulas were developed. However, with the explosion of genetic research, more accurate information is now available. For example, children who are hostile in temperament are likely to receive harsher punishment from their parents (adoptive or biological) than children with a more easygoing disposition. Also, the harsh discipline may increase the child's level of negative behavior. More is being learned about the heritability of childhood disorders like autism, schizophrenia, attention deficit hyperactivity disorder, and antisocial behavior. Rather than considering heredity and environment as providing quantitative amounts to behavior and development, it is now considered more productive to look for interventions in the environment that can alter the development of inherited characteristics (Shonkoff & Phillips, 2000; *From Neurons to Neighborhoods*, 2005).

Read the following description and explain how it fits the relationship between heredity and environment.

> When I was sixteen, my mother gave birth to my identical twin sisters. Jill was the first-born, only because Joan didn't want to stay in any longer; essentially Joan kicked Jill out. It took Joan 15 minutes to be delivered after Jill. She was not breathing at birth. The twins were approximately eight weeks early, 17 inches long, and 4.5 and 4.7 pounds, respectively. They were fully developed and healthy, with the exception of being slow eaters. Once they reached five pounds, they came home. It took one hour to feed each baby one ounce of formula. Throughout infancy and toddlerhood, they demonstrated different approaches to life. Joan (born second) was always the first to try new things. She was the first to sit up, roll over, crawl, stand, walk, run, fall down the stairs, and so on. Jill would watch Joan do the experimenting, and then do the same thing without the falls. For example, Joan crawled by wiggling on her tummy; Jill did not—she crawled on her hands and knees after carefully watching her sister struggle with the wiggling. Joan was always a "prim and proper" girl, whereas Jill was a "rough and tough" tomboy. They looked alike throughout the elementary years, but in junior high they had different circles of friends and their appearances changed to fit their different peer environments.

## GENETICS

**genetics**

The study of the factors involved in the transmission of hereditary characteristics in living organisms.

**Genetics** is the study of the factors involved in the transmission of hereditary characteristics in living organisms. Through genetic studies, scientists are able to predict the passing of a trait from one generation to the next. For example, if a blue-eyed man and a brown-eyed woman marry, a geneticist can predict how many blue-eyed and brown-eyed grandchildren they are likely to have (Wolfe, 1972, 1977). Geneticists can also predict the chance of a couple having a child with certain diseases such as phenylketonuria (PKU), an inability of the body to use protein properly, and hemophilia, a disposition to bleed heavily and easily. Tests can be done before conception to find out whether a couple's child might carry such negative traits. Tests also can be done after conception to determine the presence of these factors and others. The sex of the child can also be determined. Cole, Cole, and Lightfoot (2005) give examples of diseases or conditions that can be identified during the prenatal period:

- Down syndrome: mental and physical retardation occurs.
- Huntington's chorea: during middle age, the central nervous system and body deteriorate.
- Klinefelter's syndrome: males do not develop sexual maturity at adolescence.

- Muscular dystrophy: muscles weaken and waste away.
- Phenylketonuria (PKU): cannot digest protein in the typical way.
- Sickle-cell anemia: red blood cells are abnormal.

**germ-line gene therapy**
A procedure that doctors can use to alter the genes in women's eggs, men's sperm, or an embryo that is only a few days old.

A procedure called **germ-line gene therapy** is a method that doctors can use to alter the genes in women's eggs, men's sperm, or an embryo that is only a few days old (Joyce, 1998). The goal of this method is to eliminate genes that carry the kinds of inherited diseases and disabilities just described. For example, a woman discovered that she carried a gene that brought about early onset of Alzheimer's disease (Weiss, 2002). Her thirty-eight-year-old sister became incapacitated by Alzheimer's and her brother began to show symptoms at thirty-five. Her father died at forty-two. There was a 50 percent chance that this woman would pass the DNA on to her child. She went to a geneticist who retrieved 23 of her eggs, identified the eggs that were free from the genetic mutation, and fertilized them with her husband's sperm. Four embryos were placed in her uterus and one developed into a little girl. The use of this procedure brings up some important questions. Although it sounds wonderful to eliminate the possibility of some disabling conditions or lengthen a child's life span, it is also possible that those who can afford to do so might design their children to order.

**gene**
The biological unit of heredity.

**chromosomes**
The major units that control heredity.

**DNA**
A complex molecule that contains genetic information.

**genotype**
The set of genes an individual receives at conception that makes him or her unique.

**phenotype**
The individual's external, measurable characteristics that reflect the genotype.

As can be seen in the previous example, the study of genetics has progressed greatly since 1886, when Gregor Mendel discovered genes (Young, 1981). The **gene** is the biological unit of heredity. Genes are in specific locations on each chromosome. **Chromosomes** are the major units that control heredity. In each gene, genetic information is contained within a substance called **DNA.** A scientist named Kary Mullis (Dwyer, 1993) devised a method to actually reproduce a gene or DNA fragment. A section of DNA can be forced to copy itself. Many biological laboratories are now applying Mullis's procedure in research designed to better understand genetics.

The set of genes the individual receives at conception that makes him or her unique is referred to as the **genotype.** The individual's external appearance is referred to as the **phenotype** and is determined by both environmental and genotypical factors. Humans have 46 chromosomes in 23 pairs. All of the pairs but one have matched members. This twenty-third pair determines sex: females are X and X, and males are X and Y. The transmittal of these genes determines whether the individual will be male or female. Females inherit an X chromosome from both the mother and father. Males inherit an X chromosome from their mother and a Y chromosome from their father. Some traits, such as height, hair and eye color, and fingerprint patterns, are determined by several pairs of genes in combination.

Another area of research is the research on the human genome. The genome contains the full set of human genes (Gillis & Weiss, 2000). It is the master set of genetic instructions that governs all human biology from conception to death. Scientists are trying to decode all the information in the genome to better understand how the body works. They hope the information will lead to a better understanding of disease and improved treatments and even cures. The government's Human Genome Project is sponsored by the United States Department of Energy. The project reached its goals in 2003 (Human Genome Project, August 2005):

- Identify all of the approximately 20,000–25,000 genes in human DNA.
- Determine the sequences of the three billion chemical base pairs that make up human DNA.
- Store this information in databases.
- Improve tools for data analysis.

- Transfer related technologies to the private sector.
- Address the ethical, legal, and social issues that may arise from the project.

The project has had an impact in finding genes associate with disease. More than 30 genes have been identified and associated with breast cancer, muscle disease, deafness, and blindness. DNA sequences have been found that underlie common problems, such as cardiovascular disease, diabetes, arthritis, and other cancers. Biologists can move beyond the study of individual genes to whole genome sequences. The field of molecular genetics appears to show promise for finding specific genes that underlie specific human behaviors and characteristics. Psychology and molecular genetics working together may provide more detailed information regarding nature/nurture interaction.

What is your opinion about the possibility of modifying genes? What might be the advantages? What might be the dangers or disadvantages? If this question interests you, you might want to read Aldous Huxley's classic novel, *Brave New World*.

## GENETIC COUNSELING

The profession of genetic counseling emerged to help parents and prospective parents deal with the problems of heredity (The genetic counselor, 1977). The genetic counselor can help parents make major decisions about childbearing. For example, one couple is thinking of having a child. They know that hemophilia is a trait in the wife's family. The genetic counselor can advise them of their chance of having a child with this disease. The couple can then choose whether to try to have a child. Assume a woman wants to have prenatal information regarding the possibility of a genetic defect. She can decide to have genetic screening, choosing from among several methods of getting prenatal information (Berk, 2003). **Amniocentesis** is a commonly used method. At about 16 to 17 weeks into the pregnancy, the amniotic fluid is sampled. The amniotic fluid can reveal the sex of the child and up to 70 possible birth defects. This procedure has become common for pregnant women who are curious about the sex of the child and/or are concerned about possible birth defects. A more recently discovered method is **chorionic villus sampling (CVS)**. Using this method, a fetoscope, guided by ultrasound, is inserted through the cervix into the uterus. Cells are cut from the chorionic villi. The chorionic villi are membranous cellular projections that anchor the embryo to the uterus. At about 10 weeks, they disappear. The advantage of this procedure is that it can be done earlier than amniocentesis (during the eighth week of pregnancy), when abortion is safer. However, the risk of spontaneous abortion is twice as high (2 percent). A third commonly used method of gaining information prenatally is **ultrasound** or **sonography**. High-frequency sounds that cannot be heard by the human ear are transmitted through the mother's abdomen to the uterus. They are then reflected back from the fetus as echoes that are turned into electrical impulses. These signals display the fetal image on a television monitor. This procedure can confirm the pregnancy, determine multiple pregnancies, detect some abnormalities in development, and assist with diagnostic procedures, such as amniocentesis or intrauterine fetal treatment.

**amniocentesis**
A method of obtaining prenatal information by sampling the amniotic fluid.

**chorionic villus sampling (CVS)**
A method of obtaining prenatal information by cutting cells from the chorionic villi.

**ultrasound**
A method of gaining information by using high-frequency sounds that are turned into electrical impulses.

**sonography**
See *ultrasound*.

"One family in ten has a child born with a *serious, identifiable genetic disease*" (The genetic counselor, 1977, p. M15). If an engaged couple knows or suspects that there may be diseases, such as hemophilia, cystic fibrosis, sickle-cell anemia, Down syndrome, fragile X syndrome, or Tay-Sachs disease in their family genetic

FIGURE 9–2 The genetic counselor helps the engaged couple search their family histories for any potential hereditary problems that might affect their future children.

makeup, they can seek genetic counseling before marriage (Figure 9–2). The counselor questions the couple regarding their family history and gives them as many facts as are available about their special concern. The counselor then tries to help them make the best decision about whether or not to try to conceive. Counselors also help couples who already have a child with a genetic defect to decide whether or not to have another. Furthermore, they can help already expectant parents decide whether to go ahead with the pregnancy to full term or abort the fetus. It is always the parents' decision, however.

Richard Restak (1975) warned that dangers exist in knowing too much about genetics. Decision making in genetics is a serious matter. At first sight, it might seem wonderful to be able to reduce the number of defective babies born. However, some ethical and moral issues are involved. In a situation in which conception has occurred, the question of abortion arises. In a situation in which the parents are warned before conception, there is a question of whether to proceed with sterilization to do away with the risk of conceiving a defective child. A decision regarding aborting a fetus, even though a defective child would be produced, or to consider not ever having a child, can be very painful. Whatever the decision, it is not an easy one. When seeking genetic counseling, it is important to find the most well-trained and well-qualified counselor available who will explain with care the dangers of knowing too much and the kinds of consequences that may result from certain decisions. There are both emotional and practical considerations related to genetic testing (Ubell, 1997). The results are not always clear. Although finding answers might be lifesaving, such as with the case of cancer, emotional and financial risks abound. When one changes jobs, health insurance coverage might be limited due to having genetic information in health records. The new hope is gene therapy; as more genes are identified, the dangerous ones may be eliminated.

The consumer of genetic testing and counseling needs to beware (*The Telltale Gene*, 1990). Many obstetricians do not give adequate counseling after performing genetic tests. Many women are not told why they have had the test or what the results mean. Consumers of genetic services need to be encouraged to seek the answers to their questions.

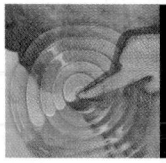

**LOOKING FURTHER**

With a classmate, prepare a debate: *Heredity or Environment–Which Has More Influence on Development?* Each of you take one side of the argument. Prepare five-minute speeches in support of each side. Present your arguments and then each take five minutes to disprove the other person's case. Have the class vote for the winner of the debate.

## ENVIRONMENTAL DANGERS

The World Health Organization actively campaigns for a safer environment for children (*World Health Day 2003*, 2005). Each year on April 7, the world celebrates World Health Day. Home, school, and community should be healthy places, but unfortunately, these places are not safe for many of the world's children. Unhealthy environments nurture germs, worms, and disease-bearing insects. Half a billion children worldwide are infected with malaria, dengue fever, cholera, and other diseases. Poverty, conflicts, natural and man-made disasters, and social inequity further enlarge the seriousness of these threats to children's health. The variety of environmental dangers includes unsafe drinking water, inadequate sanitation, indoor air pollution, insufficient food hygiene, poor housing, and inadequate waste disposal. Dangerous chemicals, toxic waste, noise and industrial pollution, and unsafe chemicals in toys and household products also may harm children. Two areas of danger that are especially rampant in the United States are substance abuse and HIV/AIDS.

## Substance Abuse

Drug and alcohol abuse provides great dangers to our children. Prevention during early childhood is the first line of defense. If children can acquire positive behaviors during early childhood, they are more likely to complete their education, avoid substance abuse, and become good citizens (*Preventing Drug Abuse Among Children and Adolescents*, 2005). Protective factors include learning self-control, having close parental monitoring, achieving academic competence, attending to antidrug policies, and having a strong neighborhood attachment. The greatest drug-abuse risk periods are during major transitions, such as leaving the family and entering school. A major source of danger that is relatively new on the scene is methamphetamine.

**methamphetamine**
or meth, "is an addictive stimulant drug that strongly activates certain systems in the brain" (*NIDA InfoFacts: Methamphetamine*, 2005).

**Methamphetamine,** or meth, "is an addictive stimulant drug that strongly activates certain systems in the brain" (*NIDA InfoFacts: Methamphetamine*, 2005). The central nervous system is activated to increased wakefulness, increased physical activity, decreased appetite, increased respiration, hyperthermia, and euphoria. Other effects can include irritability, insomnia, confusion, tremors, convulsions, anxiety, paranoia, and aggressiveness. Death may result from hyperthermia and convulsions.

The Drug Enforcement Administration (DEA) provides a *Fact Sheet* (*FACTSHEET*, 2005) about the dangers of meth. Meth is a problem everywhere, not just in the cities. The ingredients are cheap and easily obtained. Many "tabletop" labs are housed on kitchens tables and countertops, in garages, and elsewhere. It is not only dangerous to users, but also to the environment. The chemicals are very toxic and the waste may be dumped into fields and streams. The chemical vapors during cooking permeate the walls and carpets of the rooms where the cooking takes place, often making the buildings that house the labs uninhabitable. The children of meth "cooks" are in danger from the toxic environment. "More than 20 percent of the meth labs seized last year had children present" (*FACTSHEET*, 2005).

A frightening headline read, "Babies abandoned by crack cocaine addicts crowding hospitals" (July 2, 1989). Substance-abusing women of all ages are having babies. Many of these babies are abandoned. Although many of them appear healthy, as we learned in Chapter 8, they may suffer lifelong problems due to damage from the crack cocaine that entered their systems during the prenatal period. It is not unusual for these infants also to be AIDS carriers. Placing the babies in foster homes provides hope, but it is a slow process because of the amount of paperwork to be completed.

Attachment, the emotional bond between parent and child, has been the focus of much study (see Chapter 13). Rodning, Beckwith, and Howard (1989) looked at attachment and play organization in prenatally drug-exposed toddlers. The drug-exposed toddlers' performance in attachment and play situations was compared with that of toddlers who were premature at birth. Both groups lived at the poverty level. In both groups, the mothers had no or inadequate prenatal care.

The drug-exposed toddlers were found to be developmentally behind in their performance in each play situation and negative in their attachments to their caregivers. The most insecurely attached toddlers were the ones living with their biological mothers, who continued to abuse drugs. The greatest deficits appeared in spontaneous play. The drug-exposed toddlers were less able to play spontaneously and engage in representative play and were less organized in their play, had less variety, and did not follow-through with a complete activity. Although they performed more adequately in adult-structured tasks, they could not organize their own activities at a typical toddler level. Their facial expressions were bland, showing neither pleasure nor distress.

In Oakland, California, the CARE (Chemical Addiction Recovery Efforts) Clinic, part of the Center for the Vulnerable Child at Children's Hospital, is attempting to offer services for drug-exposed infants and their families to try to keep the infants with their biological parents (Tittle & Claire, 1989). The clinic offers medical services, parenting education, psychological support groups and individual counseling, and social events. So far, this model is working successfully.

### AIDS Exposure

Human immune deficiency virus (HIV) is the virus that causes acquired immune deficiency syndrome (AIDS) (*Testing HIV Positive*, 2005). HIV can be treated to prevent the onset of AIDS. AIDS results from the destruction of the immune system. Without the immune system, the body cannot fight off infections and cancer. Babies born to HIV/AIDS-infected mothers should receive an immediate checkup and treatment as needed. These infants should not be breastfed because HIV could be transmitted through the milk (*HIV Positive Women and Their Babies After Birth*, 2005).

With the increase in prenatal AIDS exposure, postnatal or pediatric AIDS (AIDS contracted by children younger than thirteen) has become a problem of epidemic proportions. These children show significant developmental delays in cognitive and motor areas. As more effective therapies have been developed, new problems have surfaced in the areas of growth, body composition, and metabolism (*Growth, Body Composition, and Metabolism*, 2005). More details will be included in chapters on physical growth, health, and nutrition. Prevention needs as much attention as we can provide. Teenagers are especially vulnerable and need to be educated regarding steps they can take to avoid HIV/AIDS, namely to abstain from sex and avoid sharing drug needles. In addition, they should avoid drugs and alcohol altogether because these substances lower resistance and cloud decision making. This advice applies to adults as well as teens; HIV/AIDS can be transmitted at any age.

## SUMMARY

At the moment of conception, hereditary factors from the mother and the father merge into a new individual. Both heredity and environment are influenced by the process of development. Although some characteristics, such as eye and hair color, are basically set, others may develop along different paths depending on the interaction of heredity and environment as the developmental process occurs.

Genetics is the study of the transmission of hereditary characteristics to living organisms. Progress in genetic study is increasing the capability to identify genetic predisposition to abnormalities or to disease before or shortly after conception. New discoveries in biotechnology are providing opportunities for gene therapy. Gene therapy can modify and even eliminate genes that may make a person prone to a particular disease or disability. The Human Genome Project has supplied us with an enormous amount of information regarding human genetics.

Genetic counselors use the information gained from genetic testing to assist couples in making decisions regarding attempts to conceive a child or carry a child with a defect to full term.

There are many dangers in the environment that can harm children. Methamphetamine and AIDS are particularly widespread and dangerous for children.

## For Further Reading


Coll, C. G., Bearer, E. L., & Lerner, R. M. (Eds.). (2004). *Nature and nurture: The complex interplay of genetic and environmental influences on human behavior and development*. Mahwah, NJ: Erlbaum.

Golombok, S., Cook, R., Bish, A., & Murray, C. (1995). Families created by the new reproductive technologies: Quality of parenting and social and emotional development of the children. *Child Development, 66*, 285–298.

Harwood, M., & Kleinfeld, J. S. (2002). Up front in hope: The value of early intervention for children with Fetal Alcohol Syndrome. *Young Children, 57*(4), 86–90.

Horowitz, F. D. (2000). Child development and the PITS: Simple questions, complex answers, and developmental theory. *Child Development, 71*(1), 1–10.

Hur, Y., & Bouchard, T. J., Jr. (1995). Genetic influences on perceptions of childhood family environment: A reared apart twin study. *Child Development, 66*, 330–345.

Lamb, M., Bornstein, M. H., & Teti, D. (2002). *Development in infancy* (4th ed.). Mahwah, NJ: Erlbaum.

Lippa, R. A. (2005). *Gender, nature and nurture* (2nd ed.). Mahwah, NJ: Erlbaum.

Marteau, T., & Richards, M. (Eds.). (1996). *The troubled helix: Social and psychological implications of the new human genetics*. New York: Cambridge University Press.

Plomin, R. (1994). *Genetics and experience*. Thousand Oaks, CA: Sage.

Plomin, R., & McClearn, G. E. (Eds.). (1994). *Nature, nurture, and psychology*. Hyattsville, MD: American Psychological Association.

Riese, M. L. (1990). Neonatal temperament in monozygotic and dizygotic twin pairs. *Child Development, 61*, 1230–1237.

Rutter, M. (2005). *Genes and behavior: The working of nature-nurture interplay*. Williston, VT: Blackwell.

Rutter, M. (2002). Nature, nurture and development: From evangelism through science toward policy and practice. *Child Development, 73*(1), 1–21.

Steinberg, S., & Avenevoli, S. (2000). The role of context in the development of psychopathology: A conceptual framework and some speculative propositions. *Child Development, 71*(1), 66–74.

Tomasello, M., & Slobin, D. I. (Eds.). (2004). *Beyond nature-nurture*. Mahwah, NJ: Erlbaum.


## Suggested Activities

1. Interview a genetic counselor. Find out whether more couples visit before marriage, after marriage but before conceiving, or after conception. Ask if many single women seek advice. Under what circumstances does the counselor believe that abortion is warranted? Share the results with the class.

2. Find a research study in one of the areas of potential prenatal danger, such as nutrition, maternal characteristics, maternal experiences, drugs, or disease. Write a report that includes the following:
   a. title
   b. author(s)
   c. journal, date, and pages
   d. a short summary
   e. an evaluation of the study and its implications
   f. a discussion of whether the study supports what is stated in this text
   g. a discussion of what you learned that helps you understand the area better

3. Make an entry in your journal.

## REVIEW

1. List the goals of the Human Genome Project.
2. Explain what is meant by the following: The adult who works with young children must be aware of each child's prior medical history.
3. Indicate which of the following characteristics is determined more strongly by heredity than environment, if the environment is a healthy one:
   a. physical size
   b. eye color
   c. hair color
   d. disposition (i.e., happy or cranky)
   e. skin color
4. Explain how heredity and environment might relate to the developmental process for the children in the following situations.
   a. Jenny and Joanie are identical twins. Jenny is delivered first. Jenny is always referred to as "the older girl." At age three, Joanie is much more active and difficult to control than Jenny. Joanie is also more babyish and less independent than Jenny.
   b. Brad's father is a professional football player, his mother, a dancer. Both parents are very concerned about good nutrition and getting plenty of physical activity.
   c. Mary's mother and father are both average in size and build. They are struggling to make ends meet and have little money for nutritious foods, such as fresh fruits and vegetables and whole-grain breads and cereals. They also tend to waste much of their meager food budget on junk foods, such as candy and potato chips.
   d. Donnie's mother was a drug and alcohol abuser before and during his pregnancy. She shared drug needles with numerous friends.
5. Define the terms *gene*, *chromosome*, *DNA*, *gene therapy*, and *genetic discrimination*. Explain how they are related.
6. Write the letter of each case that requires a genetic counselor.
   a. A pregnant woman is over 40 years of age.
   b. An engaged man has an uncle who had cystic fibrosis.
   c. A newborn is found to be deaf.
   d. A couple is curious as to whether their future children are more likely to have green eyes and red hair like the father or brown eyes and black hair like the mother.
   e. A child is born with underdeveloped legs.
7. Describe the dangers of substance abuse.

## KEY TERMS LIST

amniocentesis
behavioral geneticists
chorionic villus sampling (CVS)
chromosomes
dizygotic (DZ) siblings
DNA
environmental
gene
genetics
genotype
germ-line gene therapy
hereditary
interactionist
methamphetamine
monozygotic (MZ) siblings
nature versus nurture
phenotype
sonography
ultrasound

Additional resources for this chapter can be found on the Online Companion™ to accompany this text at http://www.earlychilded.delmar.com. Respond to "Time to Reflect" and "Looking Further" concepts, review various child development scenarios, and answer thought-provoking questions in the Critical Thinking Forum. Keep a daily journal by downloading the student journal available on this Web site. Complete the interactive matching exercises to reinforce concepts, and print out the child development assessment forms to use during your observation of development for children from birth to age eight. In addition, read the case studies on the Web site to reinforce the important concepts in each chapter, and take a look at the multitude of Web links that are available for student research on the Internet.

CHAPTER

# 10

# Birth and the First Two Weeks

## OBJECTIVES

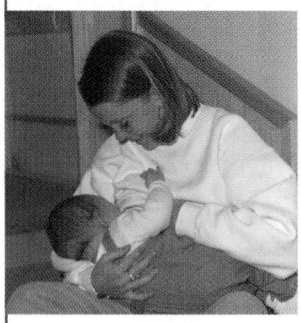

After reading this chapter, you should be able to:

- State the environmental changes that take place at birth for the newborn.
- Recognize the attributes of the Leboyer method of delivery and state its advantages.
- Identify the important aspects of the neonatal period.
- Recognize the state of arousal.
- Discuss how heredity and environment affect temperament.
- Describe how to assist the families of premature and full-term low-birth-weight infants to overcome the initial difficulties of parenting and provide needed developmentally supportive interactions.
- Discuss the responsibilities to the neonate and the neonate's family of the adult who works with the young child.

Soon-to-be Grandma waits anxiously for the first view of her newly born granddaughter, Summer Sky. Through the window overlooking the area where the newborns are checked in, she sees her son-in-law approaching, carefully cradling Summer in his arms. Mom had to have a cesarean, so Dad has the honor of introducing his daughter to the world. While it is usual for the nurse to offer a pink ribbon, dad selects a blue ribbon for his little daughter. He carries Summer into Mom, who is just waking from the anesthetic. In the hall, Grandma hears a squeal of delight. Thus, a life has begun, and parents and child form their first bond.

In another setting, a trained doula, an experienced woman who helps calm other women during the birth process, provides emotional support and bonds with a woman in labor (Tonti, 1998, TX3).

> Sensing the mother's pain, the trained doula slowly brushes aside a soft curl of this mother's hair. She soothes the mother's anguish by staying close by her side. With a calm word, the doula gently kisses the forehead of the mother-to-be.

The doula does not deliver the child, but provides support and information before, during, and after the birth of the baby to keep the mother calm and to support the initial bonding between parent(s) and child.

The parents have already developed expectations regarding their baby. The mother's competence as a caregiver is confirmed each time the baby responds to her. For example, the baby responds with cuddling when held or turns his or her head at the sound of the mother's voice (Brazelton & Cramer, 1990). These positive responses from the infant tell the mother that she is "doing the right thing" (Brazelton & Cramer, 1990, p. 46).

The first two weeks of life outside the womb are exciting and critical for the developing child, having entered the world through the process of birth. Once born, this tiny person is called a **newborn.** For the first two weeks, the term **neonate** is used; the two-week period is called the **neonatal period.** During these first two weeks, neonates must be watched closely to be sure they have a good start in life.

**newborn**
A child who has just been born.

**neonate**
A child from birth to two weeks of age.

**neonatal period**
The first two weeks of newborn life.

## BIRTH

Does the child have a pleasant experience entering the world? If not, how can it be improved? First, consider the great change that takes place from prenatal to postnatal life. The child's environment changes from the uterus and its surrounding amniotic fluid to air. The temperature changes from a relatively constant one to one that changes often. This small being moves from a state of minimal stimulation to one in which all the senses are stimulated. For nutrition, there is a change from a dependence on nutrients from the mother's blood to a dependence on food from outside and on the functioning of the neonate's own digestive system. Oxygen no longer passes from the mother's blood through the placenta to the unborn. The neonate's lungs must now operate and send oxygen to the blood. Waste materials no longer pass into the mother's bloodstream through the placenta; the neonate's own elimination system must take on this job. The neonate's own skin, kidneys, lungs, and intestinal system must start to work. Without doubt, the change from prenatal to postnatal life is a big one. The question that must be dealt with is how to make the process of birth and the move into postnatal life as comfortable as possible for the child and the parents (Figure 10–1).

Not every birth scene is warm and exciting or calm and supportive. In the past, there was criticism that certain common methods of delivery and postdelivery treatment were much too hard on both the child and parents (Newton, 1975). Negative factors included separating the mother from her family during labor and childbirth, confining the normal laboring woman to bed, stimulating labor with chemicals, routinely using forceps for delivery, and separating the mother from her newborn infant. Others included delaying the first breast-feeding, restricting infants to four-hour feeding schedules and withholding night feedings, and limiting visits by the baby's sisters and brothers.

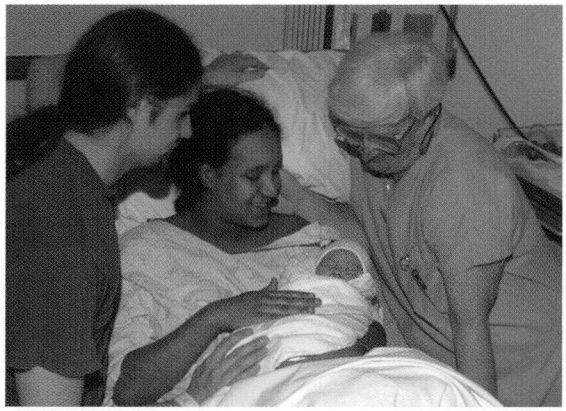

FIGURE 10–1 For everyone involved, delivery has become a much more pleasant experience than it used to be.

Leboyer (1976) believes the infant is upset by the bright lights, noise, and rough handling he or she receives just after emerging from the womb. Leboyer devised a method of delivery in which participants try to make the change from the womb to the outside world relaxed and happy, with as little environmental change as possible. The lights are dim, the baby is placed on the mother's stomach so that he or she is in contact with her body and the rhythm of her heartbeat. The umbilical cord remains attached until the baby has had some time to get used to the new surroundings. The child is gently massaged to soothe and calm him or her.

Although the pure Leboyer method has not become popular in the United States, Leboyer's ideas have prompted medical personnel to modify the atmosphere of the delivery environment. In the 1970s, home birth became popular. However, the dangers of delivering with no medical monitoring were perceived to both outweigh the advantages of women having more control over the birth process and the lower cost. As an alternative that offered a homelike atmosphere with medical safeguards, birthing centers opened around the country. Birthing center deliveries are quite popular (Fogel, 2001; Jones, 1990). At the birthing center, a midwife usually assists with the delivery, and medical assistance is available if needed. The father may bathe the mother and the newborn child. As soon as two hours after the delivery, the family may be ready to go home. In the Leboyer method, the mother is immersed in water and the infant emerges from the liquid environment of the womb into the water. Research on **water birth** indicates that it is not as safe as traditional child birth (American Academy of Pediatrics, 2002). There have been reports of deaths due to poorly managed water births and there is no evidence that the duration of labor is reduced, that there are less injuries to the birth canal, or that fewer painkillers are needed.

**water birth**

The mother is immersed in water and the infant emerges from the liquid environment of the womb into the water.

There are a number of problems that can occur during delivery. For example, breech presentation may occur (ACOG, 2002). Usually, the baby moves into a head-down position in the woman's uterus three or four weeks before birth. In about 3 percent of full-term births, the baby doesn't turn, and buttocks, feet, or both may be in place to come out first. About half the time, the doctor can turn the baby before birth. The problem with the breech birth is that the head, which is the largest and firmest part of the body, emerges last. It may be more difficult to get it through the birth canal, and the cord may get bent, cutting off the flow of blood to the baby. Cesarean delivery is probably the best option for a breech birth. Recent research has indicated that time of day for delivery may be a factor in outcomes for the newborn. Babies born at night have a greater risk of death than babies born in the daytime (ACOG, 2005). On the positive side, whereas in the past it was recommended that pregnant women engage in minimal exercise, currently 30 minutes each day of moderate exercise is recommended. Further, air travel is now considered safe for up to 36 weeks gestation (ACOG, 2001).

Birthing centers have become so popular that even hospitals are now including birthing centers as an option for parents. The work of Klaus and Kennell on parent-infant bonding has also influenced the trend toward increased humanization of infant delivery methods and improvement of the delivery room atmosphere (Goldberg, 1983). A report in the August 2002 issue of the journal *Obstetrics & Gynecology* (American College of Obstetrics and Gynecologists, 2002) indicates that newborns born at home have nearly twice the chance of dying as newborns born in a hospital. Newborns born at home also have a higher risk for low Apgar scores. Mothers were also found to have more problems, such as prolonged labor and after-birth bleeding.

There are also a number of other delivery options available to expectant mothers (Yarro, 1977). With **cesarean sections,** which are used for potentially difficult births, the baby is removed from the uterus surgically. Lamaze preparation for childbirth is very popular. The mother and her coach take a 3–12 week course that introduces them to the details of labor and delivery. The mother learns how to control and relax her muscles and what kind of physical exercise is appropriate. The father learns how to assist her during labor and delivery. There has been a movement toward **natural childbirth,** which is birth without the aid of drugs for pain reduction. Many hospitals allow older siblings to be present at birth, to visit the mother in her room, and to view their new brother or sister in the hospital nursery. Rooms are being set up in some hospitals where the whole family can

**cesarean section**

Removing the baby from the uterus using a surgical method.

**natural childbirth**

Birth without the aid of drugs for pain reduction.

participate in the delivery. Some doctors even train fathers to deliver their own children with supervision (Steinman, 1979). More hospitals are also providing rooming-in, where the baby stays in the same room as the mother.

Describe your opinion of conventional hospital delivery as compared with home and birthing center delivery.

## THE NEONATE

The newborn emerges wet with amniotic fluid (Fogel, 2001). The skin may be pale to pink (even for parents of color). The newborn may also be slightly yellow due to **normal physiological jaundice.** According to Fogel (2001), this problem is caused by unbalanced liver function and is easily treated under special lamps. The eyes usually are smoky blue and may not change to their natural color until nearly the end of the first year. The head is large compared to the rest of the body, and the newborn has little, if any, control of it. The legs are usually bowed and bent so the soles of the feet are parallel. Typically, the neck is short, there is no chin, and the nose is flat. The head may be somewhat misshapen for a short time. Newborns have six soft spots on the top of their heads. These soft spots are called **fontanels.** They allow for flexibility during birth and for brain growth. They usually close by 18 months.

**normal physiologic jaundice**
Slightly yellowish skin color caused by unbalanced liver function.

**fontanels**
The six soft spots on top of the heads of newborns.

As already described, the newborn goes through many changes in environment and bodily functions within a very short time. Once born, the child must be watched carefully, especially during the first five minutes. It is essential that the newborn's vital signs be monitored. The usual means for monitoring the vital signs is by use of the **Apgar scale** (Apgar, 1953; Apgar & Beck, 1973). With this scale, the obstetric team ensures that the infant is ready for life outside the uterus. Heart rate, respiratory effort, muscle tone, color, and reflexes are checked at one minute and five minutes after delivery (Figure 10–2). A score of four or less out of a possible 10 indicates the newborn needs immediate help. Most infants have scores of seven or above.

**Apgar scale**
The usual means for monitoring the vital signs of a newborn.

| | Apgar Score | | |
|---|---|---|---|
| Sign | 0 | 1 | 2 |
| Pulse (heart rate) | Absent | Slow (<100) | Rapid (>100) |
| Appearance (skin color) | Body is blue | Body pink, arms and legs blue | Entirely pink |
| Activity (muscle tone) | Flaccid, limp, motionless | Some movement of arms and legs but weak and inactive | Strong, active overall body motions |
| Reflexes (grimaces when slapped on the feet) | No response | Grimace or slight cry | Vigorous crying |
| Respiration (breathing) | Absent (no respiration) | Slow, irregular breathing | Effort to breathe is strong with vigorous crying |

FIGURE 10–2 The Apgar scale is used to check the readiness of the newborn to join the world. Each vital sign is rated from zero to two, with the highest possible total score being 10.

**states of arousal**

Infant degrees of being awake or asleep.

Newborn infants move in and out of five different **states of arousal** or degrees of being asleep or awake (Berk, 1998, pp. 106–107). The five states are as follows (Berk, 1998, p. 106):

1. *Regular sleep* is when the infant is at full rest. There is little, if any, body movement; the eyes are closed; breathing is slow and regular; and the face is relaxed (eight to nine hours).
2. *Irregular sleep* is characterized by gentle limb movements, occasional stirring, and facial grimaces. The eyes are closed, but some rapid eye movement (REM) may occur, and breathing is irregular (eight to nine hours).
3. *Drowsiness* is the state where the infant is either just waking up or is falling asleep. The infant is less active than in irregular sleep but more active than in regular sleep. The eyes open and close; when open, they have a glazed look. Breathing is even but faster than in regular sleep (time varies).
4. *Quiet alertness* is a state of relative inactivity, with eyes open and attentive. Breathing is even (two to three hours).
5. *Waking activity and crying is* characterized by frequent bursts of uncoordinated body activity, irregular breathing, relaxed or tense, wrinkled facial expression, and possibly crying (one to four hours).

During the first month, most of the infant's time is spent in sleep, but each infant has a unique daily rhythm that may affect adult attitudes and behavior. For example, if infants spend long periods in sleep, their caretakers can get plenty of rest and are patient with their caregiving duties. If infants spend more time awake and are fussy and crying, their caregivers may be tired, irritable, and not as calm and patient in their caregiving routines.

**bonding**

The process whereby parents and child determine they are special to each other.

Several factors concerning the newborn's emotional state are important during the first two weeks. These factors are bonding, responsiveness and sensitivity, and temperament. **Bonding** is the process whereby parents and child determine they are special to each other. When the concept of bonding was first introduced by Klaus and Kennell in the 1970s, it was thought there was a critical period immediately after birth during which bonding had to take place. For example, Summer and her Mom and Dad, as described in the beginning of this chapter, would be forming such a bond. It was believed the initial shared glance formed the basis of the bond (Spezzano & Waterman, 1977). However, this point of view has since been modified (Fogel, 2001; Goldberg, 1983; Palkovitz, 1985). Bonding does not have to take place in one critical moment. However, a strong bond is the foundation for later development of attachment (Fogel, 2001). Attachment is an enduring emotional bond between two people that develops over time and supports the development of affectionate ties with additional people during the life span. Attachment is discussed in more detail in later chapters.

From her 1983 research review, Goldberg concluded that the popularization of Klaus and Kennell's findings (1982) had both positive and negative effects on the beliefs of both medical personnel and the public. On the positive side, delivery became much more humane, especially with fathers being encouraged to participate. The evidence suggests that having the father present during delivery and providing early parent-child contacts has many positive effects on the family. However, if for some reason, such as Cesarean delivery or a premature birth, this contact is not immediately possible, it will not cause irreparable damage to the parent-child relationship. Parents have been made to feel unnecessarily guilty and upset over missing an immediate contact experience. Klaus and Kennell changed their definition of the term *bonding* to refer to the long-term development of relationships rather than to just the immediate postdelivery relationship (Goldberg, 1983). Unfortunately, the term *bonding*, defined as the development of an immediate postdelivery connection between mother and child, continued in the popular press (Wheeler, 1993). Dr. Diane Eyer, who has written a book on the scientific fictional nature of bonding, suggests the term has been so extended into a description of any close relationship that it should be done away with as a term in developmental psychology (as cited in Wheeler, 1993).

An infant with special needs results in some unique effects on the family (Fogel, 2001). Family members may feel sorrow or depression, emotionally reject the infant, have difficulty in adapting, and find their interpersonal relationships are strained. Strong emotions may be aroused, such as parents feeling like they "caused" the problem. They also may be overwhelmed by the special care needed, such as extra doctor and hospital visits, special difficulties such as soiling and wetting, special housing or equipment needs, financial hardships, special care arrangements, special clothing, and special transportation. Parental stress may carry over to other children, who may receive less attention and suffer social and emotional difficulties. Parent-infant interaction may also lack positive responses from the infant, thereby bringing less positive responses from the parent and resulting in weak bonds and weak attachment relationships. The more severe the disability, the stronger the negative effects usually are. In comparing premature infants with full-term infants, no difference in parent-child interactions is usually evident by 12 months of age. The more typical the baby's social interactions, the more likely a positive relationship with caregivers will develop.

## Premature Infants

**premature infant**
A child born before the completion of the 40-week gestation period.

The child born prior to the completion of the 40-week gestation period, the **premature infant,** most medical experts believe needs the full 40 weeks in the womb and that being born too soon is associated with some high-risk factors. Duffy, Als, and McAnulty (1990) compared healthy preterm and full-term infants at 42 weeks postconception. They found some significant differences between the two groups in several developmental areas. The preterm (premature) infants showed more stress in making the transition from sleep to wakeful behavior. They also evidenced some motor and neurological difficulties. Portions of the brain are smaller in premature children as compared with those who were full term (Portions of brain, 2004). The brain volumes of the two types of eight-year-olds were compared. Areas of the cerebral cortex that control reading, language, emotion, and behavior were reduced for the children who were born prematurely. Boys were missing more white brain material than girls. It has long been recognized that premature males have more reading and emotional problems than do premature girls. Some of the differences may be caused by medical complications that usually accompany premature delivery, whereas others may be caused by the early change of environment.

Advances continue to be made in the treatment of premature infants (Shiono & Behrman, 1995). Improvements have been made in neonatal intensive care, including advances in technology. However, low-birth-weight delivery rates continue to be high. Although all the causes of low birth weight have not been pinpointed, approximately 20 percent of low-birth-weight babies are born to mothers who smoke during pregnancy. It is disturbing to note that African American babies are twice as likely as white babies to be born with low birth weights, be preterm, and die at birth. Shiono and Behrman state that preventing prenatal smoking by the mother and improving prenatal care would cut the low-birth-weight rate considerably. Following birth, successful medical technologies need to be identified; better medical care needs to be found for the most immature, malformed, or sick infants; more programs must be made available to support parents; and society needs to be more committed to the long-term welfare of low-birth-weight and preterm infants.

Preterm neonates who received tactile stimulation while in the neonatal intensive care unit (NICU) benefitted significantly (Kilgo, Holder-Brown, Johnson, & Cook, 1988; McNichol, 1998). The tactile stimulation consisted of both stroking and motor movement exercises. Touch is an extremely powerful stimulant (Ackerman, 1990). Tiffany Field and her colleagues (Field, Hernandez-Reif, & Freedman, 2004) strongly promoted massage for stimulation of premature infants. Besides massaging, doctors have discovered that putting premature infants on small, gently swaying waterbeds makes them less irritable, enables them to sleep better, and makes them more alert and responsive. Jayne M. Standley (2002) promotes the use of music as a noninvasive nurturing stimulus that is therapeutic in the NICU environment. Music has been found to reduce the length of stay in the NICU and improve sucking rates, increase oxygen saturation, and support **homeostasis** or the tendency of an organism to maintain internal stability.

**homeostasis**

The tendency of an organism to maintain internal stability.

A form of drug assistance for very premature infants born between the twenty-fourth and thirty-second weeks of gestation has shown impressive results (Kantrowitz with Crandall, 1990). **Exosurf®** is a drug that helps babies form surfactant, a substance usually produced in the lungs by the time the fetus is 32 weeks into gestation. This substance coats the inner lining of the lungs and keeps the airspaces from collapsing. Surfactant is necessary for the baby to breathe. Premature infants often are born before enough surfactant has developed, causing serious and sometimes fatal breathing problems. Therefore, Exosurf® is a boon to infants born with lack of surfactant in the lungs.

**Exosurf®**

A drug that helps babies form surfactant to coat the inner lining of the lungs and keep the airspaces from collapsing.

Support for the parents of premature infants is essential. Brazelton and Cramer (1990) describe the feelings of the parents of a premature daughter. Clarissa was delivered at 27 weeks of gestation. She was severely distressed. At one minute, her Apgar score was five, and at five minutes, it was seven. She had severe medical complications that required surgery and antibiotics. The parents visited her regularly during her time in neonatal intensive care. They were a part of Clarissa's therapy and were involved when the **Neonatal Behavior Assessment Scale (NBAS)** was administered. (See page 191 for a description of the NBAS.) By having a close working relationship with the medical team, they were better able to handle Clarissa's developmental problems. In addition, they were able to recognize her behavioral progress and the significance of the smallest developmental increments. They also learned to view Clarissa as a challenge, rather than as a burden, and to accept her fussiness and moodiness as typical premature behavior. Because premature infants tend to be fussy, irritable, more exhausting, and less fun for their parents than full-term babies, they may not get the tactile and social stimulation they so desperately need. On the other hand, babies who are premature or otherwise stressed during delivery may be oversensitive to every stimulus in the environment and can be calmed by being placed in a low-stimulation setting (Brazelton, 1992). Barry and Singer (2001) found that a brief period of daily journal writing reduced the stress levels of mothers whose newborns had been in the NICU. Community support (Greenwald, 2003) can improve the developmental prospects for premature children. A transdisciplinary team of mental health specialists, health specialists, and developmental specialists can work together collaborating on NICU follow-up with families.

**Neonatal Behavior Assessment Scale (NBAS)**

A dynamic assessment of interactive behavior used to indicate the degree of control the newborn has over his or her sensory capacities.

Visit a hospital maternity ward, including the NICU. Through the observation windows, observe infants in the maternity nursery and in the NICU. Closely observe at least one infant in each unit. Note any differences in appearance and movements. Note the equipment used in the NICU. Are the infants responding to light, sound, touch, or any other stimuli? Describe your responses to this experience.

## Infant Sensitivity

Infant sensitivity and responsiveness should not be underestimated. Infants are not, as some once thought, "lumps of clay to be molded by their environment—for better or for worse" (Brazelton, 1977). Babies are powerful influences on their environments. Adults who understand this quality in the infant can use it to advantage in developing a relationship. The neonate has many built-in strengths. At birth, the infant responds to voices, looks at human faces, shows a preference for milk smells, and distinguishes the taste of breast milk from cow's milk. (Marlier & Schaal, 2005). Newborns are very sensitive to their environment. Touch is important for full-term as well as premature newborns (Carlson, 2005). Touch is very important for brain development. Touch helps infants manage stress, improves their physical health, and supports physical growth. Touch also supports emotional development. Parents can be shown how sensitive and responsive their newborn is, thereby viewing the child as a person to whom they can relate. This knowledge ties them more closely to their young child. Parents can learn to note and react to responses, as shown in the following examples.

> Mother shakes a rattle softly by neonate's ear. Neonate jerks as if startled and turns his head toward the sound.
>
> Dad uncovers neonate. Neonate responds by moving arms and legs about.
>
> As mother undresses neonate, she notes that he responds with resistance to the restriction of his body.
>
> When held in the arms in a cradle or shoulder position, neonate responds by cuddling.
>
> Dad enjoys playing games with neonate. Dad likes to call to him from out of his line of vision and see how he responds by turning toward his father's voice.

Thus, a reciprocal exchange is well under way within the first two weeks of life.

The adult's interpretation of the newborn's cries may be very critical in determining several aspects of the adult-child relationship. Zeskind and Marshall (1988) found that mothers are sensitive to the pitch of newborn infants' cries. Mothers rated infant cries on a seven-point scale: urgent/not urgent, distressing/not distressing, arousing/soothing, and sick/healthy. All the cries were responses to the same pain-causing stimulus. The only differences were in the intensity of each infant's response. The variability of the individual cry seemed to be the best indicator of its seriousness. Infants with more variability in their cries may receive more attention. They may also receive more positive attention and stimulation if the cry is low pitched. More negative attention might be received if the parent finds the cry irritating and stressful. An irritating cry would also have a better chance of being ignored and, thus, deprive the baby of essential stimulation.

A growing body of neonate research is documenting just how sensitive neonates are to the world around them. Brazelton and Cramer (1990) describe the five senses as they function in the newborn child. Newborns are definitely capable of being visually alert. When babies are picked up and rocked, their eyes open and they look ready for interaction. The ability to see in the delivery room may be an important factor in the bonding process. The eye-to-eye contact with the newborn reinforces attachment. Even newborns are fascinated by the human face and show a preference for real faces versus drawn faces. Newborns try to keep interesting objects in view and display tracking behavior when the objects move.

The capability of newborns to hear is also apparent at birth. They show a preference for female voices. They find auditory stimuli interesting and will look alert and turn toward a soft rattle or human voice. Right after birth, infants will synchronize their movements to their mothers' voices. Newborns are attracted to sweet smells, such as milk or sugar solutions, and turn away from unpleasant odors, such as vinegar and alcohol. They even seem to be able to distinguish the odor of their own mother's milk from other mothers' milk and from formula. Babies will resist saltwater, whereas they will suck faster for sugar water. They also appear to recognize their mothers through both sound and smell. As already mentioned, newborns are sensitive to touch. This is an important means of communication between the infant and caregiver. Slow patting is soothing, whereas fast patting alerts the baby. Touch can also heal (McNichol, 1998). It improves the status of premature infants and also increases immune function, reduces stress, and improves task-oriented behavior and social behavior of autistic children. McNichol points out that compared with other cultures, Americans are touch-deprived. The United States has one of the lowest rates of casual touch in the world, about twice per hour. Puerto Rico, on the other hand, has one of the highest rates, at 180 times per hour. Unfortunately, Americans' concern with inappropriate touch has led to "teach, don't touch" policies. Teachers are afraid even to place a hand on the shoulder of a crying child. Before birth, the infant establishes hand-to-mouth sensitivity. Contact between hand and mouth seems to serve the purposes of self-comfort, control over motor activity, and self-stimulation. The senses are all at work for the newborn. Neonates are responsive to stress experiences, according to the results of studies by Gunnar, Porter, Wolf, Rigatuso, and Larson (1995) and Davis and Emory (1995). Gunnar et al. found that, although all infants respond to stress (i.e., increased heartbeat, louder crying, and chemical responses), individual recovery time varies greatly. Davis and Emory found gender differences in comparing the physiological stress responses of males and females.

## Infant Temperament

**temperament**
Distinctive personal characteristics a child is born with that seem to stay with him or her throughout development.

**easy child**
A child who falls easily into routines, is happy, and adapts well.

**difficult child**
A child who has difficulty with routines and does not adapt easily to new experiences.

**slow-to-warm-up child**
A child who is inactive, reacts mildly to environmental stimuli, has a negative mood, and is slow to adjust to new experiences.

The quality of the relationship between the adult and infant is influenced by the child's **temperament.** The New York Longitudinal Study (Thomas & Chess, 1977, as cited in Berk, 1998) is the longest–running study of temperament. Children were followed from infancy to adulthood. They found that temperament is a major factor in children's probability of experiencing psychological problems or coping well with stresses. However, they also found that parenting practices can modify temperament. Most children fell into three types of temperament. The **easy child** (40 percent of sample) falls easily into routines, is happy, and adapts well. The **difficult child** (10 percent of sample) has difficulty with routines, does not adapt to new experiences, and tends to react negatively and intensively to anything new. The **slow-to-warm-up child** (15 percent of the sample) is inactive, reacts mildly to environmental stimuli, has a negative mood, and is slow to adjust to new experiences. The rest of the children (35 percent) did not fall strictly into any one of these patterns but demonstrated many combinations of patterns. In any case, children are born with distinctive personal characteristics that seem to stay with them as they grow. Some children are "difficult;" some are "easy." Some are active and some are passive. Neonatal temperament at the extremes tends to be positively related to later temperament (Berk, 1998). For example, Korner et al. (1993) explain that when observed during normal activity between the ages of four and eight, children who were the most active as neonates tend to still be the most active. Whether this is due to biological factors (heredity) or environmental factors, such as parent expectation, is still open to debate.

The child who is a quiet, slow reactor may not get as many positive responses from adults as the child who is outgoing and quick. The "difficult" infant is more

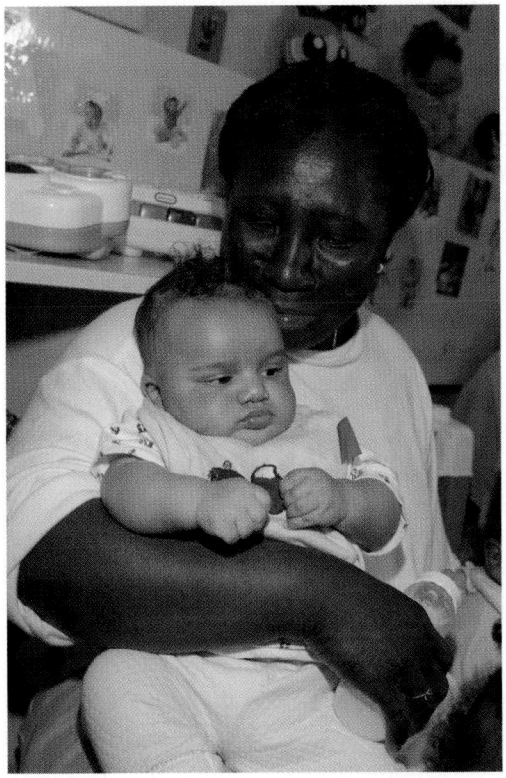

FIGURE 10–3 Early attachment forms the basis for a healthy, enjoyable relationship between parent and child.

likely to grow up with emotional problems because he or she elicits negative responses from others. Adults need to recognize that each child is born with different characteristics and should be treated as an individual, as shown in the following examples:

> Katie is a laughing, easygoing baby. She is alert and very responsive to adults. She gets a lot of adult attention. Her mother can hardly stand to stay away from her when she's awake.
>
> Mary is quiet and docile. Adults have to work hard at relating to her. Her mother takes advantage of her passiveness and spends little time in play activities with her.
>
> Gary is active and alert. At one week, his eyes dart about and his limbs always seem to be moving. His quiet, shy mother is already overwhelmed by his energy: "I can hardly change his diaper, he's so wiggly."

One mother interacts with her child, another ignores her, and the third tries, but is frustrated.

Neonates are complex individuals. They are born with their own personality characteristics. They are sensitive to their environment and ready to interact and form a bond with the adults they meet. The adult's responsibility is to get to know the newborn and be ready for the give-and-take of a close, rewarding relationship (Figure 10–3). With some adult-child pairs, attachment is immediate. For others, love grows more slowly.

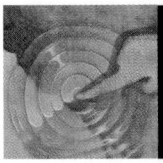

**LOOKING FURTHER**

Timmy and his mother have a cold, distant relationship. Timmy was premature and spent his first month in the NICU. His mother is expecting another child. His teacher is concerned that Timmy's mother may have the same relationship with the next child. Why might she think this way? As you read the section "Professional Responsibilities: the Neonate and the Parent," apply the information to Timmy's mother's situation and decide what you believe are the teacher's responsibilities. What kind of action plan would you suggest to the teacher?

## Neonatal Assessment

Assessment of the newborn's behavior can help caregivers understand the baby and ascertain any damage caused by prenatal environmental problems, such as discussed in Chapter 8. It has already been noted that premature birth is related to developmental difficulties. Low Apgar scores may also indicate future problems. Brazelton and Cramer (1990) believe that a thorough behavioral assessment is most useful for predicting future development. For this purpose, Brazelton and his colleagues designed the NBAS.

The NBAS is designed as a dynamic assessment of interactive behavior. The assessment incorporates the same types of stimuli parents use, such as touch, rocking, voice, facial movement, bright colors, bright light, and temperature change. The NBAS responses indicate the degree of control the newborn has over his or her sensory capacities. It is very useful for helping parents understand their baby and for identifying infants whose behavior may be difficult for parents to handle. Through understanding the difficulties their infant is having, parents can feel less discouraged and frustrated when the baby does not react as expected. Hypersensitive and disorganized babies are hard to understand and to cope with. They overreact to stimuli and change quickly from sleep to crying and back to sleep without affording the parents time for fun and play.

## PROFESSIONAL RESPONSIBILITIES: THE NEONATE AND THE PARENT

Some parents need help learning how to relate to their new baby. The adult who works with young children has the responsibility of helping parents learn about child development and how to apply this knowledge to interact with and understand their child from birth. The adult who works with young children also has the responsibility of helping parents and children get other professional help if needed. When a child is expected, you can help parents get training in how to relate to children from birth. Parents need to understand that the neonate is a complex, active person who can benefit from active involvement with people and the environment.

In his presidential address to the Society for Research in Child Development in April 1989, T. Berry Brazelton (1990) emphasized our increasing problems with damaged infants. In Boston, 25 percent of newborns were addictive at birth. With their damaged nervous systems, they did not respond positively to caregiver overtures. Caregivers must understand that damaged infants may be difficult to work with and demand a great deal of patience. Brazelton's goal is to develop both a preventative and an intervention model for attacking this problem.

Federal legislation (discussed previously in Chapter 7) mandates that each state develop a plan for providing continuous services for at-risk infants and toddlers and their families from birth through school age. However, a problem has arisen regarding which agencies are obliged to deliver which particular services at each level. For example, Cardinal and Shum (1993) surveyed NICUs in California to discover the types of services being provided to high-risk infants. They found that there was good support while the infant was in the NICU, some support for the transition from NICU to home, and very little support and follow-up after the infant was home. Surveying the research on the effectiveness of existing NICU interventions, O'Brien and Dale (1994) found very few studies had been done. The few available studies indicated that the programs focused on the infants, with little, or no, support to the families.

Hughes and McCollum (1994) interviewed mothers and fathers regarding their perceptions of what was stressful during their child's first few weeks in the NICU. Mothers identified five major stress areas: (1) infant's appearance, health, and course of hospitalization; (2) separation from infant/not feeling like a parent; (3) communications with and/or the actions of the medical staff; (4) financial concerns; and (5) the NICU environment and equipment. A large percentage of fathers also saw 1 and 2 as stressors but were more spread out across other areas in their concerns. Mothers reported significantly more stressors than did fathers. Both mothers and fathers reported stressors outside of the immediate medical situation. For example, siblings were not allowed in the NICU, so finding child care was a problem. Hence, on-site drop-in care would have been a big help. Many parents believed that their families and friends did not understand what they were experiencing. Thus, an explanatory pamphlet for distribution to family and friends would be helpful. The authors conclude that the medical staff need to be more informative and helpful and less authoritarian in its approach to parents. Meck, Fowler, Claflin, and Rasmussen (1995) interviewed mothers one and seven months after their children's discharge from the NICU. Although mothers received helpful information regarding basic infant care (e.g., bathing, feeding) upon discharge, they were at a loss regarding child development issues, the transfer of medical records, and finances. The authors recommend a stronger informational program for mothers of premature infants.

Besides premature infants, many other children are born with special needs. Educational intervention programs for these parents are essential. Fogel (2001, p. 351) believes that programs should be designed to educate parents about their children's disabilities, to provide emotional support and a support network of other parents with similar problems, and to teach parents how to respond to and anticipate the needs of their individual children. Programs that meet these criteria have been successful. Any parent or potential parent would benefit from an educational program before becoming a parent and after the birth of the baby.

Cynthia T. Garcia Coll (1990) points out that minority infants from lower socioeconomic levels are especially at risk. They are more likely to have the disadvantages associated with being economically deprived, having younger mothers, living in single-parent households, and lacking adequate prenatal care. On the other hand, they may have the advantages of greater extended family support networks. These infants are more likely to be premature, low birth weight, and vulnerable to poor health status. Overall, a larger percentage of minority newborns born into socioeconomically deprived families fall in the high-risk category. On the other hand, there are cultural differences in infants' responses to these dangers to development. Coll suggests the importance of discovering culturally sensitive intervention and prevention strategies. That is, strategies should be compatible with the customs and values of the culture.

## SUMMARY

The first two weeks are an important period in a child's life. Birth is a time of extreme environmental change for the child. In recent years, efforts have been made to make this a less traumatic event than it was in the past. Fathers are more involved in the process of birth, and family members are allowed more contact with the infant immediately following birth. Neonatal research has demonstrated that even during the first two weeks, babies are alert, aware, and sensitive to the environment. They rotate through five states of arousal: regular sleep, irregular sleep, drowsiness, quiet alertness, and waking activity and crying. Temperament characteristics appear during the neonatal period. The three most commonly identified (about 65 percent) types of temperament are the easy child, the difficult child, and the slow-to-warm-up child. Providing a stimulating, warm environment can enhance the development of the child from the time he or she first enters the outside world. During the early weeks, it is important for the primary caregiver to develop a strong bond with the infant. This bond serves as the foundation for lifelong attachments with the primary caregiver and other important people in the child's life.

Premature neonates are at high risk for several factors. Risky medical procedures may be involved in the delivery that will affect their future development, and they may have missed some of the developmental milestones that take place during the normal gestation period. A high percentage of them are the offspring of teenagers from low socioeconomic levels. Furthermore, premature and low-birth-weight, full-term infants tend to be irritable and difficult to parent, leaving them open to more negative attention and more likely to be ignored, so they do not receive the positive stimulation from others that all infants require to thrive. More family support is needed to assist families through the difficulties they may encounter in caring for a premature or full-term, low-birth-weight infant.

## For Further Reading


American Academy of Pediatrics. (2002). *New mother's guide to breastfeeding*. New York: Bantam Books.

Blacher, J. (Ed.). (2000). Families and exceptionality [Special Issue]. *Early Education and Development, 11*(4).

Burgess, T. (2000, Spring). Pre-term delivery: Impact on our families. *Today's Child*, 16–17.

Dundes, L. (2003). *The manner born: Birth rites in cross-cultural perspective*. Walnut Creek, CA: AltaMira Press.

Eyer, D. E. (1992). *Mother-infant bonding: A scientific fiction*. New Haven: Yale University Press.

Goldsmith, H. H., Buss, K. A., & Lemery, K. S. (1997). Toddler and childhood temperament: Expanded content, stronger genetic evidence, new evidence for the importance of environment. *Developmental Psychology, 33*, 891–905.

Klaus, M. H., & Kennell, J. (1982). *Parent-infant bonding* (2nd ed.). St. Louis, MO: Mosby.

Klaus, M. H., & Robertson, M. O. (Eds.). (1982). *Birth, interaction and attachment*. Piscataway, NJ: Johnson and Johnson Child Development.

Koester, L. S., & Koester, O. (2005). *Seeing babies in a new light: The life of Hanus Papousek*. Mahwah, NJ: Erlbaum.

Lewis, V. (2003). *Development and disability*. Malden, MA: Blackwell.

Marlier, L., Schaal, B., & Soussignan, R. (1998). Neonatal responses to the odor of amniotic and lacteal fluids: A test of perinatal chemosensory continuity. *Child Development, 69*, 611–623.

Murray, L., & Cooper, P. J. (1997). *Postpartum depression and child development*. New York: Guilford.

Musical lives of babies and families. (2002). *Zero to Three [Focus issue], 23*(1).

New perspectives on premature babies and their families. (2003). *Zero to Three [Focus issue], 24*(2).

O'Brien, M., Rice, M., & Roy, C. (1996). Defining eligibility criteria for preventive early intervention in an NICU population. *Journal of Early Intervention, 20*, 283–293.

Palkovitz, R. (1985). Fathers' birth attendance, early contact, and extended contact with their newborns: A critical review. *Child Development, 56*, 392–406.

Vergara, E. R., & Bigsby, R. (2004). *Developmental and therapeutic interventions in the NICU*. Baltimore: Brookes.

Widerstrom, A. H., Mowder, B. A., & Sandall, S. R. (1997). *Infant development at risk* (2nd ed.). Baltimore: Brookes.


## Suggested Activities

1. Develop a set of interview questions focusing on the various methods of infant delivery. Interview any two of the following regarding their opinions on delivery environment and procedures: (a) an obstetrician, (b) an obstetric nurse, (c) a pediatrician, (d) a pediatric nurse, (e) a doctor who has a family practice, (f ) a nurse practitioner, (g) a midwife. Evaluate the responses relevant to text and class discussion.

2. Interview six expectant mothers. Find out what kinds of plans they have for delivery.
   a. Are they taking a childbirth preparation class? If so, what are they learning? How do they feel about the class?
   b. What type of delivery is planned?
   c. What role does each see for herself and the father and/or others in her support system during the first two weeks after birth?
   d. How sensitive do they think their newborn will be to sights, sounds, smells, taste, and touch?
   e. Compare and contrast their answers.

3. Interview the married mother of a neonate. Ask questions such as the following:
   a. How did you and your husband feel when you found out you were pregnant?
   b. How did your life change?

c. When did you first start regular prenatal care? How often did you see your doctor?
d. How did the first three months go? Were there any problems?
e. How were the second three months? When did you first feel the baby kick?
f. How were the last three months?
g. Who was present during the delivery? What part did they/he/she play? When you first saw the baby, how did you feel? What did the baby look like?
h. What decision did you make regarding the place of birth? If not in a hospital, describe the setting.
i. What was your stay in the hospital like?
j. Did the baby adjust easily to feeding? How active was he or she?
k. Since you came home, have you gotten settled into a schedule?
l. How have you and your family members had to change your lives?
m. How do you feel?
n. Do you have assistance with the care of your baby? Who helps you? What kinds of things do they/he/she do?

Write an evaluation and summary of your interview.

**4.** Make an entry in your journal.

## REVIEW

**1.** Complete each statement with the environmental change that takes place at birth.
a. The environment changes from amniotic fluid to _____.
b. _____ goes from being constant to changing.
c. There is a change from minimal stimulation to one in which all the _____ are stimulated.
d. Nutrition changes from dependence on _____ to _____ and _____.
e. Oxygen no longer comes from _____ but must be processed by the neonate's _____.
f. Elimination is no longer through the placenta to the mother's bloodstream, but the baby's _____ must start to work.

**2.** Write the letter of each statement that describes the Leboyer method of delivery and treatment of the newborn.
a. Forceps are used for delivery.
b. The lights are dim.
c. The baby is placed on the mother's stomach.
d. The baby is taken away after the mother has a quick look.
e. The infant is gently massaged.
f. The lights are bright so everyone can see.

**3.** Match the definitions and descriptions in Column I with the items in Column II.

| Column I | Column II |
|---|---|
| a. Parent and newborn gaze into each other's eyes—each begins to learn the other is special. | 1. NBAS |
| b. At birth, some babies are happy and calm; others are cranky and overactive. | 2. bonding |
| c. The first two weeks of life. | 3. premature infant |
| d. Slightly yellowish skin color caused by unbalanced liver function. | 4. neonatal period |
| | 5. Apgar scale |
| | 6. surfactant |

e. Used to check on the newborn's readiness to enter the world.
f. Newborn responds to voices, faces, tastes, and smells.
g. Degree of being asleep or awake.
h. The mother is immersed in water and the infant emerges from the liquid environment of the womb into the water.
i. A scale used to obtain a dynamic assessment of newborn interactive behavior.
j. A substance that coats the inner lining of the lung and keeps the airspaces from collapsing.
k. The six soft spots on top of the heads of newborns.
l. An infant born before the completion of the full gestation period.

7. newborn sensitivity
8. infant temperament
9. state of arousal
10. water birth
11. fontanels
12. normal physiologic jaundice

## KEY TERMS LIST

Apgar scale
bonding
cesarean section
difficult child
easy child
Exosurf®
fontanels
homeostasis
natural childbirth
Neonatal Behavior Assessment Scale (NBAS)
neonatal period
neonate
newborn
normal physiologic jaundice
premature infant
slow-to-warm-up child
states of arousal
temperament
water birth

Additional resources for this chapter can be found on the Online Companion™ to accompany this text at http://www.earlychilded.delmar.com. Respond to "Time to Reflect" and "Looking Further" concepts, review various child development scenarios, and answer thought-provoking questions in the Critical Thinking Forum. Keep a daily journal by downloading the student journal available on this Web site. Complete the interactive matching exercises to reinforce concepts, and print out the child development assessment forms to use during your observation of development for children from birth to age eight. In addition, read the case studies on the Web site to reinforce the important concepts in each chapter, and take a look at the multitude of Web links that are available for student research on the Internet.

CHAPTER

# 11

# Infancy: Theory, Environment, and Culture

## OBJECTIVES

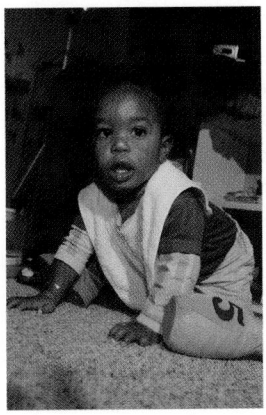

After reading this chapter, you should be able to:

- Recognize the theories of Erikson, Freud, Piaget, Vygotsky, Skinner, Bandura, Rogers, and Maslow.
- Cite examples of infant sensory competence.
- Discuss why the sensory competencies of some infants may not be as well developed as those of others.
- Recognize the factors that indicate a high-quality infant environment.
- Discuss the pros and cons of child care for infants.
- Recognize the effects of maternal employment on infant development.
- List the socioeconomic and cultural factors that may affect infant development.
- Evaluate infant caregiver behavior using an infant caregiver evaluation sheet.

A first grader wrote this description when Kate, age five months, visited her class. Even a six-year-old can see that a five-month-old is active and alert. Although the description was accurate in showing that Kate had many abilities, Kate was also totally dependent on the people in her environment to fulfill all her needs. Mother, father, brother, sister, and any other people who care for her are of great importance (Figure 11–1). What happens to her during infancy will be reflected in her behavior as a preschooler, and even as an adult.

Kate is a baby.

1. She can smile.
2. She can frown.
3. She can see.
4. She can cry.
5. She can touch.
6. She can clap.

**FIGURE 11–1** Infants are fascinated with other children, as well as with adults.

## THE THEORISTS' LOOK AT THE INFANT

Each of the theorists introduced in Chapter 2 has his own view of the infant. The views of Erikson, Freud, Bandura, Maslow, Rogers, Piaget, and Vygotsky, vary; each looks at the infant in a different way.

For Erik Erikson, the child passes through various crisis stages while developing (Miller, 2002). The crisis to be resolved during infancy is one between basic **trust** and mistrust. The child must develop trust and, with this, the basic feeling of hope that keeps human beings going in spite of the many disappointments they may meet in life. Trust develops through the relationship with the mother during the feeding experience and other activities in which the mother meets the infant's basic needs. Infants learn that they can trust their mothers to satisfy their most basic needs. This trust of the mother can then transfer to the infant's world and society as a whole. Warmth and love, along with necessary food, result in healthy affective development for the infant. If trust does not develop, the child will become fearful, suspicious, and mistrustful.

**trust**

Confidence that develops in other humans' behavior.

Freud's basic belief was that early experience had specific effects on later behavior (Miller, 2002). During infancy, the mouth and its functions are very important. Both nutritive and nonnutritive sucking experiences affect the shaping of the child's personality. Also critical during this period are close relationships with other human beings. While cuddled in a caregiver's arms, a child is fed and develops feelings of love, warmth, and dependence. Attachment to the mother is the foundation for the development of later social relationships. Attention from the mother facilitates the development of desirable behavior. Freud believed that if these experiences are not positive, the child can become anxious and develop a dependent, passive, helpless personality. Freud brought to child-rearing the idea that infants and young children should live a pleasant, nonfrustrating life in order to grow up mentally healthy (Miller, 2002).

Remember that Bandura's social cognitive theory is not a stage-governed or developmental theory but suggests how, at any age, children abstract and integrate what they find out through their social experiences (Miller, 2002). Bandura's theory does recognize that with age the environmental influences change and the child's skills in dealing with the environment change. As the infant encounters his or her first social experiences, he or she begins to build mental pictures based on these experiences. Vicarious or observational experiences are especially important for the infant. Imitation begins in the neonatal period. Infants learn the rules of behavior through observing the responses and behaviors of others. An infant learns quickly that crying can bring relief for physical discomfort. The infant observes that he or she can control others through his or her actions and, thus, begins to build a view of self as a competent individual. Social cognitive theory does not view the child as a passive receiver of knowledge but as having an active role in constructing knowledge as he figures out what his impressions from the environment mean (Miller, 2002).

Rogers (Smith, 2005) and Maslow (Boeree, 2004) emphasize the importance of parents accepting themselves and others. The parents' feelings of acceptance toward their child are critical during infancy. Parents also need to accept that it is typical to sometimes have negative feelings toward their child. That is, no parent

FIGURE 11–2 Older infants explore with their mouths.

is the perfect, loving parent all the time. Trying to deny negative feelings leads to tension and hostility and can mask positive feelings. It is also important from the beginning for parents and other caregivers to learn to read messages from children regarding their needs and to respond appropriately. The experiences that promote a positive self-concept begin at birth. Rogers (Smith, 2005), like Erikson, emphasizes the importance of the trust relationship between child and the facilitator of learning (parent or other caregiver).

In Piaget's view (Miller, 2002), the infant is in the first stage or period of cognitive development. This stage, called the **sensorimotor period**, lasts until age two. This is the period of initial learning. During this stage, children learn to use their senses—touch, taste, sight, sound, and smell—as a means to find out new things. Children also learn and grow through their motor activity. They learn about the world as they grasp, crawl, creep, stand, and walk. As they move farther and faster, they are able to learn more through their senses. When infants find something new, they look at it, hold it, smell it, and then put it in their mouths to taste, bite, and feel (Figure 11–2). For Piaget, the adult is important because it is the adult who provides the environment; however, infants have some control over what they learn as they perform their sensory and motor actions.

**sensorimotor period**

Piaget's first stage of cognitive development, lasting from birth to age two, in which children learn to use their senses as a means to find out new things.

Vygotsky viewed child development as a series of stages (Bodrova & Leong, 1996). Each stage is a period of stability that begins and ends with a crisis in development. Developmental change occurs rapidly during each crisis period and may result in educational problems because something new is developing. For Vygotsky, birth begins one of these crisis periods, which lasts for about two months. Vygotsky recognized the changes from the uterine to the outside environment described in Chapter 10 as being traumatic. This crisis, or transitional period, is the time when the first mental processes develop. Primitive mental activity takes place during these first weeks. When the child first smiles at the sound of the human voice, real reciprocal social interaction between child and adult begins. For Vygotsky, infancy extends from two months until age one. During infancy, the child is totally dependent on social interaction with others for everything and develops a specific need for this interaction. The child does not view himself or herself as separate from the adult; the child is one part of an affective bonding. At around twelve months, a new crisis develops as the child begins to walk, language appears, and affective reactions change. Vygotsky was ahead of his time in his emphasis on the value and necessity of social interaction during the first year (Bodrova & Leong, 1996).

The theorists discussed thus far look at development (the interaction of both growth and learning) as central in the child's life. Skinner (1979) gears his view of the child to learning specific behaviors in the best possible environment. His view of infant learning is reflected in the approach he used with his younger daughter. For his second daughter, Skinner decided that to simplify the care of the baby, he would build a perfect infant environment. He built what he called a **baby tender** (later called an air crib). It was a crib-sized space, enclosed like a small room, with a glass picture window on one side. Air vents were located at the bottom. The air was filtered, warmed, and moistened before it entered the crib. The infant wore only diapers and could thus move at will. No tight clothes, quilts, or covers kept her from moving freely. Deborah grew up strong and healthy in her special crib. For Skinner, "The problem is two-fold: to discover the optimal conditions for the child and to induce the mother to arrange these conditions" (Skinner, 1979, p. 31). Skinner found that some important learning took place in this environment that would not have normally occurred. For example, when wet, the diaper cooled immediately and was very uncomfortable. He felt that Deborah learned early to hold

**baby tender**

Skinner's environment for optimal conditions for the child.

FIGURE 11–3 Infants are fascinated by objects that respond to their explorations.

her urine to avoid discomfort. For Skinner, then, the right environment is the key to healthy development.

The infant is seen by these theorists as a person who actively seeks to learn about the world through the senses and motor activity. The infant's relationship with caregivers and the quality of the surrounding environment are of the utmost importance in the degree to which the individual's potential is developed. During infancy, the child moves from being dependent mainly on the senses to a combination of sensory and motor learning. This develops as children gradually move from a lying position to a sitting position and from being confined to one place to moving their own bodies. When children can sit, they can grasp objects with both hands (Figure 11–3). This opens new activities involving larger objects and coordination of two objects. For example, a favorite activity for the child who is sitting up involves putting small objects into larger objects or containers and then taking or pouring them out. When children can move on their own, a new world opens up. They explore with excitement every nook and cranny available to them.

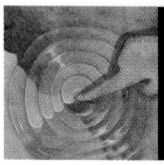

**LOOKING FURTHER**

Arrange to care for an infant for an hour or so. This can be in a friend's or relative's house, or in a family child care home or center. Record what you do, what the infant does, and your reactions to the infant. Describe how your observations and interactions relate to the theorists' views of infant development and behavior.

## THE COMPETENT INFANT

Infants are sensitive individuals who are ready and eager to interact with their environment. Research on infant competency has documented that infants are aware of much of what is going on in their environments and are ready to learn and interact (Caulfield, 1994). T. G. R. Bower (1977) summarized some of the competencies of the infant. Whereas the very young infant lacks control of body parts for motor activity, perceptual abilities serve for much early learning. **Perception** refers to the ways we know about what goes on outside our bodies. We perceive through six systems; touch, taste, smell, hearing, and sight are the five of which we are most aware. The sixth is **proprioception.** This sense tells us where the parts of our body are in relation to the whole. Babies do not perceive the world exactly as adults do because all their sense receptors, such as eyes, ears, and nose, must undergo more development. How do we know a baby is sensitive? Consider these examples of newborn behavior:

**perception**
The ways we know about what goes on outside our bodies.

**proprioception**
The sense that tells us where the parts of our body are in relation to the whole.

- Dad gently tickles infant's right leg. Infant moves his left foot toward the right leg as if to get rid of whatever is on his right leg.
- Infant is offered a choice of sugar water or milk. He chooses the sugar water.
- The smell of burning toast wafts over to baby. He turns his head to the other side.
- Big sister drops a toy on the hardwood floor of the bedroom. Baby's eyes shift in the direction of the sound.
- Mom jokingly holds a ball in her hand and moves it directly toward baby, saying, "Gonna get you, gonna get you." Baby moves her head back as if to defend herself.
- A bright plastic object hangs from a rod across baby's crib. Baby reaches out for the object again and again. Most of the time, he is close. Sometimes he touches the object.

These examples show that babies have many competencies that enable them to relate to objects. They are sensitive to touch, taste, smell, sound, and danger. They also can coordinate eye and hand movement and use their senses to relate to people. Note the following example:

> Mother is holding baby in her arms. They look directly at each other. Mother opens her mouth; baby opens his. Mother blinks her eyes; baby blinks his.

This baby seems to sense his body parts match mother's and can do the same things hers can. Infants learn by two weeks of age to coordinate their perceptions of others.

> Mother speaks directly to baby (two weeks old). He watches intently. Mrs. Jones, a stranger, talks to baby directly. His attention does not stay with Mrs. Jones. His gaze shifts away from her and back again.

This infant can perceive the difference between his mother and a strange woman.

Research on infant perception is extensive. Researchers have found that infant senses develop rapidly (Cole, Cole, & Lightfoot, 2005). Newborns are tuned into the sounds of language. They are very interested when someone speaks to them in the slow, high-pitched speech referred to as "baby talk" or "motherese." Infants are sensitive to the individual sounds of language. By six to eight months, infants' attention to sounds focuses on those in their primary language environment. Vision is at a very immature level in the newborn. By two months of age infant color discrimination reaches the adult level. Newborns are very nearsighted, but by four months they can see about as clearly as adults. Although nearsighted and lacking in acuity, infants scan from the time they are born. By 12 weeks, they scan more of an individual figure although they often miss the mark. They appear to particularly focus on the edges and angles of objects. Before two days of age, infants can discriminate among visual forms. Infants seem to prefer patterned over plain stimuli. They appear to be interested in focusing on faces almost from birth. Newborns only hours old recognize their mothers' faces when compared with a stranger's face. Neonates already have developed a keen sense of both taste and smell. They show preference for sugar water over vinegar water. They smile when presented with sweet smells and grimace when presented with garlic or vinegar.

Other factors, such as adequacy of health care and nutrition, and mother's educational level and parenting skills, may affect the child's level of sensory competence (Sameroff & Seifer, 1983). The child's physical appearance may also influence adults' assessment of the child's competence. For example, Stephan and Langlois (1984) found that European American, African American, and Mexican American adults perceived more attractive infants as more competent. It is possible that more attractive infants receive more attention, and, thus, more stimulation, and develop their perceptual competencies to a greater extent than less attractive infants. The mother's feelings about her own competence also relate to the infant's level of performance (Heinicke, Diskin, Ramsey-Klee, & Given, 1983). Heinicke et al. (1983) found that mothers who felt confident about themselves had more competent infants. All of these factors support the necessity for adults who work with infants to be knowledgeable about child development so they can provide developmental information and psychological support to parents.

For perceptual growth to take place as it should, the senses must have exercise (Figure 11–4). That is, children must have practice in perceiving: tasting, touching, hearing, smelling, and seeing. The infant is born with many perceptual competencies, but for these competencies to develop as they should, the infant must have experiences with many types of stimuli.

FIGURE 11–4 Infants like to visually examine objects.

## Special Needs and Early Intervention

Some infants are born without all the sensory and/or motor capabilities that characterize the competent infant. The learning problems of children with special needs were described in Chapter 4. Vygotsky (Berk & Winsler, 1995, p. 81) believes that "the most debilitating consequence of the problem [whether psychological or physical] for the child's development is not so much the original disability but rather how the defect changes the way the child participates in the activities of his or her culture." Disabilities can prevent the child from participating fully in cultural activities with peers and adults. According to Vygotsky, it is most important for young children with disabilities to be included in the regular activities of their culture. To alleviate these problems, **early intervention** programs have been developed. According to Karoly et al. (1998), "Early childhood interventions are formal attempts by agents outside the family to maintain or improve the quality of life of youngsters, starting with the prenatal period and continuing through entry into school (i.e., kindergarten or first grade)." Early intervention programs according to Karoly et al. include the following:

**early intervention**
Formal attempts by agents outside the family to maintain or improve the quality of life for children from the prenatal period to school entrance.

- public health programs that provide prenatal care, immunizations, or nutritional supplements
- regulations on child care quality or subsidies for child care expenses
- programs that provide safety nets (e.g., Special Supplemental Feeding Program for Women, Infants, and Children [WIC], and Early and Periodic Screening Diagnosis and Treatment [EPSDT])
- programs designed to support child development through home visits and parenting classes (e.g., Early Head Start, Head Start, or Healthy Start, and Part H infant and toddler programs under the Individuals with Disabilities Education Act, such as Early Childhood Intervention [ECI] in Texas).

Bruder & Dunst (1999/2000) describe a trend to focus early intervention on learning opportunities in natural environments. That is, instead of interventions consisting only of preplanned structured activities, interventions can take advantage of natural activities in family and community settings. Family-life learning opportunities include daily routines, play, entertainment, family rituals and celebrations, and socialization experiences. Community life opportunities include family outings, community events, recreation activities, and religious, sports, and entertainment activities. Children with disabilities can benefit from both planned and spontaneous natural experiences.

List some of the reasons that infants' sensory competence may vary. Suggest what the family might do to compensate for these conditions.

# THE INFANT ENVIRONMENT

For infants to develop fully, the environment must support their basic needs. To thrive, infants need proper nutrition, responsive caregivers with whom social attachments can be developed, and a stimulating environment that encourages them

FIGURE 11–5 Infants need space in which to move about and toys they can explore with all their senses.

to use all their senses (Caulfield, 1994; Raikes, 1996).

The infant needs an interesting and rich environment but one that is not overstimulating. They need responsive adults and exciting objects. Adults need to be aware of infant needs as outlined in Maslow's hierarchy (see Chapter 2) (Albrecht & Miller, 2001). Infants need their physiological needs (e.g., food, clothing, hygiene, health) met. They need to feel both physically and psychologically safe. They need emotional support, to feel loved, and to feel that they belong. They need to feel good about themselves. Support comes from caring adults and a well-planned environment.

Jim Greenman (2004) describes the importance of space. Space has environmental load, it affects our feelings. Crowded, highly charged spaces can give us overload and result in feelings of fear, flight, excitement, anxiety or anticipation (see Figure 11–5). For helpless infants, fear and confusion may result in a space that is too crowded and too active. A place that is soft, spacious, and not too crowded can make the infant feel calm and comfortable. At the Child Development Center at Fort George G. Meade, the area for nonmobile infants is "partitioned on one side with low movable storage units" (Friedman, 2005, p. 50). There are "soft toys, mobiles, and cushions." Windowsills have rounded edges so infants may pull themselves up safely. There is room to experiment with crawling. There is a book area with infant books that they can reach on their own.

Infants also need to experience nature in the outdoors (Torquati & Barber, 2005). During a buggy ride, the adult can talk to the infants about what they see. The infants may babble as if commenting on what they observe in their surroundings. Infants can lay on their backs on a blanket experiencing the breezes, the sun, and the leaves that may blow by. They can examine plants, trees, and grass and gaze at the sky.

The importance of quality social interaction between caregiver and child, as pointed out in previous chapters, must not be underestimated. The child's normal behaviors can be difficult for adults who do not understand their significance. According to T. Berry Brazelton (*Tots . . .*, 1984) the sudden bursts of developmental change that are normal for babies can send caregivers into a spin. Infants become obsessed with each new skill to be mastered. The author once heard her daughter, at five or six months of age, grunting and groaning in her crib. Upon entering her child's room, she found her daughter moving her body around the crib, methodically ripping off the elastics that held the crib bumpers. The baby was feeling very powerful while the mother felt vexed. Around the same time, the baby also asserted her independence by insisting on holding her bottle herself. The mother had to deal with losing an important parental function. These assertions of autonomy and independence can upset the uninformed parent or other caregiver who may not realize that asserting oneself independently is a part of normal infant development.

## Fathers' Roles

There is an increasing trend for fathers to take on more child-rearing responsibilities (Goodnough & Goodnough, 2001). Many fathers are taking on less traditional male roles in the family and becoming major nurturers of their children. In 2002, the U.S Bureau of the Census estimated that there were 105,000 at-home dads (AHD) (Cobb, 2003). These dads stay at home while their wives work. Cobb (2003) speculates that these fathers may need services, which have not yet been identified. Fathers' involvement in child-rearing increases children's self-esteem, empathy, and achievement (Goodnough & Goodnough, 2001; National Center for Fathering, 2000). Just as fathers must support the working mother, mothers must help fathers deal with the daily routines and responsibilities of parenting. Ninio and Rinott (1988) did a study that examined the extent of fathers' interactions with infants and its relationship to fathers' estimates of infants' social-cognitive competence. About half of the wives of the men in the sample worked outside the home. The fathers in this study were more likely than those in earlier studies to take responsibility for infant care. However, there was wide variation. The findings indicated the following:

- The more a father was involved in infant care, the higher were his opinions of infant capacities.
- On the average, fathers attribute less competence to their infants than do mothers.
- The more fathers are involved in infant care, the closer the match between mothers' and fathers' estimates of infant competence.

The fathers who spent less than 15 minutes per day with their infants viewed them as the least capable; the fathers who spent an hour or more per day with their infants viewed them as more capable. The views of these latter fathers were more congruent with the mothers' views. It may be that the low-interaction-time fathers are men who believe infants in general are not interesting and that children do not require social and cognitive stimulation until they reach an age at which they can communicate and interact in a more adultlike manner. The highly interactive fathers may have beliefs that value the importance of infant stimulation.

Fathers who are the primary caregiver tend to retain their playful attitude. They are also sympathetic and friendly and take pride in parenthood. Thus, male primary caregivers take on the characteristics previously believed to be female but also retain the conventional male characteristics when interacting with the infant (Berk, 2003).

Caregiving can be a complicated and traumatizing experience for separated and divorcing parents (Solomon, 2003). When a marriage fails the caregiving system is damaged. The caregiving system consists of the "psychological and behavioral strategies that an adult uses to provide protection for a specific child" (Solomon, 2003, p. 33). The caregiving system of the parent is the complement of the child's attachment system. Coparenting conflicts can disorganize caregiving. When parents feel abandoned, they may give up on parenting and leave their children feeling unattached. This circumstance is particularly difficult for infants who may be left psychologically unprotected. The transitions in care from one parent to the other are very difficult for the preverbal child whose attachment system becomes damaged and confused. Once the divorce is consummated, the parents are likely to remarry within a short time (Bullock & Forgatch, 2003). Stepparenting is not simple, especially if both parents bring children to the family. Stepparents need careful planning on dealing with each other's children, ex-spouses, and family members.

The absent father continues to be of concern. More than 25 percent of our children live in female-headed households. Of the children in these households, 40 percent have not seen their fathers in a year or more. With more mothers in the workforce, father love and care are needed more than ever. Having a nurturing father who spends time with the young child provides that child with a positive male model for development of caring and compassion (Louv, 1994). Roy and Burton (2003) did in-depth interviews with low-income level mothers who didn't have consistent father figures in the family. Forty-two percent were Latino or Hispanic, 40 percent African American, and 18 percent non-Hispanic white. All these mothers did every possible thing they could in order to obtain father figures for their children in order to provide:

- The image of the "ideal father"
- In-kind and financial resources
- Trustworthy child care
- Social support from paternal kin

Patterns were quite varied. In some cases, the biological father lived in the home or at least was a frequent visitor. In other cases, a live-in boyfriend, an uncle, or a grandfather took on the father role. Combinations of father figures changed frequently. The mothers tried very hard to have some positive father or father figure for their children and to maintain some consistency of family for their children. The National Center for Fathering (2000) published an extensive report on involving nonresident fathers in children's learning.

## Parental Employment During Infancy

There are many problems in the area of employers', parents', and children's interests (Friedman, 2001). Work schedules, child care arrangements, promotions, children's illnesses, and overtime hours can all be areas of contention. Employers are concerned about how their workers balance work and family responsibilities. Some employers have family-friendly policies, such as on-site child-care, paid leave, and flextime. However, these innovations are seldom available to the low-income workers who need them the most.

In 1997, 65 percent of mothers of children under six were in the labor force (Children's Defense Fund, 1998). Slightly more than 63 percent of married women with children under six participated in the workforce. Some mothers work because of financial necessity, others because they feel the need for a fulfilling career. In either case, the result may be a rather hectic family life.

There is a good deal of concern regarding the effects of maternal employment on child development and parent-child relations. Some research has looked at these factors from the maternal employment view. Other research has looked at these factors from the child care view. We will look first at the maternal employment view. Infant attachment has been the focus of many studies. Usually using the strange-situation method (as will be described in Chapter 13), researchers have looked at mother-infant and father-infant attachment in families with employed and nonemployed mothers. First, we will look at the results of a study that used the strange situation as the measure of attachment.

Before turning to infant child care, one more maternal employment study merits attention. Zaslow, Pedersen, Suwalsky, and Rabinovich (1989) did home observations of mothers, fathers and their one-year-old infants on weekday evenings. They observed in homes where mothers were employed outside the home and in homes where mothers were full-time homemakers. Comparing their results with the results of other studies, the authors noted the following emerging consistencies:

- When observed on weekday evenings, parents in employed-mother families tend to interact less with their infants than parents in homemaker families.

Apply your knowledge of developmentally appropriate infant care practices by evaluating Mrs. Miller's child care situation, as described below.

Ms. Miller is the head teacher with a group of 10 infants. She has been in this position for five years. She has two assistants: Mrs. Kwan, who has been with her for three years, and Mr. Peterson, who has been with her for one year. The infant section of the center is divided into two rooms. One room contains cribs and changing tables. The other room contains high chairs, walkers, a couch, and two rocking chairs. About half of the second room is a play area. There is carpeting on the floor and an assortment of play materials, such as sock animals, foam rubber blocks, rattles, and stuffed toys. Infants can move the mobile about freely. The adults observe and move in when needed. While changing one of the babies, Mrs. Kwan tickles, sings, and carries on a "conversation" with the baby. During nap time, the three teachers discuss the day's events and plan for the future. Mrs. Miller gives her assistants constructive criticism and compliments them on their skillful handling of their young charges. In the evening, as the parents arrive to pick up their children, the teachers greet each one and briefly report on the events of the day for their child.

- In mother-employed families, there is less play with objects, which may result in less-than-optimal cognitive development for the infants. Boys especially receive less of this type of attention.

It appears likely that the burden of the demands on working parents in the evening (e.g., chores, making contact with spouse) preclude providing the infant with an optimal amount of attention. It may be that working parents need to divide labor so that one does chores while the other plays with the baby. It is also possible that mothers find it difficult to change from the serious businesslike behavior of the world of work to some of the more playful behavior of parenting. Finally, it may be that infants who have been in **child care** all day are used to being autonomous and prefer independent play, thus, making it more difficult for parents to interject themselves into the play activity. More research is needed to try to identify the reasons for these differences between evening interactions in employed-mother families and homemaker-mother families.

**child care**

An arrangement in a home or center of caring for children while their adult family members are at work, school, etc.

## The Question of Child Care: Effects on Infants

A great deal of research, professional discussion, and disagreement has focused on child care for infants. Three out of five children under the age of 6 are cared for by someone other than their parents on a regular basis (CDF, 2004). Sixty-four percent of mothers of children under 6 and 78 percent of mothers with children ages 6 to 17 work outside the home. Fifty-nine percent of mothers with infants (children under age one) are in the labor force (CDF, 2001). Every day, 13 million preschoolers—including six million infants and toddlers—are in child care. This is three out of five young children. The proportion of single mothers with jobs increased from 58 percent in 1993 to 71.5 percent in 1999. In 48 states, the cost of center-based child care for a four-year-old is greater than tuition at a four-year public college. The cost for infants and toddlers can be even greater. The cost of full-day child care is $4,000 to $10,000 per year. One out of four families with young children earns less than $25,000 per year. These figures reflect a need for quality child care for infants.

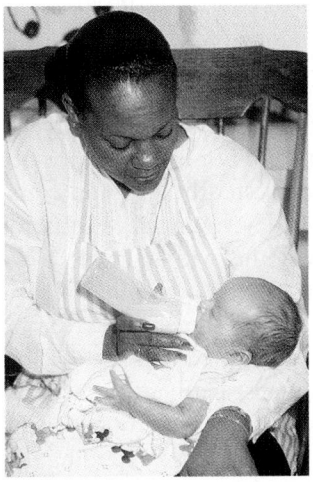

FIGURE 11–6 The child care provider can become a supplement to the family.

The quality of child care has a lasting effect on children's development (CDF, 2001). Children in poor-quality care are likely to be delayed in language and reading skills and to be more aggressive toward other children and adults. On the other hand, high-quality care can be beneficial (see Figure 11–6). Children who experienced high-quality care "demonstrated greater mathematical ability, greater thinking and attention skills, and fewer behavior problems than children in lower-quality care" (CDF, 2001, p. 2).

Thornburg, Pearl, Crompton, and Ispa (1990) looked at comparisons of child care arrangements (i.e., no child care, part-time care, and full-time care) during infancy through age five and the effects on social, intellectual, and motor development. They found no significant negative effects on the social behavior of children who had been in full-time child care as infants. Those children who were in part-time arrangements had the most social problems in kindergarten. Children who stayed home all five years were the most compliant with adults. African American children appeared to gain a cognitive advantage from the out-of-home experience as reflected in cognitive assessment test scores. These researchers had no information on the quality of child care received.

Data from the NICHD Study of Early Child Care (Brooks-Gunn, Han, & Waldfogel, 2002) indicate future negative effects for children who spend 30 hours or more in child care by the time they are nine months old. These children also experienced poorer-quality child care during their first three years than did other children. It may be that, if possible, mothers should not work full time during the child's first year. In addition, the results of the NICHD study further support the need for higher-quality care for infants and toddlers.

## Quality Infant Child Care

The Children's Defense Fund (CDF, 2001) points out the difficulty of finding good-quality child care. Child care in the United States tends to be poor to mediocre. Family care doesn't fare any better. In one study, one-third of the programs were rated as inadequate, which means the setting might be harmful to child development. Child care workers are required to have little if any training and are paid on the average $15,430 per year, so it is no wonder that it is difficult to find quality care. The recipe for quality care is simple, but costly:

> Young children benefit from care that offers them ample verbal and cognitive simulation, sensitive and responsive caregiving, and generous amounts of attention and support. These positive experiences are most prevalent when the children are in small groups, when the child-adult ratios are low, and when caregivers are educated, well-compensated, and stable in their roles (turnover among child care staff averages 30 percent per year) (Larner, Behrman, Young, & Reich, 2001, p. 16).

Korelak, Colker, and Dodge (1993, pp. 1–5) have identified seven key indicators of quality child care:

1. The program is based on an understanding of child development.
2. The program is individualized to meet the needs of every child.
3. The physical environment is safe and orderly, and it contains varied and stimulating toys and materials.
4. Children may select activities and materials that interest them, and they learn by being actively involved.
5. Adults show respect for children's needs and ideas and talk with them in caring ways.

6. Parents feel respected and are encouraged to participate in the program.
7. Staff members have specialized training in early childhood development and education.

Korelak, Colker, and Dodge (1993, p. 11) describe the developmentally appropriate infant room in the child care center as "warm and homelike" and as being staffed by caregivers who "meet infants' needs consistently, promptly, and lovingly." The caregivers encourage infants to use their developing sensorimotor skills. The environment should look like a comfortable home, with pictures at eye level, room for creeping and crawling, and appropriate materials for older infants to explore. Family child care environments should meet the same standards and present a homelike atmosphere.

Infancy is a critical time for children. If an infant must be in child care, the caregivers and the environment must include the basic ingredients proposed, and the care should be sensitive and competent (Kovach & Da Ros, 1998). Finding this quality care at an affordable cost is difficult. The need for high-quality care is urgent. Finding competent, quality care can be a hopelessly frustrating task.

## Parent Education and Support

**parent education**
Providing information and materials to the parents of children.

It is not only important for professionals to know how to design and implement a high-quality infant environment, but it is also equally important for parents to have these skills. **Parent education** has become increasingly popular as a major approach to the improvement of life for young children. Parent education can take many forms. It can be a program that is hospital-based and provides information during the prenatal and neonatal periods. It may be a parent/child learning center (Vartuli & Rogers, 1985), or it may be home-based. Parent education includes involvement in the child care center or early childhood program by attending workshops, making educational materials, volunteering to assist in the class, attending parent-teacher conferences, and participating in other related activities.

Parent education is critical for teenage parents who are ill-prepared to care for their infants and whose chances of finishing high school are poor. During the 1980s, 300 schools in 46 states started parenting programs for teens and child care centers for their children (Kantrowitz, 1990). Through these programs, children are cared for while their mothers attend class and the mothers take child development courses that help them understand their children and how to parent them. Both mother and child are provided an opportunity that greatly increases their chances of becoming productive citizens. A family support program can be beneficial to adolescent mothers. Solomon and Liefeld (1998) found that an intervention program helped first-time adolescent mothers delay becoming pregnant again and motivated them to stay in school.

Family support has been mandated for infants with disabilities (see Chapter 4). Parent support groups are a commonly used method of meeting this requirement (Krauss, Upshur, Shonkoff, & Hauser-Cram, 1993). Krauss et al. (1993) suggest being cautious in placing parents in support groups because all parents do not feel equally comfortable discussing their problems in such a public setting. Furthermore, parents who are less educated tend to be less involved in the groups. This may be because of their lack of education, lack of child care, working hours that conflict with meeting times, lack of interest, tending to be from a lower socioeconomic status (SES) level, or lack of transportation to get to the meetings.

Another method of providing for parent education, involvement, and support is the home visit. This approach provides support for parent and child in the place where they feel most comfortable. With home visits, it is especially important to be sensitive to the culture of the family. LaPoint, Boutte, Swick, and Brown (1993) suggest using a bicultural approach. Their approach uses activities that integrate the family's culture and mainstream culture.

## Infant Home Environment and Later Development

**Home Observation for Measurement of the Environment (HOME)**

A scale used to rate a home environment.

A growing body of research supports the long-term value of the kinds of environmental features discussed in this unit. For example, Bradley and Caldwell (1984) used the **Home Observation for Measurement of the Environment (HOME)** method in the homes of children when they were 12 and 24 months old. They compared the observational results with some of the same children's first-grade achievement test scores. The relationships were positive. Especially strong was the relationship between having appropriate play materials in the home at 12 and 24 months and higher school achievement. The levels of the mother's acceptance of the child and the mother's encouragement of child development were also strongly related to school achievement. Parental responsiveness did not show as strong a relationship as it did to level of cognitive development at age three. It may be that, as children become more independent of adults, the quality of materials available maintains its importance, whereas maternal responsiveness has its greatest effect during the first three years, when the child is more dependent.

The availability and use of school support, such as extended family and professionals and the sense of personal control, affect how skillful mothers are as parents (Stevens, 1988). Stevens interviewed low-income and teen African American and European American mothers. They were observed at home. Stevens obtained ratings of parenting skill, personal control, and the amount of informal and formal child-rearing support systems. The more skilled African American teen mothers were those who were willing to recognize that they had needs and sought help from extended family members. The more skilled adult African American mothers were those who expressed more personal control. The more skilled European American adult mothers felt higher levels of personal control and sought help from extended family and professionals to solve child-rearing problems. African American teens who lived with their mothers appeared to have an advantage in having advice-givers close at hand.

Teen parents and infants can also gain advantages from the presence of the teen's father in the household (Radin, Oyserman, & Benn, 1989). Teen fathers often do not have much interaction with their children; thus, these infants are deprived of male interaction. Grandfathers can serve this function. Note the playful relationship between Annie and her grandfather:

> Six-month-old Annie is sitting on the dining room table in an upright position; her grandfather is sitting on the bench. Annie and her grandfather are at eye level. Annie is observing her grandfather and all of a sudden lunges forward and grabs his tie. Once Annie has a good grasp on his tie, she tugs and pulls at it and brings it to her mouth and starts sucking on it. Annie's grandfather is laughing and talking to her. "Annie, what are you doing?" "Do you like my tie? It is soft, isn't it?" "Look at all the bright colors." "You are so silly, Annie." "Is that funny?" "Oh yes, it is funny." He spoke in a soft, exaggerated tone. When her grandfather talked to her, Annie smiled, giggled, and tried to talk herself by cooing and babbling.

Radin et al. (1989) found that high levels of interaction with nurturing grandfathers enhance infant development, especially for girls. On the negative side, the infants by age two favored the grandfathers as sources of attention and were more obedient for the grandfathers than for their mothers.

The federal welfare reform acts passed in 1996 placed limits on the amount of time mothers could stay on welfare, forcing them to move from welfare to work. Many of these mothers were teenagers. Yoshikawa, Rosman, & Hsueh (2001) looked at the long-term effects on four- to six-year-olds. Children who were in center-based care had mothers who were more likely to take advantage of self-improvement opportunities, such as education, job training, and personal development classes. Black and Latina mothers were more likely to take advantage of the advancement opportunities than were white mothers. The selection of job training and higher-quality child care by the mothers had the most positive effect on the children's cognitive development and school readiness. The low-involvement group included about half of the eligible teenage participants, which indicates a need for finding ways to motivate these mothers to take advantage of opportunities while making available more quality child care.

## SOCIOECONOMIC AND CULTURAL CONSIDERATIONS

### Socioeconomic Factors

Marian Wright Edelman (*The child's defender*, 1993), who heads the Children's Defense Fund, is a leading advocate for children's welfare in areas such as health care, teenage pregnancy, violence, and poverty. In a 1993 interview, she discussed the rising problems of poverty that demand our attention and our resources. She also discussed the problem of racial and gender bigotry. As adults, she emphasizes that we all have the responsibility to set an example of fairness and tolerance for our children. She is fearful that our country is becoming more divided into the privileged and the deprived. She also sees a resurgence of racial segregation. In her book *The Measure of Our Success: A Letter to My Children and Yours*, she expresses her concern that children are not receiving the support needed to grow up strong:

> . . . we are on the verge of losing two generations of Black children and youths to drugs, violence, too early parenthood, poor health and education, unemployment, family disintegration—and the spiritual and physical poverty that both breeds and is bred by them. Millions of Latino, Native American and other minority children face similar threats (p. 11).

Furthermore, she points out that millions of European American children are sinking also. Of the 406,000 youths who dropped out of school between October 1991 and October 1992, only 36 percent were employed (Youth indicators, 1993).

As prosperity increases, the gap between rich and poor increases (CDF, 2001). The bottom one-fifth poorest families received 4.3 percent of total U.S. family income, while the top one-fifth families received 47.3 percent. Figures from 1999 show that more than 12 million of America's children lived below the federal poverty level of $13,290 a year for a three-person family. One in six children live in poverty.

### Cultural Considerations

**cultural diversity**
Refers to differences relevant to membership in a variety of culture groups.

As indicated, our efforts to develop tolerance and understanding regarding the **cultural diversity** in our country have not yet succeeded to a large extent. Hilliard and Vaughn-Scott (1982) pointed out the negative stereotype of inferiority that goes along with the term *minority* and suggested that each cultural group should be considered according to its own special qualities. Looking at cultural groups

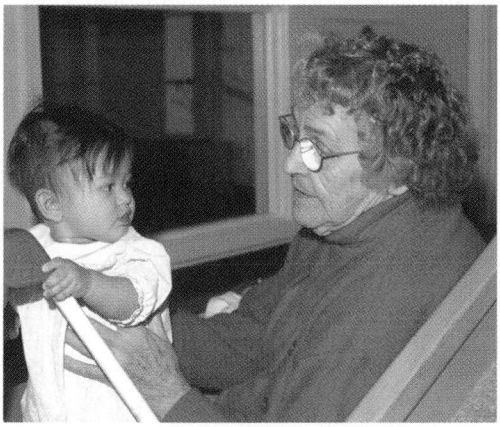

FIGURE 11–7 The caregiver needs to become familiar with the child's cultural background.

from this view can enable us to see the importance for adults who work with young children and their families to understand their cultures. Gonzales-Mena (1992) describes how to take a culturally sensitive approach in infant/toddler care programs to resolve caregiver/parent conflicts regarding child-rearing practices. Hopefully, a calm exchange of ideas can provide a solution. She suggests that adults who work with children find out what kinds of goals each parent has for the child, become clear about their own values and goals, become sensitive to anything that makes them feel uncomfortable, build positive relationships, learn to be effective cross-cultural communicators, learn how to create dialogs, use problem-solving approaches rather than power approaches when conflicts arise, and commit to educating themselves and the parents with whom they work.

It is essential to understand child development within cultural contexts (Bowman & Stott, 1994). Some research has documented cultural differences with regard to child behavior and child-rearing practices across cultures. Differences in children from different cultures are observable in newborns from each culture and their first reactions to the world (Freedman, 1982). For example, Chinese babies are more adaptable to change than European American babies. When picked up while crying, Chinese babies stop immediately, whereas European American babies stop gradually. Native American babies were observed to be even calmer and more adaptable than were the Chinese babies. Native American mothers and their infants operate very well as a unit. Researchers looked at these differences in terms of hereditary versus environmental origins. The diet common to the culture and other environmental factors may affect newborn behavior patterns even before birth. Whatever the basis for the differences, infants from different cultures are born with different characteristics (Figure 11–7). The basis is probably in both biology and culture. Parents in different cultures interact differently with their children (Paguio, Robinson, & Skeen, 1985). For example, German parents are more strict than American parents, having more rules and allowing fewer choices. Lower SES children are usually more externally oriented for control, and middle- and upper-economic-level children are more internally oriented for control.

An increasing amount of research is being done on a variety of cultural groups by researchers from those cultural groups. Hopefully, these studies will help us see which kinds of factors generalize to all children and which are specific to a given culture. Harrison, Wilson, Pine, Chan, and Buriel (1990) placed ethnic minority families in ecological context as suggested by Bronfenbrenner. They considered adaptive strategies, socialization goals, and developmental outcomes of African Americans, Native Americans and Alaskan natives, Asian Pacific Americans, and Latino Americans. These cultural groups operate under ecological challenges resulting from a history of oppression and discrimination. The gaps between minority and majority populations on social indicators, such as health care, employment opportunities, and housing, continue to widen. With the exception of Native Americans, most of these minorities live in urban areas, are younger, and have higher birth rates than majority families.

**biculturalism**

Practicing the language and customs of two different social groups.

Each minority cultural group has developed adaptive strategies to promote survival and well-being (Harrison et al., 1990). The extended family is a major strategy for problem solving and coping with stress. We have seen an example of the power of this system in the support of teen mothers' parenting skills. **Biculturalism** is another adaptive strategy. Cultural groups struggle to maintain their cultural heritage while making the needed adaptations to survive in the majority culture. Minority cultures also cope by holding onto ancestral world views. That is, they gain strength through long-term beliefs about life. Most minority peoples believe in collectivism (loyalty to the group) rather than the individualism that pervades European American culture. They also tend to have strong religious beliefs that guide their actions.

Although the mechanisms for transmitting the culture are the same in majority and minority cultures, ethnicity determines group patterns of values, social customs, language, perceptions, behavioral roles, and rules of social interaction (Harrison et al., 1990). Minority families have to find the means to maintain ethnic pride in their children while providing the tools they need to function in the majority society. Parents of successful African American children have been found to emphasize ethnic pride, self-development, awareness of racial barriers, and egalitarianism in their socialization practices. Minority socialization tends to focus on interdependence and cooperation as the route to success. This focus contrasts with the Western view of competition, autonomy, and self-reliance.

The third area examined by Harrison and her colleagues (Harrison et al., 1990) is the cognitive developmental outcomes of children raised in minority families. Infusion of biculturalism is a major goal in minority families. Achievement of this goal seems to produce children whose thinking is more flexible and who respond well to varied formats for learning. Ethnic minority children attain higher achievement in school if there is continuity between home and school expectations and environments. However, with their bicultural orientation, they are sensitive to discontinuities between home and school.

Harrison et al. (1990) point out that there is still much to be learned regarding the cultural context of child-rearing and child development in ethnic minority families. This chapter closes with examples of two studies that look at parents and infants in minority ethnic groups.

Harwood and Miller (1989) found that European American and Puerto Rican mothers have contrasting views of what can be considered appropriate attachment behaviors. Harwood and Miller (1989) had the mothers respond to examples of the three strange-situation infant responses: (A) avoidant, (B) secure, and (C) resistant. The European American mothers believed strongly that the B-type child response was the typical, acceptable response, whereas the Puerto Rican mothers viewed both the B and C responses as being typical. European American mothers evaluated behavior based on standards of independence and self-confidence, whereas Puerto Rican mothers looked at behavior as it affected others and the harmony of the situation. They were more geared to harmony and cooperation.

Maintaining the primary culture, while trying to adapt to the majority culture, can be very stressful (Stott & Halpern, 2003). A group of Mexican American mothers in Chicago shared their experiences and feelings. These mothers found it was stressful to prepare children for discrimination and for a marginal social position. They found danger everywhere and felt powerless. Their child-rearing goals focused on family unity and responsibility, and they found it difficult to cope with the American goal of independence. They emphasized respect for adults and peers and found this lacking in the United States. The need to become bilingual was a challenge. These mothers had mixed feelings about their children attending preschool. They didn't see the connection to elementary school. Through discussions with these mothers, the preschool staff gained valuable insights and understanding.

The results of a study by Lee, Ostrosky, Bennett, & Fowler (2003) indicated that early intervention professionals believe that best practices should reflect cultural appropriateness but find there are barriers in the system to meeting this challenge. There appears to be a need for more administrative support and for in-service and pre-service education.

Bornstein et al. (1992) looked at mothers' responsiveness to infants in three countries: the United States, France, and Japan. Researchers found that infant behaviors were similar in all three cultures and that the mothers responded in a similar manner in all three cultures. There appear to be some behaviors that are universal across cultures, while others are quite different. Therefore, caregivers who are responsible for other people's children must not assume that the child-rearing techniques of all cultures are identical (Bhavnagri & Gonzales-Mena, 1997; Bredekamp & Copple, 1997). Caregivers must be open to discussing differences in caregiving and childrearing customs and negotiating with families as needed.

List and describe some factors related to poverty and/or cultural diversity that might influence an infant's development. Describe any experiences you have had where your culture and another person's provided different reactions to a situation or to solving a problem.

## SUMMARY

Infants are complex individuals who develop at a rapid rate. Theorists agree that warm, loving, responsive adults are essential to ensure optimum development at this stage. Children are born with the basic competencies needed to put their senses to work in order to learn about the world. Infant research indicates that the effects of many different environmental variables can promote or diminish infant competency.

Social and cultural factors are very important influences on infant development. The infant needs a rich environment that will challenge his or her developing cognitive, social/emotional, and psychomotor abilities. Development is influenced by the objects and people that surround the infant. Both fathers and mothers add important dimensions to infant development. Additional stress on today's families results when both parents are employed outside the home and when single parents must balance work and child-rearing responsibilities. Some experts believe that infants are psychologically damaged if the mother works outside the home during the first year. Others disagree and suggest that with high-quality child care, the baby will thrive normally. The major problem with this view is that high-quality child care is difficult to find.

Parent education is increasing in scope. There is a recognition that parents need support and advice on how to parent. A home environment with appropriate play materials and nurturing caretakers provides for the best development.

Socioeconomic and cultural conditions are very important factors in infant development. The lower the income level, the greater the possibility that the family will not have access to appropriate health and nutritional care. Ethnic group is also a critical consideration. Each cultural group has its own set of values and customs and its own view of what is acceptable and unacceptable child behavior. The adult who works with infants must be knowledgeable about each infant's culture and work from a multicultural point of view: respecting each culture but also providing what the infant will need to operate in a world that may be dominated by another culture.

## For Further Reading


Albrecht, K., & Miller, L. G. (2001). *Infant & toddler development.* Beltsville, MD: Gryphon House.

Assessing and treating infants and young children with severe difficulties in relating and communicating (#145). (1997). *Zero to Three* [Special Issue].

Barrera, I. with Corso, R. M., & Macpherson, D. (2003). *Skilled dialogue: Strategies for responding to cultural diversity in early childhood.* Baltimore: Brookes.

Baum, J. (2004). *Respectful parenting: From birth through the terrific twos.* Washington, DC: Child Welfare League of America.

Behnke, A. (2004). Latino dads: Structural inequalities and personal strengths. Family focus on inequalities and families. *NCFR Report, 49*(3), F6–F7.

Berlin, L. J. (Ed.). (1998). Opening the black box: What makes early child and family development programs work? *Zero to Three, 18*(4) [Whole issue].

Borkowski, J. G., Ramey, S. L., Bristol-Power, M. (Eds.). (2002). *Parents and the child's world: Influences on academic, intellectual, and social-emotional development.* Mahwah, NJ: Erlbaum.

Bornstein, M. H. (Ed.). (2002). *Handbook of parenting* (2nd ed.). Mahwah, NJ: Erlbaum.

Bornstein, M. H., & Bradley, R. H. (Eds.). (2003). *Socioeconomic status, parenting, and child development.* Mahwah, NJ: Erlbaum.

Bremner, J. G., & Slater, A. (Eds.). (2003). *Theories of infant development.* Malden, MA: Blackwell.

Bremner, G., & Fogel, A. (2001). *The Blackwell handbook of infant development.* Williston, VT.: Blackwell.

Early Head Start: The first two years. (1997). *Zero to Three, 18*(2) [Whole issue].

Erickson, M. F., & Kurz-Riemer, K. (1999, 2002). *Infants, toddlers and families.* New York: Guilford.

Golbeck, S. L. (Ed.). (2001). *Psychological perspectives on early childhood education.* Mahwah, NJ: Erlbaum.

Hiatt-Michael, D. (Ed.). (2001). *Promising practices in family involvement.* Greenwich, CT: IAP, Inc.

Higginson, J. G. (1998). Competitive parenting: The culture of teen mothers. *Journal of Marriage and the Family, 60*(1), 135–149.

King, E. W., Chipman, M. F., & Cruz-Janzen, M. (1994). *Educating children in a diverse society.* Des Moines, IA: Longwood Division, Allyn & Bacon.

Koester, L. S., & Koester, O. (2005). *Seeing babies in a new light: The life of Hanus Papousek.* Mahwah, NJ: Erlbaum.

Lieberman, A. F., Wiedner, S., & Fenichel, E. (1997). *The DC 0-3 Casebook: A guide to the use of zero to Three's Diagnostic Classification of Mental Health and Developmental Disorders of Infancy and Early Childhood in assessment and treatment planning* (#151). Washington, DC: Zero to Three.

Lynch, E. W., & Hanson, M. J. (Eds.) (2004). *Developing cross-cultural competence.* Baltimore: Brookes.

Martini, M. (2002). How mothers in four American cultural groups shape infant learning during mealtimes. *Zero to three [Routines and rituals in the lives of infants, toddlers, and families], 22*(4), 20.

Ogbu, J. U. (1992). Understanding cultural diversity and learning. *Educational Research, 21*(8), 5–14.

Palkovitz, R. (2002). *Involved fathering and men's adult development.* Mahwah, NJ: Erlbaum.

Parlakian, R. (2003). How culture shapes social-emotional development.

*Progress in infancy research.* (Series). Mahwah, NJ: Erlbaum.

Raikes, H., & Whitmer, J. M. (2005). *Beautiful beginnings. A developmental curriculum for infants and toddlers.* Baltimore: Brookes.

Rovee-Collier, C., & Lipsitt, L. (Eds.). (Yearly). *Advances in infancy research.* Norwood, NJ: Ablex.

Sanchez, S. Y., & Thorp, E. K. (Eds.). (1998). Discovering meanings of continuity: Implications for the infant/family field. *Zero to Three, 18*(6) [Whole issue].

Tamis-LeMonda, C., & Cabrera, N. (2002). *The handbook of father involvement.* Mahwah, NJ: Erlbaum.

Wolpert, E. (2005). *Start seeing diversity: The basic guide to an anti-bias classroom.* St. Paul, MN: Redleaf Press.

Zero to Three. (2004). *Getting ready for school starts at birth.* Washington, DC: Author. (brochures)

*Zero to Three.* (2003). Partnerships for quality infant-toddler child care [Focus issue], 23(4).

*Zero to Three.* (2002). Paraprofessional in infant/family practice [Focus issue], 23(2).


## Suggested Activities

1. Describe any experiences you have had with infants. How did you feel about these babies? Is there any one of them who is (was) a favorite? Why? Any one infant to whom you had difficulty relating? Compare your experiences and reactions with those of other class members.

2. Visit a home- or center-based infant child care site. Observe a full day of activities if possible. Use the evaluation sheet in Figure 11–8 to evaluate the competence of the caregiver(s). Answer the following questions:
   a. Did the caregiver(s) have the desirable characteristics needed by an infant caregiver who is developmentally appropriate?
   b. What were the caregiver's strengths and weaknesses?
   c. In what areas should the caregiver try to improve?

3. Visit a family that includes an infant. Observe the parent(s). Rate the parent behavior using the infant caregiver evaluation sheet. Evaluate the competence of the parent(s) by answering questions a through c in Activity 2.

4. Visit a family in which the mother and father share infant care. Observe each parent separately caring for their baby. Did you note any similarities? Any differences? Repeat your observation in the homes of families with different racial and socioeconomic backgrounds. Again, compare parents with each other and with families from different cultures. Do you perceive any differences that you believe are the result of cultural differences in personality and/or customs?

5. Many agencies and groups publish pamphlets designed to help parents select high-quality child care settings. Obtain some of these and compare them with each other, particularly regarding the suggestions for choosing infant care. Visit one or more centers and see if you find the suggestions from the pamphlets to be helpful. Design your own guide for parents. To find pamphlets, check with your cooperative extension service, your state department of health, and early childhood education professional organizations, such as the NAEYC (1313 L Street, NW, Suite 500, Washington, DC 20005-4104), the Association for Childhood Education International (ACEI, 17904 Georgia Avenue, Suite 215, Olney, MD 20832-2277), or the Southern Early Childhood Association (SECA, P.O. Box 55930, Little Rock, AR 72215-5903), and local child care resource and referral programs.

6. Make an entry in your journal.

## REVIEW

1. Match each theorist in Column I with the definitions of theories or behavior in Column II.

| Column I | Column II |
|---|---|
| a. Erikson | 1. Parents need to be accepting of their children and themselves. |
| b. Bandura | 2. The infant is in the sensorimotor period. |
| c. Piaget | 3. The right environment is the key to healthy growth and learning. |
| d. Skinner | 4. The child develops a sense of trust or mistrust through his experiences during feeding. |
| e. Vygotsky | 5. During infancy, the child receives oral satisfaction while being cuddled by a caregiver. |
| f. Rogers and Maslow | 6. After a two-month crisis period, the infant settles into a stable period, during which the child develops his or her first reciprocal relationships with adults and has his or her first mental images. |
| g. Freud | 7. The infant builds mental pictures based on social interactions. Observational learning helps the child construct knowledge. |

**Infant Caregiver(s) Evaluation Rating Sheet**

For each infant caregiver behavior and characteristic, check whether the practice is observed frequently (f), occasionally (o), or not at all (n).

| Behavior or Characteristic | f | o | n | Comments |
|---|---|---|---|---|
| **Adult-Child Interaction** | | | | |
| 1. Frequent one-on-one, face-to-face pleasant contact with adult(s). | | | | |
| 2. Adult speaks in pleasant soothing voice. | | | | |
| 3. Infants are carried about and spoken to. | | | | |
| 4. Adults speak to infants during routine activities. | | | | |
| 5. Adults respond to infant vocalizations. | | | | |
| 6. Adults respond quickly to infant cries in a warm manner. | | | | |
| 7. During infant play, adult comments, makes suggestions, encourages infant exploration. | | | | |
| 8. Adult talks, sings, and reads to infant. | | | | |
| 9. Individual differences in food preferences, timing of meals, and sleeping schedules are respected. | | | | |
| 10. Infants are shown how to interact positively with each other. | | | | |
| 11. Adults play games like peek-a-boo and five little piggies. | | | | |
| 12. Adults understand that infant body movements and vocalizations are their means of communication. | | | | |
| 13. Adult's consistent responses build trust. | | | | |
| **Environmental Characteristics** | | | | |
| 14. Diapering, sleeping, feeding, and play areas are separate. | | | | |
| 15. There are many soft elements like pillows, cushions, and carpet. | | | | |
| 16. There are a variety of bright colors. | | | | |
| 17. Each infant has his or her personal crib and feeding and diapering supplies. | | | | |
| 18. Babies have a variety of play spaces: indoors and outdoors. | | | | |
| 19. The temperature and humidity are comfortable. | | | | |
| 20. Decorations include pictures of people of diverse cultures, animals, plants, etc., at infant eye level. | | | | |
| 21. Space allows for infants to roll, creep, crawl, and pull themselves up to standing. | | | | |

**FIGURE 11–8** Infant caregiver evaluation sheet.

Adapted from Lally, J. R., Provence, S., Szanton, E., & Weissbourd, B. (1987). Developmentally appropriate care for children from birth to age 3; and Lally, J. R., Griffin, A, Fenichel, E., Segal, M., Szanton, E., & Weissbourd, B. (1997, revised ed.). Developmentally appropriate practice for infants and toddlers. In S. Bredekamp (Ed.), *Developmentally appropriate practice in early childhood programs serving children from birth through age eight.* Washington, DC: National Association for the Education of Young Children.

| Behavior or Characteristic | f | o | n | Comments |
|---|---|---|---|---|
| 22. Carpet and walls are made of easy-to-clean materials. | | | | |
| 23. There are enough toys and they are nontoxic, washable, and too big to be swallowed. | | | | |
| 24. Toys and board books are on low shelves where infants can make selections. | | | | |
| 25. There are safe, well-padded climbing structures. | | | | |
| 26. Infants who are not yet mobile are routinely moved to different areas for new experiences. | | | | |
| 27. The outdoors is adjacent to the indoor area, has soft areas for mobile infants, and shady places for infants to lie on quilts or blankets. | | | | |
| 28. Infants are always supervised by an adult. | | | | |
| 29. For safety, the room is baby-proofed: electrical outlets are covered, dangerous substances are out of reach, extension cords are not exposed. | | | | |
| 30. Adults wash their hands before and after diapering and before feeding. | | | | |
| 31. Diaper changing table is sanitized after each change. | | | | |
| 32. Only healthy foods are provided, and meal time is happy and sociable. | | | | |
| 33. Infants are held and talked to when fed. | | | | |
| 34. Diapering and food preparation areas are separated. | | | | |
| **Staff-Parent Interactions** | | | | |
| 35. Pertinent information is shared daily. | | | | |
| 36. Parents are greeted warmly and treated with respect. | | | | |
| **Staff-Child Ratio** | | | | |
| 37. No more than one adult to three babies. One main and one assistant caregiver relate to each infant regularly. | | | | |
| **Staff Qualifications** | | | | |
| 38. Staff are warm, caring, and understand child development. Preferably, they have had some formal training in infant education and care. | | | | |

FIGURE 11–8 Continued

2. Name the sensory area in which the infant in each example demonstrates competency.
   a. Aunt Mary is wearing a very strong perfume. The infant turns his head toward her as she stands next to his crib.
   b. The infant smiles and becomes active as her mother peers into the crib.
   c. When offered a soft, furry toy and a hard, wooden toy, the infant feels both and then chooses the soft, furry toy.
   d. Four-year-old brother Johnny bangs on a toy drum. The infant's eyes move in Johnny's direction.
3. Name two early developing activities that coordinate motor activity and perception.
4. What are some reasons why certain infants may not fully develop their sensory competencies?
5. Select the correct statements from those that follow:
   a. The more time a father spends with his infant, the higher he is likely to rate the infant's social and cognitive capacities.
   b. Today's fathers are much more involved with infant care than was the case in the past.
   c. If possible, when both parents work, the father should share responsibility for household tasks.
   d. Parents do not find that parenting stress increases if both parents are employed.
   e. Less parent interaction with infants takes place weekday evenings in homes where both parents are employed than in homes where the mother is not employed.
   f. No problems are associated with father absence.
   g. Older women make the most sensitive caregivers for infants.
   h. According to NICHD, there are future negative effects for children who spend 30 hours or more in child care by the time they are nine months old.
   i. Father's involvement in child-rearing does not increase self-esteem, empathy, or achievement.
   j. Plenty of high-quality child care is available if parents will just take the time to look for it.
   k. Currently, parent education is very popular.
6. In your opinion, should an infant be put in a child care situation? State your reasons for or against, using material from this chapter to support your argument.
7. List some factors related to poverty and/or cultural diversity that might influence development of the infant.

## KEY TERMS LIST

baby tender
biculturalism
child care
cultural diversity
early intervention
Home Observation for Measurement of the Environment (HOME)
parent education
perception
proprioception
sensorimotor period
trust

Additional resources for this chapter can be found on the Online Companion™ to accompany this text at http://www.earlychilded.delmar.com. Respond to "Time to Reflect" and "Looking Further" concepts, review various child development scenarios, and answer thought-provoking questions in the Critical Thinking Forum. Keep a daily journal by downloading the student journal available on this web site. Complete the interactive matching exercises to reinforce concepts, and print out the child development assessment forms to use during your observation of development for children from birth to age eight. In addition, read the case studies on the Web site to reinforce important concepts in each chapter, and take a look at the multitude of Web links that are available for student research on the Internet.

CHAPTER

# 12

# Infancy: Health and Physical and Motor Skills Development

## OBJECTIVES

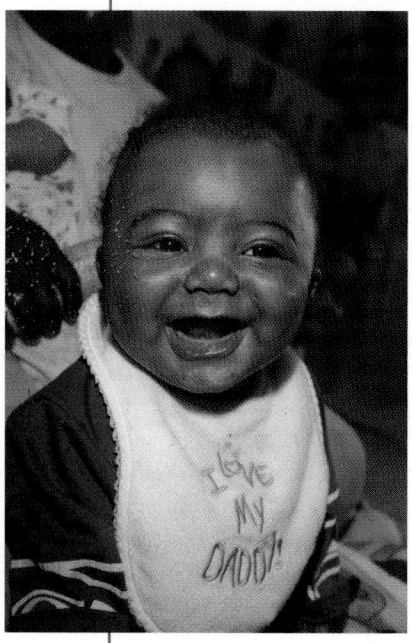


After reading this chapter, you should be able to:

- Identify the essentials that promote infant health.
- Identify potential environmental health hazards.
- Discuss the effects of nutrition on physical and motor development.
- Identify examples of basic principles of growth.
- Use a growth chart to determine if an infant's height, weight, and body proportions are within the normal range.
- Explain the relationship between physical and motor development.
- Recognize the critical factors in infant fine and gross motor development.
- Recognize the factors that influence infant motor development.
- Analyze and evaluate an infant's gross and fine motor behavior and development.
- List at least six infant motor skills.
- Explain why assessing the infant's motor skills is important.
- Describe how infants develop their motor skills.

Every child goes through the same basic patterns of physical growth and motor skills development, but in different timeframes. There is a wide range of *normal* physical and motor growth and development. How heredity and environment interact is dependent on the health support and the environmental support of development. This chapter focuses on infant health, physical development, and motor skills. The Children's Defense Fund (CDF, 2004) lists the following "Key Facts About American Children":

- 1 in 5 is born poor.
- 1 in 5 under three is poor now.

- 1 in 6 is born to a mother who did not receive prenatal care in the first three months of pregnancy.
- 1 in 8 has no health insurance.
- 1 in 8 lives in a family receiving food stamps.
- 1 in 8 has a worker in their family but is still poor.
- 1 in 13 was born with low birth weight.
- 1 in 14 lives at less than half the poverty level.
- 1 in 146 will die before their first birthday (77 each day).

It is clear that poverty and lack of proper medical care may result in poor health, poor living conditions, and poor nutrition, all of which have negative effects on development.

## INFANT HEALTH

In Chapter 8, we saw that good health begins with a healthy mother and good prenatal care. In this part of the chapter, the general health factors that apply all through childhood are reviewed including nutrition, immunization, illness and infection, safety and injury, and mental health.

### General Health

Adults who work with young children should be concerned with all aspects of children's health. According to the CDF, "millions of children have inadequate health care because of lack of insurance" (CDF, 2001). Most children without health coverage have parents who work, but who do not receive health benefits or cannot afford what is available. In 1997, landmark legislation, Children's Health Insurance Program (CHIP), was enacted to provide help for uninsured children. Gradually, CHIP is reaching children in low-income working families. There have also been Medicaid outreach programs. Due to these programs, the number of children without health insurance has begun to decrease (CDF, 2001). Under CHIP, nearly four million children and teenagers have health insurance who probably otherwise would not have insurance (American Academy of Pediatrics, 2002b).

In a 2003 review, *The Future of Children* (Lewit, Bennett, & Behrman, 2003) looked in detail at the status of health insurance for children. At that time, the rate of uninsurance for children had dropped thanks to Medicaid and CHIP. Health insurance can facilitate catching health problems before they progress too far. There are still millions of lower socioeconomic level families with no health insurance and no access to health care.

### Nutrition

The first year is the period when children's rates of growth are the most rapid (Marotz, Cross, & Rush, 2005) Babies usually double their birth weight in the first four to five months and triple it by the end of the first year. Infants are totally dependent on adults for food. Feeding should be not only a time for sustenance but also a time for socializing and for stimulation with the introduction of a variety of foods.

Because infants are growing and developing at a rapid rate, they have high needs for nutrients (Marotz, Cross, & Rush, 2005). However, their stomachs are small so they need high-nutrient food frequently. At first, calories are needed for growth but as the infant becomes more mobile, calories are needed for physical activity. If the baby is the victim of poor prenatal nutrition, he may be a **low-birth-weight (LBW) infant.** LBW babies may have serious problems, such as poor regulation of body

**low-birth-weight (LBW) infant**
A victim of poor prenatal nutrition.

temperature and increased susceptibility to infection. Children of teenage mothers, who themselves often have nutritional deficiencies, are most likely to be LBW. The Women, Infants, and Children (WIC) program provides nutritional food supplements for pregnant and breastfeeding women, infants, and children up to age five.

During the first six months, breastfeeding is the preferred feeding method. For six months, breast milk can provide all the necessary nutrients for the infant. No solid or semisolid foods should be given during the first five months. According to Marotz et al. (2005), in some situations the mother may choose to formula feed if:

- mother is ill.
- mother is taking medications.
- mother needs to be away for long periods.
- mother does not wish to nurse.
- mother uses addictive drugs.

During the first four months, it is recommended that infants be fed on demand since it can be predicted what their capacity might be. Marotz et al. (2005) suggest the following guidelines:

| | |
|---|---|
| 0–1 month | 6 feedings of 3–4 oz. each |
| 1–2 months | 6 feedings of 3–5 oz. each |
| 2–3 months | 5 feedings of 4–6 oz. each |
| 4–5 months | 5 feedings of 5–7 oz. each |
| 6–7 months* | 5 feedings of 6–8 oz. each |
| 8–12 months* | 3 feedings of 8 oz. each |

*Also receiving solid foods.

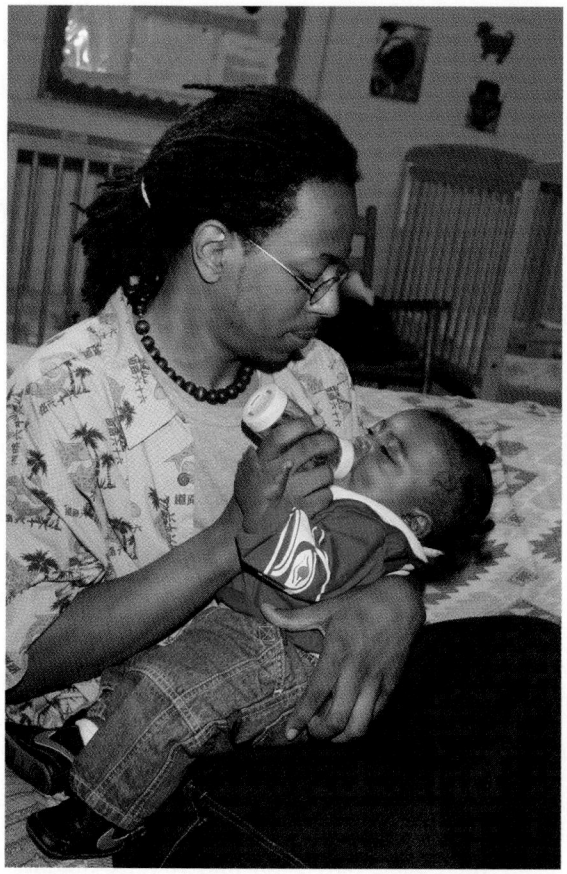

FIGURE 12–1 Feeding is a time for the adult and infant to form an attachment.

Sanitation is very important. The caregiver should wash his or her hands with soap before feeding. Formula or breast milk should be warm but not heated in a microwave. Microwaves destroy nutrients in breast milk, and the liquid in the bottle is likely to be hotter than the container and burn the infant. Marotz et al. (2005) recommend that the infant be cuddled and played with before feeding and talked to during feeding. The caretaker should stop two or three times during a feeding to burp the baby (Figure 12–1).

Infants are usually ready for semisolid foods between five and six months of age. High fluid content pureed foods, such as cereals and pureed fruits and vegetables, are appropriate. Babies' digestive systems have matured enough to digest more complex carbohydrates and proteins. By this time, children can sit up and lean toward the spoon and chew and swallow. They will also turn their heads to the side to signal they have had enough. Infants at this point enjoy feeling their food and feeding themselves by hand (Figure 12–2).

**Obesity,** weighing more than is appropriate for one's height, is a major health problem beginning in infancy (Huettig, Sanborn, DiMarco, Popejoy, & Rich, 2004). Obesity occurs when the infants take in more food than they need or growth and activity. It may occur when semisolid foods are introduced too early or cereal is fed from a bottle rather than a spoon. It is important to respect the infant's signals that he is full and not force him to finish the bottle.

**obesity**

Weighing more than is appropriate for one's height.

FIGURE 12–2 Infants enjoy the texture of their food.

It is essential that caregivers respect the infant feeding practices of every culture (Clark, 2003). Each culture has its own picture of what healthy babies should look like and what they should eat. However, some cultures may use practices that contribute to obesity beginning in infancy. In a study with Hispanic families, Clark (2003) found that children had bottles into their second year. The bottles were with them while playing and sleeping and often contained flavored milk, Kool-Aid, or juice. They might also thicken the drink with corn-based thickener, rice cereal, or raw eggs. Children were also given flavored teas. Relatives sometimes slipped infants candies for a treat. Mothers introduced all kinds of foods before the recommended five to six months. By the time their children were toddlers, they were familiar with fast food. The families believed that their way was the right way. Changing these habits cannot be accomplished in a directive way. Change to more healthy feeding can be brought about through friendly conversation with parents who trust the professional and are willing to seek an opinion.

## Immunization and Illness

**immunization**

Protection from disease through inoculation.

Many childhood diseases are preventable through **immunization** (protection from disease through inoculation). Large-scale campaigns have been instituted to try to get all infants immunized, but it is estimated that only 77 percent of children have received all the recommended age-appropriate immunizations (Marotz et al., 2005). Some states have laws requiring that children entering early care, education programs, and elementary school have all required immunizations.

**RSV**

A viral infection of the airways and lungs.

**RSV** is a viral infection of the airways and lungs occurring most often from late fall (November) until early/mid-spring (March/April), but exists throughout the year as well (Respiratory Syncytial Virus, 2005). Babies and young children are most frequently affected. Babies less than eight months of age or who have health problems are most at risk. It is easily transmitted and is very contagious. It is important to wash hands with antibacterial soap and to clean toys, pacifiers, cribs, etc., with disinfectant. At first, it may seem like a cold, but eventually it will move into mild fever, wheezing and rapid breathing, and the child should be seen by a doctor. It is best to keep babies at home and away from crowds during RSV season.

**Sudden Infant Death Syndrome (SIDS)**

Usually occurs at night during sleep.

**Sudden Infant Death Syndrome (SIDS)** is a leading cause of death among babies under one year (Kotch, 2004; Marotz et al., 2005). Most SIDS deaths occur between the second and fourth months. The victims usually appear to be in good health. The death usually occurs at night while the baby is sleeping. The exact cause is still unknown, but the following procedures are recommended (Kotch, 2004):

- Place the babies in their cribs on their backs.
- Locate the crib in a smoke-free room that is a comfortable temperature.
- Do not overdress the baby for sleep.
- Keep pillows, stuffed animals, bumpers, and toys out of the crib with the baby.

Many infants have chronic health problems, such as asthma and eczema (Aronson, 2002). An increasing number are "medically fragile." That is, they need technical medical procedures during their usual day. They may require tube feedings, endotrachial suctioning, oxygen, or other procedures. Most babies have mild illnesses. They have not yet built up their immune systems and are especially vulnerable in a group setting. Both at home and in child care, the most thorough sanitation practices must be adhered to. Adults should be observant and watch for signs of impending illness (Marotz et al., 2005):

- Unusually pale or flushed skin
- Red or sore throat

- Enlarged lymph glands
- Nausea, vomiting, or diarrhea
- Rash, spots, or open lesions
- Watery or red eyes
- Headache or dizziness
- Chills, fever, or achiness
- Fatigue or loss of appetite

A pediatrician should always be consulted if children appear to be getting sick. The doctor can often make a diagnosis over the phone or have the baby brought in if the symptoms sound serious.

## Prevention and Identification of Disease and Illness

Adults who work with young children need to know both the signs of typical, occasional illnesses and long-term or chronic illnesses (Marotz et al., 2005). They need to be able to recognize and attend to the more common problems, such as colds, diaper rash, diarrhea, earache, sore throat, stomachache, toothache, vomiting, and fever, while being alert to the possibility that any of these symptoms could indicate a more serious, chronic condition. For example, at least 71 percent of children have a serious ear infection before the age of three, and 33 percent have three or more (Watt, Roberts, & Zeisel, 1993). Ear infections can seriously impair hearing and interfere with the typical course of language development. If chronic health conditions are not diagnosed and treated, they can interfere with learning. Abnormal fatigue or poor posture can indicate underlying problems. Seizures caused by abnormal electrical impulses within the brain are symptomatic of problems, such as the effects of high fever, brain damage, central nervous system infection, and others. The greatest single cause of health problems among young children is allergies. Symptoms of allergic disorders include frequent colds and ear infections; chronic runny nose, cough, or throat clearing; headaches; frequent nosebleeds; unexplained stomachaches; and hives, eczema, or other skin rashes. Sickle-cell anemia is an inherited disorder found most often among African Americans. Early identification can indicate to parents that medical care is needed. Many of the problems mentioned go unnoticed by parents who have not had experience with other young children and do not have knowledge about typical child development and behavior.

Feeding and diapering are two routines during which it is particularly likely that disease and illness may be spread if great care is not taken (Warrick & Helling, 1997). Some examples of safe feeding procedures include the following:

- discarding leftover breast milk or leftover partial food jars if the baby has been fed directly from the jar
- ensuring that parents bring infant food to a home or center in unopened containers
- washing the tops of the containers before opening
- washing hands before preparing food
- never putting a baby down to sleep with a bottle filled with formula, milk, juice, or sweetened drinks (The sugar in these liquids can cause tooth decay. If the baby needs his or her bottle, fill it with water.)

Diapering must also be done carefully. Warrick and Helling (1997) list the guidelines supplied by the Centers for Disease Control and Prevention. Some examples include the following:

- The diapering surface should be at least three feet above the floor and be used only for diapering.
- Fecal material should be covered by folding the diaper inward and placing it in a waste container used only for that purpose.
- A disposable paper towel or roll paper should be placed under the infant's bottom.
- Adults should use moist towelettes to wipe the baby's bottom and hands and their own hands. If adults use disposable gloves, they should be discarded after every diapering.
- The diapering area should be sanitized after each changing, and the adults should wash their hands.

A major concern for those who work with young children is the advent of AIDS in young children. In most cases, the virus was acquired from the mother during gestation; a small number of cases are the result of blood transfusions with contaminated blood (Marotz et al., 2005). The incurability of AIDS has engendered emotional discussion and strong fear (Kirp & Epstein, 1989), even though HIV is not transmitted through casual contact but only through sexual contact and blood transfer (Marotz et al., 2005). School systems and child care centers need to educate staff regarding AIDS and HIV and develop policies before AIDS and HIV children arrive.

Wadsworth and Knight (1996) describe the importance of all early childhood professionals attending in-service training regarding HIV and AIDS. In-service topics should include universal health precautions against transmission, procedures for cleaning up and disposing of blood or bodily fluids in the classroom, special educational accommodations for students with HIV and AIDS, guidelines for interacting with students' families, participation on interdisciplinary teams, and how to plan and give educational programs on HIV and AIDS.

## Safety and Injury

A safe environment is a prerequisite for optimal child development. Marotz et al. (2005) outline the basic elements of an environment that promotes healthy physical, cognitive, and psychological development. Licensing and accreditation standards are designed to ensure that the environment is physically safe (Marotz et al., 2005). High-quality environmental standards should be met with regard to building facilities, outdoor play areas, staff qualifications, group size and composition, staff/child ratios, program content, health services, and transportation.

Environmental standards include allowing adequate space for the number of children; meeting fire department safety standards; and having adequate sanitary facilities, safety glass in low windows, good lighting, sturdy furniture, easily cleaned walls and floor coverings, safety electrical receptacles, and telephones located conveniently for emergency use. Outdoor space also needs to be adequate in size. It should be fenced and have a latched gate; have a variety of sturdy, safe play equipment; contain no poisonous plants or shrubs; and be well supervised at all times. A well-trained and competent staff is needed to see that standards are met and maintained (Marotz et al., 2005). See Marotz et al. (2005) for a safety checklist.

Young children may be involved in many types of accidents, including, most often, motor vehicle accidents, burns, drownings, falls, and poisoning (Marotz et al., 2005). Most accidents in early childhood settings occur during outdoor play activities, especially on equipment, such as swings, climbing apparatus, and slides. Looking at severity of injury, Aronson (1983) found climbers were by far the most dangerous equipment, followed in order by slides, hand toys, and blocks, other playground equipment (excluding swings, sandboxes, seesaws, and gliders), doors, indoor floor surfaces, motor vehicles, swings, pebbles or rocks, and pencils. Early childhood educators need to take care in choosing safe equipment, providing close supervision, and teaching children to use the equipment safely. Accidents can be prevented if adults are knowledgeable about child development and plan accordingly by following four basic principles: "advanced planning, establishing rules, careful supervision, safety education" (Marotz et al., 2005). Details on ways to implement these principles are described by Marotz et al. (2005).

There is also increasing awareness of numerous environmental hazards, such as pesticides, tobacco smoke, toxic art materials, lead, stale air, and asbestos. Many of these factors can be controlled by the alert adult. Others, such as building construction, power line location, lead content of soil and water, and pesticides and herbicides, may not be under our direct control, but we should be aware and investigate the presence of any possible health and safety hazards (Gratz & Boulton, 1993).

Bearer (1995) explains how children and adults react differently to environmental hazards. At different stages of development, children react differently to variations in the physical and biological environment. Children are most vulnerable to the increasing pollution in the environment; such levels of exposure change as they develop. For example, infants and toddlers are close to the floor and are more likely to be exposed to chemicals, such as those found in synthetic carpets or residues from pesticides.

## Housing

Habitat for Humanity founder and former president Millard Fuller (1998, p. 16) sums up the relationship of housing and health:

> Housing and health are definitely linked, and the linkage can be either negative or positive, either contrast or complementary. A poor house with a leaky roof, no insulation, or over-crowding is the antithesis of good health, while a decent house with solid walls, a good roof, and other simple but basic features that make a house a good one, promote health in a truly powerful way. A safe, secure house enables the inhabitants to sleep peacefully at night. Adequate rest promotes good health.

McLead (1998) describes some of the elements of poor housing that can make people sick. Disease and infection flourish in overcrowded housing, such as slums and squatter settlements. Lack of safe water increases the chance for disease. Lack of sanitation facilities with accompanying lack of proper disposal for waste products provides a breeding area for disease-carrying parasites, flies, and rats. Poor housing may have unhygienic dirt flooring; may contain fumes from open fires that could cause respiratory problems; may be easily destroyed by floods, fires, or landslides; and may contribute to stress, mental problems, violence, antisocial behavior, and substance abuse.

Free (1998) points out specific housing-related problems found in urban areas. In the United States, poor housing results in two major problems. First, according to a 1993 survey, more than 1.2 million U.S. families live in physically inadequate housing; second, poorer families have limited choices regarding where they can live. The major childhood health conditions directly connected to poor housing environments are lead paint poisoning, asthma and respiratory disease, physical and mental injuries, homelessness, and malnutrition.

## Mental Health

Infant mental health is a relatively new focus in the field of early childhood development. According to Leone-Getten (2005):

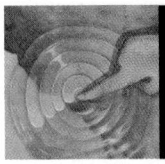

**LOOKING FURTHER**

Investigate what is being done in your community to improve housing conditions for the poor. Is there an active program and plan for improvement, such as destroying and/or upgrading poor-quality housing and building or finding adequate housing? Has Habitat for Humanity built any homes in your area? Inquire of your local government officials and look for articles in local newspapers regularly.

> The field of infant mental health focuses on relationship-based interaction, with the understanding that relationships are central to healthy development and that a child is best understood within the context of the important adults in his or her life (p. 13).

The parent/child relationship is central to infant mental health. The teacher/therapist must be caring, respectful, and nurturing in relationships with parents, modeling the behaviors parents need to use with their infants.

Infant mental health professionals focus on infants' emotional well-being (Petersen, Bair, & Sullivan (2004). Early Head Start (EHS) personnel emphasize the following guidelines (Petersen, Bair, & Sullivan, 2004, pp. 47–48):

1. Tools designed for the assessment of social-emotional development help staff to understand the child and provide a framework for discussing the topic of mental health with families.
2. The infant-parent relationship serves as a powerful and accessible point for intervention.
3. Providing support for EHS staff members helps them maintain their own emotional availability to infants, toddlers, and families within this intense and intimate work.
4. Integrating mental health concepts and strategies into every aspect of an EHS program requires thoughtful planning.

EHS staff use a variety of assessment tools that focus on environment, parents, and infants in order to arrive at an accurate picture of the family mental health situation. For example, one tool assesses infants' and toddlers' behaviors in the following areas (Petersen, Bair, & Sullivan, 2004, p. 50):

- self-regulation (capability of calming down when agitated)
- compliance (does what is asked to do)
- communication (infants' babble)
- adaptive functioning (infant is awake at least one hour during the day)
- autonomy (explores new places)
- affect (likes to be picked up and held)
- interaction with people (chooses to play near people)

Balbernie (2004) describes a British parent-infant psychotherapy program. In this program, the relationship between baby and caregiver is the "patient." The program is similar to EHS in providing services for families at the poverty level. These families face a variety of difficulties, which increasingly puts stress on the parent-baby relationship. Risk factors include severe parental mental illness, parental background of severe abuse, neglect or loss in childhood, family violence, maltreatment of the baby, and alcohol or drug abuse. Any of these factors put stress on the caregiving relationship. When caregivers have the opportunity to engage in a therapeutic relationship, they benefit from the opportunity to discuss their child, by being helped to see the child's point of view, by gaining a sense of being understood, through thinking about their relationship with the child, from gaining information on child development, and considering how past events might be influencing current behavior.

A friend comments that infants are easy to care for and understand because their needs are simple and they are not yet aware of what is going on in their environment. How might you respond?

## INFANT PHYSICAL DEVELOPMENT

Physical and motor development are closely related. Both are critical areas in the lives of children. Children who develop at a normal rate can keep up with their peers. Every child progresses through the same basic patterns of physical growth but on different time schedules. Physical growth follows seven basic principles:

1. directional growth
2. general-to-specific growth
3. differentiation/integration in growth
4. variations in growth
5. optimal tendency in growth
6. sequential growth
7. growth during critical periods

### Directional Growth

**cephalocaudal**
Growth and development proceed from head to toe.

**proximodistal**
Growth and development are from the center out.

Direction of growth is from head to toe **(cephalocaudal)** and from the center out **(proximodistal)**. Head-to-toe growth is outlined in Figure 12–3.

The sequence of growth from head to toe can be seen in the gradual change in proportions from the prenatal period to adulthood. Muscular growth is reflected in the progression of lifting the head, then the shoulders, and finally the trunk, as the infant learns to sit without aid in a step-by-step sequence. Eventually, the infant is able to stand and finally to walk as his or her trunk-to-toe development matures to the point at which the legs and feet can hold him or her up and the child can coordinate

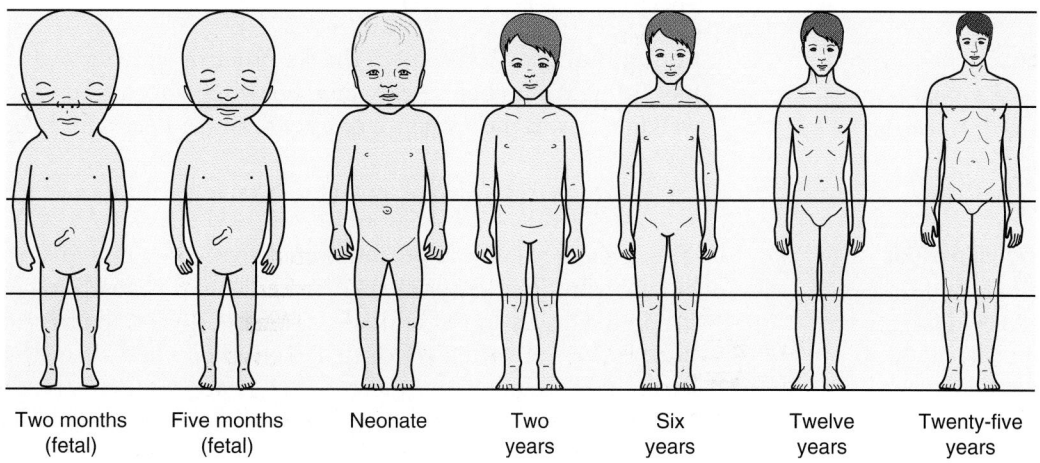


FIGURE 12–3 Changes in body proportions: prenatal to adult.

the muscles necessary for walking. The sequence from center out is reflected in the development of arm movements, first from the shoulder. Gradually, the child controls the arm at the elbow, the wrist, and then the hand and the fingers.

## General-to-Specific Growth

General-to-specific development is exemplified in the large, gross movement of the arms and legs seen in the infant to the specific movements used in walking or drawing a picture.

## Differentiation/Integration in Growth

**differentiation**
The process the child goes through as he or she gains control of specific parts of his or her body.

**Differentiation** refers to the process the child goes through while gaining control of specific parts of his or her body. Younger children often have trouble locating parts of their bodies. For example, a three-year-old boy is lying flat on the floor and is told, "Lift your head." Very likely, he will lift his shoulders and his head. If a five-year-old boy is asked to perform the same task, he usually lifts his head, leaving his shoulders still on the floor.

**integrated movements**
Combining specific movements to perform more complex activities such as walking, climbing, building a block tower, or drawing a picture.

Once the child has differentiated the individual parts of the body, he or she can develop **integrated movements.** That is, the child can combine specific movements to perform more complex activities, such as walking, climbing, building a block tower, or drawing a picture. Many integrated movements develop naturally with no special instruction. If the environment allows the child the freedom to try, he or she will crawl, walk, sit, and grasp on his or her own. Other types of integrated movements, such as opening a door, skating, or riding a bicycle, may require special help.

## Variations in Growth Rates

Children vary in their growth rate. Girls grow faster than boys until adolescence. In addition, different parts of the body grow at different rates.

## Optimal Tendency in Growth

Growth always tries to fulfill its potential. If growth is slowed down for some reason, such as lack of proper food, the body will try to catch up once it has adequate food.

## Sequential Growth

**sequential growth**
The set order in which growth proceeds.

**Sequential growth** refers to the set order in which growth proceeds. For example, sitting comes before crawling, crawling before creeping, and creeping before walking, due to the sequence of growth of the necessary bones and muscles.

## Growth During the Critical Periods

**critical periods**
The idea that growth in certain areas may be more important at particular times.

The concept of **critical periods** refers to the idea that growth in certain areas may be most important at particular times, such as is described in the prenatal period and in the discussion of brain development during the first three years.

Parents are often concerned about their child's growth rate. They wonder if he or she is too tall, too short, too thin, or too fat. Pediatric growth charts, Figures 12–4 and 12–5 answer these questions. To use the charts, follow these steps:

1. Pick the chart for the child you wish to assess: boy or girl.
2. From the chart, pick the characteristic of interest: height or weight.

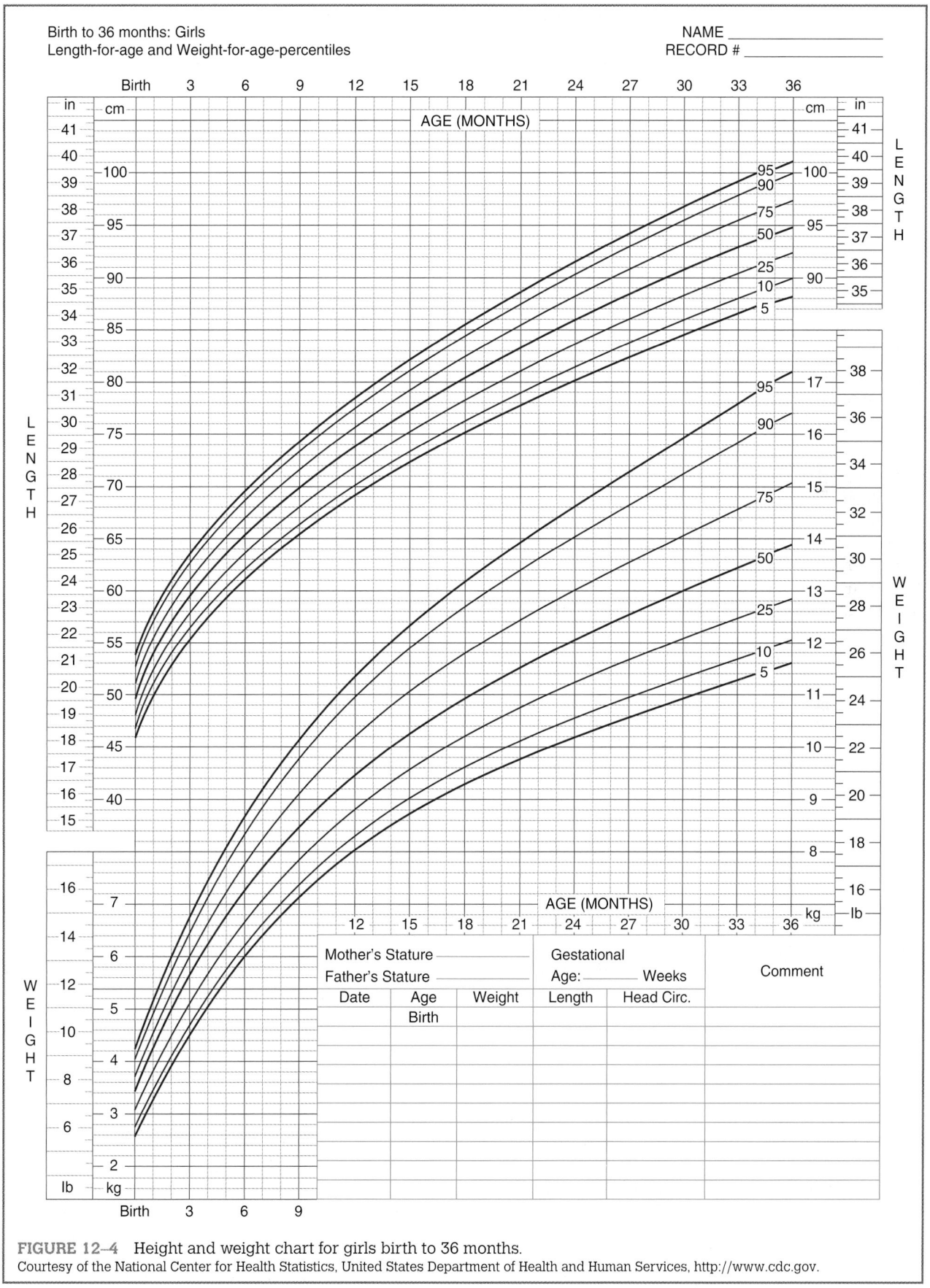


**FIGURE 12–4** Height and weight chart for girls birth to 36 months.
Courtesy of the National Center for Health Statistics, United States Department of Health and Human Services, http://www.cdc.gov.

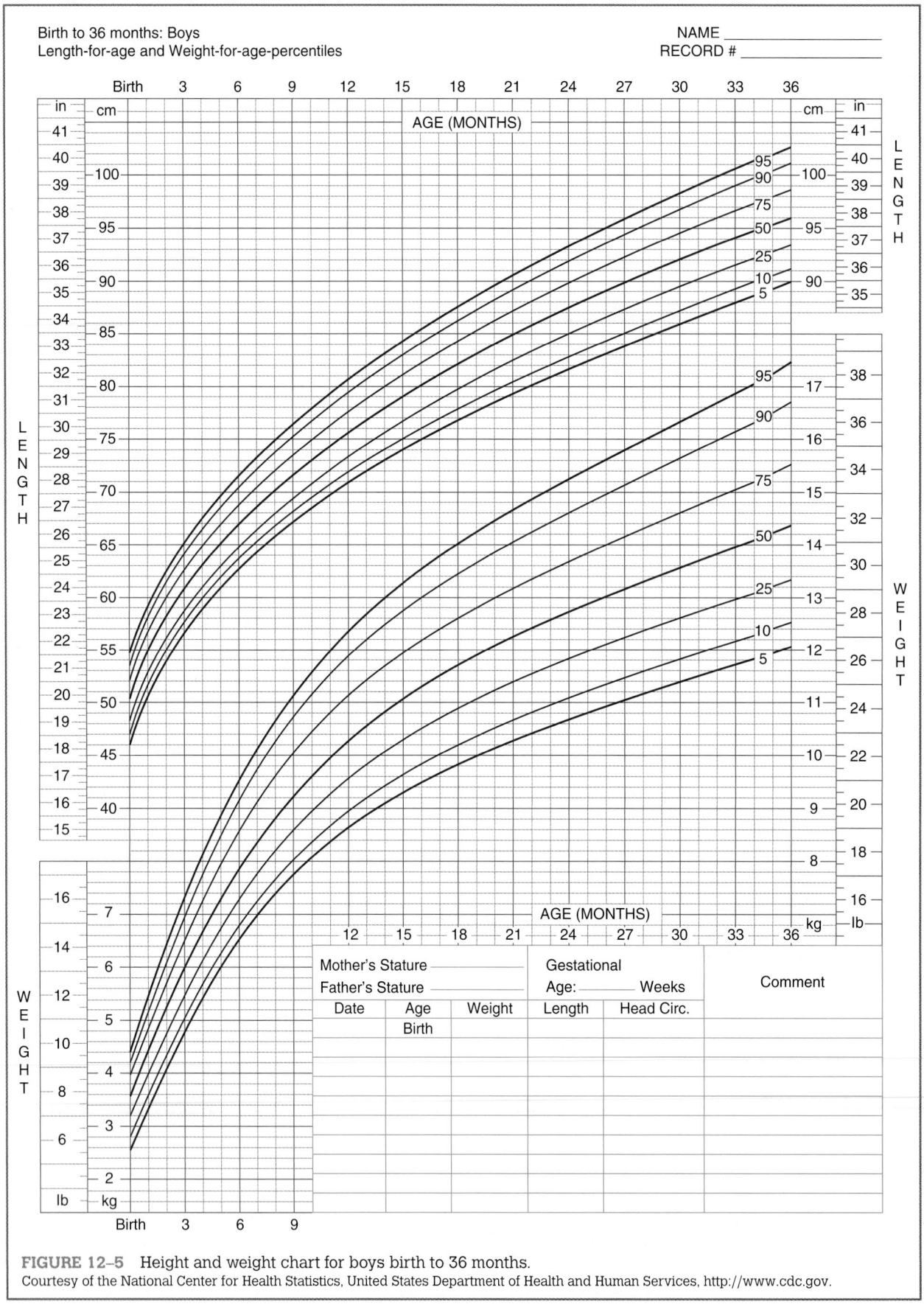


**FIGURE 12–5** Height and weight chart for boys birth to 36 months.
Courtesy of the National Center for Health Statistics, United States Department of Health and Human Services, http://www.cdc.gov.

3. Place your finger on the bottom of the graph until you come to the child's age.
4. Run your finger up the vertical line until you come to the child's height (or weight).
5. Move both fingers toward the center of the chart, the left hand horizontally and the right hand vertically, until they meet. Make a mark with pen or pencil.
6. Follow the nearest curved line to find the child's weight or height percentile. The percentile tells you where the child is compared with other children the same age. The fiftieth percent denotes that 50 percent (or half ) the children of that age are bigger and half smaller. The tenth percentile indicates that 10 percent of the children that age are smaller and 90 percent are larger.

If a child's height or weight is below the fifth percentile or if the child's weight is above the ninety-fifth percentile, then he or she is considered at high risk relative to good health. This child should be seen by a doctor.

Measurements must be taken as carefully as possible. The child should take off his or her shoes and wear light-weight clothing. The scale should be accurate. When measuring height, the child should stand against a wall.

### Delayed or Limited Physical Development

Distinguishing between what is *normal* or *typical* compared to *abnormal* or *atypical* development is not easy (Allen & Schwartz, 2001). For this reason, adults who work with young children need to have a thorough knowledge of normal or typical growth and development. This knowledge can then be used as a guide to making decisions regarding children who may have delayed or atypical developmental characteristics.

"Virtually everything a young child does is affected if physical development is delayed or limited" (Bowe, 2000). Remember, young children learn through active exploration of the world. Atypical physical growth patterns affect children's motor capabilities, which, in turn, affect their abilities to explore. Asthma; cerebral palsy; impairments of the limbs; missing body parts; traumatic brain injury; spinal cord injury or other paralysis; and arm, hand, and finger impairments limit the young child's motor activity. Causes of delays may be genetic or environmental. Many are related to poor prenatal conditions (see Chapter 8).

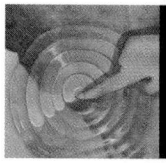

**LOOKING FURTHER**

Assess the physical development of an infant using the government height and weight charts (Figures 12–4 and 12–5) and the Infant Physical Development Chart, Figure 12-6.

## INFANT MOTOR SKILLS DEVELOPMENT

Closely aligned to physical growth is the development of motor skills. As the body grows physically, muscles develop and mature, and the child is able to perform new motor acts. Infancy is a time when children discover their body parts and explore how they work. Motor responses develop following the same patterns as physical development described earlier in this chapter. The cephalocaudal, proximodistal, and general to specific developmental patterns are also apparent in motor development. Gross motor development comes before fine motor development. Hand preference develops gradually as infants and toddlers experiment with new skills.

Observer _____ Date _____ Time _____ Place _____

Infant's name _____ Birth date _____ Age _____

| Age and Characteristic | Observed: Yes | Observed: No | Comments |
|---|---|---|---|
| **Birth to 1 month** | | | |
| Birth weight: 6.5 to 9 lbs. | | | |
| Gains average of 5 to 6 oz. per week | | | |
| Length at birth: 18 to 21 inches | | | |
| Chest appears to be same size as head | | | |
| Large head: $^1/_4$ of body length | | | |
| **1 to 4 months** | | | |
| Weighs an average of 8 to 16 lbs. | | | |
| Average length: 20 to 27 inches | | | |
| Gains $^1/_4$ to $^1/_2$ lb. per week | | | |
| Head and chest circumference are nearly equal | | | |
| Head circumference increases: $^3/_4$ inch per month until 2 months; $^5/_8$ inch per month until 4 months (indication of brain growth) | | | |
| Arms and legs are of equal length, size, and shape. | | | |
| Legs may appear slightly bowed | | | |
| Feet appear flat with no arch | | | |
| **4 to 8 months** | | | |
| Gains about 1 lb. per month | | | |
| Doubles original birth weight | | | |
| Increases length by about $^1/_2$ inch per month; average length 27.5 to 29 inches | | | |
| Increases in head circumference $^3/_8$ inch per month until 7 months; $^3/_{16}$ inch per month after 7 months (indicates brain growth) | | | |
| Begins to cut teeth-upper and lower incisors first | | | |
| **8 to 12 months** | | | |
| Height gain slows to $^1/_2$ inch per month; by first birthday $1^1/_2$ birth length | | | |
| Weight increases by about 1 lb. per month; By age 1, birth weight triples | | | |
| Teeth: about 4 upper and 4 lower incisors and 2 lower molars erupt | | | |
| Arms and hands are more developed than feet and legs; hands appear large in proportion to other body parts | | | |
| Legs may appear to be bowed | | | |
| Feet still appear to be flat | | | |

**FIGURE 12–6** Infant physical development assessment chart.
Adapted from Allen, K. E., & Marotz, L. R. (2006). *Developmental profiles: Pre-birth through twelve.* Clifton Park: NY: Delmar Learning.

Infants tend to be bilateral in that they tend to move both sides of the body at the same time. Gradually, they become unilateral and can move one side without moving the other.

## THE IMPORTANCE OF MOTOR BEHAVIOR

Michael G. Wade (1992) points out the importance of perceptual-motor development and play in the overall development of children. The motor cortex leads the way in the earliest stages of neural development. Wade (1992) believes this factor suggests ". . . movement will be the primary vehicle of discovery for the developing child" (p. 1). The infant is born with basic reflex movements that gradually develop into voluntary motor movements; motor development is closely tied to sensory development. According to Wade (1992), motor activity and play should be more than just vehicles for letting off excess energy but should be recognized as forerunners of the more formal intellectual and cognitive areas of development.

Children learn many basic concepts through movement. For example:

- *Distance:* Sammy, five months old, is lying on his back under a mobile. He swings out with his whole arm and hits one of the soft toys hanging down from the mobile. All the toys move. Sammy smiles and giggles.
- *Height:* Asad, nine months old, has crawled to the top of the stairs. He turns, looks down, and begins to cry.
- *Space:* Kachina, eleven months old, climbs into the laundry basket where she curls up for a little nap.

Sammy learns how the length of his arm relates to the distance to his mobile. Asad finds out that the height going up the stairs is a challenge and coming down is frightening. Kachina finds a comfortable space that is just right for her. All three infants are learning basic concepts as they test their motor skills.

## GROSS MOTOR DEVELOPMENT

Gross motor development proceeds through rapid and enormous developmental changes from infancy through age eight. In this part of the chapter, gross motor development in infancy is examined.

### Infant Gross Motor Development

**reflexes**

Involuntary movements present at birth. They include the eye blink, sucking, swallowing, moro reflex, Babinski reflex, crawling, rooting, and stepping.

Infant motor and physical development is influenced by the interaction of a combination of both genetic and environmental factors. Newborns move in a reflexive manner over which they have no control. **Reflexes** are involuntary movements. Some reflexes are needed for the infant's survival (Cole, Cole, & Lightfoot, 2005). The eye blink reflex protects the eyes from bright lights and foreign objects. Sucking and swallowing reflexes are needed for feeding. Cole, Cole, & Lightfoot (2005) point out that developmental psychologists disagree about the necessity for survival of the other reflexes. The grasping reflex causes the fist to close over an object pushed against the palm. The moro reflex, grasping with the arms, is a reaction to a loud noise or a feeling of being dropped. Other reflexes present at birth include:

- *Babinski reflex.* The baby's toes fan out and curl when the bottom of the foot is stroked.

- *Crawling reflex.* When placed on their stomachs and pressure is put on the soles of their feet, babies make movements as if crawling.
- *Rooting reflex.* When babies are touched on the cheek, they turn their heads and open their mouths.
- *Stepping reflex.* Held upright over a flat surface, babies will move their legs as if walking.

The focus of the first two years is development of voluntary motor control. Both internal neurological factors connecting body and brain and environmental factors, such as nutrition and opportunities for sensorimotor exploration, influence how this process takes place for individual children. However, there are normative patterns that most children follow at their own rate.

Motor and physical growth proceed in an organized way from head to toe **(cephalocaudal)** and from the center out **(proximodistal).** When the infant is born, the head is relatively large for the body compared with adult proportions. The trunk and arms and finally the legs and feet eventually catch up in growth. The infant first learns to lift the head, then the shoulders, and eventually the trunk, and is, thus, able to sit up without help. The infant next gains control of the legs, as when advancing from crawling and creeping to standing and walking. The development from center out is evident in observing the infant's arm movements. At first, infants move in a rather gross way, moving the whole arm from the shoulder. Gradually, control proceeds from shoulder to hand.

Allen and Marotz (2006) have developed a profile of infant development. They caution that when looking at such a profile it is important to keep in mind that, in reality, the child who fits the guidelines in every way does not exist. The profile is a list of developmental guidelines. They will not exactly fit every child, because there is a wide range of typical development at any age. Some examples of the typical infant characteristics described by Allen and Marotz (2006) are as follows:

> *Newborn:* Motor activity is mainly reflexive and includes behaviors such as swallowing, sucking, yawning, blinking, grasping movement, walking movement when held upright, and a startle response to sudden loud noises.
>
> *One to four months:* Average length is 20 to 27 inches and average weight 8 to 16 pounds; can grasp objects with entire hand, can raise upper body and head with arms in prone position, and, when lying down, can turn head from side to side.
>
> *Four to eight months:* Gains about one pound per month and one-half inch in length; teeth begin to appear, with increase in drooling, chewing, biting, and putting things in the mouth; uses finger and thumb (pincer grip) to pick things up; transfers objects from one hand to the other; shakes objects; puts objects in mouth; pulls body up to crawling position; rolls body from front to back and back to front.
>
> *Eight to twelve months:* Height gains average of one-half inch and weight one pound per month; continues to reach for and manipulate objects (stacks, sets side by side, drops, throws); pulls to a standing position; creeps on hands and knees; walks with adult support by the end of the first year.

Motor development is influenced by a number of factors: genetics, status at birth, size, build and composition, nutrition, rearing and birth order, social class, ethnicity, and culture (Malina, 1982).

Neonates (newborns) with respiratory problems have been found to have delayed motor development, and neonates with lower Apgar scores (indications of newborn functioning) will more likely have delayed motor development than those with higher scores. In addition, low birth weight and prematurity can lead to slower motor development; sitting, standing, and walking are usually done later by low-birth weight infants.

Undernourished and malnourished children lack the muscle strength and skeletal development necessary for typical motor activity. In addition, central nervous system dysfunction, which is usually present in the undernourished and malnourished child, limits coordination and control. Overweight babies may also have limited development. With excess weight to move, the infant may not be motivated nor physically able to develop necessary motor skills.

By age one, boys have been observed to engage in more physical activities than girls. This may be the result of environmental rather than genetic influences (Malina, 1982). Firstborn children seem to have some advantage over their siblings, possibly as a result of receiving more personal attention. "Only" children tend to be slower in motor development, perhaps because they may be overprotected. In general, children reared in more permissive environments with more opportunities for motor activity tend to be advanced.

There is only a small amount of research comparing different races and social classes. The results tend to favor the lower SES group children. It may be that the upper SES children are overprotected and do not have as many opportunities for motor activity. African American children tend to be ahead of European American children in motor development during the first year, and both have been found to be ahead of Latino infants on some motor tasks.

As mobility becomes greater, the infant gains a new view of the world (Figure 12–7). By nine months, the infant can move about.

> Travel changes one's perspective. . . . It's when you start to get around on your own steam that you discover what a chair really is. Parents who want a fresh point of view on their furniture are advised to drop down on all fours and accompany the nine- or ten-month-old on his rounds. It is probably many years since you studied the underside of a dining room chair (Fraiberg, 1959, pp. 52–53).

The infant spends hours practicing newly acquired motor skills.

Once they can move on their own, infants begin to detach from their caregivers. They are individuals with their own ideas about what to do. At this point, new problems develop for infant and adults because, for the first time, interests conflict. These are discussed in Section 4.

The onset of crawling appears to be related to milestones in cognitive development (Kermoian & Campos, 1988). Now armed with the ability to move and afforded the opportunity to exercise it, new possibilities open up for exploration and the construction of new knowledge about the world. The more efficiently the infant can move, the more he or she can learn. Bushnell and Boudreau (1993) believe that the development of motor abilities may make it possible for children to use perceptual information, such as haptic (touch/feel) and depth perception, to learn more about their environment. For example, Kermoian and Campos (1988) found that eight-and-a half-month-olds who could move around on their own were cognitively more advanced than those who could not.

**FIGURE 12–7** A new world opens up when an infant can move independently.

"Independent walking is the major developmental task of infancy" (Malina, 1982, p. 214). Walking lays the foundation for the development of other motor tasks. The child can move about without depending on his or her hands. The child's hands are then free to engage in other kinds of motor tasks. Walking at the expected time indicates that nervous system and muscle development are typical (Thelen, 1984). Walking is the landmark that indicates the end of infancy and the beginning of toddlerhood. Esther Thelen (1984) looked very closely at the development of walking. A close examination of infant kicking movements while prone showed that they are the same kinds of movements used in walking. When the infant first becomes a walker, there are many deficiencies compared to adult walking. The new walker has a wide stance, cannot stabilize on one leg for very long, has a short stride, and tends to hold his or her arms out for balance. Holding a steady posture is difficult. This may, to some extent, be the result of immature neurological development but is probably also influenced by body proportion, center of gravity, and muscle strength and tone.

Head, shoulders, hips, and chest grow faster than legs during the first 18 months. Once legs begin to grow longer and slimmer, gait matures. At the same time, the infant's leg muscles are relatively weak and lack tone. Cognitive development also has some influence on motivating walking. Zelazo (1984) believes that a spurt in cognitive development coincides with the onset of walking. He points out that talking and functional, rather than just exploratory, object use begin at about the same time as walking. See Figure 12–8 for an infant motor development chart.

## Infant Fine Motor Development

Between four and eight months, infants can use their finger and thumb in a pincer grip to pick up small objects. This is a time when caretakers must be careful to keep small objects out of the infant's reach, as the infant may put things in his or her mouth and choke or push objects into his or her nose or ears. Infants can reach with one arm and develop the capability of holding objects in one hand. They can shake, handle, and pound objects and everything goes in their mouths. They may also choose to hold their own bottle. Between eight and twelve months, they can transfer objects from one hand to another. They tend to poke with one finger when exploring something new, so outlets must be covered and electrical appliances kept out of reach. They can now pick up finger foods, stack objects, and place objects in containers. They are interested in the effects of dropping and throwing objects.

Observer _____ Date _____ Time _____ Place _____

Infant's name _____ Birth date _____ Age _____

| Age and Motor Skill | Observed: Yes | Observed: No | Comments |
|---|---|---|---|
| **Birth to 1 month** | | | |
| Motor activity is mainly reflexive. | | | |
| Maintains fetal position (back rounded with limbs drawn up to the body), especially when asleep. | | | |
| Holds hands in a fist; does not reach for objects. | | | |
| Good upper body muscle tone when supported under the arms. | | | |
| Turns head from side to side when lying down. | | | |
| Unable to coordinate eye and hand movements. | | | |
| **1 to 4 months** | | | |
| Some reflexes disappear; rooting and sucking reflexes are well developed. | | | |
| Grasps with entire hand but can't hold objects. | | | |
| Holds hands in an open or semi-open position. | | | |

**FIGURE 12–8** Infant motor development assessment chart.
Adapted from Allen, K. E., & Marotz, L. R., 2006. *Developmental profiles: Pre-birth through twelve.* Clifton Park: NY: Delmar Learning.

| Age and Motor Skill | Observed Yes | Observed No | Comments |
|---|---|---|---|
| Movements progress from large and jerky to smoother and more purposeful. | | | |
| Increased upper body movement: clasps hands above face, waves arms about, reaches for objects. | | | |
| On stomach raises head and upper body on arms. | | | |
| Turns head, and trunk follows until can roll body at will. | | | |
| By four months, can sit with support (on lap or in infant seat). | | | |
| **4 to 8 months** | | | |
| Reflexes established: Blinking, sucking, swallowing. | | | |
| Uses finger and thumb in pincer grip to pick up objects. | | | |
| Goes from reaching with both arms to reaching with one arm. | | | |
| Transfers objects from one hand to the other. | | | |
| Grasps objects using entire hand (palmar grasp). | | | |
| Handles, shakes, and pounds objects; puts everything in mouth. | | | |
| Holds own bottle. | | | |
| Can sit alone without support, head erect, back straightened, arms propped forward for support. | | | |
| Pulls into crawling position but usually doesn't move at first; but may by eight months. | | | |
| **8 to 12 months** | | | |
| Reaches with one hand to grasp an object when offered. | | | |
| Manipulates objects, transfers from one hand to the other. | | | |
| Pokes with one finger to explore new objects. | | | |
| Uses deliberate pincer grip to pick up small objects, toys, and finger foods. | | | |
| Stacks objects; places objects in containers. | | | |
| Releases objects by dropping or throwing. | | | |
| Begins pulling up to a standing position. | | | |
| Stands leaning on furniture; cruises holding on to furniture and side-stepping. | | | |
| Well balanced when sitting. | | | |
| Creeps on hands and knees; crawls up and down stairs. | | | |
| Walks holding adult hand; may walk alone. | | | |

FIGURE 12–8 Continued

Assess the motor skill development of one or more infants using the Infant Motor Skill Development Chart (see Figure 12–8).

## SUMMARY

Good health and nutrition are basic to proper physical and motor development. Physical growth follows several basic principles. The growth rate during infancy is very rapid. Concerns about a child's size compared to others of the same age are quickly answered through careful measurement of height and weight and comparison of results with U.S. government height and weight charts.

Good nutrition is the basis of rapid infant growth and development. Infants have high needs for nutrients. Breast feeding is the preferred feeding method during the first six months. Obesity is major child health problem, which can have its origins in infancy.

A number of health-related issues must be addressed with infants. Parents need to begin infant immunizations on schedule. Care should be taken not to expose infants to crowds where they might get RSV. Adult hand washing is one of the best protectors of infant health.

Adults are responsible for providing infants with an environment that is safe from hazards that may cause illness or injury. An increasing number of dangers to child health are being identified, such as the effects of prenatal substance abuse by mothers, AIDS-infected mothers, exposure to passive smoke inhalation, abusive and violent environments that threaten mental health, less-than adequate housing, and diseases transmitted in child care settings. Poverty underlies many of the dangers to infant health.

The child who is malnourished or in poor physical health because of illness or disease cannot function either physically or mentally to capacity. The adult who works with young children needs to be well-informed regarding nutrition and other health factors.

Motor skills develop in a sequence parallel to that of physical growth. Motor development supports concept development, which is closely tied to perceptual development. Gross motor skills precede fine motor skills. For example, the infant proceeds from reflexive motions, to mentally controlled arm movements, to using his or her hands to grasp objects. When infants are able to move about on their own, a whole new world of learning opens up.

## FOR FURTHER READING

American Academy of Pediatrics. (2005). *Health in child care: A manual for health professionals* (4th ed.). Elk Grove Village, IL: Author.

Aronson, S. S., & Shope, T. R. (Eds.). (2005). *Managing infectious diseases in child care and schools*. Elk Grove Village, IL: American Academy of Pediatrics.

Baxter, P. S. (Ed.). (2002). *Vitamin-responsive conditions in pediatric neurology*. Cambridge, UK: Cambridge University Press.

Caldwell, W., & Kimball, C. T. (Eds.). (2001). *Obesity sourcebook*. Holmes, PA: Omnigraphics.

Day, M., & Parlakian, R. (2004). *How culture shapes social-emotional development: Implications for practice in infant-family programs*. Washington, DC: Zero to Three.

DelCarmen-Wiggins, R., & Carter, A. S. (Eds.). (2004). *Handbook of infant, toddler, and preschool mental health assessment*. New York: Oxford University Press.

Dewey, D., & Tupper, D. E. (Eds.). (2004). *Developmental motor disorders*. New York: Guilford.

Donatelle, R. J. (2005). *Health: The basics* (6th ed.). San Francisco: Pearson.

Endres, J., Rockwell, R., & Mense, C. G. (2004). *Food, nutrition, and the young child* (5th ed.). Columbus, OH: Merrill/Prentice Hall.

Kimball, C. T. (Ed.). (2003). *Childhood diseases and disorders sourcebook*. Holmes, PA: Omnigraphics.

Kimball, C. T. (Ed.). (2003). *Healthy children source book*. Holmes, PA: Omnigraphics.

Minns, R., & Brown, K. (Eds.). (2006). *Shaken baby syndrome and other non-accidental head injuries in children*. New York: Cambridge University Press.

Roberts, M. C. (Ed.). (2003). *Handbook of pediatric psychology* (3rd ed.). New York: Guilford.

Thompson J., & Manore, M. (2005). *Nutrition: An applied approach*. San Francisco: Pearson.

## SUGGESTED ACTIVITIES

1. Visit a family or center-based infant child care facility. Note whether the suggestions for a safe and healthy environment are followed. Would you recommend this facility? Why or why not?
2. Visit a family or center-based infant child care facility. Observe the infants. Assess their physical development using the Infant Physical Development Assessment Chart (Figure 12-3).
3. At the library or on the Internet, research an issue such as the prevention of RSV, SIDS, or AIDS. Write up an information sheet that would be useful to parents.
4. Visit a family or center-based infant child care facility. Observe the infants. Find out their ages. Use the Infant Motor Development Assessment Chart (Figure 12-8) to assess their motor development.
5. Make an entry in your journal.

## REVIEW

1. Match the examples in Column II to the basic principles of growth listed in Column I.

| Column I | Column II |
|---|---|
| a. cephalocaudal | 1. Maria is able to lift her head and then her head and shoulders. |
| b. proximodistal | 2. Juan's legs are just beginning to grow longer; his proportions look more adultlike and his appearance is less squat. |
| c. general-to-specific | 3. At first, the infant seems to flail his arms wildly but soon begins directing them for specific purposes, such as grasping a toy. |
| d. differentiation | 4. Maria has just learned to walk. |
| e. integration | 5. Hold and shake a rattle. |

2. A young child is malnourished during the prenatal period and infancy but is then given a proper diet. Predict what will happen in terms of his or her height and weight, school achievement, and IQ scores.
3. Evaluate the following situations and/or comments or statements.
   a. Delayed physical development has only minimal effects on the child's abilities to learn through exploring the environment.
   b. Most child care providers are knowledgeable about health, safety, and nutrition.

c. Because they spend more time close to the floor, infants are more likely to be affected by the chemicals found in synthetic carpet fibers.
d. Children who are HIV-positive should not be allowed out of their homes to mingle with other children.
e. AIDS is easily passed on through casual contact.
f. Infants do not need mental health care—they are too young to have emotional or social problems.
g. Undernutrition is one part of the poverty problem, which includes factors such as poor housing, lack of proper medical care, parental under employment, and sometimes abuse and neglect.
h. One of the causes of increased need for health insurance for young children is that employers are cutting back on providing health benefits for employees and their families.
i. Feeding and diapering infants should follow a careful sequence of sanitation to prevent disease and illness.
j. The number of children without health insurance has been alleviated somewhat as a result of CHIP.
k. Breast feeding is the first choice over formula feeding during the first six months.

**4.** List the reflexes present at birth.

**5.** Explain the relationship between physical and motor development.

**6.** List three important infant gross motor skills and three important infant fine motor skills. Explain your selections.

**7.** Select the correct answer to the following.
The appearance of a particular skill depends on
a. maturation only.
b. environment only.
c. the interaction of maturation and environment.

**8.** Put an X by all the correct statements.
a. Both heredity and environment influence motor development.
b. African American and Hispanic infants tend to be ahead of European American infants in motor development.
c. Independent walking is a landmark that is considered the end of infancy and the beginning of toddlerhood.
d. Gross motor development precedes fine motor development.
e. Infants gradually move from unilateral to bilateral movement.
f. By the end of infancy, children develop the beginnings of voluntary motor control.
g. Between 8 and 12 months infants can transfer objects from one hand to the other, stack objects, and begin pulling to a standing position.

**9.** How old is each of the following infants?
a. Carlos pulls himself up to his feet in his playpen. He loves to eat raisins and picks them up carefully with his thumb and index finger.
b. Betsy sits propped up, turning her head from side to side as she observes the activity in the room.
c. Clancy sits on the floor rolling a ball back and forth to his sister. He seems to get bored as his glance wanders; he gets up on all fours and creeps away.

## KEY TERMS LIST

cephalocaudol
critical periods
differentiation
immunization
integrated movements
low-birth-weight (LBW) infant
obesity
proximodistal reflexes
RSV
sequential growth
Sudden Infant Death Syndrome (SIDS)

Additional resources for this chapter can be found on the Online Companion™ to accompany this text at http://www.earlychilded.delmar.com. Respond to "Time to Reflect" and "Looking Further" concepts, review various child development scenarios, and answer thought-provoking questions in the Critical Thinking Forum. Keep a daily journal by downloading the student journal available on this Web site. Complete the interactive matching exercises to reinforce concepts, and print out the child development assessment forms to use during your observation of development for children from birth to age eight. In addition, read the case studies on the Web site to reinforce the important concepts in each chapter, and take a look at the multitude of Web links that are available for student research on the Internet.

CHAPTER

# 13

# Infancy: Affective Development

## OBJECTIVES

After reading this chapter, you should be able to:

- Identify the developmental stages of adult-infant interaction.
- Identify examples of adult-infant reciprocity.
- Explain the development of stranger anxiety.
- Describe the roles of fathers with infants.
- Explain the role of infant temperament in the adult-infant relationship.
- Identify the extremes of infant temperamental reactivity.
- Understand the significance of the infant-mother reunion.
- Identify significant aspects of attachment behavior.
- Explain how infant and parent develop communication skills.
- List the primary emotions.
- Describe minority parent-child relationships and interactions.

Carlos is seven and one-half months old. He is sitting in his mother's lap facing her, when Louisa begins to make noises with her mouth and tongue. At first, Carlos laughed, then he attempted to imitate Louisa's behavior. He stuck out his tongue repeatedly. He'd stick out his tongue and then laugh. Carlos demonstrates his ability to imitate and his joyful emotion. Adults who work with young children have the opportunity to model for parents the appropriate ways of interacting with children and explain to them the factors that are important in affective development. Infant **affective development** has been the focus of a great deal of research. Rhythm and reciprocity, attachment, interactions with adults and peers, temperament, the caregiver's role, and the infant as controller of the behavior of others have all been studied.

**affective development**
The area of development that includes emotions, personality, and social behaviors.

## AFFECTIVE BEHAVIOR: ATTACHMENT AND INTERACTION

Once an initial bond, or a feeling of specialness, is developed, the infant's attachment to others must grow and deepen for healthy emotional, social, and personality development. According to Brazelton and Cramer (1990), attachment grows over time. The outcome is detachment and eventual independence of the child. The basis for attachment is the reciprocal adult-child relationship that develops from the time of birth. Four stages in the development of early interactions have been identified (Brazelton & Cramer, 1990). The first stage is during the first week to ten days. During this period, the infant learns to control his or her **emerging competencies** and gain control of his or her ability to maintain attention. The adult's job is to appreciate the emerging competencies and not overwhelm the infant with input. The second stage, from about one to eight weeks, is **prolonging attention.** With some control achieved, infants can now prolong attention and maintain communication and interaction with their most important adults. They begin to take control as they use smiles, vocalizing, facial expressions, and motor cues to signal to the adult that they are ready to interact. The adults learn to match their behaviors to the baby's. The third and fourth months are a **limit-testing** period. Infant and adult test their abilities to communicate and affect the other's behavior. Interaction should become rewarding; there should be a sense of joy in play. The fourth stage should appear around four to five months of age with the **emergence of autonomy.** Infants begin to take the lead in interactions with adults and to move their attention from the adult to other things and people in the environment. The adult needs to respect these initial signs of autonomy and to refrain from overwhelming the infant with bids to get attention back again.

**emerging competencies**
Newly developing skills or abilities.

**prolonging attention**
Maintaining communication and interaction.

**limit-testing**
Infant and adult test their abilities to communicate and affect the other's behavior.

**emergence of autonomy**
Infants begin to take the lead in the interactions with adults.

## Rhythm and Reciprocity

Brazelton and his associates (1977, 1978, 1982, 1990) studied infant and adult reciprocity by observing infants from 2 to 24 weeks of age. The infant is placed in a baby seat and is given the chance to play with an object, a parent, or a stranger. The cycle of attention to object or person is measured by examining videotapes of the infant and adult made during these play periods.

To check how the baby relates to objects, a small rubber ball is hung about 12 inches from the infant. The child tries to make movements in the direction of the ball. These movements are usually jerky. The child's attention pattern is marked by sharp periods of attention and then ignoring the object. A graphic representation of this is curve A (Figure 13–1). When a person the child knows, such as the mother, is in front of him or her, the infant's reaction is different. The cycle of attention is smoother, as in curve B (Figure 13–1). The child gradually becomes more attentive and then gradually withdraws attention in a smooth rather than jerky rhythm. The

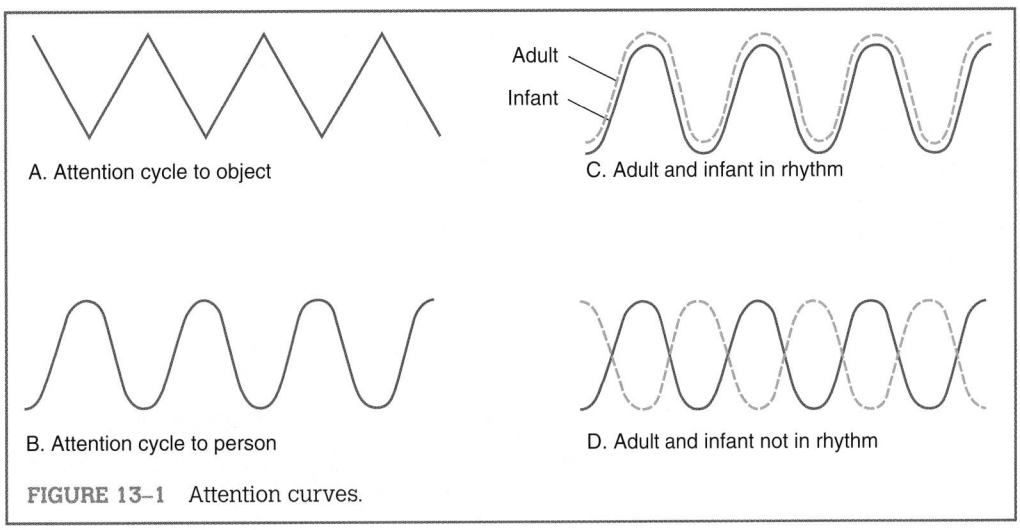


FIGURE 13–1 Attention curves.

**rhythm**

Being in a mutual exchange mode that promotes communication between adult and child.

child also moves the body forward and back with the cycle. He or she seems to want the person to approach. The parent who is in **rhythm** with the child is able to move toward and away from the child in tune with the child's attention and movements as shown in curve C (Figure 13–1). When the adult is not in tune with the child, the curves might look like curve D (Figure 13–1). When the baby finds he or she cannot get into rhythm with the adult, the baby may withdraw and even stop trying. If the mother stands in front of him or her and does not respond at all, the baby becomes jerky, as if relating to an object. If the baby gets no response, he or she soon withdraws. The child gives up and may play with his or her own body or clothing. The child seems to display a feeling of disappointment.

Mothers and fathers follow different patterns in their reciprocal interactions with their infant. These patterns develop by two or three weeks of age. Mothers tend to start out more smoothly and softly and try to find the baby's pattern. Fathers are more playful and try to carry on more of a regular conversation. Their pattern is more sharp and jerky. The baby learns this difference quickly. When Dad approaches, the child is more playful and bright eyed, as if ready for action.

When a stranger enters, both the infant and stranger may have difficulty finding the right rhythmic pattern. The stranger does not give the infant the expected response; the stranger and child may both become frustrated. They may both give up trying to get into rhythm with each other.

**reciprocity**

Communication exchange in an equal give-and-take manner.

Brazelton feels the development of **reciprocity** is absolutely necessary for not only affective development but also for cognitive and motor growth. It is through this reciprocal relationship that infants receive the social stimulation they must have. As they receive stimulation, they use their senses, sharpen them, and begin to see themselves as competent persons.

Kochanska and Aksan (2004) examined the mutual responsiveness between parents and their children at 7 and 15 months. Parental responsiveness refers to the quality of the parent's way of reacting to the child's communications toward the parent. Infant's responsiveness refers to the child's ways of responding to the parent's actions. Unlike earlier studies at 7 months, this one was done through observations of parents and children in their natural environment. Both mothers and fathers were included. Each parent and child pair was considered to consist of reciprocal partners. At 7 months, parents dominated in leading activity whereas at 15 months the children were more dominant. Parents appeared to respect the toddlers increased autonomy. Whereas mothers directed more communication to infants than did fathers, infants were equal in their bids for responses from mothers and fathers.

Rhythm appears to be a basic factor in infant development. It is important in one-to-one relationships and in physiological functioning. The total family functions better and members feel better adjusted if the infant and family are synchronized.

## Attachment and Reactions to Strangers

**attachment**

The relationship of belonging between infant and caregiver.

Child psychologists have long been interested in the development of infant behaviors that indicate attachment has developed. **Attachment** refers to the relationship of belonging between infant and caregiver. Research shows the infant goes through three steps (Schaffer, 1977). First, the infant learns to tell the difference between humans and objects. This step is learned during the first weeks of life. Second, the infant learns to distinguish mother from other humans. This step is usually accomplished before three months. It is not until the third step, at about seven months, that the infant becomes upset when mother leaves him or her and shows signs of missing mother when she is gone. Around seven to nine months, the

**stranger anxiety**
Fear of strangers.

infant may also show signs of fear of strangers, or **stranger anxiety.** When the happy, smiling seven-month-old is transferred from mother's arms into the arms of a stranger, the infant is likely to change into a crying, unhappy person. At this point, attachment has been accomplished. From this point, baby actively seeks mother (or the other primary caregiver) when she is out of sight.

Researchers are interested in the strength of the attachment relationship and how it relates to other behaviors (Bretherton & Waters, 1985). Research strongly supports the view that the mother's observed sensitivity to the infant's needs during the first months is predictive of the quality of their later relationship. Mother's sensitivity is also related to the child's later reaction in the **strange-situation** naturalistic laboratory setting, as devised by Ainsworth, Blehar, Waters, and Wall (1978 as cited in Berk, 1998, and in Fogel, 2001). This setting is one in which the infant is placed in an unfamiliar room and is allowed to explore some toys with the mother present. Mother and child play with the toys for a few minutes and then are joined by the unfamiliar adult. All three play with the toys until the mother leaves the infant with the stranger for three minutes. The stranger then leaves, and the mother returns but does not interact with the baby. The stranger then returns and the mother leaves again. Finally, the stranger leaves and the mother returns. The reunion behavior is believed to reflect the degree of security in the attachment relationship between mother and child. When the mother has been absent and returns, the observed reunion behavior has been found to be related to later behaviors.

**strange-situation**
A setting in which the infant is placed in an unfamiliar room and is allowed to explore some toys either with the mother or a stranger present.

Four patterns of reunion behavior have been identified: securely attached, insecurely attached-resistant, insecurely attached-avoidant, and disorganized-disoriented (Berk, 1998; Fogel, 2001).

1. Securely attached infants use the parent as home base for exploration of the toys and the stranger. They look for comfort from the caregiver during the final reunion but then return to their independent play.
2. Insecurely attached-resistant infants are less comfortable in the strange situation. They waver as they move from mother to toys. When they move to the toys, they are hesitant in their explorations. Attached-resistant infants are more cautious in their relationship to the stranger and get upset when the mother leaves the room. During the reunion, these infants tend to be ambivalent as they approach the mother and then push her away.
3. Insecurely attached-avoidant infants are usually not upset when left with the stranger. However, when their mothers return, they do not approach them and may even resist their attempts to comfort and hold them. These infants may even hit and push their mothers when they try to reunite.
4. Disorganized-disoriented infants display inconsistent behavior during the strange-situation experience. For example, the baby may smile and move toward the mother and then turn and move away or may sit still and stare at the wall. This reaction occurs with less frequency, but also reflects the most insecurity.

Early development of the attachment theory suggests that the caregivers' sensitivity to infants' signals for attention and attempts at communication are the foundation of secure attachment. De Wolff and van IJzendoorn (1997) analyzed 30 studies that attempted to replicate the original strange-situation research. They found that sensitivity was an important influence on attachment. However, mutuality and synchrony, stimulation, positive attitude, and emotional support are also strongly related to attachment security. Furthermore, the relationship between attachment and sensitivity is weaker in clinical and lower-class samples. Unfavorable child-rearing conditions may override the effect of sensitivity. Life's strains and stresses may overburden parental sensitivity as an influence on emotional security. Behavioral genetics studies show that inherited temperamental characteristics may also influence the development of attachment. The father's role in attachment also needs to be included. Van IJzendoorn and De Wolff (1997) also examined research in this area. They found that fathers' sensitivity influences infant attachment, but the effect is less than for the mother-infant relationship. Cowan (1997) suggests that infant attachment should be examined within the whole family system, which seems to be an especially important view as the diversity of child care and family settings increases.

A major question that has grown from the diversity of child care situations is how infant-mother attachment security may be affected by nonmaternal infant child care. The NICHD Early Childhood Care Research Network (NICHD, 1997) conducted a study that looked at the relationships between nonmaternal child care and infant-mother attachment security. Using the strange-situation as the measure of attachment security, researchers compared children who had experienced child care with those who had not and found no overall significant difference in the amount of stress exhibited when these two types of children were separated from the mother. However, maternal sensitivity and responsiveness did have some effect on the stress level. When low-maternal-sensitivity/responsiveness was associated with poor-quality child care, high amounts of child care, or more than one child care arrangement, children were less likely to be secure. On the other hand, high-quality child care appears to compensate for less maternal sensitivity/responsiveness. In addition, boys in many hours of child care and girls in minimal amounts of child care were less likely to be securely attached. The authors conclude the following:

> The results of this study clearly indicate that child care by itself constitutes neither a risk nor a benefit for the development of the infant-mother attachment relationship as measured by the strange-situation. However, poor quality, unstable, or more than minimal amounts of child care apparently added to the risks already inherent in poor mothering, so that the combined effects were worse than those of low maternal sensitivity and responsiveness alone (p. 877).

The evidence from years of research seems to indicate that the first three months is a critical time for development of an attachment relationship. Strength of attachment at 12 months has been found to be predictive of later attachment (Bretherton & Waters, 1985). Disorganized or disoriented attachment at 18 months is predictive of hostility in preschool children (Lyons-Ruth, Alpern, & Repacholi, 1993), whereas securely attached children are more likely to be viewed by their teachers as more affectively positive, more empathetic, and more compliant (Bretherton & Waters, 1985). Bretherton and Waters (1985) also noted that research indicates strength of attachment appears to be related to children's functioning. When two-year-olds were challenged with a difficult task, those identified as securely attached sought help and support from their mothers, whereas those identified as insecurely attached did not seek help.

In summary, the research indicates that children and mothers who develop a strong positive attachment in infancy will continue to show a positive relationship, and the children will display more positive behaviors in preschool.

Attachment behavior with mother as compared with father is also important (Bretherton & Waters, 1985). The quality of the two relationships may be quite different. That is, the child may be secure with one parent and not with the other. The relationship with the mother as principal caregiver seems to be more predictive of the child's later feelings of security than the relationship with the father.

Concern over separation distress in infants, toddlers, and parents increased along with the increased frequency of leaving children with a child care provider (Godwin, Groves, & Horm-Wingerd, 1993). Field et al. (1984) observed infants and parents when the children were dropped off and picked up at a child care center. Leave-taking distress increased across the two semesters. That is, it appeared to become more difficult for the infants to leave their parent as the year progressed. Girls and their mothers had the most difficulty parting, as evidenced by more crying and attention-getting behaviors by the infant and more efforts by the mother to distract the child. Mothers also tended to stay longer than fathers before finally leaving. Field et al. noted that, in another study in which parents were questioned, 75 percent of the mothers but only 35 percent of the fathers expected their infants to cry, and 40 percent of the mothers and none of the fathers were concerned about the infant's response to their departure. This finding indicates that what parents expect may be what happens. The concerned parent hesitates about leaving and this signals the infant to fuss and cry. It was also found that infants and their parents spent more time interacting before leave-taking than did preschoolers and their parents. It seems as children get older, they and their parents can separate more easily.

Another concern related to child care is the effect that the frequent turnover in child care personnel may have on infants' attachment security. Raikes (1993) found that the amount of time spent with a high-quality teacher was directly related to infants' attachment security. Nine months appears to be the critical amount of time needed to develop a secure relationship. The results from the studies of early attachment have implications for the adult who works with young children. Hopefully, this will help you understand the possible elements in the child's and parents' early relationships that may affect later behavior. Godwin et al. (1993) provide suggestions for helping infants, toddlers, and parents manage separation distress. Godwin et al. (1993) point out the importance of helping the parents as well as the child. Parents may demonstrate uneasiness because they feel guilty about leaving the infant. It is important to allow children to be left on a gradual basis, make parents feel comfortable, be reassuring, and keep the lines of communication open.

As some of the people who were observed in the strange-situation as infants grow into late adolescence and early adulthood, researchers can attempt to answer the question of whether their early attachment status continues. Waters, Weinfield, and Hamilton (2000) did such a follow-up study. They found there was a mixture of continuity and discontinuity in attachment from infancy to late adolescence and early adulthood. Attachment security remained stable for people who grew up under stable, positive conditions. A change from secure to insecure corresponded with negative life events, such as maternal depression. In another longitudinal study, Roisman, Padron, Stroufe, and Egeland (2002) examined how young adults who had very negative childhood experiences managed to attain attachment security in young adulthood. They believe one answer might be that they had some adult scaffolding that supported them in spite of their difficult experiences.

Explain why a child who would go willingly to anyone at five months cries when held by anyone but mother or father at eight months.

## Interactions with Adults and Peers

Researchers are also interested in other aspects of infant-parent interaction. Both mothers and fathers have been the focus of study. Also of interest is how infants respond to peers, or other infants.

Interaction forms the basis of communication. This mutual give-and-take is the origin of the feelings of trust essential to infant development. As already described, patterns of communication begin at birth. Parents and children develop patterns of reciprocity and rhythm in their exchanges and some degree of synchrony develops. Gazing seems to be an important aspect of this beginning communication. The longer the parent looks, the longer the infant returns the gaze. However, if infants find they are overwhelmed by too much demand for attention, they may become irritable and withdrawn. Thus, from the beginning, babies share control of the interaction.

As described in Chapter 12, much interaction takes place during routines such as feeding and diapering. Caregivers need to learn to read the infants' signals for pacing feeding time. Play also proceeds in cycles of engagement and withdrawal. Smiling involves sensitivity to signals. When the caregiver smiles, the baby observes for a while before smiling back. The caregiver needs to withdraw his or her smile to give the infant a chance for a break before beginning the cycle again. Caregiver and child learn to share experiences. They may gaze at the same object or event—caregiver talks and comments while infant looks and smiles. When the infant begins to babble and vocalize, synchrony and caregiver response are critical for good speech development. Five-month-old infants have shown they are sensitive to adult tone of voice indicating either approval or prohibition directed at themselves or to an adult (Fernald, 1993). A parent's immediate response to an infant's vocalizing encourages the infant to continue. The amount of time spent interacting with the infant, especially verbalizing, seems to be the most critical factor related to the child's later competence.

**imitation**

Doing actions one has observed another doing.

**Imitation** is an important element in parent-child interaction (Uzgiris, 1984). Adults and older peers serve as models for behavior. Imitation is a form of interpersonal communication. Imitative responses on the part of parent and child can develop into a cycle of turn-taking in which each participant influences the activity of the other. Both vocal and facial expressions are imitated. It may be from these exchanges that the infant begins to perceive the mother as a teacher. Uzgiris (1984) concludes that imitation is not only a means for developing interpersonal communications but also an essential element in cognitive growth and development.

Research has broken down some of the stereotyped views of differences between mother and father interactions with infants (Sawin, 1981). On the whole, fathers may be just as active as mothers in caregiving and affection giving with their infants. Both mothers and fathers tend to give more affectionate attention to opposite-sex infants and more attention and stimulation to same-sex infants. By 12 months of age, some well-established sex differences have been observed (Snow, Jacklin, & Maccoby, 1983). Fathers used more physical and verbal prohibitions with boys than with girls. However, boys tended to exhibit more behaviors that would need limitations. Girls tended to stay closer to the father and be held more. Fathers also played with the girls in a manner that would keep them away from forbidden objects and require less regulation behavior from the fathers. Sex stereotyping in toy use already was evident. Fathers suggested both trucks and dolls to the girls, but never suggested dolls to the boys. Fathers did, however, let their sons play with a toy vacuum cleaner, which involved the use of gross motor skills.

As mentioned in Chapter 4, a relationship with responsive caregivers is critical during the period of rapid brain growth in infancy (Shore, 1997). A strong attachment relationship appears to immunize the infant against the adverse effects of later stress or trauma. When under stress, a steroid hormone called **cortisol** that affects metabolism, the immune system, and the brain is released. Stress can impair neurological development and brain function through the release of cortisol. Babies who experience warm, nurturing care are less likely to release cortisol when experiencing stress

**cortisol**

A steroid hormone that is released under stress.

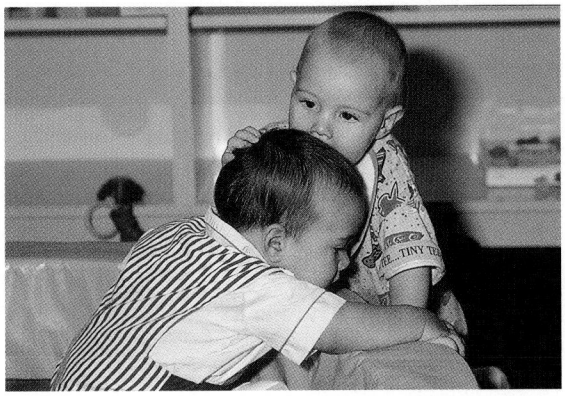

FIGURE 13–2 Peer relationships begin in infancy.

as compared with other children. This effect appears to carry into the elementary years. This research further supports the importance of positive, stimulating adult-infant interaction that is responsive to infants' moods and desires.

Infants relate socially with other infants (Fogel, 2001). At three months, they will gaze at a peer and make abrupt, jerky movements (Fogel, 2001). At six months, they are likely to look at a peer and vocalize (Fogel, 2001). From six to twelve months, peer play without objects takes place (Fogel, 2001). Babies will "explore each other with mutual touches, smile and gesture at each other, and imitate each other" (Fogel, 2001, p. 319). By age one, infants develop a kind of dialog with exchanges of tickling, touching, and laughing. They also exchange objects. Give and take is the focus of their interactions and play (See Figures 13–2 and 13–3).

## Temperament

*Temperament* may be defined as "a persistent pattern of emotion and emotion regulation in relation to people and things in the environment" (Fogel, 2001, p. 261) or "stable individual differences in the quality and intensity of emotional reaction" (Berk, 1998, p. 183). It is the major element of personality. Some people are quiet and shy, whereas others are outgoing, friendly, and assertive. Researchers are interested in how many of our temperamental qualities are inherited and how many are determined by the environment. It has already been noted that temperament appears to influence adult-neonate interaction.

The New York Longitudinal Study (Thomas & Chess, 1977, as cited in Berk, 1998, and in Fogel, 2001) is the longest-running and most extensive study of child temperament. Their results indicate that temperament greatly influences what happens to a child and is also influenced by parenting practices. Jerome Kagan and his colleagues conducted more recent research on temperament (Kagan, 1998). These researchers were interested in the temperamental extremes: the inhibited child versus the uninhibited child. They studied 500 infants who were four months old in the first phase of research. The babies were presented with several kinds of unfamiliar stimuli, such as waving a colorful mobile in front of their faces, playing an audiotape of a strange voice, and placing a cotton swab soaked in diluted alcohol under their noses. About 20 percent of the babies were "high-reactive." They became active and distressed when confronted with the unfamiliar stimuli. At the other extreme were the "low-reactive" babies, who were quiet, babbled, or laughed. The babies returned to the laboratory at 14 and 21 months of age, at which time they were introduced to novel settings. The low-reactives showed no fear, whereas the high-reactives were extremely fearful. The children were brought back to the laboratory at age seven. The high-reactive children had been observed at four months of age to be the most tense and had long, thin body types. About 15 percent of the high-reactives became shy, fearful seven-year-olds; the rest were average. Only about 15 percent of the low-reactive infants were extremely bubbly, fearless, and sociable; the majority of the low-reactives were average. The conclusion is "that temperament constrains how extreme a personality one develops. Most people move toward the middle" (Kagan, 1998, p. 57).

FIGURE 13–3 Infants need time to get involved with each other.

While the work of Thomas and Chess is classic and began an interest in temperament research, currently, temperament is viewed as a much more complex construct than it was in the early years of study (*Zero to Three*, March 2004). Leading researchers define temperament as "constitutionally based individual differences in emotional and attentional reactivity and self-regulation, influenced over time by heredity and experience" (Rothbart & Derryberry, 2000, as cited in Sturm, 2004, p. 5). Temperament is a characteristic that influences how caretakers interact and react to children.

> A model of temperament that is widely applied in current research proposes that there are two basic dimensions of temperament that interact with one another. [The first dimension,] Emotional and attentional reactivity involves the intensity and content of the child's responses to external and internal stimuli. The second dimension concerns the child's self-regulatory capacities, or the extent to which the child can manage or modulate his reactivity to meet the adaptive demands of the given situation (Sturm, p. 5).

An infant might feel a strong emotional reaction to a loud noise or have a weak reaction. The infant might respond to this feeling with a loud emotional cry or self-regulate by turning away and sucking on his fist. Children each have their own temperamental mix of reactivity and self-regulation.

In the past, temperament was measured by administering rating scales to parents and teachers. Today, new measurement tools allow researchers to look at physiological and biological views of temperament. Now, measures can be made of heart rate, stress-related cortisol levels, and brain activity. There is evidence that we inherit characteristics such as sociability, shyness, tendencies to be fearful or angry, or a tendency to be happy. However, there is so much variability in these characteristics that researchers are looking for the factors in the environment that interact with and affect these temperamental characteristics. Currently, the application of research to practice has a long way to go. There are no tools that can be used to measure infant temperament in order to predict future behavior. Research is still looking for connections.

Strum (2004) suggests that the temperamental characteristics identified by Thomas and Chess can be useful as ideas for engaging parents in trying to understand challenging, frustrating, or puzzling behavior and to guide them toward new ways to work with their child. The parents can be guided to see the child's potential strengths. Wachs (2004) identifies seven potential influences on temperament: genes, brain processes, family environment, nutrition, culture, biomedical conditions, and toxic substances.

Culture can be an important element in evaluating the adaptability of temperament (Carlson, Feng, & Harwood, 2004). Carlson, Feng, and Harwood (2004) point out that nearly 40 percent of children in the United States are members of families that may value temperament traits that are different than those valued among Anglo-American families. For example, in the United States, shy, sensitive children are often labeled as lonely and depressed. In China, shy, sensitive children are viewed as socially and academically competent, while in Sweden, they are not viewed as either positive or negative for future success. In a diverse society, each cultural group has its own views of the "ideal" baby. We need to be flexible in our evaluations and expectations regarding children's temperamental characteristics.

## Emotional Development and Mental Health

Emotional and behavioral adjustment are essential for school success (Raver, 2002). Emotional and behavioral development are as important as cognitive development. Children need to be taught to understand and regulate their emotions.

At the beginning of the chapter, you read an anecdote that is an example of infant humor. Playful exchanges between baby and adults or older children are important outlets for stress, for defining who they are in the world, and for finding silly ways to change rules (Loizou, 2004). With humor, infants can empower themselves as they control an exchange, such as in peek-a-boo. Humor is but one type of emotion. Infants may also display fear, anger, sadness, disgust, and surprise.

Many areas in the study of child development and child psychology are related to emotions: temperament, attachment, peer relations, and curiosity are examples of areas that have an emotional foundation Langlois (2004). It is through the communications during interaction with caretakers that infants identify and express emotions and learn to regulate them (Cole, Martin, & Dennis, 2005). According to Campos, Frankel, and Camras (2004), children's repertoire of emotions expands as they develop new skills, such as reaching, crawling, walking, and speaking, which provide new experiences and opportunities for more variety of emotional reactions to these experiences. Infant emotions may be rather broad and nonspecific, such as nonspecific distress, which later might result in more discrete feelings, such as anger, sadness, or fear.

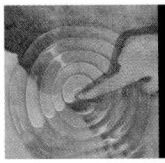

**LOOKING FURTHER**

Infant Maria Garcia is very calm and cooperative when being dressed and when sleeping. She eats at regular intervals and has regular bowel movements. She laughs and smiles during her bath. She does not seem to mind a wet diaper and enjoys trying new foods. At age two, she can play quietly, entertaining herself with her toys, music, and story tapes. She eats well at mealtime, is obedient and nonaggressive, and plays well with her siblings. In contrast, Mike Smith is wiggly when asleep, resistent when being diapered and dressed, and eats and sleeps on an irregular schedule. He cries when his diaper is wet and fusses after eating. At age two, he is very active. He climbs all over the furniture and seldom settles down to play. His bowel movements are unpredictable, making toilet training difficult. Mike stays away from strange children when he is taken to the playground. He is wiggly and resistant when his hair is cut.

- Which characteristics make these two children either easy or difficult?
- What would you predict regarding their temperamental characteristics at age seven? What kinds of environmental factors would predict Mike's future?
- Look further into temperament research to support your analysis.

Mental health is reflected in infants' emotional well-being. Alice Honig (1993) reminds adults who work with young children that besides providing infants with appropriate toys and good physical care, they need to provide love and warmth. They also need to be tuned in to signs that a baby is not thriving emotionally, such as dull eyes without sparkle, pushing away rather than cuddling up with an adult, crying inconsolably for hours, and having wild tantrums (Honig, 1993, p. 72).

More and more, mental health is being seen as an integral part of early intervention. According to Lieberman (1997), five main principles define infant mental health. The first three principles show external behavior reflecting internal behavior, and the second two principles deal with intervention.

1. *Infants are social creatures by nature.* Under normal conditions, babies build bonds of attachments with a variety of caregivers. However, some relationships are more special than others.

2. *Individual differences are an integral component of infants' functioning.* Each infant and each parent is unique. To identify mismatches in relationships, each partner's temperament, skills, areas of vulnerability, motivations, fears, wishes, and how his or her characteristics interact with the other partners need to be identified.
3. *Every individual exists in a particular environmental context that deeply affects the person's functioning.* Children are raised in ways that are influenced by their parents' upbringing and by the resources and psychological well-being of their everyday lives. Social class is a critical predictor of life circumstances. Cultural and sociological influences define the life circumstances of the family and the child.
4. *Mental health practitioners who focus on infants make an effort to understand how behaviors feel from the inside, not just how they look from the outside.* They ask questions such as, "What is the father's motivation, what is he thinking, and how is he feeling when he yells at his child? What is this mother's experience when she does not respond to her baby's crying? How does this infant feel when he or she is switched from one caregiver to another without any transition time?" (p. 4). The intervention is shaped by the answers to these questions.
5. *The intervenor's own feelings and behaviors have a major impact on the intervention.* The intervenors must be aware of how these feelings may affect the parents and, in turn, the infant. They must not make the parent feel like they are being judged. They also must avoid developing such a strong relationship with the child that the parent becomes jealous. It is important to focus on improving the parent-child relationship.

Violence in the family, on television, and in the neighborhood is identified as a source of post traumatic stress disorder that can affect infants as well as older children and adults (Special report, 1994). Unfortunately, barriers may stand between traumatized young children and the help they need (Zeanah & Scheeringa, 1996). Caregivers may be too focused on coping with their own trauma and, therefore, may not recognize the child's symptoms of stress. Furthermore, Americans tend not to accept grief and believe that it is best to ignore the child's experience and move on. Even when the child's stress is recognized, adults may not see the need for psychiatric help. Parents may bring a child in for help with aggressive behavior, not connecting the behavior with a traumatic experience, such as domestic violence, death, earthquake, or some other frightening experience. It is important to recognize and be alert to sudden changes in infant behavior that may indicate a reaction to a traumatic experience. Children may remember traumatic experiences from infancy (Gaensbauer, 2004). They may even reenact them in later years in their play.

Mothers' mental health is closely related with children's mental health. Near the end of pregnancy and during early infancy, both men and women become psychologically preoccupied with making room in their minds and lives for a new person (Mayes, 2002). Mayes (2002) reports that, through interviews, parents reported "feeling great elation, a completely altered state of being, a sense of being completely fulfilled, joyful beyond words, and of accomplishment and perfection beyond their imagination" (p. 6). On the other hand, a high percentage of parents of young infants reported concerns about bad things that might happen to the babies. About 10 percent of mothers of young infants suffer **postpartum** (occurring after birth) major depression (Epperson, 2002). Normally, most new mothers suffer postpartum **"baby blues."** The symptoms are mild and may include low mood, tearfulness, irritability, emotional ups and downs, anxiety, and sleep difficulties.

**postpartum**
Occurring after birth.

**baby blues**
A normal period of moodiness that occurs postpartum.

**postpartum depression (PPD)**
Depression occurring shortly after birth.

**postpartum psychosis (PPP)**
Psychosis occurring after the birth of a baby.

**Postpartum depression (PPD)** usually occurs in women with previous episodes of depression. Medication and/or psychotherapy can usually get the woman through PPD. Unfortunately, it is often not detected. Recurring episodes can have a negative impact on the mother-infant relationship and the child's neurodevelopment. One in 1,000 postpartum women experience **postpartum psychosis (PPP)**, which includes bizarre behaviors and may result in suicide or infanticide (killing the baby). Postpartum care must include educating the mother regarding the normality of mild depression that results from the complex interactions of normal hormone changes with neurological activity. Epperson (2002) points out the need for policy makers and the general public to be educated regarding postpartum mood changes and their biological underpinnings, which can cause delusions and even result in infanticide.

## CULTURE AND INTERACTION PATTERNS OF INFANTS AND THEIR MOTHERS AND FATHERS

Theory based on research done predominantly on European American majority children may not generalize to children from minority cultures. Cynthia T. Garcia Coll (1990) reviewed research that focuses specifically on minority infants and toddlers. Parental behaviors with their infants vary from culture to culture. For example, Navajos carry their babies on a cradle board on their backs. The use of the cradle board lowers the infants' levels of arousal and activity, resulting in less mutual give-and-take. However, this lower level of interaction does not generalize to periods when the infants are not on the boards. Navajo infants are less fearful than European American infants during the first year, but more fearful in the second year. However, there is wide variation within the Navajo population; the more interaction infants have with others, the less fearful they are.

Coll (1990) describes the results of other studies of minority mother-infant interaction. Mexican American mothers tend to be more tactile and less verbal in stimulating their infants compared with European American mothers. Mothers from various Latino groups vary in their behavior with infants: Cuban mothers talked the most and played more teaching games, and Puerto Rican and South American mothers talked less and played more social games. Compared with the Latino mothers, African American mothers talked the least and did the least infant game-playing. When questioned, the Latino mothers expressed the objective of educating their children, whereas the African American mothers expressed a fear of spoiling the infants by giving them too much attention. Native American mothers and infants were much more silent and passive when compared with African American and European American mothers.

Except for the Native American infants being more passive, there is no information on ways these different styles of interaction may affect infant-caregiver attachment or infant temperament. On the other hand, whereas large-group research of a particular culture may indicate certain cultural patterns, individual group members may vary significantly. For example, Brinker, Baxter, and Butler (1994) observed the interactions of African American mothers and infants who were participants in an early intervention program. Both low-SES and middle-SES groups were represented, and some of the mothers were drug users. They found a diversity of interaction patterns and concluded that it is important not to stereotype the members of any particular cultural subgroup.

Although the amount of research on father involvement with children is increasing, there is very little research being done on father interaction in developing countries. Meanwhile, the birthrates in developing countries are increasing, and many of these families are immigrating to the United States. Engle and Breaux (1998) point out that in many states in the United States, the proportion of ethnically diverse families is increasing at a rapid rate. Many of these recent immigrant groups have views regarding appropriate roles and behaviors of fathers that differ from those of the majority culture. To understand the broad view of the father role, it is necessary to expand the definition of **father** to that of **men** in the family. For example, in some cultures, the male in the family may not be the biological father. Engle and Breaux (1998) explain that in some cultures, such as Botswana, the mother's brother may be responsible for care of the children; in other cultures (e.g., Vietnam), some other male kin, such as the grandfather, may take on this role.

**father**

Emerging role is equally responsible as mothers for child care.

**men**

Becoming more warm and playful in interactions with children.

Engle and Breaux (1998) report the percentage of households headed by women is increasing worldwide. Within the United States, the percentage varies among ethnic groups: 23 percent of Latino families, 13 percent of European American families, and 44 percent of African American families (Engle & Breaux, 1998, p. 3). Worldwide, more mothers are employed, which places men in different positions related to mothers and children. Engle and Breaux provide examples of several cultures in which the role of father is changing. The changes in Latino families are particularly important in the United States because this is the most rapidly growing minority group. The traditional view of the Mexican family is the authoritarian man and the dependent, submissive woman. The man is the provider and disciplines the children. The wife is submissive and provides for the needs of the children through food, warmth, and affection. Due to increasing urbanization, the emergent model defines the mother and father as equals who share responsibilities. Latino fathers are likely to work long hours at low-paying jobs (Behnke, 2004). They may come home too tired to provide their children the attention they would like to give. Many Latino fathers are recent immigrants who speak little, if any, English, which impedes them from helping their children with their homework. On the other hand, Latino fathers have many strengths. They emphasize cooperation, family unity, and childrearing (Behnke, 2004). Many Latino dads are affectionate, nurturing, playful, and emotionally supportive.

Studies done in the United States and Europe show that fathers have important effects on their children's development. However, in developing countries, the expectation that fathers will interact with young children is very rare. The effect of fathers contributing economic support varies a great deal depending on the percentage of income contributed, whether the parents are married, and whether the father is abusive.

Programs are available to assist in redefining and strengthening the roles of men in families. Efforts are being made to provide more equality of roles within the family. Other programs are aimed at making men feel more responsible and gain parenting skills. In the United States, some programs are directed at unwed fathers. Preventive education focuses on broadening the definitions of gender roles while boys are still young and developing their views about parenting. Businesses and industries are being encouraged to provide paternity leave and flexible work schedules for fathers to increase father involvement. More legal protection for children of absent fathers is needed, while efforts are being made to increase men's ability to support their children.

Finding ways to deal with the male role in a world where family structures are rapidly changing is an enormous challenge. Engle and Breaux (1998, p. 17) suggest that a father might be more involved with his child if the following are true:

1. He lives in a culture that supports gender equality and father nurturance.
2. He is a coresident with his wife and child.

3. He has a harmonious relationship with the child's mother, who encourages his involvement.
4. He is part of an economic system with enough resources that he can support his children in line with society's expectations.
5. He works in a cooperative way with his wife to provide sustenance for the family.

As we look at other cultures, family structural change everywhere is increasing the need to reconceptualize the male role in the family in order to have a supportive effect on child development.

## CAREGIVER AFFECTIVE BEHAVIOR AND INVOLVEMENT

More frequently, we are beginning to see that it is the quality of the relationship more than with whom the infant has the relationship that is most important. As children develop trust during the first year, they also develop the ability to love. To be able to love others when grown up, it is essential that the child learn to love during the first months of life (Fraiberg, 1977). The "mothering" activities can be shared. Baby has an infinite amount of love to give and share (Schaffer, 1977).

Traditionally, mothers are considered the primary caregivers. However, as already mentioned, male roles are being redefined in all cultures. Just as men are more involved in the birthing process, they are beginning to take a more active role in infant caregiving.

Middle- and lower-class fathers tend to show equal interest with mothers in the newborn when observed in the maternity ward. Competence as a parent is a matter of sensitivity to the infant's needs. The competent parent can read the infant's messages correctly and respond appropriately (Figure 13–4).

Research shows that, when observed at home, men generally take on very few regular routine caregiving chores, such as feeding, bathing, and diapering the baby, although this may be changing. The man's main role is to play with the infant. Just as Brazelton observed differences in interaction, so have others (Parke & Sawin, 1977; Sawin, 1981). When fathers play, they are more physical and rough. Mothers play quieter games, like "peek-a-boo." Children whose fathers spend a lot of time playing with them are found to be better adjusted to strange situations. There is also a positive relationship between father's playing and later cognitive development. The child may get some special benefits from father that are not found with mother.

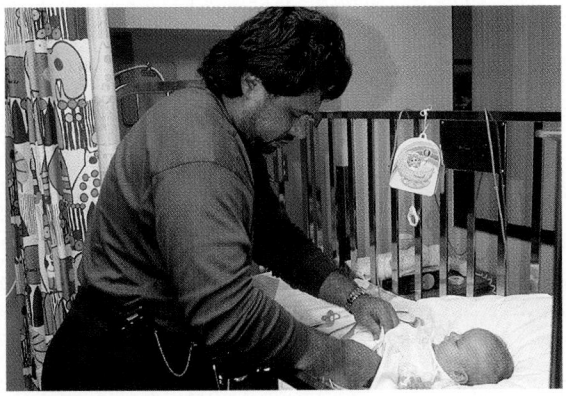

FIGURE 13–4 Father is a competent and loving caregiver.

In families that include young children with disabilities newborn to age five, responsibilities and accompanying stress increase. Gavidia-Payne and Stoneman (1997) looked at family predictors of maternal and paternal involvement in programs for young children with disabilities. The more financially secure and better educated mothers who perceived family interactions as being healthy were the most involved and had better coping abilities. Fathers who actively coped by seeking assistance and social and religious support were more involved in their children's programs. Although they did not always attend all the meetings or communicate frequently with the service providers, they did seek services. Better educated and more financially secure fathers were more involved in their children's programs. Positive family relationships were also indicative of more parental involvement. The authors believe that these results support the importance of taking an ecological view, such as suggested by Bronfenbrenner (see Chapter 3), of early intervention programs.

Describe what you perceive as the ideal parent/caretaker-infant relationship.

## SUMMARY

Infant competence is enhanced by the development of attachment and a good reciprocal relationship with caregivers. Love and warmth are basic to accomplishing these tasks. A reciprocal cycle of exchange in social interaction is a sign of a positive, sensitive relationship. Observation of the reunion between parent and child after parent absence can give clues to the strength of attachment. Interactions with both parents are important, although somewhat different. If given the opportunity, infants are interested in relating to peers as well as to adults. Temperament has some influence on whether the infant is viewed as easy or difficult. Infants, through their responses to their caregivers, control a share of the interaction and influence the caregiver's response. All the primary emotions develop during infancy. Although we know a little about cultural variations in mother-child interactions, we do not know how, or if, these variations might account for cultural differences in temperament and attachment.

Research indicates that a quality child caregiver-infant relationship does not disrupt parent-child attachment and, in fact, may enhance it. The mental health of infants continues to be a major focus in infant development. With the increasing frequency of domestic abuse, the effect on babies must be recognized and addressed. As family structures change, the role of the male in parenting and child development is being examined and redefined across cultures. Family stability and functioning is an important factor in parent involvement in programs for young children with disabilities.

## FOR FURTHER READING

Barr, R., Hopkins, B., & Green, J. (2000). *Crying as a sign, a symptom, and a signal: Clinical, emotional, and developmental aspects of infant and toddler crying.* Cambridge, UK: Cambridge University Press.

Berlin. L. J., Ziv, Y., Amaya-Jackson, L., & Greenberg, M. T. (Eds.). (2005). *Enhancing early attachments.* New York: Guilford.

Brisch, K. H. (2004). *Treating attachment disorders: From theory to therapy.* New York: Guilford.

Butterfield, P. M., Martin, C. A., & Prairie, A. P. (2004). *Emotional connections: How relationships guide early learning.* Washington, DC: Zero to Three.

Collins, R., Mascia, J., Kendall, R., Golden, O., Schock, L., & Parlakian, R. (2003). Promoting mental health in child care settings: Caring for the whole child. *Zero to Three, 23*(4), 39–45.

Day, R. D., & Lamb, M. E. (Eds.). (2004). *Conceptualizing and measuring father involvement.* Mahwah, NJ: Erlbaum.

Gerhardt, S. (2005). *Why love matters: How affection shapes a baby's brain.* New York: Psychology Press.

Gowen, J. W., & Nebrig, J. B. (2002). *Enhancing early emotional development: Guiding parents of young children.* Baltimore: Brookes.

Kristal, J. (2005). *The temperament perspective: Working with children's behavioral styles.* Baltimore: Brookes.

Lamb, M. E., Bornstein, M. H., & Teti, D. M. (2002). *Development in infancy* (4th ed.). Mahwah, NJ: Erlbaum.

Maldonado-Duran, J. M. (Ed.). (2002). *Infant and toddler mental health.* Arlington, VA: American Psychiatric Publishing.

Mathews, G., Deary, I. J., & Whiteman, M. C. (2004). *Personality traits* (2nd ed.). New York: Cambridge University Press.

Mayne, T. J., & Bonanno, G. A. (2001). *Emotions: Current issues and future directions.* New York: Guilford.

Nelson, C. A. (Ed.). (2000). *The effects of early adversity on neurobehavioral development.* Mahwah, NJ: Erlbaum.

Parlakian, R. (2003). *How culture shapes social-emotional development*. Herndon, VA: Zero to Three.

Porter, L. (2003). *Young children's behaviour: Practical approaches for caregivers and teachers*. Baltimore: Brookes.

Perinatal mental health: Supporting new families through vulnerability and change. (2002). *Zero to Three [Focus issue], 22*,(6).

Routines and rituals in the lives of infants, toddlers and families. (2002). *Zero to Three [Focus issue], 22*,(4).

Rovee-Collier, C., & Lipsitt, L. (Eds.). (Yearly.) *Advances in infancy research*. Norwood, NJ: Ablex.

Sameroff, A. J., McDonough, S. C., & Rosenblum, K. L. (Eds.). (2004). *Treating parent-infant relationship problems: Strategies for intervention*. New York: Guilford.

Shirilla, J. J., & Weatheston, D. J. (Eds.). (2002). *Infant mental health: Case studies in infant mental health*. Herndon, VA: Zero to Three.

Segal, M., Masi, E., & Liederman, R. (2002). *In time and with love: Caring for infants and toddlers with special needs* (2nd ed). Washington, DC: Zero to Three.

Shirilla, J. J., & Weatherston, D. J. (Eds.). (2002). *Case studies in infant mental health*. Washington, DC: Zero to Three.

Tamis-LeMonda, C. S., & Cabrera, N. (Eds.). (2002). *The handbook of father involvement: Multidisciplinary perspectives*. Mahwah, NJ: Erlbaum.

Vacca, J., & Bagdi, A. (2005). Relationships for life: Supporting the emotional health of infants and toddlers. *Dimensions, 33*(1), 9–16.

Waters, E., Hamilton, C. E., & Weinfield, N. S. (Eds.). (2000). The stability of attachment security from infancy to adolescence and early adulthood. [Special section]. *Child Development, 71*(3), 678–706.

## SUGGESTED ACTIVITIES

1. Observe a mother, a father, and a stranger interacting with the same infant for three to four minutes, each in turn. Describe how the mother, father, and stranger interact with the infant. Write a description of the infant's response to each. What are the similarities and differences in the infant's response to each and theirs to the infant? Are the responses what you expect from reading the text?

2. Observe two or more infants in a setting where they are free to interact if they wish. Do they seem to notice each other? Do they smile, vocalize, or reach out? If they are mobile, do they seek each other out, touch, or exchange toys? Describe exactly what happens. Share your observations in class.

3. Interview four fathers of infants (two fathers of boys and two fathers of girls, if possible). Ask the following questions:
   a. How much time do you spend playing with your baby? When? What do you do?
   b. What kinds of routine tasks do you do for your baby (e.g., feeding, changing, bathing)? How often?
   c. How did you feel when you first saw (*baby's name*)? Did the baby fulfill your expectations? Does the infant fulfill your expectations now?
   d. What do you enjoy most about babies? What, if anything, do you find most irritating or frustrating? Analyze the answers. Compare the fathers' responses. What are the similarities and differences? Are there any differences between the responses of the fathers of boys and the fathers of girls?

4. Make an entry in your journal.

## REVIEW

1. Match the stages of early interaction in Column I with the descriptions in Column II.

| Column I | Column II |
|---|---|
| a. Stage 1<br>b. Stage 2 | 1. The limit-testing period during which adult and infant test their abilities to communicate. |

c. Stage 3
d. Stage 4

2. The infant gains control of his or her emerging competencies and ability to maintain attention.
3. The infant begins to take the lead in his or her interactions—autonomy emerges.
4. The infant can prolong attention and maintain communication and interaction.

**2.** For each example below, decide whether the infant is most likely interacting with mother, father, or a stranger.
   a. Adult approaches infant and says, "Hi, Brad, old boy. Did you have a good day?" Brad is bright eyed and looks like he is ready for fun.
   b. Adult approaches, saying, "Hi, sweetheart." Brad gurgles. Adult bends closer, "Gurgly-goo to you, too."
   c. Adult approaches with, "Hi, Brad!" Brad looks at adult with a serious expression. "How about a little tickle, Brad?" Adult tickles Brad's tummy. Brad looks closely. Adult says, "It takes time to get going, doesn't it, Brad?"

**3.** Describe the two basic types of reciprocal relationships that may develop between adult and infant.

**4.** List two factors that affect infant-adult rhythmicity.

**5.** Select all the correct answers:
   a. When the mother returns to the strange-situation room, most infants are delighted.
   b. Infants who reject their mothers when they return to the strange-situation room may have mothers who are insensitive and who do not enjoy physical contact with the baby.
   c. There is no indication that the irritable infant is less attached to the mother at one year of age than the happier infant.
   d. Attachment can develop anytime during the first year.
   e. Securely attached two-year-olds will turn to their mothers when they need help.
   f. The strength of infant attachment should be considered within the whole family situation and in light of infant temperament.
   g. Fathers observed leaving their children at a child care center are likely to stay longer than mothers.
   h. Positive adult relationships developed in infancy are the basis for later competence.
   i. Under no circumstances can nonmaternal child care disrupt or weaken mother-child attachment.

**6.** Describe a situation in which infant and parent are developing communication skills.

**7.** How would you explain the fact that infants have been observed to get along very well with each other?

**8.** Define *temperament.*

**9.** Match the types of temperament listed in Column I with the characteristics in Column II.

| Column I | Column II |
|---|---|
| a. high-reactive | 1. When presented with an unexpected stimulus, they babble and laugh or are very quiet. |
| b. low-reactive | 2. When presented with an unexpected stimulus, they may be startled but are easily calmed. |
| | 3. When presented with an unexpected stimulus, they become active and distressed and appear fearful. |

**10.** Write the number of each correct statement.
   a. Mothers do a better job than fathers of caring for infants.
   b. Fathers are just as interested in their newborns as are mothers.
   c. Father's play with infants is rougher than mother's play.
   d. Both social and cognitive development seem to be given a special lift from time spent with father.
   e. Despite changes in family structure, the male role in and influence on child development have not changed.

**11.** Mrs. Clark is very upset with her relationship with two-month-old Sally. Sally is cranky, sleeps in short spurts, and never seems satisfied. Mrs. Clark feels she must be doing something wrong. What do you think?

**12.** List the primary emotions that appear during infancy.

**13.** Describe what is known about minority culture parent-child interactions.

**14.** Describe baby blues, postpartum depression, and postpartum psychosis. Discuss outcomes if parents are not educated about the possibility of depression.

## KEY TERMS LIST

affective development
attachment
baby blues
cortisol
emergence of autonomy
emerging competencies
father
imitation
limit-testing
men
postpartum
postpartum depression (PPD)
postpartum psychosis (PPP)
prolonging attention
reciprocity
rhythm
strange-situation
stranger anxiety
temperament

Additional resources for this chapter can be found on the Online Companion™ to accompany this text at http://www.earlychilded.delmar.com. Respond to "Time to Reflect" and "Looking Further" concepts, review various child development scenarios, and answer thought-provoking questions in the Critical Thinking Forum. Keep a daily journal by downloading the student journal available on this Web site. Complete the interactive matching exercises to reinforce concepts, and print out the child development assessment forms to use during your observation of development for children from birth to age eight. In addition, read the case studies on the Web site to reinforce the important concepts in each chapter, and take a look at the multitude of Web links that are available for student research on the Internet.

CHAPTER

# 14

# Infancy: Cognitive Development

## Objectives

After reading this chapter, you should be able to:

- Describe briefly the cognitive stages occurring during the first year of sensorimotor development.
- Identify the important factors in infant communication, language, and literacy development.
- Recognize factors relevant to infant categorization.
- Explain why brain lateralization is important to cognitive development.
- Know the important factors in infant object manipulation.
- Demonstrate knowledge of infant social referencing.
- Support the need for infants to have time to explore and play on their own, independent of adult intervention.
- Describe how infant play can be supported.
- Evaluate infant development using an infant development evaluation sheet.

During the first two years, cognitive, affective, and motor development are closely tied together. Chapter 13 described the affective elements of infant development, and Chapter 12 provided an overview of infant motor development.

It is a warm fall evening. The setting sun is very bright. A group of about 25 adults and children are picnicking in the park. The adults are chatting and eating. The older children are racing around playing tag. Bobby, age nine months, stands between his parents, who are seated at a picnic table. Bobby keeps his balance leaning on the bench as he munches on potato chips and observes the activity around him. He picks up his chips between his thumb and forefinger and stuffs each into his mouth. One chip falls on the ground. Bobby continues eating the rest. He finishes and indicates he wants more by pounding his fist on the bench. Mom and Dad don't respond. Bobby bends down, reaching for the chip on the ground. Mom intervenes and Dad hands him another chip. Relate this incident to what you know about pincer grip, standing, object permanence, memory, communication, and problem-solving skill development.

As described in Chapter 11, Piaget recognized this relationship in his description of the sensorimotor period of development. Whereas motor development focuses on the child's increasing control and refinement of movement activities, sensory development focuses on increasing control and refinement of perceptual or sensory (touch, taste, feel, hear, smell) skills.

**developmental biodynamics**

Research designed to consider in detail the processes that relate to sensory and motor development.

Research designed to consider in detail the processes that relate to sensory and motor development is called **developmental biodynamics.** This new view of motor development focuses not just on the sequence of motor development but on how motor development and perception through the senses interact. Most biodynamic research was done on infants from neonates to beginning walkers (Lockman & Thelen, 1993).

**cognitive development**

Changes in cognitive structure and functioning that may take place over time.

Through this integration of sensory and motor skills, the infant obtains information used to construct knowledge of the world. This construction of knowledge is called **cognitive development** and is described further in Chapter 20. Research on infant cognitive development focuses on how much babies know and how they go about learning. As discussed in Chapter 11 we now recognize that infants are much more competent than was previously thought. Sensory competencies underlie the infant's ability to progress through the various stages of cognitive development.

**substages of sensorimotor development**

Six stages that progress from reflexive action to mental problem solving.

Piaget identified six **substages of sensorimotor development** (Fogel, 2001, p. 46). Birth to two months is the stage of reflex schemes, during which inborn reflexes make the baby's first connections to the outside world. Primary circular reactions dominate the second stage from two to five months. By chance, the infant discovers connections within his own body, such as finding his mouth with his thumb. These actions are continuously repeated. The third stage, six to nine months, is the stage of secondary circular reactions. Actions that connect the infant with the environment are repeated. An example would be wiggling in his crib to make a mobile move. The fourth stage appears between ten and twelve months, when the infant can coordinate secondary circular reactions. The infant evidences goal-directed behavior, such as grasping an object for examination. Between twelve and eighteen months, during the fifth stage, tertiary circular reactions usually appear. The infant uses secondary circular reactions as the means to solve new problems, such as what happens if an object is dropped from the high chair. The sixth stage of sensorimotor development occurs between eighteen and twenty-four months. Infants invent new means through mental combinations. That is, the infant can solve problems without trial and error by thinking through a solution before acting.

## OBJECT PERMANENCE AND RECOGNITION

**object permanence**

The knowledge that objects continue to exist even when one is not seeing, hearing, or feeling it.

**object recognition**

The features the infant uses to identify objects.

During the first year, two major sensorimotor abilities proceed through the child's first developmental stages: **object permanence** and **object recognition.** Object permanence is defined as "an object continues to exist even when one cannot see, hear, or feel it" (Miller, 2002, p. 45). Children develop this knowledge through a series of six stages. Four of these stages take place during the first year. During stage one (newborn to two months), things out of sight are out of mind for the infant. The infant does not search for a hidden object or even show any sign of knowing that it has been hidden. At stage two (two to four months), the infant still does not search. The infant may, however, gaze for a few moments in the direction where a hidden toy was last seen. In stage three (four to eight months), the infant searches for an object that is partially hidden. The infant also looks for something

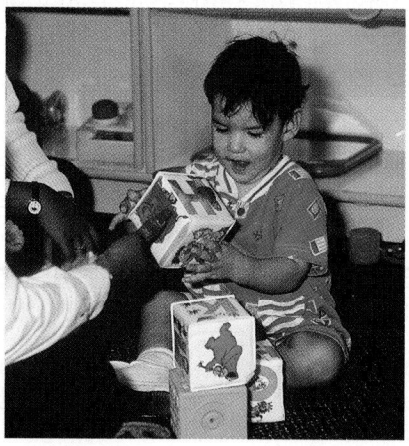

FIGURE 14–1 Manipulation of objects provides the infant with information.

that he or she has caused to disappear, such as a rattle that has been dropped. Between eight and twelve months, the fourth stage is reached. If a toy is covered by a cloth or other screen, the infant lifts it to find the toy. However, if the toy is then hidden under something else, the infant looks in the first hiding place before going to the second. The concept of object permanence is starting to develop, but it is not completely developed until the middle of the second year. At this point, the adult and child can enjoy a game of peek-a-boo.

The second sensorimotor ability, object recognition, concerns the features the infant uses to identify objects. As infants grow, they learn to use features such as color, shape, size, and texture. They seem to acquire this ability at about 16 weeks of age. The younger infant perceives the differences but does not use the information as an aid in identification (Figure 14–1).

## COMMUNICATION, LANGUAGE, AND LITERACY

Infants are also developing in the communication area. They are able communicators. In their classic studies, Condon and Sander (1974) showed through slow-motion photography that infants move in rhythm with the speech of the adults around them. They also develop a gamelike communication system with objects (Watson, 1976). That is, infants chatter happily as they watch their mobiles or bat at a rattle or ball hung from a string. This vocalizing reflects the infant's needs and mood.

From birth, babies know something about language (Gopnik, Meltsoff, & Kuhl, 1999). They enjoy sounds, such as the sound of their own sucking. One-month-old babies from a variety of cultures have been found to be able to discriminate the sounds in a diverse selection of languages. By one month, they have developed differentiated cries that indicate feeling and needs, such as hunger, sleepiness, anger, and pain. The meaning elements in language are referred to as semantics. By one year of age, infants group sounds as they hear them in their culture. Babies all around the world coo at about three months. They make little sounds like "oohh" and "aahh" as they exchange conversation with their caregivers. At seven or eight months, they babble. Babbling is the production of strings of consonant-vowel syllables, such as "dadada" or "mamama." Beyond the babbling stage, babies around the world stop sounding alike and sound more like their native language.

Around ten months, the infant tries to imitate speech. By the age of about one, sounds are made not just for fun but to refer to something. For example, Michael Halliday (1975) collected samples of his son Nigel's early vocalizations. At age one, he collected samples such as the following:

| Nigel's Word | Referent |
|---|---|
| dada | Daddy |
| da | dog |
| ba | birds |
| aba | a bus |
| ka | car |

Around age one, children move into the linguistic period where they begin to use meaningful speech.

It is vital that caregivers, both parents and teachers, spend time in conversations with infants (Bardige & Segal, 2004). Opportunities for conversation are available during routine activities, such as diaper changing, dressing, hand washing, meals, and playtime. Babies need opportunities to connect with each other. Their "conversations" consist of imitating each others actions and expressions (Bardige & Segal, 2004).

Labeling appears as an important component of cognitive development as early as 10 months of age, before children actually begin to speak conventional words (Baldwin & Markman, 1989). When a new object was labeled for infants between the ages of 10 and 14 months of age, infants attended to the object for a longer time than if no label was provided. Labeling involved showing or pointing to the object with an accompanying verbalization, such as, "See the robot. It's a robot" (Baldwin & Markman, 1989, p. 394). When given an opportunity to play with a group of toys that included a previously labeled toy, infants attended longer to the object that had been previously labeled than to the other toys. Verbal labels appear to be facilitative and stay with infants even before they speak their first word. This indicates that labeling objects is valuable for an infant's cognitive development even though speech has not yet appeared.

Read the following anecdote and explain how the incident relates to the development of the object concept. The incident takes place in the home of Tommy and his older sister Mary. Tommy is 11 months of age.

> Tommy's sister Mary was excited to see us as we walked in the door. She could not wait to show us what she had received from the Easter bunny. Immediately, she was begging her mother to get her Easter basket off the shelf where it had been safely placed out of Tommy's reach. Mary took the basket and started showing me each colorful candy item in the basket. Tommy noticed this immediately. Within seconds, he was crawling over to the bright colors being displayed on the couch. He began trying to grab anything he could from the basket. This behavior upset Mary, so she said, "No!", and took the basket away. Tommy could still see the basket and he began to cry and scream. I placed the basket behind the couch so it was out of Tommy's sight. He followed my action with his eyes while still crying. After the basket was out of sight, his crying stopped almost immediately.

Honig (1998) suggests that when an infant's attention is turned toward an object through staring and/or pointing, the adult should label the object. Infant speech develops gradually from single vowel sounds at one month of age to vowel-consonant combinations by eight months, to possibly some single words by twelve months. Understanding develops simultaneously, so that by twelve months, children usually can respond to simple directions, such as "Find the teddy bear" or "Pick up your cup" (Allen & Marotz, 2006).

While many people believe infants should not watch television, videos, or DVDs (see Chapter 4), in reality most infants are exposed to these media. Weber and Singer (2004) did a study with children ages 1 to 23 months. They found that half the children in their sample watched videos or television. On the average, they started watching videos at 6.1 months and television on the average at 9.8 months, although some began as young as one month. Nearly half the parents reported watching the programs and videos with their babies and engaging in activities, such as singing, dancing, and pointing at action on the screen. Other studies have found that parents do many language-related activities during television and video viewing, such as labeling objects on the screen and repeating dialogue. Media can support language development if watched with an active, involved adult.

Infants seem to have the ability to communicate with nonverbal gestures (Legerstee, Corter, & Kienapple, 1990). Specific hand and arm actions are consistent and convey specific meanings. When infants smiled and gazed at their responsive mothers, they gestured with pointing and open hands. When faced with an inactive mother or a doll, they gazed passively, put their arms at their sides, and curled their fingers under. The pointing and open hands appeared to indicate active communication. This natural development is being carried a step further by actually teaching preverbal babies signs beginning at about nine months of age (Walters, 1998). Walters describes how nine-month-old Sonia has learned 30 signs, such as stretching her arms out to the sides for "airplane" and placing her finger and thumb together for "Cheerios™." Research supports that signing babies learn spoken language faster. The signs do not have to be formal ones, such as American Sign Language, but can be gestures that make sense to adult and child. Children who are experiencing difficulty with speech can benefit from a combination of gesture and speech known as total communication (Armstrong, 1997). The period from nine to twelve months is a critical period in the development of communication and attentional skills that precede the onset of oral language development (Carpenter, Nagell, & Tomasello, 1998).

**literacy**

Knowledge regarding written language.

**literacy beginners**

Children ages birth to three (McGee & Richgels, 1996).

**Literacy** development is closely allied with communication and language development. Oral language development provides the foundation for the development of literacy skills (Parlakian, 2004, p. 38). McGee and Richgels (2004) identify children ages birth to three as being **literacy beginners.** Babies are not literate in the sense of being able to find meaning in written symbols, but they do exhibit literacy behavior and understanding. If given access to books and if read to regularly during infancy, babies can learn to listen to books being read, turn pages, hold books right side up, examine the pictures, and recognize and name familiar books. Sharing books with an adult or an older child connects the affective with the cognitive and provides the infant with positive feelings toward books. Schickedanz (1999) provides guidelines for selecting books that match the baby's development. For example, the youngest infants can be introduced to books with brightly colored pictures. Around four to six months, when the baby can hold his or her head upright, he or she can sit in a lap and be read to. Babies grab the books and chew and suck on them. Soft cloth and vinyl books can survive being put in the baby's mouth and can be washed. Between seven and nine months, most babies can sit on their own, hold a book in their lap, and turn the pages as they examine the pictures. Tiny board or block books with bright pictures of familiar objects are interesting to the baby and provide a medium for labeling by caregivers. By the time the baby is one year old, sharing books should be a regular routine that builds on attachment and language and literacy development. Parlakian (2004) suggests numerous ways to introduce literacy concepts to infants including reading to them, talking to them, reciting rhymes and singing songs, and describing their daily activities as they go through them.

## CATEGORIZATION

**categorization**

Sorting and grouping items according to similar attributes.

**Categorization** is another important area of early development. Categorization skills enable us to sort and group items according to similar attributes. For example, a group of toy vehicles consisting of cars, trucks, airplanes, and boats can be sorted according to type, use (land, sea, or air), color, or size. Categorizing behavior as it is observed in preschool- and kindergarten-age children is discussed in Chapter 20. Researchers have looked at infants to find the beginnings of categorization skills and concepts. Infants were found to be able to recognize categories such as stuffed animals, round fruit, human faces, colors, and shapes (Sherman, 1985). What the infants seem to learn and remember are the most obvious, consistent attributes of items in a category. For example, infants were shown a series of drawings of faces that had the same hairline and jawline. Then, after a delay, they were shown the same and similar faces. The ten-month-old infants picked hairline and jawline as the critical features for the category (Sherman, 1985).

Eimas and Quinn (1994) studied the categorization behaviors of three- and four-month-old infants. The infants were shown photographs of natural animals. The target basic categories were either horses or cats. The infants indicated that cats, zebras, and giraffes were not included in the horse category. Horses and tigers, but not female lions, were excluded from the cat category.

Younger (1993) found that ten-month-old infants can exclude items that do not fit in the category of animals they are learning. This indicates that infants actively compare the items presented to them and decide which belong in the group and which do not. Research does not tell us how infants apply this emerging capability in their everyday experiences to develop categories, only that the capability is present. It suggests, however, that infants can benefit from having experiences with many types of objects, both living and nonliving, that can serve as the basis for category building. We look further at category building as we consider cognitive development in older children.

## PLANNING

**planning**

An important human higher-level cognitive ability that enables us to consider ways to solve problems before actually embarking on a solution and thus cuts down on time lost with trial-and-error approaches.

**Planning** is an important human higher-level cognitive ability. Planning enables us to consider ways to solve problems before actually embarking on a solution and, thus, cuts down on time lost with trial-and-error approaches. Planning involves mentally going through a sequence of steps leading to a solution before actually trying out the solution. Willatts (Willatts, 1989; Willatts & Rosie, 1989) believes that infants are capable of some primitive planning behaviors and, thus, some representational thought earlier than Piaget's view of infant cognitive development. Piaget believed that planning ability and representational thought did not appear until the end of the sensorimotor period (around eighteen months to two years). Willatt's research indicates that infants show planning behavior as young as nine months of age. Infants can perceive a situation in which it was possible to remove a barrier, pull a string, and obtain an object versus a situation in which the string was not attached to the object. In the first situation, infants removed the barrier and pulled the string to get the object. In the second, they picked up the barrier and played with it. They appeared to figure out under which condition they could or could not obtain the desired object.

## BRAIN DEVELOPMENT AND LATERALIZATION

**brain research**

Research that has looked at how the brain functions.

As noted in Chapter 4, **brain research** supports the importance of infant stimulation to brain growth (*Brain Wonders*, 2001; Shore, 1997; Thompson & Nelson, 2001). Brain development begins within a week of conception and by birth the 100 billion brain cells or neurons have begun to connect (*Brain Wonders*, 2001). During infancy, the infant's senses become more acute. The developing brain influences the sequence of motor development that is so important during infancy as the means for exploring the world.

While there is no doubt that it is important to stimulate the senses during infancy, Thompson & Nelson (2001) believe we need to keep in mind that various types of brain development take place throughout life, beginning with the prenatal period. Appropriate stimulation and health care are important at every age and stage.

Zigler, Finn-Stevenson, and Hall (2002) provide a cautionary note regarding the interpretation and application of brain research to child development. First, neurological research is in its early stages. Most of the research has been done on animals, very little on humans. The popular press has exaggerated what is known about brain development, and parents have rushed to obtain materials that they believe will make their children smarter. Zigler et al. (2002) point out that the brain research just supports what we already know from years of child development research. We know that a nonstimulating environment with lack of proper nutrition and health care is harmful to child development. According to Zigler et al. (2002, p. 200), the following conclusions can be drawn:

- Brain research has confirmed what we already know from social science research: the young child's experience of the world has a profound impact on early—and continuing—development.
- A caregiving situation that emphasizes warmth, continuity of care, love, and respect gives infants and young children the elements they need for healthy and sound cognitive, social, and physical development without the need for special toys, music, or classes.
- Growth and development do not stop after infancy or toddlerhood or the school-age years, and, with few exceptions . . . windows of opportunity for learning and growth do not slam shut at preset intervals. . . . The early years of life are of critical importance for laying the foundation for a lifetime of learning and loving but that development and learning continue throughout life.

Babies need opportunities for sensorimotor exploration, such as batting at objects and mouthing appropriate toys, cooing and babbling in conversations with caregivers, exchanging funny faces with others, and having space to move about as they are able in order to support brain development (Gallagher, 2005).

**brain lateralization**

Development of both left- and right-brain functions and the communication between the two.

Another topic of study is **brain lateralization.** The brain has two distinct halves or hemispheres. It was found that each of the hemispheres of the brain controls different types of cognitive and behavioral functions. In the past, it was thought that the two central hemispheres processed distinctively different material in different ways. That is, the left side of the brain processes in a sequential, analytic, linguistic mode, while the right side processes in a parallel, holistic, spatial, nonlinguistic mode. Jensen (1998) points out that while the two sides of the brain do process differently, the position that the left side processes more academic information, such as language and mathematics, and the right side processes more creative information, such as music and art, is outdated. The right-brain left-brain distinction appears to be true for novices who are just learning. However, Jensen points out that accomplished musicians process on the left side, while accomplished mathematicians and chess players process on the right side, using the creative problem-solving function. The right side recognizes negative emotions faster, and the left side recognizes positive emotions faster. Research indicates that infants are born with this differential functioning of the two sides of the brain. To function well, there needs to be good communication between both sides.

There are gender differences in brain function (*Brain Wonders*, 2001). Male brains tend to be more lateralized. That is, the two hemispheres operate more independently

Suppose your friend tells you that it is not important to sing, chant rhymes, or read to infants because they are too young to benefit from these experiences. Respond to your friend, taking into consideration the information presented in this chapter thus far.

during some kinds of mental activities, such as speaking or navigating around the environment. Girls use their cerebral hemispheres more equally during these activities. Female infants tend to be more advanced than males in the sensory areas of vision, hearing, memory, smell, and touch. Girls also tend to be more socially tuned in and usually are ahead of boys in language and fine motor skills. Boys usually catch up by age three and are usually ahead in visual-spatial integration, the skill that supports completing puzzles and being proficient in some hand-eye coordination tasks.

It has been suggested (Cherry, Godwin, & Staples, 1989) that the brain lateralization factor has important implications for parents and teachers. Optimal brain development involves developing both left- and right-brain functions and the communication between the two. Some research indicates that left-side function in the language area can be influenced by environmental experiences. Otherwise, at this point, we have to assume that infants need a variety of experiences designed to develop both sides. Activities that should stimulate both sides of the brain include music boxes and wrist bells for auditory stimulation; mobiles and colorful pictures for visual stimulation; bells on booties or low mobiles for stimulation of kicking; plastic keys, balls, and discs on chains for finger dexterity; and nipples for sucking. The right side is often more neglected in these days of academic emphasis. It is important that infants have time to develop their own ways of dealing with the environment in order to develop their creative side, as well as their analytic and verbal side.

## OBJECT MANIPULATION

**object manipulation**
Fingering the surface of, looking at, and transferring the object from hand to hand to explore it.

The play of infants is meaningful, and meanings can be enhanced with "materials which lend themselves to manipulation, exploration, and multiple uses"(Goldhaber & Smith, 1993). The haptic (touch) aspect of **object manipulation** provides meaningful information to infants (Catherwood, 1993). The most simple, offbeat materials can capture infants' attention. For example, Goldhaber and Smith (1993) dumped crumpled paper on the floor in their infant room. The group, ranging in age from five to fourteen months, gathered around the paper and explored its properties. The crumpled pieces were picked up, mouthed, shaken, dropped, and observed as they rolled across the floor.

## SOCIAL COGNITION

**social referencing**
Infants gain information from others in order to understand and evaluate events and behave in the appropriate manner in a situation.

Social interaction and social resources are essential support for cognitive development. **Social referencing** is used by infants to gain information from others to understand and evaluate events and behave in the appropriate manner in a situation (Hornik & Gunnar, 1988). Infants have been observed seeking information and using the information as a guide for behavior. Infants may respond to affective social referencing, that is, the affective expressions of others, and to instrumental social referencing, using information about others' interactions with objects or people as a guide to their own interactions with novel objects or people. Positive affect from others facilitates positive behaviors toward novel objects and negative affect promotes avoidance (Hornik & Gunnar, 1988). As an example, consider Tony at 12 months of age:

> Tony is seated on the floor next to a cage that contains a rabbit. Tony's mother is seated nearby. Tony moves closer to the cage. He looks over at his mother who smiles and nods. Tony looks back at the rabbit with interest. He appears to want to touch it but holds back. He looks over at her again and she says, "It's okay to pat the bunny." He still holds back. Tony's mother comes over. She reaches in and pats the rabbit, "This is a sweet rabbit. He's soft and smooth. You can pat him too." Tony observes his mother's demonstration. He then leans over the cage and gently pats the rabbit just as his mother did.

This ability to gain information from others and apply it in new situations is essential in getting the most out of future educational and life experiences. Infants can retain information learned through imitation and apply it in future situations (Meltzoff, 1988).

## PLAY DURING INFANCY

The value of play as a major vehicle for learning is discussed in Chapter 5. It is by playing on their own and by playing in situations scaffolded by adults and older children that infants experience the world and build concepts through increasing brain connections (Ruhman, 1998). Both imaginative and imitative play acts begin to appear in the activities of infants.

**play**

Related to everything that children do: cognitive, affective, and psychomotor.

**Play** is the major vehicle for infant cognitive, motor, and affective development. Infants begin with mainly exploratory activity (Frost, Wortham, & Reifel, 2005). Sensorimotor intelligence develops as infants actively learn. As infant physical and motor abilities emerge, they use these abilities to grasp, bang, taste, shake, and interact with objects and people as they extend their sensory abilities and grow cognitively. Around 8 to 12 months of age, infants are beginning to walk, can coordinate play with two objects at the same time, and are beginning to use conventional words. Infants also have achieved object permanence and developed memory. They begin to engage in symbolic or pretend play. Parents and caregivers can support the infant's play by taking a role and providing toys and other materials. There are many games and activities that enrich infant play (see Helping babies play, 2003).

Analyze and evaluate the following infant play situation and infant and adult play behavior based on what you have learned thus far about infant development. Annie is six months and two weeks of age. She is at her grandmother's house.

> Annie is on her blanket on the floor playing with a few of her toys. A rattle and a teething ring have been placed on the blanket. Annie was placed on the blanket on her back. She lifts her legs up and notices her feet. She grabs her foot and pulls it into her mouth. She appears to become bored and rolls over on her stomach. She notices her rattle, which is placed within her reach. She reaches out and grasps the rattle. She shakes the rattle vigorously a few times, stops, and starts again. She is then placed in a sitting position. She leans forward on her hands and her head almost touches the blanket. Her grandmother gets down on the floor next to her and talks to her. Annie smiles and laughs at her grandmother. She waves her arms up and down and bounces her body.

## SUMMARY

Cognitive development in infancy is closely tied to sensory and motor growth and activities. Infants go through a sequence of stages in cognitive development centered on their increasing knowledge of objects in the environment and knowledge of the functions of language. The adult role is to provide the appropriate stimulation through personal interaction and providing a stimulating environment. Infants need a balance of time with other people and time to play and explore on their own in order to develop to capacity during this first part of the sensorimotor period.

Development of communication skills, which are the foundation of language and literacy, begin in infancy. Babies are also developing basic concepts, such as categorization. They also show signs of beginning to plan their activities. Focus on brain development has made us more aware of the need for providing babies with sensory and motor stimulation. The two sides of the brain have not begun to communicate but will eventually develop through infants' exploration of the environment. Infants learn through object exploration and play. They begin to show that they seek information from others. They are active learners who need time playing with others and time playing alone.

In your opinion, should an infant be placed in a child care situation? State your reasons for or against it, using material from this section on infancy (see also Chapters 11 through 13) to support your argument.

## FOR FURTHER READING

Albrecht, K., & Miller, L. G. (2000). *The comprehensive infant curriculum.* Beltsville, MD: Gryphon House.

Bardige, B. S., & Segal, M. M. (2005). *Building literacy with love: A guide for teachers and caregivers of children birth through age 5.* Washington, DC: Zero to Three.

Bremmer, G., & Fogel, A. (Eds.). (2001). *The Blackwell handbook of infant development.* Williston, VT: Blackwell.

Dupoux, E. (Ed.). (2001). *Language, brain, and cognitive development.* Cambridge, MA: MIT Press.

*Focus on Infants and toddlers.* Quarterly newsletter of the Association for Childhood Education International, 17904 Georgia Avenue, Ste. 215, Olney, MD 20832.

Gilkerson, L. (2005). *Early development and the brain.* Washington, DC: Zero to Three.

Goswami, U. (Ed.). (2002). *Blackwell handbook of childhood cognitive development.* Williston, VT: Blackwell.

Gusati, M. T. (2002). *Language acquisition: The growth of grammar.* Cambridge, MA: MIT Press.

Holyoak, K. J., & Morrison, R. G. (Eds.). (2005). *The Cambridge handbook of thinking and reasoning.* New York: Cambridge University Press.

Johnson, M. H., Munakata, Y., & Gilmore, R. (Eds.). (2002). *Brain development and cognition.* Williston, VT: Blackwell.

Lacerda, F., von Hofsten, C., & Heimann, M. (Eds.). *Emerging cognitive abilities in early infancy.* Mahwah, NJ: Erlbaum.

Landau, B., Sabini, J., Jonides, J., & Newport, E. L. (Eds.). (2000). *Perception, cognition, and language.* Cambridge, MA: MIT Press.

Lerner, C., & Dombro, A. L. (2004). *Bringing up baby.* Washington, DC: Zero to Three.

Lewis, V. (2003). *Development and disability* (2nd ed.). Williston, NH: Blackwell.

Parlakian, R. (2003). *Before the ABC's: Promoting school readiness in infants and toddlers.* Washington, DC: Zero to Three.

Rosenkoetter, S. E., & Knapp-Philo, J. (2004). *Learning to read the world: Language and literacy in the first three years.* Washington, DC: Zero to Three.

Scarlett, W. G., Naudeau, S., Salonlus-Pasternak, D., & Ponte, I. (2005). *Children's play.* Thousand Oaks, CA: Sage.

Tryphon, A., & Voneche, J. (Eds.). (2001). *Working with Piaget: Essays in honour of Barbel Inhelder.* Philadelphia: Psychology Press.

Zigler, E. F., Singer, D., & Bishop-Joseph, S. J. (2004). *Children's play: The roots of reading.* Washington, DC: Zero to Three.

## SUGGESTED ACTIVITIES

1. Observe an infant at home or at a child care site. Use an infant development evaluation sheet, as shown in Figure 14–2. Evaluate the infant's developmental level and rate of development.
   a. Overall, does the infant seem to be average, ahead of normal expectations, or slow in his or her rate of development?
   b. Are there any areas in which the infant seems to be exceptional, ahead of, or behind in development?
   c. What suggestions do you have for the parents and/or caregiver regarding this infant?

2. Find an infant under six months of age and an infant between nine and twelve months of age. Compare their development of object permanence. Try the following tasks and record their responses. Compare their reactions. At which stage of object permanence would you place each of the infants?
   a. Follow an object through space visually.
      Make a red and white bull's-eye pattern or use a bright plastic toy. Have the infant lie down or sit in an infant seat. Place yourself behind the infant so he or she concentrates on the object, not on you. Move the object in a circle around the infant's head. Do this five times. Note whether or not the infant tries to follow the object with his or her eyes and head. If the infant does follow it, does he or she follow it smoothly and through the complete circle?
   b. Reaction to a disappearing object.
      Use a brightly colored toy. Be sure the infant is looking at it. Move it slowly to a position where it is hidden. Do this three times. Note if the infant follows the object to the point where it disappears, whether he or she continues to glance at the spot where it disappeared, and whether the infant seems to be visually searching for the object at the point where it disappeared.
   c. The partially hidden object.
      Use an object, such as a toy, doll, stuffed animal, teething ring, or rattle, that the infant finds interesting. Hold the object in front of the infant and be sure he or she is looking at it. Put the object down in front of the infant where he or she can see it. Use a white cloth to cover part of the object. Note whether the infant tries to grasp the object. Does the infant try to remove the cloth or does the infant lose interest in the object when it is covered? Does he or she manage to get the object?
   d. The completely hidden object.
      Pick out a small object that you know the child finds interesting. Be sure the child watches as you hide the object completely under the white cloth. Does the child lose interest? Does he or she pick up the cloth and play with it? Does the child pick up the cloth and get the object?
   e. Two hiding places and an object.
      This time use two cloths, the white one and another one that is a dull and uninteresting color. Lay the two cloths down on the floor in front of the infant. Hide the object under one of the cloths. If the infant finds it, hide it under the other cloth. Does the infant look under the correct cloth first or under the one that was used the first time?
   f. Three hiding places and one object.
      If the infant has successfully found the hidden object with two cloths, then add a third. Note the infant's behavior as the object is hidden under the

Observer _____ Date _____ Time _____ Place _____

Infant's name _____ Birth date _____ Age _____

| Age and Cognitive Skill | Observed Yes | Observed No | Comments |
|---|---|---|---|
| **Birth to 1 Month** | | | |
| Begins to study own hand when lying on back. | | | |
| Prefers mother's voice to a stranger's. | | | |
| Often puts body movements in rhythm with speech patterns of adults. | | | |
| Communicates by crying and fussing. | | | |
| Certain music and voices can calm him/her down. | | | |
| Turns head to locate certain voices and sounds. | | | |
| Occasionally makes a sound other than crying. | | | |
| **1 to 4 Months** | | | |
| Exhibits some recognition of familiar objects. | | | |
| Does not search for objects that fall or otherwise disappear. | | | |
| Watches hands intently. | | | |
| Imitates gestures, such as bye-bye and patting head. | | | |
| Attempts to keep toy in motion by repeating arm or leg movements. | | | |
| Begins to mouth objects. | | | |
| Reacts to familiar voices. | | | |
| Will vocalize in rhythm with adult. | | | |
| Babbles or coos when spoken to or smiled at. | | | |
| Coos using single vowel sounds and imitates others. | | | |
| Laughs out loud. | | | |
| **4 Months to 8 Months** | | | |
| Focuses on small objects and reaches. | | | |
| Coordinates eyes, hand, and mouth to explore body, toys, and environment. | | | |
| Imitates actions, such as pat-a-cake, bye-bye, and peek-a-boo. | | | |
| Drops objects from high chair or crib and looks down with delight. | | | |
| Will search for hidden object. | | | |
| Handles and explores objects using multiple senses. | | | |
| Drops one toy when handed another. | | | |
| Plays actively with small toys. | | | |
| Happily bangs objects. | | | |
| Fully attached to mother or single caregiver. | | | |
| Responds to name or simple requests, such as "Wave bye-bye." | | | |

*(Continued)*

**FIGURE 14–2** Infant cognitive and language development assessment chart.
(Adapted from Allen, K. D., & Marotz, L. R., 2003. *Developmental profiles: Pre-birth through twelve.* Clifton Park, NY: Delmar Learning).

| Age and Cognitive Skill | Observed: Yes | Observed: No | Comments |
|---|---|---|---|
| Imitates nonspeech sounds, such as a cough or tongue click. | | | |
| Responds to voice tones of others. | | | |
| Produces vowels and some consonants. | | | |
| Makes different sounds to express emotions. | | | |
| "Talks" to toys. | | | |
| Babbles by repeating syllables, such as *ma, ma, ma.* | | | |
| **8 to 12 Months** | | | |
| Points at distant objects. | | | |
| Follows simple instructions. | | | |
| Puts everything in mouth. | | | |
| Drops toys intentionally. | | | |
| Shows appropriate use of everyday items: pretends to drink from cup, hugs doll, etc. | | | |
| Spatial relationships—puts block in cup when requested. | | | |
| Demonstrates functional relationships: puts spoon in mouth, turns pages of book. | | | |
| Searches for partially hidden object. | | | |
| Babbles or jabbers to initiate social interaction. | | | |
| Shakes head for "no." | | | |
| Babbles in sentence-like sequences; uses jargon (syllables with language-like inflections). | | | |
| Says "dada" and "mama". | | | |
| Enjoys rhymes and simple songs. | | | |
| Will hand toy to adult if accompanied by appropriate gesture. | | | |
| Waves "bye-bye" and claps when asked. | | | |

FIGURE 14–2 Continued

first, the second, and then the third. Does he or she successfully find the object under the third cloth?

**3.** Go to a store where infant toys are sold. Using the guidelines below, select toys that are safe and stimulating. Make a list of the six toys you think are best, the skills and concepts they support, and the cost of each toy. Design two toys you could make yourself that would support development of the same concepts and skills.

Guidelines for safe infant toys (Robertson, 2007):

- 0 to 6 months toys should be larger than $1^1/_2$ inches in diameter to avoid choking, have smooth round edges, and be soft and flexible.
- 6 months to 1 year toys should be large, unbreakable, and smooth.

Recommended toys (Robertson, 2007):

- Up to 6 months: squeeze toys, colorful mobiles, large pictures of faces or simple patterns, nonbreakable mirrors.
- 6 months to 1 year: cradle gyms, sturdy books, manipulative toys, toys that make noises, busy boards.

**4.** Discuss the following language samples with a small group in class. Analyze them and decide what stage the child is in by labeling each part of the sample according to its developmental level. Decide whether the child is vocalizing appropriately for his or her age. On a sheet of large chart paper or newsprint or on the chalkboard, list the characteristics found for each sample. Compare your results with those of the other student group groups. Note any differences and discuss them. Be sure to decide on the kind of role the adult takes in those samples that include an adult.

Sample 1. Child is two months old. She is in her crib watching a mobile and rattling a toy elephant. She bumps the mobile with her arm, which flails with excitement as she observes the mobile.

Igh* ee ee igh a
a a a a
(gutteral, like a growl) a a a
a e a
a a a
*rhymes with sigh

Sample 2. Child is five months and three weeks of age. She is crawling around the living room.

| **Mother** | **Child** |
|---|---|
| e-he-ba-ba-boo-boo | |
| Hi Hi Kate Hi | |
| The elephant goes keetsch keetsch | e-we |
| | ab awa |
| | aw aba |
| No No | ub ha |
| | h ma-ma |
| No No | uw uw he-e |
| No No | he we he me-he |
| She's after the light plug hole. | |

**5.** Make an entry in your journal.

## REVIEW

**1.** Explain why object permanence and object recognition are critical concepts that are developed during infancy.

**2.** Put an *X* by all the correct statements.

a. Infants move in rhythm with the speech of the adults around them.
b. Infants' vocalizing as they watch mobiles is meaningless and unimportant.
c. Infants usually do not discriminate their mother's voice from others until about four months of age.
d. As early as ten months of age, adult labeling of infants' actions and of objects is extremely important for later language development.
e. Single words usually do not appear before fifteen months of age.
f. Don't expect infants to comprehend simple directions before the age of fourteen months.
g. According to Honig, it is important to support language development by accompanying routines with talk, such as chants, songs, and rhymes.
h. Teaching preverbal babies signs can accelerate their language development.
i. It is not appropriate to introduce children to books before age two.

**3.** Select the correct answers.

a. In Sherman's study, infants viewed drawings of faces that all had the same hairline and jawline. When shown pairs of faces where one had the previously viewed hairline and jawline and the other had some other features,
   1. infants showed no preference for either one of the faces in the pairs.
   2. the infants remembered features other than jawline and hairline best.
   3. the infants picked hairline and jawline as the critical features in the pictures.

b. The results of Sherman's study
   1. show that infants can develop categories.
   2. indicate infants cannot develop categories.
   3. add no information to our knowledge of when children begin to learn to categorize.

c. The results of Younger's 1993 study and preceding studies indicate that
   1. by ten months of age, infants can detect and organize category features.
   2. fourteen months of age is the critical time for developing the ability to organize category features.
   3. infants became confused when shown a picture of a novel animal.

d. Willatt's research
   1. confirms that infants always use a trial-and-error approach to solve problems.
   2. confirms that infants can think through a solution to a problem before acting.
   3. supports Piaget's ideas regarding the age at which we can expect representational thought to be evident in infant approaches to problem solving.

**4.** Explain the importance of brain research to infant brain development.

**5.** Explain the importance of brain lateralization to cognitive development.

**6.** List the three types of object manipulation that seem to be necessary for the infant to achieve full cognitive capacity.

**7.** Provide an example of infant social referencing.

**8.** Describe the important factors in supporting infant play. Explain why play is an important vehicle for infant learning.

## KEY TERMS LIST

brain lateralization
brain research
categorization
cognitive development
developmental biodynamics
literacy
literacy beginners
object manipulation
object permanence
object recognition
planning
play
social referencing
substages of sensorimotor development

Additional resources for this chapter can be found on the Online Companion™ to accompany this text at http://www.earlychilded.delmar.com. Respond to "Time to Reflect" and "Looking Further" concepts, review various child development scenarios, and answer thought-provoking questions in the Critical Thinking Forum. Keep a daily journal by downloading the student journal available on this Web site. Complete the interactive matching exercises to reinforce concepts, and print out the child development assessment forms to use during your observation of development for children from birth to age eight. In addition, read the case studies on the Web site to reinforce the important concepts in each chapter, and take a look at the multitude of Web links that are available for student research on the Internet.

# SECTION IV

# The Toddler: Developing Toward Independence

## INTRODUCTION

Who are typical toddlers? During the second year, children usually enter the toddler period. By this time, they typically are walking, but their speech is limited. Their understanding of communication is beyond their speech. They are active imitators. The people in their environment serve as models. They want to do what others do. For example, a child whose mother is an accountant is observed using a calculator while the mother works with her computer spreadsheet. The toddler may be observed sitting in the laundry basket making motor noises and pretending to drive a car. Toddlers are entranced with their newly found mobility and enjoy all kinds of physical activity: running, lifting, carrying, pushing, and pulling. They also enjoy roughhousing and dancing with older children or adults.

Toddlers display many behaviors that may be viewed with delight or that may cause stress and frustration. Cognitively, they demonstrate an understanding of spoken language but cannot speak yet. They view things and events at face value, focusing on the most obvious interpretation. Motorically, they are ahead of their spoken language development. They move about their environment with ease (and often with speed), which requires adults to provide constant supervision and guidance. The second year of toddlerhood (ages two to three) is a time of transition from the sensorimotor to the preoperational period. During this stage, children develop an increased maturity that carries them over to the next cognitive developmental period. This section provides an overview of toddler development as toddlers move toward independence: autonomy and guidance, affective development, and cognitive development.

CHAPTER

# 15

# The Toddler: Autonomy and Physical and Motor Development

## OBJECTIVES

After reading this chapter, you should be able to:

- Recognize that toddlers are striving for autonomy.
- Identify major toddler characteristics from the theorists' points of view.
- Analyze and interpret toddler and adult behavior.
- Assess toddlers fine and gross motor development.
- Recommend appropriate toilet-training practices for toddlers.
- Identify important elements of toddler nutrition and health.
- List expected fine and gross motor skills attained during the toddler period.
- Explain the relationship between toddler brain and motor skill development.
- Explain the most effective guidance practices for use with toddlers.
- Understand that children with special needs also need to develop autonomy through guidance.

The toddler is a dynamo, full of unlimited energy, enthusiasm, and curiosity. . . . The toddler begins this period with the limited abilities of an infant and ends with the relatively sophisticated skills of the young child (Allen & Marotz, 2006). Toddlerhood is the time when the child begins to move from dependence to independence.

Toddlerhood is the period from one to two-and-a-half or three years; it is the time a child grows from infant to preschooler. By two-and-a-half years, Brazelton believes that children reach a time when they pull all these new skills together and are especially fun to be with as they move toward the maturity of age three:

> What fun it is to have made it with a three-year-old who can act for himself, who can think for himself, who can be gay and amusing, who can express his thoughts independently, who is beginning to realize his independence from you! How rewarding to find that at last he can afford to let himself care about you as another person—not just as an extension of himself (Brazelton, 1977, pp. 114–116).

FIGURE 15–1 The toddler enjoys using newly developed motor skills to push wheeled toys.

The major task for toddlers is to seek **autonomy** as they move toward independence (see Figure 15–1). Toddlers want to do what older children and adults do and to accomplish their goals by themselves. Toddlers present a special challenge to adults. Parents find different methods of moving toddlers toward socially acceptable independent behavior.

For example, Holden and West (1989), having observed mothers and toddlers in the naturalistic setting of the supermarket, moved into the laboratory to observe how mothers of two- and three-year-olds dealt with their toddlers' dynamic behavior. In the naturalistic setting, they observed that the children got into less trouble if their mothers used foresight to keep the children constructively busy through conversation or having them help with the shopping. Mothers who waited until their children misbehaved before they intervened had children with greater frequencies of undesirable behavior. The mothers' task in the laboratory was to keep their children from playing with attractive forbidden toys. The children were permitted to use less attractive objects. As in the naturalistic study, mothers who behaved proactively had fewer problems than those who behaved reactively. Holden and West also noted that both mothers and children were very creative in finding ways to keep away from the forbidden toys and finding interesting ways to use the less attractive objects. The mothers' creativity took a toll in mental and physical energy .". . . [the truth about the 'terrible twos' may originate in mothers' quite accurate perception of the amount of effort they expend to make their impulsive youngsters behave as cooperative partners" (Holden & West, 1989, p. 69).

**autonomy**
Growth toward independence.

Bullock and Lutkenhaus (1988) studied the development of volitional behavior in children between the ages of fifteen and twenty-five months. By volitional behavior, they referred to acts done to achieve a particular outcome or goal. Volitional skills require the child to keep the goal in mind, have the ability to stick to and follow through on the task, and keep track of progress. The toddler period is a transitional time for developing the abilities needed to be volitionally competent. The tasks used by these researchers were building a block tower, cleaning a blackboard, and dressing a doll. The results indicated that children younger than eighteen months are primarily activity-oriented; they act for the sake of pure action. After eighteen months, they start becoming outcome-oriented and show pleasure when they achieve goals. By twenty-four months, they move more directly toward the goal and have a definite stopping point in mind. It is not until about thirty months that toddlers begin to note mistakes and make corrections when in the middle of a task. Younger children might recognize a mistake but not do anything to correct it. The twenty-month-olds showed the greatest discrepancy in recognizing the standards for the task, being able to have the control to meet the standards, and actively involving the self. The authors suggest that this coordination problem underlies the typical volatile behavior frequently referred to as "**terrible twos.**" That is, young toddlers move and act for the sake of the action itself and not to achieve any specific goal. When children develop to the point where their actions are coordinated and goal directed, the sense of self as an active and competent person begins to form.

**terrible twos**
A time period when the child's active exploration and striving for independence put heavy demands on adult guidance.

The young toddler can be pictured as one who is rapidly developing new competencies in the motor, cognitive, and affective areas. However, as these competencies are developing, his or her efforts at achievement and at finding out what he or she can do demand a great deal of attention and energy from the adults providing care.

## THE THEORISTS LOOK AT THE TODDLER

Erikson, Freud, Skinner, Bandura, Piaget, and Vygotsky, each view the toddler from his own perspective. All but Skinner and Bandura place toddlers in a special stage of growth and learning.

**autonomy versus shame and doubt**

Erikson's second stage, in which the toddler must deal with this crisis.

At around eighteen months of age, toddlers enter Erikson's second stage, in which they must deal with crisis: **autonomy versus shame and doubt** (Miller, 2002). The toddler has a strong drive to push ahead and use newly developed locomotor skills. At the same time, toddlers must also develop self-control and learn to use these skills within the limits set by the environment. They learn they may climb up on the seat of the couch, but they may not climb up on the back of the couch and jump off. They learn that they are allowed to run outdoors but not in the house. Toddlers need to develop a healthy feeling of shame when they have done the wrong thing. At the same time, if feelings of shame are too strong, toddlers will doubt their own capabilities and be unable to develop a healthy sense of independence. Toddlers can be very defiant, (the "No!" stage, or exhibiting much negative behavior) or very compliant (going along with everything without ever asserting themselves). The adult has to guide toddlers through this period in such a way as to encourage autonomous behavior balanced with self-control. During much of this crisis period, behavior centers around toileting—a critical achievement in physical and motor development.

**anal stage**

Freud's second stage (congruent with the toddler period), when independent toileting is a major concern and goal.

Freud emphasized the importance of the toilet-training experience during ages one-and-a-half to three, which he labeled the **anal stage.** He found that adult psychological problems often had their roots in an improperly handled toilet-training experience. This is an important concern in our culture. The responsibility for retaining urine and feces is the first demand made on the young child to control biological and physiological needs (Miller, 2002).

From Bandura's point of view, the development of more refined motor skills and higher-level cognitive skills enables the toddler to make better use of the capacity for observational learning (Miller, 2002). The toddler moves from visual to symbolic representations, which enables the child to imitate previously observed behaviors after he or she is no longer observable. The toddler's more refined motor skills enable the accomplishment of a greater variety of tasks. Commonly, the result is finding the toddler trying out mom's makeup or dad's shaving equipment, or mixing up an original recipe in the kitchen.

**preoperational period**

May last from about the age of two until about seven; a period when the focus of development is language and speech.

In Piaget's view, the toddler goes from the latter part of the sensorimotor period into the early part of the **preoperational period.** Between eighteen months and two years of age, the child passes from sensorimotor to preoperational. Perceptually, children mature to the point at which they achieve object permanence and begin to have more adultlike mental images. Motor development ceases to dominate cognitive growth and language development takes over. Play and imitation are the major vehicles for learning. This idea is consistent with Erikson's view.

From Vygotsky's view (see Berk & Winsler, 1995, Chapter 2), the period from age one to age three is one in which the leading activities focus on manipulation of objects, the beginnings of overt private speech, and the development of self-regulation. Throughout this period, toddlers become less impulsive as they find that, to be a part of play activities, they must control their impulses and follow the rules of the activity. An important development during the toddler period is the development of autonomous speech and self-regulating private speech. Words often have no meaning out of context. Children commonly make up some of their own approximations that only the immediate family may understand. The meaning of this first speech depends on the context. According to Vygotsky, thought is not yet verbal. We explore Vygotsky's view of language and thought in later chapters.

The toddler's pressured need for activity reaches a peak between two-and-a-half and three, at which time he or she tends to settle down a bit.

The right environment is key to healthy development at any age, from Skinner's point of view.

As viewed by the developmental theorists, the toddler is typically very active and is beginning to be an independent person. Maturing muscular control enables the toddler to walk, climb, run, and toilet. Language opens up new areas of learning and communication. Play and imitation are major means for learning about the world and of the behavior expected regarding sex role, independence, aggression, differentiating right and wrong, and social actions.

Considering what you have read thus far regarding toddler behavior, why might parents become easily frustrated with their toddlers?

## NUTRITION AND HEALTH

In Chapter 12, infant nutrition and health were discussed. In Chapter 18 the food pyramid is introduced. Some general nutrition and health topics are included in this chapter.

**food security**
Access at all times to enough nourishment.

**food insecurity**
Difficulty in securing adequate food.

General health and nutrition have long been recognized as important factors affecting children's physical development and behavior. Providing adequate nutrition for young children is a serious problem in the United States. "**Food security** has been defined as access at all times to enough nourishment for an active, healthy life" (Federal Interagency Forum, 2001, p. 18). In 1999, 3.8 percent of children lived in homes where there was **food insecurity.** That is, where securing adequate food was difficult. As children get older the quality of their diet decreases mostly due to eating less fruit and drinking less milk. Low-income pregnant women, infants, and young children up to age five can receive nutritional assistance from the WIC (Women, Infants, and Children) program, which is federally funded. WIC provides for diet supplements high in nutrients, such as protein, calcium, iron, and vitamins A and C. Infants can receive iron-fortified formula and cereal. Adults can receive iron-fortified cereal, vitamin C–rich fruit and/or vegetable juice, eggs, milk, cheese, peanut butter, dried beans or peas, tuna fish, and carrots (cited in Federal Interagency Forum, 2001, p. 19) "Each year millions of American children experience hunger or lack proper nourishment" (Children's Defense Fund, 1998, p. 53). During fiscal year 1996, 13.2 million children received food stamps; during the 1997 school year, 26.9 million children received free or subsidized lunches and almost 7.1 million received a daily breakfast at school. These represent significant increases over the 1992 report. The summer food program has expanded and is currently stable. For younger children, federal funding has continued to subsidize food in center- and home-based child care, although the guidelines are now more stringent in providing funds for family child care homes in low-income areas or operated by low-income providers.

## THE ADULT ROLE IN NUTRITION AND HEALTH CARE

Adults who work with young children and their families can support the children's physical and mental development by supporting good nutrition and health care. At the school or child care center, nutritious meals and snacks should be provided. Routines such as hand washing should be emphasized. A health and nutrition education program should be developed for the students and their families.

Marotz et al. (2005) describe the need for good nutrition as the basis of good health. Adults must have knowledge about proper nutrition to serve as good models. They need to know what nutrients are needed to provide energy, materials for growth and maintenance of body tissue, and regulation of body processes. Each day, the body requires minimum amounts of nutrients obtained from the four basic food sources: dairy, protein, fruits and vegetables, and grains. **Recommended daily dietary allowances (RDA)** can be used to determine which foods to purchase and to monitor daily food intake. An RDA table can be found in Marotz et al. (2005) or can be obtained from the Food and Nutrition Board, National Academy of Sciences, National Research Council, Washington, DC.

**recommended daily dietary allowances (RDA)**

Minimum amounts of nutrients obtained from the four basic food sources that our bodies need each day.

Adults can support good child nutrition by offering children only nutritious foods. Sweets and other junk foods should not be included in the early childhood menu.

Meals should be happy, pleasant times. Serving family style can promote a pleasant atmosphere and provide an opportunity for children to develop independence (Bomba & Knight, 1993). Young children develop gradually in their eating behaviors, and their approach to eating should be respected (Figure 15–2). For example, younger toddlers will do mostly finger feeding and commonly may turn the spoon upside down on the way to the mouth. Around age two, appetite decreases and food preferences develop. Adults need to be patient with children during this period. The two-year-old enjoys self-feeding but still uses fingers along with utensils. Finger foods should be provided. From age three on, appetite usually improves along with the use of utensils, but finger foods can still make eating easier. By age three, children enjoy helping with food preparation. Children have small stomach capacities and use up a lot of energy. A nutritious snack, such as cheese cubes, fruit slices, raw vegetables, or fruit juice should be provided between meals.

FIGURE 15–2 These toddlers are just learning to feed themselves with finger foods.

Adults often use food as a reward for appropriate behavior. For example, a child picks up his or her toys and is given a cookie or a piece of candy. Using food in this way increases its preferential status (Birch, Marlin, & Rotter, 1984). Food is also used as a contingency leading to a preferred activity; for example, eating green beans and then being allowed to go outside to play. When used in this way, food becomes even less liked (Birch et al., 1984). In practice, this implies that using food as a contingency is not the way to get children to like that particular food.

Adults who work with young children are observers and appraisers of their health status. Marotz et al. (2005) suggest a scheme for health appraisal. Everyday observations of children provide an opportunity to gather information on their energy levels and motivation. Changes in activity level may indicate a problem. Daily health inspection requires only a minute or two but is very important. General appearance, scalp, face, eyes, and nose can be inspected for signs of any suspicious changes. Parents should remain with their children until the inspection is complete. This policy involves the parents and ensures that they are present if anything of special concern is noted. Health education is also important. Marotz et al. suggest that parents and children need information on topics such as toy safety, the importance of eating breakfast, the importance of nutritious snacks, the benefits of exercise, cleanliness, dressing appropriately for the weather, and dental hygiene.

## Substance Abuse

The damaging effects of substance abuse were described in Chapters 8 and 9. Drug abuse, alcohol abuse, and passive smoke inhalation continue to be sources of serious problems for young children. As will be mentioned in later chapters, we do not have enough solid data to substantiate all claims made regarding the effects of these substances. On the other hand, we cannot ignore the possibilities.

For example, Rist (1990) reports that in 1990, the first crack cocaine babies entered kindergarten. They were characterized as difficult to teach. They usually are born with birth defects and often are abandoned or go home to a crack environment. They seem unable to cope with too much sensory stimulation and are unable to respond when asked to do a complex task. Placed in the stimulating classroom environment, these children tend to either withdraw or become wild and difficult to control. Schools need to be prepared to handle these damaged children. They need an emotionally supportive, structured school/care environment beginning in infancy to counteract the chaos at home.

Although children of substance-abusing parents may not be directly affected by the substances, they may live in an emotionally damaging environment (Thompson, 1998). If drugs and/or alcohol have priority before the children, the children may feel abandoned and be unable to trust adults. "Early childhood professionals can help young children of addicts and alcoholics by developing caring relationships, maintaining consistent routines, and offering therapeutic play in the classroom" (Thompson, 1998, p. 35). These young children need to have relationships with adults who are consistent and build trust.

Lilian Katz (1994) warns that some materials being produced for use by teachers of young children for drug abuse education are not appropriate and may be confusing and even misguide them. For example, can a preschooler or kindergartner perceive the difference between an adult who drinks an occasional beer and one who is an alcoholic? How will the child who comes from a home where illegal drugs are used accept that his or her family and their friends are doing something bad? As will be seen later in this text, preschool and kindergarten students are not at a level in their mental development where they can understand the relativity underlying these situations. Rather than subjecting a whole class to inappropriate instruction, Katz suggests that early childhood teachers try to obtain assistance for individual children and families as problems are perceived. Meanwhile, adults need to find methods of drug education that fit the limits of young children's understanding.

## The Not-So-Healthy Diet

Toddlers eat semisolid and solid foods. Unfortunately, most children age two and up do not have healthy eating habits (*Report card*, 2001). Thirty-six percent of two- and three-year-olds have diets that are rated good, 60 percent rated as needs improvement, and

4 percent rated with poor diets. Toddlers often do not meet the dietary requirements for vegetables and meat. Childhood obesity is increasingly recognized as a significant problem (Fraser, 2004), and the rate of overweight preschoolers age two to five is 10.4 percent. The percentage tends to be larger for minority and low-income populations. Children are consuming more calories than they are burning off. Fraser (2004) identifies several reasons for this:

- They consume twice the amount of soft drinks.
- They eat fewer home-cooked meals and more fast food.
- They are eating more fats, sugars, and carbohydrates and fewer fruits and nonstarchy vegetables.

Children are less physically active and watch too much television. Also, while watching television and eating, children tend to eat more pizza, snack foods, meat, and caffeinated drinks and less fruits, vegetables, and juices than children who don't watch television while eating. Low-income families usually eat fewer fruits and vegetables, which are more expensive and less filling than refined grains, sugars, and fats. Overweight children face the risk of type 2 diabetes. They also can develop high levels of cholesterol, high blood pressure, and orthopedic problems due to their growing bones carrying too much weight. Families are encouraged to keep unhealthy foods out of the house, increase the amounts of milk and water and decrease the amounts of juice and caffeinated drinks, eat together as a family, not use food as a reward or punishment, adopt a physically active lifestyle, and reduce the time in front of television and videos. Schools could also do a better job of serving healthy meals. Communities could provide better sports venues (such as parks and bike paths) and offer sports activities for children.

Think about what your approach would be to provide healthy nutrition to a toddler. How could you make sure the toddler has a proper diet but doesn't get too picky?

## PHYSICAL AND MOTOR DEVELOPMENT

The general directions of physical and motor development were described in Chapter 12. The active toddler grows taller and becomes more proportional and takes great strides in gross and fine motor development.

## MOTOR DEVELOPMENT

### Toddler Gross Motor Development

At the age of seventeen months, Kate visits a second-grade class made up of many of the same students she had visited at the age of five months. One child, Shelly, describes Kate in this "toddler action story":

> Toddler Kate can walk, talk, smell, and her favorite thing is to climb. Kate can say "pop" and "milk", "DaDa", "achee", "MaMa", "cracker." Last year, Kate was five months old. But now Kate is seventeen months old and loves to do tricks but her favorite trick to do is roll. The end of Kate's story.

Shelly has noticed two major changes that characterize the toddler: Kate's increased movement and her ability to speak. Movement dominates the first year of toddlerhood, with language development dominating the second year. Selma Fraiberg describes the child just entering toddlerhood:

> The discovery of independent locomotion and the discovery of a new self usher in a new phase in personality development. The toddler is quite giddy with his new achievements. He behaves as if he had invented his new mode of locomotion (which in a restricted sense is true) and he is quite in love with himself for being so clever. From dawn to dusk, he marches around in an ecstatic, drunken dance, which ends only when he collapses with fatigue. He can no longer be contained within the four walls of his house and the fenced-in yard is like a prison to him. Given practically unlimited space, he staggers joyfully with open arms toward the end of the horizon. Given half a chance he might make it. (Fraiberg, 1959, pp. 61–62)

> The toddler is a dynamo, full of unlimited energy and enthusiasm. . . . The toddler period begins with the limited abilities of an infant and ends with the relatively sophisticated skills of a young child (Allen & Marotz, 2006).

Motorically, toddlers are quite skilled and very mobile. They are no longer quiet, passive, and content with being in a playpen or crib. They must move at all times: "Motor activity is so vital to the child of this age that interference, restriction of this activity even through another biological process, sleep, is intolerable to him" (Fraiberg, 1959, p. 59).

Toddlers' curiosity, combined with their developing motor skills, makes keeping up with their exploits a challenge to adults.

Toddlers need both indoor and outdoor environments that nurture practice of their emerging gross motor skills. Toddlers enjoy toys that they can push and pull (Frost et al., 2005). Toy vacuums and lawnmowers, small wagons and wheelbarrows, toddler ladders and slides, and outdoor room for running and jumping provide for use of gross motor skills. Toddlers may be seen running about with stuffed animals or dolls held tightly against their chests. They enjoy filling paper bags or other containers with objects, carrying them to another place and dumping the objects, then filling the containers and repeating the routine. Toddlers repeat actions as if practicing to be able to do them perfectly. The toddler gradually becomes more agile and coordinated. By age three, children become preschoolers and a great deal more motor control is evident. See Figure 15–3.

## Toileting

Achievement of appropriate toileting habits is a major physical/motor skill that is expected to be accomplished by the end of the toddler period (about age three). By age two, most children can be dry during the day, but many are not daytime dry until age three. Night dryness usually comes even later (Cole, Cole & Lightfoot, 2005). The ability to control elimination depends on maturation of the sphincter muscles, neurological maturation that enables messages to go from bladder and bowel to the brain, and desire. That is, children must get the message that it is time to toilet and control their muscles until they get to the toilet. They also must want to eliminate in the potty rather than in their pants. They can use muscular control to retain waste until they get off the toilet as well as until they get on.

Children need not only muscular maturation and desire, but also cognitive maturity. They need to be able to understand and follow instructions and retain the information between eliminations. The more casual and relaxed adults are, the more likely success will be achieved (Honig, 1993).

With increasing numbers of toddlers in child care, the toilet learning process is shared by family and out-of-home caregivers. Riblatt, Obegi, Hammons, Ganger, & Ganger (2003) investigated the degree of agreement in attitudes and practices of parents and child care professionals. They found significant differences between child

Observer _____ Date _____ Time _____ Place _____

Infant's name _____ Birth date _____ Age _____

| Age and Motor Skill | Observed: Yes | Observed: No | Comments |
|---|---|---|---|
| **One-Year-Old** | | | |
| Crawls skillfully and quickly | | | |
| Stands alone | | | |
| Gets to feet without help | | | |
| Walks unassisted by age two; falls frequently | | | |
| May use furniture to pull up to standing position or lower self to floor or may just flop down | | | |
| Enjoys pushing or pulling toys while walking | | | |
| Picks up objects and throws them | | | |
| Attempts to run; may fall | | | |
| Crawls up and down stairs | | | |
| Sits in a small chair | | | |
| Carries toys from place to place | | | |
| **Two-Year-Old** | | | |
| Walks with more erect heel-to-toe patterns; maneuvers around obstacles fairly well | | | |
| Runs more confidently; falls less often | | | |
| Squats when playing | | | |
| Climbs stairs unassisted but not with alternating feet | | | |
| Balances on one foot for a few seconds | | | |
| Begins to achieve toilet training | | | |
| Throws large ball underhand without falling | | | |
| Climbs up on chair, turns around, and sits down | | | |
| Uses feet to propel wheeled toys | | | |

**FIGURE 15–3** Toddler gross motor development assessment chart.
Adapted from Allen, K. D., & Marotz, L. R., 2006. Developmental profiles: Pre-birth through twelve. Clifton Park, NY: Delmar Learning.

care professionals and parents in the four main areas of study: age of initiation, readiness, practices, and response to accidents. For example, the majority of professionals believed training should begin after twenty-four months, and the majority of parents believed it should begin before twenty-four months. The professionals were more likely to support that there is no "magic age" of readiness. Almost 100 percent of professionals, but only about half of the parents, based their readiness assessment on development and emotional readiness, interest in the potty, asking to go to the potty or toilet, and interest in regular underwear. A similar difference appeared in practices, such as explaining expectations, having a potty chair available, using praise, being patient, and reading children books about toileting. Most professionals agreed that when accidents occurred, the child should be bathed and changed, taken to the potty chair, asked to remember next time, and engage in a discussion about how the body feels. Fewer parents believed in these kinds of responses. Riblatt et al. (2003) recommend that there should be more communication between parents and child care professionals regarding toilet training. Some of the differences may be cultural and require discussion and some agreement on procedures.

## Toddler Fine Motor Skills

Although the toddler spends a great deal of time working on gross motor skills, fine motor skills are not neglected. During the toddler years, the child progressively refines hand and finger movements (McGlaughlin & Morgan, 1981). Coordination of thumb and fingers improves and the hands are used with more precision. Small objects are manipulated with increasing dexterity. During toddlerhood, the child learns to eat independently with the fingers and then to use eating utensils. Space and movement become coordinated, so objects can be reached for and picked up with smooth movements and minimal effort. By fifteen months, a child can drop objects into and empty them out of containers, hold two objects in one hand at the same time, begin to fit objects together, turn the pages in a cardboard or cloth book, hold a crayon in a whole hand grasp, and build a tower of two or three blocks. During the rest of the toddler period, these skills are further refined. By two-and-a-half, the child can hold a pencil in the hand rather than the fist, is beginning to draw, and can pour liquids from one container to another (McGlaughlin & Morgan, 1981).

Cognitive development during the sensorimotor period is enhanced by the child's opportunities to explore objects. It is usually assumed that the more attention the child gives to this exploration, the more information the child obtains (Ruff, 1986). From the age of six months, children can clearly focus their attention on objects for measurable periods of time. The child fingers and turns the object while looking at it with an intent expression. This type of behavior is called **examining.** As fine motor development becomes more precise, the child can handle objects more dextrously during these periods of examination.

**examining**
When the child fingers and turns an object while looking at it with an intent expression.

See Figure 15–4 for toddler fine motor typical developmental capabilities.

Observer _____ Date _____ Time _____ Place _____

Infant's name _____ Birth date _____ Age _____

| Age and Skill | Observed: Yes | Observed: No | Comments |
|---|---|---|---|
| **One-Year-Old Fine Motor Skills** | | | |
| Scribbles with crayons and markers using whole arm movement | | | |
| Helps turn pages in a book | | | |
| Stacks two to four objects (such as blocks) | | | |
| Pounds wooden pegs with toy hammer | | | |
| Places three geometric shapes in a large formboard or puzzle | | | |
| **One-Year-Old Self Help** | | | |
| Helps feed himself or herself; holds spoon (often upside down) | | | |
| Drinks from glass or cup | | | |
| Often misses mouth when using utensil; frequently spills | | | |
| May still eat using fingers | | | |

*(Continued)*

**FIGURE 15–4** Toddler fine motor and self help development assessment chart.
Adapted from Allen, K. D., & Marotz, L. R., 2006. Developmental profiles: Pre-birth through twelve. Clifton Park, NY: Delmar Learning.

| Age and Skill | Observed Yes | Observed No | Comments |
|---|---|---|---|
| **Two-Year-Old Fine Motor Skills** | | | |
| Fits large pegs in pegboard | | | |
| Opens doors by turning knobs | | | |
| Grasps large crayon with fist; scribbles on large paper | | | |
| Enjoys pouring and filling (sand, water, etc.) | | | |
| Stacks four to six objects | | | |
| Puts objects together and takes them apart | | | |
| **Two-Year-Old Self Help** | | | |
| Can hold cup or glass in one hand but spills often | | | |
| Unbuttons large buttons | | | |
| Unzips large zippers | | | |
| Can feed self with increasing skill | | | |
| Tries to wash self in bath | | | |
| Tries to help dress | | | |
| Can usually remove clothing | | | |
| Stays dry longer, may show interest in toileting, may be willing to sit on potty for a few minutes | | | |

FIGURE 15–4 Continued

What is your opinion regarding toilet training? If the mother of a 20-month-old asked for your advice, what would you tell her?

## THE BRAIN AND MOTOR DEVELOPMENT

According to *Brain Wonders* (2001), in the beginning of toddlerhood walking signals the beginning of the development of a complex motor skill. The initial stiff, clumsy walk smooths out during the first year and becomes much more coordinated. It is the increased myelination of the brain's motor pathways that enables messages to be sent more clearly; along with practice, it results in smoother, better coordinated movements. More neural connections and practice result in more coordination and stronger muscles, which enable the toddler to, run, jump, and climb.

Increased myelination also influences the development of fine motor skills. The maturing of the cerebellum brings about improvement in timing and coordination. Along with practice with drawing tools, bead stringing, painting, and building with small blocks, fine motor skills improve. By 18 months, 50 percent of toddlers have a stable hand preference, but many children use both hands well into childhood.

## GUIDANCE

From the toddler's point of view, the adult, determined to socialize the toddler, is a major interference in what could be a delightful time of life. Selma Fraiberg describes the toddler point of view as follows:

> . . . They [adults] urge him to part with treasures he discovers in his travels, the rusty bolts, charred corncobs, and dried up apple cores that are so difficult to find unless you know where to look for them. They send unsolicited rescue parties to prevent him from scaling marvellous heights, from sloshing through inky puddles, or pursuing the elusive tail of the family dog. . . . They are there to interfere with the joys of emptying garbage cans and wastebaskets; and, of course, they bring in proposals of naps and bedtime at the most unfortunate moments and for reasons that are clear only to them (Fraiberg, 1959, pp. 62–64).

The toddler soon gets a reputation for being negative, as he or she resists this adult interference with his or her plans. From the adult's point of view, there are some things that are really dangerous for the toddler's health and safety and for the adult's mental health. Somehow the toddler has to begin to learn what is acceptable and what is not, while at the same time having some freedom to explore. The toddler period is a critical time for the development of self-regulation (Bronson, 2000).

Two concepts to consider when working with toddlers are prevention and behavior modification. **Prevention** involves making the environment healthy and safe for the child and minimizing the need for excessive restraint. For example, electric light sockets should be covered and poisonous substances put out of reach. Valuables that cannot be replaced if broken can be placed out of sight for a while. Some delicate but replaceable items can be left out to use as teaching tools to show the toddler how to handle things with care.

**prevention**

Involves making the environment healthy and safe for the child and minimizing the need for excessive restraint while providing room for exploration.

Prevention can also be viewed as being proactive rather than being reactive. A proactive style foresees potential problems and prevents them from happening. A reactive style waits until the problem occurs and then reacts.

## Skinner's Theory: Behavior Modification

B. F. Skinner's theory of learning has been used as the basis for a technique called **behavior modification.** Remember, toddlers understand speech to a greater extent than they can speak themselves. In behavior modification, a combination of verbal and nonverbal actions are used to help the toddler learn desired behavior and give up undesirable behaviors (Figure 15–5). As a first step, the toddler is rewarded for doing the appropriate thing.

**behavior modification**

B. F. Skinner's theory of using a combination of verbal and nonverbal actions to help the toddler learn desired behavior and give up undesirable behaviors.

FIGURE 15–5 Talking to the toddler in a pleasant tone of voice reinforces the child's cooperative behavior by providing a positive model.

A smile, a pat, and/or an attentive look can be given when toddler is doing something appropriate, such as playing nicely.

Toddlers soon learn which activities bring positive attention and comments, and they repeat those activities. A second technique of behavior modification involves the use of substitution and redirection. With substitution, toddlers are directed to do something that makes it impossible for them to do the undesirable activity. For example:

Toddler likes to open drawers and cupboards. Each time he opens one that adult doesn't want opened, adult gently helps toddler close it, saying, "Close it, you did it all by yourself!"

Redirection with toddlers involves physically changing their course of action. As a toddler moves toward an adult's bookshelf, the adult gently turns the toddler to head to the child's own bookshelf (Figure 15–6).

Eva Essa (2003) provides a sequenced approach to identifying and solving common toddler behavior problems, such as hitting, biting, not sharing, not complying

FIGURE 15–6 The toddler likes to explore adult materials. Cooking provides an excellent opportunity.

with directions, flushing objects down the toilet, throwing tantrums, and being a finicky eater. Attention is initially focused on the underlying causes of the behavior. For example, it is important to examine the environment and the people involved in the child's life to identify what may be reinforcing the unwanted behavior. Sometimes, the factors that trigger the problem can be identified and modified. For each problem, possible solutions are suggested. Finally, a specific format is described for developing a structured behavior modification plan.

## Other Factors that Influence the Effectiveness of Guidance Strategies

Helping the toddler become a socialized preschooler is not easy. It requires a great deal of patience and positive behavior on the part of the adults. This information is not new. The findings of the classic study by Sears, Maccoby, and Levin (1957) indicate that punishment alone does not help in the long-run to develop self-regulation and compliance.

Da Ros and Kovach (1998) outline strategies for dealing with toddlers in conflict situations. Conflict is a common type of toddler interaction through which they learn some rules of socialization. Conflict is often difficult for some adults to deal with, whether it takes place between children or with other adults. Da Ros and Kovach suggest that the first step in handling conflict is to accept that it is a normal and natural part of life. According to the Piagetian view, conflict is necessary for the construction of knowledge. However, adults often intervene too soon and too often neglect to teach toddlers ways of solving conflicts, and/or do not give them time to construct their own solutions. Da Ros and Kovach have identified two appropriate strategies: prevention and **intervention.** Prevention strategies include methods such as placing children in small compatible groups and giving toddlers the freedom to move, explore, and gain decision-making skills. Intervention strategies are methods adults use for conflict resolution. Caregivers need to be observant and analyze the situation before stepping in and allow enough time for natural consequences to settle the conflict. Other types of intervention are diffusion strategies, such as getting down to the child's level and explaining the situation while providing time for the toddler to work out a solution, and learning when to intercede and prevent injury if the situation appears to be dangerous. Da Ros and Kovach conclude, "Toddlers will engage in conflict. It is an integral part of how they learn social skills" (p. 30). It is the adults' responsibility to handle these situations in ways that support the learning of social skills.

**intervention**

Interceding when a situation seems dangerous or when the children need coaching to assist them in solving a problem.

The quality of the father's relationship with the toddler is also critical (Easterbrooks & Goldberg, 1984). Easterbrooks and Goldberg found that high involvement by the father related more strongly to cognitive than to emotional development. For fathers, the amount of time spent in play activities with the toddler seemed to be more important than involvement in routine caregiving, such as feeding, diapering, and bathing. When observed in a problem-solving situation, the toddlers who performed most positively tended to have fathers who were sensitive in the situation and allowed toddlers to be autonomous, were encouraging, and provided age-appropriate cues. Sensitive fathering appears to be as important as sensitive mothering.

It has become increasingly apparent that fathers need to be more involved than just at the level of basic responsibility, such as providing financial support and ensuring the children's health and welfare (McBride, 1989). Fathers also need to be involved in direct interaction and be directly accessible when needed. McBride (1989) describes the program at the Center for Young Children (CYC) at the University of Maryland, which provides help for fathers so they can learn how to be more involved with their young children. Fathers and children meet at CYC on Saturday mornings for a combination of play group and discussion activities that help the fathers learn more about child development and how to solve problems involving discipline, sibling rivalry, the influence of television, and so on. The children benefit from the interaction with their fathers and the long-term benefits of increased father involvement.

Parents and other caretakers must learn positive guidance techniques. Miller (2003) points out that children will not develop in a positive direction with no guidance, but on the other hand, they cannot be molded like clay. Adults must recognize that each child comes "equipped with individual personalities, likes, dislikes, interests, and motives" (Miller, 1990, p. 50). Miller sums up the adult role as follows:

> The role of the adult is to guide, assertively and respectfully, never forgetting that even the youngest child is truly a person with all the rights befitting any other human being [even the right to be negative and recalcitrant on occasion]. In the developmental interactionist perspective, child guidance is intended to give children feedback about the realities of their world, to allow them choices within reasonable limits, and to help them confront the logical consequences of their own actions (Miller, p. 50).

## THE TODDLER WITH SPECIAL NEEDS

Toddlers with special needs do best with quality care, whether at home or in child care settings. Booth and Kelly (2002) found that for children with special needs, the degree of adaptive ability was directly related to the quality of care. They believe that this factor provides children with special needs a better opportunity to move from more individualized infant care into larger group care.

Lewis (2003) describes the development of young children with a variety of disabilities and the variability within groups. For example, some children who are blind develop in a parallel fashion to sighted children, while others may fall behind. For example, delays in reaching for objects, becoming mobile, and engaging in stereotyped motor behaviors are not uncommon. Adults need to be perceptive to the signals for interaction of a child who is blind. Environments need to be consistent so the young child who is blind can learn them and develop autonomy. The parents of children who are deaf need to find ways to communicate limitations on behavior. Research indicates that parents of children who are deaf tend to be less permissive and are more likely to use physical punishment as a discipline technique. Communication is critical and it is important for parents who can hear to learn to sign. Children with Down syndrome are the largest group of children with learning difficulties. They tend to develop in the same sequence as typically developing children, but at a slower rate. They need a high rate of interaction as infants, even though they may be less responsive than typically developing infants. Their thought process is slower, so this demands patience from adults when making requests or setting limits. It is very important to request only actions the child can do. Children with Down syndrome tend to have inconsistent memory so they may not remember a routine or action that they seemed to have mastered the day before. Children with motor disabilities need as much assistance as possible to achieve some degree of autonomy. While typically developing toddlers provide many challenges as they try to develop autonomy, children with disabilities require even more patience and skill.

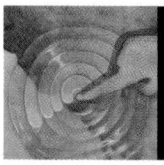

## LOOKING FURTHER

Get acquainted with a toddler. After you have spent enough time with each other so that you are good friends, take the toddler for a walk. A toddler cannot go very far, so plan a short but interesting route. Or take the toddler to a playground if one is close by. Construct a short oral or written report, including the following information:

a. Describe who the child is, the child's age, and how you happen to know the child.

b. Describe what happened on the walk. What did the toddler do and say?

c. Overall, what did you learn? What expected actions did you observe? Did any unexpected things happen?

## SUMMARY

Toddlerhood is a crucial period that bridges the time from infancy to preschool. During the period of about age one, or when the child begins to walk, until age three, toddlers develop basic motor, affective, and cognitive skills that enable them to engage in independent activity throughout life. According to both Piaget's and Erikson's theories, toddlers are striving for autonomy.

Toddlers are very active and constantly on the move. To slow down to eat, dress, toilet, or sleep is a difficult task. In this second part of the sensorimotor period, rapidly developing gross and fine motor skills enable children to gain autonomy and perform many tasks on their own. A maturing brain and lots of opportunities for practice support the development of gross and fine motor skills. Because of their constant motion and impulsive desire to explore objects and people, adults can easily become upset and frustrated with their behavior. Adults must understand that this is a natural stage of development and be calm and patient. Children need opportunities to solve their own conflicts while adults observe and are ready to move in with help and support when needed. Toddlers with special needs must also be assisted to achieve autonomy.

## FOR FURTHER READING


American Academy of Pediatrics. (2005). *Health in child care: A manual for health professionals* (4th ed.). Elk Grove Village, IL: Author.

Aronson, S. S., & Shope, T. R. (Eds.). (2005). *Managing infectious diseases in child care and schools.* Elk Grove Village, IL: American Academy of Pediatrics.

Batshaw, M. L., M. D. (2001). (Ed.). *When your child has a disability: The complete sourcebook of daily and medical care* (Rev. ed.). Baltimore: Brookes.

Baum. J. (2004). *Respectful parenting: from birth through the terrific twos.* Washington, DC: Child Welfare League of America.

Blacher, J. (Ed.). (2000). Families and exceptionality. [Special Issue]. *Early Education and Development, 11* (4).

Borkowski, J. G., Ramey, S. L., & Bristol-Power, M. (2002). *Parenting and the child's world.* Mahwah, NJ: Erlbaum.

Bornstein, M. H., & Bradley, R. H. (Eds.). (2003). *Socioeconomic status, parenting, and child development.* Mahwah, NJ: Erlbaum.

Brazelton, T. B. (1992). *Touchpoints: The essential reference.* Reading, MA: Addison-Wesley.

Caldwell, W., & Kimball, C. T. (Eds.). (2001). *Obesity source book.* Holmes, PA: Omnigraphics.

DelCarmen-Wiggins, R., & Carter, A. S. (Eds.). (2004). *Handbook of infant, toddler, and preschool mental health assessment.* New York: Guilford.

Dewey, D., & Tupper, D. E. (Eds.). (2004). *Developmental motor disorders.* New York: Guilford.

Donatelle, R. J. (2005). *Health: The basics* (6th ed.). San Francisco: Pearson.

Fagan, J., & Stevenson, H. C. (2002). An experimental study of an empowerment-based intervention for African American Head Start fathers. *Family Relations, 51*(3), 191–198.

Gartell, D. (2003). *A guidance approach for the encouraging classroom.* Clifton Park, NY: Delmar Learning. Golombok, S. (2000). *Parenting. What really counts?* Philadelphia: Psychology Press.

Grolnick, W. S. (2002). *The psychology of parental control.* Mahwah, NJ: Erlbaum.

Hamner, T. J., & Turner, P. H. (2001). *Parenting in contemporary society* (4th ed.). Boston: Allyn & Bacon.

Kimball. C. T. (Ed.). (2003). *Childhood diseases & disorders sourcebook.* Holmes, PA: Omnigaphics.

Kimball. C. T. (Ed.). (2003). *Healthy children sourcebook.* Holmes, PA: Omnigaphics.

Kohn, A. (2005). *Unconditional parenting.* New York: Atria Books.

Lerner, C., & Dombro, A. L. (2004). *Bringing up baby.* Washington, DC: Zero to Three.

Let's go outside! [Focus section]. (2002). *Young Children, 57*(3), 8–42.

Palkovitz, R. (2002). *Involved fathering and men's adult development.* Mahwah, NJ: Erlbaum.

Porter, L. (2003). *Young children's behaviour* (2nd ed.). Baltimore: Brookes.

Schock, A. M., Gavazzi, S. M., Fristad, M. A., & Goldberg-Arnold, J. S. (2002). The role of father participation in the treatment of childhood mood disorders. *Family Relations, 51*(3), 230–237.

Tamis-LeMonda, C. S., & Cabrera, N. (Eds.). (2002). *The handbook of father involvement.* Mahwah, NJ: Erlbaum.

Thompson, J., & Manore, M. (2005). *Nutrition: An applied approach.* San Francisco: Pearson.

Tortora, S., & Lerner, C. (2004). *On the move: The power of movement in your child's first three years.* Washington, DC: Zero to Three.

Turbiville, V. P., Umbarger, G. T., & Guthrie, A. C. (2000). Fathers' involvement in programs for young children. *Young Children, 55*(4), 74–79.

## SUGGESTED ACTIVITIES

1. Visit a home or center-based toddler child care facility. Observe for two or more hours. Use the gross and fine motor assessment charts in Figures 15–3 and 15–4 as guides for developing profiles of the children's developmental levels.

2. Keep a record of a toddler's food intake for a week. Evaluate the nutritional value relative to the information in the text.

3. Observe some toddlers with parents or caregivers. Note the types of guidance practices and categorize them according to the types described in this chapter.

4. Observe a toddler at home or at a child care site. Use the toddler motor development charts (see Figures 15–3 and 15–4) as appropriate to the child's age and capabilities to assess the child's developmental level in the areas of gross and fine motor and self-help development.
   a. Overall, does the child seem to be average, ahead of typical expectations, or slow in rate of development?
   b. Are there any areas where the child seems to be exceptionally ahead or behind in development?
   c. What kinds of suggestions do you have for the parents and/or the caregiver regarding this child?
   d. Support all your conclusions and recommendations with data from your developmental charts.

5. Interview three or four parents of two-year-olds regarding their experiences with toilet training. Explain that this is an assignment for your child development class and that you have been reading about toddlers and the importance of toilet training during this age period. Record the name, age, and sex of each child. Then ask the following questions:

a. Do you believe you have been pretty relaxed about toilet training or have you felt pressured to get it done in a hurry?
b. When did you first put *(child's name)* on the potty? Can you remember how old *(child's name)* was? What happened?
c. How far along is *(child's name)* now? Does he or she ever have a daytime accident? How about at night? What procedures have you used for training?
d. How did you decide how to start and when to start? Did someone give you advice? Did you read about how to do it in a book or magazine?
e. Do you find that *(child's name)* is into a period where he or she wants to do everything without help? Has this carried over into toileting?
f. What advice would you give to another parent regarding toilet training?

**6.** Observe some young children when they are on the playground or elsewhere involved in a variety of large-muscle activities. In class, list all the gross motor skills you observed. List yours on a piece of chart paper or on the chalkboard. Have other class members add others. An alternative activity: Divide the class into two or more teams. With a time limit of three minutes, see which team can list the most gross motor activities.

**7.** Supermarkets, department stores, or any large store with lots of colorful and interesting things to buy are exciting places for a child. The toddler usually finds these places interesting, but his or her desire to explore is balanced by the push for autonomy and strong attachment to the parents. Go to a supermarket, discount store, or shopping mall. Observe some children who appear to be between the ages of one and three. Observe at least four parent-child pairs for 5 to 10 minutes each. Note signs of attachment and independence. Write a detailed description of each pair observed. Did the children act as you expected after having read the text? Compare them with each other considering probable age.

**8.** Make an entry in your journal.

## REVIEW

**1.** Write the letter of each correct statement.
a. The major task for toddlers is to seek autonomy.
b. Toddlers observed in the supermarket got into less trouble if their mothers got them involved in constructive activity.
c. Mothers who act reactively have children who cause fewer problems.
d. At about 16 months of age, toddlers become goal oriented.
e. The youngest toddlers act for the sake of action with no particular goal in mind.

**2.** The developmental theorists (Erikson, Freud, and Piaget) agree on some basic characteristics of the toddler. Write the letters of the characteristics listed below with which they would all agree.
a. The toddler is quiet, compliant, and not very active.
b. The toddler's maturing muscular control is reflected in much of his or her behavior: The toddler is very active motorically while learning to walk, run, and climb.
c. Play is not very important for the toddler.
d. The toddler learns a great deal through observing others and imitating their actions.
e. The toddler is too young to understand anything about what is right and wrong.

**3.** Fill in the blanks in the statements below.
   a. _____ _____ is defined as at all times having access to enough nourishment.
   b. _____ _____ refers to the situation where there is difficulty in obtaining enough to eat.
   c. RDA refers to the _____ _____ _____ _____.
   d. _____ _____ dining is recommended for providing a pleasant atmosphere and an opportunity for independence.

**4.** List the letters of the correct statements.
   a. Toddlers should not be allowed to eat with their fingers.
   b. Nutritious snacks would be foods such as cheese, fruit, and raw vegetables.
   c. It is a good idea to use dessert as a reward for eating vegetables.
   d. It is a good idea to have a daily health inspection for signs of any sudden changes in appearance that might indicate illness.
   e. Crack cocaine children need special attention in a structured environment.
   f. Most toddlers have healthy eating habits.
   g. Obesity is becoming a problem for children as young as two.
   h. Obesity is partially due to children eating too much fast food and drinking too many soft drinks.
   i. Children today get plenty of exercise.

**5.** The environment can offer the young child ways to make the most of his or her emerging motor capabilities by
   a. having adults explain how to use materials and equipment
   b. having adults give positive reinforcement to children for using their motor skills
   c. adults stepping in and helping the child when needed
   d. being sure the toddlers have equipment, such as balls, wagons, doll buggies, short ladders, and low slides.

**6.** List the main factors to consider in child development–centered toilet training practice.

**7.** List four gross and four fine motor skills that usually develop between ages one and two.

**8.** List four gross and four fine motor skills that usually develop between ages two and three.

**9.** Consider the following situations and then evaluate each:
   a. Chan, age twelve months, sits on a blanket on the floor. He has several small objects: a rattle, a set of plastic toy keys, and a set of nesting cups. He picks each up in turn, appearing by the focus of his eyes to look closely at each as he manipulates it.
   b. Nancy, age two, says, "Do it myself!" as she sits in the bathtub, takes the soap from her mother's hand, and rubs it over her body.
   c. Theresa Garcia, eighteen months old, turns over the wastebasket and happily examines the trash.
   d. Twenty-month-old Rodney Wright knows he can open one kitchen cupboard and help himself to a healthy snack.
   e. Mary Lou Carter, thirteen months old, grabs fifteen-month-old Maria Sandoval's doll. Maria pulls on the doll's leg and Mary Lou on an arm. Teacher Jean comes over and pulls the doll away. "Mary Lou, bad girl!"
   f. Every Saturday morning, John Hardy takes his daughter, two-and-a-half-year-old Liz, to a Saturday morning play group.
   g. Sean, age two with Down syndrome, is scooting slowly to get to the toy area. The caregiver is encouraging Sean and is telling him that he is doing great and that he needs to scoot a little bit more to get to the toys.

**10.** Explain the relationship between motor skills and brain development.

**11.** Describe the guidance strategies that work best with toddlers.

## KEY TERMS LIST

anal stage
assertiveness
autonomy
autonomy versus shame and doubt
behavior modification
examining
food security
food insecurity
intervention
preoperational period
prevention
RDA
terrible twos

Additional resources for this chapter can be found on the Online Companion™ to accompany this text at http://www.earlychilded.delmar.com. Respond to "Time to Reflect" and "Looking Further" concepts, review various child development scenarios, and answer thought-provoking questions in the Critical Thinking Forum. Keep a daily journal by downloading the student journal available on this Web site. Complete the interactive matching exercises to reinforce concepts, and print out the child development assessment forms to use during your observation of development for children from birth to age eight. In addition, read the case studies on the Web site to reinforce the important concepts in each chapter, and take a look at the multitude of Web links that are available for student research on the Internet.

CHAPTER

# 16

# The Toddler: Affective Development

## OBJECTIVES

After reading this chapter, you should be able to:

- Explain Vygotsky's and Erikson's views of the toddler.
- Identify toddler exploratory play.
- Evaluate affective behaviors of the toddler and the toddler caregiver.
- Analyze and evaluate toddler social behavior.
- Describe the place of moral development during the toddler period.
- Describe the proximal, distal, and combination parenting styles.
- Identify typical toddler affective characteristics.

Toddlers' increasing independence can be seen in their play and social activities. The attachment to a caregiver and the accompanying self-trust and trust of others allow the toddler to move away from adults and try things out.

The social and emotional aspects of child behavior take a leap forward in maturity during the toddler period. Vygotsky (Berk, & Winsler, 1995; Wertsch, 1985) placed particular emphasis on the importance of social and cooperative behavior in the social context as support for cognitive development. A skilled partner, an adult or older child, supports the child's learning within the **zone of proximal development (ZPD)** (the distance between actual development and potential development at any particular time). Erikson (Miller, 2002) emphasized the social and emotional aspects of psychological development within a cultural context. Remember, he placed toddlers in a crisis of autonomy versus shame and doubt in their ongoing search for identity. During this period, children's temperaments are volatile and unpredictable, and their emotions may be expressed very strongly as they search for a definition of who they are. Gopnik, Meltzoff, and Kuhl (1999) describe the change from the "adorable" one-year-old to the two-year-old "monster." While one-year-olds think adults think the same as they do, two-year-olds know adults think differently and continuously test adult reactions as if trying to find out what the adults are thinking.

**zone of proximal development (ZPD)**
The distance between actual development and potential development at any particular time.

This chapter looks at toddler affective development in the areas of play and social relationships, social sensitivity, temperament, self-concept, and sociocultural environment.

FIGURE 16–1 Toddler play involves the independent exploration of materials such as sand.

## PLAY AND SOCIAL RELATIONSHIPS

### Play

Chapter 5 included a broad description of play as a major vehicle for children's learning. In this chapter, the play of one- and two-year-olds is the focus. Toddlers are busy children who in many ways are like small scientists as they explore and experiment in the environment (Figure 16–1).

With the development of motor skills as described in previous chapters, play becomes more complex (Frost, Wortham, & Reifel, 2005). As described in Chapter 15, toddlers like to push, pull, lift, fill, and dump. Play begins with exploration; using the senses to touch, taste, feel, smell, and grasp materials. Cognitive development also influences the development of play content. By 12 months, object permanence is achieved with the increased development of memory. Symbolic or representational play emerges, and between 18 and 24 months the toddler is able to plan play activities. By age 2, children engage in pretend play, which begins to reflect their affective (emotional, personality, and social) characteristics.

Toddler play is active and joyful. An example that demonstrates a typical toddler play activity is one in which 18-month-old Enrique plays a game with his teacher:

> Enrique gathers all the tennis balls and gives them to the teacher, then points in another direction and runs. When the teacher throws the balls, Enrique giggles and runs after them. He picks up as many as he can hold, puts them in a little plastic red wagon, and pulls the wagon around to collect the rest of the balls. When he has them all, he takes the wagon to the teacher, points, and runs as if in anticipation. When the teacher throws the balls, Enrique again runs as fast as he can after them, gathers as many as he can hold, and puts them in the red wagon. Enrique repeats this activity several times before moving on to another activity. Next, Enrique builds a tower with some small (3") blocks. When the tower is as tall as he is he pushes it and yells "Boom!" He laughs hysterically pointing at the fallen blocks and dances around for a few seconds before starting to stack the blocks again.

Enrique demonstrates typical toddler play. His play is repetitive and active, is enjoyable, and shows the beginning of pretend play as he knocks over his tower with an explosion.

Ruhman (1998) points out the importance of fostering toddlers' imitative and imaginative play. During toddlerhood, representation enters children's play. Play takes on a symbolic nature as children pretend to be adults, animals, vehicles, and other people and things. Play materials also take on a symbolic nature, such as when Enrique pretends his block tower is a building that falls with a loud boom. Representational play provides a setting for portraying ideas, thoughts, and feelings that the child might otherwise not feel comfortable about displaying. Caregivers can play along with the child, providing models of pretend activities, such as rocking the doll in the bed or helping to build a garage with blocks for the child's toy cars. Caregivers can pick up on the children's themes and demonstrate how they might be expanded. It is important to let the toddlers take the lead while the adult provides the scaffolding but does not intrude.

Toddlers are active as they use their newly developed motor skills. They need opportunities every day to throw, climb, build, paint, and dance (Wardle, 1998). They need to have balls, climbers, ladders, and bridges, paintbrushes of all sizes, tricycles, wagons, and unit and hollow blocks. These materials can provide the foundation for imaginative and imitative play.

Infants and toddlers who don't have play experiences are deprived of important affective experiences. Foster and adopted children frequently lack this early play experience (Comfort, 2005). They don't know what to do with a toy and may not even explore toys. They may dump toys out of a container and just leave them. They may not play pretend. They may lose control and become aggressive with other children or materials. Comfort (2005) states that adults must take the responsibility to join in and introduce these children to play gradually as they build trust.

## Peer Relationships

**peers**

Those who are the same age and/or developmental level.

Toddlers are interested in other children. During their second year, they may play side-by-side with other children. By age two, they might be ready to engage with their **peers** (*The Power of Play*, 2005). They have developed motor, problem-solving, and language skills. Learning social skills, such as sharing and not hitting, are the challenges of the third year. Pretend play becomes more prominent but limited. Early social activity usually involves mutual imitation (Berk, 2006). They enjoy jumping and chasing. They begin to use language to suggest play activities.

**coordinated play**

Play that involves both children doing something together.

Social activities include imitating the other child, showing the other child a toy, offering the child a toy, accepting a toy from the other child, using a toy the other child has finished with, taking a toy from the other child (when the other child does not protest), struggling over a toy (when the other child does protest), and taking part in coordinated play. **Coordinated play** involves both children doing something together. They might build a block tower, fill a bucket with water, or take turns adding blocks to a tower and knocking it down (Eckerman, Whatley, & Kutz, 1975).

Toddler-peer relationships are usually characterized as being somewhat stormy (Honig & DiPerna, 1983). Toddlers have been observed to engage in many negative social behaviors, such as grabbing other children's toys, hitting, and biting. They almost seem to explore their peers in the same way they explore objects. Also, if they are moving toward autonomy, they may find overcoming another child's will to be very fulfilling. It may seem that putting toddlers in a group is asking for trouble. However, studies such as the one by Howes (1985) indicate that if toddlers have the opportunity to interact daily and get to know each other well, they develop positive social relationships. Toddlers seem to have the most positive interactions in pairs, versus larger groups (Honig & DiPerna, 1983). This indicates that a toddler play group will run more smoothly if it is set up with several areas where one or two children can play, rather than offering limited choices, where more than two have to play in the same area. Furthermore, it has been found that interaction is more positive with gross motor equipment than with small toys. Toys should be plentiful enough so that arguments are cut to a minimum. Toddlers like to imitate each other, so there should always be duplicate toys. If a toddler can pick up an identical toy and imitate a peer, positive social development is reinforced. If there is no duplicate, the toddler will then try to take the other child's toy. As Da Ros and Kovach (1998) suggest (see Chapter 15), adults usually intervene too quickly, so toddlers do not have time to figure out how to solve their own conflicts. Adults tend to fix the problem themselves, overregulate by imposing their own solutions, promote peace without assisting toddlers in developing their own negotiation and problem-solving skills, or have the aggressor make restitution when he or she is too young to understand. Although adults should be ready to assist, they should allow time for the children to work out the solution by possibly suggesting some nonevaluative techniques, such as "You could tell her you don't want her to take your doll," or "You could tell him not to knock your blocks down."

Brownell (1990) observed previously acquainted 18-month-old and 24-month-old toddler same- or mixed-age pairs in a playroom setting. As might be expected, the older children engaged in much more complex social actions. Of more interest was the behavior of the younger toddlers when paired with an older partner as compared with a younger partner. When paired with an older partner, the 18-month-old toddlers were "more socially active, socially involved, and affectively enthusiastic" and used more advanced means to engage the older child than they used with the younger child (Brownell, 1990, p. 844). These results would support the value of mixed-age grouping. Brownell and Carriger (1990) looked at the development of cooperation between same-age peers at 12, 18, 24, and 30 months of age. Same-age pairs of peers were placed in a problem-solving situation in which the children had to work cooperatively to obtain some toys. While one worked a lever to make the toys attainable, the other could get the toys. The apparatus was designed so that one child alone could not accomplish the task. Whereas none of the 12-month-olds and few 18-month-olds could work cooperatively to get the toys, the 24- and 30-month-olds were much more able to coordinate their efforts.

Analyze the following situations and explain how you would react:

1. Johnny calls you over to where he is playing in the home center. "I'm making lunch," he explains. "I want you to eat with me."
2. Miguel is playing quietly with a bunny rabbit and a truck. He puts the bunny in the truck, drives across the room, takes the bunny out, drives around, returns, and picks up the bunny. He repeats this scenario several times. Lisa looks over and sees the bunny lying on the floor. She picks it up and gently rocks it. Miguel returns and seeing Lisa with the bunny, shouts, "Mine!" and grabs the bunny.

## Adult Influences

Adults can have a strong influence on toddlers' social behavior. For example, Howes, Hamilton, and Matheson (1994) followed a group of young children enrolled in child care as infants up until they were four years old. Howes et al. (1994) examined the interrelationships of teacher and peer behaviors as they relate to children's social competence. Toddlers who were more secure in their relationships with their teachers were less aggressive and engaged in more positive play with their peers. Teachers who approached social problems in a positive manner, such as helping the child initiate contact with a peer, monitoring contact with peers, and explaining peer behavior, tended to have children who were more highly accepted by their peers. That is, direct instruction on how to interact with peers brought positive results.

Fagot, Hagan, Leinbach, and Kronsberg (1985) observed play groups that included toddlers when they were 13 to 14 months of age and then nine to eleven months later. They recorded teachers' responses to toddlers' assertive actions. The results of the first set of observations showed that teachers were more likely to respond to girls when they sought attention in a calm, low-key way and boys when they used physical means, cried, whined, or screamed. There were actually no differences in the frequencies with which these behaviors were used by boys and by girls. During the second observations, there was a significant difference between boys' and girls' attempts to get the teacher's attention. Girls talked more, whereas boys were more often negative (whine, cry, and scream). During the first observation, both boys and girls exhibited equal amounts of assertive behaviors, such as grabbing, hitting, pushing, and kicking. Teachers were more likely to ignore girls' assertive acts and give some attention to boys' assertive acts. By the time the second set of observations was made, boys were significantly more negatively assertive than girls. Teachers now responded about the same to both boys' and girls' assertive acts. Peers, however, reacted more negatively to boys' assertive acts than to girls' acts. Teachers may expect boys to be more assertive and are more alert to their negative behaviors, while expecting girls to use more positive behaviors, thereby being more alert to these kinds of bids for attention from them. This adult attention seems to maintain these behaviors. It appears teachers need to be alert to treating boys and girls in a nonstereotyped fashion. Although teachers had dropped the **sex-stereotyped** reactions by the second round of observations, the children seemed to have adopted them in their peer interactions. Parents have also been observed to influence toddler play by selecting sexstereotyped toys (Eisenberg, Wolchik, Hernandez, & Pasternack, 1985).

**sex-stereotyped**

Treating boys and girls differently based on their sex.

**guided participation**

A vehicle through which the child learns what needs to be learned to function in a particular culture.

Rogoff and Mosier (1993) examined **guided participation** as a vehicle through which the child learns what is needed to function in a particular culture. This point of view grew out of Vygotsky's theory that social and cooperative behaviors between partners (the young child and older, more skilled partner), rather than didactic instruction, support growth in the ZPD. Rogoff and Mosier (1993) observed and interviewed four toddlers and their families who lived in Salt Lake City, Utah, and four who lived in a Mayan village in Guatemala. Their objective was to observe guided participation in cultural contexts considering the local goals for development. Adults were observed to guide children by adjusting communication and by simplifying tasks and helping them with difficult parts. When toddler and adult disagreed on what to do next, the adults usually respected the child's choice; this behavior was especially true with the Mayan mothers. The Salt Lake City mothers used more complex verbal explanations, whereas the Mayan mothers used more demonstrations, thereby reflecting a cultural difference in choice of communication mode. The Salt Lake City pairs had more face-to-face communication, even though these toddlers were more mobile. Salt Lake City parents spent time playing with their toddlers, whereas the Mayan mothers encouraged their toddlers to play alone so they could get their work done. In the Mayan culture, the children were not viewed as conversational partners as they were in the middle-class Salt Lake City culture. In the Mayan culture, the children relied on observational learning to acquire necessary skills; their attention was not managed to the same extent as the Salt Lake City children. The Salt Lake City mothers used a lot of praise, cheering, and mock excitement as motivation. Although their specific guidance techniques differed, in both cultures, the caregivers and children were collaborators in determining what would happen in a particular situation.

Providing plenty of appropriate play materials supports constructive toddler play. Toddlers can be quite content with simple play materials that help them develop fine and gross motor coordination. For example, Watson and Watson (2003) suggest many homemade toys for toddlers, such as the following examples:

- *Twelve to eighteen months:* EXPLORING TUBS. Place one solid object in a margarine tub. Put the lid on. When children shake the tub, they will hear a noise. Encourage them to remove the lid to discover what is inside. Put the lid back on. Have several tubs available with different objects inside, for example, plastic clothespins, large wooden thread spools (p. 325).

- *Eighteen to twenty-four months:* TUNNEL. Use sturdy long rectangular cardboard boxes large enough for the children to crawl through. Cut out the ends and tape the edges to keep them from scraping children and also to keep the boxes from tearing. Place several boxes end-to-end or in a zigzag pattern (p. 345).
- *Twenty-four to thirty months:* SOAP PAINT. Use one part soap flakes and one part water. Beat the mixture with a hand egg beater. Skim off soap suds to paint on a table top or shelf or freezer paper (p. 367).

The environment should also be one that makes the children feel comfortable with their own cultures (Whaley & Swadener, 1990).

Whaley and Swadener (1990) emphasize that multicultural education begins with infants and toddlers. Teachers need to learn the background and culture of each child to have continuity between home and center. Gender- or culturally stereotyped toys, books, puzzles, and puppets should be avoided. Dolls, books, music, and other materials that are authentic representations of different cultures, however, should be included. Encourage children to become competent in their first language, as well as exposing them to English in a nonpressured way. Put pictures up that show different cultures. Encourage infants and toddlers to feel good about themselves, to be empathetic, to share, and to respect the feelings of others.

> Early multicultural education is not a curriculum: it is a perspective and commitment to equity, sensitivity, and empowerment. It is something that can and should be built into the everyday experiences of young children. It is not direct teaching, but the integration of many ideas into the play experiences of the infant and toddler. Perhaps most important is the fact that children at this age can be empowered in the areas of self-esteem, acceptance, and empathy (Whaley & Swadener, 1990, p. 240).

A study by Keller et. al (2004) compared three cultures on the relationship between parenting styles at 3 months of age and the children's self-recognition and self-regulation at 18 to 20 months. The three groups compared were Cameroonian Nso farmers, Greek urban middle class, and Costa Rican middle class. Three types of parenting styles were identified:

1. Proximal style stresses body contact and body stimulation that goes along with a sociocultural style that stresses obedience and relatedness.
2. Distal style stresses face-to-face exchange and object stimulation that goes along with a sociocultural style that stresses independence, autonomy, and separateness.
3. Combination of distal and proximal styles that is related to a sociocultural emphasis on autonomy and relatedness.

The Cameroonian toddlers who experienced proximal parenting style developed self-regulation earlier. The Greek toddlers who experienced a distal parenting style developed self-recognition earlier. The Costa Rican toddlers who experienced both distal and proximal parenting styles fell between the other two groups on both self-regulation and self-recognition. The results support that parenting styles fit the cultural expectations of the sociocultural community.

Social relationships with peers and adults are well established during the toddler period. As already described, these relationships are not always positive. Although it is common for two-year-old toddlers to direct aggression toward their peers and initiate conflict situations, the degree of aggression and conflict varies greatly. That is, there is variation in the degree of internal control exhibited among individual toddlers. Rubin, Hastings, Chen, Stewart, and McNichol (1998) looked at this variability in two-year-olds as related to maternal behavior and characteristics. Mothers and toddlers were observed in a play situation and a snack situation. Overall, boys initiated more conflicts and displayed more angry aggression than did girls. Independent of toddlers' sex, emotion regulation and negative maternal dominance predicted disruptive behavior. That is, children with low levels of self-regulation skills and mothers with high rates of aversive and controlling behaviors were most likely to be aggressive toward their peers. Children with no inner control and strong outer control were the most aggressive toward others. This relationship was stronger for boys than for girls. These researchers found no relationship between observed aggression and child care experience. These findings are consistent with the NICHD Early Child Care Research Network study (1998) of 24- and 36-month-olds in child care. Mothering was found to be the strongest predictor of child behavior.

## SOCIAL SENSITIVITY

Toddlers have developed sensitivity and emotional expressiveness. As noted in the discussion of peer relationships, toddlers use expressive and protest communications in relating to peers. This increasing sensitivity is apparent also in their family relationships.

### Emotional Expression

Remember from Chapter 13 that emotional expression is well established in infancy. Malatesta, Culver, Tesman, and Shepard (1989) examined the emotional expressions observed on the faces of two-year-olds and their mothers in both stressful and nonstressful situations during infancy and toddlerhood. The strange-situation was used to elicit expressions of emotion. Malatesta et al. (1989) found that two-year-olds have adopted facial expressions, such as compressed lips, knit brow, and lip biting, that indicate efforts to control negative feelings. The mothers of the two-year-olds displayed more expressivity to girls than to boys. In particular, the girls received more smiling. During play, boys and girls displayed the same amount of anger. From seven-and-a-half to twenty-two months, the frequency of negative expressions used was significantly correlated, whereas frequency of positive expressions was not. Mothers and their two-year-old children tended to have the same emotional patterns. Mothers who showed appropriate attention to their infants' emotional states had two-year-olds who displayed more positive emotions. Mothers who ignored infant sadness and pain were more likely to have two-year-olds who displayed sadness and anger following reunions. During nonstressful interactions, secure two-year-old children were more attentive to their mothers. During stressful interactions, insecure children were more positive in their attention to their mothers in that they showed more interest. However, they also showed compressed lips with more frequency. The authors believe this indicates suppression of emotion and vigilance regarding what may happen next. The findings of the Malatesta et al. (1989) study indicates that emotional expressions are under some control by age two and that maternal emotional responsiveness during infancy influences children's development of emotional expression.

Emotional expression recognition is dependent on early experience. Parker and Nelson (2005) compared institutionalized and noninstitutionalized infants and toddlers' recognition of four facial expressions: fear, anger, happiness, and sadness.

FIGURE 16–2 Toddlers are sensitive to the feelings of their peers.

The institutionalized infants and toddlers showed less strong recognition of emotional expressions, especially fear and sadness. The researchers found that there is a breakdown in the development of brain circuitry in the less-stimulated children.

## Sensitivity and Expressiveness

Toddlers can show sympathy toward others. One-year-olds may try to give comfort and help to those in pain or distress. The toddler is very aware when someone else is upset or hurt and often responds in a helpful, sympathetic manner (Figure 16–2). Toddlers also display the beginnings of empathy as defined by attending to another person's distress (Gopnik et al., 1999; Lamb & Zakhireh, 1997). To collect data on attention to distress, Lamb and Zakhireh videotaped children in their toddler child care rooms. Each sign of distress, such as cries, whimpers, or moans, was noted and each child's response to another's distress was also noted. Prosocial behavior, such as offering a toy or patting a crying child, was also noted. Also noted were instances when a child's response to another child's distress was a distress signal. The very few observed prosocial responses were made by older children. Children most often attended to distress signals resulting from harm or interference with individual rights, such as conflicts over possessions. The louder the signal, the more attention was directed toward the signal. Crying received the most attention. Lamb and Zakhireh believe that these attention-to-distress behaviors may be the beginnings of empathy, which is a part of moral development.

When firstborn toddlers experience the arrival of a baby brother or sister, the older child often regresses to infantlike behaviors that were previously given up. For example:

> Upon the arrival of her new baby brother, two-year-old Janie's behavior at preschool changes. After snack, she is observed to get into the doll bed, burp, and curl up with her thumb in her mouth.

Children may also display signs of jealousy and a desire to get rid of the new arrival.

> A group of four three-year-old boys, all of whom have younger siblings, play firefighter every day. During the course of their activity each day, the baby dolls burn up in the oven.

Dunn and Kendrick (1980) observed some firstborns, ranging in age from eighteen to forty-three months when the study began, and their mothers. The first observation took place when the mother was pregnant. Further observations were carried out when the younger sibling was two weeks, three weeks, eight months, and fourteen months. It was found that after the sibling's arrival, the mother initiated less playful attention directed toward the older sibling, such as comments on what the child was doing. Mothers also initiated fewer verbal games and suggested new play activities less often. Overall, the mothers gave less sensitive attention. At the same time, more negative interaction occurred. Control became dominant to a greater degree in interactions between mother and child.

Dunn and Munn (1985) studied family conflicts and the development of social understanding during the second year as observed in the home. They found that during this year, there is an increasing understanding of conflict situations and their emotional aspects. During this period, there is an increase in the frequency of either supporting or teasing a sibling or parent when the sibling and parent are engaged in a conflict. By sixteen to eighteen months, children show signs of knowing that they recognize forbidden behavior. Toddlers are especially interested in noting wild behavior, rude behavior, or behavior that involves possessions and not sharing. Around eighteen months, mothers begin to provide more verbal justifications to toddlers in their responses to toddlers' unacceptable behavior. While toddlers showed more understanding of conflicts and the emotions that accompanied them, they also became more expressive; tantrums, self-abuse, destruction of objects, and physical aggression toward siblings increases during the second year. This behavior may be a reflection of their increasing awareness of themselves and their efforts to gain autonomy.

Toddlers have learned to use emotional expression to obtain support from the environment (Buss & Kiel, 2004). Twenty-four-month-old toddlers were observed during a threat situation and during a frustration situation (their mothers were present). When looking toward their mothers for help, they were more likely to use a sadness expression than to display anger or fear.

**posttraumatic stress disorder**

"reexperiencing" a violent or stressful event through play.

Toddlers also react to violence and may evidence symptoms of **posttraumatic stress disorder** such as "reexperiencing" the experience in their play, becoming emotionally subdued and withdrawn, having night terrors, shying away from persons or situations that are similar to the persons or scenes of the violent event, developing signs of anxiety such as troubled sleep or displaying disrupted eating habits and aggression, developing a limited attention span, and distorting trust relationships (Special report, 1994).

Toddlers are just beginning to develop a sense of success and failure and the emotions that accompany success and failure (Stipek, Recchia, & McClintic, 1992). Before age two, the toddlers seemed to have had an intrinsic sense of accomplishment. Around age two, they began to seek approval from adults. Children who received more praise from mothers tended to express more spontaneous positive emotions (i.e., smiling, clapping, and exclaiming) regarding their accomplishments.

Toddlers are sensitive to their own emotions and to the feelings of others. They can provide sympathy, and they can show hostility and jealousy. They enjoy feeling good about their accomplishments and learn to look to adults for confirmation. Emotion regulation begins in infancy as cooperative activity between adult and child (Campos, Frankel, & Camras, 2004). As the baby develops, he or she gradually takes over emotional regulation. It is believed that there are great changes in emotional regulation during the first 15 months.

## Humor

In Chapter 13, we saw the importance of humor for infants. Laughing and giggling are equally important during toddlerhood (Nwokah, 2003). Nwokah (2003) identified several ways that humor supports child development (p. 2):

- Improves creative thought
- Improves the learning process as a memory aid
- Teaches word meaning
- Contributes to social processes and skills
- Helps the child cope with stress and anxiety

Humor can alter a negative emotional state into a positive emotional state. Toddlers enjoy silly games, such as chase, seeing someone in a funny hat or silly, looking glasses, or an adult pretending to be a baby. By age two, when speech is developing rapidly, they enjoy word games with funny sounds or silly versions of words.

## Attachment

Toddlers and their parents can still experience separation distress (Godwin, Groves, & Horm-Wingerd, 1993). In their study of leave-takings and reunions at a child care center, Field et al. (1984) found that toddlers protested much more strongly than infants when it was time for the parent to leave. They showed more attention-getting, verbal protest, clinging, and crying behaviors. Parents of toddlers showed more hovering, distracting behaviors and did more sneaking out of the classroom. Children who received a verbal explanation for the leave-taking tended to protest less and show less stress. Those children who stayed most easily also tended to leave most easily. The adult who works with young children can be supportive of parents by helping them understand that it is normal for toddlers to protest leave-taking more than infants or preschoolers. Parents need to know that this is a part of normal development. Otherwise, they may feel they are at fault.

Toddlers eventually develop an affectional relationship with their caregiver. Affection is essential to the development of strong and healthy attachment and, thus, emotional development. In their study of toddlers' responses to affectionate teacher behavior, Zanolli, Saudargas, and Twardosz (1997) found that smiling received the most positive responses from the toddlers observed. Smiling was also the earliest affectionate teacher response to be reciprocated by the toddlers. The results of this study indicate that teachers and other caregivers can best help toddlers make the transition from home to child care through smiling. Smiling appears to signal to children that the adult cares and wants to develop a reciprocal relationship.

## Moral Development

**morality**

Ethical behavior; the development of an understanding of right and wrong.

A major concern for adults who work with young children is the development of ethical behavior and an understanding of right and wrong; that is, the development of morality. **Morality** grows out of social relationships (Damon, 1988). Adults must understand the social world of children in order to understand their special view of morality. Morality is not easy to define. Damon (1988) describes it as including the following (p. 5):

1. Morality is an evaluative orientation toward actions and events that distinguishes the good from the bad and prescribes what is good.
2. Morality implies a sense of obligation toward standards shared by others in the group.
3. Morality includes a concern for the welfare of others. It extends beyond one's own desires.
4. Morality includes a sense of responsibility for acting on one's concern for others (acts of caring, kindness, benevolence, and mercy).
5. Morality includes a concern for the rights of others (justice and fairness).
6. Morality includes a commitment to honesty.
7. When morality is not lived up to, judgmental and emotional responses occur (shame, guilt, outrage, fear, contempt).

Adults are interested in how children's views of morality and judgments of morality change with time within their unique and nonadult social context.

**shame**

A feeling of embarrassment that may occur when children feel they have not lived up to certain behavioral standards.

The early moral emotions are empathy, shame, and guilt (Damon, 1988). We already have seen that toddlers may have the beginnings of empathy or a sensitivity to the feelings of others. However, not all toddlers evidence this emotion. **Shame** is a feeling of embarrassment that may occur when children feel they have not lived up to certain behavioral standards. Remember that, according to Erikson, toddlers are striving for autonomy, but failure brings shame and doubt. Toilet training is often the focus for the toddler's first experience with this feeling. Parents may humiliate the child when success is not achieved. Guilt develops later during the preoperational period.

Toddlers are just beginning to develop morality. They are just beginning to learn about right and wrong, good and bad, and which kinds of acts fall under each label. Their values are usually situation specific. For example, just because they have learned not to pull the cat's tail does not mean they will not pull the dog's tail.

In the classroom, rules develop along two separate lines: moral and conventional (Crosser, 2004). Moral rules are those that apply in every setting and have to do with aggression (e.g., physical harm) and resource violations (e.g., taking someone else's toy). Social conventions are those that are devised to deal with a specific setting and include rules for keeping materials in order and norms for various settings and activities (e.g., not talking during a story and keeping the blocks in a special area). Smetana (1984) found qualitative differences in social interactions between the two types of transgressions. Responses to conventional transgressions were similar for one- and two-year-olds. On the whole, they paid little attention. Teachers had to repeatedly remind them to attend to basic rules, such as not talking during story time and sitting down while eating. The toddlers were more responsive to moral transgressions. They responded emotionally and physically at both ages. The older children were also likely to make a statement regarding the harm done. Whereas caregivers tended to provide a rationale for moral transgressions, they did not do so for conventional transgressions. The personal nature of moral transgressions, that is, viewing and/or feeling pain or loss, and the reasons provided by caregivers, probably support the learning of moral right and wrong earlier than conventional. Also, conventions often seem rather arbitrary from the child's point of view. "Why *not* stand up when you eat?" "Why put things away when you are finished?" Reasons for these rules are not as obvious as the consequences of pulling another child's hair.

Research studies such as those done by Kochanska and her colleagues (Kochanska, Murray, & Coy, 1997; Kochanska, Padavich, & Koenig, 1996) provide evidence of a connection between the toddler's level of inhibitory control, that is, not moving ahead with a forbidden act, and conscience development. Toddlers can develop a clear vision of right and wrong, and the ability to inhibit forbidden behavior during toddlerhood is indicative of future conscience development.

Explain how morality begins to develop during the infancy and toddler years, and describe how it relates to affective development.

## Social and Emotional Disabilities

Wittmer, Doll, and Strain (1996) describe the crucial need to identify children with social and emotional disabilities as early as possible. Intervention should begin as soon as assessment and diagnosis can be instituted. It is strongly substantiated that children's ability to create and sustain effective relationships is a strong predictor of adult mental health. The inability of a young child to express and respond appropriately and to regulate emotions is predictive of later developmental and pathological disorders. Each state is free to construct its own definition of social and emotional disorders and to develop a means for assessing a child's status. Wittmer et al., after reviewing the developmental literature, identify three target areas (p. 301):

1. cooperative and prosocial behaviors
2. active initiation and maintenance of an array of peer friendships and adult relationships
3. management of aggression and conflict

It can be seen from the descriptions of infant and toddler affective development that these behaviors should be evident during the early years.

Children with social and/or emotional disabilities are likely to experience difficulties all through school (Bowe, 2000). If behavior change is not instituted early, the problems only get worse. Social/emotional problems may be associated with disabilities in other areas. Children who are blind, motor impaired, deaf, or have other disabilities may have experienced isolation, with resulting inappropriate behavior, when they enter a prekindergarten group setting.

Emotional and social disabilities can be avoided through supporting infant and toddler mental health (Vacca & Bagdi, 2005). Vacca and Bagdi (2005) define infant mental health as follows (p. 9):

> Infant mental health is a developmental, family-driven process of providing appropriate environments for infants and toddlers to support their social and emotional growth and to serve as the foundation for resiliency in order to:
>
> - Sustain a healthy psychosocial existence;
> - Promote a positive sense of self;
> - Promote autonomous decision-making; and
> - Develop lasting relationships with others.

Both home and classroom environments must be safe and nurturing. Secure relationships enable children to meet the developmental tasks of early childhood. Secure relationships enable children to develop self-regulation skills, a positive self-concept, an internalization of rules, and a sense of right and wrong. Mothers, fathers, grandparents, other caretakers, and siblings all can provide supportive relationships. Adults need to define emotions for children and help them manage and regulate them, learn prosocial behaviors, and become a valued member of the family and classroom environment.

## TEMPERAMENT

In Chapter 13, temperament was defined and described. Just as with infants, parents of toddlers must consider children's temperamental characteristics and fit their ways of dealing with children to the children's temperaments (Sturm, 2004). Parents need to understand their own temperaments and then those of their children. By studying the child's temperament, the adult can anticipate their reactions and develop a plan for responding (Lerner & Dombro, 2004). Some types of temperament are viewed as "difficult" (Tomlin, 2004). Researchers have studied behaviors such as the following (Tomlin, 2004, p. 30):

- Negative emotionality—especially intense negative emotions, demandingness, and aggression;
- Behaviors related to impulsivity—also talked about by researchers as a "positive approach" or an "uninhibited or exuberant style";
- Persistence with undesirable behaviors, lack of compliance, or resistance to control; and
- Short attention span and low effortful control.

Often what is considered difficult "lies in the eye of the beholder" (Tomlin, 2004, p. 30). However, there are behaviors that most adults find difficult to deal with. The concern at the toddler level is that between ages two and three normal behaviors may fall into the difficult category. Hard-to-manage behaviors common to toddlers include "aggression, tantrums, and failure to comply with adult commands" (Tomlin, 2004, p. 31).

These behaviors result when the toddler wants all of something, tries to do something the caretaker feels is not safe, or just wants to have his or her own way. Adults need to keep in mind that toddlers may be limited in emotional regulation and are still developing cognitively; they may not understand expectations. They may not realize that they have hurt a person or an object. Intervention, redirection, and instruction are needed. They may not understand why they must comply, especially with "don't" commands. Attention span varies with the material and interest of the child. By 18 months, children begin to use intentionality in selecting activities. Toddlers will attend to a task of interest, but their ability to avoid distraction may be very limited. Short attention span should not be considered a problem with children under age three. The line between difficult behavior due to difficult temperament and a behavior disorder can be hard to identify. For example, a child with difficult temperament might be misdiagnosed as ADHD. The only type of noncompliance in young children associated with later behavior problems is persistent noncompliance especially with screaming, hitting, and kicking. Care must be taken in labeling a toddler's behavior. A difficult behavior may be typical of a developmental phase, a sign of difficult temperament, or a behavior disorder. The adults have the responsibility of supporting children and helping them to develop self-regulation skills.

## Self-Concept

**self-concept**
The way a person feels about himself or herself.

Through social interactions and play, young children gradually develop an idea about who they are. This picture of oneself is called a **self-concept** (Berk, 2006). The feedback received from people and objects met in the environment, no matter what culture, are reflected to the toddler in a self-concept. Each child develops an individual "self" according to the people the child chooses to imitate and the experiences in which the child chooses to participate (Figure 16–3). Play activities help the child develop as an acceptable member of the culture. As children practice what they have learned through observation in their play activities, they find out from the reactions of those around them whether they are acceptable members of their culture. If they get many positive responses, such as praise, approval, and accomplishment of tasks, they develop a positive feeling about themselves.

Pipp-Siegel and Foltz (1997) found that, by age two, toddlers distinguish themselves from other people and objects. Toddlers appear to categorize self versus others. The researchers believe that this categorization is important to the development of autonomy.

**ethnic socialization**
The developmental processes by which children acquire the behaviors, perception, values, and attitudes of an ethnic group, and come to see themselves and others as members of such groups (Phinney & Rotheram, 1987).

Of primary importance in the development of self-concept is the development of ethnic identity. Ethnic identity evolves through ethnic socialization. "**Ethnic socialization** refers to the developmental processes by which children

FIGURE 16–3 Pretending to be a grown-up is an important activity in the development of the self-concept.

acquire the behaviors, perceptions, values, and attitudes of an ethnic group, and come to see themselves and others as members of such groups" (Phinney & Rotheram, 1987, p. 11). Self-concept and self-esteem are closely tied to ethnic identity and develop through ethnic socialization. During the toddler years, children are probably assimilating some information regarding physical aspects of people, such as skin color, hair type, and hair texture. However, it is not until ages three or four that they begin to categorize and compare these differences and to place themselves in a particular category.

A major part of the self-concept is gender identity, which toddlers are just beginning to figure out. Girls may prefer female-stereotyped activities and materials and boys male-stereotyped activities and materials. Beginning in the womb, there are difference between the brains of boys and girls that may affect their choices (*Brain Wonders*, 2001). It really can't be determined "what portion of sex differences in behavior results from the biology of the brain (such as hormones) and what portion of the sex differences in behavior results from the influence of the social experiences (what we expect and provide) of young toddlers" (*Brain Wonders*, 2001). It is known that as early as seven weeks after conception the male hormone testosterone rises and begins to masculinize the brains of male fetuses. Boys and girls in general are born with different emotional styles: Girls are more social and boys more activity- and spatially oriented.

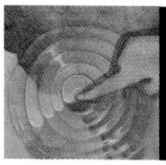

**LOOKING FURTHER**

Observe several toddlers at home, at preschool, or in child care centers. Report your observations to the class. Make a summary chart showing the range of behaviors you observed and share it with the class.

## SUMMARY

Toddlers have well-established social and personality characteristics. Toddlers play well on their own and can also play nicely with their peers in a supportive setting. Pretend play is in its early stages, but exploratory play is also prominent. Peers are just, beginning to be involved. Peer relations are often characterized by volatile, aggressive contacts on each other's bodies and play materials. Direct instruction on how to get the attention of others and how to share is helpful for making toddler play more positive. However, adults should stand back and let toddlers have time to try to solve their own problems. The responses of adults influence toddler behavior. Parenting styles have an effect on behavior. Children tend to repeat positive and negative behaviors to which adults pay attention. Toddlers show signs of sensitivity toward the feelings of others and of understanding what is happening in social conflict situations. As toddlers strive for independence, their dependence on emotional attachment to parents seems to peak. Humor is an important factor in establishing emotions of joy and happiness. Toddlers are in a stage of beginning moral development where they are learning to categorize right and wrong, especially in terms of what hurts and what does not. Abstract rules mean very little to toddlers. Temperamental characteristics tend to be stable through this period. However, it is important to note that behaviors that are difficult to deal with may not necessarily be temperament characteristics but may be typical of toddler development. Toddlers are becoming more aware of themselves and developing a broader self-concept.

## For Further Reading


Barr, R., Hopkins, B., & Green, J. (2000). *Crying as a sign, a symptom, and a signal: Clinical, emotional, and developmental aspects of infant and toddler crying.* Cambridge, UK: Cambridge University Press.

Baumeister, R. F., & Vohs, K. D. (Eds.). (2005). *Handbook of self-regulation: Research, theory, and applications.* New York: Guilford.

Berlin, L. J., Ziv, Y., Amaya-Jackson, L., & Greenberg, M. T. (Eds.). (2005). *Enhancing early attachments.* New York: Guilford.

Carpendale, J., & Lewis, C. (2004). *How children develop social understanding.* Malden, MA: Blackwell.

Crittenden, P. M., & Claussen, A. H. (Eds.). (2000). *The organization of attachment relationships.* New York: Cambridge University Press.

Day, M., & Parlakian, R. (2004). *How culture shapes social-emotional development.* Washington, DC: Zero to Three.

Gowen, J. W., & Nebrig, J. B. (2002). *Enhancing early emotional development.* Baltimore: Brookes.

Grolnick, W. S. (2002). *The psychology of parental control.* Mahwah, NJ: Erlbaum.

Grossman, K. E., Grossman, K., & Waters, E. (Eds.). (2005). *Attachment from infancy to adulthood.* New York: Guilford.

Haynes, J. (2002). *Children as philosophers.* New York: RoutledgeFalmer.

Herbert, M. (2002). *Social and antisocial development.* Williston,VT: Blackwell.

Hill, J., & Maughan, B. (Eds.). (2000). *Conduct disorders in childhood and adolescence.* New York: Cambridge University Press.

Hyson, M. (2003). *The emotional development of young children.* New York: Teachers College Press.

Killen, M., & Smetana, J. G. (Eds.). (2005). *Handbook of moral development.* Mahwah, NJ: Erlbaum.

Laible, D. J., & Thompson, R. A. (2002). Mother-child conflict in the toddler years: Lessons in emotion, morality and relationships. *Child Development, 73*(4), 1187–1203.

Lieberman, A. F., Compton, N. C., Van Horn, P., & Ippen, C. G. (2003). *Losing a parent to death in the early years.* Washington, DC: Zero to Three.

Lippa, R. A. (2002). *Gender, nature and nurture.* Mahwah, NJ: Erlbaum.

Maldonado-Durna, J. M. (Ed.). (2002). *Infant and toddler mental health.* Arlington, VA: American Psychiatric Publishing.

Matthews, G., Deary, I. J., & Whiteman, M. C. (2004). *Personality traits* (2nd ed.). New York: Cambridge University Press.

Mayne, T. J., & Bonanno, G. A. (2001). *Emotions: Current issues and future directions.* New York: Guilford.

Nelson, C. A. (Ed.). (2000). *The effects of early adversity on neurobehavioral development.* Mahwah, NJ: Erlbaum.

Osofsky, J. D. (Ed.). (2004). *Young children and trauma.* New York: Guilford.

Segal, M., Masi, E., & Leiderman, R. (2002). *In time and with love: Caring for infants and toddlers with special needs* (2nd ed). Washington, DC: Zero to Three.

Tamis-LeMonda, C. S., & Cabrera, N. (Eds.). (2002). *The handbook of father involvement: Multidisciplinary perspectives.* Mahwah, NJ: Erlbaum.

*Trajectories of physical aggression from toddlerhood to middle childhood.* (2005). Williston, MA: Blackwell.

Waters, E., Hamilton, C. E., & Weinfield, N. S. (Eds.). (2000). The stability of attachment security from infancy to adolescence and early adulthood. [Special section]. *Child Development, 71*(3), 678–706.


## Suggested Activities

1. Observe a toddler at home or at a child care site. Use the Toddler Personal-Social Development Assessment Chart (Figure 16–4) to evaluate the toddler's social development.
   a. Overall, does the toddler seem to be average, ahead of typical expectations, or slow in developmental rate?
   b. What kinds of suggestions do you have for the parents and/or caregiver regarding this toddler?
   c. Support all your conclusions and recommendations with data from your assessment chart.

Observer _____ Date _____ Time _____ Place _____

Infant's name _____ Birth date _____ Age _____

| Age and Skill/Behavior | Observed Yes | Observed No | Comments |
|---|---|---|---|
| **One-Year-Olds Personal-Social** | | | |
| Friendly toward others; less wary of strangers | | | |
| Helps pick up and put away toys | | | |
| Plays alone for short periods | | | |
| Enjoys being held and read to | | | |
| Imitates adult actions in play | | | |
| Enjoys adult attention; likes to have adult near; gives hugs and kisses | | | |
| Recognizes self in mirror | | | |
| Enjoys being with other children; usually engages in parallel play | | | |
| Asserts independence; wants to do daily routines without help (i.e., dressing, bathing, eating) | | | |
| When tired or frustrated may have a tantrum | | | |
| Very curious—can easily get into trouble if not supervised closely | | | |
| **Two-Year-Olds Personal-Social** | | | |
| Shows signs of empathy and caring when another child is upset; may offer too many hugs and kisses | | | |
| Continues to use physical aggression if frustrated or angry but is learning to verbalize anger | | | |
| Peak for temper tantrums | | | |
| Difficulty waiting or taking turns | | | |
| Enjoys "helping" with household chores; imitates everyday activities (feed a doll; toilet a stuffed animal) | | | |
| Bossy with adults | | | |
| Usually plays alone but observes and may imitate older children | | | |
| Possessive of toys although may offer a toy to another child | | | |
| Difficulty making choices; wants it both ways | | | |
| Defiant: shouts "No!" | | | |
| May be ritualistic—wants routines to stay the same, things to be in their proper place | | | |

FIGURE 16–4 Toddler personal-social development assessment chart.
(Adapted from Allen, K. D., & Marotz, L. R., 2003. *Developmental profiles: Pre-birth through twelve.* Clifton Park, NY: Delmar Learning).

2. Observe a group of toddlers playing on gross motor equipment and compare this behavior with their behavior when playing with small, individual toys. Do you note any similarities or differences when comparing play with the two types of equipment?

3. If you have not yet made friends with a toddler, do so. Take the toddler to a quiet place away from the other children. Put out 6 to 10 of the toddler's favorite toys. Make up a game where you ask him or her to do a series of tasks with the toys; for example, "Bring me your truck," "Put the baby to bed," "Roll the ball." Note how the toddler responds to these requests. Does he or she comply? If not, what is the toddler's response? Does he or she seem to enjoy the game?

4. Interview one or more parents of twelve- to twenty-four-month-olds who are walking. Ask them the following questions:
   a. What are [*child's name*] favorite play activities?
   b. Does [*child's name*] have the opportunity to play with other children? Are they the same age? What do they do?
   c. Do you find that [*child's name*] ever acts negatively? When has this occurred? Does he or she ever defy you? Say "No!" ? How do you respond?
   d. Do you feel he or she has any idea about what is right and what is wrong? How can you tell?

   Compare the responses you get with the text descriptions and with those of other students in the class.

5. Make an entry in your journal.

## REVIEW

1. Explain Vygotsky's and Erikson's views of the toddler's affective development.
2. Which of the following descriptions describes exploratory play?
   a. Maria moves a toy car across the floor, making a sound like and engine.
   b. Maria goes to the toy box and gets four cars, two trucks, and a bag of blocks. She takes the materials to the rug, builds a garage, and puts the cars in saying, "Park the car."
   c. Maria moves a car and a truck across the floor and parks them side by side.
   d. Maria picks up a toy car, looks at it, tastes it, bites it, and runs her fingers over it.
   e. Maria finds some cars and blocks on the rug. She builds a shelter around one of the cars. Then she takes the car out and pushes it around the floor.
3. Consider the following situations and evaluate each.
   a. Eighteen-month-old Maria plays alone with three stuffed bears. "Mama bear, papa bear, baby bear," she repeats.
   b. Twenty-month-old Liu Pei and eighteen-month-old Maria roll a ball back and forth to each other.
   c. Georgie and Rudy, both two-year-olds, are pulling on the arms of a teddy bear, each shouting, "Mine!"
   d. Mrs. Phung is puzzled. When eighteen-month-old Hien Phung plays with eighteen-month-old Tony, he grabs things from him and will not share. When Hien plays with two-and-a-half-year-old Lai, he shares nicely.
   e. Ms. Garcia responds more frequently to boys than to girls who seek attention by yelling, screaming, and whining.
   f. Maria, twenty months of age, is trying to put some nesting cups together. Her mother sits next to her. "Maria, find the biggest." Maria finds it. "Good

work! Now find the next biggest." Maria finds it and places it in the correct position, "Good Maria, you have the idea."

g. Dat is also twenty months old. He is trying to figure out what he can do with play dough. His mother pats it and rolls it. He watches her. Then he takes a piece of the dough and pats it.
h. Mr. Brown is surprised when seventeen-month-old Brian runs over and gently pats two-and-one-half-year-old Emily, who has just fallen down and is crying in anguish.
i. Lai has a harder time letting her mother leave the child care center now at fourteen months than she did as an infant.
j. The next time Kate heads for a flower pot, her mother takes her hand and says, "Let's go play in your sandbox."
k. Mrs. Smith, the toddler teacher, smiles at her new child, eighteen-month-old Inez.
l. Two-year-old Danny never smiles or laughs. His teacher, Mr. Jones, suggests to his parents that they have Danny assessed.

**4.** Describe the proximal, distal, and combination parenting styles.

**5.** Select the statements that are true.

a. Early social experience is necessary for the proper development of facial emotional expression recognition.
b. When seeking help from their mothers, toddlers are most likely to use an angry expression.
c. Emotional regulation emerges during the preschool period.
d. Humor supports the development of positive emotions.
e. Mental health is sustained in early childhood in safe and nurturing environments with positive social-emotional relationships.
f. If a toddler displays any difficult behaviors, he or she probably has a behavior disorder.
g. The difficult behaviors commonly displayed by the toddler are typical and probably due to immature cognitive development, which makes it difficult to discriminate right from wrong.

## KEY TERMS LIST

coordinated play
ethnic socialization
guided participation
morality
peers
posttraumatic stress disorder
self-concept
sex-stereotyped
shame
zone of proximal development (ZPD)

Additional resources for this chapter can be found on the Online Companion™ to accompany this text at http://www.earlychilded.delmar.com. Respond to "Time to Reflect" and "Looking Further" concepts, review various child development scenarios, and answer thought-provoking questions in the Critical Thinking Forum. Keep a daily journal by downloading the student journal available on this Web site. Complete the interactive matching exercises to reinforce concepts, and print out the child development assessment forms to use during your observation of development for children from birth to age eight. In addition, read the case studies on the Web site to reinforce the important concepts in each chapter, and take a look at the multitude of Web links that are available for student research on the Internet.

CHAPTER

# 17

# The Toddler: Cognitive Development

## OBJECTIVES

After reading this chapter, you should be able to:

- Name the Piagetian stages through which the toddler passes.
- Describe Vygotsky's view of toddler cognitive development.
- Identify examples of toddler concept learning.
- Analyze and evaluate toddler speech samples with regard to stage placement and context.
- Analyze and evaluate examples of toddler cognitive development.
- Describe the relationship between language and literacy development.
- Understand the importance of the sociocultural aspects of toddler cognitive and language development.

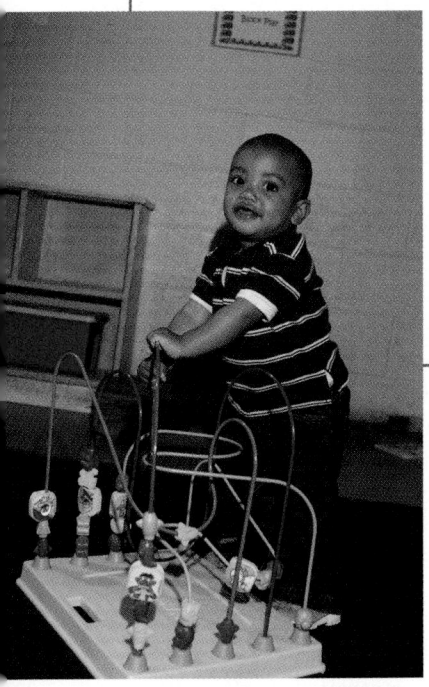

Toddlers are curious about the world. They are also developing toward independence. The combination results in a great deal of experimentation. Toddlers have been known to see what might happen if they flush a toy down the toilet, dry a wet stuffed animal in the oven, and mix up a variety of ingredients to make a cake like they have seen adults make. The combination of curiosity and independence provides for a period of development that is a challenge for adults. As described in previous chapters (see Chapters 5, 9, and 12 through 16), brain development is progressing at a rapid pace during the first three years. This chapter looks at the toddler from the views of Piaget and Vygotsky and at toddler concept development, speech and language and literacy development, concept and language interaction, and sociocultural factors.

According to Piaget, the toddler is passing through the sensorimotor to the pre-operational period of cognitive development. Before toddlerhood, sensory and motor activity are the dominant means for learning. Sensory and motor modes of learning are important all through life, but during the preoperational period, play and imitation are the dominant means for cognitive growth.

Toddlerhood continues through the last two of the six stages outlined by Piaget, which take the toddler from reflexive activity to thinking before acting (Fogel, 2001). Between 12 and 18 months of age, toddlers usually experience the fifth stage. They continue to enjoy repeating actions but also try new ways of doing things. The toddler changes from dropping the same toy out of the crib time after time in the same way, to dropping different toys in different ways. Around 18 months of age, toddlers reach Piaget's sixth and final stage, during which representational thought develops. At stage six, the child begins to think before acting, doing what is called **representational thinking.** Children are now able to represent, or think through, a problem in their minds before going into action. Suppose a toddler wants a toy on a shelf that is out of reach. The toddler tries to reach it by stretching, but stops when unable to do so and appears to think about the problem. Earlier, the child would have kept trying to climb the shelves and stretch, even though to an adult, it was obvious the attempt would fail. Now, the child represents the next move in his or her mind's eye. The child stops, thinks, gets a small chair to stand on, and is then able to reach the desired toy.

**representational thinking**

Piaget's sixth stage, when a child begins to think before acting.

At the same time, toddlers are progressing through the final two stages of object permanence. By 12 months of age, toddlers are able to solve the problem of the toy hidden under a cloth if they see it hidden and if it is always hidden in the same place. Between 12 and 18 months, they develop the ability to find an object hidden in a series of hiding places as long as they are allowed to see the object as it is being hidden. Around 18 months or shortly after, toddlers can search for objects that have been hidden without having seen which hiding place has been used. During this period, the toddler enjoys playing hidden-object games.

From Vygotsky's point of view, the toddler is in an important period in the development of language (Bodrova & Leong, 1996). Toddlers are in a critical zone of proximal development for language. Speech is essential for the development of higher mental functioning. That is, speech supports concept development. Scaffolding, support, and guidance from adults or older peers as the toddler explores his or her environment assist the toddler in reaching his or her cognitive developmental potential.

According to Bodrova and Leong (1996), the leading activity between ages one and three is the **manipulation of objects.** Toddlers learn through touching, moving, banging, and turning over objects. Whereas infants play with one object at a time, toddlers play with several. They put objects in containers and stack blocks. They discover that one object can act on another object, such as rolling a ball to knock over a block tower. During the toddler period, children begin to play on their own without immediate adult direction. As they explore, language becomes connected with the objects.

**manipulation of objects**

Toddlers learn through touching, moving, banging, and turning over objects.

Compare the views of Piaget and Vygotsky regarding toddler cognitive development. Consider how their basic ideas might apply to enhancing toddler cognitive development.

## CONCEPT DEVELOPMENT

Concepts are the building blocks of knowledge. They are the ideas that we use for thinking and problem solving.

Toddlers are busy and actively learning about concepts such as size, shape, number, classifications, comparisons, space, parts and wholes, volume, weight, length, temperature, and time (Charlesworth & Lind, 2003). As toddlers move about and work with many things in their everyday environment, they learn about the properties of objects in meaningful ways (Goldhaber & Smith, 1993). For example:

- Raymond tries to hold onto a large beach ball but finds he can hardly stretch his short little arms around it (size).
- Juan has some play dough. He pounds it, pinches it, and rolls it (shape).
- When asked how old he is, two-year-old Nathan holds up two fingers (number).
- Marnie lines up her green blocks in one row, yellow blocks in another, and red blocks in a third row (classifying by color).
- Alfredo, age two-and-a-half says, "My apple bigger" as he points at Tanya's apple and his apple (comparison).
- Aisha tries to stuff her big panda bear into a small box and finds that it does not fit (space).
- Azam breaks his cracker into two pieces, saying, "I have two crackers!" (parts and wholes).
- A group of toddlers are gathered around a tub of water. They have containers of many sizes, which they fill with water. They fill, pour, and mix (volume) (Figure 17–1).
- Chan tries to lift a box of toys, but cannot do it (weight).
- Bonnie tries to put her doll in the toy crib but the doll is too long. She finds an empty cardboard carton that is just the right size and makes a bed for the doll (length).
- Maria takes a sip of hot soup and says, "Ouch!" (temperature).
- David says, "Juice time next" (time).

The previous examples illustrate the kinds of activities and actions that support rapid and complete brain development, as described by Shore (1997). Between 12 and 18 months, an area of the brain develops that provides toddlers with new memory power (*BrainWonders*, 2002). They can now remember what they have seen and repeat it at a later time (**deferred imitation**). They thrive on repetition, which probably strengthens brain connections. Between 18 months and 24 months, many new circuits develop in the brain and areas are developing that enable toddlers to run, climb, jump, scoop, and pour (*BrainWonders*, 2002). Areas of the brain develop that provide for increased use of language and the ability to pretend. Between 24 and 36 months, toddlers are very active. Language and movement play provide for the development of problem-solving skills and thinking. New synapses are still forming, while old pathways are remodeled to allow for more speed and efficiency (*BrainWonders*, 2002). By age three, a toddler's brain is about 80 percent of adult size (*BrainWonders*, 2002).

**deferred imitation**

Toddlers between 12 and 18 months are able to remember what they have seen and repeat it at a later time.

FIGURE 17–1 Playing with water helps toddlers learn about volume.

Toddlers need opportunities to exercise their problem-solving skills. According to Segatti, Brown-DuPaul, and Keyes (2003), toddlers gain many benefits and skills as they engage in problem-solving experiences. Adults need to hold back and provide plenty of time for toddlers to solve their own problems. Adults also need to provide materials that may present problems to toddlers. Problem-solving enhances brain development and supports the learning of concepts as described in the examples previously mentioned. Both recycled items, such as various kinds of containers, plastic tubing, plastic hair curlers, keys, and purchased materials, such as blocks, beads, and puzzles, can provide challenges for toddlers.

Problem-solving experiences may emerge from toddlers' everyday activities. Febo (2005) describes how toddlers engaged in a long-term project on water that emerged from their interest in where water went when it disappeared down the sink drain. Sieminski (2005) describes how toddlers investigated light and shadow. Noting that toddlers are intrigued by light and shadow, an area of the classroom was set up with light sources: flashlights, an overhead projector, and a light table. The children engaged in an ongoing investigation of light and shadow.

Researchers have looked at toddlers' development of other specific concepts. For example, Sera, Troyer, and Smith (1988) studied two-, three-, and four-year-olds' and adults' internal representations of normative size concepts. That is, they were interested when the relative nature of *big* and *little* is understood. Big and little take on meaning relative to other members of their class (e.g., other insects, airplanes, houses, and cats). Sera et al. found that although two-year-olds could pick out shoes of appropriate sizes for adults and children, they had trouble with buttons and plates. Four-year-olds on the other hand, could easily select the correct items. It may be that the more familiar a class of objects is, the more accurately the two-year-olds are able to conceptualize the relative sizes.

Toddlers are also beginning to develop concepts in the areas of classification and categorization. That is, they are beginning to make connections between things with similar characteristics and put them into groups. It is by making categories that young children make sense of the world (Gelman, 1998). According to Gelman, "a category is any grouping of the things that are similar in some way" (p. 20). Research on children's early categories indicates that, although their thinking is different from adults, children develop an advanced category system that guides their thinking. Toddlers tend to "overextend" their categories so that they are applied very broadly: All things with wheels are cars or all small furry animals are kitties. Before age three, children tend to be deceived by appearances and do not evaluate appearance and reality simultaneously. When someone wears a costume, the toddler may not view him or her as the same person the toddler knew in his or her usual clothing. When toddlers learn that one kind of bird lives in a nest and eats a certain kind of food, they tend to generalize this information to all birds. Children may base their early classifications on incorrect information and stick by them in the face of conflicting facts. The number of generalizations children make tends to increase dramatically around two-and-a-half years of age. Adults need to label objects for children and encourage them to notice the similarities and differences; this helps children expand their knowledge.

Bornstein, Haynes, O'Reilly, and Painter (1996) examined the variations in the development of representational competence as observed during solitary and collaborative pretense play. Both Piaget and Vygotsky recognized the importance of representational play as children's first understanding and use of symbols. By twenty months of age, children engage in simple pretend play activities. They drink from empty cups, cook invisible food, and use blocks or bananas for telephones. Solitary play and play with mothers was compared by Bornstein et al. They found that play was more symbolic when toddlers played collaboratively with their mothers than when they played alone. There was also more symbolic play when the mother initiated the play. The authors concluded that higher-level symbolic play is supported, or scaffolded, when an adult collaborates with the child in the play activity. These results support the importance of adult caregivers getting down to the toddler's level and initiating pretend play.

FIGURE 17–2 As speech develops, toddlers say the names of things in picture books.

## SPEECH AND LANGUAGE DEVELOPMENT

The toddler moves into the linguistic period. That is, the child begins to use meaningful speech (Figure 17–2). As toddlers approach age two, speech develops at a fast rate (Honig, 1998) (Figure 17–3). Once toddlers say their first words, they enter the **holophrastic stage** of language development (Cole, Cole, & Lightfoot, 2005; Rathus, 2006). During this stage, the child speaks in one-word sentences called **holophrases.** These words are usually the names of familiar things, such as body parts. Things that are active are apt to be labeled first: "doggie," "car," or "kitty." Food words or names of other desired items are used in this early speech.

Children also use words that refer to a specific thing but that are not real words. One 17-month-old uses "adoo" to refer to water. She also used the approximation "mulk" for milk. Most young children substitute sounds (e.g., the *i* in milk and the *t* in tummy) or leave out some sounds, such as "minee" for vitamin, or "fust" for first. During the holophrastic and telegraphic periods, it is not unusual for a child not to articulate every sound in the English language. The child may substitute sounds or omit them. In the following samples from a 23-month-old girl, figure out what is missing or being substituted in the list on the left:

**holophrastic stage**

A stage in language development when the child speaks one-word sentences.

**holophrases**

One-word sentences.

| Child's Word | Real Word |
|---|---|
| 1. greem | green |
| 2. kik | kiss |
| 3. Chrik | Chris |
| 4. Hena | Helena |
| 5. printess | princess |
| 6. yove | love |
| 7. glakkes | glasses |
| 8. bwony | bologna |

It can be seen that *m* is substited for *n; k* for *s; t* for *s; y* for *l;* and *l* is omitted in two cases. Sometime between age two-and-a-half and four, sentences increase in length until they are complete. Meaning becomes closer to that of the adult listener, so the context is understood from the sentence itself. For example, "No bed" becomes "I no go to bed," and then "I don't want to go to bed." By age four, syntax is usually almost like that of an adult. Context, or conveying where or what, is very important at this stage. It is important to know what toddlers are referring to when they use their single-word sentences. For example, "Doggie!" might mean:

| Age | Language Characteristics | Semantic Elements |
|---|---|---|
| 12 Months | First word or wordlike combinations of sounds | Now has a referent |
| 12–18 Months (begins) | Holophrases; one-word utterances<br>Usually the names of familiar objects that act and react | Referents; context is critical |
| 18–30 Months (begins) | Telegraphic speech; two- to three-word sentences that contain only the essentials | Referents; context is very important |
| About 2 $^1/_2$ years to 4 years | Sentence length increases to four or more words | Clearer to adult listener; more detail is included |

FIGURE 17–3 The development of speech during toddlerhood.
Adapted from information in Berk, 2006; Cole, Cole, & Lightfoot, 2005; and Rathus, 2006.

"I see a doggie on TV."
"There is a doggie outside."
"I want the dog to come in."
(with tears) "Doggie knocked me down."

Toddlers usually understand more than they can say, so adults may use follow-ups such as "Show me," "Take me to ___," or "Point to ___," and so on to find out exactly what the toddler is trying to tell them. Adults also can expand on what the toddler says and note whether the toddler reacts in a way that indicates they have found the right meaning. That is, a toddler may say, "Doggie!" Mom says, "There's a doggie outside?" The toddler runs toward the living room. Mom follows and sees that there is a dog in front of the house. "There is a doggie outside," she repeats, as the toddler laughs and points with excitement.

Children learning to speak do not consciously break language down and label the parts; adults do that for descriptive purposes. Each child lives in a unique language environment to which he or she brings unique genetic characteristics. Katherine Nelson (1982) discusses some of these differences. She notes that two main types of beginning speakers, that is, one- and two-year-olds, have been identified: referential and expressive. Each type of speaker has unique characteristics:

**referential speakers**
Use mainly nouns, with some verbs, proper names, and adjectives.

**expressive speakers**
Use a diverse speech that includes a large number of combinations, such as "Stop it" and "I want it."

- **Referential speakers** use mainly nouns, with some verbs, proper names, and adjectives, whereas **expressive speakers** use much more diverse speech that includes a large number of combinations, such as "stop it" and "I want it."
- Referential speakers mainly use nouns, whereas expressive speakers use pronouns extensively.
- Although referential children do a lot of object labeling, expressive children tend to use many compressed sentences: One or two words, usually stuck together, stand for a longer sentence.
- Early speakers may use both styles but in different situations, such as referential during story time and expressive during social play.

These differences may be accounted for neurologically (brain hemisphere dominance), depending on environmental conditions (i.e., how the parents interact with the child), and in light of whether language learning is mainly a cognitive task for the child or whether the child also learns to use language appropriately in different contexts. Whatever the reasons for these individual differences, the important point is to be aware of them when evaluating the speech development of a particular child.

**strong nominals**
Those nouns that refer consistently to at least two referents.

**strong relationals**
Words that are used consistently for potentially reversible relationships.

**telegraphic sentences**
Children between eighteen months and two-and-a-half years begin to put two or three words together in sentences, which, by adult standards, are incomplete.

McCune (1989) recorded the vocal development of 10 children from the time they were nine months of age until they were sixteen months of age. There was considerable variability in the timing and the number of strong nominals and relationals the children used by sixteen months. **Strong nominals** are those nouns that refer consistently to at least two referents ( "kitty" to real and stuffed cats); **strong relationals** refer to words that are used consistently for potentially reversible relationships (e.g., "up" for "pick me up" ). At sixteen months, the range of strong words ranged from none to 27. The beginning of the use of such words occurred from fourteen-months-old on.

Sometime between eighteen months and two-and-a-half years, toddlers begin to put two or three words together in sentences. These short sentences, which are still incomplete by adult standards, are called **telegraphic sentences;** this second stage in the development of speech is the telegraphic stage. Sentences at this stage, like a telegram, contain only the essentials:

"More mulk."
"Daddy work."

Context is still important. That is, what is the child referring to when he says, "Hurty pummy" ?

"My tummy hurts."
"Teddy bear's tummy hurts."

Like detectives, adults have to look for clues to help them come up with the response the toddler has in mind.

Between eighteen months and four years, sentences become longer and more complete—more like those of an adult. "Daddy work" becomes "Daddy is at work." Two-year-olds vary a great deal in their speech. Some use holophrases, some use telegraphic speech, and some use more adultlike speech.

**private speech**

Self-talk.

Both Piaget and Vygotsky recognized that children talk to themselves as they engage in their everyday activities (Berk & Winsler, 1995). This self-talk is called **private speech.** However, Piaget and Vygotsky differed in their interpretations of the nature and function of private speech in the development of children. Piaget saw this speech as egocentric and immature. He believed it reflected the young child's inability to take another person's point of view and had no important function in development. Vygotsky, on the other hand, viewed private speech as an important factor in child development. He noted that private speech is used when working on difficult tasks and that its use reaches a peak in the preschool years, then changes to whispers and muttering, and is gradually internalized. He therefore concluded that the purpose of private speech is communication with the self for the purpose of **self-regulation.** Private speech is a tool for thought. When private speech becomes evident, usually between one and two years of age, it is used to reflect thought. As children have more social experiences, private speech mixes with social speech and eventually becomes internalized. Today, research on private speech is done from Vygotsky's point of view.

**self-regulation**

Private speech may be used to keep acuity focused.

Toddlers' private speech between ages two and three has been recorded as they begin a nap or when they first go to bed at night (Berk & Winsler, 1995). These monologs are called "crib speech." This play with language is enjoyable for children, provides time for language practice, and helps them understand their emotions and experiences. The content usually involves anticipation of a coming event, recall of a past event, or discussion of how to act according to rules for behavior.

Furrow (1984) studied two-year-olds' use of private and social speech. Private speech takes place when the child plays alone and social when involved with another person. Furrow was interested in whether two-year-olds use speech to serve the same functions in the private and social contexts. The children were studied during an informal play session in their own homes. The researcher took the role of the child's playmate when needed, letting the child take the lead in the play activity. Furrow found that speech was used differently in social and private contexts. Social speech included more regulatory (telling about something or someone not present) and attentional (seeking attention from the other person) functions. Self-regulatory speech, or speech that directs one's own activity, dominated in the private context. Overall, a much wider variety of speech functions was used in the social context (Figure 17–4).

Sixteen- to eighteen-month-old toddlers become strongly focused on speech. They suddenly lose interest in their toys. They want to be near an adult much of the time, demanding verbal interaction. They particularly demand that objects be labeled for them and they watch the adult's mouth as he or she speaks. During this period, they also may show an increased interest in books. This behavior continues until they are using words effectively in their own speech. This

FIGURE 17–4 Toddlers use their speech skills in their play.

appears to be an important activity for plunging into the period of rapid speech and language development that takes place from eighteen months of age to four years (Cawfield, 1992).

Although most children are speaking fluently by age four, a considerable number of children experience a delay and may still be speaking in one-word phrases with very limited vocabularies. Some young children evidence language disorders and may be identified as **specifically language impaired (SLI)** (Weiss, 2001). A language disorder is defined as when a child's language competencies are different from those expected considering the child's chronological age. These children should be evaluated as to speech, hearing, and general development.

**specifically language impaired (SLI)**
Children whose language competence does not meet age expectations.

## The Adult Role in Language Development

Many researchers have examined how adults affect young children's language development. The following are examples of such studies. Pan, Rowe, Singer, and Snow (2005) focused on the relationship between maternal behavior and growth in toddler vocabulary production in low-income families. They looked at the communication between mothers and their toddlers between the ages of one and three. By age three, an SES difference in number of words uttered in 10 minutes compared with middle-class children in other studies was found with the low-SES children producing fewer words. The variety of words produced by the mothers had a greater effect on the size of children's vocabulary than did the amount of mother's talkativeness. Fewell and Deutscher (2004) looked at child language during play at thirty months as a predictor of IQ at age three, verbal IQ at ages five and eight, and reading at age eight with a group of low birth-weight children. Maternal facilitation of children's language at age three and mother's level of education strongly affected the level of children's communication skills. Early expressive language was the major contributor to later verbal and reading ability. Woods, Kashintath, and Goldstein (2004) found that caregivers could be trained to include language teaching strategies during regular play routines. Inclusion of the increased language activity improved the communication skills of four toddlers with language delays. Tan and Yang (2005) examined the language development of Chinese female adoptees from 18 to 35 months old. The adoptive families were high SES. The adoptees reached typical English language expectations after living in the adoptive families for an average of 16 months. After that, the adoptees language skills moved beyond U.S. norms. From these sample studies it can be seen that communication with toddlers using a broad-based vocabulary can enhance their language development.

Conversation is also important in the child care setting (Bardige & Segal, 2004). Teachers talk with children in large groups, small groups, and individually. They ask questions; talk about feelings, expectations, and time; and help children think through their problems. Teachers can provide new and interesting vocabulary. They can also encourage children to converse with each other. Sandboxes, forts, playhouses, lofts, simple stages, and blocks elicit peer cooperation and conversation. Children with delayed language development will need special attention and encouragement.

## INTERACTION OF CONCEPTS, KNOWLEDGE, LANGUAGE, AND LITERACY

As already mentioned, concept and language development go hand in hand and interact. McCune (1989) documented a relationship among the development of the object concept, the appearance of representative play, and the onset of rapid growth in language. As the toddler learns more language, there is more material to process when thinking, and as thought capabilities become more complex, language can be used in more complex ways. Through the child's speech, we learn much about the child's thought processes. Consider the following examples from the activities of a toddler friend of the author:

> Emmett was going through a period when his interest focused on discovering the many qualities of cellophane tape. He was standing in the kitchen trying to throw some pieces of the sticky tape into the air. Unnoticed by Emmett, the piece of tape fell on the floor. Emmett noticed the tape was gone. He gazed up toward the ceiling and said, "Tape stuck in the sky."

From the example, we get a glimpse into Emmett's reasoning. As for most children his age, the most obvious solution is the answer. If you are trying to throw something sticky into the air and it disappears, it must be stuck in the sky.

Vibbert and Bornstein (1989) examined the relationships among three aspects of mother-toddler interaction and specific toddler competencies in referential language and pretense play. All toddler subjects were 13 months of age. The following interaction domains were studied:

> *Social interactions:* Affective and interpersonal communication, both nonverbal and verbal.
>
> *Didactic interactions:* Mothers' efforts to call the toddlers' attention to things in the environment.
>
> *Control actions:* Degree to which mothers or toddlers initiated and maintained activities.

Naturalistic observations of mothers and toddlers were done in their homes. Toddlers were also assessed individually on language competence and free-play competence. Mothers' didactic frequencies were strongly related to infants' noun comprehension and overall language competence. Didactic activities included actions such as pointing out objects, demonstrating how they worked, and elaborating on the properties of objects. Apparently, this makes it clear to toddlers that words stand for things. This didactic activity was accompanied by verbal social praise and encouragement. Purely social conversation does not have this effect, nor does the situation in which the toddler takes dominant control in initiating activities. Other research suggests that by the end of the second year, it is more effective if the mother switches to following the child's lead. In the area of skill at pretend play, frequent didactics combined with social interchanges were related to more pretend play skill. Mutual interaction seems to be more important than control in play skill development. The context for learning to pretend may be more casual than that for learning language. Much of the content of pretend play is learned through observation of everyday activities, such as talking on the phone and cooking.

Support for children's emerging understanding of reading and writing continues to be important during the toddler years (McGee & Richgels, 1996). The following are excerpts from a young child's toddler time literacy experiences and development (McGee & Richgels, pp. 41–42):

> By her first birthday, Kristen could hold a book right-side-up and turn the pages from front to back. Sometimes she smiled and patted the pictures or turned pages over from one side to the next, intently checking the pictures on each side of the page.

Kristen also showed an interest in coupons with familiar logos.

> A few months after her first birthday . . . She would . . . point to and ask "dat?" about animals and people pictured in her books.
>
> When Kristen was about sixteen months old, she began interrupting book reading by jumping off her father's lap to seek a toy or object in the house . . . . Each time Kristen saw a picture of crayons, for example, she would get up and find *her* crayons.
>
> At eighteen months of age, Kristen would sit by herself and look at her books, saying the name of some of the objects in the pictures while pointing at them. Kristen has several ABC books that she was particularly interested in at this time.

By age two, Kristen recognized some of her favorite logos, such as those that went with her favorite hamburger restaurants. She also began to pretend-read some of her favorite books. By age three, she was asking questions and making comments during book-reading sessions. McGee and Richgels summarized five important literacy-related concepts that Kristen learned during these early years (p. 42):

1. Literacy activities are pleasurable.
2. Literacy activities occur in predictable routines.
3. Language is an important part of reading and drawing.
4. Literacy materials are handled in special ways.
5. Literacy involves the use of symbols.
6. Literacy involves communicating meanings.

Children who have everyday book-sharing experiences are most likely to be good readers in first grade. With the appropriate language and literacy experiences, toddlers can learn that oral and written language are related (Language and literacy in the earliest years, 2004; Rosenquest, 2002). Toddlers need a variety of picture books and need to be actively involved when being read to (Jalongo, 2004). With toddlers, the adult reader should take time to let children point to and label the pictures. Toddler attention spans may be rather short so it is important to select appropriate books so that story time is a happy time that builds the motivation to read. Small reading groups (in contrast to the whole class) provide more opportunities for toddler verbal involvement through comments and questions and nonverbal involvement, such as pointing, handling books, being close to the teacher, interacting with peers, and pretending (Phillips & Twardosz, 2003).

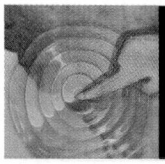

**LOOKING FURTHER**

Borrow some toddler-level books from your local public library. The librarian can help you find some appropriate books. Share the books with a one-year-old and a two-year-old. Note how they interact with you and with the books. Do they appear to have much book knowledge? That is, do they show evidence of the five things that Kristen learned during her first three years?

## SOCIOCULTURAL FACTORS

As suggested by Bronfenbrenner (1989, see Chapter 3), children need to be observed and interacted with in their communities, families, and peer groups. As described in Chapter 12, the importance of paying close attention to the growing cultural diversity in the United States is a major focus in the fields of early childhood education and development. Many risk factors are associated with poverty and are detrimental to brain growth and development (Shore, 1997). Risk factors, such as poor nutrition, lack of access to medical care, unsafe environments, family and caregiver stress, and the quality of care, predict poor school readiness and mental retardation.

Emergent literacy develops from book and other print experiences, from conversations, or from pretend play and narratives. Shared meaning is an important foundation for literacy (Howes & Wishard, 2004). When children play cooperatively they are acting out a story with its implicit narrative. When children tell stories, they are producing narratives. Pretend play narratives may be verbal or nonverbal. The important part is that the players share meaning. Howes and Wishard (2004) describe two Latino toddlers playing washing babies with no oral language but with obviously shared meaning as they go though the motions of washing, drying, wrapping, and rocking their babies. Examining the cultural setting, we can learn why the play is silent. Seven people live in a small house. The adults work different shifts so indoors the children must be quiet. They cannot go outside because the neighborhood is dangerous. These girls need some opportunity to play using oral language. Narrative development is connected to later literacy development. Through their pretend play and narratives children develop the concept of story that is important for reading comprehension. Young children need opportunities for unstructured play during which they can develop their pretend play stories. However, in assessing these experiences, the community cultural practices must be considered.

The study by Rogoff and Mosier (in Rogoff, Mistry, Goncu, & Mosier, 1993) described in Chapter 16 is a good example of contrasting toddler-parent interaction in two different cultures—a Mayan Indian town in Guatemala and a middle-class urban area in the United States. This study was part of a larger research project (Rogoff, Mistry, Goncu, & Mosier, 1993) that also included observations in a tribal village in India and a middle-class urban neighborhood in Turkey. In each culture, toddlers and caregivers developed a system of mutual collaboration for learning that included a shared understanding and adjustments to the partner's degree of and approach to involvement. Cultural variations centered on differing values and goals. Major community differences were whether children were segregated or integrated into adult activities. When segregated, caregivers had to be more formal in directly teaching, especially in the language area. Adults viewed the children as conversational partners. When children were integrated, they learned more on their own through observation with adult responsive assistance, but not planned direct instruction. The middle-class caregiver-toddler interactions were much like those in traditional school instruction. The authors suggest that non–middle-class children could benefit from having their parents learn some of the techniques that work so well at preparing middle-class children for school. On the other hand, middle-class parents and school personnel can benefit children by putting learning in a context in which children have to rely more on their own efforts and their own observational skills. In our country, we must be aware that children need to learn how to function in the majority culture without losing the values and customs of their primary culture.

Many children entering early childhood programs today have experienced very little exposure to language or exposure that is not very helpful in school. Each culture uses language in different ways. Okagaki and Diamond (2003) describe how American and Japanese mothers provide different emphasis in speaking to their infants. The Americans emphasized the names of objects while the Japanese mothers focused more on the interpersonal aspects of play (i.e., "Here is the car, I give it to you"). In English, we use terminology that may not make sense to people from other cultures. In working with second language learners, teachers must use lots of nonverbal communication, keep messages simple, emphasize the important words in the sentence, combine gestures with talk, and repeat key words (Tabors, 2003). Most importantly, families must be involved and teachers must respect the cultures of the families.

Consider the factors discussed in this chapter and in Chapters 15 and 16 regarding the toddler's physical and motor, affective, and cognitive development and the adult and cultural role with the toddler. Then analyze the following description of The Toddler Development Center.

Mrs. Sanchez discovered that there was a need for child care in her neighborhood for one- to three-year-old children. There were enough facilities for infants and a fine center for children three and older. She found an empty store in the neighborhood and converted it into The Toddler Development Center. With the help of others in the neighborhood, she was able to obtain help in remodeling the store and getting money to buy equipment. Some of the people in the neighborhood contributed their time and skills to build needed partitions, install new plumbing, and build play equipment. The big window in the front of the store was kept. The children can look out at the busy street, and the people in the neighborhood can look in. In back of the store, a former parking lot was converted into an outdoor play area.

A visit to the center finds the following activities in progress. As we enter, we find ourselves in a large area where several children are busy with large-muscle activity. Some are going up five steps and then sliding down a small slide. Others are crawling under the slide as if it were a tunnel. Some of the two-year-olds are loading big blocks in wagons, which they push or pull across the floor. A one-year-old is pulling a dog with wheels on a string. In the corner, there is a pile of cushions and pillows of many sizes. Some of the children are rolling and jumping on them, stacking them, and doing just about everything one could do with such materials.

Children go freely in and out of another room in the back, where there is quieter activity. In one area, three children are sitting on a rug working with simple form boards, puzzles, and bead stringing. One child has a big laundry basket full of small rubber balls. He has a number of containers that he fills with the balls and then pours into the laundry basket and fills again. Other activities available include working with play dough, paint and crayons, and paper and scissors. There is a corner at the back with a rug and some shelves filled with books. The sturdy cardboard books are on the lower shelves and the more delicate books on the higher shelves. The opposite side of the room has been designed as a small house. Neighbors have built a small stove, refrigerator, and sink from wood. There is a table with chairs and three cribs, also handmade. There are many rag dolls with clothes that can be put on and taken off. One of the teachers is having a pretend dinner that two of the children have made for her. Another child is feeding a "baby," which he finally tucks carefully into a crib.

One child reaches for another's play dough. The teacher in the area, Mr. Smith, notices and places a glob of play dough in the first child's hand, saying, "Here's some play dough for you, Charlie." Mr. Smith glances at the children playing with the puzzles and beads. He says, "You children are really working hard today." All the teachers give smiles, hugs, and pats on the head as they supervise the children's activities.

Some of the children are wearing diapers, while others are in training pants and some are in regular underpants. In the bathroom, there is a changing table, two small toilets, and two portable potty chairs. The staff appears to let each child proceed at his or her own pace in using the potty or toilet.

When one child falls down and scrapes his knee, several other children gather around as the teacher comforts him. One runs off and asks another teacher for a bandage while another child runs for a clean, damp cloth with which to wipe the "hurty."

There is quite a bit of talking going on. Sentences from the children range from word approximations such as "adoo" for "water," to "truck" as a child points to a toy he would like to use, to "more milk" at snack time.

## SUMMARY

During the toddler period, the child progresses from the sensorimotor to the preoperational stage of cognitive development. Representational thought appears, and the object concept develops. Object manipulation is the major activity for the toddler. Toddlers are learning about many concepts, such as size, shape, color, and space. The increasing ability to classify things into groups helps toddlers better organize what they know about the world. Their beginning representational play is their first use of symbols. They are developing problem-solving strategies and memory strategies. Toddlers learn a great deal through imitation and especially from observing demonstrations accompanied by a verbal explanation. Toddlerhood is a period when language skills develop rapidly. One-word sentences grow to four- or five-word sentences. At first, comprehension is ahead of expression but expressive language moves ahead during this period. The type of language used in social situations differs from that used in private speech when playing alone. Private speech assists the child in self-regulation of activities. The toddler's primitive level of thought is reflected in his or her language. Appropriate adult conversation is vital to language development. Adults serve as language models and as conversation partners. Oral language and pretend play are closely tied to the emergence of literacy. It is important to learn the language practices of each child's family and respect the practices of each culture.

## FOR FURTHER READING

Bardige, B. S., Segal, M. M. (2005). *Building literacy with love: A guide for teachers and caregivers of children birth through age 5*. Washington DC: Zero to Three.

Barrera, I. with Corso, R. M., & Macpherson, D. (2003). *Skilled dialogue: Strategies for responding to cultural diversity in early childhood*. Baltimore: Brookes.

Bus, A. G., Belsky, J., van IJendoorn, M. H., & Crnic, K. (1997). Attachment and bookreading patterns: A study of mothers, fathers and their toddlers. *Early Childhood Research Quarterly, 12*, 81–98.

Dupoux, E. (Ed.). (2001). *Language, brain, and cognitive development*. Cambridge, MA: MIT Press.

*Focus on Infants and Toddlers*. Quarterly newsletter of the Association for Childhood Education International, 17904 Georgia Avenue, Ste. 215, Olney, MD 20832.

Gelman, S. A., Coley, J. D., Rosengren, K. S., Hartman, E., & Pappas, A. (1998). Beyond labeling:

The role of maternal input in the acquisition of richly structured categories. *Monographs of the Society for Research in Child Development, 63* (1, Serial No. 253).

Goldin-Meadow, S. (2000). Beyond words: The importance of gesture to researchers and learners. *Child Development, 71*(1), 231–239.

Goswami, U. (Ed.). (2002). *Blackwell handbook of childhood cognitive development.* Williston, VT: Blackwell.

Gusati, M. T. (2002). *Language acquisition: The growth of grammar.* Cambridge, MA: MIT Press.

Holyoak, K. J., & Morrison, R. G. (Eds.). (2005). *The Cambridge handbook of thinking and reasoning.* New York: Cambridge University Press.

Iverson, J. M., & Goldin-Meadow, S. (Eds.). (1998). The nature and function of gesture in children's communication. *New Directions for Child Development, No. 79.* San Francisco: Jossey-Bass.

Johnson, M. H., Munakata, Y., & Gilmore, R. (Eds.). (2002). *Brain development and cognition.* Williston, VT: Blackwell.

Landau, B., Sabini, J., Jonides, J., & Newport, E. L. (Eds.). (2000). *Perception, cognition, and language.* Cambridge, MA: MIT Press.

Lynch, E. W., & Hanson, M. J. (Eds.). (2004). *Developing cross-cultural competence.* Baltimore: Brookes.

MacWhinney, B. (Ed.). (1999). *The emergence of language.* Mahwah, NJ: Erlbaum.

Mitchell, P., & Riggs, K. (2001). *Children's reasoning and the mind.* Philadelphia: Psychology Press.

Parlakian, R. (2003). *Before the ABCs: Promoting school readiness in infants and toddlers.* Herndon, VA: Zero to Three.

Rosenkoetter, S. E., & Knapp-Philo, J. (Eds.). (2004). *Learning to read the world: Language and literacy in the first three years.* Washington DC: Zero to Three.

Tryphon, A., & Voneche, J. (Eds.). (2001). *Working with Piaget: Essays in honour of Barbel Inhelder.* Philadelphia: Psychology Press.

Zentella, A. C. (1996). *Growing up bilingual: Children in elbarrio.* Cambridge, MA: Blackwell.

## SUGGESTED ACTIVITIES

1. Observe a toddler at home or at a child care site. Use the toddler cognitive and language assessment chart (Figure 17–5) to evaluate the toddler's developmental level and rate of development in the cognitive and language areas.
   a. Overall, does the toddler seem to be average, ahead of typical expectations, or slow in his or her rate of development?
   b. Are there any areas in which the toddler seems to be exceptionally ahead or behind in development?
   c. What kinds of suggestions do you have for the parents and/or caregiver regarding this toddler?
   d. Support all your conclusions and recommendations with data from your assessment chart.

2. Find a toddler between 12 and 16 months of age and one between 18 and 22 months of age. Compare their development of object permanence. Try the object permanence tasks and record their responses. With the younger child, start with part d of the second activity in Suggested Activities for Chapter 14. If the child succeeds through exercise f, proceed to the tasks that follow. Begin with exercise a of this activity for the older child. Compare the reactions of the two children. At which stage of object permanence would you place each of them? The following is a continuation of the object permanence task from the second Suggested Activity, part d, in Chapter 14.
   a. Object hidden in sequence in three hiding places.
      Find three different hiding places, such as a cloth, a box, and a hat. Have the child watch as you take a small familiar object (e.g., doll, car, cracker) and hide it first under one object; then move it between two objects. Move it under the next object, then between the two, and then under the third. Be sure the object is visible

Observer _____ Date _____ Time _____ Place _____

Infant's name _____ Birth date _____ Age _____

| Age Skill/Behavior | Observed Yes | Observed No | Comments |
|---|---|---|---|
| **One-Year-Old Cognitive** | | | |
| Enjoys playing object-hiding games | | | |
| Enjoys looking at picture books | | | |
| Recognizes objects that belong together (e.g., spoon in bowl) | | | |
| Names many everyday objects | | | |
| Begins to discriminate space and form—places objects in simple puzzles and form boards | | | |
| Places objects in a container and dumps them out | | | |
| **One-Year-Old Language** | | | |
| Produces jargon—words and sounds put together in speech-like patterns | | | |
| Uses holophrastic speech | | | |
| Follows simple directions | | | |
| Points to familiar objects when asked | | | |
| Identifies three body parts when named | | | |
| May have names for some objects and/or actions (doggie, bye-bye) | | | |
| Responds to simple questions with "yes" or "no" with appropriate head movement | | | |
| Speech is 25 to 50 percent understandable | | | |
| Uses 5 to 50 words | | | |
| Directs adult attention using gestures | | | |
| Enjoys rhymes and songs—joins in | | | |
| Seems to understand conversational exchange | | | |
| **Two-Year-Old Cognitive** | | | |
| May use objects as symbols of other objects (banana for phone) | | | |
| Completes simple classification tasks (e.g., dogs and cats) | | | |
| For self-selected tasks, attention span for increasing amounts of time | | | |
| Discovers cause and effect (squeeze cat, get scratched) | | | |
| Finds hidden object by looking in last hiding place first | | | |
| Receptive language ahead of expressive | | | |
| Names objects in picture books | | | |
| **Two-Year-Old Language** | | | |
| Enjoys being read to if allowed to participate by pointing, making relevant noises, turning pages | | | |

*(Continued)*

**FIGURE 17–5** Toddler cognitive-language development assessment chart.
(Adapted from Allen, K. D., & Marotz, L. R., 2003. *Developmental profiles: Pre-birth through twelve.* Clifton Park, NY: Delmar Learning).

| Age Skill/Behavior | Observed Yes | Observed No | Comments |
|---|---|---|---|
| Realizes can use language to get attention | | | |
| Uses 50 to 300 words—vocabulary increasing | | | |
| Receptive language is still ahead of expressive | | | |
| Uses telegraphic speech; begins to use conventional sentences | | | |
| Constructs negative statements by tacking on "no" or "not" ("no milk") | | | |
| Asks repeatedly, "What's that?" | | | |
| Uses some plurals | | | |
| Talks about objects or people not immediately in the environment | | | |
| May sometimes stammer, uses substitutions for some sounds, or uses other nonconventional speech | | | |
| Speech is 65 to 70 percent understandable | | | |

FIGURE 17–5 Continued

between hiding places. Leave it under the third hiding place. Note how the toddler goes about searching for the object. Repeat three times. If the toddler looks under the last hiding place first, he or she is ready to try a more difficult task.

The next problems involve searching under several screens placed on top of each other.

b. A favorite object hidden under three screens at the same time.
   Put three screens over the object, one at a time. Let the toddler search. If the toddler removes all the screens and finds the object, go on to the next task.
c. Object in a box with screens.
   Put the favorite object in a box with a lid that can be taken off easily. Put two cloths over the box, one at a time. Note how the child goes about the search. If the child searches until finding the object, go on to the next task.

The following problem involves the invisible hiding of an object.

d. Invisible hidden object.
   Put three cloths on a surface that will absorb sound. Use a small object that can be hidden in your hand. Hide the object in your hand. Be sure the toddler is watching. Hide your hand under each of the cloths, leaving the object under the third one. Be sure that the toddler cannot see the object when your hand is between each cloth. Show the toddler your empty hand. Observe while the toddler searches. Write down what the toddler does. Repeat two or three times. If the toddler looks directly under the last cloth and finds the object, repeat three times, hiding the object under a different cloth each time, but always putting your closed hand under each cloth in turn. If the toddler always starts with the last cloth and searches systematically in sequence, then he or she has achieved the final stage of object permanence.

**3.** Go to a store where young children's toys are sold. Make a list of toys that you think would be good for a toddler. Record the price of each. Make two toys from waste materials that would serve the same purposes but would cost less (see Watson, L. D., & Watson, M. A. [2003]. *Infants & toddlers curriculum and teaching* [5th ed.]. Clifton Park, NY: Delmar Learning.)

4. Do one of the following activities to get some firsthand information on toddler language development.

   a. Have at least three conversations with a two-year-old. Tape record the conversations each time. Later write down from the tape everything the child said. Label each sentence as holophrastic, telegraphic, or beyond telegraphic (i.e., complete sentences). Count how many of each you recorded. Using the information on language development from this chapter, describe and evaluate the child's level of language acquisition.
   b. Record on tape a conversation between a mother or father and a two-year-old. Try to get 20 to 30 minutes of talk. Transcribe the conversation later and label each of the parent's speech samples that involve prompting, echoing, or expansion. Count how many of each the parent uses. What does this tell you about the parent–child interaction? (Play dough, water, and sand are materials that the parent and child might use to produce conversation.)

5. Discuss the following language samples with a small group in class. Analyze it and decide what stage the child is in by labeling each part of the sample according to its developmental level. Decide whether the child is vocalizing appropriately for his or her age. On a sheet of large chart paper or newsprint or on the chalkboard, list the characteristics found for the sample. Compare your results with those of the other student groups. Note any differences and discuss them. Be sure to decide on the kind of role the adult takes in the samples.

   Mother and child are in the living room. Mother is trying to get child to speak. Child is 19 months old.

| **Mother** | **Child** |
|---|---|
| What's this? Where's your shoe? | |
| Where's your shoe? | my shoe |
| Shoe. Yes, shoe. | shoe |
| What's this? What's that? | ka |
| Car | ka ka |
| Another car, yes. | nother, ka, ka |
| What's this? | baby, muk |
| Milk, yes. Very good. | muk |
| Milk, yes. | digh digh digh |
| Let's look in here, Kate | |
| What's this? | bee |
| What are those? | kee |
| Key, key, yes. Hey, who is this guy? | |
| What is that? | beebee |
| Who is it? | beebee |
| Beebee (baby), yes. Let's see now. | |
| Let's look in here. | |
| Who is this? | kighkiki |
| A kitty, kitty, yes. | |

6. Put yourself in a toddler's place. Imagine you are behind a door gate looking out at a room full of interesting items. Describe what is in the room and how you might be feeling separated from the space around you. Write down what you have thought about and your reaction to taking the toddler point of view. Discuss your report with a small group in class.

7. Make an entry in your journal.

## REVIEW

**1.** Column I lists some concepts that the toddler is learning. Match the concepts with the behavioral incidents in Column II.

| Column I | Column II |
|---|---|
| a. size | 1. Maria Petey tries to put a square in a round space on a form board. |
| b. shape | 2. Josie says, "I have more cookies!" as she points to Nathan's cookies. |
| c. number | 3. Marnie tries to curl up in the laundry basket and finds that it is just the right size. |
| d. color | 4. David runs out into the snow without his mittens. Soon, he is back, crying that he is too cold. |
| e. comparisons | 5. Lisa finds she can pick up a tennis ball easily but a soccer ball is too big for her short arms. |
| f. space | 6. Nathan picks out all the blue crayons. |
| g. parts and wholes | 7. Alfredo is in the sandbox filling containers with sand. |
| h. volume | 8. Bonnie runs through the house in her pajamas shouting, "Bedtime!" |
| i. height | 9. Raymond chants under his breath, "One, two, three. One, two, three." |
| j. temperature | 10. Bonnie cuts her play dough into many small pieces. |
| k. time | 11. Marnie stands next to a tape measure that is glued on the wall and says, "Look! Marnie big girl!" |

**2.** Analyze, evaluate, and comment on each of the following examples of toddler behavior:

a. Maria, eighteen months old, is playing with an insert puzzle. She is trying to place a square shape in a circle space. She grunts as she pushes hard, not appearing to notice that she's trying to push the shape into the wrong space.

b. Two-year-old Kate has to put her teddy bear on the shelf while she eats lunch. During lunch, she often glances at the bear and at one point jumps up and runs over to look at it.

c. Mrs. Quan shows Lai how to use her new toy. Her demonstration is accompanied by an explanation. Mrs. Hopkins demonstrates the use of the same type of toy for Kate, but does it without any comments or explanation.

d. Two-and-a-half-year-old Kate's favorite doll is on the kitchen table just out of reach. She tries to stretch and reach it. Then she runs to the other side of the table and tries again. Next, she climbs on a chair and, leaning across, is able to grab the doll's leg and pull it toward her.

e. Lai, two-and-a-half, is observed retelling the story of *Goldilocks and the Three Bears* using puppets, toy dishes, her little chairs, and some boxes for beds.

f. Chan Mung, seventeen months old, refers to real and stuffed animal dogs as "doggie," to all vehicles as "car," and uses "up" to mean "pick me up," "get it off the shelf for me," and "plane in the sky."

g. Sam, thirteen months old, and his mother are playing with an assortment of toys. "Look at the truck, Sam," says his mother, pointing at a yellow dump truck. "You can carry your little blocks in the truck." "Your truck has four big wheels that run smoothly."

h. Two-year-old Amy sits quietly on the floor busily playing with her blocks. She stacks them up and knocks them down and then drops them one at a time into a plastic bowl. She then takes a large wooden spoon and stirs the blocks.

3. Analyze these toddler speech samples. For each sample, tell which stage the child is in and the importance of context in each case.
   a. "Daddy!"
   b. "Big girl!"
4. Put an *X* next to each statement below that is correct.
   a. ___ Toddler's speech development is ahead of comprehension.
   b. ___ It is expected that toddlers will use private speech when playing alone.
   c. ___ Toddler social speech includes a greater variety of language use than does private speech.
   d. ___ There is very little relationship between concept and language development.
5. For each of the following vocal samples, identify the developmental age/stage. Identify the semantic element, and evaluate whether the child is developing at a typical rate for his or her age.
   a. Kate, age two, holds her dolly tenderly, saying "hurty tummy, hurty tummy."
   b. Bobby, age seventeen months, says, "Doggy, bark!"
6. Evaluate each of the following examples:
   a. Two-year-old Juan sees a cat run across the yard. He says, "Wabbit! Wabbit!"
   b. Two-year-old Janie has a vocabulary that includes some of the following strange-sounding words:
      doy (joy)
      how (cow)
      du (duck)
      bear (bear)
      pea ba (peanut butter)
      see (sheep)
      hoay (horse)
      yellow (meow)
      boo (spoon)
      bamma (grandma)
7. Describe how oral language relates to the emergence of literacy during the toddler period.
8. Describe the sociocultural aspects of language development during toddlerhood.

## KEY TERMS LIST

deferred imitation
expressive speakers
holophrases
holophrastic stage
manipulation of objects
private speech
referential speakers
representational thinking
self-regulation
specifically language impaired (SLI)
strong nominals
strong relationals
telegraphic sentences

Additional resources for this chapter can be found on the Online Companion™ to accompany this text at http://www.earlychilded.delmar.com. Respond to "Time to Reflect" and "Looking Further" concepts, review various child development scenarios, and answer thought-provoking questions in the Critical Thinking Forum. Keep a daily journal by downloading the student journal available on this Web site. Complete the interactive matching exercises to reinforce concepts, and print out the child development assessment forms to use during your observation of development for children from birth to age eight. In addition, read the case studies on the Web site to reinforce the important concepts in each chapter, and take a look at the multitude of Web links that are available for student research on the Internet.

# SECTION V

## Physical and Motor Development: Ages Three Through Six

Chapters 12 and 15 highlighted the physical and motor development of infants and toddlers. In this section, we'll look at the physical and motor development of preschoolers (ages three through five) and kindergartners (ages five and six). As with younger children, physical development is influenced by nutrition, general health and health care, and living conditions. Motor skill development is also dependent on physical development, health, and nutrition. In this section, physical development will be examined first, followed by motor skills development.

First, let's look at a four-year-old whose mother is very health conscious. Summer's mother is a vegetarian and is very concerned about having a low-fat, nutritious diet. Summer eats no meat, but obtains her protein from other foods, such as tofu products. She has whole wheat bread, pasta, rice, fruits, and vegetables. The family is fortunate to have health insurance so her mom had regular prenatal checkups and Summer has had her regular checkups and inoculations. Summer loves her pediatrician who is very caring, and she is always excited that he gives her stickers at each visit.

From ages three to six, children develop increased skill and control in the motor area. For example,

> The adult writes three-year-old Polly's name on a piece of paper explaining that it is her name. Polly looks at it carefully and then draws curly lines on the paper as if writing letters. She appears to be copying her name. She then asks the adult, "Is A, B, huh?" "Is A, B, huh?"
>
> Miguel is a kindergartner. He is sitting at a table that is littered with crayons and blank sheets of paper. He carefully selects a green crayon and begins drawing. When he is finished, he carefully prints his name from left to right at the bottom of the page. He spelled it correctly with a capital letter *M* and the rest lowercase.

These examples illustrate the growth in fine motor skills from age three to age five. Gross motor skills also show development as illustrated in the examples that follow.

Four-year-old John is playing soccer. It is his turn to join the game. He anxiously pursues the ball ahead of the other children. He moves the ball toward the goal line with his little legs making short, swift kicks. He dribbles down the field not noticing that he has passed the goal and is running out of bounds.

Kurt and Carlos are both five years old and are in the same kindergarten class. They are both enjoying jumping on the trampoline. They are playing a game where they each take a turn to do a trick, such as a flip, somersault, land on your knees, etc. After one does a particular trick, then the other has to do that trick plus add on a new trick.

In the following chapters, the factors that underlie physical growth and motor skills development are examined.

CHAPTER

# 18

# Physical Development, Health, Safety and Nutrition: Ages Three to Six

## OBJECTIVES

After reading this chapter, you should be able to:

- Use a growth chart to determine whether a child's height, weight, and body proportions are within the normal range.
- Discuss the effects of a good diet and good health care on a child who has suffered malnutrition.
- Evaluate the nutritional appropriateness of a diet using the USDA MyPyramid guidelines.
- List the health and nutrition problems that low-income children may have when they enter school.
- Assess safety factors for young children.
- Evaluate situations involving adults' and childrens' attitudes toward physical activity, illness, and nutrition.
- Describe the basic parts of a nutrition, health, and safety education program for young children.

In Chapter 12, the highlights of infant health and nutrition were described. Also described were the principles of growth and the relationship of physical and motor development. Toddler nutrition and health were discussed in Chapter 15. In this chapter, we move ahead to the preschool/kindergarten period and the areas of physical development, health, nutrition, safety, and health education.

## PHYSICAL DEVELOPMENT

**misnourished children**

Children who get enough to eat, but their diets do not provide proper necessary nutrients.

Marcon (2003) reviewed the research on the physical development of young children. In her review, she links physical development to cognitive and social development. She points out that in the United States we have many **misnourished children.** That is, children get enough to eat, but their diets o not provide proper necessary nutrients. As children get older, their diets get worse. More two- through five-year-olds (27 percent) have good diets as compared to children ages six through nine (13 percent). An insufficient diet has negative effects on physical development, cognitive development, and social development. Marcon (2003) describes how height-for-age and weight-for-age are indicators of not only physical maturity but also cognitive maturity. Children who are at the bottom of their age group in height are also likely to be behind in cognitive development and academic achievement. Weight-for-height links with "intellectual development, cognitive reasoning, and attention" (Marcon, 2003, p. 82). Poverty affects children's nutrition, physical growth status, and cognitive development. These interrelationships are very complex. Nutritional supplements alone do not solve the cognitive deficit problems. Health care improvements, tutoring, and improvement of family living conditions are also needed. Socially undernourished children may be too weak to engage in the active play that is essential to children's growth and development. They may miss out on social as well as motoric experiences. Figures 18–1 and 18–2 provide growth charts for boys and girls ages two to twenty.

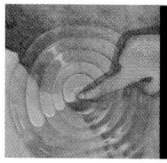

**LOOKING FURTHER**

Get together with a group of four or five other students. Each of you weigh and measure several young children ages three to five. Divide the information obtained into three groups: three-year-olds, four-year-olds, and five-year-olds. Add the heights and the weights of each group and divide by the number of children in each group to get the average height and weight. Compare your group's data with the charts in Figures 18–1 and 18–2.

## HEALTH

During the preschool/kindergarten period, children should gradually become more proportional in height and weight if they receive proper nutrition. Marotz, Cross, and Rush (2005) suggest that adults who work with young children should observe daily for any signs of health problems. For example, any of the following should be noted (Marotz, Cross, & Rush, 2005):

- General appearance: sudden weight loss, signs of fatigue, pale or flushed skin tone
- Head lice, hair loss, unclean hair
- Red eyes, tearing, or drainage
- Hearing, ear drainage
- Nose drainage
- Cavities, mouth sores
- Sudden behavior change

Many conditions may affect the health of young children. Examples are allergies (Marotz, Cross, and Rush, 2005; Holland, 2004), lead poisoning (Mulroy, Bothell, & Gaudio, 2004), asthma (Getch & Neuharth-Pritchett, 2004), diabetes (French, 2004; Marotz, Cross, & Rush, 2005) eczema, fatigue, seizure disorders, sickle cell anemia, colds and viruses (Marotz, Cross, & Rush, 2005). Washing hands is the best weapon against the spread of infectious disease and brushing teeth daily is essential to dental health (Aronson, 2002).

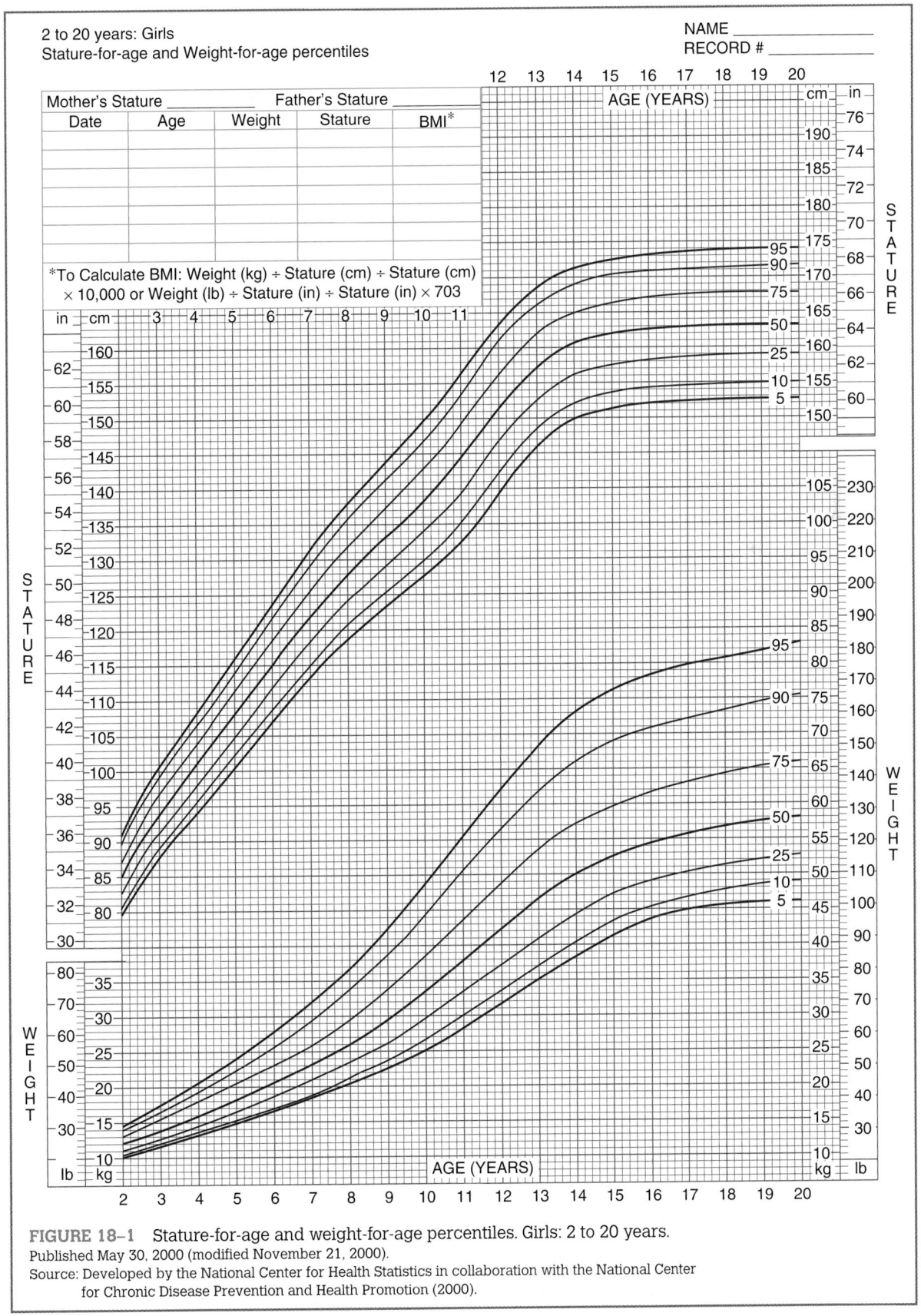


**FIGURE 18–1** Stature-for-age and weight-for-age percentiles. Girls: 2 to 20 years.
Published May 30, 2000 (modified November 21, 2000).
Source: Developed by the National Center for Health Statistics in collaboration with the National Center for Chronic Disease Prevention and Health Promotion (2000).

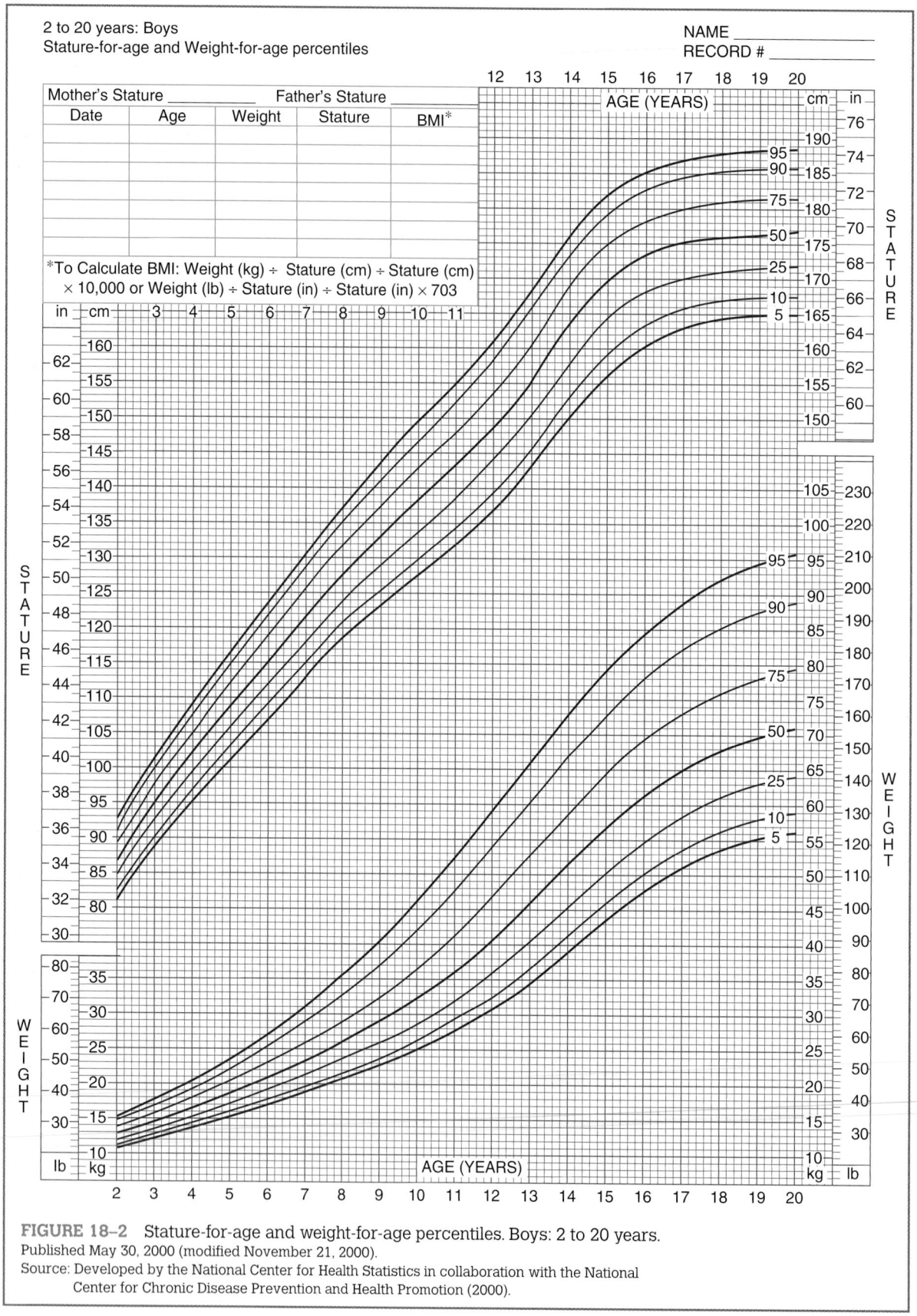


**FIGURE 18–2** Stature-for-age and weight-for-age percentiles. Boys: 2 to 20 years.
Published May 30, 2000 (modified November 21, 2000).
Source: Developed by the National Center for Health Statistics in collaboration with the National Center for Chronic Disease Prevention and Health Promotion (2000).

## Physical Fitness

Children's physical fitness is of great concern. Adults are watching their diets, running or walking regularly, and enrolling in formal exercise and fitness programs. Children, on the other hand, are being neglected (Huettig, Sanborn, DiMarco, Popejoy, & Rich, 2004). The trend toward more sit still programs for young children is increasing the prevalence of obesity. Although free-play time outdoors is not adequate, because obese children are not likely to be very active, at least they have the opportunity for some physical activity. The opportunity for motor activity has disappeared from many early childhood programs. According to Sutterby & Frost (2002, p. 37), "vigorous physical activity is much more effective than dieting in preventing and combating obesity." Outdoors is the major area for this activity and well-designed playgrounds are essential (Sutterby & Frost, 2002). Playgrounds should be designed to include children with disabilities (Flynn & Kieff, 2002). They should be modified to provide safe and valuable physical activity for children with all types of disabilities, such as visual impairments, hearing impairments, physical challenges, autism, or cognitive delays.

**physical activity play**

"A playful context combined with a dimension of physical vigor" (Pellegrini & Smith, 1998, p. 577).

**exercise play**

Gross motor movements within the context of play activity.

**rough-and-tumble play**

Happy activity; not aggressive or hostile; includes play fighting, smiling, and jumping.

Remember that play is the major vehicle through which young children learn. Pellegrini and Smith (1998) reviewed the research on **physical activity play.** They define physical activity play "as a playful context combined with a dimension of physical vigor" (p. 577). Specific examples of such activities include running, climbing, chasing, and play fighting. Smith and Pellegrini believe that physical activity play has immediate benefits for children in relation to physical, cognitive, and social development. During infancy, children engage in repeated gross motor movements such as kicking their feet and rocking their bodies. During the preschool years, children engage in **exercise play,** that is, gross motor movements within the context of their play activity. Vigorous activity distinguishes this type of play. It begins around the end of the first year when children are able to move about at will, peaks around four or five years of age, and gradually declines during the primary grades. It may include running, fleeing, wrestling, chasing, jumping, pushing and pulling, lifting, and climbing, and it may be either solitary or social. During the primary grades, children, especially boys, increasingly engage in **rough-and-tumble play.** This behavior is extremely vigorous and may include wrestling, grappling, kicking, and tumbling. The play appears to be aggressive but is characterized by a playful kind of social interaction.

Pellegrini and Smith (1998) suggest that physical activity play serves some important functions for young children. They believe that there are benefits not only for physical development but also for cognitive and social development. For infants, physical activity play improves specific motor patterns. For all young children, it may aid muscle development and general fitness and endurance. Exercise play may serve an adaptive function in the cognitive area.

## Mental Health

According to Burke and Myers (2002) one in ten U.S. children and adolescents suffers from some type of mental illness that impairs his or her functioning, only one in five receives any mental health services, including any type of special education. While teachers are not trained as psychotherapists, they can provide **relationships.** That is, teachers can provide a nurturing relationship and atmosphere that integrates education and mental health. Children need an atmosphere where they can express their feelings and act them out through creative activities, such as dramatic play, art, music, and movement.

**relationship**

Teachers can provide a nurturing relationship and atmosphere.

According to Marotz, Cross, and Rush (2005), a classroom atmosphere that is warm and nurturing contributes to young children's positive mental health. A developmentally appropriate curriculum promotes success and a positive self-concept. An inappropriate curriculum can cause stress. Research by Burts, Hart, Charlesworth, and Kirk (1990); Burts, Hart, Charlesworth, Fleege, Mosley, and Thommason (1992); and Hart, Burts, Durland, Charlesworth, DeWolf, and Fleege (1998) indicates that in some kindergartens, developmentally inappropriate instructional practices are used, such as having students sit still for long periods in large group activities and/or doing workbook or worksheet activities with a focus on abstract concepts, such as learning numerals, the alphabet, and phonics out of context. When these practices are the major means of instruction, significantly more stress behaviors are observed than in kindergartens where developmentally appropriate practices are used, such as limiting the time spent in large group activities, allowing students to move about the room, and using concrete materials rather than abstract ones. A further danger to young children's mental health is the use of paper-and-pencil standardized achievement tests. Fleege, Charlesworth, Burts, and Hart (1992) observed kindergarten students before, during, and after standardized testing sessions. The frequency of observed stress behaviors increased significantly during the testing period.

Stress can affect children's mental well-being. Stress may result from experiences such as separation from parents, moving, being placed in a child care center, mother taking a job, birth of sibling, getting a new teacher, hospitalization, parents' divorce, death of a pet or a relative, confrontations, or a hectic schedule (Marotz, Cross, & Rush 2005). Poverty and homelessness can also add to family and, thus, children's stress. According to Marotz, Cross, and Rush (2005, p. 43) "Competent parenting is, beyond a doubt, the most important and critical factor in helping children manage adversity and avoid its potentially damaging consequences."

Thinking back to your early years, can you recall any stressful events that you experienced? How did you cope? Share your experiences with two or three other students in your class.

## NUTRITION

**nutrition**
"The science of food and how it is used by the body" (Endres and Rockwell, 1994, p. 1).

"**Nutrition** is the science of food and how it is used by the body" (Endres and Rockwell, 1994, p. 1). Determining which nutrients enter the body is tied in with social, economic, cultural, and psychological factors associated with eating. Young children need foods that provide nutrients for growth and energy (Marotz, Rush, & Cross, 2005). Foods are needed from all groups (U.S. Department of Agriculture, Center for Nutrition Policy and Promotion, April 2005, available at http://www.mypyramid.gov):

- Vegetables, emphasize dark-green, such as broccoli and spinach
- Meats and beans, should be low-fat or lean meats and poultry varied with fish, beans, peas, nuts, and seeds
- Grains, at least half whole grains
- Fruits, eat a variety
- Milk, low-fat or fat-free milk, yogurt, and other milk products
- Watch calories and exercise daily

Figure 18–3 depicts the 2005 Food Pyramid.

# Anatomy of MyPyramid

**One size doesn't fit all**
USDA's new MyPyramid symbolizes a personalized approach to healthy eating and physical activity. The symbol has been designed to be simple. It has been developed to remind consumers to make healthy food choices and to be active every day. The different parts of the symbol are described below.

**Activity**
Activity is represented by the steps and the person climbing them, as a reminder of the importance of daily physical activity.

**Moderation**
Moderation is represented by the narrowing of each food group from bottom to top. The wider base stands for foods with little or no solid fats or added sugars. These should be selected more often. The narrower top area stands for foods containing more added sugars and solid fats. The more active you are, the more of these foods can fit into your diet.

**Personalization**
Personalization is shown by the person on the steps, the slogan, and the URL. Find the kinds and amounts of food to eat each day at MyPyramid.gov.

MyPyramid.gov
STEPS TO A HEALTHIER YOU

**Proportionality**
Proportionality is shown by the different widths of the food group bands. The widths suggest how much food a person should choose from each group. The widths are just a general guide, not exact proportions. Check the Web site for how much is right for you.

**Variety**
Variety is symbolized by the 6 color bands representing the 5 food groups of the Pyramid and oils. This illustrates that foods from all groups are needed each day for good health.

**Gradual Improvement**
Gradual improvement is encouraged by the slogan. It suggests that individuals can benefit from taking small steps to improve their diet and lifestyle each day.

USDA U.S. Department of Agriculture
Center for Nutrition Policy and Promotion
April 2005 CNPP-16

*USDA is an equal opportunity provider and employer.*

| GRAINS | VEGETABLES | FRUITS | MILK | MEAT & BEANS |
|---|---|---|---|---|

**FIGURE 18–3** Anatomy of MyPyramid.
U.S. Department of Agriculture Center for Nutrition Policy and Promotion.

FIGURE 18–4 After lunch, preschoolers scrape their dishes and put them in the dirty dishes tubs.

Other cultures favor different food groupings that fit their tastes and local food products. The Web site of the Southeastern Michigan Dietetic Association (SEMDA) includes a number of culturally relevant food guides, such as Arab, Chinese, Mexican, Cuban, Native American, and Indian. For more information, visit http://www.semda.org.

To be most effective, supplemental nutritional help must be available as early as possible. The effects of poor nutrition show up in early infancy in weight, length, and cognitive performance (Rose, 1994). This does not mean that food provided after age six does not have a positive effect. Although previous damage cannot be corrected, further damage can be avoided. The best procedure, however, is to provide adequate nutrition from the beginning.

A study done by Pollitt, Gorman, Engle, Martorell, and Rivera (1993) followed children into adolescence who were given supplemental nutrition from birth to seven years of age. Compared with children who had a minimal supplement and those who had none, the adolescents who had received the supplement from birth through age seven performed significantly better on a number of cognitive tasks. These results support the long-term benefits of early supplemental nutrition.

As evident in the Super et al. (1990) study and a study by Grantham-McGregor, Powell, Walker, Chang, and Fletcher (1994), it is difficult to separate the effects of malnutrition and sensory deprivation because the two often go hand in hand. Programs that provide both food and sensory stimulation are the most effective. Furthermore, it is important to keep in mind that the general health environment is also important. Children who live in poverty are often living in crowded housing with poor sanitation and may not have easy access to the best medical care.

Pollitt et al. (1996), members of an international task force on nutrition and behavioral development, concluded after reviewing the available research that the effects of undernutrition on child development are part of a larger picture. Undernutrition is only one contributor; poor social and environmental conditions are also related to depressed cognitive development. Undernourished individuals have a greater chance of exposure to additional risk factors, such as infection and lead exposure, child neglect, poor-quality schools, parental underemployment, and lack of access to medical care. To reduce the prevalence of reduced cognitive competence associated with undernutrition, the basic problems associated with poverty must also be alleviated.

## Obesity

The problem of poor eating habits, lack of physical activity, and resulting obesity was discussed in Chapter 15. Ten percent of children ages two to six in the United States are overweight (Lynn-Garbe & Hoot, 2004/2005). Obese children are more likely to suffer serious lifelong health problems, such as high blood pressure and high cholesterol levels, type 2 diabetes, and orthopedic problems due to extra stress on weight-bearing joints (Lynn-Garbe & Hoot, 2004/2005). Psychosocial problems may also result when children are teased and rejected by their peers.

Obesity probably results from a combination of genetic and environmental factors (Lynn-Garbe & Hoot, 2004/2005). Meals at home, in restaurants, and at school tend to be high in fat. In classrooms, candy is often used as an incentive and as teaching material (such as sorting and counting candies). Along with lack of nutritious foods, children are less physically active. Motor development and physical activity will be discussed in Chapters 19 and 29.

## SAFETY

Preschoolers spend time in out-of-home care and in the outdoors, where they can be exposed to different hazards. Public schools may be built on undesirable land, such as old industrial or landfill sites. Heavier chemicals, such as mercury and radon, are found closer to the floor. Proportionate to their size, infants and young children consume much more liquid than adults and are, therefore, more likely to suffer the effects of lead in tap water. Biologically hazardous substances can be absorbed through the placenta by the fetus, through the skin, through the respiratory tract, and/or through the digestive tract. Overall, infants and young children are most vulnerable to environmental hazards.

Safety education is important for both parents and students. Parents can become involved in safety education through newsletters, parent meetings, observations, class participation, assistance with field trips, and the presentation of programs themselves (Marotz et al., 2005). Children need to know the rules and regulations for the use of equipment and materials and the rationale for the rules and regulations. Units on safety can include a focus on occupations that protect us, such as firefighters, police officers, and medical personnel. Young children can also learn about bicycle/tricycle safety, pedestrian safety, vehicle safety restraints, dangerous substances, and home safety (Marotz et al., 2005).

Maria and Antonio are planning to enroll their three-year-old son, Tony, Jr., in a child care facility. They are concerned about the environmental hazards he might be exposed to. Help them by providing a set of questions they should ask and observations they should make as they investigate potential child care homes and centers.

## NUTRITION AND HEALTH EDUCATION

Once typical eating patterns are understood and necessary foods for young children are identified, the next step is to educate both children and parents regarding these factors. Furthermore, in schools for low-income children, whether full-day or part-day programs, supplemental food may be served to the children. This supplement may include just snacks or one or more meals.

National attention has been drawn to nutrition and the necessity of nutrition education for teachers, parents, and children. Research has shown that young children are capable of learning the basic concepts of good nutrition (Paguio & Resurreccion, 1987). Marilyn Church (1979) at the University of Maryland Center for Young Children performed one such study. The children were pretested regarding their food preferences. Following the pretest, a program of nutrition education that involved children and parents was carried out. The purpose of the program was to increase the children's and parents' knowledge about foods and to broaden the children's food choices. After the program, the children were tested again. It was found

FIGURE 18–5 Children feel competent when they can feed themselves.

that their food knowledge had increased significantly. There was also a trend toward broader food selection. The researchers found some incidental reactions, such as:

> Children seemed to take a genuine interest in new foods and enthusiastically participated in their preparation. Mothers were pleased and surprised to see results in the child's actions at home. (Children actually asked for asparagus and ate broccoli!) (Church, 1979, p. 64).

Children were observed talking about food during their play activities. They also often asked the teachers if particular foods were good for them.

Church concluded that young children definitely are capable of acquiring new knowledge and attitudes regarding food. She suggests that programs for young children should include multisensory experiences that involve children in looking at, tasting, touching, preparing, and eating a variety of foods (Figures 18–4 and 18–5). In addition, games, films, books, and trips should support food experiences. Charlesworth and Lind (2006, Units 22, 26, and 37) provide examples of ways food experiences can be integrated into the early childhood curriculum through dramatic play, math, science, and social studies activities. Children especially enjoy participating in preparing food, studying food sources, tasting foods, or reading about foods from different cultures.

Fuhr and Barclay (1998) point out that nutrition education should be consistent and in harmony with parents' desires for their children. Family food preferences and eating patterns need to be considered. Fuhr and Barclay provide several integrated nutrition units, including lists of food-related children's books. Information can be found online at www.kidshealth.org.

The basic concepts of health, hygiene, and safety can also be learned by young children. Nutrition education contributes to knowledge about healthful living. In addition, young children can learn basic health habits and routines, such as brushing teeth, hand washing, bathing, toileting, and dressing appropriately for the weather. Hand washing is especially critical (Figure 18–6). Germs can be spread from dirty or poorly washed hands. Young children can learn appropriate hand-washing procedures. They can also perform scientific investigations that demonstrate that hands carry germs. For example, Charlesworth and Lind (2006, Unit 37) outline an investigation using two peeled potatoes. A child who has not washed his or her hands for several hours handles one potato, which is then put in a jar labeled "unwashed hands." Another child washes his or her hands, handles the second potato, and puts it in a jar labeled "washed hands." The children then observe the day-by-day physical changes that take place.

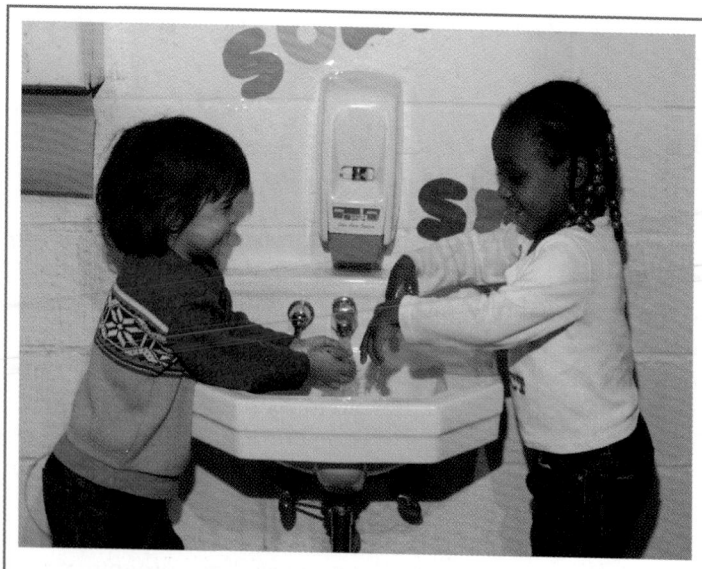

FIGURE 18–6 With a sink at their level, children can wash their hands independently.

Considering the status of health, safety, and nutrition for young children in this country, create a plan for educational programs for children and families. What would be your rationale for implementing these educational programs? What reasons could you provide to legislators and others to obtain financial and community support?

## SUMMARY

Good health and nutrition are basic to proper physical development, as well as to cognitive and affective growth. The growth rate of the preschool child slows down after the rapid pace of the prenatal and infant periods. Concerns about a child's size compared to others of the same age are quickly answered through careful measurement of height and weight and comparison of the results with U.S. government height and weight charts.

Adults are responsible for providing young children with an environment that is safe from hazards that may cause illness or injury. Children need ample opportunities for physical activity play. Life is too sedentary for young children today. Physical fitness is important, but physical education programs should be developmentally appropriate

The USDA MyPyramid food pyramid provides a guide for good nutrition. During pregnancy, infancy, and early childhood, food supplements in combination with cognitive stimulation can improve the prognosis for good physical health and cognitive growth in future years for children who live in poverty.

The child who is malnourished or in poor physical health because of illness or disease cannot function either physically or mentally to capacity. The adult who works with young children needs to be well informed regarding nutrition and other health facts. The adult also needs to be involved in nutrition and health education for the whole family.

## FOR FURTHER READING

American Academy of Pediatrics. (2005). *Health in child care: A manual for health professionals* (4th ed.). Elk Grove Village, IL: Author.

Aronson. S. S., & Shope, T. R. (Eds.). (2005). *Managing infectious diseases in child care and schools*. Elk Grove Village, IL: American Academy of Pediatrics.

Baxter, P. S. (Ed.). (2002). *Vitamin-responsive conditions in pediatric neurology*. Cambridge, UK: Cambridge University Press.

Beaty, J. J. (2004). *Safety in preschool programs*. Columbus, OH: Merrill.

Burke, R. W., & Myers, B. K. (2002). Our crisis in children's mental health [Theme issue]. *Childhood Education, 78*(5).

Caldwell, W., & Kimball, C. T. (Eds.). (2001). *Obesity sourcebook*. Holmes, PA: Omnigraphics.

DelCarmen-Wiggins, R. & Carter, A. S. (Eds.). (2004). *Handbook of infant, toddler, and preschool mental health assessment*. New York: Oxford University Press.

Donatelle, R. (2005). *Health: The basics* (6th ed.). San Francisco: Pearson.

Endres, J. (2004). *Food, nutrition, and the young child* (5th ed.). Columbus, OH: Merrill.

Frost, J. L., Brown, P., Sutterby, J. A., & Thornton, C. D. (2004). *The developmental benefits of playgrounds*. Olney, MD: Association for Childhood Education International.

Kimball, C. T. (Ed.). (2003). *Childhood diseases & disorders sourcebook*. Holmes, PA: Omnigraphics.

Kimball, C. T. (Ed.). (2003). *Healthy child sourcebook*. Holmes, PA: Omnigraphics.

Let's go outside! [Focus section]. (2002). *Young Children, 57*(3), 8–42.

Roberts, M. C. (Ed.). (2003). *Handbook of pediatric psychology* (3rd ed.). New York: Guilford.

Ryff, C. D., & Singer, B. (Eds.). (2001). *Emotion, social relationships and health*. New York: Oxford University Press.

Thompson, J., & Manore, M. (2005). *Nutrition: An applied approach*. San Francisco: Pearson.

Unintentional injuries in childhood. (2000). *The Future of Children* [Focus issue], *10*(1).

Vaca, J. J. (2001). Dealing with aftermath: Helping young children with posttraumatic stress disorder (PTSD). *Dimensions, 29*(3), 18–24.

## SUGGESTED ACTIVITIES

**1.** Follow one or more three- to six-year-olds through the day, keeping a record of what they eat. Evaluate their daily food intake. Did they eat foods in the recommended food groups? Did they eat fatty or high-cholesterol foods? Did they eat foods with high levels of sugar or sodium?

**2.** Keep a record of your food intake for a week. Go to http://www.mypramid.gov and click on Tracker. You can assess both your food intake and your physical activity online. Share your results with the rest of the class.

**3a.** Visit four or more child care centers or preschools where children are fed at least one meal each day. Try to divide your visits between centers and schools that serve lower and middle/upper economic level populations. Interview the directors/principals/teachers regarding their nutrition program. Record the date, the name of the school/center, the type of school/center (i.e., publicly or privately funded, provides child care), and the number of enrolled children five or under. Some questions you might ask include the following:

1. Does your school serve breakfast? Snacks? Lunch? If so, how are the meals financed?
2. Who plans the menus? Purchases the food ingredients? Prepares the food? What are their qualifications? Can you give me a copy of your menus for the week?
3. Are the children ever involved in any of the food planning and preparation? If so, how?
4. Is nutrition education included in your curriculum? If so, what major concepts do you teach? Can you give me some examples of learning activities that you use? Have your students provided you with any evidence of change due to your program (e.g., increased attendance, more alert behavior, more knowledge about food and nutrition, trying a wider variety of foods)?
5. Do you include any nutrition education in your parent education program? If so, describe what you do. What is the parent response?

**3b.** Summarize the results from your interview(s).

**3c.** Do you believe the programs have good nutrition education components? If not, what do you think are the weaknesses? What improvements could be made?

**4a.** Interview four parents of three- to six-year-old children. Find out what kind of health care they have for their child(ren) and themselves. Use the following questions and any others you think would be of interest.

1. Record the date, the child's name and age, and the person interviewed (e.g., mother, father).
2. Think back. Can you remember when you began prenatal care with *(child's name)?* Did you have a private obstetrician or did you go to a clinic?
3. Since your child was born, do you go to a family physician, a pediatrician, or a clinic? Do you take your child(ren) for regular checkups or just when ill? Have you found that medical care for your child(ren) has been convenient, reasonably priced, and competent? Do you think your child has had the personal attention he or she should have?
4. What about medical care for yourself? Do you get a yearly physical or just see a doctor when you are ill? Do you have a personal physician or use a rotating staff of physicians? Do you think your available health care is convenient, reasonable, and competent? Would you make any changes if you could?

**4b.** Summarize the information from your interview(s).

**4c.** Does medical care seem to be adequate for the families from whom you obtained information? If not, what seems to be the problem?

**5.** Measure the height and weight of at least 10 children. Then graph your findings and compare with the height and weight charts in this text.

**6.** Make an entry in your journal.

## REVIEW

**1.** For each of the following examples, use the growth charts in Figures 18–1 and 18–2 to find each child's percentile rank on height and weight. Decide whether each child is normal, heavy, thin, short, or tall compared with other children of the same age. Describe the child's proportions.

| | |
|---|---|
| a. Kate is four years of age. | Her height is 35 inches.<br>Her weight is 30 pounds. |
| b. Jason is five years of age. | His height is 43 inches.<br>His weight is 45 pounds. |
| c. Rudy is three years of age. | His height is 41 inches.<br>His weight is 43 pounds. |

**2.** Evaluate the following situation in terms of the safety factors discussed in this chapter. The kindergartners at John Dewey Elementary School share playground facilities with the first and second graders. Equipment consists of wooden seat swings, a 10-foot-high jungle gym, and a 12-foot-high slide. The playground is surfaced with asphalt. There are a total of 125 children in five kindergartens. Two or three classes use the playground at the same time and are supervised by one or two teacher aides.

**3.** A young child is malnourished during the prenatal period and infancy but is then given a proper diet. Predict what will happen in terms of his or her height and weight, school achievement, and IQ scores.

**4.** List the health and nutrition problems that low-income child might have when he or she enters school.

**5.** Evaluate the following situations and/or comments:

a. "It doesn't matter what the child eats as long as he eats a lot."
b. The children's dining room is noisy. Adults are yelling at children, "Watch what you are doing!" "Don't spill your food!" "Eat what's on your plate!"
c. It does not matter if a basically well-nourished child is over- or underweight. It will not affect school performance.
d. Although adults are concerned with their own physical fitness, children have been ignored.
e. Most child care providers are knowledgeable about health, safety, and nutrition.
f. Young children do not need mental health care. They are too young to have emotional or social problems.
g. The USDA Food Guide Pyramid is equally applicable to all cultures.
h. Undernutrition is one part of the poverty problem, which includes factors such as poor housing, lack of proper medical care, poor schools, child neglect, and parental underemployment.
i. It is extremely important to provide children with physical activity, especially in well-designed outdoor environments.
j. Playgrounds should provide opportunities for children with special needs.
k. Teachers can provide positive relationships for children and adolescents who suffer from some type of mental illness.

## KEY TERMS LIST

exercise play
misnourished children
nutrition
physical activity play
rough-and-tumble play
relationship

Additional resources for this chapter can be found on the Online Companion™ to accompany this text at http://www.earlychilded.delmar.com. Respond to "Time to Reflect" and "Looking Further" concepts, review various child development scenarios, and answer thought-provoking questions in the Critical Thinking Forum. Keep a daily journal by downloading the student journal available on this Web site. Complete the interactive matching exercises to reinforce concepts, and print out the child development assessment forms to use during your observation of development for children from birth to age eight. In addition, read the case studies on the Web site to reinforce the important concepts in each chapter, and take a look at the multitude of Web links that are available for student research on the Internet.

CHAPTER

# 19

# Motor Development: Ages Three to Six

## OBJECTIVES

After reading this chapter, you should be able to:

- Recognize the phases in an appropriate movement pattern sequence.
- Describe how to support fundamental motor development.
- Recognize the important values of outdoor and playground play.
- Evaluate children's progress in gross motor development.
- Analyze and evaluate a child's readiness for formal handwriting lessons.
- Recognize the developmental sequence for drawing.
- Explain why assessing the young child's motor skills is important.
- Describe how the young child learns motor skills.
- Identify examples of typical and atypical motor development.

As already described in Chapters 12 and 15, the development of motor skills is closely aligned with physical growth. As the body grows physically, muscles develop and mature, and the child is able to perform new motor acts. The preschool/kindergarten period is a time when differentiation of the various parts of the body is completed and integration becomes the primary focus. By age six, children begin to integrate movements because they arrive at a point where they can cognitively think about coordinating two or more movements, such as running and throwing or kicking a ball, tap dancing and twirling a baton, or twirling a rope and jumping over it. Preschoolers are not ready to engage in games with rules. For example, Dave Barry (November, 2004, 1D) describes his four-year-old daughter's soccer team game rules:

1. You're supposed to kick the balls.
2. You're not supposed to pick up the ball.
3. Even if you really want to pick up the ball, you're not supposed to.
4. Have to go potty, try to wait for a water break instead of just trotting off the field.
5. It can be hard to remember this sometimes, but DON'T PICK UP THE BALL, OK?

For the most part, the girls hug each other and run around randomly.

## GROSS MOTOR DEVELOPMENT: PRESCHOOL THROUGH KINDERGARTEN

**fundamental motor skills**

The foundation for more specialized motor skills that will be learned when the child is older.

**specialized movements**

Individual skills developed according to each person's particular needs and interests.

Beginning in the toddler period and extending through about age seven, fundamental motor skills develop. These skills include "locomotor skills such as running, jumping, hopping, galloping and skipping, and object control skills such as throwing, catching, striking, kicking and dribbling" (Burton, 1992, p. 3). These **fundamental motor skills** are learned by everyone and serve as the foundation for more specialized motor skills that will be learned later. By the end of early childhood, specialized skills are developed according to each person's particular needs and interests. Examples of these **specialized movements** include learning a variety of ways of pitching a baseball, spiking a volleyball, or serving a tennis ball (Burton, 1992). By age six or seven, children can begin to integrate two or more skills. That is, they can run and throw, stand on one leg and bend and pick something up, or hit a ball with a racket while maintaining their grip and balance.

Several factors affect the timing of the emergence of a particular skill. These factors include body size and physical growth, strength relative to body weight, and the maturity of the nervous system. According to Burton (1992), the maturity of the nervous system is probably the most critical factor. The nervous system is responsible for controlling each unit of movement and eventually enables the child to move smoothly without having to think about each movement. The degree to which an environment offers opportunities and encouragement for movement may also affect timing and competence level in the development of motor skills.

The first objective for the child is to gain control of each fundamental movement skill (Halverson, 1971). Once control is gained, the child can refine the quality of movements so that they are correctly sequenced, coordinated, and rhythmical. For example, when a child learns to bounce a ball, the first objective is to keep the ball near the body. "His adjustments are basically to the object, and his problems range from bouncing too hard or too far, or bending over and being hit in the nose by the bouncing ball, to chasing and trying to catch up with the ball that 'got away'" (Halverson, 1971, p. 29). When the child has mastered keeping the ball near, he or she then tries variations, such as bouncing it fast or slow or bouncing it under his or her leg. These variations are qualitative refinements. The development of fundamental skills and their refinement is very dependent on the child's perceptual development. For example, to bounce a ball, the child must perceive the rate of speed and position of the ball relative to the rate, speed, and direction of movement of his or her body. Developing motor skills is more than just eye-hand coordination (Halverson, 1971).

A review of the research on the development of motor skills led Betty Flinchum (1975, p. 12) to conclude that there is strong support for ". . . progression in the development of patterns from simple arm and leg action to highly integrated total body coordination." The progression in throwing, for example, is from elbow to shoulder. The progression in catching is from arm and body to catching with the fingers. That is, the younger child tends to throw from the elbow, whereas the older child throws with movement from the shoulder. The younger child grasps the ball to the body, whereas the older child catches it in the hands. Kicking also proceeds in a progression. First, there is no back swing. Next, there is a swing from the knee, then the hip, and last, a full-leg swing (Flinchum, 1975).

A movement pattern that follows an appropriate sequence has three phases: preparation, acting, and follow-through. Note the kicking sequence in Figure 19–1. The child lifts her leg back (preparation), kicks the ball (action),

FIGURE 19–1 A movement pattern involves a sequence of three phases: preparation, action, and follow-through.

and lets her leg go forward with the momentum from the kick (follow-through). In the throwing sequence, the arm goes back (preparation), the arm moves forward and the ball is released (action), and the arm moves through an arc back down to the body (follow-through).

As with other areas of development, guidelines determine whether a child is progressing typically. Figure 19–2 lists norms for gross motor activities. Each skill usually develops during the period listed. All children of the same age do not have exactly the same skills.

The major caution is not to allow children to overuse their developing muscles or damage their growing bones (Micheli, 1990). Simultaneously, as children begin to coordinate more than one movement, they also enter the concrete operations period. Now they can apply those motor skills to playing action games with rules. Jack Maguire (1990) has published a collection that includes the rules for games, such as hopscotch, baseball, cops and robbers, drop the handkerchief, duck-duck-goose, dodge ball, jump rope, red rover, and other old favorites.

## Motor Development of Children with Disabilities

Rosenbaum (1998) is concerned with the opportunities for physical activity play available to children with motor disorders and the effects that these opportunities might have on overall child development. What little research has been done in this area indicates that when children with disabilities attain greater independent mobility, they also show improved social, cognitive, and language development.

Because physical activity is so essential to normal development and learning, children who are limited in these capabilities are at a considerable disadvantage (Bowe, 2000). The child who moves slowly and is less effective in manipulating objects has less exploratory experience than the typically developing child. Early Childhood Special Education (ECSE) workers need to know about typical motor development to be able to identify children who are delayed in motor development. The major conditions that result in physical and motor development delay are asthma; cerebral palsy; impairments of back, feet, legs, or side; missing limbs; traumatic brain injury; spinal cord injury or other trauma that results in paralysis; and other impairments of arm, hand, or fingers, such as arthritis. Some children are identified as medically fragile and technology dependent. These children need technology, such as ventilators or machines for feeding, and may even have to have round-the-clock monitoring (Bowe, 2000). Bowe emphasizes that children with motor disorders should have opportunities to engage in active play and reap the learning benefits like other children.

Aisha was born without part of her leg. She is six years old and is in kindergarten. She is at Grandma's house playing outdoors with two other children. The three children are running around the yard playing in the leaves. Aisha comes over to where the adults are sitting. She sits down and takes off her prosthetic leg. She sets it by her and scratches her leg. She then asks her mom to help her put it on straight. After it was on, she ran off to play with the other children. What is significant about this behavior description?

Observer _____ Date _____ Time _____ Place _____

Child's name _____ Birth date _____ Age _____

| Gross Motor Skill | Observed: Yes | Observed: No | Comments |
|---|---|---|---|
| **Three-Year-Olds** | | | |
| Uses alternating feet to walk up and down stairs | | | |
| May jump from a bottom step using both feet | | | |
| Balances on one foot for two seconds | | | |
| Kicks a large ball | | | |
| Jumps in place | | | |
| Pedals a small tricycle or Big Wheel | | | |
| With both arms extended, catches a large ball | | | |
| Enjoys swinging on a swing | | | |
| Carries a cup or glass of liquid with minimal spilling | | | |
| Achieves complete bladder control | | | |
| **Four-Year-Olds** | | | |
| Walks a straight line on the floor (tape or chalk) | | | |
| Hops on one foot | | | |
| Pedals and steers a tricycle around obstacles | | | |
| Climbs ladders, trees, jungle gyms | | | |
| Jumps over objects 5 or 6 inches high and lands on both feet. | | | |
| Runs, starts, stops, and moves easily around obstacles. | | | |
| Throws a ball overhand | | | |
| **Five-Year-Olds** | | | |
| Walks backward heel to toe | | | |
| Walks upstairs alone with alternating feet | | | |
| Learns to do somersaults with instruction on the right way | | | |
| Can touch toes without bending knees | | | |
| Walks a balance beam | | | |
| Learns to skip using alternating feet | | | |
| Catches a ball thrown from three feet away | | | |
| May move up to a bicycle with training wheels | | | |
| Jumps or hops forward 10 times in a row without falling | | | |
| Balances on either foot with good control for 10 seconds | | | |

**FIGURE 19–2** Preschool/kindergarten gross motor development chart.
(From Allen, K. D., & Marotz [2003]. *Developmental profiles: Pre-birth through twelve (4th ed.).* Clifton Park, NY: Thomson Delmar Learning. Used with permission.)

## Supporting Fundamental Motor Skills Development

Susan A. Miller (2005) points out the importance of providing for young children the opportunities for gross motor activity that they need and deserve. Miller advocates for children to have opportunities to run, climb, and slide outdoors and to have big blocks for muscle building and active circle time games indoors. Zachopoulou, Tsapakidou, and Derri (2004) found in an experimental study with preschoolers that a music and movement program provided more improvements in jumping and dynamic balance than did a physical education program alone. Rhythmic accompaniment to movement activities appears to enhance motor skill development. Murata and Maeda (2002) describe a physical education program used with preschoolers with and without developmental delays. Rather than all large-group activities, they describe a center-based physical education program where children have choices of physical activities. Teachers provide guidance through questioning and making suggestions.

Developmentally appropriate physical motor activity is one means for combating childhood obesity (Huettig, Sanborn, DiMarco, Popejoy, & Rich, 2004; Lynn-Garbe & Hoot, 2004/2005). Of the children ages 2 to 5 serveyed 20.6 percent were found to be overweight or obese according to a 2000 survey reported by Huettig et al.

## Outdoor Play

Playgrounds provide the environment where children can burn off their excess weight while developing their motor skills (Sutterby & Thornton, 2005). Flat surfaces provide space for gross motor skills, such as running and jumping. Playground equipment provides opportunities for more complex movements, such as climbing, swinging, and balancing. Also important are opportunities for **brachiating**, which develops upper-body strength through the use of overhead equipment like rings and monkey bars. Besides the physical benefits, playground activity can also provide neurological benefits (Suttery & Thornton, 2005). The growth of the sensorimotor cortex in the brain, which begins in infancy and continues through adolescence, is dependent upon large-scale physical movement, such as running, hopping, jumping and climbing (Sutterby & Thornton). Thus, this is another reason for providing young children with opportunities for active play.

**brachiating**
Developing upper body strength through the use of overhead equipment.

Hurwitz (1998) provides a case for restructuring the traditional design of American playgrounds to one that will better support children's play and development. Besides the safer, more aesthetically pleasing modern play structures, Hurwitz recommends that both preschool and primary playgrounds include "large blocks of wood or plastic cubes for climbing, balancing boards, ramps, and a carpenter's bench with a supply of wood and tools for building" (p. 4). These playgrounds should also be equipped with a painting easel, sand with sand toys, balls, jump ropes, pulleys and buckets, a water table, and aesthetically pleasing landscaping with gardens and vegetation that can be explored. Teachers should know how to use the environment for teaching language, math, and science. The playground should provide curriculum integration that goes beyond just gross motor activities. The outdoors should be as carefully prepared as the indoors (DeBord, Hestenes, Moore, Cosco, & McGinnis, 2002).

Playgrounds need to be accessible to children with special needs and provide for activity and variability to be truly inclusive. Adaptations and modifications must be made to provide for the unique needs and learning styles of children with disabilities (Flynn & Kieff, 2002). Multisensory opportunities will enable children to use the senses and capabilities they have to enjoy the outdoors. Flynn and Kieff (2002) provide ideas for many possible adaptations. The child who is visually impaired or the child with blindness should be given a tour of the playground and be provided with instructions on how to use the equipment. Provided with initial support, they may become the most avid climbers. The child with deafness or the child who is hearing impaired should become visually familiar with the playground using visual gestures to communicate with them. Children with physical challenges may need broader balance beams and bigger and softer balls. Children with autism need a regular routine and repetition. Children with cognitive delays need simple directions and games that are repeated often. Other key elements in playground design are safety and developmental appropriateness. For safety, there should be resilient surfaces, such as sand, pea gravel, uniform wood chips, or rubber mats under play equipment. To be developmentally appropriate, playground environments must support creative play. If playgrounds include the variety of equipment and materials suggested by Hurwitz (1998), they will provide activities for children with a variety of capabilities and promote cooperative play among children with disabilities and typical children.

## PRESCHOOL TO PRIMARY FINE MOTOR SKILLS

Kate, age five, is carefully stringing beads. She places each one carefully, using both hands in a coordinated manner.

Theresa, age five-and-a-half, proudly shows off her clay cat. She has made two balls for the head and body and has pinched-on ears and a tail.

Five-year-old Jason prints his name on his paper.

Rudy, age three years, is building a block tower. It has eight blocks and is getting higher.

Isabel, age four, takes her painting and, using clothespins, hangs it on the line to dry.

These children are all involved in fine motor activities that are typical for their age. When their behavior is compared with the selected skills listed in Figure 19–3, it can be seen that it fits the normal expectations. Kate at age five should be able to string beads. Theresa at five-and-a-half should be able to make a clay object with at least two small parts. Rudy, at three, should be able to build an eight-block tower. Using clothespins to hang up her painting is probably a slightly advanced skill for four-year-old Isabel. Printing his first name and copying words is expected for a five-year-old like Jason. Children benefit from having many experiences that support fine motor skills. Rule and Stewart (2002) compared the development of the pincer grip in children who had opportunities to use the usual kindergarten fine motor materials as compared with materials fashioned on those developed by Montessori. The latter group of students improved the most on the pincer grip post-test.

### Writing

Fine motor development is basic for the eventual mastery of writing skills (Lamme, 1979). Writing is being taught to children at earlier ages, resulting in many children learning to write before they are ready and have all the prerequisite skills. Linda Lamme (1979) identifies six areas of prerequisite skills:

1. small-muscle development
2. eye-hand coordination
3. ability to hold a writing tool
4. ability to make basic strokes

Observer _____ Date _____ Time _____ Place _____

Child's name _____ Birth date _____ Age _____

| Fine Motor Skills | Observed Yes | Observed No |
|---|---|---|
| **Three-Year-Olds** | | |
| Feeds self with minimal assistance | | |
| Increased control of crayons or markers: makes vertical, horizontal, and circular strokes | | |
| Turns pages in a book one at a time | | |
| Builds a tower of eight or more blocks | | |
| Pounds, rolls, and squeezes clay | | |
| Begins to show hand dominance | | |
| Manipulates large buttons and zippers on clothing | | |
| Washes and dries hands | | |
| Brushes own teeth, at least partially | | |
| **Four-Year-Olds** | | |
| Builds a tower with 10 or more blocks | | |
| Forms shapes and objects out of clay: cookies, snakes, simple animals | | |
| Writes some shapes and letters | | |
| Holds a crayon or maker using a tripod grip | | |
| Paints and draws with a purpose in mind | | |
| Can hit nails or pegs with a hammer | | |
| Threads wooden beads on a string | | |
| **Five-Year-Olds** | | |
| Builds three-dimensional structures with small cubes by copying from a model | | |
| Reproduces shapes, such as square, triangle, and circle | | |
| Reproduces some letters, especially first name | | |
| Fairly good control of pencil and marker | | |
| May be able to color in the lines | | |
| Cuts on line with scissors (may not be perfect) | | |
| Hand dominance is established | | |

**FIGURE 19–3** Preschool/kindergarten fine motor development chart.
(From Allen, K. D., & Marotz [2003]. *Developmental profiles: Pre-birth through twelve (4th ed.).* Clifton Park, NY: Thomson Delmar Learning. Used with permission.)

5. letter perception
6. orientation to printed language

The first four skill areas in the list involve fine motor development.

Before children can use a writing tool, they must have control of their small muscles. That is, they must be able to control wrist and finger muscles. They can gain this control through the use of manipulative materials, such as jigsaw puzzles, construction toys, and snap beads. Children also can gain control of small muscles through play with small toys, such as peg dolls, cars, trucks, and dollhouse furniture. Materials that can be molded, such as clay, sand, play dough, and mud, support small-muscle development. Zipping, buttoning, and using scissors, crayons, and other art materials help develop finger dexterity.

Once children have developed small-muscle skills, they can coordinate the hand and eye. Most of the activities already mentioned also promote eye-hand coordination skills. The child who hammers nails straight, builds a block tower without it falling over, or copies complicated geometric designs probably has attained the eye-hand coordination needed for writing.

Some tools for writing are easier to use than others. Markers and felt-tipped pens are easiest for the child to use because they require very little pressure to achieve the desired results. Chalk is the next easiest, then crayons, and, last, pencils. Contrary to popular belief, large-diameter pencils are not necessarily easier for young children to use. Carlson and Cunningham (1990) found that some preschoolers handled large-diameter pencils better and some handled small-diameter pencils better. Therefore, they recommend that both be available and that students be allowed to select the size they can grip and control most easily. Children need opportunities to experiment with these tools for drawing before they are asked to use them for writing. Children should also have time to use paintbrushes, kitchen utensils, garden tools, sieves and strainers, and woodworking equipment. All these materials help the child learn how to hold a tool and use it to perform some act that cannot be done with the hand alone. According to Lamme, the beginning writer should be given markers and felt-tipped pens for his or her first efforts. When a child begins to select a pencil for writing, he or she then can be helped to hold it correctly.

> The pencil should be loosely gripped with the fingers above the shaved tip to about an inch from the tip. Only the index finger should remain on top of the pencil, not two or three fingers (Lamme, 1979, pp. 22–23).

Lamme cautions that the young writer should not be pressured too much about grip. He or she may become discouraged. Lamme suggests that the child who is having difficulty can be spotted by two indications:

- He or she holds the pencil too tightly, tires quickly, and is not able to write for very long. The pencil should be loose enough in the child's grip to be pulled right out.
- He or she clenches the teeth and presses hard, leaving a deep impression on the page. Or, the child may write so lightly that it can hardly be seen. Pressure should be even.

Handwriting grows out of drawing (Church, 2002a). Children experiment with drawing as they move from scribbling to symbolic drawing. They experiment the same way with writing.

> In many ways, art is the first language of the beginning reader and writer. Children usually draw or paint before they write. They use what may look like simple scribbles, squiggly lines, scratchy marks, and blobs to represent something else. The connection to writing is clear (Church, 2002a, p. 34).

By observing the child's drawing, the adult can determine whether the child is able to make the basic strokes needed for writing. Look for straight lines, circles, and curved lines. Do the lines join each other when houses, cars, people, or other figures are drawn? These strokes should not be taught during art activities; they are allowed to occur naturally. Eventually, when formal handwriting lessons

**FIGURE 19–4** A four-and-a-half-year-old makes a shopping list.

are introduced, the strokes for writing are taught. The child goes through the transition from drawing to writing slowly and gradually. Lamme (1979) suggests five guidelines to use in deciding whether a child is ready for writing:

1. The child repeats patterns (or letters or words) over and over.
2. The child goes from left to right and then return sweeps to begin again at the left.
3. The child realizes that letter elements can recur in variable patterns.
4. The child lists all of the letters (or words or symbols) he or she knows.
5. The child perceives likenesses and differences among letter elements, concepts, letters, and words (Lamme, 1979, p. 23).

Writing does not involve only small-muscle coordination. It also involves perception. The child must perceive similarities and differences, shapes and sizes, and direction. These perceptions are then integrated with small-muscle control to produce writing. It is important that children be shown standard letter models. They should also begin writing on unlined paper and continue until they have achieved a uniform size. Reversals are commonly made by beginning writers and are quite normal for the preschool and kindergarten child. Letters such as *b* and *d* and *p* and *q* are easily confused. For most children, these problems should gradually disappear as they move through the primary grades. However, some children continue to have problems with printing and writing. This condition is called dysgraphia (Allen & Marotz, 2006).

Finally, Lamme indicates that the child needs to have an orientation to printed language. That is, children must understand that printed language stands for spoken language. Children need to use their early writing skills to make books, greeting cards, and signs, and to label pictures.

Figures 19–4, 19–5, 19–6, and 19–7 are examples of early handwriting. At age four-and-a-half, Kate imitates a shopping list (Figure 19–4). She makes letterlike forms that appear to her to be like an adult's handwriting. At age five, she sits in the kitchen and copies words off cereal and detergent containers (Figure 19–5). At five-and-a-half, she writes freehand (Figure 19–6). Note the repetition and the reversals. Also at five-and-a-half, she writes a caption on her picture (Figure 19–7).

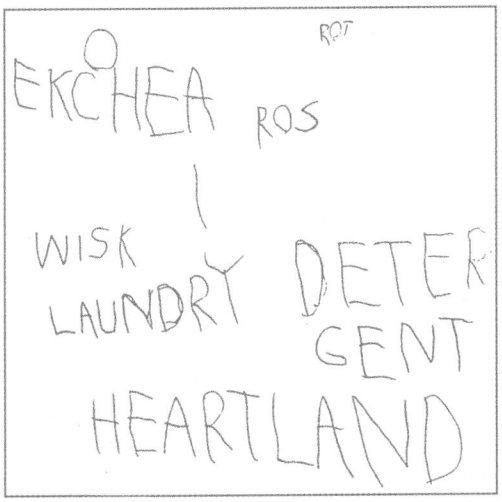


**FIGURE 19–5** A five-year-old enjoys copying print from things in the environment.

By age three, most young children express an interest in name writing. Both Hildreth (1936) and Harste, Woodward, and Burke (1984) documented the developmental sequences in name writing from ages three to six. The three-year-old uses scribbles that look like pretend cursive or mock letterlike forms. Fours usually combine letterlike forms with real letters. Five-year-olds usually can write their names correctly, including the correct letters in the right sequence, but may use all capitals or mix capitals and lowercase letters. By age six, most children can print their names correctly, with an initial capital letter followed by lowercase letters. Young children enjoy learning to write their names if given time and encouragement. They also enjoy experimenting with other words, as seen in Figures 19–4 through 19–7.

A concern for parents and other adults focuses on the question of teaching children conventional printing as used in this book and in most children's textbooks and storybooks or

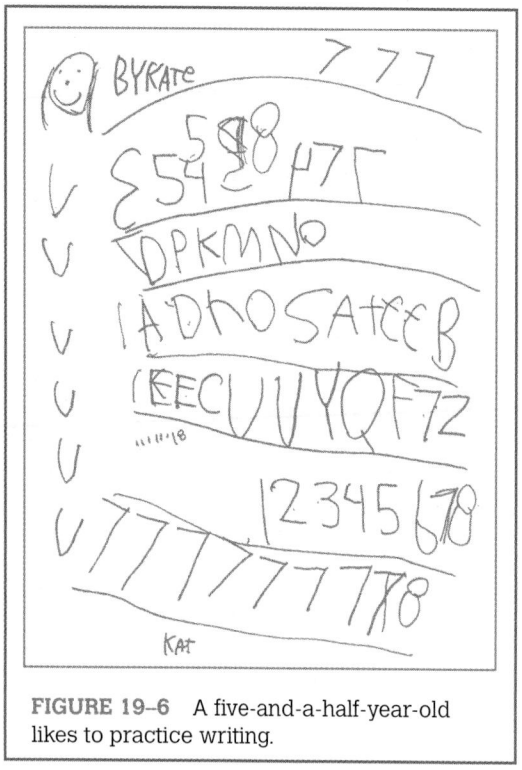


FIGURE 19–6 A five-and-a-half-year-old likes to practice writing.

FIGURE 19–7 A five-and-a-half-year-old puts a caption on her picture.

**D'Nealian alphabet**
A slanted manuscript alphabet.

teaching them a slanted manuscript alphabet, such as the **D'Nealian alphabet.** Proponents of the slanted alphabet believe use of this type of alphabet for beginning writing makes the transition to cursive writing much easier. Graham (1993/1994) reviewed the research on this question and came up with three reasons why the slanted alphabet may not be a good choice for young children. First, he found no evidence that use of the slanted manuscript makes it easier for children to learn to make the transfer to cursive. Second, both parents and teachers have to learn about the new alphabet, and teachers have to learn to write it. Finally, the most important factor probably is that most children have begun to write using traditional manuscript before coming to kindergarten. Learning a new alphabet means they have to make an extra transition that does not appear to be beneficial. Graham (1993/1994) does not recommend using a slanted alphabet in kindergarten and the early primary grades.

## Developing Drawing Skills

The development of drawing skills parallels the development of writing skills. Both skills involve many of the same lines and shapes, such as straight and curved lines, crosses, dots, and circles. For the most part, younger preschoolers are in the prewriting, prerepresentational, experimental stage. Just as they use scribbles in their writing, they also use scribbles in their drawing. The preschooler goes through two main phases or stages in his use of materials (Sevigny, 1979). The first is the *manipulatory-exploratory* stage. This is a process stage in which the child experiments to discover what can be done and not done with the materials. The child's objective is to gain some control over the materials. Children's drawing at this stage is referred to as scribbling. They do not name what they make but strictly

**communicative phase**
When children begin to name and label their drawings.

**random scribble**
The first stage in development of art when young children enjoy exploring the movement of their arms and shoulders and the resulting patterns on the paper.

**emergent diagram shapes**
Controlled scribbles that are drawn in a prescribed space.

**diagrams**
Characterized by the use of single lines to form crosses and to outline circles, triangles, and other shapes.

**aggregates**
Two or more diagrams in combination.

experiment to find out what can be done. The **communicative phase** begins when children name and label their drawings. Now children know what can be done with the material and look for configurations they can name (Sevigny, 1979).

The first stage in the development of art is seen in the **random scribble.** Young children enjoy exploring the movement of their arms and shoulders and the resulting patterns on paper. Gradually, the movement becomes more controlled. Children then proceed to "controlled pattern movement, to controlled line, to controlled shape, to named shape, to symbolic shape to art" (Sevigny, 1979, pp. 3–4). The first three stages are straight-line control, circular control, and curved-line control. All three of these stages of control are basic to handwriting skill development.

When children have achieved these three levels of control, they can combine lines, curves, and circles to make shapes. They have reached the shape control stage. They are still not trying to make anything, but simply exploring shape. Eventually, the shapes begin to remind the child of something he or she has seen earlier. The child gives the shape a name after finishing it. The child works with these presymbolic shapes, gradually working into symbolic shapes or representations of real things.

Kellogg (1970), in her major developmental study, identified a number of shapes that commonly appear in children's art. She identified 20 basic scribbles as the building blocks of art. These included dots; single and multiple vertical, horizontal, and diagonal lines; single and multiple curved lines; and loops, spirals, and circles. By age two, what Kellogg labels as **emergent diagram shapes** appear. These shapes are controlled scribbles that are drawn in a prescribed space. By three, **diagrams** usually make an appearance. Diagrams are characterized by the use of single lines to form crosses and to outline circles, triangles, and other shapes. Kellogg identified six diagrams: the rectangle and square, the oval and circle, the triangle, the Greek cross, the diagonal cross, and irregular shapes drawn with a single unbroken line. Between ages three and five, most children's art consists of **aggregates.** Aggregates consist of two or more diagrams in combination. Children gradually proceed from mandalas, which are circle shapes with crosses dividing the center space, to suns, which are circle shapes with lines sticking out, to human figures. The first human figures are usually suns with straight-line arms and primitive facial features. Children also tend to draw radials, a formation that radiates from one central point. Figures 19–10 b, d, and f are typical of early pictorial persons.

FIGURE 19–8 The young child's drawings contain just the essentials.

The young child needs plenty of time to explore materials in order to pass through these stages with the natural maturational development of muscle, bone, and conceptualization. Sevigny (1979) believes that dittos and coloring books should never be given to young children. They need big pieces of paper and room to move.

By the fourth or fifth year, the preschooler uses some symbols. These symbols are quite primitive, with the symbol for a person being most common. A figure is usually made with circles and lines; usually, it is made up of a circle for a head with lines connected for limbs. Gradually, their drawings become more like what they see in the world, but they still include only the essentials. It is not until the sixth year that more details and more realistic proportions appear. Figures 19–8 and 19–9 show drawings by a four-and-a-half-year-old girl. Note the simplicity of the three girls; yet there is no doubt that they are girls. The long hair and the dresslike

FIGURE 19–9 In this drawing of two girls on a horse, the child has used basic shapes and includes just the most essential details.

bodies are clear clues. The girls are riding on an animal (a horse, according to the artist) in Figure 19–9. We don't know if they are bareback riders or if this is just the child's sense of perspective. By the time children reach the primary grades, their drawings are usually representative and detailed. They enjoy drawing and painting to create illustrations for stories that they write, thus merging their skills.

Figure 19–10 includes pictures of families as drawn by preschoolers, kindergartners, and first graders in the fall of the school year. The author selected both an immature and a mature drawing from each level to show the wide range of development within each group, as well as the increase in complexity from preschool to first grade as more body parts and clothing details are added to the drawing.

When writing and drawing are considered, a concern with **handedness** usually surfaces. There is concern regarding whether the right-hand dominant have an advantage over the left-hand dominant and over the children who do not seem to have settled on a preference. To learn more about handedness and its relationship to motor competence in preschoolers, Tan (1985) identified two groups of four-year-olds. One group was identified as left-handed and the other as having no hand preference. Tan developed the Preschool Handedness Inventory (PHI) to assess handedness. The PHI requires the child to do tasks such as opening and shutting a packet of pens, drawing, cutting with scissors, catching and throwing a bean bag with one hand, and others. A standardized test in combination with a fine motor inventory devised by Tan was used to assess level of motor development. The left-handed children were not found to be weak in motor development. They did just as well as right-handers on the motor assessment tasks. Tan suggests that left-handed children often may be judged as lacking proper motor development because they look different when they are engaged in motor activity. On the other hand, the children with no preference did have below-average motor skills. Most of these children were boys. It is important that the adult who works with young children identify these children and help them strengthen their motor skills through developmental activities.

**handedness**

Determining the right-hand dominance, left-hand dominance, or no preference.

What kinds of physical/motor activities can you remember doing during your preschool and kindergarten years? From your current experience, do you find children are engaged in more or less of these activities than when you were a child? Share your thoughts and memories with several of your friends or classmates. Compare your experiences and opinions.

## THE ASSESSMENT OF MOTOR SKILLS

Mature performance in certain kinds of motor skills has been shown to be predictive of readiness for kindergarten and first grade. For this reason, it is important that the adult working with preschoolers be aware of these skills and how to assess them. The charts in Figures 19–2 and 19–3 may be used as guides for fine and gross motor assessment.

a. An advanced prekindergartner

b. A less advanced Prekindergartner

c. An advanced kindergartner

**FIGURE 19–10** These drawings demonstrate the wide range of motor development found in prekindergarten and kindergarten students.

(*Continued*)

d. A less advanced kindergartner

**FIGURE 19–10** Continued.

## Assessing General Motor Skill Development

An informal motor skill inventory was developed by Harriet G. Williams (1983) of the University of South Carolina. This instrument assesses four areas of perceptual-motor capacity:

1. *Gross motor control:* running, hopping, jumping, skipping, throwing, and catching
2. *Fine motor control:* cutting, pasting, manipulating objects, clapping, and using such instruments as pencils and crayons
3. *Visual perception:* coordination of eye and hand, perception of figure and ground, form constancy, position in space, and spatial relations
4. *Body awareness:* awareness of position in space, hand preference, right and left, and knowledge of body parts

Activities are suggested that aid the child's development in each area.

Williams (1983) identified a number of other motor assessment tools that are appropriate for four-, five-, and six-year-olds. She warns that motor diagnosis should be made with caution. Young children often perform a motor task incorrectly because they don't understand the instructions rather than because they are unable to accomplish what is asked. Before a formal motor assessment is administered, children should be observed during play activities and assessed with an informal checklist.

## Assessing Fine Motor Skills

The Gesell readiness tests are more formal developmental measures that have several items focusing on fine motor skills. These include copying forms, such as circle, cross, and squares; completing a picture of a man; name printing; and copying block constructions. Items concerning right and left, visual perception, and general information are also included. Claims have been made that the Gesell tests are highly predictive of school readiness (Carll & Richard, n.d.). Gesell adherents find that they have been very useful as prekindergarten and pre-first-grade placement measures. Each child is given a developmental age score that indicates whether placement should be in prekindergarten, kindergarten, pre-first-grade, or first grade. There has been a great deal of criticism about using the Gesell test as a gatekeeping instrument (Meisels, 1987). For example, Lichenstein (1990), after studying the predictive value of the Gesell, cautions that it should not be used as the primary determinant of grade placement. It can provide some valuable information about the child that could supplement other observations in making placement decisions. Lichenstein found that the Gesell predicted that more than 50 percent of the children in his sample were not ready for first grade, whereas other measures indicated the group had average capability. He also found that the more Gesell training teachers had, the more likely they were to rate children as unready for first-grade placement. He found that the test was inaccurate. For example, ratings of child performance by independent raters had unacceptably low percentages of agreement. The developmental philosophy of the Gesell test ignores environmental factors, such as lack of experience with pencil and paper and blocks and puts too much emphasis on inherited developmental time schedules as a determinant of learning readiness. A validity study on the Gesell school readiness tests done by Graue and Shepard (1989) showed similar misidentification results.

The adult who works with preschool children needs to be aware of each child's skill level in both gross and fine motor behaviors. Gross motor skills should develop as a prerequisite to the fine motor skills, which are essential for communication of knowledge.

Moving from preschool to kindergarten to primary usually means moving from concrete activities to more abstract paper-and-pencil activities. Suppose you are a kindergarten teacher and you have helped build your students' fine motor skills through the use of manipulative toys, play dough, clay, painting and drawing, and other fine motor development materials and activities. A child in your class has some knowledge, such as solving simple addition and subtraction problems, that he can express through concrete means but not with paper and pencil or workbook. You know that his first-grade teacher relies on workbooks and worksheets. What can you do to help this child?

## LEARNING AND MOTOR DEVELOPMENT

The relationship between sensory and motor development is being studied in more detail than in the past in the emerging field of developmental biodynamics. Evidence indicates that the development of motor abilities enables young children to receive more sensory information and thus learn more about their environment. Researchers in this area hope to shed light on the exact relationship between motor, perceptual, and intellectual development and functioning. Meanwhile, it appears that multisensory experiences are most likely to enhance children's learning.

Poest, Williams, Witt, and Atwood (1989) had parents and teachers of preschool children enrolled in nursery schools and child care centers respond to questionnaires designed to find out the types and frequencies of their children's physical activities. They discovered that most preschool children engage in very little high-intensity physical activity that stimulates the heart and promotes good health and optimum motor development. Although they may have excellent selections of playground equipment, most of their active play is low intensity. Children left on their own used the equipment for sociodramatic play that involved low-intensity activity that did not meet the standards of vigorousness needed to promote physical fitness. Very little time was spent in teacher-directed motor activities. Teachers with child development training did more motor instruction than those with elementary training. Children whose parents engaged in more physical activity also engaged in more physical activity. The authors conclude that more physical fitness and motor development instruction is needed in preschool and child care centers.

Poest, Williams, Witt, and Atwood (1990) suggest that a motor development program should include three major categories of focus: fundamental movement skills, physical fitness, and perceptual-motor development. Fundamental motor skills that preschool children are neurologically ready to develop include "walking, running, leaping, jumping, hopping, galloping, sliding, skipping, climbing, and tricycling; the manipulative or ball skills of throwing, kicking, punting, striking, volleying, bouncing, dribbling (hand), dribbling (foot), rolling, catching, and trapping; and the balance skills of bending, stretching, twisting, turning, swinging, upright and inverted balances, body rolling, dodging and beam walking" (Gallahue, 1982, as cited in Poest et al., 1990, p. 4). Poest et al. (1989, 1990) believe that children should not be just left on their own to develop these skills; they need adult-directed practice and instruction to ensure optimum development. Movement programs for young children must be **developmentally appropriate** (Bredekamp & Copple, 1997; Sanders, 2002). Activities must be age appropriate. For example, it's appropriate to have three-year-olds explore what they can do with a ball, but not appropriate to put them in an organized game situation. Activities must be individually appropriate, that is, they must fit each child's level of capability. For example, some four-year-olds can dribble a ball while others may only be able to practice holding and dropping a ball. Instruction must also be developmentally appropriate. The predominant teaching strategies should be "movement exploration, guided discovery, and creative problem solving" (Sanders, 2002, p. 6). Cultural appropriateness is also essential. Sanders (2002) suggests that physical activity settings provide "excellent opportunities for young children to learn to recognize differences and similarities, to work with others, and to understand that different customs and cultural habits are not barriers" (p. 6). Physical fitness "refers to the level of health development and functional capacity of the body" (Poest et al., 1990, p. 5). According to Poest et al. (1990), to be physically fit, children must maintain an adequate level of cardiovascular endurance, muscular strength, muscular endurance, flexibility, and body leanness. Perceptual-motor development involves taking information in through the senses and making a motor response. Perceptual-motor development includes "body, time, spatial, directional, visual, and auditory awareness" (Poest et al., 1990, p. 6).

**developmentally appropriate**

Age, individually, instructionally, and culturally appropriate for each child.

Poest et al. (1990) make a number of suggestions for the improvement of large muscle time. First, planning is essential. Each of the fundamental motor skills should be methodically addressed. Equipment should be set up to offer challenges for each skill. Physical fitness activities should be planned daily. Poest et al. (1990) advise that group calisthenics or exercise routines are not appropriate for young children. Perceptual-motor activities that include copying movements (like *Simon Says*) in touching body parts will develop body awareness. Time awareness can be developed through marching to a beat, to rhymes, or to chants. Spatial relations can be developed through the use of obstacle courses.

There is evidence that young children's overall learning is enhanced by using a motoric (versus an abstract) approach. For example, Herman, Kolker, and Shaw (1982) found that kindergartners' memory for location of objects in an unfamiliar environment is enhanced by motor activity. This supports having young children carefully rehearse all the routine activities at school rather than just telling and/or demonstrating the procedures.

**assistive technology**

"Any item, piece of equipment, or product system . . . that is used to increase, maintain, or improve the functional capabilities of children with disabilities" (Parette & Murdick, 1998, p. 193).

Children with physical/motor disabilities can be helped to get more out of the available learning opportunities with the use of **assistive technology** (Parette & Murdick, 1998). Assistive technology is defined by IDEA as "any item, piece of equipment, or product system, whether acquired commercially, off the shelf, modified, or customized, that is used to increase, maintain, or improve the functional capabilities of children with disabilities" (Parette & Murdick, p. 193). Examples of assistive devices that can be especially helpful to children with motor disabilities include the following:

- wheelchairs or scooters to aid mobility
- leisure and recreational materials, such as handheld electronic toys
- independent living devices, such as those that aid in buttoning or reaching
- devices, such as vinyl-covered rolls and bolsters, used to maintain proper body alignment
- adaptive toys, such as those that are battery powered and controlled by a switch
- remote controls for television or VCR
- computers that can be used for cooperative play with other children

These devices can support inclusion and enable children to achieve their academic potential.

## SUMMARY

Motor skills develop in a sequence parallel to that of physical growth. Motor development supports concept development, perceptual development, and representational competence. Gross motor development includes activities that use the large muscles: throwing, running, jumping, and pulling. Gross motor skills precede fine motor skills. The critical period for the development of fundamental motor skills begins with toddlerhood and continues until about age six or seven. Outdoor and other opportunities for active play should be available as a time to clear young minds of competing stimuli, as well as to provide chances for physical/motor exercise.

Fine motor activities make use of the small muscles, such as those in the wrist and the hand. Fine motor activities, such as bead stringing, building with construction toys, drawing, and clay modeling, serve as the basis for developing the skills that will be needed for writing. Adults who work with young children should be cautious and should not push their students into formal writing lessons too soon. Drawing materials should be readily available because drawing provides opportunities to informally practice the shapes that are included in written letters.

Because the preschool period is a critical time for the development of fundamental motor skills, the adult who works with young children should be alert to each child's developmental progress in order to assess how well each child is doing. It is important for young children to be engaged in informal teacher-planned and teacher-directed motor activities to ensure that all children have the opportunity to develop fundamental skills.

Children with physical/motor disabilities can gain the most benefit from inclusive placements with the use of assistive devices. Assistive devices can help children become more independent, be more involved in group activities, and make up for some of their lack of typical motor skills.

## For Further Reading


Barbour, A. (1999). The impact of playground design on the play behaviors of children with differing levels of physical competence. *Early Childhood Research Quarterly, 14*(1), 75–98.

Beaty, J. J. (2004). *Safety in preschool programs*. Columbus, OH: Merrill/PrenticeHall.

Dale, D., Corbin, C., & Dale, K. (2000). Restricting opportunities to be active during school time: Do children compensate by increasing activity levels after school? *Research Quarterly for Exercise and Sport, 71*(3), 240–248.

Dewey, D., & Tupper, D. E. (2004). *Developmental motor disorders*. New York: Guilford.

Diamond, A. (2000). Close interrelation of motor development and cognitive development and of the cerebellum and prefrontal cortex. *Child Development, 71*(1), 44–56.

Fernandex-Alvarez, E., & Aicardi, J. (2001). *Movement disorders in children*. Cambridge, UK: Cambridge University Press.

Frost, J. L., Brown, P., Sutterby, J. A., & Thornton, C. D. (2004). *The developmental benefits of playgrounds*. Olney, MD: Association for Childhood Education International.

Gallahue, D., & Ozmun, J. (1998). *Understanding motor development: Infants, children, adolescents, adults*. Boston: McGraw-Hill.

Herbert, M. (2002). *Typical and atypical development*. Williston, VT: Blackwell.

Leppo, M. L., Davis, D., & Crim, B. (2000). The basics of exercising the mind and body. *Childhood Education, 76*(3), 142–147.

Let's go outside! [Focus section] (2002). *Young Chilren, 57*(3), 8–42.

McLean, D. (2002). Helping Aaron navigate: Including children with physical disabilities. *Dimensions, 30*(1), 9–15.

Owen, S. E., & McKinlay, I. A. (1997). Motor difficulties in children with developmental disorders of speech and language. *Child: Care, Health and Development, 23*, 315–325.

Perry, J. P. (2001). *Outdoor play: Teaching strategies with young children*. New York: Teachers College Press.

Pica, R. (2004). *Experiences in movement with music, activities, and theory* (3rd ed.). Clifton Park, NY: Delmar Learning.

Sallo, M., & Silla, R. (1997). Physical activity with moderate to vigorous intensity in preschool and 1st grade schoolchildren. *Pediatric Exercise Science, 9*, 44–54.

Sanders, S. W. (2002). *Active for life: Developmentally appropriate movement programs for young children*. Washington, DC: National Association for the Education of Young Children.

Weikart, P. S. (2002). *Teaching movement and dance: A sequential approach to rhythmic movement* (4th ed.). Ypsilanti, MI: High/Scope Press.

Wellhousen, K. (2002). *Outdoor play everyday: Innovative play concepts for early childhood*. Clifton Park, NY: Delmar Learning.


## Suggested Activities

1. Visit a nursery school, child care center, or kindergarten. Obtain permission to try the following tasks with 4 three-year-olds, 4 four-year-olds, or 4 five-year-olds, or with one or more children from each age level.

   Task 1: Throwing and Catching a Ball

   Materials: A ball about 10 inches in diameter.

   Instructions:

   a. Stand four feet from the child. Say, "I'm going to throw the ball to you; you catch it." Throw the ball. Note the child's response to catching.
   b. Be sure the child has the ball. Say, "Now you throw the ball to me." Note the child's response.
   c. Give the ball to the child. Say, "Now throw the ball as far as you can." Note how far the child throws before the ball hits the ground. Note also how the child throws.

   Task 2: Running and Stopping

   Instructions: Measure off 10 feet. Ask the child to run the 10 feet and stop. For example, you might say, "See the chalk lines on the sidewalk. Stand at this line. Now run to the other line as fast as you can and then stop."

Task 3: Copying Shapes
Materials: Using a black marking pen, draw the following shapes on three-inch by five-inch cards: a circle, a square, a triangle, and a rectangle.
Instructions: One at a time, ask the child to copy each shape on a piece of plain white paper using a black felt pen. Say, "Look at this shape. You draw one just like it on your paper."

Task 4: Stringing Beads
Materials: A lace and 20 preschool beads.
Instructions: Give the child the lace. Say, "Here is a pile of beads. See how many you can put on your lace." (Help the child with the first one if he or she seems in doubt as to what to do.)

If you wish, make up some more tasks using Figures 19–2 and 19–3 as a guide. After you have your data, compare the children's performances with the norms in Figures. How did each of the children with whom you worked compare? How did they compare with each other?

2. If you are interested in learning more about the development of children's art, check the library for references and select a book for reading. Prepare a report for the class on *Children's Art: Its Development and Relationship to Perceptual and Motor Growth.*
3. Visit nursery school, preschool, and kindergarten, playgrounds and determine if they are designed to accommodate children with special needs.
4. Make an entry in your journal.

## REVIEW

1. Select the phases in a movement pattern that follows an appropriate sequence.
   a. preparatory, follow-through, action
   b. preparatory, approach, action, follow-through
   c. approach, action, follow-through
   d. preparation, action, follow-through
2. Describe how fundamental motor skill development can be supported.
3. Select the statements that are true regarding outdoor play:
   a. Outdoor play is an extra activity for young children.
   b. Children need outdoor flat surfaces for gross motor activities, such as running and jumping.
   c. Rings and monkey bars are dangerous and unnecessary.
   d. Large-scale physical movement has no great effect on brain development.
   e. The playground should provide more than just gross motor activities.
   f. The inclusive playground provides for the involvement of children with special needs.
4. Using the charts in this chapter, evaluate the gross motor development of the following children:
   a. Paul is five years old and is just learning to ride his tricycle.
   b. José is three years and three months old and can throw a ball underhanded six feet.
   c. Maria has just turned five and can skip quite well.
   d. Nancy is four years old and can hop twice on one foot.
   e. Paul can pull a wagon full of blocks.
   f. José can catch a bounced ball.

g. Maria has just started riding a two-wheeled bike with training wheels.
h. Nancy can bounce a ball under control.
i. Paul can bounce a ball but still has trouble catching it.

**5.** Using the charts in this chapter, decide if the following children are progressing typically, slowly, or advanced for his or her age in fine motor skills.
a. Maria is five years of age. She can print her first name, fold paper into halves and quarters, and trace around her hand.
b. Nancy is four years old. She can pour from a pitcher without spilling, cut on a line, and copy the letter X.
c. Paul is five. He can barely approximate drawing a circle, he has difficulty cutting, and every time he tries to pour from a pitcher at snack time, he spills some of the drink on the table.
d. José is three years old. He can draw a circle, cut paper, and build an eight-block tower.

**6.** Match the prewriting skill in Column I with the correct example in Column II.

| Column I | Column II |
|---|---|
| a. small-muscle development | 1. A child can hammer nails straight and copy complicated block designs. |
| b. eye-hand coordination | 2. This child's drawings include lines, curves, and circles. |
| c. hold a writing tool | 3. A child sits with an open book in his or her lap, pretending to read it. |
| d. do basic strokes | 4. This child recognizes and names all the letters of the alphabet. |
| e. letter perception | 5. These children are using construction toys, peg dolls and little cars, and clay and sand. |
| f. orientation to printed language | 6. This child can hold a pencil well with a loose grip. |

**7.** Decide whether six-year-old Bill appears to be ready for first grade. Bill likes to use writing tools. He sits for long periods repeating patterns and letters on his paper. He always goes from left to right and begins again at the left when he reaches the end of a line. He realizes that the same letters can be rearranged to make new words, such as *pan* and *nap*. He can write almost all the alphabet from memory, plus about six short words. He does not get any letters mixed up and can discriminate the few sight words he knows.

**8.** In what skill does the child develop from random scribbler to a controlled movement pattern, to controlled line, to controlled shape, to named shape, and to symbolic shape?

**9.** Why is it important for the adult who works with young children to assess the children's motor development?

## KEY TERMS LIST

aggregates
assistive technology
brachiating
communicative phase
D'Nealian alphabet
developmentally appropriate
diagrams
emergent diagram shapes
fundamental motor skills
handedness
random scribble
specialized movements

Additional resources for this chapter can be found on the Online Companion™ to accompany this text at http://www.earlychilded.delmar.com. Respond to "Time to Reflect" and "Looking Further" concepts, review various child development scenarios, and answer thought-provoking questions in the Critical Thinking Forum. Keep a daily journal by downloading the student journal available on this Web site. Complete the interactive matching exercises to reinforce concepts, and print out the child development assessment forms to use during your observation of development for children from birth to age eight. In addition, read the case studies on the Web site to reinforce important concepts in each chapter, and take a look at the multitude of Web links that are available for student research on the Internet.

# SECTION VI

## Cognitive Growth and Development: Ages Three Through Six

In this section, we look at children's cognitive development in more detail: how they think and remember, and how they learn to speak, read, and write. We also look at the question of intelligence and creativity. Young children are especially fascinating because they view the world so much differently than older children and adults. As a preview to this section, we meet Ramona Quimby, a fictional child who typifies the kinds of behaviors that make young children so special. We meet Ramona at ages four, five, and eight.

### RAMONA AT AGE FOUR

At age four, Ramona is characterized as a big problem by her big sister "Beezus" (Beatrice), who is nine years old. Ramona's character illustrates some typical four-year-old thinking and behaviors. Ramona is fixated on the book *The Littlest Steam Shovel.* She refers to the main character as "my Scoopy." She demands to have it read over and over. Her mother and father have found ways to avoid these repeated readings, so Beezus gets the brunt of the requests. Ramona has the story completely memorized word for word, and if Beezus makes any changes, she immediately corrects her. Beezus decides to take Ramona to the library to get another book. Much to Beezus's dismay, Ramona selects *Big Steve and the Steam Shovel*—another steam shovel book!

Beezus intends to check the book out on her card, but Ramona wants a card. Beezus explains that she has to be able to write her name to get a card. Ramona claims that she does know how to write her name, so the librarian fills in the necessary information. Ramona signs using mock cursive.

She has watched Beezus write *Beatrice* in cursive and from her four-year-old point of view, signing your name means making some wavy lines with dots and cross lines. Ramona's behaviors are vexing but, as we shall see, make sense in terms of what we know about how four-year-olds think and reason and how they apply their cognitive skills to an emerging knowledge of written language.

Another four-year-old characteristic demonstrated by Ramona is imagination. Her mother comments, "Oh, you know Ramona. Her imagination runs away with her" (Cleary, 1955, p. 40). Ramona sits in the middle of the living room in her empty plastic wading pool pretending she is in a boat in the middle of a lake. Ramona walks along with a string dragging behind. On the end of it is Ralph, her imaginary green lizard. Ramona uses marshmallows as powder puffs to powder her nose like a grown-up woman would. Sometimes her imagination and her literal view of things leads to what, from an adult view, is faulty reasoning. For example, pretending that she is Gretel *(Hansel and Gretel)* and her doll is the witch, she pushes the doll into the oven in which a cake is baking. Needless to say, the result is disastrous for both the cake and the doll.

To sum up, Ramona at age four views the world at face value, is showing signs of an interest in reading and writing, has a vivid imagination that is reflected in her dramatic play, and tries the patience of her sister and parents.

## RAMONA AT AGE FIVE

At five, Beezus views Ramona as not just an annoyance but as a full-blown pest. At age five, Ramona is very excited as she is entering kindergarten. She has also just learned to skip. She skips around the living room, singing as she waits to leave for school. For Beezus, this behavior is immature.

Ramona is still a literal thinker, taking everything at face value. Her kindergarten teacher, Miss Binney, tells her, "Sit here for the present." Miss Binney means "temporarily" while Ramona assumes she is a special person who will receive a gift. "Ramona wondered if her present would be wrapped in fancy paper and tied with a ribbon like a birthday present" (Cleary, 1968, pp. 17–18). The class learns a new song about "the dawnzer lee light." Ramona is puzzled because she is not sure what a "dawnzer" is. Miss Binney reads *Mike Mulligan and the Steam Shovel* to the class. Mike and his steam shovel spend the whole day digging the basement for the town hall. During the discussion after the story, Ramona has an important question. She asks, "Miss Binney, I want to know—how did Mike Mulligan go to the bathroom when he was digging the basement of the town hall?" (Cleary, 1968, p. 23). Miss Binney is rather taken aback, while the other children all seemed to have the same question in the back of their minds.

## RAMONA AT AGE EIGHT

At age eight, Ramona is in a new stage of development. She is about to enter the third grade at a new school. Reading, writing, and arithmetic are well in hand. However, Ramona's thinking, although more abstract, is still not completely out of the literal stage. She's still very concrete in her view of things. She is now overboard in the degree of accuracy she demands.

> Ramona had reached the age of demanding accuracy from everyone, even herself. All summer, whenever a grown-up asked what grade she was in, she felt as if she were fibbing when she answered "third," because she had not actually started third grade. Still, she could not say she was in the second grade since she had finished that grade in June. Grown-ups did not understand that summers were free from grades.

She can now understand the nuances of adult speech. When her teacher, Miss Whaley, says the label she has made for her fruitfly jar is "neat," Ramona knows she means extra good, not tidy.

Ramona is industrious when it comes to creative projects. For an assignment that involves giving an oral book report that "sells" the book, she writes a television commercial and constructs props for the presentation.

Now Ramona is stuck after school playing with four-year-old Willa Jean. Willa Jean does all the things Ramona did that annoyed Beezus when Ramona was four. Ramona is driven to distraction by repetition.

Ramona is now concerned with acting grown-up and mature. She has reached a level of cognitive development in which she can understand some of the problems now faced by her family. Her father has changed to part-time work so that he can attend college, and her mother has gone to work full-time. She is also more on a level with Beezus now. They can discuss their concerns and develop mutual decisions.

In the following chapters, we look at cognitive development from ages three through six. As you read each chapter, keep Ramona in mind.

**The Ramona books are authored by Beverly Cleary:**
**(1955). *Beezus and Ramona.* New York: Yearling. (Ramona, age four)**
**(1968). *Ramona the Pest.* New York: Yearling. (Ramona, age five)**
**(1981). *Ramona Quimby, Age 8.* New York: Yearling. (Ramona, age eight)**

CHAPTER

# 20

# The Cognitive System and Concept Development

## Objectives

After reading this chapter, you should be able to:

- Define *cognition.*
- Identify cognitive behaviors.
- Recognize parts of the cognitive structures and cognitive process.
- Name Piaget's periods of cognitive development and identify the major characteristics of the sensorimotor preoperational and concrete operational periods.
- Recognize and explain examples of centering.
- Draw a model of the cognitive system.
- Describe theory of mind and metacognition and provide an example of instruction that enhances metacognitive thought.
- State the significance of right- and left-brain functioning.
- Explain the significance of findings from brain research to the capabilities of entering kindergartners.
- List the highlights of Piaget's and Vygotsky's developmental theories.
- Identify the cognitive characteristics of the preoperational child.
- Identify the cognitive characteristics of the concrete operational child.
- Analyze and evaluate a child's behavior when engaged in a concept activity.
- Recognize teaching practice that is consistent with Piaget's theory.
- Explain how Vygotsky's theory helps us understand how young children develop concepts.
- Explain why technology can endanger or support concept development.

**cognitive**

Pertains to the mind and how it works.

The term **cognitive** has already been used numerous times in this text to refer to certain types of child behavior. In this section, the term is defined and described in more detail and applied to the preschool, kindergarten, and primary child's concept and language development. In this first chapter, the term *cognitive* is defined and various views of cognition described. The cognitive system, which includes cognitive development, structure, and functioning, is examined. Finally, the significance of brain development and functioning is considered.

**cognitive functioning**
Describes how the cognitive system works.

**cognitive structure**
Includes all the parts of the cognitive system; the content of the child's mind and how it is organized.

**cognitive development**
Changes in cognitive structure and functioning that may take place over time.

## COGNITIVE DEFINED

*Cognitive* pertains to the mind and how it works. The cognitive system is made up of three parts.

1. **Cognitive functioning** describes how the cognitive system works.
2. **Cognitive structure** includes all the parts of the cognitive system.
3. **Cognitive development** refers to changes in cognitive structure and functioning that may take place over time.

The term refers both to what is in the mind (what the child knows) and how the mind works (how the child thinks). Since we cannot see directly into the mind, we must guess what is happening in the child's mind from what he or she does. For example:

> Three-year-old Bill is playing with some small blocks. The blocks are several colors. Bill says, "This one is blue, this one is red, this one is green." He looks up at his mother, saying, "These blocks are all different colors."

From Bill's behavior, we can guess that he had formulated in his mind some idea about color. First, he can match the names blue, red, and green to the correct block. Second, he knows, that blue, red, and green are all colors (Figure 20–1). In Bill's mind, the ideas of blue, red, and green are stored in a place for "color"; this is an example of cognitive structure. The idea of each color enters Bill's mind first. Next, the idea of color enters and becomes the place in which to store the ideas of red, blue, and green.

In the example of Bill and the blocks, cognitive functioning denotes what happens as each color idea enters Bill's mind, is stored for future use, remembered when needed, and applied to some problem Bill wishes to solve. In this case, he matches the color names to the blocks with which he is playing. In this chapter, cognitive functioning, structure, and development are described. Structure is further elaborated through a more detailed discussion of concept development.

**formal operations period**
Piaget's fourth period; appears in early adolescence, around eleven or twelve years of age.

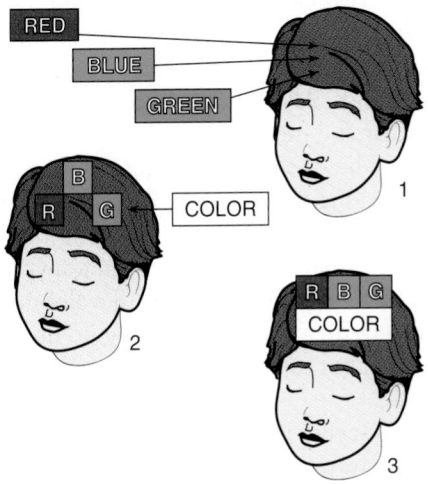


FIGURE 20–1 Bill learns that red, blue, and green are all colors.

## COGNITIVE DEVELOPMENT

Piaget found that the child uses his or her mind in a different way in each period of cognitive development. He identified four periods of cognitive development (Figure 20–2). Between the ages of three and eight, children pass through the preoperational period and enter the concrete operational period. Young children usually enter concrete operations some time between the fifth and the eighth year. The **formal operations period** usually does not appear until early adolescence, around eleven or twelve years of age.

The toddler is passing from the sensorimotor into the preoperational period. This period may last from around the age of two until about seven. Between ages five and seven, there is a transition period or time of change during which the child is moving into the next period. This stage is called the five-to-seven shift. A child may reach concrete operations at five or at seven or sometime in between. During the preoperational period, the focus of development changes from sensory

| Age | Period |
|---|---|
| Birth to two | Sensorimotor |
| Two to five | Preoperational |
| Five to seven | Transition: preoperational to concrete operations |
| Seven to eleven | Concrete operations |
| Eleven through adulthood | Formal operations |

FIGURE 20–2 Piaget's periods of cognitive development.

and motor to language and speech. The child develops almost all the speech skills he or she will use through the rest of his or her life. After the preschool period, language becomes more complex, but by four, the child usually has developed most of the basic skills.

The preoperational child learns through pretend play. The child views the world from his or her own point of view and believes only what he or she sees in the way he or she sees it. Although the child's mind works more like an adult's than does an infant's, it is still operating differently. The child comes up with many ideas that seem wrong to adults but are right within the limits of the way the young child can think. For example:

- Two-year-old Kate calls all small furry animals "ki-ki." This includes cats, dogs, rabbits, and squirrels.
- Three-year-old Bill pours his milk from a short, squat glass into a tall, thin glass and says, "Now I have more milk." The milk looks taller so there must be more of it (even though it is actually still the same amount).

**transition period**

From five to seven, when the way the child thinks changes from preoperational to concrete operational.

**concrete operational period**

When a child uses language to direct his or her own activities and the activities of others; the child is able to see another's point of view and consider it along with his or her own; the child is no longer as easily fooled by the way things look as he or she was before.

During this period, the child learns new skills through the imitation of others. He or she also begins to use one thing to represent something else. For example, the child may use sand as food, a doll as a real baby, or a stick as a gun while playing. As the child matures, the child can pretend that an object is there and does not need a real or a substitute object. He or she can eat from imaginary plates, sleep in imaginary beds, and play with imaginary friends. Also, as the child moves to the later stages of the preoperational period, he or she moves from simply imitating the actions of others to "becoming" the person he or she is imitating. That is, the child *is* the soldier, the father, or the grocer. Along with this comes play that involves acting out long, involved themes, such as going on a trip or buying things at the shopping mall. Lillard (1993a) suggests that between ages two and four, children's pretend representational play provides a zone of proximal development (ZPD) in which they participate in nonreal activities and places. They do not yet view these realities as being housed in the mind but take the behaviors and activities at face value.

The **transition period**, from age five to seven, is very important (Bartquis, Lilly, & Thomas, 2003). During this time, the way the child thinks changes from the preoperational to **concrete operational period.** We only know when this change takes place by observing and interviewing children. This is the time when most children start school. Just how ready a child is for the first grade depends on

FIGURE 20–3 In the concrete operations period, children can keep two or more things in mind at the same time and are able to play games with rules.

whether he or she has passed through the transition. The adult working with young five- and six-year-olds must help them through the transition. During this period of shift from preoperational to concrete operational thought, a number of changes take place. The child uses language to direct his or her own activities and the activities of others. The child is able to see another's point of view and to consider it along with his or her own. The child is no longer as easily fooled by the way things look.

- At age five, Kate recognizes and names many kinds of small furry animals correctly and knows that they all fall under the label *animal*.
- When Bill, now six, pours his milk into a taller, thinner glass, he knows and can tell that "the glass is taller but it is also thinner—there is the same amount of milk."

During kindergarten and the primary grades, we can expect that children will be in the transition stage from preoperational to concrete operational ways of thinking (Figure 20–3).

## Supporting Cognitive Development

Support for cognitive development may come in several forms this author finds complementary. From the Piagetian point of view, the child constructs his or her own knowledge from within. The adult acts as a guide and supplies the necessary opportunities to interact with objects and people (Kamii, 1986). Vygotskian theory emphasizes the importance of scaffolding by an adult or older child in the ZPD (Berk & Winsler, 1995). From Vygotsky's view, learning leads development as children receive instruction from more expert partners (Berk & Winsler, 1995). The instruction enables the child to move upward in the ZPD toward his or her level of potential development. Thus, the child is an active learner in an active social environment. This type of education is labeled assisted discovery; children are encouraged to discover but, at the same time, receive instruction that moves them ahead at a faster pace.

Comparing the two theories, Brown (1988) notes that Piaget and Vygotsky value both individual and social aspects of knowledge acquisition. Bandura's social cognitive theory adds a further perspective (Perry, 1989). Bandura's theory supplies a framework for "how children operate cognitively on their social experiences and how these cognitive operations, in turn, influence the child's behavior and development" (Perry, 1989, p. 3). All three theorists view the child's increasing ability to handle symbols as the crux of cognition. Children learn by constructing knowledge through acting on the environment, as a result of adult support at the right time, and through observing what others do.

Thus, Piaget and Vygotsky have some common points (Berk & Winsler, 1995):

- Natural and social development take place simultaneously and interact.
- Development is the result of experience in an environment.
- As children develop, major qualitative changes occur in their thinking. Piaget emphasizes the movement through stages, whereas Vygotsky emphasizes the

child's increased language capabilities and that more expert instruction assists children in becoming more aware and in control of their own thinking.

The essential context for cognitive development in early childhood is a play-based curriculum (Gmitrova and Gmitrov, 2003). From their research, Gmitrova and Gmitrov conclude (p. 245):

> . . . the types of cognitive skills that are demonstrated in pretense is as important (or even more important) for academic readiness and later school success than memorizing the standard set of information officially targeted as early childhood competencies.

They point out the value of younger children playing with older children as support for cognitive development as suggested by Vygotsky's theory of ZPD.

Using the information you have regarding cognitive development, analyze the following examples of young children's thinking:

- Five-year-old John is playing tag with some friends. The sun is going in and out of the clouds. One time when the sun disappeared and then reappeared, John yelled to his mother, "Mom, look! The sun is winking at me."
- Larry is six years old. "Mom, can I play outside?" Larry asked. "Did you look outside, Larry? Well, I'm sorry, honey, but it's raining; you'll have to play inside." Larry went to the door and opened it up. "Oh man, it is raining! It's not supposed to rain today, those stupid weather men, they don't know anything. They don't even know how to look outside and see if there's clouds or not. They need to go back to school."

## COGNITIVE STRUCTURE

The content of the child's mind and the way it is organized is called the cognitive structure. Within the child's mind, there are units of thought. Large units of thought are concepts. These units of thought are the bits and pieces that are used in the child's thought processes. Simple units that start to develop in infancy were called **schema** (plural: *schemata*) by Piaget. He believed that these are partial pictures of what the infant actually sees and experiences. A schema includes the highlights of what the infant perceives. For example, if the child has seen a circle once, he or she will show signs of recognition when seeing it again, but may not realize it is the same shape. As the child stores more schemata, he or she gradually develops preconcepts and then concepts. A preconcept or a concept ties several schemata or events together.

**schema**
Partial pictures of what an infant actually sees and experiences, including the highlights of what the infant perceives.

**overgeneralizations**
When a child encounters a new thing and places it in his or her mind where there is something like it.

**overdiscriminations**
When a child cannot seem to find a place for certain things that do not look the way they are expected to.

During the late sensorimotor and early preoperational periods, the child's schemata join into preconcept groups. Preconcepts may be **overgeneralizations** or **overdiscriminations**. When the child overgeneralizes, he or she encounters a new thing and places it in his or her mind in the area where there is something like it. For example, Kate has in her mind a small furry four-legged thing she calls "ki-ki." We call it a cat. She sees a new thing that is small furry and four-legged (a rabbit) and calls it "ki-ki." She then sees a skunk and next a squirrel. She calls each one "ki-ki." Another child puts a paper bag on his head, saying, "Hat." Then he puts a boot on his head and then a cardboard box. Each time he says,"Hat."

Although the child overgeneralizes with some things, he or she overdiscriminates with others. The child cannot seem to find a place for certain things that do not look the way they are expected to. For example, John meets his teacher in the supermarket. He looks shocked, hangs back, and clings to his dad. For him, this is not the same person he sees each day at nursery school. Mentally, he cannot accept his teacher out of context.

By the time the child is in the late preoperational period, he or she has acquired some simple concepts. That is, the child has begun tying schemata together into groups that have common attributes. These concept groups somewhat resemble those of adults. The child begins to store round things together, furry and feathery things together, things with wheels together, and so on. For Kate, "ki-ki" becomes "kitty" and belongs with "cats." She learns "dog" is associated with furry creatures that bark, jump on you, and lick your face. Both are animals and both are pets. Some kinds of cats are not pets—these are wild animals. Cat, dogs, pets, animals, and wild animals are all concepts.

**preconcepts**
Partial, immature concepts.

The same thing happens with the concept of animals just described. Look at Figure 20–4. As an infant, the nine schemata enter the infant's mind (1). During the preoperational period, these nine schemata develop into **preconcepts** (2) and then into concepts, such as the three groups in (3), dogs, house cats, and wild cats. Finally, these three concepts are grouped under the broad concept of "animals."

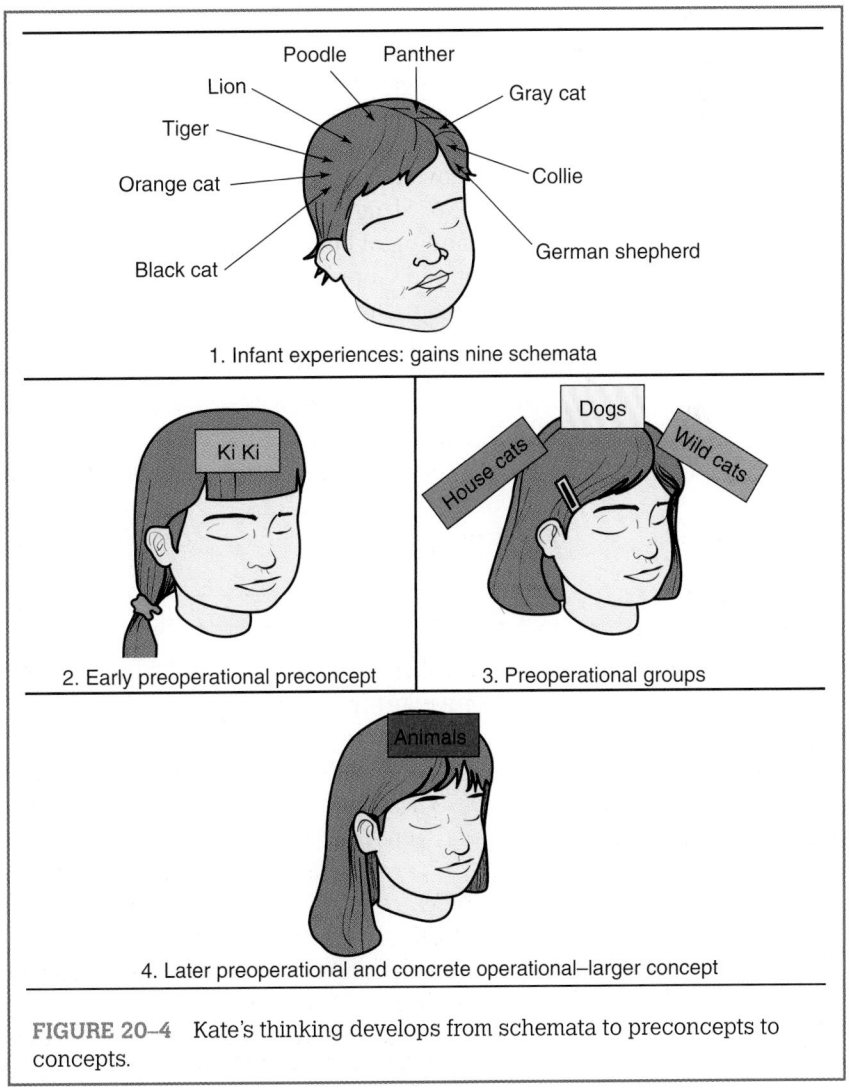


**FIGURE 20–4** Kate's thinking develops from schemata to preconcepts to concepts.

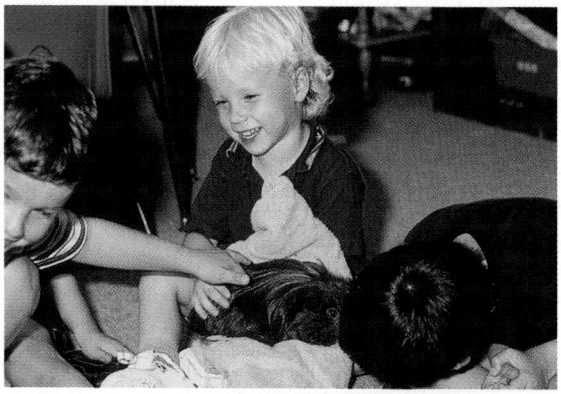

FIGURE 20–5 Eventually, the child's cognitive structure will find a space other than "kiki" for all small, furry creatures.

These concepts, the raw material that the child uses for thought, make up the cognitive structure (Figure 20–5).

An interesting area of research is identification of when and how children begin to reflect on their own thinking (Berk, 1998). Researchers are curious regarding when children begin to develop a **theory of mind.** This act of thinking about thought is called **metacognition.** As adults, we can think about our mental acts, such as those listed in Figure 20–6 (e.g., recalling, reasoning, problem solving). Berk (1998) points out that young children often use words such as *think*, *remember*, and *pretend*. They can also begin to understand that belief and reality can differ; that is, it is possible to hold **false beliefs.**

According to Wellman and Hickling (1994) and Wellman, Cross, and Watson (2001), children appear to acquire an initial *theory of mind* in the period from age three to age five. However, their view is not exactly like the adult view of mind, which perceives the mind as a separate, active thing that has a life of its own. For example, as adults, we may say, "My mind is not working well today" or "My mind is playing tricks on me." This view of the mind appears to develop from about ages six to ten. Children younger than six have some understanding of mental structure and functioning, but it is limited. By four-and-a-half or five, they may relate thinking to "seeing" but do not perceive the mind as an independent structure.

Much research focuses on children's understanding of **belief** (e.g., Murachver, Pipe, Gordon, Owens, & Fivush, 1996; O'Sullivan, Howe, & Marche, 1996; Slaughter & Gopnik, 1996). One method for ascertaining children's understanding of belief is to look at how they explain false beliefs. For example, Slaughter and Gopnik showed three- and four- year-olds things that were not what they appeared to be, such as soap that looked like golf balls and a Band-Aid® box that contained a tiny book. The children would predict what the ballshaped items were

**theory of mind**
The act of thinking about thought.

**metacognition**
Refers to knowledge and thinking about cognition.

**false beliefs**
Beliefs that do not fit reality.

**belief**
An opinion.

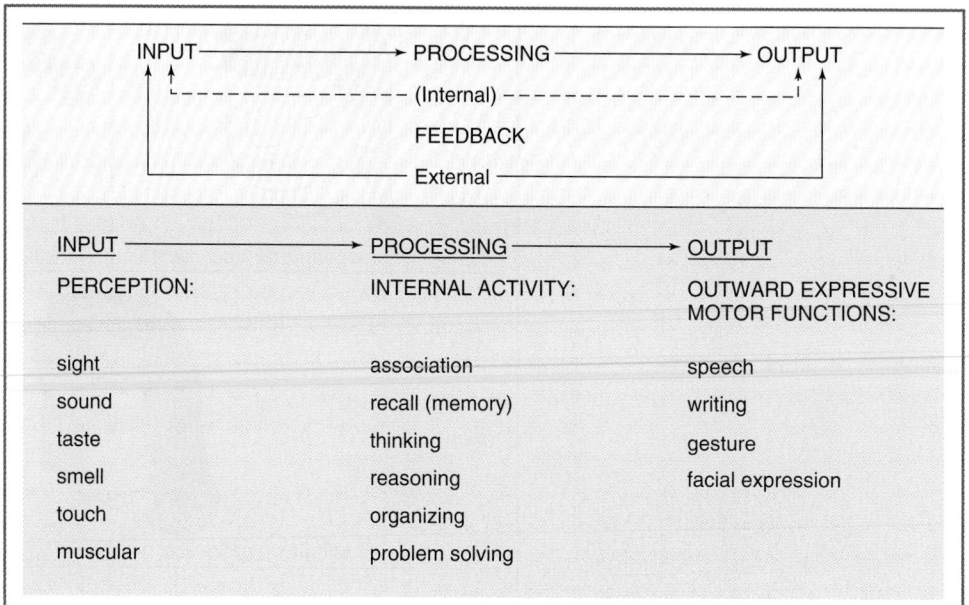


FIGURE 20–6 Model of cognitive functioning.

or what was in the Band-Aid® box. Then they would examine the item and discover that their initial belief was false. Some young children appeared to ignore that their perception led them to a false belief, whereas others demonstrated shock when provided with contradictory information. This reaction indicates they were aware that their minds had tricked them.

Lillard (1993a) reviewed the research on young children's pretend play and the relation of pretend play, especially representational play, to children's knowledge of the mind. As already mentioned, pretend play appears to be a bridge to understanding how the mind works. However, preoperational children do not appear to make the connection between pretend and mental representation. That is, they view action at face value without understanding that, for example, when a person is pretending a banana is a telephone, they have a mental representation (or picture) in their mind of the banana as food and as a pretend telephone (Lillard, 1993b).

O'Sullivan, Howe, and Marche (1996) looked at children's views of long-term memory. They found that most preschoolers could not explain that the major details of a story would be more easily remembered than the minor details, whereas third-grade children could recognize and explain this factor. Preschoolers believe that memory is an exact representation of reality; that is, they do not have the concept of false belief. Murachver et al. (1996) compared event memories acquired through direct experience, observation, and stories. The children in their study were New Zealanders of European descent, ages five and six. Their general finding was that the actual experience of acting out the story enhanced memory more than observation or just hearing a story when children were interviewed about the experience three or four days later. Flavell, Green, and Flavell (1993) asked young children if the brain is doing anything when a person is sitting still. They believed that the brain is essentially empty. Even a large percentage of six- and seven-year-olds did not perceive that the mind is continuously thinking. Young children can be helped to develop better and more efficient cognitive strategies through training in memory strategies and practice in reflecting on their ideas.

Estes (1998) looked at children's ability to describe a mental activity as an indication of their awareness of the workings of the mind. As adults, we often review events and actions in our minds, such as reviewing a book we have read or a conversation we had, and make mental plans, such as how to rearrange furniture or the route to take to get to a particular place. Estes's concern was finding out at what age children become aware of how their mind works and when they can offer a mental explanation for their thinking after they have solved a simple problem. Estes had four-year-olds, six-year-olds, and adults solve a simple rotation problem. A computer game was used. The children and adults were shown a series of paired monkeys and told to decide whether each member of the pairs was holding up the same hands. Each pair had a monkey standing upright while the second monkey might be upright, on its side, or upside down. Therefore, to solve the problem, the figures had to be rotated mentally. Most of the four-year-olds gave nonmental explanations such as "Cause, um, that monkey, he's upside down and that one's standing up, so I can tell the difference" (p. 1351). Most of the six-year-olds and adults could give mental rotation explanations, such as "Pretend your mind put them right side up. I turn this one around in my mind" (p. 1351).

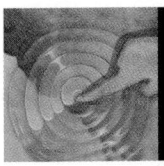

**LOOKING FURTHER**

Interview several young children ages three to seven. Prepare some false-belief materials, such as the ones described in this chapter. Have each child tell what they believe about each material and then let them examine it. Note if they can tell you what happened in their minds when they discovered the truth.

Examples of metacognitive research and practice based on metacognition research are described by Casanova (1990). Casanova (1990) makes some suggestions for practice that can help students think about what they are learning and thus be more efficient learners. For example, suppose a child comes into class with an insect specimen and asks the teacher what it is. Instead of just telling the children or looking it up, the teacher can first ask if any of the children know what the specimen is. Then the teacher can ask how they might confirm or disconfirm their ideas. The children might suggest looking it up in a book or asking their parents. Finally, after discussing the possibilities, the teacher could assign finding out the insect's name as homework. In this manner, the children learn to think about how to obtain information, weigh alternatives, obtain information, and eventually decide on an answer. When the children plan, organize information, and make decisions, they are using their metacognitive skills.

## COGNITIVE FUNCTIONING

Cognitive functioning refers to the way cognition works. The usual way to picture cognitive functioning is as a sequence that involves a stimulus and then some sort of activity in the mind followed by a response. We can observe the stimulus and the response but not the activity in the mind. All this unobservable activity is cognition. This is an information processing point of view. The stimulus is the **input**, the response is the **output**, and the internal activity is **processing**.

**input**
In cognitive functioning, this is the stimulus.

**output**
In cognitive functioning, this is the response.

**processing**
In cognitive functioning, this is the internal activity.

The model of cognitive functioning in Figure 20–6 shows there is a fourth aspect to cognitive functioning—feedback. Following the response or output, there is a response (either external or internal) that serves as another stimulus (or input). At the bottom of the diagram are definitions of input, processing, and output. Input is acquired through perception, which is the interpretation of what is sensed. Once perceived, information is processed. Processing may involve recall, thinking, reasoning, organizing, associating, problem solving, or combinations of all these processes. Output is always some kind of motor expressive activity, such as speaking, writing, gesturing, or making facial expressions.

If any of the three aspects of cognitive functioning does not work as it should, a malfunction results. For the child in the preoperational stage, perception works differently than for the older child and the adult. The preoperational child cannot attend, or pay attention, to all aspects of the information before him or her at the same time. This results in the receipt of only part of the available information. Thus, he or she often comes up with problem solutions that seem wrong from the adult point of view. Piaget refers to this process of being overwhelmed by one aspect, such as height, as **centering**. As the child gains more experience perceiving things, he or she learns more details and gains a more complete overall picture for each schema. As the child develops into concrete operations, he or she is able to attend to, perceive, and process more bits of information at the same time.

**centering**
In cognitive functioning, Piaget refers to the process of being overwhelmed by one aspect.

To show how cognitive functioning works, consider the following example. A college student, working with three-year-old Celina, gives her a digit-span test (Figure 20–7).

> . . . I used a digit span of 2-4-6, followed by 2-4-6-8-1, and the seven-digit span was 2-4-6-8-1-3-5.
>
> I began the activity with Celina. She was able to correctly repeat the first span. The second span was confusing for her. After a few seconds of deliberation, she responded with 1-8-6-2.

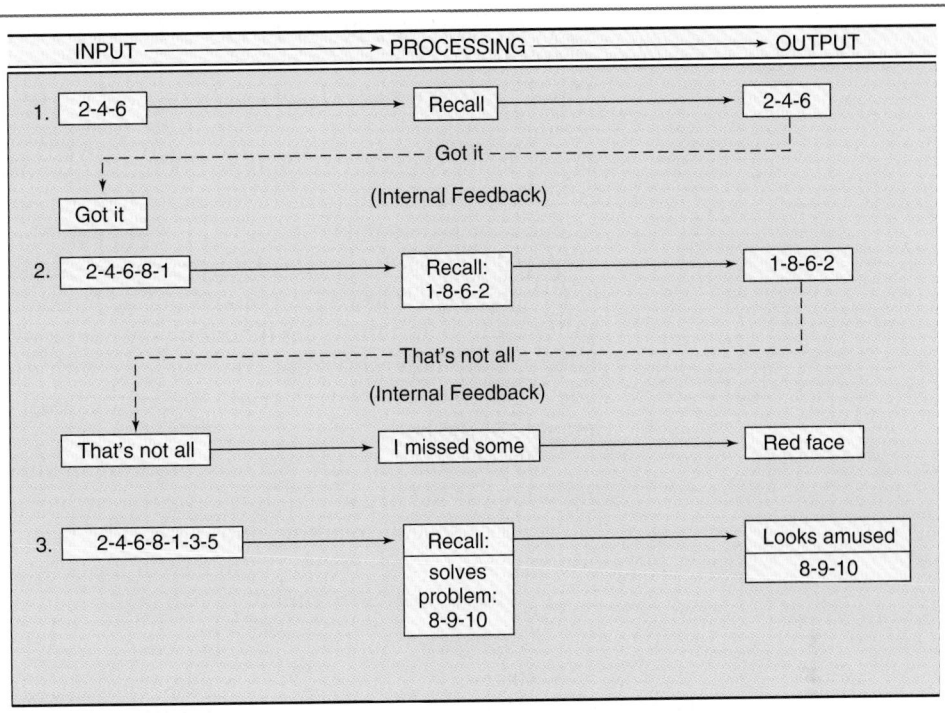


**FIGURE 20–7** Celina's cognitive functioning when presented with three-digit span problems.

> I observed a mild reaction of embarrassment. The seven-digit span was totally lost. Celina looked amused and offered her own span of 8-9-10. The last digit span seemed to go right over her head, as if she wasn't paying attention.

The input in this case, the three series of digits, was auditory. Processing involved mainly memory (recall), and output was the repeating of the digits (Figures 20–7 and 20–8). There appears to have been some internal feedback as evidenced by the look of embarrassment after her second response and the look of amusement after the third. That is, Celina perceived her own mistakes and responded with embarrassment in the first case and amusement in the second.

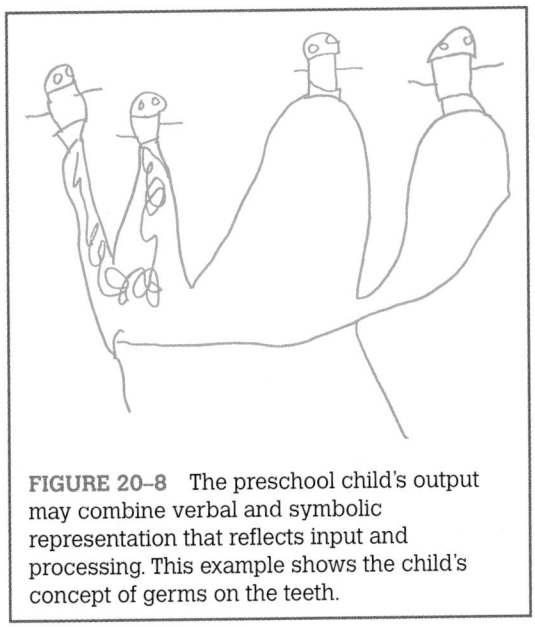

**FIGURE 20–8** The preschool child's output may combine verbal and symbolic representation that reflects input and processing. This example shows the child's concept of germs on the teeth.

In Piaget's scheme, assimilation and accommodation are the functional aspects of cognition. Assimilation is the input aspect and accommodation is the processing aspect.

Problem-solving approaches to learning support more complex cognitive functioning. Casanova's (1990) examples of metacognition-based teaching can be categorized as a problem-solving approach. Critical thinking is another name given to problem-solving approaches. Problem solving requires that students be creative and construct their own rules, rather than have rules provided by someone else. Developing and enhancing young children's thinking skills is the focus of several articles in *Young Children* (Encouraging young children to develop and enhance their thinking skills, 2003). Suggestions are made regarding board games for logico-mathematical thinking (Kamii, 2003), planning and reflection (Epstein, 2003), and principles for teaching complex thinking (Tharp & Entz, 2003).

## THE BRAIN AND COGNITION

A great deal of interest has focused on how the brain functions in cognitive processing and learning (Cherry, Godwin, & Staples, 1989; Languis, Sanders, & Tipps, 1980; Shonkoff & Phillips, 2000). Researchers have been especially interested in how different parts of the brain function in controlling different types of cognitive, sensory, and motor activity. Left- and right-side brain function has been of special interest. Each side of the brain processes in a different way, as mentioned in Chapter 14. However, as pointed out by Jensen (1998), what may appear to be either a left- or a right-brain function may not be when examined closely. The two sides operate differently, but communicate with each other. In addition, the left side of the brain controls the right side of the body, and the right side controls the left side of the body.

The brain's left side reacts to input in an analytic way. Left-brain processing is logical and organized. It is basic to learning logical ideas and skills, such as the rules of speech, reading, and math. The brain's right side controls orientation in space, creative talents, awareness of the body, and face recognition (Ornstein, 1973). The hemispheric functions can be divided as follows (Cherry et al., 1989, p. 13):

**HEMISPHERIC FUNCTIONS**

**Left Brain**

- analyzes
- uses logic
- is aware of time
- deals with events in sequence
- reduces to parts
- assembles a whole from parts
- systematic
- verbalizes and processes language
- sorts and organizes
- mathematical
- pragmatic
- cognitive
- factual
- concrete
- abstract

**Right Brain**

- responds to intuition
- uses impulses, spontaneous
- temporal unawareness
- random, lack of sequence
- holistic—no concern about separate parts
- nonverbal: associates words by touching object, not by viewing picture
- diffuses information
- recognizes faces, three-dimensional shapes, patterns
- responsive to tones, sounds
- originative, concerned with ideas
- sensory
- processes imagery, visual
- symbolic, representational

When input is taken in, each half of the brain perceives it in a different way (Cherry et al., 1989; Languis et al., 1980):

> Rudy is painting a picture. The left side of his brain reacts in a logical fashion: The tree must have a brown trunk and branches and green leaves. The right side of his brain reacts emotionally: The paint colors are bright and warm and his arm is moving in motions that feel good and bring a pleasing result on the paper.

If both sides are working together in a complementary fashion, Rudy will paint an original but realistic-looking tree. If the left side dominates, he may be obsessed more with logic than originality and satisfaction. The result might be a realistic but stereotyped tree. If the right side of the brain dominates, logic may be left behind and the tree may have a yellow trunk, purple leaves, and other original-looking features.

Languis and associates (1980) point out that educators often emphasize left-side learning and ignore right-side learning. Complete understanding involves integrating both kinds of perception and processing. To tap total creative potential, educators must provide experiences that use both sides of the brain.

Brain development has been discussed in previous chapters. The brain goes through many changes throughout life (*Brain Wonders*, 2006). Throughout middle childhood (four to eight years of age), the brain continues to remain at a peak level of synapses. From the middle of the elementary school years until the end of adolescence, the number of synapses gradually lessens. The brains of young children work very hard and reach a peak in energy level in middle childhood. Myelination continues on into the 20s in the areas of the brain that support higher order thinking.

Stimulating early experiences are essential to early brain development (*Is early experience enough?* 2002). Good positive experiences support stronger neuron connections and pruning of unnecessary connections. However, enriched experiences must continue into middle childhood for children to maintain cognitive gains.

## CONCEPT DEVELOPMENT

**concepts**
The building blocks of cognitive structure.

**Concepts** are the building blocks of cognitive structure, and they form the basic parts of the young child's cognitive structure—for example, categories, such as people, animals, cars, and houses, or attributes, such as red things, smooth things, and sweet things. Compared to the concepts of older children and adults, young children's concepts seem incomplete and even incorrect. Therefore, they may come up with responses that seem wrong to adults but are right from the children's viewpoints. For example:

> A young boy is trying to get his mother to buy him an ice cream cone. The mother is saying no. The boy wants to know why. The mother explains that she does not have enough money. Using child level logic, the boy asks, "Why don't you get some money from the wall?" (that is the bank money machine) (Goodman, 1991).

The concept that money has to be given to the bank before we can go to the "wall" and get it back is too abstract for a preschooler. It is not until second or third grade that children begin to understand where we get money and what we can do with it.

Each concept has various aspects to it. What we want to find out about young children is how far along they are in understanding the parts and putting them together.

## THE BASIC CHARACTERISTICS OF PREOPERATIONAL THOUGHT

Piaget's view of early concept development is very popular. It is meaningful to adults who work with young children and applicable to teaching and understanding the young child. Some basic concepts the young child learns (e.g., size, shape, number, classification, comparison, space, parts and wholes, volume, weight, length, temperature, and time) have previously been mentioned.

The child who is in the preoperational period thinks in a manner characteristic of that period. As the child enters the preoperational period at age two, he

FIGURE 20–9 The preoperational child views problems from his or her own point of view, centering on the obvious.

or she has acquired object permanence and has had his or her first real thoughts and insights. The child's rate of motor development has leveled off, as he or she can now walk, run, and climb and has fairly good small-muscle skills, such as self-feeding and using a crayon. Acquiring language becomes a major focus of development; representational or symbolic play becomes an essential activity.

The preoperational child's view of the world has been referred to as **egocentric**, meaning that the child centers perception on the most obvious and is bound by what he or she sees (Figure 20–9). The child also tends to feel that seeing is believing. Physical operations cannot be mentally reversed. For example, if some pennies are moved in space, such as from a row to a pile, the preoperational child cannot reverse the moving of the pennies back to the row in his or her mind. Everyone does not agree with Piaget's conclusion that preoperational children are egocentric (Lee, 1989), as young children do appear to see another's point of view in certain situations, such as offering sympathy when someone is hurt. Lee (1989) suggests that they perceive differently in social rather than in physical situations. They seem more able to decenter in social situations than in physical situations.

**egocentric**

Centers perception on the most obvious and is bound by what is seen.

Preoperational thinking is reflected in the young child's everyday actions. Cause and effect are the most obvious associations, such as in "Juanita gave me candy. She is a nice girl." Or "John won't share the clay. He is a bad boy." A person's value, good or bad, is determined by his or her most immediately observed actions. What the preoperational child sees is what he or she believes. When something happens to shake that belief, the child is cognitively unable to accept it. Bobby sees a male kindergarten teacher on television. He denies the possibility, thinking, "At my school, all the kindergarten teachers are ladies—that's the way it is supposed to be." That is the way he saw it in real life, and that is the way it is to him. The discrepancy is impossible to accept.

**operations**

Actions that take place internally as part of the organized cognitive structure.

At age five, the child may already be passing from preoperational into concrete thinking. As he or she arrives at concrete operations, he or she begins to correct the illogical ways (from the adult point of view) of thinking typical of the preoperational period.

FIGURE 20–10 The child who has reached concrete operations can keep more than one attribute of a problem in mind, such as 3 + 4 is the same as 4 + 3.

## THE BASIC CHARACTERISTICS OF CONCRETE OPERATIONAL THOUGHT

As the child enters and proceeds through the concrete operations period, the child is able to mentally reverse transformations, such as in the following conservation problems. The child relies less on the most obvious aspect of a problem and can retain several variables in mind at the same time (Figure 20–10). This period starts at about age seven and is not usually fully achieved until age eleven or even beyond (Miller, 2002).

**Operations** are actions that take place internally as part of the organized cognitive structure. Mathematics operations, when presented through concrete tasks, are easily observed. Each step, from putting sets in one-to-one correspondence to operations, such as addition, subtraction, multiplication, and division, grows through the gradual building of a system of mental actions. As we will see in later chapters, social actions also change as the child enters and proceeds through the concrete operations period (Miller, 2002). Now children can reverse thought, they can decenter, and their thinking is more in line with that of adults. It is important for adults to keep in mind that "the concrete operations are still 'concrete.' They can be applied only to concrete objects—present or mentally represented. They deal with 'what is' rather than what 'could be'" (Miller, 2002, p. 56). At best, when young children are entering the primary grades, they are only in the beginning stages of the concrete operational period.

## SOME BASIC CONCEPTS

### Classification and Logical Thinking

**classification**

The ability to classify and categorize items in the environment.

One of the most important cognitive skills is the ability to classify and categorize items in the environment. Children learn which items are red, which we use to cover our bodies, which are cars, and which are toys. They also learn that an item may belong to more than one category, such as *red*, *sweater*, and *wool*. **Classification** is also basic to understanding math and science. In math, the concept of sets or groups is fundamental. The child must understand the concept of *apples* and the concepts of *red* and *green* to use these concepts in a problem-solving situation, such as three green apples plus two red apples equals five apples. In science, categorizing is also a basic operation. For example, in geology, minerals are identified by attributes, such as color, hardness, and smoothness.

Naturalistic categorizing may become a part of everyday play activities, which can be seen in four-year-old Joanie's following actions:

> As Joanie is coloring a picture of her family, she decides to dump out the markers. She then decides to put all the same-colored markers together in a group. When the colors are all sorted into their groups, Joanie decides that each color group is a family. She gives each marker a name, and she begins to speak for each marker in a different voice. She decides that the red marker family is going to go to St. George. She puts the red marker family into a box and carries them into another room, which she has decided will be St. George.

Joanie groups the markers into logical groups according to color. Then she moves into a dramatic-play sequence, using one of her color groups to represent a family going on a trip.

The toddler and the preschool child spend a great deal of time moving objects into different groups. The following examples, noted by two university students, show the contrast between a three-year-old's sorting behavior and that of a five-and-a-half-year-old. Tito is three and Kate is five.

> Tito was given four squares, four triangles, and four circles, one each of blue, green, yellow, and red. When asked to sort the shapes into a group, he sorted them by shape. When asked to divide them another way, he spent several minutes reorganizing and came up with the same pattern.
>
> Kate had been given the same set of shapes. She also piled them first according to shape. When asked to sort them another way, she promptly sorted them by color.

Tito, being a typical preoperational thinker, sorted the shapes one way and remained centered on shape when asked to try another criteria. Kate, on the other hand, moving toward concrete operations, could decenter and change to color with ease. As already mentioned in Chapter 17, by two-and-a-half or three, young children's logical classification becomes more mature and moves from preconcepts to concepts. Gelman (1998) and her colleagues found that children make broader generalizations between two-and-a-half and four years of age. These broader categories usually focus on people and animals and are expressed by children and their mothers. Nguyen and Murphy (2003) found that three-year-olds and four- to seven-year-olds could classify items into more than one category if questioned with an open-ended task.

Underlying the ability to classify is knowledge of a number of basic concepts:

- color, shape, and size
- material, such as paper, cloth, wood, and plastic
- pattern, such as dots, stripes, or plain
- function (items share a common use, such as all are things with which to eat or to write)
- association (items are related to each other but do not perform a common function: Milk goes in a cup; matches are for lighting the candle; but you buy them both at the store)
- class names, such as food, animals, tools, people
- common elements (all have wheels, all have long hair, or all have T-shirts on)

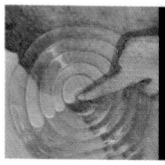

**LOOKING FURTHER**

With a group of fellow students, pool items taken at random from your purses, backpacks, or pockets. Study the array of items. Pretend you are a young child. Group the items according to the logical categories you perceive. What is the basis for your groupings, such as color, material, pattern, function, association, class names, or common elements? Compare your groupings with those of other students. See how many different kinds of groups can be developed by sorting and regrouping the items. What is the difference between what you would do as a young child and what you do as an adult?

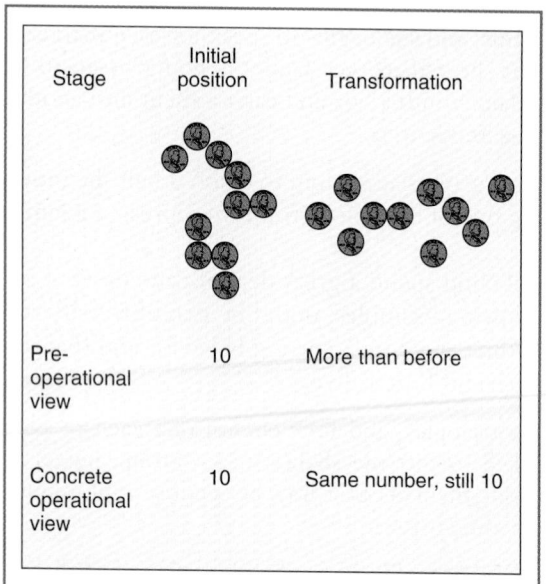


**FIGURE 20–11** A change in thinking takes place from the preoperational to the concrete operational period.

## Conservation

With the inability to decenter, the preoperational child is not yet what Piaget labeled a conserver. The attainment of **conservation** involves the ability to understand the transformation of materials without being fooled by appearances. For example (Figure 20–11), a bunch of pennies are placed in front of the child. Then a transformation is made; that is, the positions of the pennies are changed. In this case, they are spread out. When asked if the number of pennies is still the same or if there are more, the preoperational child will answer "more." The preoperational child centers on the amount of space used, not on the actual number of pennies. Also, the child cannot reverse the transformation in his or her mind. The concrete operations child, on the other hand, says, "There is still the same number, 10." This child can reverse the operation in his or her mind and is not fooled by the amount of space used in each case. He or she can think about two things at once: the number of pennies and the amount of space.

Number is typically the first conservation concept that develops, around age six or seven (Cole, Cole, & Lightfoot,

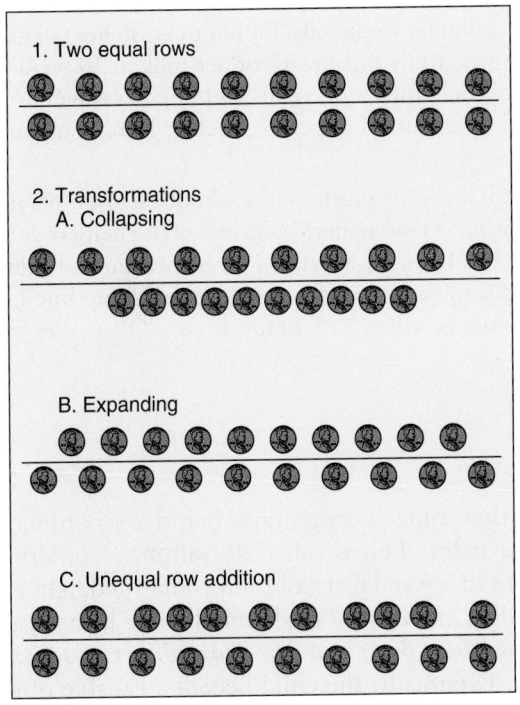


FIGURE 20–12 One-to-one correspondence (1. Two equal rows) and three transformations (2. A, B, C).

2005). To find out if the child can conserve number, he or she is first shown one row of 10 objects (7 at a minimum) and asked to make a row with the same amount, as shown in Figure 20–12. If the child is unable to construct an equal row, he or she has not developed the concept of **one-to-one correspondence** and the interview proceeds no further. The younger preoperational child spends long hours of playtime working on one-to-one correspondence (Figure 20–13). In the task described first, the child who has not developed one-to-one correspondence is likely to produce a row such as the following:

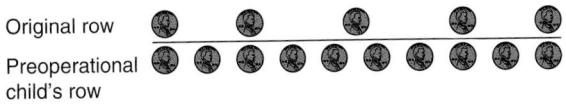


The child has centered on just length rather than length and number.

Look again at Figure 20–12. If the child demonstrates that he or she does have the concept of one-to-one correspondence, the child is then shown a series of transformations, such as in 2A, B, and C. In each case, the child first agrees that there are two equal rows. Then a transformation is made, and the child is asked, "Do both rows have the same amount or does one have more?" The preoperational child answers that the longer row in each case has more. When asked why, the child usually answers, "'Cause it's longer." The concrete operational child answers, "There's the same amount. You just moved one row." The transitional child has to check by counting or by putting the pennies back into one-to-one correspondence. As the child moves further into the concrete operations stage, he or she is able to handle transformations of additional kinds of materials, such as a ball of clay made into a pancake or snake; water poured into a tall, thin or short, fat container; or a straight path made into a curved path. In preparation for the time when the child can conserve, the preschool child works on one-to-one correspondence between objects; on parts and wholes with clay; on volume with water and sand; and on *more*, *less*, and *the same* with many kinds of materials.

**conservation**

The ability to understand the transformation of materials without being fooled by appearances.

**one-to-one correspondence**

The basis of understanding equality.

FIGURE 20–13 The preoperational child spends time matching objects so that they pair up in one-to-one correspondence.

Although the preschool child cannot solve the number conservation problem, the child does have some knowledge of mathematical concepts (Charlesworth & Lind, 2006; Golbeck & Ginsburg, 2004). For example, by age three, the child has an understanding of *more* and *less*. When shown two groups of pennies, such as six versus four or five versus nine, the child can tell which group has more. By four or five years of age, after agreeing that two groups of pennies have the same amount, when the pennies are hidden in two boxes and one or two pennies are added to one box, the child realizes that there are now more pennies in one box than in the other. When a four-year-old is shown two small groups of objects, such as three blocks and two blocks, and asked the number of total blocks, he or she should be able to solve the problem by using some form of counting. Thus, the child demonstrates the beginning of an understanding of addition.

Young children enjoy applying their increasing counting skills during their everyday activities, which is evident in the following examples:

- Carlos (age four) has a surplus of energy! He performs repeating somersaults. He counts his somersaults, "One, two, three, four, five."

- Kelly (age four) is eating lunch and is interacting with her teacher, Carrie. Kelly asks Carrie to count how long it would take for her to finish her tall glass of milk. As Carrie counts slowly, Kelly finishes all of her milk in 10 seconds. After she finishes, Kelly seems delighted and counts to 10 on her fingers. She remarks triumphantly, holding up her 10 fingers, "Teacher, I drank my milk in this many!"
- Chan is five-and-a-half. He is with his mother at a school carnival, playing the fishpond game. "Hello, what is your name?" asks one of the helpers at the fishpond game. "Brady and I'm five-and-a-half." The helper hands Brady a pole to use. "Okay, let's count to three and then throw the fishing line into the pond to see what you can get. Ready?" Brady nods. "Okay, one . . . two . . . three."

## Seriation or Ordering

**seriation**

Ordering; putting things in order according to some criterion, such as size, age, or color.

Preschool children spend much of their time putting things in order according to some criterion such as size, age, or color. This is called **seriation**, or ordering. They begin with simple comparisons of big and little, old and young, and light and dark. (See Yuzautars, 2005.) They then move on to small, middle-sized, and large. They delight in stories such as *The Three Bears* and *The Three Billy Goats Gruff*, which make use of these concepts. Eventually, the child becomes capable of ordering four or more items. For example, Tito and Kate were asked to order some circles of different sizes.

> The next task was seriation. I gave Kate seven circles and asked her to show me the biggest and smallest. She had no problem doing this. When I asked her to put them in order by size from largest to smallest, she put them in the following order:
>
> 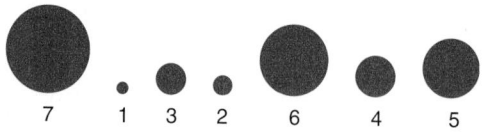
> 
>
> When I asked her to put them from smallest to largest, she put them in the following order
>
> 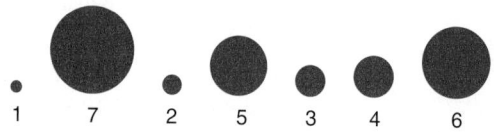
> 
>
> Each time she had the largest and smallest right next to each other.
>
> With the seriation activity for Tito came the most interesting observation. I gave him three circles: a big one, a medium one, and a small one. He pointed to the biggest and smallest ones correctly when asked. But when I asked him to put the three circles in order by size starting with the largest and going to the smallest, he picked up the smallest one and hid it under the largest one. (He did this when asked to try the task another time also.)

Tito seems to be at the comparison stage, at which he can handle only two sizes at once. Kate can see the two extremes in size but cannot yet attempt to put all the midsize circles in sequence. Another common response is the following, in which the child gets the shortest and longest sticks placed correctly but mixes up the sticks in between. The child centers on the ends of the sequence:

Seriation, or ordering, is often observed as young children engage in play activities. For example, three-year-old Isabel is lying on the floor talking to herself and her toys. She picks up every toy, of which there are about 12 to 15 individual characters, and places them into a straight, organized line, beginning with the cows. She starts with the largest cow first, all the way down to the baby cow. Next, she takes the horses and lines them up precisely as she did the cows. Next, she lines up the people, which she groups according to their gender, what they were doing, or other similarities. She places the women waving together, the little boys with hats together, and the men with curly hair and glasses together. She continues the process until all the toys are logically grouped and lined up in a row.

## Space

**spatial concepts**
Concepts that include the following: in, on, over, under, into, together, beside, between, on top, inside, outside, and below.

Development of **spatial concepts** also takes place during early childhood. Spatial concepts include concepts such as in, on, over, under, into, together, beside, between, on top, inside, outside, and below. Infants and toddlers begin to develop these concepts as they move their own bodies about and as they experiment with objects. Reifel (1984) suggests that using blocks is an excellent activity for learning about space. The toddler starts with soft, spongy blocks that he or she grasps, tastes, stuffs in containers, places next to each other, and eventually places on top of each other. Preschoolers can use wooden unit blocks as they progress from rows and piles to surfaces, enclosures, and eventually symbolic representations, such as a house or a skyscraper (Figure 20–14). As structures become more complex, children experiment with more spatial concepts placed in various combinations. Wolfgang, Stannard, and Jones (2001) found a positive correlation between preschool block performance and math achievement at the beginning of middle school (seventh grade) and in high school. The long-term, positive effect of higher-level block building appears to help the young child build the foundations for the mathematics met in the formal operations period.

FIGURE 20–14 Unit blocks provide an opportunity for children to work with spatial concepts and informal measurement.

Young children's concepts of space with regard to floor plans and maps have been studied. Uttal (1996) examined whether young children's reconstructions maintained the relative positions of objects within the configuration. The same problems were presented to four- and five-year-olds, six- and seven-year-olds, and adults. Objects were placed in parts of the room. The children and adults were asked to memorize the location of each object and then reconstruct the placement of the object on a map of the room. Generally, the younger children placed the objects farther from the target locations than the older children and the adults. The young children were more accurate with symmetric rather than with asymmetric organizations. Liben and Yekel (1996) also looked at preschoolers' understanding of maps. Four- and five-year-olds were asked to place stickers on classroom maps to show locations of objects that were visible to them. Both two-dimensional and three-dimensional plans were used. More than half of the children could explain the function of maps. However, they all had difficulty with the mapping task. They placed some items correctly and seemed to do better if they used the three-dimensional plan first.

## Causality

**causality**
Why things happen as they do in the world; "why" questions.

**animism**
Giving human characteristics to nonhuman things, such as cars, trees, wind, or the sun.

**artificialism**
The young child's feeling that everything in the world is made for people.

Young children ask adults many "why" questions. Piaget points out the importance of asking children about their view of why things happen as they do in the world from his research on **causality** (Charles, 1974). Piaget found that young children progress from realism to objectivity. Realism refers to the inability of the young child to clearly distinguish between self and others. As the child sees *I* as separate from the rest of the world, he or she reaches objectivity. The child who has not yet reached the objective stage will use animism and artificialism. **Animism** involves giving human characteristics to nonhuman things, such as cars, trees, wind, or the sun. **Artificialism** refers to the young child's feeling that everything in the world is made for people. (The sun exists to give us light and warmth, rather than we exist because we have the sun.) The three- to five-year-old may answer "why" questions in a number of ways that seem wrong from an adult point of view. For example:

1. The child may attribute human-type motivation as the cause of events. For example, we get hurt because we have been bad, or it snows because someone wants us to be cold.
2. If things are close together in time or space, they are viewed in a causal relationship.
3. Things are because they are. Dogs have tails because they are part of dogs. The rain falls because it falls from the sky.
4. A person's gestures, thoughts, and words may affect another person. Saying something bad to someone will actually hurt them.
5. Things happen because they have to happen. Airplanes fly so they will not crash. Night must end so day can begin.

The example that follows illustrates a young child's causal reasoning abilities.

| Adult | Kate, age four-and-a-half |
|---|---|
| Are you alive? | Yes. |
| Why? | Because that's the way God made us. |
| Is a cloud alive? | Yes. |
| Why? | Because God made that too. |
| Is a bicycle alive? | No, because it doesn't talk. |
| Is a car alive? | Yes, because it runs for real. |
| Is a tree alive? | No, because it sits there on the grass. |
| Is a gun alive? | No, because it doesn't talk. |

Kate refers to a higher authority as a reason for the existence of herself and clouds. In considering the manufactured items and the tree, she has a somewhat animistic interpretation. She decides whether each item is alive or not relevant to the human characteristics of being able to talk or run.

## Applications to Mathematics

The ideas and examples just described illustrate some of the basic concepts of mathematics and science (Charlesworth & Lind, 2006). The Piagetian view of cognitive development has served as the basis for a great deal of this research. Mathematics is a popular area for research on concept development.

A number of researchers have tried to accelerate mathematics learning through special training. Others have tried to show that children actually know more than Piaget gave them credit for knowing through assessing them in a different way (Price, 1982). There is disagreement as to whether the same concept is being tested if the tasks given to the children are changed. For example, Gelman and Gallistel (1983) simplified the number conservation task for two-, three-, and four-year-old children. They used much smaller groups of items, such as two to five, and showed that very young children have some concept of one-to-one correspondence and counting. However, to be conservers of number, children must be able to work with sets of 10 or more.

A great deal of the research with young children has focused on their counting skills more than on their understanding of number (Galbeck & Ginsburg, 2004). A developmental sequence for counting skills and the eventual application of counting skills to addition and subtraction has been identified. Although counting skills are important tools, they are not the sum total of early childhood mathematics. Not only are other important fundamental concepts, such as number sense (an understanding of what oneness, twoness, threeness, etc., mean), conservation, classification, and seriation involved in the process of development but also more important than just rote learning of number names is the development of an understanding of mathematics concepts (Charlesworth & Lind, 2006).

During the twentieth century, mathematics research with young children shifted from what they can't do to what they can do (Baroody, 2000). Some of the concepts that young children have include the following:

- As young as three, they have an understanding of the equivalence of small amounts, such as Δ Δ is the same amount as □ □ or Δ Δ Δ is the same amount as □ □ □.
- When children learn to count (around four years of age), they can compare larger groups and discover equivalence or nonequivalence.
- Once children understand the number sequence, such as four comes after three and is therefore more, they can make mental comparisons, usually up to five by the time they enter kindergarten and up to ten by the end of kindergarten.
- Preschoolers can solve simple addition and subtraction problems using concrete objects.
- Kindergartners can find strategies for fair-share problems that are the basis of division.

Baroody concludes that, since preschoolers have a great deal of informal mathematical knowledge, they should be involved in developmentally appropriate mathematical activities. Many opportunities for informal and structured instruction can be made available to young children (Charlesworth & Lind, 2006).

Significant research has looked at how children in different cultures develop mathematics concepts and at the factors that promote mathematics achievement in school. Both cultures within the United States and in other countries have been studied and compared. Researchers have been particularly intrigued at the advanced mathematical achievement of Asian elementary students, both in the United States and in their native countries (Stevenson & Lee, 1990) Ginsburg et al. (1989) found that within this country, it appears that upper-middle-class European-American and Asian American four-year-olds tend to be ahead, and African Americans, Latino Americans, and middle-class European Americans tend to be about equal in mathematical knowledge before they enter school.

Entwisel and Alexander (1990) assessed the beginning-of-first-grade mathematics status of large comparable samples of African American and European American students; their assessment took place in Baltimore and was measured by the California Achievement Test (CAT) administered during the fall of entrance into first grade. No significant differences were found between the two racial groups at that time. By the end of the year, the European American students had moved ahead. The researchers concluded that something is happening in school that results in this disparity. A social class difference was also noted, as performance improved among children whose parents had more economic resources. Parents' expectations were also a potent force in the level of achievement.

## APPLICATIONS OF CONCEPT DEVELOPMENT THEORY TO INSTRUCTION

This overview of concept development has outlined many of the concepts that are developing during early childhood. In this final part of the chapter, we look at how the concept development theories of Piaget and Vygotsky are related to educational practice.

### Applications of Piaget's Theory

Piaget's ideas may be applied to teaching young children in a number of ways, including applications for teaching (what the teacher does), for curriculum planning (what children can learn), and for diagnosis (where the child is at a certain point in his or her development). These applications come in the form of guiding principles rather than as specific ways to teach specific skills and concepts. Ginsburg and Opper (1979) recommend the following principles based on what they believe Piaget's work suggests for teachers:

- Learning should be child centered. It should be designed from the child's point of view rather than from the adult's perspective. Adults need to remember that children see things differently.
- Learning occurs best when it comes from self-initiated activity. This activity should include the use of real objects and the use of thought. We learn most from our reactions to our own activity. That is, the child who spends hours placing blocks in rows and putting a peg person on each one learns one-to-one correspondence from the activity itself and from his or her reactions to it. For example, finding that he or she has the same number of blocks as people, the child will repeat the activity over and over as if to confirm that this is true. The child may then label the colors of the blocks and count the number of blocks and people. Children should have opportunities for guided discovery.
- The wide range of development within a group of children underscores the need for individualized approaches to teaching and learning. Teachers need to find out where the child is to plan learning experiences that fit his or her level of development. The child needs a chance to work on his or her own.

- Social interaction assists the child in modifying his or her egocentric point of view. Through interactions with other children, the child finds that other people's opinions might differ from his or her own view. The child also learns that if he or she wants to convince others that he or she is right, a clear, logical argument must be developed.
- The child's learning is limited by the stage in which he or she happens to be. The stage also indicates which concepts the child should know or be in the process of learning.
- The interview techniques that Piaget developed tell us how the child thinks. The Piagetian interviews tell us which concept development stage a child is in.

As described by Roopnarine and Johnson (1993), Piaget's work has inspired a number of approaches to teaching practice in a constructivist framework. Leaders in this field are Constance Kamii, Rita DeVries, George Forman, and Loris Malaguzzi (Reggio Emilia in Italy). They each have their own interpretation of constructivism. Their basic differences focus on how directive the adult can be and the specificity of materials and activities. They all agree that children should work with concrete materials and should be encouraged to reflect on their actions in order to develop real understandings.

## Applications of Vygotsky's Theory

FIGURE 20–15 Sand and/or water offer open-ended experiences that can be explored by children in their own ways.

From Vygotsky's theory, as already discussed, we obtain a theoretical perspective of the importance of social interaction as support for children's learning (scaffolding) and of providing the right kind of support at the right time and the right level (the ZPD). To the Piagetian perspective of inner construction of knowledge is added an emphasis on the adult and/or other children providing support for concept development and acquisition. Vygotsky's theory provides a perspective for adding structure to children's experience and knowledge. Vygotsky provided us with the view that adult-child interdependence is central to instruction (Moll, 1990). Vygotsky's theory has been applied to preschool literacy instruction, writing instruction, instruction in the home, science instruction, and instruction for mildly retarded and learning disabled children (Moll, 1990). Combining the Piagetian-inspired views and the Vygotskian-inspired views into a post-Piagetian approach to instruction has created recommendations for "specific interactions and interventions in the process of children's knowledge construction, though they [Piagetians and post-Piagetians] similarly favor 'active methods' because of their shared constructivist view" (Berk & Winsler, 1995; Inagaki, 1992). This post-Piagetian approach to constructivism, as compared with the purely Piagetian constructivism, provides more teacher direction, such as using open-ended questions and providing materials that lend themselves to particular kinds of actions. Both Piaget and Vygotsky emphasize that play (as depicted in Figure 20–15) is the major means for concept learning (Berk & Winsler, 1995; Bodrova & Leong, 1996).

Think about how Piaget's and Vygotsky's ideas relate to your past, present, and future work with young children. Discuss your ideas with a small group in class. Develop some questions to clarify your ideas. List the questions on the chalkboard or on a large sheet of newsprint or chart paper. Present the questions to the instructor and other class members for their reactions and discussion.

## CONCEPT DEVELOPMENT AND TECHNOLOGY

The use of computer software as a means for teaching concepts is increasingly popular. Jalongo (1998a) reminds us not to be oversold on technology as the answer to all children's learning problems. She suggests that it is not always wise to be first with technology. Although technology is improving and becoming more user friendly each day, it also becomes obsolete quickly. Many software programs provide excellent information and promote thinking skills. Unfortunately, programs that provide practice on low-level skills, such as math facts, are most widely used. Jalongo concludes, "Overselling technology is just another way of underestimating our students' intellects and neglecting to prepare them for the challenges of the new millennium" (p. 222).

## SUMMARY

The term *cognitive* refers to the mind and how it works. Piaget's view of cognition is widely accepted in early childhood education and development. Other complementary views are those of Vygotsky, Bandura, and information processing. Piaget's theory of cognitive development provides four periods of mental growth. From preschool to primary, children pass from the preoperational period, through a transitional phase, and into the concrete operations period.

The cognitive structure is made up of bits of knowledge, such as schemas, preconcepts, and concepts. Metacognition, or thinking about thinking, is an area of great interest. Research indicates that those who can think about thinking can learn more efficiently and remember more. Cognitive functioning refers to the way cognition works. Information processing models can help us picture how cognitive functioning takes place. Problem-solving methods of instruction use metacognitive strategies that make the learners think about how they are learning. Another important aspect of cognition is the theory of left- and right-brain function. Left-brain function is analytic and organized and applies language to solving problems. Right-side function is more sensory and creative. School learning is conventionally dependent on left-side kinds of functions. The person who is right-brain dominant may have difficulty in adjusting to a left-brain-focused curriculum. Also critical in cognitive development is consideration of brain development during the first three years. Many children enter the three- to six-year-old period lacking necessary brain stimulation experiences during the first three years. Concepts are the cornerstones of thought. Young children actively construct basic concepts, such as classification, conservation, ordering, space, and causality.

The theories of Piaget and Vygotsky help us understand young children's concept development and acquisition. Piaget's ideas have been especially helpful in offering many ideas that can be applied by adults to their work with young children. Piaget's theory of constructivism and his periods of cognitive development have become increasingly popular as guides in designing early childhood education programs. Vygotsky's emphasis on the social aspects of learning has enriched our view of instruction.

The preschool child from ages two through four is in the preoperational period. During this period, representational activities are critical for concept development. Between ages five and seven, children progress into a transition period which takes them into concrete operations. During each period, these children have unique ways of thinking that are different from those of adults or older children. To move through each stage at the pace their capacities allow, young children need to be active in their own learning processes. Adults must provide a rich environment for exploration where children are free to construct their own knowledge.

Research in the development of mathematics concepts during early childhood provides us with some insight into how children develop their understanding in this content area. Piaget's theory has inspired the development of a number of curricular approaches. Vygotsky's conceptualizations of the ZPD and scaffolding are becoming important guides in our consideration of young children's concept learning. If software is selected with care, technology can provide intellectually challenging problems that promote concept development.

## For Further Reading

### COGNITIVE GROWTH AND DEVELOPMENT


Amsel, E., & Byrnes, J. P. (Eds.). (2002). *Language, literacy, and cognitive development.* Mahwah, NJ: Erlbaum.

Bjorklund, D. F. (2004). *Children's thinking: Cognitive development and individual differences* (4th ed.). Belmont, CA: Thomson Wadsworth.

Carver, S. M., & Klahr, D. (Eds.). (2001). *Cognition and instruction: Twenty-five years of progress.* Mahwah, NJ: Erlbaum.

Dai. D. Y., & Sternberg, R. J. (2004). *Motivation, emotion, and cognition.* Mahwah, NJ: Erlbaum.

Davidson, J. E., & Sternberg, R. J. (Eds.). (2003). *The psychology of problem solving.* New York: Cambridge University Press.

Emmorey, K. (2002). *Language, cognition, and the brain.* Mahwah, NJ: Erlbaum.

Fahle, M., & Poggio, T. (Eds.). (2002). *Perceptual learning.* Cambridge, MA: MIT Press.

Garton, A. F. (2004). *Exploring cognitive development.* Williston, VT: Blackwell.

Gauvain, M. (2000). *The social context of cognitive development.* New York: Guilford.

Gibson, E. J., & Pick, A. D. (2000). *An ecological approach to perceptual learning and development.* New York: Oxford University Press.

Gilkerson, L. (Ed.). (2005). *Early development and the brain.* Washington, DC: Zero to Three.

Hobson, P. (2004). *The cradle of thought: Exploring the origins of thinking.* New York: Oxford University Press.

Holyoak, K. J., & Morrison, R. B. (Eds.). (2005). *The Cambridge handbook of thinking and reasoning.* New York: Cambridge University Press.

Kagan, J., & Herschkowitz, N. (2005). *A young mind in a growing brain.* Mahwah, NJ: Erlbaum.

Mandler, J. M. (2004). *The foundations of mind.* Cary, NC: Oxford University Press.

McClelland, J. L., & Siegler, R. S. (2001). *Mechanisms of cognitive development.* Mahwah, NJ: Erlbaum.

Mitchell, P., & Riggs, K. (Eds.). (2000). *Children's reasoning and the mind.* Philadelphia: Psychology Press.

Nucci, L. P., Saxe, G. B., & Turiel, E. (Eds.). (2000). *Culture, thought and development.* Mahwah, NJ: Erlbaum.

Odom, S. L. (2002). *Widening the circle: Including children with disabilities in preschool programs.* New York: Teachers College Press.

Stein, N. L., Bauer, P., & Rabinowitz, M. (Eds.). (2002). *Representation, memory, and development: Essays in honor of Jean Mandler.* Mahwah, NJ: Erlbaum.

Towse, J. (2005). *Working memory and cognitive development.* New York: Psychology Press.


### CONCEPT DEVELOPMENT


Astuti, R., Solomon, G., & Carey, S. (2005). *Constraints on conceptual development.* Williston, VT: Blackwell.

DeVries, R., & Kohlberg, L. (1990). *Constructivist early education: Overview and comparison with other programs.* Washington, DC: National Association for the Education of Young Children. (Original work published 1987.)

DeVries, R., Zan, B., Hildebrandt, C., Edmiaston, R., & Sales, C. (2002). *Developing constructivist early childhood curriculum.* New York: Teachers College Press.

Friedman, W. J. (2000). The development of children's knowledge of the times of future events. *Child Development, 71*(4), 913–932.

Guralnick, M. J. (Ed.). (2001). *Early childhood inclusion: Focus on change.* Baltimore: Brookes.

Helm, J. H., & Katz, L. (2001). *Young investigators: The project approach in the early years.* New York: Teachers College Press, and Washington, DC: The National Association for the Education of Young Children.

Howes, C. (Ed.). (2005). *Teaching 4- to 8-year-olds: Literacy, math, multiculturalism and classroom community.* Baltimore: Brookes.

Kamii, C. (2003). Modifying a board game to foster kindergartners' logico-mathematical thinking. *Young Children, 58*(5), 20–26.

Kamii, C., & DeVries, R. (1978). *Physical knowledge in preschool education: Implications of Piaget's theory.* Upper Saddle River, NJ: Prentice-Hall.

Koralek, D. (Ed.). Encouraging young children to develop and enhance their thinking skills [Focus section]. *Young Children, 58*(5), 10–55.

Mix, K. S., Huttenlocher, J., & Levine, S. C. (2002). *Quantitative development in infancy and early childhood.* New York: Oxford University Press.

Newman, F. (1993). *Lev Vygotsky.* London: Routledge.

Prinz, J. J. (2002). *Furnishing the mind: Concepts and their perceptual basis.* Cambridge, MA: MIT Press.

Tolchinsky, L. (2003). *The cradle of culture and what children know about writing and numbers before being taught.* Mahwah, NJ: Erlbaum.

Vanderveer, R. (1994). *Understanding Vygotsky.* London: Blackwell.

Wiese, H. (2004). *Numbers, language, and the human mind.* New York: Cambridge University Press.

Winograd, E., Fivush, R., & Hirst, W. (Eds.). (1998). *Ecological approaches to cognition.* Mahwah, NJ: Erlbaum.

## SUGGESTED ACTIVITIES

1. Observe a child between the ages of three and eight in nursery school, kindergarten, primary classroom, or during playtime at home. Write down every behavior that indicates the child is using or learning a concept. Some concepts that might be observed are size, shape, number, classification, comparisons, space, part/whole, volume, weight, length, temperature, and time. (Refer to Chapters 4, 14, 17, and 20 for examples of these concepts.) What do your results tell you about the cognitive structure of this child? Compare your results with those of other students in the class.

2. For 30 minutes during free playtime, observe two different preschool groups consisting of children ages two to three and three to four or five. Also, observe a kindergarten class of children ages five and six. Observe 15 minutes each in two of the following areas:
   a. housekeeping
   b. sand or water play
   c. manipulative toy play (e.g., puzzles, construction toys)
   d. blocks

   Make up a chart as shown.

| Class age _____ | | Date _____ | |
|---|---|---|---|
| School _____ | | Time _____ | |
| Symbols Used | | | |
| Blocks | Housekeeping | Sand/Water | Manipulative Toys |
| | | | |

List each instance of the use of a symbol (the use of something to represent something else). Report the results in class. Which area in the chart showed the most symbolic play? What kinds of symbols were used in each area? What, if any, age differences were noted in terms of the number and kinds of symbols used?

3. Follow a child's activities for 15 minutes. Diagram his or her cognitive function. (Refer to Figures 20–6 and 20–7.) In your own words, write a description of how the child's cognitive system was functioning during your observation. Refer to your diagrams as you write.

4. Visit the library or contact your instructor for a list of resources. Find a book or an article on children's cognitive development. After reading the article, write a short summary and your reaction to the article. Include the complete bibliographic information:
title of the article or book author(s)
name of the publication (journal, magazine, book)
publisher (for books)
dates
page numbers
Make copies of your summary for the class and discuss the article during class discussion time.

5. Try the following basic concept interview tasks with two or more young children. Compare the responses from each. In which Piagetian stage would you place each child? Why? Report your results in class. Your report should include the following:
   a. the questions asked/tasks presented to each child
   b. the child(ren)'s specific responses
   c. results and conclusions:
      (1) What did you learn about each child?
      (2) Which stage is each child in?
      (3) How did you feel about the whole experience?

## PREKINDERGARTEN BASIC CONCEPT INTERVIEW TASKS

### TASK 1: CLASSIFICATION

Instructions: Place in front of the child twelve objects: two red, two blue, two green, two yellow, two orange, and two purple. Use at least four or five different kinds of objects. For example:

| Color | Object 1 | Object 2 |
|---|---|---|
| red | bead | block |
| blue | ball | block |
| green | ball | block |
| yellow | bead | car |
| orange | comb | car |
| purple | barrette | bead |

Provide the child with six to eight small containers, such as bowls, boxes, or cups. Tell the child, "Put the toys in the (bowls, boxes, or cups)."

Evaluation: Note how many groups the child makes and the criteria (e.g., color, category, shape) used.

### TASK 2: SERIATION

Instructions: Present the child with two or more objects that differ in one dimension, such as height or width. For example, cut some drinking straws so that the shortest is 2 inches, the next $2^1/_2$ inches the next 3 inches, etc. Start with two for a two-year-old and three for a three- or four-year-old.

a. For two straws: Place them in front of the child. Say, "Find the longer (taller) straw. Find the shorter straw."
b. For three or more items: Say, "Find the tallest (or shortest) straw. Put the straws in order from shortest to tallest."

Evaluation: For a, note if child can identify short and tall. For b, note if the tallest and shortest, or largest and smallest, are placed correctly and if the middle sizes are mixed up or in order.

### TASK 3: NUMBER

Instructions: Have a supply of 20 identical objects, such as coins, chips, cube blocks. Ask the child to do the following:

a. For this rote counting task, no objects are needed. Tell the child, "Count for me. Count as far as you can."

Evaluation: Note if the number names are in order, how far the child can count correctly, and how far the child counts incorrectly. Note the types of errors made.

b. Place sets of objects in front of the child. Start with two, then one, then four, then three, then five. Ask, "How many of these are there?"

Evaluation: Note if he or she can apply the number names in order, if he or she uses one-to-one correspondence, and if he or she can tell you how many are in each group.

c. If the child rote-counted over five in part a, make all the objects available. Say, "Count as many of these things as you can."

Evaluation: Note if the child can apply the number names in order, if the child uses one-to-one correspondence, and if he or she can tell you how many there are when finished.

**6.** Follow the instructions given for Activity 5.

## KINDERGARTEN/FIRST-GRADE CLINICAL INTERVIEW TASKS

### TASK 1: CLASSIFICATION

Materials: eight squares (four large and four small with one of each size red, yellow, blue, and green), eight triangles (four large and four small with one of each size red, yellow, blue, and green), and eight circles (four large and four small with one of each size red, yellow, blue, and green).

Instructions: Present the child with the cardboard shapes piled at random in front of him or her. Say, "Sort (pile) these shapes in groups any way you want to." After the child has done one sort, say, "Now sort (pile) these shapes in another way."

Evaluation: The preoperational child normally sorts one way, such as by color, shape, or size, and avoids trying any of the others. The concrete operational child will try another way.

### TASK 2: CONSERVATION OF NUMBER

Materials: 25 cube blocks, chips, coins, or any other small object that are all the same size.

Instructions: Set up a row of nine objects. Have the rest in a pile to the side. Say, "You make a row just like this one." (point to yours)

Ask the child, "Does one row have more blocks or do they both have the same amount? How do you know?" *If the child agrees to equality, go on to the transformations that follow.*

### Transformation 1

Say, "Now watch what I do." (Push yours together.)
Ask the child, "Does one row have more blocks or do they both have the same amount? Why?" Say, "Make them have the same amount again." (If the child has given a conserving answer, tell him or her, "Line them up like they were before I moved them.")

Go on to the other transformations, always being sure the child agrees to equality first.

### Transformation 2

### Transformation 3

Evaluation: The child who is not yet a conserver will center on one aspect of the problem, such as length. For transformation (1), the child will say that he or she has more because his or hers is longer or that the adult's is shorter. The transitional child will be inconsistent; that is, the child may conserve on one task and not on another. At a more advanced stage, the child may appear unsure of his or her conserving answers and have to count or do one-to-one matching to be sure there is still the same number in each row. The conserver will tell you with confidence that there is still the same number in each row and is even likely to say, "You just moved them."

## TASK 3: SERIATION

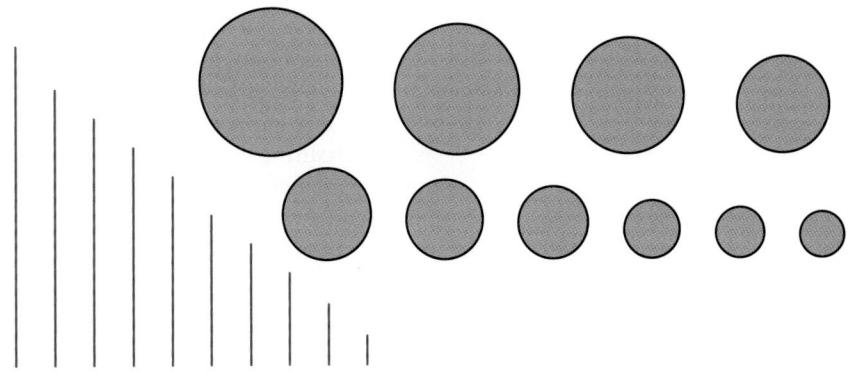

Materials: Items of the same shape, but in graduated sizes, such as 10 sticks or 10 circles as shown.

Instructions: Put the items in random order in front of the child. Start with five items. If this is too difficult, go back to three. If five is easy, try all 10. Tell the child, "Start with the largest (biggest, tallest, fattest, longest) and make a row from largest to smallest (tallest to shortest, fattest to skinniest, longest to shortest)."

Evaluation: The preoperational child will order the sticks in an approximate way, such as already shown in the unit. He or she usually focuses on the two extremes and has the middle sizes out of order. The concrete operational child can decenter and put the objects in the correct order.

### TASK 4: CAUSALITY

Materials: The following list of questions.

Instructions: Ask the following questions. Give the child plenty of time to answer. Respond with "Yes," "Uh huh," and other nonevaluative comments. Ask, "Why" or "Tell me some more" to see if he or she can expand. Try to get the child's reasons.

a. "Are you alive?"
"Is a cloud alive? Why?"
"Is a bicycle alive? Why?"
"Is a car alive? Why?"
"Is a tree alive? Why?"

b. "What makes clouds move? Why?"
"How does the sun move? Why?"
"Why don't the clouds fall down? What keeps them up?"
"What keeps the sun up in the sky?"

Evaluation: Note the kinds of reasons the child gives for his or her answers. Note whether the child uses animism or artificialism. As the child moves into concrete operations, he or she will give a more realistic answer to the questions about life. The child's answers to the questions about the things he or she cannot touch, such as the clouds and the sun, will still be illogical.

**7.** Make an entry in your journal.

## REVIEW

**1.** Write a definition of *cognition.*

**2.** Read the following example. Explain your estimation of Mary's cognitive development.

Three-year-old Mary is playing quietly alone in the kitchen. She has put all the contents of one drawer on the floor and is busily moving objects around and putting them in different piles. She has the long-handled cooking spoons in one pile and short-handled serving spoons in another. A red plastic cork, a set of red plastic measuring spoons, and a red funnel are in another pile. Another pile contains several metal cookie cutters and still another, a wooden rolling pin, a wooden spoon, and a wooden salad fork and spoon.

**3.** Indicate whether the following examples illustrate (1) cognitive functioning or (2) cognitive structure.

a. color
b. a car and a bus
c. "That animal is a dog."
d. schemata
e. thinking
f. concepts
g. preconcepts
h. memory
i. problem solving
j. perception

**4.** Write an *S* for sensorimotor, a *P* for preoperational, and a *C* for concrete operational.

a. The child learns through pretend play.
b. The child learns mainly through taste, smell, sight, and touch and through grasping, crawling, creeping, walking, and climbing.
c. The child can see another's point of view as well as his or her own.
d. The child is an explorer.

e. The child begins to use symbols, such as sand for food.
f. The child can coordinate two or more aspects of a problem at the same time.
g. The child learns through imitation.

**5.** Describe how the concept of *horse* might develop from schema to preconcept to concept.

**6.** Write the letter of each of the following that is an example of centering. State on which attribute the child has centered.

a. George looks at two groups of blocks. There are five blocks in each group. One group is pushed close together and the other group is spread out. George says there are more blocks in the bunch that is spread out.
b. A furry creature runs through Mary's yard. Mary has a gray kitten named Jet. Mary calls out, "Jet." The creature (a squirrel) keeps on running. Mary runs after it, crying.
c. Jane meets Mrs. McGee and her mother, Mrs. Clark. Mrs. Clark is several inches shorter than her daughter. Jane thinks Mrs. McGee is the mother.

**7.** Read the following behavior description. Diagram the child's activities using the cognitive functioning diagram. Tell which aspects of the description might be labeled cognitive structure. At which stage of cognitive development is this child?

Ronald is sitting at a table. It is snack time. He reaches for a pitcher of juice, picks it up, and pours some into his cup. Some juice spills on the table. Ronald frowns. He takes his napkin and wipes up the juice.

**8.** Describe metacognition and theory of mind. Explain how metacognitive skills may enhance learning. Provide an example of a problem-solving approach that makes children think about thinking.

**9.** Study the following behavioral description. Categorize Kate's behaviors as right-brained and/or left-brained.

Kate is a kindergartner. She is very quiet in class, saying very little. She chooses dramatic play and art as her favorite activities. She doesn't care for teacher-directed structured activities or tasks that involve workbook/paper and pencil. She prefers to develop her own learning experiences.

**10.** Explain the significance at kindergarten entrance of children not having needed prekindergarten experiences.

**11.** List the highlights of Piaget's and Vygotsky's developmental theories.

**12.** Select the correct answer(s) to the following. There may be more than one correct answer.

a. During most of the preschool period, the child is in the
   (1) sensorimotor stage.
   (2) preoperational stage.
   (3) concrete operations stage.
   (4) formal operations stage.
b. Developmentally, the preschool child
   (1) has acquired the object concept.
   (2) has real thoughts and insights.
   (3) has a rate of motor development that is leveling off.
   (4) is acquiring language, which is a major focus of development.
c. The preschool child's activity is characterized by
   (1) little evidence of representative or symbolic play.
   (2) learning through imitation.
   (3) a lack of egocentrism.
   (4) a focus on the most obvious parts of a problem.
d. As the young child goes into the concrete operations stage, he or she
   (1) integrates old ways of thinking into the new.
   (2) attains reversibility.
   (3) is more egocentric.
   (4) can conserve.

**13.** Look at each of the examples that follow. Analyze each one according to the child's probable Piagetian stage, the child's age, the concept or activity in which he or she is engaged, the adult response, and the evidence for your decisions. Apply the following list of terms as appropriate to each situation:

one-to-one correspondence
seriation
conservation (conserver)
classification (categorizing)
causality
preoperational
concrete operations
egocentric (centering, decentering)
reversibility
transformation
symbolic
representational
animism
artificialism
concept

a. Joe, age four, is playing with some strings of various sizes. He lines them up.

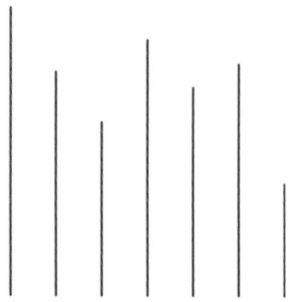

b. Doug, age five, is shown a row of 10 pennies. He is then asked to "Make a row that has the same number as this one." He does so:

Adult says, "Now watch what I do." (One row is moved):

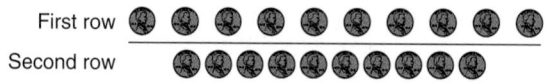


"Do both rows have the same or does one row have more?" Doug points to the first row, saying, "That row has more." "Why, Doug?" "Because it is longer," says Doug.

c. Tanya, age three-and-a-half, is playing with some sticks and stones in the backyard. She arranges the sticks and stones like this:

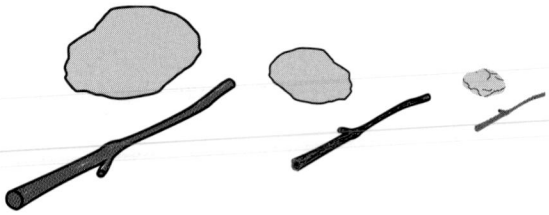

(a) (b) (c)

Each dog has a bone," she says.

d. Roger is six years old. He is shown two rows of 10 chips. He agrees that each row has the same number of chips. One row is then expanded:

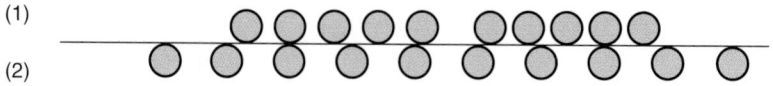

Roger is asked, "Does one row have more or do they both have the same amount?" "The same," says Roger. "At least I think they do. Maybe I better count them to be sure."

e. Derrick, age four, is asked the following questions:

| Question | Derrick's Answer |
|---|---|
| Are you alive? | Yes. |
| Why? | We have blood. |
| Is a cloud alive? | Yes. |
| Why? | Everything has blood. |
| Is a bicycle alive? | No. |
| Why? | It has a motor. |
| Is a mountain alive? | No. Because it stays wherever it is. |
| Is a tree alive? | No. Because it only moves if someone chops it down. |

**14.** In which of the following situations are adults applying Piaget's or Vygotsky's theories to practice? In which situations are they not? Give reasons for your answers.

a. Mrs. Tanaka laughs to herself as she hears Derrick tell Bill, "The rain comes so it can water our gardens."

b. "I teach to the average child in the group. Then, at least, everyone learns something."

c. Today, Mr. Santos brought in more containers for water play because he noticed the children becoming more interested in measuring, pouring, and playing with water.

d. Mrs. White Bear gives her three- and four-year-olds many materials they can use for sorting and classifying.

e. "No Tim, you are not allowed to draw a dog. Everyone is drawing oranges today."

f. "Johnny, you didn't copy the peg board design correctly. It's all wrong."

g. "Kate, I noticed you started copying the pattern for the peg board design just like it is and then changed it. Why?" Kate: "Oh, I didn't have enough green pegs so I used blue instead."

h. Mrs. Brown notices that the unit block structures are getting larger and more complex. She decides to make the block area larger.

**15.** Give an example of how concept learning is basic to math.

**16.** According to Baroody's research, explain the mathematical concepts that young children have.

**17.** Explain Jalongo's concern regarding technology and thinking.

## KEY TERMS LIST

animism
artificialism
belief
causality
centering
classification
cognitive
cognitive development
cognitive functioning
cognitive structure
concrete operational period
concepts
conservation
egocentric
false beliefs
formal operations period
input
metacognition
one-to-one correspondence
operations
output
overdiscriminations
overgeneralizations
preconcepts
processing
schema
seriation
spatial concepts
theory of mind
transition period

Additional resources for this chapter can be found on the Online Companion™ to accompany this text at http://www.earlychilded.delmar.com. Respond to "Time to Reflect" and "Looking Further" concepts, review various child development scenarios, and answer thought-provoking questions in the Critical Thinking Forum. Keep a daily journal by downloading the student journal available on this Web site. Complete the interactive matching exercises to reinforce concepts, and printout the child development assessment forms to use during your observation of development for children from birth to age eight. In addition, read the case studies on the Web site to reinforce the important concepts in each chapter, and take a look at the multitude of Web links that are available for student research on the Internet.

CHAPTER

# 21

# Oral Language Development and Use

## OBJECTIVES

After reading this chapter, you should be able to:

- Identify definitions and examples of the major kinds of language rules.
- Explain the current points of view regarding how language is learned.
- Analyze language samples according to developmental stage, semantic component, and rate of development.
- Recognize examples of normal speech development, such as pragmatic usage, use of phonemes, dialect, thought as reflected in speech, a language relationship between child and adult, and baby talk.
- Recognize some of the aspects of early childhood language use established by research.
- Categorize children's language samples using the category systems developed by Michael Halliday and Joan Tough.
- Explain how play supports academic achievement.
- Discuss the relationship of play and language use.
- Recognize private speech.

Language is a complex and important area in child development. It is necessary in several ways. Language:

- is a major means for transmitting our culture to the next generation and is an important educational tool.
- is involved in our mental processing, such as thinking, problem solving, and memory.
- serves as a means of communication.

Language symbols are arbitrary. That is, language symbols are agreed on by a group to have certain meanings that can then be used for communication. English, Chinese, Egyptian, Spanish, and other cultural groups developed their own languages, which are the dominant forms of language in certain geographic areas. Language takes a number of forms: oral, written, gestural, facial expressions, and physical position. Certain languages do not rely on oral communication but use other senses. For example, the sign language used by persons with deafness is visual; braille used by persons with blindness is tactile.

In Chapters 14 and 17, infant and toddler language development was described. In this chapter, we examine further stages of development, the rules of language, the mechanisms of language learning, the relationships of thought and language, cultural aspects of language, and how oral language is used in everyday activities. An amazing aspect of language is the speed at which it develops. The average child has achieved nearly adult language facility by the age of four.

However, although spoken language is usually well developed by age four, words are not necessarily understood as in the following example. Each year, a teacher friend of columnist Jack Smith (Smith, 1991) sent him a compilation of her kindergarten students' word definitions. These definitions provide insight into how young children decide on the meaning of new words. For some of the words, they use the word in the definition. For others, they relate to a word they already know that sounds the same or similar. For example:

Language—When you say a bad word, someone says, "Watch your language."

Adore—You go through it so you can go in and out.

Bachelor—You can flip things over with it; the things that you take off cookies with.

Marriage—You like that person and you fall in love and you get married.

Analogy—It's a germ; you get the flu; you get sick; it's your mind.

Brain—You keep your words that you want to say in there; in your head there's this thing that makes you think.

**language**
A well-ordered system of rules that each adult member of the language community tacitly comprehends in speaking, listening, and writing.

**phonemes**
The smallest units of language; the speech sounds in language.

**morphemes**
The smallest meaningful units in a language and strings of sounds that have meaning.

**syntax**
Set of rules that has to do with the way words are placed in sequence to make an acceptable sentence or phrase.

**semantics**
The study of meaning that refers to words used in the correct context and attached to the appropriate referent.

**pragmatics**
The rules for using language appropriately and to advantage.

## WHAT IS LANGUAGE?

**Language** is a well-ordered system of rules that each adult member of the language community tacitly comprehends in speaking, listening, and writing (Yussen & Santrock, 1978, p. 245). Our knowledge of language is basically unconscious. That is, it is something we learn through the natural course of everyday life (Figure 21–1).

There are three types of language rules. Some rules deal with the units we use; that is, how sounds are put together in a meaningful way. For the English speaker, the string of sounds "gato" is not a meaningful one. For the Spanish speaker, it is. While the English speaker does not respond to "g-a-t-o," he or she does respond to "c-a-t." If the three units were put together as "a-t-c" or "t-c-a," they would not be organized in a way that would make sense to an English speaker. The rules that tell us which sounds to use and how to sequence them deal with units called **phonemes** and **morphemes.** A second set of rules has to do with the way words are placed in sequence to make an acceptable sentence or phrase. This is known as **syntax.** The third set of rules defines what language means and how it can be used most appropriately in specific situations. This set of rules refers to **semantics** and **pragmatics** (Figure 21–2).

FIGURE 21–1 Language development proceeds through the same stages in every culture.

### Phonemes

Phonemes are the smallest units of language. The English language has 36 individual speech sounds. These are the phonemes of English. Specific rules in English are used to combine sounds. For example, look

| Type of Rule | Aspect of Speech That Is Governed |
|---|---|
| Phonological | The use of phonemes, the smallest units of speech |
| Morphological | The use of morphemes, the smallest meaningful units of speech |
| Syntax | The way words are put together into acceptable phrases and sentences |
| Semantic | Determines the correct use of words in context and relative to the referents used |
| Pragmatic | The degree to which language is used appropriately and to the best advantage in a particular situation |

**FIGURE 21–2** Language is a system of rules that is accepted as correct by a language community.

at the following sound combinations and decide which follow English rules and which do not:

*aq kz kl bc br*

If you said yes for *kl* and *br* and no for *aq*, *kz*, and *bc*, you were correct. However, note that *kl* and *br* carry no meaning on their own.

## Morphemes

Morphemes are strings of sounds that do have meaning. They are the smallest meaningful units in a language. Look at the following examples and decide which are morphemes:

*a gpa car drw pre- -ing*

The morphemes are *a*, *car*, *pre-*, and *-ing*. The others, *gpa* and *drw*, are not meaningful in English.

## Syntax

The syntax of a language is the set of rules for producing acceptable phrases and sentences. For example, "dog a it is" is not an acceptable English sentence. "It is a dog" and "Is it a dog?" are acceptable. Young children first invent their own syntax or rules for putting words into meaningful context (Genishi, 1987). An early rule might be as simple as noun plus another word: "Milk gone," "Daddy bye-bye," and "Water hot."

## Semantics

Semantics is the study of meaning. It refers to words used in the correct context and attached to the appropriate referent. Is a dog referred to as *dog* and a table as *table?* Are sentences put together in meaningful ways?

1. The dog ate the bone.
2. The house ate the dog.

The first sentence uses words in a meaningful way. The second does not. As children enter the elementary years, they begin to understand some of the more subtle meanings; that is, although candy and a person can be sweet, thin and skinny are similar, but they are subtly different (Genishi, 1987).

### Pragmatics

Pragmatics has to do with the rules for using language appropriately and to advantage. Which example shows good use of pragmatic rules?

1. Open the door, please.
2. (Gruff voice) Open the door!

The first example shows good social use. The request (1) is more likely to be granted than is the command (2).

## HOW ORAL LANGUAGE IS LEARNED

There are three views of how language is learned: the learning theory view, the structural-innatist view, and the interactionist view (Cole, Cole, & Lightfoot, 2005). The **learning theory** approach puts emphasis on the environment, the structural-innatist emphasizes hereditary factors, and the interactionist views language acquisition as an interaction between heredity and environment.

**learning theory**
View of language acquisition; explains language acquisition through the mechanisms of classical conditioning, operant conditioning, and imitation.

The learning theory view explains language acquisition through the mechanisms of classical conditioning, operant conditioning, and imitation. Through classical conditioning and simple associations, vocal and visual become attached. The child imitates what he or she hears and is rewarded when he or she makes a sound that sounds to others like the name of an object. Baby's first "words" may be approximations of the real word that only those in the family understand. An example of approximation is the following:

| Seventeen Months | Twenty-one Months | Twenty-four Months |
|---|---|---|
| adoo | wadder | water |

At first, the child is probably restricted by a limited use of phonemes and an incomplete recall of what he or she has heard. However, because everyone in the family responds to "adoo" with a glass of water, filling the bathtub, or turning on the hose, depending on the context, the child continues to use "adoo" until he or she is gradually able to say "water." Children learning to speak also use groups of sounds that have even less relationship to the real word than "adoo" does to water. The same child who used "adoo" used "pow" for pacifier. This term continued to be used not only by the child but also by the whole family until the last pacifier was gone. All normal children go through the same stages: from cooing to babbling to one-word, two-word, three-word, and then complete sentences. The specific language the child learns is determined by the environment in which he or she lives.

**structural-innatist theory**
Explains language acquisition as a human being born with a biological need to develop rule systems for language, while reinforcement and imitation give feedback and build vocabulary.

The **structural-innatist theory** explains language acquisition as a more complex process. It is believed that the human is born with a biological need to develop rule systems for language, while reinforcement and imitation give feedback and build vocabulary. The need to have rules is inborn, as is the sequence of development the child goes through before he or she masters his or her own language. This newer view came about for several reasons:

- Children devise sentences that they have never heard. That is, rather than learning each sentence separately, they learn rules. If they learn, "The bird is on the branch," they can apply the same rules to put together the sentence "The cat is on the fence."
- Repeated drill does not change a child's stage of development. The child will change when developmentally capable:

Sandy: Want milk!
Mother: Oh, you mean, "I want milk."
Sandy: Want milk!
Mother: Can you say, "I want milk."
Sandy: Want milk!
Mother: Sandy, please say, "I want milk!"
Sandy: *Want milk!* (Yussen & Santrock, 1978, p. 251)

Sandy is in the two-word telegraphic stage and no amount of pleading on mother's part can change what nature has set up.

- Children get positive reinforcement for incorrect or immature sentences:

| *Maria (twenty months)* | *Mr. Sanchez, her father* |
|---|---|
| "Daddy, dog big." | "Yes, the dog is big." |
| "More milk." | He pours her a glass of milk. |
| "Car blue." | "Yes, the car is blue." |

Even though children get these positive responses for sentences that use incorrect syntax, they continue to expand and eventually develop the more sophisticated syntax of adult language.

**interactionist theory**

States that the sequence and timing of speech development is biologically determined, whereas the specific language the child learns is determined by the environment in which he or she lives.

The **interactionist theory** is the most recently developed theory. It states that an interaction exists between biological and environmental factors. The sequence and timing of speech development is biologically determined, while the specific language the child learns is determined by the environment in which he or she lives (Genishi & Dyson, 1984). Some interactionists emphasize the cognitive; that is language grows out of sensorimotor thought and is mainly learning how to use words to get what you want (Cole, Cole, & Lightfoot, 2005). Learning the rules of the language is a by-product of learning to communicate more clearly. Other interactionists emphasize cultural context. Although children reinvent language, they have people who already know the language to guide the acquisition process (Cole, Cole, & Lightfoot, 2005). The chart in the following Looking Further activity provides an overview of oral language expectations for three-, four-, five-, and six-year-olds.

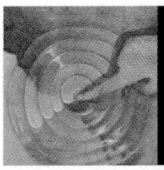

**LOOKING FURTHER**

Use the checklist below to evaluate some common developmental expectations of three-, four-, five- and six-year-old language. (Adapted from Allen, K. E., & Marotz, L. R. [2006]. *Developmental profiles: Pre-birth through twelve.* [4th ed.] Clifton Park, NY: Delmar Learning.) Reprinted with permission.

| Age/Developmental Characteristic | Yes | No | Sometimes/Comments |
|---|---|---|---|
| **By Three Years:** | | | |
| • Responds to "Put _____ in the box" and "Take the _____ out of the box." | | | |
| • Selects correct item upon request: big versus little; long versus short. | | | |
| • Identifies objects by use: "What do you wear on your feet?" | | | |

*(Continued)*

| Age/Developmental Characteristic | Yes | No | Sometimes/Comments |
|---|---|---|---|
| • Asks questions.<br>• Tells about something with functional phrases that carry meaning: "Daddy go airplane" and "Me hungry now." | | | |
| **By Four Years:**<br>• Responds appropriately to "Put it beside" and "Put it under."<br>• Responds to two-step directions: "Give me the car and put the block on the floor."<br>• Responds by selecting the correct object—for example, hard versus soft, blue versus red, and so on.<br>• Answers "if," "what," and "when" questions.<br>• Answers questions about function: "What are books for?" | | | |
| **By Five Years:**<br>• Responds to simple three-step directions: "Give me the pencil, put the book on the table, and hold the comb in your hand."<br>• Responds correctly when asked to select a penny, nickel, and dime.<br>• Asks "how" questions.<br>• Responds verbally to "Hi" and "How are your?"<br>• Tells about events using past and future tenses.<br>• Uses conjunctions to string words and phrases together—for example, "I saw a bear, a zebra, and a giraffe at the zoo." | | | |
| **By Six Years:**<br>• Uses all grammatical structures: pronouns, plurals, verb tense, and conjunctions.<br>• Uses complex sentences and carries on conversations. | | | |

## THOUGHT AND LANGUAGE

Those who study language have been interested in how language and thought relate. Those who take the environmental-learning perspective believe that much of human thought is dependent on language. Words aid in communication, but they also help children better understand the world and the things in it. Therefore, the more words the child knows, the more advanced his or her cognitive development will be (Cole, Cole, & Lightfoot, 2005).

Piaget's theory serves as the basis for the interactionist view. At the end of infancy, a new mode of representation grows out of sensorimotor schemata. Language reflects thought from the Piagetian view. Language then does not affect thought, thought determines language. Early speech, like early thought, would then be egocentric; that is, it would center on the most obvious and would ignore what others have to say (Cole, Cole, & Lightfoot, 2005).

The structural-innatists disagree that speech grows from sensorimotor cognition. They believe a built-in device in humans acquires language. Language is used to express thought, but language and thought are not interdependent (Cole, Cole, & Lightfoot, 2005).

Vygotsky developed a theory that looks at the language and thought relationship from the cultural-context point of view. Vygotsky believed that from the beginning, the child's language development is determined by the social context (Bodrova & Leong, 1996). Children first develop speech as a form of social communication. Eventually, they develop inner speech, which interconnects thought and language. Vygotsky's studies indicated that what Piaget identified as egocentric speech does have, from the children's point of view, a communicative function. Vygotsky believed that during the first two years, language and thought developed in a parallel fashion, so language occurs without thought and thought without language. At age two, they begin to join each other. Language becomes intellectual and thinking verbal. Language, even when used individually, has its roots in the social context (Cole, Cole, and Lightfoot, 2005).

Which theory is correct in its view of the language/thought relationship? This question is still not answered. However, they are certainly related and when the two most popular theories, Piaget's and Vygotsky's, are compared, a great deal of common and complementary aspects are found, especially after the first two years (Lucy, 1988). Piaget concentrated more on the representational nature of language and Vygotsky more on the social nature. At the practical level, both are certainly important.

## Thought Reflected in Language

Whatever our views of the relationship of language and thought development, listening to children is one of our major means of learning about their thinking processes and their concept development. Thinking is still preoperational at age four, whereas speech is very adultlike. That is, four-year-olds have an extensive vocabulary and their grammar is adultlike. These factors should be kept in mind when trying to communicate with young children. Although their speech may be quite articulate, their reasoning is still preoperational, as evidenced in the following example from a child who is nearing age three (*Growing Child*, 1973):

> John wants to ride along in the car when his sister goes to school. Dad explains that it's not their turn today: They belong to a car pool and their turn is tomorrow. The next day, John wants his swimming suit. When asked why, he replies, "You promised we were going in a pool."

This example reflects the preoperational "seeing is believing" approach to problems. Children take language in its most literal sense and do not have the more abstract concepts they will acquire as they approach adulthood. Children make up their own interpretations. This literal interpretation by young children must be kept in mind when communicating with them. The adult and child may be using the same words with different meanings.

Keep in mind that the vocabulary of preschoolers may be behind their ability to understand and their reasoning may be ahead of their ability to communicate clearly. Young children often seem to be oblivious to the finer nuances of language. For example, in a study by Flavell, Speer, Green, and August (1981), kindergartners did not perceive when they were given incomplete directions to follow. Flavell et al. (1981) presented a series of tasks to kindergartners and second graders in which they had to follow tape-recorded directions for building block structures. For several of the tasks, the directions were purposely incomplete and unclear. The kindergartners showed little if any recognition that some of the directions were inadequate. Even those who seemed to realize during the building process that something was wrong with the instructions always said the instructions were fine when questioned after completion of the task. Flavell et al. concluded, "It appears that children may often not understand what they see, hear, or read and yet be totally oblivious to this state of affairs" (p. 53). This research implies that adults who work with young children must be very careful in providing instructions to them and be tolerant when the children fail to recognize their own lack of understanding.

There is an increasing interest in children's awareness of language, that is, their ability to think about the structure and functions of language (Grieve, Tumner, & Pratt, 1983). Research indicates that this awareness begins to develop in early childhood. Young children have demonstrated the following signs of language awareness:

1. Young children can make judgments about language, such as the following:
   - Four-and-a-half-year-olds know that they should show interest in getting a piece of candy from an adult by saying, "I would like a piece of candy," rather than saying "I want a piece of candy."
   - Children as young as four can adjust their speech by using appropriate voices for different dramatic play roles and by simplifying their speech when talking to younger children.
   - Five-year-olds realize that adults use more complex sentences than children use.
   - Very young children can recognize that they may not articulate correctly, such as the words in the list presented in an earlier part of this chapter.
2. Young children can apply language rules:
   - They can add *s* for more than one of something.
   - They can add *ed* to show past tense.
3. Young children can correct language:
   - They may show that they realize they have made a mistake by adding a word, changing a word, or changing word order on their own.
   - They may respond to adult prompts. That is, the adult indicates that a different word is expected and the child figures out what the word should be.
4. Young children can define words by their function:
   - Broom is for sweeping.
   - Ball is for throwing.
5. Young children can identify a part of a word or a part of a sentence if the task is presented in a simple and appropriate manner.
6. As infants, children find they can control the sounds they make, and they enjoy practicing and playing with words through repetition, chants, rhymes, and plays on words.

Grieve et al. (1983) suggest some important implications for practice. First, the evidence suggests that children know a great deal about language before they enter school. Second, language awareness may be an important prerequisite for learning to read. The relationship between language awareness and beginning reading was reviewed by McGee, Charlesworth, Cheek, and Cheek (1982). A growing body of research suggests that story knowledge is an important prerequisite to learning to read. Awareness of how events and characters are common to all stories is essential. Children remember stories better if they have a basic concept that stories have a beginning, a middle, and an end. Kindergarten seems to be the critical time for development of story concepts, such as:

- Stories have a beginning, a middle, and an end.
- Stories have characters.
- Stories have a setting.
- Stories have a theme.
- Stories have a plot.

The kindergarten curriculum should include activities that will help students develop story knowledge.

## CULTURAL ASPECTS OF LANGUAGE

It is well documented that speech development proceeds in the same sequence around the world (Slobin, 1972). That is, children proceed through the cooing, babbling, one-word, two-word, and three-word stages on their way to adultlike speech. The differences between and within countries have to do with the actual sounds used and the rules for combining sounds (Munroe & Munroe, 1975). A problem arises when a child arrives in school with language that is different from that used in the school or understood by the teacher. A major difference is speaking a primary language other than English. A further difference is speaking a dialect different from that of the educational personnel. Many arguments exist regarding the best way to teach English to second-language learners. Differences in language are also associated with socioeconomic status. The language developed within different social classes varies a great deal. The following discussion centers on African American English, or Ebonics, English language learners, and socioeconomic differences in language development.

### African American English or Ebonics

**dialect**
A variation of the standard speech of a language.

A major consideration in planning instruction for African American children is whether their primary language is a dialect of English or a derivative of African languages that uses English vocabulary. A **dialect** is a variation of the standard speech of a language. There has been particular concern in the United States with the language of African Americans (Cazden, Baratz, Labov, & Palmer, 1981). Black English (BE) has been considered to be a uniform dialect of so-called Standard English (SE) and is spoken with consistent grammar from place to place. Some of the differences can be seen in the following example as a second grader, Freddie, is helping check math problems.

| Freddie, BE | SE |
|---|---|
| O kay boys and gur, take out you math bookses. We gona' check ours work. Numba' one twenty-fo, | Okay, boys and girls, take out your math books. We are going to check our work. Number one-twenty |

two is fo plus nine is thuteen.
Don't you be getten out you set.

four, two is four plus nine is thirteen. Don't you get out of your seats.

In comparison to SE, the verb tenses differ, sounds are organized differently, and sounds are substituted in a consistent, rule-governed way in the BE example. Until recently, linguists widely accepted that BE was a dialect of English. At the same time, the majority viewed BE as a lower-level slang version of English that is unacceptable in the school setting. This situation presents a controversy over BE's place in the school program. The question centers on when, how, and if SE should be taught to BE speakers. Meanwhile, another view of BE came into view. This view is that the African American language has its roots in African languages brought over by slaves. From this point of view, African American language is viewed as African grammar with English words (Smith, 1998). To clearly delineate African American English as a language in its own right with links to Africa, in 1973, a group of African American scholars came up with the label **Ebonics** (Smitherman, 1998).

**Ebonics**

African American English (USBE), a system of language that is a synthesis of African and European language traditions.

Smitherman (1998, p. 30) explains:

> Ebonics: neither "broken" English, or "sloppy" speech, nor merely "slang," nor some bizarre lingo spoken only by baggy-pants-wearing black kids. Rather the variety of Ebonics spoken in the United States (hereafter USBE) is rooted in the Black American Oral Tradition and represents a synthesis of African (primarily West African) and European (primarily English) linguistic-cultural traditions. . . . USBE can be thought of as the Africanization of American English.

Some words come directly from African language, such as *okay*, *gorilla*, *cola*, and *jazz*. However, Ebonics has its own patterns of USBE as seen in the Freddie example. Smitherman offers the following example: "The brotha be lookin good; that's what got the sista nose open!" She explains that:

- *brotha* is USBE for an African American man
- *lookin good* refers to his style, his attractive appearance
- *sista* is an African American woman
- *nose open* indicates her passionate love for the brotha
- *sista nose* indicates possession
- *be* indicates brotha's past, present, and future essence in contrast to current, which would omit the *be*

The words are similar to American English, but their usage and meaning are different. The next part of the unit looks at the development of English as a second language.

M. Mariska Malone was a college student who voiced her reflections on the section in this text on African American English. What are your reactions to the text and to Mariska's view? (The essay is included with the author's permission)

**Ebonics and Black Speech Spoken By African-Americans**

**Written by:**
**M. Mariska Malone**

I am an Early Childhood Educator and primary grade remedial tutor. I reside in a suburban community in Denver, Colorado, and I am an African-American woman. I grew up in an inner city, middle class, well kept, African-American community.

My father raised me after the death of my mother, when I was two years of age. My father has an elementary school level of education, which played a big role in my early deficiencies in education.

As a child, the language that was predominantly spoken in our household was a simplified (primary grade level) version of standard English. However, the language style was not to be mistaken with the dialect, Ebonics.

Because of my fathers lower level of education, academic preparation was not enforced in our household. The belief my father held was that he would provide our basic necessities, and our teachers would provide our education. During the tenure of my formal years of education, it was discovered that I had many deficiencies within the typical classroom environment. After six years of feeling inadequate by being placed in the lowest reading groups, I began to teach myself to read the summer after sixth grade. My reading, writing and speaking skills began to greatly improve, as I continued to practice reading aloud. Today, I am an avid reader, writer and speaker. Teaching myself to read, write and speak was an arduous, but rewarding task, that I am proud to have accomplished.

Black Speech and Ebonics spoken among African-Americans are vastly different types of speech. Some of America's most educated and prestigious Blacks may occasionally use Black Speech as a casual style of communication. Oprah Winfrey, the popular talk show host, Judge Glenda Hatchett (Judge Hatchett) and Super Model, Tyra Banks are among a few African-Americans who transition between speaking standard English and Black Speech.

The term Black Speech is a combination of English and slang. It's a communication style that many African-Americans *choose* to speak, which is associated with the Black community at large.

**Examples of Black Speech and the standard English translation:**

| Black Speech | Standard English |
|---|---|
| What's up with that? | What's going on? |
| Be straight-up with me. | Be honest with me. |
| I'll hook-up with you later. | I'll see you later. |

The dialect Ebonics is often spoken by isolated communities of mostly Blacks. The words are spoken in a syntax order that standard English speakers find difficult to understand, and in many cases the words are often mispronounced. Children who learn to speak Ebonics usually live within households where the adults have lower socioeconomic and educational levels.

**Examples of Ebonics and the standard English translation:**

| Ebonics | SE |
|---|---|
| Someone at the doh. | Someone is at the door. |
| I is. | I am. |
| Hur gon get hur pack pack. | She's going to get her back pack. |

Ebonics may be considered acceptable and useful speech among a child's home and social environment. However, the lack of proper language development often causes an otherwise typical or gifted student to experience remedial standards of learning.

*(Continued)*

The view that most African-American children grow up learning to speak Ebonics is inaccurate and unfair to an educationally and socioeconomically diverse group of people. In the wake of higher earnings for African-American women college graduates in the nation (only second to Asian-American women college graduates), there are greater numbers of middle-class African-American children who are learning to predominantly speak standard English within their households. Black Speech in these cases is considered a secondary dialect that is used informally. And Ebonics is never taught or spoken.

## English Language Learners

**English Language Learners (ELL)**

Those whose primary language is not English but who are in the process of learning English.

The school population in the United States is becoming more linguistically and culturally diverse (Tabors, 1998). Increasingly, students come from homes where English is not the primary language and thus the students are **English Language Learners (ELL).** It is expected that by 2025, "more than half of the children enrolled in U.S. schools will be members of 'minority groups,' not of European origin" (Genishi, 2002, p. 66). Large numbers of immigrants from Asia and Latin America are anticipated. Look at the example of Isabel Sanchez. At home, Mrs. Sanchez reads:

Esta es una casa grande.

Aquí vive la familia Raton.

Tambíen vive aquí un gato grande (DeHoogh, 1978, p. 1).

At school Isabel Sanchez may hear:

This is a big house.

The Mouse family lives here.

A big cat lives here too.

**bilingual**

Speaking two languages

**English-language classrooms**

Classroom in which English is the language of instruction.

If Isabel is to survive in this country, she must learn to speak English. There is, however, a good deal of difference of opinion regarding when and how Isabel should learn English. Three main types of programs are available for these children: first-language classrooms, **bilingual** classrooms, and English-language classrooms. There are very few first-language classrooms. There are many bilingual classrooms, but most ELL students are enrolled in **English-language classrooms.** We will look first at bilingual and then at English-language classrooms.

A review of research on bilingual/bicultural young children and their education by Soto (1991) explains some of the misconceptions about young children and second-language learning, describes successful bilingual education approaches, and suggests how research can be applied by early childhood educators. Soto (1991, p. 31) believes that, "Based upon existing bilingual research and what we know about how young children develop, a supportive, natural, language-rich environment, affording acceptance and meaningful interaction, appears optimal." Too often, bilingual education is set up on a deficit model, which views the children as lacking language competence rather than recognizing their strength in their first language. Garcia (1986, pp. 15–16) provides a definition of early childhood bilingualism that includes the following conditions:

1. Children are able to comprehend and produce linguistic aspects of two languages.

2. Children are exposed "naturally" in the form of social interaction to the two languages as they are used during early childhood. This condition requires a substantive bilingual environment and may occur through family, extended family, or travel experiences.
3. Development must be simultaneous in both languages. This is in contrast to the native speaker of one language, who after mastery of that language, begins on a course of second language acquisition.

Garcia applies this definition to dual language acquisition during the first five years. Soto (1991) describes the variety of terms used to label second-language learners (p. 32):

Linguistic minority student: speaks the language of a minority group.

Linguistic majority student: speaks the language of the majority group.

Limited English proficient (LEP): has a limited amount of English as a second language.

Non-English proficient (NEP): speaks the native language only.

English only (EO): refers to monolingual English speakers.

Fluent English proficient: speaks English and another language at home.

Soto points out that some of these terms, such as LEP, emphasize the children's weaknesses rather than their strengths. Too often, programs for these students are treated as compensatory rather than enriching. It is preferable to refer to these students as English Language Learners (ELL).

Soto (1991) identifies several misconceptions commonly held regarding young second-language learners. First, young children do not learn a second language more quickly than adults. People may get this impression because young children are less inhibited, have more frequent social interactions, and have an easier time with pronunciation. Second, there is no evidence that the younger the child, the easier it is to learn the second language. However, the earlier the start, the more likely the person will eventually be more proficient. Third, it is believed by some that there is one best way to acquire a second language. Individual differences must be considered as in any other type of instruction. Generally, second-language learning should be learned naturally, not in a fixed package of lessons.

## Socioeconomic Differences in Language Development

An important consideration for the adult who works with young children is socioeconomic status (SES) differences in language development and language use. Since the 1950s, many experimental early childhood programs have been developed with the major objective of improving the language skills of lower-SES children. The published versions of a number of these programs have been reviewed and evaluated by Bartlett (1981). Joan Tough (1982a) cautions that packaged programs are not the whole answer to the language curriculum for children from lower socioeconomic levels. Research indicates that lower-SES children have a good command of language but have deficiencies in language use that can only be developed through spontaneous teacher–child dialog. (This approach is described in Chapter 23.)

The British sociologist Basil Bernstein (1972) calls attention to some of the cautions that must be taken when developing programs for lower-SES children. He contends that we were too quick to coin terms such as "culturally deprived, linguistically deprived, and socially disadvantaged" (p. 135). The whole concept of compensatory education, he believes, implies a deficit or lack of something within the child's family that makes the child unable to benefit from education. This, in turn, leads to pressure for the child to drop his or her cultural identity. Bernstein cautions that we must not assume that the lower-class child is deficient in language development just because he or she uses language differently than do middle- and upper-class children. The lower-class child has developed language that is useful within his culture, family, and community, and yet has difficulty in school (Walker, Greenwood, Hart & Carta, 1994). Says Bernstein, "It is an accepted educational principle that we should work with what the child can offer. Why, then, don't we practice it?"

Think about what you would need to do to teach children from a different culture or socioeconomic level and have a successful experience for you and your students.

**talk**
The oral aspect of language.

Catherine Garvey (1990) describes the nature of children's talk. **Talk** is the oral aspect of language. Talk is a natural activity that takes place in the due course of biological development, just like walking or playing. Talk is the vehicle through which children learn language. Language develops as the child listens to others talk and as the child talks. Most talk takes place in social settings, but important talk events also take place when the child is alone. It is by listening to children's talk that we infer much regarding how they use language. Talk is the active aspect of language and goes hand in hand with learning social action and interaction. Conversation is a cooperative task in which each party has expectations as to what the other party means and what kind of response is appropriate when each party has his or her turn. The situation within which the talk takes place greatly influences the talk's meaning to the participants.

Young children gradually learn rules for forming words from sounds and sentences from words. They learn to attach words or approximations of words to referents that are understandable to other people. They learn how to communicate in a variety of everyday situations. Young children learn to use talk to protect their rights and justify their actions, to direct the behavior of others, and to obtain needed items. Eventually, talk is used to tell about the past, present, and future; to solve problems logically; to ask questions; to develop imaginative situations; to maintain social relationships; and to express feelings. Talk is an important part of young children's play. Adults have a crucial role in supporting the child's increasing skill as an oral language user.

## THE INFANT'S USE OF LANGUAGE

As already described in Chapter 14, infants develop different cries for expressing their needs for food, pain relief, sleep, and attention. Results such as the following have emerged from research that looks at the meaningfulness of infant vocalizations.

1. Meaning develops from the situations in which the infant is placed (Freedle & Lewis, 1977). That is, the amount and kind of vocalizing the infant does depends on his or her location: floor, mother's lap, playpen, or infant seat. For example, infants were observed to vocalize and communicate more intensely with mother in the infant seat than when seated on mother's lap.

2. Infants carry on a gamelike conversation with objects, such as mobiles and toys, and with people (Watson, 1976). For example, a four-month-old is in her playpen "talking" to her toy rubber dog:
   e-e ma a
   e-e-e a
   e-e a
   hav
   he-e-e
   he e-he
3. Infants respond to speech from the first day of life and possibly in utero. They have been observed to synchronize their body movements to the rhythm of adult speech (Condon, 1979). Mothers address preverbal infants with identifiably differentiated "melodies" that communicate their intent to the infant (Fernald, 1989).
4. Meaning enters infant vocalization by the middle of the first year (Halliday, 1979). The infant develops both verbal and nonverbal signs that carry specific meaning. For example, Halliday's eight-month-old son, Nigel, expressed the following:

| Meaning | Expression |
|---|---|
| | Nonverbal: |
| I want that. | Grasps an object momentarily and then lets go |
| I don't want that. | Touches object lightly for a moment |
| Do something with that for me to watch. | Touches object firmly for a longer time |
| | Vocal: |
| Let's be together. | A distinct vowel sound with a low-falling tone |
| That's interesting. | A distinct vowel sound with a mid-falling tone |

   Halliday found that by nine or ten months, his son, Nigel, was rapidly constructing a protolanguage. A **protolanguage** consists of meaningful sound combinations that are not words. At this point, the child is able to use verbal communication intentionally (Smolak, 1986). That is, the infant realizes that sound patterns can be used to influence the behavior of others.

**protolanguage**
Meaningful sound combinations that are not words.

5. Before the development of speech, infants develop mouth movements that resemble smiles, sneers, and rage. Other emotions are also expressed (Trevarthen, 1979). They also move their lips in speechlike movements that may be imitations of what they see. Furthermore, they have been observed to try to get others to respond to them. When their conversation is interrupted, they will wave their arms, grimace, and otherwise try to regain the center of attention. The infant is often the one in control in his or her vocal exchanges.

Some research indicates that speech, in a real sense, begins to develop gradually, starting at birth, continuing through early primitive communications, and progressing to some consistently meaningful vocalization by five or six months of age.

## THE TODDLER'S USE OF LANGUAGE

The development of toddler language was introduced in Chapter 17. A great deal of research examines the period around 10 to 18 months of age when the child's first words usually emerge. The following are some of the results that have come from this research:

1. When the first 50 words acquired by a sample of children between the ages of one and two were analyzed (Nelson, 1973), researchers found that beginning language usually involved the naming of objects acted upon by the child, such as a ball, or acted upon by others, such as a car.
2. Children continue in their first talk to speak about objects and their ideas regarding these objects (Bloom, Lightbown, & Hood, 1975).
3. As children move into two-word combinations, they seem to use some consistent patterns (Braine, 1976), such as the following:
   - Patterns that draw attention to something:
     See + ___ (See dog, See car, See doll)
   - Patterns that refer to specific properties of objects:
     Big/little + ___ (Big dog, Little doll)
   - Patterns concerned with having something happen again:
     More + ___ (More milk)
   - Patterns concerned with disappearance:
     All gone + ___ (All gone milk, All gone Dad)
   - Patterns expressing the negative:
     No + ___ (No milk, No bath)
   - Patterns that request:
     Want + ___ (Want milk, Want cookie)

Through this study of his son Nigel, Michael Halliday (1975) looked at the meaning of language as it functions for the child; that is, the purpose to which the child puts his or her developing language skills. Halliday views language as developing in three phases from approximately twelve months to the adultlike speech of the two-year-old:

- Phase I: The child develops his own language. By sixteen-and-a-half months, Nigel has 12 meanings. By eighteen months, he has 150 meanings and is ready to enter Phase II.
- Phase II: Transitional stage, which begins between twelve and eighteen months of age. The following examples were collected by the author of this text:

| *Mother* | *Daughter (seventeen months)* |
|---|---|
| Hey, who is this guy? | bee-bee |
| Who is that? | |
| Who is it? | bee-bee |
| Beebee (baby), yes. Let's see now. | |
| Let's look in here. (Opens book) | |
| Who is this? | kighkiki |
| A kitty kitty, yes. | |

- Phase III: Adultlike stage, which starts around age two-and-a-half. The following examples involve the author of this text and her daughter at age two years and ten months. Daughter is playing with a doll (Michael) in the bathtub.

| *Mother* | *Daughter* |
|---|---|
| No, not yet. | Michael can have some (water). Michael can have some. He could have some drink, some, some pop for me to drink and this is Kate's. |

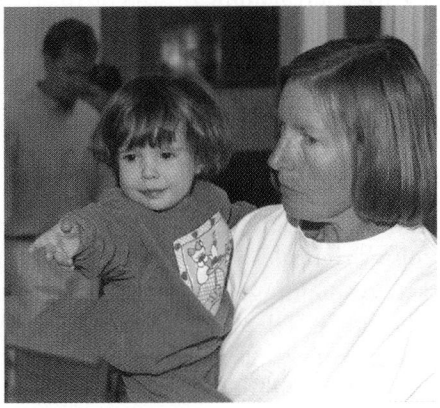

FIGURE 21–3 "That one," says the toddler, as he uses the regulatory function of language.

An amazing change has taken place in just 17 months. Language before about 18 months is very much children's own. They may or may not imitate exactly what they hear an adult say. After 18 months, they rapidly develop adult words.

Halliday developed a category system to describe the functions of language during Phases I and II prior to adultlike usage. The seven categories are as follows:

1. Instrumental: The child demands service or materials. Examples: "I want." "Where's mine?" "Give me that."
2. Regulatory (see Figure 21–3): The child uses commands or requests to control the behavior of others. Examples: "Do that." "Let's go." "Pick me up."
3. Interactional: Language is used to interact, such as to greet, call by name, respond to another. Examples: "Me and you." "Look at this." "This is for you."
4. Personal: Language is used to express uniqueness and self-awareness (such as personal feelings, interest, disgust, complaint, surprise, joy). Examples: "I'm going to." "I am . . ." "That's my . . ."
5. Heuristic: The child asks and acknowledges questions. Examples: "Tell me why." "What's that (called)?"
6. Imaginative: The child creates his or her own environment, makes up stories, plays let's pretend, and recites jingles, rhymes, or chants.
7. Informative: Gives some information that is not known by others. Examples: "I've got something to tell you."

Halliday found that prior to eighteen months of age, Nigel developed the following pattern: categories 1 through 4 were used up to twelve months of age; category 6 between fifteen and sixteen-and-a-half months; and all but the seventh appeared by eighteen months. Personal use occurred most often, followed by instrumental and regulatory use. Interactional use occurred less often, and the amount of heuristic and imaginative use was very small.

Figure 21–4 gives the results in a chart. Nigel at eighteen months is compared with the author's daughter at two-and-a-half to three-and-a-half years. It can be seen that for the older child there is much less instrumental use, about the same regulatory use, more interactional and less personal use, and an increase in heuristic

| Child | Percentage of Each of Halliday's Categories Used | | | | | | |
|---|---|---|---|---|---|---|---|
| | 1. Instrumental | 2. Regulatory | 3. Interactional | 4. Personal | 5. Heuristic | 6. Imaginative | 7. Informative |
| Nigel* (18 months) | 21.40% | 20.00% | 11.00% | 42.07% | 2.00% | 3.00% | 0% |
| Kate (30–42 months) | 1.56% | 27.00% | 29.60% | 18.60% | 14.80% | 12.50% | 4.40% |

FIGURE 21–4 Comparison of the language use of an eighteen-month-old with that of a child between two-and-a-half and three-and-a-half years shows the development toward more variety and the appearance of more mature uses.
(*Nigel's data from Halliday, M.A.K. [1975]. *Learning how to mean: Explorations in the development of language.* London, UK: Edward Arnold)

and imaginative use. Informative use has appeared. The language used by the older child is less self-centered. Conversations have more give and take.

## LANGUAGE USE FROM PRESCHOOL TO PRIMARY

Vygotsky noted that by ages two or three, children are typically skilled conversationalists (Berk & Winsler, 1995). "They follow the rules of human verbal interaction by taking turns, making eye contact, responding appropriately to their partner's remarks, and maintaining a topic over time" (Berk & Winsler, 1995, pp. 13–14). Broadened language use competency increases influence on the thinking and behavior of self and of others. Speech enables communication within the social context. From Vygotsky's view, vocalization is first used to communicate with others and later becomes a tool for controlling one's own thoughts and behaviors.

Halliday's work offers evidence of the variety of language use the child develops by the time he or she reaches the preschool stage. It is interesting to compare the child's use of language with that of an adult, another child, or with himself or herself while playing alone. Some examples from research on the preschool to primary child's use of language are as follows:

1. The child modifies his or her speech to fit the age of the listener (Shatz & Gelman, 1973). For example, the child uses longer sentences when speaking to an adult than when speaking to a child. The child seems to have some idea of what the audience expects and can understand.
2. During free-play time after age three, talk becomes less self-centered and more collaborative. Middle-class children are more likely to assert themselves and seek help from adults in school than are lower-class children (Schachter, Kirshner, Klips, Friedricks, & Sanders, 1974).
3. Young children's talk is more advanced when conversing about a familiar topic than about a nonfamiliar topic and when the child is engaged in dramatic play that centers on a familiar theme. A theme in which the child knows the roles, objects, and sequence of activities elicits higher-level speech than does an unfamiliar theme (French, Lucariello, Seidman, & Nelson, 1985). Thus, to assess the child's real oral language capability, data needs to be obtained when the child is talking about a familiar topic or playing a familiar role.
4. Children's use of language is reflected in their talk about books and about their artwork. Book experiences elicit questions and answers. Artwork elicits a description or a story (Genishi & Dyson, 1984).
5. Dramatic play is the setting for rich communication (Genishi & Dyson, 1984).
6. Kindergartners take part in complex conversation while engaged in open-ended activities, such as dramatic play, art, science, and math (Genishi & Dyson, 1984). Children seem to rely on concrete referents, such as being able to view each other's drawings, to support their conversation (Ramirez, 1989).
7. Young children often do not realize when they have sent or received an inadequate message (Beal & Belgrad, 1990; Robinson & Robinson, 1983; Sodian & Schneider, 1990).
8. Children's speech during instructional sessions reflects the emphasis made by their teachers during instruction (Lawton & Fowell, 1989).
9. Children's verbalization can affect the curriculum through opportunities to ask questions, engage in discussion, report information, and teach peers (Kessler, 1989).

10. Through dialogs with parents, children learn the strategies needed to maintain dialogs with peers (Martinez, 1987).
11. During their third year, children learn to monitor family conversations and intrude with relevant questions and information (Dunn & Shatz, 1989). These young children are already learning how to link into an ongoing dialog between an older sibling and the mother.

**private speech**

According to Vygotsky, the centerpiece of language development and use.

Berk and her colleagues continue to research the area of **private speech**, which Vygotsky viewed as the centerpiece of language development and use. According to Vygotsky, development proceeds from social speech to private speech to verbal thought. Most private speech is used for self-guidance, but it can also be used for word play, fantasizing, and some affective expression. In addition, private speech is used for verbal stimulation, play and relaxation, expression of feelings, and emotional integration of thoughts and experiences (Berk, 1985). The amount of private speech used when performing a new task is positively related to the task's future degree of success (Behrend, Rosengran, & Perlmutter, 1989).

Private speech appears to support learning if it is relevant to the task on which the child is working (Winsler, Diaz, & Montero, 1997). According to Winsler et al., children were able to solve problems presented in a laboratory setting with more success if scaffolding preceded the task. Winsler et al. concluded that private speech serves as self-collaboration that gradually replaces adult collaboration. Private speech reaches its peak at age three-and-a-half as a support to successful problem solution and decreases as children develop inner speech to support thinking. Overt private speech is replaced by more covert private speech from about five years old on (Winsler & Naglieri, 2003). For five- to eight-year-olds, overt talk is still the most prominent, but then covert talk gradually takes over. Adults should recognize that private speech serves an important self-guiding function and should be encouraged in preschool classrooms. Also, adults can learn about children's thinking through listening to the content of their private speech. Finally, Winsler et al. (1997, p. 77) suggest that the following characteristics of adult child interaction are the most effective in supporting children through the stage of private speech and encouraging maximum use of private speech:

- engages the child in collaborative, goal-directed activity
- carefully modifies task demands and adult assistance to keep the child working at an appropriately challenging level
- contingently withdraws adult control/assistance as the child's independent problem-solving ability increases
- uses leading, conceptual questions, and verbal problem-solving strategies as the primary form of teaching

Krafft and Berk (1998) observed preschoolers, ages three to five, during their classroom activities. They found that the frequency of observed private speech was greater during open-ended activities where children could engage with peers, in fantasy play, and in associative and cooperative play in comparison to activities with greater teacher involvement and assistance. Krafft and Berk conclude that the prime ingredients of curricula "are activities that promote make-believe play and peer interaction and that grant children a measure of self-determination, permitting them to establish and modify their own task goals" (p. 656).

Joan Tough (1977) did some of the most extensive research on the use of language by young children. She sampled the language of some children in England at ages three, five-and-a-half, and seven-and-a-half. At age three, the sample was

| Function | Use |
|---|---|
| 1. Directive | a. Self-directing<br>b. Other-directing |
| 2. Interpretive | a. Reporting on present and past experiences<br>b. Reasoning |
| 3. Projective | a. Predicting<br>b. Empathetic<br>c. Imaginative |
| 4. Relational | a. Self-maintaining<br>b. Interactional |

FIGURE 21–5 Tough's language categories.

obtained while the child played with a friend using a standard set of play materials for 45 to 60 minutes.

Tough found that Halliday's categories did not make fine enough distinctions for the complex talk of three-year-olds. She came up with four categories or functions of child speech (Figure 21–5). A **function** in terms of child speech is a means by which a child achieves some purpose through the use of language. Within each function are subcategories or uses. The four functions according to Tough (1977, pp. 47–69) are as follows:

**function**

A means by which a child achieves some purpose through the use of language.

1. Directive Function: The child is concerned with directing actions and operations.
   a. Self-directing language such as:
      Jimmie: This car goes down here . . . the little car.
      Pushing it down here . . . the little car.
   b. Other-directing language such as:
      James: Put your brick right on top. Be careful . . . don't push it . . .
2. Interpretive Function: Children communicate the meaning of events or situations. They are concerned with present experiences or memories of the past. They use logical reasoning.
   a. Reporting:
      Mark: That's a dog and that's a cat.
      Tim: I saw a big ship . . . and it was going on the sea.
      Tom: The garage is too small for the car to go in.
   b. Reasoning:
      Jane: And the ice cream was soft because we forgot to put it in the fridge.
      Andrew: People don't like you if you take their things. . . . I don't do that.
3. Projective Function: Children talk about situations in which they are not presently involved. They speak of things in the future; things that haven't happened and might never happen.
   a. Predicting:
      Jill: Wait until she is four or eight and then she'll go to school and she'll be a new person to go to school.
      Meg: My mom'll be cross 'cos I've got my sleeves wet.
   b. Empathetic:
      Tim: The boy wouldn't like going up and down on the see-saw. . . . It would make him feel sick.

c. Imagining:
Tom: The building's all on fire . . . a man at the top . . . can't get down . . . fire engine comes . . . er-er-er-er . . . get out the ladder . . . put it up. . . .

4. Relational Function: Children relate themselves to others through their use of language.
   a. Self-maintaining:
      "I want a biscuit."
      "Can I have a sweet?"
      "Go away you're hurting me."
      "I want a red crayon so I can draw my picture better."
      "I don't like your picture."
      "If you spoil my castle, I'll have to tell the teacher."
   b. Interactional:
      "Would you give me my car back now 'cos I'm going home?"
      (A more thoughtful, less self-centered relationship than self-maintaining)

Tough analyzed the samples of spontaneous speech of three-year-olds that she collected. She found that the amount of talk from the lower- and upper-middle-class children was about the same but that the variety was quite different. The language of lower socioeconomic class children, she indicated, "tended to be limited to the ongoing present experience and to monitoring their own activities." The upper-middle-class children used language more often for:

- analyzing and reasoning about present and past experiences, and recognizing overall structure.
- projecting beyond the present experience to future events, possible alternative courses and consequences, and into the feelings and experiences of others.
- creating imagined scenes for their play that depended on the use of language for their existence for others.

Tough concluded (1977, pp. 165–166) "[The lower socioeconomic class] child's disadvantage in school seems to stem more from a lack of motivation to think in these ways, from lack of experience in thinking in these ways and from his general lack of awareness of meaning of this kind." The problem does not stem from a lack of language resources.

## LANGUAGE USE IN PLAY

Young children spend most of their time in play activities. Play situations have proven to be a rich source of information on language use during early childhood. Research has provided the following kinds of data:

1. Observations of two- to five-year-olds indicated that during dramatic play, older children's talk reflects a more in-depth knowledge of the various roles and factors in the real-life setting that they are dramatizing. The older children carry on more mature conversations. They had better strategies for settling disagreements (Sachs, Goldman & Chaille, 1985).
2. Dramatic play is a vehicle through which young children develop the ability to construct stories that demonstrate narrative competence: That is they can tell or retell a story that ". . . combines an appropriate setting with characters that react to a central problem through a sequence of events that move to a logical conclusion" (Galda, 1984, p. 105).

FIGURE 21–6 To sustain sociodramatic play roles, children must have highly developed language skills.

3. Children who use the most complex talk during play also use the most complex talk in oral recall of familiar stories. This indicates that language used in dramatic play and language used in story-telling follow the same developmental path (Guttman & Frederiksen, 1985).
4. The skills learned in preschool dramatic play are applied by kindergarten and primary students to inform others during "Show and Tell" times. Kindergarten children tend to focus on action statements that tell what they do or what an object does (Evans, 1985).
5. Valuable experiences during dramatic play include the opportunity for exchange and turn-taking in language use, for taking another's point of view during conversation, and for modification of language to fit a partner's age level (Yawkey & Miller, 1984).
6. Planning is an important part of sociodramatic play. Two-year-olds have been observed to never preplan their dramatic play roles; three-and-a-half-year-olds spend a lot of time planning their roles, often because of disagreement regarding who will get a most desired role, and 50 percent of their talk has to do with planning action, usually regarding who will use particular play objects; five-year-olds decide on roles quickly, settle disagreements more easily, use more complex action-planning talk, and employ more complex plots. For sociodramatic play to be successful, children have to be able to pretend (Figure 21–6), take on a role, know about the theme of the play, carry out actions that go with the theme, communicate ideas, and resolve conflict. Language capability is essential to success in all the competencies, while engaging in these activities provides practice in use of language (Sachs, Goldman, & Chaille, 1984).

   Communication is a critical part of dramatic play. As children get older, their pretend play becomes more complex and each episode lasts longer (Farver, 1992).
7. Dramatic play centers, such as the kitchen area, promote higher-level fantasy play and accompanying conversation (Asquith & French, 1989). This type of communication through conversation requires good listening skills, which are, in turn, necessary for literacy development.
8. Language level is affected by the setting in which the communication takes place. For example, Benedict (1994) found that kindergartners displayed more advanced oral language facility during dramatic play than during other activities and more advanced oral language facility in a whole-language as compared with a basal-based classroom. Isbell and Raines (1991) found differences in fluency when comparing preschool children's use of language in block, housekeeping, and thematic centers. The children were most fluent in the block center, next in the thematic center, and least in the housekeeping center.
9. As mentioned earlier, children's private speech is also an important language aspect of dramatic play when children are alone or with others (Krafft & Berk, 1998; Berk, 1985).
10. Children's use of language in sociodramatic play is based on the language used in their culture. For example, when three-and-a-half to five-year-old African American girls were observed while engaged in family sociodramatic

play, the mother was dominant in language production, with twice as many utterances as other pretend characters. Mothers' talk reflected both strictness and nurturance. Daughter/big sister players spoke much like mother and changed to less complex talk when speaking to baby (versus mother). Overall, the talk was an accurate reflection of real-life talk in the African American family (McLoyd, Ray, & Etter-Lewis, 1985).

11. Strategies for second-language acquisition have been observed during sociodramatic play. For example, from observations of a preschooler who spoke Korean as a first language and was in the process of learning English through her experiences in nursery school, it was found that the dramatic play dialog the child had observed was the basis for much of her initial English talk. She tried out the dialog when playing alone and then would attempt to apply what she learned during cooperative play. Her first successes were in establishing the theme, naming characters, and setting a goal. However, she could not negotiate with her peers in English. She turned to pretend-reading to her dolls for English practice before returning, with more success, to cooperative dramatic play (Heath, 1985). Peer relationships among a group of four Korean-speaking preschoolers supported their participation in a classroom in which the teacher and the other children were English speakers. Being free to communicate in their primary language and to imitate during the normal classroom activities allowed them to become active participants in these activities (Meyer, Klein, & Genishi, 1994). Fassler (1998) studied language interaction of students in an ESL kindergarten. Children from eight different language backgrounds were enrolled in this class, and the teacher was the only native English-speaking model. Fassler documents how, given opportunities for informal conversation, these children supported each other in the use of English. Their natural desire to develop friendships motivated them to apply their growing knowledge of communication in English to forming relationships with their peers. Placement in heterogeneous native language groups helped them focus on the common language, English, as the convenient means of communication.

12. Trawick-Smith (1998b) documented the variety of verbal interactions that take place during role play but are apart from the dramatic themes being acted out. The frequency of these interactions increases with age, in this case from ages three to five. Examples of these verbalizations are as follows:

    - Announcing transformations and make-believe actions, such as "This will be the broom, all right?" or "Let's say a hunter's coming."
    - Requesting clarifications about make-believe, such as "Is the carnival starting today, James?"
    - Announcing internal mental states, such as "Let's say the mother is really angry, okay?"
    - Agreements and disagreements such as:

      J. The cow lives in the house, right?

      G. Cows can't live in a house, 'cause they make a mess.

      J. Okay, but say they live in the bedroom.

      G. Yeah.

    Trawick-Smith suggests that adults should facilitate children's conversations outside of role-playing through modeling and asking questions.

These examples demonstrate the value of sociodramatic play for oral language learning and practice.

## SUMMARY

Children are born with the ability to develop language competence in a sequence of steps that go from the simple to the complex. The rate at which the child progresses through these steps depends on inborn capacity and the response from the environment. As speech develops, what the child says reflects what he or she seems to be thinking. The adult who works with young children must be knowledgeable about the implications of cultural factors, such as nonstandard dialect, the child's first language not being English, and socioeconomic status in viewing the language development of the young child.

Meaningful speech seems to develop gradually from early infancy. By the middle of the first year, children make meaningful nonword sounds. Between ages one and two, toddlers' language develops rapidly. They use it for a variety of purposes. By two-and-a-half, children's speech is adultlike. Children learn to use language for various functions. They begin with demands, commands, and interactional talk. They gradually add questions, imagination, and informative uses. By the time they enter kindergarten, they should be able to use language for higher-level functions such as prediction, empathy, and reasoning. Sociodramatic play settings are rich in language use. In these settings, children learn how to use language functions and how to apply them to sustain social relationships. It is important to encourage children's use of private speech, which they use to direct their activities.

## FOR FURTHER READING


### LANGUAGE DEVELOPMENT

Bloom, L., & Tinker, E. (2001). The intentionality model and language acquisition. *Monographs of the Society for Research in Child Development, 66* (4, Serial No. 267).

Butler, K. G., & Silliman, E. R. (Eds.). (2002). *Speaking, reading, and writing in children with language learning disabilities.* Mahwah, NJ: Erlbaum.

Dickinson, D. K., & Tabors, P. O. (Eds.) (2001). *Beginning literacy with language: Young children learning at home and school.* Baltimore: Brookes.

Emmorey, K. (2002). *Language, cognition and the brain: Insights from sign language research.* Mahwah, NJ: Erlbaum.

Genesee, F., Paradis, J., & Grago, M. B. (2004). *Dual language development and disorders.* Baltimore: Brookes.

Gleason, J. B. (2005). *The development of language* (6th ed.). Boston: Allyn & Bacon.

Guasti, M. T. (2002). *Language acquisition: The growth of grammar.* Cambridge, MA: MIT Press.

Jaeger, J. J. (2004). *Kids' slips.* Mahwah, NJ: Erlbaum.

Landau, B., Sabini, J., Jonides, J., & Newport, E. L. (Eds.) .(2000). *Perception, cognition and language.* Cambridge, MA: MIT Press.

Lange, D. L. (Ed.). (2002). *Culture as the core: Perspective on culture in second language education.* Greenwich, CT: IAP, Inc.

Lynch, E. W., & Hanson, M. J. (Eds.). (2004). *Developing cross-cultural competence.* Baltimore: Brookes.

Masataka, N. (2003). *The onset of language.* New York: Cambridge University Press.

Oates, J., & Grayson, A. (Eds.). (2004). *Cognitive and language development in children* (2nd ed.). Malden, MA: Blackwell.

Rice, M. L., & Warren, S. F. (Eds.). (2004). *Developmental language disorders.* Mahwah, NJ: Erlbaum.

Slobin, I. (Ed.). (1986). *The cross-linguistic study of language acquisition.* Mahweh, NJ: Erlbaum.

Tomasello, M. (Ed.). (2003). *The new psychology of language.* Mahwah, NJ: Elbaum.

### LANGUAGE USE

Amsel, E., & Byrnes, J. P. (Eds.) (2002). *Language, literacy and cognitive development.* Mahwah, NJ: Erlbaum.

Ballenger, C. (Ed.). (1999). *Teaching other people's children: Literacy and learning in a bilingual classroom.* New York: Teachers College.

Bloom, L., & Tinker, E. (2001). The intentionality model and language acquisition. *Monographs of the Society for Research in Child Development, 66* (4, Serial No. 267).

Bloom, P. (2000). *How children learn the meanings of words.* Cambridge, MA: MIT Press.

Butler, K. G., & Silliman, E. R. (Eds.). (2002). *Speaking, reading, and writing in children with language learning disabilities.* Mahwah, NJ: Erlbaum.

Cockerill, H., & Carroll-Few, L. (2001). *Communicating without speech: Practical augmentative and alternative communication for children.* Cambridge, UK: Cambridge University Press.

Dickinson, D. K., & Tabors, P. O. (Eds.). (2001). *Beginning literacy with language: Young children learning at home and school.* Baltimore: Brookes.

Genishi, C. (2002). Research in review: Young English language learners: Resourceful in the classroom. *Young Children, 57*(4), 66–71.

Guasti, M. T. (2002). *Language acquisition: The growth of grammar.* Cambridge, MA: MIT Press.

Jusczyk, P. W. (2000). *The discovery of spoken language.* Cambridge, MA: MIT Press.

Landau, B., Sabini, J., Jonides, J., & Newport, E. L. (Eds.). (2000). *Perception, cognition and language.* Cambridge, MA: MIT Press.

Lange, D. L. (Ed.). (2002). *Culture as the core: Perspective on culture in second language education.* Greenwich, CT: IAP, Inc.

Lederberg, A. R., Prezbindowski, A. K., & Spencer, P. E. (2000). Word-learning skills of deaf preschoolers: The development of novel mapping and rapid word-learning strategies. *Child Development, 72*(6), 1571–1585.

Losey, K. M. (1997). *Listen to the silences: Mexican American interaction in the composition classroom and community.* Greenwich, CT: Ablex.

Meier, D. R. (2004). *The young child's memory for words.* New York: Teachers College.

Meyer, J. (2003). *Kids talking. Learning communication and culture with children.* Walnut Creek, CA: Rowman & Littlefield.

Paley, V. G. (1981). *Wally's stories: Conversations in the kindergarten.* Cambridge, MA: Harvard University Press.

Roskos, K. A., Tabors, P. O., & Lenhart, L. A. (2004). *Oral language and early literacy in preschool: Talking, reading, and writing.* Newark, DE: International Reading Association.

Sawyer, R. K. (1997). *Pretend play as improvisation: Conversation in the preschool classroom.* Mahwah, NJ: Erlbaum.

Stone, C. A., Silliman, E. R., Ehren, B. J., & Apoel, K. (Eds.). (2004). *Handbook of language and literacy.* New York: Guilford.

Tabors, P. (1997). *One child, two languages.* Baltimore: Brookes.

Weiss, A. L. (2001). *Preschool language disorders: Resource guide.* San Diego, CA: Singular.

Whithead, M. R. (2005). *Language and literacy in the early years* (3rd ed.). Thousand Oaks, CA: Sage.

Wilson, S. L. A. (2000/01). "A metaphor is pinning air to the wall": A literature review of the child's use of metaphor. *Childhood Education, 77*(2), 96–99.

Wolfram, W. (2000). Everyone has an accent. *Teaching Tolerance, 18*, 19–23.

## SUGGESTED ACTIVITIES

1. Discuss the following language samples with a small group in class. Analyze them and decide what stage the child is in by labeling each part of the sample according to its developmental level. Decide whether the child is vocalizing appropriately for her age. On a sheet of large chart paper or newsprint or on the chalkboard, list the characteristics found for each sample. Compare your results with those of the other student groups. Note any differences and discuss them. Be sure to decide on the kind of role the adult takes in those samples that include an adult.

   Sample 1. Child is now three years and eight months of age. She is in the bathtub with an assortment of toys.

| **Mother** | **Child** |
|---|---|
| | Do you like the *House on the Prairie?* |
| Yes, I like it. I like those little girls. | Well, this is on the TV. |
| Okay. What time is it on? | And it's on. |
| Oh, what time is it? | The little girls are going in the old plane and they are good and the old plane is going to crash. |
| Ah! Oh gosh! | And then they are gonna be dead. |
| Oh, No! | But their daddy and mommy and the little girls are gonna be in it. |
| Um. | And the pilot is gonna say hi to the mommy and daddy and the little girls. |
| Uh hum. | But he doesn't know that the pilot cooks something bad. |

| | |
|---|---|
| Oh! | They don't know. |
| Oh. They won't go in then. | Yes and they will fall in this wastebasket. |
| Uh hum. | And then he will say Oh Oh Oh what did I put in food. I don't like it. He will say that. |
| Uh hum. | He will throw it out for them. |
| Uh hum. | The people, the *Little House on the Prairie*, will give them the food. |
| Oh, I see. | And they don't get bad food now. |
| Oh. | They don't got more bad food. |
| | They don't got more bad food. |
| | They but they don't got more bad food. |
| I see. | But you got bad food. Do you got bad food? |
| No. | Well you got bad food. |
| Ummm. | And I don't want to eat it. |

Sample 2. Child is three years and seven months of age. She is in the bathtub with a bunch of toys—dolls, a boat, furniture. She's playing house with a Barbie doll and some horses.

The horses are gonna eat here, Lisa.
The horse, the horse.
That's a good girl.
And now you horse.
That's a good girl.
Now you horse, okay?
Good girl, horse.
And now you horse. Yeah, now you, now you Blackie.
I want some.
No you don't want some.
You sit on a chair.
I'm eating.
Okay.
(Shouts) I'm putting—I'm putting my dolly on a chair.
Barbie, Barbie, Barbie, Barbie . . . (sings this)
(High pitched) 'Cause my mommy is washing my hair today.
So I know how to do it.
I'm closing my eyes.
(High pitched) I'm not closing my eyes.

**2.** Visit a nursery school, child care center, kindergarten, or a child at home playing with his or her neighborhood friends. The child observed should be about four to five years old. Observe for about half an hour, taking down verbatim as much as possible of what the child says. Be sure that the child is engaged in play activities. If you have a choice, pick a child who is known to talk a lot while playing.

After your observation, on the same day or another day (with the teacher's or parent's permission), interview the child to find out how he or she acts in a more structured language situation. Use the following tasks. Be sure to prepare the needed materials ahead of time and be sure you have practiced the instructions.

### TASK 1: Labeling Objects

Place four common objects or pictures of four common objects in front of the child. Say, "What is this?" (Point to each object in turn.)

Sample of objects (pictures):

### Task 2: Describing Objects

Show the child each of four common objects or pictures of four common objects one at a time. Say, "Tell me about this."
Note: name, color, use, shape, parts, composition, etc.

### Task 3: Story-Telling

Present the child with some interesting objects and/or pictures. Ask him or her to tell a story (tape record it, if possible). Write a report considering the following.

(1) Include at the beginning of your report:
   a. the child's name
   b. the child's age
   c. where the child was observed and where the interview took place

(2) Include a record of everything the child said during your observation and in response to the interview tasks.

(3) Analyze the classroom observation considering the following aspects:
   a. length of sentences used
   b. dialect of non-English words used
   c. ability to use sounds (note if any sounds were substituted or omitted)
   d. size of vocabulary and correct use of words
   e. use of language in appropriate ways

(4) Analyze the interview task responses:
   a. Consider whether complete sentences, phrases, or single words were used when responding.
   b. Note length of sentences used.
   c. For the specific tasks:
      Task 1: How many of the objects did he or she label correctly? Did he or she say anything besides the names of each object?
      Task 2: Count how many descriptive terms the child used for each object.
      Task 3: Do the same analysis you used for his or her talk during play. (See Task 3 above.)

(5) Evaluate the language used during the play observation and during the interview tasks. Compare average sentence length used and the percentage of phrases and complete sentences in each situation. What similarities and differences are there? How do you account for them?

(6) Overall, what did you learn about this child's language development? Were you surprised or did he or she respond as you would expect for a child his age?

**3.** Collect language samples from different children at a variety of age levels between eighteen months and three years. Tape-record them if possible. Transcribe the results. Number each phrase or sentence.

Card 1. Age: two years, nine months.
Child is in the bathtub.
1. Oh, Monster (blows into water), I swallow you.
2. I'm fis (fish).

Card 2. Age: two years, nine months.
Child is in the bathtub.
1. You go visit Michael
2. Go there.
3. See the mommy.

Categorize each phrase or sentence using Halliday's category system. Try to get at least 25 samples from each child. Bring all the data to class. Figure out the percentage of each category used by each child. Compile the results on the black board by listing each child in order from youngest to oldest down the board. Write the numbers one to seven on the board and fill in the proportions of each category used by each child:

| Child | Phrase/ Sentence Number | Halliday Categories: Percentages Observed | | | | | | |
|---|---|---|---|---|---|---|---|---|
| | | 1 | 2 | 3 | 4 | 5 | 6 | 7 |
| | | | | | | | | |
| | | | | | | | | |

Do you find the same kind of developmental progression as in the example of Kate and Nigel in Figure 21–4? Evaluate your sample compared to what would be expected.

**4.** Collect language samples from a variety of children between ages three and six years. Tape-record them if possible. Transcribe the results. Number each phrase or sentence as in Activity 3. Categorize each phrase or sentence using Tough's category system. Try to obtain at least 25 samples from each child. Bring all the data to class. Figure the percentage of each category used by each child. Compile the results as described in Activity 3 using Tough's categories:

| Child | Phrase/ Sentence Number | Tough Categories: Percentages Observed | | | | | | | | |
|---|---|---|---|---|---|---|---|---|---|---|
| | | 1a | 1b | 2a | 2b | 3a | 3b | 3c | 4a | 4b |
| | | | | | | | | | | |
| | | | | | | | | | | |

**5.** See if you can validate the research on the uses of language in play. Observe one or more children during sociodramatic play and during art or water play. Record and transcribe the conversations. Categorize each phrase or sentence using Tough's and/or Halliday's categories. Are more language functions used during sociodramatic play than during an art activity or water play?

**6.** Make an entry in your journal.

## REVIEW

**1.** Match the definitions in Column I with the terms in Column II. Some of the terms may be used more than once.

**Column I**

a. A well-ordered system of rules that every member of a language community tacitly comprehends in speaking, listening, and writing.
b. These two types of rules deal with how sounds are put together in a meaningful way.

**Column II**

1. phoneme (phonology)
2. morpheme (morphology)
3. syntax
4. semantics
5. pragmatics
6. language

c. Examples of these types of sounds are *bar* and *-ed.*
d. These types of rules are used to put words in the proper order to make acceptable phrases and sentences.
e. According to this type of rule, it is more socially acceptable to say, "Please pass the salt" than to say, "Pass the salt!"
f. *Dog* refers to a four-legged fur-covered animal that barks and is usually a household pet.
g. Some examples are *a, b, c.*
h. Examples of this type of rule used correctly in English are *br, cl, fr.*

**2.** According to the current view, how is language learned?

**3.** For each of the following vocal samples, identify the developmental age/stage, identify the semantic element, and evaluate whether the child is developing at a typical rate for his or her age.
a. Rudy, age three, says, "Mama, I want a trike for Christmas."
b. Larry, age four, says, "Airplane go up!"

**4.** Evaluate each of the following examples:
a. Mary walks up to Laurie and says, "Give me that dolly right now!" Janie says, "No, Laurie, please give me the dolly." Laurie gives Janie the doll.
b. George inquires, "Mommy, why doesn't Daddy like pizza?" Mommy responds with the question, "Why do you say that Daddy doesn't like pizza?" After this, Georgie replies, "Daddy isn't home. He comes home late when we eat pizza." On Friday evenings, when George's father works the late shift, the family eats pizza (*Growing Child*, 1973).
c. Derrick, age five, shouts, "I wanna go to ta park."
d. Since Alfredo was a baby, his mother has always spoken to him in English and his father in Spanish. Alfredo speaks well in both languages.

**5.** Identify the statements that are true.
a. BE is a type of slang used mostly by black teenagers.
b. African American English, or Ebonics, is rooted in the languages of West Africa, with African grammar and English vocabulary.
c. Standard U.S. English should be taught as a second language to African American children.
d. Speakers of Ebonics should be constantly corrected and drilled on SE.
e. With appropriate adult scaffolding, second languages can develop naturally, much like first languages.
f. Lower-SES children enter school without the language skills needed to deal with academic content.

**6.** Select the correct answer(s) to the following. There may be more than one correct answer.
a. Research has shown the following regarding infant vocalization:
(1) The sounds that an infant makes are like the ones he or she will use when learning to speak.
(2) Infants engage in about the same amount of vocal behavior no matter what situation they are in.
(3) Infants carry on conversations with objects.
(4) Even on the first day of life, infants respond to speech.
(5) Meaning does not enter infant vocalization until at least eleven or twelve months of age.

(6) Adults can identify meaningful vocalizations in infants.
(7) Before the development of speech, infants develop mouth movements that imitate emotions, but not speech.
(8) Intentionality usually appears in infant verbal communications by nine or ten months of age.
(9) The melodic qualities of the mother's speech communicate her intent to the infant.

b. Research has shown the following regarding toddler speech:
(1) First words are usually the names of objects that the toddler acts upon, but seldom does the child use a word that is something acted upon by others.
(2) Most of the child's first talk centers on ideas about objects.
(3) Examples of some of the consistent patterns used by toddlers when they begin to put words together are: "See dog, Big dog, Hot milk, More cookie, All gone kitty, No bed, Want juice."
(4) During Halliday's Phase I of language development, the child develops his or her own language; during Phase II, the child makes wordlike vocalizations that serve as a transition to Phase III, when the child's language becomes more adultlike.

c. Research shows the following regarding preschool/primary-age children's speech:
(1) Preschool children talk to themselves while engaged in motor tasks.
(2) The child uses the same kind of speech no matter to whom he or she is talking.
(3) The child talks in shorter sentences to children than to adults.
(4) After age three, the young child's speech becomes more self-centered.
(5) Lower-SES children are less likely to assert themselves and seek help from adults in school than are middle-class children.
(6) Middle-class children exhibit a greater variety of language use than do lower-SES children.
(7) The child's real language capabilities can be observed during sociodramatic play activities.
(8) Art activities elicit little, if any, valuable talk.
(9) Dramatic play elicits no more talk than other types of play.
(10) According to Vygotsky, vocalization is used first for communication and gradually becomes a tool for controlling one's own thoughts and behaviors.
(11) Private speech is used mostly for self-guidance.
(12) Young children do not realize when they have not been given enough information to solve a problem.
(13) Private speech distracts the child from the learning task.
(14) Private speech is most supportive of learning if it is relevant to the task upon which the child is working.
(15) Private speech reaches its peak at about age six.
(16) The things children say can affect the curriculum.
(17) Parental dialogs with children have no relationship to children's capabilities in carrying on dialogs with peers.
(18) Having an older peer in the family can squelch the young child's capability to link into an ongoing conversation.
(19) The opportunity for conversation through dramatic play, such as in the kitchen area, can enhance the ability to communicate.
(20) Placing children who represent a variety of first languages in the same classroom is detrimental to their mastery of SE.
(21) Children often take timeouts from dramatic role-play to discuss elements of the play.

(22) Bodrova and Leong suggest Vygotskian-influenced methods for expanding children's use of language and for connecting oral language to print.
(23) It is a proven fact that a bilingual approach is the best method for teaching both content and SE to ELL students.
(24) Ebonics speakers' oral language should be consistently corrected or they will never master SE.

7. The following are some child language samples. Categorize each, first using Halliday's category system and then using Tough's System.
   a. They say, "Go out little piggies."
   b. And Daddy and the Big Bad Wolf was there.
   c. Where's his mommy?
   d. Gonna drink it up (pretend drink).
   e. Michael can have some.
   f. Rain is coming down.
   g. You're going down.
   h. Laura says we're gonna cook.
   i. I want that toy.
   j. What's that, mom?

## KEY TERMS LIST

bilingual
dialect
Ebonics
English-language classrooms
English Language Learners (ELL)
function
interactionist theory
language
learning theory
morphemes
phonemes
pragmatics
private speech
protolanguage
semantics
structural-innatist theory
syntax
talk

Additional resources for this chapter can be found on the Online Companion™ to accompany this text at http://www.earlychilded.delmar.com. Respond to "Time to Reflect" and "Looking Further" concepts, review various child development scenarios, and answer thought-provoking questions in the Critical Thinking Forum. Keep a daily journal by downloading the student journal available on this Web site. Complete the interactive matching exercises to reinforce concepts, and print out the child development assessment forms to use during your observation of development for children from birth to age eight. In addition, read the case studies on the Web site to reinforce the important concepts in each chapter, and take a look at the multitude of Web links that are available for student research on the Internet.

CHAPTER

# 22

# Written Language: Development and Everyday Use

## OBJECTIVES

After reading this chapter, you should be able to:

- Describe examples of reading and writing activities that are appropriate for young children.
- Recognize statements that describe normal early childhood literacy development.
- Perform informal assessments of young children's reading and writing knowledge.
- Identify and define the major elements in the development of young children's beginning reading and writing development.
- Describe sociocultural influences on young children's achievement in beginning reading and writing.

**literate**
Being able to read and write.

Learning to be a **literate** person, that is, learning to read and write, begins with experiences with books and other print media in the infant and toddler years. Such experiences were described in Chapters 14 and 17. In this unit, young children's understanding and use of print are looked at in more depth as children move through the preschool years into their first year of formal schooling in kindergarten. Learning to read and write in the primary grades is addressed in Chapter 31.

In July 1998, NAEYC and the International Reading Association published a joint position statement on developmentally appropriate practices for reading and writing instruction with young children (NAEYC/IRA, 1998). The position statement is based on a thorough review of research on early reading and writing and is designed to clarify several issues (pp. 31–32):

- It is of critical importance to teach children to read and write competently, enabling them to achieve today's high standards for literacy. More communication is done today via electronic mail (e-mail), the Internet, or facsimile (fax) transmissions than with in-person interactions or phone conversations.
- With an increasing variety of young children in programs and schools, teaching today has become more challenging. Classrooms are populated by a more diverse group, not only culturally but in terms of the amount of time spent in preschool programs and types of exceptionalities and disabilities.

- Among many early childhood teachers, a maturationist view of young children's development persists despite much opposing evidence. Many teachers still have a "readiness" view of reading development that assumes children will be "ready" for reading at a specific time in their development. Now it is evident that besides the essential story reading, many other literacy experiences during the preschool and kindergarten years can lay the foundation for formal reading instruction whenever the child shows an interest.
- Recognizing the early beginnings of literacy acquisition has often resulted in the use of inappropriate teaching practices that, although suited to older children or adults, are ineffective with children in preschool, kindergarten, and the primary grades. Inappropriate practices focus on extensive whole group instruction and use drill and practice for honing isolated skills. Appropriate practices take place in meaningful contexts and use instructional methods that fit the learning styles of young children.
- Current policies and resources do not ensure that preschool and primary teachers are qualified to support the literacy development of all children, a task requiring strong preservice preparation and ongoing professional development. Preschool teachers often lack formal education and are often paid minimum wage.

**No Child Left Behind**

A federal law passed in 2001 whose objective is that every child will be able to read by the end of third grade.

With the passage of the **No Child Left Behind** law of 2001 (Overview and Introduction, 2002; *No Child Left Behind: Expanding the promise*, 2005) increased pressure for preparation for primary-grade reading fell on preschool and kindergarten teachers. Although increasing amounts of money were poured into education by the federal government from 1996 to 2002, reading scores showed no improvement. Less than one-third of fourth graders in the United States read proficiently, according to standardized test scores. The goal of the 2001 law is to hold all schools accountable for achievement by setting up standards and instruments to assess the schools' success in meeting the standards. Only programs that have been scientifically proven to work will be funded. Just which programs have been "scientifically proven to work" is not necessarily agreed upon by government policy makers and early childhood educators. Critics such as Richard Allington (2002) believe that No Child Left Behind provides for too much federal intrusion into local autonomy. There is also the concern that No Child Left Behind promotes inappropriate testing of young children (Kauerz & McMaken, 2004).

**Early Reading First**

A federally designed reading program for preschoolers.

As part of No Child Left Behind, a federally funded program **Early Reading First** is designed to prepare preschool-age children to be prepared for school in language, cognitive and early reading skills (Early Reading First Program Description, 2005; Kauerz & McMaken, 2004). The program goals include (*Early Reading First Program Description*, 2005, p. 1):

To demonstrate language and literacy activities based on scientifically based reading, research that supports the age-appropriate development of

- Oral language (vocabulary, expressive language, listening comprehension)
- Phonological awareness (rhyming, blending, segmenting)
- Print awareness
- Alphabetic knowledge

Many early childhood educators are concerned with the emphasis on literacy as being the foundation of academic success. There is concern that the affective and psychomotor domains will be ignored. There is also concern that developmentally inappropriate teaching and assessment methods will be used. For example, the No Child Left Behind Reading First Initiative supports the use of diagnostic tests such as Dynamic Indicators of Basic Early Literacy Skills (DIBELS), which assess a limited area of reading achievement and moves instruction towards a skills-based approach and away from comprehension (Gardinier & Foster, 2004/2005). The Thirty-Seventh Annual Phi Delta Kappa/Gallup Poll of the Public's Attitudes Toward the Public Schools (2005) results indicated that 59 percent of those responding said they know little or nothing about No Child Left Behind. The majority of public school parents said they were uninformed. The public needs to be much better informed on the pros, cons, and purposes of No Child Left Behind.

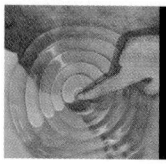

**LOOKING FURTHER**

Using the Internet and professional journal resources, obtain more information on the pros and cons of No Child Left Behind. Formulate a position regarding this legislation as it effects education at the state and local levels.

**beginning literacy**
Meaningful foundational experiences with books and writing materials.

**novice reading and writing**
Awareness that print communicates meaning.

**experimenting reading and writing**
Transitional period; children know the letters of the alphabet and attempt spelling and reading of simple words.

**conventional reading and writing**
Engaging in what society would agree is "real" reading and writing.

McGee and Richgels have identified four stages of literacy development: **beginning literacy, novice reading and writing, experimenting reading and writing,** and **conventional reading and writing** (pp. 25–29). These stages are outlined and defined as follows:

| Stage | Characteristics |
|---|---|
| Beginners | Have meaningful foundational experiences with books and writing materials—they do not yet find meaning in written symbols. |
| Novices | Aware that printed text communicates messages. They attempt to read and write in unconventional ways, however, their organization of material shows that they understand how lists, letters, and stories are organized on the printed page. They recognize some alphabet letters and logos, such as the logos on their favorite food packages or restaurants. |
| Experimenters | This is a transitional period. Children usually recognize all the letters of the alphabet, are beginning to invent spellings, and read familiar, repetitive text. |
| Conventional Readers and Writers | Read and write in ways that most people in our society would see as "real" reading and writing. |

If the environment is print-rich and supportive people are available, children gain concepts about reading and writing through naturalistic activities. National demands for educational improvement have pointed out the weaknesses in our instructional system and called for reforms. It is imperative that early childhood educators become familiar with literacy as a developmental process and understand the significance of this process in stemming the tide of inappropriate practices.

## THE BALANCED VIEW OF READING AND WRITING

Catherine Snow (2002a) makes the case for an end to the "Reading Wars." That is, the end of the argument as to whether reading instruction should begin with individual letter sounds or the meaning of words. The argument centered on phonics versus whole language as the correct approach to beginning reading instruction.

The phonics approach focuses on the relationship between letters and letter sounds. Word patterns are emphasized, and children are encouraged to sound out new words. Reading precision is emphasized (Wren, 2003), along with rules about the way words are written and spelled. It is sometimes referred to as the traditional approach.

**whole-language approach**

This approach places children and their needs at the center of the curriculum; whole language fits the cognitive-developmental or constructivist point of view.

The **whole-language approach** to reading and writing developed out of the concepts mentioned earlier. The whole-language philosophy places children and their needs at the center of the curriculum (Reutzel & Hollingsworth, 1988). Children are viewed as actively involved in their own learning. Whole language fits the cognitive-developmental or constructivist point of view. Language is considered as a whole and not cut into parts (i.e., reading, writing, spelling, listening, and speaking). Rather than beginning to learn through letter names and sounds, children learn naturally through stories, poems, and environmental print (e.g., signs and labels on cereal boxes and other containers).

In the whole-language classroom, children are learning in many different settings. Some are sitting on chairs at tables, others may be in a pillow-filled bathtub, others sit on a carpet using lap boards, and some are seated on an old couch. Writings and drawings are all over the walls. In the whole-language classroom, learning takes place in learning centers that focus on topics of interest. Children read and write about their interests. The process rather than the product is stressed. Children share ideas and review each other's work. Assessment is done through observation, interviews, discussions, video- or audiotaping of children reading, and selected samples of children's work. The teacher is a guide, an active participant, and a model who spends time engaged in his or her own reading and writing.

Snow (2002a) lists three skills that successful readers have mastered (p. 1):

1. They identify printed words using the connections between spellings and sounds.
2. They use previous knowledge and comprehension strategies to read for meaning.
3. They read fluently—they read swiftly and with understanding and enjoyment.

Some aspects of these skills relate to phonics instruction and some to whole language. The contrast between strictly phonics and strictly whole language instruction can be seen in the following writing examples:

| Spelling taught traditionally | Invented spelling encouraged |
|---|---|
| The snake is green. | WAS A PON ATIM |
| The pig is white. | TAR WAS A |
| The fish is orange. | HRNINT HWS TAR |
| George. | WAS A LITL GOST |
| | AND TAT LITL |
| | GOST WOTIDI SAM |
| | WAN TO PLA TAT |
| | LITOL GOST GOT |
| | SUM WAN TO PLAY |
| | WIT |
| | JOHN |

George plays it safe. He uses only words he is sure about. Note the careful use of periods. John is a risk taker. He is involved in the process of telling his story and feels free to spell words as they sound to him. What does his story say? In case you haven't figured it out:

ONCE UPON A TIME THERE WAS A HAUNTED HOUSE THERE WAS A LITTLE GHOST AND THAT LITTLE GHOST WANTED SOMEONE TO PLAY THAT LITTLE GHOST GOT SOMEONE TO PLAY WITH

**balanced approach to reading instruction**
Attempts to blend both phonics and whole language.

Currently, a **balanced approach to reading instruction** is emphasized—teachers attempt to blend both phonics and whole language. However, Wren (2003) points out that there is no one formula for blending or balancing. According to Wren, a balanced approach is one that fits the method to the individual child (p. 7).

> But if instruction is to be customized on individual students' learning needs, teachers need to become more adept at planning lessons to focus on areas of instructional need that were revealed through artful assessment and observation of individual students.

## The Facts about Reading According to the National Reading Panel

According to the study done by the National Reading Panel (No Child Left Behind, 2002), five key components of reading instruction have been scientifically proven to work:

**phonemic awareness**
The ability to hear and identify individual sounds and spoken words.

**phonics**
The relationship between the letters of written language and the sounds of spoken language.

**fluency**
The capacity to read text accurately and quickly.

**vocabulary**
The words students must know to communicate effectively.

**comprehension**
The ability to understand and gain meaning from what has been said.

1. **Phonemic awareness:** the ability to hear and identify individual sounds and spoken words.
2. **Phonics:** the relationship between the letters of written language and the sounds of spoken language
3. **Fluency:** the capacity to read text accurately and quickly
4. **Vocabulary:** the words students must know to communicate effectively
5. **Comprehension:** the ability to understand and gain meaning from what has been read

Certainly these are all important elements in reading. However, how do these elements connect to everyday life and to content areas, such as mathematics, science, and social studies? What about writing, listening, and speaking? The National Reading Panel Report does not support whole language and yet there is no evidence that it doesn't work, along with a balance of phonics instruction for those who need it (Krashen, 2002). In their 1998 study of the research on learning to read, Snow, Burns and Griffin conclude that children need a balanced reading program that provides for both skills in understanding letter/sound relationships and experiences with literature and language. In the following sections, we examine some of the specifics young children know about reading, writing, and print and how they learn about written language.

Read the following anecdotes. Record your response to each incident. After you have read the whole chapter, come back and look again at your reactions. Has your opinion changed? If so, how?

- The setting is a kindergarten in the fall. The whole class is working on a worksheet that instructs them to write the letter *A* and then draw four pictures of objects that begin with the letter *A*. The students then "label" their pictures using "words." Some children found words to copy, but Miss Brown does not want them to copy. She insists that they write their own labels. She encourages them to write what they think the word looks like. She reminds them that all the pictures begin with the letter *A*. Some students do not try, while others try to the best of their ability.

- Johnny and I are at his home where I am caring for him and his three siblings. Johnny is eight years old. The younger children are eager to write in my small notebook. When I ask Johnny to write in the notebook, he initially asks, "What?" Then he writes the name of the video he is watching, *Star Wars*. He appeared to be content to stop at that point. However, I provide more suggestions and he writes his name, age, and his teacher's name. When I asked him to write something else, he thinks for a minute and says, "You can't read it now. You have to wait 'til I'm done." A few moments later, he returns the notebook with two-thirds of the page filled: at the top is *Star Wars* and his name, the next third is filled with, "Bla bla bla bla bla. . . ," etc. He wrote hesitantly and his penmanship was poor for an eight-year-old second grader.

## WHAT YOUNG CHILDREN KNOW ABOUT READING

Identification of words in the environment appears to be the first step in learning to read. In a literate society like ours, most children grow up surrounded by print. In homes, there are books, magazines, letters, food and other containers, phone books, television ads, and other print materials. Only children living in very impoverished and isolated areas with parents who are illiterate may not come in contact with some environmental print during early childhood.

Research indicates that young children are very much aware of environmental print. They pay attention and can identify what the print refers to. They are especially aware of logos associated with frequently visited businesses, such as their favorite store or fast food restaurant, and commonly used products, such as their toothpaste or favorite cereal. A study by Reutzel, Fawson, Young, Morrison, and Wilcox (2002) indicates that young children's concepts about print knowledge are related to their ability to read environmental print. It is suggested that environmental print can be used as the springboard for learning other factors inherent in being able to read, such as phonics and phonemic awareness.

Young children who have contacts with printed material learn some of the conventions, or rules, of print use. For example, in English, we read left to right and from top to bottom, and we read books from front to back. By kindergarten entrance, many children have these conventions set in their minds. Whereas a toddler might be observed looking at a book that is upside down and may turn the pages from back to front, a five-year-old will usually hold it correctly and turn the pages from front to back.

By primary age, children can accurately describe what is involved in the process of reading; that is, what it means to read, what reading is used for, and how reading proceeds. Most younger children are still in the process of developing these concepts at a conscious level (McGee, Richgels, & Charlesworth, 1986). Research indicates the following (McGee et al., 1986):

- Many five-year-olds, if given a book, can explain that the print, not the pictures, is what we read and can explain that words and letters are associated with print.
- Children as young as three years old know that print carries a message.
- Young children believe that to be read, print must have at least three different letters.

FIGURE 22–1 A message written in conventional letter/word symbols is surrounded by drawn symbols representing germs. Note that many of the basic shapes found in letters appear in the germs.

- Whereas six-year-olds realize that special eye movements are needed for reading, four-year-olds do not discriminate between reading and just looking at the page.
- Whereas three-year-olds can label common print materials, such as phone books, grocery lists, letters, and maps, and tell something about how they are used, six-year-olds can give specifics about what the print in each piece of reading material is for.

It is commonly believed that letter recognition is a major prerequisite to reading. Certainly, it is an important part, but whether it is actually a prerequisite has been the subject of investigation. Research indicates that letter naming is only one of many skills that underlie reading and that children begin to develop concepts about print at the same time they are beginning to recognize letters. Teaching letter names does not in itself ensure reading success (McGee et al., 1986). McGee et al. conclude the following:

> One finding which emerges from studies detailing what young children know about reading is that they seem to learn about reading by participating in reading events. Children learn to read environmental print by observing print in all its complexity. They begin to notice how reading and writing operate in environmental print as well as in other print forms (books, directions, etc.) before and at the same time they learn to recognize letters.

## WHAT YOUNG CHILDREN KNOW ABOUT WRITING

Researchers are interested in when and how young children learn that certain kinds of marks have meaning and communicate to other people. Researchers have examined the relationships between drawing and writing, between language used during play and written language development, between the forms used in writing and attempts to use writing to communicate, and the development of alphabet writing.

Young children enjoy drawing and spend many happy hours in drawing activities (Figure 22–1). Although in the early stages their drawing and writing may look the same to the adult eye, young children seem to recognize a difference from a fairly early age. Writing and drawing seem to develop in a parallel fashion, from scribbling to representational drawing and making real letters. Some researchers believe that drawing supports writing, whereas others believe that writing supports drawing. Both are symbolic or representative; the drawings represent things and writing represents speech (Figure 22–2) (Schickedanz & Cashergue, 2004).

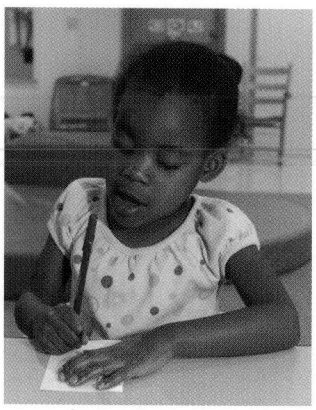

FIGURE 22–2 In the writing center, children experiment with producing different kinds of messages.

At the novice level, children are usually becoming aware of the alphabet and its relation to writing. To use the alphabet, they must be aware of sounds and their relationship to letters. Learning nursery rhymes and making up their own rhymes provide opportunities for sound awareness, which will eventually lead into letter/sound associations. A study by McBride-Chang (1998) documents the relationship between letter and sound processing, invented spelling, and decoding skills from kindergarten to first grade. Sound awareness was found to be strongly related to ability to invent spelling and to decode words. Invented spelling ability appears to be the key factor in attaining success in conventional reading, as it applies both sound awareness and letter recognition. The invented spelling test used (Tangle & Blachman, 1992, as cited in McBride-Chang) appears to be an excellent tool for predicting ending kindergartners and beginning first graders' future reading achievement.

In Chapter 21, the importance of sociodramatic play to oral language development was discussed. The relationship between make-believe play and writing has also been studied (Roskos & Christi, 2002). Play is also a symbolic activity. There is some evidence that being able to carry on a dramatic play theme is enhanced by experience with story reading, which familiarizes the child with story text and story knowledge. Dramatic play, on the other hand, affords children the opportunity to develop narratives in formats that could be used later in writing. These experiences also provide knowledge that is helpful when children are introduced to school textbooks (McGee et al., 1986). Roskos and Christie (2002) provide examples of preschoolers' literacy activities during dramatic play. The children do pretend reading and writing and move into transitional spelling as they write messages, make greeting cards, practice writing their names, make signs, and otherwise applying their growing knowledge of written language.

Children gradually develop the concepts that writing is linear and continuous and begin writing with their own names. Names are very personal, and writing one's own name is a highly motivating objective. Usually by age five, children can write their own names fairly well (McGee et al., 1986). However, within any group of five-year-olds, there will be a great deal of variation. For example, Figure 22–3 includes examples of signatures of older four-year-olds and young five-year-olds during the summer before entrance into kindergarten, Figures 22–4a and b are examples of four-year-olds signing their drawings.

Besides learning to write letters and words, young children learn that different types of messages have different formats (Figure 22–5). That is, lists, letters,

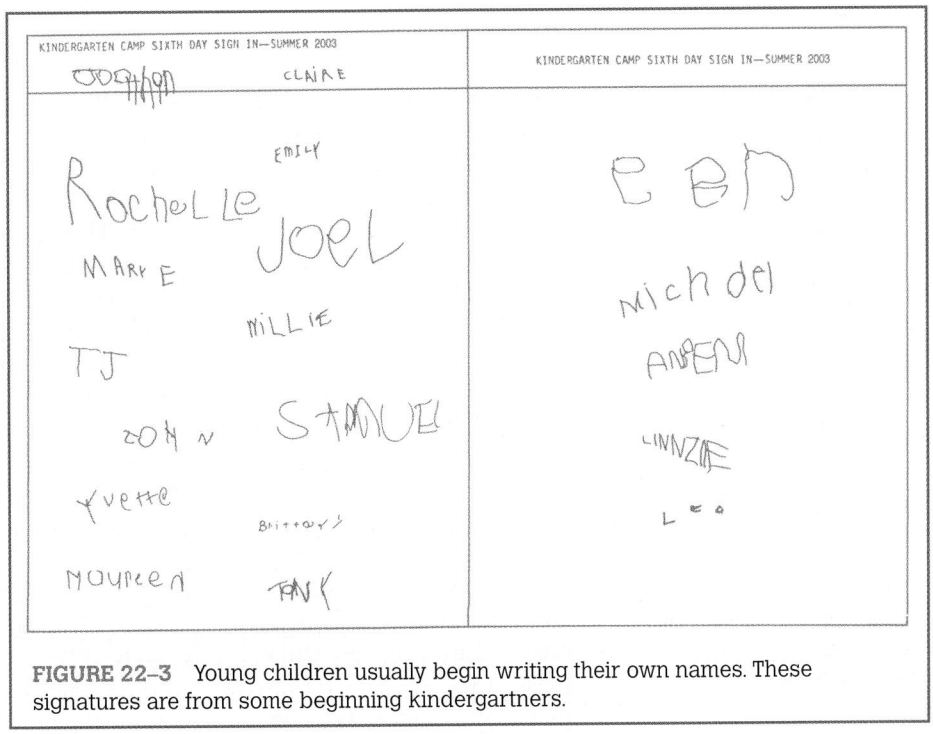


**FIGURE 22–3** Young children usually begin writing their own names. These signatures are from some beginning kindergartners.

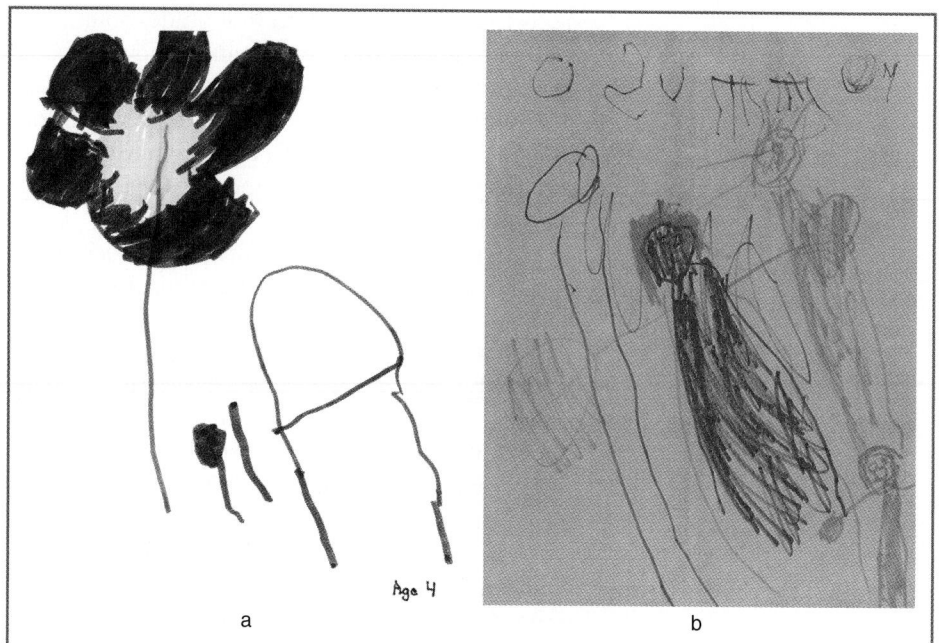


**FIGURE 22–4** Typical early signatures. Ali reverses her whole name, Summer reverses her *s*.

**FIGURE 22–5** A variety of letters were delivered to each person's mailbox during a summer program for entering kindergartners. Note the range of development. Examples a, b, c, and d were written by kindergarten campers to Dr. Charlesworth and one from Samuel to Juan, summer 1985.

and stories are each set up in a special way. For example, young children have been observed to differentiate between the formats of letters and envelopes. Children can learn to recognize and write alphabet letters naturally as they explore these various forms of written communication, rather than through alphabet-copying activities done out of the context of composing (McGee et al., 1986).

**FIGURE 22–5** *(Continued)* Examples e, f, g, and h were written by Mary, who is more advanced in her note writing.

*(Continued)*

## WHAT YOUNG CHILDREN KNOW ABOUT PRINT AND SPELLING

Researchers have also been interested in to what degree young children are consciously aware of units of language, such as individual sounds (phonemes), syllables, and words. This area is of interest because it is a type of knowledge that is not needed for speaking and listening but is necessary for reading and writing. Three areas have been investigated: (1) children's awareness of words as units of speech, (2) the relationship of such knowledge to reading ability, and (3) children's awareness of word units in print (McGee et al., 1986).

Overall, young children have been found to be confused regarding units of orally presented words. However, a transitional period occurs during kindergarten and into first grade in which individual children begin to make these auditory

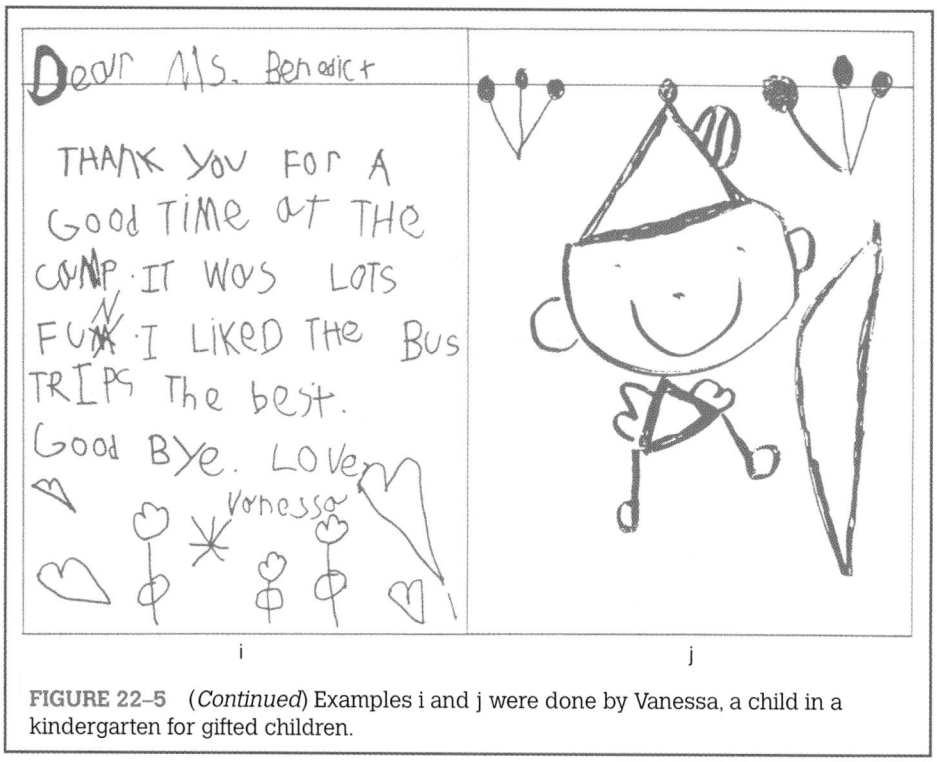


**FIGURE 22–5** (*Continued*) Examples i and j were done by Vanessa, a child in a kindergarten for gifted children.

**transitional spellings**

Moving into spelling, children invent their own spellings, usually based on the sounds of letters they are familiar with.

discriminations. Furthermore, ability to make these distinctions is positively related to the level of reading ability (McBride-Chang, 1998; McGee et al., 1986).

We know that children invent spellings. These invented spellings usually show up by kindergarten and continue through the transition period between kindergarten and first grade. Spelling gradually becomes more conventional during first grade. These invented or **transitional spellings** reflect children's understanding of how English phonology works. It is probably an unconscious knowledge, but it exists. Figure 22–6 is a Halloween picture by a kindergartner. Zach has written his own name, copied October from the calendar, and spelled *bat* conventionally on his own. He has invented spellings for two other words: *wich* (for witch) and *grav* (for grave). Zach has an excellent sense of phonology, only omitting the silent letters. In a study of preschoolers' and kindergartners' letter recognition, sound association knowledge, and invented spellings, Richgels (1986b) found that conscious awareness of letter/sound correspondence had no relationship to the ability to invent spellings. On the other hand, knowledge of letter names did aid in the ability to spell, probably because letter names may be used as clues for spelling. For example, "U R MI FRND" for "You are my friend."

**FIGURE 22–6** A beginning kindergartner combines drawing and writing in his Halloween picture.

An invented spelling assessment developed by Richgels (1986a), which is a measure superior to the usual standardized tests used for assessment of first-graders' readiness for formal reading instruction, is included in the activities section of this chapter. Richgels suggests that if adults can be tolerant and accepting of children's spellings, such as those in the examples, they can learn a lot about children's knowledge of phonology through encouraging them to write using their own spellings. Richgels (2003) makes the case for the closely intertwined nature of invented spelling and phonemic awareness. Children's invented spelling provides a picture of their conscious awareness of the relationship between phonemes and spelling.

It is evident that children acquire a great deal of knowledge about written language without much, if any, formal instruction. Examination of their invented spellings is an excellent means for finding out what they know.

Try out some of the print and writing awareness tasks in the Suggested Activities section of this chapter with some young children to obtain firsthand knowledge about what young children know about written language.

## SOCIOCULTURAL FACTORS IN READING AND WRITING

As with other areas of development, the social and cultural factors that influence written language development must be considered. For example, documented cultural differences in home literacy activities should not be used to excuse the schools' failure to educate particular groups of children (Dyson, 1993). Dyson (1993) points out that, especially in classrooms that include children from diverse backgrounds, "what and how children learn depends upon children's relationships with teacher and peers"(p. 415) within the classroom culture. A major challenge to children is not just to master how to read and write but how to use written communication to control and manage relationships. Dyson (1993) provides examples of how children attach their own social meanings to spelling and writing. This factor is also evident in a study by Mosley (1992) that documents the personal nature of kindergartners' writing and drawing and the nature of social sharing of ideas as children worked side by side in small groups. Gallas (1994) provides examples of how the writing and drawing of her diverse groups of primary students helped her see into their innermost thoughts. Another important aspect of written language development is providing literature that is not only culturally relevant but also not culturally offensive.

A great deal of research has explored children's beginning knowledge of reading and writing. For example, Korat (2005) studied a group of Israeli kindergarteners comparing low- and middle-SES skills and knowledge. Korat examined two types of literacy knowledge:

1. Contextual knowledge: How to use print material recognition of environmental print, functions, of print
2. Noncontextual knowledge: Concepts about print, phonemic awareness, letter names, emergent writing, word recognition

Korat found that the two SES groups were about equal on contextual knowledge, but the middle-SES children were ahead on noncontextual knowledge. Korat believes that the results of her study "imply that noncontextual knowledge of emergent literacy is the most important component of children's emergent word recognition and writing" (p. 234). She concludes that the noncontextual factors should receive high priority in the low-SES kindergarten curriculum.

Language and culture can be impediments to children becoming literate. In their essay on Australian Aboriginal literacy learning in early childhood settings, Simpson and Clancy (2005) demonstrate how lack of understanding of nonstandard language and different cultural customs by white teachers can provide negative feedback to young aboriginal children and impede their academic progress. Relative to instructional approaches, whites tend to teach through questioning, whereas aboriginals prefer to learn through observation and imitation.

In the United States, African American children have a history of poor reading achievement (Bowman, 2002). Almost half of all African American children live in poverty, which can be damaging to development. However, most of these children are competent and can learn. However, in the low-SES home, the skills basic to reading, such as verbal language, phonological understanding, and alphabetic knowledge, may not be promoted. Snow (2002b) describes the black/white vocabulary gap. She suggests that black parents need to understand the importance of daily conversation and other language-related activities as a foundation for literacy.

These brief examples illustrate the importance of considering the development of written language knowledge and understanding in a social and cultural context.

## SUMMARY

Research has informed our view of how young children develop and use their knowledge of written language. It is recognized that understanding and use of oral and written language develop together rather than, as believed in the past, first oral and then written language. Written language development is enhanced by a balanced approach to instruction. Early readers and writers benefit from a whole-language approach that integrates reading, writing, spelling, and oral language, balanced with work on phonemic awareness and sound-symbol relationships.

An approach that inundates children with books and other print materials and makes a variety of writing materials available can *hook* children on reading and writing, make print meaningful, and place phonics in a meaningful context. Invented spelling is a transition stage that moves children from pretend writing to conventional writing.

Another current point of view has come from research on children's writing. We now realize that writing and reading go together and that writing (composing, not penmanship) is an important part of the early childhood curriculum. Children as young as three can "write" notes, greeting cards, picture captions, and signatures at a primitive level. Accepting their scribbles as writing will encourage young children to continue their experimentation, which will develop naturally into conventional writing. Sharing ideas about what to write and reading each other's writing builds an understanding of print and provides a social and cultural context for literacy development. Sociocultural factors, such as SES and cultural customs, also effect children's success as beginning readers and writers.

## FOR FURTHER READING

Amsel, E., & Byrnes, J. P. (Eds.). (2002). *Language, literacy, and cognitive development.* Mahwah, NJ: Erlbaum.

Ballenger, C. (1999). *Teaching other peoples' children: Literacy and learning in a bilingual classroom.* New York: Teachers College Press.

Byrne, B. (1998). *The foundation of literacy: Children's acquisition of the alphabetic principle.* Philadelphia: Psychology Press.

De Oliveira, M. K., & Valsiner, J. (Eds.). (1998). *Literacy in human development.* Greenwich, CT: Ablex.

Dickinson, D. K., & Tabors, P. O. (Ed.). (2001). *Beginning literacy with language: Young children learning at home and school.* Baltimore: Brookes.

Duncan, H., & Parkhouse, S. (2001). *Improving literacy skills for children with special educational needs.* New York: Routledge Falmer.

Dyson, A. H. (2002). *The brothers and sisters learn to write: Popular literacies in childhood and social cultures.* New York: Teachers College Press.

Garan, E. M. (2002). *Resisting reading mandates: How to triumph with the truth.* Westport, CT: Heineman.

Hall, N., Larson, J., & Marsh, J. (Eds.). (2004). *Handbook of early literacy.* Thousand Oaks, CA: Sage.

Harris, J. L., Kamhi, A. G., & Pollock, K. E. (Eds.). (2000). *Literacy in African American communities.* Mahwah, NJ: Erlbaum.

Krashen, S. D. (2004). *The power of reading* (2nd ed.). Portsmouth, NH: Heinemann.

Lyytinen, H. (Ed.). (2002). The neuropsychology of developmental dyslexia [Special issue]. *Developmental Neuropsychology, 20*(2).

McCardle, P., & Chhabra, V. (Eds.). *The voice of evidence in reading research.* Baltimore: Brookes.

Meier, D. R. (2004). *The young child's memory for words.* New York: Teachers College.

Neuman, S. B., & Dickinson, D. D. (Eds.). (2001). *Handbook of early literacy research.* New York: Guilford.

Nunes, T., & Bryant, P. (Eds.). *Handbooks of children's literacy.* Hingham, MA: Kluwer.

Owocki, G. (1999). *Literacy through play.* Westport, CT: Heineman.

Raines, S. C., & Canady, R. J. (1990). *The whole language kindergarten.* New York: Teachers College Press.

Roskos, K. A., Tabors, P. O., & Lenhart, L. A. (2004). *Oral language and early literacy in preschool: Talking, reading and writing.* Newark, DE: International Reading Association.

Roskos, K. A., & Christie, J. F. (Eds.). (2000). *Play and literacy in early childhood: Research from multiple perspectives.* Mahwah, NJ: Erlbaum.

Schmidt, P. R. (1998). *Cultural conflict and struggle: Literacy learning in a kindergarten program.* New York: Peter Lang.

Schmidt, P. R., & Mosenthal, P. B. (Eds.). (2001). *Reconceptualizing literacy in the new age of multiculturalism and pluralism.* Greenwich, CT: IAP, Inc.

Serpell, R., Baker, L., Sonnenschein, S. (2005). *Becoming literate in the city: The Baltimore early childhood project.* New York: Cambridge University Press.

Smith, F. (2004). *Understanding reading* (6th ed.). Mahwah, NJ: Erlbaum.

Snowling, M. J., & Hulme, C. (Eds.). *The science of reading: A handbook.* Williston, VT: Blackwell.

Sousa, D. A. (2005). *How the brain learns to read.* Thousand Oaks, CA: Corwin.

Strauss, S. L. (2004). *The linguistics, neurology, and politics of phonics.* Mahwah, NJ: Erlbaum.

Stone, C. A., Silliman, E. R., Ehren, B. J., Apel, K. (Eds). (2004). *Handbook of language and literacy: Development and disorders.* New York: Guilford.

Sullivan, J. J. (Ed.). (2002). *Literacy and the second language learner.* Greenwich, CT: IAP, Inc.

Tolchinsky, L. (2003). *The cradle of culture and what children know about writing and numbers before being taught.* Mahwah, NJ: Erlbaum.

Whitehead, M. R. (2005). *Language and literacy in the early years* (3rd ed.). Thousand Oaks, CA: Sage.

## SUGGESTED ACTIVITIES

1. Try out the informal test of beginners' spelling abilities devised by Donald Richgels (1986a; 1986b) with several kindergartners and first graders. Compare the responses of each child with the others. Note indications that the children have begun to develop concepts of how letters and sounds fit together to make words.

### Test Instructions

**MATERIALS:** A set of movable letters (e.g., Fisher-Price magnetic letters or those developed for Montessori classrooms)

**PROCEDURE:** Interview each child individually. Say a word and give the child the meaning clue, having the child fill in the blank with the word and then spell the word using the movable letters. Record the child's spelling while the child puts the letters back in the pile. Then go to the next word.

**Invented Spelling Test Words**

| Targeted Word | Meaning Clue |
|---|---|
| JAR | Peanut butter comes in a _____. |
| PIE | One of my favorite desserts is apple _____. |
| DIRT | If I crawl around on the playground a lot, when I come inside my knees will be covered with _____. |
| NOSE | In the middle of my face is my _____. |
| FEET | At the end of my legs are my _____. |
| CRY | When I am very sad, I _____. |
| EAST | The opposite of west is _____. |
| TABLE | When I eat, I sit at a _____. |
| HAT | If my head is cold, I should wear a _____. |
| KITTEN | A baby cat is called a _____. |

## SCORING

There are 31 possible phonemes. Give the children one point for each one represented even if it is not conventional, such as using a letter name for a sound or putting in an extra letter if it makes sense. The phonemes to look for are: *j/a/r*; *p/ie*, *d/ir/t*, *n/o/se*, *f/ee/t*, *c/r/y*, *ea/s/t*, *t/a/b/le*, *h/a/t*, *k/i/tt/en*. Give credit if the phoneme is in the right place and in any spelling that conventional English spelling uses to represent that sound (such as *C* for *K*, *Y* for *I*, etc.). Extra letters are all right as long as they make sense.

a. Report your results to the rest of the class.
b. Show them the spellings and describe the range of scores.
c. Compare your results with those of other students who did this activity.

**2.** Collect writing samples from three-, four-, five-, and/or six-year-olds. Provide plain white paper and black Flair pens so that the products can be photocopied and the originals returned to the young authors. To obtain the samples, arrange with the teacher(s) to sit at a table in the classroom(s) and invite students to come and write. Use the following questions adapted from those suggested by Harste, Woodward, and Burke (1984, p. 235):

a. Write your name for me.
b. Now write, or pretend to write, anything else.
c. (To keep the child going) Can you write anything else?
d. Read me what you wrote. Show me what you wrote.

As you observe each child writing, note the following as adapted from Genishi and Dyson (1984, pp. 185–186):

## THE MESSAGE

e. Does the child believe he or she has written a message?
f. What is the message? Can the child read it?
g. Did the child create the message or copy it?
h. What is the length of the message?
i. Is there a picture on the page? How do message and picture relate?

## WRITING SYSTEM

j. Can you read the child's message?
k. Does the child seem to have a systematic way of writing, that is, arranging the letters or letterlike forms in a certain way to make words?
l. Does the child use letter names for sounds, omit vowels, or have some other systematic way of spelling?

### THE WRITTEN PRODUCT

m. Do the child's written symbols look like letters?
n. Does the child write from left to right?
o. Are the letters arranged in an organized way or haphazardly?

### THE PURPOSE OF THE WRITING

Was there a purpose such as:

- to write a message (he or she may not know what the message is)
- to show which letters he or she can write
- to add a symbol needed to complete a picture, such as a number on a house
- to label
- to write a particular thing, such as a letter, a list, or a story
- to practice how letters might fit together to make words
- to write dialog for a character in a picture the child has drawn

Take the writing samples to class and report on your analysis.

**3.** Lea M. McGee (1985) combined questions from Clay (1972) and from Goodman and Altwerger (1981) into a task designed to find out what children know about the rules that are used in written language and reading. Try an adaptation of this task with some young children ranging in age from three to six.

### CONVENTIONS OF WRITTEN LANGUAGE AND READING TASK

**MATERIAL:** A children's storybook
**PROCEDURE:**

a. What is this called? (book)
b. What do you do with this? (read)
c. What is inside this? (words, letters, story)
d. Show me the front of this.
e. (Open to a page with words and a picture.) If I were to read this to you, what would I read? (picture versus print)
f. Show me where to read on this page. (Repeat on another page.)
g. Put your finger exactly where I should begin reading. (left top)
h. Where should I go next? Next? (a left-to-right sweep)
i. Point to one word.
j. Show me one letter.
k. What is this? (period, question mark)
l. Now, I want you to take this book and show me how you would read it. (Note if the child uses book language, that is, speaks with the inflections and intonations that go with reading versus those that go with talk.)

Note if the child seems to have a good concept of how to handle and read a book.

**4.** Find out what some young children know about environmental print. Collect eight to 10 samples of items with well-known logos, such as Coca Cola, Sesame Street, McDonald's, K-Mart, and Crest, and pictures of scenes with words often seen on streets and buildings, such as stop, go, in, and out. Also write each word on a plain white card without the identifying logo or other environmental clue, such as *out* on a door. Show these to several children between the ages of three and six. First, show the items with the environmental clues and then the words written on the plain white cards. As you show each item, ask:

a. What do you think this says?
b. What things do you see that help you to know what this says?
c. Tell me some of the things you know about this (Harste et al., 1984, p. 233).

Note any age differences in the words recognized and the cues used to aid recognition. Report your findings in class.

**5.** Find out what young children know about the functions of common print items. Collect several print items such as a letter, a list, a phone book, a *TV Guide*, a map, a coupon, and/or a magazine. Ask several young children at various ages from three to six the following questions as you show them the items one at a time.

a. What is this? What do you call it?
b. What is this used for?
c. What might it say in (on) this?
d. Show me how you would you use this _____. (Let the child demonstrate.)

**6.** The checklist that follows can be used to record young children's reading and writing development. Adapted from: The continuum of children's development in early reading and writing. [1998]. (*Young Children*, *53*, 40–41.) Those using this continuum are cautioned that these are examples. The list is not exhaustive and any individual child may be at different levels of development in different areas.

**7.** Make an entry in your journal.

Child _____ Age _____ Grade _____

School _____ Teacher _____

| What Children Can Do | Assessment Dates | Comments |
|---|---|---|
| **Goals for Preschool: Awareness and Exploration** | | |
| ■ Enjoys listening to and discussing storybooks | | |
| ■ Understands that print carries a message | | |
| ■ Engages in reading and writing attempts | | |
| ■ Identifies labels and signs in the environment | | |
| ■ Participates in rhyming games | | |
| ■ Identifies some letters and makes some letter-sound connections | | |
| ■ Uses known letters or approximations of letters to represent written language | | |
| **Goals for Kindergarten: Experimental Reading and Writing** | | |
| ■ Enjoys being read to and retells simple narrative stories or informational texts | | |
| ■ Uses descriptive language to explain and explore | | |
| ■ Recognizes letters and most letter-sound connections | | |

| What Children Can Do | Assessment Dates | Comments |
|---|---|---|
| ■ Shows familiarity with rhyming and with beginning sounds<br>■ Understands basic concepts of print, such as left-to-right orientation and starting at the top of the page<br>■ Understands that spoken words can match written words<br>■ Begins to write letters of the alphabet and some high frequency words, such as their names, family names, or words such as cat, dog, and so on.<br>**Goals for First Grade: Early Reading and Writing**<br>■ Reads and retells familiar stories<br>■ When comprehension breaks down, uses a variety of strategies, such as rereading, predicting, questioning, and contextualizing<br>■ Initiates using writing and reading for his or her own purposes<br>■ Can read orally with reasonable fluency<br>■ Identifies new words through letter-sound associations, word parts, and context<br>■ Identifies an increasing number of words by sight<br>■ Can sound out and represent all the major sounds in a spelling word<br>■ Writes about personally meaningful topics<br>■ Attempts to use some punctuation and capitalization<br>**Goals for Second Grade: Transitional Reading and Writing**<br>■ Reads with greater fluency<br>■ When comprehension breaks down, uses strategies more efficiently<br>■ Uses strategies more efficiently to decode new words<br>■ Sight vocabulary increases<br>■ Writes about an increasing range of topics to fit different audiences<br>■ Uses common letter patterns and critical features to spell words<br>■ Punctuates simple sentences correctly and proofreads own work<br>■ Spends time each day reading<br>■ Uses reading to research topics | | *(Continued)* |

| What Children Can Do | Assessment Dates | Comments |
|---|---|---|
| **Goals for Third Grade: Independent and Productive Reading and Writing**<br>■ Reads fluently and enjoys reading<br>■ Uses a range of strategies when drawing meaning from the text<br>■ When encounters unknown words, uses word identification strategies appropriately and automatically<br>■ Recognizes and discusses elements of different text structures<br>■ Makes critical connections between texts<br>■ Writes expressively in different forms, such as stories, poems, and reports<br>■ Uses a rich variety of vocabulary that is appropriate to different text forms<br>■ Can revise and edit own writing during and after composing<br>■ Spells word correctly in final written drafts | | |

## REVIEW

1. Select the statements that correctly describe young children's literacy development.
   a. Before age six-and-a-half, children are able to learn very little about reading and writing.
   b. Oral language must be fully developed before written language can be at all understood.
   c. Contrary to earlier beliefs, it is now known that reading and writing develop together in a supportive fashion.
   d. There is now research that supports the view that reading and writing can be learned in a natural way, just as oral language.
   e. Identifying environmental print is an early step in learning to read.
   f. Letter recognition is a necessary prerequisite to beginning reading and writing.
   g. Literacy develops through interacting with print in a purposeful way.
   h. By age three, most children are naturally interested in writing and will experiment with it if given adult acceptance and encouragement.
   i. Research supports the conclusion that penmanship and spelling are equal in importance with composition for young children.
   j. Young children should be encouraged to invent their own spellings even though they may be incorrect by conventional standards.
   k. Drawing and writing should be clearly separate activities.
   l. During the kindergarten year, a minimum of one week of concentrated instruction should be spent on each letter of the alphabet.
   m. Too much emphasis on phonics may decrease children's interest in reading.
   n. Valuable reading and writing experiences can be incorporated into children's play activities.
   o. The beginning reading program should include a balance of attention to phonics and whole language.

2. Describe the characteristics of beginner, novice, experimenter, and conventional readers and writers.
3. Read the situations below and decide whether the adults are promoting or discouraging the literacy development process. Give a reason for your choice.
   a. Mrs. Gray Fox observes five-year-old Jason as he writes a story to go with the picture he has drawn of Superman. He writes:

      Sprman svz the good gIz. Here he
      cms now. I lIk hm the bst.

      Mrs. Gray Fox asks "Please read me what you have written, Jason." Jason reads, "Superman saves the good guys. Here he comes now. I like him the best." Miss Jones, the student teacher, looks surprised. "Mrs. Gray Fox, shouldn't we make him spell the words correctly?"
   b. It's writing time in the four-year-old group at Mrs. Miller's Child Care Center. All the children are seated at tables. Mrs. Miller has Isabel and Derrick pass each child a pencil and a ditto sheet with an uppercase *B* and a lowercase *b* at the top. The paper is lined. She explains that today they are going to practice writing *B*s.
4. Match the items in Column I with the correct definition in Column II.

| Column I | Column II |
|---|---|
| a. No Child Left Behind | 1. transitional period; children know the letter of the alphabet and attempt spelling and reading of simple words. |
| b. beginning literacy | 2. the capacity to read text accurately and quickly |
| c. comprehension | 3. engaging in what society would agree is "real" reading and writing |
| d. experimenting reading and writing | 4. the ability to hear and identify individual sounds and spoken words |
| e. Early Reading First | 5. awareness that print communicates meaning |
| f. novice reading and writing | 6. a federal law passed in 2001 whose objective is that every child will be able to read by the end of third grade |
| g. fluency | 7. meaningful foundational experiences with books and writing materials |
| h. conventional reading and writing | 8. the words students must know to communicate effectively |
| i. vocabulary | 9. a federally designed reading program for preschoolers |
| j. phonemic awareness | 10. the ability to understand and gain meaning from what has been read |

5. Describe some sociocultural factors affiliated with beginning to read and write.

## KEY TERMS LIST

balanced approach to reading instruction
beginning literacy
comprehension
conventional reading and writing
Early Reading First
experimenting reading and writing
fluency
literate
No Child Left Behind
novice reading and writing
phonemic awareness
transitional spellings
phonics
vocabulary
whole-language approach

Additional resources for this chapter can be found on the Online Companion™ to accompany this text at http://www.earlychilded.delmar.com. Respond to "Time to Reflect" and "Looking Further" concepts, review various child development scenarios, and answer thought-provoking questions in the Critical Thinking Forum. Keep a daily journal by downloading the student journal available on this Web site. Complete the interactive matching exercises to reinforce concepts, and printout the child development assessment forms to use during your observation of development for children from birth to age eight. In addition, read the case studies on the Web site to reinforce the important concepts in each chapter, and take a look at the multitude of Web links that are available for student research on the Internet.

CHAPTER

# 23

# Intelligence and Creativity

## OBJECTIVES

After reading this chapter, you should be able to:

- Identify the characteristics of the psychometric, cognitive developmental, information processing, triarchic, multiple intelligences, and ethological views of intelligence.
- List the criticisms of the use of IQ tests and IQ scores in the assessment of young children.
- Recognize the attributes of nondiscriminatory testing.
- Discuss the relationship among intelligence, creativity, and giftedness.
- Analyze children's creative behavior.

Thus far, we have examined cognition as reflected in concept development and in oral and written language development. Intelligence and creativity have an overall effect on cognitive development and cognitive processes. The adult who works with young children needs to be aware of how intelligence is defined, what kinds of criticisms have been leveled at the use of IQ tests for measurement of intelligence, and the role of environmental influences in young children's intellectual development. It is also important to be aware of the creative aspects of young children's development and work in appropriate ways to support creative growth and development. Furthermore, there needs to be an understanding of the relationship among intelligence, creativity, and giftedness. This chapter looks at various aspects of intelligence and creativity.

**intelligence**

The ability to benefit from experience, that is, the extent to which a person is able to make use of his or her capacities and opportunities for advancement in life.

## WHAT IS INTELLIGENCE?

In the broadest sense, **intelligence** is the ability to benefit from experience, that is, the extent to which a person is able to make use of his or her capacities and opportunities for advancement in life. There are a number of different points of view among those who have tried to measure, define, and study intelligence. These views include the psychometric (American), the information processing (mental representation and processing), the cognitive developmental (Piagetian), the theory of successful intelligence (Sternberg), the theory of multiple intelligences (Gardner), and the ethological (naturalistic).

**psychometric approach**

Stresses the measurement of individual differences, that is, the comparing of one person to others; also stresses acquired knowledge and language skills as those behaviors to be measured in arriving at an estimate of the individual's intelligence.

**information-processing approach**

Emphasizes the process the individual uses to try to solve problems.

**cognitive developmental approach**

Stresses stages in the development of logical thinking, reasoning, and problem solving as the indicators of the growth of intelligence.

**ethological approach**

Considers intelligence as the degree to which the individual is able to cope with and adapt to life.

**theory of successful intelligence**

The ability of the individual to apply analytic, creative, and practical abilities in society.

**theory of multiple intelligences**

Developed by Gardner; views intelligence as being potentially divided into eight types.

The **psychometric approach** stresses the measurement of individual differences, that is, the comparison of one person to others. It also stresses acquired knowledge and language skills as those behaviors to be measured in arriving at an estimate of the individual's intelligence. The **information-processing** (or cognitive science) **approach** attempts to identify all the steps taken in a problem-solving task. Rather than looking at problem solving in a global way, the information-processing view emphasizes in great detail the steps an individual takes to try to solve a problem. For example, the information-processing psychologist might seek to find exactly what mental steps are used to arrive at the answers to IQ test questions or to solve a Piagetian conservation task. The ultimate goal is to be able to simulate an individual's problem-solving tactics on a computer. The **cognitive developmental approach** stresses stages in the development of logical thinking, reasoning, and problem solving as the indicators of the growth of intelligence. The **ethological approach** considers intelligence as the degree to which the individual is able to cope with and adapt to life. The **theory of successful intelligence** approach developed by Sternberg and his associates (Sternberg, Torff, & Grigorenko, 1998) stresses using one's intelligence to achieve personal life goals. This intelligence occurs within a specific sociocultural context and involves the application of analytic, creative, and practical abilities. The **theory of multiple intelligences** developed by Gardner (1983, 1984, 1999) is, like Piaget's, biologically based. However, it views intelligence as being potentially divided into different types.

These six views are outlined in Figure 23–1 with regard to definition, how measurement is done, the major emphasis of each, and what is measured. Looking across the chart, notice the overall differences among the views: The theories range from tightly structured and specifically defined samples of behavior in the psychometric and information-processing approaches, to more open-ended samples in the cognitive developmental, triarchic, and multiple-intelligences approaches, to the total adaptation of the individual to his or her everyday life in the ethological approach.

## The Psychometric Approach

The following is an example of the psychometric approach. Lewis Terman and his colleagues translated the French test developed by Alfred Binet into English and named it the Stanford-Binet (Leslie, 2000). They developed a score that they labeled the Intelligence Quotient (IQ). For more than 80 years, the Stanford-Binet test or one of its competitors has been administered to almost every school-aged child in the United States.

A young child is taking a standardized intelligence test. The child and examiner are seated at a small table. The examiner presents the child with a series of tasks, one at a time. The tasks might include building a block tower, identifying parts of the body, or discussing what is seen in some pictures (Cole, Cole, & Lightfoot, 2005). The child is given credit according to how correct each answer is compared to acceptable types of answers as described by the test developers. The child is then compared with other children of the same age by the IQ score he or she receives. An IQ score between 90 and 110 means the child is average, according to the test results. A score above 110 indicates that the child is above average, and a score below 90 indicates below-average performance.

| | The Six Views | | | | | |
|---|---|---|---|---|---|---|
| **Aspect of Intelligence** | **Psychometric** | **Cognitive Developmental** | **Ethological** | **Information-Processing** | **Theory of Successful Intelligence** | **Multiple Intelligence** |
| Definition | What intelligent people do | Adaptations to new situations child constructs | The disposition to behave intelligently: to adapt through problem solving | Intelligence is derived from the ways people represent and process information | Using one's intelligence within a specific sociocultural context to achieve personal goals | Intelligence is composed of eight intelligences:<br>• linguistic<br>• logical-mathematical<br>• bodily-kinesthetic<br>• interpersonal<br>• intrapersonal<br>• musical<br>• spatial<br>• natural world |
| How and where measured | Measured through a structured series of tasks in a controlled situation | Measured in a controlled setting using open-ended questions | Observed in the environment as the person goes through his or her daily life tasks | One-to-one in a laboratory setting | Multiple-choice questions for assessing memory; performance assessments to measure analytical, creative, and practical achievements; and classroom activities | Unobtrusive measures used in the natural or naturalistic setting |
| Emphasis | Individual differences | Commonalities at each developmental stage of logical thinking | Identification of cognitive skills needed for adaptive problem solving | The most minute and elementary units of information processing; manipulation of symbols | Triarchic, including instruction that applies analytical, creative, and practical areas, thus capitalizing on each child's strength | Through development, achieve different levels in each area. Match individual to activities appropriate to intellectual strengths |
| What is measured | Acquired knowledge and language skills | Reasoning and problem-solving skills | Adaptive level is evaluated through observation of daily activities | Intelligent functioning in precise, testable steps related to memory and problem solving | Memory as measured in usual classroom examinations and the application of analytical, creative, and practical intelligence | Multiple intelligences as they compose parts of total intelligence |

**FIGURE 23–1** Six views of intelligence.

## The Information-Processing Approach

The information-processing approach is an attempt to overcome a major weakness in the psychometric and Piagetian measurement of intelligence (Siegler & Richards, 1982). Information processing emphasizes the process the individual uses to solve problems. Memory processes and problem solving have been the focuses of information-processing research. Memory factors, such as capacity, strategies, and organization, are studied. Problem solving is examined in terms of task analysis or breaking a task down into each substep. For example, children might be observed while trying to solve the Piagetian conservation-of-number task described earlier. Does the child examine the groups and decide that the group that takes up more space has more objects? Does the child use one-to-one correspondence to check? Does he or she count each group to check? Does the child know that changes in arrangements do not affect the number of objects present? How the child arrives at a solution is emphasized rather than the solution itself.

## The Cognitive Developmental Approach

Examples of the cognitive developmental approach are the Piagetian clinical interviews described in Chapter 20. At the University of Montreal's Institute of Psychology, some psychologists (Pinard & Sharp, 1972) developed tests of intelligence using Piaget's tasks. One of the tests involves floating and sinking objects. The examiner and child sit at a small table. On the table is a small tank of water. Various small objects are available. Pinard and Sharp (1972, pp. 66–67) describe the task given to the child. An interview might go as follows:

> The examiner picks up the nail, lets the child feel it if he wants to, and says, "If we put this nail in the water, will it go to the bottom, or will it remain on the water?"
>
> Child: It will go to the bottom.
>
> Examiner: Explain to me, why do you think it will?
>
> Child: It's heavy.
>
> Examiner: Now you may put the nail in the water and see what happens.
>
> Child puts the nail in the water and it sinks to the bottom.
>
> Examiner: Why does it go to the bottom, do you think?
>
> Child: The nail pushed itself down.

The child is given several objects. Each time he is asked to predict what will happen before he puts the object in the water. He is always asked to give his reason. There are no right or wrong answers as in the psychometric test. In the Piagetian test, the child is just assessed to find out where he is in the sequence of developmental stages. In this case, this four-and-a-half-year-old gives a typical preoperational response.

## Theory of Successful Intelligence

Sternberg and his associates' (1998) theory of successful intelligence is based on the belief that "successful intelligence involves using one's intelligence to achieve goals one sets for oneself in life, within a specific sociocultural context" (p. 668). Therefore, it is a relatively broad theory based on the degree to which individuals successfully apply their intellectual capacities. According to Sternberg et al., successful intelligence is composed of three ability areas: analytical, creative, and practical. By teaching through application of all three abilities, everyone's

**triarchic instruction**

Teaching through application of analytical, creative, and practical abilities.

strengths will be tapped, their weaknesses will be strengthened, and everyone will have an equal opportunity to retain content. This instructional method is called **triarchic instruction.** To assess achievement, multiple-choice questions are used to assess memory. Performance assessments are used to assess triarchic abilities. Analytic assessment is achieved through problem-solving tasks, tasks that involve imagination, and practical tasks that might involve organizing a project. The following are examples of third-grade performance assessment tasks for social studies (p. 669):

- *Analytical:* State why a state needs a governor, why it is a position of authority, and what its privileges and limitations are.
- *Creative:* Students are asked to imagine a place where no one tries to be a good citizen—where no one follows the rules of school or community. They are asked to write a story about a visit to this place.
- *Practical:* Students are asked to describe the steps they would take as class "election commissioner" to organize an election to choose a class president.

When taught throsugh all three methods, students do well on all three type of performance assessments and on the more conventional memory assessment. Through the use of multiple teaching strategies, all students have the opportunity to perform well in learning content.

## The Theory of Multiple Intelligences

In 1983, Howard Gardner proposed the theory of multiple intelligences. Gardner believes that while each person has an overall intelligence, this intelligence can be broken down into several parts, each contributing to the whole. Each intelligence defines a capacity, not a learning style. These talents should be cultivated in schools, not directly taught. Gardner originally identified seven intelligences:

1. *Linguistic intelligence:* mastery of language
2. *Musical intelligence:* degree of musical talent
3. *Logical-mathematical intelligence:* mastery of the world of objects and the actions that can be performed upon objects, such as counting and ordering
4. *Spatial intelligence:* ability to perceive the world accurately, to transform and modify one's initial perceptions, and to be able to recreate what one has learned through the visual modality, even without the visual stimuli present
5. *Bodily-kinesthetic intelligence:* being able to use one's body in skillful ways and to handle objects skillfully

6–7. Personal intelligences:
   (a) *Intrapersonal intelligence:* access to one's own internal feelings, such as discriminating pleasure and pain
   (b) *Interpersonal intelligence:* the ability to recognize others' moods, temperaments, motivations, and intentions

Later (Gardner, 1999), he added an eighth area:

8. *Naturalist intelligence:* the ability to recognize important distinctions in the natural world among flora and fauna and in the manufactured world among objects, such as cars or shoes

Measurement takes place in the naturalistic setting through observation of children's behavior (Gardner, 1993; Gardner & Hatch, 1989; Hatch & Gardner, 1986; Krechevsky, 1998). Gardner's premise is that standardized tests are severely limited in that they measure mainly language and logic skills. Therefore, a new method of assessment is needed that taps all areas of intelligence during culturally familiar naturalistic activities.

Gardner's proposals have been put into effect in three projects (Gardner, 1993; Gardner & Hatch, 1989). Arts PROPEL is looking for ways to assess growth and learning in the arts at the secondary level. At the elementary level, the Key School project in Indianapolis is attempting to develop assessments of all the intelligences. Project Spectrum at Tufts University has developed assessments that fit the child-centered curriculum of preschools and kindergartens. Project Spectrum assessment is done through specific activities designed to tap multiple intelligences (Gardner, 1993; Krechevsky, 1991, 1998). The activities are set up as learning centers within the regular classroom structure. Activities range from the specific, such as taking apart and assembling a meat grinder, to the open ended, such as the science discovery center. Growth is documented using many methods, such as score sheets, observation checklists, portfolios, and tape recordings. The Spectrum assessment system includes several unique dimensions (Gardner, 1993; Krechevsky, 1991, 1998):

- The line between curriculum and assessment is blurred so that assessment is integrated into everyday activities.
- Assessment is embedded into meaningful real-world activities.
- The measures used are "intelligence fair." Intelligences beyond just language and logic are tapped.
- Children's strengths are emphasized.
- Children's "working styles" are considered (e.g., persistent versus frustrated, reflective versus impulsive, confident versus tentative; responds to visual/auditory and/or kinesthetic cues).

An overall description of Project Spectrum and the project's early learning activities is included in Chen, Krechevsky, and Viens (1998) and Chen (1998). Gardner's objective is to free children from the narrow standardized-test perspective and help them discover their own intelligences and use the information as a guide to vocational and recreational choices so they can find roles where they feel comfortable and productive. Further applications to instruction are described in Chapter 24.

**FIGURE 23–2** Assessment can be done through teacher observation of children during regular classroom activities, with children's classroom work being a rich source of information for assessment.

## The Ethological Approach

In the ethological approach, rather than an examiner, there is an observer. Rather than a small room with a table and two chairs, the child is evaluated in his or her natural environment. The observer stays in the background taking note of the child's behavior. The observers might be looking for some specific kinds of adaptation, such as how the child copes with problem-solving situations (Charlesworth, 1978). Or, they might be looking for general behaviors that seem to indicate good adaptation.

Many people contend that the psychometric approach gives an unfair picture of the child's intellectual capacity (Cole, Cole, & Lightfoot, 2005). They also believe that intelligence test scores have been used in ways that have hurt children and kept them from reaching their potential (Figure 23–2).

## IQ SCORES: CRITICISMS AND CAUTIONS

Criticism of IQ tests and the uses of IQ scores has developed for several reasons (Fleege, 1997):

- Although IQ scores predict school success, they do not consider coping skills.
- IQ scores have been misused to label children as developmentally disabled who really were not; they may just have poor test-taking skills.
- IQ test content is unfair to children who may not have the English language skills nor the knowledge and experiences necessary to give correct test answers.
- The young child is inconsistent in his or her test responses from one testing to another.
- Test preparation and test taking raise stress levels.

A great deal of controversy has erupted over whether there are racial differences in intellectual capacity (Gould, 1982; Jensen, 1985; Moore, 1982, 1985) or whether the low scores obtained by minority and low-socioeconomic-status (SES) children reflect biases in the intelligence tests (Cole & Washington, 1986; McGowan & Johnson, 1984). Constance Kamii and others (1990) believe that cultural bias is a major factor limiting the usefulness of standardized tests with young children, especially if some important educational decision, such as grade retention or admission to a special program, rests on the results. Considering the nature of young children and their yet-to-be-developed capacities, adults who work with them must be cautious in using and interpreting IQ test and other standardized test scores. Multiple measures should be reviewed before making any decisions about placement or retention.

Think back to when you were a child. Can you ever remember having your intelligence assessed? If so, can you remember the purpose of the assessment? Describe what you remember about your feelings during the assessment. Compare your experience with the experiences of other class members.

## INTELLIGENCE: ENVIRONMENTAL AND CULTURAL INFLUENCES

The adult who works with the young child needs to consider the question of assessing the intellectual capacity of the child to plan and evaluate an instructional program. The teacher should consider classroom, home, and neighborhood performance along with any information from formal or informal testing. The Council for Exceptional Children (Policy, *Exceptional Children*, 1977) has formulated suggested policies for nondiscriminatory evaluation of individual children. Some of the suggested policies include the following:

- Assessment instruments should be appropriately adapted when used with children of impaired sensory, physical, or speaking skills and must consider each child's age and socioeconomic and cultural background.
- Specialists implementing evaluation procedures must be familiar with local cultural, language, and social patterns and practices.
- Tests and similar evaluation materials should be administered in the child's primary language, when appropriate.

- Interpreters, in the native language and/or in sign language, may be used throughout all phases of the evaluation.
- All communication with parents and the child should be in the native language of the home.
- Instruments should be administered only by trained personnel according to the producer's instructions.
- Instruments should assess specific abilities, not merely produce a single IQ score.
- No one result should determine placement.

Evaluation of groups of children in classrooms or schools can also go beyond IQ scores and make better use of informal interviews with children, checklists, classroom observations, and portfolios of children's work (Fleege, 1997; Kamii, 1990; McAfee, Leong, & Bodrova, 2004; Shores & Grace, 1998). Information for authentic assessment should be obtained when children are engaged in their regular daily activities rather than in artificial individual or group testing situations, through examination of developmentally appropriate student work, or during individual interviews where developmentally appropriate tasks are used. For future guidance, see the NAEYC/ NAECS/SDE position statement (1991).

An important consideration for teachers of young children is long-term program effects. Teachers of young children deal with the child's first school experience. Will or can the teacher have an effect on a child in the long term? Will the child be able to cope with life any better than if he or she had not received early educational experience? The long-term follow-up on children who participated in the infant and preschool programs of the 1950s and 1960s and further studies of those and other models look very encouraging (Bracey, 1994; Bracey & Stellar, 2003; Campbell & Ramey, 1994; Farnsworth, Schweinhart, & Berrueta-Clement, 1985; Frede & Barnett, 1992; Lazar, Darlington, Murray, Royce, & Snipper, 1982; Miller, 1984; Miller & Bizzell, 1983; Schweinhart, Barnes, & Weikart, 1993; Schweinhart, 2002; Schweinhart & Weikart, 1985, 1997; Schweinhart, Weikart, & Larner, 1986). For example, these children have had less special education placement during their school careers. They were also less likely to be retained in a grade than children who had not had a preschool experience. The children had short-term IQ score gains that held through the third grade. It may be that the preschool programs taught the children the language and concept skills they needed to cope successfully with the early years of school. This also enabled them to go through school with a better set of reading, writing, and arithmetic skills. The adult who works with young children can be confident that the child is being taught some basic skills and attitudes that will help in dealing with future school experiences.

Children from minority groups are often penalized when assessed with standardized IQ tests (Brooks-Gunn, Klebanov, & Duncan, 1996; Gonzalez, 1996; Ogbu, 1994). Gonzalez points out how sociocultural factors, such as formal schooling, home environment and SES, have a major influence on intelligence. Efforts to develop culturally fair instruments have been unsuccessful. As already mentioned, both Gardner and Sternberg are experimenting with other kinds of assessment measures. Research shows that younger children who are just learning language perform better on the nonverbal parts of the tests than on the verbal. Gonzalez suggests that we need to understand the following:

- Verbal and nonverbal procedures are complementary, not alternative, criteria for assessing young majority and minority children's cognition.
- Both verbal and nonverbal tasks should be administered to bilingual children using their first and second languages.

- Different theoretical and assessment models need to be developed for language-minority children, resulting in new alternative measures.

As currently measured, intelligence focuses on language and logico-mathematical knowledge, and not on children's overall potential.

Commenting on Terman's long-term study of the predictive value of IQ tests, Hastorf explains that he believes the tests do pretty well at identifying "school bright" children (Leslie, 2000). That is, the tests predict how well children will do in school, but other factors, such as genetics, biological health, and motivation, also affect school success. Children with equal IQs may differ in achievement due to differences in persistence, confidence, and early parental involvement.

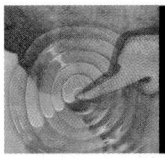

**LOOKING FURTHER**

The class should divide into two groups. Have one group list reasons for heredity having a stronger influence on intelligence than environment. Have the other group list the reasons why environment has a stronger influence on intelligence than heredity. Have each group list its reasons on a large piece of newsprint, the chalkboard, or an overhead transparency. Finally, after presenting both positions, have the groups try to arrive at a consenus position.

## WHAT IS CREATIVITY?

Are the children in the examples in Figure 23–3 creative? How about Kate's drawing in Figure 23–4 of a girl riding a horse? Are young children really creative in the same sense as an older child or adult, or do they just seem creative because of their preoperational view of the world? Something may be considered creative for young children if it is new to them, even if it may not be new to adults. **Creativity** is an aspect of behavior that reflects originality, experimentation, imagination, and a spirit of exploration (Figure 23–5).

**creativity**
An aspect of behavior that reflects originality, experimentation, imagination, and a spirit of exploration.

Both Piaget and Vygotsky have contributed to the theoretical understanding of the concept of creativity (Ayman-Nolley, 1988). Both viewed creativity as emerging from children's imaginative play. Children's imaginative play pulls away from reality and is a reflection of the distortions caused by their preformal operational way

Sandy is caring for Janice, age five. As the observer, I took a notebook for recording anecdotal accounts. Janice observed me taking notes and asked me to let her write. I obliged her request on more than one occasion and found the results very interesting. The first time I gave her a page from my notebook, she wrote her name, the names of two of her siblings, her phone number, her age, and the message, "Don't forget me." The second time, I gave her my whole notebook. She filled the pages with the names of her family members, friends, cousins, and anything else she could think to write. She drew pictures of boys, girls, me, and a graveyard (it was near Halloween) spontaneously, informing me of everything she drew.

Tyler, age eight, has just returned from a duck-hunting trip with his uncle and cousin. He has been telling his dad about the trip. Tyler goes into the house and comes out with paper and colored pencils. "Do you want to see what the ducks look like?" he says to his dad. He draws a picture of a duck that resembles a duck fairly closely. He colors green around the edges and adds purple and red. Then he draws the pond and the duck blinds (where you hide when waiting for the ducks to appear). After he has finished the drawing, he labels all the areas he has drawn. He gives the finished picture to his dad.

FIGURE 23–3 Are these young children creative? Evaluate their activities based on the criteria described in this chapter.

FIGURE 23–4 Children are being creative when they draw what to them is original, such as this "girl on a horse."

of thinking. According to Piaget and Vygotsky, true creative imagination develops when abstract thinking and conceptualization are possible in adolescence and adulthood. Both theorists apply their ideas to artistic behavior, but say relatively little about scientific inventions. According to Isenberg & Jalongo (2006, 4th ed.), to be considered creative, a behavior must meet four basic criteria related to the child's thinking process:

1. **Originality:** The behavior reflects a new idea or a new combination of ideas and has a low probability of happening.
2. **Appropriate and Relevant:** The behavior is relevant to a goal the child has.
3. **Fluency:** Ideas that are easily developed from previous knowledge
4. **Flexibility:** Seeing a new use for an idea or material that no one else figures out

Use these criteria when evaluating a child's behavior as being creative or noncreative.

Analyze the following incident using information from this chapter.

Dana and Katie are both three years old. As soon as the children sit down, Katie grabs a Q-tip, dips it in the paint, and begins painting. Dana watches her. After she observes, she selects a Q-tip, dips it in the paint, and begins painting. Dana seems content using one color until she sees Katie using different colors and even mixing colors. Dana appears to observe Katie closely so that she can follow each of her moves. Throughout the entire activity time, Dana's eyes shift back and forth from her paper to Katie's in hopes of doing the identical thing that Katie does. Katie starts gluing macaroni on her paper; Dana follows. Katie uses the markers first: Dana follows. They proceed in this manner until they are finished.

**gifted person**

A person who exhibits, or has the potential for a high performance level in at least one area.

FIGURE 23–5 Creativity is reflected in the young child's imaginative, original explorations of materials in their environment.

## What Is Giftedness?

According to the National Association for Gifted Children (n.d.), a "**gifted person** is someone who shows, or has the potential for showing, an exceptional level of performance in one or more areas of expression." Some aspects of giftedness may be very general, but giftedness may be found in special talents, such as intellectual ability, creative thinking, leadership, visual/performing arts, or specific academic ability.

Walker, Hafenstein, Crow-Enslow (1999) and Renzulli (2002) explain that the concept of giftedness is moving beyond the traditional emphasis on general advanced academic achievement. Research with preschoolers documents giftedness in specific areas, such as science, art, and music. Gifted children show advanced knowledge and skills in one or more areas to the extent they need some differentiated educational programming. Walker et al. describe the characteristics in the cognitive, affective, and physical development areas that may indicate an intellectually gifted child (p. 33):

**originality**

A behavior that reflects a new idea or a new combination of ideas and that has a low probability of happening.

**appropriate and relevant**

A behavior relevant to a goal the child has.

**fluency**

Ideas that are easily developed from previous knowledge.

**flexibility**

Seeing a new use for an idea or material that no one else figures out.

- *Cognitive characteristics:* high level of language development, accelerated pace of thought, ability to generate original ideas and solutions, sensitivity to learning, and the ability to synthesize and think abstractly. They may have exceptional attention spans for topics or activities that particularly interest them.
- *Affective characteristics:* tend to want to organize people, may invent complex games to organize their playmates, are emotionally sensitive, are very aware of their environment, may be social isolates if they do not have opportunities to socialize with intellectual equals.
- *Physical development:* fine motor skills may lag behind intellectual development so they may not be able to draw or construct what they have in mind.

According to Karnes and Schwedel (1983), young gifted children may also be exceptionally curious, ask more questions than other children, be excellent problem solvers, and exhibit more resourcefulness.

It is important to keep in mind that gifted children are gifted all day (Rotigel, 2003). They need to have appropriate experiences at school and at home all day. Intellectually gifted children sometimes hide their gifts so they can fit in with their peer group since their social and emotional development may be at a level typical for their age, while intellectually they are ahead. They may need peer groups at different levels to meet their intellectual, emotional, and social needs.

Defining and measuring giftedness is a controversial problem (Hoge, 1988). Selecting the best measure for deciding who is "gifted" and who is "not gifted" presents many difficulties. There are problems in defining giftedness and problems in finding valid and reliable means for identifying the gifted child. While definitions of giftedness may include constructs such as motivation and creativity, actual selection usually rests on an IQ test score. Such means of selection ignores other qualities that may be equally indicative of giftedness and ignores the weaknesses of IQ tests. Jackson and Sacks (1994) point out that in 25 of our largest cities, the majority populations are culturally diverse and, in a large percentage, non-English-speaking. The procedures for identifying gifted students have not kept up with these changing populations. According to Jackson and Sacks (p. 8), the identification of gifted African American and Latino children has been held back for several reasons: "(1) preponderantly narrow definitions of giftedness; (2) a heavy reliance on IQ test scores or achievement test scores; and (3) many school personnel's low expectations of these students in predominantly European American school districts." A survey of 12 predominantly nonwhite school districts revealed that minority students were underrepresented in gifted programs. Jackson and Sacks recommend that before minority low-SES children are tested, they receive an infusion of intellectual stimulation designed to develop their thinking skills and better prepare them to demonstrate what they can really accomplish.

A paper (*Talent & Diversity*, 1998) published by the Office of Educational Research and Improvement of the U.S. Department of Education discusses the underrepresentation of limited-English-proficient (LEP) speakers in gifted education programs. However, this paper indicates that there is increasing acceptance of Gardner and Sternberg's theories of intelligence and movement away from the IQ score as the major means of identifying gifted and talented children. Meanwhile, LEP students are affected most severely by the application of conventional identification procedures. The following are barriers for LEP students (p. 14):

- teachers' inability to recognize indicators of potential giftedness
- teachers' prejudicial attitudes (i.e., taking it for granted that LEP students, especially if they are low-SES, do not have the benefit of educational activities at home)

An expanded view of intelligence and ability related to cultural norms, along with new methods of assessment, are needed to include LEP students in gifted education programs.

## Creativity, Intelligence, and Giftedness

The definitions of creativity and giftedness overlap. However, the two do not necessarily go hand in hand. That is, a person may be highly intelligent but not very creative, or highly creative but not of outstanding intelligence. Children may also be low in both creativity and intelligence. They can be gifted in one area but not in others.

Creativity and intelligence, then, do not necessarily go hand in hand. Each child must be looked at individually and helped to develop creatively in his or her own way in whatever areas he or she finds interesting.

## Creativity, Curiosity, and Problem Solving

Problem-solving skills and curiosity behavior are important elements in the definition of creativity. Torrance (1983) identified several types of creative thinking skills that he believes all children develop to some degree by the time they enter school. Creative thinking skills help children develop new combinations and relationships in organizing symbols, objects, numerals, people, places, and words. Natural curiosity extends children's knowledge as they develop more mature question-asking skills. These thinking skills support the young child's curiosity and problem-solving activities. If placed in an environment with peers who are explorers, children's exploratory behavior is increased (Moore, 1985). The presence of a supportive adult also helps bring out the natural inquisitiveness of young children (Schmidt, 1985).

Early childhood classrooms can provide impetus to exploration by offering a rich array of interesting materials for both spontaneous and planned activities. Changing the environment often excites children's curiosity and entices them to explore and find out what's new. Science investigations lend themselves to exploration of questions such as the following:

- How long does it take a bean plant to sprout from a seed?
- Which kinds of objects are attracted by a magnet?
- Where does steam come from?

Adults must be sensitive about when to intrude with a question and when to leave children alone to work on their own projects and problems (Clark, 1985).

Consider the following incident, applying what you have just read about creativity, curiosity, and problem solving.

> Janice, age five, takes a child-size chair into the bathroom. She then puts a towel on the closed toilet lid. She places a toy cup and other accessories on this towel. She then puts water in the cup and pretends to drink. When asked what she is doing, she explains that she is drinking coffee. She assigns her younger sister, Kayla, to the role of servant. She also holds a conversation with an imaginary guest.

## Artistic Development

According to R. Craig Sautter (1994), integrating the arts into the school curriculum can encourage positive changes in the curriculum. Whereas the arts are conventionally an integral part of prekindergarten and kindergarten programs, school becomes more textbook driven and drill and practice oriented from the primary grades on. Opportunities to create through writing, music, art, drama, and dance can greatly enhance student motivation and provide an outlet for the creativity evident in all young children (Davis, 1993; Gardner, 1993).

The visual arts can be easily integrated into other content areas (Colbert, 1997; Mayesky, 2006; Schirrmacher, 2006; & Thompson, 2005). In programs for young children in Reggio Emilia, Italy, a teacher trained in the visual arts works closely with the teachers and children in the preprimary schools (Althouse, Johnson, & Mitchell, 2003; Hendrick, 1997). In the Reggio schools, "... children's use of media is not a separate part of the curriculum but an inseparable, integral part of the whole cognitive/symbolic expression involved in the process of learning" (Hendrick, p. 21). If young children are given daily opportunities for creativity during the elementary grades, creativity might not disappear until it appears again in adult artists.

"The drawings, paintings, and sculptures children produce offer tangible evidence of their thoughtful planning, their perceptual and conceptual development, their individuality, and their interests" (p. 202). That is, they offer a view into the minds of children. Artistic behavior is always intriguing to adults because the child's products give us something tangible that reflects planning, perceptual and conceptual development, and communication skills (Taunton & Colbert, 1984; Thompson, 2005). Drawings have been studied a great deal. As already described in Chapter 8, the first stage in drawing consists of scribbles. At this stage, the child explores the implements and enjoys the kinesthetic experience as much as the tangible results of the activity. Between the ages of three and five, representational drawings usually appear. The first ones are usually human figures with just a head and leglike appendages (Figure 23–6a). Young children seem to focus at first from the top down in reconstructing their mental image of human figures. Figure 23–6b

**FIGURE 23–6a** Kindergartners' drawings of their fathers: from early representational to more mature representational.

**FIGURE 23–6b** First graders' drawings of their fathers: from early representational to more detailed, proportional versions.

compares human figures drawn by kindergarten and first-grade students. All are capable of drawing representationally, but the developmental differences are wide within each grade, and development overlaps between the children at the two grade levels. Overall, the first-graders' drawings are more mature. Pictures inspire descriptive verbalizations and, as mentioned in Chapter 22, drawing also develops written language (Figure 23–7).

**FIGURE 23–7** In a burst of creative energy, Summer drew three figures on notepads.

## SUMMARY

Six views of intelligence were described in this chapter. These views are psychometric, information-processing, cognitive developmental, the theory of successful intelligence, multiple intelligences, and ethological. The first three view intelligence as reflected in responses to standard questions. The theory of multiple intelligences and the ethological view look at intelligence as reflected in everyday life activities. The theory of successful intelligence views intelligence as the response to everyday living, but attempts to measure it in standardized situations. Many critics believe that the psychometric approach (i.e., use of the IQ test) is an unfair assessment of intellectual capacity. IQ tests are believed to be especially unfair to the minority child because of cultural biases and different language experiences. Test scores should be used with caution and combined with other measures and observational materials when a child or program is being evaluated.

Creative behavior is usually defined in terms of originality, high levels of curiosity, and frequent problem seeking. Giftedness refers to the potential for showing an exceptional level of performance in one or more areas of expression. Creativity may accompany high intelligence, but this is not always the case. Children of lower intelligence may be creative, and children of high intelligence are not necessarily creative. The gifted individual may be advanced intellectually or creatively or both.

## FOR FURTHER READING


Bartholemew, D. J. (2004). *Measuring intelligence: Facts and fallacies.* New York: Cambridge University Press.

Dreary, I. J. (2000). *Looking down on human intelligence: From psychometrics to the brain.* New York: Oxford University Press.

Fish, J. M. (Ed.). (2002). *Race and intelligence: Separating science from myth.* Mahwah, NJ: Erlbaum.

Ford, D. Y., & Harris, J. J., III. (1999). *Multicultural gifted education.* New York: Teachers College Press.

Gardner, H. (1982). *Art, mind and brain.* New York: Basic Books.

Gardner, H. (1983). *Frames of mind: Theory of multiple intelligences.* New York: Basic Books.

Gross, M. U. M. (2003). *Exceptionally gifted children.* New York: RoutledgeFalmer.

Heilman, K. M. (2005). *Creativity and the brain.* New York: Psychology Press.

Kincheloe, J. L. (2004). *Multiple intelligences reconsidered.* New York: Peter Lang.

Kogan, E. (2001). *Gifted bilingual students: A paradox?* New York: Peter Lang.

Meadows, S. (2005). *The child as thinker* (2nd ed.). New York: Psychology Press.

Millar G. E. (1995). *Paul Torrance: "The creativity man": An authorized biography.* Narwood, NJ: Ablex.

Raina, M. K. (1998). *The creativity passion: E. Paul Torrance's voyages of discovering creativity.* Greenwich, CT: Ablex/JAI.

Runco, M. A. (2004). *Creativity. Theories and themes: Research, development and practice.* St. Louis, MO: Elsevier.

Smith, N., and the Drawing Study Group. (1998). *Observation drawing with children.* New York: Teachers College Press.

Smutny, J. F. (Ed.). (1998). *The young gifted child.* Cresskill, NJ: Hampton Press.

Sternberg, R. J. (Ed.). (2004). *International handbook of intelligence.* New York: Cambridge University Press.

Sternberg, R. J., & Davidson, J. E. (2005). (Eds.). *Conceptions of giftedness* (2nd ed.). New York: Cambridge University Press.

Sternberg, R. J., & Cianciolo, A. T. (2004). *Intelligence: A brief history.* Malden, MA: Blackwell.

Sternberg, R. J., & Pretz, J. (Eds.). (2004). *Cognition and intelligence.* New York: Cambridge University Press.

Sternberg, R. J., & Grigorenko, E. L. (Eds.). (2002). *The general factor of intelligence: How general is it?* Mahwah, NJ: Erlbaum.

Sternberg, R. J., & Kaufman, J. C. (Eds.). (2002). *The evolution of intelligence.* Mahwah, NJ: Erlbaum.

Sternberg, R. J., & Zhang, L. (Eds.). (2000). *Perspectives on thinking, learning, and cognitive styles.* Mahwah, NJ: Erlbaum.

Taylor, L. M. (2005). *Introducing cognitive development.* New York: Psychology Press.

Valdes, G. (Ed.). (2002). *Expanding definitions of giftedness: The case of young interpreters of immigrant background.* Mahwah, NJ: Erlbaum.

Wilhelm, O., & Engle, R. W. (Eds.). *Handbook of understanding and measuring intelligence.* Thousand Oaks, CA: Sage.

Willats, J. (2005). *Making sense of children's drawings.* Mahwah, NJ: Erlbaum.

Winnicott, D. W. (2005). *Playing and reality.* New York: Psychology Press.

## SUGGESTED ACTIVITIES

1. With a small group in class, discuss the statement "Intelligence testing of young children does more harm than good." Report your decision to the rest of the class.
2. In the library, find an article on intelligence testing. Write a report using the following format:
   a. Bibliographic information: author(s), title, name of periodical (or book), volume number, publisher, date published, and page numbers
   b. A short summary of the article: the main point the author(s) is (are) trying to make and the support presented for the point of view
   c. A reaction that tells your opinion of the material presented in the article: Does the material have any practical applications? What are they? Do you agree with the ideas presented? Why or why not?
3. Discuss with a small group in class: Which would be best, to be highly intelligent or highly creative? Why? Discuss the advantages and disadvantages of both. What is your personal preference? Are you now stronger on intelligence or creativity?
4. Visit an early childhood classroom. Record all the creative acts you observe during a 45-minute period. Group them according to the areas in which each creative act took place (e.g., Social Studies, Science, Mathematics, Writing, Art, Blocks, Dramatic Play). Discuss activities that you could develop that would promote creativity.
5. Make an entry in your journal.

## REVIEW

1. Match the view of intelligence in Column I with the correct definition in Column II.

| Column I | Column II |
|---|---|
| a. psychometric view | 1. Intelligence is reflected in adaptations to new situations. |
| b. cognitive developmental view | 2. Adaptations occur through problem solving. |
| c. ethological view | 3. The behavior of intelligent people. |
| d. information-processing view | 4. Intelligence is made up of seven types of different intelligences. |
| e. theory of successful intelligence | 5. Intelligence is derived from the ways people represent and process information. |
| f. multiple intelligences | 6. Intelligence includes analytic, practical, and creative applications to everyday problems. |

2. Decide for each of the following examples whether the assessment is psychometric (P), cognitive developmental (CD), ethological (E), information processing (IP), theory of successful intelligence (TSI), or multiple intelligence (MI).

a. **Adult:** Here are some cups and some saucers. Is there a saucer for each cup? (There are 10 cups and 9 saucers. They are lined up in two rows so the rows are of equal length).
**Rudy:** Yes.
**Adult:** How do you know?
**Rudy:** My mother told me.
**Adult:** (Concludes that three-year-old Rudy is in the early part of the preoperational stage of intellectual development since he is fooled by appearance and cannot give a logical reason.)

b. **Adult:** (Speaking to child seated across the table from him) Point to your nose.
**Derrick:** (Points to his nose.)
**Adult:** (Marks *correct* on his scoring sheet.)

c. **Adult:** I have a bunch of blocks over here. I want you to count them for me.
**Hien Phung:** (He starts out by taking one block at a time.) One, two, three, four, five, six, seven, eight, nine, ten, twelve, fourteen, sixteen, seventeen, . . . that's as far as I can go.
**Adult:** (Notes that Hien Phung has the concept of one-to-one correspondence, proceeds in an orderly manner, and knows when he has reached his limit.)

d. **Adult:** Take these blocks and build a tower just like mine.
**Child:** (Builds structure but it does not match the adult's.)
**Adult:** (Marks *incorrect* on his scoring sheet.)

e. **Adult:** (Watches as Theresa struggles to reach a toy on a high shelf. After no success, Theresa gets a small chair, puts it by the shelf, and climbs up. She gets the toy.)
(Adult notes that Theresa has managed to cope with a problem situation and find a solution on her own.)

f. Mrs. Brown observes each of the children carefully as they go about their activities in her preschool classroom. She notes that each child has a unique pattern of intellectual strengths. She will use this information in planning her instructional program.

g. **Adult:** Sorry, Kate, you can't play with that glass bowl. You will have to find something else to do.
**Kate:** I just want to look at it. Could you hold it, and I could look?
**Adult:** Good idea, Kate. Here, I'll get it.
(Adult notes that Kate was able to arrive at a solution that was agreeable to the adult and to herself.)

**3.** List the criticisms of the use of IQ tests and IQ scores.

**4.** Write the number of each statement that is consistent with suggestions for non-discriminatory testing developed by the Council for Exceptional Children.
a. Every assessment instrument used must be adapted to each child's socioeconomic, cultural, and language background.
b. A single IQ score can be used for decision making as long as the test is administered by a qualified examiner.
c. Assessment should be broad and look at each area of child development.
d. Communication with parents and child could be carried out in the family's language.
e. It is not necessary for those who set up assessment programs to be familiar with local culture and customs.

**5.** Discuss the relationship among intelligence, creativity, and the gifted person.

**6.** Discuss the four criteria of behavior that is considered creative, according to Isenberg & Jalongo (2001, 3rd ed.).

## KEY TERMS LIST

appropriate and relevant
cognitive developmental approach
creativity
ethological approach
flexibility
fluency
gifted person
information-processing approach
intelligence
originality
psychometric approach
theory of multiple intelligences
theory of successful intelligence
triarchic instruction

Additional resources for this chapter can be found on the Online Companion™ to accompany this text at http://www.earlychilded.delmar.com. Respond to "Time to Reflect" and "Looking Further" concepts, review various child development scenarios, and answer thought-provoking questions in the Critical Thinking Forum. Keep a daily journal by downloading the student journal available on this Web site. Complete the interactive matching exercises to reinforce concepts, and printout the child development assessment forms to use during your observation of development for children from birth to age eight. In addition, read the case studies on the Web site to reinforce the important concepts in each chapter, and take a look at the multitude of Web links that are available for student research on the Internet.

CHAPTER

# 24

# The Adult Role and Cognitive Development

## OBJECTIVES

After reading this chapter, you should be able to:

- Explain how concepts are developed along with language.
- Explain the important factors in the adult's role in the child's oral language development.
- Understand the opposing views regarding which instructional strategies are best for developing Standard English (SE) proficiency in English Language Learners (ELL) and speakers of Ebonics or African American English.
- Discuss the adult role in the literacy development of young children.
- Evaluate whether adults are promoting or discouraging young children's literacy development.
- Describe how the adult who works with young children can have a long-term effect on their school success.
- Evaluate the creative aspect of adult-child interaction.

In this section we have looked at the factors in young children's development in the cognitive areas of concept development, oral and written language, and intelligence and creativity. In this chapter, the focus is the adult's role in these areas. Adults influence children's cognitive development in many ways, such as in the examples below.

**Preschooler.** Kofi, age four, is playing in the sand. He is crouching down. At first, he picks up some sand in one hand and lets it spill from between his fingers. Then, using his finger, he demonstrates how he can write letters he learned in preschool. He looks over and sees a stick that has fallen from a tree. He rushes over to get it, then takes the stick back to the sand, and writes letters with it. Then, he writes his name in the sand with the stick. He explains that the stick is his imaginary pencil.

**Kindergartner.** Marta is a student in Mrs. Wood's kindergarten class. Marta and the rest of the children were instructed to draw a picture of a dog and write one or two words about what they would do if they had a dog. All the students had their own ideas regarding what they would do with their dog. Mrs. Wood went around the classroom asking some of the students about their ideas and wrote some of them on the chalkboard. Marta wanted to walk her dog. She drew a picture of the dog being walked and wrote out the word *walk*.

These two young children demonstrate their knowledge of print and writing words. Kofi learned about writing his name in his preschool class. Kofi also demonstrates his imagination. Marta demonstrates her concept of dog as she does an assignment in kindergarten that relates to drawing and writing.

In Chapter 20 we examined the cognitive system and concept development. Support for cognitive development was described as coming from the theories of Piaget and Vygotsky. Adults are responsible for scaffolding the child's movement through the zone of proximal development (ZPD) while providing an environment for exploration that supports the child's construction of knowledge. In this chapter, school and home adult support for cognitive development through language, literacy, and creative expression is described.

## THE ADULT ROLE IN ORAL LANGUAGE DEVELOPMENT

Adults need to support children whose first language is English and those for whom English is a second language. This is one of the foremost adult responsibilities today.

### Supporting Second Language Learners

FIGURE 24–1 Reading to children provides experience connecting oral language with print.

Soto (1991) describes successful approaches to bilingual instruction. The three most commonly used approaches are the transitional, the maintenance/developmental, and the two-way bilingual. Transitional approaches begin with instruction in the native language and move as quickly as possible into instruction in English. The maintenance/developmental approach builds language skills in the native language while simultaneously moving toward mastery of English. The two-way approach is designed for both language minority and language majority speakers, with the expectation that both groups will be academically successful and become bilingual. Overall, the research evaluating bilingual early childhood programs indicates that children from programs that develop proficiency in both languages hold the advantage in achievement in both languages and in the development of divergent thinking ability and cognitive flexibility (Figure 24–1).

Soto (1991, pp. 34–35) offers seven suggestions for teachers of young children:

1. Be aware of individual differences—do not push children too fast into becoming second-language proficient.
2. Be accepting of whatever the children say. Opportunities for trial and error are very important. Children should have time to converse in both languages. Adults should not dominate the conversation but should listen and support the efforts of the children. Children should be given plenty of opportunities for informal conversation during dramatic play, stories, cooking, and so on.

3. Use an additive approach. That is, add on new language skills while maintaining and enriching first-language skills.
4. Provide a stimulating, developmentally appropriate curriculum, not teacher-directed, scripted instruction.
5. Include experiences that would be culturally responsive to any child.
6. Informal observation should be used to obtain information needed for planning.
7. The classroom environment should be accepting and value culturally and linguistically diverse young children.

Soto (1992) and Genishi (2002) advocate supporting bilingual education in spite of the English-only proponents. Children are at a great advantage intellectually if their education is bilingual and if their primary language and culture are maintained at home, in the community, and in school.

Learning English becomes more complex in a multilingual setting, that is, where several native languages are spoken. In this case, teaching in the native languages and English is usually not possible. For example, Solorzano (1986) describes a school in Falls Church, Virginia, where 55 different languages are spoken. In this setting, bilingual education as described by Soto (1991) is impractical. In this type of situation, an **English as a Second Language (ESL)** or immersion program is the only possibility. These approaches can be successful if there is ample time for informal conversation in English, not just rote teacher-directed activities. Genishi, Dyson, and Fassler (1994) have observed that children in multilingual and bilingual classrooms develop communication proficiency rapidly in a climate where conversation with both peers and teacher is continuously encouraged.

**English as a Second Language (ESL)**

Specific techniques for teaching English to learners whose primary language is not English.

Zheng He, a native of the People's Republic of China, was interested in observing an ESL class attended by a kindergartner whose primary language was Chinese. He was concerned because her English was not improving very rapidly. The following excerpts are from his observations:

> Ten children are in the class. They come from 10 different countries. There is a teacher and an assistant. They use an immersion approach that incorporates small group and one-to-one activities for instruction. The small-group activities are teacher directed. The program uses a six-stage ESL program for children. The program has a Sesame Street theme.
>
> For the first part of the daily whole-class lesson, the teacher asks the children to close their books and prepares them for what they will see and hear on the page. Picture cards are presented to introduce new vocabulary.
>
> In the second part of the lesson, the children are asked to open the books and look at the assigned page. The teacher describes the pictures for the children. The teacher points out certain objects and characters and helps the children review vocabulary. Four steps are used in each lesson. The first is listen, look, and point. As the children listen to a tape or the teacher, they point to the appropriate pictures. The second step is to speak in a chorus, repeating a song, chant, conversation, poem, or story line by line after the teacher. In the third step, the children are grouped into pairs and practice the conversational exchanges they have just learned. For the fourth step, the pairs role-play the conversation.
>
> For the third phase of the daily lesson, children are provided opportunities to relate the new language to themselves and their daily lives through games, role-playing, and art projects. They also work on individual work sheets. In one-to-one activity, the teacher and the aide help each of the children read their books individually according to their reading levels. They correct pronunciation and

intonation and explain what the book is about. The children spend 50 minutes in the group activity and 30 minutes in the one-to-one and games, role-playing, and art projects. There is no time for play with concrete materials or for the informal spontaneous conversation that facilitates learning a second language as documented by Genishi et al. (1994).

In some cases, a teacher may have only one or two students who speak a language other than English at home. Just as in the bilingual and multilingual groups, the teacher needs to provide plenty of time for informal conversation and trial and error and encourage everyone to be a good listener. The author had the opportunity to observe a Vietnamese child, who had never spoken English, enter a regular kindergarten class in January and by May read to the rest of the class in English. The teacher and other students were welcoming and accepting, supported her efforts to learn English, and she was very successful.

Courtney Cazden (1990) provided the following description of what is done by teachers who are helpful to young second-language learners:

1. They engage the children in one-to-one conversation.
2. They adapt the conversation to the children's stages of English language development.
3. They include the children in structured activities with English-speaking peers:
   a. repetitive rhymes, songs, and fingerplays
   b. literacy activities, that is, picture-book reading
   c. manipulative activities (e.g., puzzles, construction toys, clay) with an adult who used the activity with consistent accompanying language
4. The teacher shows appreciation for the children's language-learning strategies. Second-language learners go through a distinct set of language acquisition stages:
   a. They try what they have and if it does not work, they drop it: a trial-and-error approach.
   b. When their first language does not work, they lie low and do some guessing.
   c. They begin to communicate using gestures and approximations.
   d. They learn useful things to say (important labels and phrases) and try to communicate with peers.
   e. If their efforts are accepted and get results, they keep on talking.

Keeping these developmental stages and techniques in mind, a teacher can feel at ease with second-language learners enrolled in the class.

As Tabors (1998) and Genishi (2002) point out, it is essential to work with parents. As already mentioned in earlier chapters, teachers need to learn about the linguistic and cultural backgrounds of families. Through a questionnaire or interview, teachers can find out about language and cultural practices, eating habits, child care arrangements, and parents' expectations. In turn, parents may be willing to share some of their customs and language in the classroom.

## Supporting Language Development

The basic role of the adult is to provide scaffolding for the young child's language development. Vygotsky suggested that young children need adult guidance to support them until they reach understanding. This guidance enables the young child to proceed through the stages of language development as easily and rapidly as his or her capacity allows. The adult serves as model, provider of language experiences, and interactor as the child participates in the give-and-take of conversation. According to Tough (1982b), the adult provides an environment that promotes thinking through the use of meaningful dialog between teacher and children. Through the use of divergent questions—questions that do not have one right answer—the adult encourages the child to construct concepts through his or her own language experiences. Adults need to let children know they are interested in what the children are thinking. Adult-child interaction has been the focus of extensive research. Researchers have examined the roles of adult and child from a number of different points of view and at a variety of ages and stages during infancy and early childhood.

These critical roles begin in infancy. The infant responds to speech from the first day of life (Condon, 1979), when he or she can be observed synchronizing body movements into rhythm with adult speech. Furthermore, infants whose mothers always respond to their early vocalizing have been found to be at an advantage in speech development at age two (Freedle & Lewis, 1977). From about age one to age four, adults use what is called **baby talk (BT)**. BT is a simplified form of speech with short, simple sentences and simple vocabulary that is within the child's realm of experience. It is often rather high pitched and consists of a lot of questions and commands. BT has been found to be used everywhere in a variety of cultures. It seems to serve several functions in language acquisition (Ferguson, 1977, pp. 209–235)

**baby talk (BT)**

A simplified form of speech with short, simple sentences and simple vocabulary that is within the child's realm of experience.

- BT enables good, clear communication and self-expression.
- It is suited to teaching language to a young child in the early stages of speech development.
- Children learn social values through the frequent use of words such as *pretty*, *good*, *bad*, and *dirty*.
- The child learns socially acceptable "cute" terms for referents that may be taboo, such as for some body parts.

Throughout the developmental period, the adult's listening behavior serves as reinforcement for the child's increased use of speech. Newport, Gleitman, and Gleitman (1977) found that even responses such as "mm-hmmm" seem to serve as powerful reinforcers of the child's speech. The "mm-hmmm" signals the child that what he or she has said is worth listening to and, thus, worth saying.

Children do not learn language in the same way in every community. Each community has its own expectations and customs. In her classic study Shirley Brice Heath (1983) studied language-development environments in two communities. Trackton was an all-black community of two-family rental homes whose residents considered themselves "respectable" and on the way up and transients who settled for a short time while waiting to go north or move into a public housing project. Most of the residents of Trackton worked at decent-paying but seasonal jobs. Although the outside of their homes looked run-down, inside they were comfortably and nicely furnished. Roadville was a neighborhood of small, individually owned homes inhabited by white mill workers. The homes were neat and well kept. Although their incomes were fairly good, having the right appliances and other material goods usually kept the families on a financial tightrope.

Roadville parents believed that it was important for the baby to have his or her own room. The first year was spent in a colorful environment with many toys and opportunities for language and literacy experiences. The infant heard nursery rhymes and played with many objects that provided experiences with color, shape, and texture. Conversations with infants were frequent. So-called BT was commonly used. Mothers were cautioned not to pick up their babies too soon or too much, and they learned to listen for sounds that told them the infant really needed something. Babies were given time alone to explore and play with sounds. Mothers listened closely for any sound that approximated the first word. Mothers were home alone a great deal of the time and spent a lot of time talking with their infants. As soon as word approximations were picked up by adults, the adults addressed verbal responses to the infant using these words. They also began to label items for the infant, such as "Milk, say milk." Toddlers developed their own vocabulary that was picked up by the adults. Infants were encouraged in their monologs and adults expanded and extended what they heard the children say. Adults picked up on nouns used by children and used each noun as the topic of a lengthy discourse. Adults viewed themselves as language teachers for their young children and used every opportunity to teach labels, ask questions, and expand on the child's vocalizations. From the age of two on, boys and girls were segregated in their play and provided with sex-stereotyped toys. Adults and older children played social games, such as pat-a-cake and peek-a-boo. Most adult-child play centered on a book or a toy. By age four, this play activity ended and most children went to nursery school for their educational activities. Moral education became dominant at home after four, and children learned that there is one right way for everything. Thinking about alternatives was discouraged.

In contrast to Roadville infants, Trackton infants were surrounded by adults and older children night and day. They were almost never left alone to coo and babble on their own. They were constantly held and were in the midst of conversation and other household noises except when everyone went to bed. They were in the midst of communication between and among others, but communication was rarely, if ever, directed at them. They were talked about but not talked to. Adults believed that infant vocalization was not meaningful and that it was not necessary to respond to it. Adults believed that a child would talk when ready; they could not teach children to talk. Even when infants began to make their wants and needs known with meaningful sounds, adults ignored them, believing that they could best determine the infant's needs.

Toddlers were watched while they explored. Adult vocalizations usually were warnings of danger ("dos" or "don'ts"). Toddler boys had special status and were included in adult conversations because conversational skill was considered of special value for males. Boys were teased and taunted by adults and between 16 and 24 months usually picked up a special phrase that they used to respond to their tormentors. For example, 16-month-old Teggie used "Go on, man" to mean "No," "Give it to me," and so on. Early on, Trackton children learned to judge from nonverbal behaviors just what role they should take with others. Posture and gesture were important means of communication because they told the child whether to tease, defy, boss, baby, or scold. In problem situations, they were often provided with a question, "What you gonna do if . . . ?" and forced to think of their own solution.

In Trackton, young children were not viewed as conversational partners. Children were not information givers; they were knowers. That is, they paid attention and learned. Toddler vocalization usually consisted of repetition of parts of the conversation going on around them. Eventually, these vocalizations developed into monologs parallel to the conversation they heard. Eventually, young children attempted to become conversationalists by breaking into the adults' conversation. Trackton parents did a lot of correcting and never used simplified speech or clarifications, such as talking slower. Girl talk followed the same stages as boy talk but at a later time for each stage. Boys started trying to enter conversations around 14 to 18 months, whereas girls began to participate around 22 months. Girls were not included in challenges

**fussing**

Female interchanges.

but were included in female interchanges called **fussing** and in playsong games with older children. Playsong games are spontaneous rhymes and chants. They are much like nursery rhymes and guessing games middle-class mainstream adults play with their infants and toddlers. Young children were not expected to ask questions. Adults asked them questions. The most common questions were analogies designed to see if the child could transfer information from one situation to another: "What's dat like?" Trackton children centered on the smallest details of what they experienced. For example, when sorting items, they tended to focus on some tiny detail like a slight blemish rather than on color, shape, or size. They could not answer questions regarding why they sorted as they did. Adults seldom asked them *why* questions. Most of the children's questions to adults had to do with context "Whose is this?" and "You buy dese?"

In both communities, children learned to talk, but in vastly different language environments. Trackton infants "come up," whereas Roadville infants are "brought up." Trackton infants are surrounded constantly by others and have no particular routines, whereas Roadville infants spend most of their time alone or with their mothers and follow a predictable daily routine. Roadville parents converse with their infants and toddlers and use direct instruction; Trackton parents talk about their children and expect them to learn on their own.

When enrolled in a preschool program, both groups presented language-related problems to their teachers. Both groups had dialects that did not fit the teachers' standards for speech. However, this did not bother the teachers as much as the ways children used language. Teachers could understand the words, but not the meanings. The Trackton children did not answer questions, and the Roadville children gave very minimal answers. On the children's part, both groups had some difficulty in understanding indirectly stated rules such as, "Is this where the scissors belong?" versus "The scissors belong in this basket." During group discussions, the Trackton children interrupted and chatted with their neighbors. Teachers recognized that they had to take on new role behaviors to successfully teach these children. For example, they learned to give directions in direct ways and to be very specific. They based questions on children's own experiences and things in their neighborhoods. As teachers changed, so did the children, and everyone felt more satisfied and involved in school.

Heath's research documents how important it is for effective teachers to understand the language environment of their students' community and to find methods to work with what the children bring to school. Home values and methods may not prepare children for mainstream, middle-class-oriented expectations. Heath documented this in another aspect of her research (Heath, 1982). Heath observed the classroom teachers at home interacting with their own children. She found that questions dominated their conversations with their preschool-age children. As parents, the teachers believed that this was the only way to ensure a response from the children, and they achieved success. It was not surprising that they proceeded with the same strategy in the classroom.

Snow, Dubber, and DeBlauw (1982) suggest this lack of school language preparation for nonmainstream children might stem from variations in parents' values regarding the kind of verbal facility that is important, lack of time and energy to work closely with the child during the early stages of language development, and/or use of different teaching styles. Research supports the conclusion that an interactive style is the best preparation for school. The role of the parent is to take turns interacting with the child in what Snow et al. refer to as **routines.** Snow et al. describe three types of routines: formal games played by mothers and infants, such as peek-a-boo; instructional games played by mothers and infants during the second year, such as pointing to body parts and asking "What's this?";

**routines**

Formal games, instructional games, and joint book-reading.

and joint book-reading during the third year accompanied by particular types of question-asking by the mother. Snow suggests that the greatest language value comes from these routines when they are played over and over to the point where the child takes over and controls the game.

Mothers who are unaware of how to enrich their children linguistically can be trained to use language-enrichment activities with their young children. For example in a study by McQueen and Washington (1988), a group of African American adolescent mothers were given extensive training, which included the following activities:

- The mothers enrolled in mathematics, English, child development, and parent education classes; they were taught methods of working with their children and served as teaching assistants in their child's classroom at the parent-child center (PCC).
- Mothers and children met at the PCC and worked together making toys, such as puzzles, felt boards, and musical instruments. Verbal mother-child conversation was stimulated during these sessions.
- At the PCC, mothers read stories to their children and learned to follow up by asking questions and listening to the answers, discussing the story with the children, and having the children retell the stories to their classmates.

This intensive parent education program had significant positive effects on the children's performance on language tests as compared with children whose mothers had less extensive or no training in how to support children's language development. All these strategies encourage the child to become a conversationalist and engage in the give and take of dialog.

Genishi and Dyson (1984) describe the kinds of teacher talk that foster oral language development for preschoolers, kindergartners, and primary-age children. For example, the teacher can step into preschoolers' dramatic play and ask a question that will make the children think of ways to expand and extend their activity:

- Tell me about . . .
- What's going on here?
- Maybe you need . . .
- That's a good idea.
- Call me when you are finished so I can see . . .
- What does a . . . do?
- How can you fix the . . . ?

Teachers can also answer informational questions posed by children.

Kindergartners can apply language even further. Kindergartners also enjoy spontaneous conversation (Genishi & Dyson, 1984). Adults need to offer opportunities one to one, in small groups, and in large groups to fit each child's preferred setting for talk. Even in more formal, teacher-directed discussions, an informal, conversational tone should be used that allows for each child's contribution. As with preschoolers, adults can insert questions and comments into dramatic play activities. Science and mathematics provide opportunities for children to observe and to describe, analyze, and predict—all activities that enhance language development.

By the primary grades, children can become very skillful in communicating orally (Genishi, Dyson, & Fassler, 1994; Genishi & Dyson, 1984). Teachers only need to create situations that promote talking. At this age, children can communicate well with each other and can be paired into teams with one child helping another. They can also work in small groups if given a clearly focused task. Large group discussions demand skillful teaching. Teachers need to ask open-ended questions: "Why?" "How do you know?" "Tell us what you mean" questions.

Parents naturally compare their child's language development with that of other children. If they feel concerned, they should seek the advice of a speech-language pathologist certified by the American Speech-Language-Hearing Association. A professional assessment can determine whether or not a child may need some special help. Just how long to wait before getting professional help is difficult to decide. However, early diagnosis for language problems increases the chances for improvement and prevention of later problems with behavior, learning, reading, and social interaction (ASHA, 2002, p. 9).

Looking back, describe what you believe are the important factors in the adult role in child language development. Provide reasons for your choices.

## THE ADULT'S ROLE IN EXPANDING THE CHILD'S USE OF ORAL LANGUAGE

As already described in Chapter 21, adults can foster young children's language development in many ways (Figure 24–2). Conversation takes on a powerful role in the support of children's language learning (Koralek, 2002). In the introduction to a special focus section on supporting language learning, Koralek (2002) reminds the reader that the articles authors' focus on "the pure joy of language . . . demonstrates how language is linked to healthy social and emotional development, reading and writing abilities, creativity, and learning content areas such as science and social studies" (p. 8). When conversing with a child, adults can inform, explain, talk about feelings, project into the unknown, talk about the future, and pretend or imagine. Adults can begin in infancy with a conversational give-and-take that should continue all through early childhood. They also provide peers with whom the young child can practice and expand oral language skills. Finally, adults provide many social and informational experiences that give children something to talk about in situations, such as sociodramatic play, dialog with adults or other children, and school discussion settings, such as show-and-tell. Young children must learn to use language for a variety of purposes. Adults can help children become reflective and carry on an inner dialog. They can help children think aloud and extend their imaginative play through language. Adults can offer opportunities for children to report, to go beyond the observable, immediate situation by use of imagination, and to reason and solve problems. Adults assess where the child is in the development of language use, that is, ZPD, and provide the experiences that serve as the scaffolding to enable the child to move to the limits of the current ZPD.

FIGURE 24–2 Adult scaffolding supports children's language use.

Suppose you are a kindergarten teacher. Several parents are critical of you because you provide time for children to engage in social activity, such as dramatic play and conversation, while they work in a variety of centers. The parents believe that dramatic play is a waste of time for kindergartners. They also believe that a quiet classroom is one where the students are engaged in "real" learning. The parents want more time spent on "academics." Develop an argument to support the cognitive and social values of dramatic play and conversation.

Bodrova and Leong (1996, pp. 105–107) suggest several ways that adults can use language in the classroom from the Vygotskian approach. They suggest the following methods:

1. *Make your actions and the children's actions verbally explicit.* Label your actions and the children's actions. For example, "Hand me the small red block" or "When you pay attention, your legs are like a pretzel and your eyes are looking at the book."
2. *Model your thinking and the strategies you are using aloud.* For example, "What is in this bag?" Children do not respond. "I wonder how I can figure this out. I know, I can feel through the bag, maybe that will give me a clue."
3. *When introducing a new concept, be sure to tie it to actions.* You are introducing a thermometer. You have a large cardboard model. "This measures the temperature; when the red goes higher, it is warmer; when it goes down, it is colder."
4. *Use thinking while talking to check children's understanding of concepts and strategies.* Encourage children to think out loud directly to you and to their peers.
5. *Use different contexts and different tasks as you check whether or not children understand a concept or strategy.* They may only be able to accomplish the task in one context. For example, have them count many different objects and people to arrive at different objectives.
6. *Encourage the use of private speech* (as described earlier).
7. *Use mediators to facilitate private speech.* For example, tell the children that to put something in their "memory bank," they need to repeat it out loud at least three times.
8. *Encourage "thinking while talking."* Talking through problem solutions can help children identify mistakes.

The following strategies, which are discussed in Chapter 22, connect oral language with written language.

9. *Encourage children to communicate through writing, even if it is scribbling.* The child can read you what they wrote, and you can write down what they say.
10. *Encourage the use of written speech in a variety of contexts.* Use writing in all content areas, not just for journals or a writers' workshop.
11. *Revisit the children's writing and reprocess their ideas.* Revisit the children's writings, even if they are pictures with scribbles and dictated translations. Encourage them to expand and revise.
12. *Incorporate writing into play.* Place writing tools and materials in the dramatic play area.

Jeffrey Trawick-Smith (1994) describes the importance of having authentic dialog with children, that is, a dialog in which "children and adults talk to each other about interesting, relevant matters" (p. 10). Trawick-Smith believes that these conversations provide natural opportunities for adults to model language that is slightly beyond the children's current ability. Trawick-Smith describes some critical features of "teacher talk." Responding is critical as long as it is geared to the meaning of the children's talk and not to the form (i.e., correcting grammar). The adult should expand on the topic of the children's remarks, not correct them or change them. Verbal elaboration that is carefully done can also be valuable. Adults can make comments or ask questions regarding the children's activities that invite responses, not make statements or ask questions designed to control the activity. Questions also facilitate language development if they are open-ended versus closed, one-answer questions. It is important to allow time for children to think through their answers. **Adult-to-child language (ACL)** is a special form of speech that adults use when speaking with children. It tends to be slower and more deliberate and contain shorter sentences than adult-to-adult language. It should be just beyond the children's current complexity level in their own use of language.

**adult-to-child language (ACL)**

A special form of speech that adults use when speaking with children; tends to be slower and more deliberate and tends to contain shorter sentences than adult-to-adult language.

Another critical factor under the control of adults is the way the classroom is set up, such as the room arrangement and the materials and activities available. Pellegrini (1984) observed the language behavior of two-, three-, and four-year-olds as they involved themselves in various activity centers provided in their preschool classrooms. He categorized the children's talk using Halliday's categories. Housekeeping centers and blocks elicited a large amount of imaginative language. A great deal of social interactional and multifunctional language was used in the housekeeping center, which supported group sociodramatic imaginary themes. In contrast, the activity is individual and conversation is not needed to sustain play in art and water play centers. Isbell and Raines (1991) also found that the type of center in which a dialog took place affected language production.

Pellegrini also looked at the effect of adult presence in the centers. Although the presence of adults increased younger children's talk, it decreased the older children's talk. It may be that the older children had reached a level where they could sustain their own play and no longer needed adult support. For the two- and three-year-olds, adult presence was necessary. The results of this study suggest that dramatic play centers are essential for providing opportunities to use language fully. It also suggests that teachers should be cautious about involvement in older children's sociodramatic play. If the play is proceeding well and the children are using imaginative and multifunctional language, the adult should stay out.

Pellegrini's classroom conclusions are supported by research focusing on parent scaffolding. Behrend, Rosengran, and Perlmutter (1989) found that parental interactive style had a strong effect on children during a researcher-designed play session. Although stronger parental control seemed to be helpful to the three-year-olds, it lowered the level of performance of five-year-olds.

Adults also take the role of assessor of language use. Through observation, adults can obtain samples of child language and find out if children are using language for a variety of functions. Genishi and Dyson (1984) suggest several ways adults can record and assess young children's language development: handwritten notes, tape recordings, observation forms and checklists, and specific language interview tasks. Lane and Bergan (1988) looked at the effects of instructional variables on the language ability of preschoolers enrolled in Head Start. They found that the students who received more direct language instruction and whose teachers did the best job of assessing what they needed when they planned instruction evidenced the highest levels of language competence.

It is clear that adults can enhance the oral language competence of young children through making an assessment of the child's strengths and weaknesses and planning for a variety of oral language experiences with adults and peers.

Develop your own explanation for the importance of supporting child talk and provide suggestions for how adults can support children's use of language. Imagine you are speaking with parents and/or with other teachers.

## CULTURAL DIVERSITY AND LANGUAGE USE

Some options for adult promotion of oral language use with young children from diverse cultures and with diverse language backgrounds were described in Chapter 21 and earlier in this chapter. Providing a variety of opportunities for oral language use for all children is of critical importance. However, there are disagreements regarding how oral-language use should be developed. The major problems are pointed out in the following section.

### How Should We Teach English Language Learners?

The 2001 Federal Interagency Forum on Child and Family Statistics (FCFS) indicators of the well-being of America's children support the need to focus on children whose primary language is not English. The percentage of children who are European American has decreased from 74 percent in 1980 to 64 percent in 2000. The number of Latino children has increased rapidly, from 9 percent in 1980 to 16 percent of the child population in 2000. It is projected that, by 2020, more than one in five children in the United States will be of Latino origin. By 2020, it is expected that 6 percent of U.S. children will be of Asian/Pacific Islander origin. The percentage of African American, European American, and Native American/Alaska Native children has been stable at about 18 percent. In 1999, the number of school-age children (ages five through seventeen) whose primary home language was other than English was 2.6 million, double what it was in 1979. The largest percentage of these children are in the West. In 1999, 23 percent of children of Latino origin and 12 percent of children of Asian or other origin had difficulty speaking English. Federal law requires that children with limited English ability must be evaluated and provided with appropriate services. The problem is deciding what type of instruction is most effective.

According to Giacchino-Baker (1995), while second-language learning takes place in stages similar to first-language learning, the actual proficiency is divided into the following two types:

1. Basic Interpersonal Communication Skills **(BICS)**: the language used in everyday social activity
2. Cognitive Academic Language Proficiency **(CALP)**: the language of academics

**Basic Interpersonal Communication Skills (BICS)**

Language use to accomplish basic interpersonal communication skills; the language used in everyday social activity.

**Cognitive Academic Language Proficiency (CALP)**

The language of academics.

It is estimated that BICS proficiency can be achieved in two years, whereas CALP proficiency takes about seven years. Those in favor of a bilingual approach to education base their views on the BICS/CALP model. That is, if children can learn the academics first in their primary language, they can transfer to English later. However, there is disagreement regarding the efficacy of bilingual education versus the English immersion approach for ELL students. (See for example, Baker, 1998, and Krashen, 1996, for the arguments for each instructional approach.)

As mentioned previously a bilingual (BL) approach will work well in a setting with a large number of minority language (ML)-speaking students and a teacher who speaks their primary language. On the other hand, Necochea and Cline (1993) point out the dangers of taking BL as the only approach to promoting oral language use. First, there are not enough bilingual teachers to meet the needs of all ML students. Second, in most classrooms, these students are the minority and many speak low-incidence languages, such as Hmong, Vietnamese, and Laotian. Necochea and Cline believe that many English-speaking teachers feel helpless in the shadow of the bilingual philosophy and believe that they cannot be effective. On the other hand, Necochea and Cline describe creative and effective practices that teachers have developed for working with ML students. The best of these practices emphasizes integration and inclusion "for ML students plus the modification of the delivery of instruction to provide comprehensive input, thus allowing students to participate in the core instructional mainstream program" (p. 407). The kindergarten described by Fassler earlier in the chapter provides an example of children in a multicultural classroom helping each other use English. Mari Riojas-Cortez (2001) describes the prekindergarten classroom of Alma Perez, who uses a constructivist approach with her Mexican American bilingual students. Alma examines their strengths and weaknesses and teaches to their needs. She communicates in the children's language of choice so they can have rich conversations in her classroom and increase vocabulary. The play-centered curriculum provides scaffolding for language development. Children learn English not through drill and practice, but through dramatic play, music, finger plays, and conversation.

## How Should We Teach Standard English to Culturally Diverse Students Who Speak Ebonics as a First Language?

In Chapter 21, the origins of Ebonics were explained. Many African American children grow up learning to speak Ebonics. They may even translate Standard English (SE) into Ebonics when reading aloud. Delpit (1998) points out that we should not confuse learning a new language form with reading comprehension. When Ebonics speakers are constantly corrected, they learn to dislike reading and speaking. On the other hand, editing is a requirement for good writing; hence, it makes more sense to edit written products. Children can be taught the relationship between Ebonic and SE grammar and spelling in a nondegrading manner that objectively points out the similarities and differences between the two. In Oakland, California, the Standard English Proficiency (SEP) program was developed (What . . . , 1998). This program respects Ebonics. Carrie Secret, an Oakland fifth-grade teacher, explains that she emphasizes reading to her students and has them read both informational and fiction books of their own choosing.

Blake (1994) documented the language use of three young African American children and their mothers. Blake found that African American mothers and children use language differently than European American mothers and children. African Americans emphasize the emotional functions of language. Language use focuses on likes, dislikes, and feelings. Therefore, these children enter school with a cultural emphasis on the socioemotional use of language. Most American teachers may not recognize this difference in communicative style and, rather than building on it, may downplay it.

Evidence supports the conclusion that African American children can benefit from a standard English-rich language environment. For example, Benedict (1994) found that low-SES African American kindergartners were as advanced in oral language use as middle-SES European American kindergartners when both groups were enrolled in a whole-language kindergarten, and also more advanced than comparable African American children enrolled in a basal-based kindergarten. As pointed out by Mariska Malone (Chapter 21), children who grow up with African American dialect need to master SE.

## HOW YOUNG CHILDREN LEARN ABOUT WRITTEN LANGUAGE

Young children do not learn about print just because it is available. Reading and writing are learned because they can be used to achieve goals. What happens in the context of social learning that promotes literacy development? Print is used as a contact between family members and friends:

- Lists of friends are made.
- Notes and letters are written to friends and family members.
- Signs are made for a lemonade stand.

### Reading and Writing at Home

Heath (1980, 1983) studied a group of professional-class families. They used reading in the ways already mentioned, plus in a critical/educational way. They read to increase knowledge. When they read, they expanded the story-reading activity by relating the story to past activities. The adults also made many comments about the stories and encouraged the children, when old enough, to do the same. Other researchers have found that parents encourage literacy by encouraging children in written language activities and developing in them an interest in books and written language in general. Young children learn about print through supportive literacy experiences with family and friends (McGee et al., 1986). Look back at the letters in Figure 22–5. These letters were sent and delivered through a classroom mail system by children the summer before entering kindergarten. The children were very inspired to write through this exchange of letters. They were thrilled when they received a letter, and they were just as excited when the recipient received theirs. The writing achieved the goal of making a social contact with a friend.

Children have developed strategies to learn about writing while they are writing. Children usually talk before, during, and after writing. They may use talk to get information they need for their writing, to comment while they are writing, or to read what they have written. Children seem to enhance their writing by talking with each other and reading their writing to each other. They also apply what they have learned in other language situations, both oral and written, to their writing. Most important, for young children to write, they have to be willing to take risks and experiment. After all, most adults do not look upon writing as a task for preschoolers and kindergartners and do not encourage this experimentation. Note that early readers and writers always have an older person in the home who encourages their early literacy efforts. If adults can be accepting of invented spellings and nonconventional sentences, as they are with oral language, children will learn on their own how to manage written language (McGee, Richgels, & Charlesworth, 1986; Bissex, 1985).

Researchers have attempted to find out the characteristics of adult-child interactions that seem critical to the encouragement of literacy development. A review of this research indicates that the following factors are supportive (McGee et al., 1986):

- Warm-up questions asked before a book is read
- Verbal interactions during story reading that relate the content of the story to the child's past experiences
- Positive reinforcement of the child's responses
- Asking evaluative questions after the book is read
- Beginning dialog during book reading in infancy before the child is even capable of responding, treating infants' prelinguistic responses as if they were conventional responses, and then rewarding approximations and finally conventional words used for labels
- In dialog with infants, mothers labeling important parts of the illustrations
- Encouraging infants to model their responses from what the adult does

These type of interactions seem to offer a strong basis for success in school literacy activities. The behaviors listed are more likely to be observed with professional and upper-middle-class parent-child pairs than with working-class or lower-class pairs. Lower-class mothers use less talk and a more limited vocabulary than do middle-class mothers during story reading. Both story-reading and writing sessions seem to be of the most value to children if there is reciprocal interaction and reinforcement of the child's use of both oral and written language and encouragement of the child's experimentation, rather than directions and criticism from the adult.

As mentioned numerous times in this chapter, question asking is a critical factor in the development of literacy. Questions from readers to nonreaders are important. Equally important are the questions of children directed toward readers. Children ask questions about many aspects of print (McGee et al., 1986):

- They ask about letters. (What is this letter?)
- They ask about words. (What does this say?)
- They ask for information. (Do people come from eggs, too?)
- They ask about print. (Where does it say _____?)

FIGURE 24–3 Children need to be provided with a library of books from which to select.

There has been some speculation regarding why children are prompted to ask these questions. One reason may be that this is how children were introduced to reading during infancy and toddlerhood and, therefore, they are modeling adult behavior. Also, book illustrations often have prominent print, such as a road sign or a sign on a building, that may catch children's attention. Furthermore, as they learn some letters, they may be drawn to these in the text and wonder what words say that have these known letters (Figure 24–3).

Technology can also provide an avenue for acquiring knowledge of early reading and writing. Computer software provides beginning reading and writing programs. Television provides many programs designed to teach children about alphabet letters and their sounds, sight words, and literature. PBS's Teacher Source (2002) provides suggestions for literacy-related activities based on children's programs such as *Arthur, Barney, Clifford, Caillou, Mr. Rogers' Neighborhood, Dragon Tales, Jay Jay the Jet Plane, Sagwak, Sesame Street,* and *Zoboomafoo.* PBS developed *Between the Lions,* a program specifically geared to kindergarten literacy (Rath, 2002; St. Clair, 2002). *Reading Rainbow* introduces children to classic literature.

## Reading and Writing in School

**letter names**

Names of alphabet symbols.

**letter sounds**

Sounds associated with alphabet symbols.

Conventional kindergarten curricula focus much attention on **letter names** and **letter sounds**. It is essential to understand how children learn letter names and letter sounds to plan age-appropriate experiences. Treiman, Tincoff, Rodriguez, Mouzaki, and Francis (1998) examined how young children learn letter sounds. Their study focused on preschool and kindergarten students. Young children usually learn letter names before they make specific sound associations. However, as we saw in the work by McBride-Chang (1998) as described in Chapter 22, children apply their knowledge of letter names in their initial attempts at spelling. Treiman et al. documented that children use their knowledge of letter names to learn letter sounds. The most easily learned sound-symbol relations are made for letters that have their sound as the initial sound in their name, such as the letter *b*. The next easiest are letters that have their sound at the end of their name, such as l. Letters that contain a clue to the sound, such as *f*, are easier to learn than letters that contain no sound clue, such as *w*. The authors conclude that "children . . . do not memorize letter-sound links as rote paired associates. Rather, they try to make sense of these relations based on what they know about the letters' names and the sounds the names contain" (p. 1537). The authors suggest that the common practice of spending the same amount of time on each letter in our kindergartens does not make sense in light of their findings. Less time could be devoted to the easily learned sounds and more time to the more difficult sounds.

A strong motivator for learning the alphabet are children's names (Kirk & Clark, 2005). Children's first sight word is their name:

> Summer sits at Grandma's computer "writing a book." The book begins "Summer" followed by lines of random letters and numbers.

Children have a strong attachment to their own names and eventually to the names of their friends. Kirk and Clark suggest using names in meaningful contexts, such as name labels on cubbies, names on children's work, names on jobs charts, and names to copy when signing in to class each day. In a preschool class, the job chart motivated children to recognize their classmates names and to begin to note the similarities and differences, such as in a class where there was *John*, *Jane*, *Jim* and *Jon*.

**phonics**

Focus on sound-symbol relationships.

Jalongo (1998b) attacks the **phonics**-only approach to reading instruction, which focuses on learning sound-symbol relationships as the key to learning to read. Instruction usually involves a lot of flashcard drill and workbook activities. Except for children with auditory difficulties, a knowledge of phonics is helpful in its application to decoding new words. However, as Jalongo points out, a focus on phonics misses the real objective of reading—understanding. It also decreases motivation to read for enjoyment and for information. Children need to learn about reading and its function; then they can learn phonics as an important tool in literacy. The first step in reading is exposing children to books and other print media. As mentioned earlier, this is a major concern regarding the No Child Left Behind requirements.

**drawing**

Using a tool to create a picture.

**handwriting**

Using a tool to make letters or letterlike forms.

We have already seen that **drawing** and **handwriting** are closely connected. Drawing can also be a connection to writing as composing. Oken-Wright (1998) provides the steps for enhancing children's drawing, while at the same time guiding them into creative writing. The first step is to ask the right questions about the drawing. Oken-Wright suggests that "What's happening [in the picture]?" is the best question for getting children to expand their verbalizations. The teacher must begin with taking dictation, proceed to the child copying the dictation, and then move on to independent writing. See also Thompson (2005).

**play**
The actions and activities through which children construct knowledge.

Remember that **play** is the major medium through which young children learn (see Chapter 5). It is essential to infuse opportunities to interact with print into play experiences (McGee & Richgels, 2004). Besides the reading and writing centers, other play centers can include print material. The home center should include magazines, a *TV Guide*, a phone book, and some children's picture books. It should also contain a supply of Post-it® Notes, plain paper pads, pencils, and pens for taking phone messages and making shopping lists. The kitchen shelves should be stocked with empty food cartons. Other dramatic play centers should be similarly supplied with print materials. Play should be a major activity not only in the preschool classroom but also in kindergarten. Kindergartners' notemaking, list writing, and sign making become even more important. Dramatization of stories is an essential play opportunity that extends well into the primary grades.

Children can learn to read and write through developmentally appropriate activities that spark their creativity and develop understanding of written language. For further guidelines see Greenberg's discussions of reading, writing, and spelling (1998a, 1998b, & 1998c) and McGee and Morrow (2005) for suggested kindergarten literacy instruction.

## THE ADULT ROLE IN EARLY READING AND WRITING DEVELOPMENT

After reviewing the research on the early stages of learning to read and write, McGee et al. (1986) concluded that children need a multitude of print experiences to support emerging literacy. They need more than identifying and discriminating sounds and letters, learning rhymes, and developing oral language skills. Early childhood educators need to develop curricula for home and school that include many kinds of print experiences (Coe & Shelby, 1998; Dickinson & DeTemple, 1998; Dickinson & Tabors, 1991; Duke & Kays, 1998; Holmes, 1993; Lonigan & Whitehurst, 1998; Marvin & Mirenda, 1993; McGee & Morrow, 2005; McMackin, 1993; Neuman and Roskos, 1993; Ratner & Olver, 1998; Rosow, 1994/95; Rosenkoetter 2001a & 2001b; Scher, 1998; Vasquez, 2000) McGee et al. (1986, pp. 63–65) suggest the following:

1. Call attention to the conventions of print while writing down children's dictation.
2. Point out the uses of print materials, such as phone books, storybooks, shopping lists, greeting cards, menus, and magazines as children use these materials in dramatic play.
3. Model reading behavior by reading when the children are reading, such as during a library or rest period.
4. Have children read signs during field trips.
5. Read children's dictation and have them read their dictation.
6. Encourage writing and drawing and label the products.
7. Draw attention to letters in context, such as when writing the child's name, labeling a picture, or taking dictation.
8. Provide a variety of writing implements and materials, such as lined and unlined paper, large and small paper, pens, markers, pencils, chalk and chalkboard, and paint and paintbrushes.
9. Encourage children to write and accept their products no matter how distant they are from conventional writing.

FIGURE 24–4 A listening center provides an opportunity for listening to stories and following the narrative in the book.

10. Provide props and print materials that will stimulate role-playing and story reenactments.
11. Encourage cooperative social interaction during play and during writing activities.
12. Provide movable letters and encourage experimentation (e.g., matching, sorting, sequencing).
13. Motivate children by encouraging them to write words that are personally important to them (e.g., their own names, names of friends and family members, names of their pets, or favorite play materials).
14. Provide opportunities to write letters; make greeting cards, lists, labels, and captions; and write stories.
15. Call attention to print in familiar stories by pointing to the words as they are read.
16. Write messages to children (e.g., "I like you," "You are a good helper," "Thanks for playing nicely today," "Time to wash your hands").
17. Let the children see adults using written language (e.g., making lists, writing captions and notes).
18. Encourage questions and discussion during story reading, especially by relating story content to the children's past experiences.
19. Enlist the aid of parents, volunteers, and older children to be trained as story readers to provide individual story-reading time.
20. Develop a parent education program designed to provide parents with techniques for enhancing learning at home.
21. Provide opportunities for and encourage "pretend" reading by modeling easy-to-learn stories, such as those found in predictable and pattern books.
22. Provide an abundance of reading material, including children's literature, wordless picture books, newspapers, phone books, catalogs, cartoons, menus, coupons, junk mail, and children's magazines.

The materials and activities listed will provide a print-rich environment for young children. Applying the information in this chapter in such a print-rich environment, adults can enhance literacy development by encouraging children to construct their own concepts of print and their own reading and writing skills (Figure 24–4).

Respond to the following statement:

"The major role of the adult in young children's reading and writing development is to provide a print-rich environment, to encourage children's reading and writing attempts in accepting and encouraging ways, and to stand back and observe the literacy process."

## HOW THE ADULT CAN FOSTER CREATIVITY IN THE YOUNG CHILD

**reflective learning**

Learning that takes place from the inside out.

The Association for Childhood Education International (ACEI) developed a position paper on the child's right to the expressive arts (Jalongo, 1990). The paper presents arguments for including the expressive arts of music, art, drama, dance, and writing in the curriculum. The expressive arts foster **reflective learning** (from the inside out). They enhance symbolic development and growth in all areas of development, and the child is viewed as one who constructs and makes meaning. The expressive arts can be integrated into all content areas, providing a means for the child to create and construct. The adult role is to provide the materials and the impetus for the children to feel free to use them (Figure 24–5).

Adults can foster children's creativity by encouraging their personal expressions and providing materials, time, space, and support (Moyer, 1990). For beginning artists, adults can provide a variety of materials so children can select the kind of material over which they believe they have the most control. The objective of much early artwork is finding out what can be done with various kinds of materials. Children should be encouraged to decide on their own topic and should have plenty of time to work at their own pace, experimenting and exploring the material without feeling bound by the need to produce a specific product. Teachers may comment as the children work, discussing concepts such as color, line, mass or volume, pattern, shape or form, space, and texture. Ditto and pattern art are not appropriate because they devalue the children's ideas, making them afraid to take risks and express themselves. For young children, it is the artistic process, not the product, that is the focus of creativity (Edwards & Nabors, 1993). "Creativity is feeling free to be flexible and original, to express one's *own* ideas in one's *own* way" (p. 79), not following a teacher's step-by-step directions in a craft-type project. Artwork created and selected by young artists should be prominently displayed in their classrooms.

**FIGURE 24–5** A collaboration: Summer has Grandma draw a picture of her, which Summer completes with arms and legs; and Summer draws Grandma and her mother.

When children are well into the representational stage, usually around age five, teachers can integrate art into unit topics and projects as a means for students to represent what they have learned and experienced, still allowing plenty of opportunity for children to work on a sudden inspiration. Nancy Smith (1982, 1983) developed an approach for providing a topic that still leaves children free to be creative. Smith believes that as children become skilled at representational drawing and have experimented with various media extensively, the teacher

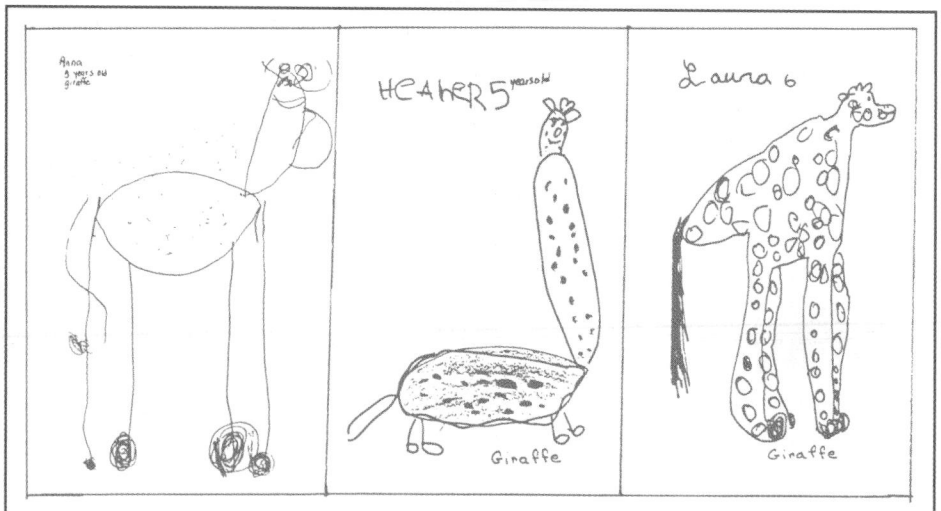


**FIGURE 24–6a** Observational drawings of a giraffe by three kindergarteners illustrate three levels of development in moving from stick drawings to drawings with shape, contour, and pattern.

no longer has to stay in the background. Smith's procedure is designed to promote observational art for children who are ready for it; that is, children age five and older. She has found that children can produce more detailed artwork if they are encouraged to observe the object of their drawing rather than having to draw completely from recall. Figures 24–6a and b contain some observational drawings done by kindergartners (Koenig, 1986). The models were plastic animals commonly available for dramatic play in preschool and kindergarten classrooms and a real crawfish. Before having the children draw, the adult discussed the visual characteristics of the animals with the children: the contours, the shapes, and the body parts. The resulting drawings were very detailed and representational. Compared with data collected by Smith, these children were quite advanced, including many kinds of details usually found mainly in drawings done by older children.

Creativity is nurtured by social interactions. The seeds of original ideas often come from interactions with peers and adults (Wolf, 1989). Mosley (1992) observed that kindergartners shared ideas about basic graphic elements, such as birds, rainbows, houses, and people, but incorporated the elements into their drawings in original ways. Thompson (1990) reviewed the theory and research on children's talk and drawing development. Before age three, the act of learning what the implement can do usually takes all the child's attention. From around age three and beyond, children talk about their drawings. It is at this point that the adult and child can enter into discussion centered on the artwork. This adult support enhances the children's development as artists, bringing us again to Vygotsky's concept of scaffolding. Adult comments should be responses to child comments and should focus on shape, color, texture, and so on, not on an interrogation regarding the topic or on pressure to tell a story. Examples of appropriate comments would be: "You must like bright colors" or "You must like to make circles."

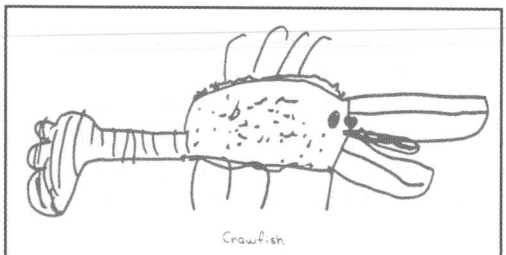


**FIGURE 24–6b** An observational drawing of a crawfish by a kindergartener shows unusual attention to detail for a child of this age.

Also ask children questions that promote creative thinking, such as the following:

- What if an elephant had no trunk?
- What would you do if you looked out the window in the morning and there was a dinosaur in your yard?

Encourage imagination. When the child says "There's an alligator in my bedroom," go along with it. Ask the child questions, such as, "What is he doing? Is he hungry? What's his name?" This type of game taps the child's creative potential and encourages the child to use his or her imagination. Keep children curious, allow them to explore, and guide them to discover answers on their own. Every child has some capacity for creativity; the adult who looks for it will find it. Many excellent resources are available for promoting creativity such as Koralek, 2004, Mayesky, 2006, and Schirrmacher, 2006.

Analyze the adult role in the following example of the interaction between Timmy, age four, and his preschool teacher:

Timmy drew a picture and took it to his teacher, Miss Mary. Mary responded, "Wow, Timmy, this is great, would you like to tell me about it?" Timmy answered, "It's you, Miss Mary!" Mary responded, "Yes, I can see it is. I can see my head and arms and legs. Thank you, this is wonderful."

Timmy went back to the art table and drew another picture. Again he took it to Miss Mary. This time he had drawn her with eyes, a nose, a mouth, and hair. She responded in a manner similar to the first time. Timmy and Miss Mary repeated this interaction three more times. Each time, Timmy added more details to his drawing. The final picture included the pencil that was stuck in Miss Mary's hair.

## SUMMARY

The adult's role in language development is to provide scaffolding experiences that support language development. The adult serves as a language model and provides language experiences and language interaction. Give-and-take conversation with a competent adult and with peers seems to be the most critical factor in successful early childhood language development.

Adults have a critical role in developing children's abilities to engage in talk. The adults provide an environment that promotes talk and provides initial conversational experiences. With infants, toddlers, two-year-olds, and three-year-olds, adults need to make a conscious effort to engage in conversation and promote the give-and-take of dialog. With four- and five-year-olds, the adult pulls back, observes, and lets children take over their own talk. However, if children are not displaying multifunctional language in their talk, the adult may step in and provide the spark to conversation. It is also important to encourage young children's private speech, which they use to direct and control their activities between the ages of two and five. Private speech bridges children's early attempts at oral language with their later ability to engage in verbal thought. Children from diverse cultures can expand their oral language use through extensive experiences with conversation. However, opinions differ regarding whether mastery of SE can be attained best through a bilingual experience or an immersion experience.

When a child enters school, he or she already knows a great deal about written language that teachers can capitalize on, just as they can capitalize on what the child has learned about oral language. The early childhood classroom should be a print-rich environment in which children are encouraged to construct their own knowledge about reading and writing. Children from print-rich homes come to school recognizing environmental print, knowing how to handle books, recognizing all or part of the alphabet, being able to write their own names and probably some other words, and knowing the use and format of letters, notes, lists, and other printed material. They have had many story-reading sessions at home, during which they were asked questions and encouraged to ask their own questions. A print-rich classroom can move these children ahead toward conventional reading and writing. For those children who enter school with little print experience, the print-rich classroom can introduce the world of reading and writing in the naturalistic way that other children have experienced at home.

The adult who works with young children can encourage creative behavior by providing an environment in which original and unusual ideas can be pursued.

## For Further Reading


Bardige, B. S., & Segal, M. M. (2004). *Building literacy with love.* Washington, DC: Zero to Three.

Bennet, K. K., Weigel, D. J., & Martin, S. S. (2002). Children's acquisition of early literacy skills: *Examining family contributions. Early Childhood Research Quarterly, 17*(3), 295–317.

Bloom, P. (2000). *How children learn the meanings of words.* Cambridge, MA: MIT Press.

Compton-Lilly, C. (2003). *Reading families: The literature lives of urban children.* New York: Teachers College Press.

Dickinson, D. K., & Tabors, P. O. (Eds.). (2001). *Beginning literacy with language: Young children learning at home and at school.* Baltimore: Brookes.

Duffy, B. (1998). *Supporting creativity and imagination in the early years.* Bristol, PA: Taylor and Francis.

Fassler, R. (2003). *Room for talk: Teaching and learning in a multilingual kindergarten.* New York: Teachers College Press.

Ford, D. Y., & Harris, J. J. (1999). *Multicultural gifted education.* New York: Teachers College Press.

Garcia, E. E. (2005). *Teaching and learning in two languages. Bilingualism and schooling in the United States.* New York: Teachers College.

Gardner, H. (1982). *Art, mind, and brain.* New York: Basic Books.

Gardner, H. (1983). *Frames of mind: theory of multiple intelligences.* New York: Basic Books.

Genishi, C. (2002). Research in review. Young English language learners: Resourceful in the classroom. *Young Children*, 57(4), 66-71.

Kogan, E. (2001). *Gifted bilingual students: A paradox?* New York: Peter Lang.

Lachat, M. A. (2004). *Standards-based instruction and assessment for English Language Learners.* Thousand Oaks, CA: Corwin.

Lange, D. L. (Ed.). (2002). *Culture as the core: Perspective on culture in second language education.* Greenwich, CT: IAP, Inc.

Martinez, M. (Ed.). (2000). *Education as the cultivation of intelligence.* Mahwah, NJ: Erlbaum.

McGee, L. M., & Richgels, D. J. (2003). *Designing early literacy programs: Strategies for at-risk preschool and kindergarten children.* New York: Guilford.

Morrow, L. M., & Gambrell, L. B. (2004). *Using children's literature in preschool: Comprehending and enjoying books.* Newark, DE: International Reading Association.

Mountain, L. (2000). *EARLY3Rs: How to lead beginners into reading, writing and arithme-TALK.* Mahwah, NJ: Erlbaum.

Ray, K. W. (2004). *About the authors: Writing workshop with our youngest writers.* Portsmouth, NH: Heinemann.

Schickdanz, J. A., & Casbergue, R. M. (2004). *Writing in preschool: Learning to orchestrate meaning and marks.* Newark, DE: International Reading Association.

Smith, N., and the Drawing Study Group. (1998). *Observation drawing with children.* New York: Teachers College Press.

Strickland, D. S., & Schickedanz, J. A. (2004). *Learning about print in preschool: Working with letters, words, and beginning links with phonemic awareness.* Newark, DE: International Reading Association.

Stuart, D. (Ed.) (2002). *Start with the Arts.* Baltimore: Brookes.

Venn, E. C. & Jahn, M. D. (2004). *Teaching and learning in preschool: Using individually appropriate practices in early childhood literacy instruction.* Newark, DE: International Reading Association.

Vukelich, C., & Christie, J. (2004). *Building a foundation for preschool literacy: Effective instruction for children's reading and writing development.* Newark, DE: International Reading Association.

Wolfe, P., & Nevills, P. (2004). *Building the reading brain, PreK–3.* Thousand Oaks, CA: Corwin.

Wolfram, W., Christian, D., & Adger, C. (1998). *Dialects in schools and communities.* Mahwah, NJ: Erlbaum.


## Suggested Activities

1. Visit a preschool and/or kindergarten classroom. Observe the teachers in each setting and record everything they and the children say. Use a tape recorder with the teacher's permission. Analyze the verbalizations of the teachers and the children, keeping in mind the factors discussed in this chapter regarding the adult role. Which techniques did the adults use? Was there give-and-take dialog? Is there conversation? If possible, observe a parent and child at home, record the language used, and analyze it. Compare your results with those of other students in the class.

2. Divide the class into groups. Have the members of each group look through issues of one of the journals listed from 2000 through the current issue. Students should look for articles describing activities that promote literacy development in early childhood classrooms. Have each group select 10 activities to share with the rest of the class, set up the activities in the format given, and provide a copy for each member of the class.

**FORMAT FOR LITERACY ACTIVITIES**

AREA: Literacy
ACTIVITY:
OBJECTIVE:
MATERIALS:
PROCEDURE:

Journals to search: *Young Children*, *Dimensions of Early Childhood Education*, *Early Childhood Education Journal*, *Childhood Education*, *Reading Teacher*, and *Language Arts*.

Discuss the following questions in class:
a. Which journals seemed to have the most useful articles?
b. How many suggested activities did you find that were based on the ideas in this chapter?
c. Did you find any activities that you think are inappropriate?
d. Look over all the activities. Which do you think are best? Why?

3. With another student, plan and present a debate on the merits of teaching dialect-speaking and/or non-English-speaking young children using a programmed drill method versus an activity-centered method. As preparation, do some additional background reading on the pros and cons of each method. Have a third student serve as moderator. After each of you has spent 10 minutes presenting a case for each side of the issue, open the floor to questions and comments from the class. Each debater should then give a three-minute summation. Finally, have the class members vote on which method they believe is best.

4. Choose an activity from a book of creative activities for preschool children (such as suggested in this chapter). Obtain whatever materials are needed and try the activity with three to six preschool children. Write a description of what each child does during the activity. Evaluate each child's degree of creativity using the following scale.

**CREATIVITY SCALE**

| 1 | 2 | 3 | 4 | 5 |
|---|---|---|---|---|
| **Low Creativity** (Lacks originality, flexibility, curiosity, willingness to explore—may look to see what other are doing and copy exactly) | | **Somewhat Creative** (Has some characteristics of creativity, but not all) | **High Creativity** (Demonstrates originality, flexibility, curiosity, willingness to explore—does what he, or she wants to do—not greatly influenced by others) | |

If possible, try another activity with the same children individually. Rate their degree of creativity. Were any differences observed when each child worked alone as opposed to when he or she worked with a group? What were these differences? What seemed to make the difference?

**5.** Make an entry in your journal.

## REVIEW

**1.** Match the items in Column I with the correct definition in Column II.

| Column I | Column II |
|---|---|
| a. letter sounds | 1. Using a tool to create a picture. |
| b. phonics | 2. Actions and activities through which children create meaning. |
| c. drawing | 3. Sounds associated with alphabet symbols. |
| d. handwriting | 4. The relationship between the letters of written language and the sounds of spoken language. |
| e. play | 5. Using a tool to make letters or letter-like forms. |
| f. adult-to-child language (ACL) | 6. Specific techniques used to teach persons whose primary language is not English. |
| g. baby talk | 7. A simplified form of speech with short, simple sentences and simple vocabulary that is within the child's realm of experience. |
| h. Cognitive Academic Language Proficiency (CALP) | 8. Games and joint book-reading are examples. |
| i. Basic Interpersonal Communication Skills (BICS) | 9. Special form of adult-to-child speech. |
| j. fussing | 10. Female interchanges. |
| k. reflective learning | 11. The language of everyday social activity. |
| l. English as a Second Language (ESL) | 12. The language of academic activities. |
| m. letter names | 13. Name of alphabet symbols. |
| n. routines | 14. Learning from within. |

**2.** Explain the relationship between language and concept development.

**3.** Can the adult who works with young children have a long-term effect on children's school success? What evidence is there to support your answer? Look also through previous chapters.

**4.** Decide whether each adult is promoting creativity in the following situations. Give a reason for each of your answers.

a. The teacher passes out a worksheet with a picture of a fish on it and asks each child to color his or her fish carefully, using orange as the main color.

b. The teacher places paints, crayons, paper, glue, and other materials on the table. She tells the children to think about their trip to the Tropical Fish Shop and then create a picture of the kind of fish they would like to have.

c. Derrick says he doesn't want to make a fish. He liked the snails best. Mrs. Chen responds, "Go ahead, Derrick. I look forward to seeing your snail."

## KEY TERMS LIST

adult-to-child language (ACL)
baby talk (BT)
Basic Interpersonal Communication Skills (BICS)
Cognitive Academic Language Proficiency (CALP)
drawing
English as a Second Language (ESL)
fussing
handwriting
letter names
letter sounds
phonics
play
reflective learning routines
routines

Additional resources for this chapter can be found on the Online Companion™ to accompany this text at http://www.earlychilded.delmar.com. Respond to "Time to Reflect" and "Looking Further" concepts, review various child development scenarios, and answer thought-provoking questions in the Critical Thinking Forum. Keep a daily journal by downloading the student journal available on this Web site. Complete the interactive matching exercises to reinforce concepts, and printout the child development assessment forms to use during your observation of development for children from birth to age eight. In addition, read the case studies on the Web site to reinforce the important concepts in each chapter, and take a look at the multitude of Web links that are available for student research on the Internet.

# SECTION VII

## Affective Growth and Development: Ages Three Through Six

This section looks at children's affective development in more detail: how they develop in the areas of emotions, personality, and social behavior. Young children's development in the affective areas is closely tied to their development in the cognitive areas. Their views of their own feelings, of themselves, and of others are different from those of adults and older children. As a preview to this section, we will again meet Ramona Quimby and introduce several other fictional children who typify the kinds of affective thinking and behavior that make young children so special.

Let's look at Ramona first. At age four, young children are just beginning to incorporate a sense of right and wrong. With their preoperational logic, they may do things that appear to be misbehavior, but that really reflect they are victims of their immature logic. For example, Ramona does not want to return *Big Steve and the Steam Shovel* to the library. From her preoperational point of view, the library *gave* her the book, and she writes her name on every page to prove it.

From preschool to primary, young children learn the limits of their initiative. Having grappled with autonomy, they can take on more specific projects. For example, Peter (Keats, 1964) wants to learn how to whistle so that he can whistle for his dog, Willie. He views being able to whistle as a sign of maturity and even puts on his father's hat so that he will feel more grown-up. He keeps trying and eventually reaches his goal.

Young children are just learning to deal with strong feelings. Alexander during his terrible, horrible, no good, very bad day is faced with a variety of problems and disappointments from waking up with gum in his hair to having his best friend change to some other best friends to lima beans for supper (Viorst, 1972). From preschool to primary is a time when young children learn to face a variety of fears. Monsters may lurk anywhere but grown-ups may not understand. Harry's mother goes into the basement even though Harry knows there is something terrible down there (Gackenbach, 1977). It is left up to Harry to protect his mother from the Terrible Whatzit. Because it is also important to be strong and brave, Harry manages to overcome his fears and overcome the Terrible Whatzit. With the advent of real-time television news, children see war and disaster firsthand.

Peer relationships are very important to young children. Ramona has her best friend, Howie. They have their ups and downs, but maintain their friendship. In kindergarten, Ramona chases Davy around the school yard threatening to kiss him. She can't resist pulling Susan's curls and finds herself in trouble.

In the following chapters, we look at affective development from ages three through six. As you read each chapter, keep Ramona, Peter, Alexander, and Harry in mind.

**Books referred to:**

**Cleary, B. (1955). *Beezus and Ramona.* New York: Yearling. (Ramona, age four)**

**Cleary, B. (1968). *Ramona the pest.* New York: Yearling. (Ramona, age five)**

**Gackenbach, D. (1977). *Harry and the terrible whatzit.* New York: Scholastic.**

**Keats, E. J. (1964). *Whistle for Willie.* New York: Viking.**

**Viorst, J. (1972). *Alexander and the terrible, horrible, no good, very bad day.* Hartford, CT: Anthenum.**

CHAPTER

# 25

# The Nature of Affective Development: Theory, Emotion, and Personality

## OBJECTIVES

After reading this chapter, you should be able to:

- Define *affective*.
- Recognize the interests of major theorists in the affective area.
- Identify affective behaviors of a young child.
- Identify the major areas of interest of the theorists discussed in the chapter.
- Discuss the importance of ego development during early childhood.
- State why the young child has a "right to feel."
- Understand the importance of emotional intelligence.
- Identify the major aspects of attachment.
- Recognize examples of dependence and independence.
- Describe the relationship between independence and responsibility.
- Explain what might be done to handle children's fears and reduce stress.
- Discuss what the child must learn about handling angry feelings.
- Know the developmental aspect of the recognition and regulation of emotions.
- Recognize the major factors in the acquisition of sex-role standards and gender-role behaviors.
- Determine what stage a child is in regarding his or her knowledge of sex and birth.
- Provide developmentally appropriate knowledge regarding sexuality and sex roles.
- Identify the major factors in the development and description of the self-concept.
- Discuss whether there are cross-cultural differences in personality characteristics.

FIGURE 25–1 Affective behavior is seen in the expression of both positive and negative feelings.

**affective**

The area that centers on the development of social, emotional, and personality characteristics and the self-concept.

**Affective** is defined as the area that centers on the development of social, emotional, and personality characteristics and self-concept. Each of the major theorists has some interest in affective growth. For Freud, Erikson, Rogers, and Maslow, affective growth is the center of attention. Freud's theory is concerned with personality development. Erikson's psychosocial theory centers on the effect of social environment on personality development. Rogers' theory emphasizes self-concept development. Maslow also emphasizes self-concept development through self-actualization. Bandura's social learning theory focuses on the emotional and motivational aspects of thinking (Miller, 2002). Piaget's social theory focuses on the relationship between the individual and the social "in sociomoral, affective, and intellectual development" (DeVries, 1997, p. 4). Vygotsky views cognition as a social activity, with social experiences shaping how people think (Berk & Winsler, 1995) (Figure 25–1).

As previously discussed, in infancy, a bond is formed that is the basis for attachment and future independence. Between ages one and three, the toddler is off on his or her own. As the child interacts with others, he or she demonstrates an interest in social activity and a need to develop positive self-regard, and even shows kind feelings toward those in trouble or in pain. Thus, the preschool child has already progressed through two stages of affective development.

**Phallic Stage**

Freud stated that children ages three to six are in this stage, in which the child concentrates on sex-role identification and conscience development.

**Crisis III: Initiative versus Guilt**

A stage in Erikson's theory of development through which children pass between the ages three and six; children deal with the crisis that results from a desire to make their own choices but meet the demands of their developing consciences.

## THEORETICAL VIEWS

To Freud, children ages three to six are in the **Phallic Stage,** during which the child concentrates on sex-role identification and conscience development. In Erikson's view, the period from ages three to six is the time for working through **Crisis III: Initiative versus Guilt.** Rogers and Maslow emphasize the importance of the child's personal experience and its effect on self-concept development. For Sears, the child continues through Phase II: Secondary Behavioral Systems. In the Piagetian system, the child is in the latter part of the preoperational stage and for Vygotsky he or she is in the stage of early childhood. Gesell identified a sequence of stages from age three to five at half-year intervals characterized by equilibrium at three, four, and five, and disequilibrium at three-and-a-half and four-and-a-half. For Skinner, there is no special stage of affective development during the preschool years; the child merely continues to learn and to have his or her behavior modified by environmental forces. For Bandura, increased cognitive skills affect how the child uses social knowledge.

| Stage | Age | Focus |
|---|---|---|
| Oral | Infancy | Emotional facets of the feeding experiences |
| Anal | 1½–3 years | Emotional facets of the toilet-training experience |
| Phallic | 3–6 years | Sex-role identification and conscience development |
| Latency | 7–13 years | Consolidation of previous stages of development |

FIGURE 25–2 Freud's stages of early childhood personality development. It is important that the young child learn to handle the kinds of problems presented in each stage in a positive way.

## Freud

**Crisis IV: Industry versus Inferiority**

A stage in Erikson's theory of development through which children pass during middle childhood and cope with the need to be productive and successful and not be overwhelmed by failure and inferiority.

Freud's theory (Miller, 2002) describes five stages through which children pass as they develop from birth to adolescence. As already described, the infant is in the Oral Stage and the toddler in the Anal Stage. The three- to six-year-old is in the Phallic Stage. The seven- to twelve-year-old is in the Latency Stage. These four stages are outlined in Figure 25–2. During the Phallic Stage, according to Freud, the child becomes aware of himself or herself as male or female and must successfully deal with the identification process. Through this process, the child takes on the behaviors of the same-sex parent. The young child also develops a conscience, the sense of right and wrong, as his or her superego develops (this is discussed further in the description of Erikson's theory) (Figure 25–3).

## Erik Erikson

Erikson's theory (Miller, 2002) includes eight stages through which each person passes as he or she develops from birth through old age. As already described, the infant deals with the crisis of Trust versus Mistrust and the toddler with the crisis of Autonomy versus Shame and Doubt. The preprimary child faces the crisis of Initiative versus Guilt during Stage III. During the primary years, children enter **Crisis IV: Industry versus Inferiority.** Each crisis has its roots in infancy and continues to affect future development. Erikson's stages of early childhood are listed in Figure 25–4. None of the crises are ever resolved; the conflicts stay with us throughout life. The person who copes successfully at each step learns to handle these conflicts in a positive and healthy way.

FIGURE 25–3 Preprimary children become increasingly independent and do more on their own.

The preprimary child now has a sense of purpose in what he or she does. The child plans and then attacks a task for the sake of the activity. He or she loves to investigate and explore, but at the same time the child has to learn the limits of his or her initiative. The child must begin to detach from the parents and do things independently. Independence is given gradually by adults; the young child must learn what is considered acceptable and unacceptable behavior. The conscience, or sense of right and wrong, begins to develop during this stage. The ego, or self-concept, works on perfecting basic skills in the psychomotor, perceptual, communicative, and social areas. Children become increasingly independent and do more

| Stage | Conflict That Is Faced |
|---|---|
| I. Infancy | Basic Trust versus Mistrust |
| II. Toddlerhood | Autonomy versus Shame and Doubt |
| III. Preprimary | Initiative versus Guilt |
| IV. Primary | Industry versus Inferiority |

FIGURE 25–4 Erikson's theory centers on the eight stages through which people progress during the life span. Each stage presents the person with a new conflict to be handled. Each conflict has its beginning in infancy and continues to influence the person's behavior throughout life. The four stages of early childhood are listed here.

things for themselves, such as dressing, getting their own snacks, and making projects using wood, clay, and other materials. At the same time, they begin to develop inner control of their behavior.

During the preprimary period, the foundations of the child's sex-role identity are built. Boys and girls learn who they are in relation to being male and female, respectively. Play is the young child's major activity, serving as a means for trying out dreams and working through conflicts. Through play, the child can carry out activities that are not otherwise available. The child can do what adults do through dramatic play and stories. The child becomes very aware that adults have privileges he or she does not have. Through activities with toys and tools or through responsibilities for younger children, preschool children practice some of these adultlike behaviors.

The preprimary child who passes through this period successfully learns how to take initiative within the limits of society. The child develops a conscience but is not so overwhelmed by guilt at his or her desire to do grown-up things that he or she is not able to do anything. The child's new sense of control helps him or her stay within realistic boundaries.

As children enter the primary years, they also enter the stage of Industry versus Inferiority. Success and productivity are necessary in order for them not to develop feelings of inferiority. They seek to be productive not only through cognitive activities, such as those in the school setting, but also through projects, such as crafts and collections, physical activities, such as sports and dance, and artistic endeavors, such as art and music.

**id**

To Freud, this is present at birth and contains the person's unconscious motives and desires and operates on the pleasure principle.

**ego**

To Freud, this is characterized by reason and common sense and operates on the reality principle.

**superego**

To Freud, this begins to develop around the age of four; the conscience or the part of the personality that holds on to the moral values of society.

By the preprimary period, the child's personality has developed three major structures: the id, the ego, and the superego (Figure 25–5). The **id** is present at birth and contains the person's unconscious motives and desires. It operates on the pleasure principle; that is, it is concerned with the comfort and well-being of the child. At birth, the **ego** begins to develop. The ego develops as the child begins to discover he or she is separate from the environment. The ego is characterized by reason and common sense and operates on the reality principle; that is, the ego interprets reality to the child. The **superego** begins to develop around the age of four. This is the conscience—the part of the personality that holds on to the moral values of society.

The ego, id, and superego are in constant conflict. The id tells the child to go ahead and engage in pleasureful activities: Take the cookie even though mother said not to; grab a toy from another child because you want to play with it now. The superego says be good: Do not get angry; do not take the cookie; never take someone else's belongings. The ego must mediate between the two so that the child is not dominated by one or the other. Through the ego, the child develops a sense of self so that he or she can take initiative with confidence but not overstep

| Personality | Age at Which Development Begins | Example Characteristics | When in Control |
|---|---|---|---|
| Id | Present at birth | • Unconscious motives<br>• Pleasure principle<br>• Acts in terms of most basic desires, such as hunger and comfort | Child is hungry. Takes a cookie even though he or she has been told to take fruit if he or she wants a snack because the child likes cookies better. |
| Ego | Begins to develop right after birth | • Reason and common sense<br>• Reality principle<br>• Mediates between id and superego; tries to keep both under control | Child is hungry. Wants a cookie, but knows that only fruit is allowed. The child chooses an apple. |
| Superego | Begins to develop around four years of age | • Conscience; incorporation of society's moral values | Child is hungry. Afraid to take any food without checking with adult first. If adult is not available, continues being hungry rather than taking the initiative. |

FIGURE 25–5 The structure of personality: psychoanalytic view.

society's boundaries. At one extreme, id-dominated children think only of their own pleasures and desires and behave accordingly. At the other extreme, superego-dominated children may be so fearful of doing wrong that they are afraid to take chances and as a result do not develop a sense of purpose and initiative.

## Rogers and Maslow

As discussed in Chapter 2, Rogers and Maslow are not stage theorists. Both focus on the process of achieving a positive self-concept. The child moves toward self-actualization supported by love from parents and positive peer interactions. Between ages three and six, children begin the move from focusing on parents to focusing on peers, so interactions with peers take on more importance than previously for these two theorists.

Rogers emphasizes the importance of the child focusing on personal experiences. Children need to make full use of their physical and mental faculties to get the most out of their daily experiences. Rogers and his followers emphasize counseling approaches to child rearing, that is, approaches that involve discussing the problem. Emotionally healthy people can see their emotions and the emotions of others clearly; they can bring them to the symbolic level and can speak about them. Parents are in a critical position. They need to learn to accept themselves and their feelings about their children. They have to accept that it is all right not to be "perfect." They have to accept that it is all right not to always feel positive and accepting toward everything their child does.

**hierarchy of needs**

To Maslow, a series of levels a person must fulfill to achieve self-actualization.

Maslow also emphasizes self-knowledge. He developed a **hierarchy of needs** that the person must deal with and satisfy to be self-actualized. Each lower-level need must be satisfied to reach the upper-level needs. The needs include, starting with the lowest and most basic:

1. *Physical/Organizational*
   - Survival—to be able to eat, breathe, and live
   - Security—predictability, assurance that tomorrow will come

2. *Affiliation/Social*
   - Belonging—being part of a group
   - Esteem—being valuable and unique
3. *Achievement/Intellectual*
   - Knowledge—wanting to know about things, symbols, and so forth
   - Understanding—putting small bits of knowledge together into a larger picture
4. *Aesthetic*
   - Aesthetic—a sense of order, balance, and beauty; love for all
5. *Self-Actualization*
   - Being a fully functioning person
   - Being one's true self

It can be seen that affective needs are the most basic after survival. Both of these sets of needs have to be fulfilled before the child will be motivated to seek knowledge and understanding, essential motivations when he or she enters school.

## Jean Piaget

Although Piaget is best known for his cognitive theory, he also acknowledged the importance of social development and constructed a social theory (DeVries, 1997). Piaget believed that, just as knowledge of the object world is constructed by the child, psychosocial knowledge is also constructed. Furthermore, he believed that affective bonds serve as motivation for social and moral development. Finally, Piaget believed that an equilibrating, or self-regulating, process acts in the social and moral development areas just as it does in the cognitive.

**sociomoral development**
Development of the moral rules and regulations of society.

**anomy**
Unregulated behavior.

**heteronomy**
Regulation of behavior by others.

**autonomy**
Regulation of behavior by one's self.

**affectivity**
Piaget believed that feelings are closely associated with cognitive development and that these feelings are the fuel that makes intelligence work.

**social reciprocity**
The give and take of social relationships.

Piaget's social theory has a particular focus on **sociomoral development** (DeVries, 1997). Sociomoral development progresses through the following three phases:

1. **anomy**—nonregulation by others or the self
2. **heteronomy**—regulation by others
3. **autonomy**—self-regulation

Reaching the third stage requires a cooperative adult-child relationship. Within this relationship, children are encouraged to make their own decisions in the best interests of everyone involved. Adults show respect for children and their ideas and actions. Adults provide moral rules and foster the child's thoughtful application in specific situations. In child-child relationships, children have the opportunity to practice autonomous decision making, which can support perspective taking and decentering.

Integrated with Piaget's theory of sociomoral development is his theory of affective and personality development (DeVries, 1997). Piaget viewed **affectivity** as the fuel that makes intelligence work. As children interact in more social situations, their personalities gradually develop. Feelings are related to cognitive acts. That is, when we act on or with objects and other people, we develop positive or negative feelings about that act. The critical element in relationships is **social reciprocity.** Through reciprocal interactions, children learn to coordinate different points of view and cooperate with others. If children have cooperative reciprocal relationships with adults, they can develop similar relationships with peers. The development of cooperative social relationships follows the same developmental pattern as cognitive relationships, such as conservation. Children conserve roles in play just as they conserve number or substance. If Jimmy says, "Let's play space explorers," and Jenny says, "Okay" and follows through on the space explorer role, she has conserved the agreement.

DeVries (1997) believes that the implication of the Piagetian view for education is that a socially interactive classroom should be valued in which cooperative social exchanges happen. Devries and Zan (1994) state that the first principle of constructivist education is "to cultivate a sociomoral atmosphere in which mutual respect is continually practiced" (DeVries, 1997, p. 14). DeVries identifies the following five principles of **cooperative teaching:**

**cooperative teaching**
Instructional methods that promote cooperation and positive interactions among students.

1. Relate to children in cooperative ways.
2. Promote peer friendship and cooperation, including conflict resolution.
3. Cultivate a feeling of community and construct collective values.
4. Appeal to the children's interests and engage their purposes.
5. Adapt to children's understanding.

Unnecessary coercion should be minimized and respect and cooperation maximized. The objective for all children is the development of self-regulation or inner control. Although he puts it in different terms, Vygotsky's theory focuses on the same objective in the affective area.

## Lev Vygotsky

Vygotsky's concern with the social components of learning were described in earlier chapters. He focuses on language as a critical tool of behavior regulation (Bodrova & Leong, 1996). Adults use language to communicate their wishes, such as "Time to listen to the story," "Build the blocks only up to your shoulder," or "Use words to tell your friend you are angry." Children then transfer these words to their behavior and to their interactions with their peers. Through **shared activities,** such as working together on a project or through reciprocal language exchange, children share their mental functions. Shared activities provide a setting for meaningful learning. Through play interactions and explanations of problem solutions, children clarify what they have learned about the world. During reciprocal interactions in shared activities, the roles of other-regulator and self-regulator are exchanged. At age three, children are usually other-regulators, seeing rules as applying only to others. As they proceed toward age six, they gradually become self-regulators. They perceive that rules apply to them as well as to others.

**shared activities**
Students working together on a project or discussing a problem solution.

## B. F. Skinner

Skinner's operant-conditioning theories have been used to develop ways to modify the behavior of young children. They have been particularly useful for stopping unwanted behaviors, such as temper tantrums and aggression, and increasing the frequency of positive behaviors, such as sharing and cooperation.

As reviewed in Chapter 15, Skinner's theory inspired the behavior modification approach to child guidance. This approach (discussed further in Chapter 27) is especially effective with toddlers. It is also widely used to modify the behavior of older children.

Fields and Fields (2006) explain how artificial reward systems are set up in order to control children's behavior externally. Behavior modification has been very popular in schools as a means to control large groups of children. Behavior modification is based on the premise that rewards (verbal and tangible) will effectively cause children to behave in a desired manner. Fields and Fields do not recommend this method.

### Albert Bandura

Bandura's theory provides a framework for the acquisition of appropriate affective behaviors. Observing others provides knowledge of expectations for appropriate emotional, personality, and social behaviors (Miller, 2002). Children create some of their own environment through their behavior and choice of activities. Children who are kind and generous with others receive reciprocal responses from others, whereas those who are hostile and selfish are ignored or treated negatively by others. Children who watch television see different models than those who spend more time with other children. As children mature cognitively and are able to manipulate symbols, they can also mentally manipulate the social roles they have observed and coordinate the behaviors into their own particular behavior. Imitation is not necessarily a one-to-one correspondence to what is observed. Cognition also serves a role in the degree to which children perceive themselves as competent in dealing with the environment. Children must not only have the skills to accomplish specific tasks but also view themselves as capable of using their skills to achieve mastery.

### Conclusions

Each of these theorists has some interest in affective development. The affective area encompasses the development of the self-concept, ego and superego, sex-role identification, aggression, dependency, moral judgment, social behavior with peers, and the content of play activities. Psychoanalyst Selma Fraiberg (1959) believes that at the center of child development during the early years is the development of "I." For children to reach age six with good mental health, they must have an ego that is capable of dealing with conflict, tolerating frustration, adapting, and finding solutions to problems that satisfy both inner needs and outer reality. "These qualities of the ego are the product of the child's bonds to his parents, the product of the humanizing process" (Fraiberg, 1959, p. 302).

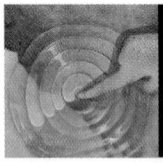

**LOOKING FURTHER**

As you consider each theorist, which one(s) do you prefer? Explain the reasons for your choices. Select one theory and look further into how the theory may be applied to working with young children. Start with the references in the For Further Reading section of this chapter.

## EMOTIONAL DEVELOPMENT

What kinds of feelings do I have in relation to other people and in relation to things? How do I express these feelings? What purposes do these feelings serve? The answers to these questions are found in the study of the area of emotional development. The emotional area includes feelings such as anxiety, fear, sadness, anger, happiness, love, and affection. Young children have a well-developed set of emotional responses by the time they reach the preschool period. These responses come from feelings children have within themselves about other people, things, and events in the environment. For children's mental health, it is important that they have opportunities and methods for expressing their feelings. They also need to learn that having feelings is normal. Adults in our culture often deny feelings and may lead children to hold their feelings in check. As Fraiberg expresses it, the young child has "the right to feel"(Fraiberg, 1959, p. 273).

For example, Fraiberg describes an incident in which a mother wants to buy a substitute hamster before her son finds out that his hamster is dead. Fraiberg feels that the boy has a right to experience the feeling of loss: "In our efforts to protect children from painful emotions we may deprive them of their own best means of mastering painful experiences" (Fraiberg, p. 274). She believes that if the child can experience mourning a hamster, it will help him when the time comes to face the loss of a friend or a family member. Furthermore, holding feelings inside is not mentally healthy. He will also be able to work through his feelings about death and dying.

Lewis and Michalson (1983) did an in-depth study of emotions and their development in early childhood. Whereas emotional and cognitive development are conventionally viewed as separate processes, Lewis and Michalson suggest a model that interrelates the two areas. They choose to view emotional behavior and feelings as cognitive processes. The model they propose is much like the Model of Cognitive Functioning shown in Chapter 20 of this text. According to the model, an internal or external event would be perceived as input, then processed internally to develop an internal response or feeling, and followed by output through facial expression, vocalization, posture or gesture and/or motor behavior. Internal and/or external feedback would set the sequence moving again.

For example:

Anger:

1. Jason accidentally knocks down the unit block building he has been working on for 20 minutes (external event).
2. Jason feels his elbow hit the building and sees it topple over (tactile and visual perception).
3. Jason thinks, "Oh no! It's falling!" (processing).
4. Jason feels hot and his body feels stiff (internal response).
5. He throws himself to the floor, flailing and crying (output, external response, motor and vocal).

Dealing with emotions is an important aspect of working with young children. Adults must be aware that children have had different experiences that will shape their individual emotional reactions and behaviors and be prepared to act accordingly (Elkind, 1993).

Historically, emotional development was the major focus of the early childhood curriculum: "Traditionally, early childhood programs have emphasized the emotional nature of teacher-child relationships, the selection of activities to meet children's emotional needs, the open expression of feelings by children and adults, the development of positive affective dispositions, and adult awareness of children's emotional responses" (Hyson, 1996, p. 5). Hyson points out that in its beginnings, early childhood education was strongly influenced by the theories of Freud, Erikson, and others who viewed development from a humanistic point of view. In recent years, the focus on emotions has faded. Observation has revealed "widespread insensitivity, detachment, and harshness among caregivers in child-care programs" (Hyson, 1996, p. 5). Furthermore, classrooms that foster very little talk about feelings appear emotionally sterile. Fear of being accused of sexual abuse and increased attention to academics have probably contributed to this change. Unfortunately, more children are arriving in school "with high levels of anxiety, stress, and emotional vulnerability" (p. 6), and, therefore, are very much in need of emotional support.

**emotional intelligence**

Goleman's view of the ability to understand and manage emotions.

Daniel Goleman (*Daniel Goleman talks about emotional intelligence*, 1999) has refocused attention on emotions with his work on **emotional intelligence.** Emotional intelligence is set up much like Gardner's theory of multiple intelligences, which was discussed in Chapter 23. According to Goleman (1999, p. 29), emotional intelligence is made up of the following five domains:

1. *Knowing one's emotions:* being self-aware and recognizing an emotion when it happens
2. *Managing emotions:* handling feelings appropriately
3. *Motivating oneself:* emotional self-control—delaying gratification and stifling impulsiveness
4. *Recognizing emotions in others:* empathy—the fundamental "people skill"
5. *Handling relationships:* skill in managing relationships in others

According to Goleman (p. 29), "These abilities combine to foster self-esteem and leadership and interpersonal effectiveness." During the first three years, when the brain is growing at a rapid rate, emotional intelligence must be learned. Adults support this learning through their positive responses to children's needs. The basic lesson children must learn "is that all feelings are okay to have; however, only some reactions are okay" (p. 30). It is essential that children learn the language of emotions (Novick, 2002). Sullivan and Strang (2002/2003) suggest that bibliotherapy can be very effective in helping children develop emotional intelligence. Literature is used as the basis for learning effective social techniques.

The emotions and their development in the young child discussed in this chapter include attachment dependency, fear and anxiety, stress, hostility and anger, and happiness. Also discussed are teachers' beliefs and recognition and regulation of emotions.

## Attachment

Attachment is a lifelong commitment between child and caregiver that builds from birth and evidences specific features around six months of age when the infant perceives the caretaker as a special person (Stroufe, 1991). (Refer to Chapters 13 and 16.) Terri Smith (1991) describes some of the effects that lack of secure attachment may have on children's social behavior. Four-year-old best friends have been found to have a more happy and harmonious relationship if both are securely attached to their mothers. Insecurely attached six-year-old boys were rated by teachers and peers as less competent, not as well liked by peers, and as having more behavior problems than securely attached boys. The results of other studies (Barnett, Kidwell, & Leung, 1998; Chisholm, 1998; Verschueren & Marcoen, 1999) support the importance of attachment relationships to children's behavior. Siblings who have secure attachments also have better relationships. Those who work with young children must help parents develop secure attachments and provide that secure attachment if they are working with young children in a caretaking/instructional role. Attention must all be focused on the importance of fathers in children's emotional, as well as academic, development (Gadsden & Ray, 2002). The various aspects of emotional development described in the following discussion are of equal importance and are an integral part of the cognitive developmental factors described in Section VI.

FIGURE 25–6 The preschool child becomes physically independent but remains emotionally dependent on adults.

## Dependency

Newborns are completely dependent on the other people in their environment to fulfill all of their needs. Two types of dependency develop. One type is an **emotional dependency** that springs from the development of attachment. The other type is a **physical dependency.**

Physical dependency involves basic needs, such as nourishment, comfort, and elimination. Young infants are totally dependent on others to care for their needs. However, physical dependency changes rapidly with age. Children enter a helpless stage, then a stage during which they cooperate and accept help, and finally a stage in which they do it themselves. By the time children reach preschool age, they have become independent in eating, toileting, building, and walking and are becoming independent in dressing. During the preschool period, children's play and social behaviors become increasingly independent.

Emotional dependency develops in a different way than does physical dependence (Figure 25–6). Whereas hugging, kissing, and clinging are acceptable behaviors for infants or toddlers, how they show and receive affection and love will change as children develop through the preschool period. That is, they are less public in their expression and decrease their clinging behavior. From wanting to be picked up and hugged when coming home from nursery school, the preschooler develops toward a verbal greeting, a smile, and maybe a quick hug. Cuddling is saved for the privacy of home. The objective is not to make the child independent of emotional attachments but to change the way the child shows love. Furthermore, children are encouraged to widen their emotionally dependent attachments to others: peers, relatives, and teachers, for example. To get reassurance that they are still loved, preschoolers turn more to verbal attention seeking:

**emotional dependency**
The need for affiliation with others; develops from early bonding and attachment.

**physical dependency**
Relying on others to care for one's basic needs, such as nourishment, comfort, and elimination.

"Look what I can do!" (as the child tries a somersault)

"Look at my picture!" (as the child holds up a drawing)

"Help me, please." (as the child tries to rearrange the furniture in his or her bedroom)

"Isn't this a pretty dress?"(as she comes in wearing a new outfit)

Some adults believe it is not good to reinforce dependent behavior. However, the child's emotional needs continue to require fulfillment. This requirement is accomplished by giving attention when the child is independently performing a physical act. Punishment for dependency may only increase children's desire for it and the frequency with which they seek attention, reassurance, and affection.

The development of physical independence enables children to develop responsibility for their own actions (Veach, 1979). This is accomplished through offering the child the opportunity to make more complex choices.

Independence supports increasing feelings of competence. Lewis and Michalson (1983) define competence as "the ability to participate in a set of age-related tasks, which is accompanied by a positive feeling" (p. 344). Research indicates that these feelings may begin to appear as early as 10 weeks of age. Once feelings of competence, or its opposite, helplessness, are established, they seem to stay with the child as he or she enters each new situation.

Considering what you have just read about dependence and independence, analyze and evaluate Kerry's behavior:

> Kerry, age five, climbed onto the counter so she could watch her mother make sandwiches. Her mother started to spread the slices of bread with Miracle Whip®. Kerry immediately said that she wanted to help. Her mother handed her the knife and told Kerry not to get too much Miracle Whip® on the bread. It took her about five minutes to get it just right. Her mother then told her, "Good job, sweety." Kerry smiled and continued building her sandwich. She put on some mustard, a slice of cheese, and a piece of lettuce. Then she took the other piece of bread and put it on top. She looked at the sandwich and said, "I now need to cut it in four pieces just like you do, Mom." Smiling, her mom handed her a butter knife. Kerry took the knife and cut the sandwich in half and then in half again. Grinning broadly, she put the sandwich on a plate. She bit into it and said, "This is the best sandwich I've ever eaten." Her mom gave her a big hug and told her how proud she was.

## Fear and Anxiety

Young children typically develop fears and anxieties as they proceed through the preschool period (Robinson & Gladstone, 1993). Robinson and Gladstone found that monsters were the fears mentioned most often by three- to five-years-olds. School-related fears appear around four or five years of age. Children in the Robinson and Gladstone study mentioned fear of not learning to read, of not being able to talk in class, and of being sent to detention. Overall, 80 different feared objects were mentioned. Young children are concerned about monsters in the closet and goblins under the bed. They may be afraid of going down the bathtub drain or being sucked into the toilet. They may be afraid of new situations and new people. Wind, thunder, and lightning may also be frightening. Working through these fears enables the child to be a mentally healthy person. By working through these childhood fears, the child strengthens his or her feelings of power in relation to the world. The young child has the mental equipment to deal with danger. If adults teach the child how to use that equipment to deal with goblins and witches, the child will be able to apply those skills later when he or she meets real danger. The child will also learn how to handle things that are realistically anxiety and fear provoking, such as having a tooth filled, getting an injection at the doctor's office, or wondering what happens when an animal or a person dies.

**fear**

Develops most likely through a combination of genetic and learned factors that are acquired through conditioning and observational learning.

Most likely, **fear** develops through a combination of genetic and learned factors. Fears have been shown to be acquired through conditioning and observational learning. Fear may also depend on the child's perception of whether the fearful person is real. For example, infants who have been around a lot of people and realize that people come in many sizes and shapes are less likely to develop a fear of strangers.

The normal fears of the young child can be handled by facing them instead of pretending they do not exist (Hyson, 1979; Robinson & Gladstone, 1993; Smith, Allen, & White, 1990). Hyson (1979) makes the following suggestions:

FIGURE 25–7 Talk to children about their fears.

- Talk about the fears. Help the child put the fear into words and/or pictures (Figure 25–7).
- Provide opportunities for dramatic play. Sometimes by taking the role of one who is feared, such as the doctor, the bad wolf, or the witch, the child can lessen his or her anxiety.
- Use desensitization or gradually build up to the feared object or experience. Have the child play with a puppy if he or she is afraid of full-grown dogs; let the child play in a small swimming pool if he or she is afraid of a big one.
- If the child's fear is centered on a personal need, it may be best to work on that need. For example, the child who is afraid of a monster may really have a problem of needing to be aggressive.
- Help the child learn skills for coping with fear. For example, prepare through books and dramatic play for a trip to the hospital. Do not tell the child that "It won't hurt" when it will.

Death is an especially difficult concept with which to deal. Most young children encounter death in some form whether a dead bug, a pet, or a relative. These experiences provide a component of understanding and feelings about death (Essa & Murray, 1994). Essa and Murray reviewed the research on children's understanding of (the concept level) and feelings about (the emotional level) death. Understanding the concept of death is more advanced if children have experienced a death.

Some young children may have to face their own death. It is important for adults not to transfer their own fears to the terminally ill child. They should treat death as a part of life. Preschoolers usually do not understand that death is permanent, but think it is like what they see in cartoons, where the victim may come back to life. They may see their illness as punishment for something they thought or did and will need to be reassured that this is not the case. (Lucile Packard Children's Hospital, n.d.).

Children younger than age five or six have a restricted view of death. A clearer concept develops during the five-to-seven transition period to concrete operations. During the elementary years, children begin to understand that everyone will eventually die, but they do not see the personal relevance. Understanding of death includes four basic components:

1. *Finality:* Death cannot be reversed. Preschoolers often believe that magic or medicine can reverse the process.
2. *Inevitability:* All living things will eventually die. Young children tend to believe that death can be avoided.
3. *Cessation of bodily functions:* Death ends movement, feeling, and thought. Preschoolers may view death as a type of sleep.
4. *Causality:* Understanding how death may occur. Younger children tend to focus on outside factors, such as guns or accidents, whereas older children perceive that internal factors, such as illness or old age, may be the cause.

The first three factors usually become understood between ages five and seven. Causality seems to be a more difficult concept and is understood later.

Other factors that must be considered besides cognitive development are culture, experience, and environment. Seeing characters on television rise from the dead may distort young children's concepts of death. Different cultures may vary in their views of death. For example, some cultures view death as a "deathman." Children who live in an environment that is war torn or who live in a violence-prone inner-city neighborhood have early firsthand experiences with death (Alat, 2002; Essa & Murray, 1994).

At the emotional level, mourning and grief are normal reactions, but so are anxiety and fear. As children get older, it is not unusual for their anxiety to increase. The death of a close friend or relative provokes deep emotional reactions in young children. They may even withdraw from and/or deny the fact. Adults have the responsibility of handling these situations in sensitive and supportive ways (Essa & Murray, 1994; Hogan and Graham, 2002).

Natural disasters can provoke fear and anxiety. Tidal waves, hurricanes, and fires can be very frightening for young children. In the summer of 2005, Hurricanes Katrina and Rita devastated the U.S. Gulf Coast. The city of New Orleans was nearly wiped out, and for miles on each side there was devastation. Aghayan, Schellhaas, Wayne, Burts, Buchanan, and Benedict (2005) describe how a group of preschool children, some refugees from New Orleans and some from Baton Rouge, play out their experiences and fears following Katrina. They dramatized their experiences and concerns through dramatic play and art processes and products. Their teachers provided them with emotional support, information, and attention to their fears.

The threat of war can also cause confusion and fear for young children. During the 1980s, nuclear war was of great concern to children (Beardslee & Mack, 1986). Television news and programs that depict the nuclear threat may be very frightening to children. Understanding nuclear threat appears to develop in a sequence parallel to that of death. Children ages four to six can be frightened without really understanding the phenomenon; by third or fourth grade, they begin to understand and need accurate information to come to terms with their concerns. Young children can be reassured, but extensive explanations will only confuse them (Children's Nuclear Fears, 1984).

Today, war can be with us in our living rooms through on-the-spot live action reporting. In 1999, the reporting of the air war over Serbia demonstrated the power of modern communications technology. It also brought to adult attention the fearful nature of war as perceived by young children. After the September 11, 2001, terrorist attack, the threat of terrorism provoked fear in young children. Well-known experts (Brazelton, 1991; Rogers & Sharapan, 1991) were called on to offer advice on dealing with children's fears. At this writing, the war in Iraq is affecting the lives of families and children. Adults must be honest about the danger and reassure children that they will take care of them and keep them safe. It is also more important to listen to children and help modify their misinterpretations than to offer long explanations that may only confuse and frighten them. Through discussion and dramatic play, young children's fears about the danger of war can be calmed. Finally, television viewing and radio listening should be kept to a minimum so that children are not overwhelmed by the apparent nearness of the conflict. Hogan and Graham (2001) provide an overview of possible reactions of children to tragic events and suggestions for helping children to cope.

**stress**

"Nonspecific response of the body to any demand that exceeds the person's ability to cope, a person-environment relationship that threatens or taxes personal resources, and a mental state in response to strains or daily hassles" (Honig, 1986, p. 51).

## Stress

An element closely related to fear and anxiety is **stress** (Honig, 1986; Mills & Spooner, 1988; Swick, 1987). Stress has been defined in various ways (Honig, 1986, p. 51), such as *nonspecific response of the body to any demand that exceeds the person's ability to cope, a person-environment relationship that threatens or taxes personal*

Considering what you have read about fear and anxiety, comment on the following incidents:

- Kayla is three-and-a-half years old. Kayla is asked to get a dishcloth from the basement. She initially agrees and goes to the top of the stairs. She then comes running back to her aunt and says, "I can't go down there." Her aunt responds, "Why not?" Kayla, "It's scary." Her aunt, "Could you go if Johnny (her older brother) went with you?"

  One minute later.

  "Did you get it?" asks her aunt. "It's scary (voice quivering), will you come with me?"
- Carlos is four years old. Carlos wanted to go outside to play. Because he lives in a single-parent family with a mother who works full time, Carlos rarely gets an opportunity to go outside. Either his mother is tired from working all day, or it is dark by the time they get home from work and child care. His sitter thought it would be fun for him to go outside. He was not very active at first, even though other children were playing in the vicinity. Before long, he was interacting somewhat with the neighborhood children. A boy who was about eight years old decided to climb a nearby tree. Carlos watched him closely, but became panicked the higher the boy climbed. The sitter thought he was worried about the boy possibly falling out of the tree. As they watched, Carlos became more and more agitated. His sitter asked him what was wrong. Carlos answered, "The tree is going to tip over!"

*resources, and a mental state in response to strains or daily hassles.* Stressors may come from illnesses, fear of failure, teasings about physical appearance, fear of loss of love, poverty, catastrophe, hospitalization, disasters, (e.g., a storm or an earthquake), nuclear threat, war, terrorism, birth of a sibling, death, separation and divorce, and step families. Each child reacts differently to the same or similar stressors depending on what the stressor personally means to the child (Honig, 1986). The stress response is made up of several stages (Honig, 1986):

- *Stage of alarm:* Physiological changes, such as changes in blood pressure or heart rate, come with the initial feeling of not being able to cope. Often, psychosomatic symptoms develop into illness, so stressed children may get sick more often than other children.
- *Stage of appraisal:* The same event may or may not be identified as stressful by different children, depending on their beliefs and previous experiences.
- *Stage of searching for a coping strategy:* Some strategies are adaptive and some are not. Tears and tantrums are not very adaptive. Ignoring, compromising, or finding a substitute activity are adaptive.
- *Stage of implementing coping responses:* Coping responses are the means used to deal with stress. They can take on different forms:

  a. Defensive strategies may be used to distort or deny that there is something disturbing the child. They may act compulsively or rigidly.
  b. Externalization is a process in which children attribute control to fate or to other people. They cope with stress by lashing out and blaming others for their problems.
  c. Problem solving may be used to try to find a way to lessen the stress.
  d. Instrumental coping involves using skills and knowledge to improve the situation.

Adults can help children by protecting them (i.e., reducing stress in the environment) and by helping children learn about how to deal with stress (Cadiz, 1994; Honig, 1986).

Today's young children are exposed to numerous stressors in the world, at home, in the community, and at school (Witkin, 1999). Because stress has a cumulative effect, as Honig (1986) has suggested, adults need to try to eliminate as many stressors as possible. Research by Burts, Hart, Charlesworth, and Kirk (1990); Burts, Hart, Charlesworth, Fleege, Mosley, and Thomassen (1992); and Hart, Burts, Durland, Charlesworth, DeWolf, and Fleege (1998) indicates that developmentally inappropriate instructional practices (as defined in Bredekamp, 1987, and Bredekamp & Copple, 1997) produce significantly more observed stress behaviors (e.g., lying on the desk, playing with body parts or clothing, playing with objects) in kindergartners than does more developmentally appropriate instruction. Workbook/worksheet curriculum is more stressful than hands-on/concrete experiences curriculum. Additional stress is added by the use of inappropriate assessment practices that require young children to take standardized group paper-and-pencil tests (Fleege, Charlesworth, Burts, & Hart, 1992). This research suggests that eliminating developmentally inappropriate instructional and assessment practices could greatly reduce school-based stress for young children.

Stressed young children are a concern in other countries. For example, Bagdi (2004) describes the widespread prevalence of stress in India. Children ages eight to fourteen are so stressed by academic pressure that 35 percent need clinical help. Children as young as four years old are pressured to complete homework, attend coaching classes, and take exams. "School is no longer merely challenging, but distressing, competitive and anxiety-provoking" (p. 204). Further, there is no time for play, which could provide outlets for stress and time for relaxation.

Adults who work with young children can help them develop the resilience to cope with stress and trauma in their lives. Children who survive stressful childhoods and traumatic events either have families or other adults, such as teachers, who provide needed support and understanding (McCormick, 1994; Melson, Windecker-Nelson, & Schwarz, 1998; Novick, 1998; Zimmerman & Arunkumar, 1994).

## Hostility and Anger

**hostility**

Emotion that underlies aggressive behavior.

**anger**

See *hostility*.

**Hostility** and **anger** are the emotions that underlie aggressive behavior. Infants may appear angry when they cry loudly, flail their arms and legs, get red in the face, and breathe heavily. We do not know for sure that the baby feels anger in the same way as the older child or adult, but he or she appears, at least, to be angry. The behavior mimics later temper tantrums. The problem for the young child is to learn to control the expression of these angry, hostile feelings. The child has the right to feel anger, but it is necessary to learn socially acceptable modes of expression. Dealing with hostility and anger is discussed further in Chapters 26 and 27.

Gun violence has particularly affected young children. The Children's Defense Fund's 2005 *Gun Report* states that one American child or teen is killed by gunfire nearly every three hours. Nearly 2,867 children and teens died from gunfire in the United States in 2002. In 1993, NAEYC published a position paper on violence in the lives of children (NAEYC, 1993). Efforts are being made to teach children at an early age that there are peaceful alternatives to solving problems with violence (Bernat, 1993; Boyatziz, 1997; Cain & Boher, 1997; Jackson, 1997; Marion, 1997; Parry, 1993).

Research on anger has looked at the factors that make some children react negatively when hostile feelings are aroused, whereas others act in a positive manner. Strength of emotionality and controllability of emotions and actions have been studied. Eisenberg, Fabes, Nyman, Bernzweig, and Pinuelas (1994) examined constructive and nonconstructive factors in the anger behavior of middle-class preschoolers. Children who had overall constructive ways of coping with problems and who reacted with low-intensity emotions were more likely to use verbal methods to deal with their anger. Children who used nonconstructive coping strategies and reacted with strong emotions were more likely to react to anger with aggression. Young children who have been maltreated and/or exposed to violence between adults are likely to have poorly regulated emotional patterns and symptoms of anxiety and depression (Maughan & Cicchetti, 2002).

After reading the previous description of stress behaviors in school settings, analyze the following situation:

> The setting is a kindergarten classroom. The students are working on a worksheet. They are instructed to write the letter *A* and then draw four pictures of objects whose names begin with *A*. Finally, the students are to "label" (at the teacher's direction) their pictures using "words." The children at Molly's table were working quietly when one of the girls called out to the teacher, "Mrs. Brown, Molly messed up!" Mrs. Brown went over to investigate and found that Molly was crying. Molly had not written her *A*s within the lines and was distraught. Mrs. Brown tried to rectify the situation by giving Molly a new worksheet but discovered she did not have any additional sheets. She put her hand on Molly's shoulder and said she would get her another worksheet that Molly could work on at home. This pacified Molly, who dried her eyes and continued her coloring.

## Happiness and Humor

**happiness**
The expression of positive emotions, such as pleasure, joy, and delight.

**Happiness** is the expression of positive emotions, such as pleasure, joy, and delight (Lewis & Michalson, 1983). Smiling is the most popular cue to happiness. We have already described the development of the smile. Whether early smiles are really a reflection of happiness, we do not know, but they definitely give the caregiver a positive signal. About a month to as long as 12 months after smiling for the first time, laughing usually appears. Lewis and Michalson did not find any developmental trend in happiness: It was either there or not there. Children older than nineteen months showed more happiness than younger children. Hestenes, Kontos, and Bryan (1993) found that children in higher-quality child care centers with teachers who displayed more smiling and laughing smiled with greater intensity than children in lower-quality centers.

**humor**
Understanding (jokes, riddles, etc.) that requires a higher level of cognitive development than that required as a response to tickling and peek-a-boo games that provoke laughter in infants.

Understanding **humor** (e.g., jokes, riddles) requires a higher level of cognitive development than responses that provoke laughter in infants. Infant smiling and laughing is provoked by tickling, bouncing, and peek-a-boo games (Poole, 2005). Toddlers also enjoy hide-and-seek and chase and tease. Toddlers enjoy imitating silly things that adults do. Three- and four-year-olds enjoy being silly (Miller, 2005). They like to make funny noises, make up funny stories, and do silly things. Four-year-olds may be getting into "Knock-Knock" jokes, which they learn from older children. They may have one joke, which they tell over and over. By kindergarten age, children are usually compiling a collection of Knock-Knock jokes (Church, 2005). The predictable pattern in Knock-Knock jokes makes them easy to remember and repeat. Their increasing vocabulary enables them to use language in a variety of ways that appear humorous to them. Kindergarteners enjoy entertaining with silly movements and slapstick falls. They tend to share bathroom humor with their close friends. Being silly and laughing together is a major social activity. Laughter feeds the brain with blood, which increases the receptivity to learning by energizing the mind and increasing alertness.

## Teacher's Beliefs

Research by Hyson and Lee (1996) focused on early childhood practitioners' beliefs about emotions. The practitioners were teachers of children ages four through six. A teacher sample from the United States and Korea responded to a questionnaire regarding their beliefs about emotions. Findings indicated that education level is an important factor. American teachers with more education strongly believed that a strong emotional bond should exist between adults and children, that adults should talk with children about emotions, that children have the ability to control their emotions, and that it is less essential to protect children from unpleasant or strong emotions. Teachers with degrees in early childhood education agreed more strongly that teachers should be emotionally expressive and that children should be able to display their emotions in acceptable ways. Korean teachers were more likely than American teachers to believe that teachers should avoid emotional demonstrativeness and that children should be protected from emotionally distressing events.

## Recognizing and Regulating Emotions

Developmentally, children learn to recognize their own emotions before learning to interpret those of others. Children also recognize positive emotions before negative ones.

Lewis and Michalson (1983) found that when children as young as two years of age were requested to make faces, indicating specific emotions, they could make several different kinds of faces, such as happy, sad, angry, and surprised. By age four, they could make happy, sad, angry, funny, surprised, and scary faces. The difference may reflect that two-year-olds have less well-developed muscular control, have fewer labels, and/or become bored with the game sooner than four-year-olds. The two-year-olds could also identify pictures of happy, sad, angry, and disgusted faces as they fit a story they were told. Lewis and Michalson conclude that by age six, children know when and how to express emotions.

Carroll and Steward (1984) investigated the role of cognitive development in children's understanding of their own feelings. They looked at the relationship between performance on classification and conservation tasks and understanding of feelings with four- and five-year-olds and eight- and nine-year-olds. The children were asked questions such as, "How do you know when you are feeling happy?" and "How do I know when you are feeling happy?" Carroll and Steward found that preoperational children explained feelings in situational rather than more generalized terms. That is, preoperational children saw happiness as having an ice cream cone, while concrete operational children would refer more to situations and inner feelings. Younger children with high verbal intelligence also gave more sophisticated answers.

Besides recognizing emotions, children also need to learn how to regulate them. Katz and McClellan (1997) define emotional regulation as being able to meet experiences with a range of socially acceptable emotions and to delay reactions when needed. Emotions serve as motivation for problem-solving and other activities. Emotional patterns are well established by the preschool period and are indicative of future social success (Eisenberg, Fabes, Shepard, Murphy, Guthrie,

Jones, Friedman, Poulin, & Maszk, 1997). Children move from relying on parental regulation to regulating themselves. Some children overregulate their emotions and, therefore, do not take part in social situations that might arouse emotions. Children with high-quality social functioning have a high level of regulation competency. Children with low-level regulation competency have low-level social functioning.

## PERSONALITY

**personality traits**

Develop from initial genetic temperament characteristics as children experience their environment.

Characteristics such as cute, funny, happy, well adjusted, confident, aggressive, shy, feminine, and masculine are what we usually think of as **personality traits.** In Chapters 10 and 13, infant temperament was discussed. Research indicates that infants are born with definite temperamental characteristics that may be modified by parental child-rearing practices. While temperament places some constraints on how the most extreme personalities develop, children tend to move toward the middle as they grow. This chapter examines several characteristics and areas of development that contribute to personality development: sex roles and sex-typing, sexuality, self-concept, and cultural differences in personality development.

### Sex-Typing and Gender Roles

A major aspect of the individual's personality is reflected in how he or she perceives himself or herself as either male or female. Maier (1978) states that "young individuals begin to notice sex and other role differences among those in their environment, which affect both their own self-definition and the course they must pursue according to the social demands of their society." The girl must identify with the female and the young boy with the male. Each has to take on the behaviors society says are appropriate for males and females.

The question of nature versus nurture and their effect on personality development continues to be studied. Sex-typing and gender roles have been the focus of much research. Lehman (1997) describes the complexity of gender roles and questions of nature and nurture influence. According to Lehman, **sex** and **gender** are defined as follows (p. 47):

**sex**

The anatomical and physiological characteristics we call male and female.

**gender**

The social and cultural overlay that makes a man "masculine" and a woman "feminine."

> . . . "sex" describes biology—the anatomical and physiological characteristics we call male and female. "Gender" signifies the social and cultural overlay that makes a man "masculine" and a woman "feminine."

Sex is a fixed characteristic, except by surgery and hormones, whereas gender is socially and culturally created. Gender refers to the roles and characteristics associated with males and females across time and across cultures. Since ancient times, Western cultures have applied the same characteristics to men and women (Lehman, 1997, p. 49; How to understand, n.d.):

> Masculine traits still include strength, courage, independence, competitiveness, ambition, and aggression. Feminine qualities still include emotional sensitivity, patience, caution, nurturance, passivity, and dependence. Men are taught to place higher value on power, and women to place higher value on interpersonal relationships.

The nature, or biological, view perceives male and female role differences as genetic, whereas the nurture, or cultural, view perceives these differences as more affected by cultural and societal beliefs.

The development of sex roles is a complex process. We will examine the development of sex-role standards or stereotypes, sex differences, and sex-typing.

**sex-role standards**

Behaviors that society regards as appropriate for males and females.

**Sex-role standards** are those behaviors society regards as appropriate for males and females. Since the 1970s, there has been a growing concern that expectations for males and females are stereotyped; that is, society has set up pictures of males and females that are not necessarily true, fair, or needed. During the late twentieth century, women led a movement to break down these stereotypes and to open more options for careers and combining careers with parenthood.

Jalongo (1989) reviewed the research on career education and sex-role stereotypes. She found that sex-role stereotypes in career awareness take hold in early childhood and become stronger as children grow older. By second grade, boys were found to be more knowledgeable regarding their fathers' occupations and were able to identify twice as many career options as girls. Although older girls are aware of many career options, they tend to perceive themselves in more stereotyped positions. Maternal employment influences females' perceptions of career options. Mothers who are satisfied with their careers tend to have daughters who have higher career aspirations. Fathers are also influential. By the end of high school, both boys and girls tend to identify with the career attitudes of their fathers. Brookins (1985) found that African American children whose mothers worked had a more egalitarian view of sex roles than comparable children whose mothers were not employed. Children whose mothers were in higher-level occupations expressed a broader range of occupational choices than children of mothers in lower-level occupations. Jalongo (1989) concludes that career education should begin with preschoolers and be integrated throughout the educational process. More efforts need to be aimed at breaking down stereotypes and encouraging boys and girls to survey the variety of choices available, not only occupationally but in other interests and activities as well.

**gender equity**

Treating both males and females with fairness.

Consideration of gender roles is an important element in the classroom. Evans (1998) points out some of the gender-related factors observed through research in early childhood classrooms. This research indicates that much gender inequity is present in early childhood classrooms. Evans also outlines guidelines for promoting **gender equity.** Girls are more likely to be praised for appearance, cooperation, and obedience, and boys for achievement. Furthermore, boys may be praised for playing with blocks, while girls are praised for playing with dolls and cooking in the housekeeping center. Boys tend to get first choice on the more active playground equipment and more playground space. Children's literature, both storybooks and textbooks, have been cited for promoting gender inequity by depicting males as strong and assertive and females as passive and nurturing. Evans suggests the following guidelines for combating gender inequity:

- Use unbiased literature that reflects diversity and does not promote stereotypes.
- Promote unbiased play activities. Encourage boys to take on nurturing roles and girls to take on assertive roles. Dramatic play props should include equal amounts of materials that promote a variety of role taking and should be available to both boys and girls.
- The curriculum should be unbiased and provide a variety of experiences that involve both boys and girls.

Trepanier-Street and Romatowski (1999) reexamined the influence of children's literature on children's gender-role perceptions. Previous studies demonstrated the short-term effects of decreased stereotypical views of gender roles through the use of unbiased children's literature. Trepanier-Street and Romatowski looked at young children's views and choices of occupational roles. Their sample included preschool through first-grade boys and girls. Six unbiased books were selected and served as the focus for related classroom activities. The results reflected less biased selections of either strictly male or female occupations and an increase in selections of occupations as being appropriate for both sexes.

Television has been examined as an influence on gender role socialization and the preservation of stereotypes (Signorielli, 1998; Witt, 2000). Signorielli pointed out that women are consistently underrepresented and are younger than men, with an emphasis on the women's good looks. Witt (2000) points out additional gender bias (p. 322);

- Men usually dominate women.
- Men are portrayed as being strong, smart, violent, and having other powerful characteristics.
- Women are portrayed as being sensitive, attractive, submissive, and having other nonpowerful characteristics.
- Marriage is emphasized for women, but not for men.

Men are portrayed in professions, whereas the majority of working women are in low-paying, unskilled jobs. Males dominate children's programming. Children who watch television have more gender-stereotyped views than those who don't watch television.

A popular stereotype views girls as having less capability than boys in skills related to mathematics and technology. To examine this view, Yelland (1999) devised an experiment where she paired young children about six years of age boy–boy, girl–girl, and boy–girl. Each pair took part in "Get the Toys," a computerized maze activity in which a turtle had to be directed to pick up a toy. The children were required to draw a picture of the most efficient route. The girl pairs were much more successful in solving the problems. The girls exhibited more forethought and planning in finding solutions. They evaluated each step. On the other hand, the boys were more impulsive and physical, jockeying for position at the computer. They tended not to reflect on their moves and usually stuck with each move rather than making modifications that might put the turtle in a better position.

Consider the following anecdotes. How do the children's activities and views relate to what you have read about gender roles?

- Jennifer enters her kindergarten classroom to select some toys to play with. She looks around at the toys for a minute. She picks up some trucks and then puts them down. Next, she examines a ball. Finally, she picks up a doll. She moves its arms and tries to pull hair off the doll's face. She then looks for some doll clothes. After finding some suitable clothing, she spots some purses. She picks out a purse and announces that she and her doll are going shopping.
- Preschooler Kayla, age five, and two friends are playing at the water table, washing clothes. The three girls take turns washing and laying out the clothes to dry. They are having fun, laughing and talking. George also wants to play. Kayla tells George that washing clothes is for girls and boys do not wash clothes. George argues back saying, "I can wash the clothes if I want to!" Kayla persists in stating that washing clothes is what girls do, not boys. Her friends agree and tell George the same thing. The girls and George argue for a few minutes until George decides it is not worth the fight. He leaves and goes over to the LEGO® table and begins to build cars with the boys.

**sex differences**

Examined from a variety of aspects to determine which are biologically determined and which are socially determined.

**Sex differences** have been examined from a variety of aspects to determine which are biologically determined and which are socially determined. Shapiro (1990) interviewed researchers regarding their findings. The long-standing differences in verbal behaviors (favoring girls) and mathematics (favoring boys) have been narrowing. However, some differences do seem to hold up. Boys, for example, tend to be more active, but the differences are very small during the early preschool years. By age four or five, children seem to adopt stereotypic roles no matter how hard their parents may try to leave all avenues open to them. Boys work out their aggressive impulses through active gun play; girls by using verbal put-downs and being socially cruel (i.e., "We don't want to play with you"). By the time children reach elementary school, they usually select playmates of the same sex. They may have contests that place the boys against the girls, engage in pollution rituals (i.e., one sex is contaminated by the others), or invasion rituals (i.e., one sex teases or interrupts the other sex's games). Overall, boys engage in more play with motion and include more conflict in their play. Girls tend to solve their problems in more low-key ways (Garvey, 1990).

Other sex differences (Hales, 1998) have been discovered between the brains of females and males. Neuroscience research shows that male and female brains differ in size, structure, and sensitivities. When females engage in any activity, their neuron activity is widely spread, whereas male brain activity is focused on specific areas. While females may be monitoring several activities at once, males shut out all but their current interest. Female brains respond more intensely and accurately to emotions. When the brain is at rest, male brains relax in the area that is geared to expressions of emotion, such as aggression and violence. Female brains rest in a different region, one that is related to symbolic forms of expression, such as gestures and words. Men appear to be emotionally primitive. They are more likely to attack when aroused, whereas women are more likely to say, "I'm angry with you." Girls speak sooner, learn to read earlier, and have fewer learning disabilities than boys. It may be because girls use neurons on both the left and right sides of the brain, whereas boys draw only from the left side. Girls can draw on both the logical and creative parts of the brain. Females have more acute vision, more sensitive hearing, and sharper memories than males. This may be because females can categorize more clearly by attaching emotional factors, as both the right and left sides of the brain are used simultaneously. Finally, the female brain is more intuitive. The frequent right–left crossovers may enable females to make connections that would never occur to males. Females are more adept at reading what others' behavior may mean.

It is difficult to separate the effects of societal forces on male and female behavior. For example, when it comes to aggression, girls are more likely to receive a verbal explanation, and boys are more likely to be punished with no explanation. This factor might account for the fact that boys misbehave more often than girls. Even in book reading, gender differences have been observed; parents use more emotion words with girls than with boys. Although the study of women has been popular, it may be men who are in need of study. Males are more aggressive, as evidenced in the higher rates of male homicides and male homicide victims. An emerging body of research indicates that the parental model may be the key. When fathers take an equal or even full-time role in the nurturant aspects of child rearing, boys are more nurturing and girls have a broader view of the roles they can aspire to in the future.

**sex-typing**

Influenced from infancy through old age by environmental factors and experience; these sex labels often influence how adults treat babies.

**Sex-typing** is influenced from infancy through old age by environmental factors and experiences. Several studies have documented that sex labels influence how adults treat babies (Honig, 1983). Infants are treated differently according to whether they have a male or female name or are wearing stereotyped male or female clothing (Honig, 1983). In one study, the same infant was dressed in pink and identified by a girl's name and then dressed in blue and identified by a boy's name. Each adult who played with the baby viewed the infant as definitely showing typical male or female characteristics depending on the identifying name and outfit. When adults thought the baby was a girl, they offered her dolls to play with, commented on the baby's "femininity" and sweetness, and were more nurturing. When adults thought the baby was male, they commented on the baby's strength and size, did not offer dolls to play with, and gave more encouragement for physical activity. Adults who work with preschool children in child care centers were observed to behave in the same way as the adults in the laboratory setting. For example, they offered more nurturance to girls and encouraged boys to be more physically active.

It has been documented that as children move through the elementary grades, boys and girls are treated differently by their teachers. Gradually, boys' self-esteem increases and girls' decreases. Girls, it appears, are being short-changed. For example, boys get more specific, helpful comments on their work; boys are encouraged to use computers but girls are not; boys demand more attention and get it, whereas girls tend to sit back in silence (Chira, 1994).

Awareness of self as a male or female, that is, exhibiting interest in masculine and feminine activities and behaviors, is observable in the child's earliest years. A two-year-old girl may want to use mommy's perfume and lipstick and wear dresses with lace trim. Preschool girls may perceive themselves as Disney princesses. A boy of the same age may confine his play to trucks, cars, and blocks. In these earliest years, children go back and forth in their interests but usually move gradually toward the behaviors expected by society as they reach age six or seven. Studies of preschoolers (Hyun & Choi, 2004) and kindergartners (Blaise, 2005) document that they already are deeply into socially constructed gender roles. A number of forces shape the child's sex-role behavior. These forces come from family, television, teachers, and peers. From the time blue booties are put on boys and pink booties on girls, boys and girls are treated differently by adults and reinforced for imitating same-sexed models (Figure 25–8).

**sexuality**

"Includes the biological nature of the person, the physical aspects of sex relations, and many other aspects of sex-linked behavior" (Lively & Lively, 1991, p. 21).

Children can be taught either gender-biased or unbiased views. Keener (1999) examined variations in gender-equitable teaching practices across early childhood classrooms and the relationship between gender-equitable teaching practices and other program variables that indicate quality. Keener found that the higher the environment is rated regarding furnishings, personal care routines, and interactions, the more likely that classroom practices are gender equitable. Higher-quality programs are more likely to use gender-equitable teaching practices.

FIGURE 25–8 In an accepting environment, young girls and boys will play together.

## SEXUALITY

The development of the child into an adult who feels comfortable and satisfied in his or her role as a male or female begins in infancy (Lively & Lively, 1991). "**Sexuality** is the term that includes the biological nature of the person, the physical aspects of sex relations, and many other aspects of sex-linked behavior" (Lively & Lively,

Think back to your early childhood years. Who do you think had the most influence on your gender-role development? Was it your parents, brothers and sisters, peers, or others? If you had siblings of the opposite sex, were you treated differently? Were there different rules and expectations? Compare your experiences with the experiences of others in the class.

1991, p. 21). Learning about anatomy and reproduction are important aspects of the child's developing sexuality. Lively and Lively (1991) emphasize that the primary focus for the adult in supporting the development of children's sexuality is taking a positive and natural approach that demonstrates love and acceptance to children, not specific sex instruction (Figure 25–9).

Anatomy is ordinarily learned in the home as the child sees other family members when they are not wearing clothes. If not, it may be learned at nursery school or from neighborhood playmates. In preschool groups, there are usually some very curious children who consistently follow their peers to the bathroom for observation. In a group of two-year-olds, a crowd of children will gather each time a child has to be changed after wetting his or her pants. This is normal and natural behavior for this age, based on curiosity. Thackeray and Readdick (2003–2004) questioned four-year-olds regarding their knowledge of the names of sex-related anatomical body parts. They found that most children did not know the correct names. They suggest that young children should be taught the correct names rather than slang terms or no names in order to develop positive attitudes. The trust built with parents and other caregivers during the infant and toddler years prepares the child for healthy sex education during the preschool period (*The Development of Sexuality*, 2006). Child sexuality develops gradually with individuals moving at their own rate.

Around age three, children become interested in reproduction. It is around this age that they will ask, "Where did I come from?" or "How do people get babies?"

Anne Bernstein (1976) asked 60 boys and girls, all of whom had younger brothers and sisters and all of whom were white and middle or upper class, "How do people get babies?" One-third of the children were preoperational three- and four-year-olds, one-third were concrete operational seven- and eight-year-olds, and one-third were eleven- and twelve-year-olds who were just entering formal operations. The children answered her question at six developmental levels, as outlined in Figure 25–10. Most of the preschool children were at Level one, geography, or Level two, manufacturing.

**FIGURE 25–9** Many activities are enjoyed by both girls and boys.

The child at Level One answers the question as if it were a geography question. That is, the child's explanation is in terms of where he or she thinks babies are located. Some examples from Bernstein (1976, p. 32) include the following:

- "You got to go to a baby store and buy one."
- "From tummies."
- "From God's place."

The Level-One child believes that each baby has always existed somewhere, just as he or she believes that all the people he or she is acquainted with have always been around, including himself or herself. The child knows

| Age Years | Stage | Parallel Piaget Stage | Characteristics |
|---|---|---|---|
| 3–4 | Geography (Level One) | Preoperational | Babies are in locations, such as a store, a stomach, or "God's place." They have always existed. |
| 3–5 | Manufacturing (Level Two) | Preoperational | Babies are put together or manufactured, just like appliances, cars, or toys. They may be perceived as placed in the mother's stomach by the father. |
| 5–7 | Transitional Physiology and Technology (Level Three) | Transitional | Realizes that love and marriage, sexual intercourse, and union of sperm and ovum are involved, but cannot get the whole process put together. |
| 8–12 | Concrete Physiology (Level Four) | Concrete Operations | Can explain conception, but does not understand why it happens the way it does. |
| 8–12 | Preformation (Level Five) | Concrete Operations | Tries to explain conception, but believes that the baby comes preformed from one of the germ cells. (The baby is sometimes thought to be the sperm itself, which is fed and sheltered by the egg.) |
| 121 | Physical Causality (Level Six) | Formal Operations | Everything starts to come together for the child. Begins to realize that both parents contribute genetically to the baby and that conception can take place without marriage. |

FIGURE 25–10 Anne Bernstein found six stages in the development of children's understanding of sex and birth. (Adapted from Bernstein, A.C. [1976, Jan.]. How children learn about sex and birth. *Psychology Today*, 31–35+.)

that babies grow in mothers' tummies but seems to have a picture of babies moving from one stomach to another as they are needed.

The Level-Two child sees babies as being manufactured, just as a car, a stove, or a toy is. The child now realizes that a baby has not always existed. For example:

> When people are already made, they make some other people. They make the bones inside and blood. They make skin. They make skin first and then they make blood and bones. They paint the blood, paint the red blood and the blue blood (Bernstein, 1976, p. 33).

Being egocentric, they can solve problems only in terms of their own experience. They know that a "seed" gets into the mother's stomach, grows, and comes out as a baby. They often adopt the **digestive fallacy.** That is, they think the baby is swallowed, develops in the mother's stomach, and then is eliminated—a process just like the one their food goes through. At this level, the child may begin to bring the father into the picture but cannot conceptualize how he gets the seed into the mother's stomach to unite with the egg. The child thinks that somehow the father unzips or unbuttons the mother's stomach and puts the seed inside.

**digestive fallacy**

Children believe a baby is swallowed, develops in the mother's stomach, and is then eliminated.

At Level Three, children are in a transition from preoperational to concrete operational thought. They might reach this level at age five but more likely will reach it around six or seven. At this stage, they realize that "social relationships such as love and marriage; sexual intercourse; and the union of sperm and ovum" (Bernstein, 1976, p. 33) are involved, but they cannot put all this information together into one coherent picture.

Preschool and kindergarten children demonstrate curiosity about reproduction, but their understanding is limited by their preoperational thinking. For this reason, the adult must be careful not to give the young child more information than he or she can handle. Too many details just confuse the child and give him or her more information to distort. Bernstein recommends that the adult first respond with questions to find out where the child is in thinking ability:

- How do people get babies?
- How do mommies get to be mommies?
- How did your daddy get to be your daddy?

She believes that children can be given explanations one level above their understanding. It is important not to laugh or make them feel stupid when they give their mixed-up explanations. For the preoperational child, what the child says is perfectly logical from his or her point of view. Bernstein suggests the following approaches for the Level One and Level Two child:

> Level-One child: The child believes that babies have always existed. The child might be told, "Only people can make other people. To make a baby person, you need two grown-up people, a woman and a man, to be the baby's mommy and daddy. The mommy and daddy make the baby from an egg in the mommy's body and a sperm from the daddy's body."

> Level-Two child: The child believes babies are manufactured. The child could be told, "That's an interesting way of looking at things. That's the way you make a doll. You could buy a head and some hair and put it all together. But making a real live baby is different from making a doll or a cake or an airplane." It can then be explained that the ingredients for making the baby are inside the mother and father's bodies. The child can also be asked to consider whether the father could really put his hand into the mother's stomach or whether there might be some other method to bring about the meeting of sperm and egg.

Bernstein cautions regarding the use of some of the available sex-education books with the preoperational child because the child often becomes confused by the amount of detail presented.

Knowledge of reproduction also comes from firsthand experiences with pets. At home or at school, mice, gerbils, dogs, cats, rabbits, or fish can offer firsthand experience with the processes of conception, pregnancy, and birth. The most important factor is to answer the young child's questions honestly and simply and accept the child's interpretations as normal for his or her age. Honest discussion of sex roles, sex differences, anatomy, and reproduction helps the young child develop healthy feelings about himself or herself as male or female.

Some topics are difficult to address. Communicating about masturbation, sex talk, and sex play is not easy (Kostelnik, Stein, Whiren, Soderman, & Gregory, 2002; Lively & Lively, 1991; *The Development of Sexuality*, 2006). Parents should be the major sex educators, but teachers also have to deal with these problems at school. Communication must be open and honest. Punishment and scolding for masturbation can cause feelings of anxiety and fear for the young child. Masturbation is not physically harmful but may hurt the child psychologically. Occasional masturbation can be ignored. Frequent masturbation may be a sign of an emotional problem that warrants professional help. Adults are also concerned with "sex talk" and "sex play"(Lively & Lively, 1991). Adults can make it clear in an honest, straightforward, nonpunishing manner that certain words are not acceptable at school. Although at age three an interest in the anatomy of others is natural curiosity and expressed openly, by age five or six children learn that adults find their interest in comparing anatomy unacceptable and they will try to conceal their activities (Lively & Lively, 1991). When caught in the act of exploring each other's bodies, children should not be made to feel guilty. It is best to just suggest another activity. This might also be an opportunity to explain that some parts of the body are private and should not be looked at or touched by others. Teachers can assist parents in their task of promoting the development of healthy sexuality in their children by offering help and advice when needed and by providing an accepting and healthy environment at school.

In summary, behaviors and teaching objectives suggested during the preschool years by the Society of Obstetricians and Gynaecologists of Canada are (*The Development of Sexuality*, 2006, p.3):

**Common Behaviors**

- Occasional masturbation (soothing or relaxing, not sexual arousal or pleasure)
- Consensual exploration of same-age playmates' bodies in a playful, curiosity-focused manner (e.g., playing doctor)
- Enjoyment of nudity
- Using slang terms for body parts and functions

**Learning Objectives**

- Teach the basics of reproduction (e.g., babies grow in the uterus of the woman, male and female are required for reproduction).
- Teach basic rules around privacy.
- Teach child that "your body belongs to you."
- Teach child the difference between appropriate and inappropriate touching.

## THE YOUNG CHILD'S SELF-CONCEPT

Shirley C. Samuels (1977) points out that early childhood is a critical period for self-concept development. The young child is still open regarding his or her feelings, and the adults who work with him or her can assess more easily how the young child feels. As children get older, they mask their feelings and it becomes harder to get underneath and find out what is really going on. Adults can help young children develop a positive **self-concept;** that is, they can help them to feel good about themselves.

**self-concept**
A person's idea about who he or she is.

The way the child handles development in the emotional and personality areas adds bits and pieces to his or her concept of himself or herself. Samuels divides the self-concept into several dimensions.

- *Body Image:* how the child views himself or herself, how he or she looks physically, and how his or her body reacts and acts
- *Social Self:* the racial, ethnic, cultural, and religious self
- *Cognitive Self:* the self as viewed in the child's mental development and aptitudes
- *Self-Esteem:* how the person evaluates his or her self-concept; how much respect the person has for himself or herself

Curry and Johnson (1991) expanded the view of self-esteem. They view **self-esteem** as a life-long developmental process. "How children feel and think about themselves is integrally tied to their physical, social, moral, emotional, cognitive, and personality development" (Curry & Johnson, 1991, p. 5). Just as children are viewed as constructors of their cognitive side, they are also now viewed as actively involved in constructing their sense of self. Their view of themselves causes them

**self-esteem**
How a person evaluates his or her self-concept; how much respect the person has for himself or herself.

to behave in certain ways. Behavior brings a response from the environment, which in turn is interpreted by the child and incorporated into the self-concept. Preschoolers have consolidated a sense of self during infancy and toddlerhood and are in a period where they are testing and evaluating that self as they strive for acceptance, power and control, moral worth, and efficacy and competence. Kindergarten and primary students are entering a new era. They are entering concrete operations and the stage of industry versus inferiority. Relationships become more complex as they venture out into the neighborhood and as they become involved in sports, scouts, camps, hobbies, and lessons. The search for power, competence, acceptance, and moral worth becomes much more complex as the child strives to meet the demands of formal schooling. We look more closely at the primary child in Chapters 30 and 31.

Self-evaluation underlies self-esteem. How one feels about one's competencies affects motivation to achieve. Stipek, Recchia, and McClintic (1992) performed a series of studies designed to examine the development of self-evaluation of achievement in children ages one to five years old. They were interested in finding out just when children begin to evaluate their own competencies and when they develop emotional responses; that is, feeling good or feeling bad. They found that self-evaluation appears to develop in three stages. In the first stage, children are not yet self-reflective and do not anticipate others' reactions to their accomplishments. They may smile when they succeed but do not show any response that would suggest pride. Just before age two, they enter a second stage in which they begin to anticipate adult reactions to their performance. They seek praise for their successes and try to avoid negative reactions to failure. At the third stage, sometime after age three, children gradually internalize external reactions to their successes and failures. They begin to evaluate their performance and react at an emotional level independent of what they may expect from adults. Stipek et al. suggest that children seem to have some concept of success and failure by age two and, therefore, adults should not impose rigid standards that might lead to young children developing a low self-evaluation and, in turn, a lack of motivation to achieve.

Schools are concerned about enhancing children's self-esteem. Formal school programs have been developed that are specifically designed to build self-esteem. Katz (1993) suggests that these programs tend to provide young children with an unrealistic and out-of-context view of themselves by providing superficial flattery and rewards, such as stars and happy faces. According to Katz (p. 1), "Esteem is conveyed to children when adults and peers treat them respectfully, consult their views and preferences . . . , and provide opportunities for children to make decisions and choices about things that matter to them." Self-esteem is built through everyday constructive activity that provides opportunities to deal with both success and failure. These experiences at school are especially critical for children who are not having positive self-esteem fostered at home.

## Children with Special Needs

Children with special needs may need extra support to enhance their self-concepts. Children with learning disabilities are especially vulnerable when they enter school (Elbaum & Vaughn, 1999). Their disabilities often do not show up until they enter kindergarten or primary grades. Programs for working with these students are described in Chapter 30. As a group, gifted students feel as good about themselves as do nongifted students (Hoge & Renzulli, 1991). Moving gifted children out of the mainstream may lower their self-esteem. It is important that children with any type of disability feel positive about themselves and that their strengths are recognized (Figure 25–11).

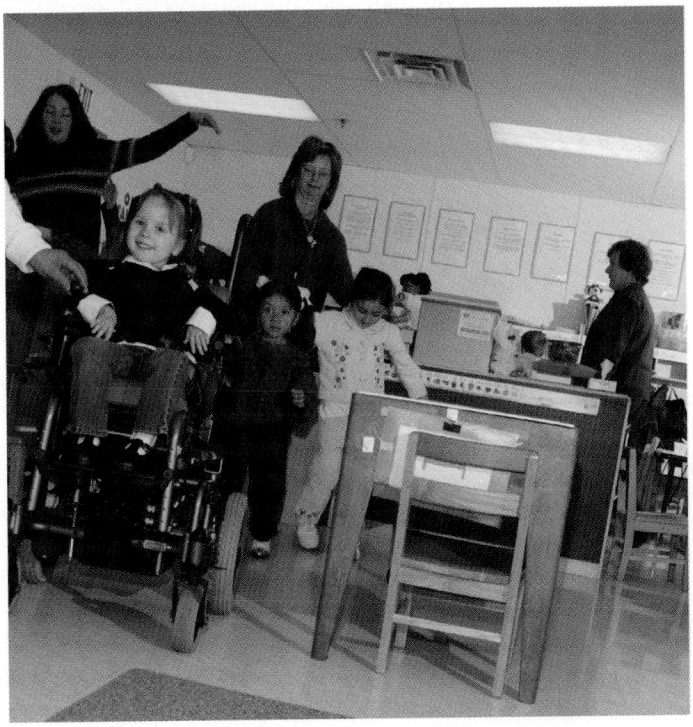

FIGURE 25–11 A young girl with a disability is happily integrated into a regular classroom.

## Racial and Social Class Factors and Self-Concept

Samuels (1977) found in looking through available research that by age two-and-a-half, children develop a racial consciousness and a sense of racial identity. The acquisition of feelings of positive self-esteem at home can give a child from a minority racial group and/or lower-class status group the strength to counter the prejudice he or she may meet outside the family. Teachers can help these children achieve their potential by supporting and maintaining their positive feelings about themselves. Social class may be an even more significant factor in self-concept than race. For example, lower-class African American children seem to have higher self-esteem than middle-class African American children.

It may be that as the child becomes integrated into mainstream society, he or she begins to make comparisons he or she would not have the opportunity to make while segregated. It may also be that the child's cultural roots are diluted and/or ignored. This implies an especially strong need for giving support to minority group children in integrated settings. The minority child can easily become lost in the crowd in a setting where it is most important that his cultural pride be reinforced. In studying the interaction patterns of African American middle-income fathers and their children, McAdoo (1979) found that the fathers were for the most part warm, supportive, and nurturing and their children had positive self-esteem. McAdoo (1979) believes that for African American children to maintain their self-esteem and achieve their potential, their fathers should have more input into their children's preschool programs.

Respect for the culture of the child must include not only language and customs but also the cultural self-concept. The self is a part of the view of one's group. For example, the African American has his roots in the African perspective regarding the self. This culture does not emphasize individuality as does the mainstream culture of North America. Nobles (1977, p. 164) states the contrast as follows:

> Self-awareness or self-conception is not, therefore, limited (as in Euro-American tradition) to just the cognitive awareness of one's uniqueness, individuality and historical finiteness. It is, in the African tradition, awareness of self as the awareness of one's historical consciousness (collective spirituality) and the subsequent sense of "we" or being one.

Cross (1985) points out the importance of the distinction between personal identity and identification with a reference group. Early studies using measures of reference group identification of African American children came up with a negative self-concept. More recent studies have used personal identity measures, and the results have been in favor of a positive self-concept for African American children. The most recent approach is to look at both types of identity as they contribute to self-concept. The results indicate that the two types of identity are not directly linked. That is, African American children with high self-esteem (personal identity) could be identified more with the African American or the European American reference group or equally with both. The troublesome factor in the findings from ethnic identity research is that minority group children tend to show a preference for white skin (Spencer & Mardstrom-Adams, 1990). Very young children appear to perceive white as being of more value. Spencer and Mardstrom-Adams (1990) cite research where young African American children were trained to a pro–African American bias; a European American experimenter was more effective than an African American experimenter. They conclude that intervention is necessary to develop a pro–African American bias.

Another factor that needs to be considered in measuring children's concepts regarding racial identity is their cognitive developmental level (Semaj, 1985; Spencer, 1985). Currently, it is believed that the negative results from the early studies of African American children's self-image resulted from neglecting the cognitive developmental factor; that is, not considering how preoperational children think. In these early studies, children were usually asked if they would prefer to play with a dark-skinned or a light-skinned doll without considering the child's reasons for his or her choice. Alejandro-Wright (1985) used a cognitive-developmental approach to examine how young African American girls develop racial categories. She designed her study from a Piagetian developmental perspective. She looked at children's spontaneous grouping in addition to researcher-imposed groupings. The children were asked to group photos of European white, African black, and Asian people by putting together the people whom they felt belonged together. The three-, four-, five-, and six-year-olds tended to use criteria other than color for their groupings. When the researcher asked them to group by black, Negro, white, and Chinese, the three- and four-year-olds picked only the darkest-skinned people (although there were darker-skinned people that adults would identify as black). The five- and six-year-olds broadened their categorization to include medium-complected people, but called these people brown. The three- to six-year-olds used only color as a criteria, ignoring hair texture and facial features. Negro was sorted in a similar way, although the three- and four-year-olds did not seem to be familiar with the term. Not until age ten did children show an understanding of these labels in the biological/physiological sense. For these young children, white included Asians and some light-complected African Americans. All except the three-year-olds could pick the Chinese correctly, but could not verbalize a reason for their choice. Until age eight, they perceived the Chinese as a European American subgroup. There was a clear developmental sequence from purely color identification through a transitional phase to an adultlike understanding. Young children seem to look at racial identity in a qualitatively different fashion than adults, guided in their understanding by their preoperational way of perceiving the world.

Racial stereotypes (both positive and negative) are already imbedded in European American preschoolers' thinking (Bigler & Liben, 1993). Bigler and Liben found that when preschoolers were presented with counterstereotyped material, they tended to distort it to fit their preconceived stereotype. Bigler and Liben conclude that just presenting children with nonstereotypic material is not enough to break down stereotypes and may even confirm the stereotype in their minds. Their research supports the need for an antibias approach, as described in Chapter 6, by all caregivers during the child's earliest years to avoid negative stereotyping.

Evaluate the following situation considering what you have learned about racial awareness and racial and cultural differences:

> Kerry, age five, and her mother are in the kitchen preparing an afternoon snack. Kerry sits on a bar stool next to the kitchen counter while her mom looks through the refrigerator to find something to eat. They discuss Kerry's day at school. Kerry says, "We had a new girl in class today. Her name is Hannah. But mom (pause), her skin is black. Why? She's not hurt is she? Was she burnt in a fire?" Kerry's mom looked surprised by the question. She stopped what she was doing and went and sat on a bar stool next to Kerry. She explained to Kerry that people come from different cultures and races. She said, "Even though some people look different from others, they are still people just like us." Kerry smiled. Kerry's mom then said, "Would you like Hannah to come over after school one day to play?" Kerry smiled and said, "Sure, you really mean it?"

## Cross-Cultural Differences in Personality Development

In Chapter 6, sociocultural factors and the adult role in learning were described. Some of these factors are reviewed briefly here because they include apparent personality differences.

African American children have been characterized as having a strong self-concept, strong motivation to achieve, and a strong religious orientation. They are people oriented and sensitive to feelings and emotions. Thus, they may respond best to a learning process that stresses human interaction rather than interaction with objects (Hale, 1978, 1981). They also need a setting that will accept an assertive personality style.

Because they are reared to show courtesy to others and respect for authority figures, Mexican American children may tend to be quiet and unassertive in school. They are affectively oriented and learn best if they like what they are doing. They work best cooperatively rather than competitively. Mexican American children have also been characterized as "field sensitive." That is, they are unusually sensitive to the environment and those in it (Cortes, 1978).

The Native American personality is characterized as self-confident, serene, and nonaggressive. This personality contrasts with the assertive, independent one emphasized in European American culture. Emotionally, Native Americans learn that shame as embarrassment, rather than guilt, is the punishment for bad behavior. Their learning style is affective; teaching is by example and cooperation and emphasizes readiness. Native Americans respond best to private rather than public recognition and a child-centered approach (Burgess, 1978).

Another cultural complication occurs when children move from one culture to another. Minoura (1993) describes the difficulties experienced by Japanese children who spent their elementary years in the United States. When they returned to Japan to live, they found they had problems relating to their Japanese peers and teachers. The Japanese custom of providing indirect communication seemed ambiguous to the Americanized Japanese, while the more direct communication of the Americanized Japanese seemed too assertive and impolite to the Japanese.

Lower-socioeconomic-level European Americans are a group about which we know relatively little. They seem to have a different cognitive style, different language patterns, and different motivations from those of middle-class European Americans.

As pointed out in Chapter 6, all these descriptions are very general. Within any one cultural group, there is wide variation and many subgroups. There are many Latino groups. Within the Native American group are many tribes, each with its own unique lifestyle, language, and values. We must also be aware of individual differences within cultural groups and be careful about making assumptions about individuals based on their membership in a cultural group.

## SUMMARY

The affective area of development can be defined by examining the theories of several psychologists: Sigmund Freud, Erik Erikson, Carl Rogers, Abraham Maslow, Jean Piaget, Lev Vygotsky, B. F. Skinner and Albert Bandura. During the early years, affective growth centers on the development of the child's picture of self. By the age of six, the child is ready to begin to look at others and society as they relate to himself or herself and to each other as they develop their egos. Early childhood is a crucial period in emotional development. Young children are learning to feel for themselves and recognize in others emotions, such as anxiety, fear, sadness, anger, happiness, and love. The attachments they make to others serve as a foundation to take the initiative and move toward independence. Children experience many kinds of fear, such as fear of monsters and goblins, death, and war. Coping with imaginary fears helps them gain the skills needed to cope with fears that have a basis in reality. Young children have to learn how to handle their emotions in socially acceptable ways. Research indicates that throughout early childhood, children are gradually learning how to label, define, and understand their own emotional behavior and that of others. The personalities of young children are reflected in their gender, their sex-role learning experiences, and their self-concepts. Although children are born with identifiable temperament characteristics, experience can have a powerful effect on their future behavior. The early years are critical ones in the development of sex-role behaviors. An unbiased education can provide children with alternatives to stereotyped views of appropriate and expected behaviors. Sex education includes the acquisition of acceptable (although non-stereotyped) sex-role behaviors, sex-role standards, and awareness of self as male or female. The young child also gains knowledge of anatomy and reproduction.

Preschool children's self-concepts continue to develop. Their racial and social class membership affects the way they perceive themselves. The adult who works with the preschool child needs to demonstrate respect for the child's unique racial and cultural characteristics.

## FOR FURTHER READING

### THEORIES

Davidson, R. J., Scherer, K. R., & Goldsmith, H. H. (Eds.). (2002). *Handbook of affective sciences.* New York: Oxford University Press.

DeVries, R., & Zan, B. (1994). *Moral classrooms, moral children: Creating a constructivist atmosphere in early education.* New York: Teachers College Press.

Kostelnik, M. J., Stein, L. C., Whiren, A. P., & Soderman, A. K. (2002). *Guiding children's social development* (4th ed.). Clifton Park, NY: Delmar Learning.

Lomax, E. M. R., Kagan, J., & Rosenkrantz, B. G. (1978). *Science and patterns of child rearing.* San Francisco: W. H. Freeman.

Maier, H. W. (1978). *Three theories of child development* (3rd ed.). New York: Harper & Row.

Mead, D. E. (1976). *Three approaches to child rearing.* Provo, UT: Brigham Young University Press.

Miller, P. H. (2002). *Theories of developmental psychology* (4th ed.). New York: Worth.

Stroul, B. A. (Ed.). (1996). *Children's mental health: Creating systems of care in a changing society.* Baltimore: Brookes.

Talay-Ongan, A. (1998). *Typical and atypical development in early childhood.* New York: Teachers College Press.

Vasta, R. (Ed.). (1992). *Six theories of child development.* London & Philadelphia: Jessica Kingsley Publishers.

Wadsworth, B. J. (1996). *Piaget's theory of cognitive and affective development* (5th ed.). New York: Longman.

## EMOTION


Brandstatter, H., & Eliasz, A. (Eds.). (2001). *Persons, situations, and emotions.* New York: Oxford University Press.

Brazelton, T. B., & Sparrow, J. D. (2001). *Touchpoints three to six: Your child's emotional and behavioral development.* Cambridge, MA: Perseus.

Brewer, M. B., & Hewstone, M. (Eds.). (2003). *Emotion and motivation.* Malden, MA: Blackwell.

Christ, G. H. (2000). *Healing children's grief: Surviving a parent's death from cancer.* New York: Oxford University Press.

Cooper, C. L., & Dewe, P. (2004). *Stress: A brief history.* Malden, MA: Blackwell.

Crittenden, P. M., & Claussen, A. H. (Eds.). (2000). *The organization of attachment relationships: Maturation, culture and context.* New York: Cambridge University Press.

Elkind, D. (2001). *The hurried child.* (3rd ed.). Boulder, CO: Perseus.

Gimpel, G. A., & Holland, M. L. (2003). *Emotional and behavioral problems of young children.* New York: Guilford.

Golden, B. (2002). *Healthy anger: How to help children and teens manage their anger.* New York: Oxford University Press.

Goldstein, S., & Brooks, R. (Eds.). (2005). *Resilience in children.* New York: Springer.

Harvey, J. H., & Fine, M. A. (2004). *Children of divorce.* Mahwah, NJ: Erlbaum.

Hyson, M. (2003). *The emotional development of young children.* New York: Teachers College Press.

Kristal, J. (2005). *The temperament perspective.* Baltimore: Brookes.

LaGreca, A. M., Silverman, W. K., Verbverg, E. M., & Roberts, M. C. (Eds.). (2002). *Helping children cope with disasters and terrorism.* Washington, DC: American Psychological Association.

Manstead, A. S. R., Frijda, N., & Fischer, A. (Eds.). (2003). *Feelings and emotions: The Amsterdam symposium.* New York: Cambridge University Press.

Mayne, T. J., & Bonanno, G. A. (Eds.). (2001). *Emotions: Current issues and future directions.* New York: Guilford.

Nelson, C. A. (Ed.). (2000). *The effect of early adversity on neurobehavioral development.* Mahwah, NJ: Erlbaum.

Oatley, K. (2004). *Emotion: A brief history.* Malden, MA: Blackwell.

Osofsky, J. D. (Ed.). (2004). *Young children and trauma.* New York: Guilford.

Silverman, W. K., & Treffers, P. D. A. (Eds.). (2001). *Anxiety disorders in children and adolescents.* New York: Cambridge University Press.

Stanford, B. H., & Yamamoto, K. (Eds.). (2001). *Children and stress: Understanding and helping.* Olney, MD: Association for Childhood Education International.

Thacker, V. J., Strudwixk, D., & Babbedge, E. (2002). *Educating children with emotional and behavioral difficulties.* New York: Routledge Falmer.

Webb, J. T. (1994). *Nurturing the social-emotional development of gifted children.* Eric EC Digest, #E527. Retrieved November 3, 2002, from http://www.kidsource.com/content2/social deveopment gifted.html.

Webb, N. B. (Ed.). (2004). *Mass trauma and violence: Helping families and children cope.* New York: Guilford.

Zeece, P. O., & Stolzer, J. (2002). Creating literature safety zones for young children. *Early Childhood Education Journal,* 30(1), 47–52.

Zubenko, W. N., & Capozzoli, J. (Eds.). (2002). *Children and disasters: A practical guide to healing and recovery.* New York: Oxford University Press.


## PERSONALITY


*AAUW Report: How schools shortchange girls.* (1992). Annapolis Junction, MD: American Association of Women.

Bornstein, R. F., & Masling, J. M. (Eds.). (2002). *The psychodynamics of gender and gender role.* Washington, DC: American Psychological Association.

Bracken, B. (Ed.). (1995). *Handbook of self concept: Developmental, social, and clinical considerations.* New York: Wiley.

Chrisman, K., & Couchenour, D. (2002). *Healthy sexuality development: A guide for early childhood educators and families.* Washington, DC: National Association for the Education of Young Children.

Damio, C. (2001, Fall/Winter). Instilling pride for both sides: Raising your biracial child. *Today's Child,* 43–45.

Ding, S., & Littleton, K. (Eds.). *Children's personal and social development.* Williston, VT: Blackwell.

Kohnstamm, G. A., Halverson, C. F., Mervie, I., & Havill, V. L. (Eds.). (1998). *Child personality.* Mahwah, NJ: Erlbaum.

Kohnstamm, G. A., Halverson, C. F., Mervie, I., & Havill, V. L. (Eds.). (1998). *Parental descriptions of child personality.* Mahwah, NJ: Erlbaum.

Lippa, R. A. (2002). *Gender, nature, and nurture.* Mahwah, NJ: Erlbaum.

Paley, V. G. (1986). *Boys & girls: Superheroes in the doll corner.* Chicago: University of Chicago Press.

Schmidt, L. A., & Schulkin, J. (Eds.). (1999). *Extreme fear, shyness, and social phobia.* New York: Oxford University Press.

Shields, S. A. (2002). *Speaking from the heart: Gender and social meaning of emotion.* New York: Cambridge University Press.

Stroufe, L. A., Egeland, B., Carlson, E. A., & Collins, W. A. (2005). *The development of the person: The Minnesota study of risk and adaptation from birth to adulthood*. New York: Guilford.

Swann, W. B., Jr., Langlois, J. H., & Gilbert, L. A. (Eds.). (1998). *Sexism and stereotypes in modern society: The gender science of Janet Taylor Spence*. Washington, DC: American Psychological Association.

Westenberg, P. M., Blasi, A., & Cohn, L. D. (Eds.). (1998). *Personality development*. Mahwah, NJ: Erlbaum.

## SUGGESTED ACTIVITIES

1. Organize a group discussion on childhood fears. On the chalkboard or on a sheet of chart paper, group members can list the childhood fears that they can remember and/or fears that their friends or relatives might have had. The list is divided into those fears that were imaginary and those that were real. How were the fears handled? Are there any lasting effects? Consider each of the following ways to handle a child's fears. Which would be the best? the worst? The group can then rank these alternatives from best to worst.
   a. Force the child to face the fear straight on. That is, make the child hold a snake or put the child in the swimming pool.
   b. Point out to the child that if he or she wants to be "grown up," he or she must stop being afraid.
   c. Help the child by developing experiences that enable him or her to gradually experience the fearful situation or object.
   d. Be a strong model. Demonstrate that you are not afraid.
   e. Ignore the fear. Say, "It will go away."
   f. Explain to the child which dangers are realistic and which are imaginary.

   Develop a rationale for the decisions.

2. Read articles and/or books that explain how to handle the subject of death with a young child. Organize a small group discussion. Have the students discuss the following list of ways to tell a young child that his or her grandmother has died. Have the group members rank each method from best to worst. From your reading, you should be able to help the group see why some of the methods might even be dangerous to the child's emotional development:
   a. Grandmother got very old and she died.
   b. Grandmother went to heaven.
   c. Grandmother died, just like your pet kitten died.
   d. Grandmother went to sleep forever.
   e. Grandmother has gone on a long trip.
   f. Grandmother was very sick and then she died.

3. Observe for 60 minutes a young child at home or a group of young children at a nursery school, child care center, kindergarten, or primary classroom. Write a description of any behaviors that indicate children are experiencing emotions, such as fear, anger, sadness, or happiness. Write a summary of the kinds of emotions you observed. What kinds of events seemed to bring about each type of emotional reaction? What kinds of behaviors gave you the clues needed to label each emotion? If you observed in a group setting, did you notice any differences between male and female behaviors?

4. Make three columns on a sheet of paper. In the first column, list three gifts you might buy if you were going to a baby shower before the baby was born. In the

second column, write down what you would buy if you knew the baby was a boy. In the third column, write down what you would buy if you knew the baby was a girl. Compare your lists. Are there any items that are the same in the three lists? With a small group in class compile your lists by writing the items in three columns on the chalkboard or on a sheet of chart paper. Decide if, as a group, you used sex stereotypes in choosing gifts.

5. Many experts believe that education has tended to support sex-role stereotypes too strongly. Do some reading on the topic and formulate a report for the class on sex-role stereotyping and early childhood education.

6. Interview some young children regarding their knowledge of sex and birth using the questions suggested by Anne Bernstein. Interview five three-year-olds, five four-year-olds, and five five-year-olds. If you do not know enough children at each age level, collaborate with some other students in the class and combine information. Ask each child individually:
"Where do babies come from?"
If the first question does not get a response, try:
"How do people get babies?"
"How do mommies get to be mommies?"
"How did your daddy get to be your daddy?"
Write down or tape-record what each child says. Compare each child's response with Bernstein's stages. Do the children you and your classmates interviewed fit into Bernstein's stages? Were there any problems in assigning a stage to the responses? Were any of the children ahead of what Bernstein found from her interviews? Any behind? What did you learn from this experience?

7. Make an entry in your journal.

## REVIEW

1. Define *affective*.
2. Match each of the theorists in Column I with their interest from Column II.

| Column I | Column II |
|---|---|
| a. B. F. Skinner | 1. Social and personality development within the social context. |
| b. Jean Piaget | 2. Self-actualization through satisfying a hierarchy of needs. |
| c. Erik Erikson | 3. Observational learning of affective-related behaviors. |
| d. Carl Rogers | 4. The interrelationships of cognitive, sociomoral, and affective development. |
| e. Abraham Maslow | 5. Modification of behavior, including affective. |
| f. Sigmund Freud | 6. The role of language in developing self-regulation through shared activities. |
| g. Lev Vygotsky | 7. Personality development, especially the development of sex-role identification and conscience. |
| h. Albert Bandura | 8. Self-concept development. |

3. Identify the affective behaviors in the following example from a case study of a five-year-old preschool child named Sean.

When he played alone, he was quiet and fully involved, yet he just did not seem as happy as the other children. Later, when Sean began playing associatively with children, he smiled more, laughed more, and even began to talk more.

From the beginning, Sean has been willing to share and take turns with others. He is very patient and considerate. Sean has extremely good manners and courtesy. Although Sean is a good listener, especially to adults, he lacks skill in communicating with others. . . . He also seems to find it hard to stand up for his own rights, as can be seen in the many times Sean passively allowed another child to take his toy, his chair, or his tricycle. He seemed to fear other children and would not use any type of skills to ease the situation.

He shows pride in his accomplishments and can get the attention of adults in socially acceptable ways. Sean will express feelings of hostility to peers occasionally but will never express affection. I did not note a single time when Sean expressed either hostility or affection to adults. Sean never destroyed anything or used any acts of physical or verbal violence toward another child. Like many four- and five-year-olds, Sean shows dependency by seeking approval and attention. Many times he has exclaimed, "See what I did!"

Sean has demonstrated fear by withdrawing. He will not answer questions and speak to the teachers in a natural, relaxed way. He withdraws when he is uncomfortable or in unfamiliar surroundings.

**4.** Write the letter of each correct statement.
   a. For Erikson, the preschool period is a time during which the child must deal with Crisis III: Initiative versus Guilt.
   b. The crises that Erikson describes are never resolved but are handled successfully if the child is able to deal with them in a positive way.
   c. Maslow's hierarchy of needs is based on the belief that some needs are more basic than others and, therefore, must be satisfied first.
   d. During Erikson's Stage III, the conscience, or sense of right and wrong, begins to develop.
   e. In Erikson's scheme, the child typically does not develop much in the way of independent behaviors until he or she is of school age.
   f. Freud's stage theory runs parallel to Erikson's stage theory and includes the same theory of personality structure: id, ego, and superego.
   g. The child who successfully completes Crisis III knows how to take initiative and do things independently without overstepping the boundaries and limitations set by society.
   h. The id operates on the pleasure principle and the ego on the reality principle.
   i. The moral values of society are held in the ego.
   j. The child's understanding of personal experiences is critical to Rogers' theory.
   k. Vygotsky is more concerned with the cognitive than with the social aspects of the adult's interaction with the child.
   l. For Bandura, the cognitive aspects of observational learning are not important.

**5.** Discuss why ego development is important from ages three to six.

**6.** Why does the young child have a "right to feel?" What does a "right to feel" mean? Relate it to emotional intelligence.

**7.** Write the letter of each correct statement.
   a. The smiles of newborns are reflexive.
   b. Children laugh and smile more often if they receive a lot of positive responses from others when they display joy and pleasure.
   c. Smiling and laughing are of minimal importance in the development of attachment.
   d. Early attachments are needed for the child to be socially successful later.
   e. Even cognitive development seems to be affected by the strength of attachments.

**8.** Indicate which of the following examples illustrate physical dependence (PD), physical independence (PI), emotionally dependent immaturity (EDI), and emotionally dependent maturity (EDM):
   a. Eighteen-month-old Maria drinks from a cup on her own with no help.
   b. Five-year-old Jason greets his mother with a smile and shows her the picture he painted in preschool today.
   c. Two-year-old Kate cuddles up on mother's lap for a story.
   d. Infant Tony is picked up by Mr. Smith and carried to the car.
   e. Three-year-old Carlos clings to his father and refuses to go into the child care group by himself.
   f. Four-year-old Isabel puts on her own coat, hat, and boots before going outside.
   g. Two-year-old Carmelita says, "No! No! Do it myself."
   h. Three-year-old Rudy stops to give his teacher, Mr. Santos, a hug before going off to build with blocks.

**9.** How are physical independence and responsibility related?

**10.** What should the adult do in each of the following situations?
   a. The child's pet kitten is run over and killed while the child is at preschool.
   b. Derrick, age four, runs in the house every time he sees the neighbor's big dog outside. The dog is friendly and loves children.
   c. Rudy, age three, wants a night-light left on in his room to scare off the ghosts and goblins.
   d. Seven-month-old Karen is introduced to a new baby sitter. Mother has taken her to the sitter's home.
   e. Rudy, age three-and-a-half, is about to go to the hospital for minor surgery.
   f. Three-year-old Rudy's grandfather has passed away. Rudy asks, "When will Grandpa be back? Do you think he misses us?"
   g. Derrick, age four, is sitting with his father watching the evening news. The reporter is telling about a disaster at a nuclear power plant far away. That night Derrick has a nightmare about the local nuclear plant blowing up.
   h. A child attends a kindergarten that is pressuring the students to use math and read workbooks and do them correctly. She becomes cranky, has frequent tantrums, and comes down with more colds than usual.

**11.** Discuss the statement "The child must learn not to become angry."

**12.** Recognition of emotions is a developmental occurrence.
   a. Can the young child recognize others' emotions as early as he can recognize his own?
   b. Which does the young child recognize first, positive or negative emotions?
   c. By age six, what milestones would you expect in the child's understanding of emotions?

**13.** Explain emotional regulation.

**14.** Write the letter of each correct statement.
   a. Infant temperament has no relationship to later personality characteristics.
   b. Sex refers to the biological characteristics and gender to the social and culturally determined characteristics that identify a person as male or female.
   c. It is not important for boys and girls to take on the approved sex-role behaviors defined by society as a whole.
   d. Those behaviors that society says are appropriate for males and females are called sex-role standards.
   e. In the United States, standards for males and females are not very different.
   f. It is usually expected that females are more passive, loving, sensitive, and supportive.
   g. Sex-role stereotypes that set up male and female standards with no common elements have been highly criticized.
   h. Young children's gender roles may be influenced by teaching practices in their classrooms.

i. Children's literature can be a powerful tool in promoting equitable gender-role perception.
j. Sex-role stereotypes in career awareness do not appear until around twelve years of age.
k. Logically, it is impossible for a person of either sex to be both warm and nurturing and assertive and competitive—the characteristics just do not mix.
l. Research now indicates that the differences in favor of boys compared to girls on math achievement are disappearing.
m. Of great concern regarding sex differences is the increasing incidence of men's aggression resulting in murder.
n. There is strong research evidence that, in early childhood, girls are more dependent, fearful, timid, and anxious than boys.
o. Boys have been found to have higher achievement motivation and to be more competitive than girls.
p. Boy pairs are better, more logical planners than pairs of girls when faced with a problem to solve.
q. Neuroscientists have discovered that females use much more of their brain than males do.
r. The female role in our culture is more clearly defined than the male role.
s. Lower-class children take on stereotyped male and female sex-role behaviors earlier than do middle-class children.
t. It appears that children whose mothers are employed may have a broader view of the career possibilities open to them.
u. Most people tend to treat boys and girls exactly the same.
v. We can expect to find kindergarten girls playing with girls and kindergarten boys playing with boys.
w. The most feminine girls usually play with each other.
x. Gender-segregated play during nursery school and kindergarten is detrimental to girls' adjustment in first grade.
y. Evidence of male- or female-type behavior does not usually appear before the age of four.
z. Television influences gender-role socialization and the preservation of stereotypes.
aa. Children who watch television are not affected by gender stereotypes when compared to children who do not watch television.

**15.** Match the stages in Column II with the children's answers in Column I. The children have been asked "Where do babies come from?" Each stage may be used more than once (or not at all).

| Column I | Column II |
|---|---|
| a. You go to the store and buy the head, legs, arms, body, hair, and everything, and then put it together. | 1. geography |
| b. The mother swallows the seed and it finds the egg in her stomach. Then it comes out. | 2. manufacturing |
| c. God sends one down when you need it. | 3. transitional |
| d. The baby is in the sperm. The sperm gets to the egg and then the baby can stay there and grow. | 4. concrete physiology |
| e. You go to the hospital and buy one. | 5. preformation |
| f. You get married and then the father puts the sperm in the egg some way—I'm not sure just how. | 6. physical causality |

**16.** A three- or four-year-old asks you, "Where do babies come from?" Describe how you would respond.

**17.** Select the correct answer to the following. There is only one correct answer for each.

a. How the child views himself or herself physically and motorically is referred to as
(1) social self. (3) body image.
(2) cognitive self. (4) self-esteem.

b. How the person evaluates his or her self-concept is referred to as
(1) social self. (3) body image.
(2) cognitive self. (4) self-esteem.

c. The racial, cultural, ethnic, and religious self is called the
(1) social self. (3) body image.
(2) cognitive self. (4) self-esteem.

d. In comparing race and social class and their effect on self-esteem,
(1) social class may be a stronger factor than race.
(2) race may be a stronger factor than social class.
(3) race and social class are about equal in their effects.

e. African American children may have a unique self-concept because of
(1) the struggle that African Americans have had in this country.
(2) their African heritage.
(3) their desire to not be white.

f. Past studies of African American children's self-concept have been criticized because
(1) only reference-group identity was considered.
(2) only personal identity was considered.
(3) reference-group and personal identity were considered.

g. Recent research that examined young African American children's concept of race from a cognitive-developmental point of view
(1) indicates that African American children view race differently than European American children.
(2) indicates that young children view "African American" as referring to very dark skin color rather than to a particular group.
(3) demonstrates that by six years of age, children understand the biological/physiological basis of race.

h. Sometimes a minority group child may be forced to disregard his or her cultural inheritance to succeed in the educational system.
(1) This never happens.
(2) Usually the child is allowed to carry through with both cultures.
(3) This happens often.

i. Children with
(1) a family may need extra support to enhance self-concept.
(2) siblings may need extra support to enhance self-concept.
(3) special needs may need extra support to enhance self-concept.

**18.** Discuss whether you believe that real cross-cultural differences exist in personality characteristics. Support your position.

## KEY TERMS LIST

affective
affectivity
anger
anomy
autonomy
cooperative teaching
Crisis III: Initiative versus Guilt
Crisis IV: Industry versus Inferiority
digestive fallacy
ego
emotional dependency
emotional intelligence
fear
gender

gender equity
happiness
heteronomy
hierarchy of needs
hostility
humor
id
personality traits
Phallic Stage
physical dependency
self-concept
self-esteem
sex
sex differences
sex-role standards
sex-typing
sexuality
shared activities
social reciprocity
sociomoral development
stress
superego

Additional resources for this chapter can be found on the Online Companion™ to accompany this text at http://www.earlychilded.delmar.com. Respond to "Time to Reflect" and "Looking Further" concepts, review various child development scenarios, and answer thought-provoking questions in the Critical Thinking Forum. Keep a daily journal by downloading the student journal available on this Web site. Complete the interactive matching exercises to reinforce concepts, and print out the child development assessment forms to use during your observation of development for children from birth to age eight. In addition, read the case studies on the Web site to reinforce important concepts in each chapter, and take a look at the multitude of Web links that are available for student research on the Internet.

CHAPTER

# 26

# Social Development

## OBJECTIVES

After reading this chapter, you should be able to:

- Describe theoretical views of social development.
- Identify the important factors regarding social relationships, social competence, and self-regulation.
- Recognize aspects of social strategies, positive and negative social responses, and how children become friends.
- Identify characteristics of sibling relationships.
- Recognize ways of helping unpopular children.
- Recognize moral realism and moral autonomy.
- Recognize and categorize examples of prosocial and aggressive behaviors.
- Know how to help children improve their social skills.
- Identify methods of supporting the moral development of young children.
- Understand important factors relevant to the social behaviors of children with disabilities in inclusive settings.

Young children are both sociable and becoming socialized during their development. They spend as much time as they can with other children if they are available. During the preschool period, young children develop enhanced oral language skills that they can use to facilitate social interactions. They become more capable of getting others to comply with their desires. The complex relationships that develop among child, family, and peers influence the child's degree of social competence. This chapter looks at some of the complexities involved in children's social development. Theoretical views, the general area of relationships, social competence, peer relationships, moral development, and social relationships in inclusive settings are examined.

## THEORISTS' VIEWS OF SOCIAL DEVELOPMENT

Erikson, Piaget, Maslow, and Rogers have all focused on the social development of the young child from one or more aspects. For Erikson (Miller, 2002), the child in Stage III centers his or her activity on play. From Erikson's point of view, play serves as a vehicle for children to work through their feelings about life. The major social task of preschool children is to develop their relationships with others. They become less socially dependent on their families and move out into the neighborhood and very often into a preschool group. Piaget (Miller, 2002) also looks at play as an important vehicle of learning for the young child. According to Piaget, play is the preschool child's major means for assimilating and adapting. Confrontations with other children are of major importance for the child's cognitive development in that they help him or her move out of his or her egocentric view of incidents. That is, confrontations force the child to see the other person's point of view. Piaget's social theory was described in Chapter 24. Piaget recognized the importance of affective bonds and social interactions (DeVries, 1997).

Vygotsky (Musatti, 1986) believed that social interaction plays a critical part in the young child's learning. Vygotsky focused on the adult as the provider of cultural knowledge and was not specifically concerned with the role of peers. However, he believes that play is related to the development of representational abilities and that play creates a ZPD that stimulates the child to overcome cognitive limitations (Musatti, 1986). Because so much play time is spent with peers, a relationship must exist between the social interaction that is included in play with peers and cognitive development.

Moral development of the young child is also seen as critical by Piaget. Piaget's social theory focuses on sociomoral development as the child moves toward autonomy and self-regulation (DeVries, 1997). The child's conceptions of good and bad and right and wrong take shape during the preoperational period. Although young children may at times do what they know is wrong, they still look upon adults as the ultimate authority and they respect that authority.

Maslow and Rogers (Mead, 1976), like Erikson, view early childhood as a time when children strive for autonomy but have difficulty giving up dependence. They still need love, acceptance, and security from adults. Social interaction is essential for young children to work on the development of a healthy *self*-concept. As children learn to adjust to others, they begin to realize that they are not the only ones in the world: The points of view of others need to be considered. Bandura's social cognitive theory also provides a view of how social behaviors are learned (Miller, 2002). From the social cognitive view, children acquire social behaviors through reinforcement or through observing and imitating models. They attend to models that they view as being attractive and/or as having power. Although parents are the earliest models, peers and teachers gain more attention as children grow older.

Some researchers from the disciplines of developmental psychology, social psychology, anthropology, and sociology have attempted to apply cognitive theory to social development. From this interest has developed an area called social cognition, made up of researchers interested in children's understanding of social events (Ruble, Higgins, & Hartup, 1983). The social cognition point of view is constructivist (refer to Piaget). That is, children take an active role in their own social development. Social cognition attempts to relate the social situation to social understanding (cognition) to the resulting social behavior. The focus is on children's views of social situations and the reasoning that leads to their behavioral responses. For example, Porath (2003) looked at how four- and five-year-olds understood "their own and others' intentions, roles, relationships, and activities in early childhood classrooms" (p. 469) Porath's study was based on Gardner's interpersonal intelligence concept (see Chapter 23). The results indicated that children who understood the roles and intentions of others were better at analyzing classroom relationships. Kindergarten students were much better at understanding others than were preschoolers.

## RELATIONSHIPS

From the pioneering work of Willard W. Hartup, considering relationships "in terms of ongoing behavioral interdependencies" has come to the forefront of social development (Collins, 1999). Rather than just looking at processes operating within or on the child, developmental change is viewed as a complex of relationships that involve the children and those with whom they associate most. In essence, changes in children affect and are affected by those persons with whom they interact. Social development is a constant give-and-take among biological growth factors and a multitude of environmental factors. While we look at specific parts, we also have to consider the interactions that surround children as they grow and develop. For example, the complex relationships among family and peer influences and interactions have been identified. However, each individual relationship is a one-to-one relationship and varies on four dimensions: similarity or difference in expertise, power, trust or distrust, and similar or opposite goal orientations (van Lieshout, Cillessen, & Haselager, 1999). How the relationship proceeds depends on the support between the two participants. Parent-child relationships, friendships, and bully-victim relationships all have their own ways of operating. Relationships within groups, such as families or schools, also have their own complexities. Therefore, as we examine a particular child, we should consider the social context of relationships within which the child is functioning.

## SOCIAL COMPETENCE

**social competence**
A characteristic that grows from and with children's relationships with others.

**Social competence** is a characteristic that grows from and with children's relationships with others. Research supports the importance and value of developing positive relationships with others during early childhood. (This research is discussed later in this chapter.) The better children get along with others, the more likely they will make a healthy and constructive adaptation to adult life. Katz and McClellan (1997) define social competence as follows (p. 1):

> . . . the competent individual is a person who can use environmental and personal resources to achieve a good developmental outcome—an outcome that makes possible satisfying and competent participation in and contributions to the groups, communities, and larger society to which one belongs.

Social competence is viewed as an essential component of children's overall competence. For example, Raver and Zigler (1997) propose a social competence model that could be used as a dimension for evaluating the success of the Head Start program. Raver and Zigler describe three types of social skills: regulation of one's emotions, social cognition (mentioned later in this chapter), and social interaction with peers (also discussed in this chapter).

**self-regulation**
The ability to control emotions, interact in positive ways with others, avoid inappropriate or aggressive actions, and become a self-directed learner.

**Self-regulation** is an essential aspect of social competence. Bronson (2000) describes a number of ways that self-regulation is defined. It basically refers to children's increasing capabilities to "control their emotions, interact in positive ways with others, avoid inappropriate or aggressive actions, and become self-directed learners" (Bronson, 2000, p. 32). Sociodramatic play settings can serve as the major stage for developing self-regulation (Elias & Berk, 2002).

Social relationships and social competence were the focus of a great deal of research during the latter part of the twentieth century (Collins & Laursen, 1999). The following sections describe what has been learned from this research.

Read the following anecdote before and after reading the rest of this chapter. Record your initial responses and thoughts about Molly's social competence and compare them with the specific applications you can make after reading the chapter.

Molly chatted sweetly with the little girl next to her. She said, "I like your colors." During story time, she interacted beautifully with the teacher and was more than willing to participate. The teacher asked the children questions about the story, such as, "Why was Matty so hungry?" Molly spoke up very quickly and answered, "Because he did not eat his breakfast."

## PEERS

Peers are those persons of equal status (i.e., age, grade, and developmental level) with whom we interact regularly. For the child in school, they are usually children of the same age. At home and in the neighborhood, they may be older, younger, or the same age. Peers serve as play companions, reinforcers, models, and friends. Learning how to enter peer groups and be accepted and attain popularity are important skills that children explore from preschool to primary age. Peers can serve as models of acceptable and unacceptable social behavior. Peers are very important to young children (Figure 26–1). When a child is unpopular and/or socially isolated, it is usually a cause for concern. Siblings (i.e., brothers and/or sisters) also have a role in peerlike social development.

It was thought at one time that peers were children only of about equal age. More recently, peers have been defined as children who interact at about the same developmental level in their play. The preschool child, confined to his or her neighborhood, may play with a wider range of children than the school-aged child who meets a variety of children of the same age in school.

Hartup and Moore (1990) provided a rationale for the importance of peer relationships and their contribution to child development. Unlike relationships with adults, child-child relationships are fairly egalitarian. That is, there is always the possibility of being dominant as well as submissive, whereas in the adult-child relationship, the adult always has the last word. Child-child interaction provides

**FIGURES 26–1a & b** Peer interaction and activity are of major importance in the social development of young children all over the world.

wider opportunities to deal with a variety of social behaviors and situations, such as cooperation, competition, aggression, disagreement, and negotiation, that may not be available in adult-child relationships. The first two years are spent mainly learning to relate to adults, whereas from age two on, peers take on increasing importance as resources not only for fun but for learning about how to get along in the social world. Longitudinal studies indicate that childhood friendships and good peer relations are necessary precursors of later mental health and adjustment.

## Peer Reinforcement and Peer Popularity

**peer reinforcement**

A critical role in children's behavior is determined by positive or negative reinforcement given by peers.

**peer popularity**

Children who gave the most positive reinforcement were likely to be very well liked by their peers.

**Peer reinforcement** plays a critical role in children's social behaviors. Giving positive reinforcement not only shapes the behavior of others but also is associated with degree of **peer popularity.** Two related studies, one by Charlesworth and Hartup (1967) and one by Hartup, Glazer, and Charlesworth (1967), defined social reinforcement and collected information on its frequency and power. Both positive and negative reinforcement categories were defined and used (The Hartup-Charlesworth System, 1973):

### Positive Reinforcements

I. Positive attention and approval. Examples: "Here, Bobby, it's coming" as Ronnie pushes a toy car to Bobby (giving directions).

   Ronnie smiles at Bobby (smiling or laughing with no accompanying verbalization).

II. Giving affection and personal acceptance. Examples: Ronnie sits between Bobby and Derrick. Bobby puts his arm around Ronnie and kisses him. The three all have their arms around each other and Ronnie hugs Derrick (physical attention and acceptance).

   Ronnie says, "I like you, Bobby" (verbal affection) "You can be the boss" (verbally giving status).

III. Submission. Examples: Ronnie gets an idea to put the ramps a different way. Bobby agrees with him (accepts another's idea).

   Ronnie drives his car with the steering wheel. He shows Bobby, and Bobby does it, too (imitation).

   Ronnie and Bobby work together to build a garage for their cars (cooperation).

IV. Giving tokens. Example: Bobby gives Ronnie two cars (voluntarily and spontaneously gives a toy to another child).

### Negative Reinforcements

V. Negative reinforcements. Examples: Ronnie and Chuck will not let Bobby and David play (noncompliance: rejection, denies an activity to another).

   Andy, frustrated and angered, says, "Get off" and "Stand up." He pulls the boys off his block building (rejects and attacks).

   Building with blocks, Andy says, "This is not the door, David" (derogation and disapproval).

It was found that four-year-olds gave more positive reinforcements than did three-year-olds (Charlesworth & Hartup, 1967). This finding is not surprising, since younger children engage in less social play with peers than do older children. The older children also gave reinforcements to more different children than did the younger children. Girls tended to reinforce girls, and boys reinforced boys. Those who gave the most positive reinforcement received the most.

FIGURE 26–2 During cooperative dramatic play, children give each other a great deal of positive social reinforcement.

More positive reinforcement was given during dramatic play than during other types of activities (Figure 26–2). The least positive reinforcement was given during participation in table activities, such as art or playing with manipulative toys, and when a child was wandering around the room.

Giving positive reinforcement was linked to popularity (Hartup et al., 1967). That is, the children who gave the most positive reinforcement were likely to be very well liked by their peers. Overall, relatively little negative reinforcement was given compared to the amount of positive reinforcement. This research indicates that, by the preschool period, reinforcement from peers becomes a powerful social factor.

Going beyond the classroom, some researchers believe that the playground provides a more natural and less restrictive context for studying children's social behavior (Hart, 1993). Ladd and Price (1993) describe a number of studies that examined the play styles of accepted and rejected children on playgrounds. Popular preschoolers appear to be those who start the year as skilled cooperative players. Preschoolers who begin the year in an argumentative fashion tend to be more likely to be rejected throughout the year. Older children follow a similar pattern. Children selected on a sociometric measure by peers as most liked demonstrate more cooperative and social play on the playground. Children rejected by peers on the sociometric measure tend to spend more time on the playground in unoccupied behavior.

Popular children are better at negotiating disagreements with peers. Black (1989) found that the children most often selected as *liked* by their peers also used positive negotiation strategies in their social interactions during laboratory play sessions. Positive strategies included acts such as agreeing to and extending peer ideas, soliciting clarification of peer suggestions, and explaining ongoing play to newcomers. Liked children were able to insert their own ideas by attaching them to peers' ideas rather than rejecting the peers' ideas outright and insisting on their own.

Ladd (1990) investigated the relationship between kindergartners' peer relationships during the first two months of school, their attitudes toward school, and their degree of academic success at the end of the kindergarten year. Ladd found that children who achieved the most satisfactory peer relationships were more successful academically and had more positive attitudes toward school. Children who were rejected early were more likely to have negative views of school and to experience less academic success. The results indicate that if children can be placed in kindergartens with preschool friends, they have a better chance of maintaining those old friendships and making a good adjustment to school. The results also point out the importance of making social skills development an integral part of the kindergarten curriculum.

## Friendship

**friendships**
Special relationships that develop with other people.

**Friendships** are special relationships that develop with other people. Friendships serve special functions for young children. Young children's friendships center on enjoyment, entertainment, and satisfaction. The goals are stimulation and excitement through high levels of fantasy play. Children repeat the same themes, such as danger-rescue, over and over again. They learn to develop means for communicating, managing conflicts, negotiating, and taking other's perspectives as they engage in dramatic play (Hart, McGee, & Hernandez, 1993). Friendships serve four major functions (Hartup, 1991, pp. 1–2):

1. Emotional resources for having fun and adapting to stress
2. Cognitive resources for both problem solving and knowledge acquisition
3. Contexts in which basic social skills are acquired or elaborated
4. Forerunners of subsequent relationships (as reported by Ladd previously)

Friendships may be viewed based on the child's view of friendship, developmental changes with age, conflict resolution, and effects on peer status.

Selman and Selman (1979) explored the development of children's ideas regarding friendship. Younger children tend to be egocentric and cannot see the other person's point of view. They have difficulty separating and seeing both a physical action and the intention behind it. When someone grabs a toy from young children, they cannot comprehend that the other person may feel he or she has the right to take the toy.

> Friends are valued for their material and physical attributes, and defined by proximity. As one child told us, "He is my friend." Why? "He has a giant Superman doll and a real swing set" (Selman & Selman, 1979, p. 71).

The child at this stage looks at what seems to adults as the most obvious physical characteristics in deciding whom he or she likes:

- Girls with long hair are nice.
- My teacher is nice because she has a cat.
- He is my friend because he gives me candy.

As children move to a higher level, they can begin to differentiate between their point of view and the point of view of others, but still may not understand the need for give and take. A good friendship usually involves one person doing what the other person wants him or her to do:

> Said one child, "She is not my friend anymore." Why? "She wouldn't go with me when I wanted her to" (Selman & Selman, 1979, pp. 71–72).

Considering that the preschool child is in the beginning stages of forming friendships, it is not surprising to find young children's friendships characterized by the following:

- one person taking the lead and another following more often than there being a real give-and-take relationship
- breaking down friendships when the follower decides not to follow
- difficulty on the part of the young child in understanding the other person's point of view

Berndt (1983) looked at social cognition, or how children view friendship, and social behavior. Sharing and helping seem to be critical factors in marking the difference between friendships and nonfriendships. Sharing and helping make a relationship special. Younger children tend to be more competitive with friends. Sharing and helping increase with age. Even in early childhood, conflicts arise between the child's desire to do what a friend wants in order to maintain the friendship and the desire for independence. Overall, to survive, friendships must be sources of gratification for both participants.

Some researchers have been interested in how friendships develop. Studies by Smollar and Youness (1982) and Gottman (1983) shed some light on this area.

Smollar and Youness (1982) looked at friendship development as it relates to social development. They found that from ages six to ten, children indicated that strangers would become friends if they did something together, such as play or talk, and/or if they shared or helped each other. Not interacting or interacting in a negative fashion means strangers will not become friends. Children over age twelve rely more on getting acquainted through talking rather than the action-oriented techniques of younger children. Maintaining a friendship for younger children depends on positive interaction. Cooperation is the means for sustaining a relationship. Children do not base friendships on personal qualities until adolescence.

How conflicts are handled is influenced by the friendship levels of the participants. Hartup, Laursen, and Stewart (1988) compared the handling of conflicts by preschoolers who were either friends or nonfriends. Conflicts between friends tended to be less "heated" than those between nonfriends. In addition, friends were more likely to end the conflict by disengaging, or turning away, rather than standing firm or negotiating. Friends neutralized the conflict by avoiding the standing-firm alternative that would end in a winner-loser outcome. Friends were also more likely to remain near each other after the conflict.

Children who are more mature at handling conflicts with friends at age three continue to be more mature at age six (Dunn, 1999).

Analyze the following friends' quarrel, applying what you have just read regarding friendships:

> Susan and Jackie, both five-year-olds, are in the front yard roller skating. After playing for some time, Susan shouts, "Fine! Then you're not my friend anymore!" and Jackie leaves for home crying. Susan runs to her mother and explains that Jackie hurt her feelings and that she did not want to play with her anymore. The quarrel centered on the fact that Jackie was bragging about her recent trip to Disneyland. Within about 20 minutes, they were friends again, and the problem appeared to be resolved.

## Siblings

**siblings**
Brothers and sisters.

**Siblings** (brothers and sisters) constitute another important social network for young children. Pepler, Corter, and Abramovitch (1982) analyzed sibling relationships and compared the relationships between siblings with those between peers. Sibling interaction consisted of both positive and negative behaviors. Siblings expressed empathy for each other. There was also frequent helping, cooperation, and affection. On the other hand, there were object struggles, verbal insults, and physical aggression. However, twice as many positive as negative behaviors were observed. Older siblings exhibited more prosocial behaviors than younger siblings. The older siblings also exhibited most of the negative behaviors. Older siblings usually retaliated to younger siblings' aggression, whereas younger siblings were more likely to give in to older siblings. Younger siblings engaged in much more frequent imitation than older siblings. This supports the importance of older siblings as models for their younger brothers and sisters. Same-sex sibling pairs exhibited more imitation than mixed-sex pairs. Younger siblings have an important role in maintaining the relationship by responding positively to their older siblings.

In comparing the sibling and peer relationships of young children, Pepler et al. (1982) looked at several factors. Mixed-age peer interaction is similar to sibling interaction in that the older child can direct the social activity and the younger child has an opportunity to imitate a more competent playmate. Sibling interaction provides an opportunity for positive and negative interactions and thus may provide a situation in which more complex social exchanges occur. Sex differences are insignificant in sibling interactions but not in peer interactions. Siblings may be so close that familiarity overrides sex differences. Pepler et al. concluded that siblings provide a unique social experience that cannot be matched by peers.

Downey & Condron (2004) looked at the relationship between being a sibling and children's social and interpersonal skills. These researchers looked at children from the Early Childhood Longitudinal Study—Kindergarten Class of 1998 through 1999. They found that children with one or more siblings did have an advantage in social and interpersonal skills as rated by their kindergarten teachers. The children with siblings were rated higher on self-control. It does appear that children learn some important social skills from interacting with their siblings.

In her studies of siblings and friends, Dunn (1999) focused on children's understanding of other's thoughts and emotions in conflict situations. She and her colleagues followed a group of children in Pennsylvania from ages two-and-a-half to four, and in England from early childhood to adolescence. High-quality play with an older sibling and engagement in pretend play with an older sibling appear to strongly affect the child's ability to understand other persons' thinking and emotions. DeHart (1999) also compares sibling and peer relationships. She particularly focuses on conflicts. Like Dunn, DeHart notes that a qualitative continuity is present in sibling-peer relationships. Children tend to have more positive feelings toward friends than toward siblings after a conflict. However, peer relationships are more likely to suffer as the result of frequent conflict. Frequent sibling conflict is associated with low-quality friendships. In her own research, DeHart has studied sibling and friend conflict and averted conflict. She found a higher frequency of social involvement between friends compared with siblings. Conflicts and averted conflicts occurred at about the same frequency with friends and with siblings. When only social engagement was considered, siblings had more conflicts and more averted conflicts per minute than friends did. Sibling conflicts were also more likely to include aggression. The only direct links from sibling-friend interaction were the number of turns per conflict and the number of aggressive acts per conflict. DeHart concludes the following (p. 299).

> Sibling relationships and friendships provide substantially different interaction contexts for young children and require them to use different social skills and strategies for managing conflict. Siblings tend to be less motivated to maintain interaction with each other than friends are, and their interactions contain more oppositions, both mutual and unreciprocated, than friends' interactions do.

Overall, sibling conflicts are more aggressive and involve less positive conflict resolution strategies than do peer conflicts.

Based on the information you have just read, analyze the following sibling interactions:

> Three-year-old Kayla is invited to play by her five-year-old sister, Joanie. Joanie was acting out a complex imaginative dramatic play situation in which she was several characters in a neighborhood setting. Her characters interacted with each other and other imaginary characters. It appeared like a one-person play. Joanie invited Kayla to play. Kayla entered the scene as various characters imitating Joanie. The play continued for several minutes.

## Social Isolation and Unpopularity

**social isolates**

Persons who seldom, if ever, interact with peers, or may attempt to interact but are rejected.

As already indicated, when children are in groups, differing degrees of popularity are apparent early in the school year. Some unpopular children may be **social isolates** who seldom, if ever, interact with peers, whereas others may be children who attempt to interact but are rejected (Roopnarine & Honig, 1985). An unpopular child may be shy and withdrawn or disruptive and aggressive. The unpopular child is the one whom other children choose least often as being someone with whom they would like to play. This has become an important area for study since it has been discovered that peer rejection during the elementary school years is predictive of school dropout, antisocial behavior, delinquency, sexual disorder, and psychopathology in adolescence and early adulthood (Rubin, 1982). If children who are isolated and unpopular can be discovered early, they may be helped to develop social skills. However, although we can probably be assertive in working with children who are aggressive and/or have difficulty in entering play groups, caution should be taken with children who are shy. It is estimated that approximately 15 percent of all children are born with a predisposition to shyness (Bullock, 1993). Adults must be supportive of these children because they are even more likely to back off from new situations if they are pushed (Bullock, 1993).

In a review of research on unpopularity, Roopnarine and Honig (1985) found that popular children tend to play with other popular children, and unpopular children play with other unpopular children. Thus, unpopular children have little, if any, opportunity to observe the behavior of popular children. Unpopular children spend their time differently than popular children. Rejected children spend more time in verbal and physical aggression. When they try to make social contacts, they are rejected. Rejected children wander, look on, and hover on the edge of activities. When they do enter a group, they are often ignored. Popular children give and receive more positive reinforcement than unpopular children.

Research indicates that children with good early family relationships "often are more popular in nursery school, tend to engage frequently in more social contact, and are more effective in offering guidance and suggestions to others. . . . Poor family relationships are also accompanied by dependence on the teacher and poor impulse controls" (Hartup & Moore, 1990, p. 10). Rejected children, with their inept modes of interacting, meet persistent and recurring social failure and diminish the number of opportunities to attain more positive social skills.

Rubin (1982) targeted isolated preschoolers and observed their play behaviors. He found that their play was less cognitively mature. They played fewer social games and participated in less dramatic play. Both of these kinds of play correlate with higher-level cognitive functioning. In this sample of children, in contrast to their more aggressive peers, the social isolates were just as popular as the more sociable children. When placed in a situation with another child, the isolates were more likely to talk to themselves. Their speech was at a more egocentric level. They also talked more to inanimate objects than did more sociable children. The more social group had higher mental ages than the isolate children. The isolates' mental ages could be depressed due to a lack of social play experiences that enhance cognitive development.

Coplan, Rubin, Fox, Calkins, and Stewart (1994) looked in more detail at children who spend most of their time alone. These researchers defined three types of withdrawal behavior:

1. *Solitary passive play* involves playing quietly with objects and/or constructive activity while playing alone. This type of play is reinforced by adults and accepted favorably by peers during early childhood.

2. *Solitary active play* involves repeated motor activity with or without objects and/or solitary dramatizing. This type of play is usually associated by adults with being aggressive, impulsive, and immature and is associated with peer rejection.
3. *Reticent behavior* is defined as looking at others without any accompanying play, that is, onlooking and unoccupied. It seems to indicate anxiety about joining a group, possibly due to fear of rejection or lack of confidence regarding how to enter.

The Coplan et al. (1994) study involved observations of preschoolers in play groups of four to see if the three types of solitary behavior defined actually would occur. The results of the study confirmed that social withdrawal comes in more than one form. The author's concern is that if these children continue to spend most of their time in solitary activity, they will be rejected by their peers by the time they reach middle childhood.

In an article in *USA Weekend* (January 15–17, 1999) headlined "Which are better . . . SMART kids or GOOD kids?" popular radio and TV psychologist "Dr. Laura" Schlessinger says it is more important for children to be honorable, less important that they be on the honor roll. What do you think about this point of view? What does Dr. Laura's point appear to be? Record your immediate reaction, then read this part of the chapter and come back and evaluate your response.

## MORAL DEVELOPMENT

**morality**
Ethical behavior; the development of an understanding of right and wrong.

**Morality** does not have a universal definition (Damon, 1988). Morality is constantly evolving and changing. However, Damon (1988, p. 5) lists several facets that are usually included in the conceptualization of morality:

- An evaluative orientation toward actions and events that distinguishes good from bad and prescribes good conduct consistently
- A sense of obligation toward standards shared by a social collective
- A concern for others' welfare
- A sense of responsibility for acting on one's concern for others through acts of caring, benevolence, kindness, and mercy
- Concern for the rights of others; a concern for justice and fairness
- A commitment to honesty as the norm in interpersonal dealings
- Awareness that violations may result in emotional responses, such as shame, guilt, outrage, fear, and contempt

Moral values are learned from parents, caretakers, peers, teachers, and television. Moral reasoning is the cognitive aspect of morality that leads the person to make a moral judgment. That is, the person considers his or her values compared to a problem situation and then judges what should be done in that situation. For example, one five-year-old child takes a toy away from another five-year-old child. The first child has been taught to value self-control and generosity but wants the toy back. This child also has been taught to value obedience, so he controls his impulse to grab the toy (self-control). Searching through his values, he comes to honesty. He runs to his mother and tells her that the other child has stolen his toy.

Because he has been taught that stealing is wrong, he sees this as a way out of his dilemma. The nature of "stealing" versus "borrowing" is not a distinction he has made yet. Running to mother comes under the third aspect of morality: action. Action is the young child's follow-through on the reasoned judgment.

**conscience**

Inner control; an emotional element that includes feelings of guilt and anxiety.

Moral development also has an emotional element, the **conscience.** This emotional element includes feelings of guilt and anxiety. In the previous example, the child felt some anxiety about grabbing the toy back or attacking the other child due to fear of punishment and loss of approval from his mother. This led him to search further for a way to retrieve his toy. If he had attacked the other child and gotten away with it, he would likely feel guilty. That is, he would feel uncomfortable because he had not done what was consistent with the values he had been taught. The development of conscience, or inner control, is the major objective of moral training during the preschool period (Berkowitz, 1998).

**moral reasoning**

When a person considers his or her values compared to a problem situation and then judges what should be done in that situation.

**moral judgments**

Decisions made regarding solutions to moral dilemmas.

Much of the research on moral development focuses on developing **moral reasoning** and making **moral judgments.** The work of Piaget (1965) and Kohlberg (1968) have been examined most closely. Basically, for Piaget and Kohlberg, as the person becomes less egocentric, his or her moral judgments become more mature. The preschool child is still in the preoperational period and, therefore, egocentric and perception bound. Three-, four-, and five-year-olds:

- are relatively hedonistic; that is, they are most interested in their own welfare and pleasure.
- are controlled by external sanctions; that is, they fear punishment and loss of approval.
- have values that are situation specific; that is, what is right or wrong in one situation is not necessarily generalized to another situation.
- are able to verbalize good behavior, but good actions depend on the need for approval and the threat of punishment.

How often the adult says of the young child, "I know he knows better!" And the adult is right; the child does "know better" but is not yet able to reason and act consistently with his knowledge. It is not until children are close to age six that they begin to develop standards, to generalize, and to internalize sanctions so that they act morally not just to avoid punishment but because they *should* act that way.

Piaget constructed a two-stage theory of moral reasoning (Figure 26–3). In the first stage, moral realism (age four to age ten), the child's evaluation centers on the degree of damage and not intent. The four-year-old in the example reacts

| Age | Stage | Characteristics |
|---|---|---|
| 4–7 | Moral Realism (Preoperational) | • Centers on consequences of act.<br>• Rules are unchangeable.<br>• Punishment for breaking rules is automatic. |
| 7–10 | Transition (Concrete Operational) | • Gradually changes to second-stage thinking. |
| 11+ | Moral Autonomy, Realism, Reciprocity (Formal Operations) | • Considers intentions.<br>• Realizes rules are arbitrary conventions.<br>• Punishment is socially determined, not inevitable. |

FIGURE 26–3 Piaget's two-stage theory of moral development, with transition period.

exactly this way. From seven to ten, the child experiences the transition as evidenced by consideration of each child's intentions. The child is able to consider both the amount of damage and the intentions. The preschool child, besides focusing on the consequences, is also characterized by viewing rules as unchangeable and viewing punishment for rule breaking as automatic. The preschool child considers rules as always having existed rather than as being invented by people. Not considering intentions, the child feels that any and all transgressions must be punished; forgiveness is not yet in the child's domain. It is only gradually during Piaget's transition period, which coincides with concrete operations, that the child begins to see that rules are arbitrary and ever changing and that punishment is socially determined and not automatic.

During the early years, the child learns the values of people in his or her environment but does not yet reason and act in the same ways as an adult. The preschooler needs help to see intentionality. Through cooperative effort and responsibility, the child can be helped to move to the next stage.

In Piaget's view, merely following a morality of obedience will not result in the internalization of autonomous rules of moral judgment (DeVries & Kohlberg, 1990; DeVries & Zan, 1994; DeVries, Hildebrandt, & Zan, 2000; DeVries, Zan, & Hildebrandt, 2002). As with other concepts, the child needs the freedom to develop moral rules through his or her own cognitive actions. The child needs autonomy to figure out how to apply rules in different situations.

DeVries and Zan (1994) provide a model for classrooms that support children's opportunities to exercise their autonomy. Their approach requires a great many teacher skills, a teacher who models understanding and fairness, and a sustained commitment. DeVries and Zan (1994) describe how to develop a classroom community for young children. Research done by DeVries and her colleagues (DeVries, Halcyon, & Morgan, 1991; DeVries, Haney, & Zan, 1991) and by Schmidt (1993) contrasts the behavior of children enrolled in more democratic classrooms, where positive guidance strategies are used that support students constructing their own solutions to problems, and more authoritarian classrooms, where more negative guidance strategies are used that promote obedience through fear. The results from both studies document the more advanced sociomoral behaviors of children from the more democratic classrooms.

With so many young children spending most of their day in child care settings, it is important to try to find out what effect, if any, this experience has on their conceptions of moral and social rules. Siegal and Storey (1985) compared the moral judgments of preschoolers who had been in child care for at least 18 months with the judgments of recently enrolled preschoolers. They were interested in whether the children with more experience dealing with social rules would be able to discriminate better between moral rules, rules that generalize across situations, and social rules, arbitrary rules that are specific to the situation. Moral rules are rules that apply in every situation, such as sharing, not hitting, not shoving, not throwing things at another child, and not taking another child's possessions. Social rules are situation specific, such as having to participate in show and tell, sitting in a certain place at story time, putting toys away in the correct place, and putting personal belongings in the correct place. Both the preschool veterans and the newly enrolled viewed moral transgressions as equally unacceptable. The preschool veterans were more tolerant of social transgressions. They seemed to feel these transgressions were to be expected and that the children would find solutions without adult intervention. The child care experience seemed to give children a higher level of understanding so they could discriminate between standard and arbitrary rules.

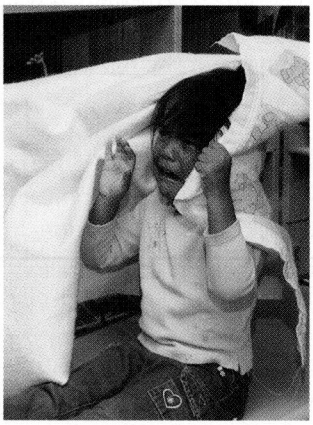

FIGURES 26–4a & b Young children display both positive and negative feelings.

The child's values are reflected in his or her moral reasoning and judgments. Equally important, however, are actions. The child may be able to talk about a positive moral solution and yet when it comes to his or her behavior, the child may not follow through. Two related areas of behavior that are of concern to those who work with young children are prosocial and aggressive behaviors.

## Prosocial Behavior

The outward manifestations of positive moral development are seen in **prosocial behaviors** that reflect generosity, nurturing, sympathy, empathy, and helping (Figure 26–4). They involve attempts to join another person, collaborate with another, offer suggestions, follow the lead of another, and engage in conversations. Research supports the conclusion that young children are capable of and demonstrate the use of prosocial behaviors (Buzzelli, 1992; Moore, 1977) and that parents and teachers can promote prosocial behavior through prosocial curricula (DeVries, Halcyon, & Morgan, 1991; DeVries, Haney, & Zan, 1991; Doescher & Sugawara, 1989; Kim & Stevens, 1987; Schmidt, 2005). For example, Schmidt asked children from positive guidance (PG) and negative guidance (NG) kindergartens, "What would you do if a friend got hurt on the playground?" The PG children answered consistently that they would try to help their friend by getting a Band-Aid®, consoling the friend, or staying with the friend until the friend felt better. The NG children all responded that they would go get the teacher. The PG children showed a mature level of sociomoral development; the NG children's responses reflected a lack of knowledge of moral responsibility.

**prosocial behaviors**
Outward manifestations of positive moral development that reflect generosity, nurturing, sympathy, empathy, and helping.

**Empathy** is an important aspect of moral development (Berkowitz and Grych, 1998; Flatter et al., 2006). Empathy is a feeling that occurs when individuals put themselves in the other person's position. They experience the same feelings as another person. While it is not until age six or seven that children really understand what is going on in another person's mind, younger children do pick up on the feelings of others. It is very important to take notice of children's empathetic behavior in order for them to know that it is important. It is also important for adults to be open about their feelings when they are happy, angry, sad or upset. In summary (Flatter et al., 2006, p. 5), from two to six:

**empathy**
A feeling that occurs when individuals put themselves in the other person's position.

- Preschoolers can empathize with feelings, such as happiness, sadness or anger. They cannot empathize with more complicated emotions, such as frustration or embarrassment, because they have not yet identified those feelings in themselves.
- Adults should reinforce empathic behavior by praising a child for sharing or showing concern for others.

## Violence and Aggression

The headlines tell the story: "Teenage homicides become deadly epidemic" (Bayles, 1993). A kindergartner draws a picture of a homicide in her journal—she had witnessed her aunt shooting her mother. Children's Defense Fund (CDF) states (Children's Defense Fund, 1999, p. 107):

> While many of the broader statistics show marked improvement [regarding children's Safe Start] over previous years, and the reasons behind these gains provide much hope for future progress, the tragic fact remains that too many children are denied a Safe Start in Life.

- Too many children in America live in communities where violence and gunfire are a stark, everyday reality.
- Too many children are the victims of crime and violence.

Furthermore, children who appear to live in safe and affluent circumstances are becoming so angry that they are shooting their peers and their teachers in middle schools and high schools.

The Children's Defense Fund (2004, August) ranks the United States last among industrialized countries in protecting our children against gun violence. The CDF reports additional frightening information. According to the Centers for Disease Control (Children's Defense Fund, 2004, August), children in the United States under the age of 15 are:

- 9 times more likely to die in a firearms accident
- 11 times more likely to commit suicide with a gun
- 12 times more likely to die from gunfire
- 16 times more likely to be murdered with a gun

than children in 25 other industrialized countries *combined*. In America, every three hours a child or teen is killed by a firearm, and every six hours a child is killed by abuse or neglect. Children exposed to this **violence** are more likely than their classmates to experience depression, low self-esteem, excessive crying, and worries about dying or being injured. Many inner-city children who are exposed to excessive violence develop psychological defense mechanisms that inhibit their ability to learn in school and may cause them to be aggressive. Poverty is the strongest predictor of criminal activity. With 40 percent of African American children living in poverty, it is no surprise that African American males are the largest group of both offenders and victims. Children have easy access to weapons and they have experience with violence, not only in their neighborhoods but also on television and in video games.

**violence**

Exertion of physical force to injure or abuse; destructive force or action; a child's exposure to violence can result in depression, low self-esteem, excessive crying, and worries about dying or being injured.

In response to this epidemic of violence, the NAEYC published a position statement on violence in the lives of children in 1993 that states: "Schools and child care programs can be vitally important support systems by strengthening children's resilience and providing resources for parents so they can serve as psychological buffers to protect their children" (NAEYC position statement on violence in the lives of children, 1993, p. 81). Chapter 27 looks at some of the steps parents and other adults can take to protect young children. This chapter closes with a description of some of the research on aggressive behavior and the effects on young children's current and future social development.

**aggressive**

Opposite of prosocial behavior; has the purpose of hurting another.

**Aggressive** behavior is the other side of the coin from prosocial behavior. One of the foremost challenges for adults who work with young children is helping them handle their hostile feelings in positive ways while developing more prosocial behavior.

For young children, *aggressive* behavior is defined as that which a person commits in order to hurt another (Cole, Cole, & Lightfoot, 2005). There are two major types of aggression:

1. *Instrumental aggression:* aggression designed to unblock a blocked goal, such as getting back an object, territory, or privilege.

The following story is abbreviated from *Starting Small* (1997) published by the Teaching Tolerance Project, Southern Poverty Law Center, Montgomery, Alabama. What is your reaction before reading the following section of the chapter? After reading the following section of the chapter?

Cedric's Story. Four-year-old Cedric, as described in Chapter 1, came into his classroom one day anxious to tell his story. During Circle Time, he described in detail how the night before he, his mother, his father, and his father's friend went for a ride. The dad and his friend were drinking and smoking reefers. The police chased them down the freeway while his mother yelled at them to stop. They were finally pulled over. His dad was pulled out of the car and the police officers threw him on the hood of the car, cuffed him, and dragged him to the police car. On the following days, Cedric and his friends replayed the incident in their dramatic play. Finally the teacher made herself the family protector and suggested that the children drive somewhere else, such as a pizza place or an amusement park. The play changed, but the teacher believed Cedric might still be feeling the trauma of having one of his protectors removed from him. Said his teacher, "for the kids who come from more violent homes, there is a difference in how they interact with others and what methods they use to solve problems. They know what they're supposed to do to conform to this environment. When I say to them, 'What should you do when someone snatches your toy or hits you?' They say, 'Use your words. Tell them I don't like that. Tell the teacher.' They have all the pat answers, but when something happens to them, when they get angry and frustrated, they can't do it because their home environment is so overwhelming."

2. *Hostile aggression:* aggression that is person oriented—the act is intended to hurt the person physically or psychologically (criticism, ridicule, tattling, or verbal disapproval).

**relational aggression**

That part of hostile aggression that includes hostile actions, such as excluding another child from play, threatening a child if they don't follow instructions, and trying to get others to reject a child who wants to play.

There is a current research focus on **relational aggression**, that part of hostile aggression that includes hostile actions, such as excluding another child from play, threatening a child if they don't follow instructions, and trying to get others to reject a child who wants to play, (Ostrov & Crick, 2005). Nelson, Robinson, and Hart (2005) found that relationally aggressive preschool children were also popular and very sociable, whereas physically aggressive children, especially girls, were not seen as socially acceptable. Girls displayed more frequent relational aggression.

Bullying is a behavior that has been focused on with older children but is now also viewed as a problem in preschool and kindergarten (Holland 2004b). Bullies are children who repeat aggressive actions toward others over and over (Holland, 2004b). They tend to use both instrumental and hostile approaches. Bullies tend to pick specific victims for continuous aggressive approaches.

The young child needs to learn to develop positive social skills that will preclude the need to be excessively aggressive. At times, events will cause the child to be angry. For the young child, these events are most likely someone taking something he or she has or not giving the child something he or she wants, not letting the child join in an activity, not sharing materials, hurting the child's feelings, or hurting the child physically. The child must gradually learn control and compromise to solve these problems. Chapter 27 looks at some of the means being used to help children develop nonviolent procedures for handling problems. The rest of this unit looks at a number of areas that relate to violence and aggression: socioeconomic status (SES) and conduct, classroom conflict, rough-and-tumble play, and young children's views of authority.

## Socioeconomic Status and Conduct

Dodge, Pettit, and Bates (1994) followed 585 children, of whom 51 were from the lowest SES, from preschool through third grade. The purpose of the study was to find the process in socialization that might explain the relationship between early SES and later child behavior problems. The results indicated that the lower the children's SES at the preschool level, the more likely they were to be rated by teachers and peers as being aggressive. Poverty-related factors in early childhood that predicted later behavior problems included harsh discipline, neighborhood and family violence, more transient peer groups (thus no stable friendships), and less cognitive stimulation in the home. Furthermore, their mothers tend to be less warm, experiencing a relatively high level of family stressors, perceive that they have less social support and feel relatively isolated, and likely to approve of aggression as a way to solve problems. It is not that these parents want their children to be aggressive, but they perceive that aggression is the only means of survival in a violent neighborhood. On the other hand, harsh discipline has the strongest relationship to later behavior problems, suggesting that the children learn from aggressive models. The authors conclude that these factors make the poverty-level environment "a breeding ground for aggressive behavior development" (p. 662).

Campbell, Pierce, March, Ewing, and Szumowski (1994) conducted a study with middle-class and upper-middle-class boys at ages four and six. The results indicated that children identified by teachers and/or parents as "having problems" experience basic difficulties in controlling activity, impulsivity, noncompliance, and aggression that they could not control in any situation. The most extreme cases were still problems when followed up at age six.

## Classroom Conflict

Peer conflict is another area that is a major focus for research. In her review of research on peer conflict in the classroom, Wheeler (1994) found that problems of peer conflict have led to an interest in teaching children how to resolve conflicts independent of adult assistance. Wheeler (1994) notes that peer conflicts have a structure that can be identified (p. 296):

- Issues are the arguable event and the initial opposition.
- Strategies are the ways children deal with the mutual opposition.
- Outcomes are the endings to the conflict.

Typically, issues involve control of the physical or social environment. The most common disputes for the youngest children center on possessions. As children get older, conflicts center on issues of morality (physical harm, psychological harm, distribution of toys and rights) and social order (rules about how things should be done). Strategies may be physical or verbal and aggressive or nonaggressive. The outcomes may be unresolved, the result of an adult-imposed solution, submission of one child to another, or a compromise arrived at through mutual discussion.

Some other points of interest emerged from Wheeler's (1994) review. In looking at the contexts of conflict, children who are engaged in cooperative or associative play use less aggression than children who are engaged in onlooker, solitary, or parallel play. Friends have more frequent but less intense conflicts than nonfriends. If left alone by adults, children can generate their own conflict solutions. When parents intervene, they are usually inconsistent and biased. If the first move toward resolution is aggressive, the follow-up responses are aggressive. If the first move is conciliatory, there is more likelihood that a peaceful solution will be reached. It appears that in terms of outcomes, most conflicts are unresolved; that is, they are just dropped.

### Rough-and-Tumble Play

Rough-and-tumble play (R&T) is a type of play that may appear aggressive but actually serves constructive purposes for young children (MacDonald, 1992). R&T involves playful wrestling, chasing, mock attacks, and is generally boisterous and lively. It has been most extensively studied at the elementary school level, where it is most prevalent (see Chapter 30), but it does emerge at the preschool level (McBride-Chang & Jacklin, 1993). McBride-Chang and Jacklin (1993) found a relationship between fathers' amount of R&T with their children and children's amount of R&T. MacDonald's (1992) concern is that with closer supervision of children's out-of-school activities, children do not have the opportunity to engage in the fun and excitement of R&T that they had in the past.

### Views of Authority

Considering that children are becoming more aggressive and less under control, it is important to look at their relationships with authority. Laupa (1994) found that preschoolers consider both adult status and social position of authority in relation to particular situations. That is, they do not view the need to be obedient to just any adult. For example, they give more authority to teachers than to other adults. They are also willing to accept peers as authorities in the context of play. Although preschoolers still see teachers as major authorities, they are beginning to differentiate among authority figures based on their position and the context.

As our world becomes more violent, children are exposed to more aggression and they are displaying more aggressive and violent behaviors. No longer can it be assumed that they will learn moral behaviors through being told standards. Teaching children to live in peace is more complex than it was in the past. We explore the adult role further in Chapter 27.

## INCLUSION AND SOCIAL BEHAVIOR

In Chapter 4, the social learning advantages of inclusive classroom placement for children with special needs were described. Odom, Zercher, Li, Marquart, and Sandall (1998) examined the social relationships in a cross-national sample of inclusive preschool settings. Children with disabilities engaged in positive social interactions with peers at a lower frequency than typically developing children. About 70 percent of the children with disabilities were rated as meeting social acceptance criteria for positive social interactions. Approximately 30 percent were identified as rejected due to negative behaviors, such as conflicts with peers and disruption in class. A study by Okagaki, Diamond, Kontos, and Hestenes (1998) supported the conclusion that participation in an inclusive preschool class helps typical children accept diversity in others. Although the children with disabilities engaged in more parallel play than social play, the authors believe that parallel play affords a gateway into typical social life. Hundert, Mahoney, Mundy, and Vernon (1998) examined the social interactions of children with severe disabilities in inclusive preschool settings. They found that these children gained very little socially, whether segregated or integrated, but developed at a higher rate in integrated settings. Overall, there continues to be support for inclusive placement, with thoughtful attention to a setting's use of best practices (Hanline & Daley, 2002). Odom (2002) suggests that we need to look more closely at what types of benefits children with different types of disabilities may gain from inclusion.

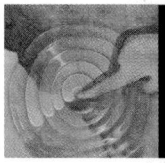

**LOOKING FURTHER**

Spend at least an hour observing children during play activities. Note both positive and negative social interactions. Apply the Parten, Smilansky, or combined-play categories designed by Rubin and the social reinforcement categories devised by Hartup and Charlesworth. Summarize your findings.

## SUMMARY

Erikson, Piaget, Maslow, and Rogers all included a focus on social development in their theories.

Between toddlerhood and school age, children make great strides in social development. Development of social competence is an essential task during the preschool period. They learn to develop more complex relationships with peers, who serve as play companions, reinforcers, models, and friends. Siblings also serve as important sources of social interaction. Children who are not popular may be isolates or may exhibit behaviors unacceptable to others. These children need special adult attention to help with the development of appropriate social skills. Young children begin to acquire moral values, to reason about problems of right and wrong, to develop judgments, and to act according to these judgments. They learn that positive behaviors are "right" and that aggressive behaviors are "wrong."

With both neighborhood and community environments becoming more violent and family life becoming more stressful, adults who work with young children are facing more aggressive behaviors and serious behavioral and emotional problems. Helping children develop positive behavior patterns is a greater challenge than ever. Children with disabilities can benefit socially from placement in a setting with nondisabled children.

## FOR FURTHER READING


Baumeister, R. F., & Vohs, K. D. (2005). *Handbook of self-regulation*. New York: Guilford.

Bell, S. H., Carr, V. W., Denno, D., Johnson, L. J., Phillips, L. R. (2004). *Challenging behaviors in early childhood settings*. Baltimore: Brookes.

Bloomquist, M. I., & Schnell, S. V. (2002). *Helping children with aggression and conduct problems*. New York: Guilford.

Bronson, M. B. (2000). *Self-regulation in early childhood*. New York: Guilford.

Bukowski, W. M., Newcomb, A. F., & Hartup, W. W. (Eds.). (1996). *The company they keep: Friendships in childhood and adolescence*. New York: Cambridge University Press.

Carpendale, J., & Lewis, C. (2004). *How children develop social understanding*. Malden, MA: Blackwell.

Children, youth, and gun violence [Focus issue]. (2002). *The Future of Children, 12*(2).

Corsaro, W. A. (2003). *We're friends, right? Inside kids' culture*. Washington, DC: Joseph Henry Press.

Dunn, J. (2004). *Children's friendships*. Malden, MA: Blackwell.

Forgas, J. P. (Ed.). (2001). *Handbook of affect and social cognition*. Mahwah, NJ: Erlbaum.

Goodwin, M. (2005). *The hidden life of girls*. Williston, VT: Blackwell.

Guerin, S., & Hennessey, E. (2002). *Aggression and bullying*. Williston, VT: Blackwell.

Hart, C. H., Nelson, D. A., Robinson, C. S., Olsen, S. F., McNeilly-Choque, M. K., Porter, C. L., & McKee, T. R. (2000). Russian parenting styles and family processes: Linkages with subtypes of victimization and aggression. In K. A. Kerns, J. M. Contreras, & A. M. Neal-Barnett. (Eds.), *Family and peers: Linking two social worlds*. Westport, CT: Praeger.

Howe, N., Rinaldi, C. M., Jennings, M., & Petrakos, H. (2002). "No! The lambs can stay out because they got cozies": Constructive and destructive sibling conflict, pretend play, and social understanding. *Child Development, 73*(5), 1460–1473.

Killen, M., & Smetana, J. G. (Eds.). (2005). *Handbook of moral development*. Mahwah, NJ: Erlbaum.

Kostelnik, M. J., Stein, L. C., Whiren, A. P., Soderman, A. K., & Gregory, K. (2002). *Guiding children's social development*. Clifton Park, NY: Delmar Learning.

Loeber, R., Farrington, D. P., Stouthamer-Loeber, M., & Van Kammen, W. B. (1998). *Antisocial behavior and mental health problems*. Mahwah, NJ: Erlbaum.

Meyer, L. H., Park, H., Grenot-Scheyer, M., Schwartz, I. S., & Harry, B. (Eds.). (1998). *Making friends: The influences of culture and development*. Baltimore: Brookes.

NICHD Early Child Care Research Network. (2005). *Trajectories of physical aggression from toddlerhood to middle childhood*. Williston, MA: Blackwell.

Reid, J. B., Patterson, G. R., & Snyder, J. J. (Eds.). (2002). *Antisocial behavior in children and adolescents*. Washington, DC: American Psychological Association.

Smith, P., & Hart, C. H. (Eds.). (2002). *Blackwell handbook of childhood social development*. Williston, VT: Blackwell

Sullivan, K. (2000). *The anti-bullying handbook*. New York: Oxford University Press.

## SUGGESTED ACTIVITIES

1. Do your own survey to find out who the peers of some young children are. Interview three mothers of children at each of at least three of the following age levels: three, four, five, six, and/or seven. Do they play more with children in their neighborhood? From their school? Do the mothers arrange playmates for them?
2. Discuss with a small group in class: Should we always expect young children to obey their parents? Why or why not? Relate the discussion to the young child's developmental stage.
3. Observe three children with disabilities in inclusive settings and analyze their social behaviors.
4. Make an entry in your journal.

## REVIEW

1. Match the theorists in Column I to their views in social development in Column II.

| Column I | Column II |
|---|---|
| a. Erikson | 1. Views play as an important vehicle for learning for the young child. |
| b. Maslow & Rogers | 2. Views children's play as a vehicle to work through their feelings about life. |
| c. Piaget | 3. Views social interaction as having a critical part in the young child's learning. Play is related to the development of representational abilities and that play creates a ZPD. |
| d. Bandura | 4. Views early childhood as a time when children strive for autonomy. |
| e. Vygotsky | 5. Views children acquiring social behaviors through reinforcement or through observing and imitating models from a social cognitive perspective. |
| f. Social Cognitionists | 6. View children taking an active role in their own social development and focus on children's social situations and reasoning that leads to their behavior responses. |

2. Describe what a peer is.
3. Categorize each of the following examples of child play behavior. Rate each according to the Hartup and Charlesworth behavioral categories.

| Charlesworth/Hartup Category | Incident Example |
|---|---|
| | a |
| | b |
| | c |
| | d |
| | e |
| | f |

   a. Janie comes over to the block area and moves one of the blocks. Aaron sees her and exclaims, "Janie wrecked it!" They argue between themselves until Janie walks away. Aaron goes on building with the blocks. Two other children are building near him.
   b. The blocks have fallen down. Aaron sees Andy start to build and he does the same next to Andy. They share the blocks and compare buildings.
   c. As Carmen watches the children fish, she blurts out, "Get the hook in him, David!"
   d. Miguel gives the yellow car to Bill. Bill then follows Miguel.
   e. Ronnie suggests that they all pile leaves. "Come on, get in here," he shouts. Six children are piling leaves.
   f. Maria and her friends are all riding bikes. She slows herself by dragging her feet. Her friends do, also.
4. Identify the predominant criteria regarding relationships:
   a. Relationships are best looked at from the individual child's point of view.
   b. Developmental changes in relationships are best looked at as a complex of relationships that involve children and the other people with whom they interact.
   c. Families and peers must both be considered when looking at relationships.
   d. Social context is not an important influence on relationships.
5. Select the important elements regarding social competence:
   a. Social competence grows out of the young child's relationships with others.
   b. Socially competent young children are likely to be successful adults.
   c. Social competence should be assessed just as academic competence is assessed.
   d. There is no need for further research on social competence.
6. In the research by Charlesworth and Hartup and Hartup et al., information was collected on positive and negative reinforcement. Write the letter of each correct statement concerning the research results.
   a. Four-year-olds gave more positive reinforcements than three-year-olds.
   b. Younger children gave reinforcement to more children than did older children.
   c. Dramatic play activities brought forth a lot of positive reinforcement.
   d. Popular children usually were the ones who gave the most positive reinforcement.
   e. Almost as much negative reinforcement as positive reinforcement was given.
7. For each of the following examples, write either *0* for friendship stage *0*, or *1* for friendship stage 1.
   a. "She is my friend. She gives me popcorn."
   b. "Girls who wear dresses are nice."
   c. "I'm mad at Nora. She always wants to be boss."
   d. "Bob is my friend. He lets me ride his trike."
   e. "Johnny, you are nice. You share toys and play the games I like."

**8.** Consider the following two examples. Decide which child, Isabel or Jamilla, is most likely to develop prosocial behaviors. Explain why.

a. Isabel and Theresa are playing. Suddenly Isabel yells to Theresa, "Give me my dolly or I'll hit you." Theresa holds on tightly to the dolly. Isabel hits her. Theresa cries. Isabel's mother, Mrs. Sanchez, comes in and asks, "What's going on, girls?" She finds out what happened as she comforts Theresa. She explains to Isabel that hitting is not the way to get her dolly back. She then explains to Theresa that that particular doll is very special to Isabel. She then gets the girls to agree that Theresa will play with the doll for 10 minutes and then give it to Isabel.

b. Jamilla and Kato are playing. Jamilla takes Kato's truck. Kato is crying and runs to get his mother. She comes in looking angry. She says, "Jamilla, you are a bad girl. Give that truck back to Kato. You go sit on that chair for 10 minutes and then I expect you to come back and play nicely."

**9.** Select the items that are true regarding sibling and peer relationships.

a. Play with an older sibling can provide the skills for understanding the thoughts and emotions of others.

b. After conflicts, children tend to have more positive feelings toward siblings than toward peers.

c. A high frequency of sibling conflicts is associated with low-quality friendships.

d. Siblings, provide a social advantage.

**10.** Decide which of the following examples show instrumental aggression and which show hostile aggression. Mark *I* for instrumental and *H* for hostile.

a. "Mommy, Mommy, Janie took a cookie!"

b. "Jason, you look ugly."

c. Jason pushes Rudy off the chair that he wants.

d. Isabel tries to pull Maria off the swing because she feels it is her turn.

e. "You don't know how to do it right."

Which of the examples above are most likely to involve preschool children? Why?

**11.** Select the correct answer(s) to the following. There may be more than one correct answer or no correct answers.

a. The results of Ladd's kindergarten study indicated the following regarding early peer relationships:

(1) Children who have high status in the group at the beginning of kindergarten will have high status at the end.

(2) Children who were rejected early in the kindergarten year were likely to remain rejected at the end of the year.

(3) Popular children tend to have a positive attitude toward school.

(4) Less popular children tend to have a positive attitude toward school.

b. Peers serve an important function as models for other children. The children most likely to be imitated are those who

(1) are warm and rewarding.

(2) are powerful.

(3) control resources.

(4) the child perceives as being similar to himself or herself.

c. The playground has been selected as an excellent place for observing children's social behavior because

(1) there is more room for the researchers.

(2) it is more natural and less restrictive.

(3) the children tend to go wild.

(4) researchers are no longer allowed in classrooms.

d. Berndt (1983) found that children's views of what is special about friendship are related to age and development in several ways. According to Berndt,

(1) the importance of sharing and helping increases with age.

(2) older children are more competitive with their friends.

(3) a desire for independence is usually subordinated to the desire to maintain a friendship.
(4) children will persevere even when a friendship is not gratifying.

e. Younger children are likely to become friends if
(1) they interact, share, and/or help each other.
(2) the guest child agrees with the host.
(3) the children can agree on a common-ground activity.
(4) they can successfully exchange information.

f. Some factors that research has documented regarding children's friendships are
(1) friendships are special relationships that develop with other people and serve several functions for young children, such as being an emotional resource, a cognitive resource, a context in which basic social skills are learned, and a forerunner of future relationships.
(2) friends resolve conflicts more calmly than nonfriends.
(3) children who enter elementary school with preschool friends are more likely to feel satisfied with school and maintain those friendships.
(4) children who start out aggressive at the beginning of kindergarten usually attain popularity by the end of the year.

g. Sibling relationships are unique in that
(1) due to sibling rivalry, there are more negative than positive interactions.
(2) younger siblings rarely imitate older siblings.
(3) sibling relations are usually more positive than peer relations.
(4) children with siblings play better with their peers.

h. Unpopular young children are most likely children who
(1) are withdrawn and isolated.
(2) are aggressive.
(3) spend time observing popular children to learn techniques for making friends.
(4) will drop out of school in adolescence, display antisocial behavior, become delinquents, etc.

i. Coplan et al. discovered
(1) children who spend most of their time alone during preschool usually have many friends by the end of third grade.
(2) there are three types of children who spend most of their time alone: solitary passive, solitary active, and reticent.
(3) solitary active play by preschoolers is usually looked upon favorably by adults.
(4) solitary passive play by preschoolers is usually looked upon favorably by adults.

j. Morality includes
(1) values and actions.
(2) judgments and values.
(3) values, judgments, and actions.
(4) reasoning, thinking, and acting.

k. Research by DeVries and her colleagues and by Schmidt indicates that
(1) more democratic approaches to classroom guidance support children's moral development.
(2) children from positive guidance classrooms are more likely to help a friend who is in trouble than those from negative guidance classrooms.
(3) children from more authoritarian classrooms are more obedient and have a better understanding of good behavior.
(4) children from authoritarian classrooms are better at constructing their own solutions to problems.

l. Young children may not always obey, even though they know what the rules and expectations for behavior are because
(1) young children are innately bad.
(2) they have not been well disciplined.

(3) their parents are not good models.
(4) developmentally, they have not reached the point at which they are able to act in a way consistent with what they have been taught.

m. Select the true statements:
(1) Every three hours, a child or youth younger than age twenty is killed by a firearm.
(2) Every two hours, a child or youth younger than age twenty is a homicide victim.
(3) Incidents of crime and violence are decreasing.
(4) Every six hours, a child is killed by abuse or neglect.

n. Regarding SES and school behavior problems,
(1) family context is a stronger influence than SES on the chances a child will be a behavior problem in school.
(2) the lower a child's SES is when he or she starts school, the more chance the child will be identified as a behavior-problem student.
(3) a multitude of predictive factors, such as harsh discipline in the home, violence in the neighborhood, and mothers who feel isolated and stressed, are part of the poverty picture.
(4) SES level is not a good predictor of school problem behavior.

o. Several other factors related to aggressive acts are that
(1) poverty is not the only factor in the development of problem behaviors: middle- and upper-middle-class boys may demonstrate problem behaviors in preschool and at home that continue into the elementary grades.
(2) peer conflict has an identified structure: issues, strategies, and outcomes.
(3) young children nearly always arrive at a satisfactory outcome for their conflicts.
(4) rough-and-tumble play is dangerous and should never be allowed.
(5) preschool children already discriminate between levels of adult authority.

p. Self-regulation is
(1) the ability to control behavior.
(2) the ability to become a self-directed learner.
(3) the ability to control emotions.
(4) the ability to interact in positive ways with others.

q. Development of self-regulation takes place
(1) in music activities.
(2) in sociodramatic play indoors.
(3) in sociodramatic play outdoors.
(4) in drawing activities.

## KEY TERMS LIST

aggressive
conscience
empathy
friendships
moral judgments
moral reasoning
morality
peer popularity
peer reinforcement
prosocial behaviors
relational aggression
self-regulation
siblings
social competence
social isolates
violence

Additional resources for this chapter can be found on the Online Companion™ to accompany this text at http://www.earlychilded.delmar.com. Respond to "Time to Reflect" and "Looking Further" concepts, review various child development scenarios, and answer thought-provoking questions in the Critical Thinking Forum. Keep a daily journal by downloading the student journal available on this Web site. Complete the interactive matching exercises to reinforce concepts, and printout the child development assessment forms to use during your observation of development for children from birth to age eight. In addition, read the case studies on the Web site to reinforce the important concepts in each chapter, and take a look at the multitude of Web links that are available for student research on the Internet.

CHAPTER

# 27

# The Adult Role in Affective Development

## OBJECTIVES

After reading this chapter, you should be able to:

- Explain the NAEYC guidelines for adult decision making.
- Recognize the major components of love and affection.
- Identify examples of various types of guidance techniques.
- State the advantage of using the inductive method of guidance.
- Recognize the characteristics of the authoritative, authoritarian, permissive, and harmonious parenting approaches.
- State which guidance methods can be labeled as positive and list the negative effects of punishment.
- Identify examples of shaping, modeling, and coaching.
- Understand the factors that underlie the development of moral autonomy.
- Explain how crisis-oriented literature can be used.
- Analyze discrepancies in beliefs and actions regarding teacher affective behavior.
- Explain how the affective curriculum is implemented.

As described thus far in this section, children's development in the affective areas is complex and closely integrated with their cognitive and psychomotor development. Children are currently faced with lifestyles that were not traditional in the past, as well as with increasing violence. Children are asked to deal with an unpredictable world. Adults who work with young children have an ever greater challenge in fulfilling their responsibility for supporting the affective development of children.

The developmentally appropriate practice guidelines for adult decision making (Bredekamp & Copple, 1997) include the following (pp. 16–23):

- *Creating a caring community of learners:* Relationships with others are consistent and positive; opportunities are available for the development of social relationships; and children's psychological safety is protected so they feel "secure, relaxed, and comfortable rather than disengaged, frightened, worried, or stressed."

- *Teaching to enhance development and learning emphasizes that "teachers respect, value, and accept children and treat them with dignity":* Teachers get to know their students well, listen to their students, plan individually, are alert to signs of stress and trauma, and are aware of strategies to reduce stress and develop resilience. Teachers work to develop children's self-regulatory and responsibility capabilities.

The NAEYC guidelines are designed to promote the development of competent young children. Competence has multiple origins in genetic factors, attachment bonds, and parenting styles (Schneider, 2000). (Competence was discussed in Chapter 26.) Jambunathan, Burts, and Pierce (1999) believe that developmentally appropriate practice will enhance young children's perception of their own competence. Jambunathan et al. interviewed preschool children regarding their perception of their self-competence and also observed their classrooms. From these observations and interviews, they arrived at a rating for developmentally appropriate practice. These researchers found that appropriate curriculum, teaching, and guidance strategies, as well as promotion of intrinsic motivation, were related to a high perception of peer acceptance. Considering the importance of peer relationships for young children, this study supports the conclusion that developmentally appropriate classroom practice makes children feel more satisfied about their peer relationships.

When following the NAEYC guidelines, adults also need to keep in mind that another important aspect is establishing reciprocal relationships with families. An important element of this guideline is that "teachers acknowledge parents' choices and goals for children and respond with sensitivity and respect to parents' preferences and concerns without abdicating professional responsibility to children" (Bredekamp & Copple, p. 22).

Adults should also keep in mind the specific experiences and cultural backgrounds of the children. Background factors, such as economic hardship (McLoyd, 1990), family ecology (Harrison, Wilson, Pine, Chan, & Buriel, 1990), and racial/ethnic socialization (Lin & Fu, 1990; Thornton, Chatters, Taylor, & Allen, 1990), influence the affective development of young children. For example, some cultural groups, such as Mexican Americans, emphasize the affective domain to a greater extent than others, resulting in some children entering school with a greater sensitivity to their own and others' feelings. Some cultures, such as Native Americans, may emphasize self-reliance and independence more than others. Different ethnic, cultural, and socioeconomic groups may have different views on selection of guidance and discipline strategies, on definitions of acceptable behavior, and on the place of authority figures (Gonzalez-Mena & Shareef, 2005). Adults who work with young children need to be considerate of cultural customs and negotiate with parents when differences appear to present problems (Bredekamp, 1997). Adults who work with young children also need to be aware of the increasing numbers of families with gay, lesbian, and transsexual parents. Research supports that the children in these families are as socially and emotionally healthy as children in the general population (Child Welfare League of America, 2006; Cianciotto & Cahill. 2003; National Adoption Information Clearinghouse, 2000). Any problems these children experience in the social and emotional areas come from teasing and bullying outside the family, not from within the family unit.

## LOVE AND AFFECTION

All children need to feel loved and cared for. Through the attachment that grows during infancy and the sense of trust that is basic to attachment, children feel loved (Watson, 2003). Children who are insecurely attached may present

**love and affection**

Fondness or caring for another.

behavior problems. They need to be approached in a caring and supportive manner. Expressing **love and affection** to young children may be a more complex procedure than we might think at first. Alan Fogel (1980) points out the complexities of giving affection. He believes that the emotional aspects of affection giving, that is, what each person feels, are as important or possibly even more important than the observed behavior, such as tickling, cuddling, and kissing. Fogel identifies three main aspects of affection giving. Children need love from a warm and accepting adult. Love helps children feel competent and secure. Adults' past experiences affect their reactions to children's needs for love. One adult may warmly accept a child whom another adult cannot tolerate. Some adults feel ambivalent or uncertain about expressing love to children. To be effective, the adult must feel that the child needs affection at the same time the child feels the need for affection.

Fogel goes on to point out that, although young children need to achieve autonomy and move ahead toward independence, they also need to learn to trust that adults will offer support and help when needed. Children need adults they can count on for love and respect even when they are out of control. At the same time, adults must work through their feelings with other adults, because young children are not at a point where they can serve this function for adults.

Adults need to be cautious in relation to the value of love. Love is a spontaneous and natural feeling that cannot be turned on and off at will. Acceptance and respect come first. Love for a particular child or adult does not necessarily follow. Rita M. Warren (1977, p. 4) warns, ". . . indiscriminate hugs, back-patting and head-touching may be unrelated to love and may dilute instead of strengthen the child's growing understanding of relationships between people." An adult can have a positive relationship with a child without necessarily feeling or expressing love and affection. Acceptance and respect are the most necessary ingredients for a good relationship (Figure 27–1).

FIGURE 27–1 A supportive adult is there when needed.

Usually, the most effective way to start a relationship with a small child is to stand back, be low key, and let the child make the first move when he or she feels comfortable. The overzealous, effusive adult too often scares off and overwhelms the small child. Touching is important in relating to the preschool child, but it must be done on the child's terms. Some preschoolers need hugs and cuddling on adult laps. Others gain the same positive feelings from a pat on the shoulder or a minute or two of undivided adult attention to their conversation and/or their activity.

Although research indicates that closeness and physical affection are necessary for healthy affective development, a problem regarding the giving of physical affection has emerged from concerns about child sexual abuse. ". . . [P]ublicity about sexual abuse may be creating unwarranted negative attitudes toward normal physical affection" (Hyson, Whitehead, & Prudoe, 1988, p. 55). Hyson et al. (1988) demonstrated through an experimental study that knowledge of the prevalence and effects of sexual abuse can lower adults' level of approval for physical affection giving to young children; on the other hand, knowledge of the need for closeness and physical affections can raise the level of approval. Their research indicates the need to clarify for adults the difference between sexual abuse and good touches.

Think back to your childhood. Write a short essay using the following questions as a guide:

What can you remember about your need for love and affection? Do you feel you were loved and respected? Did you receive love and affection through outward demonstrations, such as hugging, kissing, tickling, and holding? Would you characterize your family as very warm, moderately warm, or cool when it comes to expressing affection? How do you feel about expressing and accepting affection? How would you react if you were a teacher and one of the children clung to you and demanded constant attention? How would you feel if a child you really liked seemed to freeze every time you came near?

## DISCIPLINE AND GUIDANCE

**discipline**

The original meaning is "to teach"; today, it means to teach techniques of socially appropriate behavior.

**guidance**

Techniques used by adults to teach children socially appropriate behavior.

What is discipline? The term **discipline** is often associated with punishment. For some adults, the terms are synonymous. Discipline is a much broader concept of which punishment is only one part.

The term *discipline* has lost much of its original meaning and has become a rather negative term. It had respectable origins in a Latin root that established its connections with learning and education. It still retains its connections with education in the dictionary: "training that develops self-control, character, an orderliness and efficiency." However, today it is used synonymously with punishment, most particularly corporal punishment (Gartrell, 2004). In teaching the child to be a disciplined, self-controlled individual, various techniques can be used. Today the term **guidance** is used to distinguish positive techniques from the negative connotation of the term *discipline*. According to Hyson and Christiansen (1997), the guidance view in early childhood education grew out of the psychoanalytic theories of Freud and Erikson, Rogers' humanistic view, and Gesell's maturationist theory. "The term 'guidance' reflected a belief that children's impulses were maturally healthy, and that the adults' role was gently to direct or 'guide' those impulses into socially acceptable, developmentally healthy outlets" (p. 288). Those theorists influenced by Piaget "have regarded 'guidance' as one part of a process in which children actively construct understanding about appropriate, productive ways of behaving in classroom settings" (p. 288). Some people use the terms *classroom management* and *behavior management*. These terms "suggest a more directive approach to the task, with more focus on adult-selected goals" and include techniques of environmental management, modeling, and systematic reinforcement. Developmentally appropriate practice is carried out from the guidance perspective.

The most common guidance and disciplinary techniques are outlined in Figure 27–2. These techniques fall into two major categories:

1. Child behavior is inhibited.
2. Child behavior is directed.

There are two types of inhibiting techniques: power assertive and psychological. Both of these techniques inhibit or stop the child from proceeding with the unacceptable activity in which he or she is engaged. Power-assertive techniques include physical punishment, such as spanking, verbal punishment, such as shouting and threats, and physical inhibition, such as holding the child or restricting his or her activities. Psychological techniques include love withdrawal and guilt-producing

| Child Behaviors | Practices |
|---|---|
| Inhibited | 1. Power Assertive<br>• physical punishment<br>• shouting<br>• threats<br>• physical inhibition<br>2. Psychological<br>• love withdrawal and guilt production<br>• induction (reasons, consequences stressed) |
| Directed | 3. Modeling<br>• observational learning<br>• modeling statements<br>4. Reinforcement |

FIGURE 27–2 Guidance and discipline techniques.

strategies, such as shaming or making the child feel he or she has lost the adult's love and approval. The second psychological technique is the use of induction. Inductions include reasoning and stressing consequences (Figure 27–3). That is, the child is told why he or she cannot be allowed to do what he or she is doing, and any negative consequences are described.

The directing techniques include the behaviorist approaches of modeling and reinforcement. Modeling includes observational learning and modeling statements. Through observational learning, the child watches what other children do and then does the same to receive positive reinforcement and self-satisfaction. Modeling statements are used by the adult to clarify for children exactly which models are behaving appropriately:

"Good, Jason, you are putting the blocks back on the bottom shelf."

"I can see that Carlos has his coat on and is ready to go outside."

"Isabel and Theresa, you are sharing the dolls."

FIGURE 27–3 With the inductive method of inhibiting undesirable behavior, reasons are given and consequences explained.

Adult reinforcement can be powerful, not only in terms of the behavior of the child to whom it is directed but also for the children who observe the reinforcement and use that child as a model. Modeling statements can be a powerful technique in directing children's behavior.

After reviewing the research on guidance goals, Hyson and Christiansen (1997) suggested the following four key guidance goals (p. 301):

1. *Self-regulation:* This goal helps children control and regulate their impulses and use these tools to live in their social and cultural world.
2. *Self-efficacy and self-respect:* This goal helps children feel capable, worthy, and ready to tackle difficult and challenging problems.
3. *Emotional understanding:* This goal helps children develop sensitivity to their own feelings and others' feelings (see emotional IQ, Chapter 25).

| Style | Parent Behavior | Child Outcome |
|---|---|---|
| Authoritarian | Low on nurturance and sympathy. Uses less rational control methods and more threats than others. | Discontented, withdrawn, distrustful. |
| Authoritative | Controlling but warm and has good communication. | Mature: independent, responsible, and assertive. |
| Permissive | Disorganized and not in control. Withdraws love or ridicules. | Immature. |
| Harmonious | Encourages independence and individuality. | Girls: very competent. Boys: low in competence. |

FIGURE 27–4 Baumrind's four parenting styles.

4. *Sociocultural competence:* This goal helps children work within the classroom community toward common group goals. Conflicts are handled in productive ways.

Adults are faced with many varieties of challenging behaviors. The most common behavior problems include "high levels of negative and angry feelings, an unwillingness to comply, defiance with parents and other adults, frequent squabbles with other children that may involve physical aggression, failure to follow directions, and problems getting along with peers" (Campbell, 2005, pp. 7–8). Deciding which approach to take with an individual child is not easy but there are many approaches from which to select (See the References at the end of the book and for Further Reading section in this chapter). Parents, teachers, and other adults are faced with many challenges.

**parental styles**

Parental discipline techniques identifying four styles of parenting: authoritarian, permissive, authoritative, and harmonious.

How do parental discipline techniques affect child behavior? Some of the best-known studies of **parental styles** have been done by Diana Baumrind and her colleagues (1975, 1978). Baumrind identifies four styles of parenting, outlined in Figure 27–4. The three most common types of approaches to parenting are authoritarian, permissive, and authoritative. A few parents use the harmonious style.

Parents who used authoritative control techniques were controlling yet warm and communicated clearly with their children. The children were judged to be the most mature. Parents insisted on mature and obedient behavior. The children were independent, responsible, and assertive. The authoritarian parents were less nurturant and sympathetic toward their children. They used less rational methods of control and more threats. The children of these parents were more discontented, withdrawn, and distrustful. The children of the permissive parents tended to be the most immature. These parents tended to use withdrawal of love or ridicule as punishment techniques. The permissive parents were not as well organized and controlling as the others.

The harmonious parents were nonconformists. They did not display control types of behaviors and yet their children seemed to know what was expected and to follow through. In general, these parents were well educated, provided their children with enriched environments, and encouraged independence and individuality. When their children disobeyed, they looked on it more as a difference of opinion than as "bad behavior." Baumrind found only eight families of this type. The girls were highly competent; the boys were low in competence.

The authoritative approach seemed to have the most positive overall effect on child behavior. Children of authoritative parents tended to be the most mature and well adjusted. These parents had a balance of high expectations for their children with clear communications concerning their expectations and strong, warm relationships with them. They mainly used inductive methods of control. They listened to the child's opinions when they disagreed and always gave clear reasons for their decisions.

There has been increasing interest in looking further at how parental discipline styles, as defined by Baumrind, affect child behavior. Power-assertive, or authoritarian, mothers of preschool children tend to have children who view hostile methods as being the successful means for solving peer conflict and use more antisocial behaviors in their play (Hart, DeWolf, & Burts, 1992). Inductive, or authoritative, mothers tend to have children who believe positive strategies will bring success in resolving conflicts and exhibit more prosocial and positive behaviors during playground play (Hart, DeWolf, & Burts, 1992). Children of inductive mothers were also more popular with their peers (Hart, DeWolf, Wozniak, & Burts, 1992). The results of these two studies support the advantage for children of inductive, or authoritative, discipline.

**teaching styles**

May affect children's behavior; guidance-oriented, authoritarian, and developmentally appropriate practice are examples of various teaching styles.

It is apparent from the results of the study by Jambunathan, Burts, and Pierce (1999) that **teaching styles** may also affect children's behavior. Other studies support the idea that a guidance-oriented approach develops a positive social climate and results in students being better disciplined and self-regulatory than those children in authoritarian-type classrooms (Hart, Burts, & Charlesworth, 1997; Marcon, 1993, 1994; Pfannenstiel & Schattgen, 1997; Stipek, Feiler, Byler, Ryan, Milburn, & Salmon, 1998). McMullen (1999) found that early childhood teachers who believe in developmentally appropriate practice and apply this philosophy in their classrooms tend to believe in their own competence and their power to control what happens in their classrooms. The more developmentally appropriate teachers also had degrees in early child education, coursework in child development, and/or experience teaching preschool, rather than degrees in elementary education.

**punishment**

Disciplining children; punishment is a controversial issue.

**Punishment** is an area of discipline that merits attention. The use of corporal, or physical, punishment has been a controversial issue (Ispa & Halgunseth, 2004; Richardson & Evans, 1993). Corporal punishment in schools was banned by law in 22 states as of 1993 (Richardson & Evans, 1993). However, corporal punishment is still inflicted in many schools and is used by many parents, although research indicates that is has no long-term positive effects and correlates with a number of negative effects, such as delinquency, vandalism, and poor grades (Cryan, 1987; Ramsburg, 1997). Other documented negative effects of corporal punishment include the following (Corporal punishment, 1981):

- Hitting children makes them more aggressive.
- Corporal punishment does not develop self-control. It lets the child know which kind of behavior is inappropriate but does not let him or her know what is appropriate.
- Corporal punishment is often applied unfairly.
- The line separating punishment from abuse is a thin one.

Children who received physical punishment at home acted out more in school, according to the results of a study with kindergartners and their parents (Michels, Pianta, & Reeve, 1993). Kindergartners who received nonphysical punishment (e.g., time out, attention to the misbehavior from the parent) exhibited relatively little acting-out behavior in school. Weiss, Dodge, Bates, and Pettit (1992) found that the degree of harsh discipline ("severe, strict, and often physical," p. 1324) used by parents was directly related to the amount of aggressive behaviors exhibited by children in school. That is, the harsher the discipline, the higher the children were rated by their teachers on aggressive behavior in the classroom.

Discipline styles of child care givers are also of concern. Scott-Little and Holloway (1992) found that caregivers who blamed misbehavior on internal factors used more power-assertive methods of discipline than caregivers who considered external causes that were out of the child's control. These researchers point out the need for caregivers to look more in-depth at the causes of children's misbehavior.

Recent research indicates that in both low-income and middle-income households, mild or moderate physical punishment is not harmful to children. In spite of the focus of child development specialists on avoidance of the use of physical punishment, most parents still use it (Ispa & Halgunseth, 2004). Ispa and Halgunseth did an in-depth study of nine low-income African American mothers' perspectives on corporal punishment. They focused on discovering the reasons the mothers continued to use physical punishment. The mothers might add the positive guidance techniques to their repertoires but did not give up physical punishment in spite of their Early Head Start home visitors promoting other procedures. Several reasons surfaced from the researchers' conversations with the mothers:

1. Mothers found the positive guidance techniques didn't work to their satisfaction. Children didn't seem to take the milder forms of discipline seriously.
2. Other family members pressured for the use of physical punishment.
3. The mothers felt that physical punishment worked during their own childhoods.
4. Although mothers felt it was natural for toddlers to test limits, they believed toddlers would not change their behavior without physical punishment.
5. These families live in dangerous neighborhoods. The mothers believed children had to learn early to avoid the temptations of early sex, drugs, and crime.
6. The mothers also believed that their children need to be prepared for self-defense—prepared to fight back. Therefore, an aggressive model is necessary.

The nonphysical methods of punishment may not be accepted in every culture, even though child development experts believe they are more effective in the long run.

Nonphysical methods of punishment, such as deprivation of privilege or isolation, are considered preferable to physical punishment by child development experts. However, punishment is most effective if accompanied by an explanation (inductive approach). The preferred and most effective discipline methods are those that are preventive. These are **positive guidance techniques** that teach children what the expected behaviors are and how to solve their conflicts using words rather than physical force. Inductive methods use positive statements that tell the child exactly what he or she is supposed to do and why. For this reason, they are most likely to support long-term generalization as discussed in Chapter 26.

**positive guidance techniques**

Teach children what the expected behaviors are and how to solve their conflicts using words rather than physical force.

**time out**

involves "a brief social isolation and temporary suspension of usual activity" (Readdick & Chapman, 2000).

Time out has been a frequently used method to decrease children's unacceptable behavior. **Time out** involves "a brief social isolation and temporary suspension of usual activity" (Readdick & Chapman, 2000, p. 81). The objective of time out is to help children learn to not continue using inappropriate behaviors and to learn appropriate ones. However, in a study of time-out effects on two-, three-, and four-year-olds, Readdick and Chapman (2000) found that children gained very little insight regarding inappropriate behavior. Also, children felt alone, disliked by the teacher, ignored by peers, and sad and afraid. Time out was viewed as punishment, not as a learning experience. That is, it is most frequently a response to behaviors such as biting, spitting, splashing water, and not staying seated during story time. Further, during time out, children were not mulling over the cause of their misbehavior. Readdick and Chapman (2000) recommend that time out be used only when a child is "wildly out of control or an imminent threat to other children" (p. 87).

Fields and Fields (2006) provide examples of less stringent time-out procedures. That is, where children may decide themselves to go to another area of the room to calm down and return when they are ready to behave appropriately in the group. In one example, the teacher has the students select and decorate a private space where they can go when they feel the need to cool down.

Time out is one of several behavior modification approaches (Fields & Fields, 2006). As mentioned in Chapter 25, behavior modification is an outgrowth of Skinner's operant conditioning theory. Rewards are used to modify (or change) behavior. Alfie Kohn is a major critic of behavior modification. Kohn believes that children deserve our unconditional love. They shouldn't have to earn our love by receiving it only when they please us. His point of view is that adults need to ask themselves "What does my child need—and how can I meet those needs?" (p. 118) A child's every need cannot be fulfilled, but can be respected. Kohn believes children should be taken seriously and that this can be accomplished through three specific methods (p. 119):

1. Expressing unconditional love.
2. Giving children opportunities to make decisions.
3. Imagining how things look from the child's point of view.

We will look next at some views of positive guidance applied in the early childhood classroom.

**LOOKING FURTHER**

Observe a preschool, kindergarten, or first-grade teacher for approximately 60 minutes. Write down everything the teacher does. Write a running description of your observations. Identify all the teacher's actions that can be categorized as disciplinary or guidance approaches as defined in this chapter. Categorize each approach by using the categories outlined in Figure 27–1. Which types of techniques did the teacher use most often? Evaluate the teacher's skill in the guidance/discipline area. Explain if you believe the children were learning appropriate behaviors, self-regulation, and independence. Does this teacher follow the NAEYC guidelines? Does this teacher fit in any of Baumrind's categories?

## TEACHING FOR DEMOCRACY, NONVIOLENCE, AND MORAL DEVELOPMENT

Teaching for democracy, nonviolence, and moral development begins with positive guidance. Historically, the concept of positive guidance goes back to 1950 and the publication of the first edition of Katherine Read Baker's textbook *The Nursery School: A Human Relationships Laboratory.* Baker presented her view of the nursery school as a human relationships laboratory, where guides or simple rules give support (Read, 1992). With this approach, the adult takes a low-key, positive, consistent role as a guide rather than as a director. The emphasis is on telling the child what he or she should be doing, not what he or she should not be doing.

Josh is throwing blocks. The guidance-oriented teacher say, "The blocks are used for building, Josh," rather than "Stop throwing those blocks!"

Isabel is washing dolls in a tub of soapy water. Water is dripping on the floor. The guidance-oriented teacher says, "Keep the water in the tub, Isabel," rather than "Isabel! Don't be so messy. You are spilling water all over the floor."

What about the adult's and the child's feelings? Both adult and child may at times display strong feelings. These feelings can be difficult to cope with when displayed as anger. We accept the child's right to be angry, but the child cannot be allowed to destroy property and hurt other people. The child needs to know that adults have feelings, too. Therefore, the child needs to know when an adult disapproves of his or her behavior and feels angry. Disapproval has to be open and direct to let the child know that he or she has done something wrong. It is through receiving disapproval from a respected adult that the child develops those guilt feelings needed for self-control. The adult does not need to yell and degrade the child but can let him or her know how he or she feels in a firm, constructive way:

Isabel refuses to help clean up the materials she has been using. She says to Mrs. Sanchez, "You're a dummy!" "Isabel," says Mrs. Sanchez firmly, "I don't like being called a dummy. Just do your job and then you can go play with your friends."

In this case, Mrs. Sanchez is direct and to the point, so Isabel knows that she disapproves but does not reject Isabel as a person.

## Teaching for Democracy

Articles by Joanne Hendrick (1992), Polly Greenberg (1992a, 1992b) and Suzanne Miller (2005) remind us that we live in a democratic country. Both Hendrick and Greenberg point out that preparation for democratic participation should begin in early childhood. Hendrick (1992) suggests that during the preschool years we begin to transfer some adult power to children by encouraging them to make decisions (the power to choose), by building autonomy (the power to try), and by fostering competence (the power to do) (p. 51). This does not mean adults should step back and let children run wild. It means that adults provide realistic choices, such as selecting which center to go to, encouraging children to try new things (in the ZPD), and supporting children when they tackle difficult problems (provide scaffolding). In this atmosphere, children can learn to value themselves and others, trust adults, and trust their peers.

In the first article, Greenberg describes how developmentally appropriate practice supports democratic living based on the ideas of John Dewey (1992a). Just as with parenting, teaching that is autocratic or too permissive is not supportive of child development. She also supports a democratic approach that develops democratic character in children. Greenberg states, ". . . democratic character is a cluster of characteristics, interests, and motivations in an individual that add up to a habit of acting in a way that's at once self-fulfilling and of benefit to the group" (p. 59). In Greenberg's second article (1992b), she describes how to institute some simple democratic practices in the classroom that will develop democratic character. Her suggestions include using preventive discipline, providing positive guidance, never shaming or demeaning a child (e.g., making threats, labeling a child "bad," ignoring needs for help), and teaching personal and social responsibility throughout the day. Miller (2005) also suggests that the classroom should be a democratic community. She suggests supporting cooperation rather than competition, using nonviolent conflict resolution skills, providing prosocial models, promoting service learning projects, and guiding children to appreciate diversity.

## Teaching for Nonviolence

Adults who work with young children have an opportunity to counteract some of the negative effects of violence in the family and the community (Osofsky, 1995; Quick, Botkin, & Quick, 1999). Wallach (1993, p. 7) suggests, "Child care centers, recreation programs, and schools can be resources for children and offer them alternative perceptions of themselves, as well as teaching them skills." Professionals in these settings can offset some of the negative effects of violence. Wallach (1993, pp. 7–8) provides the following guidelines for professionals:

- Make sure that your program provides opportunities for children to develop meaningful relationships with caring and knowledgeable adults.
- Organize schedules and time with the children to provide as much consistency as possible.
- Provide clear structure, expectations, and limits.
- Offer children many opportunities to express themselves.

Opportunities for involvement in play, art, and storytelling can be therapeutic by offering an opportunity to express feelings. Most important is collaboration with the children's families.

Parry (1993) describes "Choosing Nonviolence," the Rainbow House educational program for helping children survive in a violent world. It has been used in Head Start, child care, and primary classrooms. It is an approach that teaches children that they have a choice. There are three key concepts in the program (p. 14):

1. Understand what violence is and be able to name it in their lives, their toys, their choices, and so forth.
2. Realize they have the power to choose and control how they will act and how they will be.
3. Learn the power of language so that they can use it to say how they feel and to protect and defend themselves without being violent. They learn to speak out and find alternatives to violence for settling conflicts.

According to Wallach (1993) and Parry (1993), adults who work with young children can provide a therapeutic haven and alternative behaviors for children who live in a violent environment.

Some children come from homes and communities where violence is the only problem-solving tool they have learned. Lourdes Ballestereos-Barron, in her first teaching position, found herself in a classroom with 30 hitting, pushing, and name-calling first-graders (Teaching Tolerance Project, 1997). She soon found herself yelling, pointing out wrongdoing, writing names on the board, handing out "frowny faces," and placing children in detention. She realized that this was not the way to teach. She took a course with the Peace Education Foundation in Miami, Florida, and changed her teaching methods. She learned to teach in the opposite manner of her first-year behavior. She speaks softly, arranges her kindergarten room for cooperative activity, and posts "I care" rules. She pays attention to positive behaviors and gives specific praise. There is a "peace table" in the room where children go when they need to negotiate differences. Her class is a safe place filled with happy students who have learned alternatives to violent behavior.

## Teaching for Moral Development

There is a growing constructivist movement based on Piaget's theory. Kamii (1984) describes the basic constructivist philosophy as it bears on guidance practices. Kamii believes, from the Piagetian perspective, that reward and punishment have only short-term effects. Punishment leads to finding ways to get away with unacceptable behavior without getting caught, blind conformity, and revolt. Rewards keep the adult in the power position and never give the children opportunities to think for themselves. The crux of the Piagetian approach is reciprocity, or exchange of viewpoints between adult and child, and allowing children an opportunity to make their own decisions. These two elements enable the child to develop personal values and achieve moral autonomy. Children can learn about decision making only by making and living with their own decisions. For young children, these decisions are simple ones, such as which clothing to wear today or which activity to choose at school. By five years of age, children are capable of making many decisions for themselves if they have been given the opportunity for trial and error in previous years. With five-year-olds, the teacher should be able to leave the room for a few minutes without having chaos result; the children can govern themselves. If the teacher has approached problems with "What do you think we should do?" soon the children will do the same. Self-governance with small decisions will generalize to bigger ones. According to Kamii, this approach supports moral development, as well as intellectual development in general, because it forces children to think about different points of view.

**moral classrooms**

Classrooms in which the sociomoral atmosphere supports and promotes children's development.

**community in the classroom**

A classroom in which there is an atmosphere of respect among teachers and students.

The constructivist approach was elaborated on in more detail by DeVries and Zan (1994). DeVries and Zan developed guidelines and a plan for "moral classrooms." They define **moral classrooms** as "classrooms in which the sociomoral atmosphere supports and promotes children's development" (p. 7). These are not classrooms in which children are indoctrinated with values through specific lessons on character; they are classrooms in which a feeling of **community in the classroom** prevails and where the teacher is a friendly mentor. The basic atmosphere is one of respect. The teacher respects the children's ideas and consults them when there is a problem in the classroom. The teacher uses positive strategies to engage children in learning, making threats and punishments unnecessary. In moral classrooms, teachers use what DeVries and Zan refer to as "persuasive strategies," such as making suggestions, elaborating on children's ideas, reminding children of the reasons for rules, offering choices, encouraging the generation of ideas, and upholding the value of fairness. In the moral classroom, there are "moral children." Moral children deal with questions of right and wrong and good and bad in relation to their everyday activities. They worry about how people are treated, about aggression, and about questions of fairness. "They construct their morality out of daily life experiences" (p. 28). DeVries and Zan documented the success of this type of classroom in the research described in Chapter 26.

The constructivist approach can be carried from preschool and kindergarten into the primary grades. Castle and Rogers (1993/94) explain how children can learn through constructing their own classroom rules. Discussions on creating rules provide opportunities for active involvement, reflection, making meaningful connections, developing respect for rules, developing a sense of community, experiencing problem solving through negotiation, experiencing cooperation, having opportunities for inductive thinking, and acquiring a sense of ownership for the rules developed. See *Young Children*, March 1998, for a variety of ideas for building community in classrooms (Classroom Community Building, 1998).

Teaching for democracy, nonviolence, and moral classrooms are all positive procedures designed to develop the whole child. Other methods for helping children in the emotional, personality, and social development areas focus on more specific behaviors and behavior change and can be adopted as needed.

## Other Strategies for Affective Development

Several strategies have been used successfully to teach skills to children (Asher, Oden, & Gottman, 1977). These methods include shaping, modeling, and coaching. As previously described, shaping involves giving positive reinforcement each time a child demonstrates any behavior close to the desired behavior to increase the probability that the child will behave in the same way again. For the isolate, this involves first observing and finding out how often the child interacts with other children. Then, the teacher must be sure someone is watching the child at all times so that reinforcement can be given immediately every time the child interacts with another child. At first, the child may be reinforced for just being next to or near another child. Once there is some contact, he or she is reinforced for interaction only. General reinforcement has been found to be most effective. For example, four boys are playing in the sandbox. The adult says, "You boys are playing nicely." This approach avoids the possibility of embarrassing the target child by mentioning him specifically. Once the isolate is playing close to other children, he or she needs to develop some interaction skills. Modeling and coaching are ways of giving direct instruction. Sometimes from viewing filmed examples, children learn long-lasting skills that they had not been able to learn by watching their peers in the classroom. It may be that the film narration that calls their attention to the skills is necessary to make them focus on the most relevant and basic behaviors.

Shaping and modeling and other aspects of the behaviorist approach are described in detail by Eva Essa (2003) in her book *A Practical Guide to Solving Preschool Behavior Problems.* Even though this approach usually does not have long-term results, it is a way to get children started on the right track through achieving externally controlled changes in behavior. By gradually accompanying this approach with the inductive approach as the child is able to handle it, the inductive methods can eventually take over. Some children are too extreme in their use of inappropriate behaviors to deal with them inductively in the beginning. For the child who is very aggressive, antisocial, disruptive, destructive, overly emotionally dependent, and/or isolated, the adult can shape more appropriate behavior first, then move gradually to inductive, reciprocal, and discussion approaches.

Children can be taught directly how to interact with others. That is, they can be coached on how to play with other children. Children have been taught various kinds of prosocial behavior, such as sharing and taking turns. Much coaching comes through the use of inductive control methods because these define social rules quite clearly. Coaching has helped aggressive children to be more prosocial and isolated children to be more popular.

Another method that has become widely used in all areas of social development is using literature as a means for helping children solve problems in appropriate ways. For example, Krogh and Lamme (1983) describe a developmental approach to teaching sharing behavior through literature. As pointed out in Chapter 26, sharing is an important aspect of young children's definitions of friendship. Krogh and Lamme view literature as a vehicle for taking the abstract concept of sharing and putting it into a more concrete context. Children can hear about someone else's experiences with sharing, discuss how they themselves would solve the problem, and give their opinions on how the character in the book goes about solving the problem. Krogh and Lamme (1983, p. 191) suggest asking questions such as the following:

- Do you have a toy (or whatever fits the story) you don't like to share?
- How do you feel about sharing?
- How do you think the boy in our story felt after he decided to share?
- How do people feel when they share?

Children with special needs in the affective areas may need special attention in order to achieve behavior change. For example, children identified as ADHD (described in Chapter 4) are likely to display many unacceptable behaviors such as hyperactivity and impulsivity in the elementary grades, but they may be difficult to identify during the preschool years (Phillips, Greenson, Collett, & Gimpel, 2002). In their research on identification of ADHD symptoms in preschoolers, Phillips et al., (2002) found that parents were more likely than teachers to identify their children as having ADHD symptoms and males were rated as having higher levels of ADHD than females. A major problem in identifying ADHD in preschoolers is that many behaviors viewed as problems in elementary school (i.e., high levels of physical activity, short attention span, etc.) are viewed as typical of preschoolers. Therefore, caution should be taken in labeling preschoolers as ADHD, while focusing on increasing self-regulatory behavior through developmentally appropriate guidance procedures.

Many methods have been developed for helping children learn appropriate and satisfying social skills. Several of the articles and books listed in the For Further Reading section at the end of the chapter contain positive methods for helping children develop social skills.

## GIVING SUPPORT IN TIMES OF CRISIS

An important responsibility for adults in the child's affective development is helping the child through crises. In Chapter 25, we looked at children's emotional development. Among the areas considered were fear, anxiety, and stress. Whereas moderate amounts of each of these can be motivational, large amounts can be detrimental to the child's functioning. Children's concepts of death and fears regarding war were discussed. In our modern, fast-paced culture, children also have to cope with many changes that center on the family. Events, such as moving, divorce, working mothers, and other immediate social changes, can be traumatic for the young child (Sunal & Hatcher, 1985). Young children may have difficulty understanding and discussing these traumatic events. Crisis-oriented books can be used to help young children through these experiences (Jalongo, 1983; Sunal & Hatcher, 1985), just as they can be used as instructional support for social skills. Several resources for crisis-oriented children's books are included in the For Further Reading section at the end of this chapter. Also, resources are available on the World Wide Web. The late Fred Rogers (2001) provided advice on helping children deal with scary feelings and national tragedies (2001–2002). NIMH (The National Institute of Mental Health, 2001) provides information on helping children and adolescents cope with violence and disasters. The site for the National Center for PTSD includes many resources for working with post-traumatic stress disorder. For example, Hamblen (2002) provides facts regarding the effects of terrorist attacks on children.

### Listening to Children

Crucial to the adult role in affective development is listening closely to children. Adults need to be observant and attentive. In the book *Listen to the Children* (Zavitkovsky,

Baker, Berlfein, & Almy, 1986), a series of anecdotes with accompanying photographs and analyses are presented centering on five areas for listening: (1) when they (the children) trust an adult to understand, (2) developing self-control, (3) figuring things out, (4) interacting with others, and (5) listening to parents. Each anecdote and accompanying commentary and questions to consider provide powerful food for thought for the adult who works with young children. For example, in "Hit him!" (p. 16), the teacher explains that even though Kevin is angry with Greg, he must use words, not fists, to express his anger. Then, she asks Kevin what he would like to do; he responds, "Hit him!" and that is exactly what he does. This story reminds us of how careful we must be in what we do and say. The author of the commentary suggests that the teacher should have gone a step further and had Kevin devise a solution other than hitting. She points out that children can be very clever and creative in solving their own problems and are more likely to live with a solution they have developed themselves. In "I just helped her cry" (p. 38), a young boy explains to his mother that when his friend's doll broke he could not fix it but he could help her cry. The incident reflects this boy's developing understanding of another's feelings and how he can help. As reflected in this collection of delightful and touching anecdotes, most of the affective curriculum is based on spontaneous, unplanned events, the adult's sensitivity to what children mean and what they feel, and the ability to respond in a sensitive manner.

Teachers also need to spend more time listening to and reflecting on their own thoughts and behaviors (Bowman & Stott, 1989). Young children are easily hurt and embarrassed by sarcastic and insensitive remarks and actions, especially when they are shamed in front of their peers or in the presence of other adults. It is very important for teachers and other adults who work with young children to be reflective practioners.

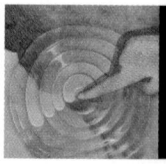

**LOOKING FURTHER**

Explore some of the positive guidance books and/or articles listed in the For Further Reading section. Select the strategies you think would be most effective. Develop a booklet containing a positive guidance plan that could be used by parents and/or teachers.

## SUMMARY

The adult has a variety of roles in the child's affective development. The NAEYC guidelines include two major elements for adult support of affective development: (1) creating a caring community of learners, and (2) respecting, valuing, and accepting children and treating them with dignity. Love and affection giving, early experiences, discipline, and teaching social skills and values are all critical areas that enter into affective development. Love is built on a foundation of acceptance and respect. Inner feelings are more important than outward behaviors. Once inner feelings have been established, observable expressions of love come spontaneously.

Positive responses from other people are necessary for normal affective development during early childhood. These responses must begin at birth for optimum development to occur. As children develop beyond infancy, they must learn self-control or self-regulation. Self-control comes about through the techniques of discipline used by adults to help children learn the difference between appropriate and inappropriate behavior. An authoritative approach to discipline, where demands are high but where there is warmth and reinforcement for independent behavior, seems to be most effective. Punishment may have an immediate effect on stopping an unwanted behavior, but it has no long-term positive effects. Harsh punishment may even be harmful by presenting an aggressive model for the child to imitate when solving problems. The commonly used time-out approach may do more psychological harm to young children than is commonly believed.

To combat the increasingly violent nature of our society, it is suggested that preventive teaching be done, using positive guidance approaches, such as teaching for democracy, teaching nonviolent techniques for solving problems, and creating a moral classroom. These techniques all include discussion, reflection, negotiation strategies, and other positive ways to resolve conflict. Children with good positive social skills are most likely to feel good about themselves. Social skills can also be taught through shaping, modeling, and coaching.

Affective aspects are reflected in all adult-child interactions. Although we may look at cognitive and affective development as separate areas for purposes of study, in reality, they are interrelated and need to be recognized as such by adults who work with young children. The affective curriculum comes mostly from day-to-day incidents. Adults need to be observant, listen to children, and be sensitive to what their actions and responses mean.

## For Further Reading


Aylward, G. P. (2003). *Practitioner's guide to behavioral problems in children*. New York: Kluwer Academic/Plenum Publishers.

Barber, B. K. (Ed.) (2002). *Intrusive parenting: How psychological control affects children and adolescents*. Washington, DC: American Psychological Association.

Baumeister, R. F., & Vohs, K. D. (2004). *Handbook of self-regulation*. New York: Guilford.

Bell, S. H., Carr, V. W., Denno, D., Johnson, L. J., & Phillips, L. R. (2004). *Challenging behaviors in early childhood settings*. Baltimore: Brookes.

Borkowski, J. G., Ramey, S. L., Bristol-Power, M. (Eds.). (2002). *Parenting and the child's world*. Mahwah, NJ: Erlbaum.

Bornstein, M. (Ed.). (2002). *Handbook of parenting*. (2nd ed.). Mahwah, NJ: Erlbaum.

Cameron, J., & Pierce, W. D. (2002). *Rewards and intrinsic motivation: Resolving the controversy*. Westport, CT: Greenwood.

Grieshaber, S. (2004). *Rethinking parent and child conflict*. New York: RoutledgeFalmer.

Grolnick, W. S. (2002). *The psychology of parental control*. Mahwah, NJ: Erlbaum.

Hiatt-Michael, D. (Ed.). (2002). *Promising practices in family involvement*. Greenwich, CT: IAP, Inc.

Omer, H. (2004). *Non-violent resistance: A new approach to violent and self-destructive children*. New York: Cambridge University Press.

Paley, V. G. (1993). *You can't say, "You can't play"*. Cambridge, MA: Harvard University Press.

Rogoff, B. (2003). *The cultural nature of human development*. New York: Oxford University Press.

Rogovin, P. (2004). *Why can't you behave?* Portsmouth, NH: Heinemann.

Sigsgaard, E. (2005). *Scolding. Why it hurts more than it helps*. New York: Teachers College.

Tamis-LeMonda, C. S., & Cabrera, N. (Eds.). (2002). *The handbook of father involvement: Multidisciplinary perspectives*. Mahwah, NJ: Erlbaum.


### POSITIVE GUIDANCE: BOOKS


Adams, S., & Baronberg, J. (2005). *Promoting positive behavior: Guidance strategies for early childhood settings*. Columbus, OH: Merrill/Prentice Hall.

Baker, K. R., Gardner, P., & Mahler, B. (1993). *Early childhood programs: A laboratory for human relationships* (8th ed.). New York: Harcourt, Brace, Jovanovich.

Brazelton, T. B., & Sparrow, J. D. (2001). *Touchpoints three to six*. Cambridge, MA: Perseus.

Cherry, C. (1981). *Think of something quiet*. Belmont, CA: David S. Lake.

Cherry, C. (1983). *Please don't sit on the kids*. Belmont, CA: David S. Lake.

Clemens, S. G. (1983). *The sun's not broken: A cloud's just in the way*. Mt. Rainier, MD: Gryphon House.

Essa, E. (2003). *A practical guide to solving preschool behavior problems* (5th ed.). Clifton Park, NY: Delmar Learning.

Fields, M. V., & Fields, D. (2006). *Constructive guidance and discipline* (4th ed.). Columbus, OH: Merrill/PrenticeHall.

Gartell, D. (2004). *The power of guidance*. Clifton Park, NY: Delmar Learning.

Gartrell, D. (2003). *A guidance approach for the encouraging classroom* (3rd ed.). Clifton Park, NY: Delmar Learning.

Howes, C., & Richie, S. (2002). *A matter of trust: Connecting teachers and learners in the early childhood classroom*. New York: Teachers College.

Kaiser, B., & Rasminsky, J. S. (2003). *Challenging behavior in young children: Understanding, preventing, and responding effectively.* Boston: Allyn & Bacon.

Marion, M. (2002). *Guidance of young children* (6th ed.). New York: Merrill/Prentice-Hall.

Orange, C. (2000). *25 biggest mistakes teachers make and how to avoid them.* Thousand Oaks, CA: Corwin.

## POSITIVE GUIDANCE: ARTICLES

Blaska, J. K., & Lynch, E. C. (1998). Is everyone included? Using children's literature to facilitate the understanding of disabilities. *Young Children, 53,* 36–38.

Bloch, J. (2005). Helping very young children with developmental disabilities make friends. *Focus on Inclusive Education, 2*(3), 1–5, 7

Ferrario, R. C. (2003). Classroom meetings in a kindergarten community. *Utah Journal of Reading & Literacy, 8*(1).

Flicker, E. S., & Hoffman, J. A. (2002). Developmental discipline in the early childhood classroom. *Young Children, 57*(5), 82–89.

Gartrell, D. (2002). Replacing time-out: Part one—Using guidance to maintain an encouraging classroom. *Young Children, 56*(6), 8–16.

Gartrell, D. (2002). Replacing time-out: Part two—Using guidance to maintain an encouraging classroom. *Young Children, 57*(2), 36–43.

Hong, Y. (2003). An ethnographic study of Korean kindergartners' reasoning during group moral discussions. *Early Childhood Education Journal, 30*(3), 151–156.

Hong, Y. (2004). Cultural meaning of group discussions on problematic moral situations in Korean kindergarten classrooms. *Journal of Research in Childhood Education, 18*(3), 179–192.

Joseph, P. B., & Efron, S. (2005). Seven worlds of moral education. *Phi Delta Kappan, 86*(7), 525–533.

McClurg, L. G. (1998). Building an ethical community in the classroom: Community meeting. *Young Children, 53,* 30–35.

## HELPING WITH CRISES, FEARS, AND FEELINGS

Alat, K. (2002). Traumatic events and children: How early childhood educators can help. *Childhood Education, 79*(1), 2–8.

Chen, D. W. (2003). Preventing violence by promoting the development of competent conflict resolution skills: Exploring roles and responsibilities. *Early Childhood Education Journal, 30*(4), 203–208.

Dettore, E. (2002). Children's emotional growth: Adults' role as emotional archaeologists. *Childhood Education, 78*(5), 278–281.

Fallin, K., Wallinga, C., & Coleman, M. (2001). Helping children cope with stress in the classroom setting. *Childhood Education, 78*(1), 17–24.

Gilbert, S. (2005, Fall). Helping traumatized children. *The Director's Link,* 1–3.

Gross, T., & Clemens, S. G. (2002). Painting a tragedy: Young children process the events of September 11. *Young Children, 57*(3), 44–51.

Helping young children in frightening times. (2001). *Young Children, 56*(6), 6–7.

Hopkins, A. R. (2002). Children and grief: The role of the early childhood educator. *Young Children, 57*(1), 40–47.

Kirova, A. (2001). Loneliness in immigrant children: Implications for classroom practice. *Childhood Education, 77*(5), 260–267.

Willis, C. A. (2002). The grieving process in children: Strategies for understanding, educating and reconciling children's perceptions of death. *Early Childhood Education Journal, 29*(4), 221–226.

Zeece, P. D., & Stolzer, J. (2002). Creating literature safety zones for young children. *Early Childhood Education Journal, 30*(1), 47–52.

Zeece, P. D. (1998). Books for children. Disasters! *Early Childhood Education Journal, 25,* 189–192.

Zeece, P. D. (2001). Meeting children's needs with quality literature. *Early Childhood Education Journal, 28*(3), 175–180.

Zeece, P. D. (2001). Meeting children's needs with quality literature: Part two. *Early Childhood Education Journal, 28*(4), 237–241.

# SUGGESTED ACTIVITIES

1. Read an article or book on early emotional or social experience. Write a short review and reaction to the article including:
   a. title and author
   b. publisher and title of journal or book

c. date of publication and pages
d. a statement of the main message of the author(s)
e. the subpoints the authors presented to support the main message
f. What did you learn from reading this article (or book)? How does the information relate to your own experience and other things you have read? Was the article of value to you? Why?
g. Develop three discussion questions. Use the questions as a guide as you lead a small group discussion in class.

**2.** Interview four sets of parents of young children. Ask them how they define *discipline*. Ask them what kinds of methods they use. Compare your results with those obtained by the students described in this chapter. What conclusions can you draw regarding parents' views and techniques of discipline? Compare your results with those of other students who may have done the same activity.

**3.** Have you ever heard the expression "Practice what you preach"? Observe a teacher for two or three 60-minute periods. Fill out a form like the following one with information on what you observed the teacher doing. Then have the teacher fill out the form. Compare your responses with the teacher's. Were there any discrepancies? Would you say this teacher follows the expression above? If not, what are the differences between what the teacher says and what he or she actually does?

**WHAT YOU VALUE IN THE AFFECTIVE AREA: A SELF-CHECKLIST**
**Mark each item as it applies to you and your teaching.**

**A = Always F = Frequently S = Sometimes O = Occasionally N = Never**

| | | A | F | S | O | N |
|---|---|---|---|---|---|---|
| (1) | I accept children's feelings, both positive and negative. | | | | | |
| (2) | I reinforce physical independence; that is, I give children opportunities to do things for themselves. | | | | | |
| (3) | I reinforce emotional dependence by giving children all the affection and attention they need. | | | | | |
| (4) | When a child is afraid, I try to provide comfort and help the child find a way to cope with his or her fear. | | | | | |
| (5) | When a child is angry, I try to help the child find a way to handle angry feelings without making him or her feel that it is wrong to be angry. | | | | | |
| (6) | I consciously try to make my classroom and my actions not be those that encourage sex-role stereotypes. | | | | | |
| (7) | When children ask about the parts of the body or about reproduction, I give them honest but simple answers based on their level of understanding. | | | | | |
| (8) | I try to help the children develop self-esteem and a positive self-concept. | | | | | |
| (9) | I respect the children's culture, customs, and behaviors. | | | | | |
| (10) | I encourage good peer relationships and opportunities for peer interaction. | | | | | |
| (11) | I provide settings for dramatic play and give the children help in developing more mature levels of play interaction. | | | | | |
| (12) | I discuss rules and expectations with the children, providing the reasons for all limits and restrictions. | | | | | |

4. Obtain an early childhood storybook that deals with a potential crisis or social problem situation that young children might face, such as moving, starting school, sharing, death, sibling rivalry, or joining a blended family. See the resource list under the For Further Reading section.

   The children's librarian can also help you. Most libraries have lists of crisis-oriented children's books. Read the book to a small group of preschool or kindergarten students. Discuss the book with them, asking questions regarding what they think about the characters, their feelings and their actions. Find out if any of them have had experiences like those in the story. How did they solve their problem? Discuss the children's responses in class.

5. Make an entry in your journal.

## REVIEW

1. Write the letter of each correct statement.
   a. Outward expressions of love, such as tickling, hugging, and squeezing, are the most important of the components of the adult-child affectional relationship.
   b. The emotional aspects of affection (what the person feels) may be more important than the outward expression of affection.
   c. The child's need for love is a feeling of emptiness that needs to be filled in order for him or her to feel competent and complete.
   d. Usually, an adult will be able to emphathize and feel the same feelings the child feels.
   e. It is uncommon for an adult to feel ambivalent about expressing feelings to a child.
   f. The adult who achieves success in working in the affective area with young children is one who works through his or her personal feelings outside of the school setting with other adults.
   g. Love cannot be turned on and off whenever one feels like it: It is spontaneous and natural.
   h. Love and affection are not essential to a positive adult-child relationship; acceptance and respect are equally, if not more, important.
2. Decide whether the disciplinary technique(s) used in each of the following examples are power assertive (physical punishment, shouting, threats, or physical inhibition), psychological (love withdrawal or induction), modeling (observational learning or modeling statements), or reinforcement.
   a. "I can't stand it when you do that. I'm going in the other room until you can behave yourself."
   b. "Mary and Janie, you are picking up the toys and putting them away in the right places. You're working hard."
   c. "The children at Jose's table are all seated and look like they are ready to eat."
   d. "Larry! How could you make such a mess! Now you get a spanking and if you ever do this again you'll get an even harder spanking."
   e. "I just can't let you pick up that hot kettle. It's too big and heavy and you may burn yourself. If you would like to cook, we have plenty of other pans your size."
   f. Jack watches as Isabel is praised by the teacher for washing out paintbrushes. Jack then proceeds to do the same.
   g. "You didn't clean up your room. No TV for you tonight."

3. What is the advantage of using the inductive method for discipline?
4. Describe the negative effects of corporal/harsh punishment.
5. Discuss the advantages and disadvantages of time out.
6. According to the Piagetian view of discipline, what is the advantage of adult and child exchanging viewpoints and allowing children to make their own decisions?
7. Match the characteristics in Column I to the parenting approaches listed in Column II.

| Column I | Column II |
|---|---|
| a. This type of technique produces the most mature children. | 1. authoritative |
| b. The children whose parents use this type of technique tend to be the most immature. | 2. authoritarian |
| c. The children whose parents used this technique always seem to know what their parents expect without being told. | 3. permissive |
| d. Boys reared under this type of parenting approach tend to be low on competence, whereas girls are very high on competence. | 4. harmonious |
| e. Children of these parents are independent, competent, and assertive. | |
| f. These parents are not very nurturant or sympathetic and use threats. | |
| g. The children of this type of parent are likely to be discontented, withdrawn, and distrustful. | |
| h. These parents use withdrawal of love or ridicule as punishment techniques. | |
| i. These parents tend to be very well educated. | |
| j. This method seems to be the most positive overall, according to Baumrind. | |

8. Which disciplinary methods are considered positive approaches according to the text?
9. Select the correct answer to the following. There is only one correct answer for each.
   a. "If you want to play in the sandbox with the other children, you have to take turns and share the trucks and cars." This is an example of
      (1) shaping.
      (2) modeling.
      (3) coaching.
   b. Rudy is an isolate. He never plays with any other children. Mrs. Chen takes some movies of the other children playing. One day, she takes Rudy to another room and shows him the film. She points out some of the social skills used by the other children. This is an example of
      (1) shaping.
      (2) modeling.
      (3) coaching.
   c. "Let's think about what cowboys do. Anyone have any ideas?" "Yes, they ride horses and herd cows." "Now let's pretend we are cowboys." This is an example of
      (1) shaping.
      (2) modeling.
      (3) coaching.
   d. Bill has been engaged in solitary play only. One day, he moves close to a group and looks on as they play. Mr. Brown smiles at him and pats him on

the shoulder. Bill begins to spend more time near other children observing. This is an example of
(1) shaping.
(2) modeling.
(3) coaching.

**10.** Mrs. Ramirez learns that Kate is going to have her appendix removed. She finds a book about a little girl name Madeleine who also has her appendix removed. She plans to read it to Kate and discuss it with her. Is this a good idea? Why?

**11.** Mrs. Harper goes through the values self-checklist included in the Suggested Activities section of this chapter. She rates herself either *always* or *frequently* on each item. You observe her as she works with the children in her family child care home. The following describes what you observe. Decide whether Mrs. Harper's beliefs are consistent with her practices. Give reasons for your answers.

The children are engaged in play activities. Two children are playing house and dressing up in grown-up clothes. They are the mother and father and have a baby doll who they refer to as "Baby Mindy." Both children are girls. "Mrs. Harper, Mrs. Harper," says the girl playing Mother, "How do the babies get in the mothers' tummies?" Mrs. Harper looks embarrassed and says, "That's something you should ask your Mommy." Sally wants to go to the bathroom. She starts in the door but stops and runs to Mrs. Harper. "Please turn the light on in the bathroom for me; it's dark and scary." "Okay," says Mrs. Harper, "but let me show you, you can reach around from outside like this and turn it on yourself." Mrs. Harper notices that Pete is trying to feed the bird. Birdseed is falling on the floor. Mrs. Harper says, "Pete, I know it's your turn today, but I can't let you do it when you are so messy."

**12.** Think about the following statement: "The affective curriculum can be planned in a developmental sequence just like the psychomotor and the cognitive." Is this true? Explain your response.

**13.** Explain what is meant by preventive discipline/guidance approaches.

## KEY TERMS LIST

community in the classroom
discipline
guidance
love and affection
moral classrooms
parental styles
positive guidance techniques
punishment
teaching styles
time out

Additional resources for this chapter can be found on the Online Companion™ to accompany this text at http://www.earlychilded.delmar.com. Respond to "Time to Reflect" and "Looking Further" concepts, review various child development scenarios, and answer thought-provoking questions in the Critical Thinking Forum. Keep a daily journal by downloading the student journal available on this Web site. Complete the interactive matching exercises to reinforce concepts, and print out the child development assessment forms to use during your observation of development for children from birth to age eight. In addition, read the case studies on the Web site to reinforce the important concepts in each chapter, and take a look at the multitude of Web links that are available for student research on the Internet.

# SECTION VIII

## The Primary Child: Growth and Development Ages Six Through Eight

Ideally, children enter the primary grades with six years of life experience. This experience prepares them to learn the academics that will ensure that they exit third grade able to apply the basics of reading, writing, and arithmetic as they move on through school. Making the connection from preschool to kindergarten to the primary grades is a focus of much concern. Of major interest is the status of children when they first enter the public school system at the kindergarten level. This concept of readiness for school continues to be a national concern.

In 1989, President Bush and the members of the National Governors' Conference adopted the goal "by the year 2000, all children will start school ready to learn." This statement generated a great deal of response. To clarify the implications of the stated national goal and define readiness, the NAEYC issued a position statement on school readiness (NAEYC Position Statement on School Readiness [1990]. *Young Children*, *46* [1], 21–23.) This position statement was designed to address what appears to be an oversimplification of the concept of readiness as included in Goal 1. The preamble to the NAEYC Position Statement states the problem:

> State and local efforts for educational reform and improved accountability have prompted considerable concern regarding children's "readiness" to enter kindergarten and first grade. The issue gained national prominence when the President and the nation's governors adopted it as a national education goal, vowing that "by the year 2000, all children will start school ready to learn." The construct of school readiness is based on the assumption that there is a predetermined set of capabilities that all children need before entering school. Therefore, any discussions of school readiness must consider at least three critical factors:
>
> 1. the diversity and inequity of children's early life experiences
> 2. the wide range of variation in young children's development and learning
> 3. the degree to which school expectations of children entering kindergarten are reasonable, appropriate, and supportive of individual differences.

The NAEYC position is that these three factors must be considered when planning for children as they enter school. The point is that children are ready to learn, but schools must be ready to receive them where they are.

Chapter 28 considers three areas critical to early school success: continuity, readiness, and assessment. As already indicated in this text, developmentally appropriate instructional practices have the power to provide for school success and eliminate the "fourth-grade slump" (Marcon, 1995). Chapters 29, 30, and 31 describe the physical/motor, affective, and cognitive development of primary-grade children and the implications for developmentally appropriate schooling.

CHAPTER

# 28

# Preschool to Primary: Bridging the Gap

## OBJECTIVES

After reading this chapter, you should be able to:

- Explain why continuity is needed in educational programs from prekindergarten to primary.
- Assess whether a classroom has the characteristics of developmental appropriateness.
- Identify the basic factors in the concept of readiness.
- List the major factors to consider in the assessment of readiness.
- Identify skills and knowledge that children have usually acquired by the end of kindergarten.
- List the skills a child probably will need to deal with the world of the future.

As mentioned in the introduction to Section VIII, on January 20, 1990, in his second State of the Union message, President Bush formally announced the national education goals (Boyer, 1993). During the first years of Bill Clinton's presidency, the national education goals were modified and labeled "Goals 2000 Program." Each state was charged with developing standards to meet the year 2000 goals. On January 8, 2002, President George W. Bush signed into law the *No Child Left Behind Act* of 2001 (No Child Left Behind, 2002; Friedrich, 2002). As with the previous legislation goals, No Child Left Behind established among them that all children should be able to read by the end of third grade. No Child Left Behind also focuses on reading, but begins with prekindergarten. However, No Child Left Behind includes four basic education reform principles: stronger accountability for results, increased flexibility and local control, expanded options for parents, and an emphasis on teaching methods that have been proven to work. This legislation has caused concern about the increased testing associated with the focus on accountability and with the definition of research-based teaching methods (Popham, 2005; St. Pierre, 2002).

The concept of readiness is still in the spotlight. The national goals statement built on the traditional concept of readiness, which, as you will see later in this chapter, is now outdated (Kagan, 1990; NAEYC Position Statement on School

FIGURE 28–1a Symbolic activity supports the shift to the use of abstract symbols, such as those representing numbers.

Readiness, 1990; Willer & Bredekamp, 1990). This concept of readiness, among other faults, tends to promote the view that preschool, kindergarten, and primary are separate entities, with their only relationship being that each exists to ready children for the next level. This factor has tended to promote the belief that an imaginary gap exists between each level. This chapter examines the case for bridging that imaginary gap by looking at early childhood as a continuum of growth and development rather than as separate stages related only by a vague concept referred to as "readiness."

From the cognitive developmental or constructivist point of view, early childhood is a unique period in child development that merits consideration beyond the conventional readiness point of view. Remember particularly that the period from age five to age seven is a time when a cognitive shift takes place as children pass from preoperational to concrete operational thought processes. Early childhood educators are becoming increasingly concerned with the movement to include more prekindergarten children in public education and at the increase in inappropriate academic pressures being placed on young children (Kagan, 1990; NAEYC Position Statement on School Readiness, 1990; Willer & Bredekamp, 1990).

## CONTINUITY

**continuity**

Development is a continuous process that needs to be recognized as programs are planned for children as they move from grade to grade.

In the early years of schooling, kindergarten and primary, young children are passing through the second transition period. Symbolic play serves as a vehicle that supports children's development from purely concrete activity to connecting the concrete with the abstract (Figures 28–1a and 28–1b). Unfortunately, play is not a part of many of today's kindergarten programs and is seldom included in the primary grades (Wasserman, 1990). Lack of play opportunities represents one of the major factors that create the gap between preschool, kindergarten, and primary education. (To review how play serves as the major vehicle for young children's learning, look back at Chapter 5.) Chafel (1997) perceives that there is a so-called hidden curriculum in schools beginning in kindergarten that separates play from work. By fifth grade, children perceive play as pleasurable and work as not pleasurable. For children in grades one through five, play is an activity that breaks up the monotony of the required work. Play is not perceived by teachers or students as a vehicle for learning. Learning activities are designated as work and not perceived as creative or enjoyable.

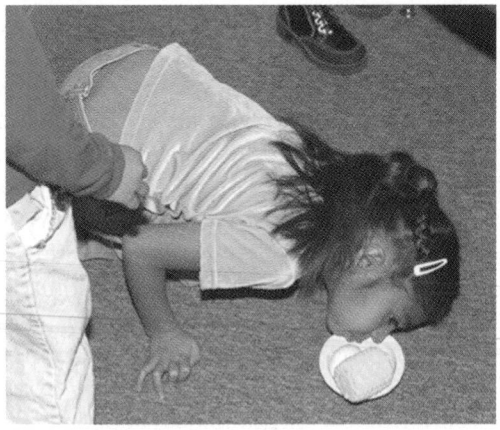

FIGURE 28–1b Young children engage in symbolic activity in their representational dramatic play. This young girl is pretending to be an animal and is eating food off the plates.

The question of **continuity** is by no means a new one. For example, Dorothy H. Cohen (1972) expressed concern regarding preschool to kindergarten continuity, and Betty Caldwell (1978) was concerned about the chasm between kindergarten and primary. Cohen's conclusion that "Children of four, five, six, and seven are continuations of themselves" is as relevant today as it was in 1972. As an example, consider Kate's reactions at different ages and stages on a trip to the zoo:

At age three, Kate goes to the zoo. Back at the Child Development Center, she shows her response to the trip by painting a yellow-and-black blob, which she tells us is a tiger. She also shows an interest in leafing through an assortment of animal books that are available, and pointing out some of her favorites. In addition, she is observed in a wooden packing crate growling and begging for food just as she had seen the tigers do at the zoo during feeding time. When asked to dictate a story about the trip to the zoo, she responds, "I like the tiger at the zoo. He eats meat. He growls. That's all."

At age four, Kate visits the zoo again. At preschool the next day, she paints a cagelike design with a yellow-and-black animal-like figure. She tells us to write on her picture that this is a hungry tiger. She requests that several animal stories be read to her. She is observed playing zoo animals with two other children; one child is the keeper and the other two are being fed. Later, they build some square structures with the unit blocks and put all the small rubber animals in the enclosure. When asked to dictate a story about the zoo, Kate responds, "We went on the little yellow bus to the zoo. First we saw the wild animals. I liked the tigers best. Then we went to the petting zoo. I liked the horses and the rabbits. Then we ate a picnic lunch. We came home on the bus."

At age five, Kate again visits the zoo. Back at school she paints a picture of a tiger in a cage that is fairly recognizable to the adult eye. She also asks for a large piece of drawing paper and with markers and crayons draws a larger overview of the zoo with several cages, each containing one of her favorite animals. On each cage she draws a rectangle and asks the teacher how to spell the names of each of the animals so she can label each cage. With some help from her teacher, she makes a zoo book with captions such as "This is a tiger" and "The rabbit wiggles his nose." She leafs through all the zoo storybooks and soon has her favorite stories memorized. She is observed pretending to read a story to one of her classmates. Kate and three other children build a rather elaborate zoo with the unit blocks. They each take responsibility for different roles, such as the zookeeper who feeds the animals, the zookeeper who cleans, the zoo doctor, and the snack-stand salesperson. Kate also displays curiosity with follow-up questions regarding the animals.

At age six, Kate visits the zoo again. In her first-grade class she enjoys again reliving the experience. She writes and illustrates her own zoo storybook. She reads some books about the zoo and zoo animals. She asks her teacher to read the class some informational books. From these books they learn how much each animal eats in a day and proceed to figure out their intake per week. The books also tell them statistics, such as the weight and height of each animal, so they can compare the sizes. She and the other children work together to build a miniature zoo, using boxes to make cages and clay to make the animals. In her developmental classroom, there is a dramatic play center. The class members relive their zoo experience using large boxes for cages. They make signs for each cage. Each sign has the name of the animal and a brief description of its habits and lifestyle.

The examples of Kate's behavior demonstrate that as Kate grows and matures, her responses to the same experience and the same raw materials also grow and mature. Her growth in curiosity, in perceptual-motor ability (i.e., drawing, painting, and building), in language, and in sociodramatic play capacity is reflected in her response at each level.

Cohen warned that cutting children's early years into small, unrelated pieces can only damage them. Today, her warning is becoming a reality. Children approach learning as their developmental levels lead them, supported by adult scaffolding at the right moments. Unfortunately, some of the concerns of the 1970s regarding moving first-grade curriculum into kindergarten and kindergarten curriculum into prekindergarten curriculum has become reality. Efforts have been made to increase continuity (Barbour & Seefeldt, 1999; Edson, 1994; Kohler, Chapman, & Smith, 1994; Fiflik, 2003; La Daro, Kraft-Sayre, & Pianta, 2003; Vail & Scott, 1994) and overcome the barriers to smooth transitions. In previous chapters, some of the barriers to smooth transitions and continuity have been described. **Barriers** include instructional strategies that are not consistent with the principles of child development, such as sit-still workbook/worksheet and large group instruction; inappropriate placement procedures, such as extra-year readiness classes before kindergarten and transitional classes after kindergarten (Bredekamp, 1990; Brewer, 1990; Patton & Wortham, 1993; Uphoff, 1990); common evaluation procedures (Charlesworth, Fleege, & Weitman, 1994; Fleege, 1997; Kamii, 1990); retention and other practices that doom children to failure (McGill-Franzen & Allington, 1993; Smith & Shepard, 1988); and lack of teachers and school administrators qualified and/or certified in child development and early childhood education (Burts, Campbell, Hart, & Charlesworth, 1991).

**barriers**

Instructional strategies that are not consistent with the principles of child development; inappropriate placement procedures.

## Efforts Aimed at Achieving Continuity

Programs that attempt to sustain continuity from prekindergarten through the primary educational years have been developed. One example was the major national effort called Follow Through. Follow Through attempted to extend the types of programs developed for preschool children attending Head Start through to compulsory kindergarten and primary education (Hodges & Sheehan, 1978; Maccoby & Zellner, 1970). A number of program models that could be used as the basis for continuity grew out of these efforts (Roopnarine & Johnson, 2004). Although some of the national evaluation results interpret the success of the program as being only moderate, the individual sponsors believe that much was learned. They believe that the national evaluation studies were of such poor quality that they are of questionable value (Hodges & Sheehan, 1978). Follow Through's objective is to disseminate its models to school systems where there is a high risk of children failing (Walgren, 1990).

Since the publication of the NAEYC guidelines (Bredekamp, 1987) and their revision (Bredekamp & Copple, 1997), interest has increased in developing programs that provide continuity. The NAEYC guidelines for developmentally appropriate practice and those for developmentally appropriate curriculum and assessment (NAEYC, 1991) have provided a nationally recognized justification that ties education from birth through age eight together in one continuous developmental sequence. The NAEYC documents have provided support for those who wish to attempt reform of early education practices.

In 1990, the Head Start Transition Project was created by the U.S. Congress in the Head Start reauthorization legislation (*Santa Clara*, 1992). "The Head Start Transition Project is a research and demonstration project [designed] to test the hypothesis that *the provision of continuous and comprehensive services, developmentally appropriate curriculum, and parent involvement will 'sustain the gains' of Head Start children after they leave Head Start*" (*Santa Clara*, p. 2). In 1997, at the annual meeting of the American Educational Research Association (AERA), a symposium was presented on the progress of several Head Start transition projects. The presenters documented the difficulty of breaking into the elementary grades with developmentally appropriate practice. High/Scope has created a developmentally appropriate elementary model that provides continuity (Brickman, 1998). This model is based on the same active learning philosophy as the High/Scope preschool program. Other researchers are examining how transitions from preschool to kindergarten take place. A symposium at the 1998 AERA meeting reported on a national survey of school-entry transition practices. Researchers found that the lower the socioeconomic-status (SES) level and the more minority population families, the more difficult it was to make successful transitions. The most common method was a whole-group activity after the start of school. Letters to the families were also commonly used; individual meetings, such as home visits, were rare. A number of barriers were perceived to successful implementation of a transition plan, such as receiving class lists too late, doing summer work with no additional pay, not having a comprehensive plan, and not having time. Overall, transitions into grade school were not reported to be done in a nurturing fashion.

Early, Pianta, Taylor, and Cox (2001) focus on the need for schools to be ready to transition children into kindergarten. Successful transitions include activities and events designed to provide continuity so as not to disrupt children's learning and development. A national survey of transition practices showed that most practices involved some kind of group activity. Rarely is there one-to-one contact with children and families prior to the first day of school and yet this type of transition practice would be very beneficial for children with disabilities (as well as other children).

Valeski & Stipek (2001) interviewed kindergarten and first-grade students regarding their feelings about school. First-graders' relationships with their teachers correlated with their academic performance. This indicates that children who enter first grade "unready" are at a double disadvantage, as they begin behind and may never catch up. Kindergartners in highly structured, teacher-directed classrooms felt less satisfaction with school as compared with those who were in classrooms where there was some freedom and some choice. Kindergartners still need opportunities to move freely about the classroom while first-graders are more accepting of a more rigid classroom structure. A developmentally appropriate classroom structure, as described next, appears to provide the best transition into kindergarten, which will result in a positive attitude toward school.

## The Developmentally Appropriate Classroom

Developmentally appropriate classrooms have some common elements that ensure that instruction fits the students' developmental levels. Constance Kamii (1984) reminds us that the stage concept is not the core of Piaget's contribution to a developmental view of education. For Piaget, the aims of education were intellectual and moral autonomy. Autonomy is the ability to govern oneself. Moral autonomy is achieved through exchanging points of view regarding moral issues, rather than through externally determined rewards and punishments (as discussed in Chapter 27). Intellectual autonomy comes through constructing knowledge from within, rather than internalizing it directly from outside (see Section VI). Children are not pressured to arrive at "correct" answers but are encouraged to think autonomously and discover relationships on their own. Kamii points out that most of our education is not based on developing autonomous learning but on the belief that all knowledge comes out of the teacher's head. Social interaction is an invaluable process in the development of intellectual autonomy. Comparing answers, judgments, and hypotheses forces children to question, evaluate, and think about what they are doing. They also remember their conclusions and learn about the process of problem solving. Play is an important component in young children's learning and should not be cut off after kindergarten. As children move into concrete operations, they naturally become interested in games with rules (Figure 28–2). These games can be very effective for teaching (Kamii, 1985) and a much more natural and developmentally appropriate method than work sheets. For example, Kamii has found that first-grade arithmetic can be taught successfully with group games using cards or dice. She has found that "worksheets are harmful for first

FIGURE 28–2 Six-year-olds are ready to play games on their own. They can now integrate information to keep track of the rules of the game, take turns, and see another's point of view regarding the play of the game.

graders' development of arithmetic while play is highly beneficial" (Kamii, 1985, p. 6). This statement applies to pre–first grade also.

Teachers in developmentally appropriate classrooms understand and apply child development theories to their practice as described in earlier chapters. Teachers consider individual and age appropriateness as they relate to development and culture (New, 1994; Williams, 1994). For example, they are warm and affectionate toward the children, use positive discipline strategies, encourage exploration and independence, are sensitive to the needs of families, and take time to observe and record observations while children are working independently. The physical environment is arranged in interest centers that provide individual and group learning experiences; there are concrete materials, an area for messy play, and furniture is sized appropriately for the children and is movable. Centers might include writing, library, mathematics, manipulatives and games, art, dramatic play, blocks, music, science, social studies, and gross motor. Block centers and sand play are a part of the primary classroom as well as the preprimary (Ewing & Eddowes, 1994; Harris, 1994). Centers can be combined and integrated to support project work.

Developmentally appropriate practice is supported by constructivist theoretical views. Some of the models that particularly fit the DAP criteria are the moral classroom (DeVries & Zan, 1994), the constructivist classroom (DeVries, Zan, Hildebrandt, Edmiaston, & Sales, 2002), the High Scope cognitively oriented curriculum, and the Bank Street model. (For descriptions, see Roopnarine & Johnson, 2004.)

## THE CONCEPT OF READINESS

**readiness**

An end point that is reached during a certain age or stage that enables the child to move on to the next level.

The term **readiness** is commonly used to describe an end point that is reached during a certain age or stage that then enables the child to progress to the next level. In the 1980s, the use of this term became extremely questionable (Charlesworth, 1985). The meaning of the term changed from *letting* children get ready through the normal course of development, with appropriate adult support and guidance, to *making* them ready. For example, Graue (1992) believes that the popular conceptions of readiness as biologically determined and/or the result of environmental stimulation and as a fixed sequence of developments is inaccurate. Furthermore, the current views of readiness have European American middle-class roots, which means they may not be applicable to all cultures. In addition, readiness cannot be accurately measured, and when such measures are made and used for making ready/not-ready decisions, children may be placed in the wrong grades and/or in the wrong special programs. Graue's point of view is that readiness is a culturally defined term. Every community of adults has a personal view of readiness that determines when children are "ready" to enter school and/or move on to the next grade in that community. From this view, readiness is a socially constructed concept rather than a characteristic of children. That is, each community of adults defines readiness in its own way. Graue does not believe that we can throw away the idea of readiness—it is too deeply ingrained in our culture. Somehow all those concerned, academic, policy, and parent communities, must come to a consensus. Although there is much concern about developing standards, most states have

created guidelines (or standards) for what children should know and be able to do upon kindergarten entrance (Kagan and Scott-Little, 2004). Kagan and Scott-Little provide three reasons for concern:

1. Young children's development is not standardized, but is uneven and individual.
2. Experience strongly effects development.
3. The content of standards may be too academically oriented.

States have felt pressure from local concerns about investment in prekindergarten education and pressure from the No Child Left Behind legislation and its demands for accountability. Kagan and Scott-Little are concerned that state guidelines may be used to make high-stakes decisions rather than as guides to improve instruction.

Viewing variability in development and lack of readiness as deficits is a mistake (Graue, 1998). Graue presents the case of shy, immature Edward, who is taken home from preschool to wait until he is "ready." Preschool presented a challenge to Edward, but Graue suggests that it would have been more appropriate and more helpful to Edward in the long run to find a way to help him feel comfortable in this new setting. Because no accurate measurement of readiness and no successful interventions have been discovered, Graue believes that Edward should not be held entirely responsible for his own "readiness." Instead, Edward's teacher should work out a way to support Edward's adjustment to his new environment. Graue's view is that "Readiness is in the eye of the beholder as much as in the skill, maturity, and abilities of those we behold" (p. 14). Furthermore, homogenizing classrooms by removing the Edwards supports the pressure to move the curriculum down.

A major problem for early educators is parental pressure for more formal academics for their young children. Early childhood teachers often have difficulty coming up with a defense for the developmentally appropriate program. Barbara Simmons and JoAnn Brewer (1985) developed answers to frequently asked questions from parents who did not understand how children learn through a developmentally appropriate program. The results of a national survey (Lewit & Baker, 1995a) indicated that although kindergarten teachers viewed being physically healthy, rested, and well nourished as the most important factors in readiness for school (with social characteristics next), parents were more likely to judge academic skills, such as knowing the alphabet, as most important.

Willer and Bredekamp (1990) proposed that redefining readiness was an essential requisite to educational reform. They expressed concern that readiness is being used as an exclusionary device. That is, by setting up certain prerequisites for school entry, readiness becomes a gatekeeping concept. The blame for not being ready is placed on the children rather than on the possibility that expectations placed on the children may not be appropriate. Willer and Bredekamp suggest that schools need to be ready to help children succeed at learning. They describe a number of assumptions (Figure 28–3) that underlie the gatekeeping point of view and explain why these assumptions are inaccurate and how they hinder reform efforts (pp. 22–24). Willer and Bredekamp (1990) suggest four reform strategies for ensuring that children are ready to succeed (p. 24):

1. Lay the foundation for school success by eradicating childhood poverty.
2. Prepare schools and teachers to respond to individual needs rather than trying to mold every child to be the same as they move down the assembly line of education.
3. Make schools places where developmentally appropriate practice predominates.
4. Invest the resources needed to accomplish these goals.

| Inaccurate Assumptions | Rationale for Inaccuracy |
|---|---|
| Learning occurs only in school. | Learning occurs before children enter school, both at home and in various early childhood settings outside the home. Many conditions, such as poverty, drugs, and poor health care, work against children's natural desire to learn. |
| Readiness is a special inherent condition within the child. | Environmental factors and inherent variations interact to produce a variety of developmental patterns in children. |
| Readiness is a condition that is easily measured. | Readiness for school is not easily measured due to a variety of factors, such as the lack of valid and reliable assessment instruments and the nature of the assessment situation. |
| Readiness is mostly a function of time; some children need more time than others. | Adults cannot just wait for children to blossom, but need to facilitate development by providing an environment in which children can construct knowledge. |
| Children are ready to learn when they can sit quietly at a desk and listen to the teacher. | Children are active learners who construct knowledge through concrete activities and interaction with peers and adults. |
| Children who are not ready do not belong in school. | It is those children who are most likely labeled as unready who most need the advantages of developmentally appropriate schooling. This assumption leads to homogenizing classrooms so that only those who fit a specific readiness mold are let in. They are then put under pressure as they are taught inappropriate curricula using inappropriate practices. |

**FIGURE 28–3** Countering the gatekeeping point of view.
Adapted from Willer & Bredekamp, 1990.

As Sharon L. Kagan (1990, p. 276) states, "instead of individualizing entry and homogenizing services, we should homogenize entry and individualize services." Readiness needs to be redefined to include every aspect of children's development and children's lives, both inside and outside of school.

Because a clear understanding of the term *readiness* is essential to working constructively with young children, the *NAEYC Position Statement on School Readiness*, which summarizes the essential aspects of the term *readiness* as it applies to schooling, should be read and reread by those who work with young children. Whether child readiness is defined from inside the child and/or from the social context of the community, it is important to keep in mind that children are born learning; they need to be in a setting that is ready to nurture their learning (Children are born learning, 1993).

An important element in the area of school readiness is consideration of ethnic and cultural differences. Rouse, Brooks-Gunn, and McLanahan (2005) describe concerns with the gap in achievement between whites, blacks, and Hispanics that surface at kindergarten entrance. The spring 2005 issue of *The Future of Children* is devoted to the various prekindergarten factors that influence the skills of entering kindergartners: academic, social/emotional, health, genetic, neurological, etc. In the late 1990s a national survey of over 3,500 kindergarten teachers found that forty-six percent of the teachers said that at least half of their students were "having problems following directions, some because of poor academic skills and others because of difficulties working in a group" (Rouse, Brooks-Gunn, and McLanahan, p. 6). These problems were more frequent for black and Hispanic children than for whites. There is not much data regarding the causes of these gaps. Research is needed to document factors such as SES, environmental stress, health, parenting

styles, prekindergarten educational programs, and genetics, which are all factors that account for most of the racial and ethnic gaps. Rouse, Brooks-Gunn, and McLanahan conclude that "the most promising strategy [for closing the ethic and cultural gap] is to increase access to high-quality center-based early childhood education programs for all low income three- and four-year-olds" (p. 12). Besides quality education, these programs should provide teachers who are trained to identify children with serious learning and/or behavior problems, parent-training components, health components, and integration with kindergarten programs that the children will enter.

| Behavior | Observed | Comments |
|---|---|---|
| | Yes or No | |
| **Cognitive** | | |
| • See Chapter 22 for reading and writing benchmarks | | |
| • Sorts objects by color, shape, or function | | |
| • Names most letters and numerals | | |
| • Rote counts to 20 and beyond | | |
| • Rational counts 10 or more objects | | |
| • Recognizes groups from 1–5 | | |
| • Draws a person with head, trunk, legs, arms, and features; may add some clothing | | |
| • Follows the rules of a simple board game | | |
| • Makes recognizable structures with LEGOS® or other construction materials | | |
| • Completes a 15-piece puzzle | | |
| • Communicates well verbally | | |
| **Affective** | | |
| • Takes turns playing a simple board game | | |
| • Takes turns playing an active motoric game | | |
| • Engages in cooperative play with other children | | |
| • Shares materials | | |
| • Demonstrates empathy and sympathy | | |
| • Acts on knowledge of right and wrong | | |
| • Makes independent decisions | | |
| • Works on a cooperative project with one other child | | |
| • Expresses hostility and anger verbally rather than physically | | |
| **Gross and Fine Motor** | | |
| • Walks across a balance beam | | |
| • Skips with alternating feet | | |
| • Hops for several seconds on one foot | | |
| • Incorporates gross motor skills into a game | | |
| • Climbs well | | |
| • Cuts out simple shapes | | |
| • Writes name in a recognizable fashion | | |
| • Handedness is well established | | |
| • Uses computer keyboard | | |
| • Zips, buttons, and ties shoes with coaching | | |

Developmental expectations for the end of kindergarten.
(Sources: Previous chapters and Allen & Marotz, 2006; and Bredekamp & Copple, 1997, pp. 102, 105, 109, 117)

### End-of-Kindergarten Developmental Expectations

Although developmental benchmarks or expectations should not be used for gatekeeping, they can be helpful for developing instructional goals and objectives and, thus, guiding instruction for individual children. In previous chapters, developmental checklists were included for this purpose. The checklist on the previous page includes some of the major developmental landmarks that children usually reach by the end of kindergarten.

Look over the developmental expectations checklist. Note any other expectations you believe are equally important and any listed that you believe are not essential for success in first grade. Discuss your opinions with a small group in class.

## ASSESSMENT PRACTICES

In 1990, Kamii described how early childhood assessment practices at that time included approaches that are dangerous to child growth and development (Kamii, 1990). The administration of inappropriate group paper-and-pencil standardized achievement tests to young children has escalated to an almost universal point. Administering these tests to young children is stressful, is not a valid and reliable measure of the children's achievement, and encourages teaching to the test, which narrows down the scope of the curriculum. Furthermore, test preparation, time spent taking the tests, and recovery from the test-taking experience use up valuable instructional time. In addition, the results are often used to make a variety of decisions about children and their educational futures:

- making decisions regarding grade placement, instructional level, and/or need for special help or eligibility for an enrichment program
- evaluating effectiveness of instruction
- evaluating teacher effectiveness
- comparing schools and districts
- satisfying public and administrative demands for accountability

Another practice, already mentioned, involves the misuse of the results from group paper-and-pencil achievement and readiness tests and from individually administered achievement, readiness, and screening instruments as the sole criteria for making important decisions about the placement of children. Decisions might include placement in regular or so-called "developmental" kindergarten, placement in transition classes or special education, retention in a grade, or providing Chapter 1/Title I or other special services.

Several points need to be considered about the misuse of tests and test scores. First, paper-and-pencil test taking is very stressful for young children. Children demonstrate increased frequencies of stress behaviors, respond with wrong answers to questions they could answer correctly under other circumstances, and copy answers from other students' test booklets (Charlesworth, Fleege, & Weitman, 1994; Fleege, Charlesworth, Burts, & Hart, 1992; Fleege & Charlesworth, 1993).

The pressure to perform well on the tests forces teaching to the test. This practice "dummies down" instruction by narrowing the instruction to fit the specific skills included on the test. Drill and practice, workbooks/worksheets, flash cards, and large-group instruction take over as methodology. Reading and math skills are emphasized, leaving little, if any, time for science, social studies, art, music, and play (Charlesworth et al., 1994; Madaus, 1988). Results of a study by Burts, Charlesworth, and Fleege (1991) indicated that students from teach-to-the-test classrooms did not obtain significantly higher scores on the *California Achievement Test (CAT)* than children from more developmentally appropriate classrooms.

Readiness and screening instruments have been used increasingly to implement the homogenizing of classes by determining placement of students in classes with other students of similar apparent capabilities. Screening and readiness instruments are not designed for use in making placement decisions (Meisels & Atkins-Burnett, 2005). The purpose of screening instruments is to identify children who may need in-depth diagnosis. The purpose of readiness instruments is to provide information that will assist in planning instruction (NAEYC and NAECS/SDE, 1991; NASBE, 1990). Readiness instruments are unreliable and are invalid predictors of school success (see studies by Graue & Shepard, 1989; Lichtenstein, 1990).

Unfortunately, with the standards movement and the accountability requirements of No Child Left Behind, developmentally inappropriate testing practices are again surfacing (High stakes testing position statement, 2001; Hyson, 2002; Kohn, 2001; Meisels, 2000; Wesson, 2001). A major example of inappropriate assessment is the National Reporting System (NRS), which developed a test for 400,000 Head Start students (Children's Defense Fund, May 17, 2005). This test contains inappropriate items, has not been shown to be reliable or valid, and poses a danger that it may be used to make high-stakes decisions. It also may lead to a narrowing of the curriculum and to "teaching to the test" for preschoolers. Next, we'll examine the factors that define developmentally appropriate assessment.

## Developmentally Appropriate Assessment

**inappropriate assessment procedures**

Addresses misuse of readiness test results and the elimination of paper-and-pencil, whole-group achievement testing through third grade.

**appropriate assessment procedures**

Authentic evaluation of educational achievement that directly measures actual performance in the subject area

In the 1990s, there was a nationwide movement to eliminate the use of **inappropriate assessment procedures** with young children, especially misuse of readiness test results and the elimination of paper-and-pencil whole-group achievement testing through third grade. Simultaneously, alternative **appropriate assessment procedures** were being developed (Krechevsky, 1998; Meisels, 1993, 1994; Schweinhart, 1993). This type of assessment is called authentic evaluation. "Authentic evaluation of educational achievement directly measures actual performance in the subject area. Standardized multiple-choice tests, on the other hand, measure test-taking skills directly, and everything else either indirectly or not at all" (Pett, 1990, p. 8). Authentic evaluation is also referred to as performance, appropriate, alternative, or direct evaluation. A wide variety of techniques may be used, such as teacher observations recorded as anecdotes or on checklists, portfolios of student work (Grace & Shores, 1992; Shores & Grace, 1998; McAfee, Leong, & Bodrova, 2004; Vavrus, 1990), performances while investigating a problem in science or math (Helm, Beneke, & Steinheimer, 1998; Shavelson, Carey & Webb, 1990), written compositions and reports, drawings and paintings, structures, and audio and videotapes. Skills can be observed as children engage in typical developmentally appropriate activities and through direct interviews, using concrete materials rather than paper-and-pencil tests. As documented in the Fleege et al. (1992) study, children may be able to apply concepts in concrete situations that they cannot deal with on a group-administered, paper-and-pencil, multiple-choice test. These various forms of authentic evaluation can be placed on a scale or summarized numerically in some way for assembling data on performance to report to administrators.

In his introduction to a special *Phi Delta Kappan* section on assessment, Eisner (1999) states his beliefs regarding performance assessment. He points out the developmental variability that exists among any group of children of the same age. Optimal teaching would enhance this variability by supporting each student's individual talents. Unfortunately, our traditional methods of instruction are based on standardization, uniformity, and homogenization, with students moving through a fixed pattern of grade levels toward fixed goals. The objective of performance assessments is to provide students an opportunity to demonstrate their individual talents. However, it would take a major change in the public's attitude to fully accept more authentic assessments.

A developmentally appropriate readiness instrument can be helpful in providing directions for curriculum and instruction. Such an instrument should be selected with care, using the following criteria:

1. The instrument should be designed to be individually administered. A test that has been designed and normed for group administration is not appropriate.
2. Required child responses should be mainly motoric (e.g., pointing, constructing, sorting), verbal (e.g., naming an object or a pictured object, answering a question) or require responses to auditory stimuli (e.g., following directions, sound discrimination). Paper and pencil should be used only as a check of perceptual-motor functioning (e.g., copy a shape, write his/her name, draw a person). Concrete materials and pictures should be the main media for obtaining responses.
3. The instrument should be broad in scope, sampling a variety of developmental areas: expressive and receptive language, reasoning, auditory reception, gross and fine motor development, perceptual development, and general behavior.
4. The instrument should be relatively short, taking no more than 30 minutes to administer.
5. The instrument should provide information that will be useful for further diagnosis and curriculum planning.
6. The instrument should be normed on a large representative sample of children.
7. Information on validity and reliability should be in the instrument's manual.
8. Instruction for administration should be clear and specific so that a teacher, parent, or teacher aide can easily administer the instrument.
9. A follow-up curriculum guide would be a valuable feature.
10. Other valuable features would include a parent questionnaire and reasonable cost.

Much of the assessment can be done through observation of students during their regular activities, but some must be done through individual interviews. Appropriate tasks for use with young children have been included throughout this text.

In their report from the Goal 1 assessment resource group, Shepard, Kagan, and Wurtz (1998) and Shepard (2000), indicate that assessment of young children should be an integral part of teaching. The resource group identified the following four kinds of reasons for assessment (p. 52):

1. To promote children's learning and development
2. To identify children for health and special learning services

3. To monitor trends and evaluate programs and services
4. To assess academic achievement and hold individual students, teachers, and schools accountable

None of these assessments should be used to make high-stakes decisions before age eight. "High stakes assessments intended for accountability purposes should be delayed until the end of third grade (or preferably fourth grade)" (p. 53). The authors conclude "Ultimately the goal is to set high expectations for early learning and development, to make sure that no child who falls behind goes unnoticed, and at the same time to help parents and the public understand how varied are the successful paths of early learning, depending on the rate of development, linguistic and cultural experiences, and community contexts" (p. 54).

Think about your past and recent assessment experiences. Note your feelings about being assessed and how you reacted to receiving the results. What high-stakes decisions have been made for you as a result of standardized test scores?

## PREPARING CHILDREN FOR THE FUTURE

In 1977, Karen Hartman, then a teacher of four-year-olds, asked herself the following question:

> [Considering what she and those before her had been doing with four-year-olds] How relevant was this routine, this philosophical regime, initiated by Caroline Pratt in 1914, for children who would ultimately cope with future shock, both externally and internally? (Hartman, 1977, p. 32).

She then proceeded to perform a self-evaluation of the manner in which she was teaching preschool children and whether it was teaching them the skills they would need in the future. She found she was teaching the following skills, which should help children deal with an increasingly complex world as they develop toward adulthood:

- By teaching children to focus on a task with few materials at a time, she was helping them develop the focusing skill necessary to deal with the highly stimulating world outside.
- By offering a carefully selected limited supply of materials in the classroom, she was helping the children develop decision-making ability before being faced with many choices in the future.
- By coping effectively with the environment provided for them, they were learning independence.
- Through offering firsthand rather than vicarious experiences, she was keeping their curiosity and inner resources alive.

FIGURE 28–4 Hopefully, some of the skills children learn during their early years will help them cope with an increasingly stimulating world of sights, sounds, and technology.

Hopefully, learning to focus on a task, make independent decisions, and maintain curiosity and creativity will enable today's young children to deal with our increasingly complex technological environment in the future (Figure 28–4).

Looking to the future, what skills and what kinds of knowledge can be acquired during the early childhood years that will help children deal with the world's increasing complexity as they progress toward adulthood?

## SUMMARY

The concept of readiness as preparation for the next level tends to underlie the belief that prekindergarten, kindergarten, and primary levels of education are totally separate periods. This concept was reflected in the goal set forth by the first President Bush and the nation's governors that, by the year 2000, all children in America would enter school ready to learn. Actually, preschool through primary should be treated as a continuous period of development. From this view, the transitions from preschool to kindergarten to primary education programs can be made smooth using familiar materials and activities as children progress from one level to another. Developmentally appropriate classrooms should be available for all young children.

It is time to redefine readiness, not as a gatekeeping concept used to keep so-called "not ready" children out of programs, but as the concept that we must help children be ready to succeed in schools that are ready to accept them as they are. As part of this redefining, readiness assessment should function as a means of finding out where to begin instruction, not as a gatekeeper for deciding who is let in and who is kept out of classrooms.

Besides reforming readiness assessment, the whole area of assessment of young children is in need of change. Paper-and-pencil, multiple-choice, group-administered, standardized achievement tests should not be used with young children. They increase stress level, use up valuable instructional time with preparation, and are too abstract to provide reliable or valid measures of young children's academic achievement. In addition, they overlook areas such as social development, motor development, problem solving, and thinking. Authentic evaluation procedures that provide information from naturally occurring learning experiences are appropriate. Preparation for the future in a technological world demands a workforce of creative thinkers and problem solvers, not test takers.

## FOR FURTHER READING

Adcock, S. G., & Patton, M. M. (2001). Views of effective early childhood educators regarding systemic constraints that affect their teaching. *Journal of Research in Childhood Education, 15*(2), 194–208.

Assessment [Special section]. (2002). *Phi Delta Kappan, 83*(10), 758–765.

Assessment for learning. (2004). [Special section]. *Phi Delta Kappan, 86*(1), 8–27.

Bagnato, S. J., Neisworth, J. T., & Munson, S. M. (1997). *Linking assessment and early intervention: An authentic curriculum-based approach.* Baltimore: Brookes.

Block, P., Harrison, C. Lee, C., Marshall, V., & Wilam, D. (2005). *Assessment and learning: Putting it into practice.* New York: Open University Press.

Dever, M. T., & Barta, J. J. (2001). Standardized entrance assessment in kindergarten: A qualitative analysis of the experiences of teachers, administrators, and parents. *Journal of Research in Childhood Education, 15*(2), 220–233.

FairTest. (1990). *Standardized tests and our children: A guide to testing reform.* Cambridge, MA: Author.

FPG working to define, assess and promote school readiness. (2001). *Early Developments, 5*(1), 6–10.

Golbeck, S. L. (Ed.). (2001). *Psychological perspectives on early childhood education.* Mahwah, NJ: Erlbaum.

Graue, M. E. (1993). *Ready for what? Constructing meanings of readiness for kindergarten.* Albany, NY: SUNY Press.

Graue, M. E., & DiPerna, J. (2000). Redshirting and early retention: Who gets the "gift of time" and what are its outcomes? *American Educational Research Journal, 37*(2), 509–534.

Gullo, D.F. (2005). *Understanding assessment and evaluation in early childhood education* (2nd ed.). New York: Teachers College.

Hatch, J. A. (2002). Accountability shovedown: Resisting the standards movement in early childhood education. *Phi Delta Kappan, 83*(6), 457–462.

Hirsh-Pasek, K., Kochanoff, A., Newcombe, N. S., & de Villiers, J. (2005). Using scientific knowledge to inform preschool assessment: Making the case for "Empirical validity." [Focus issue]. *SRCD Social Policy Report, 19*(1).

Hyson, M. (2002). Curriculum and assessment in early childhood programs: Yesterday, today, and tomorrow—with your help. *Young Children, 57*(3), 56–57.

Lopez, E. J., Salas, L., & Flores, J. P. (2005). Hispanic preschool children: What about assessment and intervention? *Young Children, 60*(6), 48–54.

Montessori, M. (2004). *The Montessori method* (edited by G.L. Gutek). Blue Ridge Summit, PA: Rowan & Littlefield.

National Association for the Education of Young Children. (2005). *NAEYC early childhood program standards and accreditation criteria.* Washington, DC: Author.

Neil, M., & Medina, N. J. (1989). Standardized testing: Harmful to educational health. *Phi Delta Kappan, 70*(9), 688–697.

*Phi Delta Kappan* [Special section on assessment]. (1999). 80(9).

Position statement of the American Educational Research Association concerning high-stakes testing in preK–12 education. (2000). *Educational Researcher, 29*(8), 24–25.

Raver, C. C. (2002). Emotions matter: Making the case for the role of young children's emotional development for early school readiness. *SRCD Social Policy Report, 16*(3), 3–17.

Raver, C. C., & Knitzer, J. (2002). *Ready to enter: What research tells policymakers about strategies to promote social and emotional school readiness among three- and four-year-old children: Policy paper #3.* New York: National Center for Children in Poverty. http://www.nccp.org/ProEmoPP3.html.

Raywid, M. A. (2002). Accountability: What's worth measuring? *Phi Delta Kappan, 83*(6), 433–436.

Rhodes, M., Feldman, J., & LaCount, M. (2006). Leaps and bounds: Preparing parents for kindergarten. *Young Children, 61*(1), 50–51.

Sameroff, A. J., & Haith, M. M. (1996). *The five to seven year shift: The age of reason and responsibility.* Chicago: University of Chicago Press.

Schweinhart, L. J., & Weikart, D. P. (1997). *Lasting differences: The High/Scope pre-school curriculum.* Ypsilanti, MI: High/Scope.

Scott-Little, C., & Niemeyer, J. (2001). *Assessing kindergarten children: What school systems need to know.* Greensboro, NC: SERVE.

Shepard, L., Kagan, S. L., & Wurtz, E. (Eds.). (1998). *Principles and recommendations for early childhood assessments.* Washington, DC: National Education Goals Panel.

Stipek, D. (2002). At what age should children enter kindergarten? A question for policy makers and parents. *SRCD Social Policy Report, 16*(3), 3–17.

Walmsley, B. B., & Wing, D. R. (2004). *Welcome to kindergarten.* Portsmouth, NH: Heinemann.

## SUGGESTED ACTIVITIES

1. Review the previous chapters. Make your own list of the skills that should be developed by young children by the end of the preoperational period. Compare your list with the end-of-kindergarten list included in this chapter. What differences do you find? Explain these differences.

2. Obtain some copies of readiness, screening, and/or achievement assessment instruments commonly used with young children. Your instructor can provide a list of assessment, readiness, and screening instruments that are commonly used. Using the list of criteria in this chapter, individually or in small groups, analyze each test. Also, compare the items included with the list in this chapter and/or the list you devised (Activity #1).
   a. Note which skills each assessment instrument included or did not include.
   b. Compare the strengths and weaknesses of each assessment instrument based on content and the selection criteria from this chapter. Rank the tests from the one you feel is best and would be most useful to the one you feel would be least useful. State the reasons for your decisions.

3. Try some of the assessment tasks suggested in the text (see especially Chapters 12, 15, 19, 20, 21, 22, 23, 29, 31) or use one or more of the readiness, screening, and/or assessment instruments reviewed for Activity 2 with one or more five-year-old prekindergarten or kindergarten children. If possible, videotape the assessment session. Play the videotape for the class and have the class members evaluate the child(ren)'s performance and your interviewing technique. Prepare a report including the name, age, and sex of the child interviewed, a description of what you did, the results, and your analysis and evaluation.

4. Read about some of the Follow Through model programs. Information on resources can be obtained in your library through the reference librarian. Some of the more highly publicized models are:

American Montessori Society (AMS)
281 Park Avenue South, 6th Floor
New York, NY 10010-6102

Behavior Analysis Model
Support and Development Center for Follow Through
Department of Human Development
University of Kansas
Lawrence, KS 66044

Cognitively Oriented Curriculum
High/Scope Educational Research Foundation
600 N. River
Ypsilanti, MI 48197

Bank Street Model
Bank Street College of Education
610 W. 112th Street
New York, NY 10025

Direct Instruction Model
University of Oregon
Department of Special Education
College of Education
Eugene, OR 97403

Language Development Approach
Southwest Educational Development Laboratory (SEDL)
Follow Through Division
211 E. Seventh Street
Austin, TX 78701

Compare the objectives and instructional approaches of each program reviewed. Evaluate each based on what you have learned about child development from this text. Do you think each program follows through at a level and in a way that works with the child as he or she leaves the preschool period and enters the shift to middle childhood? Share what you discover with a small group in class.

5. Make an entry in your journal.

## REVIEW

1. How would you explain to a kindergarten teacher that continuity is needed between your program for prekindergartners and his or her program? Or to a first-grade teacher that continuity is needed between your kindergarten program and his or her first-grade curriculum?
2. Select the correct responses.
   a. According to Elizabeth Graue, "readiness"
      (1) refers to what must be mastered before moving on to the next grade in school.

(2) refers to indicators of having acquired end-of-grade skills.
(3) is variable and its definition depends on who is defining readiness as much as on the child's skills, maturity, and abilities.

b. The core of Piaget's contribution to education is that
(1) intellectual and moral autonomy are the aims of education.
(2) education should follow a developmental pattern.
(3) children develop according to the stage concept.

c. Constance Kamii believes that
(1) worksheets are useful if young children are mature enough to use a pencil.
(2) worksheets with good, clear art work can supplement concrete activities.
(3) worksheets are harmful, even in the primary grades.

d. The traditional definition of the term *readiness* is based on the concept that
(1) each level of early childhood is designed to ready the child for the next stage.
(2) learning of a particular type may be done whenever the teacher is ready.
(3) schools should be ready to teach the variety of children they receive.

e. Willer and Bredekamp (1990) propose a new definition of readiness that emphasizes
(1) children developing at individual rates; readiness is mostly a function of time.
(2) that readiness is a special inherent condition within the child.
(3) that we need to ensure that children enter school ready to succeed and that schools are ready to help all children succeed.

f. Homogenizing the classroom refers to
(1) making sure each classroom has a wide variety of children at different levels of development.
(2) using readiness test scores to group children so that those of similar abilities are in the same classes.
(3) using readiness test scores as the basis for ensuring that all teachers get a fair share of students at every level of ability.

g. Using readiness as a gatekeeper refers to
(1) keeping those evaluated as unready out of the grade level for which they are eligible according to their age.
(2) making sure all children who are ready have a class to enter.
(3) ensuring that all children are ready to learn when they enter school.

h. If we push a child too hard to learn new things,
(1) it motivates him or her that much more to master the task.
(2) the child develops a stronger will to achieve and gain our approval.
(3) the child may become turned off to learning and not want to try new things.

i. An important factor regarding learning is that it
(1) only takes place in school.
(2) takes place not only in school but also at home and in various other settings out of the home.
(3) is not natural for children to want to learn.

j. By offering the child tasks that can be mastered through self-instruction,
(1) we make learning too easy and the child loses motivation.
(2) the child develops self-reinforcement while learning through his or her own activity.
(3) the child may make a lot of mistakes that we might miss, meaning that he or she does not really learn the task.

**3.** Write the letter of each correct statement.

a. Standardized achievement tests offer the most accurate and valid means for assessing the achievement of young children.

b. Through the use of authentic assessment methods, teachers can document children's real progress more accurately than the information obtained from group standardized tests.
c. During the administration of a group paper-and-pencil standardized test, young children show increased frequencies of stress behaviors.
d. Selecting a readiness test is an easy task since there are many that fit all the selection criteria.
e. It is all right to individually administer a test designed for group administration.
f. By age five, a child should have no problems dealing with a group-administered, standardized, paper-and-pencil test.
g. Child test responses should be motoric, verbal, or require a response to auditory stimuli.
h. Paper-and-pencil tasks have no place in a test used with young children.
i. A test used with young children should be broad in scope.
j. A test used with young children should be completed in 30 minutes or less.
k. According to the Goal 1 Assessment Resource group report, high-stakes assessments intended for accountability purposes should not be administered until the end of third grade at the earliest.
l. According to the No Child Left Behind Act of 2001, all children should be able to read by the end of third grade.

**4.** List the four skills Karen Hartman believes should be developed by preschool children so they will be able to deal with future shock.

## KEY TERMS LIST

appropriate assessment procedures
barriers
continuity
inappropriate assessment procedures
readiness

Additional resources for this chapter can be found on the Online Companion™ to accompany this text at http://www.earlychilded.delmar.com. Respond to "Time to Reflect" and "Looking Further" concepts, review various child development scenarios, and answer thought-provoking questions in the Critical Thinking Forum. Keep a daily journal by downloading the student journal available on this Web site. Complete the interactive matching exercises to reinforce concepts, and print out the child development assessment forms to use during your observation of development for children from birth to age eight. In addition, read the case studies on the Web site to reinforce the important concepts in each chapter, and take a look at the multitude of Web links that are available for student research on the Internet.

CHAPTER

# 29

# The Primary Child: Physical and Motor Development

## OBJECTIVES

After reading this chapter, you should be able to:

- Use the Food Guide Pyramid (MyPyramid) to evaluate a child's daily food intake.
- Evaluate the nutritional quality of a school lunch program.
- Measure the height and weight of six-, seven-, and eight-year-olds and evaluate their proportions.
- Evaluate the gross and fine motor developmental levels of six-, seven-, and eight-year-olds.
- List the food groups in the Food Guide Pyramid (MyPyramid).
- List the motor skills that improve in the primary ages.
- Recognize the pros and cons of young children engaging in organized sports.
- Explain the importance of fine motor skill development in the primary grades.

In previous chapters (12, 15, 18, and 19) the physical, health, and motor development of infants, toddlers, and preschool/kindergarten children have been described. In this chapter, these areas are examined relative to the special characteristics of six- through eight-year-olds. The following are examples of some primary grade children involved in the gross motor activities that are so vital for their good health.

> Sophia (seven years old), Anna (six years old), Mary (eight years old), Mike (six years old), and Ruben (six years old) are playing outside, engaged in physically, active dramatic play. Sophia, Anna, and Mary are playing house. Mike and Ruben are playing on the jungle gym, which they are using as a ship. The girls are using the trampoline as their swimming pool. The girls yell "Help!" as they jump into the water. The boys run over to the trampoline, "Quick, get on our ship!" shouts Mike. Sophia gets on, and the other girls follow. The game of house has ended as they are all pirates on the ship.

The elementary school soccer field is alive with laughing, excited children running across the field at their soccer practice. The girls seem happy to be there to enjoy their friends, not necessarily for the soccer practice. They have a hard time paying attention, but soon it is their turn to kick the soccer ball into the goal, which they love to do. Dianna (eight years old) is engaged in the after-school soccer practice. The coach is having them do different activities each time they line up. Dianna tries several times to get a shot before she finally makes it. She returns to the back of the line with a great grin on her face full of excitement that she has made the shot.

Fine motor development is also essential and enables children to engage in writing and drawing activities both at school and at home.

Ngu (seven years old) is sitting at her desk in her living room. She is working on a homework sheet, writing her alphabet letters. She calls out to her mother, telling her she wants to write a story. "Do you have something I can make a book out of?" Mother replies that she has some index cards. After Ngu gets the cards, she sits down and proceeds to work diligently for about 2 to 25 minutes. She draws, colors, and writes. She looks up and says, "I need the stapler." She staples the cards together and gives the book to her mother. She is grinning from ear to ear. The title of the book is *The Book of Ngu.*

## PHYSICAL DEVELOPMENT AND HEALTH

### Growth

During the primary years, growth continues slowly but steadily (Allen & Marotz, 2006). Children gain weight as muscle mass increases. Arms and legs become longer in proportion to the rest of the body (see the chart in Figure 12-1). The "baby teeth" are lost, and the permanent teeth come in. By seven, some girls may become taller than boys. As arms and legs get longer, seven-year-olds appear thinner. Height and weight charts can be found in Chapter 18. Although the weight of the brain only increases by about 10 percent during middle childhood, some brain structures continue to develop (Berk, 2005). Areas that control consciousness, impulse control, planning, spatial abilities, and communication between the hemispheres continue to become more complex.

### Health

Children in the primary grades are now in school all day. Therefore, according to Marotz, Cross, and Rush (2005), teachers play an important role in children's health. Teachers need to collaborate with other professionals and parents in early identification and assisting families to obtain appropriate medical treatment and encouraging a healthy lifestyle. Teachers need to be alert to sudden changes in children's behavior and appearance, which might indicate an illness or other health problem. Teachers need to be observant for signs of colds and fever. Answers to questions regarding children's health can be found on Web sites such as KidsHealth, for which there is a link in the Online Companion.

#### Nutrition

The 2005 Food Guide Pyramid (MyPyramid.gov) was introduced in Chapter 18. The pyramid guidelines apply to everyone over the age of two. Therefore, as children reach the primary ages, they continue to need a good diet and plenty of physical exercise in order to have a proper **energy balance** and avoid obesity (*Dietary Guidelines,* 2005). To have an energy balance, the body must burn as many calories

**energy balance**
When the body burns as many calories as are taken in.

FIGURE 29–1a Children need a nutritious lunch.

as are taken in. The Dietary Guidelines are used for planning federally funded nutrition programs, such as school lunch, and for planning nutrition education and information programs. Keep in mind that each day, and at all ages, people should have foods from all the food groups on the pyramid. Children four to eight years old need grains (4 to 5 ounces), vegetables (1½ cups), fruits (1½ cups), dairy and calcium-rich foods (2 cups), proteins (3 to 4 ounces), and small amounts of fats and oils (such as from salmon or tuna or olive oil, corn oil, soybean oil, or sunflower oil) plus exercise (The New Food Guide Pyramid, 2005). Note that sweets are no longer included. See Figures 29–1a and 29–1b. Malnutrition, food insecurity, obesity, and other negative nutritional factors were discussed in Chapter 18.

### Injury

Parents and teachers are responsible for prevention of unintentional childhood injuries (Marotz et al., 2005). Adults need to provide a safe environment, health and safety education, and have emergency procedures. Adults in centers and schools should be trained in CPR and basic first aid and have basic first aid supplies on hand. There should be written procedures for handling both minor and serious injuries (see Marotz et al., 2005). Parents need to obtain junior car seats for their older children who have outgrown infant seats so that vehicle seatbelts fit correctly.

## Health Education

Children need to learn about proper nutrition and correct hand-washing and tooth-brushing procedures.

As already mentioned, AIDS education is also important. Teachers, children, and parents need to be educated, especially if an HIV-positive child is enrolled in the class. Parents with HIV-positive children want to have the problem out in the open (Ryan, June 1997). For example, Pat Broadbent discovered that her adopted daughter Hydeia was HIV-positive. Pat was honest with her daughter about her condition and even eventually took her on a nationwide speaking tour. Hydeia is quoted as telling her audiences:

> "With kids, I say they make life choices, and they have to be careful it is the right choice" . . . "I tell adults to help educate our kids, because they're our future. I talk to church groups about compassion. I remind them that they might not like AIDS, but God might not like some of the things they do either, but he still lets them come to church" (Ryan, June 1997).

FIGURE 29–1b Children need an after-school snack.

Drug education is also an area of great importance. Evans and Bosworth (1997) explain that besides being knowledgeable about principles of prevention, individuals who develop curriculum must also know how to deliver lessons to children. One-way communication, such as lecturing, is not effective. Interactive techniques, such as role-playing, small-group activities, brainstorming, simulations, cooperative learning, and discussions, engage children's interests and involvement. Parents and young children who have been affected by drug abuse need support from early childhood professionals (Rice & Sanoff, 1998). Early childhood professionals need to know the facts about addiction to provide informed support and a therapeutic relationship that focuses on parent, caregiver, and teacher concern for the child.

### Mental Health

Robert Burke (2005) reports that the 1999 Surgeon General's report on children's mental health indicated that only about one-third of America's children and youth who need mental health services actually receive them. It can be concluded that the other two-thirds are enrolled in elementary schools. Burke suggests that teachers should have more mental health training through more emphasis on development of relationships. Classrooms are stressful settings, and teachers need someone to relate to as well as skill for relating in a positive manner with their students. Principals need to take a more proactive role in mentoring their staff and talking openly about teacher stress and teacher concerns about children's mental health status.

## MOTOR DEVELOPMENT

Frost, Wortham, and Reifel (2005) point out that by school age gross motor skills improve as evident in more flexibility, balance, and agility. School-age children can participate in organized sports and games that require coordinated movement and thinking in order to remember the rules of the game. Fine motor skills develop to meet the requirements of school activities, such as writing and drawing. Computers and video games also require fine motor skills.

Play and physical development are closely related. Opportunities for physical activity support children's healthy physical development and provide for social interaction and learning to play fair and take turns. Cognitive development is also related to motor development (Marcon, 2003). Caterino and Polak (1999) looked at the effects of physical activity on concentration level of children in grades second through fourth. They found that children who experienced physical activity before the test achieved higher scores than those who sat quietly before the test. These results suggest that the following procedures will increase student achievement (p. 1):

- Fifteen minutes of stretching and physical activity prior to the administration of tests requiring concentration
- Physical activity as stress management for academic performance
- Daily physical education as stress management for academic performance
- Daily recess in addition to daily physical education as stress management for academic performance

Young children typically have relatively short attention spans. They have a difficult time controlling information input; thus, their short-term memory becomes cluttered with irrelevant information. Frequent changes to different academic tasks may not be as beneficial to learning as a play break. The drastic change of activity and stimulus material during a physically active play break may clear their minds so they can tackle the next academic task. At the primary level, rough-and-tumble play provides for physical development and an opportunity for social dominance. Children learn how to assess the strength of others.

Pellegrini and Perlmutter (1988) observed kindergartners, second graders, and fourth graders during rough-and-tumble play on the playground. They discovered that rough-and-tumble play was positively related to social competence. They found it often led to children's involvement in cooperative games with rules and reduced the frequency of aggressive play. It had especially positive effects on boys. Pellegrini and Perlmutter believe that teachers should help boys who do not get involved in rough-and-tumble play to do so. Rough-and-tumble play, while providing some needed physical activity, also serves an important function in social development.

## Gross Motor Development

During school age, children's skills, such as running, jumping, hopping, and ball handling greatly increase (Berk, 2005). Children run faster and skipping becomes more coordinated. Vertical jumping and height and broad jumping length increase. Distance and accuracy of throwing, ability to catch a ball, kicking speed and accuracy, batting skill, and dribbling all become more refined (see Figures 29–2a and 29–2b).

## Youth Sports and Recess

Adult-organized youth sports are an ever-increasing area of activity for children (Berk, 2005). There is some concern that adult control is removing opportunities for children to explore and experiment in developing their own games. Further, children may be pushed beyond their developmental capabilities. Some coaches are so critical rather than encouraging and put so much emphasis on winning that the joy is taken

**FIGURES 29–2a & b** During the primary grades, children develop more complex motor skills, such as being able to jump rope and use more advanced playground equipment.

out of playing the game. Also, the less capable players may experience emotional suffering. Every child should have an opportunity to play if they wish to. Adaptations can be made for children with disabilities (Adaptations for Physical Activities, 2006).

As previously mentioned, physical activity improves concentration. As pressure for academic instruction in order to achieve higher test scores brings even more pressure, there has been much controversy over whether or not there is still time for recess (Council for Physical Education for Children, 2001; Maintaining Recess, 2006). Children need breaks. The Council on Physical Education for Children (2001) published a position paper supporting recess as an essential component of the school day (p. 1):

> Recess provides children with discretionary time and opportunities to engage in physical activity that helps to develop healthy bodies and enjoyment of movement. It also allows elementary children to practice life skills such as conflict resolution, cooperation, respect for rules, taking turns, sharing, using language to communicate, and problem solving in real situations. Furthermore, it may facilitate improved attention and focus on learning in the academic program.

Recess should be a supplement to the more structured physical education program. Unfortunately physical education is no longer required in many elementary schools (Berk, 2005).

With the increase in the prevalence of obesity, there is a great deal of concern with physical fitness (Sanders, 2002). According to Sanders, there is a critical period for gross motor development—from prenatal to five—and for fine motor skills—from birth to age nine. These are critical periods for the brain to gather and store information regarding movement activities. Fitness suggestions for parents of elementary school-age children can be found on the KidsHealth Web site (Fitness and Your 6- to 12-year-old, 2005). It is recommended that school-age children:

- Get 60 minutes or more of physical activity every day
- Accumulate activity throughout the day, which can be broken down into parts of 15 minutes or more
- Avoid periods of inactivity of 2 hours or more

Parents can work activity into daily routines and serve as models by participating in activities, such as walking, bike riding, hiking, or sports such as tennis, golf, or soccer. Children can be encouraged to participate in team sports, but some children don't care for them (Fitness for Kids Who Don't Like Sports, 2005). Some children can't develop the skills needed for a team sport or may be shy about joining a group. They can still get physical activity on their own playing tag, jumping rope, or taking dancing. They might also prefer individual sports, such as horseback riding, skating, martial arts, or gymnastics.

We also need to be concerned with young children and sports injuries (Micheli, 1990). Organized sports have worked their way down to the primary grades, replacing free play and sandlot sports. Dr. Lyle E. Micheli, Director of Sports Medicine at Boston Children's Hospital since 1974, has noted an increase in the number of children with the types of injuries that previously affected only

Mr. Gregory, a second-grade teacher, explains that, because of increased pressure to obtain higher standardized test scores, the other second-grade teachers are deleting recess and physical education periods for the month before testing to have more time for test practice. He asks your advice regarding the pros and cons of this plan. What advice would you give Mr. Gregory? What support could you give for your advice?

professional athletes. These injuries occur from playing when hurt or from overtraining. They may develop slowly in growing children but result in permanent problems. Many volunteer coaches are not trained in safe training techniques. Parents need to be sure that coaches are certified before letting their children participate in organized sports.

Children don't think about what will happen 20 years later when their teen injuries result in a painful middle age (Lampros, 2006). Lampros (2006) reports that the *Journal of the American Academy of Pediatrics* lists the following factors as contributing to sports injuries in youth:

- Hazardous playing fields
- Playing while tired
- Weather conditions
- Improper playing techniques
- Improper or poorly fitting equipment

The most common body areas injured are ankle, knees, head, elbow, and groin. Cheerleaders also are having an increase in injuries as stunts get more dangerous (see Figure 29–3).

| Six-Year-Old | Seven-Year-Old | Eight-Year-Old |
|---|---|---|
| • Increased muscle strength<br>• Can maintain body in space while bending, stretching, twisting, and turning | • Balances on either foot<br>• Continues to maintain body in space while bending, stretching, twisting, and turning | • Enjoys activities such as dancing, rollerblading, swimming, wrestling, riding a bike, or flying a kite |
| • Movements are more precise and deliberate<br>• Increased body awareness<br>• Increased spatial awareness (direction and location) | • Runs up and down stairs with alternating feet<br>• Can change from one movement to another, such as hopping to skipping | • Gets into team activities and games, such as soccer, baseball, and kickball<br>• Can combine various ways of moving and travel in various ways |
| • Enjoys and performs vigorous physical activity: running, jumping, climbing, catching, and throwing.<br>• Can throw various objects underhand at a target (such as a bean bag through a hoop)<br>• Can catch objects of various kinds below the waist using two hands<br>• Can jump forward with control | • Throws and catches smaller balls<br>• Can kick a stationary ball, with either foot, to a partner or a large target<br>• While moving, can bounce a ball with either hand<br>• Can dribble a ball with their feet over a short distance<br>• Can jump and land safely<br>• Can balance both on and off equipment while stationary or moving | • Can catch a tennis ball, walk across a balance beam, and hit a ball with a bat<br>• Can throw a ball overhand using two hands to a partner or a target.<br>• Can catch various objects using two hands both above and below the waist<br>• Can hit a moving object (such as a ball or a balloon), toward a partner or a large target<br>• Can jump over low objects<br>• Can move their body under, over, through, and around equipment |
| • Constantly moving—hard time sitting still | • Practices new motor skill until mastered and moves on to the next one | • Possesses seemingly endless energy |

**FIGURE 29–3** Selected gross motor skills for six-, seven-, and eight-year-olds.
From Allen, K. E., & Marotz, L. [2006]. Developmental profiles: Pre-birth through twelve (5th ed.). Clifton Park, NY: Delmar Learning. Used with permission.

## Fine Motor Development

Fine motor skills become more focused upon in the primary grades as children must write words and numerals. Drawings become more detailed as children gain control of their fine motor skills (see Figure 29–4). However, as can be seen in Figure 29–5, there is a range of skill (see also Figure 29–6).

Two school programs are described next. Knowing what you know now about physical health, safety, nutrition, and gross motor development, evaluate the two programs. Do you think Westchester might benefit from a program like the one at Carver?

On the north side of the city, we visit Carver Elementary. Carver is located in a lower socioeconomic section. Most of the families are headed by single mothers and are supported by welfare allotments. All the children are eligible for the federally funded free breakfast and lunch program. The school houses two four-year-old classrooms, four kindergartens, and three each of first through fifth grade. Observing at recess on the kindergarten playground, we see one teacher on duty supervising the 78 kindergartners. The children have a selection of balls and jump ropes to use but no climbing equipment, swings, or sandbox. Mostly, they run randomly in small groups pretending to be superheroes, heroines, or persons in distress. Inside, we interview "Coach," the physical education teacher. He explains that he has time to work with the prekindergarten, kindergarten, and primary children only one hour per week. During that time, he works with them on basic skills, such as throwing, catching, and kicking balls or running from one fixed point to another. With the primary children, he introduces simple games with rules, such as dodge ball.

Advanced first grader.

Less advanced first grader.

**FIGURE 29–4** First graders' drawings may reflect a range of fine motor skill.

After school, we have an opportunity to meet with the principal and some of the teachers. We ask them what kinds of things they do to promote health and nutrition in the school. They explain that they have become increasingly concerned about the health and physical development of their students. Just providing breakfast and lunch and one period of physical education per week is not enough. Therefore, they are gradually developing a physical fitness curriculum that includes daily teacher- directed movement activities and instructional units on good health and nutrition practices. They have communicated their objectives to the parents. The children and teachers are planning a health fair for the spring as a vehicle for getting parents more involved and concerned about their children's health, nutrition, and motor development. Through the local medical society, they have located two doctors

| Six-Year-Olds | Seven-Year-Olds | Eight-Year-Olds |
|---|---|---|
| Enjoys art projects, wood working, construction toys | Uses knife and fork appropriately but inconsistently | Increasing accuracy in copying words and numbers from blackboard |
| Writes numbers and letters with varying degrees of precision and interest; may reverse or confuse some letters: *b/d, p/g, g/q, t/f* | Holds pencil in tight grasp near the tip; rests head on forearms, lowers head almost to the table top when doing pencil-and-paper tasks | Good eye-hand coordination—may begin to learn cursive writing |
| Traces around hand and other objects | Produces letters and numbers in a deliberate and confident fashion | Draws representative figures in pictures with increasing detail |
| Folds and cuts paper into simple shapes | Written characters are increasingly uniform in size and shape; may run out of room on the line or page | Can easily accomplish six- and seven-year-old skills |
| Most can tie own shoes | Draws representative figures in pictures with increasing detail | |
| Draws representative figures in pictures | Can easily accomplish six-year-old skills | |

**FIGURE 29–5** Selected fine motor skills for six-, seven-, and eight-year-olds.
From Allen, K. E., & Marotz, L. [2006]. Developmental profiles: Pre-birth through twelve (4th ed.). Clifton Park, NY: Delmar Learning. Used with permission.

who are willing to volunteer half a day per month to provide health education activities and consultation for parents and children. The principal and teachers are very excited about this new program and believe it will have a positive impact on the students and their families.

A few days later, we visit Westchester Elementary located in the eastern section of the city. The area is middle- and upper-middle socioeconomic level. No students are eligible for federally supported breakfast and/or lunch programs. Most of the families have two parents in the home. About 60 percent of the mothers work full time. The school houses six kindergartens and four or five classes at each grade level up through fifth. Many of the students are enrolled in a before- and after-school program conducted at the school. The program was started by the parents and is run by a parent board. There is a tuition fee for this service. We visit the primary playground, which we note has some excellent permanent equipment purchased with a combination of money from Parent Association fund-raising activities and donations from businesses in the community. The students are supervised by three teachers, one teacher from each of the primary grades, who are performing their assigned playground duty for that day. Some children are observed in vigorous physical activity: climbing, jumping, and running. Most are engaged in sociodramatic play, pretending that the playground equipment is a spaceship or a house. They are active but do not engage in sustained physical activity. Some children sit on

**FIGURE 29–6** Primary grade students' fine motor skill development enables them to write and to do more detailed, controlled drawings.

benches and watch their more active peers. We talk with the physical education teacher, Mrs. Phillips. She also can meet with each class only once each week and follows the same program as Coach.

We meet with the principal and some of the kindergarten and primary teachers after school. They voice their concerns about the physical fitness of their students and the health care they receive. Many of the parents are very health conscious and make sure their children eat nutritious food, have regular medical and dental checkups, and get plenty of outdoor exercise. On the other hand, many are either ignorant or too busy to monitor their children's health. They send them to school hungry or with a nonnutritious breakfast picked up at the local doughnut shop. At home, they watch television for hours. Many attend a nearby child care center before they enter kindergarten at Westchester. The center is convenient but offers no teacher-planned physical activity nor any nutrition and health education. They have suggested that the after-school program might provide some adult-directed physical activities, but most of the parents are not interested. They have their children enrolled in the local soccer league in the fall and winter and T-ball or softball in the spring and summer and believe that is enough. The teachers are concerned that some of the coaches are pushing the children too hard—making them overuse their developing muscle and bone structures and sending them back onto the field of play without checking that injuries are completely healed. They are considering the development of a physical fitness program at the school.

We have just visited two elementary schools in two different neighborhoods. The schools are fictitious, but the situations described represent what is happening with our young children today. Consider what we learned from our observations and our discussions with the principals and teachers. Reflect on some of the problems that seem to be present as threats to the health and welfare of the students. After reading this section, look back at these descriptions and evaluate what is going on in each of the two settings. Explain where, in your opinion, the schools are on the right track and where they could be doing a better job.

## SUMMARY

Physical development, health, and motor development are interrelated elements. During the primary grade years, children's bodies become more proportional with arms and legs lengthening. They are in school all day so teachers need to be aware of signs of illness. Nutrition continues to be an important factor. To avoid obesity, the body must burn as many calories as it takes in. The new Food Pyramid (MyPyramid) continues to be an important guide for proper nutrition. Children are prone to unintentional injuries. Adults need to have first aid supplies and a plan for action for serious injuries. Health education for children and parents is essential. More attention needs to be paid to the mental health of elementary grade students.

Gross motor skill improvements enable primary grade children to get involved in organized sports and games. Active, vigorous play is an important gross motor activity. Recess is a vital part of the school day. An activity break improves children's ability to concentrate. Elementary schools should include both recess and a structured, daily physical education program. Parents also need to be sure their children get the exercise needed to maintain physical fitness. The number of childhood sports injuries is increasing. Children are sometimes pushed beyond what their growing bodies can handle. Fine motor skills are focused on in the classroom as children perfect their writing skills.

## For Further Reading


American Academy of Pediatrics. (2005). *Health in child care: A manual for health professionals* (4th ed.). Elk Grove Village, IL: Author.

Aronson. S. S., Shope, T. R. (Eds.). (2005). *Managing infectious diseases in child care and schools*. Elk Grove Village, IL: American Academy of Pediatrics.

Baxter, P. S. (Ed.). (2002). *Vitamin-responsive conditions in pediatric neurology*. Cambridge, UK: Cambridge University Press.

Burke, R. W., & Myers, B. K. (2002). Our crisis in children's mental health [Theme issue]. *Childhood Education, 78*(5).

Caldwell, W., & Kimball, C. T. (Eds.). (2001). *Obesity sourcebook*. Holmes, PA: Omnigraphics.

Clay, D. L. (2004). *Helping children with chronic health conditions*. New York: Guilford.

Dewey, D., & Tupper, D. E. (Eds.). (2004). *Developmental motor disorders*. New York: Guilford.

Donatelle, R. J. (2005). *Health: The basics* (6th ed.). San Francisco: Pearson.

Endres, J. (2004). *Food, nutrition, and the young child* (5th ed.). Columbus, OH: Merrill.

Frost, J. L., Brown, P., Sutterby, J. A., & Thornton, C. D. (2004). *The developmental benefits of playgrounds*. Olney, MD: Association for Childhood Education International.

Kimball, C. T. (Ed.). (2003). *Childhood diseases & disorders sourcebook*. Holmes, PA: Omnigraphics.

Kimball, C. T. (Ed.). (2003). *Healthy child sourcebook*. Holmes, PA: Omnigraphics.

Let's go outside! [Focus section]. (2002). *Young Children, 57*(3), 8–42.

Natasi, B. K., Moore, R. B., & Varjas, K. M. (2004). *School-based mental health services*. Washington, DC: American Psychological Association.

Pellegrini, A. D. (2005). *Recess: Its role in education and development*. Mahwah, NJ: Erlbaum.

Roberts, M. C. (Ed.). (2003). *Handbook of pediatric psychology* (3rd ed.). New York: Guilford.

Ryff, C. D., & Singer, B. (Eds.). (2001). *Emotion, social relationships and health*. New York: Oxford University Press.

Shannon, J. B. (Ed.). (2002). *Sports injuries sourcebook* (2nd ed.). Holmes, PA: Omnigraphics.

Thompson, J., & Manore, M. (2005). *Nutrition: An applied approach*. San Francisco: Pearson.

Unintentional injuries in childhood. (2000). *The future of children* [Focus issue], *10*(1).

Vaca, J. J. (2001). Dealing with aftermath: Helping young children with post-traumatic stress disorder (PTSD). *Dimensions, 29*(3), 18–24.


## Suggested Activities

1. Follow one or more six- to eight-year-olds through the day, keeping a record of what they eat. Using the Food Guide Pyramid (MyPyramid) (Chapter 18), evaluate their daily food intake. Did they eat from the recommended food groups? Did they eat high-fat or high-cholesterol foods? Did they eat foods with high levels of sugar or sodium?

2. Keep a record of your food intake for a week. Categorize each item to see if you ate from all the basic food groups and the recommended amounts. Give yourself one point per day for each group from which you ate each day. Did you also get an adequate amount of exercise? Would you be a good model for children?

3. Visit one or more elementary schools where both breakfast and lunch are served. Interview whoever is in charge of the cafeteria. Ask questions such as the following, and write up a summary of what you find out:
   (1) How are breakfast and lunch financed?
   (2) Who plans the menus? Purchases the food? Prepares the food? What are their qualifications? Can you give me a copy of your menus for the week?
   (3) Is nutrition education included in your curriculum? May I see the curriculum? Do you believe having meals at school improves children's learning?

What are the strengths and weaknesses of the program(s)? [Use the Food Guide Pyramid (MyPyramid), in Chapter 18.] Can you suggest any improvements?

4. Measure the height and weight of 5 six-year-olds, 5 seven-year-olds, and 5 eight-year-olds. Graph your findings and compare with the height and weight charts in the text (Chapter 18).

5. Observe a six-, seven-, or eight-year-old at home or at school. Use the gross and fine motor skills charts (Figures 29–3 and 29–5) to assess the child's developmental level in the areas of gross and fine motor development.
   a. Overall, does the child seem to be average, ahead of typical expectations, or slow in rate of development?
   b. Are there any areas where the child seems to be exceptionally ahead or behind in development?
   c. Support all of your conclusions and recommendations with data from your developmental charts.

6. Observe some primary grade children on the playground or in the neighborhood involved in a variety of vigorous physical activity. In class, list all the gross motor skills you observed on a piece of chart paper or on the chalkboard. Have other class members add theirs. An alternative activity: Divide the class into two or more teams. With a time limit of three minutes, see which team can list the most gross motor activities on the board.

7. Have a primary grade child write letters, numbers, or a story and draw a picture. Assess the level of his or her fine motor skills.

8. Visit an elementary school playground and determine if it is designed to accommodate children with disabilities.

9. Make an entry in your journal.

## REVIEW

1. Look back to the beginning of the chapter. Relate the behaviors of the children in the three anecdotes (dramatic play group, soccer players, and Ngu the writer) to the material on motor development in the chapter.
2. For each of the following examples, use the growth charts in Figures 18–1 and 18–2 to find each child's percentile rank for height and weight. Decide whether each child is average, heavy, thin, short, or tall compared with other children of the same age. Describe the child's proportions.

| | |
|---|---|
| a. Jason is six years of age | His height is 32 inches<br>His weight is 55 pounds |
| b. Anne is eight years of age | Her height is 34 inches<br>Her weight is 38 pounds |
| c. Thuy Phung is seven years of age | Her height is 40 inches<br>Her weight is 36 pounds |

3. Decide if the following statements are true or false.
   a. By seven girls may be taller than boys.
   b. The brain does not develop in the areas of impulse control and planning during middle childhood.
   c. Teachers need to be alert to the health of their students.
   d. Energy balance is the state where calories taken in equal the amount of energy used.

e. Adults in centers and schools should be trained in CPR and basic first aid.
f. Once children reach 40 pounds, they no longer need a special booster seat in the car.
g. It is important for young children and their parents to receive education in good health practices.

**4.** List the food groups in the Food Pyramid.
**5.** Describe some of the developments in motor skills achieved by elementary age.
**6.** Identify the statements that are true.
a. Play and physical development are closely related.
b. Physical/motor activity before a test will make the child too tired to do well.
c. Daily physical education will increase academic performance.
d. There is no evidence that recess is a worthwhile activity.
e. Rough-and-tumble play supports young children's motor development.
**7.** List some of the skills that increase for school-age children.
**8.** Select the statements that are true.
a. Children may spend too much time in organized sports.
b. Children need time to engage in physical activity that encourages exploration and experimentation.
c. There is a danger that in youth sports children will be pushed beyond their capabilities.
d. Seldom do coaches treat the less capable players unfairly.
e. A structured physical education program is not necessary.
f. Exercise for physical fitness can help fight obesity.
g. Children need at least 60 minutes of physical activity each day.
h. Adults don't need to be models of physical activity.
i. All children must engage in team sports.
j. Too many young children and teens are getting sports injuries that may result in a painful middle age.
**9.** List factors that may contribute to youth sports injuries.
**10.** Describe the importance of fine motor skills in the primary grades.

## KEY TERMS LIST

energy balance

Additional resources for this chapter can be found on the Online Companion™ to accompany this text at http://www.earlychilded.delmar.com. Respond to "Time to Reflect" and "Looking Further" concepts, review various child development scenarios, and answer thought-provoking questions in the Critical Thinking Forum. Keep a daily journal by downloading the student journal available on this Web site. Complete the interactive matching exercises to reinforce concepts, and print out the child development assessment form to use during your observation of development for children from birth to age eight. In addition, read the case studies on the Web site to reinforce the important concepts in each chapter, and take a look at the multitude of Web links that are available for student research on the Internet.

CHAPTER

# 30

# The Primary Child: Affective Development

## OBJECTIVES

After reading this chapter, you should be able to:

- Recognize the affective characteristics of primary-level children.
- Give an example of how social interaction can benefit children in primary classrooms.
- State how primary-level children might experience stress.
- Understand the important factors related to self-esteem and moral development in the primary years.
- Identify the important factors in middle childhood sexuality.
- Identify the symptoms of ADHD in school-age children.
- Describe the adult role with primary-age children.

Eight-year-old Tyler is wearing hiking boots, a sweatshirt, and jeans. He recently returned from duck hunting with his cousin and uncle. He took his dog, Rumbo, with him. His dog's travel kennel is in the garage by the car. Tyler is helping his dad clean out the car. He says, "Ben shot at one of the ducks that was in the water. He aimed down at the duck and you could see the B-Bs spread out." "Really?" his Dad says. Tyler is emptying things out of the trunk of the car. He picks up some marbles and throws them into the street. He climbs into the trunk and retrieves the rest of the marbles for his father. He walks over to his dog's travel kennel. "I need some new straw for Rumbo, Dad. After taking him duck hunting this morning, he needs new straw." His dad says okay. His dad tells Tyler to plug in the shop vacuum. Tyler unwinds the extension cord and plugs it in. His dad tells him to vacuum all the car floor mats. "Why me?" says Tyler. "Because you can help out and do something," says his dad. So Tyler starts vacuuming the floor mats. Tyler says, "This morning when we were shooting the guns, you could see fire come out of them." Tyler moves away from vacuuming the floor mats and vacuums the old straw from his dog's travel kennel. "Dad, when we say 'kennel,' Rumbo jumps right in, huh Dad?" Tyler stands and watches his dad vacuum the trunk. Tyler shows an interest in being a buddy with his dad as he relates his hunting experience, demonstrates responsibility for care of his dog's kennel, and helps his dad clean the car.

FIGURE 30–1 Primary children enjoy working together independent of adults.

This chapter explores some of the characteristics of the six- through eight-year-old children who are students in primary classrooms (i.e., grades one through three). First, however, there is a general overview of the primary child's developmental characteristics.

In the **primary grades,** grades one through three, we find children from ages six through eight. It is a period when development in the physical, cognitive, social, and emotional areas becomes integrated and all areas begin to work together in a coordinated manner (Allen & Marotz, 2006; Bredekamp & Copple, 1997). Gross motor skills are well developed and integrated with newly developed concrete operational cognitive skills, enabling children to begin to play games that have rules and that require complex combinations of motor skills (see Chapter 29). Fine motor skills are also integrated with cognitive skills, as writing skills are refined and used to express inner thoughts. Physical and motor characteristics were discussed in Chapter 29. Both perceptual and cognitive development reach the point at which children can be expected to attain some expertise in conventional reading and connect concrete experiences in arithmetic with abstract symbols. Primary-level children usually have attained almost adultlike use of speech. Play is still an important activity for children. Both cognitive and social development continue to be supported through play. Children are into Erikson's stage of Industry versus Inferiority (see Chapters 2 and 25). Being productive is very important to primary-age children, and they are deeply affected by experiences that make them feel inferior and unproductive.

**primary grades**
Grades one through three.

Peers are of increasing importance and provide conversation and work partners. Primary children work well in small cooperative groups (Figure 30–1). In this stage of Industry versus Inferiority, successful accomplishment of tasks provides feelings of self-esteem and self-worth as a basis for further development. Before this period, children have learned the rules of appropriate and inappropriate behavior. Now, adults must offer them support in achieving self-control by providing opportunities for independence and responsibility, as well as necessary adult guidance. Inappropriate practices can destroy children's self-esteem and their motivation to learn (Nuttall, 1993).

This chapter examines some of the affective characteristics of primary children, the adult role with primary children, and some sociocultural factors.

## AFFECTIVE CHARACTERISTICS: SOCIAL AND EMOTIONAL DEVELOPMENT

The primary period is the gateway to increasing self-consciousness and sensitivity, which reach their peak in adolescence. Alan Shapiro (n.d.) writes about the meaning of the daily sharing period, such as show-and-tell, bring and brag, or news time, when individual children have their time in the limelight in front of the whole class. He presents the following examples of this sensitivity:

> It feels embarrassing when you go up front. You have to talk and you feel scared and frightened (a female third grader) (p. 31).
>
> It feels crazy when you stand in front of the room . . . everybody looks at you (female third grader) (p. 32).

Although these children find getting up in front of the class a risky business, others find it an exciting and worthwhile experience:

> Oh, I like it because I like to tell about me and what I do, and what I have and what my cousins do (male first grader) (p. 35).
>
> When they say things, I like to know what they say . . . and I say something and they know what I say (female third grader) (p. 35).

Children's self-evaluations continue to provide their degree of self-esteem. Children with learning disabilities (LD) are especially vulnerable to poor self-concept. These students benefit from a combination of academic and affective interventions (Elbaum & Vaughan, 1999).

It can be seen from these examples that the same type of activity results in different feelings for each child. We will look at the highlights of development during the primary grades in the areas of peer relationships, social interaction, self-esteem, and moral development.

Read the following anecdotes and analyze what you believe these children are thinking and feeling.

- We are in church for the children's program. Edward, age seven, is sitting behind me. He calls my name. When I turn around, he says, "Do you have a part in the program?" "No," I reply. "Lucky!" he says sincerely. He seems nervous. Later, when it is his turn to take the podium, he does so conscientiously. He recites his part accurately and carefully and returns to his seat, appearing relieved.
- Carl and Keely, third graders, are about to give oral book reports in class. When asked by their teacher who will give their report first, Keely quickly points to Carl and Carl quickly points to Keely. Other students pipe up, "Who is older?" Carl announces that he is older so he gives his report first.

## Peer Relationships

Peer relationships become increasingly important during the primary years. Hart, McGee, and Hernandez (1993) review some of these factors. Peer popularity in grade school continues to be related to friendly approaches, nurturing, cooperation, conversation, and positive reinforcement, just as it was during the preschool period. Both aggressive and withdrawn children are rejected by peers. Popular grade-school children engage in more cooperative play and less onlooker behavior when observed on the playground. As with younger children, group entry is accomplished most successfully by approaching the group silently, hovering, and then imitating the behavior of the group members. "Starting young and continuing through adulthood, friendships are among the most important activities of life" (Gurian & Pope, 2001). Friendships are essential to social and emotional development. Children learn the give and take of life through interactions with their peers.

They have opportunities for decision making and experience the range of emotions. They experience winning and losing. They learn to understand that other people have different points of view. Friends provide support when times are tough. Friends are necessary for mental health. In the elementary years, children tend to choose friends who are similar to themselves and who have the same interests. They tend to join groups with girls in smaller more intimate groups than boys. Children who enter first grade with friends tend to enjoy school and do better academically.

In Chapter 29 there was a description of how grade-school children, especially boys, enjoy rough-and-tumble (R&T) play and use it as a means to develop games with rules (Hart et al., 1993). R&T play also affords opportunities to improve social problem-solving skills. This appears to be an especially important factor for boys. R&T also includes affective aspects as reported by primary-grade boys (Reed & Brown, 2000). When interviewed, primary-grade boys interpreted their R&T play as a vehicle for expressing care, fondness, and friendship toward each other. Also described was the importance of daily recess breaks. Adequate recess time is especially important for aggressive children, who need adult modeling and coaching to assist them in learning the difference between R&T play and aggression. Pellegrini and Smith (1993) and Pellegrini and Bjorklund (1996) have reviewed research that provides support for the cognitive and social values of recess.

Barbour (1996) studied the play activities of eight second-grade students during recess. The students were identified as high physical competence (HPC) or low physical competence (LPC). HPC children were able to engage in more of a variety of play activities that provided them with more opportunities to acquire social knowledge than were available to the LPC students. Barbour concludes that improving physical competence could have positive effects for socially isolated children. Participation in organized sports and games is a means for second-grade boys to attain popularity. LPC boys are more likely to participate in dramatic play with domestic themes and avoid organized games. HPC girls are more likely to play organized games, such as sports, chase, or tag. LPC boys are also more likely to play with girls, an activity considered unacceptable by HPC boys.

Play is an important activity for primary-level children. It also directly enhances academic development. For example, Stone and Christie (1996) observed children in a multiage (kindergarten through second grade) primary classroom engaged in literacy learning during dramatic play. Several activity centers were situated in the classroom. Children were observed in the home center, which contained play furniture, props such as a phone and dishes, and dolls. A variety of literacy props were also included: children's books on open shelves and writing materials, such as markers, pens, pencils, and paper. Most of the groups that selected this center were mixed age. A great deal of literacy behavior was identified, such as environmental print reading, reading for fun, writing for a purpose, and writing skill practice. Seventy-five percent of the literacy activity was collaborative, taking place in pretend dramatic play situations. The older children were helpful to the younger children. The center provided a place for both literacy learning and social interaction. Schneider (2000) reviewed the research looking at affective and cognitive factors in schooling. His conclusion is that "social interaction facilitates cognitive development and academic achievement" (p. 76). Agreements and disagreements between friends facilitate cognitive development while providing opportunities for affective development. The research supports the value of using cooperative learning groups in the classroom (as described later in this chapter) (Schneider, 2000).

Evaluate how the following children's physical motor play activities fit in with Barbour's research conclusions.

- Jack, age seven, is a member of a soccer team. Earlier in the season, he was not doing well. He was not going after the ball and seemed a little tentative. Jack is tall for his age and, therefore, has an advantage over the other players. Today, Jack played exceptionally well. As he and his parents were leaving, the coach came up to him and told him that he had played great and that he could tell that he had practiced and played his very best. Jack was beaming from ear to ear.
- A group of neighborhood children, ages five to seven, are playing follow-the-leader. They are all lined up, except Brittany, who says she hates the game. Brittany sits down on the ground. The other children tell her she does not have to play. The first leader hops around the yard, and the others follow. Brittany watches and sees that they are having fun. She jumps up and joins them. Instead of just following the leader, Brittany exaggerates her movements and starts laughing. All the children stop to watch her and also start laughing. Brittany continues to play with the group.
- A group of 10 first-grade girls are on the playground with a large jump rope. The teacher holds one end of the rope while one of the girls holds the other end. Everyone gets plenty of turns. Some of the girls "jump in" while the teacher and the classmate turn the rope. Other girls start out by the still rope and then start jumping when the rope is turned. Some girls turn their bodies (spin around) while they jump, and others just jump in place the entire time. Some of the girls even jump in pairs. They sing chants as the girls jump. Each time Sharon jumps, she cannot even jump once before the rope trips her up. She always jumps too soon or too late, so her turns last about two seconds. After Sharon goes through the line three or four times, she gets a small jump rope and starts jumping by herself. She can do it!

Popular children seem to have a better grasp on the goals and strategies that are appropriate to peer situations (Hart et al., 1993). Unpopular children may actually believe that unfriendly strategies will result in social success. Furthermore, unpopular children tend to misread cues from others and believe an attack is called for when the other child actually intended no harm (Hart et al. 1993). Popular children tend to generate more than one solution to a social problem and make their selection after consideration of these alternatives.

Some children lack frequent social interaction due to shyness (Brophy, 1996; Malouff, 2002–2006). According to Malouff (2002–2006), shyness occurs in social situations due to anxiety and behavioral inhibition. It usually occurs in new situations or situations where the child is in the spotlight. Shy children may want to interact with other children but are afraid. The positive side of shyness is that shy children tend to get into less trouble than more outgoing children. The shy child may be concerned about others' opinions of them. On the other hand, they may be less socially skilled because they have less practice in socializing. Malouff suggests 17 strategies that parents and teachers can use to help the shy child overcome shyness (pp. 3–12). Some examples are:

- Tell the child about times when you acted bashful.
- Explain the benefits of being more outgoing.
- Show empathy when the child feels afraid to interact.
- Don't use the label *shy*.

- Be a model of outgoing behavior.
- Pair the shy child with an outgoing child in some situations.

Loneliness is a problem for some primary-grade students (Hart et al., 1993). As early as first grade, rejected children have been identified as feeling lonely. Loneliness may be related to behaviors such as aggression, disruptiveness, or shyness. Less-accepted children tend to attribute their social failure to their own incompetence rather than to traits of the rejector. Nonbehavioral factors, such as physical attractiveness, social class, name, and handicapping conditions, appear to affect popularity.

For grade-school children, proximity is the major factor in friendship choice. Most of their closest friends live in their neighborhood. They usually have mixed-age friendships, with skill levels, mutual interests, and social status being more important than age. Cooperation is the major factor in developing and maintaining friendships. When conflict does occur, friends are able to arrive at an agreement. Friends serve multiple functions for children: play, teaching, nurturance, intimacy, protection, and caregiving. They also support feelings of self-worth, provide companionship, pass on social norms, and serve as models of social skills (Hart et al., 1993).

In our multicultural society, peer relationships of children from different ethnic groups in the same school setting are of interest. Howes and Wu (1990) point out that school integration is based on the idea that everyday contacts between children from different ethnic groups will decrease stereotyped views.

## Antisocial Behaviors

Antisocial behavior may be aggressive or nonaggressive. Aggressive antisocial behavior includes physical acts of aggression, such as bullying or fighting, whereas non-aggressive antisocial behavior includes delinquent behaviors, such as truancy and theft (Eley, Lichtenstein, & Stevenson, 1999). These behaviors increase greatly in adolescence and occur more commonly in boys than in girls. The aggressive type of anti-social behavior has been found to be present in preschoolers and is correlated with degree of later aggressive behavior. The nonaggressive behaviors are related to peer relationships in adolescence. Eley et al. compared the two types of antisocial behavior in samples of twins ages seven to sixteen. They concluded that aggressive antisocial behavior, although having some environmental influences, has a strong inherited element, whereas nonaggressive antisocial behavior is influenced by environmental factors. Deater-Deckard and Plomin (1999) had parents and teachers rate adopted and nonadopted sibling pairs on externalizing behavior problems at ages seven, nine, ten, eleven, and twelve. Consistent with other studies, both teachers and parents reported higher levels of both types of antisocial behavior in boys as compared with girls. The differences between boys and girls were greater for adoptees. As for the question of inherited versus environmental causes, the results indicated some of each, with aggression showing a stronger inherited factor and delinquency being more influenced by environment.

Special attention has been paid to bullies (Sanders & Phye 2004). Sanders cites Olweus' (1993) definition of bullying ". . . a student is being bullied or victimized when he is exposed repeatedly and over time to negative actions on the part of one or more other students" (Olweus, 1993, p. 9). According to Sanders, the problem in Olweus' definition is the definition of *negative actions*. Many people only think of physical harm, forcing people to do something they do not want to do, and threats as bullying; but many other behaviors can be included that are more subtle, such as social and emotional abuse. Sanders lists the following major characteristics of bullies and of victims as indicated by experts in the field.

> Bullies: control others through threats and physical actions, are quicker to anger and use force sooner than others, tend to have little empathy for others, often have been exposed to models of aggressive behavior, inappropriately perceive others as hostile, are angry and revengeful, use aggression to protect their self-image, may experience inconsistent discipline procedures at home.
>
> Victims: believe they can't control their environment, have poor social and interpersonal skills, are less popular, have underlying fears of personal inadequacy, feel socially isolated, are afraid to go to school, are physically, younger, smaller, and weaker than peers.

Gottfredson (2004) emphasizes the importance of interventions. Usually school-wide approaches are the most effective. School-wide interventions are designed to improve the school climate and create communal feelings and, thus, reduce and prevent bullying. Samples (2004) evaluated curriculum-based intervention programs. Prevention should begin in the early years to develop children's prosocial attitudes and behaviors. There are curriculum-based programs that have been used successfully in the primary grades:

- Primary school (K–2, ages five through seven) Bullying Prevention Program by Olweus
- Bully Proofing your School (School-wide, K–12)
- Lions-Quest (K–12); PATHS, Promoting Alternative Thinking Strategies focuses on self-control, self-esteem, emotional understanding, relationships, and interpersonal problem-solving skills (K–5) with lessons sequenced by grade level
- Quit It! (K–3)
- Second Step can be used as young as age three (and up) and is designed to reduce aggression, increase prosocial behavior, and reduce conflict.

Changing school policy is essential to success in decreasing and eliminating bullying.

Some researchers have looked at the early childhood factors that appear to influence later behavior. For example, Eisenberg et al. (1997) found that levels of emotionality and regulation at ages four to six predicted social functioning at ages six to eight and eight to ten in school and at home. The ability to control emotions is related to the ability to control behavior. Schwartz, Dodge, Pettit, and Bates (1997) examined the early socialization experiences of boys who were both aggressive and the victims of aggression. Mothers were interviewed when the boys were five years old to assess the boys' preschool home environments. Four to five years later, their aggressive behavior and peer victimization in school classrooms were assessed. Boys who were victims of aggression in third and fourth grade came from homes with negative environments during the preschool period. That is, their homes tended to be harsh, disorganized, and potentially abusive. Mother–child interactions were hostile, restrictive, or overly punitive. Mothers and their spouses or partners tended to have conflict relationships. Boys who were aggressors but not victims usually were exposed to hostility and violence in the home, but were not abused.

Research on maladaptive behavior reflects the significance of early experience and underscores the importance of helping young children develop higher levels of emotional intelligence (Daniel Goleman, 1999), as described in Chapter 25. Young children need to be supported in developing awareness of their own emotions, learning to manage their emotions so they are less impulsive, learning to be aware of others' emotions, and learning how to handle social relationships.

Students with learning disabilities also tend to have difficulties with social interactions (Gresham & MacMillan, 1997). In their review of research, Gresham and MacMillan found that students classified as having mild disabilities, such as specific learning disabilities, mild mental retardation, behavior disorders, and attention deficit-hyperactivity disorder, had difficulties with both peers and teachers. They also tend to have poorer social skills, exhibit more interfering problem behaviors, and are poorly accepted or rejected by their peers. Children with specific language impairment (SLI) are at risk for social problems as well (Fujiki, Brinton, Morgan, & Hart, 1998). These children tend to exhibit higher levels of withdrawal and lower levels of social behavior than their typical peers. The children with SLI were rated as more reticent, as indicated by anxiety, fear, and inept entry skills, even though they wanted to be involved in peer activities.

As discussed in earlier chapters, today's media is frequently cited as a source for learning antisocial behaviors (Hamilton, 2002). Children have a multitude of electronic equipment, such as stereos, televisions, computers, video games, portable televisions, and cassette and CD players. Unsupervised television viewing alone provides children with a multitude of examples of sex and violence. Thirty-two percent of children ages two to seven, and 26 percent of children ages two to four have televisions in their bedrooms. Two-thirds of children aged eight and older have their own televisions. Some studies have shown that children spend 70 percent of their television-viewing time watching shows meant for adults.

## Social Interaction: Benefits in the Classroom

As described in Chapter 25, before entering the primary grades, children are developing a view of culturally acceptable gender roles. Further development takes place during middle childhood (ages five to twelve years). Serbin, Powlishta, and Gulko (1993) found evidence of both cognitive and affective development aspects of children's views of sex roles as they progress through middle childhood. The general level of cognitive development was related to children's flexibility of views and knowledge about sex-role stereotypes. Affective aspects in terms of preferred roles, professions, and activities related to sex-typing in the home. Affective and cognitive aspects were related in that children with flexible views about sex-typed roles were less sex-typed in their stated preferences. During middle childhood, children tend to see their own sex as having the most positive characteristics.

**cooperative learning**
"The process whereby small, heterogeneous groups of students work together to achieve mutual learning goals" (Ajose & Joyner, 1990, p. 198).

FIGURE 30–2 Primary children benefit from the social interaction that takes place as they perform their daily activities.

Children's natural interest in and attachment to peers can be valuable factors in planning and organizing the primary classroom. It is apparent that opportunities for social interaction are necessary for normal social development (Figure 30–2). As already mentioned, cooperative learning strategies are recommended for school instruction (Ajose & Joyner, 1990; Schneider, 2000). **Cooperative learning** can be defined as "the process whereby small, heterogeneous groups of students work together to achieve mutual learning goals" (Ajose & Joyner, 1990, p. 198). Students, usually in groups of two to four, are provided with a problem to solve. They are required to work together to arrive at a solution. Through cooperative learning, children gain both cognitive and social skills and benefit more than in competitive or individualistic learning settings. Cooperative learning also provides a way to integrate children from different ethnic groups and to integrate children with special needs.

Primary-grade children enjoy inventing their own games. For example, they like to invent board games. Castle (1990) describes the variety of games children invent. Game invention puts children in a position of power as they decide on the game to invent, select needed materials, and set up the rules. This process provides a valuable educational experience as they use skills they have learned in school: writing (e.g., rules, game labels), arithmetic (scoring), and incorporation of theme or unit topics as the focus of the game. Working together on game development provides opportunities for cooperation, negotiation, and problem solving. Children learn how to resolve conflicts without relying on the teacher. Children enjoy working on and playing the games because they can talk and play with friends and do something interesting.

Examine the following situation based on what you have just read:

Third-grade teacher Mrs. Brown has told the students to get into small groups of three or four to work on some math games. As the students are attempting to get their partners and gather supplies, it is noticeable that the girls seem to use this time for social interaction and the boys use this time to run and roughhouse. When the groups are organized and the games begin, the groups are drawn by gender lines; the boys are with boys and the girls with girls.

Positive social interaction in classrooms can be supported through community-building activities. "A community is a group of individuals who have a serious stake in each other's well-being and who can accomplish together that which they could not do alone" (Katz & McClellan, 1997, p. 17). Children have a deep need for community. DeVries and Zan (1994) provide a total program for community building. Other educators suggest some specific activities that can build community. Classroom meetings (McClurg, 1998; Vance & Weaver, 2002), creating reflective memory walls (Scharmann, 1998), or creating settings that can support inclusion of children with special needs (Blaska & Lynch, 1998; Elgas & Peltier, 1998) or a multitude of other strategies (Krall & Jalongo, 1998/99) can support community building.

## Stress

Stress continues to be a problem beyond the kindergarten level. The results of a study by Gonzali and Crase (1991) that involved upper-elementary-grade children and adolescents indicated that academic stress and low self-concept were correlated. Children with moderate amounts of academic stress received better grades than those with the lowest or highest amounts of academic stress. A survey of children younger than age twelve (Witkin, 1999) indicated that their top stresses are as follows:

- *school concerns:* grades and homework
- *worries about family and parents:* health, money, and moods
- *peer pressures:* bullies, gangs, popularity, fickle friends, and teasing
- *world concerns:* inequality, justice, and human cruelty

They are scared most when parents fight, get angry, or lose emotional or physical control. Millions of children each year are victims of physical and emotional abuse, which results in feelings of stress. Parents who responded to the survey underestimated how much stress their children were experiencing. A major concern is the overload of homework being given to elementary school children. Large amounts of homework do not affect standardized test results until junior high and high school. Elementary children should be given minimal homework and allowed more time for sports, hobbies, and relaxation.

Dr. Bruce Perry is an authority on children in crisis. *Scholastic*'s Web site (http://teacher.scholastic.com/professional/bruceperry) provides links to Dr. Perry's advice regarding a multitude of crisis situations. After the Twin Towers disaster on September 11, 2001, children's responses to violence and disaster and fears regarding terrorist attacks became a focus of concern for mental health workers. In Chapter 25 the reaction to Summer 2005's Hurricane Katrina was described. Many suggestions for helping children and adolescents can be found on the Internet (Hamblen, 2002; Helping children and adolescents cope with violence and disasters, 2001). Reporting on a conference on school-based mental health, Robert W. Burke (2002) emphasizes the importance of schools educating for resiliency. **Resiliency** is the essential ability to "bounce back" from difficult circumstances. Goldstein and Brooks (2005, p. xiii) describe the life of Ray Charles. He saw his five-year-old brother drown. At five he developed glaucoma. His family was too poor to provide medical help. His parents died when he was a teenager, and he was sent to an institution for the blind. As an African American he was not allowed to participate in activities, such as music, but despite all these problems, he became a world-renowned musician. How could this happen? How and why do some overcome and others don't? The authors believe that all children should acquire resilient characteristics: "dealing effectively with stress and pressure, coping with everyday challenges, bouncing back from disappointments, adversity and trauma, developing clear and realistic goals, solving problems, relating comfortably with others, and treating oneself and others with respect" (p. xiv) are important ingredients for a satisfying lifestyle. Adults must focus on strengthening children's assets versus just fixing deficits. Wright & Masten (2005) state that at different points in development, children have different vulnerabilities and different protective systems. Infants are vulnerable but also lack understanding of traumatic events. As children mature, school and community provide new avenues for trauma but also increased skills for coping. Wright and Masten provide examples of assets and protective factors, such as:

**resiliency**

The essential ability to "bounce back" from difficult circumstances.

- social and adaptable temperament in infancy
- good cognitive abilities and problem-solving skills
- effective emotional and behavioral regulation strategies
- a positive view of self and life
- a stable and supportive family life and involved parents
- a high-quality neighborhood, effective schools, and health care
- connections to caring adult mentors and prosocial peers

A culture/society that is protective of children values education and has a low acceptance of physical violence. We have to work with families, professionals, and the community to provide children with the skills needed for resilience.

## Self-Esteem

During the primary-grade period, as children enter concrete operations, they also enter the stage of Industry versus Inferiority. Primary children venture out into new social worlds (e.g., sports, lessons, hobbies) that contribute to their identities and their feelings of competence. However, school is the place where they spend the most out-of-home time. In school, they meet the challenge of many new standards against which they evaluate themselves. Entering first grade, they are expected to act with more autonomy and responsibility, act more mature, be task directed, and display self-control (Curry & Johnson, 1991). Children become capable of comparing themselves with others and, therefore, new possibilities open up for developing feelings of inferiority. Curry and Johnson (1991, p. 69) categorize four components of self-esteem: competence, power, acceptance, and virtuousness.

Young children, as noted by Stipek and MacIver (1989) in Chapter 31, are quite flexible in their beliefs about academic success. They begin school feeling smart and feeling that hard work will pay off in success. Curry and Johnson (1991) point out that sometimes this extreme optimism can mask feelings of inferiority. Social-emotional maturity probably contributes to school success to a greater degree than self-expectations. The trend to try to fit children to the curriculum rather than the curriculum to the children impedes developing feelings of competence. A number of means, such as changing the age of school entrance, keeping children out of school for an extra year, placing children in transition classes, and retaining children in kindergarten or first grade, have been used to give children time to get ready. None of these means has shown overall success, especially when children are placed in classrooms that are boring and/or stressful. Adjusting the child's pace through the system does not compensate for inappropriate instructional practices (Curry & Johnson, 1991). Parents tend to have high expectations for their children's school success, but may not have the skills to support their children's learning. Many teachers are aware of child development but tend to place too much weight on age and view immature children as learning disabled. Early educational experiences have been criticized for being "too demanding, too lax, or too insensitive" (Curry & Johnson, 1991, p. 76). "Too demanding" means pushing down academics to lower levels, resulting in children being asked to perform in ways that are not developmentally appropriate. "Too lax" refers to a lack of challenge: Spending a whole year on boring worksheets lacks intellectual excitement. "Insensitivity" refers to the lack of recognition of children's developmental needs: Learning is presented as an isolated, passive activity, rather than something that is intellectually and socially active.

According to Johnson and Curry (1991), power assessment is a critical component of self-esteem during middle childhood. Power is assessed based on others and based on an inner sense of power and control. When success is based on competitive comparisons, it can be hard on the ego. When success is based on hard work and doing one's best through interest, effort, and collaboration, learners can develop feelings of power over their own accomplishments. Supporting autonomy (Rodgers, 1998) and providing opportunities for classroom responsibility (Ellsworth, 1997) can build self-esteem.

Peer rejection is one of the best predictors of later maladjustment. Children do not have to be extremely popular to feel accepted, but they do have to feel good about themselves.

Everyone needs a social place in the classroom, but Curry and Johnson (1991) caution that shyness should not be confused with rejection. Shyness appears to be an inherited characteristic to some extent, but also seems to be triggered by stressors in the environment (Crowley, 1991). Some children are just slower to warm up and, if nurtured and allowed to move at their own pace, will eventually enter social situations (Crowley, 1991).

Finally, virtue or moral worth is an important component of self-esteem (Curry & Johnson, 1991). School-age children evaluate themselves according to new standards of moral worth. Being good or bad in the classroom and being a nice friend are newly defined. Fairness is of primary concern. Moral development is discussed further in the next section of this chapter.

## Moral Development

According to Damon (1988), sharing is a very significant moral behavior that underlies children's understanding of distributive justice. The division of the world's goods is understood through the basic understanding of the concept of sharing that develops from the child's earliest naturally occurring interactions with others. By the elementary years, children begin to have an objective idea about fairness. The first aspect of fairness that elementary children use regularly is equality. Their major concern is the concept of equal shares. Concerns with merit and benevolence as the basis of justice enter their thoughts during middle or late elementary school.

Damon (1988) explains that the most important aspect of moral development that the family contributes is respect for authority. A close affectionate attachment to parents is the strongest element in building respect for authority. Moral rules and values are introduced in the family in many different ways. Preschoolers obey because they have to, "I clean my room because my mother says I have to." As children get into middle childhood, obedience becomes a sign of respect for adults, "I clean my room because my mother wants me to, and she is the person who cares for me."

According to Damon (1988), the peer group is the ideal setting for moral development. This is the only place where children interact with equals. Cooperative play in the peer group is necessary for the development of moral standards. It is in this setting that children try out the moral rules they have learned in the family. With friends, fairness is natural. Children only realize the value of the norms of fairness and honesty when they discover them in their social play. Reciprocity, or give-and-take, is the primary norm of childhood. The standards learned through interaction with peers are the basis for lifelong moral standards. Truth and honesty are especially important components of children's friendships. As children become more skilled in perspective taking, seeing another's point of view, they become better able to act on their moral knowledge.

Character development was a focus of many educational programs at the end of the twentieth century (Rusnak & Ribich, 1997). These programs promise to improve children's values, morals, and ethics. Rusnak and Ribich conclude that these programs have accomplished very little. They suggest that character education should be integrated into every subject and everyday, routine activities, rather than being taught as a separate subject.

## Sexuality

Freud's theory that middle childhood (ages five through eight) was a period of sexual latency has long been discarded (Society of Obstetricians and Gynecologists of Canada, 2006). Throughout childhood, children's development and interest in sexuality continues. While children select same-sex friends, they maintain an interest in the opposite sex. They also are old enough to understand the basics of reproduction. Adults should explain reproduction as children can acquire many misconceptions from their peers. Their natural curiosity may cause them to engage in sex play. If it is extensive, this should be a cause for concern. It needs to be explained that their bodies belong to themselves, no one else. Children will also use slang terms to describe body parts and sexuality.

### Attention Deficit Disorder

ADHD was described in Chapter 4. It is difficult to identify before school age, probably because we expect preschoolers to be active and to have relatively short attention spans. Once children enter elementary school, they are expected to be able to sit still and take turns speaking. The child who is hyperactive, inattentive, and/or impulsive soon stands out. Children may display all or combinations of these behaviors (National Institute of Mental Health, 2003). Treatment for ADHD varies with each child. Several stimulant medications that work have been approved for children six and older: Concerta, Focalin, Metadate ER, Metadate CD, Ritalin, Ritalin SR, and Ritalin LAS. The child and the family may benefit from some behavior intervention. Some benefits from psychotherapy can help them learn to understand and work with their problems. Behavior therapy (BT) is designed to change behavior using behaviorist approaches. Social skills training can also help children change behavior through modeling and explaining appropriate ways to interact with others. Parent support groups and parent education may also be effective interventions.

Look back through what you have learned about affective development. Select the components that you believe are most critical for parents and teachers to understand. Outline a plan for informing parents and teachers.

## THE ADULT ROLE WITH THE PRIMARY-AGE CHILD

The overall role of adults with children of any age is to promote self-esteem and moral worth. Curry and Johnson (1991) describe the following six principles that underlie the development of children's self-esteem (pp. 91–95):

1. Adult feedback must be authentic. Praise must be given for real accomplishments. Too much empty praise can actually lower self-esteem. Too many stickers and/or comments such as "good job" or "well done" may cause children to rely on outside judgments rather than on their internal judgment of the quality of their accomplishments. Children need to learn to recognize and deal with their own errors and develop an acceptance that things do not always turn out as expected. When praise is given, it should be specific, (i.e., "The story you wrote is very interesting").
2. Adults and children need goodness of fit. Adults should work with children at a developmental level that they find interesting and challenging. Primary children are reaching for independence and for abstract ideas and need adults who can support these efforts.
3. Scaffolding supports autonomy. Adults must gauge the amount of support and challenge necessary for children's optimal growth.
4. Individuals are different. Adults must consider temperamental and cultural differences when working with children.
5. Self-esteem is multifaceted. Acceptance, power and control, competence, and moral virtue must all be considered.
6. Children are resilient. Adults make mistakes and children normally run into problems. Part of good mental health is learning how to deal with conflict and frustration through discovering solutions to the problems that life presents.

Damon (1988) suggests the following principles for fostering moral growth (pp. 117–119):

1. Moral awareness is built from within by children through natural encounters with their peers, not by imposition from outside.
2. Moral awareness is shaped by natural encounters with others and natural emotional reactions to these encounters. For example, empathy supports moral compassion and prosocial behavior; shame, guilt, and fear support obedience and rule following; and love for and attachment to adults supports respect for authority.
3. Through their relationships with adults, children learn social standards, rules, and conventions. "*Authoritative* adult-child relations, in which firm demands are made of the child while at the same time there is clear communication between adult and child about the nature and justification of these demands, yield the most positive results for the child's moral judgment and conduct."
4. It is through peer relations that children are introduced to norms of direct reciprocity and to standards of sharing, cooperation, and fairness. It is with peers that children can experiment and discover new ways of interacting with others.
5. Social influence shapes children's morality. This influence varies from culture to culture. However, every culture has some kind of standards for values, such as truth, human rights, human welfare, and justice.
6. "Moral growth in school settings is governed by the same developmental processes that apply to moral growth everywhere." That is, moral values are acquired through interaction with adults and peers, not through listening passively to lectures or lessons. Children learn democratic values by participating in a democratic setting.

**respectful engagement**

Moral education based on a cooperative relationship between adult and child; the adult must respect the child's initiatives and reactions.

The context for children's full participation and moral learning is created by adults who "practice a **respectful engagement** with the child" (p. 119). Moral education is based on a cooperative relationship between adult and child. The adult must respect the children's initiatives and their reactions. The situation is not one of extreme permissiveness or strict authoritarian indoctrination. Adults should serve as models by openly discussing their feelings about moral issues that come up in their lives and discussing with children their reactions and feelings to the moral issues they face. Young children can gain experience in introspection, self-monitoring, and recognizing and discussing the feelings of others. Most important, children must be given real and appropriate responsibilities through which they can learn what it means to be a responsible member of society (Figure 30–3).

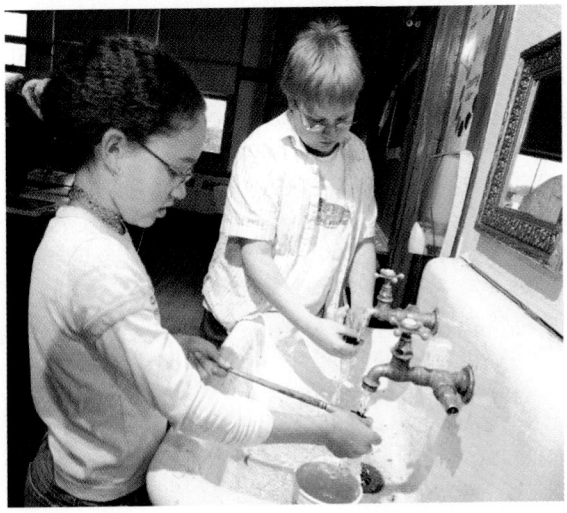

FIGURE 30–3 Primary children's moral development is supported by opportunities for real and appropriate responsibilities in the classroom.

## Research on Parental Factors

Hart, Ladd, and Burleson (1990) looked at the relationships between maternal disciplinary styles, children's expectations of the outcomes of social strategies, and children's peer status. The subjects were mothers of first and fourth-graders and their children. Children of mothers who were more power assertive (authoritarian) were found to be less well accepted by their peers. They expected that aggressive assertive methods, such as threatening to hit another child, would solve social conflicts.

Cohn (1990) found that for first-grade boys, maternal attachment was related to peer acceptance and teacher ratings of behavior. Boys who had less secure attachment relationships with their mothers were viewed by teachers and peers as less socially competent. The results of both of these studies are consistent with the recommendations that parental love and an authoritative approach to discipline support positive social adjustment out of the home.

Some adults believe that yelling, speaking in a stern voice, and/or spanking will make children well behaved, even though these methods do not have long-term positive effects on behavior. A study by Zambarano (1991) sheds some light on why shouting and physical punishment do not curb behavior effectively. Dramatized incidents were created with a parent and child involved in various situations in which child behavior needed to be changed. The incidents varied according to the tone of the adult voice (loud or soft), and whether the child was spanked or not. The voice messages and to some extent the spanking behavior made the parent's message clear to adult and twelve-year-old viewers. However, for the four- to eight-year-olds, the messages were not clear. Although yelling and spanking may seem like clear messages to adults, this research indicates that for young children, speaking in a clear and careful manner gets the message across best. **Zero tolerance** (Zero evidence for zero tolerance, 2001) is another popular method the effectiveness of which has not been proven. Zero tolerance includes harsh punishments, such as suspension and expulsion, for nondangerous, but unacceptable, behavior. The research indicates that it increases the risk that children will be removed from school and may not return. There is no evidence that a zero-tolerance policy improves student behavior or ensures school safety. A report on zero-tolerance research is available from the Indiana Education Policy Center Web site (www.indiana.edu/~iepc). As described in Chapter 27, inductive methods work best.

**zero tolerance**

Involves suspension and expulsion for nondangerous, but unacceptable, behavior.

Apply the criteria for adult-child relationships to the following situation:

Tonja is seven years old. She, her aunt, and two younger children have been to a softball game in the park. They stop at a convenience store to get some treats. When they walk inside the doorway, all the children dash in different directions trying to find the Slurpy machine. When it is found, they are all disappointed that it is out of order. The two younger children point at the machine saying, "I want blue!" Tonja asks if they could get something else. They rush over to the large case full of popsicles and ice cream treats. Aunt Kay notices a pink and a purple container with "Slurpy" written on the outside. She lifts the younger children up, and they select the pink ones. Tonja says happily, "I guess I want a purple one." They pay for their items, throw the wrappings in the trash, and head for the car. As they are leaving, Aunt Kay notices Tonja is extra quiet, licking her treat very slowly. She says, "Aunt Kay, what is this flavor?" Kay turned and read the label, "Cola." She asks Tonja if she likes it and she says, "Yeah, it's okay." Her tongue barely touches the treat as she licks it. Kay takes a closer look and tells her she will buy her a different flavor if she does not like that one. Tonja again says, "It's okay." After a few moments, Kay tells her to pick out something else; it does not matter if they throw the cola flavor away. Tonja smiles and rushes inside, relieved to get another choice. She picks out a pink one. The cashier has watched this whole event and kindly refuses money for the replacement. As we drive away, Tonja says to the younger girls, "That purple Slurpy wasn't grape, and it was yucky!"

## SOCIOCULTURAL INFLUENCES ON CHILD DEVELOPMENT AND BEHAVIOR

Phinney and Rotheram (1987) express concern about the problems of ethnic socialization of children, that is, the process of acquiring ethnic identity. Ethnic identity refers to the acquisition of ethnic group patterns. According to research described by Aboud (1987), children gradually learn to recognize members of other ethnic groups. By age seven, children begin to recognize that ethnicity is unchangeable, but this does not seem to be stable knowledge until about age ten. Primary children are still in the process of attaining an understanding of their own ethnic identity and those of other groups.

Phinney and Rotheram (1987) describe several themes in ethnic socialization. First, different ethnic groups are distinguished not just by easily observed characteristics, such as skin color, hair texture, and food preferences, but also by attitudes, values, and behaviors. They believe that it is important to help young children develop positive attitudes about these differences through positive interaction. Although biculturalism can be stressful, children can be helped to feel proud of being able to function well in two cultures. Second, young children perceive ethnicity in concrete ways. It is not until adolescence that children can consider the choices they have in terms of selecting an identity. Third, when children are in the minority, they are made very aware of this fact by their fewer numbers in a group and by the need to follow majority customs and rules. Majority children may be shielded from ethnic differences or see them in a stereotyped fashion. Finally, the environmental and sociocultural contexts influence children's ethnic socialization. Family and community factors are important influences. With an ever-increasing emphasis on pluralism, children from diverse cultures are more aware of their cultural heritage, and hopefully majority children are becoming more aware of how diverse our society is.

McCracken (1993) points out several reasons why we value diversity: It is the right thing to do, appreciation of each other will lead to a more harmonious world, and it is illegal to discriminate. As primary children delve deeper into content, it is essential to celebrate diversity by making it a part of the total curriculum, as suggested in the **antibias approach** (McCracken, 1993).

**antibias approach**
Celebrating diversity, making it part of the total curriculum.

Phinney and Rotheram (1987) point out several implications of ethnicity for education. Multicultural education is very important. Learning about ethnic diversity and the promotion of interethnic relations must be expanded. Such programs need to fit the developmental levels and interests of children. Because young children learn by experience and think concretely, firsthand experience with members of other groups is essential. McCracken (1993) describes how the diverse primary curriculum should look.

Phinney and Rotheram (1987) point out that each cultural group needs to learn about its own culture to build personal self-esteem. In integrated settings, interaction between ethnic groups will not necessarily just happen. Designing work groups that force children of different ethnic backgrounds to work together cooperatively has proven to be successful in promoting cross-ethnic interaction. Younger children select friends according to interests and, therefore, are the most open to cross-ethnic interaction.

Nelson-Le Gall and Jones (1990) observed average-achieving African American third- and fifth-grade children as they worked on a multitrial verbal task. These researchers were interested in learning more about which factors influence African American children to seek help when needed. When children thought they were responding correctly, they did not seek help. When they believed their responses were incorrect, they tended to seek help. However, there was a difference in the kind of help they sought. Academically confident children sought hints that would help them figure out the solutions on their own. Children who were not academically confident sometimes asked for hints and other times tried to get answers. Younger children were much less consistent about seeking help. This study provides normative information on average-achieving African American children and their courses of action under conditions of perceived failure and perceived success. It shows that the African American children studied did not give up under conditions in which they thought they were failing and sought help when needed.

Rotherham-Baron and Phinney (1990) compared patterns of social expectations among African American and Mexican American third- and sixth-grade children. These children were asked to respond to eight videotaped scenes of everyday social situations with the same ethnic, unfamiliar peers in a school setting. Mexican American children, more frequently than African American children, reported an expectation for sharing and for relying on adults when solving social problems. African American children relied more on apologizing, getting angry, and initiating action than did their Mexican American counterparts. For both groups, socially desirable responses increased and emotional responses decreased with age. The groups were more alike at the third-grade level than at the sixth-grade level. Girls tended to use apology more often than boys. Children with the highest self-esteem were the most similar to their own ethnic group. The authors suggest these differences in social expectations may account for a decrease in cross-ethnic friendships and increase in self-segregation as children move into higher grades. They recommend that these differences in reactions be openly discussed as part of the multicultural education program.

## SUMMARY

Developmentally, primary-level children are in many ways more like kindergartners than they are like upper-elementary students. They are still in the process of integrating the physical, motor, affective, and cognitive skills and concepts that developed during the preoperational periods, and they are just entering concrete operations. They still learn best through concrete experience, which they are just beginning to associate with abstract symbols, such as letters and numbers.

Primary-level children are entering a period of self-consciousness that peaks in adolescence. Peer relationships are very important to them; they are more important than academics. Opportunities to interact in the classroom can enhance learning and build social skills that can only be learned through give-and-take interaction with peers.

Self-esteem continues to develop as children enter the period of Industry versus Inferiority. They meet new standards for maturity when they enter first grade. As they measure themselves against these standards, new avenues open for developing higher or lower levels of self-esteem, depending on how they perceive themselves as compared to their peers. Children need to feel competent, powerful, socially accepted, and morally worthy. Moral worth is an extremely important part of self-esteem. Moral worth is measured according to such attributes as good and bad, meeting social standards, degree of concern for others, caring, benevolence, kindness, mercy, justice and fairness, honesty, and reactions to moral violations, such as shame, guilt, outrage, fear, and contempt. Adults have the responsibility of providing an environment that promotes self-esteem and moral worth. Adults need to be appropriate models who show respect for the children. Adults have the responsibility of clarifying the facts related to children's continued development and interest in sexuality. When children enter school, those who are ADHD are likely to be identified.

A growing body of research supports the child development value of an authoritative parental discipline style. Physical punishment and yelling do not send clear messages to young children and have no lasting positive effects on their behavior.

Sociocultural influences continue to be vital considerations in child development. Primary children are still in the process of attaining an understanding of their own ethnic identity and those of other groups. Multicultural education continues to be a necessary component of the school environment and curriculum. Current research is breaking down many of the ethnic group stereotypes about school achievement. Risk factors, such as low socioeconomic status, damage children from any ethnic group.

## For Further Reading


Anderson, L. W., & Bourke, S. F. (2000). *Assessing affective characteristics in the schools* (2nd ed.). Mahwah, NJ: Erlbaum.

Bierman, K. L. (2004). *Peer rejection*. New York: Guilford.

Bloomquist, M. I., & Schnell, S. V. (2002). *Helping children with aggression and conduct problems*. New York: Guilford.

Bornstein, R. F., & Masling, J. M. (Eds.). (2002). *The psychodynamics of gender and gender role*. Washington, DC: American Psychological Association.

Brandstatter, H., & Eliasz, A. (Eds.). (2001). *Persons, situations, and emotions*. New York: Oxford University Press.

Bronson, M. B. (2000). *Self-regulation in early childhood*. New York: Guilford.

Children, youth, and gun violence [Focus issue]. (2002). *The Future of Children, 12*(2).

Christ, G. H. (2000). *Healing children's grief: Surviving a parent's death from cancer*. New York: Oxford University Press.

Cowan, P. A., Cowan, C. P., Ablow, J. C., Johnson, V. K., & Measelle, J. R. (Eds.). (2005). *The family context of parenting in children's adaptation to elementary school*. Mahwah, NJ: Erlbaum.

Craig, W. M. (Ed.). (2000). *Childhood social development: The essential readings*. Oxford, UK: Blackwell.

Dunn, J. (2004). *Children's friendships*. Malden, MA: Blackwell.

Edwards, R. (Ed.). (2002). *Children, home and school: Regulation, autonomy, or connection?* New York: Routledge-Falmer.

Epps, S., & Jackson, B. J. (2000). *Empowered families, successful children: Early intervention programs that work*. Washington, DC: American Psychological Association.

Forgas, J. P. (Ed.). (2001). *Handbook of affect and social cognition*. Mahwah, NJ: Erlbaum.

Golden, B. (2002). *Healthy anger: How to help children and teens manage their anger*. New York: Oxford University Press.

Guerin, S., & Hennessey, E. (2002). *Aggression and bullying*. Williston, VT: Blackwell.

Harwayne, S. (2002). *Messages to ground zero: Children respond to September 11, 2001*. Portsmouth, NH: Heinemann.

Jackson, P. W., Boostrom, R. E., & Hansen, D. T. (2000). *The moral life of schools*. Indianapolis: Jossey-Bass.

Killen, M., & Smetana, J. G. (2005). *Handbook of moral development*. Mahwah, NJ: Erlbaum.

Kline, F. M., & Silver, L. B. (Eds.). (2004). *The educator's guide to mental health issues in the classroom*. Baltimore: Brookes.

Kohn, A. (2005). *Unconditional parenting*. New York: Atria Books.

LaGreca, A. M., Silverman, W. K., Vernberg, E. M., & Roberts, M. C. (Eds.). (2002). *Helping children cope with disasters and terrorism*. Washington, DC: American Psychological Association.

Lippa, R. A. (2002). *Gender, nature, and nurture*. Mahwah, NJ: Erlbaum.

Mayne, T. J., & Bonanno, G. A. (Eds.). (2001). *Emotions: Current issues and future directions*. New York: Guilford.

McLaughlin, M. W., Irby, M. A., & Langman, J. (2001). *Urban sanctuaries: Neighborhood organizations in the lives and futures of inner-city youth*. Indianapolis: Jossey-Bass.

Nucci, L. (2001). *Education in the moral domain*. New York: Cambridge University Press.

Schmidt, L. A., & Schulkin, J. (Eds.). (1999). *Extreme fear, shyness, and social phobia*. New York: Oxford University Press.

Smith, P., & Hart, C. H. (Eds.). (2002). *Blackwell handbook of childhood social development*. Williston, VT: Blackwell.

Smith, P. K., Pepler, D., & Rigby, K. (Eds.). (2004). *Bullying in schools. How successful can interventions be?* New York: Cambridge University Press.

Stanford, B. H., & Yamamoto, K. (Eds.). (2001). *Children and stress: Understanding and helping*. Olney, MD: Association for Childhood Education International.

Sullivan, K. (2000). *The anti-bullying handbook*. New York: Oxford University Press.

Zins, J. E., Weissberg, R. P., Wang, M. C., & Walberg, H. J. (Eds.). (2004). *Building academic success on social and emotional learning*. New York: Teachers College.

# UGGESTED ACTIVITIES

1. Observe some six-, seven-, and/or eight-year-olds in a social situation. Note whether their interactions are congruent with the descriptions and criteria in this chapter.

2. Analyze the following adult-child interaction based on what you have read in this chapter. Jake, age seven, enters the kitchen, where his mom is preparing dinner. He asks, "Can we take that game to play?" His mom answers, "No, you are not even supposed to have a friend over today, remember?" Jake responds, "I want to teach Andy how to play." Mom says, "No, you need to go outside. I am busy right now. You are grounded today. Do you remember why?" Jake says, "But I want to play it now." Mom says, "Jake, we'll talk about the game after dinner. Right now you and Andy need to go outside. Otherwise he will have to go home." Jake says, "I want to play it right now." Jake turns to go back outside. He is outside for a few minutes talking to Andy and then he comes back inside with his friend. They walk through the living room, not visible to his mom, who is still in the kitchen, and go to his room to play.

3. Assess the affective development of a six-, seven-, or eight-year old using the following list of developmental expectations.

| Behavior | Observed | Comments |
|---|---|---|
| | Yes or No | |
| **Six-Year-Old Expectations** | | |
| • Plays cooperatively with other children | | |
| • Completes cooperative projects with other children | | |
| • Takes turns when playing simple board or electronic games | | |
| • Evidences self-control of emotions, especially anger | | |
| • Uses good negotiation strategies when a plan arises with peers | | |
| • Demonstrates concern for fairness and justice | | |
| • Feels comfortable in gender role | | |
| • Enjoys and interacts well in team activities | | |
| • Values friendships | | |
| • Handles stress in a positive and constructive manner | | |
| • Shows respect for and interest in adults, including parents, teachers, and others | | |
| **Seven-Year-Old Expectations** | | |
| • Makes friends easily | | |
| • Shows control of anger, using words rather than physical aggression | | |
| • Participates in play that requires teamwork and rule observance | | |
| • Engages in completing cooperative projects with other children | | |
| • May make up own game rules to increase chances of winning | | |
| • Seeks adult approval for efforts | | |
| • Values friendships | | |

| Behavior | Observed | Comments |
|---|---|---|
| | Yes or No | |
| • Handles stress in a positive and constructive manner<br>• Shows respect for and interest in adults, including parents, teachers, and others<br>• Seeks adult attention and approval<br>• Seeks and enjoys opportunities to take on responsibilities<br>• Demonstrates concern for fairness and justice<br>• Feels comfortable in gender role | | |
| **Eight-Year-Old Expectations** | | |
| • Demonstrates patience and handles frustrations about own performance<br>• Interacts, plays, and works cooperatively with other children<br>• Engages in completing cooperative projects with other children<br>• Participates in group activities, such as games, sports, and plays<br>• Enjoys school—disappointed if has to miss a day<br>• Accepts responsibility and completes work independently<br>• Handles stressful situations without becoming overly upset<br>• Has one or more hobbies or collections<br>• Values friendships<br>• Shows respect for and interest in adults, including parents, teachers, and others<br>• Seeks adult attention and approval<br>• Demonstrates concern for fairness and justice<br>• Feels comfortable in gender role<br>• Describes what he or she likes and does not like about himself or herself—has generally positive self-concept and moderate to high self-esteem<br>• Has developed a sense of competence or industry—is willing to practice and master skills and has one or more areas where he or she feels successful | | |

4. Interview several primary teachers. Find out what they are doing to incorporate multicultural education in their classrooms. Also, ask them what methods they use to promote positive self-esteem and moral worth in their students.

5. Make an entry in your journal.

1. Select the statements that describe affective characteristics of primary-level children.
   a. Primary-level children are not especially sensitive about specific situations, such as talking in front of the rest of the class.
   b. Peers become less important to children as they proceed from first to third grade.

c. Aggressive but not withdrawn children are usually rejected by peers.
d. If a child hovers silently and then enters a play group by imitating what the group members are doing, the group entry is most likely to be successful.
e. Rough-and-tumble play includes running, jumping, laughing, chasing, and other physically active acts.
f. Rough-and-tumble play is dangerous and should never be allowed because it has no value for young children.
g. Recess is not necessary for primary children. It is a waste of time.
h. Children who master appropriate social strategies are most likely to be popular with their peers.
i. Bullies need to be taught appropriate methods for reacting to anger.
j. Friends serve many functions for young children. Besides being playmates, they support feelings of self-worth and provide nurturance and intimacy.
k. In ethnically diverse groups, children tend to stick with friends from their own group.

**2.** Give an example of a way social interaction can benefit children in the primary classroom.

**3.** Describe a situation in which a young child might feel stressed.

**4.** Select the correct answer for each of the following questions.

a. Self-esteem includes the way children feel about themselves in the following areas:
(1) physical
(2) social and moral
(3) emotional
(4) cognitive
(5) all of the above

b. According to Erikson, during the primary grades, children enter
(1) the preoperational period.
(2) the period of Initiative versus Guilt.
(3) the period of Industry versus Inferiority.
(4) the period of concrete operations.

c. According to Piaget, during the primary grades, children enter
(1) the preoperational period.
(2) the period of Initiative versus Guilt.
(3) the period of Industry versus Inferiority.
(4) the period of concrete operations.

d. Self-esteem, according to Curry and Johnson, consists of four components:
(1) power, happiness, acceptance, and love.
(2) competence, power, acceptance, and virtuousness.
(3) competence, power, love, and virtuousness.
(4) acceptance, competence, power, and dominance.

e. The best way to ensure that children will feel competent in school is to
(1) fit the curriculum to the child.
(2) fit the child to the curriculum.
(3) change the age of school entrance.
(4) place children in transition classes.

f. One of the following will *not* help children feel powerful and in control:
(1) Success is based on hard work.
(2) Success is based on doing your best.
(3) Success is based on beating out the competition.
(4) Success is based on collaborative learning.

g. Moral worth is an important component of self-esteem. Some of the facets of moral worth are
(1) not having a positive feeling about being a good person.
(2) kindness, mercy, justice and fairness, and honesty.

(3) meanness, carelessness, cheating, and lying.
(4) trying to win by competing with others.

h. Sharing is a significant moral behavior that is learned
(1) from the time of the child's first naturally occurring interactions.
(2) from direct instruction provided by significant adults.
(3) from being forced to divide groups of toys equally with peers.
(4) during interactions that begin during the primary period.

i. "I take out the trash because Dad wants me to, and he is one of the people who cares for me." This is an example of
(1) obeying because one has to.
(2) obeying as a sign of respect for adults.
(3) obeying as it occurs in adolescence.
(4) obeying as it occurs during the preoperational period.

j. One of the following is not true:
(1) The peer group is the ideal setting for moral development.
(2) In the peer group, children have the opportunity to try out moral rules with equals.
(3) Children gain an understanding of norms of fairness as they discover them during their play.
(4) Truth and honesty are not important components in the friendships of young children.

k. Zero tolerance is a method that
(1) involves detention.
(2) involves commitment.
(3) involves suspension and expulsion from school for nondangerous but unacceptable behavior.
(4) involves suspension of parents.

l. Resiliency is defined as
(1) the essential ability to engage.
(2) the essential ability to "bounce back" from difficult circumstances.
(3) the essential ability to argue.
(4) the essential ability to disagree.

m. During middle childhood, sexuality
(1) enters a period of latency.
(2) is of no interest to children.
(3) should be discussed and explained by adults.
(4) should be left to peers for providing information.

n. ADHD symptoms are always
(1) hyperactivity.
(2) inattentiveness.
(3) impulsivity.
(4) any combination of the above.

**5.** Describe in your own words and in no more than one page the components of the adult's role with the primary child that you believe to be most important.

**6.** Explain "ethnic identity" and why it is important.

## KEY TERMS LIST

antibias approach
cooperative learning
primary grades
resiliency
respectful engagement
zero tolerance

Additional resources for this chapter can be found on the Online Companion™ to accompany this text at http://www.earlychilded.delmar.com. Respond to "Time to Reflect" and "Looking Further" concepts, review various child development scenarios, and answer thought-provoking questions in the Critical Thinking Forum. Keep a daily journal by downloading the student journal available on this Web site. Complete the interactive matching exercises to reinforce concepts, and printout the child development assessment forms to use during your observation of development for children from birth to age eight. In addition, read the case studies on the Web site to reinforce the important concepts in each chapter, and take a look at the multitude of Web links that are available for student research on the Internet.

CHAPTER

# 31

# The Primary Child: Cognitive Development and Schooling

## OBJECTIVES

After reading this chapter, you should be able to:

- List the characteristics of a classroom setting that is developmentally appropriate for primary-level children.
- Analyze and evaluate the extent to which a primary classroom supports the development of young children.
- Identify the typical cognitive characteristics of six- through eight-year-old children.
- Explain how primary children move from the concrete to the symbolic.
- Explain the function and value of private speech.
- Recognize strategies commonly used by beginning readers.
- Explain the difference between guidance and discipline.
- Explain the functions of writing and drawing in promoting self-esteem.
- Identify key factors in Piaget's and Vygotsky's views of primary-level children's cognitive development.
- Describe the place of superheroes in the primary classroom.
- List the problems associated with having computers in schools.
- List the important factors that affect level of achievement for primary-level children.
- Develop a vision of the ideal primary classroom setting.
- Identify the characteristics of the caring curriculum and the hidden curriculum.

This chapter looks at some of the cognitive characteristics of six- through eight-year-old children who are students in primary classrooms (grades one through three). Let's begin by looking in on two primary-grade classrooms:

> In Mr. Marcos' class, we observe children in various learning centers. There is the soft buzz of conversation as they concentrate on their activities and projects. The class appears to include children of an unusually broad range of sizes. Mr. Marcos

> explains that at the primary level in this school, children are randomly assigned to classes across the conventional grade levels. Only about one-third of his students were new to him this year; the rest have been with him one or two years. As we look around the room, we note that some children are using dry lima beans to develop their own math problems. Another group is measuring the growth of their bean plants and recording the results on graphs. Still others are building unit block structures to house a variety of miniature farm animals and farm equipment. Mr. Marcos is working with a group that is drawing pictures and writing and/or dictating their own versions of *Jack and the Beanstalk* for a class book. Still others are in the library area looking at various fiction and nonfiction books about plants. We also notice that, in all of the centers, children are helping each other.
>
> Next, we go to another school in the same district. As we enter Ms. Brown's class, we are immediately struck by the difference in atmosphere. First, we note the silence as the children sit working at their individual desks. One group is filling in workbook pages, another has several ditto worksheets to complete, and a third group sits with Ms. Brown and takes turns reading from a basal reader. We note that some of the children doing workbook and worksheet exercises do not seem to know what they are supposed to do, but appear to be trying hard to look busy. The children with Ms. Brown who are waiting for a turn to read seem restless and bored. Ms. Brown explains that, in this school, children are given a readiness test when they enter kindergarten and then are grouped homogeneously according to their test scores. This year she has the "lowest" group.

Which classroom is an example of developmentally appropriate practice? Which is an example of developmentally inappropriate practice? Relate these classroom practices to the developmental characteristics of primary-level children described in this and other chapters.

School is a major aspect of the primary child's life. As the NAEYC guidelines suggest, instruction for primary children should fit their developmental characteristics (Bredekamp & Copple, 1997). For example, primary-level children are physically active. They find it difficult to sit for long periods. They still need to engage in active learning rather than in passive kinds of activities. Cognitively, primary children are in the process of moving into concrete operations. They are beginning to be able to mentally manipulate objects, but they still need concrete experiences through which they can make the connections to symbols. Their fascination with school is reflected in their dramatic play. Jane relates the following anecdote:

> Aunt Jane arrives home to find her two nieces, Diane, age seven, and Ann, age five, writing on the marker board. The minute Aunt Jane walks in, Diane asks her if she wants to play school. Aunt Jane says she would be glad to, and Diane then proceeds to teach her how to count, add, and draw. When she asks Jane to count her numbers, she whispers to her, "Pretend you don't know numbers, okay?" When Jane says the wrong number, Diane says, "That's okay. Let's count to that number." She is very much a little teacher in the making. People who choose to be teachers frequently say they were influenced by special teachers when they were in elementary school (White, Buchanan, Hinson & Burts, 2001).

This chapter examines some of the cognitive characteristics of primary-level children, and the place of schooling in their lives.

## COGNITIVE CHARACTERISTICS

As already described, during the primary years, young children pass through the transition period and enter the concrete operations period. As a result, they begin to be able to handle more complex cognitive problems and to connect symbols

| PIAGET'S PERIODS OF COGNITIVE DEVELOPMENT | DEVELOPMENTALLY APPROPRIATE PRACTICE |
|---|---|
| Preoperational<br><br>Language and cognitive development are rapid as learning takes place through imitation, play, and other self-initiated activities (ages 3–7). | •integrated curriculum<br>•a caring community<br>•concrete learning experiences<br>•opportunities to plan and select activities<br>•opportunities for conversation<br>•teacher support of play<br>•opportunities for collaboration |
| Transitional (ages 5–7) | •continuity with preoperational fitting age, individual, and family and cultural aspects |
| Concrete Operations<br><br>Abstract symbols and ideas can be applied to concrete experience (ages 7–13). | •integrated curriculum providing knowledge of basic concepts in all content areas<br>•caring, democratic community<br>•instruction that is adapted to individuals<br>•active, intellectually engaging teaching strategies, such as in-depth project work<br>•curriculum containing ongoing project work based on students' interests as they emerge |

**FIGURE 31–1** Piaget's periods of cognitive development and developmentally appropriate practice.

with concrete experiences. Being in a transitional period, primary-level children still enjoy dramatic play, but it takes on more structure and complexity than previously, as can be seen in the example that follows. Remember, primary-level children are in the transitional stage from preoperational to concrete operational thought. Figure 31–1 outlines the relationship between these developmental periods and developmentally appropriate practice in the classroom. Children are also making the transition into elementary school (Axelrod, Goldstein, LaGrange, Lever, & Burke, 2002).

Remember that Vygotsky also outlined stages of cognitive development (see Chapter 2). During the preschool period (ages three to seven), the leading activity is play and overt private speech develops self-regulation. During school age (seven to thirteen), the leading activity is learning and silent private speech serves to regulate task-related behavior and performance. Around age seven, children stop talking to themselves out loud and begin talking silently as they play and work. In the classroom, discussion and problem solving are the major strategies of instruction (Berk & Winsler, 1995).

## Concept Development

In Chapter 20, fundamental concept development was described. Remember that conservation of number is usually the first conservation problem solved as children enter concrete operations. As they proceed through concrete operations, they reach points where they can solve other conservation problems that involve other types of physical changes, such as liquid volume, solid volume, area, and weight. Two of these other problems are illustrated in Figure 31–2. Children need to be conservers to attain a true understanding of mathematical operations.

| Original | Physical Change | Question | Nonconserving Response | Conserving Response |
|---|---|---|---|---|
| Child agrees that the same amount of drink is contained in each glass. | | Is there still the same amount of drink in each glass, or does one glass have more? | No, they are not the same; there is more in the tall glass. | Yes, they have the same amount; you just put the drink in a different size glass. It is taller, but it is also thinner. |
| Child agrees each ball contains the same amount of clay. | | Is there still the same amount of clay in the ball and the snake, or does one have more? | No, there is more clay in the snake because it is longer (or more in the ball because it is fatter). | Yes, they have the same amount. You just rolled one ball out in a different shape. |

**FIGURE 31–2** Physical changes in conservation tasks.

Describe what the following example tells you about these children's interests and their knowledge. Consider both their social and cognitive development.

Ed and Kent are both eight years old. They are on the school playground. "Ed, you be Charles Barkley and I'll be Karl Malone. Then we can switch, okay?" Ed agrees, and the two boys begin playing basketball. Kent plays cautiously, following the rules of the game. Kent starts to take a step but realizes that he cannot because it is against the rules. He regains his balance, pivots, and takes a shot at the basket. Ed guards Kent, and Kent becomes frustrated. He says, "What the heck are you doing, Ed? Do you have to keep your hands on my back the whole time?" As they make baskets, they are careful about throwing the ball back in the game correctly. Kent has another idea: "I'll shoot baskets until I make one, and then you can, okay?" He then moves to another basket so he can practice shooting on his own. After missing several shots in a row, Kent mumbles to himself, "Come on. I have to focus. I have to pay attention." He continues to shoot until he makes a basket.

**learning activity**

Vygotsky views these leading primary activities as formalized, structured, and culturally determined.

From the Vygotskian view, the leading activity during the primary grades is the **learning activity** (Bodrova & Leong, 1996). "*Learning activity* is adult-guided activity around specific content that is formalized, structured, and culturally determined" (p. 60). In Western culture, the content centers on literacy, mathematics, science, social studies, art, and physical education. Language is the major means of transmitting content and processes in learning activity. During the primary period, children develop the beginnings of *theoretical reasoning*, which enables them to understand the fundamental properties of science that may not be evident.

For example, they may learn that dolphins have certain attributes that categorize them as mammals rather than as fish, even though they swim and live in the water. This development to true theoretical reasoning is not complete until age 18 or older and is much like moving from concrete to formal operations for the Piagetian. A second developmental accomplishment is the emergence of *higher mental functions.* Planning, monitoring, evaluative thinking, and deliberate memory develop. Children begin to evaluate their own thought processes and actions when solving problems. A third accomplishment is the emergence of *intrinsic motivation.* Through their participation in learning activities, children become interested in learning for its own sake. Praise or other rewards from the teacher are not needed. Gradually, children make a transition from play to learning. Whereas Vygotsky views the preprimary child's major form of learning as being through play, during the primary years, a distinction develops as children learn there are standards for learning (i.e., correct responses) that make learning different from play. Errors are not left for self-correction; rather, the teacher points them out and helps the students make corrections.

Jensen (1998) points out the importance of brain-compatible learning, that is, instruction presented in a manner that fits the developing brain and its ways of processing. In Chapter 4, we looked at how learning takes place and in Chapter 20 at the cognitive system and concept development. Learning takes place as neurons in the brain make new connections. Our intelligence grows as more neuron connections are made. All children can benefit from an enriched environment ( Jensen, 1998). All children can benefit from challenge, novelty, and specific feedback. Enrichment can come through reading and language, motor stimulation, thinking and problem solving, and the arts. Jensen (1998, p. 40) states:

> Two rules come from the field of brain research and enrichment. One is to eliminate threat, and the other is to enrich like crazy. Before we understood the collective impact of an enriched environment, it may have been acceptable to justify a minimalist classroom. Gone are the days in which any teacher could justify a barren classroom with one-way lecture as the only input.

The growing brain needs a variety of enriched input (Solomon & Hendren, 2003).

Consider how the following event might relate to Piaget's and Vygotsky's views of cognitive development during the primary period. The setting is a third-grade classroom. Carson is seven years old.

> The teacher is in the front of the room explaining a new math concept. Each child has a math book and they are working together as a class as the teacher shows them step by step the process of making an organized list to find combinations. One of the problems is as follows:
>
> Tara may choose to have a peanut butter sandwich or a cheese sandwich for lunch. With her sandwich she can have an apple, a pear, or grapes. How many possible combinations can she choose from?
>
> Carson answered five right after the teacher asked the question. The teacher then showed the children how to make an organized list to solve the problem. After they made the list, Carson realized the answer was six. He listened very closely and wrote down everything the teacher wrote on the board.

## The Child's View of Personal Intellectual Competence

Stipek and MacIver (1989) reviewed studies that examined how children view their own intellectual competence. Preschool through first graders tend to focus on social behavior rather than on academic achievement as the criteria for "smartness." That is, sharing is smart, and hurting another child is not smart. Social relationships are more important than knowing the alphabet or being able to count, read, or write. By second grade, children perceive work habits, such as being neat and putting forth effort, as indications of intelligence. Being good and following rules may also be seen as indicators of intellectual ability. By age seven, children seem to understand the concept of effort and how it can affect success, but do not perceive differences in ability as affecting success. By second grade, children begin to understand the concept of task difficulty; that is, a hard task is one that most children cannot do. However, the perception that ability is a stable trait does not seem to really take hold until the fifth or sixth grade, when repeated failure causes task persistence to decrease.

According to Stipek and MacIver (1989), most younger children feel pretty good about their intellectual competence, no matter how they actually perform. Young children seem to view their competence in terms of their successes rather than their failures. They appear to believe that with effort, they will eventually succeed. Younger children are also very responsive to positive social reinforcement. That is, praise makes them feel more successful than stickers or other concrete rewards. Apparently, praise is more salient to preoperational children, who can process only one idea at a time. It seems children need to be well into concrete operations to be able to consider both praise and other forms of reward simultaneously. Younger children also tend to receive praise at face value, whereas older children weigh it in terms of the task they have accomplished. When symbols are used to denote success, younger children can relate to stars and happy faces, but not to letter grades. Letter grades do not seem to affect children's perception of ability until the third or fourth grade. This is probably because, to really understand letter grades, one has to be able to understand an ordinal scale.

For younger children, effort is a primary indicator of intellectual competence. Being a hard worker and practicing a lot is also being "smart." Comparisons with peers take on increasing importance during the primary grades. Preschoolers through second graders are inconsistent in the way they use information about how well others are doing. At some point in the period between third and fifth grade, comparison with peers takes on great importance. In summary, primary-level students still respond to adult approval and to task success, whether easy or difficult, as criteria for their intellectual competence. Consequently, it is relatively easy to promote an atmosphere that enables them to feel good about themselves as learners.

Stipek and MacIver (1989) suggest several factors within the classroom setting that may account for the change in children's views of intellectual competence as children progress from preschool to primary to upper elementary. In a preschool, usually any product is accepted if the child has demonstrated reasonable effort in working on it. As children proceed through the grades, they are given more tasks to complete that have either right or wrong answers. Their accomplishments with these tasks provide specific, concrete feedback. However, during the primary grades, teachers emphasize good work habits and appropriate conduct, so these aspects may appear more salient to the primary-level child than actual academic performance. Stipek and MacIvers (1989, p. 535) conclude that educators should consider the way children evaluate intellectual competence at different ages and design "instructional practices that maximize self-confidence and positive motivation for children" for each age group. An important consideration is that, cognitively, primary-level children are more similar to preschool and kindergarten children than to upper-elementary students. They still respond best to and feel more confident in doing tasks that are open-ended and emphasize process rather than product. Their confidence can be eroded quickly by adult responses that indicate they are not making progress.

## Concept Development: Problem Solving in Mathematics

Providing children with problems to solve is a major strategy for concept development in mathematics and science. Buschman (2002) observed problem-solving strategies in his classroom of first, second, and third graders. He identified seven stages of problem-solving development:

1. *Concrete Stage.* Display solutions with concrete objects.
2. *Readiness Stage.* Use fingers rather than real objects. Reasoning is circular from problem to answer with no steps in between.
3. *Copying Stage.* Imitate what others do and may use trial and error. Reasons are obscure.
4. *Mechanical Stage.* Select one method, which they use over and over. They may see their errors but continue to use the same strategy.
5. *Novice Problem-Solver Stage.* Use past experience to solve problems if they are similar to previous problems. Use creative methods but can't explain their logic.
6. *Apprentice Problem-Solver Stage.* Can modify previously used strategies to solve new problems. Use formal logic in explanations.
7. *Problem-Solver Stage.* Use creative solutions or new solutions. Children can explain the logic of their solutions.

Children develop at different rates and at different times. Some skip a stage and some regress. Buschman found that if allowed time to develop strategies, the children's natural problem-solving abilities emerged.

## Private Speech

Bivens and Berk (1989) conducted a longitudinal study of the development of private speech from first through third grade. Their observations support Vygotsky's theory that overt private speech gradually becomes internalized private speech during this period. Along with this internalization, an increasing degree of physical self-control and an increase in on-task behavior also develops. The interaction of private speech and increased physical control seem to facilitate each other's development and result in more appropriate school learning behavior. By third grade, the cumulative effect of private speech use and increased self-control appears to be related to higher levels of achievement.

## Literacy and Language

Chapter 28 included a description of the No Child Left Behind legislation. This legislation is intended to ensure that children, by third grade, are able to read conventionally and apply their reading skills to the learning of content material, such as social studies, science, English language arts, and mathematics. There has been much criticism of No Child Left Behind and its emphasis on assessment, unfair standards, and pressure to dumb-down the curriculum to meet a narrow set of outcomes (i.e., Houston, 2005; Lewis, 2005; Popham, 2005; Thomas, 2005). It is not easy for teachers to use developmentally appropriate practice under the pressure of No Child Left Behind, but it is possible. Developing literacy skills is a major focus of the primary educational program. A study by McIntyre (1990) provides a picture of how this development took place in a whole-language first-grade classroom where storybook reading by the teacher, with child involvement and interaction encouraged, took place daily. McIntyre observed these first graders during their independent reading time in the classroom reading center. The reading center contained more than 1,200 books from which the children could make independent selections. Children could read independently and/or with other students during a daily 60- to 90-minute reading and writing period. She found several strategies children used:

1. *Reading the pictures with oral-like language:* That is, as the children "read," they used language that was more like conversation than like written story-book language.
2. *Reading pictures with textlike language:* The children used textlike language, although the text was not exactly memorized.
3. *Saving the text from memory:* The children used the text language they remembered and read in a chantlike rhythm. Their eyes were focused on the pictures rather than on the print.
4. *Reading the text from memory:* The readers' eyes were focused on the print as they read a familiar book from memory.
5. *Reading the text, skipping words:* Children read the words but skipped so many words and pages that the story did not make sense. The reader looked for the familiar, rather than reading for meaning.
6. *Reading the text:* The children actually read the text with minimal or no help.
7. *Repeated reading:* Children repeated what another child had read or tried to read along with the reader.
8. *Browsing:* No reading was going on, but there was interaction with books, such as flipping through them, carrying them around, fighting over a book, grabbing a book, or passing a book on to someone else.

Strategies 1 through 6 tend to be developmental, but may be intermixed. The last two strategies were used by all the children observed throughout the course of reading development. These observations demonstrate how, under the right classroom conditions, first graders can become conventional readers following their natural developmental capabilities and strategies.

During the primary grades, children are expected to master reading. All children are expected to read conventionally by the end of first grade (McGee & Richgels, 2004). They are expected to learn many new skills that support reading. According to McGee and Richgels, the major elements to be learned are:

- Being able to comprehend stories and information texts
- Learning the meanings of new words
- Recognizing several hundred sight words
- Being able to use sound-letter relationships to identify unknown words
- Being able to spell words
- Being able to create a variety of written works

Children entering first grade vary in their levels as readers. Some are already conventional readers, others catch on quickly, and others are slow to acquire the ability to read. With a good start in first grade, children can expand their experiences with reading and writing as they move into second grade and beyond.

Besides exhibiting a natural readiness in learning to read, primary-level children are also eager authors. Anne Haas Dyson (1989) has documented in detail the worlds of child writers in her three-year study in a multicultural primary (kindergarten through grade three) language arts classroom. In this classroom, writing was observed to grow out of the children's drawing and talking. Talking and drawing were the tools the children initially used to organize the world. Writing gradually became a part of their symbolic toolbox. Dyson (1989) and Salyer (1994) emphasize the importance of the classroom as a community where social interaction supports literacy development. Daily journal writing was an especially significant activity that afforded the children opportunities to express themselves freely. Experiences from home and school could be recorded. Children repeated themes that were the most salient to them. Their drawings and writings became more elaborate with each repetition. Unlike the often-observed rote repetition drill and practice that stifle children's initiative, this child-controlled repetition reflected increasing initiative and growing cognitive abilities. The children's writings reflected their increasing mastery of written language and the use of symbols. Writing also provided a vehicle for building self-esteem. This open-ended approach provided success for everyone at their own developmental level.

Continuing her immersion in the early grades, Dyson (1998) spent several years immersed in the writings of a culturally diverse second-grade classroom located in a lower-socioeconomic-level urban school. She dealt with the question of promoting writing, which builds on children's experiences out of school but brings their superheroes into the classroom. Many people believe that superheroes provide children with dangerous ideas that should not be brought into schools. Each day in this classroom, there is a period of "free writing" and "author's theater." The children's writing is filled with good guy/bad guy characters who are presented in their authors' theater dramatizations. The author's theater provides an opportunity for the more structured dramatic play that primary-level children enjoy and that affords them an opportunity to work through their need for power and to express the complexities of their social lives and the human relations involved. Although there is much criticism of commercial media (see Chapter 4), Dyson believes that because it is central to contemporary children's lives, it provides children with common story material. Dyson speaks to the children's stories that may appear unimaginative and dangerous to many adults, but which she finds important in their growth as writers (p. 166):

> "Innocent" children, adults may feel, should be free from such complexities, free to play on playground and paper. But children's imaginative play is all about freedom from their status as powerless children. Tales about good guys and bad ones, rescuers and victims, boyfriends and girlfriends allow children to fashion worlds in which *they* make decisions about characters and plots, actors and actions. Thus, for children, as for adults, Freedom is a verb, a becoming; it is experienced as an expanded sense of agency, of possibility for choice and action.

Dyson's book contains a wealth of child writing and acting examples that support self-motivation of young children to express their thoughts, experiences, and wishes.

Unfortunately, school systems are adopting assessments like DIBELS (see Chapter 22), which is quick, easy, and narrow in focus. Kamii and Manning (2005) compared literacy achievement as measured by DIBELS with other means of assessment and found it lacking as an instrument for measuring literacy instruction.

When I was a young child, I often acted the part of the good guy in dramatic play. I was Dale Evans, the female cowgirl heroine who assisted my other heroes, Roy Rogers, Gene Autry, and Hopalong Cassidy. I was also the American female heroine spy out to stop the wicked WWII aggressors. I was often saved from arch villains by Superman. However, I don't remember ever having the opportunity to write about or act out these characters at school, except on the playground.

Think back and reflect on your primary years. Who were your heroes and heroines? What was the content of your dramatic play? Did you ever write stories about your imaginary adventures? Write a short essay describing your experiences and your thoughts about bringing popular culture into the classroom.

Primary-grade students still learn through play (Kaplan, 2000; Kieff & Casbergue, 2000; Ritchie, 2000). Owocki (1999) presents examples of how children grow and develop in literacy through play in the primary grades. Allington (2002) describes exemplary reading instruction as instruction that fits children's individual needs. Research indicates that the teacher is more important than the materials or any packaged curriculum.

> It has become clearer that investing in good teaching—whether through making sound hiring decisions or planning effective professional development—is the most "research based" strategy available. If we truly hope to attain the goal of "no child left behind" we must focus on creating a substantially larger number of effective, expert teachers. (Allington, 2002, p. 740)

Allington, through classroom observation of exemplary teachers, found six common features or the six *T*s:

1. Time—At least 50 percent of each day was spent on reading and writing activities.
2. Texts—Books were supplied that provided successful reading experiences for all children, no matter what their achievement levels were. Basal readers were often ignored. These teachers recognized that motivation to read was based on reading success.
3. Teaching—These teachers frequently gave direct instruction in cognitive strategies that good readers use. They realized that students don't learn from work sheets.
4. Talk—Purposeful talk was encouraged. More open-ended questions were posed.
5. Tasks—Assignments were longer. Children might work several days on the same writing assignment or book. Assignments were complex, and students could make choices.
6. Testing—Grades were assigned based more on effort and improvement rather than on just level of achievement.

Expert teachers are more important than so-called proven programs in reaching reading success.

Students need time to engage in challenging reading and writing projects, such as keeping an author's notebook (Roberts, 1999), using cooking to connect literature and mathematics (Richardson, Hoag, Miller, & Monroe, 2001), writing to pen pals (Kirylo, Millet, Luckett, & Guindon, 2001), or attaining an understanding of aging, through literature (Crawford, 2000). They also need time to apply language to meaningful discussion. Further, they can benefit from the opportunity to learn a second language (Araujo, 2001).

In Chapter 22, reading and writing development and basic instructional strategies were discussed. The NAEYC/IRA goals for reading and writing (1998) were listed. The NAEYC/IRA position for primary reading and writing supports the integration of the two areas and the critical importance of looking at reading and writing development as a continuum: "IRA and NAEYC believe that goals and expectations for young children's achievement in reading and writing should be developmentally appropriate, that is *challenging but achievable*, with sufficient adult support" (p. 38). Most children will learn to read by age six or seven, but some need a great deal of individual support to read by age eight or nine. Educators must be prepared to apply a variety of strategies to ensure success for this range of learning and development. They also need to be prepared to work with children with special needs and second-language learners and to respect the home cultures of their students.

## TECHNOLOGY

As already described in this text (see Chapter 4), technology, including computers, television, and video games, is now an important element in the lives of young children. As just described, superheroes can motivate children's writing and dramatizing. On the other hand, the amount and type of violence on television is of great concern. In Springfield, Oregon, teacher Susan Colonna decided to have her second graders tackle violence head-on (Evans, 1996). They studied Martin Luther King, Jr., and nonviolence; discussed violence; collected data on television violence, planned activities to promote nonviolence through an action plan; and were interviewed by the media. Computers open the door to the Internet and to dangers previously not imagined (Burris, 1997). Although e-mail can be an exciting means for conversing with people in other areas of the world, talking to strangers on the Internet may be as dangerous as talking to strangers on the street. Children need some rules for the Internet. For example, if they receive a scary e-mail message, they should do the following (Burris, p. 3):

- Tell a parent, teacher, or other trusted adult immediately.
- Do not respond to the message without a parent's or teacher's permission.
- Report the incident to the online or Internet service provider, or call the police if they feel threatened.

Children also need to be protected from Internet sites that promote obscenity and pornography. Adults need to carefully monitor children's Internet connections and provide clear limits on their access. Technological methods are becoming available to block access. An abundance of educational material can be of great value to children, and they need to know which sites are acceptable and how to access them.

An overall question regarding computers is whether they really help children learn (Winik, 1997). They are widely available in schools, and computer literacy is considered essential for today's young people. However, there are questions about their value and their placement (lab versus classroom). For example, quantity of time is not always quality. In one study, preschoolers who spent time using computer drill programs designed to develop reading skills dropped 50 percent in creativity and showed no significant improvement in reading. Computer-assisted instruction (CAI) appears to be only moderately helpful in teaching beginning readers (Blok, Oostdam, Otter, & Overmaat, 2002). On the other hand, the opportunity to use computers can be very motivating for hard-to-reach students. A big problem, however, is money. Purchasing computers and wiring buildings for the Internet is expensive. Many problems need to be solved, such as developing school plans for installation and use of computers, using the computers for educational purposes that are valuable for student learning, training teachers, monitoring the Internet, and obtaining quality software.

Read the following descriptions of activities taking place in an after-school computer lab program. Give your opinion of the activities and the instructors' teaching strategies. José is six years old and Becky is eight years old.

- José runs into a problem with his computer game. He comes to a screen where he cannot determine how to move on or go back. He calls out the instructor's name. The instructor is reluctant to rush over and push the "magic button" that would automatically solve the problem. Instead, he acts as a guide as he probes the child on the basic rules they had learned previously in the computer orientation class. The instructor verbally cues the child by reminding him of the basic computer knowledge that he had been taught but may have forgotten. José eventually solves his problem and feels successful.
- Becky is working busily in a print-shop program. She is typing friendly messages to her friends and parents. She is placing pictures on the notes to make them more decorative. Becky comes to an instructor with a concerned look on her face and tells her that her note cards are not printing. The instructor asks her to show her the process she was using to print her projects. She grabs the mouse and moves the arrow over to the edit option at the top of her screen and scrolls down to the word copy. She had not been instructed in how to print and apparently her logic told her that copy was like photocopy, a familiar term.

FIGURE 31–3 Friendship ignores gender, cultural, and ethnic differences.

## SCHOOL ACHIEVEMENT AND ADJUSTMENT

School achievement and adjustment are critical concerns for educators and parents. Two factors are examined in this section: culture and fears.

### Cultural Factors

Of great concern to educators at all levels are the variable degrees of achievement of children from different ethnic groups and socioeconomic levels (Figure 31–3). Slaughter-Defoe, Nakagawa, Takanishi, and Johnson (1990) express concern that research promotes stereotypes of Asian American students as more likely to be high achievers and African American students as more likely to be low achievers in school. They believe that the research is at fault for not differentiating among subgroups with different cultural, language, immigration, and economic backgrounds. This point should be carefully considered when looking at the results of cross-cultural research on school achievement.

Cross-cultural comparison of school achievement has been of increasing interest to child development researchers. A few studies in this area are briefly described here. Patterson, Kupersmidt, and Vaden (1990) report the results of a study that looked at income level, gender, ethnicity, and household composition as predictors of children's competence in school. Their subjects were African American and European American elementary students enrolled in second through fourth grades. Household income level and gender were the best predictors of competence in conduct and peer relations. That is, boys and children from low-income homes were likely to be the least competent. Income level and ethnicity were the best overall predictors of academic achievement. Because African American children were more likely to live in lower-income families, they were also more likely to be among those with lower competence in school. A caution in looking at these results is a consideration of whether poverty, per se, causes lower achievement and more conduct problems or whether those who teach low-income children have a preconceived picture of these children as poor achievers and as lacking in appropriate school social skills.

Luster and McAdoo (1991) looked at a sample of six- to nine-year-old African American children included in the National Longitudinal Survey of Youth. More than half of these children lived in conditions that would put them "at risk": born to mothers who are under 20 years old, living below the poverty line, and often having less than a twelfth-grade education. Consistent with other studies, children who did well on the achievement tests had mothers who were relatively intelligent and well educated, lived in financially secure families with relatively small numbers of children, and had relatively supportive home environments. The likelihood of children having behavior problems in school was associated with a mother with low self-esteem and relatively low intelligence, low income level, large family size, low-quality home environment, and absence of a male partner in the home. The results of this study show clearly that being African American does not doom a child to school failure. It demonstrates the diversity among African American children and documents that African American children who live under conditions of low risk do well academically and have few behavior problems.

The results of the LSU studies (Charlesworth, Hart, Burts & DeWolf, 1993) shed some light on a possible reason for the trend found by Entwisle and Alexander (1990). Charlesworth et al. (1993) found that African American children who attended more developmentally appropriate kindergartens (DAP) did better than African American children who attended less developmentally appropriate kindergartens (DIP). Twice as many stress behaviors were observed in the DIP kindergartens as in the DAP ones (Burts, Hart, Charlesworth, & Kirk, 1990; Burts, Hart, Charlesworth, Fleege, Mosley, & Thomasson, 1992). A portion of the children observed in kindergarten were followed up in first grade to determine their academic status (Burts, Hart, Charlesworth, DeWolf, Ray, Manuel, & Fleege, 1993). The results indicated that the first-graders who had attended the more developmentally appropriate kindergartens had higher reading grades on their report cards than students who had attended the less developmentally appropriate kindergartens. There were no significant differences in report card grades between the high and low-SES children who had attended developmentally appropriate kindergartens, whereas higher-SES students had an advantage over the lower-SES students if they had attended the more developmentally inappropriate kindergartens. Similar results were obtained for achievement test scores. Furthermore, first-grade students who had attended the more developmentally inappropriate kindergartens were rated by their first-grade teachers as being more hostile and aggressive, more anxious and fearful, and more hyperactive and distractible than the children who attended the more developmentally appropriate kindergartens (Charlesworth et al., 1993). A follow-up through third grade (Hart, Yang, Charlesworth, & Burts, 2003) indicated that students who experienced a DIP kindergarten had an increase in hostility and aggression through third grade and slower growth in understanding of mathematics compared with students who attended DAP kindergartens. Boys were hurt most in reading and language arts by having attended a DIP kindergarten. The results of these studies suggest that a DAP kindergarten experience can have positive effects on academic achievement and social behavior in the primary grades.

### School Related Fears

As already described in Chapter 30, children have many fears that may result in undue stress reactions. Many of these fears are school related.

Fears centering on achievement are common from ages six to eleven (King & Ollendick, 1989). Estimates of text anxiety range from 10 percent to 30 percent of the school-age population. School phobia, depression, and other anxiety disorders are not uncommon among school-age children (King & Ollendick, 1989). Unfortunately, teachers often perceive behaviors that reflect anxiety as noncompliance. King and Ollendick (1989) suggest that teachers use teaching practices conducive to fear reduction. If the climate of the classroom is low-anxiety-producing, students will be able to face fear-provoking situations with minimal anxiety. For example, some students, (as shown in the Chapter 30 examples), fear speaking in front of others. These children should have other options for demonstrating their communication skills.

**learned helplessness**
When failure is attributed to external factors rather than lack of effort.

Fincham, Hokoda, and Sanders (1989) conducted a longitudinal analysis of learned helplessness, test anxiety, and achievement. Children were studied in the third grade and then again in the fifth grade. Children who exhibit **learned helplessness** attribute failure to external factors rather than effort. They tend to do worse after each failure experience. Test-anxious children are those who experience unpleasant emotional feelings in the test situation and perform more poorly than children who do not have these unpleasant feelings. In their study, Fincham et al. (1989) found that learned helplessness and achievement were positively related over time and that teacher ratings were accurate indicators of children's degrees of learned helplessness. Unlike previous investigations, they did not find that test anxiety was directly related to achievement test scores. They concluded that the measure of test anxiety they used was unreliable. The significant factor that those who work with primary-level children should be aware of is that learned helplessness is well established by third grade. This factor makes it even more important that primary teachers build on the young child's eagerness to learn and provide as many success experiences as possible through developmentally appropriate individualized instructional practices. Hyun (1998) proposes a model that is both developmentally and culturally appropriate (DCAP). She provides detailed descriptions and procedures for providing a developmentally appropriate program for children from a variety of cultures.

## SCHOOLING

**caring**
A reciprocal relationship that should underlie teaching and learning.

As children enter elementary school, they enter a formalized system that has many critics. At the foundational level, Nel Noddings (2005) is known for her view that education and educators should be more **caring**. Noddings defines three types of *care.* There are those teachers who are cruel and uncaring. There are those who "care" in the sense of being conscientious and trying their best to make their students learn. The third type of caring teacher cares in a relational way that builds a trust relationship with students. "In a caring relation or encounter, the cared-for recognizes the caring and responds in some detectable manner. . . . Without an affirmative response from the cared-for, we cannot call an encounter or relation caring" (Noddings, p. 3). A caring relationship involves give-and-take between the caregiver and the cared-for. Teachers and students are partners in the educational experience. Teachers can no longer know everything—the world is too complex. There are some basic skills and concepts that everyone needs to know, but the caring teacher also supports students in reaching their personal goals. With a foundation of trust, students are more likely to be open to learning. Caring teachers pay attention to their students and learn what their interests are. Caring relationships build moral character and motivation to learn. Noddings believes that if education was more caring, students would learn more and there would be less need for formal testing. "The present insistence on more and more testing—even for young children—is largely a product of separation and lack of trust . . . fear and competition take the place of eager anticipation and shared delight in learning" (Noddings, p. 7).

**hidden curriculum**

What students learn outside of the schools' stated curriculum.

Along with the lack of true caring relationships, schools are characterized as having a **hidden curriculum.** The hidden curriculum includes what students learn outside of the schools' stated curriculum (Wikipedia, 2006). The knowledge gained from the hidden curriculum has social, political, and cultural underpinnings that are the basis of many of the major criticisms of educational activities. John Gatto is a major critic of the hidden curriculum, and Duen His Yen (2005) has compiled some of Gatto's quotes. Gatto believes our school system is designed to keep the population as ignorant as possible. His collected essay collection is entitled *Dumbing Us Down: The Hidden Curriculum of Compulsory Education.* Gatto saw public schooling as designed to regulate the poor through obedience to authority with no place for independent thinking and creativity. As you look at the research described in this part of the chapter, you will see that evidence indicates that children who are provided opportunities for independent choices and creativity do better in the long run. Yet this type of education is not currently supported by mandated outcomes and continuous testing.

**FIGURE 31–4** In the DAP classroom, students have time to explore activities at their own pace.

Looking back at the beginning of the chapter, note that Mr. Marcos' class with its active child involvement, individual and small group activities, and communication among students is appropriate for primary children (Figure 31–4). Ms. Brown's classroom, on the other hand, is developmentally inappropriate, as children work individually and silently on abstract assignments. A number of age/grade organizations have been recommended for kindergarten and the primary grades. These include multiage groupings (Charlesworth, 1989; Stone, 1998), looping or keeping the same group of students for two or more years (Bellis, 1999; Chapman, 1999; Kuball, 1999), and continuous progress (Charlesworth, 1989). Connell (1987) provides a delightful description of her ungraded primary classroom, which combined kindergarten, first grade, and second grade, and for which she designed a curriculum that fit the needs and developmental levels of the students.

In her book *Schooling* (1990), Sylvia Farnham-Diggory presents an overview of the way our schools today are built on old theories of learning that do not incorporate

FIGURE 31–5 The primary classroom's formality contrasts with the preschool classroom's organization.

our current knowledge about how children grow and develop and how they learn. She points out how the school reforms of the 1980s (which are in vogue again in the twenty-first century) were bureaucratic: tougher standards, more testing, homogeneous grouping, and a more fractionated skill-and-drill curriculum. Only in a few instances was attention paid to child development and to practices that better fit the curriculum to the students. Classrooms have become places in which children are forced to fit into a nonchildlike mold. Farnham-Diggory suggests a plan where schools become a place for a cognitive apprenticeship, "a place where people go to develop skills in learning to learn, problem solving, and the creative application of ideas" (p. 56). (See Figures 31–5 and 31–6). The apprenticeship model operates on several principles:

1. Human minds are designed for complex, situated learning. Human minds are designed to deal with rich environments that provide many concrete experiences the mind can investigate and organize.
2. Education must begin where the student is.
3. Human learning is a social enterprise.

The teacher uses a variety of instructional techniques: modeling, coaching, scaffolding, articulation (summaries, critiques, or dialogs), reflection, and exploration. These are facilitative techniques, not didactic or "pour in the knowledge" techniques. They open up the classroom to students constructing their own knowledge. Here and there, individual teachers, small groups of teachers, and occasionally whole schools have adopted developmentally appropriate practices and made them work.

FIGURE 31–6 Primary-grade children benefit from a well-stocked library and enjoy listening to stories.

A question currently being examined is why some teachers manage to institute developmentally appropriate practice and others do not. A study done by Mary McMullen (1999) was described in Chapter 27. Buchanan, Burts, Bidner, White, and Charlesworth (1998) examined the beliefs and practices of first-, second-, and third-grade teachers. A number of variables were found to be predictive of DAP and of **developmentally inappropriate practice (DIP).** Class variables that predicted DIP included the number of children on free and reduced-cost lunch, grade level taught (first-grade teachers used more DAP), and number of children in the class. Having children with disabilities in the class also predicted DAP. The most predictive teacher variable was the amount of influence they believed they had regarding planning and curriculum implementation. Teachers who were more DIP believed outside forces, such as principals and parents, had more control over what happens in their classrooms. Teachers certified in elementary education were more likely to

**developmentally inappropriate practice (DIP)**

Instructional practice that does not meet the student's developmental levels.

use inappropriate practices than those with early childhood certification. Amos Hatch interviewed three K–3 teachers regarding how they functioned under the demands for accountability (McDaniel, Isaac, Brooks, & Hatch, 2005). All three teachers are finding ways to teach in a developmentally appropriate manner but still meet the demands for achievement. All three were trained in early childhood programs and two in a program combined with special education. This background provides them with a rationale for finding ways to meet the needs of individual children. Further research is needed to pinpoint exactly which factors account for DAP teachers.

The Kentucky Department of Education reports the results of a study done to assess the degree of success of legislated reform toward more developmentally appropriate practice in the primary grades (McCormick, Anderman, Brown, Privett, Hemmeter, Gerry, & Rous, 2001). High-performing, improving, and low-performing schools were selected based on fourth-grade achievement test results. A questionnaire was administered to 138 teachers, teachers were interviewed, and observations were done in their classrooms. The teachers in the high-performing schools used more developmentally appropriate practices. There was more open-ended discussion and use of hands-on materials, students were directly involved in decision making, the room arrangement provided more opportunities for student independence and self-management, and the curriculum was more individualized. In the low-performing classrooms, discipline strategies tended to be more punitive, buildings were in poor condition, arts and humanities were absent, and most teachers used ability grouping. Overall, the study supported the effectiveness of developmentally appropriate practice.

## Classroom Guidance and Management

In Chapter 27, the major factors of the adult/child relationship were discussed. Types of discipline were described, including parenting styles. It was suggested that the guidance view, and authoritative parenting were superior in the long run to the discipline view which has become too closely associated with punishment. Related topics in Chapter 27 included challenging behavior, physical punishment, timeout, and developing a democratic community in the classroom that supports moral development. In reviewing these topics, one must consider if the guidance approaches described will work with older children in the elementary grades. The answer is yes according to experts such as Fields and Fields (2006) and Gartrell (2004). The older children get more responsibility they should be able to handle and the more articulate and capable they should be in using negotiating strategies and in expressing their opinions. Gartrell (2004) suggests that there should be positive guidelines rather than rules in the primary classroom. Rules tend to be stated negatively whereas guidelines are phrased in a positive way that tells what to do rather than what not to do. Gartrell suggests the following kinds of guidelines for the primary classroom (p. 71):

- Friendly touches only
- Sometimes we need to stop, look, and listen
- We all need to take care of our room
- We are friendly to each other and to ourselves
- Making mistakes is OK—we just try to learn from them

Gartrell also points out the importance of an encouraging program. An encouraging program is designed to fit the needs and development of the students. Conflicts are reduced to a minimum because the room arrangement and activities are developmentally appropriate and culturally responsive. The daily schedule is consistent, and transitions are organized in a way the students can handle them. The room is arranged in centers, and the children work in small groups. Large group activities involve everyone with very little wait time for turn-taking. The guidance approach described by Gartrell promotes a positive learning environment for each child.

### Inclusive Schools

The importance of inclusive education for students with disabilities has been previously discussed. Success of inclusion depends on several factors (McLeskey & Waldron, 2002);

- Change to more inclusive practices must be supported by both teachers and administrators.
- Schools must be empowered to manage their own change—successful change can't be mandated.
- For inclusion to succeed, the whole school must undergo major changes.
- Changes should not just be an "add on," but should be integrated into the total school program.
- Differences among students should become an ordinary part of classroom life.
- If one change is made, other changes will have to follow.
- Change must be designed for each individual school—there is no one model.
- Professional development must be provided to enable teachers to take on new responsibilities.
- There will always be some resistance to change. The questions posed by resistant teachers can lead to important insights.
- The work of developing an inclusive school is an ongoing project.

Making a school truly inclusive cannot be done in a short time, but is worth pursuing for everyone's sake: children, teachers, and families.

### Schooling that Supports Development

James P. Comer, noted psychiatrist (2005, 2004, 2001), advocates schools that develop children. He advocates for schools that focus on both social and psychological development, as well as academic development. Comer emphasizes the importance of applying child development knowledge to education. Hopefully, schools can become communities and safe havens for children (Rogoff, Turkanis, & Bartlett, 2001; Stone, 2001; Vance & Weaver, 2002).

## SUMMARY

Cognitively, primary-grade children are in the five-to-seven shift period. They are moving from preoperational to concrete operational thinking in the Piagetian theoretical view and from play-focused to adult-guided formal learning experiences in the Vygotskian view. From the Vygotskian view, children are beginning a shift to higher mental functioning. They are still in the process of integrating their cognitive processes with their physical motor and affective skills and knowledge. Private speech becomes internalized and guides learning. They still learn best through concrete experience, which they are just beginning to associate with abstract symbols, such as letters and numbers.

School is the center of existence for primary-level children. They are still at a level in which they believe they can learn no matter what their native ability, socioeconomic status, and ethnic group. They respond best to open-ended tasks and activities. One-right-answer tasks to which they may not respond correctly can quickly bring on feelings of failure. Learning reading, writing, and arithmetic naturally provides the success that will support them in later schooling. School is a major source of fear and anxiety for young children. Opportunities for creative writing can alleviate their anxiety. Writing about superheroes, for example, can make them feel strong.

A growing body of research supports the value for child development of an authoritative discipline style. Our approach to schooling for primary children is in need of reform. Developmentally appropriate instructional practices are gradually taking hold, but the traditional worksheet/workbook/basal curriculum still dominates our schools with the advent of No Child Left Behind. The school curriculum should be caring and supportive of learning rather than impeding it.

## For Further Reading


Abbot, C. (Ed.). (2002). *Special education needs and the internet.* New York: RoutledgeFalmer.

Alderman, M. K. (2004). *Motivation for achievement* (2nd ed.). Mahwah, NJ: Erlbaum.

Barrera, I. with R. M. Corso & D. Macpherson. (2003). *Skilled dialogue: Strategies for responding to cultural diversity in early childhood.* Baltimore: Brookes, and Washington, DC: Zero to Three.

Barth, R. S. (2001). *Learning by heart.* Indianapolis: Jossey-Bass.

Bergen, D., & Coscia, J. (2001). *Brain research and childhood education: Implications for educators.* Olney, MD: Association for Childhood Education.

Branscombe, N. A., Castle, K., Dorsey, A. G., Surbeck, E., & Taylor, J. B. (2000). *Early childhood education: A constructivist perspective.* New York: Houghton Mifflin.

Brophy, J. (2004). *Motivating students to learn* (2nd ed.). Mahwah, NJ: Erlbaum.

Click, P. M., & Parker, J. (2002). *Caring for school-age children* (3rd ed.). Clifton Park, NY: Delmar Learning.

Compton-Lilly, C. (2003). *Reading families: The literature lives of urban children.* New York: Teachers College Press.

Connolly, P. (2004). *Boys and schooling.* New York: RoutledgeFalmer.

Dragan, P. B. (2003). *Everything you need to know to teach first grade.* Portsmouth, NH: Heinemann.

English, L. D. (2004). *Mathematical and analogical reasoning of young learners.* Mahwah, NJ: Erlbaum.

Erlauer, L. (2003). *The brain compatible classroom: Using what we know about learning to improve teaching.* Alexandria, VA: ASCD.

Gatto, J. T. (2002). *Dumbing us down: The hidden curriculum of compulsory schooling.* Gabriola Island, BC: New Society Publications.

Grisham-Brown, J., Hemmeter, M. L., & Pretti-Frontczak, K. (2005). *Blended practices for teaching young children in inclusive settings.* Baltimore: Brookes.

Gurian, M. (2001). *Boys and girls learn differently!* Indianapolis: Jossey-Bass.

Helm, J. H., & Katz, L. (2001). *Young investigators: The project approach in the early years.* New York: Teachers College, and Washington, DC: National Association for the Education of Young Children.

Kohn, A. (2000). *What to look for in a classroom and other essays.* Indianapolis: Jossey-Bass.

Koplow, L. (2002). *Creating classrooms that heal: Real life solutions.* New York: Teachers College.

Kostelnik, M. J., Onaga, E., Rohde, B., & Whiren, A. (2002). *Children with special needs.* New York: Teachers College Press.

Kostelnik, M. J. (2004). *Developmentally appropriate curriculum: Best practices in early childhood education* (3rd ed.). Columbus, OH: Merrill/Prentice Hall.

Lambert, N. M., & McCombs, B. L. (Eds.). (1998). *How students learn: Reforming schools through learner-centered education.* Washington, DC: American Psychological Association.

McIntyre, E., Rosebery, A., & Gonzalez, N. (Eds.). (2001). *Classroom diversity: Connecting curriculum to students' lives.* Westport, CT: Heinemann.

McNary, S. J., Glasgow, N. A., & Hicks, C. D. (2005). *What successful teachers do in inclusive classrooms.* Thousand Oaks, CA: Corwin.

Pellegrini, A., & Blatchford, P. (2000). *The child at school: Interactions with peers and teachers.* New York: Oxford University Press.

Pressley, M., Dolezal, S. E., Raphael, L. M., Mohan, L., Roehrig, A. D., & Bogner, K. (2003). *Motivating primary-grade students.* New York: Guilford.

Reider, B. (2005). *Teach more and discipline less.* Thousand Oaks, CA: Corwin.

Rogoff, B., Turkanis, C. G., & Bartlett, L. (2001). *Learning together: Children and adults in a school community.* New York: Oxford University Press.

Schofield, J. W., & Davidson, A. L. (2002). *Bringing the internet to school.* Indianapolis: Jossey-Bass.

Slavin, R. E., & Calderon, M. (Eds.). (2000). *Effective programs for Latino students.* Mahwah, NJ: Erlbaum.

Sousa, D. A. (2001). *How the special needs brain learns.* Thousand Oaks, CA: Corwin.

Sprenger, M. (2002). *Becoming a "Wiz" at brain-based teaching.* Thousand Oaks, CA: Corwin.

Stone, R. (2005). *Best classroom management practices for reaching all learners.* Thousand Oaks, CA: Corwin.

Trumbull, E., Rothstein-Fisch, C., Greenfield, P. M., & Quiroz, B. (2001). *Bridging cultures between home and school.* Mahwah, NJ: Erlbaum.

Watson, M. (2003). *Learning to trust: Transforming difficult elementary classrooms through developmental discipline.* San Francisco: Jossey-Bass.

Watson, R. J., & Watson, R. S. (2002). *The school as a safe haven.* Westport, CT: Greenwood.

Zimmerman, B. J., & Schunk, D. H. (Eds.). (2001). *Self-regulated learning and academic achievement.* Mahwah, NJ: Erlbaum.

## SUGGESTED ACTIVITIES

1. Using the checklist format that follows, list some of the attributes you believe would fit under appropriate and inappropriate practice. Bring your checklist to class to compare with the checklists devised by other students. Discuss both checklists and construct a class checklist that can be shared by everyone. Select characteristics mentioned in the text and/or obtain a copy of Bredekamp and Copple (1997) and select items from Part 3. You do not have to limit your checklist to four items in each section.

| Appropriate Practice | Mixed (Describe briefly) | Inappropriate Practice |
|---|---|---|
| Classroom Organization and Materials | | Classroom Organization and Materials |
| ___ 1. | | ___ 1. |
| ___ 2. | | ___ 2. |
| ___ 3. | | ___ 3. |
| ___ 4. | | ___ 4. |
| Teacher Behavior | | Teacher Behavior |
| ___ 1. | | ___ 1. |
| ___ 2. | | ___ 2. |
| ___ 3. | | ___ 3. |
| ___ 4. | | ___ 4. |
| Activities for Students | | Activities for Students |
| ___ 1. | | ___ 1. |
| ___ 2. | | ___ 2. |
| ___ 3. | | ___ 3. |
| ___ 4. | | ___ 4. |

2. Arrange to visit two or more primary classrooms. Observe for one hour or more in each class. Take notes on what you see. After you leave, take a copy of your checklist of developmentally appropriate practices. Put a (+) for items observed and a (–) for items not observed. Evaluate the degree of developmental appropriateness of each classroom. Explain where you found positives and on which items improvements could be made. Share your findings with the class.

3. In the library, look through recent issues of journals, such as *Young Children, Dimensions, Childhood Education, Science and Children, Teaching Children Mathematics,*

| Behavior | Observed | Comments |
|---|---|---|
| | Yes or No | |
| **Six-Year-Old Expectations**<br>• See Chapter 22 for reading and writing goals<br>• Sorts objects on one or more dimensions, such as color, shape, form, or function<br>• Names most letters and numerals<br>• Counts by rote to 10 or more and tells which number comes next<br>• May solve one or more conservation problems<br>• Has some concept of clock time relative to daily schedule<br>• Draws a person with head, trunk, legs, arms, and features; may add clothing details<br>• Builds recognizable structures with blocks or other construction toys/materials<br>• Completes a 15-piece puzzle<br>• Uses all grammatical structures: pronouns, plurals, verb tenses, and conjunctions<br>• Uses complex sentences<br>• Carries on conversations<br>• Identifies familiar coins: pennies, nickels, dimes, and quarters | | |
| **Seven-Year-Old Expectations**<br>• See Chapter 22 for reading and writing goals<br>• Asks many questions<br>• Uses correct verb tenses, word order, and sentence structure in conversation<br>• Enjoys reading and being read to<br>• Uses writing implement to write words and numbers<br>• Draws pictures with many details and a sense of proportion<br>• Shows some understanding of cause-and-effect concepts<br>• Understands concepts of space and time: knows a year is a long time and 100 miles is far away<br>• Tells time by the clock and understands calendar time<br>• Is interested in counting and saving money<br>• Is probably able to solve more than one conservation problem | | |
| **Eight-Year-Old Expectations**<br>• See Chapter 22 for reading and writing goals.<br>• Expresses relatively complex thoughts in a clear and logical fashion<br>• Shows interest in creative expression, such as writing, dramatizing, drawing, and telling stories<br>• Knows how to tell time<br>• Looks forward to going to school—hates to miss even one day<br>• Demonstrates expected skills in reading, writing, and math; adds and subtracts multiple-digit numbers and is learning multiplication and division<br>• Has collections that are organized and displayed; bargains with peers to obtain additional items<br>• Has achieved understanding of several conservation problems | | |

Cognitive development expectations for six-, seven-, and eight-year olds.
(Sources: Allen & Marotz, 2006; and Bredekamp & Copple, 1997, Part 5.)

and *Language Arts*. Select five articles that describe developmentally appropriate instructional practices for primary classrooms. Write a summary of each article. Share what you find out with the class.

4. Assess the cognitive development of a six-, seven-, or eight-year-old using the list of developmental expectations on page 667.
5. Make an entry in your journal.

## REVIEW

1. Look back at the beginning of the chapter. Write an analysis of Mr. Marcos' and Ms. Brown's classrooms based on how well what is described does or does not fit the developmental characteristics of primary-level students. Compare the two classrooms.
2. Select the items below that describe typical cognitive characteristics for six- through eight-year-old children.
   a. During the primary period, children begin to see good work habits as indications of intelligence.
   b. Being good and following rules are viewed as evidence of being smart.
   c. Primary-level children can usually understand that no matter how hard you work, you are limited by your innate ability.
   d. Young children perform better with constructive criticism than with praise.
   e. Primary children do not weigh praise against task difficulty.
   f. Primary children should receive letter grades because they are meaningful to them.
   g. Comparisons with peers do not take on great importance until between the third and fifth grades.
   h. It is relatively easy to make primary-level children feel good about themselves because they are very responsive to adult approval.
   i. During the primary period, children move into being able to use abstract symbols without connecting them to the concrete.
   j. Primary-level children are in the cognitive developmental period called the five-to-seven shift.
   k. According to Vygotsky, around age seven, play becomes a formal learning activity.
   l. According to Vygotsky's theory, around age seven, higher-order mental functions begin to emerge.
   m. The primary period is the critical time for development of intrinsic motivation, according to Vygotsky.
3. Using time as an example, explain how primary-level children move from the concrete to the symbolic.
4. Visiting a first-grade classroom, you notice that many of the children talk to themselves as they work. Is this expected behavior? Is this activity of any value?
5. Match the descriptions below with the reading strategies described by McIntyre (1990):
   a. Bill sits on a pillow in the reading center. He holds the book *The Little Engine That Could* on his lap. His eyes focus on the pictures as he reads in a chantlike voice, "I think I can—I think I can—I think I can. Up, up, up. Faster and faster the little engine is climbing. At last they reach the top of the mountain." His teacher notices that he uses words very close to the book's exact language.
   b. Mr. Marcos hands Lai a book she has never seen before. "I think you will like *Fish is Fish*." Lai opens the book, she looks at the pictures, her eyes focus on

the print, and she reads aloud as follows: "At the end of the woods there was a pond, and there a minnow and a tadpole swam among the weeds. They were in-sep-ar-able friends." Mr. Marcos notes that she reads exactly what the book says.

c. Kate selects *Fish is Fish*. Her eyes focus on the pictures and she reads, "A minnow and a tadpole are in the pond in the woods. They were friends and swam in the weeds."

6. Explain why and how writing and drawing promote literacy and self-esteem.
7. Explain Dyson's view of how and why superheroes have a place in the primary-level classroom.
8. List the major problems and considerations concerning technology in schools.
9. List the factors you believe have the greatest effect on school achievement. Explain why each of these factors is important.
10. Describe what you envision as the ideal primary school setting that would strongly support child development.
11. Explain the six *T*s for exemplary teachers.
12. Discuss developmentally appropriate practices in the primary grades.
13. Discuss the factors for success in inclusion, according to McLeskey and Waldron (2002).
14. Select the statements that are correct.
    a. Nel Noddings believes education and educators should be caring.
    b. Noddings believes there are no teachers that are cruel and uncaring.
    c. Caring is a reciprocal relationship between teacher and students.
    d. If students feel trusted, they are more likely to be motivated to learn.
    e. Noddings believes it is important to use testing as a motivator of learning.
    f. The hidden curriculum in schools includes material children are not taught but are tested on.
    g. The hidden curriculum has a social, political, and cultural agenda.
    h. John Gatto believes the hidden curriculum is designed to do away with independent thinking and creativity.
15. Explain the difference between discipline and guidance in the primary grades.

## KEY TERMS LIST

caring
developmentally inappropriate practice (DIP)
hidden curriculum
learned helplessness
learning activity

Additional resources for this chapter can be found on the Online Companion™ to accompany this text at http://www.earlychilded.delmar.com. Respond to "Time to Reflect" and "Looking Further" concepts, review various child development scenarios, and answer thought-provoking questions in the Critical Thinking Forum. Keep a daily journal by downloading the student journal available on this Web site. Complete the interactive matching exercises to reinforce concepts, and printout the child development assessment forms to use during your observation of development for children from birth to age eight. In addition, read the case studies on the Web site to reinforce the important concepts in each chapter, and take a look at the multitude of Web links that are available for student research on the Internet.

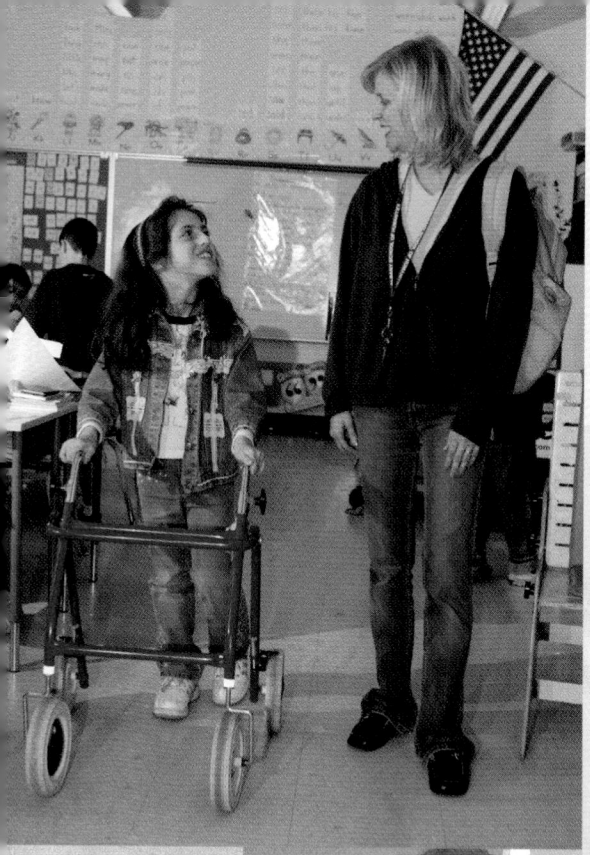

# SECTION IX

## The Whole Child

To have a complete understanding of child development, we need to look at the whole child, that is, the child in the context of home, school, and community. Almost daily, the popular press has stories about the problems facing today's children and families. If this information is newsworthy, then there must be some concern and interest in the population in general about the well-being of children and families in the United States. The introduction to this section looks at children and families in the context of the community as they appear in the daily newspaper. Stories regularly appear about the economic status of families, the changing appearance of families, technology and children, child care and schooling, childhood dangers, and child health. The following are a selection of such stories that appeared in daily newspapers.

### NEWS ABOUT FAMILIES

KIDS OF DYSFUNCTIONAL FAMILIES MORE IMPORTANT THAN PUPPIES (*Standard-Examiner*, Ogden, UT, May 5, 2002). The Dee Elementary Families, Agencies, Community Together (FACT) team deals with the dangers faced by children in families where the danger is guns, sex, and drugs. Families with parents on meth, children with cavities, a father who is a drug dealer shot, an eight-year-old who is smoking pot. Frustrated with the lack of ability to save these children because the laws are weak, one person comments that they have better laws for puppies—at least they have to be leashed.

POVERTY OVERCOME BEST WHEN MOMS NURTURE OUTGOING KIDS. (*Standard Examiner*, Ogden, UT, May 31, 2004). A study of children living in poverty indicates that outgoing, sociable children with nurturing mothers are most likely to overcome the negative effects of poverty.

UNMARRIED MOMS NOT JUST TEENS. (*Standard-Examiner*, Ogden, UT, October 29, 2005). The percentage of unmarried teen mothers has decreased, and the percentage in their 20s has increased.

## TECHNOLOGY

HILLARY VS. XBOX: THE KIDS WITH THEIR GAMES ARE CLEAR WINNERS by Steven Johnson. (*Standard-Examiner*, Ogden, UT, August 1, 2005). Steven Johnson suggests that video games offer a release of aggression and support children's problem-solving skill development.

## CHILD CARE

UTAH'S DAY CARE: A BIG ROLE TO PLAY by Rosemary Winters. (*The Salt Lake Tribune* online, August 18, 2005, retrieved from www.sit.com). Availability of child care provides support to the economy by allowing parents to work and support their families while providing needed employees for business and industry.

EMPLOYERS FILL CHILD CARE NEEDS (*Standard-Examiner*, Ogden, UT, November 17, 2002). More companies are viewing child care assistance as a way to keep employees. Larger companies may have on-site child care centers. The number of licensed child care slots compared to the number of working parents is pitifully small.

## SCHOOLING

'COMMUNITY SCHOOLS' BROADEN SERVICES. (*Standard-Examiner*, Ogden, UT, November 17, 2002). A small but growing number of full-service schools are springing up across the country. These schools fill community needs, such as offering dental and medical care, after-school activities, parenting courses, and family counseling. Some even stay open on weekends, offering sports, arts, and other recreation programs.

'CUSSING AND DISCUSSING': SYMPOSIUM FOCUSES ON EDUCATIONAL CHALLENGES FACING AMERICAN INDIANS by Blair Dee Hodges. (*Standard-Examiner*, Ogden, UT, February 10, 2006). Arvol Looking Horse, spiritual leader for the Lakota, Dakota, and Nakota People, and Forrest Cuch, executive director of the Utah Office of Indian affairs, spoke to the educational plight of young Native Americans at a symposium in Ogden, Utah. Current education does not fit the culture of Native Americans.

SCHOOLS' NEED FOR DISCIPLINE GROWS by Cynthia L. Garza. (*Standard-Examiner*, Ogden, UT, August 23, 2004). Today's kindergartners are suffering more emotional and behavioral problems than previous generations. Young children are hitting, spitting, kicking, biting, and cursing.

HISPANIC DROPOUT RATE SOARS IN UTAH: CENSUS REPORTS TREND ACROSS THE NATION. (*Standard-Examiner*, Ogden, UT, October 12, 2002). According to the Census Bureau, the number of Hispanics who dropped out of or never attended high school in Utah more than doubled in the 1990s (11.9% up to 29.9%). Across the country, the rate increased by more than 50%. The South and West have the highest dropout rates. In 2000, the national average was 33.8%. Many of the parents have very little education, so they cannot even read to their children in Spanish or English. It is essential to make the parents and children feel comfortable in school.

## CHILDHOOD DANGERS

FRONT-SEAT FATALITIES INVOLVING CHILDREN DECLINE, STUDY FINDS by Ken Thomas. (*Standard-Examiner*, Ogden, UT, August 18, 2005). The campaign to have children sit in the backseat and be belted in seems to be gaining success.

TOO YOUNG TO BODY TRAIN? MEDICAL EXPERTS SEEING INCREASE IN SPORTS INJURIES IN CHILDREN by Wina Sturgeon. (*Standard-Examiner*, Ogden, UT, August 23, 2005). A sports medicine physician is seeing children as young as six years old with serious overuse injuries. He also notes emotional problems, such as tiredness when it is time to practice, irritability, sleeping difficulties, and moodiness.

REPORT: COACHES, PARENTS NEED BETTER TRAINING TO PREVENT SOCCER INJURIES. (*Standard-Examiner*, Ogden, UT, May 1, 2002). Soccer can be dangerous. It can lead to concussions and other head injuries. Parents and coaches need training in how to identify life-threatening head injuries. Children's brains are still developing, so they may be more at risk than adults.

GET HEAVY WEIGHT OFF CHILDREN'S LIVES IN REGARD TO BACKPACKS. (*Standard-Examiner*, Ogden, UT, June 11, 2002). Children's days are so filled with structured activities and homework that their backpacks are full to overflowing. Our competitive society has pushed us into pressuring our children. Further, young children are at risk for physical injury (BACKPACKS: IT'S ALL IN THE BAG, *USA Weekend*, August 25–27, 2000). A backpack should weigh no more than 10 percent of the child's weight to avoid risk of neck or back strain.

## HEALTH

STUDY: WIC PLAN PROGRAM HELPS INFANTS. (*Standard-Examiner*, Ogden, UT, August 5, 2002). University of Utah research shows babies have higher birth weight.

FORUM: TOO MANY KIDS SEDENTARY by Jamie Lampros (*Standard-Examiner*, Ogden, UT, August 18, 2005). Childhood obesity continues to be a health problem. One out of four Utah children are overweight. Parents are advised to limit children's television-viewing time. School systems are putting more healthy snacks in vending machines.

EXPERTS DECRY CHUBBY YOUTH. (*Standard-Examiner*, Ogden, UT, August 25, 2002). Universities and corporations are trying to provide healthier lifestyles to stop the fatty trend. Fourteen percent of youth are classified as obese or overweight.

SLEEP TROUBLE IN SCHOOL-AGE KIDS. (*USA Weekend*, November 15–17, 2002). Up to 30 percent of children don't get enough sleep. The fallout includes problems with behavior, learning, health, and safety. Toddlers should have 13 to 15 hours of sleep, four- to twelve-year-olds 10 hours, and teens 8 1/2 to 9 1/2 hours.

## CHILDREN AT RISK OR AT PROMISE?

The headlines indicate that our children and families face many risk factors in their daily lives. Many of these factors focus on low-income and minority children and families. Swadener and Lubeck (1995) believe that the term *at-risk* has become a popular buzzword and that the assumptions underlying its usage have gone largely unexamined. They believe *at-risk* has come to be equivalent to meaning dysfunctional, poor families. They believe that "the generalized use of the 'at-risk' label is highly problematic and implicitly racist, classist, sexist, and ablest, a 1990s version of the cultural deficit model, which locates problems or 'pathologies' in individuals, families, and communities rather than in institutional structures that create and maintain inequality" (p. 3). Swadener and Lubeck prefer the term *at promise*. The at-promise view is an alternative that looks at how policy and practice can be transformed to facilitate the promise of all children.

Washington and Andrews (1998), in looking ahead to 2010, point out that during the twenty-first century, we will reach a point where no single racial or ethnic group will constitute a majority of the U.S. population. "This means that democracy will require an unprecedented level of cooperation, communication, and teamwork among people who are different" (p. 1). Washington and Andrews point out the importance of treasuring each child and breaking down the barriers that have kept many children from access to the opportunities available to others. Social change will be necessary if we are to preserve our democracy in the new millennium. Chapter 32 closely examines the whole child in context. In Chapter 33, we will examine the ways you, as an individual concerned with young children and their development, can promote public policy action that will make life better for children and their families.

CHAPTER

# 32

# A Look at the Whole Child

## Objectives

After reading this chapter, you should be able to:

- List the factors that make up the whole child.
- Explain your view of the status of American children.
- Describe the American family of today.
- Evaluate the quality of child care, kindergarten, and primary programs.
- Identify important factors we have learned from research on the quality of child care.
- Identify important factors that support the need for concern regarding elementary-level schooling.
- Understand the need for parent involvement in the education of young children.
- Know why social class, economic status, and racism are relevant to the development of young children.

We have now looked at young children's development from conception through age eight. We have seen that young children are complex and at times puzzling persons identified as infants, toddlers, three-, four-, five-, six-, seven-, and eight-year-olds. We have looked at young children as they strike out on their own, developing more initiative and relying less on constant adult supervision.

Adults who work with young children must keep in mind the children's histories, their present status, and their probable future needs. Throughout this text, readers have been encouraged to view children not as isolated individuals, but as persons acting and reacting within a context of family, community, and a larger society. Child development includes these factors as they interact with affective, cognitive, and psychomotor development to obtain a picture of **the whole child.**

**the whole child**

Viewing children not as isolated individuals, but as persons acting and reacting within a context of family, community, and a larger society; in the development of children, it includes affective, cognitive, and psychomotor development.

Joe L. Frost (2003) described what he labeled as "gaps" in child rearing that indicate we are failing our young. These gaps have been discussed in earlier chapter and are summarized by Frost:

- Gaps in child rearing, which result in gaps in the lives of children due to family disruption such as divorce, teen pregnancy, single-parent families, extended parent absence, child abuse, lack of quality child care outside the home, excessive television watching, changing sexual mores, violence, and illicit drug use" (p. 29).

- The child obesity gap, which is due to poor eating habits and lack of proper exercise.
- The standardized testing gap, which has made our schools into "academic factories—factories that sort both children and teachers into 'winners' and 'losers' and grade children like chickens on the assembly line going to market" (p. 30).
- The pill generation gap, which has focused on prescription of psychiatric drugs, such as Ritalin, rather than looking for the causes of behavior.
- The crime and violence gap, which finds even young children more aggressive than in years past.
- The morals and ethics gap is reflected in adult models who steal and cheat and the increasing number of children who cheat and lie.
- International gaps are reflected in the increasing gaps between haves and have-nots.

Frost states that it is the responsibility of adults—parents, teachers, and community members, such as school boards and politicians—to close these gaps. He also believes we need to develop more caring attitudes and actions and help those in need, and we need to rediscover ethics and morals.

In order to obtain a clearer picture of child health and development from birth to age 21, *The National Children's Study* (2006, 2004) will collect data on 100,000 children in the United States. In 2006, the first phase of the study is just beginning. It is expected that preliminary results will be available in 2008–2009.

## THE STATUS OF AMERICA'S CHILDREN

From interviews with adults and children in his community, Edward Pratt, an African American newspaper reporter, writes about some of the emotional moments that particularly stuck with him (Pratt, 1992):

- There was a little eight-year-old boy, whose busted sneakers barely touched the floor when he sat, who coolly told a schoolmate how to commit murder and get away with it.
- I watched a nine-year-old boy ignore several requests from a school teacher to sit down. The boy just folded his arms and stared at her. He finally sat down after she grabbed his shoulders and tried to force him into his chair. I can't imagine doing that when I was that age.

Pratt was very disturbed by the attitudes of three teenage boys incarcerated in the local juvenile facility. They said that they felt no qualms about shooting people. "Their attitude was, 'get them before they get you'" (p. 7). Pratt found that it was not just European Americans but also most of the African American middle class that was ignoring these African American children living in poverty and violence. There were some bright spots: teachers and counselors that really cared, industries that donated their employees as tutors on company time, and community groups working on substance-abuse problems.

The Children's Defense Fund (CDF) each year provides facts and figures regarding the State of America's Children. Each year CDF publishes a chart "Moments in America for Children" (2004). Some of the moments in 2004 included:

- Every 9 seconds, a high school student drops out.
- Every 13 seconds, a public school student is corporally punished.
- Every 23 seconds, a baby is born to an unmarried mother.
- Every 36 seconds, a baby is born into poverty.

- Every 42 seconds, a baby is born without health insurance.
- Every minute, a baby is born to a teen mother.
- Every 4 minutes, a child is arrested for drug abuse.
- Every 8 minutes, a child is arrested for a violent crime.
- Every 42 minutes, a child or youth under twenty dies from an accident.
- Every three hours and 20 minutes, a child or youth under age twenty is killed by a firearm.
- Every 6 hours a child is killed by abuse or neglect.

In 2004, the Children's Defense Fund listed 25 "Key Facts About American Children." Among these facts are the following:

- Three in five preschoolers' mothers are in the labor force.
- One in two will live in a single-parent family at some point in childhood.
- One in three is born to unmarried parents.
- One in three will be poor at some point in their childhood.
- One in four lives with only one parent.
- One in five was born poor.
- One in five is poor now.
- One in six is born to a mother who did not receive prenatal care in the first three months of pregnancy.
- One in twelve has a disability.
- One in thirty-five lives with a grandparent (or other relative) but neither parent.

There is no doubt that children and families are in crisis. CDF (1999) calls for America to be fair to its children and invest leadership, attention, and resources at the same level we do with corporate and military interests. In this time of economic strength, "*every* child should be assured enough to eat, a place called home to sleep, health care to prevent and treat illness, the opportunity to get ready for and learn in school through quality early childhood experiences, and to be safe and positively engaged after school" (Children's Defense Fund, 1999, p. x). CDF continues to call for action and outlines a plan in their action guide *Stand Up for Children Now!* (Children's Defense Fund Action Council, 2005).

**FIGURE 32–1** Young children need time to grow and develop with minimal stress in a healthy and developmentally appropriate environment.

What effects are these crisis conditions having on our schools? According to Reed and Sautter (1990), teachers are alarmed at the rise in health and social problems they see reflected in their classrooms. They report that surveys of teachers indicate the following:

> Teachers worry about constant pupil turnover, about students' health problems, and about students' preoccupation with health problems. . . . Such concerns are more common among teachers of children from low-income families. Guidance counselors report that, even at the elementary level, they find themselves "dealing with one crisis after another" in a child's life (p. K7).

Teachers are also seeing more children with learning disabilities, low self-esteem, and a belief that they cannot learn (see Figure 32–1).

FIGURE 32–2 What happened to the traditional family?

What can be done to alleviate these problems? At the federal level, programs like Head Start have documented a positive impact on the later lives of young children. For example, in one study, nearly 60 percent of Head Start graduates were employed at age nineteen, compared with 32 percent for the control group. Federal Chapter 1/Title I funds are being steered more in the direction of working with younger children. However, these programs serve fewer than half of the eligible children. Programs for four-year-olds are increasing in number through funding by states and by local school districts to identify and alleviate problems before they have gone too far.

School systems across the country are trying to attack the problems brought on by increasing poverty in two ways: by mobilizing parents and by integrating community health resources into the schools (Reed and Sautter, 1990). Parental involvement is discussed later in this chapter.

## TODAY'S FAMILY

**family**
Those persons who inhabit the same living area.

As we look at today's **family** and the forecast for the future in the twenty-first century, the so-called traditional family, as depicted by a kindergartner in his family drawing in Figure 32–2, is becoming more and more just one of many types of American families (Footlick, 1990). Families continue to split and sometimes recombine, the rate of births to single mothers has continued to increase, there is an increasing number of homeless families, and the number of gay and lesbian households are on the rise. An increasing variety of family types (Figure 32–3) is becoming common:

- the traditional working father and nonworking mother
- families blended from two families after remarriage by both parents
- gay and lesbian couples heading families
- extended families made up of relatives and/or nonrelatives in the same household
- two-parent families with both parents working

FIGURE 32–3 Today's family may be any one of a variety of configurations.

- two-parent families with father at home and mother working
- homeless families
- single-parent families, parents divorced
- single-parent families, mother unmarried
- single-parent families, child(ren) adopted
- foster care families
- child(ren) and grandparent(s)
- children with no family

More mothers of young children are working outside the home, more parents are separated or divorced, and there is an increasing number of stepfamilies, families in which the parents are not married, and families that include grandmother, teenage mother, and child(ren) (grandchildren). The number of families in which mothers are raising children and grandchildren is increasing rapidly in the poverty areas of our big cities. Teenage mothers are not mature enough to fulfill the needs of a young child. The risks of child abuse and neglect are very high. The factor that keeps a great many of these children thriving is that there is often a strong extended family network of older siblings, aunts, mother, and grandmothers to give support. The constant missing element is a father.

Fathers are gradually becoming more involved in their children's lives (Stambor, 2005). In a review of research, Stambor notes that the affection of fathers and their involvement in children's lives promotes children's social and emotional development. Between 1948 and 2001, the percentage of employed working-age women increased from 33 percent to more than 60 percent. Simultaneously, the degree of father involvement in child care increased. Father love is essential to children for developing meaningful relationships in later life. Current research is breaking down cultural stereotypes. In a comparison of Hispanic, black, and white fathers' ideas about caregiving, there was little variation. However, there were differences in what fathers actually do. For example, black fathers more frequently cared for their infants' physical needs and more frequently prepared meals than did Hispanic or white fathers. Further, Mexican American fathers are more egalitarian than was commonly thought.

Evans and Fogarty (2005) suggest that fathers play five roles, the Five *P*s. These five roles are the ones fathers most commonly define for themselves.

1. *Participator/Problem-solver.* Fathers help children make decisions and solve problems.
2. *Playmate.* Fathers spend a lot of time in high-energy, physical play. They do more R&T activity.
3. *Principled guide.* Fathers used to be mainly punishers. However, if they use positive guidance strategies, they can have a significant positive effect on the child. Mom and Dad must agree on strategies.
4. *Provider.* Men still are identified as the dominant provider for the family although an increasing number of men are taking on the major child-care role and have wives who have higher-paying jobs.
5. *Preparer.* Fathers view one of their roles as preparing children for the future. This role begins in early childhood as they provide moral guidance and practical life lessons.

Increasingly, grandparents are becoming the primary caregivers for their grandchildren (see Figure 32–4). More than 2.5 million grandparents are raising grandchildren without either of the biological parents in the home (Bickmayer,

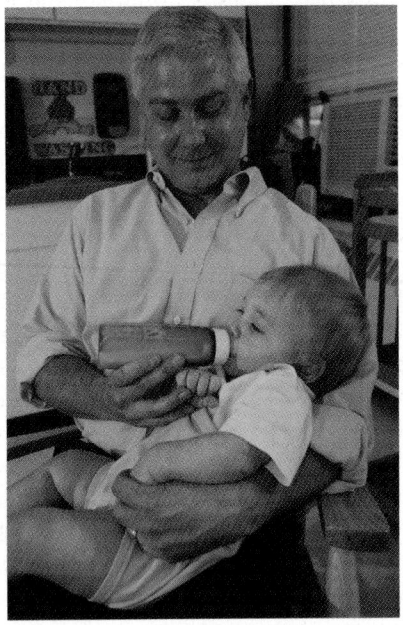

**FIGURE 32–4a, b, c** Fathers and grandparents are taking on more child-rearing responsibilities.

Cohen, Jensen, & Variano, 2005). Many other grandparents provide part-time care. Vandell, McCartney, Owen, Booth, and Clarke-Stewart (2003) identified four types of care provided by grandparents during the first three years: extended full-time care, extended part-time care, sporadic care, and no routine care. Bickmayer et al. point out that grandparents frequently take over due to tragic circumstances, such as parental substance abuse, divorce, mental and physical illness, child abuse and neglect, parental incarceration, or even death. Parenting the second time can be a great hardship. Grandparent-parents need support and assistance in obtaining information, such as regarding community and legal services.

The numbers of gay and lesbian headed families is also increasing. According to the 2000 census, gay and lesbian families live in 99.3 percent of all U.S. counties (Child Welfare League of America, 2006). Research supports that lesbian, gay, bisexual, and transsexual parents (LGBT) do as well raising children as heterosexual parents. Their children are as well developed in all areas as children of heterosexual parents. When there are problems, they are usually created by outside prejudices (COLAGE, 2006). Children of gay parents report being harassed at school as much as students who are themselves gay. No evidence supports that children of LGBT parents have any more chance of being homosexual than children of heterosexual parents.

In the introduction to his edited book on nontraditional families, Michael Lamb (1982) reminds us that the traditional family as we once knew it was of fairly recent origin. Shared economic and child care responsibilities have been known in cultures throughout history. Up until the industrial revolution, we were an agrarian society. Everyone shared in the economic life of the family. Prior to the 1830s, children were the father's property and went to him if the marriage was dissolved. The only long-lasting traditional belief is that mothers should have the predominant responsibility for child rearing. Lamb concludes that, overall, we have been very flexible about learning to manage as family styles have come and gone. Although divorce, single-parenting, and stepparenting are all difficult for adults and children, so is an unhappy traditional marriage. In the twenty-first century, a wide variety of family types is the norm and will likely continue to be so. Adults who work with young children need to be aware of family structure and tailor parental contact, education, and involvement to fit that structure. Footlick (1990) points out that many people still have some difficulty defining family. Some want to retain the 1950s family of mother, father, and children, with mother staying home and caring for the children, and then reject all other groups living together as ineligible for the "family" label. However, those who are in daily contact with young children realize this definition is no longer viable and realistic. Another changing aspect of family demographics is the number of ethnic groups within our society. According to Zill (reported in *U.S. children and their families*, 1991), by 2010, the percentage of African American and Latino youths will increase from 27 percent to 33 percent of the child population, with a disproportionate number of these children living in families at the lowest socioeconomic levels.

Family issues must be faced and addressed for the social and economic future of the country (Footlick, 1990). We can no longer ignore the growing underclass that lives in poverty. The numbers of working poor are increasing (Children's Defense Fund, 2001). Some sectors believe that a national family policy must be developed that includes the following (Footlick, 1990, p. 20):

- child and family allowances, with payments scaled to the number of children in each family
- guarantees to mothers of full job protection, seniority, and benefits upon their return to work after maternity leave
- pay equity for working women
- cash payments to mothers for wages lost during maternity leave
- full health care programs for all children
- national standards for child care

All Americans do not support these suggestions, mainly because of the increased burden they would bring to taxpayers. American businesses will need to employ even more women to fill the needs for workers in the future, while many mothers will continue to work due to personal choice and others due to financial need. The family will continue to take on new aspects that we cannot even foresee at this point. Meanwhile, we need a national policy that will support families and child development.

Look back through the descriptions of children and families. As an individual, what can you do to plan and implement improvements?

## EXTENDING THE FAMILY

Now we will look at the two locations where young children today spend a large portion of their time out of the home: in child care and in school. Furthermore, we will examine factors in parental involvement in both of these out-of-home institutions.

In 1988, Valora Washington (1988a, 1988b) described the trends in demographics and in instruction in early childhood. We have already examined some of these factors, such as changing family configurations, the increasing number of young children living in poverty, the increase in the percentage of minorities in the ranks of young children, and the problems related to developmentally appropriate versus inappropriate instructional practices. Washington also calls attention to the need to deal with the problems of licensing requirements and staff qualifications. Rust and Williams (1989) point out how the field of early childhood has expanded from a concern with the development and education of three-, four-, and five-year-olds to encompass infants, toddlers, and primary-age children also. This expanded focus has taken early educators into many new settings where children can be found. "These settings now range from the infants' own homes or homes of other caregivers to informal and formal public and private school classrooms, as well as a variety of nonschool situations, such as workplace or employer-provided facilities, and hospital and hospice programs" (pp. 334–335). Education has become an essential part of care, whatever the location.

## Child Care

In the past, when supplemental care was needed for young children, the nuclear family was extended by hiring a caregiver who came in each day or actually lived in the home. Now this "Mary Poppins" figure is a fantasy of the past except for those families at the upper-income levels. Today, supplemental care is usually in an out-of-home location. The National Center for Educational Statistics (2002) reports the characteristics of early childhood programs in 2001. Children of the non-poor are more likely to be enrolled in center-based preschool programs than those of the poor (59 percent versus 47 percent). Sixty-four percent of black, 59 percent of white, and 40 percent of Latino three- to five-year-olds were enrolled. Twice as many children are enrolled in center-based programs as in home-based programs. Programs for after-school care for school-age children are also growing in number. Fifty percent of kindergarten and primary children are left on their own for part of the day (Click & Parker, 2002). It is estimated that in the future, 34 million school-age children will need child care.

Today, as indicated in previous chapters, the search for the factors that define quality child care is the focus of a great deal of research. Phillips and Howes (1987) summarized the results of this work. The pioneering study in this area was the National Day Care Study (Ruopp, 1979). The major finding regarding quality indicated that two factors were present in high-quality programs for preschool children: relatively small groups of children and the caregivers having child-specific education/training. Well-trained teachers with a small ratio of children per teacher brought the most positive outcome in classroom behaviors and test scores for the children. This leads to higher salaries for teachers and a higher cost for the consumer. According to Phillips and Howes (1987), research conducted since the National Day Care Study has confirmed some of the results, contradicted others, and looked into new areas. Quality is not an easy concept to define, but researchers continue to try to pin it down.

Studies that have looked at child care in a global fashion, that is, high quality compared with low quality, have confirmed that better child care has more positive effects on children's cognitive and social development. Other studies have looked at specifics such as adult/child ratio, group size, and caregiver training and experiences. The results have supported that lower child/staff ratios have positive effects on verbal interaction, opportunities for play, and nurturant, nonrestrictive caregiver behavior. Group size is also a significant factor, with smaller group size appearing "to facilitate constructive caregiver behavior and positive developmental outcomes for children" (Phillips & Howes, 1987, p. 6). The more recent research indicates that both the amount of specialized child development/early childhood education training and years of experience teaching tend to relate to more positive teacher behavior and better outcomes for children. However, this is a complex area that warrants a great deal more study. Research on stability of the caregiver has provided a mixed picture. When the child remains in the same setting, having a stable caregiver does appear to be a plus for development. On the other hand, studies that examined the number of changes in settings children experienced showed no association with child outcomes. A more recent area of research has been an examination of the joint effects of family and the child care setting. For example, families who select low-quality care tend to have more stressful lives and to be less involved and invested in what is happening with their children. Mothers' attitudes toward the use of child care, in terms of whether they are comfortable with the idea or not, also appear to be important in influencing child behavior. The possible effects of child care appear to be the result of the interaction of a number of variables within home and child care settings that are still in need of much more study. Clarke-Stewart, after examining five major child-care studies, concludes that "the best predictors of advanced child development, and hence our best clues as to indexes of quality child care, are (Clarke-Stewart, 1987, p. 118) a licensed program (usually in a center)" in which:

- the child's interaction with the caregiver is frequent, verbal, and educational, rather than custodial and controlling.
- children are not left to spend their time in aimless play together.
- there is an adequate adult/child ratio (for older preschoolers probably not less than 1:12) and a reasonable group size (probably no larger than 25).
- the caregiver has balanced training in child development and some degree of professional experience in child care, and has been in the program for some period of time.

A critical element in child care quality is the regulation of homes and centers through standards that are usually provided by licensing agencies in each state. Phillips, Lande, and Goldberg (1990) compared licensing regulations among the states. Stringency varies greatly among states and within states. That is, even within states, regulations may be stringent on one item, such as the number of children allowed in a child care home, and lax on another, such as staff/child ratio. Some states, overall, have very low standards that do not even meet the minimums suggested by national organizations or federal departments. Licensing has become increasingly important, as more mothers of young children have had to leave welfare due to the welfare reform act and enter the labor force (Regulation of Child Care, 2002). Most of these children are in poor-quality unlicensed care. Only 14 percent of centers and 13 percent of family child care homes in the United States are rated as good quality. It is imperative that more attention be paid to upgrading the quality of child care through increased regulation. If federal standards, such as those developed by the Department of Health and Human Services, were imposed, many states would have to make drastic changes in upgrading their licensing requirements, with resulting increases in the cost of care. Phillips et al. (1990) found that the median level of standards was similar to the Accreditation Guidelines of NAEYC's National Academy of Early Childhood Programs and the Accreditation Profile of the National Association for Family Day Care (NAFDC), which are less stringent than the federal guidelines. Phillips et al. (1990) recommend a gradual upgrade of regulations to meet at least the NAEYC and NAFDC standards through a cooperative federal and state effort. Enforcement procedures would also need to be improved, along with opportunities for staff training to upgrade instructional practices. With more training, salaries and costs would increase. Specific information on the cost of quality care is the content of an NAEYC publication edited by Barbara Willer (1990). At present, the average child care worker earns an amount below the poverty line. Providing quality care and eliminating harmful care is an enormous and important challenge for the future.

Within communities, parents need guidance in finding the best care for their young children. Bradbard and Endsley (1980) found that parents were usually at a loss as to how to go about finding a good child care setting for their child and that professionals offer little help. Bradbard and Endsley developed and field tested a guide that can be used by parents to rate child care facilities. Checklists and guides to use in selecting quality child care are available from many sources, such as the Southern Early Childhood Association (SECA) and NAEYC and their affiliate groups, Child Care Resource and Referral, and from state licensing agencies and local service and action groups. See Chapters 11 and 15 for infant and toddler care checklists.

## Schooling

Teachers have reported informally that one of the strongest impediments to developmentally appropriate practice is the principal's point of view. The results of a study by Burts, Campbell, Hart, Charlesworth, DeWolfe, and Fleege (1991) that looked at the relationship between kindergarten teachers' beliefs and practices and principals' beliefs support this view. The results found that equal numbers of principals in the samples had developmentally appropriate and developmentally inappropriate beliefs. Most principals did not believe that active exploration and adjusting instruction for individual interests and abilities were important. There was little relationship between principals' beliefs and teachers' beliefs. Older principals, who most likely had taken their teacher education courses when socialization was the objective of kindergarten, had more appropriate beliefs than younger principals, who had probably been educated with an emphasis on academic achievement and skills training. Principals certified in kindergarten or who had in-service training in early childhood education had more appropriate beliefs overall than those who were not knowledgeable about the field. The results of this study support the need for principals to have early childhood education training if developmentally appropriate practices are to become widespread.

Efforts are being made to improve the quality of education for young children. For example, at the preschool level, there is a great deal of interest in the programs developed in Reggio Emilia, Italy (Bredekamp, 1993; Gandini, 1993; Hendrick, 1997; Malaguzzi, 1993). The **Reggio Emilia** is an all-day program that combines care, education, and social services. A unique factor is that the public schools of Reggio Emilia were literally built from the ground up by parents after World War II. In Italy, free programs are open to all three- to six-year-olds. Parents pay a fee for infants and toddlers. The Reggio philosophy is based on theories such as those of Dewey, Piaget, and Vygotsky. A set of basic principles includes, for example, that children have the preparedness, curiosity, and interest to construct their own knowledge; parent participation is essential; the layout of the school encourages communication and peer interaction; time is not set by the clock; teachers work in partnerships; teachers view themselves as researchers collecting information on each child; the curriculum is emergent; project work is promoted; and art is a central focus.

**Reggio Emilia**

An all-day program in an Italian city that combines care, education, and social services free to all three- to six-year-olds, with parents paying a fee for infants and toddlers.

Bredekamp (1993) found the experience very thought provoking and particularly picked up on the core of the Reggio philosophy: *the image of a competent child who has rights.* She believes that the challenge for American educators is to reclaim this image. She also hopes we can somehow incorporate some of the approaches to instruction that provide teacher assistance as needed while children move toward their self-selected goals.

The state of Missouri, in consultation with Rheta DeVries, has developed Project Construct, a process-oriented curriculum and assessment framework designed for working with children ages three through seven. It is a program based on principles derived from constructivist theory. Thus, children are viewed as competent to take the lead in constructing their own knowledge through meaningful activities provided by the teacher (*Understanding the possibilities*, 1992).

There are many other developmentally appropriate early childhood models, such as High/Scope, Bank Street, and Montessori (see Roopnarine & Johnson, 2004, and Goffin & Wilson, 2001, for model descriptions). Maria Montessori developed an educational method in Italy in 1907. Her method, which focused on all the senses, was initially used with students identified as retarded but eventually was incorporated into schools for low-socioeconomic-status children of normal intelligence. Montessori incorporated a strong element of parent involvement. Her curriculum is individualized and based on child development principles. The Bank Street School developed the Developmental-Interaction Approach. This approach grew initially along with the progressive approach of John Dewey. The major focus was on the social-emotional development of the whole child. Cognitive development was important but not laid out in a specific plan, such as Montessori. The Bank Street curriculum is developed from the children's individual needs and interests. The High/Scope model is based on Piagetian theory. High/Scope grew out of the Perry Preschool Project whose students have been followed up into adulthood. In its current format, it focuses on children gaining positive dispositions toward learning, gaining a sense of responsibility and independence, and becoming goal-oriented. The central focus is "plan-do-review." Children plan their activities for the day, follow through on their plan, and report back to the group on what they did. These models provide a variety of approaches to early childhood instruction from which individuals can make a selection.

## Parent Involvement

As mentioned earlier in this chapter, parents are the child's first and most significant teachers. However, in today's society, from infancy on, children may spend more time with other adults than with their parents. Therefore, getting parents involved through a partnership with caregivers or teachers should be one of the primary goals in our nation (Epstein, 1991; Reed & Sautter, 1990). Unfortunately, those children most in need of **parent involvement** are least likely to benefit from it. Parents in poverty may not feel comfortable or capable of becoming fully involved in their children's school. (Reed & Sautter, 1990) Head Start has been the model for successful parent involvement (Zigler & Styfco, 1993).

**parent involvement**

Various means through which parents collaborate in and support their children's education.

Epstein (1991) describes national, state, district, and individual school initiatives promoting parent involvement. At the national level, Chapter 1/Title I includes an emphasis on parent involvement. FIRST (Fund for the Improvement and Reform of Schools and Teaching) grants fund local programs designed to create, develop, and implement new school/family/community partnerships. Even Start links the education of young children with the education of their underachieving parents.

A five-year study of the Centers on Families, Communities, Schools, and Children's Learning has been completed (Epstein, 2005). Eight "essential elements" were identified for effective leadership and programs of school, family, and community partnerships. These elements are leadership, teamwork, action plans, implementation of plans, funding, collegial support, evaluation, and networking.

Schools and districts that included these elements had the most success in developing partnerships. Student behavior and achievement showed improvement and was better than that of matched nonpartnership schools.

## SOCIOLOGICAL FACTORS

A number of factors regarding the relationship between sociocultural status and child development have been discussed. Some of these factors include the following:

- The current focus is on celebrating diversity, multicultural education, and antibias curriculum.
- Adults who work with young children and families from a culture different than their own should learn about the children's and families' cultures and respect and incorporate the customs and language.
- Caution is needed in applying developmental theories to culturally diverse children.
- Lower-socioeconomic-level parents may not recognize the infant's need for motor activity and sensory stimulation and may not be able to provide proper nutrition, with the child then possibly showing signs of neurological impairment.
- Adults who feel powerless have fewer resources, less time, and less energy to give their infant.
- The child's behavior and development in language are affected by factors, such as dialect, mother tongue, and parental use and reinforcement of the child's use of language.
- Discrimination based on faulty use and interpretation of intelligence and achievement test results has resulted in mislabeling and misplacing children in special education classes.
- Lower-class families usually have less access to needed health care facilities and often lack the means for supplying their children with adequate nutrition.

Children often arrive at school with a learning style that does not fit the school's instructional approaches. As discussed previously, the importance of learning styles cannot be overemphasized.

We have a long way to go in providing the best educational opportunities for all our young children. Racism and classism still underlie many of our educational policies and practices (Banks, 1993; Bowman & Stott, 1994; Comer, 1989; Hyun, 1998; Kessler, 1992; Pine & Hilliard, 1990; Swadener & Lubeck, 1995). For the adult who works with young children, a time comes when these questions must be faced and important educational decisions made. Whatever the outcome, if teachers, parents, and allied workers cooperate and develop policies that fit the values identified by the group the program serves, the program stands a better chance of enhancing the development of the whole child.

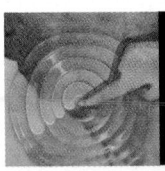

**LOOKING FURTHER**

Look through the selections in this chapter listed in "For Further Reading." Select a book that interests you. Obtain a copy. After you have read the book, write an essay describing your reactions to the ideas and information included.

## SUMMARY

The whole child is more than the sum of his or her parts; personal history, present status, and affective, cognitive, and psychomotor components determine what the child is today, but the child has the potential for becoming more. Children also are affected by, and affect, their family and society. In the twenty-first century, our children are in a perilous situation. An ever-increasing proportion live in poverty and are likely to face early mortality due to poor prenatal care, poor nutrition, and lack of proper medical attention.

Today, the family is a different and more diverse entity than it was in the past. The number of families made up of working father, nonworking mother, and one or more children is rapidly shrinking. Adults need to be prepared to work with these different types of families. With more working mothers, the family has extended out of the home to the child care provider. Federal, state, and local government agencies are focusing increasingly on early development and education programs. Quality child care and developmentally appropriate practices in preschool and elementary school instruction are goals for the twenty-first century. A further objective is to get families more involved in the education of their children and to make the school a community center where education, family, and community work together for the benefit of children. Increasing numbers of minority and female-headed households trying to survive below the poverty level make the job of adults who work with young children more challenging. Sociocultural status has an immense impact on the child and the family.

## FOR FURTHER READING


Annie B. Casey Foundation. (2005). *2005 Kids count data book*. Baltimore: Author.

Ayers, W. (2003). *On the side of the child: Summerhill revisited*. New York: Teachers College.

Bogenschneider, K. (2002). *Family policy matters: How policy making affects families and what professionals can do*. Mahwah, NJ: Erlbaum.

Bornstein, M. H., & Bradley, R. H. (Eds.). (2003). *Socioeconomic status, parenting, and child development*. Mahwah, NJ: Erlbaum.

Bugental, D. B. (2003). *Thriving in the face of childhood adversity*. New York: Psychology Press.

Cadwell, L. B. (2002). *Bringing learning to life*. New York: Teachers College Press.

Carey. (2003). *The whole child: Restoring wonder to the art of parenting*. Walnut Creek, CA: Alta Mira Press.

Christopherson, E. R., & Mortsweet, S. L. (2003). *Parenting that works: Building skills that last a lifetime*. Washington, DC: American Psychological Association.

Clinton, H. R. (1996). *It takes a village and other lessons children teach us*. New York: Simon and Schuster.

Comer, J. P., Joyner, E., & Ben-Avie, M. (Eds.). (2004). *Six pathways to healthy child development and academic success*. Thousand Oaks, CA: Corwin.

Connelly, R., DeGraff, D. S., & Willis, R. A. (2004). *Kids at work. The value of employer-sponsored on-site child care centers*. New York: Guilford.

Crouter, A. C., & Booth, A. (Eds.). (2004). *Work-family challenges for low-income parents and their children*. Mahwah, NJ: Erlbaum.

Cryer, D., & Clifford, R. M. (Eds.). *Early childhood education & care in the USA*. Baltimore: Brookes.

Donaldson, S. I., & Scriven, M. (Eds.). (2002). *Evaluating social programs and problems*. Mahwah, NJ: Erlbaum.

Epstein, J. L. (2001). *School, family and community partnerships*. Boulder, CO: Westview.

Family Support America. (2004). *Drawing from the data: Working effectively with Latino families*. Chicago: Author.

Gandini, L., Hill, L., Cadwell, L., & Schwall, C. (Eds.). (2005). *In the spirit of the studio: Learning from the Atelier of Reggio Emilia*. New York: Teachers College.

Ganong, L. H., & Coleman, M. (2003). *Stepfamily relationships*. New York: Springer.

Garan, E. M. (2004). *In defense of our children: When politics, profit, and education collide*. Portsmouth, NH: Heinemann.

Hanson, M. J., & Lynch, E. W. (2004). *Understanding families: Approaches to diversity, disability, and risk*. Baltimore: Brookes.

Heineman, T. V., & Ehrensaft, D. (2005). *Building a home within: Meeting the emotional needs of children and youth in foster care*. Baltimore: Brookes.

Hiatt-Michael, D. (Ed.). (2002). *Promising practices in family involvement*. Greenwich, CT: IAP, Inc.

Jeynes, W. (2002). *Divorce, family structure, and the academic success of children*. New York: Haworth Press.

Landy, S., & Menna, R. (2005). *Early intervention with multi-risk families*. Baltimore: Brookes.

Maton, K. I., Schellenbach, C. J., Leadbeater, B. J., & Solarz, A. L. (Eds.). (2004). *Investing in children, youth, families, and communities*. Washington, DC: American Psychological Association.

NICHD Study of Early Care and Youth Development. (2005). *Child care and child development*. New York: Guilford.

Oser, C., & Cohen, J. (2003). *America's babies: the Zero to Three policy center data book*. Herndon, VA: Zero to Three.

Phillion, J., He, M. F., & Connelly, E. M. (Eds.). *Narrative and experience in multicultural education*. Thousand Oaks, CA: Sage.

Pryor, J., & Rodgers, B. (2001). *Children in changing families*. Williston,VT: Blackwell.

Prout, A. (Ed.). (2004). *The future of childhood*. New York: RoutledgeFalmer.

Rogoff, B. (2003). *The cultural nature of human development*. New York: Oxford University Press.

Saracho, O. N., & Spodek, B. (2002). *Contemporary perspectives on curriculum for early childhood education*. Greenwich, CT: IAP, Inc.

Swick, K. (2004). *Empowering parents, families, schools, and communities during the early childhood years*. Champaign, IL: Stipes.

Weiss, H. B., Kreider, H., Lopez, M. E., & Chatman, C. M. (Eds.). (2005). *Preparing educators to involve families*. Thousand Oaks, CA: Sage.

Willie, C. V., & Reddick, R. J. (2003). *A new look at black families* (5th ed.). Walnut Creek, CA: AltaMira Press.

## SUGGESTED ACTIVITIES

1. To find out how well acquainted typical American citizens are with the realities of family life today, look back through the chapters and select 10 facts about today's families. List them numbered 1 through 10 in a true/false format, such as follows:

**TODAY'S FAMILY QUIZ**

**Decide whether each of the following statements is true (T) or false (F). Circle your response to each statement.**

**T F 1. By 2010, the percentage of African American and Latin youth will increase from 27 percent to 33 percent of the U.S. child population. Most of these children will live in poverty-level families.**

**(List nine more statements about families in the format above.)**

Make 10 or more copies of your quiz. Administer the quiz to 10 friends and/or relatives. Bring your results to class for discussion.

2. Visit two or more child care centers that enroll infants and toddlers. Use the checklist in Chapter 11 (infant caregiver) and the checklist in Chapter 15 (toddler caregiver) to evaluate each facility and its staff. Compare the centers. Which seemed best? Why? Did you find the checklists were helpful? Why or why not? Report your findings in class.

3. Looking through the text, make a list of factors that would indicate a program for preschoolers, kindergartners, and primary students was developmentally appropriate. Visit two preschool, kindergarten, and/or primary classrooms that enroll children who live in poverty. Use your list of factors to evaluate the programs. Find out if there is a parent-involvement program. Report your findings in class.

4. Make an entry in your journal

## REVIEW

1. List the factors that make up the whole child.
2. Explain your view of the status of America's children today using the information in the chapter as the basis for your opinion.
3. Describe "today's American family."
4. Evaluate the following description of a child care center using what you have learned about the factors that indicate quality child care for young children.

   The First Avenue Child Development Center is located in a working-class neighborhood of a midsized city. The director, Mrs. Tanaka, has a bachelor's degree in child development. The two teachers, Ms. Miller and Mr. Santos, have associate's degrees in early education. All three are actively involved with the children and they smile, pat, and hug children and give verbal approval frequently. The children smile and laugh, and there is a relaxed feeling in the center.

   A flexible approach to grouping is used with the 35 enrolled children, ages two-and-a-half to five-and-a-half. Sometimes each teacher and the director takes a group, and sometimes the children are divided into two groups, depending on the objectives and activities for the day. During the afternoon nap and the play period following, two high school students who have taken a child development course offered at their high school work at the center, allowing each of the regular staff a chance for a break and filling in when the teacher who has opened up in the morning leaves in midafternoon.

   Lots of materials, such as toys, games, and art materials, are available on low shelves where the children can easily reach them. Indoor equipment includes dolls, dress-up clothes, DVDs and DVD players, blocks, and books. The room is arranged so that areas for the use of each type of material are not clearly defined. The outdoor play area is small and includes a sandbox, a slide, and a small jungle gym. Inside, the children play well and rarely bicker over materials, as plenty are available for everyone. Outside, there is not quite enough room (although only half the group usually uses the playground at one time). The equipment is crowded. Teachers must intervene often to stop pushing and shoving and to make sure everyone gets his or her turn.

   The program seems to include both free play and structured small group activities. Sometimes the whole group gets together for a film or a special visitor. The schedule indicates that the children will take a trip to the farm next week and will begin a gardening project the next day on a small plot in the play yard.

   The center is very clean. The walls are yellow and sunlight streams in the large windows. Bulletin boards contain teacher information and interesting, colorful pictures and displays for the children. Many of the children's paintings are used to decorate the room. Near the entrance is a small office with a room off to the side that is used both as a teacher's lounge and a place to isolate sick children. In case of the need for emergency medical care, all parents have signed a release allowing their child(ren) to be treated by the staff at the clinic down the street. Menus for the week follow government guidelines for nutrition. Observing the lunch period, we find the food is served family style. Several children have helped bake cookies that are served for dessert.

   When the parents arrive to pick up their children, one of the teachers makes a point of talking with each one and passing along some information regarding the parent's child. Today, Mrs. Tanaka is trying to arrange times for parent visits and conferences.
5. Select the statements below that are true.
   a. The field of early childhood education has expanded from its concern with mainly three-, four- and five-year-olds to a concern with the whole period from birth through age eight.

b. Most child care for young children takes place in the child's own home.
c. It is not clear whether high- versus low-quality care makes any difference in the development of children.
d. When selecting child care, it should be kept in mind that both the amount of specialized child development/early childhood education training and years of staff experience are critical factors related to quality.
e. Child care licensing standards in most states are above the minimum recommended by NAEYC and other professional organizations.
f. We should be just as concerned about the quality of later, more formal, schooling as we are about early child care.
g. The principal's point of view is critical in determining whether or not classroom instruction is developmentally appropriate.
h. Schools need to develop programs that focus on community and parental involvement in children's education.
i. The best parent involvement programs require that each parent volunteers some time to participate in the school program.
j. Racism and classism have been eliminated from educational programs.

## KEY TERMS LIST

family
parent involvement
Reggio Emilia
the whole child

Additional resources for this chapter can be found on the Online Companion™ to accompany this text at http://www.earlychilded.delmar.com. Respond to "Time to Reflect" and "Looking Further" concepts, review various child development scenarios, and answer thought-provoking questions in the Critical Thinking Forum. Keep a daily journal by downloading the student journal available on this Web site. Complete the interactive matching exercises to reinforce concepts, and printout the child development assessment forms to use during your observation of development for children from birth to age eight. In addition, read the case studies on the Web site to reinforce the important concepts in each chapter, and take a look at the multitude of Web links that are available for student research on the Internet.

CHAPTER

# 33

# Action for Children

## Objectives

After reading this chapter, you should be able to:

- List and describe some of the current policy issues relevant to young children and their families.
- Know how to obtain materials for planning an advocacy action.
- Understand why young children need advocates.
- Identify the conditions that describe the area of public policy for children and families.
- Explain what the 101st Congress accomplished for young children and their families.
- Describe what advocates for children might do in taking action for them.

**child advocates**
Adults who work to see that children's rights are protected.

Adults who work with young children may feel helpless in the face of what appear to be insurmountable national problems. During the 1970s, we lost many battles in the fight for our children and families because we did not have the skills, knowledge, and experience to mount strong advocacy campaigns. Whereas adult special interest groups (e.g., gun ownership advocates, farmers, industrialists) can campaign firsthand for their interests, children cannot. Consequently, it is left up to caring adults to protect their interests and welfare. **Child advocates** are adults who work to see that children's rights are protected. They work through the political system for child-centered public policy. They also work for public awareness so parents and other adults are informed about policy issues and can join the advocate ranks. During the 1980s, adults who worked with young children realized that they would have to pull some of their energies away from their immediate daily work with children to seek changes in social policies and services.

In the 1990s, various stakeholders formed coalitions on issues affecting children. For example, "in September 1993, nearly 300 early childhood professionals, business leaders, researchers, parents, community planners, health and human service professionals, clergy, fenders, and local, state, and federal policy makers gathered in Washington, DC, for the first Forum on State and Community Planning in Early Childhood Education" (Galinsky, Shubilla, Willer, Levine, & Daniel, 1994). A cross-section of stakeholders in promoting sound early childhood development and education came together to share ideas and strategies. Their purpose was to go beyond coming up with a list of recommendations to actually collaborating to create new systems for high-quality early childhood service delivery. They identified eight components that need to be addressed to achieve systemic reform: creating linkages, using data in planning, improving the quality of programs, developing a coordinated professional development system, financing the system, creating new systems of governance, building public awareness, and developing a public policy agenda. To achieve these goals, a planning group must have a clear mission and convince a cross-section of influential players to buy into the mission. The Forum will continue meeting each year to work on long-term goals and actions for reform.

## THE GRASSROOTS LEVEL

Advocacy at its worst is a time-consuming, exhausting, and often disappointing effort. Advocacy at its best is made up of both large and small victories: a large victory being one that changes or develops new policy at the federal, state, or local levels; small victories occur when one parent, one teacher, or one other person who is concerned with young children perceives the need for change and joins in the advocacy struggle. The author, after being involved at the local level in a national child care awareness campaign, realized that the general public in her city probably did not perceive there was a problem and for the most part ignored the campaign. It was evident that a successful public awareness campaign in an area with a population of more than 400,000 would require grassroots support and a great deal of labor by enthusiastic and persistent community volunteers.

Laura Smith (fictitious name) is a mother and a teacher. She held a position as a special education home-based teacher working with preschoolers with disabilities. She worked with the children individually in their homes or in their child care centers. She was appalled by some of the things she saw going on in the name of early education and child care. Laura, feeling ill-equipped to address the problem, took a leave of absence and returned to school to obtain her master's degree. During the course of her studies, she found herself in a seminar with a focus on issues of public policy. The following, in Laura's own words, is the story of how she instituted action for children in her community.

### Laura's Story: A Grassroots Effort

In the beginning, there was a discussion in class about the lack of knowledge that persists in the general public about what constitutes high quality in an early childhood program. I immediately envisioned that educating the community was going to take longer than seven days! However, I decided I would take on the responsibility of looking at the problem.

The initial approach was to enlist the help of organizations that would disseminate information on quality early childhood programs. As I began gathering information prior to approaching interested organizations and persons, it became apparent that most of the information in the community dealt only with surface issues, such as cleanliness, staffing, and furnishings. It did not address the fundamentals and content knowledge of child development and the way it is applied to early childhood programs and practices. At this point, I realized that a full understanding of development as it relates to early childhood education could not be accomplished solely through the distribution of flyers and pamphlets.

I wanted to raise the community's awareness of the need for high-quality, developmentally appropriate early childhood programs. Also, I felt that organizations

**INTEREST SURVEY**

Volunteer organization: _____

Contact person and phone number: _____

Address: _____

Interest level: Interested _____ Moderately interested _____ Need more information _____

Present involvement in education issues:

_____

_____

_____

_____

As an interested organization, the possible allocation of our resources are:

1. Manpower, volunteers _____
2. Financial support _____
3. Participation in planning committee _____

Comments:

**FACTS**

- Nearly 80 percent of the mothers with preschool-age children will be in the workforce by 1990.
- A typical American family will pay $3,000 to $5,000 per child for child care a year.
- Presently in Baton Rouge, the average consumer has very little information on how to determine **quality** in early childhood programs.

What should the consumer look for in order to determine **quality** in an early childhood program?

The **National Association for the Education of Young Children** (NAEYC) believes that a high-quality early childhood program provides a safe and nurturing environment that promotes the physical, social, emotional, and cognitive development of young children while responding to the needs of families. A major determinant of program quality is the extent to which knowledge of child development is applied in program practices—the degree to which the program is **developmentally appropriate.** NAEYC believes that high-quality, **developmentally appropriate programs** should be available to all children and their families.

The purpose of the attached interest survey is to determine the interest level of community organizations or persons interested in educating the Baton Rouge community on the current knowledge of child development and how it relates to quality early childhood programs.

FIGURE 33–1 This interest survey, with accompanying fact sheet, served as a vehicle for encouraging dialog with potential advocates.
(Used with permission of the Quality Early Education Coalition, 910 Marquette, Baton Rouge, LA 70806).

and individuals should be surveyed to determine the level of interest and support within the community. Therefore, I developed a short interest survey (Figure 33–1) that could be used to survey those persons or organizations interested in educating the community by becoming volunteers, providing financial support, or participating on a planning committee. I surveyed a community cross-section, including representatives from organizations such as the YWCA, the Junior League, a hospital, the local public school system, local private schools, a local industry, a pediatrician, media personnel, university professors, and parents of young children. Each person was contacted first by phone, and an appointment was made to discuss the survey and answer any questions.

Every person contacted, with one exception, was very interested. However, each had a specific focal point. For example, industry wanted to educate its employees, the YWCA had specific groups, such as teen parents, that it wanted to target, and a church-affiliated preschool wanted to inform other church preschools and network among them.

With such a positive response and the support of my classmates, I decided to move ahead. I foresaw a long-term project, with the initial step being the formation of an Executive Committee to develop a Mission Statement (Figure 33–2), form a Planning Committee, create by-laws, obtain nonprofit status, and establish goals and objectives. Realistically, I knew it would take at least two years to become operational.

Looking back, what have we accomplished? We have become a viable, active, and recognized group in the community. Probably our most difficult task was obtaining nonprofit status. This required the services of an accountant and a lawyer and took two years to accomplish. Fortunately, the lawyer volunteered his services and the accountant kindly agreed to work for a small portion of her normal fee. With the aid of many volunteers, a Membership Action Grant from NAEYC, and support services for design, typesetting, and printing from a local hospital's publication department, we developed an initial one-page flyer (Figure 33–3). Later we created a professional-quality brochure defining developmentally appropriate practices for children from infancy through age eight. We also developed a checklist for selecting an early childhood program and a one-page flyer warning parents about the dangers of inappropriate assessment practices. We disseminated these citywide. QEEC members gave presentations on developmentally appropriate practice to many groups of parents and professionals, worked with individual schools to make changes, instituted a fall workshop for teachers and a spring information session for parents looking for criteria for kindergarten selection, answered a multitude of requests for information, participated in community activities for children, and collaborated with other organizations in child advocacy activities. Our long-term goal is to serve as a model that other communities can use in developing advocacy and public information campaigns.

## PUBLIC POLICY

In 1979, Kenneth Keniston, commenting on the conclusions from a study of public policy by the Carnegie Council on Children, stated that public policy was letting the family down. He believed that we were not very protective of children and their families. He stated that we needed to use more preventive policies rather than the usual after-the-fact policies. According to Keniston, family policy must put "greater emphasis on changing the social and economic factors that contribute so massively to family problems . . ." The council recommended that parents be stronger advocates for children and more powerful in making child-rearing choices. The council recommended that seven changes be made in national family policy:

1. Parents need jobs. Something needs to be done to ensure that all parents have work.
2. The benefits of working should be distributed fairly by doing away with discriminative recruiting and unfair job qualifications.
3. Parents need assurance of a minimally decent income from their jobs.
4. Parents need more flexible work schedules and maternity and paternity leave.
5. Parents need access to and some control over decent medical, dental, social, and psychological services.

## MISSION STATEMENT of THE QUALITY EARLY EDUCATION COALITION

The Quality Early Education Coalition is a nonprofit organization composed of citizens concerned with:

1. creating an awareness within the Baton Rouge community about high-quality, developmentally appropriate early childhood programs.
2. initiating and supporting change within the existing structure of early childhood education.
3. developing a model for community action.

The Coalition was formed in response to the recent prevalence of inappropriate academic instruction for children from birth to age eight in the Baton Rouge community. We believe this trend has developed as a result of a lack of information regarding appropriate practice. Thus, the Coalition seeks to inform the community as to the nature and importance of developmentally appropriate practice (DAP).

The Quality Early Education Coalition is committed to the expansion of developmentally appropriate practice and program quality in the Baton Rouge community according to the definitions that follow. The National Association for the Education of Young Children (NAEYC) has defined "developmentally appropriate practice" as a safe and nurturing environment that promotes the physical, social, emotional, and cognitive development of children from birth to eight, while responding to the needs of families.

The chart below contrasts appropriate practice with inappropriate practice.

| Appropriate Practice | Inappropriate Practice |
|---|---|
| Infants are held and carried frequently. The adults talk to the infant before, during, and after moving the infant around. | Infants are wordlessly moved about at the adult's convenience. Nothing is explained to the infant. |
| Diapering, sleeping, feeding, and play areas are separate to ensure sanitation and provide quiet, restful areas. | Areas are combined and are noisy and distracting. |
| Children are expected to be physically and mentally active. They choose from among activities the teacher has set up or the children spontaneously initiate. | Children are expected to sit down, watch, be quiet, and listen, or do paper-and-pencil tasks for long periods of time. A major portion of time is spent passively sitting, listening, and waiting. |
| Objects children can manipulate and experiment with, such as blocks, cards, games, woodworking tools, and arts and crafts materials, including paint and clay, are readily accessible. Tables are used for children to work alone or in small groups. A variety of work places and spaces is provided and flexibly used. | Available materials are limited primarily to books, workbooks, and pencils. Children are assigned permanent desks and desks are rarely moved. Children work in a large group most of the time, and no one can participate in a playful activity until all work is finished. |

Program quality is the extent to which knowledge of child development is applied in program practices—the degree to which the program is developmentally appropriate.

Once awareness throughout the Baton Rouge community has been established, the Coalition will seek to initiate and support change in early education through organizing volunteers, soliciting financial support, and providing consultation.

Through our efforts, The Quality Early Education Coalition will develop a model for community action that will be disseminated to other interested communities, not only in our state but also nationwide.

The goal of The Quality Early Education Coalition is to develop and implement a plan of action to accomplish the above mission.

**FIGURE 33–2** Quality Early Education Coalition Statement.
(Used with permission of the Quality Early Education Coalition, 910 Marquette, Baton Rouge, LA 70806).

## THE QUALITY EARLY EDUCATION COALITION PURPOSE

The Quality Early Education Coalition is a nonprofit organization composed of citizens concerned about high-quality, developmentally appropriate early childhood programs. Our work initiates and supports change within the existing structure of early childhood education.

## DEVELOPMENTALLY APPROPRIATE PRACTICE

The National Association for the Education of Young Children (NAEYC) has defined "developmentally appropriate practice" as a safe and nurturing environment that promotes the physical, social, emotional, and cognitive development of children from birth to age eight while responding to the needs of families. Appropriate environments provide children challenges, support, and success based on individual needs, interests, and learning abilities.

## HOW CHILDREN LEARN

Children learn through activities that:

- Are interesting
- Yield success and satisfaction
- Encourage independence
- Require hearing, seeing, tasting, smelling, and feeling things
- Are child-initiated
- Foster creativity
- Are supported by adults
- Require active exploration of real things

## CHILDREN LEARN BY DOING

- Dancing, singing, playing music
- Painting, cutting, pasting, squeezing, and pounding clay
- Scribbling, drawing, writing
- Counting objects, sorting, and classifying
- Exploring sand and water, planting seeds, caring for pets
- Talking, listening, role playing
- Hearing stories and looking at books
- Doing puzzles, stringing beads, building with blocks
- Pretending to be adults, fantasy persons, or animals

## WHAT PARENTS CAN DO

- Provide appropriate activities for learning
- Provide opportunities for children to learn by doing
- Look for and support developmentally appropriate practices in schools

## CHILDREN AT THEIR BEST

Adults who understand normal child development can provide personal and academic support through developmentally appropriate practices. The result is children who are happy, confident, and successful.

**FOR INFORMATION:** Write, QEEC, 910 Marquette Ave., B.R., LA 70806

Production of this flyer funded by a Membership Action Grant from the National Association for the Education of Young Children and by Woman's Hospital. The contents and views presented reflect the work of this Membership Action Group and do not necessarily represent the position of the National Association for the Education of Young Children or Woman's Hospital.

**FIGURE 33–3** This brief handout provides basic information about QEEC and child development.
(Used with permission of the Quality Early Education Coalition, 910 Marquette, Baton Rouge, LA 70806).

6. The health care system needs to be altered to stress preventative measures.
7. Parents and children need changes in the laws and legal practices that affect families. More effort needs to be put into noninstitutional placement of children and support for keeping families together.

Keniston suggests that government maintain a more protective role and enlarge people's freedom of choice. Parents, he believes, should be given more resources so they can do a better job. Looking at the statistics accumulated during the next decade, it is apparent that our country has continued with the same policies that Keniston and the Carnegie Council saw as outdated in the 1970s. Families are in more danger than ever as we proceed into the twenty-first century.

In 1994 (15 years later), a report was released from another Carnegie-funded group: the task force on Meeting the Needs of Young Children (*Starting points*, 1994). The Task Force focused particularly on the needs of our youngest children, three years old and younger, and their families. The task force identified four key areas that need to be addressed immediately as a step toward improving life for young children and their families: promote responsible parenthood, guarantee quality child care choices, ensure good health and protection, and mobilize communities to support young children and their families. They called on all segments of the nation and its communities to take action to achieve the identified goals.

As already mentioned, minority families, and particularly African American families, are at the highest degree of risk. Valora Washington (1985, 1988, 1989) has written extensively on our public policy for children and for African American children in particular. Overall, she supports Keniston's view that, while we have talked a lot about valuing children and families, our policies do not reflect such values. Politically, we have tended to take a noninterventionist position based on a belief that parental rights take precedence over children's needs. On the other hand, Washington (1985) points out that in emergencies, such as the 1930s Depression when federally supported child care centers were opened, we have intervened. A number of programs have also been provided for poor children and their families in the areas of income support, health care, protection from abuse, nutritional assistance, and child care. Historically, most of these programs have served only a small fraction of those needing their services. Some programs, such as free and partial school lunch subsidies and Chapter 1/Title I educational benefits, are available on a fairly broad basis. By the mid-1980s, the enthusiasm of the war-on-poverty years of the 1970s had died out, and with harder times, politicians became less supportive of governmental assistance to children and families. Washington (1985) suggests that our best strategy, because we have a basic belief of noninterference in the family, is to help parents do more for their children rather than offering only direct services to children.

When considering support for minority families, the problems presented by race and racism must also be recognized (Washington, 1988, 1989). Prejudiced points of view and lack of attention to ethnic differences in family lifestyles affect policy decisions. For example, African Americans more than European Americans are more likely to be looked on as the undeserving poor who are in poverty through their own fault and, therefore, undeserving of assistance. In setting up assistance guidelines, the fact that African Americans are more likely than European Americans to live in an extended family group is not considered. Washington (1988) concludes that, with the projected increases in our populations' African American and other minority ethnic groups, these groups will be more essential resources in our economy and our political arena. More opportunities must be made available for these children so they can grow up to be productive citizens.

Children not only need to be fed, clothed, and kept safe and healthy, they also need to be provided with educational opportunities (Washington, 1989). African American parents in general have high educational aspirations for their children, but their children are at great risk for educational failure. Washington believes that studies of African American children can shed light on the link between education and public policy. For example, so-called compensatory education programs have not considered the African American child's family configuration or learning style. The color-blind approach to policy development assumes that problems of African American learners can be solved in the same way as problems of white learners. "This approach has led to educational policy solutions indifferent to the fact that both poverty and educational failure among blacks often result from political, instructional, and economic systems that condone and foster institutional racism" (Washington, 1989, p. 287). Washington points out that equal educational opportunity programs have "focused on changing individual children who were expected to accommodate to the schools, rather than adapting to the needs of the children and their communities" (p. 289). As described earlier in the text, each cultural group has a distinct learning style that needs to be considered in planning educational programs.

Washington (1989) believes that the risk to African American learners can be reduced by linking research, policy, and practice. That is, policy and practice should be based on what has been found from studies of African American child development. The deficit view of African American, as well as other minority group, students must be dropped, and a view that emphasizes instruction based on cultural and learning style and family involvement must replace it. Washington (1989) asserts the need for policy to be based on a multicultural perspective.

In the twenty-first century, it is apparent that public policy has not taken into consideration the development of children in the context of their families, their cultures, and their true educational needs. The next part of the chapter will provide an overview of recent and future policy issues.

How would you feel about starting a local grassroots organization like QEEC in your community? Why do you think it might not work? Explain how you might apply some of Laura's ideas.

## Issues

A patchwork of public policy issues in many areas has appeared in this and other chapters. As already mentioned, it has been a recent phenomenon for those who work with young children to become actively engaged in public policy activities. A massive, well-organized grassroots effort finally achieved success in 1990 (Mann, 1991). The payoff for all this time and effort came through with the 101st Congress in 1990 (Willer, 1991). In the January 1991 Public Policy Report in *Young Children*, Barbara Willer reported on "The Children's Congress" that enacted historic legislation on child care, Head Start, and children's television. In 1971, former President Nixon vetoed the first effort at comprehensive child care legislation. Twenty years later, a freestanding federal child care program finally was at last a reality. Head Start was reauthorized with a larger budget and provision for full funding to serve all eligible three- through five-year-olds by 1994. The Earned Income Tax Credit was increased, providing income support to low-income working families with children. Two additional new tax credits were enacted. One provides credit for children's health insurance expenses and the other for families with children younger than one year of age.

Issues often resurface, as authorizations are for a limited time period. When reauthorization becomes due, such as for Head Start and for federally supported child care programs, advocates have to be ready to deal with the issues again. Other issues involve lengthy battles, discussion, and debate, with little or no benefit to children and families resulting. From the National Association of Child Advocates' (NACA) (NACA, 2001) compilation of national legislative and policy priorities, the highest priority was increasing child care subsidies. Other priorities included gaining support for afterschool programs; increasing access to health care; increasing tax credits for families with children; providing support for economic/family security; ensuring school readiness; providing universal prekindergarten and full-day kindergarten; including mental and oral health care in health policies; providing more services to foster children; providing health care coverage up to age twenty-one; providing postsecondary education assistance; and improving compensation for early childhood education workers.

Look carefully through the issues just described. Which one would you advocate? Explain why you made this selection.

In a 1991 talk, Joan Lombardi warned us that all the success we have had in promoting advances in early education and care do not mean we can become complacent. For example, we know what developmentally appropriate practice is, but now we need policies that support it. Lombardi recommended a number of actions that child advocates need to take:

**Federal**

- Ensure that Congress authorizes full funding for child care and Head Start.
- Ensure that training monies are readily available.
- Work for parental maternity/paternity leave legislation, such as that passed in other countries.
- Ensure that Congress authorizes full funding for WIC and for maternal and child health services.
- Invite your legislators to visit quality programs.

**State**

- Develop coalitions of groups and organizations. For example, in one state, 14 organizations have organized the Coalition for Families and Children, with the mission of ensuring practical and creative use of that state's share of the Child Care Block Grant.
- Speak at hearings on child and family issues.
- Reach out to the business community as partners.
- Have press conferences to address issues.
- Keep in touch with other states.

**Community**

- College and university personnel should document the plight of our children.
- Speak up and have the courage of your convictions.
- Within organizations, provide training for new leaders.
- Teach teachers how to speak with parents and empower them to stand up for their convictions.
- Reach out to doctors. They are our natural allies, but they are not well informed.
- Get more involved politically. Run for local office.

FIGURE 33–4 Professionals work together to plan activities for young children and their families.

- Gain influence with parents by showing them you care.
- Be model professionals, support each other, work together, and show that we love and respect children (Figure 33–4).

Now we know that organization and hard work can affect the content of social policy legislation. The final section of the chapter presents some of the "hows" of advocacy.

## CHILD ADVOCACY

Because advocacy is an accepted activity for those who work with young children, a wealth of advocacy materials are available. All the major early childhood education organizations publish policy reports that keep members up-to-date on policy issues and developments. They publish inexpensive informational pamphlets that can be used to support advocacy activities. They also have developed materials that provide step-by-step procedures for advocacy.

In the 1980s, organizations concerned with the development and education of young children were forced to become deeply and actively involved in the politics of child advocacy. For example, journals such as *Young Children* (NAEYC) and *Dimensions* (SECA) have regular public policy reports. They also send out special policy alerts to members, alerting them to contact their legislators regarding laws that may be pending. Organizations such as the Children's Defense Fund, the National Latino Children's Institute, and the National Black Child Development Institute monitor events in Washington, DC, and elsewhere and publish informational material. The Society for Research in Child Development publishes a quarterly *Policy Report* that relates research in child development to policy issues pending in Congress.

Adele Robinson and Deborah R. Stark (2002) suggest a number of strategies for child advocacy. They outline three forms of advocacy: personal advocacy, public policy advocacy, and private sector advocacy. The form selected by individuals depends on their comfort in speaking out, their passion for the issue, and their time and energy. **Personal advocacy** involves sharing our views with others. It is usually spontaneous and informal and may involve getting an informal group together to solve a problem, such as cleaning litter out of the neighborhood playground. **Public policy advocacy** has the goal of influencing public policies and practices to improve children's lives. Public policy advocates challenge legislators, school boards, and other agencies. For example, they might work to enact laws to raise standards for child care facilities. **Private sector advocacy** has the goal of improving private sector policies and practices to support children and families. Private sector advocates work for more child- and family-friendly workplace policies, such as maternity and paternity leave and child care subsidies. They may also work for improved products, such as toys, videos, and car seats.

**personal advocacy**
Involves sharing our views with others.

**public policy advocacy**
The goal is to influence public policies and practices to improve children's lives.

**private sector advocacy**
The goal is to improve private sector policies and practices to support children and families.

Robinson and Stark (2002) suggest several strategies an individual might select:

- share research information with teachers and parents
- join an organization that works for changes in public policy
- write a letter to the editor of your local newspaper or to a legislator

- join a local advocacy group's public policy committee
- do the background research and develop a position statement on an issue
- volunteer to be a speaker on an issue
- conduct a survey on a local issue, such as the cost of child care

## A LOOK TO THE FUTURE

Washington and Andrews (1998) conclude their description of the vision for the future of children in 2010 by stating that the major focus should be on making access to opportunity fairer and more accessible. Advocacy is needed at the local level to develop community agendas. All our diverse groups need to develop partnerships for collaboration and thus develop a louder and stronger voice. The book concludes with a letter to the children of 2010 and this final statement:

> Even caring parents and other concerned adults cannot create a problem-free America. As always, there will also be plenty of problems remaining for you to solve, but we hope they won't be the same ones with which we are wrestling in 1998! (p. 161)

Near the conclusion of the book *Children of 2010* (Washington & Andrews, 1998), a number of suggestions and questions are listed. Look through the following selection of statements and ideas adapted from the list and write a response to as many as you can:

1. Write a list of facts, ideas, and insights that you have discovered in this chapter and in your study of child development.
2. If you have regular contact with parents, ask them what improvements they would like to see for the children of 2010.
3. Explain what you see as the role parents should play in creating a good future for their children.
4. How could mass media improve opportunities for children?
5. What is your assessment of the public schools? What solutions do you propose?
6. Why isn't there better continuity between preschool, kindergarten through high schools, and post-secondary education?
7. Outline your own vision statement for the children of 2010.
8. What can you do to implement your vision?
9. Are you planning any action or changes for the children of 2010?

## SUMMARY

Advocacy for children and families has become a normal part of the activities of adults who work with young children. During the 1980s, we realized that we could not just sit back and wait for government to develop family-centered/child-centered policies. Public policy changes through legislation do not just happen. Many hours of organized volunteer work are needed to get things done. Advocacy begins at the grassroots level with community groups and coalitions, builds at the state level, and becomes a force to be reckoned with at the national level. All the major early childhood development and education organizations can provide assistance in helping advocates plan action for children and families.

## For Further Reading

Babies, practitioners, and public policy [Focus issue]. (2001). *Zero to three, 21*(3).

Bowman, B., Donovan, & Burns, M. S. (Eds.). (2000). *Eager to learn: Educating our preschoolers.* Washington, DC: National Academy Press.

*CDF Reports.* Newsletter of the Children's Defense Fund, P.O. Box 7584, Washington, DC 20077–1245.

Clinton, H. R. (1996). *It takes a village and other lessons children teach us.* New York: Simon & Schuster.

Federal Interagency Forum on Child and Family Statistics. (2001). *America's children: Key national indicators of well-being 2001.* Washington, DC: Author. Available at http://childstats.gov.

Flekkoy, M. G., & Kaufman, N. H. (1997). *The participation rights of the child: Rights and responsibilities in family and society.* Bristol, PA: Kingsley.

Gestwicki, C. (2004). *Home, school, and community relations* (5th ed.). Clifton Park, NY: Delmar Learning.

Haupt, J. H., & Ostlund, M. F. (1997). Informing parents, administrators, and teachers about developmentally appropriate practices. In C.H. Hart, D.C. Burts, and R. Charlesworth (Eds.), *Integrated curriculum and developmentally appropriate practice: Birth to eight* (pp. 417–447). Albany, NY: SUNY Press.

Huston, A. C. (2005). Connecting the science of child development to public policy. *SRCD Social Policy Report, 19*(4).

Rickel, A. U., & Becker, E. (1997). *Keeping children from harm's way: How national policy affects psychological development.* Washington, DC: American Psychological Association.

Robinson, A., & Stark, D. R. (2002). *Advocates in action: Making a difference for young children.* Washington, DC: National Association for the Education of Young Children.

Shaheen, J. C., & Spence, C. C. (2002). *Take charge: Advocating for your child's education.* Clifton Park, NY: Delmar Learning.

*The State of America's Children* (yearly publication). Children's Defense Fund, 25 E Street, NW, Washington, DC 20001.

## Suggested Activities

1. Read some recent policy reports, such as the Public Policy Report in *Young Children, The Black Child Advocate* (National Black Child Development Institute), or *Social Policy Report* (Society for Research in Child Development). Report to the class on the important current issues in public policy for young children and their families.

2. Using guidelines from materials referred to in the chapter, plan an advocacy action activity designed to change a policy or to inform the public. (See Robinson & Stark, 2002.) Discuss the proposed activity with a group of students in class. Obtain their opinions and suggestions. Consider actually following through on your plan. Possibly some of the other students will join you.

3. Obtain an appointment with one of your local policy makers, such as a school board member, a city council member, the mayor, a state legislator, or a U.S. Congressperson. Interview him or her regarding opinions on child and family issues you have read about in this book or elsewhere that you believe are relevant to your city, state, and nation.

4. Find out which groups in your community are active child advocates. Check with the local affiliates of the following: NAEYC, SECA, Council for Exceptional Children, League of Women Voters, Junior League, Kiwanis International, Head Start Association, Parent-Teachers Association, the YMCA, and the YWCA. Make appointments to interview the presidents/directors of at least three of these groups. Find out what kinds of policy issues they are working on. Report back to the class on the results.

5. Look back through your journal. Note any comments you made that may provide a lead to some policy issue(s) that should be acted upon in your community, state, and/or the nation. Research the issue so you are thoroughly familiar with the pros and cons of the problem. Consider joining or building a coalition to work on the issue.

## REVIEW

1. Explain the role of the child advocate. Why is it necessary for children to have advocates?
2. Select the statements that describe the conditions of public policy for children and families:
   a. Historically, public policy in the United States has supported the child and the family.
   b. Our policies are usually developed after the fact rather than as preventive measures.
   c. Family policy should help parents provide a better life for their children and feel more empowered.
   d. During the 1980s, policy makers tried diligently to overcome the faults described by the Carnegie report.
   e. African American and other minority children and their families have been the victims of public policy guided by race and racism.
   f. So-called compensatory education programs have not considered the racial and cultural factors in the lives of children and families.
   g. There has been a national effort to reduce institutional racism as it influences policy for children and families.
   h. Child development research probably will not offer much help in developing educational policies for African American children.
3. Explain why the 101st Congress is referred to as "The Children's Congress." What did they accomplish for young children and their families?
4. Describe some of the actions that adults who work with young children can take to advocate for young children.
5. Explain strategies for child advocacy.

## KEY TERMS LIST

child advocates
personal advocacy
private sector advocacy
public policy advocacy

Additional resources for this chapter can be found on the Online Companion™ to accompany this text at http://www.earlychilded.delmar.com. Respond to "Time to Reflect" and "Looking Further" concepts, review various child development scenarios, and answer thought-provoking questions in the Critical Thinking Forum. Keep a daily journal by downloading the student journal available on this Web site. Complete the interactive matching exercises to reinforce concepts, and print out the child development assessment forms to use during your observation of development for children from birth to age eight. In addition, read the case studies on the Web site to reinforce the important concepts in each chapter, and take a look at the multitude of Web links that are available for student research on the Internet.

# GLOSSARY

## A

**accessibility**—The degree of availability to the child.

**accommodation**—The means for changing the old concepts to fit a new piece of learning.

**acquired immunodeficiency syndrome (AIDS)**—A communicable disease caused by a virus that attacks the immune system.

**adult-to-child language (ACL)**—A special form of speech that adults use when speaking with children; tends to be slower and more deliberate and tends to contain shorter sentences than adult-to-adult language.

**affective**—The area that centers on the development of social, emotional, and personality characteristics and the self-concept.

**affective development**—The area of development that includes emotions, personality, and social behaviors.

**affective growth**—Centers on the self-concept and the development of social, emotional, and personality characteristics.

**affectivity**—Piaget believed that feelings are closely associated with cognitive development and that these feelings are the fuel that makes intelligence work.

**aggregates**—Two or more diagrams in combination.

**aggressive**—Opposite of prosocial behavior; has the purpose of hurting another.

**Americans with Disabilities Act (ADA)**—"States that people with disabilities are entitled to equal rights in employment, state and local public services, and public accommodations, such as child care and early childhood education programs" (Chandler, 1994).

**amniocentesis**—A method of providing prenatal information by sampling the amniotic fluid.

**amnion**—A sac lining the uterus.

**amniotic fluid**—The liquid that fills the amnion.

**amplification**—The provision of greater challenge within the zone of proximal development.

**anal stage**—Freud's second stage (congruent with the toddler period), when independent toileting is a major concern and goal.

**anger**—See hostility.

**animism**—Giving human characteristics to nonhuman things, such as cars, trees, wind, or the sun.

**anomy**—Unregulated behavior.

**anoxia**—The stage in which the oxygen supply in the blood dips below the safe level.

**antibias approach**—Celebrating diversity, making it part of the total curriculum.

**Apgar scale**—The usual means for monitoring the vital signs of a newborn.

**appropriate and relevant**—a behavior relevant to a goal the child has.

**appropriate assessment procedures**—Authentic evaluation of educational achievement that directly measures actual performance in the subject area.

**artificialism**—The young child's feeling that everything in the world is made for people.

**assertiveness**—To attain one's goals with perseverance but not aggression.

**assimilation**—An incorporation process in which new ideas and concepts are fit into old ideas or concepts.

**assistive technology**—"Any item, piece of equipment, or product system . . . that is used to increase, maintain, or improve the functional capabilities of children with disabilities" (Parette & Murdick, 1998, p. 193).

**at-risk**—Children with special needs.

**attachment**—The relationship of belonging between infant and caregiver.

**attention**—A critical aspect of perception involving ignoring irrelevant information and finding relevant information.

**attention deficit disorder (ADD)**—A condition in which most of the hyperactivity symptoms are present with or without hyperactivity.

**autonomy**—Children will be able to explore and think through problem solutions and construct knowledge independently through their own actions; growth toward independence; regulation of behavior by one's self.

**autonomy versus shame and doubt**—Erikson's second stage, in which the toddler must deal with this crisis.

**axon**—An output fiber that sends information to other neurons.

## B

**baby biographies**—Diary records of interesting things a particular child does each day.

**baby blues**—a normal period of moodiness that occurs postpartum.

**baby talk (BT)**—A simplified form of speech with short, simple sentences and simple vocabulary that is within the child's realm of experience.

**baby tender**—Skinner's environment for optimal conditions for the child.

**balanced approach to reading instruction**—Attempts to blend both phonics and whole language.

**barriers**—Instructional strategies that are not consistent with the principles of child development; inappropriate placement procedures.

**beginning literacy**—Meaningful foundational experiences with books and writing materials.

**behavior modification**—B. F. Skinner's theory of using a combination of verbal and nonverbal actions to help the toddler learn desired behavior and give up undesirable behaviors.

**behavioral geneticists**—Those who are concerned with heredity and environment as a two-way interaction and influence.

**behaviorist theories**—Ideas emphasizing change that originates in the environment through learning.

**belief**—An opinion.

**BICS**—Language used to accomplish basic interpersonal skills; the language used in everyday social activity.

**biculturalism**—Practicing the language and customs of two different social groups.

**bilingual**—Speaking two languages.

**bonding**—The process whereby parent and child determine they are special to each other.

**brachiating**—Developing upper-body strength through the use of overhead equipment.

**brain lateralization**—Development of both left- and right-brain functions and the communication between the two.

**brain research**—Research that looks at how the brain functions.

## C

**CALP**—Cognitive Academic Language Proficiency; the language of academics.

**caring**—A reciprocal relationship that should underlie teaching and learning.

**categorization**—Sorting and grouping items according to similar attributes.

**causality**—Why things happen as they do in the world; "why" questions.

**CD-ROM**—Compact disc software that contains great varieties of information and activities in an easy-to-store format.

**centering**—In cognitive functioning, Piaget refers to the process of being overwhelmed by one aspect.

**cephalocaudal**—Growth and development proceed from head to toe.

**Caesarean section**—Removing the baby from the uterus using a surgical method.

**child advocates**—Adults who work to see that children's rights are protected.

**child care**—An arrangement in a home or center of caring for children while their adult family members are at work, school, etc.

**child science**—The child's gradual acquisition of the knowledge that some constants exist in the world and that there are reasons for these constants.

**children-first language**—Involves mentoring the child before the disability.

**chorionic villus sampling (CVS)**—A method of providing prenatal information by cutting cells from the chorionic villi.

**chromosomes**—The major units that control heredity.

**classical conditioning**—Learning takes place through the association of a stimulus and a response.

**classification**—The ability to classify and categorize items in the environment.

**cognitive**—Pertains to the mind and how it works.

**cognitive development**—Changes in cognitive structure and functioning that may take place over time.

**cognitive developmental approach**—Stresses stages in the development of logical thinking, reasoning, and problem solving as the indicators of the growth of intelligence.

**cognitive functioning**—Describes how the cognitive system works.

**cognitive growth**—Centers on the mind and how the mind works as the child grows and learns.

**cognitive structure**—Includes all the parts of the cognitive system; the content of the child's mind and how it is organized.

**communicative phase**—When children begin to name and label their drawings.

**community in the classroom**—A sense of group belongingness.

**comprehension**—The ability to understand and gain meaning from what has been read.

**conception**—The moment when fertilization takes place.

**concepts**—The building blocks of cognitive structure.

**concrete operational period**—When a child uses language to direct his or her own activities and the activities of others; the child is able to see another's point of view and consider it along with his or her own; the child is no longer as easily fooled by the way things look as he or she was before.

**conscience**—Inner control; an emotional element that includes feelings of guilt and anxiety.

**conservation**—The ability to understand the transformation of materials without being fooled by appearances.

**constructivism**—A belief that learning takes place based on the process of stage change brought about as the child constructs knowledge.

**constructivist**—A believer in the idea that children construct their own knowledge through interaction with the environment.

**context of play**—Interaction with peers that takes place within a play context.

**continuity**—Development is a continuous process that needs to be recognized in planning programs for children as they move from grade to grade.

**conventional reading and writing**—Engaging in what society would agree is "real" reading and writing.

**cooperative learning**— "The process whereby small, heterogeneous groups of students work together to achieve mutual learning goals" (Ajose & Joyner, 1990, p. 198).

**cooperative teaching**—Instructional methods that promote cooperation and positive interactions among students.

**coordinated play**—Play that involves children doing something together.

**cortisol**—A steroid hormone that is released under stress.

**creativity**—An aspect of behavior that reflects originality, experimentation, imagination, and a spirit of exploration.

**Crisis III: Initiative versus Guilt**—A stage in Erikson's theory of development through which children pass between the ages three and six; children deal with the crisis that results from a desire to make their own choices but meet the demands of their developing consciences.

**Crisis IV: Industry versus Inferiority**—A stage in Erikson's theory of development through which children pass during middle childhood and cope with the need to be productive and successful and not be overwhelmed by failure and inferiority.

**critical periods**—The idea that growth in certain areas may be more important at particular times.

**critical theory**—Encourages teachers to examine the power relationships in the classroom.

**cultural diversity**—Refers to differences related to membership in a variety of culture groups.

**cultural stereotyping**—Believing that all members of certain groups have identical beliefs and behaviors.

**cultural style**—The personality of a group.

## D

**deferred imitation**—Toddlers between twelve and eighteen months are able to remember what they have seen and repeat it at a later time.

**dendrites**—Short, hair-like fibers that receive information.

**developmental biodynamics**—Research designed to consider in detail the processes that relate sensory and motor development.

**developmental theories**—Ideas that explain changes in the child due to interaction between growth and learning.

**developmentally and culturally appropriate practice (DCAP)**—An elaboration of DAP that focuses more strongly on cultural appropriateness (Hyun & Marshall, 1997).

**developmentally appropriate practices (DAP)**—Instructional practice that is age, individually, and culturally appropriate as defined by the NAEYC (Bredekamp & Copple, 1997).

**developmentally inappropriate practice (DIP)**—Instructional practice that does not meet the student's developmental levels.

**diagrams**—Characterized by the use of single lines to form crosses and to outline circles, triangles, and other shapes.

**dialect**—A variation of the standard speech of a language.

**differentiation**—The process the child goes through as he or she gains control of specific parts of his or her body.

**difficult child**—A child who has difficulty with routines and does not adapt easily to new experiences.

**digestive fallacy**—Children believe a baby is swallowed, develops in the mother's stomach, and is then eliminated.

**direct engagement**—Direct contact through play, caretaking, and leisure time activities.

**discipline**—The original meaning is "to teach"; today, it means to teach techniques of socially appropriate behavior.

**discrimination**—Perceiving differences.

**dizygotic (DZ) siblings**—Twins who develop from separate eggs fertilized at the same time.

**DNA**—A complex molecule that contains genetic information.

**D'Nealian alphabet**—A slanted manuscript alphabet.

**dramatic play**—Play that centers on the social world and includes characters, dramatic themes, and a story line.

**drawing**—Using a tool to create a picture.

## E

**early intervention**—Formal attempts by agents outside the family to maintain or improve the quality of life for children from the prenatal period to school entrance.

**Early Reading First**—A federally designed reading program for preschoolers.

**easy child**—A child who falls easily into routines, is happy, and adapts well.

**Ebonics**—African American English (USBE), a system of language that is a synthesis of African and European language traditions.

**ecological research model**—Viewing children in all their roles in all the areas of their environment.

**ego**—To Freud, this is characterized by reason and common sense and operates on the reality principle.

**egocentric**—Centers perception on the most obvious and is bound by what is seen.

**embryo**—The second stage of the gestation period; usually lasts from about three to eight weeks.

**emergence of autonomy**—Infants begin to take the lead in interactions with adults.

**emergent diagram shapes**—Controlled scribbles that are drawn in a prescribed space.

**emerging competencies**—Newly developing skills or abilities.

**emotional dependency**—The need for affiliation with others; develops from early bonding and attachment.

**emotional intelligence**—Daniel Goleman's (1999) view of the ability to understand and manage emotions.

**empathy**—A feeling that occurs when individuals put themselves in the other person's position.

**energy balance**—When the body burns as many calories as are taken in.

**English as a Second Language (ESL)**— Specific techniques for teaching English to learners whose primary language is not English.

**English-language classrooms**—Classroom in which English is the language of instruction.

**English Language Learners (ELL)**—Those whose primary language is not English but who are in the process of learning English.

**environmental**—Factors that begin to play a role as soon as conception occurs.

**equilibration**—Brought about through the balance between assimilation and accommodation.

**ethnic socialization**—The developmental processes by which children acquire the behaviors, perceptions, values, and attitudes of an ethnic group, and come to see themselves and others as members of such groups (Rotheram & Phinney, 1990).

**ethological approach**—Considers intelligence as the degree to which the individual is able to cope with and adapt to life.

**examining**—When the child fingers and turns an object while looking at it with an intent expression.

**exercise play**—Gross motor movements within the context of play activity.

**Exosurf®**—A drug that helps babies form surfactant to coat the inner lining of the lungs and keep the airspaces from collapsing.

**exosystem**—A child's interactions and relationships with local government, parents' workplace, mass media, and local industry.

**experimenting reading and writing**—Transitional period; children know the letters of the alphabet and attempt spelling and reading of simple words.

**expressive speakers**—Use a diverse speech that includes a large number of combinations, such as "stop it" and "I want it."

**extinction**—Unlearning; if a behavior is not rewarded, it gradually is no longer used.

**extrinsic rewards**—Concrete and social rewards.

## F

**false beliefs**—Beliefs that do not fit reality.

**family**—Those persons who inhabit the same living area.

**family-centered practice**—Educational plans and practices developed from the family's point of view (versus the professionals').

**father**—The male figure in the child's life, who may be related legally or nonlegally; emerging role as equally responsible as mothers for child care.

**fear**—Develops most likely through a combination of genetic and learned factors and is acquired through conditioning and observational learning.

**fertility**—The ability to contribute successfully to fertilization or conception.

**fertilization**—The joining of sperm and egg.

**fetal alcohol effects (FAE)**—A condition related to FAS where children do not usually have the identifiable physical characteristics, but may be hyperactive as infants.

**fetal alcohol syndrome (FAS)**—A group of child behaviors associated with maternal alcohol intake during the fetal period.

**fetus**—The third stage of the gestation period; usually lasts from nine weeks until birth.

**flexibility**—Seeing a new use for an idea or material that no one else figures out.

**fluency**—The capacity to read text accurately and quickly; with regard to creativity, ideas that are easily developed from previous knowledge.

**follicle**—Fluid-filled sac that houses the ovum.

**fontanels**—The six soft spots on top of the heads of newborns.

**food insecurity**—Difficulty in securing adequate food.

**food security**—Access at all times to enough food.

**formal operations period**—Piaget's fourth period; appears in early adolescence, around eleven or twelve years of age.

**four *Rs***—Factors common to the roles of parent and teacher as reflected in our knowledge of child development: (1) responsiveness, (2) reasoning, (3) rationality, and (4) reading.

**friendships**—Special relationships that develop with other people.

**full inclusion**—All of the services and support needed by children are present and available in the schools the children would normally attend.

**function**—A means by which a child achieves some purpose through the use of language.

**fundamental motor skills**—The foundation for more specialized motor skills that will be learned when the child is older.

**fussing**—Female interchanges.

## G

**gender**—The social and cultural overlay that makes a man "masculine" and a woman "feminine."

**gender equity**—Treating both males and females with fairness.

**gene**—The biological unit of heredity.

**generalization**—The process of finding similarities among things.

**genetic counseling**—Assessment of maternal and paternal genetic makeup and its possible effects on offspring.

**genetics**—The study of the factors involved in the transmission of hereditary characteristics in living organisms.

**genotype**—The set of genes an individual receives at conception that makes him or her unique.

**germ-line gene therapy**—A procedure that doctors can use to alter the genes in women's eggs, men's sperm, or an embryo that is only a few days old.

**gestational period**—The period of pregnancy; usually lasts about nine and a half calendar months.

**gifted person**—A person who exhibits, or has the potential for, a high performance level in at least one area.

**growth**—A series of steps or stages the child goes through on the way to becoming an adult.

**guidance**—Techniques used by adults to teach children socially appropriate behavior.

**guided participation**—A vehicle through which the child learns what needs to be learned to function in a particular culture.

## H

**habituation**—A feature of getting used to something.

**handedness**—Determining right-hand dominance, left-hand dominance, or no preference.

**handwriting**—Using a tool to make letters or letterlike forms.

**hapatic**—Sensing through touch.

**happiness**—The expression of positive emotions, such as pleasure, joy, and delight.

**hereditary**—Factors determined at conception.

**heteronomy**—Regulation of behavior by others.

**hidden curriculum**—Includes what students learn outside of the schools' stated curriculum.

**hierarchy of needs**—To Maslow, a series of levels a person must fulfill to achieve self-actualization.

**high-risk**—Children who are at-risk for school failure and possibly even for survival due to various environmental, mental, physical, and/or emotional problems.

**holophrases**—One-word sentences.

**holophrastic stage**—A stage in language development when the child speaks one-word sentences.

**Home Observation for Measurement of the Environment (HOME)**—A scale used to rate a home environment.

**homelessness**—Having no stable place to call home.

**homeostasis**—The tendency of an organism to maintain internal stability.

**hostility**—Emotion that underlies aggressive behavior.

**HOX gene**—Establishes the head-to-tail axis.

**humor**—Understanding (jokes, riddles, etc.) that requires a higher level of cognitive development than that required as a response to tickling and peek-a-boo games that provoke laughter in infants.

## I

**id**—To Freud, this is present at birth and contains the person's unconscious motives and desires and operates on the pleasure principle.

**IDEA 97**—The Individuals with Disabilities Act Amendments greatly improved educational opportunities for children with disabilities.

**ideals**—The goals of practitioners.

**imitation**—Doing actions one has observed another doing.

**immigrants**—Individuals from one country who settle in another country.

**immunization**—Protect from disease through inoculation.

**inappropriate assessment procedures**—Addresses misuse of readiness test results and the elimination of paper-and-pencil, whole-group achievement testing through third grade.

**inclusion**—The commitment to educate each child, to the maximum extent appropriate, in the school and classroom he or she would otherwise attend; involves bringing the support services to the child and requires only that the child benefit from being in the class.

**individual education plan (IEP)**—A set of objectives that must be written for every special education student.

**individualized family service plan (IFSP)**—A plan with specific objectives that must be developed for all families enrolled in birth to three-year-old special education programs.

**infant**—Child from birth to approximately one year of age.

**information-processing approach**—Emphasizes the process the individual uses to try to solve problems.

**input**—In cognitive functioning, this is the stimulus.

**inside intervention**—Sociodramatic play in which the adult is involved in the play activity.

**integrated movements**—Combining specific movements to perform more complex activities such as walking, climbing, building a block tower, or drawing a picture.

**intelligence**—The ability to benefit from experience, that is, the extent to which a person is able to make use of his or her capacities and opportunities for advancement in life.

**interactionist**—One who views the child as entering the environment with a variety of potential behaviors that may or may not be exhibited depending on the process of development and the opportunities presented in the environment.

**interactionist theory**—States that the sequence and timing of speech development is biologically determined, whereas the specific language the child learns is determined by the environment in which he or she lives.

**Internet**—the worldwide computer connection.

**intervention**—Interceding when a situation seems dangerous or when children need coaching to assist them in solving a problem.

**intrinsic rewards**—The development of a desire within the child to learn through internal motivation.

**IVF (in vitro fertilization)**—Egg and sperm are united in a sterile medium in the laboratory and implanted in the uterus.

## K

**kindergartners**—Children enrolled in kindergarten classrooms; usually between the ages of four-and-a-half and six years.

## L

**language**—A well-ordered system of rules that each adult member of the language community tacitly comprehends in speaking, listening, and writing.

**learned helplessness**—When failure is attributed to external factors rather than lack of effort.

**learning**—Behavior change that results from experience.

**learning activity**—Vygotsky views these leading primary activities as formalized, structured, and culturally determined.

**learning styles**—The methods by which a child acquires knowledge.

**learning theory**—Explains language acquisition through the mechanisms of classical conditioning, operant conditioning, and imitation.

**letter names**—Names of alphabet symbols.

**letter sounds**—Sounds associated with alphabet symbols.

**limit-testing**—Infant and adult test their abilities to communicate and affect the other's behavior.

**literacy**—Knowledge regarding written language.

**literacy beginners**—Children ages birth to three (McGee & Richgels, 1996).

**literate**—Being able to read and write.

**love and affection**—Fondness or caring for another.

**low-birth-weight (LBW) infant**—Victim of poor prenatal nutrition.

## M

**macrosystem**—A child's interactions and relationships with the dominant beliefs and ideologies of the culture.

**manipulation of objects**—Toddlers learn through touching, moving, banging, and turning over objects.

**memory**—The mental capacity of retaining and reviving impressions.

**men**—Becoming more warm and playful in interactions with children.

**mesosystem**—The interactions and relationships between and among the child's home, school, neighborhood, peer groups, and church.

**metacognition**—Refers to knowledge and thinking about cognition.

**methamphetamine, or Meth**—"An addictive stimulant drug that strongly activates certain systems in the brain" (*NIDA InfoFacts: Methamphetamine*, 2005).

**microsystem**—A child's relationship to home, school, neighborhood, peer group, and church.

**misnourished children**—Children who get enough to eat but their diets do not provide proper necessary nutrients.

**monozygotic (MZ) siblings**—Twins who develop from one egg that has divided into two or more parts after fertilization, so the same hereditary characteristics are present in each.

**moral classrooms**—"Classrooms in which the sociomoral atmosphere supports and promotes children's development" (DeVries & Zan, 1994, p. 7).

**moral judgments**—Decisions made regarding solutions to moral dilemmas.

**moral reasoning**—When a person considers his or her values in a problem situation and then judges what should be done in that situation.

**morality**—Ethical behavior; the development of an understanding of right and wrong.

**morphemes**—The smallest meaningful units in a language and strings of sounds that have meaning.

**motor development**—The development of skill in the use of the body and its parts.

**multicultural education**—Teaching with respect to the diversity within our culture.

**myelin**—A white, fatty material that protects Axons.

## N

**NAEYC**—National Association for the Education of Young Children.

**natural childbirth**—Birth without the aid of drugs for pain reduction.

**natural family planning**—A form of contraception; the couple charts ovulation and avoids intercourse during that period.

**nature versus nurture**—The relative influence of heredity and environment in a child's development

**Neonatal Behavior Assessment Scale (NBAS)**—A dynamic assessment of interactive behavior used to indicate the degree of control the newborn has over his or her sensory capacities.

**neonatal period**—The first two weeks of newborn life.

**neonate**—A child from birth to two weeks of age.

**neurons**—Small cells that are the building blocks of the brain.

**newborn**—A child who has just been born.

**No Child Left Behind**—A federal law passed in 2001 whose objective is that every child will be able to read by the end of third grade.

**nonthematic**—The use of open-ended materials and various types of realistic props.

**normal physiologic jaundice**—Slightly yellowish skin color caused by unbalanced liver function.

**normative/maturational view**—A way of looking at development that stresses certain norms.

**norms**—What most children do at a certain age.

**novice reading and writing**—Awareness that print communicates meaning.

**nutrition**—"The science of food and how it is used by the body" (Endres & Rockwell, 1994, p. 1).

## O

**obesity**—Weighing more than is appropriate for one's height.

**object manipulation**—Fingering the surface of, looking at, and transferring the object from hand to hand to explore it.

**object permanence**—The knowledge that objects continue to exist even when one is not seeing, hearing, or feeling them.

**object recognition**—The features the infant uses to identify objects.

**observation**—A means by which children obtain information about social behavior.

**one-to-one correspondence**—The basis of understanding equality.

**operant conditioning**—Behavior is shaped by careful use of reinforcements (rewards) for appropriate behavior and at the same time, inappropriate behavior is ignored so that it is not rewarded with attention.

**operations**—Actions that take place internally as part of the organized cognitive structure.

**originality**—A behavior that reflects a new idea or a new combination of ideas and that has a low probability of happening.

**output**—In cognitive functioning, this is the response.

**outside intervention**—Sociodramatic play in which the adult stays outside of the play but offers questions, suggestions, directions, and clarifications that will help children enhance their dramatic play roles.

**overdiscriminations**—When a child cannot seem to find a place for certain things that do not look the way they are expected to.

**overgeneralizations**—When a child encounters a new thing and places it in his or her mind where there is something like it.

**ovum**—Female egg cell.

## P

**parent education**—Providing information and materials to the parents of children.

**parent involvement**—Various means through which parents collaborate in and support their children's education.

**parental styles**—Parental discipline techniques identifying four styles of parenting: authoritarian, permissive, authoritative, and harmonious.

**pediatrician**—A physician who specializes in the care of children from birth to age twenty-one.

**peer popularity**—Children who gave the most positive reinforcement were likely to be very well liked by their peers.

**peer reinforcement**—A critical role in children's behavior is determined by positive or negative reinforcement given by peers.

**peers**—Those who are the same age and/or developmental level.

**perception**—The ways we know about what goes on outside our bodies.

**perinatologist**—A physician who specializes in the care of women who are at high risk during pregnancy.

**personal advocacy**—Involves sharing our views with others.

**personality traits**—Develop from initial genetic temperament characteristics as children experience their environment.

**Phallic Stage**—Freud stated that children ages three to six are at this stage, in which the child concentrates on sex-role identification and conscience development.

**phenotype**—The individual's external, measurable characteristics that reflect the genotype.

**phonemes**—The smallest units of language; the speech sounds in language.

**phonemic awareness**—The ability to hear and identify individual sounds and spoken words.

**phonics**—Focus on sound–symbol relationships. The relationship between the letters of written and the sounds of spoken language.

**physical activity play**—"A playful context combined with a dimension of physical vigor" (Pellegrini & Smith, 1998, p. 577).

**physical dependency**—Relying on others to care for one's basic needs, such as nourishment, comfort, and elimination.

**physical growth**—Development of the body and its parts.

**PL 94–142**—The Education of All Handicapped Children Act of 1975, which ensures that all children with special needs, ages five to twenty-one, have equal opportunity education.

**PL 99–457**—The Education of the Handicapped Act Amendments; Title I, Programs for Infants and Toddlers with Handicaps; gave states five years to institute a program for serving children with disabilities from ages three through five.

**PL 101–476**—Revision of PL 94–142. IDEA 97 made further improvements.

**placenta**—The covering that protects the developing infant and serves as a medium of exchange for food and oxygen.

**planning**—An important human higher-level cognitive ability that enables us to consider ways to solve problems before actually embarking on a solution and thus cuts down on time lost with trial-and-error approaches.

**plasticity**—Abundance of synapses accounts for why the young child's brain learns new skills quickly.

**play**—Related to everything that children do: cognitive, affective, and psychomotor; the actions and activities through which children construct knowledge.

**portfolio**—An ongoing record of a child that includes information collected by the teacher and the student.

**positive guidance techniques**—Teach children what the expected behaviors are and how to solve their conflicts using words rather than physical force.

**postpartum**—Occurring after birth.

**postpartum depression (PPD)**—Depression occurring shortly after birth.

**postpartum psychosis (PPP)**—Psychosis occurring after the birth of the baby.

**posttraumatic stress disorder**—"Reexperiencing" a violent or stressful event through play.

**pragmatics**—The rules for using language appropriately and to advantage.

**preconcepts**—Partial, immature concepts.

**premature infant**—A child born before the completion of the 40-week gestation period.

**preoperational period**—May last from about the age of two until about seven; a period when the focus of development is language and speech.

**preschoolers**—Three-, four-, and some five-year-olds who have not yet entered elementary school.

**prevention**—Involves making the environment healthy and safe for the child and minimizing the need for excessive restraint, while providing room for exploration.

**primary grades**—Grades one through three.

**primary period**—Children ages six through eight or grades first through third.

**principles**—Guides for conduct that can help solve ethical problems.

**private sector advocacy**—The goal is to improve private sector policies and practices to support children and families.

**private speech**—Self-talk; according to Vygotsky, the centerpiece of language development and use.

**processing**—In cognitive functioning, this is the internal activity.

**prolonging attention**—Maintaining communication and interaction.

**proprioception**—The sense that tells us where the parts of our body are in relation to the whole.

**prosocial behaviors**—Outward manifestations of positive moral development that reflect generosity, nurturance-giving, sympathy, and helping.

**protolanguage**—Meaningful sound combinations that are not words.

**proximodistal**—Growth and development are from the center out.

**psychometric approach**—Stresses the measurement of individual differences, that is, the comparing of one person to others; also stresses acquired knowledge and language skills as those behaviors to be measured in arriving at an estimate of the individual's intelligence.

**public policy advocacy**—The goal is to influence public policies and practices to improve children's lives.

**punishment**—Disciplining children; punishment is a controversial issue.

## R

**RSV**—A viral infection of the airways and lungs.

**random scribble**—The first stage in development of art when young children enjoy exploring the movement of their arms and shoulders and the resulting patterns on the paper.

**readiness**—An end point that is reached during a certain age or stage that enables the child to move on to the next level.

**reciprocity**—Communication exchange in an equal give-and-take manner.

**recommended daily dietary allowances (RDA)**—Minimum amounts of nutrients obtained from the four basic food sources that our bodies need each day.

**referential speakers**—Use mainly nouns with some verbs, proper names, and adjectives.

**reflective learning**—Learning that takes place from the inside out.

**reflexes**—Involuntary movements present at birth. They include eye blink, sucking, swallowing, Moro, Babinski, crawling, rooting, and stepping.

**Reggio Emilia**—An all-day program in an Italian city that combines care, education, and social services free to all three- to six-year-olds, with parents paying a fee for infants and toddlers.

**reinforcements**—Positive consequences that are likely to increase positive behavior; rewards.

**relational aggression**—That part of hostile aggression that includes hostile actions, such as excluding another child from play, threatening children if they don't follow instructions, trying to get others to reject a child who wants to play, etc.

**relationship**—Teachers can provide a nurturing relationship and atmosphere.

**representational thinking**—Piaget's sixth stage when a child begins to think before acting.

**resiliency**—The essential ability to "bounce back" from difficult circumstances.

**respectful engagement**—Moral education based on a cooperative relationship between adult and child; the adult must respect the child's initiatives and reactions.

**responsibility**—Degree of meeting emotional, social, and economic needs.

**rewards**—Positive consequences that are likely to increase positive behavior; reinforcements.

**Rh factor**—A substance found in 85 percent of humans; when present, it is referred to as Rh positive; when absent, Rh negative.

**rhythm**—Being in a mutual exchange mode that promotes communication between adult and child.

**rough-and-tumble play**—Happy activity; not aggressive or hostile; includes play fighting, smiling, and jumping.

**routines**—Formal games, instructional games, and joint book reading.

**running record**—A naturalistic observation done by an outside person that describes what the child did in a factual way and in great detail; also called a specimen record.

## S

**scaffolding**—A process through which an adult supports the child's learning, providing support as the child moves from the current developmental level to a higher level; assistance supplied by an adult or an older child that supports movement through the ZPD.

**schema**—Partial pictures of what an infant actually sees and experiences that include the highlights of what the infant perceives.

**self-concept**—The way a person feels about himself or herself; a person's idea about who he or she is.

**self-esteem**—How a person evaluates his or her self-concept; how much respect the person has for himself or herself.

**self-regulation**—The behavior control needed to be accepted by peers into a play activity and, in a broad sense, the ability to control emotions, interact in positive ways with others, avoid inappropriate or aggressive actions, and become a self-directed learner.

**semantics**—The study of meaning that refers to words used in the correct context and attached to the appropriate referent.

**semen**—Liquid ejaculated from the male's reproductive organs.

**sensorimotor period**—Piaget's first stage of cognitive development, which lasts from birth to age two, in which children learn to use their senses as a means to find out new things.

**sensory integrative dysfunction**—A condition where the senses do not provide accurate or clear messages.

**sensory involvement**—Using all the senses as a bridge from the concrete to the abstract.

**sequential growth**—The set order in which growth proceeds.

**seriation**—Ordering; putting things in order according to some criteria such as size, age, or color.

**sex**—The anatomical and physiological characteristics we call male and female.

**sex differences**—Examined from a variety of aspects to determine which are biologically determined and which are socially determined.

**sex-role standards**—Behaviors that society regards as appropriate for males and females.

**sex-stereotyped**—Treating boys and girls differently based on their sex.

**sex-typing**—Influenced from infancy through old age by environmental factors and experience; these sex labels often influence how adults treat babies.

**sexuality**—"Includes the biological nature of the person, the physical aspects of sex relations, and many other aspects of sex-linked behavior" (Lively & Lively, 1991, p. 21).

**shame**—A feeling of embarrassment that may occur when children feel they have not lived up to certain behavioral standards.

**shaping**—Gradual acquisition of a learned behavior.

**shared activities**—Students working together on a project or discussing a problem solution.

**shows**—Calling attention to something by pointing.

**siblings**—Brothers and sisters.

**slow-to-warm-up child**—A child who is inactive, reacts mildly to environmental stimuli, has a negative mood, and is slow to adjust to new experiences.

**social competence**—A characteristic that grows from and with children's relationships with others.

**social isolates**—Persons who seldom, if ever, interact with peers, or may attempt to interact but are rejected.

**social reciprocity**—The give-and-take of social relationships.

**social referencing**—Infants gain information from others in order to understand and evaluate events and behave in the appropriate manner in a situation.

**sociomoral development**—Development of the moral rules and regulations of society.

**software**—Individual programs installed for use on the computer.

**sonography**—See *ultrasound*.

**spatial concepts**—Concepts that include the following: in, on, over, under, into, together, beside, between, on top, inside, outside, and below.

**specialized movements**—Individual skills developed based on each person's particular needs and interests.

**Specifically Language Impaired (SLI)**— Children whose language competence does not meet age expectations.

**specimen record**—See *running record*.

**sperm**—Male reproductive cell.

**sperm microinjection**—A process through which sperm are injected directly into the ovum.

**states of arousal**—Infant degrees of being awake or asleep.

**strange-situation**—A setting in which the infant is placed in an unfamiliar room and is allowed to explore some toys either with the mother or a stranger present.

**stranger anxiety**—Fear of strangers.

**stress**—"Nonspecific response of the body to any demand that exceeds the person's ability to cope, a person-environment relationship that threatens or taxes personal resources, and a mental state in response to strains or daily hassles" (Honig, 1986, p. 51).

**strong nominals**—Those nouns that refer consistently to at least two referents.

**strong relationals**—Words that are used consistently for potentially reversible relationships.

**structural-innatist theory**—Explains language acquisition as a human being born with a biological need to develop rule systems for language, while reinforcement and imitation give feedback and build vocabulary.

**substages of sensorimotor development**—Six stages that progress from reflexive action to mental problem solving.

**successive approximation**—Gradual learning in discrete steps.

**Sudden Infant Death Syndrome (SIDS)**—Usually occurs at night during sleep.

**superego**—To Freud, this begins to develop around the age of four; the conscience or the part of the personality that holds on to the moral values of society.

**synapses**—The connection of brain cells to each other.

**syntax**—Set of rules that has to do with the way words are placed in sequence to make an acceptable sentence or phrase.

## T

**talk**—The oral aspect of language.

**task analysis**—A procedure through which learning tasks are broken down into smaller steps for children with learning disabilities.

**teacher researcher**—A classroom teacher who does a carefully planned and documented study of action designed to solve a classroom instructional problem or introduce a new teaching practice; often done in collaboration with university personnel.

**teaching styles**—May affect children's behavior; guidance-oriented, authoritarian, and developmentally appropriate practice are examples of various teaching styles.

**telegraphic sentences**—Children between eighteen months and two-and-a-half years begin to put two or three words together in sentences, which, by adult standards, are incomplete.

**temperament**—Distinctive personal characteristics a child is born with that seem to stay with him or her throughout development.

**terrible twos**—A time period when the child's active exploration and striving for independence put heavy demands on adult guidance.

**thalidomide**—A drug taken by pregnant women in the early 1960s for the relief of morning sickness that caused retarded limb development when taken during the embryonic period.

**the whole child**—Viewing children not as isolated individuals, but as persons acting and reacting within a context of family, community, and a larger society; in the development of children, it includes affective, cognitive, and psychomotor development.

**thematic**—The use of set play centers that suggest specific roles to be taken, such as a home center, medical center, or a firefighter center.

**theories**—Ideas designed to show one plan or set of rules that explains, describes, or predicts what happens and what will happen when children grow and learn.

**theory of mind**—The act of thinking about thought.

**theory of multiple intelligences**—Developed by Gardner; views intelligence as being potentially divided into eight types.

**theory of successful intelligence**—The ability of the individual to apply analytic, creative, and practical abilities in society.

**time out**—Involves "a brief social isolation and temporary suspension of usual activity" (Readdick & Chapman, 2000).

**toddlers**—Children from age one to age three.

**transition period**—From five to seven, when the way the child thinks changes from preoperational to concrete operational.

**transitional spellings**—Moving into spelling, children invent their own spellings, usually based on the sounds of letters they are familiar with.

**triarchic instruction**—Teaching through application of analytical, creative, and practical abilities.

**trust**—Confidence that develops with regard to other humans' behavior.

## U

**ultrasound**—A method to gain information by using high-frequency sounds that are turned into electrical impulses.

**umbilical cord**—The cord that connects the developing child to the mother.

## V

**vehicles for play**—Play with motion and interaction, objects, language, and social materials.

**violence**—Exertion of physical force to injure or abuse; destructive force or action; a child's exposure to violence can result in depression, low self-esteem, excessive crying, and worries about dying or being injured.

**vocabulary**—The words students must know to communicate effectively.

## W

**water birth**—The mother is immersed in water and the infant emerges from the liquid environment of the womb into the water.

**Web sites**—Internet sites that offer opportunities for many activities.

**whole-language approach**—This approach places children and their needs at the center of the curriculum; whole language fits the cognitive-developmental or constructivist point of view.

## Y

**young children**—Children from birth through eight years of age.

## Z

**zero tolerance**—Involves suspension and expulsion for nondangerous but unacceptable behavior.

**zone of proximal development (ZPD)**—The distance between actual development and potential development at any particular time.

**zygote**—The cell that is formed by the uniting of the ovum and sperm.

# R·E·F·E·R·E·N·C·E·S


Aboud, F. E. (1987). The development of ethnic self-identification and attitudes. In J. S. Phinney & M. J. Rotheram (Eds.), *Children's ethnic socialization* (pp. 32–55). Newbury Park, CA: Sage. **30**

*About pregnancy/birth: Pregnancy by month*. Retrieved July 20, 2005, from http://pregnancy.about.com. **8**

Ackerman, D. (1990, Mar. 25). The power of touch. *Parade*, 4–5. **11**

*Adaptations for Physical Activities*. (2006). Retrieved January 22, 2006, from http://www.pecentral.org **29**

Aghayan, C., Schellhaas, A., Wayne, A, Burts, D. C., Buchanan, T. K., & Benedict, J. (2005). Project Katrina. *Early Childhood Research and Practice*, 7(2). **25**

Ainsworth, M. D. S., Blehar, M. D., Waters, E., & Wall, S. (1978). *Patterns of attachment*. Hillsdale, NJ: Erlbaum. **13**

Ajose, S. A., & Joyner, V. G. (1990). Cooperative learning: The birth of an effective teaching strategy. *Educational Horizons*, *68*, 197–207.

Alat, K. (2002). Traumatic events and children: How early childhood educators can help. *Childhood Education*, *79*(1), 2–7. **25**

Albrecht, K., & Miller, L. G. (2001). *Infant & toddler development*. Beltsville, MD: Gryphon House. **11**

Alejandro-Wright, M. N. (1985). The child's conception of racial indentification: A socio-cognitive developmental model. In M. B. Spencer, G. K. Brookins, & W. R. Allen (Eds.), *Beginnings: The social and affective development of black children* (pp. 185–200). Mahwah, NJ: Erlbaum. **26**

Alexander, M. (2001). Best-seller, co-authored by Stipek, helps parents encourage children's learning. *Stanford Report*. Retrieved January 15, 2004, from http://www.stanford.edu **6**

Allen, K. E., & Marotz, L. R. (2006). *Developmental profiles: Pre-birth through twelve* (5th ed.). Clifton Park, NY: Delmar Learning. **1, 8, 14, 15, 20, 29, 30, 31**

Allen, K. E., & Schwartz, I. S. (1999). *The exceptional child: Inclusion in early childhood education* (4th ed.). Clifton Park, NY: Delmar Learning. **4, 5**

Allen, K. E., & Schwartz, I. S. (2001). *The exceptional child: Inclusion in early childhood education* (4th ed.). Clifton Park, NY: Delmar Learning. **12**

Alliance for Childhood. (n.d.). *Fool's gold: A critical look at computers in childhood*. Retrieved August 6, 2002, from http://www.allianceforchildhood.net/projects/computers/computer reports.htm **4**

Allington, R. L. (2002). What I've learned about effective reading instruction from a decade of studying exemplary elementary classroom teachers. *Phi Delta Kappan*, *83*(10), 740–747. **31**

Allington, R. L. (2002). *Big brother and the national reading curriculum*. Portsmouth, NH: Heinemann. **22**

Althouse, R., Johnson, M. H., & Mitchell, S. T. (2003). *The colors of learning*. Washington, DC: National Association for the Education of Young Children. **23**

Ambron, S. R. (1978). *Child development* (2nd ed.). New York: Holt, Rinehart, & Winston. **23**

American Academy of Pediatrics. (2002). *Television: How it affects children*. Retrieved July 16, 2005, from http://www.aap.org **7**

American Academy of Pediatrics. (2002). *Television—positive Actions for parents*. Retrieved July 16, 2005, from http://www.aap.org **7**

American Academy of Pediatrics. (2002). *Television—what children see and learn*. Retrieved July 16, 2005, from http://www.aap.org **7**

American Academy of Pediatrics. (2002, August 5). *Water birth—A near-drowning experience*. Retrieved August 17, 2002, from http://www.aap.org/advocacy/release/augwater.htm **11**

American Academy of Pediatrics. (2002, August 1). *State children's health insurance program turns five-years old*. Retrieved August 17, 2002, from http://www.aap.org/advocacy/release/augschip.htm **7**

American College of Obstetricians and Gynecologists (ACOG). (2002). *If your baby is breech*. Retrieved August 9, 2005, from http://acog.com **10**

American College of Obstetricians and Gynecologists (ACOG). (2002, September 1). *Healthy babies born to young girls more likely to die before their first birthday*. Retrieved September 8, 2002, from http://www. acog.com/from_home/publications/press_releases/nr-09-01-02-1.cfm **9**

American College of Obstetricians and Gynecologists (ACOG). (2002, July 31). *Home births double risk of newborn death*. Retrieved September 8, 2002, from http://www.acog.com/from_home/publications/press-releases/nr07-31-02-3.cfm **11**

American College of Obstetricians and Gynecologists (ACOG). (December 12, 2001). *ACOG news release: ACOG addresses latest controversies in obstetrics.* Retrieved August 9, 2005, from http://acog.com **10**

American College of Obstetricians and Gynecologists (ACOG). (August 1, 2005). *ACOG news release: evening deliveries have worse outcomes for newborns.* Retrieved August 9, 2005, from http://acog.com **10**

American Educational Research Association (AERA). (2005). *Ethical Standards.* Retrieved June 17, 2005, from http://www.aera.net **3**

*The AmFAR Report.* (1993, Jan.). [Special Edition.] New York: American Foundation for Aids Research. **8**

Anderson, D. R., Huston, A. C., Schmitt, K. L., Linebarger, D. L., & Wright, J. C. (2001). Early childhood television viewing and adolescent behavior. *Monographs of the Society of Research in Child Development, 66* (1 Serial No. 264). **4**

Annis, L. (1978). *The child before birth.* Ithaca, NY: Cornell University Press. **9**

Apgar, V. A. (1953). A proposal for a new method of evaluation of the newborn infant. *Current Researches in Anesthesia and Analgesia, 32,* 260–267. **11**

Apgar, V. A., & Beck, J. (1973). *Is my baby alright?* New York: Trident Press. **11**

Araujo, L. (2001). Other than English in elementary schools: Fostering communicative competence in a second language. *ACEI Focus on Elementary, 13*(3), 1–3. **31**

Armstrong, M. B. (1997). Total communication in early care, education and intervention: An augmentative and alternative communication (AAC) strategy. *Focus on Infants and Toddlers, 10*(2), 1–4. **14**

Arnold, M. S. (1995). Exploding the myths: African American families at promise. In B. B. Swadener & S. Lubeck (Eds.), *Children and families "at promise"* (pp. 143–162). Albany, NY: SUNY Press. **6**

Aronson, S. S. (1983). Injuries in child care. *Young Children, 38*(6), 19–20. **7**

Aronson, S. S. (Ed.). (2002). *Healthy young children.* Washington, DC: National Association for the Education of Young Children. **18**

ASHA (American Speech, Language, and Hearing Association). (2002). *Language and literacy development.* Retrieved October 6, 2002, from http://www.asha.org/speech/development/lang_lit.cfm **24**

Asquith, P., & French, L. (1989, April). *Talking while playing: Fantasy in the kitchen.* Paper presented at the meeting of the American Educational Research Association, Kansas City, MO. **21**

Axelrod, J., Goldstein, J., LaGrange, R., Lever, N., & Burke, R. W. (2002). Students navigating school-based transitions: Practical strategies for teachers. *ACEI Focus on Elementary, 15*(1), 1–7. **31**

Ayman-Nolley, S. (1988). Piaget and Vygotsky on creativity. *The Quarterly Newsletter of the Laboratory of Comparative Human Cognition, 10,* 107–111. **23**

Bagdi, A. (2004). Too young to be stressed. *Childhood Education, 80*(4), 202–205. **25**

Baker, K. (1998). Structured English immersion: Breakthrough in teaching Limited-English-Proficient students. *Phi Delta Kappan, 80,* 199–204. **24**

Balbernie, R. (2004). An infant mental health service for Sure Start programs: A British colleague's chronicle. *Zero to Three, 24*(6), 54–59. **12**

Baldwin, D. A., & Markman, E. M. (1989). Establishing word-object relations: A first step. *Child Development, 60,* 381–398. **14**

Banks, J. A. (1993). Multicultural education: Development, dimensions, and challenges. *Phi Delta Kappan, 75,* 22–28. **33**

Banks, J. A., Cookson, P., Gay, G., Hawley, W. D., Irvine, J. J., Nieto, S., Schofield, J. W., & Stephan, W. G. (2001). Multicultural education. *Phi Delta Kappan, 83,* 196–203. **5**

Barbour, A. C. (1996). Physical competence and peer relations in 2nd-graders: Qualitative case studies from recess play. *Journal of Research in Childhood Education, 11*(1), 35–46. **30**

Barbour, N. H., & Seefeldt, C. (1999). *Developmental continuity across preschool and primary grades: Implications for teachers.* Association for Childhood Education International. **28**

Bardige, B., & Segal, M. (2004). Conversations in child care. *Zero to Three, 25*(1), 16–22. **14, 17**

Barnett, D., Kidwell, S. L., & Leung, K. H. (1998). Parenting and preschooler attachment among low-income urban African American families. *Child Development, 69,* 1657–1671. **25**

Baroody, A. J. (2000). Research in review: Does mathematics instruction for three- to five-year-olds really make sense? *Young Children, 55*(4), 61–67. **19**

Barry, D. (2003, July 20). It's a doll world, after all. *Ogden Utah Standard-Examiner,* D1. **1**

Barry, L. M., & Singer, G. H. S. (2001). Reducing maternal psychological distress after the NICU experience through journal writing. *Journal of Early Intervention, 24*(4), 287–297. **11**

Bartgis, J., Lilly, A. R., & Thomas, D. G. (2003, July). Event related potential and behavioral measures of attention in 5-, 7-, and 9-year olds. *Journal of General Psychology.* Retrieved December 6, 2005, from http://www.findarticles.com **20**

Bartlett, E. J. (1981). Selecting an early childhood language curriculum. In C. B. Bazden (Ed.), *Language in early childhood education* (Rev. Ed.) (pp. 83–96). Washington, DC: National Association for the Education of Young Children. **20**

Baumrind, D. (1975). *Early socialization and the discipline controversy.* Morristown, NJ: Programs Modular Series. **28**

Baumrind, D. (1978). Note: Harmonious parents and their preschool children. In J. K. Gardner (Ed.), *Readings in developmental psychology* (pp. 140–144). Boston: Little, Brown. (Originally published in *Developmental Psychology,* 1971, *4,* 99–102.) **28**

Baumrind, D. (1993). The average acceptable environment is not good enough. A response to Scarr. *Child Development, 64*, 1299–1317. **9**

Bayles, F. (1993, August 1). Teen-age homicides become deadly epidemic. *Baton Rouge Morning Advocate*, 1A, 8A. **27**

Beal, C. R., & Belgrad, S. L. (1990). The development of message evaluation skills in young children. *Child Development, 61*, 705–712. **21**

Beardslee, W. R., & Mack, J. E. (1986, Winter). Youth and children and the nuclear threat. *Newsletter of the Society for Research in Child Development*, 1–2. **25**

Bearer, C. F. (1995). Environmental health hazards: How children are different from adults. *Future of Children: Critical Issues for Children and Youths, 5*(2), 11–26. **7**

Beckoff, A. G., & Bender, W. N. (1989). Programming for mainstream kindergarten success in preschool: Teachers' perceptions of necessary prerequisite skills. *Journal of Early Intervention, 13*, 269–280. **5**

Behnke, A. (2004). Latino dads: Structural inequalities and personal strengths. *NCFR Reports: Family Focus, 49*(3), F6–F7. **13**

Behrend, D. A., Rosengran, K. S., & Perlmutter, M. (1989, Apr.). *Parental scaffolding and private speech: Relations between two sources of regulation.* Paper presented at the meeting of the Society for Research in Child Development, Kansas City, MO. **24**

Bellis, M. (1999). Look before you loop. *Young Children, 54*(3), 70–73. **31**

Benedict, J. (1994). *A comparative study of the oral language of students in basal-based and whole language kindergartens.* Unpublished doctoral dissertation, Louisiana State University, Baton Rouge, LA. **21**

Bentzen, W. R. (2004). *Seeing young children: A guide to observing and recording behavior* (4th ed.). Clifton Park, NY: Delmar Learning. **3**

Bergen, D., & Coscia, J. (2000). *Brain research and early childhood education.* Olney, MD: Association for Childhood Education International. **5**

Berk, L. E. (1985). Why children talk to themselves. *Young Children, 40*(5), 46–52. **21**

Berk, L. E. (1998). *Development through the lifespan.* Boston: Allyn & Bacon. **8, 9, 11, 13, 20**

Berk, L. E. (2006). *Child development* (7th ed). Boston: Allyn & Bacon. **8, 11, 16**

Berk, L. E., & Winsler, A. (1995). *Scaffolding children's learning: Vygotsky and early childhood education.* Washington, DC: National Association for the Education of Young Children. **2, 12, 15, 16, 17, 20, 21, 24, 31**

Berk, L. E. (2005). *Infants and children* (5th ed.). Boston: Allyn & Bacon. **29**

Berkowitz, M. W., & Grych, J. H. (1998). Fostering goodness: Teaching parents to facilitate children's moral development. *Journal of Moral Education, 27*(3), 371–391. Retrieved May 28, 2006, from http://parenthood.library.wisc.edu. **26, 30**

Berliner, D. (1990). Play is the work of childhood. *Instructor*, March, 22–23. **5**

Bernat, V. (1993). Teaching peace. *Young Children, 48*(3), 36–39. **25**

Berndt, T. J. (1983). Social cognition, social behavior, and children's friendships. In E. T. Higgins, D. N. Ruble, & W. W. Hartup (Eds.), *Social cognition and social development* (pp. 158–189). New York: Cambridge University Press. **26**

Bernstein, A. C. (1976). How children learn about sex and birth. *Psychology Today, 9*, 31–35+. **25**

Bernstein, B. (1972). A critique of the concept of compensatory education. In C. B. Cazden, V. P. John, & D. Hymes (Eds.), *Functions of language in the classroom* (pp. 135–151). New York: Teachers College Press. **20**

Bers, M. U., New, R. S., & Boudreau, L. (2004). Teaching and learning when no one is expert: Children and parents explore technology. *Early Childhood Research and Practice, 6*(2). **7**

Bhavnagri, N. P., & Gonzalez-Mena, J. (1997). The cultural context of infant caregiving. *Childhood Education, 74*(1), 2–8. **12**

Bigler, R. S., & Liben, L. S. (1993). A cognitive-developmental approach to racial stereotyping and reconstructive memory in Euro-American children. *Child Development, 64*, 1507–1518. **25**

Birch, L. L., Marlin, D. W., & Rotter, J. (1984). Eating as the "means" activity in a contingency: Effects on young children's food preferences. *Child Development, 55*, 431–439. **15**

Birckmayer, J., Cohen, J., Jensen, I. D., & Variano, D. A. (2005). Kyle lives with his granny—where are his mommy and daddy? Supporting grandparents who raise grandchildren. *Young Children, 60*(3), 100–109. **32**

Bissex, G. L. (1985). Watching young writers. In A. Jaggar & M. T. Smith-Burke (Eds.), *Observing the language learner* (pp. 99–114). Newark, DE: International Reading Association. **24**

Bivens, J. A., & Berk, L. E. (1989, April). *A longitudinal study of the development of elementary school children's private speech.* Paper presented at the meeting of the Society for Research in Child Development, Kansas City, MO. **31**

Black, B. (1989, March). *Negotiation in social pretend play: Strategy use as a function of social status.* Presentation at the meeting of the American Educational Research Association, San Francisco, CA. **26**

Blaise, M. (2005). A feminist poststructuralist study of children "doing" gender in an urban kindergarten classroom. *Early Childhood Research Quarterly, 20*(1) 85–108. **25**

Blake, I. K. (1994). Language development and socialization in young African-American children. In P. M. Greenfield & R. R. Cocking (Eds.), *Cross-cultural roots of minority child development* (pp. 167–195). Mahwah, NJ: Erlbaum. **24**

Blaska, J. K., & Lynch, E. C. (1998). Is everyone included? Using children's literature to facilitate the understanding of disabilities. *Young Children, 53*(2), 36–38. **30**

Bloch, M. N., Tabachnick, B. R., & Espinosa-Dulanto, M. (1994). Teacher perspectives on the strengths and achievements of young children: Relationship to ethnicity, language, gender, and class. In B. L. Mallory & R. S. New (Eds.), *Diversity and developmentally appropriate practices* (pp. 223–249). New York: Teachers College Press. **6**

Blok, H., Oostdam, R., Otter, M. E., & Overmaat, M. (2002). Computer-assisted instruction in support of beginning reading instruction: A review. *Review of Educational Research, 72*(1), 101–130. **31**

Bloom, L., Lightbown, P., & Hood, L. (1975). Structure and variation in child language. *Monographs of the Society for Research in Child Development, 40* (2, Serial No. 160). **21**

Bloom, P. J. (2005). Dedication doesn't have to mean deadication. *Exchange*, no. 164, 74–76. **6**

Bodrova, E., & Leong, D. J. (1996). *Tools of the mind: The Vygotskian approach to early childhood education.* Upper Saddle River, NJ: Merrill/Prentice Hall. **2, 4, 5, 6, 11, 17, 19, 24, 31**

Bodrova, E., Leong, D. J., Hensen, R., & Henninger, M. (2000). Imaginative, child-directed play: Leading the way in development and learning. *Dimensions, 28*(4), 25–30. **6**

Bodrova, E., & Leong, D. J. (2003a). Learning and development of preschool children from the Vygotskian perspective. In A. Kozulin, B. Gindis, V. S. Ageyev, & S. M. Miller (Eds.), *Vygotsky's educational theory in cultural context* (pp. 156–176). New York: Cambridge University Press. **4, 5**

Bodrova, E., & Leong, D. J. (2003b). Chopsticks and counting chips: Do play and foundational skills need to compete for the teachers' attention in an early childhood classroom? *Young Childen, 58*(3), 10–17. **5**

Bodrova, E., & Leong, D. J. (2004/05). The importance of being playful. In K. M. Paciorek & J. H. Munro. (Eds.), *Annual editions: Early childhood education 04/05* (pp. 86–87). Dubuque, IA: McGraw-Hill/Dushkin. **5**

Boeree, C. G. (2004, Revised). *Abraham Maslow.* Retrieved August 13, 2005, from http://www.ship.edu. **11**

Bomba, A. K., & Knight, K. B. (1993). Family style dining in the child care center: Yes, it can work! *Day Care and Early Education, 21*(1), 4–5. **15**

Booth, C. L., & Kelly, J. F. (2002). Child care affects on the development of toddlers with special needs. *Early Childhood Research Quarterly, 17*(2), 171–196. **15**

Bornstein, M. H., Haynes, O. M., O'Reilly, A. W., & Painter, K. M. (1996). Solitary and collaborative pretense play in early childhood: Sources of individual variation in the development of representational competence. *Child Development, 67*, 2910–2929. **17**

Bornstein, M. H., Tamis-LeMonde, C. S., Tal, J., Ludemann, L., Toda, S., Rahn, C. W., Pecheux, M., Azuma, H., & Vardi, D. (1992). Maternal responsiveness to infants in three societies: The United States, France, and Japan. *Child Development, 63*, 808–821. **12**

Boutte, G. (2000). Multiculturalism: Moral and educational implications. *Dimensions, 28*(3), 9–16. **6**

Bowe, F. G. (2000). *Birth to five: Early childhood special education.* Clifton Park, NY: Delmar Learning. **7, 8**

Bower, T. G. R. (1977). *The perceptual world of the child.* Cambridge, MA: Harvard University Press. **12**

Bowman, B. T., & Stott, F. M. (1989). Self-reflection as an element of professionalism. *Teachers College Record, 90*(3), 444–451. **28**

Bowman, B. T., & Stott, F. M. (1994). Understanding development in a cultural context: The challenge for teachers. In B. L. Mallory & R. S. New (Eds.), *Diversity and developmentally appropriate practices* (pp. 119–133). New York: Teachers College Press. **12, 32**

Bowman, B. (Ed.). (2002). Love to read. *Essays in developing and enhancing early literacy skills of African American children.* Washington, DC: National Black Child Development Institute, Inc. **22**

Boyatzis, C. J. (1997). Of Power Rangers and V-Chips. *Young Children, 52*(7), 74–79. **25**

Boyer, E. L. (1993). Ready to learn: A mandate for the nation. *Young Children, 48*(3), 54–57. **28**

Bracey, G. W. (1994). Research: More on the importance of preschool. *Phi Delta Kappan, 75*, 416–417. **23**

Bracey, G. W., & Stellar, A. (2003). Long-term studies of preschool: Lasting benefits far outweigh costs. *Phi Delta Kappan, 84*(10), 780–783, 797. **23**

Bradbard, M., & Endsley, R. (1980). Educating parents to be discriminating day care consumers. In S. J. Kilmer (Ed.), *Advances in early education and day care* (Vol. 1) (pp. 187–201). Greenwich, CT: JAI Press. **32**

Bradley, R. H., & Caldwell, B. M. (1984). The relation of infants' home environments to achievement test performance in first grade: A follow-up study. *Child Development, 55*, 803–809. **12, 13**

Bradley, R. H., Corwyn, R. F., Burchinal, M., McAdoo, H. P., & Coll, C. G. (2001). The home environments of children in the United States Part II: Relations with behavioral development through age thirteen. *Child Development, 72*(6), 1868–1886. **6**

Braine, M. D. S. (1976). Children's first word combinations. *Monographs of the Society for Research in Child Development, 41* (1, Serial No. 164). **21**

*BrainWonders.* (2001). Retrieved September 4, 2005, from http://www.zerotothree.org **13, 16, 31**

*BrainWonders.* (2002). Retrieved September 22, 2002, from http://www.zerotothree.org/brainwonders **17**

*BrainWonders.* (2006). *Brain development: Frequently asked questions.* Retrieved May 25, 2006 from http://www.zerotothree.org **20**

Brazelton, T. B. (1977). From dependence to independence: The toddler comes of age. In *Readings in Early Childhood Education 77/78.* Guilford, CT: Dushkin. **11, 13, 15**

Brazelton, T. B. (1977, November). *Why must we think about a passive model for infancy?* Keynote address presented at the annual meeting of the National Association for the Education of Young Children, Dallas, TX. **13**

Brazelton, T. B. (1978). Early parent-infant reciprocity. In J. K. Gardner (Ed.), *Readings in developmental psychology* (pp. 71–78). Boston: Little, Brown. Reprinted from V. C. Vaughn & T. B. Brazelton (Eds.) (1976). *The family—Can it be saved?* Chicago: Year Book Medical Publishers. **13**

Brazelton, T. B. (1982). Behavioral competence of the newborn infant. In J. K. Gardner (Ed.), *Readings in developmental psychology* (2nd ed.) (pp. 7990). Boston: Little, Brown. **13**

Brazelton, T. B. (1990). Saving the bathwater. *Child Development, 61*, 1661–1671. **11, 13**

Brazelton, T. B. (1991, Feb. 25). What parents need to say. *Newsweek, 117*(8), 52. **25**

Brazelton, T. B. (1992). *Touchpoints: The essential reference.* Reading, MA: Addison-Wesley. **9, 11**

Brazelton, T. B., & Cramer, B. G. (1990). *The earliest relationship: Parents, infants, and the drama of early attachment.* Reading, MA: Addison-Wesley. **13**

Bredekamp, S. (Ed.) (1987). *Developmentally appropriate practice in early childhood programs serving children from birth through age eight.* Washington, DC: National Association for the Education of Young Children. **25**

Bredekamp, S. (1990). Extra-year programs: A response to Brewer and Uphoff. *Young Children, 45*(6), 20–21. **28**

Bredekamp, S. (1993). Reflections on Reggio Emilia. *Young Children, 49*(1), 1317. **32**

Bredekamp, S. (1997). Developmentally appropriate practice: The early childhood teacher as decisionmaker. In S. Bredekamp & C. Copple (Eds.), *Developmentally appropriate practice in early childhood programs* (Rev. Ed.) (pp. 33–54). Washington, DC: National Association for the Education of Young Children. **28**

Bredekamp, S., & Copple, C. (Eds.). (1997). *Developmentally appropriate practice in early childhood programs* (Rev. Ed.). Washington, DC: National Association for the Education of Young Children. **1, 2, II Introduction, 4, 5, 7, 11, 26, 27, 28, 30, 31**

Bretherton, I., & Waters, E. (Eds.) (1985). *Growing points of attachment theory and research. Monographs of the Society for Research in Child Development, 50*, 1–2. **13**

Brett, A. (1994). Online for new learning opportunities. *Dimensions of Early* Childhood Education, 22(3), 10–13. **5**

Brewer, J. (1990). Transitional programs: Boom or bane? *Young Children, 45*(6), 15–18. **28**

Brickman, S. (1998, Winter). Taking a look at a High/Scope elementary program. *High/Scope Resource*, 1, 4–5. **28**

Brinker, R. P., Baxer, A., & Butler, L. S. (1994). An ordinal pattern analysis of four hypotheses describing the interactions between drug-addicted, chronically disadvantaged, and middle-class mother-infant dyads. *Child Development, 65*, 361–372. **13**

Bronfenbrenner, U. (1979). *The ecology of human development.* Cambridge, MA: Harvard University Press. **3**

Bronfenbrenner, U. (1989, April). *The developing ecology of human development: Paradigm lost or paradigm regained.* Presentation at the biennial meeting of the Society for Research in Child Development, Kansas City, MO. **3**

Bronfenbrenner, U. (1992). Ecological systems theory. In R. Vasta (Ed.), *Six theories of child development* (pp. 187–250). London and Philadelphia: Jessica Kingsley. **3**

Bronson, M. B. (2000). Research review: Recognizing and supporting the development of self-regulation in young children. *Young Children, 55*(2), 32–37. **15, 26**

Brookins, G. K. (1985). Black children's sex-role ideologies and occupational choices in families of employed mothers. In M. B. Spencer, G. K. Brookins, & W. R. Allen (Eds.), *Beginnings: The social and affective development of black children* (pp. 257–272). Mahwah, NJ: Erlbaum. **26**

Brooks-Gunn, J., Han, W., & Waldfogel, J. (2002). Maternal employment and child cognitive outcomes in the first three years of life: The NICHD study of early child care. *Child Development, 73*(4), 1052–1072. **12**

Brooks-Gunn, J., Klebanov, P. K., & Duncan, G. J. (1996). Ethnic differences in children's intelligence test scores: Role of economic deprivation, home environment, and maternal characteristics. *Child Development, 67*, 396–408. **23**

Brophy, J. (1996). *Working with shy or withdrawn children.* Retrieved February, 5, 2006, from http://www.kidsource.com **30**

Brown, N. S., Curry, N. E., & Tittnich, E. (1971). How groups of children deal with common stress through play. In *Play: The child strives toward self-realization* (pp. 26–28). Washington, DC: National Association for the Education of Young Children. **4**

Brown, T. (1988). Why Vygotsky? The role of social interaction in constructing knowledge. *The Quarterly Newsletter of the Laboratory of Comparative Human Cognition, 10*, 111–117. **20**

Brownell, C. A. (1990). Peer social skills in toddlers: Competencies and constraints illustrated by same-age and mixed-age interaction. *Child Development, 61*, 838–848. **16**

Brownell, C. A., & Carriger, M. S. (1990). Changes in cooperation and self-other differentiation during the second year. *Child Development, 61*, 1164–1174. **16**

Bruder, M. B., & Dunst, C. J. (1999/2000). Expanding learning opportunities for infants and toddlers in natural environments: A chance to reconceptualize early intervention. *Zero to Three, 20*(3), 34–40. **12**

Buchanan, T., Burts, D., Bidner, J., White, V. F., & Charlesworth, R. (1998). Predictors of the developmental appropriateness of the beliefs and practices of first, second, and third grade teachers. *Early Childhood Research Quarterly, 13*, 459–484. **31**

Buckleitner, W., & Kalinowski, M. (2005). Trends in software for children under six. *Exchange*, no. 161, 66–70. **6**

Bullock, B. M., & Forgatch, M. (2003). Parenting together after divorce: Navigating the winds of change. *Zero to Three, 23*(3), 38–43. **11**

Bullock, J. (1993). Supporting the development of shy children. *Day Care and Early Education, 20*(4), 8–10. **26**

Bullock, J. R. (1990). Child-initiated activity: Its importance to early childhood education. *Day Care and Early Education, 18*(2), 14–16. **4**

Bullock, M., & Lutkenhaus, P. (1988). The development of volitional behavior in the toddler years. *Child Development, 59*, 664–674. **15**

Burchinal, M., Lee, M., & Ramey, C. (1989). Type of day-care and preschool intellectual development in disadvantaged children. *Child Development, 60*, 128–137. **6**

Burgess, B. J. (1978). Native American learning styles. In L. Morris (Ed.), *Extracting learning styles from social/cultural diversity* (pp. 41–53). Southwest Teacher Corps Network, Austin, TX. **25**

Burke, R. W. (2002). Report from the seventh national conference on advancing school-based mental health programs. *ACEI Focus on Elementary, 15*(2), 1–6. **30**

Burke, R. (2005). The integration of teacher education and expanded school mental health. *Focus on Elementary, 17*(3), 1, 4, 7. **29**

Burke, R. W., & Myers, B. K. (2002). Our crisis in children's mental health: Frameworks for understanding and action. *Childhood Education, 78*(5), 258–260. **18**

Burris, L. (1997). Safety in the cybervillage: Some internet guidelines for teachers. *ACEI Focus on Elementary: Ages 710, 10*(2). **31**

Burton, A. W. (1992). The development of motor skills. *Early Report, 19*(2), 3–4. **8**

Burts, D. C., Campbell, J., Hart, C. H., & Charlesworth, R., DeWolf, M., and Fleege, P. O. (1991, April). *Comparison of principals' beliefs and kindergarten teachers' beliefs and practices.* Paper presented at the American Educational Research Association, Chicago, IL. **28, 32**

Burts, D. C., Charlesworth, R., & Fleege, P. O. (1991, April). *Achievement of kindergartners in developmentally appropriate and developmentally inappropriate classrooms.* Presentation at the Society for Research in Child Development, Seattle, WA. **28**

Burts, D. C., Hart, C. H., Charlesworth, R., DeWolf, D. M., Ray, J., Manuel, K., & Fleege, P. O. (1993, Fall/Winter). Developmental appropriateness of kindergarten programs and academic outcomes in first grade. *Journal of Research in Childhood Education, 8*(1), 23–31. **31**

Burts, D. C., Hart, C. H., Charlesworth, R., Fleege, P. O., Mosley, J., & Thomasson, R. H. (1992). Observed activities and stress behaviors of children in developmentally appropriate and inappropriate kindergarten classrooms. *Early Childhood Research Quarterly, 7*, 297–318. **18, 25, 31**

Burts, D. C., Hart, C. H., Charlesworth, R., & Kirk, L. (1990). A comparison of the frequencies of stress behaviors observed in kindergarten children in classrooms with developmentally appropriate vs. developmentally inappropriate instructional practices. *Early Childhood Research Quarterly, 5*(3), 407–423. **8, 25, 31**

Buschman, L. (2002). Becoming a problem solver. *Teaching Children Mathematics, 9*(2), 98–103. **31**

Bushell, D., Jr. (1982). The behavior analysis model for early education. In B. Spodek (Ed.), *Handbook of research in early childhood education* (pp. 156–184). New York: The Free Press. **5**

Bushnell, E. W., & Boudreau, J. P. (1993). Motor development and the mind: The potential role of motor abilities as a determinant of aspects of perceptual development. *Child Development, 64*, 1005–1021. **8**

Buss, K. A., & Kiel, E. J. (2004). Comparison of sadness, anger, and fear facial expressions when toddlers look at their mothers. *Child Development, 75*(6), 1761–1773. **16**

Buzzelli, C. A. (1992). Research in review. Young children's moral understanding: Learning about right and wrong. *Young Children, 47*(6), 47–53. **26**

Cadiz, S. M. (1994). Food for thought: Striving for mental health in the early childhood center setting. *Young Children, 49*(3), 84–86. **25**

Cain, B., & Boher, C. (1997). Battling Jurassic Park: From fascination with violence toward constructive knowledge. *Young Children, 52*(7), 71–73. **25**

Caldwell, B. M. (1978). Bridging the chasm between kindergarten and primary. In *Readings in early childhood education, 77/78.* Guilford, CT: Dushkin Publishing Group. **28**

Cameron, J., & Pierce, W. D. (1994). Reinforcement, reward, and intrinsic motivation: A meta-analysis. *Review of Educational Research, 64*, 363–424. **5**

Campbell, E. N., & Foster, J. E. (1993). Play centers that encourage literacy development. *Day Care and Early Education, 21*(2), 22–26. **4**

Campbell, F. A., & Ramey, C. T. (1994). Effects of early intervention on intellectual and academic achievement: A follow-up study of children from low-income families. *Child Development, 65*, 684–698. **23**

Campbell, K. C., & Arnold, F. D. (1988). Stimulating thinking and communicating skills. *Dimensions, 16*(2), 11– 13. **5**

Campbell, S. B., Pierce, E. W., March, C. L., Ewing, L. J., & Szumowski, E. K. (1994). Hard-to-manage preschool boys: Symptomatic behavior across contexts and time. *Child Development, 65*, 836–851. **26**

Campbell, S. B. (2005). Understanding common problem behaviors in young children. *OCD Developments, 19*(2), 5–8. **27, 28**

Campos, J. J., Frankel, C. B., & Camras, L. (2004). On the nature of emotion regulation. *Child Development, 75*(2), 377–394. **13, 16**

Cannella, G. S. (1993). Learning through social interaction: Shared cognitive experience, negotiation strategies, and joint concept construction for young children. *Early Childhood Research Quarterly, 8*, 427–444. **4**

Cardinal, D. N., & Shum, K. (1993). A descriptive analysis of family-related services in the neonatal intensive care unit. *Journal of Early Intervention, 17*, 270–282. **11**

Carll, B. & Richard, N. (no date). *One piece of the puzzle: A practical guide for schools interested in implementing a school readiness program.* Lumberville, PA: Modern Learning Press. **8**

Carlson, F. M. (2005). Significance of touch in young children's lives. *Young Children, 60*(4), 79–85. **10**

Carlson, V. J., Feng, X., & Harwood, R. L. (2004). The "Ideal Baby": A look at the intersection of temperament and culture. *Zero to Three, 24*(4), 22–28. **13**

Carlson, K., & Cunningham, J. L. (1990). Effect of pencil diameter on the graphomotor skill of preschoolers. *Early Childhood Research Quarterly, 5*, 279–293. **8**

Carlton, M. P., & Winsler, A. (1998). Fostering intrinsic motivation in early childhood classrooms. *Early Childhood Education Journal, 25*, 159–166. **5**

Carpenter, M., Nagell, K., & Tomasello, M. (1998). Social cognition, joint attention, and communicative competence from 9 to 15 months of age. *Monographs of the Society for Research in Child Development, 63* (4, Serial No. 255). **14**

Carr, K. S. (1988). How can we teach critical thinking? *Childhood Education, 65*(2), 69–73. **5**

Carroll, J. J., & Steward, M. S. (1984). The role of cognitive development in children's understandings of their own feelings. *Child Development, 55*, 1426–1492. **25**

Carta, J. J., Atwater, J. B., & Schwartz, I. S. (1991, Apr.). *The effects of classroom survival skills intervention on young children with disabilities: Results of a two year follow-up.* Presented at the meeting of the Society for Research in Child Development, Seattle, WA. **5**

Caruso, D. A. (1988). Play and learning in infancy: Research and implications. *Young Children, 43*(6), 63–70. **14**

Casanova, U. (1990). Helping kids learn how to learn: Casanova on practice. *Instructor, 99*(5), 16–17. **18**

Cassidy, D. J. (1989). Questioning the young child: Process and functioning. *Childhood Education, 65*, 146–149. **5**

Castle, K. (1990). Children's invented games. *Childhood Education, 67*, 82–85. **30**

Castle, K., & Rogers, K. (1993/94). Rule-creating in a constructivist classroom community. *Childhood Education, 70*, 77–80. **28**

Caterino, M., Polak, E. (1999). Effects of two types of activity on the performance of second, third, and fourth grade students on a test of concentration. *Perceptual and Motor Skills, 89*, 245–248. Retrieved January 22, 2006, from http://www.pecentral.org **29**

Catherwood, D. (1993). The robustness of infant haptic memory: Testing its capacity to withstand delay and haptic interference. *Child Development, 64*, 702–710. **14**

Caughy, M. O., DiPietro, J. A., & Strobino, D. M. (1994). Daycare participation as a protective factor in the cognitive development of low-income children. *Child Development, 65*, 457–471. **6**

Caulfield, R. (1994). Infants' sensory abilities: Caregiving implications and recommendations. *Day Care and Early Education, 21*(4), 31–35. **12**

Cawfield, M. E. (1992). Velcro time: The language connection. *Young Children, 47*(4), 26–30. **17**

Cazden, C. B. (1990, Nov.). *Cultural capital in the preschool: Teacher education for language and literacy.* Presentation at the annual meeting of the National Association of Early Childhood Teacher Educators, Washington, DC. **24**

Cazden, C. B., Baratz, J. C., Labov, W., & Palmer, F. H. (1981). Language development in day care programs. In C. B. Cazden (Ed.), *Language development in early childhood education* (Rev. Ed.) (pp. 107–125). Washington, DC: National Association for the Education of Young Children. **21**

Celebrating Head Start's 25th Anniversary. (1990). Special section. *Young Children, 45*(6). **6**

Chafel, J. A. (1997), Schooling, the hidden curriculum, and children's conceptions of poverty. *SRCD Social Policy Report, XI*(1), 1–18. **28**

Chandler, P. A. (1994). *A place for me: Including children with special needs in early care and education settings.* Washington, DC: National Association for the Education of Young Children. **1, 5**

Chapman, J. (1999). A looping journey. *Young Children, 54*(3), 80–83. **31**

Charles, C. M. (1974). *The teacher's petit Piaget.* Belmont, CA: Fearon. **19**

Charlesworth, R. (1985). Readiness: Should we make them ready or let them bloom? *Day Care and Early Education, 12*(3), 25–27. **28**

Charlesworth, R. (1998a). Is developmentally appropriate practice for everyone?—YES! *Childhood Education, 74*(5), 274–282. **2**

Charlesworth, R. (1998b). Response to Sally Lubeck's "Is DAP for everyone?" *Childhood Education, 74*(5), 293–298. **2**

Charlesworth, R. (1989). Behind before they start? Dealing with the problems of kindergarten failure. *Young Children, 44*(3), 5–13. **4, 31**

Charlesworth, R., Fleege, P. O., & Weitman, C. J. (1994). Research on the effects of group standardized testing on instruction, pupils and teachers: New directions for policy. *Early Education and Development, 5*, 195–212. **28**

Charlesworth, R., Hart, C. H., Burts, C. C., & DeWolf, M. (1993). The LSU Studies: Building a research base for developmentally appropriate practice. In S. Reifel (Ed.), Perspectives on developmentally appropriate practice. *Advances in Early Education and Day Care, 5*, 3–28. **31**

Charlesworth, R., & Hartup, W. W. (1967). Positive social reinforcement in the nursery school peer group. *Child Development, 38*, 993–1002. **26**

Charlesworth, R., & Lind, K. K. (1995). Whole language and primary grades mathematics and science: Keeping in step with national standards. In S. Raines (Ed.), *Whole language across the curriculum: Grades 1, 2, and 3* (pp. 156–178). New York: Teachers College Press. **18**

Charlesworth, R., & Lind, K. K. (2007). *Math and science for young children* (5th ed.) Clifton Park, NY: Delmar Learning. **17, 18, 20**

Charlesworth, W. R. (1978). Ethology: Understanding the other half of intelligence. *Social Science Information, 17*, 231–277. **23**

Chen, J. (Ed.). (1998). *Project Spectrum: Early learning activities.* New York: Teachers College Press. **23**

Chen, J., Krechevsky, M., & Viens, J. (1998). *Building children's strengths: The experiences of Project Spectrum.* New York: Teachers College Press. **23**

Cherry, C., Godwin, D., & Staples, J. (1989). *Is the left brain always right?* Belmont, CA: David S. Lake. **14, 20**

Chess, S. (1990). Comments: "Infant day care: A cause for concern." In M. A. Jensen & Z. W. Chevalier (Eds.), *Issues and advocacy in early education* (pp. 196–197). Boston: Allyn & Bacon. **12**

*Child Abuse and Neglect Fact Sheet.* (2005, August). Children's Defense Fund. Retrieved September 16, 2006 from http://www.childrensdefense.org. **7**

Child health talk. (1997). *Nutrition.* [Special issue], *VI* (4). **7**

Child Welfare League of America. (2006). *Position statement on parenting of children by gay, lesbian, and bisexual adults.* Retrieved May 16, 2006, from http://www.cwla.org. **32**

Children are born learning. (1993). *Dimensions of Early Childhood, 22*(1), 5–8. **29**

Children's Defense Fund. (1994). *The state of America's children: Yearbook 1994.* Washington, DC: Author. **7**

Children's Defense Fund. (1998). *The state of America's children: Yearbook 1998.* Washington, DC: Author. **6, 7, 8, 12, 15, 32, 33**

Children's Defense Fund. (1999). *The state of America's children: Yearbook 1999.* Washington, DC: Author. **26, 32, 33**

Children's Defense Fund. (2001). *The state of America's children: Yearbook 2001.* Washington, DC: Author. **7, 8, 12, 32**

Children's Defense Fund Action Council. (2005). *Stand up for children NOW!* Washington, DC: Author. **32**

Children's Defense Fund (CDF). (2005, May 17). *New Government Report Backs CDF in Questioning Reliability and Validity of NRS Test Given to Children in Head Start.* Retrieved August 14, 2005, from http://www.childrensdefense.org **28**

Children's Defense Fund (CDF). (2005, January). *Bush Administration polices exacerbate growing housing crisis for families with children.* Retrieved July 18, 2005, from http://www.chidrensdefense.org **7**

Children's Defense Fund (CDF). (2004). *Key facts about American children.* Retrieved July 18, 2005, from http://www.chidrensdefense.org **12**

Children's Defense Fund (CDF). (2004, July). *The state of America's children 2004: A continuing portrait of inequality fifty years after Brown v. Board of education.* Retrieved August 14, 2005, from http://www.chidrensdefense.org **11**

Children's Defense Fund (CDF). (2005, June). *2005 Gun Report.* Retrieved June 19, 2005, from http://www.chidrensdefense.org **25**

Children's Defense Fund (CDF). (2004, August). *Where America stands.* Retrieved June 19, 2005, from http://www.chidrensdefense.org **26**

Children's Defense Fund (CDF). (2002). *Family Income and Jobs.* Retrieved May 19, 2006, from http://www.chidrensdefense.org **7**

Children's Defense Fund (CDF). (2001, April). *Child care basics.* Retrieved August 14, 2005, from http://www.chidrensdefense.org **11**

Children's nuclear fears: What parents can do about them. (1984). *Today's Child, 32*(4), 6. **25**

The child's defender. (1993). *Teaching Tolerance, 2*(1), 8–12. **12**

Chira, S. (1994). How boys and girls learn differently. In K. M. Paciorek & J. H. Munro (Eds.), *Early Childhood Education 93/94* (pp. 78–80). Guilford, CT: Dushkin. (Originally published in *Redbook,* Sept. 1992, 191–192, 194–195. **25**

Chisholm, K. (1998). A three year follow-up of attachment and indiscriminate friendliness in children adopted from Romanian orphanages. *Child Development, 69,* 1092–1106. **25**

Christie, J. F. (1982). Sociodramatic play training. *Young Children, 37*(4), 25–32. **5**

Christie, K. (2005). Changing the nature of parent involvement. *Phi Delta Kappan, 86*(9), 645–646. **7**

Church, E. B. (2005a, March). A closer look at children's art and writing. *Early Childhood Today,* 34–42. **19**

Church, E. B. (2005b, March). Developmental ages and stages: The importance of humor, 5 to 6. *Early Childhood Today,* 32–33. **25**

Church, M. (1979). Nutrition: A vital part of the curriculum. *Young Children, 35*(1), 61–65. **18**

Cianciotto, J., & Cahill, S. (2003). *Education Policy Issues Affecting Lesbian, Gay, Bisexual and Transgender Youth.* New York: The National Gay and Lesbian Task Force Policy Institute. Available at: http://www.thetaskforce.org **27**

Clabaugh, G. K. (1993). The cutting edge: The limits and possibilities of multiculturalism. *Educational Horizons, 71,* 117–119. **6**

Clark, L. (2003). Making new choices possible: Understanding differences in infant feeding practices between Latina mothers and Anglo health care providers. *Zero to Three, 23*(5), 22–27. **12**

Clark, P. (1985). Curiosity in the classroom. *Early Report, 12*(3), 3–4. **23**

Clarke-Stewart, A. (1984). Day care: A new context for research and development. In M. Perlmutter (Ed.), *Parent-child interaction and parent-child relations in child development* (pp. 61–100). Mahwah, NJ: Erlbaum. **6**

Clarke-Stewart, A. (1987). In search of consistencies in child care research. In D. Phillips (Ed.), *Quality in child care: What does research tell us?* (pp. 105–120). Washington, DC: National Association for the Education of Young Children. **32**

Classroom community building. (1998). *Young Children* [Special section], *53*(2), 17–39. **28, 29**

Clay, M. (1972). *Sand—The concepts about print test.* London: Heinemann. **22**

Click, P., & Parker, J. (2002). *Caring for school age children.* (3rd ed.) Clifton Park, NY: Delmar Learning. **32**

Cobb, L. (2003). Providing services for at-home dads. Family focus on marriage. *NCFR Report, 48*(3), F10–F11. **11**

Coe, G., & Shelby, D. (1998). Relative efficacy of parent and child involvement in a shared-reading intervention for preschool children from low-income backgrounds. *Early Childhood Research Quarterly, 13,* 293–294. **22**

Cohen, D. H. (1972). Continuity from prekindergarten to kindergarten. In K. R. Baker (Ed.), *Ideas that work with young children.* Washington, DC: National Association for the Education of Young Children. **28**

Cohen, S. (1993/94). For parents particularly: Television in the lives of children and their families. *Childhood Education, 70,* 103–104. **6**

Cohen, S., Semmes, M., & Guralnick, M. J. (1979). Public Law 94–142 and the education of preschool handicapped children. *Exceptional Children, 45*, 279–290. **5**

Cohn, D. A. (1990). Child-mother attachment of six-year-olds and social competence at school. *Child Development, 61*, 152–162. **30**

Colbert, C. (1997). Visual arts in the developmentally appropriate integrated curriculum. In C. H. Hart, D. C. Burts, & R. Charlesworth (Eds.), *Integrated curriculum and developmentally appropriate practice: Birth to age eight* (pp. 201–223). Albany, NY: SUNY Press. **23**

COLAGE (Children of Lesbians and Gays Everywhere). (2006). *Facts and Figures About Kids with Gay Parents.* Retrieved May 16, 2006, from http://www.colage.org **32**

Cole, M., Cole, S. R., & Lightfoot, C. (2005). *The development of children* (5th ed.). New York: Worth. **4, 7, 8, 9, 11, 15, 17, 20, 21, 23, 26**

Cole, P. M., Martin, S. E., & Dennis, T. A. (2004). Emotion regulation as a scientific construct: Methodological challenges and directions for child development research. *Child Development, 75*(2), 317–333. **13**

Cole, O. J., & Washington, V. (1986). A critical analysis of the assessment of the effects of Head Start on minority children. *Journal of Negro Education, 55*(1), 91–106. **23**

Coll, C. G., Lamberty, G., Jenkins, R., McAdoo, H. P., Crnic, K., Wasik, B. H., & Garcia, H. V. (1996). An integrative model for the study of developmental competencies in minority children. *Child Development, 67*, 1891–1914. **2**

Coll, C. T. G. (1990). Developmental outcome of minority infants: A process oriented look at our beginnings. *Child Development, 61*, 270–289. **11, 13**

Collins, W. A. (1999). Willard W. Hartup and the new look in social development. In W. A. Collins & B. Laursen (Eds.), *Relationships as developmental contexts* (pp. 3–12). Mahwah, NJ: Erlbaum. **26**

Collins, W. A., & Laursen, B. (Eds.). (1999). *Relationships as developmental contexts.* Mahwah, NJ: Erlbaum. **26**

Comer, J. P. (1989). Racism and the education of young children. *Teachers College Record, 90*, 352–361. **33**

Comer, J. P. (2001). Schools that develop children [Electronic version]. *The American Prospect, Inc., 12*(7). Retrieved March 14, 2003, from http://www.prospect.org/print/V12/7/comer-j.html **31**

Comer, J. P. (2004, July). *Overview of the School Development Program.* Retrieved February 10, 2006, from http://www.med.yale.edu **31**

Comer, J. P. (2005). A missing element in school reform. *Phi Delta Kappa, 86*(10). 757–763. **31**

Comfort, R. L. (2005). Work in progress: Learning to play: Play deprivation among young children in foster care. *Zero to Three, 25*(4), 50–53. **16**

Condon, W. S. (1979). Neonatal entrainment and enculturation. In M. Bullowa (Ed.), *Before speech: The beginnings of interpersonal communication* (pp. 131–148). Cambridge, UK: Cambridge University Press. **24**

Condon, W. S., & Sander, S. W. (1974). Synchrony demonstrated between movements on the neo-nate and adult speech. *Child Development, 45*, 256–262. **14**

Connell, D. R. (1987). The first 30 years were the fairest: Notes from the kindergarten and ungraded primary (K–12). *Young Children, 42*(5), 30–39. **32**

Cook, D. A., & Fine, M. (1995). "Motherwit" childrearing lessons from African American mothers of low income. In B. B. Swadener & S. Lubeck (Eds.), *Children and families "at promise"* (pp. 118–142). Albany, NY: SUNY Press. **6**

Coplan, R. J., Rubin, K. H., Fox, N. A., Calkins, S. D., & Stewart, S. L. (1994). Being alone, playing alone, acting alone: Distinguishing among reticence and passive and active solitude in young children. *Child Development, 65*, 129–137. **26**

Corporal punishment: Effects on children. (1981). *ERIC/EECE Newsletter, 13*(6), 1, 3. **28**

Cortes, C. E. (1978). Chicano culture, experience and learning. In L. Morris (Ed.), *Extracting learning styles from social/cultural diversity* (pp. 29–40). Southwest Teachers Corps Network, Austin, TX. **25**

Council on Physical Education for Children. (2001, July). *Position paper: Recess in Elementary Schools.* **29**

Cowan, P. A. (1997). Beyond meta-analysis: A plea for a family systems view of attachment. *Child Development, 69*, 601–603. **13**

Cowles, M. (1971). Four views of learning and development. *Educational Leadership, 28*, 790–795. **5**

Crawford, P. A. (2000). In the gap: Bridging the generation through literature and learning experiences. *ACEI Focus on Elementary, 12*(4), 1–6. **31**

Cross, W. E. (1985). Black identity: Rediscovering the distinction between personal identity and reference group orientation. In M. B. Spencer, G. K. Brookins, & W. R. Allen (Eds.), *Beginnings: The social and affective development of black children* (pp. 155–172). Mahwah, NJ: Erlbaum. **25**

Crosser, S. (2004). What's the difference between right and wrong: Understanding how children think. *Early childhood education 04/05.* Dubuque, IA: McGraw Hill/Dushkin. **16**

Crowley, G. (1991). Children in peril. *Newsweek* [special edition]. **30**

Cryan, J. R. (1987). The banning of corporal punishment: In child care, school and other educative settings in the U.S. *Childhood Education, 63*, 146–153. **28**

Curry, N. E., & Johnson, C. N. (1991). *Beyond self esteem: Developing a genuine sense of human value.* Washington, DC: National Association for the Education of Young Children. **25, 30**

Damon, W. (1988). *The moral child: Nurturing children's natural moral growth.* New York: The Free Press. **16, 27, 30**

Daniel Goleman talks about Emotional Intelligence. (1999, Jan.). *Scholastic Early Childhood Today*, 29–30. **25, 30**

Da Ros, D. A., & Kovach, B. A. (1998). Assisting toddlers & caregivers during conflict resolutions: Interactions that promote socialization. *Childhood Education, 75*, 25–30. **15, 16**

David, J. L. (1994). School-based decision making: Kentucky's test of decentralization. *Phi Delta Kappan, 75*, 706–712. **32**

Davis, M., & Emory, E. (1995). Sex differences in neo-natal stress reactivity. *Child Development, 66*, 14–27. **11**

Davis, J. (1993). Why Sally *can* draw. *Educational Horizons, 71*, 86–93. **23**

Deater-Deckard, K., & Plomin, R. (1999). An adoption study of the etiology of teacher and parent reports of externalizing behavior problems in middle childhood. *Child Development, 70*, 144–154. **30**

DeBord, K., Hestenes, L. L., Moore, R. C., Cosco, N., & McGinnis, J. R. (2002). Paying attention to the outdoor environment is as important as preparing the indoor environment. *Young Children, 57*(3), 32–35. **8**

DeHart, G. B. (1999). Conflict and averted conflict in preschoolers' interactions with siblings and friends. In W. A. Collins & B. Laursen (Eds.), *Relationships as developmental contexts* (pp. 281–304). Mahwah, NJ: Erlbaum. **26**

DeHoogh, E. (1978). *Poniendo la campana al gato* (*Belling the cat*) (Vol. 1). Skokie, IL: National Textbook Company (Spanish and English versions). **20**

Delgado-Gaitan, C. (1994). Socializing young children in Mexican-American families. In P. M. Greenfield & R. R. Cocking (Eds.), *Cross-cultural roots of minority child development* (pp. 55–86). Mahwah, NJ: Erlbaum. **6**

DeLoache, J. S., Cassidy, D. J., & Brown, A. L. (1985). Precursors of mnemonic strategies in very young children's memory. *Child Development, 56*, 125–137. **17**

Delpit, L. (1998). What should teachers do? Ebonics and culturally responsive instruction. In T. Perry & L. Delpit (Eds.), *The real Ebonics debate* (pp. 17–28). Boston: Beacon Press. **24**

de Melendez, W. R., & Ostertag, V. (1997). *Teaching young children in multicultural classrooms: Issues, concepts, and strategies.* Clifton Park, NY: Delmar Learning. **1, 6, 7**

Derman-Sparks, L. (1993). Revisiting multicultural education. *Dimensions of Early Childhood, 21*(2), 6–10. **6**

Derman-Sparks, L. (1993/94). Empowering children to create a caring culture in a world of difference. *Childhood Education, 70*, 66–71. **6**

Derman-Sparks, L., & the ABC Task Force. (1989). *Anti-bias curriculum: Tools for empowering young children.* Washington, DC: National Association for the Education of Young Children. **6**

DeVries, R. (1997). Piaget's social theory. *Educational Researcher, 26*(2), 4–17. **2, 25**

DeVries, R., Halcyon, R., & Morgan, P. (1991). A study of children's enacted interpersonal understanding. *Early Childhood Research Quarterly, 6*, 473–517. **26**

DeVries, R., Haney, J., & Zan, B. (1991). Socio-moral atmosphere in direct-instruction, eclectic, and constructivist kindergartens: A study of teachers' enacted interpersonal understanding. *Early Childhood Research Quarterly, 6*, 449–471. **26**

DeVries, R., Hildebrandt, C., & Zan, B. (2000). Constructivist early education for moral development. *Early Education & Development, 11*(1), 313–343. **27, 28**

DeVries, R., & Kohlberg, L. (1990). *Constructivist early education: Overview and comparison with other programs.* Washington, DC: National Association for the Education of Young Children. (Original work published in 1987.) **2, 4, 6, 26**

DeVries, R., & Zan, B. (1994). *Moral classrooms, moral children: Creating a constructivist atmosphere in early education.* New York: Teachers College Press. **24, 26**

DeVries, R., Zan, B., & Hildebrandt, C. (2002). Issues in constructivist early moral education. *Early Education & Development, 13*(3), 9–35. **26**

DeVries, R., Zan, B., Hildebrandt, C., Edmiaston, R., & Sales, C. (2002). *Developing constructivist early childhood curriculum.* New York: Teachers College Press. **2, 5, 31**

DeWolff, M. S., & van IJzendoorn, M. H. (1997), Sensitivity and attachment: A meta-analysis on parental antecedents of infant attachment. *Child Development, 68*, 571–591. **13**

Dickinson, D. K., & DeTemple, J. (1998). Putting parents in the picture: Maternal reports of preschoolers' literacy as predictors of early reading. *Early Childhood Research Quarterly, 13*, 241–261. **22**

Dickinson, D. K., & Tabors, P. O. (1991). Early literacy: Linkages between home, school and literacy achievement at age five. *Journal of Research in Childhood Education, 6*(1), 30–46. **22**

*Dietary Guidelines for Americans* (2005). Retrieved August 18, 2005, from http://wwwmypyramid.gov **29**

Disabled children: A population vulnerable to maltreatment (1994, Mar.). *Developments, 8*(1), 10. **6**

Divoky, D. (1989). Ritalin: Education's fix-it drug. *Phi Delta Kappan, 70*, 599–605. **4**

Dixon, G. H. (1980). Child development in the family health care center. *Young Children, 35*(3), 49–56. **7**

Dodge, K. A., Pettit, G. S., & Bates, J. E. (1994). Socialization mediators of the relation between socio-economic status and child conduct problems. *Child Development, 65*, 649–665. **26**

Dodge, M. K., & Frost, J. L. (1986). Children's dramatic play: Influence of thematic and non-thematic settings. *Childhood Education, 62*, 166–170. **5**

Doescher, S., & Sugawara, A. I. (1989). Encouraging prosocial behavior in young children. *Childhood Education, 65*, 213–216. **26**

Dokecki, P. R., Baumeister, A. A., & Kupstas, F. D. (1989). Biomedical and social aspects of pediatric AIDS. *Journal of Early Intervention, 13*, 99–113. **10**

Donmoyer, R., & Kos, R. (1993). At-risk students: Insights from/about research. In R. Donmoyer & R. Kos (Eds.), *At-risk students* (pp. 7–36). Albany, NY: SUNY Press. **6**

Downey, D. B., & Condron, D. J. (2004). Playing well with others in kindergarten: The benefits of siblings at home. *Journal of Marriage and Family, 66*(2), 333–350. **26**

Duarte, G., & Rafanello, D. (2001). The migrant child: A special place in the field. *Young Children, 56*(2), 26–34. **6**

Duffy, F. H., Als, H., & McAnulty, G. B. (1990). Behavioral and electrophysiological evidence for gestational age effects in healthy preterm and fullterm infants studied two weeks after expected due date. *Child Development, 61*, 1271–1286. **11**

Duke, N., & Kays, J. (1998). "Can I say 'Once upon a time'?" Kindergarten children developing knowledge of information book language. *Early Childhood Research Quarterly, 13*, 295–318. **22**

Dunn, J. (1999). Siblings, friends, and the development of social understanding. In W. A. Collins & B. Laursen (Eds.), *Relationships as developmental contexts* (pp. 263–280). Mahwah, NJ: Erlbaum. **26**

Dunn, J., & Kendrick, C. (1980). The arrival of a sibling: Changes in patterns of interaction between mother and first-born child. *Journal of Child Psychology and Psychiatry, 21*, 119–132. **16**

Dunn, J., & Munn, P. (1985). Becoming a family member: Family conflict and the development of social understanding in the second year. *Child Development, 56*, 480–492. **16**

Dunn, J., & Shatz, M. (1989). Becoming a conversationalist despite (or because of ) having an older sibling. *Child Development, 61*, 399–410. **21**

Dwyer, J. (1993, Oct. 10). The quirky genius who is changing our world. *Parade Magazine, 8*, 10. **13**

Dyson, A. H. (1989). *Multiple worlds of child writers: Friends learning to write.* New York: Teachers College Press. **31**

Dyson, A. H. (1993). From invention to social action in early childhood literacy: A reconceptualization through dialogue about difference. *Early Childhood Research Quarterly, 8*, 409–426. **22**

Dyson, A. H. (1998). *Writing superheroes: Contemporary childhood, popular culture, and classroom literacy.* New York: Teachers College Press. **31**

E-learning for educators. (2004). *Young Children* [Focus section], *59*(3), 10–44. **4**

Early, D. M., Pianta, R. C., Taylor, L. C., & Cox, M. J. (2001). Transition practices: Findings from a national survey of kindergarten teachers. *Early Childhood Education Journal, 28*(3), 199–206. **28**

*Early Reading First. Program Description.* Retrieved December 26, 2005, from http://www.ed.gov/print/programs/earlyreading/index.html **22**

Easterbrooks, M. A., & Goldberg, W. A. (1984). Toddler development in the family: Impact of father involvement and parenting characteristics. *Child Development, 55*, 740–752. **15**

Eckerman, C. O., Whatley, J. L., & Kutz, L. S. (1975). Growth of social play with peers during the second year of life. *Developmental Psychology II* (pp. 42–49). Reprinted in Smart, R. C. (Ed.) (1977). *Readings in child development and relationships* (2nd ed.) (pp. 81–92). New York: Macmillan. **16**

Eddowes, E. A. (1994). Schools providing safer environments for homeless children. *Childhood Education, 70*, 271–273. **6**

Edelman, M. E. (1992). *Measure of our success: A letter to my children and yours.* Boston, MA: Beacon Press. **12**

Edson, A. (1994). Crossing the great divide: The nursery school child goes to kindergarten. *Young Children, 49*(5), 69–75. **28**

Edwards, L. C., & Nabors, M. L. (1993). The creative arts process: What it is and what it is not. *Young Children, 48*(3), 77–81. **24**

Eimas, P. D., & Quinn, P. C. (1994). Studies on the formation of perceptually based basic-level categories in young infants. *Child Development, 65*, 903–917. **14**

Eisenberg, N., Fabes, R. A., Nyman, M., Bernzweig, J., & Pinuelas, A. (1994). The relations of emotionality and regulation to children's anger-related reactions. *Child Development, 65*, 109–128.

Eisenberg, N., Fabes, R. A., Shepard, S. A., Murphy, B. C., Guthrie, I. K., Jones, S., Friedman, J., Poulin, R., & Maszk, P. (1997). Contemporaneous and longitudinal prediction of children's social functioning from regulation and emotionality. *Child Development, 68*, 642–664. **25, 30**

Eisenberg, N., Wolchik, S. A., Hernandez, R., & Pasternack, J. F. (1985). Parental socialization of young children's play. A short-term longitudinal study. *Child Development, 56*, 1506–1513. **16**

Eisner, E. W. (1999). The uses and limits of performance assessment. *Phi Delta Kappan, 80*, 658–660. **29**

Elbaum, B., & Vaughn, S. (1999). *Can school-based interventions enhance the self-concept of students with learning disabilities?* Retrieved November 8, 2002, from http://www.ncld. org/research/ncld self concept.cfm **26, 30**

Eley, T. C., Lichtenstein, P., & Stevenson, J. (1999). Sex differences in the etiology of aggressive and nonaggressive antisocial behavior: Results from two twin studies. *Child Development, 70*, 155–168. **30**

Elgas, P. M., & Peltier, M. B. (1998). Jimmy's journey: Building a sense of community and self-worth through small-group work. *Young Children, 53*(2), 17–21. **30**

Elias, C. L., & Berk, L. E. (2002). Self-regulation in young children: Is there a role for sociodramatic play? *Early Childhood Research Quarterly, 17*(2), 216–238. **26**

Elkind, D. (1993). *Images of the young child.* Washington, DC: National Association for the Education of Young Children. **2, 25**

Elkind, D. (2003). Thanks for the memory: The lasting value of true play. *Young Children*, 58(3), 46–50. **5**

Elkind, D. (2005). Viewpoint. Early childhood amnesia: Reaffirming children's need for developmentally appropriate programs. *Young Children, 60*(4), 38–49. **4**

Ellsworth, J. (1997). Enhancing student responsibility to increase student success. *Educational Horizons, 76*(1), 17–22. **30**

Embracing Ebonics and teaching Standard English: An interview with Oakland teacher Carrie Secret. In T. Perry & L. Delpit (Eds.) (1998). *The real Ebonics debate* (pp. 79–88). Boston: Beacon Press. **21**

Encouraging young children to develop and enhance their thinking skills. [Focus section]. (2003). *Young Children, 58*(5), 10–55. **20**

Endres, J. B., & Rockwell, R. E. (1994). *Food, nutrition, and the young child.* New York: Merrill/Macmillan. **18**

Endsley, R., & Bradbard, M. (1981). *Quality day care: A handbook for parents and caregivers.* Upper Saddle River, NJ: Prentice Hall. **32**

Engle, P. L., & Breaux, C. (1998). Fathers' involvement with children: Perspectives from developing countries. *SRCD Social Policy Report, XII*(1). **13**

English, D. J. (1998). The extent and consequences of child maltreatment. *The Future of Children: Protecting Children from Abuse and Neglect, 8*(1), 39–53. **6**

Entwisle, D. R., & Alexander, K. L. (1990). Beginning school math competence: Minority and majority comparisons. *Child Development, 61*, 454–471. **20**

Epperson, N. (2002). Postpartum mood changes: Are hormones to blame? *Zero to Three, 22*(6), 17–23. **13**

Epstein, A. S. (2003). How planning and reflection develop young children's thinking skills. *Young Children, 58*(5), 28–36. **20**

Epstein, J. (2005). *Developing and sustaining research-based programs of school, family and community partnerships: Summary of five years of NNPS research.* Retrieved February 19, 2006, from http//www.csos.jhu.edu **32**

Epstein, J. (1997, Sept./Oct.). Six types of school-family-community involvement. *Harvard Education Letter: Research Online.* Retrieved March 14, 2003, from http://www.edletter.org/past/issues/1997-so/sixtypes.shtm1 **6**

Epstein, J. L. (1991). Paths to partnership: What we can learn from federal, state, district and school initiatives. *Phi Delta Kappan, 72*, 344–349. **6, 32**

Essa, E. L., & Murray, C. I. (1994). Research in review: Young children's understanding and experience with death. *Young Children, 49*(4), 74–81. **25**

Essa, E. (2003). *A practical guide to solving preschool behavior problems* (5th ed.). Clifton Park, NY: Delmar Learning. **15, 28**

Estes, D. (1998). Young children's awareness of their mental activity: The case of mental rotation. *Child Development, 69*, 1345–1360. **20**

Evans, A., & Bosworth, K. (1997, Dec.). Building effective drug education programs. *Phi Delta Kappa Research Bulletin*, No. 19. **7**

Evans, G. D., & Fogarty, K. (2005). *The Common Roles of Fathers: The Five Ps.* Retrieved February 18, 2006, from http://edis.ifas.ufl.edu **32**

Evans, K. S. (1998). Combating gender disparity in education: Guidelines for early childhood educators. *Early Childhood Education Journal, 26*, 83–88. **25**

Evans, M. A. (1985). Play beyond play: Its role in formal informative speech. In L. Galda & A. D. Pellegrini (Eds.), *Play, language and stories* (pp. 129–146). Norwood, NJ: Ablex. **21**

Evans, W. (1996, May). Addressing TV violence in the classroom. *Phi Delta Kappa Research Bulletin*, No. 16. **31**

Ewing, J., & Eddowes, E. A. (1994). Sand play in the primary classroom. *Dimensions of Early Childhood, 22*(4), 24–25. **29**

*FACTSHEET: Facts About Meth.* (2005). From DEA Ongoing Programs. Retrieved August 5, 2005, from http://www.usdoj.gov.8o **9**

Fagella, K., & Horowitz, J. (1990). Different child, different style. *Instructor, 100*, 49–54. **4**

Fagot, B. I., Hagan, R., Leinbach, M. D., & Kronsberg, S., (1985). Differential reactions to assertive and communicative acts of toddler boys and girls. *Child Development, 56*, 1499–1505. **16**

Farnham-Diggory, S. (1990). *Schooling.* Cambridge, MA: Harvard University Press. **31**

Farnsworth, M., Schweinhart, L. J., & Berrueta-Clement, J. R. (1985). Preschool intervention, school success and delinquency in a high-risk sample of youth. *American Educational Research Journal, 22*, 445–464. **23**

Farver, J. A. M. (1992). Communicating shared meaning in social pretend play. *Early Childhood Research Quarterly, 7*, 501–516. **21**

Fassler, R. (1998). Room for talk: Peer support for getting into English in an ESL kindergarten. *Early Childhood Research Quarterly, 13*, 379–409. **24**

Febo, S. (2005). Where does the water go? Emergent curriculum with toddlers. *Focus on Infants & Toddlers, 17*(3), 1–4, 6. **17**

Federal Interagency Forum on Child and Family Statistics (FIFCF). (2001). *America's Children: Key national indicators of well-being 2001.* Washington, DC: U.S. Government Printing Office. **9, 15, 24**

Feeney, S., & Freeman, N. K. (1999). *Ethics and the early childhood educator: Using the NAEYC code.* Washington, DC: National Association for the Education of Young Children. **3**

Fein, G. G., & Fox, N. A. (Eds.). (1988a). Infant day care, Part I: Empirical studies [Special issue]. *Early Childhood Research Quarterly, 3*(3). **12**

Fein, G. G., & Fox, N. A. (Eds.). (1988b). Infant day care, Part II: Empirical studies [Special issue]. *Early Childhood Research Quarterly, 3*(4). **12**

Feldman, H. M., Dale, P. S., Campbell, T. F., Colborn, D. K., Kurs-Lasky, M., Rockette, E., & Paradise, J. L. (2005). Concurrent and predictive validity of parent reports of child language at ages 2 and 3 years. *Child Development, 76*(4), 856–868. **17**

Ferguson, C. A. (1977). Baby talk as a simplified register. In C. E. Snow & C. E. Ferguson (Eds.), *Talking to children* (pp. 209–235). Cambridge, UK: Cambridge University Press. **24**

Fernald, A. (1989). Intonation and communicative intent in mothers' speech to infants: Is the melody the message? *Child Development, 60*, 1497–1510. **21**

Fernald, A. (1993). Approval and disapproval: Infant responsiveness to vocal affect in familiar and unfamiliar languages. *Child Development, 64*, 657–674. **13**

Fewell, R., & Deutscher, B. (2004). Contributions of early language and maternal facilitation variables to later language and reading abilities. *Journal of Early Intervention, 26*(2), 132–145. **17**

Field, T., Gewirtz, J. L., Cohen, D., Garcia, R., Greenberg, R., & Collins, K. (1984). Leave-takings and reunions of infants, toddlers, preschoolers, and their parents. *Child Development, 55*, 628–635. **13, 16**

Field, T., Hernandez-Reif, M. & Freedman, J. (2004). Stimulation programs for preterm infants. *SRCD Social Policy Report, 18*(1). **10**

Fields, M. V., & Fields, D. (2006). *Constructive guidance and discipline* (4th ed.). Upper Saddle River, NJ: Merrill/Prentice Hall. **25, 27, 28, 31**

Fincham, F. D., Hokoda, A., & Sanders, R., Jr. (1989). Learned helplessness, test anxiety, and academic achievement: A longitudinal analysis. *Child Development, 60*, 138–145. **31**

Firlik, R. (2003). Early years summit: Preschool-Kindergarten collaboration makes a difference. *Young Children, 58*(1), 73–78. **28**

Fischer, M. A., & Gillespie, C. W. (2003). One Head Start classroom's experience: Computers and young children's development. *Young Children, 58*(4), 85–91. **6**

*Fitness and Your 6- to 12-year-old.* (2005, June). Retrieved January 22, 2006, from http://www.kidshealth.org **29**

*Fitness for Kids Who Don't Like Sports.* (2005, August). Retrieved January 22, 2006, from http://www.kidshealth.org **29**

Fitzgerald, L. M., & Goncu, A. (1993). Parent involvement in urban early childhood education: A Vygotskian approach. In S. Reifel (Ed.), *Advances in early education and day care: Perspectives on developmentally appropriate practice* (pp. 197–212). Greenwich, CT: JAI Press. **6**

Five commentaries: Looking to the future. (2000). *The future of children: Children and computer technology, 10*(2), 168–180. **4**

Flatter, C., Herzog, J. M., Tyson, P., & Ross, K. (2006). *Empathy.* Retrieved May 28, 2006, from http://www.sesameworkshop.org **30**

Flavell, J. H., Green, F. L., & Flavell, E. R. (1993). Children's understanding of the stream of consciousness. *Child Development, 64*, 387–398. **20**

Flavell, J. H., Speer, J. R., Green, F. L., & August, D. L. (1981). The development of comprehension monitoring and knowledge about communication. *Monographs of the Society for Research in Child Development, 46*, (5, Serial No. 192). **21**

Fleege, P. (1997). Assessment in an integrated curriculum. In C. H. Hart, D. C. Burts, & R. Charlesworth (Eds.), *Integrated curriculum and developmentally appropriate practice: Birth to age eight* (pp. 313–334). Albany, NY: SUNY Press. **23, 29**

Fleege, P. O., & Charlesworth, R. (1993). "Teacher, Why am I failing? I know the answers" : The effects of developmentally inappropriate assessment. In R. Donmoyer & K. Kos (Eds.), *At-risk students: Portraits, policies, programs, and practices* (pp. 219–228). Albany, NY: SUNY Press. **1, 2, 28**

Fleege, P. O., Charlesworth, R., Burts, D. C., & Hart, C. H. (1992). Stress begins in kindergarten: A look at behavior during standardized testing. *Journal of Research in Childhood Education, 7*(1), 20–26. **18, 25, 28**

Flinchum, B. M. (1975). *Motor development in early childhood.* St. Louis, MO: Mosby. **19**

Flynn, L. L., & Kieff, J. (2002). Including everyone in outdoor play. *Young Children, 57*(3), 20–26. **18, 19**

Foerster, L. M., & Little Soldier, O. (1978). Learning centers for young Native Americans. *Young Children, 33*(3), 53–57. **6**

Fogel, A. (1980). Expressing affection and love to young children. *Dimensions, 8*(2), 39–44. **28**

Fogel, A. (2001). *Infancy: Infant, family, and society* (4th ed.). Belmont, CA: Wadsworth. **11, 13, 14, 17**

Footlick, J. K. (1990). What happened to the family? *Newsweek* [Special edition]. **32**

FNS online. (2002). *WIC at a Glance.* Retrieved July 30, 2002, from http://www.fns.usda.gov/wic/programinfo/WIC-ataglance.htm **12**

Fraiberg, S. (1959). *The magic years.* New York: Charles Scribner's Sons. **15, 24, 25, 28**

Fraiberg, S. (1977). How a baby learns to love. In P. Cantor (Ed.), *Understanding a child's world.* New York: McGraw-Hill. [Reprinted from *Redbook*, 1971, May, pp. 123–133] **13**

Franke, J., & Geist, E. A. (2003). The effects of teaching play strategies on social interaction for a child with autism: A case study. *Journal of Research in Childhood Education, 18*(2), 125–140. **5**

Fraser, J. (2004). Childhood obesity: Alarming trends, the risks overweight children face, and how families, schools, and communities can help. *University of Pittsburgh OCD Developments, 18*(3), 5–10. **15**

Frede, E., & Barnett, W. S. (1992). Developmentally appropriate public school preschool: A study of implementation of the High/Scope curriculum and its effects on disadvantaged children's skills in first grade. *Early Childhood Research Quarterly, 7*, 483–500. **23**

Free, K. (1998, Aug./Sept.). Millions are worried sick about housing. Shelter and health: A critical connection. *Habitat World*, 79. **7**

Freedle, R., & Lewis, M. (1977). Prelinguistic conversations. In M. Lewis & L. A. Rosenblum (Eds.), *Interaction, conversation and the development of language* (pp. 157–185). New York: John Wiley. **24**

Freedman, D. G. (1982). Ethnic differences in babies. In J. K. Gardner (Ed.), *Readings in developmental psychology* (pp. 110–118). Boston: Little, Brown. **12**

French, K. (2004). Supporting a child with special health care needs. *Young Children, 59*(2), 62–63. **18**

French, L. A., Lucariello, J., Seidman, S., & Nelson, K. (1985). The influence of discourse content and context on preschoolers' use of language. In L. Galda & A. D. Pellegrini (Eds.), *Play, language and stories* (pp. 1–28). Norwood, NJ: Ablex. **21**

Friedman, D. E. (2001). Employer supports for parents with young children. *Future of Children, 11*(1), 63–78. **11**

Friedman, S. (2005). Environments that inspire. *Young Children, 60*(3), 48–58. **11**

Friedrich, S. (2002). No Child Left Behind—What it means to teachers. *NCTM News Bulletin, 39*(4), 4. **29**

*From Neurons to Neighborhoods: The Science of Early Childhood Development*. (2005). Retrieved from the National Academic Press July 21, 2005, http://www.nap.edu **9**

Froschl, M., & Sprung, B. (1999). On purpose: Addressing teasing and bullying in early childhood. *Young Children, 54*(2), 70–72. **30**

Frost, J. L., Wortham, S. C., & Reifel, S. (2005). *Play and child development* (2nd ed.). Upper Saddle River, NJ: Merrill/Prentice Hall/Pearson. **5, 14, 15, 16, 29**

Frost, J. L. (2003). Bridging the gaps: Children in a changing society. *Childhood Education, 80*(1), 29–34. **32**

Frost, J. L. (1992). *Play and playscapes*. Clifton Park, NY: Delmar Learning. **4, 5**

Fuchs, D., & Fuchs, D. L. (1998). Competing visions for educating students with disabilities: Inclusion vs. full inclusion. *Childhood Education, 74*(5), 309–316. **4**

Fuhr, J. E., & Barclay, K. H. (1998). The importance of nutrition and nutrition education. *Young Children, 53*(1), 74–80. **18**

Fujiki, M., Brinton, B., Morgan, M., & Hart, C. H. (1998). *Withdrawn and sociable behavior of children with specific language impairment*. Manuscript submitted for publication. **30**

Fuller, M. (1998, Aug./Sept.). Health and home. Shelter and health: A critical connection. *Habitat World*, 14. **7**

Furrow, D. (1984). Social and private speech at two years. *Child Development, 55*, 355–362. **17**

Gadsden, V., & Ray, A. (2002). Engaging fathers: Issues and considerations for early childhood educators. *Young Children, 57*(6). 32–41. **25**

Gaensbauer, T. J. (2004). Telling their stories: Representation and reenactment of traumatic experiences occurring in the first year of life. *Zero to Three, 24*(5), 25–31. **13**

Galda, L. (1984). Narrative competence: Play, story telling, and story comprehension. In A. Pellegrini & T. Yawkey (Eds.), *The development of oral and written language in social context* (pp. 105–118). Norwood, NJ: Ablex. **21**

Galinsky, E., Shubilla, L., Willer, B., Levine, J., & Daniel, J. (1994). National Institute: State and community planning for early childhood systems. *Young Children, 49*(2), 54–57. **33**

Gallagher, K. C. (2005). Brain research and early child development: A primer for developmentally appropriate practice. *Young Children, 60*(4), 12–20. **5, 14**

Gallas, K. (1994). *The languages of learning: How children talk, write, dance, draw, and sing their understanding of the world*. New York: Teachers College Press. **22**

Gandini, L. (1993). Fundamentals of the Reggio Emilia approach to early childhood education. *Young Children, 49*(1), 4–8. **32**

Garber, H. L., & Slater, M. (1983). Assessment of the culturally different preschooler. In K. D. Paget & B. A. Bracken (Eds.), *The psychoeducational assessment of preschool children* (pp. 443–471). New York: Grune & Stratton. **6**

Garcia, E. E. (1986). Bilingual development and the education of bilingual children during early childhood. In B. Spodek (Ed.), *Today's kindergarten* (pp. 15–31). New York: Teachers College Press. **20**

Gardner, H. (1983). *Frames of mind: Theory of multiple intelligences*. New York: Basic Books. **23**

Gardner, H. (1984). Assessing intelligences: A comment on 'Testing intelligence without IQ tests'. *Phi Delta Kappan, 65*, 699–700. **23**

Gardner, H. (1993). *Multiple intelligences: The theory in practice*. New York: Basic Books. **23**

Gardner, H. (1999). *Intelligence reframed: Multiple intelligences for the 21st century*. New York: Basic Books. **4**

Gardner, H., & Hatch, T. (1989). Multiple intelligences go to school: Educational implications of the theory of multiple intelligences. *Educational Researcher, 18*(8), 4–9. **23**

Gartrell, D. (2004). *The power of guidance: Teaching social-emotional skills in early childhood classrooms*. Clifton Park, NY: Delmar learning. **27, 31**

Garvey, C. (1990). *Play* (Enlarged ed.). Cambridge, MA: Harvard University Press. **4, 20, 25**

Gavidia-Payne, S., & Stoneman, Z. (1997). Family predictors of maternal and paternal involvement in programs for young children with disabilities. *Child Development, 68*, 701–717. **13**

Geist, E., & Baum, A. C. *Yeah, But's* that keep teachers from embracing an active curriculum: Overcoming the resistance. *Young Children, 60*(4), 28–32, 36. **4**

Gelfer, J. I., & Perkins, P. G. (1992). Constructing student portfolios: A process and product that fosters communication with families. *Day Care and Early Education, 20*(2), 9–13. **3**

Gelman, S. A. (1998). Research in review. Categories in young children's thinking. *Young Children, 53*(1), 20–25. **17, 19**

The genetic counselor. (1977, Apr.). *The exceptional parent*, M14–M17. **10**

Genishi, C. (2002). Research in review. Young English language learners: Resourceful in the classroom. *Young Children, 57*(4), 66–72. **20**

Genishi, C., & Dyson, A. H. (1984). *Language assessment in the early years*. Norwood, NJ: Ablex. **20, 24**

Genishi, C., Dyson, A. H., & Fassler, R. (1994). Language and diversity in early childhood: Whose voices are appropriate? In B. L. Mallory & R. S. New (Eds.), *Diversity and developmentally appropriate practices* (pp. 250–268). New York: Teachers College Press. **20, 24**

Gesell, A., Ilg, F., Ames, L. B., & Rodell, J. (1974). *Infant and child in the culture of today* (Rev. Ed.). New York: Harper & Row. **24**

Getch, Y. Q., & Neuharth-Pritchett, S. (2004). Asthma management in early care and education settings. *Young Children, 59*(2), 34–41. **18**

Giacchino-Baker, R. (1995, Apr.). *Preparing teachers for multilingual/multicultural classrooms: Competencies, knowledge bases, curricula, and strategies*. Workshop presented at Weber State University, Ogden, UT. **24**

Gillis, J., & Weiss, R. (2000, May 22). Q & A. *Washington Post*. Retrieved June 5, 2002, from http://www.washingtonpost.com/wp-dyn/articles/A51750-2000May22.html **10**

Ginsburg, H. P., Lopez, L., Chung, Y. E., Netley, R., Chao-Yuan, C., McCarthy, C., Cordero, M., Blake, I., Song, M.,

Baroody, A., & Jaegers, R. (1989, Apr.). *Early mathematical thinking: Role of social class, racial, and cultural influences.* Presentation at the biennial meeting of the Society for Research in Child Development, Kansas City, MO. **19**

Ginsburg, H. P., & Opper, S. (1979). *Piaget's theory of intellectual development* (2nd ed.). Upper Saddle River, NJ: PrenticeHall. **19**

Glascott, K. (1994). A problem of theory for early childhood professionals. *Childhood Education, 70,* 131–132. **2**

Glink, P. (1998). The Chicago Doula Project: A collaborative effort in perinatal support for birthing teens. *Zero to three, 18*(5), 44–50. **11**

Gmitrova, V., & Gmitrov, J. (2003). The impact of teacher-directed and child-directed pretend play on cognitive competence in kindergarten children. *Early Childhood Education Journal, 30*(4), 241–246. **20**

Godwin, L. J., Groves, M. M., & Horm-Wingerd, D. M. (1993). "Don't leave me" : Separation distress in infants, toddlers, and parents. *Day Care and Early Education, 20*(3), 13–17. **13, 16**

Goffin, S. G., & Lombardi, J. (1988). *Speaking out: Early childhood advocacy.* Washington, DC: National Association for the Education of Young Children. **33**

Goffin, S. G., & Wilson, C. S. (2001). *Curriculum models and early childhood education.* Columbus, OH: Merrill. **32**

Golbeck, S. L., & Ginsburg, H. P. (Eds.). (2004). Early learning in mathematics and science. [Special issue]. *Early Childhood Research Quarterly, 19*(1). **20**

Goldberg, M. F. (1997). Maintaining a focus on child development: An interview with James Comer. *Phi Delta Kappan, 78*(7), 557–559. **3**

Goldberg, S. (1983). Parent-infant bonding: Another look. *Child Development, 54,* 1355–1382. **11**

Goldhaber, J., & Smith, D. (1993). Infants and toddlers at play: Looking for meaning. *Day Care and Early Education, 20*(3), 9–12. **14, 17**

Goldman, R. L. (1993). Early education special education: Sexual abuse of young children with special needs. Are they safe in day care? *Day Care and Early Education, 20*(4), 37–38. **6**

Goldstein, S., & Brooks, R. B. (Eds.) (2005). *Handbook of resilience in children.* New York: Kluwer. **30**

Gonzalez, V. (1996). Do you believe in intelligence? Sociocultural dimensions of intelligence assessment in majority and minority students. *Educational Horizons, 75,* 45–52. **23**

Gonzalez-Mena, J. (1992). Taking a culturally sensitive approach in infant-toddler programs. *Young Children, 47*(2), 4–9. **12**

Gonzalez-Mena, J., & Shareef, I. (2005). Discussing diverse perspectives on guidance. *Young Children, 60*(6), 34–38. **27**

Gonzali, E., & Crase, S. J. (1991, April). *Academic stress among school age children and early adolescents in the United States and Indonesia.* Paper presented at the biennial meeting of the Society for Research in Child Development, Seattle, WA. **30**

Goodman, E. (1991, Jan. 11). Let's treat people as well as banks. *Baton Rouge, LA, Morning Advocate,* 8B. **19**

Goodman, Y. M., & Altwerger, B. (1981). *A study of the development of literacy in preschool children.* Program in Language and Literacy Occasional Paper No. 4. Tucson, AZ: University of Arizona. **22**

Goodnough, G. E., & Goodnough, L. E. (2001). Mothers returning to the work force: The father's role in the transition. *Focus on Infants and Toddlers, 14*(2), 1–2, 4. **12**

Gootman, M. E. (1993). Reaching and teaching abused children. *Childhood Education, 70,* 15–19. **6**

Gopnik, A., Meltzoff, A. N., & Kuhl, P. K. (1999). *The scientist in the crib: What early learning tells us about the mind.* New York: Perennial. **14, 16, 18**

Gordinier, C. L., & Foster, K. (2004/05). What stick is driving the reading hoop? *Childhood Education, 81*(2), 94–O. **3, 22, 31**

Gottfredson, D. C. (2004). Schools and bullying. In C. E. Sanders & G. D. Phye (Eds.), *Bullying: Implications for the classroom* (pp. 159–176). Boston: Elsevier. **30**

Gottfried, A. E. (1983). Research in review. Intrinsic motivation in young children. *Young Children, 39*(1), 64–73.

Gottman, J. M. (1983). How children become friends. *Monographs of the Society for Research in Child Development, 48* (3, Serial No. 201). **27**

Gould, S. J. (1982). Racist arguments and IQ. In J. K. Gardner (Ed.), *Readings in developmental psychology* (2nd ed.). (pp. 233–235). Boston: Little, Brown. **23**

Grace, C., & Shores, E. F. (1992). *The portfolio and its use.* Little Rock, AR: Southern Early Childhood Association.

Graham, S. (1993/94). Reviews of research: Are slanted manuscript alphabets superior to the traditional manuscript alphabet? *Childhood Education, 70,* 91–95. **8**

Grantham-McGregor, S., Powell, C., Walker, S., Chang, S., & Fletcher, P. (1994). The long-term follow-up of severely malnourished children who participated in an intervention program. *Child Development, 65,* 428–439. **18**

Gratz, R. R., & Boulton, P. (1993). Taking care of kids: A director's concerns about environmental hazards. *Day Care and Early Education, 21*(2), 29–31. **7**

Gratz, R. R., & Boulton, P. J. (1996). Erikson and early childhood educators: Looking at ourselves and our profession developmentally. *Young Children, 51*(5), 74–78. **24**

Graue, M. E. (1992). Meanings of readiness and the kindergarten experience. In S. Kessler & B. B. Swadener (Eds.), *Reconceptualizing the early childhood curriculum* (pp. 62–92). New York: Teachers College Press. **28**

Graue, M. E. (1998). What's wrong with *Edward the Unready*? Our responsibility for readiness. *Young Children, 53*(2), 12–16. **28**

Graue, M. E., & Shepard, L. A. (1989). Predictive validity of the Gesell School Readiness Tests. *Early Childhood Research Quarterly, 4,* 303–315. **28**

Greenberg, P. (1992a). Why not academic preschool? Part 2. Autocracy of democracy in the classroom? *Young Children, 47*(3), 54–64. **27**

Greenberg, P. (1992b). Ideas that work with young children. How to institute some simple democratic practices pertaining to respect, rights, responsibilities, and roots in any classroom (without losing your leadership position). *Young Children, 47*(5), 10–17. **27**

Greenberg, P. (1998a). Some thoughts about phonics, feelings, Don Quixote, diversity, and democracy: Teaching young children to read, write, and spell (Part 1). *Young Children, 53*(4), 72–83. **24**

Greenberg, P. (1998b). Warmly and calmly teaching young children to read, write, and spell: First thoughts about the first four of twelve well-known principles (Part 2). *Young Children, 53*(5), 68–82. **24**

Greenberg, P. (1998c). Thinking about goals for grown-ups and young children while we teach reading, writing, and spelling (and a few thoughts about the "J" word) (Part 3). *Young Children, 53*(6), 31–42. **24**

Greenberg, P. (2001). The irreducible needs of children: An interview with T. Berry Brazelton, M.D., and Stanley I. Greenspan, M.D. *Young Children, 56*(2), 6–14. **1**

Greenman, J. (2004, Jan./Feb.). The experience of space, the pleasure of place. *Child Care Information Exchange*, 34–35. **11**

Greenwald, S. (2003). Special start: A collaborative project designed to support premature babies and their families. *Zero to Three, 24*(2), 38–44. **10**

Gresham, F. M., & MacMillan, D. L. (1997). Social competence and affective characteristics of students with mild disabilities. *Review of Educational Research, 67*, 377–415. **30**

Grieve, R., Tumner, W. E., & Pratt, C. (1983). Language awareness in children. In M. Donaldson, R. Grieve, & C. Pratt (Eds.), *Early childhood development and education.* Oxford, UK: Blackwell. **21**

*Growing Child.* (1973). 22 North Second Street, Lafayette, IN 47902. **21**

*Growth, Body Composition, and Metabolism.* Retrieved August 5, 2005, from http://www.hivguidelines.org **9**

Gunnar, M. R., Porter, F. L., Wolf, C. M., Rigatuso, J., & Larson, M. C. (1995). Neonatal stress reactivity: Predictions to later emotional temperament. *Child Development, 66*, 1–13. **11**

Gurian, A., & Pope, A. (2001). *Do Kids Need Friends?* Retrieved February 5, 2006, from http://www.med.nyu.edu **30**

Gutierrez, J., & Sameroff, A. (1990). Determinants of complexity in Mexican-American and Anglo-American mothers' conceptions of child development. *Child Development, 61*, 384–394. **6**

Gutierrez, J., Sameroff, A., & Karrer, B. M. (1988). Acculturation and SES effects on Mexican-American parents' concepts of development. *Child Development, 59*, 250–255. **6**

Guttman, M., & Frederiksen, C. H. (1985). Preschool children's narratives: Linking story comprehension, production and play discourse. In L. Galda & A. D. Pellegrini (Eds.), *Play, language and stories.* (pp. 99–128). Norwood, NJ: Ablex. **21**

Hale, J. (1978). Cultural influences on learning styles of Afro-American children. In L. Morris (Ed.), *Extracting learning styles from social/cultural diversity* (pp. 7–28). Southwest Teacher Corps Network, Austin, TX. **25**

Hale, J. (1981). Black children: Their roots, culture, and learning styles. *Young Children, 36*(2), 37–50. **25**

Hale-Benson, J. (1990). Visions for Children: African-American early childhood education program. *Early Childhood Research Quarterly, 5*, 199–213. **6**

Hales, D. (1998, May). The female brain. *Ladies Home Journal*, 128, 173, 176, 184. **25**

Halliday, M. A. K. (1975). *Learning how to mean: Explorations in the development of language.* London, UK: Edward Arnold. **14, 21**

Halliday, M. A. K. (1979). One child's protolanguage. In M. Bullowa (Ed.), *Before speech: The beginnings of interpersonal communication* (pp. 171–190). Cambridge, UK: Cambridge University Press. **14, 21**

Halverson, L. E. (1971). The significance of motor development. In G. Engstrom (Ed.), *The significance of the young child's motor development* (pp. 17–33). Washington, DC: National Association for the Education of Young Children. **8**

Hamblen, J. (2002). *Terrorist attacks and children.* Retrieved November 17, 2002, from http://www.ncptsd.org/facts/disasters/fs children disaster. html. **28, 30**

Hamilton, J. O'C. (2000, Dec.) The question is: What are the costs? *Stanford Magazine*, 52–58. **8**

Hamilton, J. O'C. (2002, Nov./Dec.). Spoiling our kids [Electronic Version]. *Stanford Magazine.* **30**

Hanline, M. F., & Daley, S. (2002). 'Mom. Will Kaelie always have possibilities?' The realities of early childhood inclusion. *Phi Delta Kappan, 84*(1), 73–76. **26**

Harris, T. (1994). The snack shop: Block play in a primary classroom. *Dimensions of Early Childhood, 22*(4), 22–23. **29**

Harrison, A. O., Wilson, M. N., Pine, C. J., Chan, S. Q., & Buriel, R. (1990). Family ecologies of minority children. *Child Development, 61*, 347–362. **12, 28**

Harste, J. C., Woodward, V. A., & Burke, C. L. (1984). *Language stories and literacy lessons.* Portsmouth, NH: Heinemann. **8**

Hart, C. H. (Ed.). (1993). *Children on playgrounds: Research perspectives and applications.* Albany, NY: SUNY Press. **26**

Hart, C. H., Burts, D. C., & Charlesworth, R. (1997). Integrated developmentally appropriate curriculum: From theory and research to practice. In C. H. Hart, D. C. Burts, & R. Charlesworth (Eds.), *Integrated curriculum and developmentally appropriate practice: Birth to age eight* (pp. 1–28). Albany, NY: SUNY Press. **5, 28, 29**

Hart, C. H., Burts, D. C., Durland, M. A., Charlesworth, R., DeWolf, M., & Fleege, P. O. (1998). Stress behaviors and activity type participation of pre-schoolers in more and less developmentally appropriate classrooms: SES and sex differences. *Journal of Research in Childhood Education, 12*(2), 176–196. **18, 25**

Hart, C. H., DeWolf, D. M., & Burts, D. C. (1992). Linkages among preschoolers' playground behavior, outcome expectations, and parental disciplinary strategies. *Early Education and Development, 3*, 265–283. **27**

Hart, C. H., DeWolf, D. M., Wozniak, P., & Burts, D. C. (1992). Maternal and paternal disciplinary styles: Relations with preschoolers' playground behavioral orientations and peer status. *Child Development, 63*, 879–892. **24**

Hart, C. H., Ladd, G. W., & Burleson, B. R. (1990). Children's expectations of the outcomes of social strategies: Relations with sociometric status and maternal discipline styles. *Child Development, 61*, 127–137. **30**

Hart, C. H., McGee, L. M., & Hernandez, S. (1993). Themes in the peer relations literature: Correspondence to outdoor peer interactions portrayed in children's storybooks. In C. H. Hart (Ed.), *Children on playgrounds: Research perspectives and applications* (pp. 371–416). Albany, NY: SUNY Press. **27, 30**

Hart, C. H., Yang, C., Nelson, L. J., Jin, S., Olsen, J. A., Nelson, D. A., Wu, P., Olsen, S., Robinson, C. C., & Porter, C. (1998, July 1–4). *Peer acceptance in early childhood and subtypes of socially withdrawn behavior in China, Russia, and the United States.* Paper presented at the 15th Biennial Meetings of the International Society for the Study of Behavioral Development, Bern, Switzerland. **27**

Hart, C. H., Yang, C., Charlesworth, R., & Burts, D. C. (2003, Apr.). *Kindergarten Teaching Practices: Associations with Later Child Academic and Social/Emotional Adjustment to School.* Paper presented at the biennial meeting of the Society for Research in Child Development, Tampa, FL. **31**

Hartman, K. (1977). How do I teach in a future shocked world? *Young Children, 32*(3), 32–36. **29**

Hartup, W. W. (1991). Having friends, making friends, and keeping friends: Relationships in educational contexts. *Early Report, 19*(1), 1–2. **26**

The Hartup-Charlesworth System. (1973). In E. G. Boyer, A. Simon, & G. R. Karafin (Eds.), *Measures of maturation* (pp. 1009–1045). Philadelphia: Research for Better Schools. **26**

Hartup, W. W., Glazer, J. A., & Charlesworth, R. (1967). Peer reinforcement and sociometric status. *Child Development, 38*, 10017–10024. **26**

Hartup, W. W., Laursen, B., & Stewart, M. I. (1988). Conflict and friendship relations of young children. *Child Development, 59*, 1590–1600. **26**

Hartup, W. W., & Moore, S. G. (1990). Early peer relations: Developmental significance and prognostic implications. *Early Childhood Research Quarterly, 5*, 1–17. **26**

Harwood, R. L., & Miller, J. G. (1989, Apr.). *Perceptions of attachment: A comparison of Anglo and Puerto Rican mothers.* Presented at the biennial meeting of the Society for Research in Child Development, Kansas City, MO. **12**

Hasselbring, T. S., & Glaser, C. H. W. (2000). Use of computer technology to help students with special needs. *Future of Children, 10*(2), 102–122. **5**

Hatch, T. C., & Gardner, H. (1986). From testing intelligence to assessing competencies: A pluralistic view of intellect. *Roeper Review, 8*(3), 147–150. **23**

Haugland, S. (1992). Computers and young children: Maintaining an anti-bias curriculum. *Day Care and Early Education, 20*(2). **5**

Haugland, S. (1993). Computers and young children: The outstanding developmental software. *Day Care and Early Education, 21*(2). **5**

Haugland, S. (1994). Computers and young children: Selecting software that facilitates developmental gains. *Day Care and Early Education, 21*(4). **5**

Haugland, S. W. (1999). What role should technology play in young children's learning? *Young Children, 54*(6), 26–31. **5**

Haugland, S. W. (2000). Early childhood classrooms in the 21st century: Using computers to maximize learning. *Young Children, 55*(1), 12–27. **5**

Haugland, S. W., & Shade, D. D. (1990). *Developmental evaluations of software for young children.* Clifton Park, NY: Delmar Learning. **4, 5**

Haugland, S. W., Bailey, M. D., & Ruiz, E. A. (2002a). The outstanding developmental software and web sites for 2001. *Early Childhood Education Journal*, 29(3), 191–200. **6**

Haugland, S. W., & Ruiz, E. A. (2002b). Empowering children with technology: The outstanding developmental software for 2002. *Early Childhood Education Journal*, 30(2), 125–132. **6**

Hauser, M. E., & Thompson, C. (1995). Creating a classroom culture of promise: Lessons from a first grade. In B. B. Swadener & S. Lubeck (Eds.), *Children and families "at promise"* (pp. 210–223). Albany, NY: SUNY Press. **6**

Hauser-Cram, P. (1998). Research in review. I think I can, I think I can: Understanding and encouraging mastery motivation in young children. *Young Children, 53*(4), 67–71. **4**

Heath, S. B. (1980). The function and uses of literacy. *Journal of Communication, 30*, 123–133. **24**

Heath, S. B. (1982). Questioning at home and at school: A comparative study. In G. Spindler (Ed.), *Doing the ethnography of schooling* (pp. 102–131). New York: Holt, Rinehart, & Winston. **24**

Heath, S. B. (1983). *Ways with words.* New York: Cambridge University Press. **24**

Heath, S. B. (1985). Narrative play in second language learning. In L. Galda & A. D. Pellegrini (Eds.), *Play, language and stories* (pp. 147–166). Norwood, NJ: Ablex. **21**

Heinicke, C. M., Diskin, S. D., Ramsey-Klee, D. M., & Given, K. (1983). Pre-birth parent characteristics and family development in the first year of life. *Child Development, 54*, 194–208. **12**

Helping babies play. (2003). *Young Children, 58*(3), 52–53. **14**

Helm, H. H., Beneke, S., & Steinheimer, K. (1998). *Windows on learning: Documenting young children's work.* New York: Teachers College Press. **29**

Helping children and adolescents cope with violence and disasters. (2001). National Institute of Mental Health. Retrieved November 17, 2002, from http://www.nimh.nih.gov/publicat/violence.cfm **30**

Hendrick, J. (1992). Where does it all begin? Teaching the principles of democracy in the early years. *Young Children, 47*(3), 51–53. **28**

Hendrick, J. (Ed.). (1997). *First steps toward teaching the Reggio way.* New York: Merrill/Prentice Hall. **23, 32**

Henkens-Matzke, A., & Abbott, D. A. (1990). Game playing: A method for reducing young children's fear of medical procedures. *Early Childhood Research Quarterly, 5*, 19–26. **4**

Herman, J. F., Kolker, R. G., & Shaw, M. L. (1982). Effects of motor activity on children's intentional and incidental memory for spatial locations. *Child Development, 53*, 239–244. **8**

Hernandez, D. J. (2004). Demographic change and the life circumstances of immigrant families. *The Future of Children, 14*(2), 17–47. **7**

Hestenes, L. L., Kontos, S., & Bryan, Y. (1993). Children's emotional expression in child care centers varying in quality. *Early Childhood Research Quarterly, 8*, 295–308. **25**

Hidden Curriculum. (2006). *Wikipedia.* Retrieved February 10, 2006, from http://en.wikipedia.org **31**

*High Stakes Testing Position Statement.* (2001). Retrieved August 6, 2002, from http://www.allianceforchildhood.net/histakes test position statement.htm. **28**

Hildreth, G. (1936). Developmental sequences in name writing. *Child Development, 7*, 291–302. **19**

Hilliard, A. G., III. (1989). Teachers and cultural styles in a pluralistic society. *NEA Today, 7*(6), 65–69. **6**

Hilliard, A. G., III. (1994). How diversity matters. *Kappa Delta Pi Record, 30*, 114. **6**

Hilliard, A. G., & Vaughn-Scott, M. (1982). The quest for the "minority" child. In S. G. Moore & C. R. Cooper (Eds.), *The young child: Reviews of research* (Vol. 3) (pp. 175–189). Washington, DC: National Association for the Education of Young Children. **6, 12**

Hinnant, H. A. (1997). Unplugging. *KDP Record, 34*(1), 17. **5**

Hirshberg, L. M., & Svejda, M. (1990). When infants look to their parents: I. Infants' social referencing of mothers compared to fathers. *Child Development, 61*, 1175–1186. **12**

*HIV Positive Women and Their Babies After Birth* from the U.S. Department of Health and Human Services AIDS info. Retrieved August 5, 2005, from http://.www.aidsinfo.nih.gov **9**

Hodges, W. L., & Sheehan, R. (1978). Follow Through as ten years of experimentation: What have we learned? *Young Children, 34*(1), 4–14. **28**

Hogan, N., & Graham, M. (2001). Helping children cope with disaster. *Focus on PreK & K, 14*(2), 1–6. **25**

Hogan, N., & Graham, M. (2002). Helping children cope with grief. *Focus on PreK & K, 15*(1), 1–6. **25**

Hoge, R. D. (1988). Issues in the definition and measurement of the giftedness construct. *Educational Researcher, 17*(7), 12–16. **23**

Hoge, R. D., & Renzulli, J. S. (1991). *Self-concept and the gifted child.* Retrieved November 8, 2002, from http://www.gifted.uconn.edu/hogerenz.html **26**

Holden, G. W., & West, M. J. (1989). Proximate regulation by mothers: A demonstration of how differing styles affect young children's behavior. *Child Development, 60*, 64–69. **15**

Holland, M. (2004a). "That food makes me sick!" Managing food allergies and intolerances in early childhood settings. *Young Children, 59*(2), 42–46. **18**

Holland, M. (2004b). Surviving the playground king and the recess queen: Using storybooks to prevent bullying in early childhood. *Focus on Pre-K & K, 17*(1), 1–5, 8. **26**

Holliday, B. G. (1985). Towards a model of teacher-child transactional processes affecting black children's academic achievement. In M. B. Spencer, G. K. Brookings, & W. R. Allen (Eds.), *Beginnings: The social and affective development of black children* (pp. 117–130). Mahwah, NJ: Erlbaum. **6**

Holloway, S. D. (1988). Concepts of ability and effort in Japan and the United States. *Review of Educational Research, 58*(3), 327–345. **6**

Holmes, J. G. (1993). Teachers, parents, and children as writing role models. *Dimensions of Early Childhood, 2*(3), 12–14. **22**

Honig, A. S. (1983). Sex role socialization in early childhood. *Young Children, 38*(6), 57–70. **4, 25**

Honig, A. S. (1984). Developmental effects on children of pregnant adolescents. *Day Care and Early Education, 12*(1), 36–42. **9**

Honig, A. S. (1986). Stress and coping in children, Part I. *Young Children, 41*(4), 50–63. **25**

Honig, A. S. (1993a). Mental health for babies: What do theory and research tell us? *Young Children, 48*(3), 69–76. **13**

Honig, A. S. (1993b). Toilet learning. *Day Care and Early Education, 21*(1), 6–9. **15**

Honig, A. S. (1998, Aug./Sept.). The sounds of language. *Early Childhood Education Today.* **14, 17**

Honig, A. S., & DiPerna, C. (1983). Peer relations of infants and toddlers. *Day Care and Early Education, 10*(3), 36–39. **16**

Hornik, R., & Gunnar, M. R. (1988). A descriptive analysis of infant social referencing. *Child Development, 59*, 626–634. **14**

Horowitz, F. D. (1989). Nature-nurture. In M. R. Gunnar & E. Thelen (Eds.), *Systems and development: The Minnesota Symposium on child psychology* (Vol. 22) (pp. 211–218). Mahwah, NJ: Erlbaum. **9**

Houston, P. D. (2005). NCLB: Dreams and nightmares. *Phi Delta Kappan, 86*(6), 469–470. **31**

*How to understand gender-role development* (n.d.). Retrieved November 8, 2002, from http://psychology. about.com/library/howto/htgender.htm **25**

Howard, G. R. (1993). Whites in multicultural education: Rethinking our role. *Phi Delta Kappan, 75*, 36–41. **6**

Howes, C. (1985). Sharing fantasy: Social pretend play in toddlers. *Child Development, 56*, 1253–1258. **16**

Howes, C. (1989). Research in review: Infant child care. *Young Children, 44*(6), 24–28. **12, 16**

Howes, C., Hamilton, C. E., & Matheson, C. C. (1994). Children's relationships with peers: Differential associations with aspects of the teacher-child relationship. *Child Development, 65*, 253–263. **16**

Howes, C., & Wu, F. (1990). Peer interactions and friendships in an ethnically diverse school setting. *Child Development, 61*, 537–541. **30**

Howes, C., & Wishard, A. G. (2004). Linking shared meaning to emergent literacy: Looking through the lens of culture. *Zero to Three, 25*(1), 10–15. **17**

Hrncir, E. J., & Eisenhart, C. E. (1991). Use with caution: The "At-risk" label. *Young Children, 46*(2), 23–27. **4**

Huettig, C., Sanborn, C. F., DiMarco, N., Popejoy, A., & Rich, R. (2004). The O generation: Our youngest children are at risk for obesity. *Young Children, 59*(2), 50–55. **12, 18, 19**

Hughes, M., & McCollum, J. (1994). Neonatal intensive care: Mothers' and fathers' perceptions of what is stressful. *Journal of Early Intervention, 18*, 258–268. **11**

*Human Genome Project.* (2005, August). Retrieved August, 2005, from http://www.orn.gov/hgmis **10**

Humphryes, J. (1998). The developmental appropriateness of high-quality Montessori programs. *Young Children, 53*(4), 4–16. **4**

Hundert, J., Mahoney, B., Mundy, F., & Vernon, M. L. (1998). A descriptive analysis of developmental and social gains of children with severe disabilities in segregated and inclusive preschools in Southern Ontario. *Early Childhood Research Quarterly, 13*, 49–65. **27**

Hurwitz, S. C. (1998). Today's playground—A look at the past to prepare for the future. *ACEI Focus on PreK & K, 10*(3), 1–5. **8**

Hyland, C. R. (1989). What we know about the fastest growing minority population: Hispanic Americans. *Educational Horizons, 67*, 131–135. **6**

Hymes, J. L., Jr. (1990). *The year in review: A look at 1989.* Washington, DC: National Association for the Education of Young Children. **8**

Hyson, M. C. (1979). Lobster on the sidewalk. In L. Adams & B. Garlick (Eds.), *Ideas that work with young children* (Vol. 2) (pp. 183–185). Washington, DC: National Association for the Education of Young Children. **25**

Hyson, M. C. (1996). Emotional development and early education. *Early Education and Development* [Special Issue], 7(1), **25**

Hyson, M. C. (2002). "Huh!" "Eek!" "Help!" Perspectives on early childhood assessment. *Young Children, 57*(1), 62–63. **28**

Hyson, M., & Christiansen, S. L. (1997). Developmentally appropriate guidance and the integrated curriculum. In C. H. Hart, D. C. Burts, & R. Charlesworth (Eds.), *Integrated curriculum and developmentally appropriate practice: Birth to age eight* (pp. 285–312). Albany, NY: SUNY Press. **28**

Hyson, M. C., Hirsh-Pasek, K., Rescorla, L., Cone, J., & Martell-Boinske, L. (1989). *Building the scaffold: Parents' involvement in young children's learning.* Unpublished manuscript, University of Delaware, Newark, DE. **6**

Hyson, M. C., & Lee, K. (1996). Assessing early childhood teachers' beliefs about emotions: Content, contexts, and implications for practice. *Early Education and Development,* 7(1), 59–78. **25**

Hyson, M. C., Whitehead, L. C., & Prudoe, C. M. (1988). Influences on attitudes towards physical affection between adults and children. *Early Childhood Research Quarterly, 3*, 55–75. **28**

Hyun, E. (1998). *Making sense of developmentally and culturally appropriate practice (DCAP) in early childhood education.* New York: Peter Lang. **31, 32**

Hyun, E., & Marshall, J. D. (1997). Theory of multiple/multi-ethnic perspective-taking ability for teachers' developmentally and culturally appropriate practice (DCAP). *Journal of Research in Childhood Education, 11*(2), 188–198. **2**

Hyun, E., & Choi, D. H. (2004). Examination of young children's gender-doing and gender-bending in their play dynamics: A cross-cultural exploration. *International Journal of Early Childhood, 36*(1), 49–64. **25**

Inagaki, K. (1992). Piagetian and post-Piagetian conceptions of development and their implications for science education in early childhood. *Early Childhood Research Quarterly, 7*, 115–133. **19**

Infants and children at risk: A symposium report. (1992). *Early Report, 20*(2). **9**

International Reading Association and National Association for the Education of Young Children. (1998). Learning to read and write: Developmentally appropriate practices for young children. *Young Children, 53*(4), 30–46. **22**

*Is early experience enough?* (2002). Better Brains for Babies. Retrieved May 21, 2006, from https://www.fcs.uga.edu **20**

Irvine, J. J. (1990). Transforming teaching for the twenty-first century. *Educational Horizons, 69*(1), 16–21. **6**

Isbell, R. T., & Raines, S. C. (1991). Young children's oral language production in three types of play centers. *Journal of Research in Childhood Education, 5*, 140–146. **24**

Isenberg, J. P., & Jalongo, M. R. (2006). *Creative thinking and arts-based learning* (4th ed.). Upper Saddle River, NJ: Pearson/Merrill Prentice Hall. **23, 24**

Ispa, J. M., & Halgunseth, L. C. (2004). Talking about corporal punishment: Nine low-income African American mothers' perspectives. *Early Childhood Research Quarterly, 19*(3), 463–484. **27**

Jackson, B. R. (1997). Creating a climate for healing in a violent society. *Young Children, 52*(7), 68–73. **25**

Jackson, C. L., & Sacks, A. (1994, Apr./May). Minority gifted: Not so minor. *Pi Lambda Theta Newsletter, 38*(6), 8. **23**

Jackson, J. F. (1993). Human behavioral genetics, Scarr's theory, and her views on interventions: A critical review and commentary on their implications for African-American children. *Child Development, 64*, 1318–1332. **9**

Jacobson, S. W., Fein, G., Jacobson, J. L., Schwartz, P. M., & Dowler, J. K. (1985). The effect of intrauterine PCB exposure on visual recognition memory. *Child Development, 56*, 853–860. **9**

Jalongo, M. R. (1983). Using crisis-oriented books with young children. *Young Children, 39*(2), 64–74. **27**

Jalongo, M. R. (1998a). On behalf of children: Overselling technology, underestimating thinking. *Early Childhood Education Journal, 25*, 219–222. **19**

Jalongo, M. R. (1998b). On behalf of children: "The phuss over phonics." *Early Childhood Education Journal, 26*, 1–6. **24**

Jalongo, M. R. (1989). Career education. *Childhood Education, 66*, 108–115. **26**

Jalongo, M. R. (1990). The child's right to expressive arts: Nurturing the imagination as well as the intellect. *Childhood Education, 66*, 195–201. **24**

Jalongo, M. R. (2004). *Young children and picture books* (2nd ed.). Washington, DC: National Association for the Education of Young Children. **17**

Jambunathan, S., Burts, D. C., & Pierce, S. (1999). Developmentally appropriate practice as predictors of self-competence among preschoolers. *Journal of Research in Childhood Education, 13*, 167–174. **28**

Jensen, A. R. (1985). Compensatory education and the theory of intelligence. *Phi Delta Kappan, 66*, 554–558. **23**

Jensen, E. (1998). *Teaching with the brain in mind.* Alexandria, VA: Association for Supervision and Curriculum Development. **14, 18, 31**

Joe, J. R. (1994). Revaluing Native-American concepts of development and education. In P. M. Greenfield & R. R. Cocking (Eds.), *Cross-cultural roots of minority child development* (pp. 107–114). Mahwah, NJ: Erlbaum. **2**

Johnson, J. E., Christie, J. F., & Wardle, F. (2005). *Play, development, and early education.* Boston: Pearson/Allyn & Bacon. **5**

Jones, E. (2003). Viewpoint: Playing to get smart. *Young Children*, 58(3), 32–36. **5**

Jones, J. (1990, July 3). Low-tech birthing centers gaining acceptance in high-tech medical world. *Baton Rouge, LA, Morning Advocate*, 11A. [Reprinted from the *Los Angeles Times.*] **11**

Joos, S. K., Pollitt, E., Mueller, W. H., & Albright, D. L. (1983). The Bacon Chow study: Maternal nutritional supplementation and infant behavioral development. *Child Development, 54*, 669–676. **8**

Jordan, A. B., & Woodward, E. H., IV. (2001). Electronic childhood: The availability and use of household media by 2- to 3-year-olds. *Zero to Three, 22*(2), 4–9. **4**

Joshi, A. (2005). Understanding Asian Indian families: Facilitating meaningful home-school relations. *Young Children, 60*(3), 75–83. **7**

Joyce, C. (1998, Apr. 24–26). Should we "fix" nature's genetic mistakes? *USA Weekend*, 16. **10**

Kagan, J. (1994, Oct. 5). The realistic view of biology and behavior. *The Chronicle of Higher Education*, A64. **9**

Kagan, J. (1998, Sept./Oct.). How we become. *Networker*, 52–63. **13**

Kagan, S. L. (1990). Readiness 2000: Rethinking rhetoric and responsibility. *Phi Delta Kappan, 72*, 272–279. **28**

Kagan, S. L., & Scott-Little, C. (2004). Early learning standards: Changing the parlance and practice of early childhood education. *Phi Delta Kappan, 85*(5), 388–396. **28**

Kamii, C. (1984a). Autonomy: The aim of education envisioned by Piaget. *Phi Delta Kappan, 65*, 410–415. **28**

Kamii, C. (1984b). Obedience is not enough. *Young Children, 39*(4), 11–14. **28**

Kamii, C. (1985). Leading primary education towards excellence—Beyond worksheets and drill. *Young Children, 40*(6), 3–9. **28**

Kamii, C. (1986). Cognitive learning and development. In B. Spodek (Ed.), *Today's kindergarten* (pp. 67–90). New York: Teachers College Press. **4, 5, 20**

Kamii, C. (Ed.) (1990). *Achievement testing in the early grades: The games grown-ups play.* Washington, DC: National Association for the Education of Young Children. **23, 28**

Kamii, C., & Ewing, J. K. (1996). Basing teaching on Piaget's constructivism. *Childhood Education, 72*, 260–264. **5**

Kamii, C. (2003). Modifying a board game to foster kindergartners' logico-mathematical thinking. *Young Children, 58*(5), 20–26. **20**

Kamii, C., & Manning, M. (2005). Dynamic Indicators of Basic Early Literacy Skills (DIBELS): A tool for evaluating student learning. *Journal of Research in Childhood Education, 20*(2), 75–90. **31**

Kantor, R., Elgas, P. M., & Fernie, D. (1993). Cultural knowledge and social competence within a pre-school peer-culture group. *Early Childhood Research Quarterly, 8*, 125–148. **27**

Kantrowitz, B. (1990). [Special Issue.] High school homeroom. *Newsweek*, 50–54. **12**

Kantrowitz, B., with Crandall, R. (1990, Aug. 20). A vital aid for preemies. *Newsweek*, 70. **11**

Kaplan, J. S. (2000). Making classrooms come alive: Drama as play. *ACEI Focus on Elementary, 13*(2), 1–3, 5–6. **31**

Karnes, M. B., & Schwedel, A. M. (1983). Assessment of preschool giftedness. In K. D. Paget & B. A. Bracken (Eds.), *The psychoeducational assessment of preschool children* (pp. 473–507). New York: Grune & Stratton. **23**

Karoly, L. A., Greenwood, P. W., Everingham, S. S., Hoube, J., Kilburn, M. R., Rydell, C. P., Sanders, M., & Chiesa, J. (1998). *Investing in our children: What we know and don't know about the costs of investing in our children.* Santa Monica, CA: Rand. **12**

Katz, L. (1996). Resolving differences between teachers and parents. *ERIC/EECE Newsletter, 8*(1), 2–3. **6**

Katz, L. G. (1993). Self-esteem in early childhood programs. *ERIC/EECE Newsletter, 5*(2), 1–2. [Adapted from Katz, L. G., *Distinctions between self-esteem and narcissism: Implications for practice.* Urbana, IL: ERIC/ EECE.] **25**

Katz, L. (1994). Misguided intentions in drug abuse prevention. *Young Children, 49*(3), 2–3. **15**

Katz, L. G., & McClellan, D. E. (1997). *Fostering children's social competence : The teacher's role.* Washington, DC: National Association for the Education of Young Children. **5, 25, 26**

Kauerz, K., & McMaken, J. (2004). *Implications for the Early Learning Field. No Child Left Behind Policy Brief.* Denver, CO: Education Commission of the States. **22**

Keener, J. (1999, Apr.). *Are Early Childhood Classrooms Gender Equitable?* Paper presented at the annual meeting of the American Educational Research Association, Montreal, Canada. **25**

Keller, H., Yovsi, R., Borke, J., Kartner, J., Jensen, H., & Papaligoura, Z. (2004). Developmental consequences of early parenting experiences: Self-recognition and self-regulation in three cultural communities. *Child Development, 75*(6), 1745–1760. **16**

Kellogg, R. (1970). *Analyzing children's art.* Palo Alto, CA: National Press Books. **8**

Kemple, K. M. (1996). Teachers' beliefs and reported practices concerning sociodramatic play. *Journal of Early Childhood Teacher Education, 17*(2), 19–31. **5**

Keniston, K. (1979, Spring/Summer). Children and politics? *Forum*, 10–11. **33**

Kermoian, R., & Campos, J. J. (1988). Locomotor experience: A facilitator of spatial cognitive development. *Child Development, 59*, 908–918. **8**

Kessler, S. (1989). Boys' and girls' effect on the kindergarten curriculum. *Early Childhood Research Quarterly, 4*, 479–503. **21**

Kessler, S. (1992). The social context of early childhood curriculum. In S. Kessler & B. B. Swadener (Eds), *Reconceptualizing the early childhood curriculum: Beginning the dialogue* (pp. 21–42). New York: Teachers College Press. **33**

*Key Facts About American Children.* (2004, August). Retrieved June 16, 2005, from http://www.childrensdefense.org **32**

Kieff, J. E., & Casbergue, R. M. (2000). *Playful learning and teaching.* Boston: Allyn & Bacon. **31**

Kilgo, J., Holder-Brown, L., Johnson, L. J., & Cook, M. J. (1988). An examination of the effect of tactile-kinesthetic stimulation on the development of pre-term infants. *Journal of the Division of Early Childhood, 12*, 320–327. **11**

Kim, Y., & Stevens, J. H., Jr. (1987). The socialization of prosocial behavior in children. *Childhood Education, 63*, 200–206. **26**

King, N. J., & Ollendick, T. H. (1989). Children's anxiety and phobic disorders in school settings: Classification, assessment, and intervention issues. *Review of Educational Research, 59*, 431–470. **31**

Kirk, E. W., & Clark, P. (2005). Beginning with names: Using children's names to facilitate early literacy learning. *Childhood Education, 81*(3), 139–144. **24**

Kirp, D. L., & Epstein, S. (1989). AIDS in America's school houses: Learning the hard lessons. *Phi Delta Kappan, 70*, 584–593. **7**

Kirylo, J. D., Millet, C., Luckett, A., & Guindon, M. (2001). The pedagogy of meaningful writing: A pen pal project between 1st-graders in a Louisiana public school and early childhood education majors at the University of Alabama at Birmingham. *ACEI Focus on Elementary, 13*(4), 1–6. **31**

Kitano, M. K. (1982). Young gifted children: Strategies for preschool teachers. *Young Children, 37*(4), 14–24. **6**

Klaus, M. H., & Kennell, J. (1982). *Parent-infant bonding* (2nd ed.). St. Louis, MO: Mosby. **11**

Klein, T. P., Wirth, D., & Linas, K. (2003). Play: Children's Context for development. *Young Children, 58*(3), 38–45. **5**

Knutson, J. (1993). Comment: Diversity in American schools—Past and present. *Educational Horizons, 72*, 114. **6**

Kochanska, G., Murray, K., & Coy, K. C. (1997). Inhibitory control as a contributor to conscience in childhood: From toddler to early school age. *Child Development, 68*, 263–277. **16**

Kochanska, G., Padavich, D. L., & Koenig, A. L. (1996). Children's narratives about hypothetical moral dilemmas and objective measure of their conscience: Mutual relations and socialization antecedents. *Child Development, 67*, 1420–1436. **16**

Kochanska, G., & Aksan, N. (2004). Development of mutual responsiveness between parents and their young children. *Child Development, 75*(6), 1657–1676. **13**

Koenig, G. (1986). *Observation drawing.* Unpublished manuscript, Louisiana State University, College of Education, Baton Rouge, LA. **24**

Kohlberg, L. (1968). The child as a moral philosopher. *Psychology Today, 2*, 25–30. **26**

Kohler, P., Chapman, S., & Smith, G. (1994). Transition procedures for preschool children. *Dimensions of Early Childhood, 22*(3), 26–27. **28**

Kohn, A. (2001). Fighting the tests: Turning frustration into action. *Young Children, 56*(2), 19–24. **28**

Kohn, A. (2001). Five reasons to stop saying "Good job." *Young Children, 56*(5), 24–28. **6**

Kohn, A. (2004). Standards and testing. In A. Kohn, *What does it mean to be well educated?* (pp. 65–74). Boston: Beacon Press. **28**

Kohn, A. (2005). *Unconditional parenting: Moving from rewards and punishments to love and reason.* New York: Atria Books. **27**

Kontos, S., & Wilcox-Herzog, A. (1997a). Influences on children' competence in early childhood classrooms. *Early Childhood Research Quarterly, 12*, 247–262. **5**

Kontos, S., & Wilcox-Herzog, A. (1997b). Research in review. Teachers' interactions with children: Why are they so important? *Young Children, 52*(2), 4–12. **5**

Kontos, S., & Wilcox-Herzog, A. (2001). How do education and experience affect teachers of young children? *Young Children, 56*(4), 85–91. **5**

Koralek, D. (2002). The power of conversations: Supporting children's language learning. *Young Children, 57*(2), 8–9. **24**

Koralek, D. G., Colker, L. J., & Dodge, D. T. (1993). *What, why, and how of high quality early childhood education: A guide for on-site supervision.* Washington, DC: National Association for the Education of Young Children. **12**

Koralek, D. (Ed.). (2004). Exploring the creative arts with young children [Focus Section]. *Young Children, 59*(4). **24**

Koralek, D. (Ed.). (2004). E-learning for Educators [Focus Section]. *Young Children, 59*(3). **4**

Korat, O. (2005). Contextual and non-contextual knowledge in emergent literacy development: A comparison between children from low SES and middle SES communities. *Early Childhood Research Quarterly, 20*, 220–238. **22**

Korner, A. F., Zeanah, C. H., Linden, J., Berkowitz, R. I., Kraemer, H. C., Kostelnik, M. J., Stein, L. C., Whiren, A. P., & Soderman, A. K. (1993). *Guiding children's social development* (2nd ed.). Clifton Park, NY: Delmar Learning. **11**

Kostelnik, M. J., Stein, L. C., Whiren, A. P., & Soderman, A. K. (2002). *Guiding children's social development* (4th ed.). Clifton Park, NY: Delmar Learning. **25**

Kotch, L. (2004). Preventing SIDS in child care: What can you do? *Young Children, 59*(2), 48. **12**

Kovach, B. A., & Da Ros, D. A. (1998). Respectful, individual, and responsive caregiving for infants: The key to successful care in group settings. *Young Children, 53*(3), 61–64. **12**

Krafft, K. C., & Berk, L. E. (1998). Private speech in two preschools: Significance of open-ended activities and make-believe play for verbal self-regulation. *Early Childhood Research Quarterly, 13*, 637–658. **21**

Krall, C. M., & Jalongo, M. R. (1998/99). Creating a caring community in classrooms: Advice from an intervention specialist. *Childhood Education, 75*, 83–89. **30**

Kramer, L., & Schaefer-Hernan, P. (1991, Apr.). *What's real in children's fantasy play?* Presented at the meeting of the Society for Research in Child Development, Seattle, WA. **4**

Krashen, S. (2002). Whole language and the great plummet of 1987–92: An urban legend from California. *Phi Delta Kappan, 83*(10), 748–753. **24**

Krashen, S. D. (1996). *Under attack: The case against bilingual education.* Culver City, CA: Language Associates. **24**

Krasnor, L. R. (1982). An observational study of social problem solving in young children. In K. H. Rubin & H. S. Ross (Eds.), *Peer relationships and social skills in childhood* (pp. 113–132). New York: Springer-Verlag. **27**

Krauss, M. W., Upshur, C. C., Shonkoff, J. P., & Hauser-Cram, P. (1993). The impact of parent groups on mothers of infants with disabilities. *Journal of Early Intervention, 16*(4), 8–20. **12**

Krechevsky, M. (1991). Project Spectrum: An innovative assessment alternative. *Educational Leadership, 48*(5), 43–48. **23**

Krechevsky, M. (1998). *Project Spectrum: Preschool assessment handbook.* New York: Teachers College Press. **23, 29**

Krogh, S. L., & Lamme, L. L. (1983). Learning to share: How literature can help. *Childhood Education, 59*, 188–192. **28**

Kuball, Y. E. (1999). A case for developmental continuity in a bilingual K2 setting. *Young Children, 54*(3), 74–79. **31**

Ladd, G. W. (1990). Having friends, keeping friends, making friends, and being liked by peers in the classroom: Predictions of children's early school adjustment? *Child Development, 61*, 1081–1100. **26**

Ladd, G. W., & Price, J. (1993). Playstyles of peer-accepted and peer-rejected children on the playground. In C. H. Hart (Ed.), *Children on playgrounds: Research perspectives and applications* (pp. 130–161). Albany, NY: SUNY Press. **26**

Lamb, M. E. (Ed.). (1982). *Nontraditional families: Parenting and child development.* Mahwah, NJ: Erlbaum. **32**

Lamb, S., & Zakhireh, B. (1997). Toddler's attention to the distress of peers in a day care setting. *Early Education and Development, 8*(2), 105–118. **16**

Lamme, L. L. (1979). Handwriting in early childhood curriculum. *Young Children, 35*(1), 20–27. **8**

Lampros, J. (2006, January 24). Pain of the game. *Ogden Utah Standard-Examiner*, 1A, 10A. **29**

Landau, S., & McAninch, C. (1993). Research in review. Young children with attention deficits. *Young Children, 48*(4), 49–58. **4, 28**

Lane, S., & Bergan, J. R. (1988). Effects of instructional variables on language ability of preschool children. *American Educational Research Journal, 25*, 271–283. **21**

Langlois, J. H. (2004). Emotion and emotion regulation: From another perspective. *Child Development, 75*(2), 315–316. **13**

Language and literacy in the earliest years. (2004). *Zero to three* [Focus issue], *25*(1). **17**

Lansford, J. E., Dodge, K. A., Pettit, G. S., Bates, J. E., Crozier, J., & Kaplow, J. (2002). A twelve-year study of the long-term effects of early child physical maltreatment on psychological, behavioral, and academic problems in adolescence [Electronic version]. *Archives Pediatric and Adolescent Medicine, 156*(8), 824–830. **6**

LaParo, K. M., Kraft-Sayre, M., & Pianta, R. C. (2003). Preschool to kindergarten transition activities: Involvement and satisfaction of families and teachers. *Journal of Research in Childhood Education, 17*(2), 147–158. **28**

LaPoint, S. A., Boutte, G. S., Swick, K. J., & Brown, M. H. (1993). Cultural sensitivity: How important is it for effective home visits? *Day Care and Early Education, 20*(4), 11–14. **12**

Larkin, J. M. (1993). Rethinking basic skills instruction with urban students. *The Educational Forum, 57*, 413–419. **4**

Larner, M., Behrman, R. E., Young, M., & Reich, K. (2001). Caring for infants and toddlers: Analysis and recommendations. *Future of Children, 11*(1), 7–20. **11**

Laupa, M. (1994). Who's in charge? Preschool children's concept of authority. *Early Childhood Research Quarterly, 9*, 1–18. **26**

Lauritzen, P. (1992). Facilitating integrated teaching and learning in the preschool setting: A process approach. *Early Childhood Research Quarterly, 7*, 531–550. **4**

Lawton, J. T., & Fowell, N. (1989). A description of teacher and child language in two preschool programs. *Early Childhood Research Quarterly, 4*, 407–432. **21**

Lazar, I., Darlington, R. B., Murray, H., Royce, J., & Snipper, A. (1982). Lasting effects of early education: A report from the consortium for longitudinal studies. *Monographs of the Society for Research in Child Development, 47* (23, Serial No. 195). **23**

Leboyer, F. (1976). *Birth without violence.* New York: Knopf. **11**

Lee, C. L., & Bates, J. E. (1985). Mother-child interaction at age two years and perceived difficult temperament. *Child Development, 56*, 1314–1325. **16**

Lee, G. (2003). Understanding immigrated Korean children's educational needs. *Kappa Delta Pi Record, 39*(4), 168–172. **7**

Lee, H., Ostrosky, M. M., Bennett, T., & Fowler, S. A. (2003). Perspectives of early intervention professionals about culturally-appropriate practices. *Journal of Early Intervention, 25*(4), 281–295. **11**

Lee, P. C. (1989). Is the young child egocentric or sociocentric? *Teacher's College Record, 90*, 375–391. **19**

Lefrancois, G. R. (1992). *Of children: An introduction to child development* (7th ed). Belmont, CA: Wadsworth. **4**

Legerstee, M., Corter, C., & Kienapple, K. (1990). Hand, arm, and facial actions of young infants to a social and nonsocial stimulus. *Child Development, 61*, 774–784. **14**

Lehman, S. (1997, May/June). Woman. *Stanford Today*, 47–52. **25**

Leiter, J., & Johnsen, M. C. (1997). Child maltreatment and school performance declines: An event-history analysis. *American Educational Research Journal, 34*, 563–589. **6**

Leone-Getten, M. B. (2005, Spring). Relationship builders. *University of Minnesota Link*, 12–17. **12**

Lerner, C., & Dombro, A. (2004). Finding your fit: Some temperament tips for parents. *Zero to Three, 24*(4), 42–45. **16**

Leslie, M. (2000, July/Aug.). The vexing legacy of Lewis Terman. *Stanford Magazine*, 45–51. **23**

Levin, D. E. (1998). *Remote control childhood? Combating the hazards of media culture.* Washington, DC: National Association for the Education of Young Children. **5**

Levin, D. E., & Carlsson-Paige, N. (1994). Developmentally appropriate television: Putting children first. *Young Children, 49*(5), 38–44. **4**

Lewis, A. C. (2005). Washington commentary: States feel the crunch of NCLB. *Phi Delta Kappan, 86*(5), 339–340. **31**

Lewis, M., & Michalson, L. (1983). *Children's emotions and moods.* New York: Plenum. **25**

Lewis, M., Sullivan, M. W., Stanger, C., & Weiss, M. (1989). Self development and self-conscience emotions. *Child Development, 60*, 146–156. **13**

Lewis, V. (2003). *Development and disability.* Malden, MA: Blackwell. **15**

Lewit, E. M., & Baker, L. S. (1995a). School readiness. *The Future of Children: Critical Issues for Children and Youth, 5*(2), 128–133. **28**

Lewit, E. M., & Baker, L. S. (1995b). Child indicators: Health insurance coverage. *The Future of Children: Long-Term Outcomes of Early Childhood Programs, 5*(3), 192–204. **12, 15**

Lewit, E. M., & Kerrebrock, N. (1997). Childhood hunger. *The Future of Children: Welfare to Work, 7*(1), 128–137. **7**

Lewit, E. M., Bennett, C., Behrman, R. E. (2003). Health insurance for children: Analysis and recommendations. *Future of Children, 13*(10), 5–30. **12**

Liben, L. S., & Yekel, C. A. (1996). Preschoolers' understanding of plan and oblique maps: The role of geometric and representational correspondence. *Child Development, 67*, 2780–2796. **19**

Lichtenstein, R. (1990). Psychometric characteristics and appropriate use of the Gesell School Readiness Screening Test: *Early Childhood Research Quarterly, 5*, 359–378. **28**

Lieberman, A. F. (1997). An infant mental health perspective. *Zero to Three, 18*(3), 3–5. **13**

Lillard, A. S. (1993a). Pretend play skills and the child's theory of mind. *Child Development, 64*, 348–371. **20**

Lillard, A. S. (1993b). Young children's conceptualization of pretense: Action or mental representational state? *Child Development, 64*, 372–386. **20**

Lin, C. C., & Fu, V. R. (1990). A comparison of child-rearing practices among Chinese, immigrant Chinese, and Caucasian-American parents. *Child Development, 61*, 429–433. **28**

Lindsey, G. (1989/99). Reviews of research: Brain research and implications for early childhood education. *Childhood Education, 75*, 97–100. **18**

Little Soldier, L. (1992). Working with Native American children. *Young Children, 47*(6), 15–21. **6**

Lively, V., & Lively, E. (1991). *Sexual development of young children.* Clifton Park, NY: Delmar Learning. **25**

Lockman, J. J., & Thelen, E. (1993). Developmental biodynamics: Brain, body, behavior connections. *Child Development, 64*, 953–959. **14**

Loizou, E. (2004). Funny babies: Humor and power in infancy. *Zero to Three, 24*(3), 17–21. **13**

Lomax, E. M. R. (1978). *Science and patterns of childrearing.* San Francisco: Freeman. **12**

Lombardi, J. (1991, Mar.). *New directions for early childhood advocacy.* Presentation at the meeting of the Southern Association on Children Under Six, Atlanta, GA. **33**

Lombardi, J., & Goffin, S. G. (1986). IDEAS! Child advocacy at the state level: Strategies for success. *Dimensions, 14*(2), 15–18. **33**

Lonigan, C. J., & Whitehurst, G. J. (1998). Relative efficacy of parent and teacher involvement in a shared-reading intervention for preschool children from low-income backgrounds. *Early Childhood Research Quarterly, 13*, 263–290. **22**

Losey, K. M. (1995). Mexican American students and classroom interaction: An overview and critique. *Review of Educational Research, 65*, 283–318. **6**

Louv, R. (1994). The crisis of the absent father. In K. M. Paciorek & J. H. Munro (Eds.), *Early Childhood Education 94/95* (pp. 49–51). Guilford, CT: Dushkin. Originally published in Louv, R. (1993). *Father love.* New York: Pocket Books. **12**

Lubeck, S. (1998a). Is DAP for everyone? *Childhood Education, 74*(5), 283–292. **2**

Lubeck, S. (1998b). Is DAP for everyone? A response. *Childhood Education, 74*(5), 299–301. **2**

Lucile Packard Children's Hospital. (n.d.). *Care of the Terminally Ill Child.* Retrieved October 12, 2002, from http://www.lpch.org/DiseaseHealthInfo/HealthLibrary/terminallyill/concept.html **25**

Lucy, J. A. (1988). The role of language in the development of representation: A comparison of the views of Piaget and Vygotsky. *The Quarterly Newsletter of the Laboratory of Human Cognition, 10*, 99–103. **20**

Luster, T., & McAdoo, H. P. (1991, Apr.). *Factors related to the achievement and adjustment of young black children.* Paper presented at the meeting of the Society for Research in Child Development, Seattle, WA. **31**

Lynn-Garbe, C., & Hoot, J. L. (2004/05). Weighing in on the issue of childhood obesity. *Childhood Education, 81*(2), 70–76. **18, 19**

Lyons-Ruth, K., Alpern, L., & Repacholi, B. (1993). Disorganized infant attachment classification and maternal psychosocial problems as predictors of hostile-aggressive behavior in the preschool classroom. *Child Development, 64*, 572–585. **13**

Maccoby, E. E., & Zellner, M. (1970). *Experiments in primary education: Aspects of project Follow-Through.* New York: Harcourt Brace Jovanovich. **28**

MacDonald, K. (1992). A time and place for everything: A discrete systems perspective on the role of children's rough-and-tumble play in educational settings. *Early Education and Development, 3*, 334–335. **26**

Madaus, G. F. (1988). The influence of testing on the curriculum. In L. N. Tanner (Ed.), *Critical issues in curriculum* (pp. 83–121). Chicago: National Society for the Study of Education, distributed by the University of Chicago Press. **28**

Maguire, J. (1990). *Hopscotch, hangman, hot potato, & hahaha: A rulebook of children's games.* New York: Prentice Hall. **8**

Maier, H. W. (1978). *Three theories of child development* (3rd ed.). New York: Harper & Row. **5, 12, 15, 25, 27**

Maintaining recess in elementary schools. (2006, Jan.). *Elementary Physical Education, 8*(1), 1. Retrieved from http://www.pelinks4u.org. **29**

Malaguzzi, L. (1993). For an education based on relationships. *Young Children, 49*(1), 9–12. **32**

Malatesta, C. Z., Culver, C., Tesman, J. R., & Shepard, B. (1989). The development of emotion expression during the first two years of life. *Monographs of the Society for Research in Child Development, 54* (1–2, Serial No. 219). **13, 16**

Malina, R. M. (1982). Motor development in the early years. In S. G. Moore & K. Cooper (Eds.), *The young child: Reviews of research* (Vol. 3, pp. 211–229). Washington, DC: National Association for the Education of Young Children. **8**

Mallory, B. L., & New, R. S. (Eds.). (1994). *Diversity & developmentally appropriate practices.* New York: Teachers College Press. **2**

Malouff, J. (2002–2006). *Helping young children overcome shyness.* Retrieved February 5, 2006, from http://www.une.edu.au **30**

Mangelsdorf, S., Gunnar, M., Kestenbaum, R., Lang, S., & Andreas, D. (1990). Infant-proneness-to distress temperament, maternal personality, and mother-infant attachment: Associations and goodness of fit. *Child Development, 61*, 820–831. **13**

Mann, J. (1991). Public policy report. Congress remembers the children—finally. *Young Children, 46*(2), 81. **33**

Marazon, R. E. (1994). *Mr. Rogers' Neighborhood*—As affective staff development for teachers of young children: A story of conflict, conversion, conviction, and celebration. *Young Children, 49*(5), 34–37. **5**

Marcon, R. A. (1993). Socioemotional versus academic emphasis: Impact on kindergartners' development and achievement. *Early Child Development and Care, 96*, 81–91. **28**

Marcon, R. A. (1995, May 17). The fourth-grade slump: The cause and cure. *Principal*, 19–20. **28**

Marcon, R. A. (2003). Research in review. Growing children: The physical side of development. *Young Children, 58*(1), 80–87. **18, 29**

Marlier, L., & Schaal, B. (2005). Human newborns prefer human milk: Conspecific milk odor is attractive without postnatal exposure. *Child Development, 76*(1), 155–168. **10**

Marion, M. (1997). Research in review. Guiding young children's understanding and management of anger. *Young Children, 52*(7), 62–67. **25**

Marotz, L. R., Cross, M. Z., & Rush, J. M. (2005). *Health, safety, and nutrition for the young child* (6th ed.). Clifton Park, NY: Delmar Learning. **12, 15, 18, 29**

Martinez, M. A. (1987). Dialogues among children and between children and their mothers. *Child Development, 58*, 1035–1043. **21**

Marvin, C., & Mirenda, P. (1993). Home literacy experiences of preschoolers enrolled in Head Start and special education programs. *Journal of Early Intervention, 17*, 351–367. **22**

Matheny, A. P., Jr., Wilson, R. S., & Nuss, S. M. (1984). Toddler temperament: Stability across settings and over ages. *Child Development, 55*, 1200–1211. **16**

Maughan, A., & Cicchetti, D. (2002). Impact of child maltreatment on children's emotion regulation abilities and socioemotional adjustment. *Child Development, 73*(5), 1525–1542. **25**

Mayes, L. C. (2002). Parental preoccupation and perinatal mental health. *Zero to Three, 22*(6), 4–9. **13**

Mayesky, M. (2006). *Creative activities for young children* (8th ed.). Clifton Park, NY: Delmar Learning. **23, 24**

McAdoo, J. L. (1979). Father-child interaction patterns and self-esteem in black preschool children. *Young Children, 34*(1), 46–53. **25**

McAfee, O., Leong, D. J., & Bodrova, E. (2004). *Basics of assessment: A primer for early childhood educators.* Washington, DC: National Association for the Education of Young Children. **3, 23, 28**

McBride, B. A. (1989). Interaction, accessibility, and responsibility: A view of father involvement and how to encourage it. *Young Children, 44*(5), 13–19. **15**

McBride, S. L., Brotherson, M. J., Joanning, H., Whiddon, D., & Demmitt, A. (1993). Implementation of family centered services: Perceptions of families and professionals. *Journal of Early Intervention, 17*, 414–430. **6**

McBride-Chang, C. (1998). The development of invented spelling. *Early Education and Development, 9*, 147–160. **24**

McBride-Chang, C., & Jacklin, C. N. (1993). Early play arousal, sex-typed play, and activity level as precursors to later rough-and-tumble play. *Early Education and Development, 4*, 99–108. **26**

McClurg, L. G. (1998). Building an ethical community in the classroom: Community meeting. *Young Children, 53*(2), 30–35. **30**

McCormick, K. M., Anderman, L. H., Brown, J. G., Privett, N., Hemmeter, M. L., Gerry, G. B., & Rous, B. (2001). *Characteristics and attributes of effective primary programs and practices in Kentucky.* Louisville, KY: University of Louisville. **31**

McCormick, P. (1994). How kids survive trauma. In K. M. Paciorek & J. H. Munro (Eds.), *Early Childhood Education 94/95* (pp. 183–185). Guilford, CT: Dushkin. **25**

McCracken, J. B. (1993). *Valuing diversity: The primary years.* Washington, DC: National Association for the Education of Young Children. **30**

McCune, L. (1989, Apr.). *Toward an integrative theory of early language acquisition: Evidence from longitudinal trends in vocal behavior.* Presented at the biennial meeting of the Society for Research in Child Development, Kansas City, MO. **17**

McDaniel, G. L., Isaac, M. Y., Brooks, H. M., & Hatch, A. (2005). Confronting K–3 teaching challenges in an era of accountability. *Young Children, 60*(2), 20–26. **31**

McGee, L. M. (1985). *Evaluation of East Baton Rouge, Louisiana, preschool program.* (Report to the State Department of Education). Louisiana State University, Baton Rouge. **22**

McGee, L. M., Charlesworth, R., Cheek, M., & Cheek, E. (1982). Metalinguistic knowledge: Another look at beginning reading. *Childhood Education, 59*, 123–127. **20**

McGee, L. M., & Richgels, D. J. (2004). *Literacy's beginnings: Supporting young readers and writers* (4th ed.). Boston: Allyn & Bacon. **14, 17, 22, 24**

McGee, L. M., Richgels, D., & Charlesworth, R. (1986). Emerging knowledge of written language: Learning to read and write. In S. J. Kilmer (Ed.), *Advances in early education and day care* (Vol. IV) (pp. 67–121). Greenwich, CT: JAI Press. **24**

McGee, L. M., & Morrow, L. M. (2005). *Teaching literacy in kindergarten.* New York: Guilford. **24**

McGill-Franzen, A., & Allington, R. L. (1993). Flunk'em or get them classified: The contamination of primary grade accountability data. *Educational Researcher, 22*(1), 19–22. **28**

McGinn, D. (2004/05). Guilt free TV. In K. L. Freiberg (Ed.), *Human Development 04/05* (pp. 51–55). Guilford, CT: McGraw-Hill/Dushkin. **7**

McGlaughlin, B. N., & Morgan, N. L. (1981). Fine motor development. In M. Tudor (Ed.), *Child Development* (pp. 427–430). New York: McGraw-Hill. **15**

McGonigel, M. J., Kaufman, R. K., & Johnson, B. H. (1991). A family-oriented process for the individualized family service plan. *Journal of Early Intervention, 15*, 46–56. **6**

McGowan, R. J., & Johnson, D. L. (1984). The mother-child relationship and other antecedents of childhood intelligence: A causal analysis. *Child Development, 55*, 810–820. **23**

McInerney, D. M., Roche, L. A., McInerney, V., & Marsh, H. W. (1997). Cultural perspectives on school motivation: The relevance and application of goal theory. *American Educational Research Journal, 34*(1), 207–236. **4**

McIntyre, E. (1990). Young children's reading strategies as they read self-selected books in school. *Early Childhood Research Quarterly, 5*, 265–277. **31**

McLead, M. (1998, Aug./Sept.). Remedy for ill health: decent shelter. Shelter and health: A critical connection. *Habitat World*, 2–3. **7**

McLean, D. (2002). Helping Aaron navigate: Including children with physical disabilities. *Dimensions, 30*(1), 9–15. **5**

McLean, J. E. (1997), Teacher empowerment through action research. *KDP Record, 34*(1), 34–38. **3**

McLean, S. V. (1993). Learning from teachers' stories. *Childhood Education, 69*, 265–268. **3**

McLesky, J., & Waldron, N. L. (2002). School change and inclusive schools: Lessons learned from practice. *Phi Delta Kappan, 84*(1), 65–72. **31**

McLoyd, V. (1990). The impact of economic hardship on black families and children: Psychological distress, parenting, and socioemotional development. *Child Development, 61*, 311–346. **28**

McLoyd, V. C. (1983). The effects of the structure of play objects on the pretend play of low-income preschool children. *Child Development, 54*, 626–635. **5**

McLoyd, V. C., Ray, S. A., & Etter-Lewis, G. (1985). Being and becoming: The interface of language and family role knowledge in the pretend play of young African girls. In L. Galda & A. D. Pellegrini (Eds.), *Play, language, and stories* (pp. 29–44). Norwood, NJ: Ablex. **4, 21**

McMackin, M. D. (1993). The parent's role in literacy development: Fostering reading strategies at home. *Childhood Education, 69*, 142–145. **22**

McMullen, M. B. (1999). Characteristics of teachers who talk the DAP talk and walk the DAP walk. *Journal of Research in Childhood Education, 13*, 216–230. **28**

McNichol, T. (1998, Feb. 6–8). The power of touch. *USA Weekend*, 22. **11**

McQueen, A. B., & Washington, V. (1988). Effect of intervention on the language facility of poor, black adolescent mothers and their preschool children. *Early Child Development and Care, 33*, 137–152. **24**

Mead, D. E. (1976). *Six approaches to child rearing.* Provo, UT: Brigham Young University Press. **26**

Meck, N. E., Fowler, S. A., Claflin, K., & Rasmussen, L. B. (1995). Mothers' perceptions of their NICU experience 1 and 7 months after discharge. *Journal of Early Intervention, 19*, 288–301. **11**

Meddin, B. J., & Rosen, A. (1986). Child abuse and neglect: Prevention and reporting. *Young Children, 41*(4), 26–30. **6**

Meisels, S. J. (1987). Uses and abuses of developmental screening, and school readiness testing. *Young Children, 42*(2), 4–6, 68–73. **8**

Meisels, S. J. (1993). Remaking classroom assessment with the work sampling system. *Young Children, 48*(5), 34–40. **29**

Meisels, S. J. (1994). Designing meaningful measurements for early childhood. In B. L. Mallory & R. S. New (Eds.), *Diversity and developmentally appropriate practices* (pp. 202–222). New York: Teachers College Press. **29**

Meisels, S. J. (2000). On the side of the child: Personal reflections on testing, teaching, and early childhood education. *Young Children, 55*(6), 16–19. **28**

Meisels, S. J., & Atkins-Burnett, S. (2005). *Developmental screening in early childhood: A guide* (5th ed.). Washington, DC: National Association for the Education of Young Children. **28**

Melson, G. F., Windecker-Nelson, E., & Schwarz, R. (1998). Support and stress in mothers and fathers of young children. *Early Education and Development, 9*, 261–281. **25**

Meltzoff, A. N. (1988). Infant imitation and memory: Nine-month-olds in immediate and deferred tests. *Child Development, 59*, 217–225. **14**

Meltzoff, A. N., & Moore, M. K. (1983). Newborn infants imitate adult facial gestures. *Child Development, 54*, 702–709. **12**

Meyer, C. A., Klein, E. L., & Genishi, C. (1994). Peer relationships among four preschool second language learners in "Small Group Time." *Early Childhood Research Quarterly, 9*, 61–86. **21**

Micheli, L. J. (1990, Oct. 29). Children and sports. *Newsweek*, 12. **8, 29**

Michels, S., Pianta, R. C., & Reeve, R. E. (1993). Parent self-reports of discipline practices and child acting-out behaviors in kindergarten. *Early Education and Development, 4*, 139–144. **28**

Mills, B. C., & Spooner, L. (1988). Preschool stress and the three R's. *Dimensions, 16*(2), 8–10. **25**

Miller, D. F. (2003). *Positive child guidance.* (4th ed.) Clifton Park, NY: Delmar Learning. **15**

Miller, L. B. (1984). Long-term effects of four preschool programs: Ninth- and tenth-grade results. *Child Development, 55*, 1570–1589. **23**

Miller, L. B., & Bizzell, R. B. (1983). Long-term effects of four preschool programs: Sixth, seventh, and eighth grades. *Child Development, 54*, 727–741. **23**

Miller, P. H. (2002). *Theories of developmental psychology* (4th ed.). New York: Freeman. **2, 4, 6, 14, 15, 16, 19, 24, 26**

Miller, S. (2005). Building a peaceful and just world—Beginning with children. *Childhood Education, 82*(1), 14–18. **27**

Miller, S. A. (2005). Reflections on kindergarten: Giving young children what they deserve. *Childhood Education, 81*(5), 256–260. **19**

Miller, S. A. (2005, March). Don't forget to laugh: The importance of humor, 3 to 4. *Early Childhood Education Today*, 30–31. **25**

Minoura, Y. (1993). Culture and personality reconsidered: Theory building from cases of Japanese children returning from the United States. *The Quarterly Newsletter of the Laboratory of Comparative Human Cognition, 15*, 63–71. **25**

Mizokawa, D. T., & Ryckman, D. B. (1988, Apr.). *Attributions of academic success and failure to effort or ability: A comparison of six Asian-American ethnic groups.* Presented at the annual meeting of the American Educational Research Association, New Orleans, LA. **6**

Moll, L. C. (1990). *Vygotsky and education.* New York: Cambridge University Press. **5, 19**

*Moments in America for Children.* (2004, Aug.). Retrieved June 16, 2005, from http://www.childrensdefense.org **32**

Monaghan, P. (1985, Apr.). *The development of symbolic expression in preschool play and language.* Paper presented at the meeting of the American Educational Research Association, Chicago, IL. **4**

Moore, E. G. J. (1982). Language behavior in the test situation and the intelligence test achievement of transracially and traditionally adopted black children. In L. Feagans & D. C. Farran (Eds.), *The language of children reared in poverty* (pp. 141–162). New York: Academic Press. **23**

Moore, S. G. (1977). The effects of television on the prosocial behavior of young children. *Young Children, 32*(5), 60–65. **26**

Moore, S. G. (1985). Social effects of peers on curiosity. *Early Report, 12*(3), 1–2. **23**

Morrison, J. W., & Bordere, T. (2001). Supporting biracial children's identity development. *Childhood Education, 77*(3), 134–138. **6**

Morrison, J. W., & Rodgers, L. S. (1996). Being responsive to the needs of children from dual heritage backgrounds. *Young Children, 52*(1), 29–33. **6**

Morrow, L. M. (1990). Preparing the classroom environment to promote literacy during play. *Early Childhood Research Quarterly, 5*, 537–554. **4, 5**

Morrow, R. D. (1989). What's in a name? In particular, a Southeast Asian name? *Young Children, 44*(6), 20–23. **4, 6**

Mosley, J. G. (1992). *A comparison of language and graphic products of students from kindergarten classrooms differing in developmental appropriateness of instruction.* Unpublished doctoral dissertation, Louisiana State University, Baton Rouge. **22, 23**

Moyer, J. (1990). Whose creation is it anyway? *Childhood Education, 66*(3), 130–131. **24**

Mukhopadhyay, C., & Henze, R. C. (2003). On race, biology, and society. *Phi Delta Kappan, 84*(9), 669–678. **7**

Mulroy, M. T., Bothell, J., & Gaudio, M. (2004). First steps in preventing childhood lead poisoning: The role of child care practitioners. *Young Children 59*(2), 20–25. **18**

Munroe, R. L., & Munroe, R. H. (1975). *Cross-cultural human development.* Monterey, CA: Brooks/Cole. **21**

Murachver, T., Pipe, M., Gordon, R., Owens, J. L., & Fivush. (1996). Do, show, and tell: Children's event memories acquired through direct experience, observation, and stories. *Child Development, 67*, 3029–3044. **20**

Murata, N. M., & Maeda, J. K. (2002). Structured play for preschoolers with developmental delays. *Early Childhood Education Journal, 29*(4), 237–240. **5, 19**

Murray, B. (2006, May). Understanding brain development and early learning. *FACSNET*. Retrieved May 16, 2006, from http://www.facsnet.org. **4**

Musatti, T. (1986). Early peer relations: The perspectives of Piaget and Vygotsky. In E. Mueller & C. Cooper (Eds.), *Process and outcome in peer relations* (pp. 25–53). New York: Academic Press. **26**

NAEYC (National Association for the Education of Young Children) & NAECS/SDE (National Association of Early Childhood Specialists in State Departments of Education). (1991). Guidelines for appropriate curriculum content and assessment in programs serving children ages 3 through 8. *Young Children, 46*(3), 21–38. **23, 28**

NAEYC. (1996). Technology and young children. *Early years are learning years*, #9. **6**

NAEYC/IRA. (1998). Learning to read and write: Developmentally appropriate practices for young children. A joint position statement of the International Reading Association (IRA) and the National Association for the Education of Young Children (NAEYC). *Young Children, 53*(4), 30–46. **22, 31**

NAEYC's Code of Ethical Conduct: Guidelines for responsible behavior in early childhood education. (1996). *Young Children, 51*(3), 57–60. [NAEYC.org]. **3**

NAEYC joins task force on media violence. (1993). *Young Children, 48*(5), **48**

NAEYC position statement on media violence in children's lives. (1990). *Young Children, 45*(5), 18–21. **4**

NAEYC position statement on school readiness. (1990). *Young Children, 46*(1) 21–23. **28**

NAEYC position statement on violence in the lives of children. (1993). *Young Children, 48*(6), 80–84. **4, 25, 26**

*NIDA InfoFacts: Methamphetamine*. Retrieved August 5, 2005, from http://www.nida.nih.gov **9**

Nash, J. M. (2004/05). Inside the womb. In K. L. Freiberg (Ed.), *Human Development 04/05* (pp. 16–20). Guilford, CT: McGraw-Hill/Dushkin. **8**

National Adoption Information Clearinghouse (NAIC). (2000). *Gay and Lesbian Adoptive Parents: Resources for Professionals and Parents*. Retrieved May 16, 2006, from http://naic.acf.hhs.gov **27**

National Association for Gifted Children (n.d.). *Who are the gifted?* Retrieved October 27, 2002, from http://www.nagc.org/parentinfo. **23**

National Association of Child Advocates (NACA). (2001). *2001 NACA member legislative reference guide*. Retrieved November, 2002, from http://www.childadvocacy.org/2003briefingbook.pdf **33**

National Association of State Boards of Education. (1990). *Right from the start: The report of the NASBE task force on Early Childhood Education*. Alexandria, VA: Author. **27**

National Center for Early Development & Learning (NCEDL). (2002). *Regulation of child care, 2*(1).

National Center for Education Statistics. (2002). *Characteristics of children in early childhood programs*. Retrieved October 20, 2002, from http://nces.ed.gov/ fastfacts/display.asp?id=78 **32**

National Center for Fathering. (2000, Sept.). *Involving non-resident fathers in children's learning*. Retrieved August 6, 2002, from http://fatherhood.hhs.gov/involv-non-res00 **12**

National Center for Infectious Diseases. (2005). *Respiratory Syncytial Virus*. Retrieved May 19, 2006, from http://www.cdc.gov **12**

*The National Children's Study*. Retrieved February 19, 2006, from http://nationalchildrensstudy.gov. **32**

National Gay and Lesbian Task Force. (2003). *Lesbian, Gay, Bisexual and Transgender (LGBT) Parents and Their Children*. Retrieved May 16, 2006, from http://www.thetaskforce.org **27**

National Institute of Mental Health. (2003). *Attention Deficit Hyperactivity Disorder*. Retrieved May 9, 2006, from http://www.nimh.nih.gov **30**

National Institute of Mental Health (NIMH). (2001). *Helping children and adolescents cope with violence and disaster*. Retrieved November 17, 2002, from http://www.nimh.nih.gov/ publicat/violence.cfm **27**

Nazario, S. (1997, Nov. 16). Orphans of addiction. *Los Angeles Times*, p. **1**

Necochea, J., & Cline, Z (1993). Building capacity in the education of language minority students. *The Educational Forum, 57*, 402–412. **24**

Nelson, B., & Fritschi, J. (2004). Tour, inventory, and retool—assistive technology for all children. *Focus on inclusive education*, [an ACEI publication] *2*(2), 1–7. **6**

Nelson, D. A., Robinson, C .C., & Hart, C. H. (2005). Relational and physical aggression of preschool-age children: Peer status linkages across informants. *Early Education and Development, 16*(2), 115–140. **26**

Nelson, K. (1973). Structure and strategy in learning to talk. *Monographs of the Society for Research in Child Development, 38* (12, Serial No. 38). **21**

Nelson, K. (1982). Individual differences in language development: Implications for development and language. In J. K. Gardner (Ed.), *Readings in developmental psychology* (2nd ed). Boston: Little, Brown. **17**

Nelson-Le Gall, S., & Jones, E. (1990). Cognitive-motivational influences on the task-related help-seeking behavior of black children. *Child Development, 61*, 581–589. **30**

Neuman, S. B., & Roskos, K. (1993). Access to print for children of poverty: Differential effects of adult mediation and literacy-enriched play settings on environmental and functional print tasks. *American Educational Research Journal, 30*, 95–122. **4, 5, 22**

New, R. S. (1994). Culture, child development, and developmentally appropriate practices: Teachers as collaborative researchers. In B. L. Mallory & R. S. New (Eds.), *Diversity and developmentally appropriate practices* (pp. 65–83). New York: Teachers College Press, **3, 28**

New, R. S., & Mallory, B. L. (1994). Introduction: The ethics of inclusion. In B. L. Mallory & R. S. New (Eds.), *Diversity & developmentally appropriate practices* (pp. 1–13). New York: Teachers College Press. **2**

The New Food Guide Pyramid. (2005, April). *KidsHealth*. Retrieved January 22, 2006, from http://www. kidshealth. org **29**

*The new American Webster handy college dictionary*. (1995). (3rd ed.). New York: Penguin Books. **4**

Newport, E. L., Gleitman, H., & Gleitman, L. R. (1977). Mother, I'd rather do it myself: Some effects and noneffects of maternal speech style. In C. E. Snow & C. A. Ferguson (Eds.), *Talking to children* (pp. 109–149). Cambridge, UK: Cambridge University Press. **24**

Newton, N. (1975). Putting the child back in childbirth. *Psychology Today, 9*, 24–25. **11**

Nguyen, S. P., & Murphy, G. L. (2003). An apple is more than just a fruit: Cross-classification in children's concepts. *Child Development, 74*(6), 1581–1593. **20**

NICHD Early Childhood Care Research Network. (1997). The effects of infant child care on infant-mother attachment security: Results of the NICHD study of early child care. *Child Development, 68*, 860–879. **13**

NICHD Early Childhood Care Research Network. (1998). Early child care and self-control, compliance, and problem behavior at twenty-four and thirty-six months. *Child Development, 69*, 1145–1170. **16, 18**

Nicolich, L. M. (1977). Beyond sensorimotor intelligence: Assessment of symbolic maturity through analysis of pretend play. *The Merrill-Palmer Quarterly, 23*, 89–99 **16**

Nicolson, S., & Shipstead, S. G. (1994). *Through the looking glass: Observations in the early childhood classroom*. New York: Merrill/Macmillan. **3**

Ninio, A. & Rinott, N. (1988). Fathers' involvement in the care of their infants and their attributions of cognitive competence to infants. *Child Development, 59*, 652–663. **12**

*No Child Left Behind*. (2002). Retrieved November 22, 2002, from http://www.nochildleftbehind.gov. **22, 28**

*No Child Left Behind: Expanding the Promise*. (2005). Retrieved December 26, 2005, from http://www.ed.gov/ **22**

Nobles, W. W. (1977). Extended self: Rethinking the so-called Negro self-concept. In M. Coleman (Ed.), *Black children just keep on growing* (pp. 159–165). Washington, DC: National Black Child Development Institute. **26**

Noddings, N. (2005). Caring in education. *The Encyclopedia of Informal Education*. Retrieved February 10, 2006, from http://www.infed.org **31**

Notar, E. (1989). Children and commercials. *Childhood Education, 66*, 66–67. **4, 6**

Novick, R. (1998). The comfort corner: Fostering resiliency and emotional intelligence. *Childhood Education, 74*, 200–204. **25**

Novick, R. (2002). Learning to read the heart: Nurturing emotional literacy. *Young Children, 57*(3), 84–89. **25**

Nuttall, D. (1993). Letters I never sent to my daughter's third grade teacher. *Young Children, 48*(6), 6–7. **30**

Nwokah, E. E. (2003). Giggle time in the infant/toddler classroom: Learning and connecting through shared humor and laughter. *Focus on Infants and Toddlers, 16*(2), 1–7. **16**

O'Brien, M., & Dale, D. (1994). Family-centered services in the neonatal intensive care unit: A review of research. *Journal of Early Intervention, 18*, 78–90. **11**

O'Brien, S. Put your kids on a TV diet. (2005, June 17–19). *USA Today*. **4**

Odom, S. (2002). Narrowing the question: Social integration and characteristics of children with disabilities in inclusion settings. *Early Childhood Research Quarterly, 17*, 167–170. **26**

Odom, S. L., & Diamond, K. E. (1998). Inclusion of young children with special needs in early childhood education: The research base. *Early Childhood Research Quarterly, 13*(1), 3–26. **4**

Odom, S. L., Zercher, C., Li, S., Marquart, J., & Sandall, S. (1998). *Social relationships of preschool children with disabilities in inclusive settings*. Paper presented at the annual meeting of the American Educational Research Association, San Diego, CA. **26**

Ogbu, J. U. (1994). From cultural differences in cultural frame of reference. In P. M. Greenfield & R. R. Cocking (Eds.), *Cross-cultural roots of minority child development* (pp. 365–392). Mahwah, NJ: Erlbaum. **6, 23**

Okagaki, L., Diamond, K. E., Kontos, S. J., & Hestenes, L. L. (1998). Correlates of young children's interactions with classmates with disabilities. *Early Childhood Research Quarterly, 13*, 67–86. **26**

Okagaki, L., & Sternberg, R. J. (1993). Parental beliefs and children's school performance. *Child Development, 64*, 36–56. **6**

Okagaki, L., & Diamond, K. E. (2003). Responding to cultural and linguistic differences in beliefs and practices of families with young children. In C. Copple, (Ed.), *A world of difference: Readings on teaching young children in a diverse society* (pp. 2–15). Washington, DC: National Association for the Education of Young Children. **1, 17**

Oken-Wright, P. (1998). Transitions to writing: Drawing as a scaffold for emergent writers. *Young Children, 53*(2), 76–81. **22**

Olweus, D. (1993). *Bullying at school: What we know and what we can do*. Cambridge, MA: Blackwell. **30**

O'Neil, D. K., & Astington, J. (1990, Apr.). *Young children's understanding of the role sensory experiences play in knowledge acquisition*. Presented at the annual meeting of the American Educational Research Association, Boston, MA. **4**

Ornstein, R. E. (1973). Right and left thinking. *Psychology Today, 6*, 87–92. **18**

Osofsky, J. D. (1995). Children who witness domestic violence: The invisible victims. *SRCD Social Policy Report, IX*, 3. **28**

Ostrov, J. M., & Crick, N. R. (2005). Introduction to the special issue: Current directions in the study of relational aggression during early childhood. *Early Education and Development, 16*(2), 109–114. **26**

O'Sullivan, J. T., Howe, M. L., & Marche, T. A. (1996). Children's beliefs about long-term retention. *Child Development, 67*, 2989–3009. **20**

Owocki, G. (1999). *Literacy through play*. Portsmouth, NH: Heinemann. **31**

Paguio, L. P., & Resurreccion, A. V. A. (1987). Children's food preferences: Development and influences. *Childhood Education, 62*, 296–300. **18**

Paguio, L. P., Robinson, B. E., & Skeen, P. (1985). Review of research: A cross-cultural view of parental child-rearing practices. *Dimensions, 14*(1), 22–23. **12**

Paley, V. G. (1995). *Kwanzaa and me.* Cambridge, MA: Harvard University Press. **1**

Palkovitz, R. (1985). Fathers' birth attendance, early contact, and extended contact with their newborns: A critical review. *Child Development, 56*, 392–406. **11**

Pan, B. A., Rowe, M. L., Singer, J. D., & Snow, C. E. (2005). Maternal correlates of growth in toddler vocabulary production in low-income families. *Child Development, 76*(4), 763–782. **17**

Pang, V. O. (1990). Asian-American children: A diverse population. *The Educational Forum, 55*(1), 49–60. **6**

Papert, S. (2004). Child psychologist: Jean Piaget. In K. L. Freiberg (Ed.), *Human Development 04/05* (pp. 65–66). Guilford, CT: McGraw-Hill/Dushkin. **2**

Parette, H. P., Jr., & Murdick, N. L. (1998). Assistive technology and IEPs for young children with disabilities. *Early Childhood Education Journal, 25*, 193–198. **8**

Parke, R. D., & Sawin, D. B. (1977). Fathering: Its major role. *Psychology Today, 11*, 108–112. **13**

Parke, R. D. (2004). The Society for Research in Child Development at 70: Progress and promise. *Child Development, 75*(1), 1–24. **3**

Parker, S. W., & Nelson, C. A. (2005). The impact of early institutional rearing on the ability to discriminate expressions of emotion: An event-related potential study. *Child Development, 76*(1), 54–72. **16**

Parlakian, R. (2004). Early literacy and very young children. *Zero to Three, 25*(1), 37–44. **14**

Parry, A. (1993). Children surviving in a violent world—"Choosing non-violence." *Young Children, 48*(6), 13–15. **25, 28**

Parten, M. B. (1932). Social participation among pre-school children. *Journal of Abnormal and Social Psychology, 27*, 243–269. **27**

Patterson, C. J., Kupersmidt, J. B., & Vaden, N. A. (1990). Income level, gender, ethnicity, and household composition as predictors of children's school-based competence. *Child Development, 61*, 485–494. **31**

Patton, M. M., & Wortham, S. C. (1993). Transition classes, A growing concern. *Journal of Research in Childhood Education, 8*, 32–42. **28**

Pausell, D., & Nogales, R. (2003). The community consolidated child care pilot services program, El Paso County, CO. *Zero to Three*, 23(4), 11–16. **1**

*PBS Teacher Source* (n.d.). Retrieved October 26, 2002, from http://www.pbs.org/teachersource **22**

Pekkanen, J. (2004/05). The mystery of fetal life: Secrets of the womb. In K. L. Freiberg (Ed.), *Human Development 04/05* (pp. 21–29). Guilford, CT: McGraw-Hill/Dushkin. **8**

Pellegrini, A. D. (1984). The effects of classroom ecology on preschoolers' functional use of language. In A. Pellegrini & T. Yawkey (Eds.), *The development of oral and written language in social contexts* (pp. 129–144). Norwood, NJ: Ablex. **24**

Pellegrini, A. D. (1985). The relations between symbolic play and literate behavior: A review and critique of the empirical literature. *Review of Educational Research, 55*, 107–121. **4**

Pellegrini, A. D. (1991). *Applied child study.* Mahwah, NJ: Erlbaum. **3**

Pellegrini, A. D., & Bjorklund, D. F. (1996). The place of recess in school: Issues in the role of recess in children's education and development, An introduction to the theme issue. *Journal of Research in Childhood Education, 11*(1), 5–13. **30**

Pellegrini, A. D., & Perlmutter, J. C. (1988). Rough-and-tumble play on the elementary school playground. *Young Children, 43*(2), 1417. **7, 29**

Pellegrini, A. D., Perlmutter, J. C., Galda, L., & Brody, G. H. (1990). Joint reading between black Head Start children and their mothers. *Child Development, 61*, 413–453. **6**

Pellegrini, A. D., & Smith, P. K. (1993). School recess: Implications for education and development. *Review of Educational Research, 63*, 51–68. **30**

Pellegrini, A. D., & Smith, P. K. (1998). Physical activity play: The nature and function of a neglected aspect of play. *Child Development, 69*, 577–598. **18**

Pepler, D., Corter, C., & Abramovitch, R. (1982). Social relations among children: Comparison of sibling and peer interaction. In K. H. Rubin & H. S. Ross (Eds.), *Peer relationships and social skills in childhood* (pp. 209–227). New York: Springer-Verlag. **26**

Perez, S. (2004). Shaping new possibilities for Latino children and the nations future. *The Future of Children: Children of Immigrant Families*, 14(2), 122–126. **7**

Perez, S. A. (1994). Responding differently to diversity. *Childhood Education, 70*, 151–153. **6**

Perlmutter, J. C., & Laminack, L. L. (1993). Sociodramatic play: A stage for practicing literacy. *Dimensions of Early Childhood, 21*(4), 13–16. **4**

Perry, D. G. (1989, Apr.). *Social learning theory.* Presentation at the biennial meeting of the Society for Research in Child Development, Kansas City, MO. **5, 12, 20**

Perry, T., & Delpit, L. (Eds.). (1998). *The real Ebonics debate: Power, language and the education of African-American children.* Boston: Beacon Press. **21**

Persson-Blennow, I., & McNeil, T. F. (1980). Questionnaires for measurement of temperament in one- and two-year-old children: Development and standardization. *Journal of Child Psychology and Psychiatry, 21*, 37–46. **16**

Petersen, S., Bair, K., & Sullivan, A. (2004). Emotional well-being and mental health services: Lessons learned by Early Head Start Region VIII programs. *Zero to Three, 24*(6), 45–53. **12**

Petroski, H. (2004/05). Early education. In K. M. Paciorek & J. H. Munro. (Eds.), *Annual editions: Early childhood education 04/05* (pp. 29–32). Dubuque, IA: McGraw-Hill/Dushkin. **5**

Pett, J. (1990). What is authentic evaluation? Common questions and answers. *Fair Test Examiner, 4*(1), 8–9. **29**

Pfannenstiel, J., & Schattgen, S. F. (1997, Mar.). *Evaluating the effects of pedagogy informed by constructivism: A comparison of student achievement across constructivist and traditional classrooms.* Paper presented at the annual meeting of the American Educational Research Association, Chicago. IL. **28**

Phillips, C. B. (1994). The movement of African-American children through sociocultural contexts: A case of conflict resolution. In B. L. Mallory & R. S. New (Eds.), *Diversity and developmentally appropriate practices* (pp. 137–154). New York: Teachers College Press. **6**

Phillips, D., Lande, J., & Goldberg, M. (1990). The state of child care regulation: A comparative analysis. *Early Childhood Research Quarterly, 5*, 151–179. **32**

Phillips, D., McCartney, K., Scarr, S., & Howes, C. (1990). Selective review of infant day care research: A cause for concern! In M. A. Jensen & Z. W. Chevalier (Eds.), *Issues and advocacy in early education* (pp. 190–195). Boston: Allyn & Bacon. **12**

Phillips, D. A., & Howes, C. (1987). Indicators of quality in child care: Review of research. In D. A. Phillips (Ed.), *Quality in child care: What does research tell us?* (pp. 1–20). Washington, DC: National Association for the Education of Young Children. **32**

Phillips, D. A., Voran, M., Kisker, E., Howes, C., & Whitebook, M. (1994). Child care for children in poverty: Opportunity or inequity. *Child Development, 65*, 472–492. **6**

Phillips, L. B., & Twardosz, S. (2003). Group size and storybook reading: Two-year-old children's verbal and nonverbal participation with books. *Early Education and Development, 14*(4), 453–478. **17**

Phillips, P. L., Greenson, J. N., Collett, B. R., & Gimpel, G. A. (2002). Assessing ADHD symptoms in preschool children: Use of the ADHD Rating Scale. *Early Education and Development, 13*(3), 283–300. **28**

Phillipsen, L. C., Burchinal, M. R., Howes, C., & Cryer, D. (1997). The prediction of process quality from structural features of child care. *Early Childhood Research Quarterly, 12*, 281–304. **5**

Phinney, J. S., & Rotheram, M. J. (1987). *Children's ethnic socialization: Pluralism and development.* Thousand Oaks, CA: Sage. **16, 30**

Piaget, J. (1965). *The moral judgement of the child.* New York: The Free Press. **26**

Piaget, J. (1966). *The child's conception of physical causality.* Totowa, NJ: Littlefield-Adams. **3**

Piaget, J. (1971). *Science of education and the psychology of the child.* New York: Viking Press. **5**

Pianta, R. C., Nimetz, S. L., & Bennett, E. (1997). Mother-child relationships, teacher-child relationships, and school outcomes in preschool and kindergarten. *Early Childhood Research Quarterly, 12*, 263–280. **5**

Pinard, A., & Sharp, E. (1972, June). IQ and point of view. *Psychology Today, 6*, 65+. **23**

Pine, G. J., & Hilliard, A. G., III. (1990). RX for racism: Imperatives for America's schools. *Phi Delta Kappan, 71*, 593–600. **33**

Pinon, M. F., Huston, A. C., & Wright, J. C. (1989). Family ecology and child characteristics that predict young children's educational television viewing. *Child Development, 60*, 846–856. **6**

Pipp-Siegel, S., & Foltz, C. (1997). Toddlers' acquisition of self/other knowledge: Ecological and interpersonal aspect of self and other. *Child Development, 68*, 69–79. **16**

Planned Parenthood. (2005). *Your contraceptive choices.* Retrieved July 20, 2005, from http://www.plannedparenthood.org **8**

Poest, C. A., Williams, J. R., Witt, D. D., & Atwood, M. L. (1989). Physical activity patterns of preschool children. *Early Childhood Research Quarterly, 4*, 367–376. **8**

Poest, C. A., Williams, J. R., Witt, D. D., & Atwood, M. L. (1990). Challenge me to move: Large muscle development in young children. *Young Children, 45*(5), 4–10. **12, 15**

Policy regarding nondiscriminatory evaluation. (1977). *Exceptional Children, 43*, 403. **23**

Pollitt, E., Golub, M., Gorman, K, Grantham-McGregor, S., Levitsky, D., Schurch, B., Strupp, C., & Wachs, T. (1996). A reconceptualization of the effects of undernutrition on children's biological, psychosocial, and behavioral development. *SRCD Social Policy Report, X*(5), 1–21. **18**

Pollitt, E., Gorman, K. S., Engle, P. L., Martorell, R., & Rivera, J. (1993). Early supplementary feeding and cognition. *Monograph of the Society for Research in Child Development, 58* (No. 7, Serial No. 235). **18**

Poole, C. (2005, Mar.). Developmental ages and stages: The importance of humor, 0 to 2. *Early Childhood Education Today*, 29–30. **25**

Popham, W. J. (2005). How to use PAP to make AYP under NCLB. *Phi Delta Kapppan, 86*(10), 787–791. **28, 31**

Porath, M. (2003). Social understanding in the first years of school. *Early Childhood Research Quarterly, 18*, 468–484. **26**

Porter, P. (2006). *Early Brain Development.* Retrieved May 16, 2006, from http://www.educarer.com **4**

Portions of brain are smaller in children born prematurely. (2004 Aug. 18). *Stanford Report.* **10**

Posey, J. D. (1997, Oct.). *Exploring indigenous pedagogies: Why is this knowledge important to today's educators?* Paper presented at the annual meeting of the Northern Rocky Mountain Educational Research Association, Jackson Hole, WY. **6**

*The Power of Play.* Retrieved September 24, 2005, from http://www.zerotothree.org **16**

Pratt, E. (1992, June 3). Can we save our black children? *The Advocate*, Baton Rouge, LA. **32**

*Preventing Drug Abuse among Children and Adolescents.* From the National Institute on Drug Abuse. Retrieved August 5, 2005, from http://www.nida.nih.gov **9**

Provenzo, E. (1991). *Video kids: Making sense of Nintendo.* Cambridge, MA: Harvard University Press. **4**

Quick, D. S., Botkin, D., & Quick, S. (1999). Helping young children deal with family violence. *Dimensions of Early Childhood, 27*, 3–10. **27**

Radin, N., Oyserman, D., & Benn, R. (1989, Apr.). *The influence of grandfathers on the young children of teen mothers.* Presented at the biennial meeting of the Society for Research in Child Development, Kansas City, MO. **11**

Rafferty, Y., & Griffin, K. W. (2005). Benefits of reverse inclusion for preschoolers with and without disabilities: Perspectives of parents and providers. *Journal of Early Intervention, 27*(3), 173–192. **4**

Raikes, H. (1993). Relationship duration in infant care. Time with a high ability teacher and infant-teacher attachment. *Early Childhood Research Quarterly, 8*, 309–325. **13**

Raikes, H. (1996). A secure base for babies: Applying attachment concepts to the infant care setting. *Young Children, 51*(5), 59–67. **11**

Ramirez, J. D. (1989, Apr.). *The role of extralinguistic context in egocentric speech production.* Paper presented at the meeting of the Society for Research in Child Development, Kansas City, MO. **21**

Ramsburg, D. (1997, Mar.). *ERIC Digest. The debate over spanking.* Champaign, IL: ERIC Clearinghouse on Elementary and Early Childhood Education. **28**

Raspberry, W. (1985, July 15). Too little 'lap time.' *Morning Advocate, Baton Rouge, LA.* **13**

Rath, L. K. (2002). Get wild about reading: Using *Between the Lions*™ to support early literacy. *Young Children, 57*(2), 80–87. **24**

Rathus, S. A. (2006). *Childhood and adolescence* (2nd ed.). Belmont, CA: Thomson/Wadsworth. **17**

Ratner, N. K., & Olver, R. R. (1998). Reading a tale of deception, Learning a theory of mind? *Early Childhood Research Quarterly, 13*, 219–240. **22**

Raver, C. C. (2002). Emotions matter: Making the case for the role of young children's emotional development for early school readiness. *SRCD Social Policy Report, 16*(3). **13**

Raver, C. C., & Zigler, E. F. (1997). Social competence: An untapped dimension in evaluating Head Start's success. *Early Childhood Research Quarterly, 12*, 363–386. **26**

Read, K. H. (1992). The nursery school: A human relationships laboratory. *Young Children, 47*(3), 4–5. **28**

Readdick, C. A., & Chapman, P. L. (2000). Young children's perceptions of time out. *Journal of Research in Childhood Education, 15*(1), 81–87. **28**

Reed, S. (1983). Preschool computing. What's too young. *Family Computing, 1*(3), 55–68. **6**

Reed, S., & Sautter, R. C. (1990). Children of poverty: The status of 12 million young Americans. *Phi Delta Kappan, 71*, K1–K12. **32**

Reed, T., & Brown, M. (2000). The expression of care in the rough and tumble play of boys. *Journal of Research in Childhood Education, 15*(1), 104–116. **30**

Regulation of child care. (2002). *National Center for Early Development and Learning Briefs, 2*(1).

Reifel, S. (1984). Block construction: Children's developmental landmarks in representation of space. *Young Children, 40*(1), 61–67. **19**

Renzulli, J. S. (2002). Expanding the conception of giftedness to include co-cognitive traits and to promote social capital. *Phi Delta Kappan, 84*(1), 33–40, 57–58. **23**

*Report Card on the Diet Quality of Children Ages 2 to 9.* (2001, Sept.). Retrieved August 18, 2005, from http://www.cnpp.usda.gov. **15**

*Respiratory Syncytical Virus.* (2005). National Center for Infectious Diseases. Retrieved May 19, 2006, from http://www.cdc.gov. **12**

Restak, R. (1975). The dangers of knowing too much. *Psychology Today, 9*, 21+. **10**

Reutzel, D. R., Fawson, P. C., Young, J. R., Morrison, T. G., & Wilcox, B. (2002, Apr.) *Reading environmental print: What is the role of concepts-of-print in discriminating young readers' responses?* Roundtable presentation at the annual meeting of the American Educational Research Association, New Orleans, LA. **22**

Reutzel, D. R., & Hollingsworth, P. M. (1988). Whole language and the practitioner. *Academic Therapy, 23*, 405–416. **22**

Reynolds, A. J., & Robertson, D. L. (2003). School-based early intervention and later child maltreatment in the Chicago longitudinal study. *Child Development, 74*(1), 3–26. **7**

Riblatt, S. N., Obegi, A. D., Hammons, B. S., Ganger, T. A., & Ganger, B. C. (2003). Parents' and child care professionals' toilet training attitudes and practices: A comparative analysis. *Journal of Research in Childhood Education, 17*(2), 133–146. **15**

Rice, K. F., & Sanoff, M. K. (1998). Growing strong together: Helping mothers and their children affected by substance abuse. *Young Children, 53*(1), 28–33. **7**

Richardson, M. V., Hoag, C. L., Miller, M. B., & Monroe, E. E. (2001). Children's literature and mathematics: Connections through cooking. *ACEI Focus on Elementary, 14*(2), 1–6. **31**

Richardson, R. C., & Evans, E. D. (1993). Empowering teachers to halt corporal punishment. *Kappa Delta Pi Record, 29*, 39–42. **28**

Richey, D. D., & Wheeler, J. J. (2000). *Inclusive early childhood education.* Clifton Park, NY: Delmar Learning. **4**

Richgels, D. J. (1986a). Beginning first graders' "invented spelling" ability and their performance in functional classroom writing activities. *Early Childhood Research Quarterly, 1*, 85–97. **22**

Richgels, D. J. (1986b). An investigation of preschool and kindergarten children's spelling and reading abilities. *Journal of Research and Development in Education.* **22**

Richgels, D. J. (2003). Invented spelling, phonemic awareness, and reading and writing instruction. In S. B. Neuman & D. K. Dickinson, (Eds.), *Handbook of early literacy research* (pp. 142–155). New York: Guilford. **22**

Riojas-Cortez, M. (2000). It's all about talking: Oral language development in a bilingual classroom. *Dimensions, 29*(1), 11–15. **24**

Rist, M. C. (1990, July). The shadow children: Preparing for the arrival of crack babies in school. *Phi Delta Kappa Research Bulletin* (No. 9). **15**

Ritchie, G. V. (2000). Meeting state and county standards and objectives with a play-based classroom. *ACEI Focus on PreK & K, 12*(3), 1–7. **31**

Roberts, S. K. (1999). Creating an author's notebook. *ACEI Focus on Elementary, 12*(2), 1–6. **31**

Robertson, C. (2007). *Safety, nutrition and health in early education*. Clifton Park, NY: Delmar Learning. **12**

Robinson, A., & Stark, D. R. (2002). *Advocates in action: Making a difference for young children*. Washington, DC: National Association for the Education of Young Children. **33**

Robinson, E. J., & Robinson, W. P. (1983). Ways of reacting to communication failure in relation to the development of the child's understanding about verbal communication. In M. Donaldson, R. Grieve, & C. Pratt (Eds.), *Early childhood development and education* (pp. 83–103). Oxford, England: Blackwell. **21**

Robinson, S. L., & Gladstone, D. H. (1993). *Dimensions of Early Childhood, 22*(1), 23–25. **25**

Roche, A. F. (Ed.). (1979). Secular trends in human growth, maturation, and development. *Monographs of the Society for Research in Child Development, 44* (Nos. 3 & 4). **12**

Rockwell, R. E., Andre, L. C., & Hawley, M. K. (1996). *Parents and teachers as partners*. Fort Worth, TX: Harcourt Brace. **6**

Rodgers, D. B. (1998). Research in review. Supporting autonomy in young children. *Young Children, 53*(3), 75–80. **30**

Rodning, C., Beckwith, L., & Howard, J. (1989). *Characteristics of attachment organization and play organization in prenatally drug exposed toddlers*. Manuscript submitted for publication. **10**

Rogers, C. S., & Sawyers, J. K. (1988). *Play in the lives of children*. Washington, DC: National Association for the Education of Young Children. **4, 5**

Rogers, F. (2001–2002). *Helping children deal with scary news*. Retrieved November 17, 2002, from http:// www.pbskids.org/rogers/parents/sept11.htm **28**

Rogers, F., & Sharapan, H. B. (1991). Helping parents, teachers, and caregivers deal with children's concerns about war, *Young Children, 46*(3), 12–13. **25**

Rogers, M. (1990). Nintendo and beyond. *Newsweek, 115*(25), 62–63. **4**

Rogoff, B., & Mosier, C. (1993). IV. Guided participation in San Pedro and Salt Lake. In B. Rogoff, J. Mistry, A. Goncu, & C. Mosier (Eds.), Guided participation in cultural activity by toddlers and caregivers. *Monograph of the Society for Research in Child Development* (pp. 59–101), *58* (No. 8, Serial No. 236). **16, 17**

Rogoff, B., Turkanis, C. G., & Bartlett, L. (2001). *Learning together: Children and adults in a school community*. New York: Oxford University Press. **31**

Roisman, G. I., Padron, E., Stroufe, L. A., & Egeland, B. (2002). Earned-secure attachment status in retrospect and prospect. *Child Development, 73*(4), 1204–1219. **13**

Roopnarine, J. L., & Honig, A. S. (1985). The unpopular child. *Young Children, 40*(6), 59–64. **26**

Roopnarine, J. L., & Johnson, J. E. (2004). *Approaches to early childhood education*. New York: Merrill/Macmillan. **19, 28, 32**

Rose, L. C., & Gallup, A. M. (2005). The 37th Annual Phi Delta Kappa/Gallup Poll of the public's attitudes towards the public schools. *Phi Delta Kappan, 87*(1), 41–57. **22**

Rose, S. A. (1994). Relation between physical growth and information processing in infants born in India. *Child Development, 65*, 889–902. **7**

Rosenbaum, P. (1998). Physical activity play in children with disabilities: A neglected opportunity for research? *Child Development, 69*, 607–608. **8**

Rosenkoetter, S. (2001a, March). Emergent literacy: Developmentally appropriate experiences with language and literacy yield long-term benefits. *Collaborative Ties: Oregon State University Child Development Center*, 1–2. **22**

Rosenkoetter, S. (2001b, March). Effective strategies for emergent literacy. *Collaborative Ties: Oregon State University Child Development Center*, 3–5. **22**

Rosenquest, B. B. (2002). Literacy-based planning and pedagogy that supports toddler language development. *Early Childhood Education Journal, 29*(4), 241–250. **17**

Roskos, K. A., & Christie, J. F. (Eds.). (2002). "Knowing in the doing"—Observing literacy learning in play. *Young Children, 57*(2), 46–54. **22**

Rosow, L. V. (1994/95). How schools perpetuate illiteracy. In K. M. Paciorek & J. H. Munro (Eds.), *Early childhood education 94/95* (pp. 101–103). Guilford, CT: Dushkin. [Originally printed in *Educational Leadership, 49*(1), 41– 44, 1991.] **22**

Rosser, P. L. (1977). Child development theory: Physiological development. In M. Coleman (Ed.), *Black children just keep on growing* (pp. 169–178). Washington, DC: Black Child Development Institute. **7**

Rotigel, J. V. (2003). Understanding the young gifted child: Guidelines for parents, families and educators. *Early Childhood Education Journal, 30*(4), 209–214. **23**

Rotherham-Baron, M. J., & Phinney, J. S. (1990). Patterns of social expectations among Black and Mexican-American children. *Child Development, 61*, 542–556. **30**

Rouse, C., Brooks-Gunn, J., & McLanahan, S. (2005). Introducing the issue. *The Future of Children, 15*(1), 5–14. **28**

Roy, K., & Burton, L. (2003). Kinscription: Mothers keeping fathers connected to children. *Zero to Three, 23*(3), 27–32. **11**

Rozycki, E. G. (1993). From the trenches. Immigrants in the New America: Is it time to heat up the melting pot? *Educational Horizons, 71*, 126–127. **6**

Rubin, K. H. (1977). Play behaviors of young children. *Young Children, 32*(6), 16–24. **27**

Rubin, K. H. (1982a). Nonsocial play in preschoolers: Necessary evil? *Child Development, 53*, 651–657. **27**

Rubin, K. H., Hastings, P., Xinyin, C., Stewart, S., & McNichol, K. (1998). Intrapersonal and maternal correlates of aggression, conflict, and externalizing problems in toddlers. *Child Development, 69*(6), 1614–1629.

Ruble, D. N., Higgins, E. T., & Hartup, W. W. (1983). What's social about social-cognitive development? In E. T. Higgins, D. N. Ruble, & W. W. Hartup (Eds.), *Social cognition and social development* (pp. 3–12). New York: Cambridge University Press. **26**

Ruff, H. A. (1986). Components of attention during infants' manipulative exploration. *Child Development, 57* 105–114. **8**

Ruhman, L. H. (1998). Fostering the imitative and imaginative play of infants and toddlers. *Focus on Infants and Toddlers, 10*(3), 1–4. **14, 16**

Rule, A. C., & Stewart, R. A. (2002). Effects of practical life materials on kindergartners' fine motor skills. *Early Childhood Education Journal, 30*(1), 9–14. **19**

Rule, S., Innocenti, M. S., Coor, K. J., Bonem, M. K., & Stowitschek, J. J. (1989). Kindergartners' preacademic skills and mainstream teachers' knowledge: Implications for special educators. *Journal of Early Intervention, 13*, 212–220. **5**

Ruopp, R. R. (1979). *Children at the center.* Cambridge, MA: Abt Books **32**

Rusnak, T., & Ribich, F. (1997). On balance: The death of character education. *Educational Horizons, 76*(1), 10–13. **30**

Rust, F. C., & Williams, L. R. (1989). The care and education of young children: Expanding contexts, sharpening focus. *Teachers College Record, 90*, 334–336. **32**

Ryan, F. J. (1993). The perils of multiculturalism: Schooling for the group. *Educational Horizons, 71*, 134–138. **6**

Ryan, M. (1997, March 9). 'That baby is loved.' *Parade Magazine*, 8–9. **8**

Ryan, M. (1997, June 29). The child who teaches compassion. *Parade Magazine*, 12–13.

Ryan, S., & Grieshaber, S. (2004). It's more than child development: Critical theories, research and teaching young children. *Young Children, 59*(6), 44–52. **2**

Sachs, J., Goldman, J., & Chaille, C. (1984). Planning in pretend play: Using language to coordinate narrative development. In A. Pellegrini & T. Yawkey (Eds.), *The development of oral and written language in social contexts* (pp. 119–128). Norwood, NJ: Ablex. **4**

Sachs, J., Goldman, J., & Chaille, C. (1985). Narratives in preschoolers' sociodramatic play: The role of knowledge and communicative competence. In L. Galda & A. D. Pellegrini (Eds.), *Play, language and stories* (pp. 45–62). Norwood, NJ: Ablex. **21**

Salomon, G., Perkins, D. N., & Globerson, T. (1991). Partners in cognition: Extending human intelligence with intelligent technologies. *Educational Researcher, 20*(3), 2–9. **4, 6**

Salyer, D. M. (1994). Noise or communication? Talking, writing and togetherness in one first grade class. *Young Children, 49*(4), 42–47. **31**

Sameroff, A. J., & Seifer, R. (1983). Familial risk and child competency. *Child Development, 54*, 1254–1268. **12**

Samples, F. L. (2004). Evaluating curriculum-based intervention programs: An examination of preschool, primary and elementary school intervention programs. In C. E. Sanders & G. D. Phye (Eds.), *Bullying: Implications for the classroom* (pp. 203–227). Boston: Elsevier. **30**

Samuels, S. C. (1977). *Enhancing self concept in early childhood.* New York: Human Sciences Press. **25**

Sandall, S. R. (2003). Play modifications for children with disabilities. *Young Children, 58*(3), 54–55. **5**

Sanders, C. E., & Phye, G. D. (2004). (Eds.). *Bullying: Implications for the classroom.* Boston: Elsevier. **30**

Sanders, G. E. (2002). *Fitness begins in early childhood.* Retrieved November 20, 2005, from http://www.earlychildhood.com **29**

Sanders, S. W. (2002). *Active for life: Developmentally appropriate movement programs for young children.* Washington, DC: National Association for the Education of Young Children. **8**

*Santa Clara County Head Start Transition Project: Bridges to the Future.* (1992). San Jose, CA: Santa Clara County Office of Education. **28**

Sautter, R. C. (1994). An arts education school reform strategy. *Phi Delta Kappan, 75*, 432–437. **23**

Sawin, D. B. (1981). Fathers' interactions with infants. In B. Weissbourd & J. S. Musick (Eds.), *Infants: Their social environments* (pp. 169–184). Washington, DC: National Association for the Education of Young Children. **13**

Scarr, S. (1993). Biological and cultural diversity: The legacy of Darwin for development. *Child Development, 64*, 1333–1353. **9**

Schacter, F. F., Kirshner, K., Klips, B., Friedricks, M., & Sanders, K. (1974). Everyday preschool interpersonal speech usage: Methodological, developmental, and sociolinguistic studies. *Monographs of the Society for Research in Child Development, 39* (3, Serial No. 156). **21**

Schaffer, R. (1977). *Mothering.* Cambridge, MA: Harvard University Press. **13**

Scharmann, M. W. (1998). We are friends when we have memories together. *Young Children, 53*(2), 27–29. **30**

Scher, P. J. (1998). Shared reading intervention. *Early Childhood Research Quarterly, 13*, 291–292. **22**

Schickedanz, J. A. (1999). *Much more than the ABCs.* Washington, DC: National Association for the Education of Young Children. **14**

Schickedanz, J. A., & Casbergue, R. M. (2004). *Writing in preschool.* Newark, DE: International Reading Association. **22**

Schirrmacher, R. (2006). *Art and creative development for young children* (5th ed.). Clifton Park, NY: Delmar Learning. **23, 24**

Schmidt, J. (2003). Let's just play. *Teaching Tolerance, 24*, 19–25. **5**

Schmidt, D. (1985). Adult influences on curiosity in children. *Early Report, 12*(3), 2–3. **23**

Schmidt, H. M. (2005). *Impact of teacher guidance strategies on children's interpersonal relations.* Unpublished manuscript, Louisiana State University, Baton Rouge, LA. **26**

Schneider, B. H. (2000). *Friends and enemies: Peer relations in childhood.* New York: Oxford University Press. **30**

Scholars question conventional analyses of Chicano child-rearing practices. (1994, Apr.). *Stanford School of Education, 3.* **6**

Schrader, C. T. (1990). Symbolic play as a curricular tool for early literacy development. *Early Childhood Research Quarterly, 5,* 79–103. **4, 15**

Schwartz, D., Dodge, K. A., Pettit, G. S., & Bates, J. E. (1997). The early socialization of aggressive victims of bullying. *Child Development, 68,* 665–675. **30**

Schweinhart, L. J. (1993). Observing young children in action: The key to early childhood assessment. *Young Children, 48*(5), 29–33. **29**

Schweinhart, L. J. (2002, June). How the High/Scope Perry Preschool study grew: A researcher's tale. *Phi Delta Kappa Research Bulletin,* 7–9. **23**

Schweinhart, L. J., Barnes, H. V., & Weikart, D. P. (1993). *Significant benefits: The High/Scope Perry Preschool study through age 27.* Ypsilanti, MI: High/Scope. **23**

Schweinhart, L. J., & Weikart, D. P. (1985). Evidence that good early childhood programs work. *Phi Delta Kappan, 66,* 545–551. **23**

Schweinhart, L. J., & Weikart, D. P. (1997). The High/Scope preschool curriculum comparison study through age 23. *Early Childhood Research Quarterly, 12,* 117–143. **23**

Schweinhart, L. J., Weikart, D. P., & Larner, M. B. (1986). Consequences of three preschool curriculum models through age 15. *Early Childhood Research Quarterly, 1,* 15–46. **23**

Scott-Little, M. C., & Holloway, S. D. (1992). Child care providers' reasoning about misbehaviors: Relation to classroom control strategies and professional training. *Early Childhood Research Quarterly, 7,* 595–606. **28**

Segal, M., & Adcock, D. (1976). *From one to two years.* Rolling Hills Estates, CA: B. L. Winch. **16**

Segatti, L., Brown-DuPaul, J., & Keyes, T. L. (2003). Using everyday materials to promote problem solving in toddlers. *Young Children, 58*(5), 12–8. **17**

Selman, R. L., & Selman, A. P. (1979). Children's ideas about friendship. *Psychology Today, 13,* 71–80+. **26**

Semaj, L. T. (1985). Afrikanity, cognition and extended self-identity. In M. B. Spencer, G. K. Brookins, & W. R. Allen (Eds.), *Beginnings: The social and affective development of black children* (pp. 173–184). Mahwah, NJ: Erlbaum. **25**

Sera, M. D., Troyer, D., & Smith, L. B. (1988). What do two-year-olds know about the sizes of things? *Child Development, 59,* 1489–1496. **17**

Serbin, L. A., Powlishta, K. K., & Gulko, J. (1993). The development of sex typing in middle childhood. *Monographs of the Society for Research in Child Development, 58* (No. 2, Serial No. 232). **30**

Sevigny, M. J. (1979, Mar.). A look at the art of young children. In A. B. Johnson, D. J. Radeloff, J. Dermer, & E. Roemer (Eds.), *Young children internationally.* Proceedings of the Second Annual Early Childhood Conference, Bowling Green State University, Bowling Green, OH. **8**

Sexuality and U. (2006). *The Development of Sexuality from Infancy to Puberty: Developmental Outcomes, Common Behaviors, Concerns, and Learning Objectives.* Retrieved May 26, 2006, from http://www.sexualityandu.ca **25**

Sexuality and U. (2006). *Early Childhood (2–5).* Retrieved May 28, 2006, from http://www.sexualityandu.ca **25**

Sexuality and U. (2006). *Middle Childhood (5–8).* Retrieved May 28, 2006, from http://www.sexualityandu.ca **30**

Shade, D. D. (1993). Computers and young children: Peace of mind for teachers and parents—Fun for kids? *Day Care and Early Education, 20*(4), 39–41. **5**

Shade, D. D. (1994). Computers and young children: New frontiers in computer hardware and software *or* what computer should I buy? *Day Care and Early Education, 21*(3), 39–41. **5**

Shade, D. D. (1996). Computers and young children: Are you ready to teach young children in the 21st century? *Early Childhood Education Journal, 24*(1), 43–44. **4**

Shapiro, A. (n.d.). Show'n tell—It's a window on their lives. In M. van Manen (Ed.), *Texts of teaching* (pp. 31–36), Human Sciences Research Project, 441 Education South, Faculty of Education, University of Alberta, Edmonton, Canada, T6G 2G5. **30**

Shapiro, L. (1990, May 28). Guns and dolls. *Newsweek,* 56–65. **25**

Shatz, M., & Gelman, R. (1973). The development of communication skills: Modifications of the speech of young children as the function of listener. *Monographs of the Society for Research in Child Development, 38* (5, Serial No. 152). **21**

Shavelson, R. J., Carey, N. B., & Webb, N. M. (1990). Indicators of science achievement: Options for a powerful policy instrument. *Phi Delta Kappan, 71,* 692–697. **29**

Shepard, L. A. (2000). The role of assessment in a learning culture. *Educational Researcher, 29*(7), 4–14. **29**

Shepard, L. A., Kagan, S. L., & Wurtz, E. (1998). Public policy report. Goal 1: Early childhood assessments resource group recommendations. *Young Children, 53*(3), 52–54. **29, 33**

Sherman, T. (1985). Categorization skills in infants. *Child Development, 56,* 1156–1573. **14**

Shields, M. K. (Ed.) (2004) *The Future of Children: Children of Immigrant Families,* 15(2). **7**

Shim, S., Herwig, J. E., Shelley, M. (2001). Preschoolers' play behaviors with peers in classroom and playground settings. *Journal of Research in Childhood Education, 15*(2), 149–163. **27**

Shiono, P. H., & Behrman, R. E. (1995). Low birth weight: Analysis and recommendations. *The Future of Children. Low Birth Weight, 5*(1), 4–18. **11**

Shonkoff, J. P., & Phillips, D. (Eds.). (2000). *From neurons to neighborhoods: The science of early child development.* Washington, DC: The National Academies Press. **9, 20**

Shore, R. (1997). *Rethinking the brain.* New York: Families and Work Institute. **4, 13, 14, 17**

Shores, E. F., & Grace, C. (1998). *The portfolio book.* Beltsville, MD: Gryphon House. **3, 23, 29**

Siegal, M., & Storey, R. M. (1985). Day care and children's conceptions of moral and social rules. *Child Development, 56*, 1001–1008. **27**

Siegler, R. S., & Richards, D. D. (1982). The development of intelligence. In R. J. Sternberg (Ed.), *Handbook of human intelligence* (pp. 901–974). New York: Cambridge University Press. **23**

Sieminski, J. (2005). Can I touch it? Can I taste it? Toddlers' investigation of light and shadow. *Focus on Infants and Toddlers, 18*(1), 1–4. **17**

Signorielli, N. (1998). Television and the perpetuation of gender-role stereotypes. *AAP News* [Electronic version]. Retrieved November 8, 2002, from http://www.aap.org/advocacy/sign298.htm **25**

Silvern, S. B., & McCary, J. C. (1986). Computers in the educational lives of children: Developmental issues. In J. Hoot (Ed.), *Computers in early childhood education* (pp. 6–21). Upper Saddle River, NJ: PrenticeHall. **4**

Simmons, B., & Brewer, J. (1985). When parents of kindergartners ask, "Why?" *Childhood Education, 61*, 177–184. **28**

Simpson, L., & Clancy, S. (2005). Enhancing opportunities for Australian aboriginal literacy learners in early childhood settings. *Childhood Education, 81*, 327–337. **22**

Skeen, P., & Hodson, D. (1987). AIDS: What adults should know about AIDS (and shouldn't discuss with very young children). *Young Children, 42*(4), 65–71. **8**

Skinner, B. F. (1979). My experiences with the baby-tender. *Psychology Today, 12*, 28–40. **12**

Slaughter, V., & Gopnik, A. (1996). Conceptual coherence in the child's theory of mind: Training children to understand belief. *Child Development, 67*, 2967–2988. **20**

Slaughter-Defoe, D. T., Nakagawa, K., Takanishi, R., & Johnson, D. J. (1990). Toward cultural/ecological perspectives on schooling and achievement in African- and Asian-American children. *Child Development, 61*, 363–383. **6, 31**

Slobin, D. I. (1972). Children and language: They learn the same way all around the world. *Psychology Today, 6*, 71–74+. **21**

Smetana, J. G. (1984). Toddlers' social interactions regarding moral and conventional transgressions. *Child Development, 55*, 1767–1776. **16**

Smilansky, S. (1968). *The effects of sociodramatic play on disadvantaged children: Preschool children.* New York: John Wiley. **27**

Smith, D. G. (no date). *Living with children. Texts of childhood.* Edmonton, Canada: University of Alberta Human Science Research Project. **30**

Smith, D. J., Allen, J., & White, P. (1990). Helping preschool children cope with typical fears. *Dimensions, 19*(1), 20–21. **25**

Smith, E. (1998). What is Black English? What is Ebonics? In T. Perry & L. Delpit (Eds.), *The real Ebonics debate: Power, language and the education of African-American children* (pp. 49–58). Boston: Beacon Press. **20**

Smith, J. (1991, Jan. 23). Words from kindergartners. *Baton Rouge, LA, Morning Advocate*, 9B. **21**

Smith, M. K. (Revised 2005, Jan. 30). *Carl Rodgers, core conditions and education.* Retrieved August 13, 2005, from http://www.infed.org. **11**

Smith, M. L., & Shepard, L. A. (1988). Kindergarten readiness and retention: A qualitative study of teachers' beliefs and practices. *American Educational Research Journal, 25*, 307–333. **28**

Smith, N. R. (1982). The visual arts in early childhood education. In B. Spodek (Ed.), *Handbook of research in early childhood education* (pp. 295–317). New York: The Free Press. **23**

Smith, N. R. (1983). *Experience and art: Teaching children to paint.* New York: Teachers College Press. **23**

Smith, T. (1991). A look at recent research on attachment. *Early Report, 18*(2), 7. **25**

Smitherman, G. (1998). Black English/Ebonics: What it be like? In T. Perry & L. Delpit (Eds.), *The real Ebonics debate: Power, language and the education of African-American children* (pp. 29–37). Boston: Beacon Press. **21**

Smolak, L. (1986). *Infancy.* Upper Saddle River, NJ: Prentice Hall. **21**

Smollar, J., & Youness, J. (1982). Social development through friendship. In K. H. Rubin & H. S. Ross (Eds.), *Peer relationships and social skills in childhood* (pp. 279–298). New York: Springer-Verlag. **27**

Snow, C. E., Burns, M. S., & Griffin, P. (Eds.). (1998). *Preventing reading difficulties in young children.* Washington, DC: National Academy Press. **22**

Snow, C. E., Dubber, C., & DeBlauw, A. (1982). Routines in mother-child interaction. In L. Feagans & D. C. Farran (Eds.), *The language of children reared in poverty* (pp. 53–74). New York: Academic Press. **21, 24**

Snow, C. E. (2002a). *An End to the Reading Wars.* Retrieved October 26, 2002, from http://www4.nationalacademies.org **22**

Snow, C. E. (2002b). Ensuring reading success for African American children. In B. Bowman (Ed.), *Love to read. Essays in developing and enhancing early literacy skills of African American children.* Washington, DC: National Black Child Development Institute, Inc. **22**

Snow, M. E., Jacklin, C. N., & Maccoby, E. E. (1983). Sex-of-child differences in father-child interaction at one year of age. *Child Development, 54*, 227–232. **13**

Sodian, B., & Schneider, W. (1990). Children's understanding of cognitive cuing: How to manipulate cues to fool a competitor. *Child Development, 61*, 697–704. **21**

Solarz, A. L. (1988). Homelessness: Implications for children and youth. *SRCD Social Policy Report, 3*(4). **6**

Solomon, J. (2003). Caregiving systems for separated and divorcing parents. *Zero to Three, 23*(3), 33–37. **11**

Solomon, M., & Hendren, R. L. (2003). A critical look at brain-based education. *Middle Matters, 12*(1), 1–3. Retrieved May 21, 2006, from http://www.naesp.org **31**

Solomon, R., & Liefeld, C. P. (1998). Effectiveness of a family support center approach to adolescent mothers: Repeat pregnancy and school drop-out rates. *Family Relations, 47*, 139–144. **12**

Solorzano, L. (1986, Mar. 31). Educating the melting pot. *U.S. News and World Report*, 20–21. **20**

Soto, L. D. (1991). Research in review: Understanding bilingual/bicultural young children. *Young Children, 46*(2), 30–36. **21, 24**

Soto, L. D. (1992). The politics of early bilingual education. In S. Kessler & B. B. Swadener (Eds.), *Reconceptualizing the early childhood curriculum: Beginning the dialogue* (pp. 189–204). New York: Teachers College Press. **21**

Special report: Infants and toddlers exposed to violence. (1994). *Developments, 8*(2), 5–8. **13, 16**

Spencer, M. B. (1985). Cultural cognition and social cognition as identity correlates of black children's personal-social development. In M. B. Spencer, G. K. Brookins, & W. R. Allen (Eds.), *Beginnings: The social and affective development of black children* (pp. 215–230). Mahwah, NJ: Erlbaum. **25**

Spencer, M. B., & Mardstrom-Adams, C. (1990). Identity processes among racial and ethnic minority children in America. *Child Development, 61*, 290–310. **25**

Spezzano, C., & Waterman, J. (1977). The first day of life. *Psychology Today, 11*, 110–116. **11**

St. Clair, J. P. (2002). Using *Between the Lions*™ in a kindergarten classroom. *Young Children, 57*(2), 87–88. **24**

St. Pierre, E. A. (2002). "Science" rejects postmodernism. *Educational Researcher, 31*(8), 25–27. **28**

Stambor, Z. (2005, Dec.). Meet the renaissance dad. *APA Monitor, 36*(11). Retrieved February 18, 2006, from http://www.apa.org **32**

Standley, J. (2002) Music therapy in the NICU: Promoting the growth and development of premature infants. *Zero to Three, 23*(1), 23–30. **10**

Starting points: Executive summary of the report of the Carnegie Corporation of New York Task Force on Meeting the Needs of Young Children. (1994). *Young Children, 49*(5), 58–61. **33**

Stegelin, D. A. (2005). Making the case for play policy: Research-based reasons to support play-based environments. *Young Children, 60*(2), 76–85. **5**

Steinman, C. (1979, Feb. 25). Caesarean births: A new perspective. *Toledo Blade*, E1, E6. **11**

Stephan, C. W., & Langlois, J. H. (1984). Baby beautiful: Adult attributes of infant competence as a function of infant attractiveness. *Child Development, 55*, 576–585. **12**

Stephens, L. C. (1997). Sensory integrative dysfunction in young children. *News Exchange, 2*(1). Retrieved May 16, 2006, from http://www.tsbvi.edu **4**

Sternberg, R. J., Torff, B., & Grigorenko, E. (1998). Teaching for successful intelligence raises school achievement. *Phi Delta Kappan, 79*, 667–679. **23**

Stevens, J. H., Jr. (1988). Social support, locus of control, and parenting in three low-income groups of mothers: Black teenagers, black adults, and white adults. *Child Development, 59*, 635–642. **12**

Stevenson, H. W., & Lee, S. (1990). Contexts of achievement. *Monographs of the Society for Research in Child Development, 55* (12, Serial No. 221). **19**

Stipek, D., & Byler, D. J. (1997). Early childhood education teachers: Do they practice what they preach? *Early Childhood Research Quarterly, 12*, 305–326. **5**

Stipek, D. J., Feiler, R., Byler, P., Ryan, R., Milburn, S., & Salmon, J. M. (1998). Good beginnings: What difference does the program make in preparing young children for school? *Journal of Applied Developmental Psychology, 19*, 41–66. **28**

Stipek, D. J., Feiler, R., Daniels, D., & Milburn, S. (1995). Effects of differential instructional approaches on young children's achievement and motivation. *Child Development, 66*, 209–223. **5**

Stipek, D., & MacIver, D. (1989). Developmental change in children's assessment of intellectual competence. *Child Development, 60*, 521–538. **30, 31**

Stipek, D., Recchia, S., & McClintic. (1992). Self-evaluation in young children. Monographs of the Society for Research in *Child Development, 57*, (No. 1, Serial No. 226). **16, 25**

Stone, J. G. (2001). *Building classroom community.* Washington, DC: National Association for the Education of Young Children. **31**

Stone, S. J. (1998). Defining the multiage classroom. *ACEI Focus on Elementary: Ages 7–10, 10*(3), 1–6. **31**

Stone, S. J., & Christie, J. F. (1996). Collaborative literacy learning during sociodramatic play in a multiage (K2) primary classroom. *Journal of Research in Childhood Education, 10*, 123–133. **30**

Stott, F., & Bowman, B. (1996). Child development knowledge: A slippery base for practice. *Early Childhood Research Quarterly, 11*(2) 169–184. **2**

Stott, F., & Halpern, R. (2003). Listening to the voices of families: Thoughts, hopes and fears in a Latino community. *Zero to Three, 23*(5), 16–21. **11**

Stroufe, L. A. (1991). Sorting it out: Attachment and bonding. *Early Report, 18*(2), 3–4. **25**

Sturm, L. (2004). Temperament in early childhood: A primer for the perplexed. *Zero to Three, 24*(4), 4–11. **13, 16**

Sullivan, A. K., & Strang, H. R. (2002/03). Bibliotherapy in the classroom: Using literature to promote the development of emotional intelligence. *Childhood Education, 79*(2), 74–80. **25, 27**

Sunal, C. S., & Hatcher, B. (1985). A changing world: Books can help children adapt. *Day Care and Early Education, 13*(2), 16–19. **28**

Super, C. M., Herrera, M. G., & Mora, J. O. (1990). Long-term effects of food supplementation and psychosocial intervention on the physical growth of Colombian infants at risk of malnutrition. *Child Development, 61*, 29–49. **7**

Sutterby, J. A., & Thornton, C. D. (2005). It doesn't just happen! Essential contributions from playgrounds. *Young Children, 60*(3), 26–30, 32–33. **19**

Sutterby, J. A., & Frost, J. L. (2002). Making playgrounds fit for children and children fit on playgrounds. *Young Children, 57*(3), 36–41. **18**

Swadener, B. B., & Lubeck, S. (Eds.). (1995). *Children and families "at promise."* Albany, NY: SUNY Press. **IX, 6, 32**

Swick, K. J. (1987). Managing classroom stress. *Dimensions, 15*(4), 9–11. **25**

Swick, K. J., & Bailey, L. B. (2004). Communicating effectively with parents and families who are homeless. *Early Childhood Education Journal, 32*(3), 211–215. **7**

Tabachnick, B. R., & Bloch, M. N. (1995). Learning in and out of school: Critical perspectives on the theory of cultural compatibility. In B. B. Swadener & S. Lubeck (Eds.), *Children and families "at promise"* (pp. 187–209). Albany, NY: SUNY Press. **6**

Tabors, P. (1998). What early childhood educators need to know: Developing effective programs for linguistically and culturally diverse children and families. *Young Children, 53*(6), 20–26. **21**

Tabors, P. O. (2003). What early childhood educators need to know: Developing effective programs for linguistically and culturally diverse children and families. In C. Copple (Ed.), *A world of difference* (pp. 17–23). Washington, DC: National Association for the Education of Young Children. **17**

Takanishi, R. (2004). Leveling the playing field: Supporting immigrant children from birth to eight. *The Future of Children, 14*(2), 61–79. **7**

*Talent and diversity.* (1998). Washington, DC: Office of Educational Research and Improvement, U.S. Department of Education. **23**

Tamis-LeMonda, C. S., & Cabrera, N. (Eds.). (1999). Perspectives on father involvement: Resarch and policy. *Social Policy Report: Society for Research in Child Development, 13*(2). **6**

Tan, T. X., & Yang, Y. (2005). Language development of Chinese adoptees 18–35 months old. *Early Childhood Research Quarterly, 20*(1), 57–68. **17**

Tan, L. E. (1985). Laterality and motor skills in four-year-olds. *Child Development, 56*, 119–124. **8**

Tangle, D. M., & Blachman, B. A. (1992). Effect of phoneme awareness instruction on kindergarten children's invented spellings. *Journal of Reading Behavior, 24*, 233–258. **22**

Taunton, M., & Colbert, C. (1984). Artistic and aesthetic development: Considerations for early childhood educators. *Childhood Education, 61*, 55–63. **23**

Teaching Tolerance Project. (1997). *Starting small: Teaching tolerance in preschool and the early grades.* Montgomery, AL: Southern Poverty Law Center. **1, 28**

Tello, J. (1995, Nov./Dec.). The children we teach. *Scholastic Early Childhood Today*, 38–39. **1**

Temperament in early development. (2004). *Zero to Three* [Focus issue], *24*(4). **13**

*Testing HIV Positive—Do I Have AIDS?* Retrieved from http://www.aidsinfo.nih.gov **9**

Thackeray, A. D., & Readdick, C. A. (2003/04). Preschoolers' anatomical knowledge of salient and non-salient sexual and non-sexual body parts. *Journal of Research in Childhood Education, 18*(2), 141–148. **25**

Tharp, R. (1994). Intergroup differences among Native Americans in socialization and child cognition: An ethnogenetic analysis. In P. M. Greenfield & R. R. Cocking (Eds.), *Cross-cultural roots of minority child development* (pp. 87–106). Mahwah, NJ: Erlbaum. **6**

Tharp, R., & Entz, S. (2003). From high chair to high school: Research-based principles for teaching complex thinking. *Young Children, 58*(5), 38–44. **20**

*The Development of Sexuality from Infancy to Puberty: Developmental Outcomes, Common Behaviours, Concerns, and Learning Objectives.* (2006). Retrieved May 16, 2006, from http://www.sexualityandu.ca **25**

The Society of Obstetricians and Gynecologists of Canada. (2006). *Middle Childhood (5–8).* Retreived May 28, 2006, from http://wwwsexualityandu.ca **30**

The telltale gene. (1990). *Consumer reports, 55*(7), 483–488. **10**

Thelen, E. (1984). Learning to walk: Ecological demands and phylogenetic constraints. In L. P. Lipsitt & C. Rovee-Collier (Eds.), *Advances in infancy research* (Vol. 3). Norwood, NJ: Ablex. **8**

Thomas, A., & Chess, S. (1977). *Temperament and development.* New York: Bruner/Mazel. **11, 13**

Thomas, B. (1984). Early toy preferences of four-year-old readers and nonreaders. *Child Development, 55*, 424–430. **5**

Thomas, J. (2005). Calling a cab for Oregon students. *Phi Delta Kappan, 86*(5), 385–388. **31**

Thompson, C. M. (1990). "I make a mark": The significance of talk in young children's artistic development. *Early Childhood Research Quarterly, 5*, 215–132. **23**

Thompson, R. A., & Nelson, C. A. (2001). Early brain development. *American Psychologist, 56*(1), 5–15. **14**

Thompson, S. H. (1998). Working with children of substance-abusing parents. *Young Children, 53*(1), 34–37. **12**

Thompson, S. C. (2005). *Children as illustrators. Making meaning though art and language.* Washington, DC: National Association for the Education of Young Children. **23, 24**

Thornburg, K. R., Pearl, P., Crompton, D., & Ispa, J. M. (1990). Development of kindergarten children based on child care arrangements. *Early Childhood Research Quarterly, 5*, 27–42. **6, 12**

Thornton, M. C., Chatters, L. M., Taylor, R. J., & Allen, W. R. (1990). Sociodemographic and environmental correlates of racial socialization by black parents. *Child Development, 61*, 401–409. **28**

Tittle, B., & St. Claire, N. (1989). Promoting the health and development of drug exposed infants through a comprehensive clinic model. *Zero to Three, 9*(5), 18– 20. **10**

Tonti, J. (1998, Aug. 20). Doulas offer special support for mothers-to-be. *Ogden Standard Examiner*, TX3. **11**

Torquati, J., & Barber, J. (2005). Dancing with trees: Infants and toddlers in the garden. *Young Children, 60*(3), 40–48. **11**

Torrance, E. P. (1983). Preschool creativity. In K. D. Paget & B. A. Bracken (Eds.), *The psychoeducational assessment of preschool children* (pp. 509–519). New York: Grune & Stratton. **23**

Tots' normal development is rough on families. (1984). *Growing Child Research Review, 3*(2), 3. **12**

Tough, J. (1977). *The development of meaning.* London, UK: Allen & Unwin. **21**

Tough, J. (1982a). Language, poverty and disadvantage in school. In L. Feagans & D. C. Ferran (Eds.), *The language of children reared in poverty* (pp. 3–18). New York: Academic Press. **20**

Tough, J. (1982b). Teachers can create enabling environments for children and then children will learn. In L. Feagans & D. C. Ferran (Eds.), *The language of children reared in poverty* (pp. 265–268). New York: Academic Press. **20, 24**

Trawick-Smith, J. (1985). Developing the dramatic play enrichment program. *Dimensions, 13*(4), 7–10. **4, 5**

Trawick-Smith, J. (1994). Authentic dialogue with children: A sociolinguistic perspective on language learning. *Dimensions of Early Childhood, 22*(4), 9–16. **29**

Trawick-Smith, J. (1998a). A qualitative analysis of metaplay in the preschool years. *Early Childhood Research Quarterly, 13*, 433–452. **21**

Trawick-Smith, J. (1998b). Why play training works: An integrated model for play intervention. *Journal of Research in Childhood Education, 12*, 117–129. **5**

Treiman, R., Tincoff, R., Rodriguez, K., Mouzaki, A., & Francis, D. J. (1998). The foundations of literacy: Learning the sounds of letters. *Child Development, 69*, 1524–1540. **24**

Trepanier-Street, M. L., & Romatowski, J. A. (1999). The influence of children's literature on gender role perceptions: A reexamination. *Early Childhood Education Journal, 26*, 155–160. **25**

Trevarthen, C. (1979). Communication and cooperation in early infancy: A description of primary intersubjectivity. In M. Bullowa (Ed.), *Before speech: The beginnings of interpersonal communication* (pp. 321–347). **21**

Tudge, J. (1990). Vygotsky, the zone of proximal development, and peer collaboration: Implications for classroom practice. In L. C. Moll (Ed.), *Vygotsky and education: Instructional implications and applications of sociohistorical psychology.* New York: Cambridge University Press. **4**

Tudge, J., & Caruso, D. (1988). Cooperative problem solving in the classroom: Enhancing young children's cognitive development. *Young Children, 44*(1), 46–52. **5**

Ubell, E. (1995, Oct. 8). If you are trying to have a child . . . *Parade Magazine*, 12–13. **8**

Ubell, E. (1997, Jan. 12). Should you consider gene testing? *Parade Magazine*, 8–9. **10**

*Understanding the possibilities: A curriculum guide for Project Construct.* (1992). Columbia, MO: Project Construct National Center. **32**

U.S. children and their families: Current conditions and recent trends. (1991, Winter). *SRCD Newsletter, 13*. **32**

U.S. Department of Agriculture. (April, 2005). *Food Pyramid.* Retrieved November 1, 2005, from http://www.mypyramid.gov **18**

Unique strengths, shared strengths. (2003). *Insights and Evidence*, 1(2). Retrieved from www.searchinstitute.org **1**

Uphoff, J. K. (1990). Extra-year programs: An argument for transitional programs during transitional times. *Young Children, 45*(6), 19–20. **28**

Uttal, D. H. (1996). Angles and distances: Children's and adults' reconstruction and scaling of spatial configurations. *Child Development, 67*, 2763–2779. **19**

Uzgiris, I. C. (1984). Imitation in infancy: Its interpersonal aspects. In M. Perlmutter (Ed.), *Parent-child interaction and parent-child relations in child development* (pp. 1–32). Mahwah, NJ: Erlbaum. **13**

Vacca, J., & Bagdi, A. (2005). Relationships for life: Supporting the emotional health of infants and toddlers. *Dimensions, 33*(1), 9–16. **16**

Vail, C. O., & Scott, K. S. (1994). Transition from pre-school to kindergarten for children with special needs; Issues for early childhood educators. *Dimensions of Early Childhood Education, 22*(3), 21–25. **28**

Valeski, T. N., & Stipek, D. J. (2001). Young children's feelings about school. *Child Development, 72*(4), 1198–1213. **28**

Van Der Veer, R. (1986). Vygotsky's developmental psychology. *Psychological Reports, 59*, 527–536. **12**

van Ijzendoorn, M. H., & De Wolff, M. S. (1997). In search of the absent father—meta-analyses of infant-father attachment: A rejoinder to our discussants. *Child Development, 68*, 604–609. **13**

van Lieshout, C. F. M., Cillessen, A. H. N., & Haselager, G. J. T. (1999). Interpersonal support and individual development. In W. A. Collins & B. Laursen (Eds.), *Relationships as developmental contexts* (pp. 37–60). Mahwah, NJ: Erlbaum. **26**

Vance, E., & Weaver, P. J. (2002). *Class meetings: Young children solving problems together.* Washington, DC: National Association for the Education of Young Children. **30, 31**

Vandell, D. L., McCartney, K., Owen, M. T., Booth, C., & Clarke-Stewart, A. (2003). Variations in child care by grandparents during the first three years. *Journal of Marriage and Family, 65*, 375–381. **32**

Vann, K. R., & Kunjufu, J. (1993). The importance of an Afrocentric multicultural curriculum. *Phi Delta Kappan, 74*, 490–491. **6**

Vartuli, S., & Rogers, P. (1985). Parent-child learning centers. *Dimensions, 14*(1), 11–14. **12**

Vasquez, V. (2000, May). Negotiating a critical literacy curriculum with young children. *PDK Research Bulletin, 29*, 7–10. **22**

Vavrus, L. (1990, Aug.). Put portfolios to the test. *Instructor*, 48–53. **29**

Veach, D. M. (1979). Choice with responsibility. In L. Adams & B. Garlick (Eds.), *Ideas that work with young children* (Vol. 2) (pp. 45–48). Washington, DC: National Association for the Education of Young Children. **25**

Veciana-Suarez, A. (1992, Oct. 23). Parents urged to monitor use of video games. *The Advocate*, Baton Rouge, LA, 2C. **4**

Vernon, P. E. (1979). *Intelligence: Heredity and environment.* San Francisco: Freeman. **23**

Verschueren, K., & Marcoen, A. (1999). Representation of self- and socioemotional competence in kindergartners: Differential and combined effects of attachment to mother and to father. *Child Development, 70,* 183–201. **25**

Vibbert, M., & Bornstein, M. H. (1989). Specific associations between domains of mother-child interaction and toddler referential language and pretense play. *Infant Behavior and Development, 12,* 163–184. **17**

Votruba-Drzal, E., Coley, R. L., & Chase-Lansdale, P. L. (2004). Child care and low-income children's development: Direct and moderated effects. *Child Development, 75*(1), 296–312. **7**

Wachs, T. D. (2004). Temperament and development: The role of context in a biologically based system. *Zero to Three, 24*(4), 12–21. **13**

Wade, M. G. (1992). Motor skills, play, and child development: An introduction. *Early Report, 19*(2), 1–2. **12, 18**

Wadsworth, D. E., & Knight, D. (1996). Meeting the challenge of HIV and AIDS in the classroom. *Early Childhood Education Journal, 23*(3), 143–148. **7**

Walgren, C. (1990). Introducing a developmentally appropriate curriculum in the primary grades. *High/Scope Resource, 9*(2), 4–10. **28**

Walker, B., Hafenstein, N. L., & Crow-Enslow, L. (1999). Meeting the needs of gifted learners in the early childhood classroom. *Young Children, 54*(1), 32–36. **23**

Walker, D., Greenwood, C., Hart, B., & Carta, J. (1994). Prediction of school outcomes based on early language production and socioeconomic factors. *Child Development, 65,* 606–621. **20**

Wallach, L. B. (1993). Helping children cope with violence. *Young Children, 48*(4), 4–11. **28**

Walters, L. S. (1998, Apr. 23). Before they talk, they can sign. *The Christian Science Monitor,* 12. **14**

Wardle, F. (1987). Are you sensitive to interracial children's special identity needs? *Young Children, 42*(2), 53–59. **6**

Wardle, F. (1998, Aug./Sept.). Physical play, all day. *Early Childhood Today, 36.* **16**

Wardle, F. (2001). Viewpoint: Supporting multiethnic and multiracial children and their families. *Young Children, 56*(6), 38–39. **6**

Warren, R. M. (1977). *Caring.* Washington, DC: National Association for the Education of Young Children. **28**

Warrick, J., & Helling, M. K. (1997). Meeting basic needs: Health and safety practices in feeding and diapering infants. *Early Childhood Education Journal, 24*(3), 195–200. **12**

Wartella, E., Caplovitz, A. G., & Lee, J. H. (2004). From Baby Einstein to Leapfrog, from Doom to the Sims, from instant messaging to Internet chat rooms: Public interest in the role of interactive media in children's lives. *Social Policy Report, 18*(4). **4**

Washington, V. (1985). Social and personal ecology influencing public policy for young children. In C. S. McLoughlin & D. F. Gullo (Eds.), *Young children in context: Impact of self, family and society on development* (pp. 254–274). Springfield, IL: Charles C. Thomas. **33**

Washington, V. (1988). Historical and contemporary linkages between black child development and social policy. In D. T. Slaughter (Ed.), *Black children and poverty: A developmental perspective* (pp. 93–105). San Francisco: Jossey-Bass. **6, 33**

Washington, V. (1988). The black mother in the United States: History, theory, research, and issues. In B. Birns & D. F. Hay (Eds.), *The different faces of motherhood* (pp. 185–213). New York: Plenum. **33**

Washington, V. (1988a). Trends in Early Childhood Education. Part I: Demographics. *Dimensions, 16*(2), 4–7. **32**

Washington, V. (1988b). Trends in Early Childhood Education. Part II: Instruction. *Dimensions, 16*(3), 47. **32**

Washington, V. (1989). Reducing the risks to young black learners: An examination of race and educational policy. In J. B. Allen & J. M. Mason (Eds.), *Risk makers, risk takers, risk breakers: Reducing the risks for young literacy learners* (pp. 281–294). Portsmouth, NH: Heineman. **33**

Washington, V., & Andrews, J. D. (Eds.). (1998). *Children of 2010.* Washington, DC: National Association for the Education of Young Children. **32, 33**

Wasserman, S. (1990). *Serious players in the primary classroom: Empowering children through active learning experiences.* New York: Teachers College Press. **4, 28**

Waters, E., Weinfield, N. S., & Hamilton, C. E. (2000). The stability of attachment security from infancy to adolescence and early adulthood: General discussion. *Child Development, 71*(3), 703–706. **13**

Watson, J. (1976). Smiling, cooing, and "The Game." In J. Bruner, A. Jolly, & K. Sylva (Eds.), *Play: Its role in child development and evolution* (pp. 268–276). New York: Basic Books. **14, 21**

Watson, L. D., & Watson, M. A. (2003). *Infants & toddlers curriculum and teaching* (5th ed.). Clifton Park, NY: Delmar Learning. **16, 18**

Watson, M. (2003). Attachment theory and challenging behaviors: Reconstructing the nature of relationships. *Young Children, 58*(4), 12–20. **27**

Watt, M. R., Roberts, J. E., & Zeisel, S. A. (1993). Ear infections in young children: The role of the early childhood educator. *Young Children, 49*(1), 65–72. **7**

Weber, D. S., & Singer, D. G. (2004). The media habits of infants and toddlers: Findings from a parent survey. *Zero to Three, 25*(1), 30–36. **14**

Weiss, A. L. (2001). *Preschool language disorders: Resource guide.* San Diego, CA: Singular/Thomson Learning. **17**

Weiss, B., Dodge, K. A., Bates, J. E., & Pettit, G. S. (1992). Some consequences of early harsh discipline: Child aggression and a maladaptive social information processing style. *Child Development, 63,* 1321–1335. **28**

Weis, D. L. (2006). *Interpersonal Heterosexual Behaviors: Childhood Sexuality.* Retrieved May 16, 2006, from http://www2.hu-berlin.de **30**

Weiss, R. (2002, Feb. 27). Alzheimer's gene screened from newborn. Retrieved by topic March 15, 2003, from http://www.nl.newsbank.com/archives/ **10**

Wellman, H. M., Cross, D., & Watson, J. (2001). Meta-analysis of theory-of-mind development: The truth about false belief. *Child Development, 72*(3), 655–684. **20**

Wellman, H. M., & Hickling, A. K. (1994). The minds's "I" : Children's conception of the mind as an active agent. *Child Development, 65*, 1564–1580. **20**

Wesson, K. A. (2001). The "Volvo effect"—Questioning standardized tests. *Young Children, 56*(2), 16–18. **28**

West, B. (1983). The new arrivals from Southeast Asia: Getting to know them. *Childhood Education, 60*, 84–89. **6**

West, B. (1986). Culture before ethnicity. *Childhood Education, 62*, 175–181. **6**

West, M. M. (2001). Teaching the third culture child. *Young Children, 56*(6), 27–32. **6**

Weston, C. R., Ivins, B., Zuckerman, B., Jones, C., & Lopez, R. (1989). Drug exposed babies: Research and clinical issues. *Zero to three, 9*(5), 1–7. **8**

Whaley, K., & Swadener, E. B. (1990). Multicultural education in infant and toddler settings. *Childhood Education, 66*, 238–242. **16**

What is the Standard English Proficiency Program? (1998). In T. Perry & L. Delpit (Eds.), *The real Ebonics debate* (pp. 154–155). Boston: Beacon Press. **24**

Wheeler, D. L. (1993, Mar. 10). Psychologist deflates the modern craze of 'Baby Bonding.' *Chronicle of Higher Education*, A6–A7, A13. **11**

Wheeler, E. J. (1994). Reviews of research: Peer conflicts in the classroom: Drawing implications from research. *Childhood Education, 70*, 296–299. **26**

White, B. P., & Phair, M. A. (1986). "It'll be a challenge!" Managing emotional stress in teaching disabled children. *Young Children, 4*(2), 44–48. **5**

White, C. J. (1995). Native Americans at promise: Travel in borderlands. In B. B. Swadener & S. Lubeck (Eds.), *Children and families "at promise"* (pp. 163–184). Albany, NY: SUNY Press. **6**

White, V. F., Buchanan, T. K., Hinson, J. M., & Burts, D. C. (2001). Primary teachers: Five portraits. *Young Children, 56*(1), 22–32. **31**

Widerstrom, A. H., Mowder, B. A., & Sandall, S. R. (1991). *At-risk and handicapped newborns and infants: Development, assessment, and intervention.* Upper Saddle River, NJ: Prentice Hall. **6**

Wikipedia. (2006). *Hidden Curriculum.* Retrieved February 10, 2006 from http://en.wikipedia.org. **31**

Wilds, M. (2001). It's about time! Computers as assistive technology for infants and toddlers with disabilities. *Zero to Three, 22*(2), 37–41. **4, 5**

Willatts, P. (1989, Apr.). *Development of planning in infants.* Paper presented at the annual conference of the British Psychological Society, St. Andrews, Scotland. **14**

Willatts, P., & Rosie, K. (1989, Apr.). *Planning by 12-month-old infants.* Paper presented at the biennial meeting of the Society for Research in Child Development, Kansas City, MO. **14**

Willer, B. (Ed.) (1990). *Reaching the full cost of quality.* Washington, DC: National Association for the Education of Young Children. **32**

Willer, B. (1991). Public policy report. 101st Congress: The children's Congress. *Young Children, 46*(2), 78–80. **33**

Willer, B., & Bredekamp, S. (1990). Public policy report. Redefining readiness: An essential requisite for educational reform. *Young Children, 45*(5), 22–24. **28**

Williams, C. K., & Kamii, C. (1986). How do children learn by handling objects? *Young Children, 42*(1), 23–26. **4**

Williams, D. (2004). Parenting: How students' families can challenge stereotypes on television. *Teaching Tolerance, no. 25*, 16–17. **7**

Williams, H. G. (1983). Assessment of gross motor functioning. In K. D. Paget & B. A. Bracken (Eds.), *The psychoeducational assessment of preschoolchildren* (pp. 225–260). New York: Grune & Stratton. **18**

Williams, L. R. (1994). Developmentally appropriate practices and cultural values: A case in point. In B. L. Mallory & R. S. New (Eds.), *Diversity and developmentally appropriate practices* (pp. 155–165). New York: Teachers College Press. **28**

Winik, L. W. (1997, Feb. 2). Do computers help children learn? *Parade Magazine*, 8–9. **31**

Winsler, A., Diaz, R. M., & Montero, I. (1997). The role of private speech in the transition from collaborative to independent task performance in young children. *Early Childhood Research Quarterly, 12*, 59–79. **21**

Winsler, A., & Naglieri, J. (2003). Overt and covert problem-solving strategies: Developmental trends in use, awareness, and relations with task performance in children aged 5 to 17. *Child Development, 74*(3), 659–678. **21**

Winsler, A. (Ed.). (2003). Vygotskian perspectives in early childhood education [Special Issue]. *Early Education and Development 14*(3). **4**

Witkin, G. (1999, Feb. 5). Kid stress. *USA Weekend*, 7. **25, 30**

Witt, S. D. (2000). Review of research: The influence of television on children's gender socialization. *Childhood Education, 76*(5), 322–324. **25**

Wittmer, D., Doll, B., & Strain, P. (1996). Social and emotional development in early childhood: The identification of competence and disabilities. *Journal of Early Intervention, 20*(4), 299–319. **16**

Wolf, D. (1989, Spring). Novelty, creativity, and child development. *SRCD Newsletter*, 1–2. **23**

Wolfe, P. (1977). Heredity or environment. Excerpt from *Pregnancy, birth, and the newborn baby.* (1972). Delacorte Press. Reprinted in Cantor, P. (Ed.), *Understanding a child's world* (pp. 15–25). New York: McGraw-Hill. **9**

Wolfgang, C. H., Stannard, L. L., & Jones, I. (2001). Block play performance among preschoolers as a predictor of later school achievement in mathematics. *Journal of Research in Childhood Education, 15*(2), 173–180. **19**

Woods, J., Kashinath, S., & Goldstein, H. (2004). Effects of embedding caregiver-implemented teaching strastegies in daily routines on children's communication outcomes. *Journal of Early Intervention, 26*(3), 175–193. **17**

*World Health Day 2003: Healthy Environments for Children*. Retrieved August 5, 2005, from http://www.webhealthcentre.com **9**

Wren, S. (2003). *Developing Research-based Resources for the Balanced Reading Teacher.* Retrieved November 26, 2004, from http://www.balancedreading.com. **22**

Wright, M. O., & Masten, S. S. (2005). Resilience processes in development. In S. Goldstein & R. B. Brooks (Eds.). *Handbook of resilience in children*. New York: Kluwer. **30**

Yamamoto, K. (1972). *The child and his image.* Boston: Houghton-Mifflin. **16**

Yang, K. (2004). Southeast Asian American children: Not the "Model Minority." *The Future of Children, 14*(2), 127–137. **7**

Yarro, B. (1977, June). The changing world of child birth. *Detroit Free Press*, 1C, 3C. **11**

Yawkey, T. D., & Miller, T. J. (1984). The language of social play in young children. In A. Pellegrini & T. Yawkey (Eds.), *The development of oral and written language in social contexts* (pp. 95–104). Norwood, NJ: Ablex. **21**

Yelland, N. (1999). "Would you rather a girl than me?" : Aspects of gender in early childhood contexts with technology. *Journal of Australian Research in Early Childhood Education, 1*, 141–152. **25**

Yen, D. H. (2005). *Dumbing us down*. Retrieved February 10, 2006, from http://www.noogenesis.com **31**

Yoshikawa, H., Rosman, E. A., & Hsueh, J. (2001). Variation in teenage mothers' experiences of child care and other components of welfare reform: Selection processes and developmental consequences. *Child Development, 72*(1), 299–317. **12**

Young, V. M. L. (1981). Human genetics: Blueprint for development. In M. Tudor (Ed.), *Child Development* (pp. 47–61). New York: McGraw-Hill. **10**

Younger, B. A. (1993). Understanding category members as "the same sort of thing": Explicit categorization in ten-month infants. *Child Development, 64*, 309–320. **14**

*Youth indicators 1993: Trends in the well being of American youth.* Washington, DC: U.S. Department of Education, Office of Educational Research and Improvement. **12**

Yussen, S. R., & Santrock, J. W. (1978). *Child development.* Dubuque, IA: W. C. Brown. **4, 21**

Yuzawa, M., Bart, W. M., Yuzawa, M., & Junko, I. Young children's knowledge and strategies for comparing sizes. *Early Childhood Research Quarterly, 20*(2), 239–253. **20**

Zachopoulou, E., Tsapakidou, A. & Derri, V. (2004). The effects of a developmentally appropriate music and movement program on motor performance. *Early Childhood Research Quarterly, 19*(4), 631–642. **19**

Zambarano, R. J. (1991, Apr.). *Effects of tone-of-voice and physical punishment on children's and adults' interpretation of a brief disciplinary prohibition.* Paper presented at the meeting of the Society for Research in Child Development, Seattle, WA. **30**

Zanolli, K. M., Saudargas, R. A., & Twardosz, S. (1997). The development of toddlers' responses to affectionate teacher behavior. *Early Childhood Research Quarterly, 12*, 99–116. **16**

Zaslow, M. J., Pedersen, F. A., Suwalsky, J. T. D., & Rabinovich, B. A. (1989). Maternal employment and parent-infant interaction at one year. *Early Childhood Research Quarterly, 4*, 459–478. **12**

Zavitkovsky, D., Baker, K. R., Berlfein, J. R., & Almy, M. (1986). *Listen to the children.* Washington, DC: National Association for the Education of Young Children. **28**

Zeanah, C. H., & Scheeringa, M. (1996). Evaluation of post-traumatic symptomatology in infants and young children exposed to violence. *Islands of Safety.* Washington, DC: Zero to Three. **13**

Zelazo, P. R. (1984). "Learning to walk": Recognition of higher order influences? In L. P. Lipsitt & C. Rovee-Collier (Eds.), *Advances in infancy research* (Vol. 3) (pp. 251–256). Norwood, NJ: Ablex. **12, 18**

Zero evidence for zero tolerance: New report finds no support for harsh discipline. (2001). *ACEI Focus on Elementary Education, 13*(5), 7. **30**

*Zero to three.* (2004, March). Temperament in early development [focus issue], 24(4).

Zeskind, P. S., & Marshall, T. R. (1988). The relations between variations in pitch and maternal perceptions of infant crying. *Child Development, 59*, 193–196. **11**

Zigler, E., & Styfco, S. J. (Eds.). (1993). *Head Start and beyond: A national plan for extended childhood intervention.* New Haven, CT: Yale University Press. **32**

Zigler, E. F., Finn-Stevenson, M., & Hall, N. W. (2002). *The first three years and beyond*. New Haven, CT: Yale University Press. **14**

Zimmerman, M. A., & Arunkumar, R. (1994). Resiliency research: Implications for schools and policy. *Social Policy Report: SRCD, 8*(4). **25**

Zvetina, D. (2000). Redefining fatherhood in low-income communities. In *Father Care* (Erikson Institute publication), no. 2, 1, 9–17. **7**

# INDEX

The letter *f* following a page number indicates a figure.


## A

Abuse and neglect, 142–144
Accessibility, 122
Accommodation, 51
ACL (adult-to-child language), 487
ADA (Americans with Disabilities Act), 107
ADD. *See* Attention deficit disorder
Adults. *See also* Parents and families; Teachers
  affective development, role in, 570–585
  bilingual education, role in, 478–480
  cognitive development, role in, 477–497
  creativity, role in, 497
  infants and, 247–249
  intervention by, 100–101
  language development, role in, 320
  learning, role in, 51–52, 90–113
  neonates and, 189–190, 192–193
  oral language development, role in, 478–488
  play and, 100–106
  prenatal development, role in, 164–166
  primary children and, 636–638
  responsibility for children, 675–676
  technology and, 103–106
  toddlers and, 280–282, 298–301
  written language development, role in, 490–495
  young children and, 7
Adult-to-child language (ACL), 487
Advocacy for children, 691–701
AERA (American Educational Research Association), 36
Affection. *See* Love and affection
Affective, definition, 506
Affective development, 16f, 17f
  adult role in, 570–585
  definition, 242
  in infants, 242–256
  in preschoolers and kindergartners, 505–536
  in primary children, 624–641
  sociocultural factors and, 571
  theories of, 506–512
  in toddlers, 295–308
Affective growth, 14. *See also* Affective development
Affective values checklist, 587f
Affectivity, 510
African American English, 415–418, 489–490
African Americans, 135–136. *See also* Sociocultural factors
Aggregates, 359
Aggression, 16f, 559–560, 629. *See also* Violence
Aggressive, 559
AIDS (acquired immunodeficiency syndrome), 160f, 164, 178. *See also* HIV-positive status
Alcohol, prenatal development and, 160f, 161–162, 164
American Educational Research Association (AERA), 36
Americans with Disabilities Act (ADA), 107
Amniocentesis, 175
Amnion, 158
Amniotic fluid, 158
Amplification, 94
Anal stage, 17f, 278
Anecdotal record method of child study, 32
Anger, 520
Animism, 392
Anomy, 510
Anoxia, 160f, 161
Antibias approach, 639
Antisocial behaviors, 629–631
Anxiety, 516–518
Apgar scale, 185
Apgar score, 184, 185f
Appropriate and inappropriate practices checklist, 666
Appropriate and relevant, 469
Appropriate assessment procedures, 603. *See also* Assessment and assessment practices
Artificialism, 392
Artistic development, 471–472
Arts PROPEL, 464
Asian Americans, 136–138. *See also* Sociocultural factors
Assertiveness, 278
Assessment and assessment practices
  developmentally appropriate, 603–605
  Dynamic Indicators of Early Literacy Skills (DIBELS), 35, 439–440, 655
  inappropriate, 35–36, 54–55, 439–440, 602–603
  for school readiness, 602–605
  standardized testing, 35, 54
Assessment of motor skills, 360–363
Assets, developmental, 2
Assimilation, 51
Assistive technology, 59, 106, 365
Associative play, 81f, 82, 83
At-risk children, 61–62. *See also* High-risk children; Sociocultural factors; Socioeconomic factors; Special needs
  neonates, 192–193
Attachment, 212, 242–243, 244–247. *See also* Bonding
  definition, 244
  in preschoolers and kindergartners, 514
  substance abuse and, 177–178
  in toddlers, 304
Attention, 47

Attention deficit disorder (ADD), 47–48, 62f, 636
  definition, 47
Authoritarian style, 575
Authoritative style, 575
Authority, preschoolers and kindergartners and, 562
Autism, 62f
Autonomy, 17f, 93, 243, 277, 278, 510
Axon, 46

B

Babinski reflex, 233
Baby biographies, 29
Baby blues, 252
Baby talk (BT), 481
Baby tender, 199
Balanced approach to reading instruction, 442
Bandura, Albert, 15, 16f, 20, 22f, 91, 94–95, 198, 278, 512
Barriers, 596
Basic Interpersonal Communication Skills (BICS), 488
Beginning literacy, 440
Behavior modification, 286–287
Behavioral disturbance, 62f
Behavioral geneticists, 172
Behaviorist theories, 13, 16f, 45, 91, 94–96
Belief, 380–381
BICS (Basic Interpersonal Communication Skills), 488
Biculturalism, 211–213
Bilingual, definition, 418
Bilingual education, 418–419, 478–480
Birth, 183–185
  stages of children's understanding of, 529f
Bodily-kinesthetic intelligence, 463
Body size, 16f
Bonding, 186–187. *See also* Attachment
Brachiating, 353
Brain
  attention, 47
  cognition, 384–385
  hemispheric functions, 384
  memory, 49–50
  perception, 46–47
Brain development
  in infants, 265–267
  in toddlers, 286
Brain function, 46
  gender differences in, 266–267
Brain lateralization, 266
Brain research, 265
Breastfeeding, 221
Breech presentation, 184
Brothers. *See* Siblings
BT (baby talk), 481
Bullying, 560, 629–630
Burnout, 111–112

C

CALP (Cognitive Academic Language Proficiency), 488
Caregivers. *See* Nonparental care; Parents and families
Caring, 660–661
Carnegie Council on Children, 694–695, 697
Categorization, 264–265, 316
Causality, 392
CD-ROM, 105
Centering, 382
Cephalocaudal, 227, 233
Cesarean section, 184
Charts and checklists
  affective area values checklist, 587
  appropriate and inappropriate practices checklist, 666
  creativity scale, 499
  developmental expectations for the end of kindergarten checklist, 601
  height and weight charts, 229, 230, 337, 338
  infant caregiver evaluation sheet, 216–217
  infant cognitive and language development assessment chart, 271–272
  infant motor development assessment chart, 236–237
  infant physical development assessment chart, 232
  interest survey for child advocates, 693
  language development checklist, 411–412
  learning environment checklist, 115
  preschool/kindergarten fine motor development chart, 355
  preschool/kindergarten gross motor development chart, 352
  primary children affective development checklist, 642–643
  primary children cognitive development checklist, 667
  reading and writing development checklist, 454–456
  toddler cognitive-language development assessment chart, 327–328
  toddler fine motor and self help development assessment chart, 285–286
  toddler gross motor development chart, 284
  toddler personal-social development assessment chart, 310
Checklists. *See* Charts and checklists
Child abuse. See *Abuse* and neglect
Child advocates, 691–701
  definition, 691
Child care, 682–684. *See also* Nonparental care
  definition, 206
  infants and, 206–208
Child interview method of child study, 33
Child study
  history of, 28–31
  methods of, 31–36
Childbirth, 183–185
Children-first language, 61
Children's Defense Fund, 210, 676–677
Chorionic villus sampling (CVS), 175
Chromosomes, 174
Classical conditioning, 50
Classification, 387–388
Classroom. *See also* School; Teachers
  conflict in, 561–562
  developmentally appropriate, 597–598
  inclusive, 63, 107–108, 562–563
  management of, 663–664
Cognitive, defined, 374–375
Cognitive Academic Language Proficiency (CALP), 488
Cognitive decentering, 79
Cognitive development, 16f, 17f, 375
  adult role in, 477–497
  definition, 261
  in infants, 260–269
  play and, 78–79
  in preschoolers and kindergartners, 374–397
  in primary children, 647–658
  in toddlers, 313–325
Cognitive developmental approach, 460, 462
Cognitive functioning, 375, 380f, 382–383
Cognitive growth, 13
Cognitive level of play, 81–83
Cognitive structure, 375, 378–382
Communication. *See* Language and language development
Communicative phase, 359

Community in the classroom, 581
Competence, 99–100
  in infants, 200–201
  in primary children, 652–653
Comprehension, 442
Computers, 58–59, 60–61, 104–106, 657
  in the home, 129–130
Concept development, 16f
  in preschoolers and kindergartners, 385–397
  in primary children, 649–651
  technology and, 396
  theories of, 394–396
  in toddlers, 314–316, 321–322
Conception, 154–156
  definition, 155
  heredity and, 170–172
Concepts, 385
Concrete operational period, 376–377
Concrete operational thought, 386–387, 388f
Concrete operations, 17f
Conscience, 556
Conservation, 388–390
Constructive play, 82
Constructivist, definition, 93
Constructivist theories, 18, 53, 92–94
Context of play, 81–83
Continuity, 594–597
Contraception, 156, 162–163
Conventional reading and writing, 440
Cooperation, 16f
Cooperative learning, 631–632
Cooperative play, 81f, 82, 83
Cooperative teaching, 511
Coordinated play, 297
Cortisol, 248–249
Counting, 389–390, 393
Crack cocaine, 177–178
Crawling, 235
Crawling reflex, 233
Creativity, 467–472. *See also* Intelligence
  adult role in, 495–497
  criteria for, 468
  definition, 467
  giftedness and, 468–470
Creativity scale, 499
Crisis, 583–584
Crisis III: Initiative versus Guilt, 506
Crisis IV: Industry versus Inferiority, 507
Critical periods, 228
Critical theory, 18
Cultural differences. *See* Sociocultural factors
Cultural diversity, definition, 210
Cultural stereotyping, 140–142
Cultural style, 140–142
Culture. *See* Sociocultural factors
Curiosity, 470
CVS (chorionic villus sampling), 175

## D

DAP. *See* Developmentally appropriate practices
Death, 517–518
Decision making, guidelines for, 570–571
Deferred imitation, 315
Democracy, teaching and, 579–580
Dendrites, 46
Dependency, 16f, 515–516
Development. *See* Growth; *specific kinds of development*
Developmental and learning theories, 13–25, 45
  applied, 19–24
  behaviorist theories, 13
  developmental theories, 13
  sociocultural factors and, 18, 23–24
Developmental assets, 2
Developmental biodynamics, 261
Developmental expectations for the end of kindergarten checklist, 601f
Developmental psychology, 13–17
Developmentally and culturally appropriate practice (DCAP), 13. *See also* Developmentally appropriate, definition, 364
Developmentally appropriate practices (DAP)
Developmentally appropriate assessment. *See* Assessment and assessment practices
Developmentally appropriate classroom, 597–598
Developmentally appropriate practices (DAP), 7, 112, 438–439, 570–571, 662–663, 684.
  challenge to, 12–13
Developmentally inappropriate practice (DIP), 662–663
Diagrams, 359
Dialect, 415
Diary method of child study, 33
DIBELS. *See* Dynamic Indicators of Early Literacy Skills (DIBELS)
Differentiation, 228
Difficult child, 190
Digestive fallacy, 529
DIP (developmentally inappropriate practice), 662–663
Direct engagement, 122
Directing techniques, 573–574
Directive function, 426
Disabilities. *See* Special needs
Discipline, 573–578
Discrimination, 51
Disease and illness, 222–224, 336. *See also names of specific conditions*
Diversity. *See* Sociocultural factors
Divorce of parents, 204
Dizygotic (DZ) siblings, 171
DNA, 174
D'Nealian alphabet, 358
Doubt, 17f
Down syndrome, 173
Dramatic play, 77–78, 82
  definition, 77
Drawing, 358–360
  definition, 492
  handwriting and, 492
Drug abuse. *See* Substance abuse; *names of specific substances*
Drug exposure, 62f
Drugs, prenatal development and, 163–164
Dynamic Indicators of Early Literacy Skills (DIBELS), 35, 439–440, 655

## E

Early intervention, 202
Early Reading First, 439–440
Easy child, 190
Ebonics, 415–418, 489–490
  definition, 416
Ecological research model, 30–31
Ecological-systems approach, 19
Ecological theory, 18–19
Edelman, Marian Wright, 210
Ego, 508–509
Egocentric, 386
Eight-year-olds. *See* Primary period
ELL. *See* English Language Learners
Embryo, 156, 158–159
Emergence of autonomy, 243
Emergent diagram shapes, 359
Emerging competencies, 243
Emotional dependency, 515
Emotional development
  in infants, 250–253
  in preschoolers and kindergartners, 512–523
  in primary children, 632–636
  in toddlers, 301–304
Emotional disturbance, 62f

Emotional intelligence, 514
Emotions, recognition and regulation of, 522–523
Empathy, 558
Employment of parents, infants and, 205–206
Energy balance, 612
English as a Second Language (ESL), 479. *See also* Bilingual education
English-language classrooms, 418–419
English Language Learners (ELL), 418–419, 488–489. *See also* Bilingual education
Environment
  development and, 170–179
  effects on prenatal development, 160–164
  heredity and, 172–173
  for infants, 202–210
  intelligence and, 465–467
  learning environment checklist, 115f
  for play, 102–103
Environmental dangers, 176–177
Environmental factors, 170
Equilibration, 51
Erikson, Erik, 15, 16f, 17f, 20, 22f, 73, 74, 91, 198, 278, 507–509, 545, 546
ESL. *See* English as a Second Language
Ethnic socialization, 307–308, 639. *See also* Racial identification
Ethnicity. *See* Sociocultural factors
Ethological approach, 460, 464
European Americans, 138–139. *See also* Sociocultural factors
Examining, 285
Exercise play, 339
Exosurf®, 188
Exosystem, 30, 31f
Experimenting reading and writing, 440
Exploration, in play, 75–76
Expressive speakers, 318
Extinction, 51
Extrinsic rewards, 95–96

## F

FAE (fetal alcohol effects), 164
False beliefs, 380
Families. *See* Parents and families
Family, definition, 678
Family-centered practice, 126–127
Family planning, 156
FAS (fetal alcohol syndrome), 164
Fathers, 122, 203–205, 209, 679. *See also* Adults; Parents and families
  infants and, 254–256
  toddlers and, 288–289
Fear, 516–518
Fertility, 155
Fertilization, 155
Fetal alcohol effects (FAE), 164
Fetal alcohol syndrome (FAS), 164
Fetal development. *See* Prenatal development
Fetus, 157, 159
Fine motor skills. *See* Motor development
Five-year-olds. *See* Kindergartners; Preschoolers
Flexibility, 469
Fluency, 442, 469
Follicle, 154
Fontanels, 185
Food, as reward, 280
Food insecurity, 279
Food pyramid, 341f, 612–613
Food security, 279
Formal operations period, 375
Four-year-olds. *See* Preschoolers
Freud, Sigmund, 15, 16f, 17f, 20, 22f, 29, 73, 74, 91, 198, 278, 506, 507
Friendships, 550–552
Full inclusion, 63
Fuller, Millard, 225
Function, 426
Functional play, 82
Fundamental motor skills, 350
Fussing, 483

## G

Games, 73
  with rules, 82
Gardner, Howard, 463–464
Gay parents. *See* Nontraditional families
Gender, definition, 523
Gender equity, 524
Gender identity, 308
Gender roles, 523–527
Gene, 174
Generalization, 51
Genetic counseling, 164–165, 175–176
Genetics, 173–175
Genital herpes, 160f
Genotype, 174
Germ-line gene therapy, 174
Gesell readiness tests, 32–363
Gesell, Arnold, 15, 16f, 17f, 20, 22f, 29, 91
Gestational period, 156
Gifted person, 468, 469
Giftedness, 62f, 468–470
Grandparents, 679–680
Gross motor development. *See* Motor Development
Group entry techniques, 83
Growth. *See also specific kinds of development*
  definition, 13
  in primary children, 612
  sequential, 228
Growth rate (body), 16f
Guidance, 573–578
  of toddlers, 286–289
Guided participation, 299
Guilt, 17f, 506

## H

Habitat for Humanity, 225
Habituation, 51
Hall, G. Stanley, 29
Halliday, Michael, 422, 423, 424
Handedness, 360
Handicaps. *See* Special needs (children with)
Handwriting, 492
Happiness, 521–522
Haptic, 107
Harmonious style, 575
Head Start, 678
Health education, 343–344, 613–614
Hearing impairment, 62f
Heath, Shirley Brice, 481–483
Height and weight charts, 229f, 230f, 337f, 338f
Hemophilia, 173
Heredity
  conception and, 170–172
  development and, 170–179
  environment and, 172–173
Hereditary factors, 170
Heteronomy, 510
Hidden curriculum, 661
Hierarchy of needs, 509–510
High-reactive, 249
High-risk children, 1–2. *See also* At-risk children
Hispanic Americans, 132–134. *See also* Sociocultural factors
HIV-positive status, 62f. *See also* AIDS (acquired immunodeficiency syndrome)
Holophrases, 317
Holophrastic phase, 317
HOME (Home Observation for Measurement of the Environment), 209

Home Observation for Measurement of the Environment (HOME), 209
Homelessness, 144–145
Homeostasis, 188
Hostility, 520–521
Housing, 225
HOX gene, 159
Human Genome Project, 174–175
Humor
  definition, 521
  in primary children, 521_522
  in toddlers, 303–304
Huntington's chorea, 173

I

Id, 508–509
IDEA, 97, 107
Ideals, 36
IEP (individual education plan), 48
IFSP (individualized family service plan), 126
Illness. *See* Disease and illness
Imitation, 248
Immigrants, 130–131, 132
Immunization, 222
In vitro fertilization (IVF), 156
Inappropriate assessment procedures, definition, 603. *See also* Assessment and assessment practices
Inclusion, 63, 107–108, 562–563, 664
Individual education plan (IEP), 48
Individualized family service plan (IFSP), 126
Industry, 17f, 507
Infant caregiver evaluation sheet, 216–217
Infant cognitive and language development assessment chart, 271–272f
Infant motor development assessment chart, 236–237f
Infant physical development assessment chart, 232f
Infants, 4–5, 41–42. *See also* Neonates
  adults and, 247–249
  affective development of, 242–256
  attachment in, 242–243, 244–247
  brain development of, 265–267
  child care and, 206–208
  cognitive development of, 260–269
  competence in, 200–201
  cultural diversity and, 210–213
  definition, 3
  early intervention, 202
  emotional development of, 250–253
  employment of parents and, 205–206
  fathers and, 203–205
  health of, 220–227
  infant caregiver evaluation sheet, 216–217
  language development of, 262–264, 420–421
  low-birth-weight (LBW), 220–221
  media and, 263
  mental health in, 225–227
  motor development of, 231–238
  nutrition for, 220–222
  parent education and, 208–209
  peers and, 247–249
  perception in, 200–201
  physical development of, 227–231
  physical environment for, 202–203
  play and, 268
  posttraumatic stress disorder (PTSD) and, 252
  proprioception in, 200–201
  sensorimotor development of, 200–201
  social cognition in, 267–268
  sociocultural factors and, 253–256
  special needs in, 202, 208, 255–256
  temperament in, 249–250
  theories of infant development, 198–200
  trust development of, 198
Inferiority, 17f, 507
Information-processing approach, 460, 462
Inhibiting techniques, 573–574
Initiative, 17f, 506
Injury. *See* Safety
Input, 382
Inside intervention, 100–101
Integrated movements, 228
Intellectual development, 16f
Intelligence, 459–467. *See also* Creativity
  definition, 459
  environmental and cultural factors, 465–467
  giftedness and, 468–470
  IQ tests, 465
  multiple intelligences, 53, 460, 463–464
  views of, 461f
Interactionist, 171
Interactionist theory, 411
Interest survey for child advocates, 693
Internet, 105, 657
Interpersonal intelligence, 463
Interpretive function, 426
Interracial children, 139–140
Intervention, 100–101, 288
Intrapersonal intelligence, 463
Intrinsic rewards, 95–96
IQ tests, 465
IVF (in vitro fertilization), 156

K

Key School, 464
Kindergartners, 4, 6, 42–43
  affective development of, 505–536
  authority and, 562
  cognitive development of, 375–397
  cognitive functioning of, 382–383
  cognitive structure of, 378–382
  concept development of, 385–397
  definition, 4
  drawing and, 358–360
  emotional development of, 512–523
  health of, 336–340
  mental health of, 339–340
  moral development of, 555–562
  motor development of, 349–365
  nutrition and, 335–336, 340–342
  oral language development of, 407–430
  peers and, 548–555, 561–562
  personality of, 523–527
  physical development of, 335–345
  play and, 353–354
  self-concept in, 531–536
  sex-typing and gender roles and, 523–527
  sexuality and, 527–531
  social development of, 545–563
  special needs in, 351, 365, 532, 562–563, 583
  violence and, 558–561
  writing and, 354–358
  written language development of, 438–450
Klinefelter's syndrome, 173

L

Labeling, 263
Language, 407–410. *See also* Language development
  infants' use of, 420–421
  kindergartners' use of, 424–427
  play and, 427–429
  play with, 76–77
  preschoolers' use of, 424–427
  rules of, 409f
  sociocultural factors, 415–419
  thought and, 412–415
  toddlers' use of, 421–424
Language and speech disorders, 62f

Language development. *See also* Language
adult role in oral language development, 478–488
adult role in written language development, 490–494
of infants, 262–264
play and, 79–80
of preschoolers and kindergartners, oral language, 407–430
of preschoolers and kindergartners, written language, 438–450
of primary children, written language, 653–657
reading instruction and, 440–445
sociocultural factors and, 449–450, 481–484, 488–490
socioeconomic factors and, 419–420
theories of, 16f, 410–411, 412–413
of toddlers, 317–322
Language development checklist, 411–412f
Latency stage, 17f
Latino Americans. *See* Hispanic Americans; Sociocultural factors
LBW (low-birth-weight) infants, 220–221
Learned helplessness, 54, 660
Learning activity, 650–651
Learning disabilities, 62f
Learning environment checklist, 115f
Learning styles, 53
Learning theories. *See* Developmental and learning theories
Learning theory (of language), 410
Learning, 44–64
adult role in, 51–52, 90–113
classical conditioning, 50
computers and, 58–59, 60–61
definition, 44
memory and, 49–50
motivation and, 54–55, 96–97
motor development and, 363–365
observation and imitation, 50–51
operant conditioning, 50
peer support of, 51–52
play and, 52, 72–85
prenatal, 159–160
sensory involvement and, 48–49
technology and, 55–61
television and, 55–57
theories of. *See* Theories; *see also specific kinds of theories*
video games and, 57
LEP. *See* Limited-English-proficient
lesbian parents. *See* Nontraditional families
Letter names, 492
Letter sounds, 492
Limited-English-proficient (LEP), 469–470. *See also* Bilingual education
Limit-testing, 243
Linguistic intelligence, 463
Listening to children, 583–584
Literacy, 79–80, 101, 264, 322, 440. *See also* Assessment and assessment practices; Language development; Reading
Literacy beginners, 264
Literate, 438
Logical-mathematical intelligence, 463
Love and affection, 571–573
Low-birth-weight infant (LBW), 220–221
Low-reactive, 249

## M

Macrosystem, 30, 31f
Make-believe. *See* Play
Manipulation
of objects, 267, 314
in play, 75–76
Manipulatory-exploratory stage, 358–359
Maslow, Abraham, 15, 16f, 20, 22f, 91, 198–199, 509–510, 545, 546
Masturbation, 530
Maternal characteristics and prenatal development, 160f, 161–163
Mathematics, 392–394, 653
Maturationist theories, 91
Media. *See specific kinds of media*
Medical conditions, 62f
Medically fragile, 222
Memory, 49–50
Men, 254. *See also* Fathers
Mental health
of infants, 225–227
of preschoolers and kindergartners, 339–340
of primary children, 614
of new mothers, 252–253
Mental retardation, 62f. *See also* Special needs
Mesosystem, 30, 31f
Metacognition, 380–382
Methamphetamine, 177
Microsystem, 30, 31f
Migrant workers, 145
Minority children. *See* Sociocultural factors; *see also specific minority group*
Misnourished children, 335–336
Mistrust, 17f
Monozygotic (MZ) siblings, 170–171
Moral classrooms, 581
Moral development
of preschoolers and kindergartners, 555–562, 581–582
of primary children, 635
of toddlers, 304–305
Moral judgments, 556
Moral reasoning, 556
Morality, 304, 555
Morphemes, 408, 409
Mothers, 122. *See also* Adults; Parents and families
maternal characteristics and prenatal development, 160f, 161–163
mental health of, 252–253
Motion and interaction, in play, 74
Motivation, 16f, 54–55, 96–97
Motor development, 16f, 17f
definition, 14
of infants, 231–238
of kindergartners, 349–365
learning and, 363–365
of preschoolers, 349–365
of primary children, 614–620
special needs and, 351
of toddlers, 282–286
Motor skills. *See* Motor development
Motor skills assessment, 360–363
Movement pattern, 351f
Multicultural education, 131–132
Multiple intelligences, 460, 463–464
Multisensory learning, 48
Muscular dystrophy, 174
Musical intelligence, 463
Myelin, 46
MyPyramid.gov, 341f, 612–613

## N

NAEYC. *See* National Association for the Education of Young Children
National Association for the Education of Young Children (NAEYC), 3, 36
developmentally appropriate practices (DAP). *See* Developmentally appropriate practices (DAP)
Position Statement on School Readiness, 591–592, 593–594, 600
principles of, 112
software guidelines, 129
television and, 55–56
National Reading Panel, 442–443
Native Americans, 21, 134–135. *See also* Sociocultural factors

Natural childbirth, 184
Natural disasters, 518
Natural family planning, 156
Naturalist intelligence, 463
Nature versus nurture, 171
NBAS (Neonatal Behavior Assessment Scale), 188, 191–192
Neglect. *See* Abuse and neglect
Neonatal assessment, 188, 191–192
Neonatal Behavior Assessment Scale (NBAS), 188, 191–192
Neonatal period, 183
Neonates, 183, 185–193. *See also* Birth; Infants
  adults and, 189–190, 192–193
  assessment of, 188, 191–192
  bonding, 186–187
  parent stress and, 192–193
  physical characteristics of, 185–186
  premature, 187–188, 192–193
  sensitivity of, 189–190
  temperament of, 190–191
  touch and, 190
Neurological impairment, 62f
Neurons, 46
Newborn, definition, 183. *See also* Neonates
No Child Left Behind, 439, 653–654. *See also* Readiness (for school)
Nonparental care, 123–124, 679–680. *See also* Child care
Nonthematic, 102
Nontraditional families, 121, 678–681
Nonverbal gestures, 264
Nonviolence, teaching and, 580
Normal physiological jaundice, 185
Normative/maturational view, 13
Norms, 13
Novice reading and writing, 440
Nutrition
  definition, 340
  of infants, 220–222
  prenatal, 160–161
  of preschoolers and kindergartners, 335–336, 340–342
  of primary children, 612–613
  sociocultural factors, 342
  of toddlers, 279–282
Nutrition education, 343–344

O

Obesity, 342–343
  definition, 221
  in infants, 221–222
Object manipulation, 267, 314
Object permanence, 261–262
Object recognition, 261–262
Objects, play with, 75–76
Observation, 91
One-to-one correspondence, 389
One-year-olds. *See* Toddlers
Onlooker activity, 81f, 82
Operant conditioning, 50
Operations, 386–387
Oral language, 407–430
Oral stage, 17f
Ordering, 390–391
Organized supplementary play, 82
Originality, 469
Orthopedic disability, 62f
Output, 382
Outside intervention, 100–101
Overdiscriminations, 378–379
Overgeneralizations, 378–379
Ovum, 154

P

Pacific Islander Americans, 136–138. *See also* Sociocultural factors
Parallel play, 81f, 82
Parent education, 208–209
Parent interview method of child study, 33
Parent involvement, 685–686
Parental styles, 575–576
Parents and families. *See also* Adults; Fathers; Mothers; Siblings
  abuse and neglect and, 142–144
  African Americans, 135–136
  Asian Americans, 136–138
  education, involvement in, 124–126
  education of, 124–126
  employment of parents, 205–206
  European Americans, 138–139
  extended family, 681–682
  Hispanic Americans, 132–134
  homelessness, 144–145
  immigrants, 130–131, 132
  interracial children, 139–140
  learning, role in, 120–123
  migrant workers, 145
  neonates and, 192–193
  news reports about, 671–674
  nonparental care, 123–124
  nontraditional family, 121, 678–681
  Pacific Islander Americans, 136–138
  parent interview method, 33
  parent-child and teacher-child interactions, 109–110
  primary children and, 637–638
  sociocultural factors and, 121–125, 130–142, 253–256
  socioeconomic factors and, 2, 144–145
  special needs and, 126–127
  status today, 678–681
  technology and, 127–130
  toddlers and, 288–289
  traditional family, 121
Pediatrician, 165
Peer popularity, 549–550, 554–555
Peer reinforcement, 549–550
Peers, 51–52, 81–83, 247–249
  definition, 297
  kindergartners and preschoolers and, 548–555, 561–562
  primary children and, 626–629
  toddlers and, 297–298
Perception, 46–47, 200–201
Perinatologist, 165
Permissive style, 575
Personal advocacy, 700
Personal intelligences, 463
Personality, 523–527
Personality development, 17f
  sociocultural factors and, 535–536
Personality traits, 523
Phallic stage, 17f, 506
Phenotype, 174
Phenylketonuria (PKU), 173, 174
Phonemes, 408–409
Phonemic awareness, 442
Phonics, 440–442, 492
  definition, 442
Physical activity play, 339
Physical dependency, 515
Physical development, 16f, 17f
  delayed, 231
  of infants, 227–231
  of kindergartners, 335–345
  of preschoolers, 335–345
  of primary children, 611–614, 620
Physical fitness, 339, 616
Physical growth, definition, 14
Piaget, Jean, 15, 16f, 17f, 20, 22f, 29, 73, 74, 91, 92–93, 199, 278, 313–314, 375, 377, 394–396, 413, 467–468, 510–511, 545, 546, 556–557, 649
PKU (phenylketonuria), 173, 174
PL 101-476, 107, 126
PL 94-142, 107, 126
PL 99-457, 107, 126
Placenta, 157
Planning, 265
Plasticity, 46
Play
  associative, 81f, 82, 83
  cognitive development and, 78–79

Play (*continued*)
cognitive level of, 81–83
constructive, 82
cooperative, 81f, 82, 83
definition, 268
disabilities and, 80–81
dramatic, 77–78, 82
environment for, 102–103
as exercise, 339
functional, 82
games, 73
infants and, 268
kindergartners and, 353–354
with language, 76–77
language development and, 79–80
language use in, 427–429
learning and, 52, 72–85
with motion and interaction, 74
with objects, 75–76
outdoor, 353–354
parallel, 81f, 82
practice, 73
preschoolers and, 353–354
primary children and, 627–628, 656
reading and writing and, 493
representational, 73
rough-and-tumble, 339, 562
social development and, 80
sociocultural factors and, 83–85
solitary, 81f, 82
symbolic, 73
theories of, 73–74
toddlers and, 296–297
value of, 85
vehicles for, 74
Popularity, 549–550, 554–555, 628–629. *See also* Peers
Portfolio systems, 31–34
definition, 32
Positive guidance techniques, 577
Postpartum depression (PPD), 253
Postpartum psychosis (PPP), 253
Postpartum, 252
Posttraumatic stress disorder (PTSD)
definition, 303
infants and, 252
toddlers and, 303
Poverty. *See* Socioeconomic factors
PPD (postpartum depression), 253
PPP (postpartum psychosis), 253
Practice, in play, 75–76
Pragmatics, 408, 410
Preconcepts, 379–380
Pregnancy. *See also* Prenatal development
age, 162–163, 165
Premature infants, 187–188, 192–193
Prenatal development, 156–164
adult role in, 164–166
alcohol and, 160f, 161–162, 164
disease and, 164
drugs and, 163–164
environmental effects on, 160–164
learning during, 159–160
maternal characteristics and, 160f, 161–163
nutrition and, 160–161
physical, 156–160
smoking and, 160f, 161
Prenatal testing, 173–174
Preoperational period, 17f, 278
Preoperational thought, 385–386, 388f
Preschool/kindergarten fine motor development chart, 355
Preschoolers, 5–6, 42
affective development of, 505–536
authority and, 562
cognitive development of, 375–397
cognitive functioning of, 382–383
cognitive structure, 378–382
concept development of, 385–397
definition, 4
drawing and, 358–360
emotional development of, 512–523
health of, 336–340
mental health of, 339–340
moral development of, 555–562
motor development of, 349–365
nutrition and, 335–336, 340–342
oral language development of, 407–430
peers and, 548–555, 561–562
personality in, 523–527
physical development of, 335–345
play and, 353–354
self-concept in, 531–536
sex-typing and gender roles and, 523–527
sexuality and, 527–531
social development of, 545–563
special needs in, 351, 365, 532, 562–563, 583
violence and, 558–561
writing and, 354–358
written language development of, 438–450
Preschoolers/kindergartners gross motor development chart, 352f
Prevention, 287, 288
Primary children affective development checklist, 642–643f
Primary children cognitive development checklist, 667
Primary children
adults and, 636–638
affective development of, 624–641
antisocial behaviors and, 629–631
cognitive development of, 647–658
competence and, 652–653
concept development of, 649–651
emotional development of, 632–636
mental health in, 614
moral development of, 614–620, 635
peers and, 626–629
physical development of, 611–614, 620
play and, 627–628, 656
readiness for school, 591–606
schooling and, 658–665
self-esteem in, 633–635
sexuality and, 635
social development of, 625–632
sociocultural factors and, 639–640
special needs in, 631, 636
sports and, 615–617
stress and, 632–633
technology and, 657–658
written language development of, 653–657
Primary grades, 625
Primary period, 6–7, 43. *See also* Primary children
definition, 4
transition to, 593–606
Principals (school), 684
Principles, 36
Private sector advocacy, 700
Private speech, 319, 425, 653
Problem solving, 16f, 98–100, 316, 470
Processing, 382
Professional ethics, 36
Project Spectrum, 464
Projective function, 426–427
Prolonging attention, 243
Proprioception, 200–201
Prosocial behaviors, 558
Protolanguage, 421
Proximodistal, 227, 233
Psychometric approach, 460
PTSD. *See* Posttraumatic stress disorder
Public policy, 694–700
Public policy advocacy, 700
Punishment, 576–577

## Q

Quality Early Education Coalition, mission statement, 695–696

## R


Racial identification, 533–535
Random scribble, 359
RDA (recommended daily dietary allowances), 280
Readiness (for school), 591–606
  assessment practices and, 602–605
  definition, 598
  sociocultural factors and, 600–601
Reading and writing development checklist, 454–456
Reading development, 440–445
  primary children and, 653–657
  reading at home, 490–491
  reading at school, 492–493
  sociocultural factors and, 449–450
Reading First Initiative, 35
"Reading Wars," 440
Recess, 615–617
Reciprocity, 244
Recommended daily dietary allowances (RDA), 280
Reference group identification, 533–534
Referential speakers, 318
Reflective learning, 495
Reflexes, 233
Reggio Emilia, 684–685
Relational aggression, 560
Relational function, 427
Relationships
  definition, 339
  preschoolers and kindergartners and, 547–548
Repetition, in play, 76
Representational thinking, 314
Resiliency, 633
RESOLVE, 156
Respectful engagement, 637
Responsibility, 122
Rewards, 95–96
Rh factor, 160f, 161
Rhythm, 243–244
Roadville, 481–483
Rogers, Carl, 15, 16f, 20, 22f, 91, 198–199, 509–510, 545, 546
Role-playing, 80
Rooting reflex, 233
Rough-and-tumble play, 339, 562, 627
Routines, 483–484
RSV, 222
Rubella, 160f
Running record method of child study, 33–34, 35


## S


Safety, 224–225, 343, 613, 617, 638, 657
Sanitation. *See* Disease and illness
Scaffolding, 19, 51–52, 94. *See also* Adults
Schema, 378
School. See also Classroom; Teachers
  criticisms of, 660–662
  developmentally appropriate and inappropriate practice and, 662–663, 684–685
  fear about, 660
  inclusive, 664
  parent involvement, 685–686
  primary children and, 658–665
  principals, 684
  readiness for, 591–606
  sociocultural factors and, 658–660, 686
Sears, Robert R., 29
Second language learners. *See* Bilingual education
Self-concept, 14, 16f, 307
  definition, 531
  in preschoolers and kindergartners, 531–536
  sociocultural factors and, 533–535
  special needs and, 532
Self-esteem, 531–532
  in primary children, 633–635
Self-regulation, 101, 319, 547
Self-talk, 319
Semantics, 408, 409
Semen, 154
Sensitivity, of neonates, 189–190
Sensorimotor development, 261. *See also* Cognitive development
Sensorimotor period, 17f, 199
Sensory development, 47
  prenatal, 159–160
Sensory integrative dysfunction, 48–49, 48
Sensory involvement, 48–49
Separation distress, 247
Sequential growth, 228
Seriation, 390–391
Seven-year-olds. *See* Primary period
Sex differences, 526–527
Sex
  definition, 523
  stages of children's understanding of, 529f
"Sex play," 530–531
Sex-role standards, 524
Sex-stereotyped, 299
Sex-typing, 523–527
  definition, 526
Sexual abuse, 143
Sexuality, 527–531, 635
Shame, 17f, 305
Shaping, 51
Shared activities, 511
Siblings, 552–553
Sickle-cell anemia, 174
SIDS. *See* Sudden Infant Death Syndrome
Sisters. *See* Siblings
Six-year-olds. *See* Kindergartners; Primary period
Skinner, B. F., 15, 16f, 20, 22f, 91, 94–95, 199–200, 286–287, 511–512
SLI (specifically language impaired), 320
Slow-to-warm-up child, 190
Smoking, prenatal development and, 160f, 161
Social cognitive theory, 91–92
Social competence, 547–548
Social development, 17f
  play and, 80
  of preschoolers and kindergartners, 545–563
  of primary children, 625–632
  theories of, 545–547
  of toddlers, 301–306
Social isolates, 554
Social reciprocity, 510
Social referencing, 267
Social roles, play and, 80
Sociocultural factors, 8, 21, 31. *See also* Socioeconomic factors
  affective development and, 571
  African Americans, 135–136
  Asian Americans, 136–138
  biculturalism, 211–213
  cultural diversity, 210–211
  cultural style, 140–142
  developmental and learning theories and, 18, 23–24
  developmentally and culturally appropriate practice (DCAP), 13
  ethnic socialization, 307–308
  European Americans, 138–139
  families and, 121–125, 130–142
  fathers and, 254–256
  giftedness and, 469–470
  head of household, 254
  Hispanic Americans, 132–134
  homelessness, 144–145
  immigrants, 130–131, 132
  infants and, 253–255

Sociocultural factors (*continued*)
intelligence and, 465–467
interracial children, 139–140
language and, 415–419
language development and, 481–484, 488–490
mathematics and, 393–394
migrant workers, 145
motivation and, 54
multicultural education, 131–132
Native Americans, 21, 134–135
neonates and, 193
nonparental care, 123–124
nutrition, 342
Pacific Islander Americans, 136–138
personality development and, 535–536
play and, 83–85
primary children and, 639–640
public policy and, 697–698
readiness for school and, 600–601
reading and writing and, 449–450
school and, 658–660, 686
self-concept and, 533–535
as special needs, 62f
stereotyping, 128–129
stress and, 520
temperament and, 250
toddlers and, 300, 323–324
Socioeconomic factors, 144–145, 210, 219–220, 676–678. *See also* Sociocultural factors
food and, 279–280
language development and, 419–420
violence and, 561
Sociomoral development, 510
Software, 104
Solitary play, 81f, 82
Sonography, 175
Space, 391–392
Spatial concepts, 391
Spatial intelligence, 463
Special needs, 61–64, 106–108. *See also specific conditions*
abuse and, 143
assistive technology, 59, 106, 365
children-first language, 61
early intervention, 202
emotional disabilities, 305–306
inclusive settings, 63, 107–108, 562–563, 664
individual education plan (IEP), 48
individualized family service plan (IFSP), 126
infants with, 255–256
kindergartners with, 351, 365, 532, 562–563, 583
motor development and, 351
neonates with, 193
parent and family involvement, 126–127
play and, 80–81
preparation for elementary grades and, 108
preschoolers with, 351, 365, 532, 562–563, 583
primary children with, 631, 636
self-concept and, 532
social disabilities, 305–306
specifically language impaired (SLI), 320
technology and, 59, 106
toddlers with, 289–290, 305–306, 320
types of, 62f
Specialized movements, 350
Specifically language impaired (SLI), 320
Specimen record method of child study, 34, 35
Speech development. *See* Language and language development
Spelling development, 447–449
Sperm, 154
Sperm microinjection, 156
Sports, 615–617
Standardized testing. *See* Assessment and assessment practices
States of arousal, 186
Stepping reflex, 233
Stereotypes, 128–129, 140–142, 524–525
Strange-situation, 254
Stranger anxiety, 245
Stress, 518–520, 632–633
Strong nominals, 318
Strong relationals, 318
Structural-innatist theory, 410–411
Substages of sensorimotor development, 261
Substance abuse, 142, 160f, 161, 177–178
attachment and, 177–178
prenatal development and, 160f, 161, 163–164
toddlers and, 281
Successful intelligence, 460, 462–463
Successive approximation, 51
Sudden Infant Death Syndrome (SIDS), 162, 222
Superego, 508–509
Synapses, 46
Syntax, 408, 409
Syphilis, 160f

## T

Talk, 420
Task analysis, 107
Teacher researchers, 34–35
Teachers
beliefs of, 110–111, 522
burnout and, 111–112
parents and, 109–110
teacher-child interactions, 109–110
Teaching styles, 576
Technology. *See also specific kinds of technology*
assistive, 59, 106, 365
concept development and, 396
future of, 59–61
in the home, 127–130
learning and, 55–61, 103–106
primary children and, 657–658
Teen Outreach Program (TOP), 165
Teen parents, 208, 209–210. *See also* Pregnancy, teenage
Teenage pregnancy. *See* Pregnancy, teenage
Telegraphic sentences, 318–319
Television
education and, 55–57, 103–104
in the home, 127–129
Temperament, 190
of infants, 249–250
of toddlers, 306–308
Terrible twos, 277
Thalidomide, 163
Thematic, 102
Theories. *See also specific subjects of theories; names of theorists*
of affective development, 506–512
definition, 12
of infant development, 198–200
of language development, 16f, 410–411, 412–413
of play, 73–74
practice and, 91–92, 97–98
of social development, 545–547
of toddler development, 278–279
Theorists. *See names of theorists*
Theory of mind, 380
Theory of multiple intelligences, 460, 463–464
Theory of successful intelligence, 460, 462–463

Thinking
language and, 412–415
representational, 314
and thinking skills, 98–100
Thought. *See* Thinking
Three-year-olds. *See* Preschoolers; Toddlers
Time out, 577–578
Tobacco. *See* Smoking
Toddler cognitive-language development assessment chart, 327–328f
Toddler fine motor and self help development assessment chart, 285–286f
Toddler gross motor development chart, 284f
Toddler personal-social development assessment chart, 310f
Toddlers, 5, 42, 276–278
affective development of, 295–308
attachment in, 304
brain development of, 286
cognitive development of, 313–325
concept development of, 314–316, 321–322
definition, 4
emotional development of, 301–304
fathers and, 288–289
gender identity and, 308
guidance of, 286–289
humor in, 303–304
language development of, 317–322, 421–424
moral development of, 304–305
motor development of, 282–286
nutrition and, 279–282
peers and, 297–298
play and, 296–297
posttraumatic stress disorder (PTSD) and, 303
social development of, 301–306
sociocultural factors and, 300, 307–308, 323–324
special needs in, 289–290, 305–306, 320
substance abuse and, 281
temperament of, 306–308
theories of toddler development, 278–279
toileting and, 283–284
Toileting, toddlers and, 283–284
TOP (Teen Outreach Program), 165
Touch, 190
Tough, Joan, 425–427
Toys, emotional attachment to, 76
Trackton, 481–483
Traditional families, 121, 678–679
Transition period, 376–377
Transitional spellings, 448
Triarchic instruction, 463
Trust, 17f, 198
Two-year-olds. *See* Toddlers

## U

Ultrasound, 175
Umbilical cord, 157
Unoccupied activity, 81
Unpopularity. *See* Popularity; Peers

## V

Vehicles for play, 74
Video games, 57
Violence, 676–678
infants and, 252
in media, 55–56
preschoolers and kindergartners and, 558–561
socioeconomic factors and, 561
teaching nonviolence, 580
Visual impairment, 62f
Vocabulary, 442
Vygotsky, Lev, 15, 16f, 17f, 20, 22f, 73, 74, 91, 93–94, 199, 278–279, 314, 377–378, 394–396, 413, 424, 425, 467–468, 511, 546, 649

## W

Walking, 235–236
War, 518
Water birth, 184
Web sites, 105
Welfare, 210
Whiting, John, 29
Whole child, 675–687
definition, 675
Whole-language approach, 441–442
Writing development, 354–358, 444–447
sociocultural factors and, 449–450
writing at home, 490–491
writing at school, 492–493
Written language, 438–450

## Y

Young children, 3–7
definition, 3

## Z

Zero tolerance, 638
Zone of proximal development (ZPD), 295, 378
ZPD. *See* Zone of proximal development (ZPD)
Zygote, 155, 157